THE OXFORD ENCYCLOPEDIA OF
AMERICAN SOCIAL HISTORY

THE OXFORD ENCYCLOPEDIA OF
AMERICAN SOCIAL HISTORY

Lynn Dumenil

EDITOR IN CHIEF

VOLUME 1
ABOR–MEDI

OXFORD

UNIVERSITY PRESS

OXFORD
UNIVERSITY PRESS

Oxford University Press, Inc., publishes works that further
Oxford University's objective of excellence
in research, scholarship, and education.

Oxford   New York
Auckland   Cape Town   Dar es Salaam   Hong Kong   Karachi
Kuala Lumpur   Madrid   Melbourne   Mexico City   Nairobi
New Delhi   Shanghai   Taipei   Toronto

With offices in
Argentina   Austria   Brazil   Chile   Czech Republic   France   Greece
Guatemala   Hungary   Italy   Japan   Poland   Portugal   Singapore
South Korea   Switzerland   Thailand   Turkey   Ukraine   Vietnam

Copyright © 2012 by Oxford University Press

Published by Oxford University Press, Inc.
198 Madison Avenue, New York, NY 10016
www.oup.com

Oxford is a registered trademark of Oxford University Press

Library of Congress Cataloging-in-Publication Data

The Oxford encyclopedia of American social history / Lynn Dumenil, editor in chief.
    p. cm.
  Includes bibliographical references and index.
  ISBN 978-0-19-974336-0 (alk. paper)
  1. United States–Social conditions–Encyclopedias. 2. United States–Social life and
customs–Encyclopedias. 3. Social history–Encyclopedias. I. Dumenil, Lynn, 1950- II.
Title: Encyclopedia of American social history.
  HN57.O94 2012
  306.0973–dc23

2011034907

1 3 5 7 9 8 6 4 2

Printed in the United States of America
on acid free paper

EDITORIAL AND PRODUCTION STAFF

CONTENTS

LIST OF ENTRIES

INTRODUCTION

The Oxford Encyclopedia of American History carries on a tradition of scholarly publishing by Oxford University Press that began in 1478, fourteen years before Christopher Columbus set out from Palos de la Frontera in Spain and sailed westward across the Atlantic. As for American history, Oxford's first contribution was John Smith's annotated *Map of Virginia*, published in 1612, five years after 104 English men and boys had founded the Jamestown settlement.

This tradition has continued over the centuries, including *The Oxford Companion to United States History* (2001), affectionately called "OCUSH," which I had the pleasure and privilege of editing along with a distinguished group of associates. To this long and noteworthy record, Oxford now proudly adds this new work. Building on the one-volume *Companion*, this twelve-volume set of six encyclopedias offers a far more capacious format, making it possible to include a greater number of entries and to provide more detailed, in-depth coverage than was possible in the briefer compass of the *Companion*.

The rationale for such a work is obvious. Awareness of, and interest in, our collective past is part of what makes us human, and the recording of history has characterized every great civilization. The case for this specific set of encyclopedias is equally compelling. From the time when the first human beings made their way from present-day Siberia across a now-vanished land bridge to what we call North America, the history of the peoples of this great geographic region has been rich in its diversity and interest. From the late sixteenth century onward, the various settlements in what Europeans called first the New World and then, after 1776, the United States have loomed large on the world stage—first in the realm of the imagination and then, increasingly, as unavoidable reality. The nation's political, social, economic, and cultural lives have always roused interest, sometimes as the target of criticism and ridicule, sometimes as an ideal to be envied and emulated. As Johann Wolfgang von Goethe wrote in an 1827 poem (in Daniel Platt's translation):

America, you've got it better
Than our old continent. Exult!
You have no decaying castles
And no basalt.
Your heart is not troubled,
In lively pursuits,
By useless old remembrance
And empty disputes.

The actual America of 1827, distracted by controversy over the tariff and by angry feuds within John Quincy Adams's unpopular and dysfunctional presidential administration, was, of course, irrelevant to Goethe. As others have done before and since, he was conjuring up a finer America of his dreams, a fresh, new society uncorrupted by the all-too-human flaws of tired, old Europe. (That strange reference to "basalt," some scholars believe, may be a metaphorical allusion to volcanoes as symbols of social unrest and revolutionary turmoil.) Of more substantive, less abstract interest has been America's global military, diplomatic, economic, and strategic role, which has grown steadily more significant and inescapable over the years. In short, for a variety of reasons, the case for a comprehensive reference work covering all of American history is clear.

But is such a work really needed in the twenty-first century, given the tsunami of "information" endlessly churning through the media, accessible at a keystroke? The answer is a decisive, "Yes." This set of encyclopedias arose from a core assumption shared by the editors at Oxford University Press, by the gifted scholars constituting the editorial teams, and certainly by me. In an era in which the production and dissemination of knowledge have become wholly diffuse, often anonymous and unsourced, and frequently idiosyncratic and unreliable, we are convinced that there is still a place—indeed, a vital necessity—for a historical reference work that is authoritative, carefully planned, analytically sophisticated, written by scholars familiar with the latest findings, and carefully edited for accuracy, clarity, and readability.

Grounded in these basic principles, *The Oxford Encyclopedia of American History* is chronologically comprehensive, from the earliest human settlements to the twenty-first century, from the Stone Age to the Computer Age. The work is topically comprehensive as well. This is a daunting task, particularly because the field of American history has expanded dramatically in recent decades: the field has come to include much more extensive coverage of social, cultural, scientific, medical, and demographic topics than was true in the past. Recent scholarship has vastly broadened our knowledge of the historical experience of all Americans of the past, not just the elite figures who once dominated the story. This set of encyclopedias fully reflects this broader understanding of the American past.

HISTORY: AN ANCIENT DISCIPLINE, YET EVER NEW

History is among the oldest of the scholarly disciplines, tracing its origins to West African griots, ancient Chinese chroniclers, and Mesopotamians who combined the skills of historian, elocutionist, scribe, and stonemason, celebrating the exploits of their rulers in viva voce orations and on steles and tablets for future generations to transcribe and wonder at. The Greek historian Herodotus, who lived in the fifth century BCE, wrote an account of successive rulers of Persia, with whom Greece fought several wars. Filling his narrative with stories about the peoples and places he had heard about, he was an early practitioner of what is now called social and cultural history. Herodotus's younger contemporary Thucydides devoted his great talents to a history of the Peloponnesian war, the long conflict between Athens and Sparta. Focusing on battles and diplomacy and avoiding Herodotus's charming penchant for digression, Thucydides nevertheless recognized the importance of personality traits and social factors, such as the terrible plague that struck Athens in the midst of the war. In an authorial decision that would place him at odds with some participants in modern America's culture wars, Thucydides strictly excluded divine intervention from his causal forces, and he avoided suggesting that the gods favored one side or another in the conflict he was describing.

But history writing, this ancient pursuit, is also ever new, which helps account for its appeal to so many bright young scholars. It continually reinvents itself, not only because more things keep happening, but also because historians' understanding of their field, and of what merits their attention, is continually shifting and enlarging. In former times, the historian typically focused his attention (and it almost invariably was a "he") on politics, war, law, and diplomacy. Together with industrialization, finance, and other economic matters, these were considered history's driving forces, and thus the historian's proper subject matter.

But gradually a broader understanding emerged. George Bancroft, the prolific nineteenth-century historian, famously included a chapter on social history in his monumental ten-volume history of the United States (1834–1874). Henry Adams began his multivolume *History of the United States during the Administrations of Thomas Jefferson and James Madison* (1889–1891) with a chapter each on the "popular characteristics" of the American people, on "American ideals," and on the intellectual life of New England, the middle-Atlantic states, and the South. By offering new approaches to the history of ideas, Vernon L. Parrington's *Main Currents in American Thought* (1927) and Merle Curti's *The Growth of American Thought* (1943) helped create a new field, combining history and literature, that came to be known as American Studies.

Later scholars have vastly expanded these initiatives. The twenty-first century's historians recognize that the history of social groups, class conflict, sexuality, popular culture, ideas and ideology, religious belief, literature, music, and the arts, as well as developments in science, medicine, technology, and the economy, all lie within their purview and merit careful attention and study. The traditional areas of politics, the law, military history, and foreign relations remain central, of course, but these fields, too, have been enriched by attention to the broader sociocultural context within which elections, legislative battles, legal decisions, wars, and diplomatic maneuverings unfold.

Indeed, all these subfields are interconnected. One cannot understand the social and military history of colonial America, for example, without understanding the devastating effects of the bacteria and viruses that the European newcomers unwittingly brought with them: lacking the immunity to these bacteria and viruses that comes with long exposure, native peoples were decimated by disease. The history of slavery remains incomplete without attention to the changing technology of cotton production. One cannot grasp the full impact on America of World War I without also grasping the impact of the virulent influenza virus (the precise point of origin remains uncertain) that spread across the battlefields of Europe and home-front military bases, causing a global pandemic that took at least 50 million lives. The nation's military and political history is enriched by attention to the ways in which perceptions of wars, battles, elections, and political careers are shaped by the popular culture, from ballads and broadsides to cartoons, films, and television programs. Our picture of working-class America is enriched if we examine workers' families, leisure activities, religious lives, and consumption patterns, as well as their voting habits and participation in labor unions—important as voting patterns and unions obviously are. On and on the list could go, illustrating that American history, like all history, is really a seamless web, however we divide it into subfields for analytic and pedagogical purposes.

Along with the subject matter of history, the demographic profile of the profession of American history itself has changed. Once the domain of white males of British or northern European ancestry, in the twenty-first century the profession is far more diverse in terms of gender, race, and ethnicity. This has made for a livelier and more stimulating intellectual environment, as well as for a greater sensitivity to the diverse historical experience of the many subgroups within American society.

Historians' understanding of America's place in the world has evolved as well. In the past, U.S. historians tended to stress the uniqueness of the American experience. Underlying this view was the notion that America was not only different from, but superior to, other nations, and that it was somehow immune to the historical processes that could be seen in the rise and decline of other once-powerful civilizations and nation-states, from Babylon, Greece, and Rome to Spain, Portugal, Sweden, the Netherlands, and Great Britain. Sometimes, as in the writings of the New England Puritans, this view of America's uniqueness took on explicitly religious overtones. Even George Bancroft, a liberal Unitarian with a European education including a PhD from Germany's University of Göttingen, saw America as enjoying God's special favor. Such explicitly supernaturalist understandings of American history gradually faded, but notions of American exceptionalism survived, shaping historians' approach to their subject. This, too, has changed since the later twentieth century. U.S. historians now recognize that the forces shaping American history are hardly unique to the United States, but replicate processes also observable in other societies. This broader comparative dimension has both enriched American historical scholarship and added a chastening note of humility.

The heightened transnational awareness has not been only at the abstract level. American historians have vastly benefited from the work of foreign scholars, including the British historian E. P. Thompson, whose book on the making of the English working class was pathbreaking, and the French historians Lucien Febvre, Marc Bloch, Fernand Braudel, and Emmanuel Le Roy Ladurie, who did pioneering work in social history and founded the so-called *Annales* school, with its shift from providing a narrative of passing events to focusing on the *longue durée*, or long-term, processes that shape human societies over centuries.

Influential, too, has been the Italian historian Carlo Ginzburg, with his attention to the illuminating insights to be gained from "microhistory," the close analysis of specific events or small communities. Ginzburg's *Il formaggio e i vermi: Il cosmo di un mugnaio del*

Cinquecento (1976; English trans., *The Cheese and the Worms: The Cosmos of a Sixteenth-Century Miller*, 1980), based on detailed Inquisition records that Ginzburg discovered in long-neglected archives of the Catholic Church, told of an obscure miller, Domenico Scandella, better known as Menocchio, burned at the stake in 1600 in the northeastern Italian town of Montereale for beliefs that he summed up this way:

> I have said that in my opinion, all was chaos . . . and out of that bulk a mass formed—just as cheese is made out of milk—and worms appeared in it, and these were the angels. There was also God, he too having been created out of that mass at the same time.

Such heresy shocked church authorities, and Menocchio went to his fiery death. In writing about this forgotten event in an obscure town, Ginzburg offered a wealth of fresh insights into the procedures and processes of the Inquisition, late medieval folk belief and oral culture, and the ramifications of the Counter-Reformation in Italy. Such scholarship proved appealing to American historians, who explored microhistories of their own to see what they would reveal. Laurel Thatcher Ulrich's Pulitzer Prize–winning *A Midwife's Tale* (1991) offered a biography of Martha Ballard, an obscure Maine midwife of the turn of the nineteenth century, based on Ballard's diary recording the unremarkable routines of her life. In the diary's "exhaustive, repetitive dailiness," Ulrich argued, lay its value as a historical document.

As this suggests, American historians' methodologies and sources have expanded as well. While retaining a strong sense of the value of their traditional text-based approaches, historians have learned from sociologists and political scientists the value of quantification in illuminating the past. Census records, voting data, tax lists, and many other forms of quantified information have yielded rich results. Such pathbreaking books using quantified data as Lee Benson's *The Concept of Jacksonian Democracy: New York as a Test Case* (1961) and Stephan Thernstrom's *Poverty and Progress: Social Mobility in a Nineteenth Century City* (1964) provided a means of testing cherished American myths about the "era of the common man," "rags to riches," and the United States as a "land of opportunity"—myths reinforced by Horatio Alger stories and the oft-told biographies of exceptional figures like Andrew Carnegie. (That Thernstrom's book was pathbreaking is indicated by its being relegated by the *American Historical Review* to a brief notice in a section called "Other Recent Publications" and by its being overlooked entirely by the *Journal of American History*, whose editor assumed that it was a work of sociology.)

Fully aware that statistically based findings must be interpreted for and presented in prose accessible to people who are not mathematicians, historians are in little danger of becoming computing automatons, spewing out numbers, statistics, and formulas. And the profession has learned that statistical data, like any other form of evidence, can be fudged and misrepresented and thus must be approached with due skepticism. Nevertheless, American historians have grown more conscious of the rich resources buried in the nation's vast repositories of quantified data. So, too, have they discovered the research value of material-culture products, visual materials, industrial designs, fashion shows, television commercials, and mundane everyday objects from toys, comic books, tombstones, and toilets to domestic structures. Approached with insight and imagination, such materials are invaluable historical sources.

To be sure, all this ferment and change within the profession of American history has raised troublesome questions. If historians focus too exclusively on subgroups within society, how can they formulate a larger conception of *American* history? Put another way, what meaning does the familiar phrase "one nation indivisible" from the original Pledge of Allegiance to the flag ("under God" was inserted later) retain in the twenty-first century, apart from the banal point that a second secession movement like that of 1861 would be unlikely to succeed? Or, again, if historians adopt a snapshot approach, documenting the experience of specific groups during one brief period of their history, how can they explain change over time? Other questions have been raised as well. As historians, from wholly laudable motives, turned their attention to the poor, disenfranchised, and disinherited—doing "history from the bottom up," as it was called—did they risk losing sight of the important role of powerful elites and interest groups in society? In abandoning the notion of American exceptionalism as self-serving and parochial, did they risk missing what might, in fact, be distinctive and unique about the American experience? At the practical level, could historians successfully integrate quantified statistical data and other new forms of evidence with the written sources upon which they have traditionally relied? Such questions have for decades energized the profession of American history, and echoes of these questions will be found in the pages of this set of encyclopedias.

THE OXFORD ENCYCLOPEDIA OF AMERICAN HISTORY: A REFERENCE WORK FOR THE TWENTY-FIRST CENTURY

All these trends—the greater diversity of the profession of American history, historians'

broader understanding of the discipline's scope and available range of sources and methodologies, the greater openness to multicultural and transnational perspectives—have informed the planning and execution of *The Oxford Encyclopedia of American History*. This becomes immediately evident as one looks at the basic structure of the work. The effort to bring organizational and intellectual coherence to such a vast and unwieldy topic has been formidable indeed. We have been reminded more than once of Immanuel Kant's much-quoted observation: "Out of the crooked timber of humanity, no straight thing was ever made." Yet we have given it a try—with, we hope, some success. To make this set of encyclopedias of maximum benefit to its users, we have divided the sprawling, almost boundless field of American history into six topical subcategories, each comprising two volumes and each with its own editor or editors in chief. Here are these six subcategories, with the name of the editor or editors in chief and his or her academic affiliation:

The Oxford Encyclopedia of American Business, Labor, and Economic History
Editor in Chief
Melvyn Dubofsky
Binghamton University, State University of New York

The Oxford Encyclopedia of American Cultural and Intellectual History
Editors in Chief
Joan Shelley Rubin
University of Rochester

Scott E. Casper
University of Nevada, Reno

The Oxford Encyclopedia of American Military and Diplomatic History
Editor in Chief
Timothy J. Lynch
University of Melbourne

The Oxford Encyclopedia of American Political and Legal History
Editors in Chief
Donald T. Critchlow
Arizona State University

Philip R. VanderMeer
Arizona State University

The Oxford Encyclopedia of the History of American Science, Medicine, and Technology
Editor in Chief
Hugh Richard Slotten
University of Otago

The Oxford Encyclopedia of American Political and Legal History
Editor in Chief
Lynn Dumenil
Occidental College

These editors, distinguished scholars all, have been assisted by teams of associate editors, ranging from prominent senior scholars to gifted younger scholars. Through extended discussions, these teams carefully formulated their entry lists to ensure comprehensive coverage of the core topics in their field, supplemented by mid-length and shorter entries on topics of interest. The editors then solicited entries from historians who had relevant expertise. This great project would be impossible without the participation of hundreds of scholars who welcomed the opportunity to offer an account of their work to a broader public, beyond the circle of colleagues who routinely review their books, evaluate their research proposals, and share panels at scholarly meetings. The specialization and compartmentalization of the profession of history can be rewarding, as one exchanges ideas with others who share one's specific interests, but it can also seem confining and a bit

claustrophobic. Participation in a large-scale collaborative project like *The Oxford Encyclopedia of American History* provides an opportunity to move beyond one's professional comfort zone and to share one's research with an interested worldwide readership.

Incorporating the most recent research and interpretive approaches, the entries are designed to be of value to scholars, advanced students, and all those seeking high-level analytic treatment of key topics in American history. The entries include essential facts, of course—names, dates, and so on—but they go further, contextualizing the topic, conveying its human dimensions, suggesting its larger historical significance, and addressing matters of controversy or interpretive disagreement.

Along with matters of content, methodology, and scope, we have given high priority to the entries' organization and style. Historians have long hovered ambivalently between the social sciences and the humanities, unwilling to abandon the social scientists' commitment to methodological rigor, but also determined to retain the humanities' concern for clarity and persuasiveness of presentation. For all the changes since the days of Herodotus and Thucydides—and Edward Gibbon, Voltaire, Francis Parkman, George Bancroft, Henry Adams, and scores of other historians admired for their writing style—historians still take pride in writing lucid, accessible, even elegant prose. They pay attention not only to the information being conveyed, but to the manner in which it is conveyed.

In choosing our contributors, describing their assignments, and editing their entries, therefore, we have emphasized style as well as content. Lewis Mumford once rather cattily observed that reading John Dewey was like riding on the Boston subway: one eventually got to one's destination, but considerably the worse for wear. We have made every effort to ensure that such a criticism will not be leveled against the contributors to this set of encyclopedias. Acquiring historical knowledge should not be the intellectual equivalent of a visit to the dentist.

USING THE ENCYCLOPEDIA

Taken together, the twelve volumes of *The Oxford Encyclopedia of American History* include more than 3,500 entries, arranged in alphabetical order within each two-volume topical set, for ease of research. Composite entries gather together discussions of similar or related topics under one entry title. For example, under the entry "Internal Migration" in *The Oxford Encyclopedia of American Social History*, the reader will find four subentries: "Colonial Era," "Nineteenth-Century Westward," "Twentieth Century and Beyond," and "African Americans." A headnote listing the various subentries introduces each composite entry.

A selective bibliography at the end of each entry directs the reader who wishes to pursue a topic in greater detail to the most important recent scholarly work. Most entries include references at the end that guide interested readers to related entries. Blind entries direct the user from an alternate form of an entry title to the entry itself. For example, the blind entry "Mormon Rebellion" tells the reader to look under "Utah War."

Throughout the planning and execution of this work we have been guided by a single goal: to make the full panorama of American history accessible and understandable to the maximum number of users. We hope that we have succeeded in this purpose.

Finally, the editors would like to extend sincere thanks to the professionals at Oxford University Press who aided immeasurably in the preparation of this work: Grace Labatt, who patiently and cheerfully oversaw the process of selecting the editors in chief; Stephen Wagley, executive editor, who shared his wisdom and experience and saw the project successfully launched; Damon Zucca, editorial director, and Alixandra Gould, senior editor, who aided us in thinking about the emerging world of online reference; and Eric Stannard and Andrew Jung, the development editors, who with unfailing good humor moderated early discussions among the editors over where specific entries should go, dealt with problems as they arose, and gently prodded us to maintain the pace. Our thanks to one and all.

Paul S. Boyer
Merle Curti Professor of History Emeritus
University of Wisconsin–Madison
July 2011

PREFACE

In the mid-twentieth century, an encyclopedia devoted to U.S. social history would have been unthinkable. The term "social history" was not even in common use. By the 1960s, however, scholars in the United States and abroad had begun the transformation that would alter the stuff of history. Rejecting the notion that all that was important about the past were the actions of political and military leaders and the ideas of elite intellectuals, these historians insisted upon the value of the experiences of ordinary people. Often called "history from the bottom up," social history included the study of marginalized people whose voices had been largely missing from the history books and covered a wide span of activities embracing, as William H. Sewell Jr. has put it, "the whole range of ordinary people's life experience: work, child rearing,

disease, recreation, deviant behavior, kinship, sociability, procreation, [and] popular religion" (quoted in Geoff Eley and Keith Nield, *The Future of Class in History: What's Left of the Social?* [Ann Arbor: University of Michigan Press, 2007], p. 40). Social historians looked at individuals in the context of social categories—a rich scholarship emerged on indentured servants, slaves, women, and workers, for example—and explored the ways in which social structures, such as economic organization, technological innovation, legal constructions, and the family, affected them. To do so, the historians consciously drew upon the methods and theories of social scientists, especially sociologists, and this led to increased sophistication in methodology. "Above all," as Paula Fass has argued, "social history provided us with a sharp set of analytic tools, questions about social organization and social function, and a series of defined methods that emphasized systematic research" ("Cultural History/Social History: Some Reflections on a Continuing Dialogue," *Journal of Social History* 37, no. 1 [2003]: 42).

This new approach required an interdisciplinary rethinking not only of who was important in the past, but also of how scholars might uncover these people's lives. Wills and other legal documents laid bare the social structure of colonial life, plantation records revealed much about the lives of both slaves and slaveholders, U.S. Census figures tracked social mobility in particular communities, oral histories shed light on the experiences of Mexican migrant workers, and diaries contained a wealth of insights on the lives of westward-migrating frontier women. Ethnic newspapers, as well as ship registries, uncovered the world of immigrants. Court records of divorce cases revealed the changing nature of middle-class marriage in the early twentieth century. Although much of the new social history relied upon statistics and quantitative methods, its openness to a wide range of subjects and sources made for a rich scholarship of the American experience, broadly conceived.

The drive to examine the social worlds and relationships of marginalized groups was a central motivation of the scholars who produced the new social history. It is not accidental that this field of historical scholarship emerged as the civil rights movement reached its height in the 1960s and as antiwar protest and the counterculture flourished. The women's movement, too, had a powerful influence. As Americans challenged all manner of entrenched hierarchies, many groups, especially racial and ethnic minorities and women, sought to find a so-called usable past through historical inquiry. Social history reflected

that challenge to hierarchy and the desire to uncover the agency of ordinary people as they struggled against the power structures—slavery, corporations, the patriarchal family—that constrained their lives.

Though the turmoil of the 1960s fed the imperative of social history, other factors were also important. U.S. historians were very much indebted to the work of European scholars, especially those associated with the French *Annales* school, which began with the founding in 1929 of the journal *Annales d'histoire économique et sociale* but did not have significant influence in the United States until the editorship from 1957 to 1967 of Fernand Braudel. Braudel's two pathbreaking works, *La Méditerranée et le monde Méditerranéen à l'époque de Philippe II* (1949; English trans., *The Mediterranean and the Mediterranean World in the Age of Philip II*, 1972–1973) and *Civilisation matérielle, économie, et capitalisme, XVe–XVIIIe siècle* (3 vols., 1967–1979; English trans., *Civilization and Capitalism, 15th–18th Century*, 1979), had a profound impact on thinking about broad sources of change, especially in material life, over what was called the *longue durée*, or long term. As Geoff Eley has noted, the richness of Braudel's approach came from its inclusion of such diverse factors as "landscape, climate, demography, deep patterns of economic life, long-run norms and habits, the reproduction of social structures, the stabilities of popular understanding, and the repetitions of everyday life" (*A Crooked Line: From Cultural History to the History of Society* [Ann Arbor: University of Michigan Press, 2005], p. 37).

Equally important were British Marxists, particularly Eric Hobsbawm and E. P. Thompson. Thompson's masterly *The Making of the English Working Class* (1963) had an enormous impact and helped expand labor historians' focus beyond the narrow institutional study of labor unions to the quality of life and leisure of working-class people, as well as their political consciousness. Labor history was perhaps the most significant of early social-history writings in the United States, a fact that underscores the centrality of social class and the lives of working people to the project of writing American social history.

By the late 1980s, social history had significantly permeated the scholarship and teaching of American history. According to Joyce Appleby, Lynn Hunt, and Margaret Jacob, in twenty years, between 1958 and 1978, the number of doctoral dissertations in social history increased fourfold and outpaced those of political history (*Telling the Truth about History* [New York: W. W. Norton and Company, 1994], p. 147). U.S. survey texts supplemented traditional narrative with the stories of workers, women, African Americans, and immigrants, among others. In the 1980s and 1990s, however, even as it rose to prominence, social history was challenged by another emerging historical approach, the new cultural history. Influenced by postmodernism and particularly by the work of Michel Foucault, some cultural historians challenged the social groupings that social historians had embraced: these cultural historians argued that all such categories were social constructs and that social historians had not sufficiently analyzed the ways in which many of the sources they used were created. This critique promoted heated debate, and in the long run, social history has been enriched by cultural history's attention to textual analysis and the social construction of identity. In particular, social historians have broadened the scope of their inquiry to take into account the broader cultural context, as well as the purposes and meaning of the sources they use. At the same time, social historians have been influenced by the argument that politics, and particularly the power of the state, are important to understanding social experience; the drive to

"bring the state back in," as it were, has led to valuable studies that combine social and political history. The result has been a richer framework for social history, one in which other historical approaches and topics are embraced. This increased fluidity among fields in history is reflected in the entries presented in *The Oxford Encyclopedia of American Social History*.

This encyclopedia's entries are organized alphabetically, but its framework is based on a number of conceptual categories that the editors felt would best represent the main contemporary directions in social history. (For these categories, see the Topical Outline at the end of volume 2.) Although critics of social history in its early phases complained that the attention to specific groups or individual communities led to a fragmented sense of the past, many social historians have situated their work in a larger context. Reflecting that trend, the encyclopedia includes sixteen major entries on chronological periods, from "Exploration, Conquest, and Settlement in North America" to "Modern America (1980 to Present)." These entries offer a long view of social change and its relationship to the political and economic developments of specific periods, with attention to the impact on various groups of Americans.

The category "Places" includes both entries about regions, such as the entries "Southwest, The" and "New England," and entries about major cities. "Place" is a particularly apt category for this encyclopedia, because social historians have generally paid careful attention to the specificity of locale for shaping human experiences. The complex interplay among politics, climate, location, economic infrastructure, and class and racial composition inform these entries on pivotal places and regions in American history.

Population movement and organization are together another valuable entryway into social history. Major entries in the category "Settlement and Migration" run the gamut from "Rural Life and Society" and "Cities and Suburbs" to "Immigration" and "Internal Migration." The entries on rural areas and cities analyze transformations in American life as the nation became more urban and as class and racial divides began to define the modern city. The entries assess the factors that shaped Americans' lives: technological factors such as railways, elevators, electric lights, mechanized farm equipment, and automobiles, as well as political and economic factors. The entries on immigration and migration, which center on issues of race, ethnicity, and class, explore fundamental aspects of the American experience and address the wide range of factors that encouraged people to immigrate to the United States or to move within the nation's boundaries. The composite entry "Internal Migration" encompasses both the westward movement of settlers and farmers in the eighteenth and nineteenth centuries and the so-called Great Migration of African Americans in the first half of the twentieth century, whereby millions of black southerners moved to the cities of the North and, later, the West. Supporting entries on these topics include "Native American Removal," about a corollary of westward expansion; "Borderlands," about the contested and fluid nature of frontier areas in the American past; "Chinatowns," about both the reality of life in these urban ethnic enclaves and the power of anti-Asian stereotypes to construct a specific exotic imagery of them; and "Sunbelt," about a post–World War II concept that reflects both the rising political power of the Sunbelt region and the economic transformations brought about by the decline of older manufacturing regions and the rise of those relying on service, technology, and defense industries.

Because social history has focused extensively on the diversity of the American people, the encyclopedia also includes entries on prominent American ethnic and racial groups, including a major entry on Native Americans that spans the long history of this diverse group of peoples. Entries about particular ethnic groups address the construction of ethnicity, as well as the particular characteristics and historical experience of such diverse groups as German Americans, Puerto Rican Americans, Chinese Americans, Mexican Americans, Hmong Americans, and—reflecting important recent trends—multiracial and multiethnic Americans. Also included are an entry addressing the broad topic of race and ethnicity and an entry on the more recent phenomenon of transnational identity.

Social history's contribution both to our understanding of slavery and emancipation and also to the inclusion of these topics in the grand narrative of American history has been significant—perhaps more significant than its contribution to any other topic. The encyclopedia's entries reflect the current understanding of slavery as a dynamic system of labor that underwent constant change and that also varied tremendously across geographic space. Entries address topics like diet, childbirth, family life, and health, always with attention to regional variation and historical development. Scholars also have recognized that multiple slave trades existed to and within North America. The composite entry "Slave Trades," covering the Native American slave trade, the transatlantic slave trade, the internal slave trade, and the illegal slave trade, reflects the current understanding that slavery was embedded in larger national, regional, and world economies, rather than being a singular, exceptional aberration confined to certain, distinctive regions. Current scholarship also emphasizes how, despite severe constraints, enslaved persons constantly strove to negotiate the terms of their lives and labor. Entries on slave resistance and runaways, as well as the entries covering significant individuals and groups, cast light on the many ways slaves contested their situation. Entries on black soldiers, freedmen and freedwomen, and others illustrate that emancipation was the culmination of a broad social movement that was carried forward by the actions of ordinary men and women.

The history of work and workers has also been an integral part of social-history scholarship. The major entry "Work" not only traces the transformation of work through time, but reflects the extraordinary diversity in types of work and types of workers— from child laborers to factory laborers, from domestic servants to white-collar clerks. A related entry, "Working-Class Life and Society," addresses communities of workers in the context of class, ethnicity, race, and family. Social historians' shattering of the image of workers as being primarily white and male and their exploration of the importance of gender to understanding the work experience of Americans are also evident in several entries, most notably "Women Workers." Paralleling the study of work has been that of leisure, which has given social historians an avenue for offering a broader accounting of workers' lives and experiences. Social historians recognized that the organization of labor, be it blue collar or white collar, created defined times for leisure. The major entry "Leisure," as well as the entries on sports, film, Disney amusement parks, and vaudeville, among others, reflects scholars' interest in how leisure time became not only central to Americans' lives, but heavily commercialized as well.

Though often downplayed by earlier historians, social unrest has been a constant of American history. The category "Social Order and Disorder" addresses this history by exploring efforts to challenge the social order, whether from below or from above, or to shore it up. Many varied phenomena—from the heterogeneity of the American population

to war to natural disasters and much more— have revealed or resulted from fissures in American society. These entries examine clashes as diverse as food riots, race riots, and the Stonewall riots that sparked the gay liberation movement, along with the underlying factors and motivations, often unacknowledged at the time, that shaped them. They also examine the efforts by varied groups of Americans to maintain social order. Entries on eleemosynary institutions such as philanthropic organizations and on topics such as mental health probe the economic, social, and cultural developments that led Americans to seek to understand and address problems in particular ways at particular times. The entries "Health and Healing, Eighteenth and Nineteenth Centuries" and "Medicine, Popular and Non-Western," meanwhile, delve into how people have taken care of themselves and tried to make sense of their suffering.

Closely related to the category "Social Order and Disorder" is the category "Movements and Social Reform." Although they exhibit social historians' emphasis on human agency, these entries also reflect the fluidity of the division between social and political history. Entries on such diverse topics as the civil rights movement, feminism, the woman suffrage movement, Prohibition, antislavery, the Ku Klux Klan, the antilynching movement, the modern conservative movement, counterculture, and the consumer movement stress the social forces that underlay these movements and evaluate their impact on diverse groups of Americans. The entry "Mexican American Civil Rights Movement," for example, traces the history of Mexican immigrants' experience of discrimination and the significance of labor unions, middle-class activism, World War II, and the social ferment of the 1960s for the development of organizations such as the League of United Latin American Citizens (1929) and the Raza

Unida Party (1969). The "Antebellum Reform" entry, which covers a wide range of interconnected reform movements including those addressing education, labor, prisons, temperance, abolition, and women's rights, explores the efforts of men and women to bring about change in the context of vast economic and political changes. Entries on key individual reformers, such as Lucretia Mott, William Lloyd Garrison, Frances Perkins, Ida B. Wells-Barnett, Rosa Parks, and Martin Luther King Jr., form another part of the encyclopedia's focus on social movements.

Perhaps no area of social history has received more attention from historians than that of religious movements. Indeed, the history of religion and religious movements, such as revivals, along with their impact on social organization and class relations, was among the early topics explored by social historians. The major entry "Religion" spans America's religious history from the pre-Columbian era onward and reflects current directions in American historiography by attending both to areas of the French and Spanish empires that became part of the United States and to Native American spirituality past and present. Assessing such topics as utopian hopes, church organization, westward migration, African American Christianity, and the impact of immigration on religion, the entry explores how religious pluralism has always been a source of social and political contestation in America. Additional entries include "Women and Religious Institutions," which highlights the role of women as leaders in American society and culture even when they did not hold formal power, and "Clergy," which traces the nature of clerical authority through upheavals in American life such as the Great Awakening and the civil rights movement.

The category "Women, Men, and Family" has at its center the major entry "Family," which builds upon an extraordinarily rich scholarly literature to examine both changes in the family through time and also the diversity in family formation, from Native Americans to slaves and from white middle-class Victorians to same-sex couples. Specialized entries such as "Marriage and Divorce," "Adoption," and "Adolescence" further explore the family in American life. Other entries address sexuality and reproduction, the social construction of gender, and gay, lesbian, and transgendered communities.

Another theme central to social history—one of the encyclopedia's categories and the title of one of its articles—is "Everyday Life." The major entry in this category explores so-called landscapes of everyday experience, from colonial houses to modern technology. It weaves together discussions of sanitation, time, the body, electric light, sound, clothing, and the household to offer a complex understanding of the ways in which daily life has changed and the forces underlying these changes. Additional entries such as "Housing, Public," "Automobiles," "Guns," and "Coffeehouses and Coffee" further enhance an understanding of the contours of Americans' everyday life. Another way of understanding daily life is to examine the organizations that give shape to individuals' social and political activity. Entries in the category "Organizations" run the gamut of voluntary associations, including those that promote visions of patriotism, such as the United Daughters of the Confederacy or the American Legion; those that focus on ethnic or religious identity, such as the Knights of Columbus or B'nai B'rith; and those that have charitable or religious aims, such as the Salvation Army or the Society for the Propagation of the Gospel in Foreign Parts. Also included are extensive entries on organizations that have served political ends, such as the National Rifle Association, the National

Association for the Advancement of Colored People, or the National Organization for Women. All these entries focus less on an institutional history per se and more on the ways in which people used these organizations to further their goals and interests.

In short, the entries gathered in these volumes, written by leading scholars in the field, offer the most comprehensive survey available anywhere of the full spectrum of American social history in all its rich diversity, interpreted from the most sophisticated contemporary analytical and theoretical perspectives.

The encyclopedia is addressed to users— whether general readers, college and high school students, or scholars—seeking information, definitions, ideas for research papers, an overview of recent scholarship, or an introduction to the many aspects of social history.

There are some 450 entries in *The Oxford Encyclopedia of American Social History*, arranged in alphabetical order letter by letter. Composite entries gather together discussions of similar or related topics under one entry title. For example, under the entry "Internal Migration" the reader will find four subentries: "Colonial Era," "Nineteenth-Century Westward," "Twentieth Century and Beyond," and "African Americans." A headnote listing the various subentries introduces each composite entry.

The contributors have sought to write in clear language with a minimum of technical vocabulary. The entries give important terms and titles in their original languages, with English translations when needed. A selective bibliography at the end of each entry directs the reader who wishes to pursue a topic in greater detail to the most important recent scholarly work.

To guide readers from one entry to related discussions elsewhere in the encyclopedia, cross-references appear at the end of entries. Blind entries direct the user from an alternate form of an entry title to the entry itself. For example, the blind entry "Bars" tells the reader to look under "Taverns and Bars." Readers interested in finding all the entries on a particular subject, such as everyday life or religion, may consult the Topical Outline at the end of volume 2. A comprehensive index at the end of volume 2 lists all the topics covered in the encyclopedia, including those that are not entry titles themselves. Also at the end of volume 2 is a directory listing the encyclopedia's contributors.

I would like to thank my two associate editors, Matthew Warner Osborn and Amanda B. Moniz, for their valuable help on the project. They not only helped conceptualize the themes of the encyclopedia, but wrote entry descriptions, identified potential contributors, and edited entries. They also helped develop this preface. Many colleagues and friends—indeed, too many to list here— offered their assistance in identifying contributors and fine-tuning entry descriptions. Series editor Paul Boyer has offered exceptionally insightful assistance along the way and development editor Eric Stannard was a model of efficiency and patience. The contributors themselves are a remarkable group of scholars, and they were extraordinarily patient with requests for revisions and produced outstanding work that is both accessible to a wide range of readers and sophisticated in its analysis.

Lynn Dumenil

COMMON ABBREVIATIONS USED IN THIS WORK

b.	born		**l.**	line (plural, ll.)
BCE	before the Common Era (= BC)		**n.**	note
c.	*circa*, that is, about, approximately		**n.d.**	no date
CE	Common Era (= AD)		**no.**	number
cf	*confer*, that is, compare		**n.p.**	no place
d.	died		**p.**	page (plural, pp.)
diss.	dissertation		**rev.**	revised
ed.	editor (plural, eds.), edition		**ser.**	series
f.	and following (plural, ff.)		**vol.**	volume (plural, vols.)
fl.	*floruit*, that is, flourished			

THE OXFORD ENCYCLOPEDIA OF
AMERICAN SOCIAL HISTORY

A

ABORTION

The legal status of abortion in the United States has undergone dramatic shifts, while its practice has been consistent. Throughout American history, many women have relied on abortion to manage their reproductive lives to their own ends. Before the mid-nineteenth century, abortion prior to quickening (the moment when the pregnant woman feels fetal movement) was a legal and accepted practice, especially for young, unmarried women. By midcentury the commercialization of abortion gave greater visibility to its prevalence among married, white, native-born women. This increased visibility coincided with growing agitation by women for inclusion in public life and with increased immigration of ethnically diverse people, both of which provoked concern about the nation's changing character. Thus when physicians pursued the criminalization of abortion in an effort to stabilize their professional standing in contrast to midwives, their proposals resonated with legislators' gender, ethnic, and nationalist fears. In the twenty years between 1860 and 1880, with little public debate, every state made abortion illegal, except when performed by a licensed physician to save the life of the pregnant woman. In this same period, federal and state laws also prohibited the distribution of contraceptive information and devices.

During the one hundred years when abortion was illegal, women continued to procure abortion despite the risks, and the practice maintained a degree of public acceptance. During the Depression of the 1930s, abortion providers operated more openly, contributing to an estimated eight hundred thousand abortions a year. The procedure was still quite risky. Induced abortions accounted for 14 percent of maternal mortality. After World War II, hospitals tightened their rules for therapeutic abortion, leading to a dramatic reduction in hospital abortions. Police raids on the independent clinics that had thrived in the 1930s made abortion even more difficult and dangerous to obtain. Abortion deaths doubled between 1951 and 1962, with the risk falling most heavily on women of color: these women were four times more likely than white women to die from abortion.

Political challenges to abortion restrictions were rare before the 1960s. The birth control movement led by Margaret Sanger did not contest abortion restrictions, instead pointing to injury and death from criminal abortion as a compelling reason to decriminalize contraceptive information and devices. As repression of abortion increased through the 1950s and deaths from criminal and self-induced abortion rose, however, physicians and women began to seek reform of abortion laws. The resurgent women's movement, argued that the fundamental right of women to control their bodily processes included the decision to terminate a pregnancy. By 1973, through legislative and court actions, the abortion reform/repeal movement won changes in nineteen state laws.

This activism culminated in the 1973 Supreme Court landmark decision, *Roe v. Wade*. Based on the 1965 Court decision, *Griswold v. Connecticut*, which had established the right to privacy in contraceptive decision-making, *Roe* established a fundamental right to abortion. Except to ensure maternal health, the Court held, states could not restrict abortion before fetal viability, the point in pregnancy when the fetus is "capable of meaningful life outside the womb" (roughly the end of the second trimester). After *Roe*, maternal mortality rates dropped by nearly half.

Efforts to overturn *Roe* began almost immediately. Small groups opposed to abortion reform blossomed into the "pro-life" movement, arguing that abortion violated the fetus's right to life. Initially led by the American Roman Catholic Church, the movement expanded as social conservatives and Protestant fundamentalists took up the issue. Early efforts by the pro-life movement included the 1976 Hyde Amendment that banned federal funding of abortion, as well as various state laws that required teenagers to secure parental consent. Organized campaigns to disrupt abortion services also emerged, the goal of which was to make abortion difficult, if not impossible, to obtain. Since 1977 violence against abortion clinics and providers has included 8 murders, 17 attempted murders, 6,100 reported acts of violence (bombings, arson, death threats, and assaults), and more than 100,000 disruptions of services. Overt violence declined after passage of the Freedom of Access to Clinic Entrances Act (FACE) in 1994. However, campaigns of intimidation directed at abortion providers continue, including protests at their homes and publication on websites of their personal information. Abortion opponents have also intensified efforts to dissuade women from seeking abortion. In addition to the long-standing use of images and rhetoric that personify the fetus and depict abortion procedures as horrific, opponents have begun to claim that abortion is bad for women themselves. Since the late 1990s, false claims that abortion damages future fertility, causes an increased risk of cancer, and leads to depression (the so-called post-abortion syndrome) have been widespread. Although debunked by national medical authorities, such claims have influenced public perceptions of abortion risk.

In 1992 and 2007, the Supreme Court retreated somewhat from its holding in *Roe*. In the 1992 *Planned Parenthood of Southeastern Pennsylvania v. Casey* decision, which upheld various Pennsylvania abortion regulations including mandatory waiting periods and state-mandated counseling, the Court ruled that the state's interest in protecting potential life permitted some restrictions on abortion throughout pregnancy, so long as the restrictions did not impose an undue burden on women. Although the decision reaffirmed women's right to abortion as a matter of individual liberty (the freedom from unwarranted government intrusion), it no longer described abortion as a fundamental right, and the lower standard of "undue burden" gave greater leeway to limit its practice. Since 1992, legislatures have enacted a number of restrictions that limit the timing, reasons, and procedures for performing abortions. In the 2007 *Gonzales v. Carhart* decision, the Court upheld the 2003 federal ban on so-called partial-birth abortion, even though the prohibited procedures were vaguely defined and the law, the Partial-Birth Abortion Ban Act, omitted an exemption to protect women's health. Supporters of abortion rights fear that this decision will lead to even greater restrictions.

For much of the post-*Roe* era, abortion has been a surgical procedure. However, chemically induced abortion, an abortion pill, has become increasingly widespread since its approval by the Food and Drug Administration in 2000. The abortion pill, also known as "RU486," is often confused with emergency contraception, known as the "morning-after pill." The pills were approved and marketed at about the same time, despite organized opposition by abortion opponents. Yet they are distinct. Emergency contraception, marketed as "plan B" and available over the counter since 2005, contains a concentrated dose of the same hormones as the birth control pill and simply prevents pregnancy after intercourse. The abortion pill, sold only to doctors, is an entirely different chemical compound that terminates an existing pregnancy. Introduction of the abortion pill has increased the proportion of early abortions, those before nine weeks of pregnancy, but expectations that it would increase overall access to abortion have not been realized.

Thus despite continued controversy in the twenty-first century, abortion remains legal in the United States. However, practical access to it has been increasingly constrained. In response to harassment, intimidation, and legislative restrictions, many hospitals and practitioners have stopped providing abortions. An estimated 87 percent of U.S. counties and 97 percent of nonmetropolitan areas have no abortion provider. As in the past, young women and women of limited income —who have less access to health care and birth control in general—bear the greatest burden of abortion restrictions.

[*See also* **Antiabortion Movement; Birth Control and Family Planning; Hospitals and Dispensaries; Infanticide; Law and Society; Planned Parenthood; Pregnancy; Rape;** *and* **Reproductive Rights Movement.**]

BIBLIOGRAPHY

"Abortion." MedlinePlus. U.S. National Library of Medicine, National Institutes of Health. http://www.nlm.nih.gov/medlineplus/abortion.html.

Brodie, Janet Farrell. *Contraception and Abortion in Nineteenth-Century America.* Ithaca, N.Y.: Cornell University Press, 1994.

Garrow, David J. *Liberty and Sexuality: The Right to Privacy and the Making of "Roe v. Wade."* New York: Macmillan, 1994.

Gordon, Linda. *The Moral Property of Women: A History of Birth Control Politics in America.* 3rd ed. Urbana: University of Illinois Press, 2002.

Mohr, James C. *Abortion in America: The Origin and Evolution of National Policy, 1800–1900.* New York: Oxford University Press, 1978.

Reagan, Leslie J. *When Abortion Was a Crime: Women, Medicine, and Law in the United States, 1867–1973.* Berkeley: University of California Press, 1997.

Carole R. McCann

ACADIANS

See Cajun (Acadian) Americans.

ADDAMS, JANE

(1860–1935), Progressive Era political activist. Jane Addams was one of the nation's most admired and effective Progressive political activists; she fought for social justice for more than four decades. Engaged in many social movements and the author of ten books, including *Twenty Years at Hull-House* (1910), Addams was the first American woman to receive the Nobel Peace Prize.

She came to her interest in politics through her father, a wealthy agricultural businessman, abolitionist, and Illinois state senator. Her mother, Sarah Weber Addams, a woman beloved for her neighborly kindness in their small town of Cedarville, died when Jane, the youngest of four surviving siblings, was two years old.

Although expected to devote herself to family and local charity as her mother had done, Jane Addams possessed a fierce ambition to become a person of accomplishment. She was one of the first generation of women to earn a college degree and used the money she inherited after her father's death to cofound the nation's first settlement house, Hull-House, in Chicago, in 1889 with her friend Ellen Gates Starr. The settlement was mostly modeled on the world's first, the all-male Toynbee Hall in London. Prosperous single women, seeking ways to live independently, were drawn to Hull-House to live (they were called "residents") or to volunteer. Men, too, volunteered from the beginning; when the first male resident arrived in 1891, Hull-House became the world's first coed settlement house.

The settlement was conceived as a center for social and educational activities for working people in their predominantly immigrant, industrial neighborhood and as a place where prosperous women and men could learn about the obstacles that working people faced. Some historians, mindful of the traditional reason such women had contact with the poor, have thought that the settlement's original purpose was charity—that is, to assuage physical suffering of those in poverty—but as Addams's and Starr's correspondence shows, they always had broader goals in mind.

Addams's childhood interest in politics resurfaced as she gained a sense of solidarity with working people. She was drawn into political reform in 1893 by the activism of women's labor union leaders, including Mary Kenney O'Sullivan, women's club leaders in the city, and her good friend and Hull-House resident Florence Kelley, a social reformer from Philadelphia. In time Addams became a leading spokesperson for the view that upper-middle-class people should be the political allies of working people and advocate for their issues. Over the years Addams pushed to end child labor and supported widows' pensions (the precursor to Social Security), unemployment insurance, the minimum wage, labor organizing rights, affordable housing, special courts for juveniles, and freedom of speech. Between 1911 and 1914 she was a leader of the women's suffrage movement for the same reason: to support working women's efforts to gain the vote.

Addams recognized the evil of racism as early as 1892, when she condemned the social segregation imposed on African Americans, and the next year Hull-House became the first settlement house in a white neighborhood to have an African American resident. Although Addams has been rightly criticized for failing to acknowledge that the rape charges often invoked by white men to justify lynching African Americans were false, she spoke out against lynching at the invitation of her fellow Chicagoan Ida B. Wells-Barnett, invited W. E. B. Du Bois to speak at Hull-House, and was a cofounder of the National Association for the Advancement of Colored People (NAACP) in 1909. As African Americans moved in greater numbers to Chicago and the Hull-House neighborhood after World War I, they were welcomed at the settlement house. When she was seventy, Addams called the problem of race "the gravest situation in American life," and she warned, "[T]o continually suspect, suppress or fear any large group in a community must finally result in a loss of enthusiasm for [democracy]" (Jane, Addams, *The Second Twenty Years at Hull-House* [New York: Macmillan, 1930], p. 401).

Addams worked through local, state, and national groups to achieve the social reforms that she thought so necessary. She was a member of the National Child Labor Committee, a cofounder and board member of the Women's Trade Union League, a member of the Chicago Board of Education, a vice president of the Illinois Equal Suffrage Association, a vice president of the National American Woman Suffrage Association, the first woman president of the National Conference of Charities and Correction (now the National Conference of Social Welfare), a founding board member of the NAACP and the American Civil Liberties Union, and a member of the executive committee of the Progressive Party's national committee. The highpoint of her involvement in organized politics occurred in 1912 when she seconded the nomination of Theodore Roosevelt for U.S. president at the Progressive Party Convention and then campaigned for him in the midwestern states, although she herself could not vote. Her embrace of partisanship shocked those—and they were many—who thought women should be nonpartisan. If Roosevelt had been elected, he was planning to name her to his cabinet.

Addams joined the small and struggling Chicago Peace Society in 1893, and across the remaining decades of her life she came to devote more and more of her energies to the peace movement. Initially she was drawn to the movement because of her belief in nonresistance, or the power of moral force, a belief inspired less by her father's mildly Quaker leanings than by her reading of Leo Tolstoy's Christian writings. It was some years before she grasped the political implications of her philosophy of nonresistance. She took her first public stance against war in a speech about the settlement movement in December 1898, a few months after the United States had fought and won the short Spanish-American War over Cuba.

In opposing World War I, Addams argued that pacifists were patriots, too, and that there had to be a better way to resolve international disputes than for governments to force the people of the earth to kill each other. In 1915 she cofounded both the Woman's Peace Party in the United States, whose agenda was peace and women's rights, and the

Women's International League for Peace and Freedom (as it was eventually called), which was based in Geneva, Switzerland. She served as the league's president until a few years before her death. Addams was the first American woman and the second woman in the world to receive the Nobel Peace Prize, in 1931. Addams's commitment as a political activist, her skill as a cooperator, her unflagging persistence despite many setbacks, and her wisdom as a social critic and visionary made her an effective fighter for social justice and the most accomplished political woman of her era.

[*See also* Anti-child-labor Movement; Charity Organization Movement; Feminist Reforms in the Progressive Era, Maternal; Social Work; War Resisters; Woman Suffrage Movement; *and* Working-Class Life and Society.]

BIBLIOGRAPHY

Elshtain, Jean Bethke, ed. *The Jane Addams Reader*. New York: Basic Books, 2002. A useful selection of Addams's writings, some of them chapters from her books.

Fischer, Marilyn, Carol Nackenoff, and Wendy Chmielewski, eds. *Jane Addams and the Practice of Democracy*. Urbana: University of Illinois Press, 2009. A diverse selection of essays by leading Addams scholars from several disciplines.

Knight, Louise W. *Citizen: Jane Addams and the Struggle for Democracy*. Chicago: University of Chicago Press, 2005. An in-depth examination of Addams's formative years, with an extensive bibliography and an afterword on the history of Addams scholarship.

Knight, Louise W. *Jane Addams: Spirit in Action*. New York: W. W. Norton and Company, 2010. The first biography of Addams's full life in thirty-seven years, it includes a short essay on further reading about Addams.

Louise W. Knight

ADOLESCENCE

The modern concept of "adolescence"—the word comes from the Latin *adolescere*, meaning "to grow up"—dates back to an early twentieth-century American psychologist, G. Stanley Hall. Though historians in the 1960s affirmed the early twentieth-century origins of adolescence, later scholarship established that youth in premodern Europe and colonial New England engaged in age-specific cultural practices. Subsequent research on the history of youth demonstrates that adolescence has long been recognized as a developmental phase and, moreover, that adolescence is neither unchanging nor uniform. Historical forces, developmental factors, and the agency of youth have varied the boundaries of adolescence, the experiences of adolescents, and the nature of youth cultures in the United States.

Early America. Early America was characterized by a diversity of adolescent experiences. For millennia, young Native American males underwent vision quests and other rites of passage on their way to adulthood. Though first menstruation—which usually occurred between the ages of twelve and seventeen—marked girls' entry into womanhood, Native American female adolescents often exercised social power as Pocahontas did. Not long after she famously saved the life of a settler, a migration of youthful indentured servants, most of them between the ages of fifteen and twenty-four, displaced the indigenous population. Yet tobacco planters hindered the freedom of English males unable to marry and heightened the risks for females, who experienced high rates of out-of-wedlock pregnancies. By the end of the seventeenth century, the enslavement of brutalized young African males replaced the servitude of abused immigrant youth.

In seventeenth-century New England, Puritan youth by age fourteen were no longer seen as children but were not yet regarded as adults. In order to diminish generational tensions within patriarchal families, adolescents lived with neighbors, who taught them gender-appropriate skills and reinforced religious precepts. Yet "placing out," church organizations, apprenticeships, and controlled courtships failed to contain youthful resistance to religious expectations and Puritan conventions. The diminishing of property inheritances that had prolonged dependence well into adulthood eventually enabled male youth to defy their fathers and migrate to other regions in search of opportunity. The flight of bachelors heightened insecurity among home-bound adolescent girls, who experienced intense anxiety—widely interpreted as witchcraft possession among New Englanders troubled by the rapidly changing social order.

Adolescents constituted more than half the population in the eighteenth century, a time when the rise of the African American family, the decline of the patriarchal family, geographic mobility, a market economy, and the Enlightenment all contributed to the autonomy of adolescents. Although at adolescence they were forced to begin work in the fields, African American youth found ways to manage their enslavement. In New England, as romantic love replaced property exchange as a basis for marriage, rates of premarital pregnancy rose, and sisters married out of birth order. Responding to new opportunities for learning, labor, and liberty, college students and apprentices migrated to commercializing cities, where they participated in recreational, religious, and revolutionary activities. Politicized "daughters of liberty" boycotted British goods, staged spinning bees, sewed homespun, and served as cooks and spies.

Nineteenth Century. In antebellum America, industrialization, urbanization, republican ideals, and gender ideology influenced adolescents' experiences and adults' understandings of youth. The decline of apprenticeship led native-born migrant and European immigrant males to flout moral conventions and adult authority. Middle-class sons challenged parents and teachers for prolonging their dependence and expecting deference. Although some boys complied with adults who sought to control them by establishing reform associations, expanding education, and promoting mothers' moral authority, others resisted.

Feminine ideals such as domesticity, piety, purity, and submission influenced the experiences and limited the expectations of middle-class girls, for whom teaching typically preceded marriage. Farmers' daughters strapped for cash found employment in New England textile mills, and immigrant and working-class adolescents labored as domestics, as pieceworkers, and in casual prostitution. Working girls who donned flashy clothing, lived in boardinghouses, and enjoyed urban recreations disregarded daughterly obligations and shunned prevailing notions of feminine decorum. Enslaved African American girls forced into more demanding work roles at adolescence also faced their greatest sexual dangers at that time. Slave girls were widely perceived as licentious, and the innocence of the archetypal adolescent "southern belle" served to deflect attention from white males' sexual abuse of enslaved female adolescents.

The expansion of high schools after the Civil War laid the foundation for "young ladies" to develop modern identities as "girls," although Indian boarding schools imposed strict domestic standards on Native Americans. Apprehensions about the sexual dangers facing girls—whose age of menarche dropped to fifteen years old—stirred adults to publish advice books, establish sex-segregated organizations such as the Young Women's Christian Association, and raise the age of consent. The rapid social transformations of the late nineteenth century that also accelerated the assertions of adolescent males exacerbated the anxieties of adults, who in response provided boys with character building and physical training at the Young Men's Christian Association and other sex-segregated organizations.

Widespread unease about commercial amusements, labor exploitation, sexual immorality, and a heterosocial subculture fashioned by immigrant and working-class youth prompted turn-of-the-century reformers to establish educational, scouting, and athletic organizations. Following the publication in 1904 of G. Stanley Hall's influential study *Adolescence: Its Psychology and Its Relations to Physiology, Anthropology, Sociology, Sex, Crime, Religion, and Education*, school attendance soared to include half of all American youth by the late 1920s. Instead of protecting students from the temptations that might activate their "storm and stress," however, high school homogeneity spread modern beliefs and behaviors across lines of class, gender, race, ethnicity, and region. During the 1920s, adults struggled to contain what was labeled "the girl problem," the consumer-based youth culture that redefined female adolescence. Attempts to control the so-called youth crisis failed to end the sharing of innovative teen principles, social rituals, and the commodities that reinforced group identity among Depression-era adolescents, the majority of whom attended high school by the late 1930s.

"Teenagers."   During the 1940s, military service, a war economy, and limited parental surveillance stoked adolescents' assertions of personal freedom and forged their identity as "teenagers." Among the many adolescents who entered the military were those who found a supportive gay community. Leaving internment camps for employment and education freed Japanese American girls from the rigid patriarchal structure of traditional family life. American girls' more brassy behaviors provoked a moral panic among adults anxious about elevated rates of "juvenile delinquency." Latino and African American working-class youth who claimed a distinct generational and ethnic identity by wearing transgressive "zoot suits" met violent resistance, as in Los Angeles in 1943.

In the 1950s, efforts to halt the spread of juvenile delinquency intensified. Despite pressures from above, teenagers with more time and more money fueled the market for goods and gadgets. Rock and roll, inspired by rhythm and blues, voiced the desires and concerns of most teenagers, while defining works such as J. D. Salinger's novel *Catcher in the Rye* (1951) and the film *Rebel without a Cause* (1955) expressed the angst, confusion, and alienation of white male adolescents. Though the vast majority of young people went steady and married in their late teens, novels such as Vladimir Nabokov's *Lolita* (1955) and *Spring Fire* (1952), written by Marijane Meaker under the pseudonym Vin Packer, provoked changing presumptions about female adolescent sexuality and sexual orientation. Debuting in 1959, the sexually provocative Barbie doll personified the shift from the postwar consumer-driven "teen" to the emergent freedom-seeking young "woman."

Later Twentieth Century.   The millions of baby boomers who came of age in the 1960s transformed a vast commercial "teen culture" into a culturally rebellious "youth culture," especially following the U.S. tour of the Beatles in 1964. Increasingly critical of cultural conventions, a repressive sexual system, racism, sexism, classism, homophobia, and the war in Vietnam, young people created a vibrant and varied counterculture that valued autonomy, egalitarianism, and individuality. Building on the activism of African American teens during the 1950s, students organized political protests and built mass movements for social change, from civil rights to Black Power, from antiwar to the New Left, and from gay rights to the American Indian Movement (AIM) and the women's movement.

During the 1970s, feminists actively pursued an agenda that influenced notions of female adolescence and impacted girls' lives. The passage of Title IX of the Education Amendments of 1972 (amending the Civil Rights Act of 1964) banned discrimination of girls in schools and athletics. In key decisions that broadened girls' access to sex education, birth control, and abortion, the Supreme Court validated girls' sexual identity—indeed, 76 percent of girls were sexually active by age seventeen—and reproductive autonomy. A backlash against rising rates of pregnancy among white teens, however, led conservatives troubled by an alleged epidemic of teenage pregnancy to alter policies, slash programs, and, by the 1980s, stigmatize so-called welfare queens.

Simultaneous with the rise of a "girl crisis" discourse generated by feminist academics in the 1980s, adolescent girls with a new sense of agency reinvented girls' culture. Many pioneers of "punk" created new musical paradigms and professional roles for young women in the music industry. As the music flowed from the cultural margins to the mainstream, Madonna appropriated punk girls' antifeminine fashions and antipatriarchal lyrics and gave voice to ordinary girls' claims to independence. "Empowerment" became a

defining feature of American girlhood thanks to (1) the influence of the underground feminist "riot grrrl" movement, which challenged the gender domination of boys' musical subculture, (2) the rise of Third Wave feminism, which focused attention on the victimization of girls, and (3) the emergence of the "girl power" ethos. The marketing of a globalized culture of teen girls' and the declining age of menstruation (to slightly less than thirteen years old) further blurred the borders among teens, "girls" in their twenties, and the new consumer niche of preadolescent "tweens."

Though the accelerated sexualization of younger girls heightened the concerns of social conservatives and feminists alike, it was males who became the focus of an intense discourse on adolescence at the end of the century. Following a series of school shootings that culminated in those at the high school in Columbine, Colorado, in 1999, experts condemned the culture of boyhood—for instance, hypermasculine rap and rock and roll, violent video games—and the proliferation of cliques, from jocks to geeks, controlled by male bullies.

The variety of youthful experiences, individual identities, and subcultures in the new millennium reveal that adolescence continues to be a dynamic social category and not a static developmental stage. An array of forces—from the economy to electronics, from divorce to drugs, from race to religion, from gender to gangs—have affected adolescence by accelerating the transition to adulthood for some and by delaying development for others. Decreasing college attendance among males, the waning importance of marriage, and soaring unemployment among youth, especially minority males, have all contributed to the emergence of the postadolescent "boomerang kid" and the reframing of adolescence in the twenty-first century.

[*See also* Counterculture; Courtship and Dating; Family; Juvenile Delinquency; Life Stages; Music, *subentry on* Popular Music; Pregnancy; Scouting; Sex Education; Sexual Reform and Morality; *and* YMCA and YWCA.]

BIBLIOGRAPHY

Austin, Joe, and Michael Nevin Willard, eds. *Generations of Youth: Youth Cultures and History in Twentieth-Century America*. New York: New York University Press, 1998.

Cahn, Susan K. *Sexual Reckonings: Southern Girls in a Troubling Age*. Cambridge, Mass.: Harvard University Press, 2007.

Hall, G. Stanley. *Adolescence: Its Psychology and Its Relations to Physiology, Anthropology, Sociology, Sex, Crime, Religion, and Education*. New York: Appleton, 1904.

Hunter, Jane H. *How Young Ladies Became Girls: The Victorian Origins of American Girlhood*. New Haven, Conn.: Yale University Press, 2002.

Kett, Joseph F. *Rites of Passage: Adolescence in America, 1790 to the Present*. New York: Basic Books, 1977.

Mintz, Steven. *Huck's Raft: A History of American Childhood*. Cambridge, Mass.: Belknap Press of Harvard University Press, 2004.

Schrum, Kelly. *Some Wore Bobby Sox: The Emergence of Teenage Girls' Culture, 1920–1945*. New York: Palgrave Macmillan, 2004.

Thompson, Roger. *Sex in Middlesex: Popular Mores in a Massachusetts County, 1649–1699*. Amherst: University of Massachusetts Press, 1986.

Miriam Forman-Brunell

ADOPTION

Since ancient times and in all human cultures, children have been transferred from adults who would not or could not be parents to adults who wanted them for love, labor, and property. Adoption's close association with humanitarianism, upward mobility, and infertility is, however, modern and, some contend, uniquely American. An especially prominent and historically unprecedented feature of recent adoption history has been matching: the set of social practices that aimed to substitute one family for another so carefully, systematically, and completely that natal kinship was rendered invisible and irrelevant.

During the early history of the United States, no adoption laws existed. People with means used wills and indentures to forge legal ties with children born to others, typically for the purpose of inheritance. But most adoptions during the colonial era and early republic were informal, including the children and adults of European descent captured and "adopted" by native tribes. These kin relations all existed beyond the law. In the nineteenth century, state legislatures began passing adoption statutes. The 1851 Massachusetts Adoption of Children Act is considered the first modern adoption law because it identified children's welfare as adoption's core purpose. Equivalent reforms in other Western nations lagged by many decades. Observers have frequently attributed the early acceptance of adoption in the United States to its compatibility with national traditions from immigration to democracy. According to this way of thinking, solidarities achieved on purpose are more powerful—and more quintessentially American—than are solidarities ascribed to blood.

Adoption has always been more significant symbolically than statistically, touching only a tiny minority of U.S. citizens, even since the earlier twentieth century. In 1900, formalizing adoptive kinship in a court was rare. By 1970, the year of the numerical peak of twentieth-century adoption, 175,000 adoptions were finalized annually. "Stranger" or "nonrelative" adoptions have predominated over time, and most people equate adoption with families in which parents and children lack genetic ties. In the early twenty-first century, however, a majority of children are adopted by natal relatives and stepparents, a trend that corresponds to the rise of divorce, remarriage, and blended families. Conservative estimates suggest that 5 million Americans alive in the early twenty-first century are adoptees, that 2 to 4 percent of all families have adopted, and that 2.5 percent of all children under the age of eighteen are adopted. Adoptions steadily rose in number, especially after 1945, but remained exceptional.

Adoptive kinship has been atypical as well as unusual. Adoptive families are more racially diverse, better educated, and more affluent than families in general are. This is known because in 2000, "adopted son/daughter" was included in the U.S. Census for the first time in U.S. history.

Since World War II, adoption has globalized. From Germany in the 1940s and Korea in the 1950s to China and Guatemala in the more recent past, countries that export children for adoption have been devastated by poverty, war, and genocide. Because growing numbers of adoptions are transracial or international or both, many adoptive families have made adoption literally more visible than it was in the past. This new visibility has made it difficult to appreciate that adoptions in the United States have declined since 1970 to approximately 125,000 children annually.

Waves of reform have tried to surround placement with legal, scientific, and bureaucratic safeguards. In 1917, Minnesota passed the first law requiring that children and adults be investigated and that adoption records be shielded from public view. By midcentury, virtually all states in the country had revised their laws to incorporate such minimum standards as preplacement inquiry, postplacement probation, and confidentiality and sealed records. These standards promoted

child welfare, while also reflecting eugenic anxieties about the quality of adoptable children and making adult tastes and preferences more decisive in adoption than children's needs.

Since 1950, several major shifts have occurred. First, "adoptability" expanded beyond "normal" children to include older, disabled, and nonwhite children, as well as children with special needs. Second, since 1970, earlier reforms guaranteeing confidentiality and sealed records have been forcefully criticized, and movements to encourage search, reunion, and so-called open adoption have mobilized sympathy and support. The adoption "closet" has been replaced by an astonishing variety of adoption communities and communications. Adoption is visible online, in popular media, and in grassroots organizing.

Like so many other issues related to childhood and family, adoption illustrates that public and private issues are historically inseparable. Beliefs about blood and belonging, nature and nurture, needs and rights are not the exclusive by-products of free individual choices. They have been decisively shaped by changes in law, public policy, and culture, which in turn have altered Americans' ordinary lives and the families in which they live and love.

[*See also* **Family;** *and* **Orphanages and Orphans.**]

BIBLIOGRAPHY

The Adoption History Project. http://pages.uoregon.edu/adoption.

Briggs, Laura. *Somebody's Children: The Politics of Transnational and Transracial Adoption.* Durham: Duke University Press, forthcoming 2012.

Dubinsky, Karen. *Babies without Borders: Adoption and Migration across the Americas.* New York: New York University Press, 2010.

Herman, Ellen. *Kinship by Design: A History of Adoption in the Modern United States.* Chicago: University of Chicago Press, 2008.

Ellen Herman

AFFIRMATIVE ACTION

The term "affirmative action" first appeared in a legislative context in the 1935 National Labor Relations Act and was later written into state laws prohibiting racial discrimination in employment. But the term, implying simply that government agencies should try to prevent discrimination against African Americans, initially attracted little notice. Prior to the 1960s, virtually no one saw affirmative action as a way of giving minorities preferential treatment in hiring, promotions, and admissions.

More than anything else, the civil rights movement helped change the meaning of the term "affirmative action." In 1964, after years of black protest, Congress passed the landmark Civil Rights Act, which among other things created new agencies run by officials eager to bring minorities into the mainstream of American life. By 1965, with the passage of the Voting Rights Act, the legal barriers to integration began to crumble, and government and civil rights leaders began to confront a new, more difficult issue: how to give under-privileged minorities a fair shot at economic and social equality.

One answer was affirmative action. In 1965, President Lyndon B. Johnson issued an executive order establishing the Office of Federal Contract Compliance, which, along with the Equal Employment Opportunity Commission, began requiring companies for the first time to set numerical racial hiring goals. The trend toward quotas, goals, and timetables continued into the late 1960s as the administration of Richard M. Nixon also supported this new, more radical interpretation of affirmative action.

The nation's major institutions, under pressure from consumers, employees, students, and federal bureaucrats and aware of recent U.S. Supreme Court decisions supporting race and gender preferences, quickly began devising their own affirmative action programs. By 1978 when the Supreme Court ruled in *Regents of the University of California v. Bakke* that universities could use race as a plus factor in admissions, affirmative action had become deeply entrenched in American society.

By the late twentieth century, however, affirmative action had become a source of great controversy. Opponents tended to see racial preferences as unjust—as an unfair government program that exacerbated an already large racial divide, harming whites and stigmatizing blacks as needing preferential treatment. Opponents also contended that affirmative action mainly aided more privileged African Americans and did little to help poor ones.

In the 1990s, Republican Party politicians and activists lobbied hard against affirmative action, both helping pass Proposition 209, a 1996 California initiative to abolish racial and gender preferences, and also backing the regents of the University of California, who in 1995 voted to end affirmative action in hiring and admissions. That same year, President Bill Clinton tried to stake out a middle ground on the issue, arguing that affirmative action was a flawed though necessary response to centuries of discrimination against women, blacks, and other groups.

Many in the civil rights community went further in their defense of affirmative action, arguing that white males still held a disproportionate number of powerful positions in society, and that laws and programs mandating preferences were one way to combat that imbalance. These supporters also argued that racism and sexism were still rampant, and that affirmative action was a small but just part of national social policy.

The Supreme Court addressed the issue in two important 2003 cases involving the University of Michigan, *Grutter v. Bollinger* and *Gratz v. Bollinger*. In *Grutter*, by a 5 to 4 vote the Court upheld the Michigan law school's admissions policy, which took race and ethnicity into consideration without using hard-and-fast quotas. On the other hand, in *Gratz* the justices, by a 6 to 3 vote, found that Michigan's undergraduate-admissions system, favoring African Americans, Hispanics, and American Indians through a system that automatically awarded them points toward admission, violated the equal protection clause of the Fourteenth Amendment. The National Association for the Advancement of Colored People hailed the rulings as "a strong endorsement of the constitutionality of affirmative action with the proviso that institutions have to . . . structure these programs the right way."

[*See also* **Conservative Movement; Desegregation; Great Society Reform Programs; Law and Society;** *and* **Racism.**]

BIBLIOGRAPHY

Cahn, Steven M., ed. *The Affirmative Action Debate.* New York: Routledge, 1995.
Graham, Hugh Davis. *The Civil Rights Era: Origins and Development of National Policy, 1960–1972.* New York: Oxford University Press, 1990.

Matthew Dallek; updated by Paul S. Boyer

AFRICAN AMERICAN EMIGRATION

Two powerful and recurring motifs have marked the African American experience in the United States, resistance and flight: resistance against the structures and conditions of oppression and the flight—escape—from them. From the earliest years of African enslavement on the North American continent, much of the flight took place internally, with the enslaved and formerly enslaved moving from one region or state to another in search of freedom and a fuller life. But the movement of African Americans was not always voluntary; frequently it was coerced. Against the classic slave narrative of escape and freedom in the North—Frederick Douglass's, for instance—ought to be set the more somber tale of black family breakup, separation, sale, and forced migration from the upper South to the Deep South and Southwest during the cotton revolution of the early nineteenth century. More than a million African Americans are estimated to have endured this so-called second Middle Passage between 1790 and 1860.

Thus although African Americans appear, in hemispheric terms at least, relatively sedentary compared to their highly peripatetic Caribbean cousins, for instance, the reality is that they have engaged in and experienced remarkable mobility, albeit within the borders of the United States. But given the United States's unparalleled and enormous political and economic variability, its sheer geographic size and economic and social dynamism, this is not so surprising. And this is especially so when one bears in mind the cost, danger, and other challenges of black emigration over the centuries. Viewed in comparative perspective, however, what is striking about the African American population in the United States is the extent to which, rather than cross the borders of its native land, it has remained within them.

Despite this fact, however, there have been notable movements abroad by African Americans—albeit on a relatively small scale, and episodically—beginning with the nation's tumultuous birth. For remarkably, during the Revolutionary era, African American mobility took the form not only of migration, but also of emigration, with African Americans moving abroad in unprecedentedly large numbers. Canada, the Caribbean, and Britain were key destinations. From the late eighteenth century right into the twentieth century, this movement expanded to include destinations in West Africa, especially Liberia.

Movements Abroad. The American Revolution spawned the first significant and large-scale African American emigration. During that conflict, African Americans forged alliances, including with the British, that enhanced their prospects of freedom. Although there is considerable debate over the numbers involved, as many as twenty thousand may have gained their freedom and moved abroad under British auspices. A significant proportion settled in British colonies, most notably Canada, Jamaica, Saint Lucia, and the Bahamas, as well as Britain itself. Many loyalists, whose slave property was generally protected by the British, also evacuated with their slaves, most notably to the Bahamas. The American Revolutionary authorities augmented this international scattering of African Americans by selling some of the captured runaways to the Caribbean.

The War of 1812 also contributed to a further dispersal of some four thousand African Americans, including fighting men and their families. Like their counterparts in the Revolutionary War, they sought escape from their former masters by lending support to the British who promised them freedom. The British evacuated them from the Atlantic and Gulf coasts to Nova Scotia and Bermuda, with about a thousand ending up in Trinidad, where they settled in free villages and became known locally as "Merikens."

African Americans sought refuge in numerous countries in the nineteenth century.

Although accurate figures about the size and composition of the black population of nineteenth-century Canada do not exist (the censuses are notoriously unreliable), it has been plausibly estimated that on the eve of the Civil War, Canada West (modern-day Ontario), the key site of black settlement in the country, had about forty thousand black residents. Of these, three-quarters, or thirty thousand, were fugitive slaves and their children.

The next major nineteenth-century destination was Liberia, founded in 1822. But despite the efforts of the colony's founder, the American Colonization Society (ACS)—a combination of slaveholders and humanitarians aimed at aiding the removal of the free people of color from the United States—fewer than twenty thousand, including those sent by independent state societies, such as Maryland, had emigrated there by the end of the century. Meanwhile, black enthusiasm for Haiti and the encouragement of the Haitian government resulted in the migration of some six thousand African Americans to Haiti in the 1820s and another two thousand in the late 1850s and early 1860s. Many of the migrants were from cities on the Atlantic Seaboard. Unprepared and ill-equipped for the rigors of agricultural life in Haiti and dogged by disorganization and unfulfilled promises, the majority returned to the United States disillusioned by the experience.

Missionary societies sponsored other emigrations aimed at providing black ministers to Africa. Some of these ministers emerged as important intellectuals in the formation of black-nationalist and Pan-Africanist thought, most notably Edward Wilmot Blyden and Alexander Crummell. Others, such as John Brown Russwurm, went under the auspices of the ACS and served as educators and government officials in Liberia. Still others emigrated under their own steam. Robert Campbell, for instance, who had previously worked in Philadelphia's black schools, accompanied Martin Delany on an exploratory trip to Nigeria in 1859 and later decided to settle there.

An even smaller number of African Americans emigrated from the United States during the twentieth century than during the nineteenth. The efforts of the black-nationalist Universal Negro Improvement Association in the 1920s to facilitate the large-scale emigration of African Americans to Africa were abortive. Even more than the movement during the eighteenth and nineteenth centuries, African American emigration in the twentieth century was largely the preserve of its disaffected intelligentsia and political activists. Few, in fact, were emigrants proper, the majority having been sojourners and temporary political exiles rather than genuine settlers abroad. And a significant proportion— probably the majority—of those who left the United States in the heady days of African political independence in the 1950s and 1960s eventually returned to the United States. The same holds true for those who left during the time of disillusionment and persecution that followed the civil rights and Black Power movements. Some, fugitives from justice, returned despite the certainty of imprisonment on reentering the United States.

Small Scale. What emerges from this brief survey is that African American emigration, considering the size of the black population in the United States, has operated on a relatively small scale. African Americans have been reluctant emigrants and have largely left the United States through repulsion rather than by positive attraction elsewhere—pushed rather than pulled. The hatred of slavery propelled the evacuation with the British in the aftermath of the American Revolution, as it did at the end of the War of 1812, not the positive attraction of Nova Scotia, Jamaica, or England, places of which they knew little. Later, Liberia and Haiti provided both escape from oppression and the promise of a fuller life. Both were destinations widely debated in the African American community during the nineteenth century. But the power of domestic repulsion rather than foreign attraction was underlined by the distinct spurt in emigration from the United States after the passage of the Fugitive Slave Bill in 1850: Liberia, Haiti, and Canada all experienced increased African American immigration in its wake. Even the more positive attraction of an independent Ghana and Tanzania in the 1960s and 1970s could not be separated from the brutal political assassinations in the 1960s—Malcolm X, Martin Luther King Jr., Robert Kennedy—the unending Vietnam War, and the relentless persecution of the Black Panthers, all of which combined to make the United States a singularly unattractive place to be and to be black in.

Likewise, throughout history, as political prospects in the United States improved, black emigration declined. Once the Civil War commenced, for instance, African American spirits lifted, and the movement to Liberia and Canada came to a virtual halt overnight. Thus unlike the international black migration elsewhere in the Americas, that from the United States was overdetermined by political rather than strictly economic considerations, by the desire for liberty rather than bread.

[*See also* **African Americans; Black Nationalism; Caribbean; Colonization Movement, African; Emancipation of Slaves; Internal Migration,** *subentry on* **African Americans; Liberia, Colonization of; Maroon Societies; Missions, Foreign; Slave Resistance; Underground Railroad;**

and **Universal Negro Improvement Association.**]

BIBLIOGRAPHY

Campbell, James T. *Middle Passages: African American Journeys to Africa, 1787–2005.* New York: Penguin Press, 2006. A thoughtful and comprehensive overview of the subject.

Cohen, William. *At Freedom's Edge: Black Mobility and the Southern White Quest for Racial Control, 1861–1915.* Baton Rouge: Louisiana State University Press, 1991. A comprehensive overview of the struggle over black mobility from the Civil War to World War I.

Frey, Sylvia R. *Water from the Rock: Black Resistance in a Revolutionary Age.* Princeton, N.J.: Princeton University Press, 1991. The most authoritative overview of the black struggle during the American Revolution.

Pybus, Cassandra. *Epic Journeys of Freedom: Runaway Slaves of the American Revolution and Their Global Quest for Liberty.* Boston: Beacon Press, 2006. An ambitious and wide-ranging analysis of the experience of the African American diaspora that emerged out of the American Revolution.

Shick, Tom W. *Behold the Promised Land: A History of Afro-American Settler Society in Nineteenth-Century Liberia.* Baltimore: Johns Hopkins University Press, 1980.

Winks, Robin W. *The Blacks in Canada: A History.* 2d ed. Montreal and Buffalo, N.Y.: McGill-Queen's University Press, 1997. First published in 1971, it remains the most comprehensive and authoritative overview of the subject.

Winston James

AFRICAN AMERICANS

The African American community has its roots in the great migration of peoples from the Old World to the New. Unlike European, Asian, and Latino Americans, however, Africans entered the New World in chains.

Despite the Revolutionary War and the emergence of the United States as an independent republic, most African Americans remained in bondage until the Civil War and Reconstruction. In the 1860s and 1870s, African Americans gained freedom and citizenship, but the rise of racial segregation soon undercut this achievement. By World War I, the United States had institutionalized new patterns of class and racial inequality in its politics, culture, and economy. The Jim Crow system, as it was called, persisted through the mid-twentieth century.

As the nation instituted different forms of inequality and as African Americans confronted ongoing status and social-class conflicts within their own communities, they nonetheless staged both individual and collective resistance to discrimination, and they shaped the nation's history in the process. The black freedom struggle culminated in the rise of the modern civil rights movement and what has been called the Second Reconstruction in the 1950s and 1960s. Although the civil rights struggle demolished the legal underpinnings of Jim Crow, it failed to translate such changes fully into material improvements in the lives of poor and working-class blacks. As these gaps in the civil rights agenda became clearer, black activists launched the Black Power movement and advocated new and more autonomous strategies for social change. With the demise of the industrial economy in the 1970s and 1980s, whites intensified their resistance to the gains of the Second Reconstruction, as well as to the Black Power movement. By the close of the twentieth century, African Americans again searched for appropriate strategies to counteract new forms of inequality.

The Era of Enslavement. When Europeans arrived on the West African coast during the fifteenth and sixteenth centuries, they had already established the economic and technological foundations for the international slave trade. Between 1433 and 1488, Portuguese mariners used new knowledge of ocean currents to navigate Africa's western coast, establish trade relations on the so-called Gold Coast, and set up sugar plantations on the northwest African islands of Madeira, Príncipe, and São Tomé. Portugal was soon importing some five hundred to a thousand Africans per year to work its island plantations. As early as 1502, the Spanish imported Africans to work on their New World sugar plantations in Hispaniola (modern Haiti and Dominican Republic). By century's end, the Spanish colonies imported an average of about eighty thousand Africans each year. Following a brief decline during the 1790s, the number of slave imports peaked during the early nineteenth century. No fewer than 10 million Africans landed in the Americas during the era of the slave trade. Another 2 million died in the infamous Middle Passage en route to the New World. The European colonies of the Caribbean and Latin America absorbed more than 90 percent of these Africans.

Although some Africans had entered the present-day United States with Spanish explorers and helped to establish Saint Augustine, Florida—the first permanent non-Indian community in North America—the British colonies became the center of African American settlement in North America. The first Africans entered British North America in 1619 when a Dutch man-of-war deposited some twenty Africans at Jamestown. Initially the black population increased only slowly, comprising no more than 170 in 1640. Until the late seventeenth century, indentured servitude rather than enslavement "for life" defined the labor system of the tobacco-growing Chesapeake colonies of Virginia and Maryland. Early Africans like Anthony and Richard

Johnson won their freedom, legally married, purchased property, gained redress in courts of law, and sometimes imported their own black and white servants. By the early eighteenth century, however, both Virginia and Maryland had passed statutes pronouncing Africans or black servants slaves "durante vita," or "for life." The rice- and indigo-producing colonies of South Carolina and Georgia soon followed suit. By the late eighteenth century, the black population had grown through a combination of imports and natural increase to nearly eight hundred thousand.

As Africans made the transition from a less rigid form of servitude to bondmen and bondwomen "for life," colonial authorities reinforced their enslavement with so-called slave codes. Borrowing from Caribbean precedents, the new legislation redefined human beings as property by eliminating the right of blacks to bear arms, engage in trade, own property, move about freely, peaceably assemble, or seek legal redress. Such codes also legalized the maiming and even killing of enslaved persons as part of the owners' "property right." Although such laws were most prevalent in the South, the northern colonies also enacted statutes restricting the lives of bondmen and bondwomen, including laws mandating the whipping of blacks who "attempted to strike" a white person.

Technological changes and the opening of new agricultural land in the Deep South intensified the demand for slave labor in the early national era. The cotton gin enabled planters to increase production from less than three hundred thousand bales in 1820 to nearly 4.5 million in 1860. Slave-produced cotton dominated the nation's foreign exports and fueled the early industrialization both of Great Britain and of New England mill towns like Lowell and Waltham, Massachusetts. Under the impact of cotton production, nearly a million blacks experienced forced migration from the declining tobacco-growing states of the upper South to the booming Deep South states of Georgia, South Carolina, Alabama, Mississippi, and Louisiana. Whereas the majority of blacks had lived in the Chesapeake region during the eighteenth century, the Deep South claimed nearly 60 percent of all African Americans by 1860.

From the outset of their enslavement in the New World, Africans and their American descendants acted on their own behalf. As bondmen and bondwomen, they built formal and informal religious, social, and political networks, ran away, rebelled, and plotted to rebel. Such revolts and plots include the Stono Rebellion (1739), Gabriel Prosser's plot (1800), Denmark Vesey's plot (1822), and Nat Turner's rebellion (1831). African Americans also shaped the advent and outcome of the American Revolution and the Civil War. Some 180,000 blacks, enslaved and free, served in the Union forces and helped transform the war between the states into a war of liberation.

Civil War to World War II. Following the Civil War, some 4 million African Americans gained their freedom and made the transition from slave to citizen. The Thirteenth, Fourteenth, and Fifteenth Amendments to the Constitution granted blacks citizenship and equal rights under the law. Yet in the late nineteenth and early twentieth centuries, African Americans experienced what the historian Rayford Logan called the "nadir" of their history (*The Negro in American Life and Thought: The Nadir, 1877–1901*, 1954): economic exploitation under the sharecropping, crop-lien, and convict-lease systems; lynchings; disenfranchisement; and institutional segregation. Southern white-supremacist groups like the Knights of the White Camelia and the Ku Klux Klan encouraged and carried out mob attacks on African Americans and their communities. In 1896 the Supreme Court upheld racial segregation in its landmark *Plessy v. Ferguson* decision. Jurists, scholars, and popular writers justified the subordination of blacks, further undermining the promise of Reconstruction. Racist publications and portrayals of black life proliferated, culminating in D. W. Griffith's film *The Birth of a Nation* (1915).

As the promise of freedom faded, the black leaders Booker T. Washington and W. E. B. Du Bois offered divergent strategies for action. Ordinary African Americans, meanwhile, used their newly won geographic mobility to resist limitations on their rights as citizens and workers. Beginning gradually during the late nineteenth and early twentieth centuries, during World War I and its aftermath the population movement of blacks turned into the Great Migration. The proportion of blacks living in cities rose from about 2.6 million, or 27 percent, in 1910 to 6.4 million, or 49 percent, in 1940 to more than 18 million, or more than 80 percent, in 1970—10 percent higher than the figure for the population at large.

Although African Americans improved their lot by taking jobs in urban industries, they nonetheless entered the industrial economy at the lowest rungs of the occupational ladder. Moreover, as their numbers increased in northern and western cities, they faced growing residential and educational restrictions and limitations on access to social services and public accommodations. Responding to the impact of such class and racial restrictions, African Americans intensified their institution building and their cultural, political, economic, and civil rights activities. They founded mutual aid societies, fraternal orders, and social clubs; established a range of new business and professional services; and launched diverse political, labor, and civil rights organizations, including the National Association for the Advancement of Colored People (NAACP), founded in 1909.

Urbanization and northern migration profoundly affected African American cultural life as well. Black churches, including those of the Baptist, Pentecostal, and African Methodist Episcopal (AME) denominations, ranging from struggling storefronts to large establishments with thousands of members, provided spiritual and social support to urban newcomers. From the black communities of New Orleans, Kansas City, Chicago, and other cities emerged vibrant new adaptations of musical traditions rooted in the past, including ragtime, gospel, the blues, and jazz. New York City's black community of the 1920s produced a rich flowering of literary, dramatic, and artistic activity, the so-called Harlem Renaissance, including such writers, performers, and intellectuals as Langston Hughes, Zora Neale Hurston, Paul Robeson, and Alain Locke. In *Native Son* (1940), the novelist Richard Wright offered a searing picture of race relations and life among the black underclass in Depression-era Chicago.

African American activism in these years included Marcus Garvey's mobilization of the urban black masses in the 1920s, participation in the Democratic Party's New Deal coalition during the 1930s, and, before and during World War II, A. Philip Randolph's March on Washington movement, which demanded an end to discrimination in defense industries, and the NAACP's so-called Double V campaign, for victory over fascism abroad and over racism at home.

Partly because of black voters' overwhelming support of the New Deal, President Franklin Delano Roosevelt in 1941 issued Executive Order 8802: the order banned racial discrimination in industries with government contracts and set up the federal Fair

Employment Practices Committee (FEPC) to monitor the process. For the first time, African Americans broke the job ceiling and moved into jobs above the "unskilled" and "semiskilled" categories. Though the wartime struggle against inequality entailed substantial tensions and conflicts within the African American community between elites and workers, between urban newcomers and older residents, and between men and women, it nevertheless formed the communal, institutional, and leadership foundation for the rise of the postwar civil rights movement.

The Civil Rights Movement. Building upon their wartime militancy, African Americans moved their struggle to the streets during the 1950s and 1960s, adopting nonviolent direct-action strategies for social change. Grassroots organizations like the Montgomery Improvement Association in Alabama initiated boycotts, sit-ins, Freedom Rides, and voter-education projects across the South and parts of the North and West.

The Supreme Court's landmark 1954 *Brown v. Board of Education* decision outlawing racial segregation in public schools intensified the impetus for change, while black writers such as Ralph Ellison and James Baldwin contributed to the heightened sense of identity and group consciousness within the postwar African American community.

Though their actions were rooted in their own local community-based institutions and national organizations like the Southern Christian Leadership Conference, African Americans gained the support of white allies in federal agencies and diverse peace and freedom organizations, including the New York–based Fellowship of Reconciliation. With their white allies, African Americans achieved a Second Reconstruction with passage of the Civil Rights Acts of 1964 and 1968 and the Voting Rights Act of 1965. This legislation demolished the legal pillars of discrimination in employment, housing, and the voting booth and sought to reverse centuries of inequality by setting up affirmative action programs in employment and institutions of higher education.

Though the Second Reconstruction destroyed the legal foundations of the segregationist system, it also highlighted the further and more difficult challenge of translating legal victories into real change. Moreover, the 1968 assassination of Martin Luther King Jr. removed a key symbol and source of unity in the nonviolent freedom struggle. According to one activist, King was "the one man of our race that this country's older generations, the militants, and the revolutionaries and the masses of black people would still listen to." As the limitations of the civil rights movement became more apparent, growing numbers of young African Americans advocated Black Power as an alternative to nonviolent direct-action strategies. Partly because revolutionary black organizations like the Black Panther Party, formed in 1966, emphasized the mass mobilization of poor and working-class blacks, armed struggle, and opposition to the Vietnam War, they came under the combined assault of federal, state, and local authorities. Under the weight of official and unofficial white resistance, the Black Power movement fragmented and gradually dissipated by the early 1970s.

Late Twentieth-Century Developments. As the civil rights and Black Power movements weakened, white resistance to the gains of the Second Reconstruction intensified. Opposition to affirmative action policies in employment and education were closely related to the deindustrialization of the nation's economy. The loss of jobs to mechanization and low-wage overseas factories affected all industrial

workers, black and white, but the persistence of overt and covert discriminatory employment practices rooted in white kin and friendship networks made black workers and their communities especially vulnerable to economic downswings. African American unemployment rates persisted at well over the white rate, especially among young black males. At the same time, the beneficiaries of existing affirmative action programs—the middle class and better-educated members of the black working class—experienced a degree of upward mobility and moved into outlying urban and suburban neighborhoods. They left working-class and poor blacks, disproportionately single women with children, concentrated in the central cities, where violence, drug addiction, and class-stratified social spaces intensified, causing acute tensions in day-to-day intraracial as well as interracial relations.

Perhaps even more than the industrial era had, the postindustrial era challenged African Americans to develop new strategies for coping with social change and the persistence of inequality. Some of their emerging responses built upon earlier struggles. Institution building, marches, participation in electoral politics, and migration in search of better opportunities all continued to express black activism and resistance to social injustice. Yet much had changed in the nation and in African American life, and such time-tested strategies took on different meanings in the 1980s and 1990s. Rising numbers of southern-born blacks returned to the South during the 1970s. After declining for more than a century, the proportion of blacks living in the South increased by 1980. Other African Americans rallied behind the Rainbow Coalition and supported the Reverend Jesse Jackson's bids for the Democratic Party's presidential nomination in 1984 and 1988. Still others endorsed the Nation of Islam minister Louis Farrakhan's Million Man March (MMM) in 1995. Calling the march a "day of atonement" for black men, leaders of the MMM encouraged black men to earn and reclaim a position of authority in their families and communities. Two years later, many black women responded to the MMM's gender bias with their own Million Woman March, which emphasized the centrality of women in the ongoing black freedom struggle. Through these various actions and many more, African Americans continued to resist shifting forms of inequality and gave direction to their own lives as a new century began.

These same years saw the emergence of a new generation of African American academics, musicians, performers, sports figures, and writers. Such diverse men and women as the scholars and public intellectuals Henry Louis Gates Jr., Cornel West, and Stephen L. Carter; the basketball superstar Michael Jordan and the track-and-field athlete Jackie Joyner-Kersee; the film actors Eddie Murphy and Denzel Washington; the jazz musicians Joshua Redman, Herbie Hancock, and Wynton and Bradford Marsalis; the television celebrity Oprah Winfrey; and an array of novelists and writers including Maya Angelou, Alice Walker, and Toni Morrison enriched American life and gave voice to the black experience.

By the 1990s the nation's more than 30 million African Americans, representing about 12 percent of the total population, had transformed themselves from a predominantly rural people into an overwhelmingly urban people; from a southern regional group to a national population living in every part of the nation; and, perhaps most important, from a group confined to southern agriculture, domestic service, and general labor to a workforce with representation in every sector of the nation's economy.

[See also African American Emigration; African Immigrants, Recent; Allen, Richard; Antilynching Movement; Antislavery; Baker, Ella; Bethune, Mary McLeod; Black Nationalism; Black Panthers; Brownsville Incident; Buffalo Soldiers; Carmichael, Stokely; Civil Rights Movement; Colonization Movement, African; Congress of Racial Equality; Crack Cocaine; Delany, Martin; Desegregation; Douglass, Frederick; Emancipation of Slaves; Equiano, Olaudah; Father Divine's Peace Mission Movement; Fitzhugh, George; Forten, James; Free Communities of Color; Freedmen's Bureau; Haynes, Lemuel; Hemings, Sally; Internal Migration, subentry on African Americans; Jacobs, Harriet; King, Martin Luther, Jr.; Liberia, Colonization of; Lynching; Malcolm X; March on Washington; Maroon Societies; Military Personnel, subentry on Civil War, African Americans; National Association for the Advancement of Colored People; National Association of Colored Women; National Black Feminist Organization; National Council of Negro Women; National Urban League; Occom, Samson; Parks, Rosa; Racism; Segregation, Racial; Slave Families and Communities; Slave Rebellions; Slave Resistance; Slavery; Slaves and Childbirth; Slave Trades; Smalls, Robert; South, The; Student Nonviolent Coordinating Committee; Tubman, Harriet; Tuskegee University; Underground Railroad; Universal Negro Improvement Association; Voluntary Associations, subentry on African American; and Wells-Barnett, Ida B.]

BIBLIOGRAPHY

Bennett, Lerone, Jr. Before the Mayflower: A History of Black America. 8th ed. Chicago: Johnson, 2007.

Berry, Mary Frances, and John W. Blassingame. Long Memory: The Black Experience in America. New York: Oxford University Press, 1982.

Christian, Charles M. *Black Saga: The African American Experience.* Boston: Houghton Mifflin, 1995.

Franklin, John Hope, and Alfred A. Moss Jr. *From Slavery to Freedom: A History of African Americans.* 8th ed. New York: Alfred A. Knopf, 2000.

Hine, Darlene Clark, and Kathleen Thompson. *A Shining Thread of Hope: The History of Black Women in America.* New York: Broadway Books, 1998.

Horton, James Oliver, and Lois E. Horton, eds. *A History of the African American People: The History, Traditions, and Culture of African Americans.* Detroit, Mich.: Wayne State University Press, 1997.

Kelley, Robin D. G., and Earl Lewis, eds. *To Make Our World Anew: A History of African Americans.* Oxford: Oxford University Press, 2000.

Smallwood, Arwin D., with Jeffrey M. Elliot. *The Atlas of African-American History and Politics: From the Slave Trade to Modern Times.* Boston: McGraw-Hill, 1998.

Trotter, Joe W., Jr. *The African American Experience.* Boston: Houghton Mifflin, 2001.

Joe W. Trotter Jr.

AFRICAN COLONIZATION MOVEMENT

See Colonization Movement, African; Liberia, Colonization of.

AFRICAN IMMIGRANTS, RECENT

By the early twenty-first century, Africans had a full presence in the new global migration circuits. According to the U.S. Department of Homeland Security, at the end of 2008 nearly a million Africans had entered the United States during the last four decades either voluntarily or as involuntary migrants or refugees forced to flee from wars and conflicts. Factors within Africa are behind Africans' exodus and migration to the United States. Chronic unemployment and underemployment among high school and college graduates is a major push factor. Additionally, rural neglect and the failure to develop their rural towns continue to impel rural youths to urban areas in search of nonexistent jobs. The continent's economic problems are aggravated by the persistent erosion of democratic institutions and the absence of the rule of law and adherence to constitutional principles. With their countries unable to sustain robust economic and industrial development programs to provide jobs for the masses, people are left with no choice but to look outside the continent for economic and cultural opportunities.

This mass emigration has been dubbed the "brain-drain saga" and is seen as forming a neo-African diaspora. The emigrants include refugees, young and old, educated and uneducated, and skilled and unskilled. Skilled Africans who cannot find work in Africa look to the United States and the West for employment. Those with advanced credentials in the arts and sciences successfully transition from nonimmigrant to immigrant status. The U.S. Immigration Reform and Control Act of 1986 made it possible for thousands of Africans to gain residency status, a first step toward naturalization and citizenship. Most Africans in the United States come from Egypt, Nigeria, Sudan, Ghana, South Africa, and Kenya, as well as Ethiopia, Somalia, Cape Verde, and Liberia. The first wave of African immigrants to enter the United States came from Egypt, Ghana, and Nigeria during the late 1950s.

Most African immigrants to the United States have settled along the East Coast, particularly New York, Maryland, the District of Columbia, Virginia, North Carolina, Georgia, and Florida. Sizable cohorts of Africans have also settled in the northern Illinois and

Indiana upper corridor, with huge settlements in Chicago. Since 1980 African immigrants and refugees have settled in midwestern states such as Minnesota, Iowa, Ohio, Missouri, and Wisconsin.

There are noticeable cultural and economic differences between African-born and American-born blacks. African immigrants tend to separate themselves from American-born blacks, preferring instead to maintain social and cultural affinities with fellow Africans or immigrants from the Caribbean. Intra- and interethnic associations have become a principal way for immigrants to establish strong ties with other immigrants from the same town, ethnic or tribal group, community, or nation. These associations may cross ethnic or tribal affiliations to include fellow alumni from high schools and colleges. Other associations are formed to represent the national identity of the immigrants. Pan-African continental associations are also formed to represent the interests of the continent at large. Once formed, these various associations serve as mutual-benefit or benevolent societies providing economic, cultural, social, and psychological support for their members; some also provide regular economic and cultural development support for their respective hometowns, schools, and nations.

Participation in the labor force is an essential form of economic integration for African immigrants. Those with advanced degrees have been successful in obtaining access to well-paying jobs in academics, business, health care, and technology. Others are able to find employment as parking-ramp attendants, taxi drivers, and private security officers, as well as in hospitality management (custodial and janitorial services). Only a few take jobs in farming, agriculture, and food processing.

Like American-born blacks, African immigrants are concerned about the persistence of racism and discrimination. The violent shooting death of Amadou Diallo, an African immigrant from Guinea, at the hands of New York City police officers on 5 February 1999 is still etched in the collective memory of the immigrants. While noting that discrimination is unavoidable, most of the immigrants minimize its deleterious impact by relying on their strong family bonds. For the African immigrant, the family is an economic and cultural unit of production whose assets are the kinship bonds of its members. Resources of family networks are harnessed to assist members in need. Elaborate parties and celebrations are organized during child-naming ceremonies for the deceased, puberty rites for adolescents, and national Independence Day celebrations.

Africans will continue to form a growing part of the American immigration experience. Future migrations will hinge on geopolitical and economic conditions within Africa coupled with American public sentiments regarding legal and undocumented migrations.

[*See also* **African Americans** *and* **Immigration.**]

BIBLIOGRAPHY

Arthur, John A. *Invisible Sojourners: African Immigrant Diaspora in the United States.* Westport, Conn.: Praeger Press, 2000.

Martin, Daniel C., and Michael Hoefer. "Refugees and Asylees: 2008." Annual Flow Report, June 2009. United States Office of Immigration Statistics, Policy Directorate, Department of Homeland Security. http://www.riwn.org/uploads/files/1248761397_DHS%20OIS%20Annual%20Flow%20Report%20Refugee%20and%20Asylees%202008.pdf.

Owusu, Thomas Y. "The Role of Ghanaian Immigrant Associations in Toronto, Canada." *International Migration Review* 34, no. 4 (2000): 1155–1181.

John A. Arthur

ALASKA

Alaska was purchased by the United States in 1867 from Russia. It had been a Russian colony since being claimed in the 1740s by Russian explorers. Its indigenous population in historical times consisted of many ethnic and linguistic groups. Some, such as the Inuit, arrived as recently as 1000 CE. The Eskaleuts were the most recent at 7,000–6,000 years ago while the Tlingit and Haida peoples of the Southeast Panhandle may have been resident since ca. 8000 BCE. The groups on the northern, western, and southwestern coasts Yupiit are the Inupiaq Inupiat (Inuit Inupiaq speakers who inhabit the northern-most regions), Alaskan Yupik (the Yupiit speak Yup'ik), Alutiiq (also Yupik actually Sugpiak speakers of Yup'ik), and Aleut Unangan (the people of the Aleutian Islands). Groups on the southern and southeastern coast are the Tlingit, Haida, Tsimshian, and Eyak. The interior regions of Alaska are populated by almost a dozen Athabascan or Dena dialect groups, related to Cree peoples in Canada. The Unangan (also called Aleut) and Alutiiq people were most heavily affected by Russian colonization and intermarried at the highest rates, resulting in the creation of a Creole population and the mixing of native and Russian Orthodox cultures. The peoples of the southeast, living in a resource-rich rainforest ecosystem, were highly organized and far more successful at resisting Russian influence both culturally and militarily.

Before Statehood.   After 1867 the white population of Alaska remained small, and American presence was limited to scattered commercial trading posts and the capital, which was moved from Sitka to Juneau in the 1880s. Alaska's legal status was poorly defined. It remained a department of Washington

Territory until 1912. It was administered by the U.S. Army for the first ten years of American rule, then by the Navy from 1876 to 1884. As such it had no standing law code beyond the fiat of local officers. The dangers of this situation were illustrated in 1882 when a conflict between natives and white whalers led a navy cutter to shell and then burn the native village of Angoon. The resulting congressional inquiry led in 1884 to the adoption of the First Organic Act, which gave Alaska its first law code. Prior to 1898, however, white presence and public interest in Alaska were limited.

Extractive industries shaped Alaska's modern history and culture more than any other factor. Early European and American interest was primarily in furs, especially seal and otter. Salmon packing, however, has proved the most consistent and commercially viable industry. The first canneries were built in 1878 by companies based in San Francisco, though by the 1900s packing companies based in Seattle dominated the industry. Seattle's commercial hold on Alaska was cemented by the 1890s. Before statehood, control over Alaska's fisheries was bitterly contested between large companies and local fishermen. Nevertheless, salmon canneries helped sustain communities in southeast Alaska through a constant influx of labor. Early cannery workers were a mixture of Alaska natives, Chinese, Japanese, Filipinos, Scandinavians, and southern Slavs. Over time, Filipinos came to dominate the workforce and proved one of the most enduring ethnic communities in southeast Alaska.

Gold was discovered near the Klondike River in the Yukon in 1896. The resulting Klondike gold rush of 1898 inspired many of the popular images of Alaska as what was called "The Last Frontier," immortalized by authors like Jack London and in scores of dime novels and popular songs. Although the most famous goldfields were in Canada, the main routes to the Klondike went from Seattle via the Alaska boomtown of Skagway. Other gold strikes were made in Nome and Fairbanks shortly thereafter. Prospectors poured into the state, though few made any money. Ignored prior to 1898, Alaska became a symbolic frontier in the American consciousness, permanently standing in for an idea that would otherwise have been relegated to a vanishing past.

Other extractive industries also proved lucrative. The Kennecott copper strike of 1900 in central Alaska was one of the richest copper deposits ever found. Nevertheless, throughout Alaska's history, extractive industries have left the state at the mercy of fluctuating commodity prices, high transportation costs, and the economic decisions of business and government leaders far removed from the state. Resources like timber or coal were often cost-prohibitive to exploit, and sometimes the rights to them were purchased by corporate interests only to keep them off the market.

Alaska's most sustained boom came during World War II and the Cold War. Responding to Japanese aggression and later to the Soviet threat, the federal government invested heavily in Alaska's infrastructure, including the Alaska Highway and a rapid expansion of seaports, airports, and communications. Anchorage became a major population center during the 1940s, growing from a town of about 1,000 to a city of 40,000 by 1950. This shifted the center of economic and political gravity away from the southeast panhandle with its ties to the Seattle canning industry and set the stage for statehood in 1959. By the end of the twentieth century, 60 percent of Alaska's population lived in the greater Anchorage area.

Statehood. The struggle for statehood highlighted the problems of unresolved native land claims. Because native communities in Alaska had never been granted reservations—with the exception of a community of Tsimshian on Annette Island in the southeast panhandle—the question of native rights remained open. From the 1930s, native Alaskans were increasingly active, using both the federal courts and the political process to press for land rights. The discovery of oil in the North Slope region of Alaska in 1967 set the stage for a comprehensive effort at resolution. In 1971, in the face of a morass of native claims and a political climate more favorable to indigenous rights, Congress passed the Alaska Native Claims Settlement Act (ANCSA). This landmark agreement between native Alaskans and the state and federal governments moved native claims away from the land-trust model, instead creating native corporations whose shareholders could reap the economic benefits of Alaska's natural-resource-based economy. Although ANCSA did not resolve all issues, it represented an effort at greater economic justice for indigenous groups and opened the way for the creation of Alaska's modern oil-based economy.

By the early twenty-first century, Alaska's economy continued to be based on the extraction of natural resources and on tourism. It had no state income tax, and residents received a yearly dividend check from the earnings of a fund based on oil royalties. Alaska was the only state in which a significant (though declining) proportion of residents depended on subsistence hunting, fishing, or gathering. Although government spending accounted for a significant proportion of the economy—in part because the federal government owns 69 percent of the land—Alaskans viewed themselves as individualists, and the state continued to attract migrants based on the imagery of Alaska's being the last frontier.

[*See also* **Borderlands; Eskimos; Frontier, The; Gold Rushes;** *and* **Tourism and Travel.**]

BIBLIOGRAPHY

Arnold, David F. *The Fishermen's Frontier: People and Salmon in Southeast Alaska.* Seattle: University of Washington Press, 2008.

Borneman, Walter R. *Alaska: Saga of a Bold Land.* New York: HarperCollins, 2003.

Haycox, Stephen. *Alaska: An American Colony.* Seattle: University of Washington Press, 2002.

John Radzilowski

ALCATRAZ ISLAND, OCCUPATION OF (1969)

On 20 November 1969, more than eighty American Indians from the organization Indians of All Tribes (IAT) claimed Alcatraz, an island in San Francisco Bay, as Indian land by right of discovery. The occupation lasted a total of nineteen months as thousands of indigenous people from all across the Americas made their collective stand for treaty and human rights on Alcatraz.

Two of the most important leaders for the IAT were college students: Richard Oakes, an Akwesasne Mohawk from San Francisco State College, and LaNada Means, a Shoshone-Bannock from the University of California, Berkeley. The occupation emerged from an intertribal coalition of local college students and urban Indian leaders from San Francisco's Mission District. Sophisticated and highly organized, the IAT championed a nonviolent call for direct action to transform the former prison at Alcatraz into a new cultural center, intertribal university, ecological center, and museum. The occupiers also distributed a national newsletter, maintained a hospital, hosted their own radio show, and established their own school system on Alcatraz. They relied on public support and the international media in their effort to overturn anti-Indian federal policies such as the Bureau of Indian Affairs' Operation Relocation (1952) and House Concurrent Resolution 108 (1953), part of the government's so-called termination policy.

Metaphorically the abandoned federal prison highlighted the failure of federal Indian policy: like most reservation lands, the island lacked employment, running water, plumbing, fertile land for agricultural development, education, health care, and the basic resources necessary for survival. Alcatraz was a potent symbol for the Red Power movement and inspired hundreds of similar takeovers from Seattle to New York. As a direct result of the occupation of Alcatraz, more than twenty-six pieces of self-determination legislation were passed, giving native nations greater sovereignty.

[*See also* **American Indian Movement; Native American History and Culture,** *subentry on* **Since 1950;** *and* **Wounded Knee, Occupation of (1973).**]

BIBLIOGRAPHY

Johnson, Troy R. *The American Indian Occupation of Alcatraz Island: Red Power and Self-Determination.* Lincoln: University of Nebraska Press, 2008.

Smith, Paul Chaat, and Robert Allen Warrior. *Like a Hurricane: The Indian Movement from Alcatraz to Wounded Knee.* New York: New Press, 1996.

Wilkinson, Charles F. *Blood Struggle: The Rise of Modern Indian Nations.* New York: W. W. Norton and Company, 2005.

Kent Blansett

ALCOHOL AND ALCOHOL ABUSE

Alcohol looms large in American history, and attitudes toward it have been linked to myriad reformist causes, have reflected many social concerns, and have mirrored the prevailing cultural, political, and economic climate of successive eras.

Alcoholic beverages, whether rum distilled from West Indian sugar, home-brewed beer, or imported wines, were widely consumed in colonial America, and the physician-statesman Benjamin Rush targeted them in his widely reprinted *Inquiry into the Effects of Ardent Spirits upon the Human Body and Mind* (1784). Fearful for the new republic, Rush recoiled at the prospect of intoxicated voters shaping its destiny—no small concern at a time when elections often featured heavy drinking. Annual per capita consumption of absolute alcohol when Rush wrote ranged between four and six gallons (twice the rate of that in 2000), and evidence suggests a further sharp rise between 1800 and 1830. The profitability of corn whiskey, heavy frontier drinking, the spread of saloons in cities, and the immigration of beer-drinking Germans and whiskey-using Irish all encouraged the nation's bibulous tendencies.

Temperance Reformers. These tendencies elicited a reaction within the Protestant churches, however, which linked salvation with temperance and other reforms. The American Society for the Promotion of Temperance (ASPT), founded by evangelical clergymen in 1826, also gained support from farmers, industrialists, and homemakers. Indeed, the temperance campaign—really a series of reform drives—constituted the nineteenth century's longest and largest social-reform movement. Alcohol was seen as imperiling capitalist enterprise, domestic tranquility, and the national virtue. By 1836 the ASPT, renamed the American Temperance Society, advocated total abstinence. In the early 1840s, Americans thronged temperance rallies, "took the pledge" for sobriety, and in record numbers lobbied to end the licensing

of saloons. The Washingtonian movement, a grassroots total-abstinence campaign, sponsored parades and speeches; offered recruits financial and moral assistance; and established institutions for inebriates—Washingtonian Homes—that relied on moral suasion to keep residents sober. The Washingtonian enthusiasm soon gave way to better-organized temperance fellowships, such as the Good Templars and the Blue Ribbon societies. The late antebellum era also saw renewed middle-class drives for local and state prohibition. In the 1850s eleven states passed prohibitory legislation, although most of it was soon repealed.

The brewing and distilling industries expanded after the Civil War, and alcohol consumption, especially in the immigrant cities, remained high. But the temperance movement revived as well, linking "demon rum" to concerns about immigration, workplace efficiency, social welfare, and urban political corruption. Frances Willard's Woman's Christian Temperance Union (WCTU) redefined temperance, along with other reforms, as a women's issue involving home protection. At the WCTU's prompting, Congress mandated the inclusion of "scientific" temperance instruction in high school physiology texts.

This era of social reorganization and professionalization also brought the first widespread attempt to medicalize drunkenness. The American Association for the Cure of Inebriates (AACI), founded in 1870 by physicians and reformers, promoted the concept of inebriety as a hereditary disease exacerbated by chronic debauchery. As their drinking progressed, the AACI contended, inebriates lost control of their actions and required restorative medical and moral treatment. Envisioning a new medical specialty to address this ailment, the AACI built a network of private institutions to treat habitual drunkards. California, Iowa, Massachusetts, New York, and other states followed suit.

In this age of industrial capitalism, the goal was to restore inebriates' economic productivity as well as their willpower. The AACI faded as the prohibition movement grew, however; by 1920, most of the inebriate institutions had closed, and habitual drunkenness was again viewed as primarily a moral, political, and legal issue.

Prohibition and After. The church-based Anti-Saloon League (ASL), meanwhile, founded in Ohio in 1893, expanded nationally in 1895, and supported by industrialists like Henry Ford and Pierre du Pont, spearheaded the prohibition drive. Under its superintendent, Wayne Wheeler, the ASL's innovative bipartisan lobbying approach secured prohibitory state legislation and, in 1919, ratification of the Eighteenth Amendment, establishing nationwide prohibition. A World War I reaction against German American–owned breweries and fears that alcohol would undermine the nation's military contributed to this success.

But many Americans, especially in the cities, rejected prohibition; speakeasies flourished and bootleg liquor flowed freely in many municipalities. With repeal in 1933, the nation entered what some scholars have called an age of ambivalence about alcohol. The reopened breweries and distilleries advertised heavily to win new customers. As old taboos faded, alcohol consumption spread widely. In the later twentieth century, wine connoisseurship spread, and U.S. wine production flourished in California and elsewhere. Though the major breweries dominated the beer market, imported brands and local microbreweries also flourished.

Simultaneously, however, antialcohol sentiment remained powerful in evangelical Protestantism; in such organizations as Alcoholics Anonymous (AA), founded in 1935, and Mothers against Drunk Driving (MADD),

founded in 1980 and boasting some six hundred chapters nationwide by 2000; and in heightened concern about college binge drinking, alcohol-related domestic abuse, and fetal alcohol syndrome. Beginning in the early 1980s, these efforts, coupled with health and fitness concerns, spurred a slow decline in per capita alcohol consumption.

These years also saw renewed debate over the nature of alcoholism. The AA founders William Wilson and Robert Smith, a physician, along with the National Committee for Education on Alcoholism, led a crusade to treat alcoholism as a disease. In the 1950s the biostatistician E. M. Jellinek of the Yale Center of Alcohol Studies promoted a multistage model of alcohol addiction based on his research on AA members. But the disease concept met criticism as well. The American Medical Association in the 1960s and 1970s encouraged physicians to treat alcoholism's "medical aspects" but argued that labeling alcoholism a disease did not relieve individuals of responsibility for their intoxicated behavior. The Supreme Court concurred, declining to exonerate persons for actions committed while drunk. Although the National Institute on Alcohol Abuse and Alcoholism (NIAAA) was established in 1971, lending federal support and funding to alcoholism studies, some social scientists, including ones funded by the NIAAA, mustered evidence discrediting the disease model. The 1970s and 1980s witnessed the emergence of a broad-based public-health approach oriented toward preventing excessive drinking.

By the end of the twentieth century, what some called a neo-temperance movement gained momentum, linked to the antitobacco and antidrug campaigns. Nevertheless, the nation still had nearly thirty thousand liquor stores, many supermarkets and convenience outlets sold beer and wine, and more than half of adult Americans regularly drank alcoholic beverages. Alcohol's central role in American culture, if somewhat diminished, seemed firmly entrenched.

[*See also* Antebellum Reform; Anti-Saloon League; Disease; Drugs, Illicit; Leisure; Prohibition; Taverns and Bars; Twenties, The; War on Drugs; Woman's Christian Temperance Union; *and* Working-Class Life and Society.]

BIBLIOGRAPHY

American Association for the Cure of Inebriates. *Proceedings, 1870–1875.* New York: Arno Press, 1981.

Blocker, Jack S., Jr. *American Temperance Movements: Cycles of Reform.* Boston: Twayne, 1989.

Conrad, Peter, and Joseph W. Schneider. "Alcoholism: Drunkenness, Inebriety, and the Disease Concept." In their *Deviance and Medicalization: From Badness to Sickness*, pp. 73–109. Rev. ed. Philadelphia: Temple University Press, 1992.

Lender, Mark Edward, and James Kirby Martin. *Drinking in America: A History.* Rev. ed. New York: Free Press, 1987.

Reinarman, Craig. "The Social Construction of an Alcohol Problem: The Case of Mothers against Drunk Drivers and Social Control in the 1980s." *Theory and Society* 17 (1988): 91–120.

White, William L. *Slaying the Dragon: The History of Addiction Treatment and Recovery in America.* Bloomington, Ill.: Chestnut Health Systems/ Lighthouse Institute, 1998.

Sarah W. Tracy

ALIENS DURING WARTIME

The wartime experience of aliens—or noncitizens—in the United States has varied considerably since the country's independence from Great Britain: America's foreign relations affected aliens' social and material well-being, but racial and ethnic discrimination played a role as well. In reaction to the Atlantic world upheavals of the 1790s, including the French and Haitian revolutions, the United States, like Great Britain and France, passed laws to control the influx of foreigners. The 1790 Naturalization Act, which stipulated that only "free white persons" were eligible for citizenship, barred nonwhite aliens from political participation. The 1798 Alien and Sedition Acts, passed by Congress during the so-called Quasi-War with France, subjected aliens and their sympathizers to government surveillance, prohibited certain forms of political protest, and authorized the president, in times of war, to arrest and deport aliens from the United States.

The Sedition Acts expired under President Thomas Jefferson in 1801, but the 1798 Alien Enemies Act, which authorized the wartime arrest and deportation of "enemy aliens," remained intact. James Madison, who had opposed the acts in the 1790s, became the first president to invoke the Alien Enemies Act: he did so against the British in the War of 1812. An estimated ten thousand British subjects in the United States were required to register with the government as "enemy aliens." Nevertheless, for the remainder of the nineteenth century, the federal government did little to regulate alien activity, which remained under the jurisdiction of individual states. Only after the 1882 Chinese Exclusion Act did the United States develop a bureaucratic regime—known at first as the Immigration Service and later as the Immigration and Naturalization Service—to police the internal spaces of the nation.

During World War I, President Woodrow Wilson invoked the Alien Enemies Act to restrict the wartime activities of those considered enemy aliens and detained thousands of Germans and Austro-Hungarians suspected of subversive activity at so-called internment camps such as Hot Springs, North Carolina. Nearly all internees were men; hundreds were merchants and seamen transferred to the United States from Panama and the Philippines and detained on a technical charge for violating immigration law. In October 1917, Wilson appointed Alexander Mitchell Palmer to the position of Alien Property Custodian to hold in trust enemy assets until the end of the war. Most individual investments in real property and securities were returned, but— to the benefit of the American chemical industry—corporate investments in industries like chemicals and textiles, including valuable patents, were not.

After World War I, Americans pursued an anti-Communist campaign in which the government used immigration law to combat radicalism. In order to avoid the formal legal procedures that would have been required to prosecute citizens under the Espionage Act (1917) or Sedition Act (1918), Mitchell Palmer, then attorney general, focused his attention on aliens and arrested hundreds of suspected radicals, often without warrants. The controversial 1919–1920 "Palmer Raids" turned a fear of Communism into an attack against the foreign-born population of the United States. During the 1930s the development of fascism and communism abroad heightened Americans' concerns over national security. Aliens continued to be targets of suspicion, which led the United States in 1940 to transfer the Immigration and Naturalization Service from the Labor Department to the Justice Department.

In World War II, policy makers referred to the World War I experience as a model for how to handle aliens. The Alien Registration Act of 1940, also known as the Smith Act, required all noncitizen adult residents to register with the federal government. After the Japanese attack at Pearl Harbor, President Franklin Delano Roosevelt invoked the Alien Enemies Act to declare nine hundred thousand of the 5 million foreigners in the United States "enemy aliens." Mostly Germans, Japanese, and Italians, they were subject to travel restrictions and curfews and were prohibited from carrying guns, short-wave radios, and cameras. Based on a so-called custodial detention list generated by the Federal Bureau of Investigation, the Justice and War Departments held more than thirty thousand enemy aliens at detention stations and internment camps in locations such as Crystal City, Texas. Among those internees, thousands were transferred to the continental United States from Alaska and Hawai'i and from countries in Central and South America. By contrast, the War Relocation Authority held more than one hundred thousand Japanese Americans, two-thirds of them United States citizens, who were forced to relocate from the West Coast when Roosevelt issued Executive Order 9066 in February 1942.

Early in the Cold War, the United States reformulated its immigration policies to target Communists, rendering all but invisible the line that separated alien from citizen. Senator Pat McCarran led the charge, insisting that immigration policy was a matter of "internal security." "The Communist movement in the United States," a Senate subcommittee reported, was an "alien movement, sustained, augmented, and controlled by European Communists and the Soviet Union." Accordingly, the 1950 Internal Security Act provided for the exclusion, deportation, and denaturalization of Communists. President Harry Truman, whose veto had been overruled, declared the bill "the greatest danger to freedom of speech, press, and assembly since the Alien and Sedition Laws of 1798."

After the terrorist attacks of 11 September 2001, the United States did not invoke the

Alien Enemies Act, which requires a formal declaration of war. But key elements of history informed the government's approach to national security, including the use of immigration law. From September 2001 to August 2002 the government detained 738 foreigners on immigration charges, the inspector general of the Justice Department later revealed, merely because of their association with Arab and Muslim groups. Since immigration proceedings were a matter of administrative and not criminal law, the government claimed authority to detain noncitizens without interference from the courts. Perhaps most controversially, the United States military held hundreds of foreigners with alleged ties to the Taliban or al-Qaeda at its military base in Guantánamo Bay, Cuba. In a departure from the past, these detainees were not "enemy aliens" but "enemy combatants," a new term that legal scholars warned extended to any individual, whether alien or citizen.

Elected in 2008, President Barack Obama promised to reexamine the situation at Guantánamo, but struggled, at least in the early years of his presidency, to find a tenable solution. Americans continued to debate the perceived trade-off between liberty and security and the treatment of aliens in a far less well-defined wartime.

[*See also* **Angel Island Immigration Station; Deportations and Repatriations; Immigration; Japanese Americans, Incarceration of; Terrorism, Domestic; World War I, Home Front;** *and* **World War II, Home Front.**]

BIBLIOGRAPHY

Cole, David. *Enemy Aliens: Double Standards and Constitutional Freedoms in the War on Terrorism.* New York: New Press, 2003.

Kennedy, David M. *Over Here: The First World War and American Society.* New York: Oxford University Press, 1980.

Ngai, Mae M. *Impossible Subjects: Illegal Aliens and the Making of Modern America.* Princeton, N.J.: Princeton University Press, 2004.

Robinson, Greg. *A Tragedy of Democracy: Japanese Confinement in North America.* New York: Columbia University Press, 2009.

Zolberg, Aristide R. *A Nation by Design: Immigration Policy in the Fashioning of America.* Cambridge, Mass.: Harvard University Press, 2006.

Stephen Mak

ALLEN, RICHARD

(1760–1831), founder of the African Methodist Episcopal Church. Richard Allen was born in 1760, probably in colonial Pennsylvania. Enslaved to the jurist Benjamin Chew, Allen lived in a world that sanctioned bondage as a vital legal, political, and economic institution. By the time of his death in 1831, Allen was known throughout the Atlantic world as a leading abolitionist and advocate of black equality. Part of a generation of black leaders who came of age during the American Revolutionary era, Allen believed that the Declaration of Independence was the moral foundation of the American republic, securing liberty across the color line. As an evangelical Methodist, Allen also believed that Christianity promulgated equality in God's eyes. Allen fused these secular and sacred ideologies into a prophetic view of African American reform that linked American and African American destinies.

Allen's prophetic sensibility took shape as a young man. After being sold from his first master to a Delaware man named Stokeley Sturgis, Allen was separated from several family members. He found succor in Methodist revivals that envisioned a spiritual life beyond bondage. Allen eventually convinced his master that slavery was a sin; after buying his own freedom from Sturgis in 1783, Allen set out to transform black life regionally and nationally. By 1787, Allen had moved to Philadelphia, where his dynamic preaching attracted a host of new black worshippers to Saint George's Methodist Church. Yet Allen discovered that whites wanted to segregate them in separate church pews. Allen then led a famous walkout, after which he created Bethel Church in 1794. After roughly fifteen years of struggle, Allen secured full independence from white Methodists in 1816. In that same year, he helped form the African Methodist Episcopal (AME) denomination, which by the 1830s had become the largest institution in African American culture. As head of the AME, Allen also became North America's first black bishop.

Allen was a lifelong activist who struggled against racism in a variety of forms. He authored several abolitionist pamphlets— including a stinging rebuke of slaveholders in the 1794 pamphlet *A Narrative of the Proceedings of the Black People, during the Late Awful Calamity in* Philadelphia, coauthored with Absalom Jones—and a crafty eulogy of George Washington in 1799 that attacked slavery as a blight on the American character. He supported several black organizational initiatives, including the Free African Society, a mutual aid group that he helped form in 1787, and the inaugural gathering of black leaders at Bethel Church in 1830—a distant precursor to the National Association for the Advancement of Colored People (NAACP).

Medium in height and having a fierce gaze, Allen was a resolute man who did not back down from challenges. Though an early advocate of voluntary African emigration in the 1810s, he soon opposed the American Colonization Society for its slaveholding leadership. During the 1820s, Allen flirted with Haitian emigration when he believed that American society had betrayed its emancipatory promises. But in his autobiography, published posthumously in 1833, Allen recounted his struggles to build the black church within the United States and thus African Americans' prophetic mission to reform American democracy. In one way or another, that belief has influenced black leaders from Frederick Douglass to Martin Luther King Jr.

[*See also* **African American Emigration; Antislavery; Clergy; Free Communities of Color; Jones, Absalom;** *and* **Religion.**]

BIBLIOGRAPHY

Newman, Richard S. *Freedom's Prophet: Bishop Richard Allen, the AME Church, and the Black Founding Fathers.* New York: New York University Press, 2008.

Raboteau, Albert J. *A Fire in the Bones: Reflections on African-American Religious History.* Boston: Beacon Press, 1995.

Richard Newman

AMATEUR SPORTS

See **Sports, Amateur.**

AMERICAN ASSOCIATION OF RETIRED PERSONS

The American Association of Retired Persons (AARP) arose out of an effort by a prominent Los Angeles high school principal to improve the status of retired schoolteachers. Dr. Ethel Percy Andrus founded the National Retired

Teachers Association (NRTA) in 1947 to lobby for health-insurance coverage and increases in state pensions for retired educators. The NRTA's membership, twenty thousand in 1955, soared after Andrus arranged with Leonard Davis, an insurance agent, to offer NRTA members insurance coverage; the pair established the AARP so that others might be eligible. Chartered in 1958, the combined NRTA-AARP retained separate boards of directors but shared office space and staff.

Membership grew from a hundred and fifty thousand to a million between 1959 and 1969. By 1982 the American Association of Retired Persons had outgrown its parent organization, and the NRTA became a division within the AARP. More than 33 million members belonged to the AARP by the mid-1990s, making it, after the Roman Catholic Church, the nation's second-largest voluntary association.

The AARP offers members a variety of services, from travel advice and discounts on mail-order prescriptions to auto, life, and insurance programs. Concern over its ties to Leonard Davis's Colonial Penn insurance company in the late 1970s led the AARP to choose other underwriters for its insurance plans. By the end of the twentieth century and well into the twenty-first, the AARP had become a key voice for older Americans in Washington, D.C., lobbying against age discrimination and for health-care reform. Its influence, however, was mixed, as it experienced difficulty in mobilizing its membership in a consistent manner.

[*See also* **Life Stages** *and* **Retirement Communities.**]

BIBLIOGRAPHY

Pratt, Henry J. *Gray Agendas: Interest Groups and Public Pensions in Canada, Britain, and the United States.* Ann Arbor: University of Michigan Press, 1993.

Van Tassel, David D., and Jimmy Elaine Wilkinson Meyer, eds. *U.S. Aging Policy Interest Groups: Institutional Profiles.* New York: Greenwood Press, 1992.

W. Andrew Achenbaum

AMERICAN INDIAN MOVEMENT

Of the various forms of ethnic and racial nationalism in the 1960s and 1970s, the American Indian Movement (AIM) emerged as the best-known "Red Power" organization. AIM got its start in 1968 when charges of police brutality in Indian neighborhoods in Minneapolis led the Chippewas Dennis Banks and George Mitchell to assemble "red patrols" to follow police and witness arrests.

AIM soon evolved into a national group patterned after the Black Panthers, with chapters appearing in many cities. Especially popular among urban Indians, it quickly became a powerful force in the politics of many reservations as well. Members styled themselves as traditional warriors but drew on tactics of the larger civil rights movement. Russell Means, an Oglala Sioux, became AIM's principal spokesperson by staging attention-grabbing actions, such as the 1972 demonstrations in Gordon, Nebraska, to protest the murder of Raymond Yellow Thunder, and the Trail of Broken Treaties caravan that same year, which concluded in a six-day occupation of the offices of the Bureau of Indian Affairs in Washington, D.C. In 1973, Means was involved in AIM's dramatic seventy-one-day siege of the village of Wounded Knee, South Dakota, site of an 1890 massacre of Indians, as well as in a fracas between AIM members and police in the courthouse of Custer County, South Dakota. In 1975, armed

AIM members took over an electronics factory on the Navajo reservation in New Mexico.

By the late 1970s, AIM's popularity was fading as its militant, sometimes violent tactics became increasingly controversial. The government cracked down, imprisoning key leaders, and internal dissension split the ranks. Nonetheless, AIM's long-term influence far surpassed its short life span. AIM not only contributed to a sense of pan-Indian unity and to pride in Indian identity and heritage, but also drew national attention to Indian issues.

[*See also* **Native American History and Culture,** *subentry on* **Since 1950; Sixties, The;** *and* **Wounded Knee, Occupation of (1973).**]

BIBLIOGRAPHY

Johnson, Troy, Joane Nagel, and Duane Champagne, eds. *American Indian Activism: Alcatraz to the Longest Walk.* Urbana: University of Illinois Press, 1997.

Matthiessen, Peter. *In the Spirit of Crazy Horse.* New York: Viking, 1983.

Smith, Paul Chaat, and Robert Allen Warrior. *Like a Hurricane: The Indian Movement from Alcatraz to Wounded Knee.* New York: New Press, 1996.

Larry Burt

AMERICANIZATION MOVEMENT

The Americanization movement aimed to bring new immigrants into citizenship and to acculturate them to American society. It emerged in response to the wave of immigration that transformed American life in the early twentieth century. Between 1900 and 1920, 15 million people, many of them Catholics or Jews from southern or eastern Europe, arrived in the United States. These newcomers swelled the size of cities; in some places, immigrants and their children constituted the majority of the population. They also increased the country's heterogeneity as they brought new religious and cultural traditions.

Some observers worried that these immigrants were ignorant of the ideals and civic traditions of their new home and that their presence would undermine American democracy. Inspired in part by the broader Progressive Era, in the 1910s and 1920s reformers looked for ways to incorporate newcomers into American national identity. In order to speed the process of assimilation and to instill particular behaviors and values, they created Americanization programs that emphasized English-language proficiency, knowledge of U.S. history, loyalty to the nation, allegiance to democratic principles, naturalization to citizenship, and informed participation in the political process.

The Americanization movement included a broad range of organizations and activities. School boards, factories, unions, settlement houses, philanthropic groups, and patriotic associations offered adult-education classes teaching the English language and American civics. Religious organizations, women's groups, public libraries, and chambers of commerce also sponsored classes and events. The federal Bureaus of Education and of Naturalization established divisions for immigrant education, while state governments passed laws requiring Americanization programs and established agencies of their own. National organizations, including the National Americanization Committee, promoted activities across the country. When World War I raised Americans' suspicions about the loyalty of immigrant groups, the movement became increasingly prominent. Americanization education gained urgency during the push for wartime unity and continued after the war's end.

Reformers at the time celebrated Americanization as an effective means of bringing newcomers into national life. But later historians criticized it as a coercive process that forced immigrants to abandon Old World ways. These critics charged that Americanizers fostered a repressive cultural hegemony; they scorned native language, clothing, foods, and traditions as they insisted that newcomers cast off the customs of their homelands in order to assimilate to middle-class Protestant values. Some critics charged, too, that Americanization aimed to create workers willing to accept their place in urban industrial capitalism.

Since the later twentieth century, historians have emphasized the contested nature of Americanization. They have described it as a complex movement in which diverse participants advocated various ideas and methods and in which immigrants exerted influence of their own. Leaders of the Americanization movement understood assimilation, cultural diversity, and nationalism in a variety of ways. Similarly, rather than simply acquiescing to a narrow definition of American culture offered by elites, immigrant communities adjusted Americanization education to meet their own needs and aspirations. Immigrants found ways to retain elements of their ethnic cultures even as they embraced American identity and citizenship.

[*See also* Anti-Catholicism; Anti-Semitism; Nativist Movement; Race and Ethnicity; Transnational Identity; *and* World War I, Home Front.]

BIBLIOGRAPHY

Barrett, James R. "Americanization from the Bottom Up: Immigration and the Remaking of the Working Class in the United States, 1880–1930." *Journal of American History* 79 (December 1992): 996–1020.

Mirel, Jeffrey E. *Patriotic Pluralism: Americanization Education and European Immigrants.* Cambridge, Mass.: Harvard University Press, 2010.

Ziegler-McPherson, Christina A. *Americanization in the States: Immigrant Social Welfare Policy, Citizenship, and National Identity in the United States, 1908–1929.* Gainesville: University Press of Florida, 2009.

Diana Selig

AMERICAN LEGION

The American Legion, an organization open to all military wartime veterans, was founded in 1919 by a handful of World War I officers, including Theodore Roosevelt Jr. Within a year, the organization boasted 840,000 former officers and enlisted men—mostly middle-class whites—and was well on its way to becoming a highly influential association. Espousing a rhetoric of love of country and duty to uphold the nation's principles, it became a nationalistic defender of "one hundred percent Americanism." During the 1919–1920 Red Scare, legionnaires promised to be "the greatest bulwark against Bolshevism and anarchy." Legion posts throughout the country helped to institute loyalty oaths for teachers and prevented individuals whom they viewed as radicals from speaking in their local communities, sometimes by running the offenders out of town.

The legion pursued its mission as the self-proclaimed protector of American "justice, freedom, and democracy" throughout the twentieth century. During World War II, legionnaires were active in organizing local civil defense. In addition, the legion became officially associated with the Federal Bureau of Investigation, assisting government agents in investigating enemy aliens. At war's end, an infusion of new veterans swelled the membership roster to 3.5 million. In keeping with their anti-Communist stance, legionnaires during the Cold War adamantly insisted upon the need to roust "subversives" from government service and other positions of authority, and it vehemently supported the U.S. anti-Soviet foreign policy.

In addition to promoting nationalistic patriotism, the legion has been one of the most powerful lobbying agencies in the nation's history. It was instrumental in the establishment in the 1920s of the Veterans Bureau, the predecessor of the Department of Veterans Affairs. The Servicemen's Readjustment Act of 1944 (the GI Bill of Rights), the government's generous package of benefits to veterans, was drafted by the former legion commander Harry W. Colmery and was vigorously supported by legion lobbyists. By the early twenty-first century the American Legion had nearly 3 million members in almost fifteen thousand posts worldwide.

[*See also* **Fraternal Organizations; Military Personnel; Servicemen's Readjustment Act;** *and* **Veterans' Rights Movement.**]

BIBLIOGRAPHY

Pencak, William. *For God and Country: The American Legion, 1919–1941*. Boston: Northeastern University Press, 1989.

Lynn Dumenil

AMERICANS DISABLED FOR ACCESSIBLE PUBLIC TRANSPORT

Americans Disabled for Accessible Public Transport, or ADAPT, was founded in Denver, Colorado, in 1983 as an outgrowth of the Atlantis Community. Its goal was to have public transportation systems become accessible for all people with impairments. In 1990, after the Americans with Disabilities Act (ADA) mandated the implementation of some of its demands, ADAPT changed the meaning of its acronym to Americans Disabled for Attendant Programs Today, and it changed its focus to personal-assistance services. Its demand became that people with impairments should be able to use their Medicaid money for home- or community-based services, rather than only in institutional settings, and that they should have control over hiring the people to provide those services. Nevertheless, even after ADAPT changed its name and its mission, it still conducted protests that focused on transportation issues, especially the enforcement of ADA regulations. But overall, in its shift from demands for rights to demands for services, ADAPT transmogrified itself to stay in line with the rest of the disability movement—and to stay relevant.

ADAPT was the first disability activist organization to focus on a single issue that appealed to a variety of impairment groups rather than on a single impairment. Despite the change of mission in 1990, ADAPT retained its single-issue, multiple-impairment focus. It was never, however, a truly cross-disability organization.

ADAPT has been the disability activist organization most involved in contentious political actions—that is, protests—in the United States. Of 756 U.S. disability protests identified by this author that occurred between 1970 and 2005, ADAPT conducted almost 35 percent. No other single organization conducted more than 1 percent of the protests. In the years 1985–1988 and 1997–1998, ADAPT conducted more than half of the disability protests.

ADAPT's protests were usually disruptive and sometimes violent—unlike, for example, those related to blindness, in which one of the most prominent national organizations had very radical ideas but conducted traditional, noncontentious political actions. In a number of ADAPT's early street actions, protesters chained themselves to buses or blockaded bus stations; in their later protests, long-term building takeovers occurred several times. Overall, ADAPT's protests were statistically significantly more likely than other disability protests were to use at least one disruptive tactic, to have police present, or to result in arrests.

ADAPT and its protests served as models for other disability organizations. ADAPT showed the disability community how to conduct disruptive protests, and it showed that disruptive protests were successful. ADAPT was initially criticized for the disruptiveness of its actions. However, after the passage of the ADA, such criticisms were muted. It is likely that ADAPT's influence was both direct and indirect through its success and through the dispersion of its tactics.

[*See also* **Disability Rights Movement.**]

BIBLIOGRAPHY

Barnartt, Sharon, and Richard Scotch. *Disability Protests: Contentious Politics 1970–1999*. Washington, D.C.: Gallaudet University Press, 2001.

Tarrow, Sidney. "Social Movements in Contentious Politics: A Review Article." *American Political Science Review* 90, no. 4 (1996): 874–883.

Sharon N. Barnartt

AMUSEMENT PARKS AND THEME PARKS

Prior to World War I, there were more than fifteen hundred amusement parks in the United States. They often went by such fanciful names as White City, Luna, Wonderland, and Dreamland. They evolved out of the amusement areas of turn-of-the-century international expositions, seaside bathing resorts, country fairs, and European pleasure gardens. Amusement parks were so widespread because new electric streetcar and interurban railroad companies built the parks at the end of their rail lines. Some charged admission, and some did not: the primary goal, however, always was to encourage ridership on the rail line, and the parks served as desirable destinations at the ends of traction companies' lines. Big cities like New York and Chicago each had as many as eight parks operating at a time. Medium-size cities like Cleveland, Pittsburgh, and Washington, D.C., had at least three apiece at any given time during this period. Even rural states almost always featured at least one amusement park on the outskirts of towns with populations of at least twenty thousand.

Features. Amusement parks, also called "electric parks" or "trolley parks," featured mechanical thrill rides, games of chance, dancing, band concerts, disaster shows, live acts and ethnographic displays, motion pictures, fireworks shows, food and drink, and swimming pools or beaches. The architecture of the parks often provided fanciful, exotic backdrops with ornate electrified towers, boldly painted facades, brilliant flags waving, and vividly colored gardens. The parks' atmosphere was filled with visual and auditory excitement, a showcase of new mechanical technologies, and crowds of diverse peoples. Amusement parks helped to define a new concept of urban modernism: the celebration of motion and speed, the beauty of industrial technologies, and the experience of the crowd. Their modernity lay not in any specific style of architecture but in their sensory overstimulation—their bombardment and exaggeration of sight, sound, and motion.

Most parks were indeed "white cities": amusement parks, like other public and private recreational facilities at the turn of the twentieth century, were racially segregated. Some southern parks ran separate late-autumn seasons for African Americans after they closed their seasons for whites. In the North, amusement parks practiced de facto segregation. Big-city amusement parks increasingly adopted the practice of admitting African Americans only on special days, called "Jim Crow Days" or "Colored Days."

In both the North and the South there were also a number of "colored only" amusement parks, as they were called, that admitted African Americans. Sometimes these African American parks were located next to a white park. But more often, African American parks were at the end of city trolley lines, and for the same reason that their white counterparts were located at such places: local traction companies built parks at the ends of streetcar lines that went through black neighborhoods in order to stimulate more fares on those routes, too. Occasionally, African American businessmen built and operated amusement parks. For example, in Nashville, Tennessee, the undertaker Preston Taylor ran Greenwood Park from 1905 to 1949. His park featured a swimming pool, rides, and a baseball diamond. At these parks, swimming pools and exhibition baseball games were central, because these were the very recreations to which African Americans were otherwise denied access.

Meanings. Amusement parks were important targets for debate about modern culture and a focus for defining what counted as social values. For some, the amusement park's commingling of immigrants and different classes symbolized the democratic ideals of a melting-pot society. For Progressive reformers, however, the parks' cheap sensations and sale of alcohol contributed to the relaxation of codes of conduct and immoral sexual behavior, which they believed could result only in a devalued mongrel culture. In particular, prominent social workers like Jane Addams and Belle Israels concluded that the parks were dangerous because they fed young girls' desire for entertainment, while fostering a new sexually relaxed courtship between relative strangers that was tantamount to sexual bartering: young men "treated" the girls to the park's concessions and expected sexual "favors" in return. Social workers reasoned that a carnivalesque atmosphere that encouraged loosened inhibitions, combined with the consumption of alcohol, led to promiscuity and female immorality. As both a commercialized perversion of play and a playground for voyeurism and unchaperoned sexual liaisons, amusement parks were both branded as a vice and likened to a disease.

Although studies of temperance rhetoric tend to focus on how alcohol in the neighborhood saloon made workers and family men wastrels, abusive fathers and husbands, and unproductive citizens, amusement parks, too, were at the center of national fights about the evils of alcohol. Most parks did indeed serve beer, although many had to respond to temperance campaigns. Their response was not uniform. Some, like Palisades Park and Olympic Park in northern New Jersey, banned alcohol and gambling and billed themselves as "family parks." In the Midwest, where temperance advocates and strict Christian beliefs dominated, from the beginning many parks did not serve alcohol, and they advertised that fact. Indeed, when Alamo Park, which was open from 1906 to 1910 in Cedar Rapids, Iowa, revoked its ban on alcohol and gambling, it actually lost business: patrons boycotted it for admitting vice, and the park shut down the following season.

Interestingly enough, the traction companies' response to temperance campaigns—at least philosophically—was to build more parks. One reason that many traction companies in medium to large cities may have owned more than one amusement park was not just to drop an excuse for travel to the end of each of their lines but to sort out amusement parks by class and "standards." In a city where a family-oriented, alcohol-free park might trumpet its wholesomeness, there would likely be another park at the end of a nearby trolley line that admitted alcohol and other "cheap sensations."

Many parks also relied upon their arrangement of attractions within the park grounds as a strategy for differentiating the wholesome parts of the park from the more lascivious, as well as higher-class audiences from lower-class ones. Parks often located movie theaters and dance halls next to beer gardens and cafés, thus allowing alcohol service to be extended to the entertainment venues. On the other hand, assigning a vaudeville or movie theater a location nearer the picnic grounds and exhibiting only higher-class types of fare for a higher ticket price could also raise the standards for audience behavior. Rearranging the crowds into more homogeneous social groups shored up rather than broke down class, racial, and ethnic divisions—as was also being done, of course, through the segregationist practices employed by amusement parks across the country.

Most amusement parks went out of business between the end of World War I and the Depression in the 1930s. Various factors led to their demise: devastating fires and mismanagement were major causes. Park land also became increasingly valuable real estate for suburban development as cities grew to their boundaries. But the chief factor was that the railroad companies that had built the parks generally went out of business or became public utilities. Competition from the automobile proved too much for the streetcar and interurban railroad companies that had been running the parks only to attract people to ride on their trains. By the Depression, only about four hundred amusement parks were left across North America, and most of these succumbed to the poor economy in the 1930s.

[*See also* Circuses; Cities and Suburbs; Courtship and Dating; Dance Halls; Disney Amusement Parks; Holidays and Festivals; Jim Crow Era; Leisure; Segregation, Racial; *and* Tourism and Travel.]

BIBLIOGRAPHY

Adams, Judith A. *The American Amusement Park Industry: A History of Technology and Thrills.* Boston: Twayne, 1991.

Addams, Jane. *The Spirit of Youth and the City Streets.* New York: Macmillan, 1909.

DeBlasio, Donna. "The Immigrant and the Trolley Park in Youngstown, Ohio, 1899–1945." *Rethinking History* 5, no. 1 (2001): 75–91.

Immerso, Michael. *Coney Island: The People's Playground.* New Brunswick, N.J.: Rutgers University Press, 2002.

Israels, Belle Lindner. "The Way of the Girl." *Survey* 22 (3 July 1909): 486–497.

Kahrl, Andrew W. " 'The Slightest Semblance of Unruliness': Steamboat Excursions, Pleasure Resorts, and the Emergence of Segregation Culture on the Potomac River." *Journal of American History* 94, no. 4 (March 2008): 1108–1136.

Kasson, John F. *Amusing the Million: Coney Island at the Turn of the Century.* New York: Hill and Wang, 1978.

Nasaw, David. *Going Out: The Rise and Fall of Public Amusements.* New York: Basic Books, 1993.

Peiss, Kathy. *Cheap Amusements: Working Women and Leisure in Turn-of-the-Century New York.* Philadelphia: Temple University Press, 1986.

Rabinovitz, Lauren. *For the Love of Pleasure: Women, Movies, and Culture in Turn-of-the-Century Chicago.* New Brunswick, N.J.: Rutgers University Press, 1998.

Lauren Rabinovitz

ANGEL ISLAND IMMIGRATION STATION

During its years of operation, 1910–1940, an estimated three hundred thousand immigrants and travelers from eighty countries were processed at the Angel Island Immigration Station in San Francisco Bay. Although most were from China and Japan, significant numbers came from Russia and other countries of the Pacific Rim, as well as from Europe and the Middle East. Class, gender, and race as well as international politics figured in the enforcement of the Chinese exclusion laws and the general immigration laws so that immigrants' experiences varied, even among compatriots. Under both sets of laws and because of the common practice of attempting entry as "paper sons," the one hundred thousand Chinese applicants for entry (new immigrants, returning residents, and U.S. citizens) endured longer interrogations and detentions than did members of other groups, making them a majority at the station. However, the extensive use of the legal system by the Chinese resulted in successful appeals and an exclusion rate of about 7 percent. The eighty-five thousand arrivals from Japan, including "picture brides," the most numerous group, experienced less intensive questioning and much shorter detentions. Only 1 percent were excluded, mostly because of the Japanese government's ability to look after the interests of its citizens

abroad and its desire to cooperate with the United States. Encouraged by California's Asian Exclusion League and sanctioned by officials in Washington, D.C., Angel Island inspectors excluded South Asians by strict medical exams and a loose interpretation of the clause in the 1882 Immigration Act that denied entry to those likely to become a "public charge." The mostly farmers and laborers from the Punjab were excluded at a rate of 54 percent, the highest of any immigrant group.

World War I brought increasing numbers of non-Asians to Angel Island, including refugees from the Mexican revolution and Russian Jews fleeing conscription and the turmoil of fighting on the eastern front. Between April 1917 and May 1919 more than eight hundred German and Austro-Hungarian alien enemies came into custody at Angel Island. German seamen and nationals resident in the Philippine Islands, discharged noncitizen U.S. Army soldiers, and passengers from enemy countries, as well as resident aliens, were interrogated and detained until they were deported, transferred to internment camps, or paroled for work.

Despite the quota laws of the 1920s, refugees from the Bolshevik revolution and civil war and Nazi persecution managed to arrive via Siberia. Most of the former and about a quarter of the latter were detained for processing and sometimes detained.

In addition to arrivals, the population at Angel Island included resident aliens whom the government sought to deport. Inspectors took an active role in several national campaigns against alleged prostitutes and procurers and political radicals, as well as in the repatriation of more than two thousand Filipinos under the Tydings-McDuffie Act (1934), which gave the Philippines independence from the United States. Heightened concern during the Depression about illegal and jobless aliens turned the immigration station into a hub for deportation and repatriation.

After it was moved to the mainland and the site abandoned after occupation during World War II by the U.S. Army, the Angel Island Immigration Station faded from public memory. Discovery in 1970 of Chinese poems carved onto the walls of the detention building galvanized activists in San Francisco's Chinese community and saved the buildings from demolition. Forty years of organizing and scholarship resulted both in the station's being given National Historic Landmark status (1997) and also in a large-scale preservation project.

[*See also* **Aliens during Wartime; Chinese Americans; Deportations and Repatriations; Ellis Island; Immigration;** *and* **Japanese Americans, Incarceration of.**]

BIBLIOGRAPHY

Lee, Erika, and Judy Yung. *Angel Island: Immigrant Gateway to America.* New York: Oxford University Press, 2010.

Sakovich, Maria. "When the 'Enemy' Landed at Angel Island: San Francisco Immigration Station Sought to Bar Hostile Aliens and Deport Resident Radicals during World War I." *Prologue* 41, no. 2 (Summer 2009).

Maria Sakovich

ANTEBELLUM ERA

At the end of the War of 1812, the United States already looked significantly different from how it had looked at the end of the American Revolution, but the changes wrought by the decades after 1815 were so substantial as to render its contours practically unrecognizable compared with what they had been at the founding. Large and potentially powerful from the moment of its creation, by the end of the 1840s the United States had become a sprawling continental empire with a rapidly multiplying and increasingly diverse population. It had assumed a place as one of the most important economic producers in the world, its citizens had acquired confidence in themselves as individuals and collectively as a nation, and it seemed to demonstrate the brilliant if raucous possibilities for republican government.

Yet the unanticipated social changes unleashed by territorial expansion and economic development also were met with considerable ambivalence as they realigned the familiar arrangements and understandings that people had of their lives: many people found all the changes disorienting and disturbing. Moreover, although Americans everywhere saw and experienced similar kinds of changes, the impact of those changes had regionally disparate effects that could not be reconciled. Ultimately, as the nineteenth century reached its midpoint, the evolution of the United States had the paradoxical effect of both enhancing nationalism and deepening economic integration and also, at the same time, sowing the seeds of sectionalism that led to the country's dismemberment and nearly to its destruction in the war that retrospectively gave the antebellum era its name.

Expansion, Expulsion, and War. In 1815 the nation comprised eighteen states, just five more than had had signatories to the Declaration of Independence. Only Louisiana sat west of the Mississippi River or occupied space beyond the boundaries of the United States that had been established by the Treaty of Paris at the end of the Revolutionary War. The Spanish claimed Florida and a large portion of the western half of the continent, England claimed sizable territory in the

Pacific Northwest, and even though several of the groups had suffered major military setbacks during the War of 1812, various groups of Native Americans inhabited land both east and west of the Mississippi.

In remarkably short order, however, the United States used a combination of diplomacy, negotiation, threats, and no small amount of brute force to extend its geographic reach dramatically. A year after Andrew Jackson, then a general, created an international incident in 1818 by invading Florida, Spain ceded the territory. Upon assuming the presidency early in 1829, meanwhile, Jackson made the removal of tens of thousands of Native Americans living east of the Mississippi among his administration's leading priorities. Skeptical of the prospects for white and Indian coexistence and solicitous of white Americans who desired Indian land, Jackson instituted policies that led by the end of the 1830s to the displacement and expulsion of tribes ranging from the Sauk and the Fox in what is now the upper Middle West to the Seminole, Creek, Choctaw, Chickasaw, and Cherokee in what is now the Southeast.

By the 1840s, American ambitions extended across the Mississippi River to the Pacific Ocean, the successes of the early nineteenth-century expansions having given rise to an ideological conviction, popularly known as Manifest Destiny, that continental conquest and the spread of white American civilization were nothing less than expressions of divine will. Among the initial tangible results of this mind-set was a treaty signed with England that secured division of the disputed Oregon Country at the forty-ninth parallel. Disappointing to some politicians who blustered about warfare unless the British conceded American claims extending practically to Alaska, peaceful settlement of the Oregon question allowed the United States to focus attention on its escalating conflict with Mexico.

Though tensions between the two countries had been charged since the middle of the 1830s—when, over Mexican objections, the United States recognized the breakaway Mexican province of Texas as an independent republic—they finally boiled over in 1846 after American troops provoked Mexican forces into an attack, providing the pretext for a congressional declaration of war. Seen as an effort to take by military might territory that Mexico had refused to sell, the war was an unambiguous success. When it ended in 1848, the United States acquired more than half a million square miles of land, comprising roughly one-third of Mexico and including California; President James K. Polk had declared such an acquisition among his principal goals when running for office in 1844. The nearly hundred thousand Mexican and hundred and fifty thousand Indian inhabitants of the ceded territory, meanwhile, in time found much of their power, rights, and land claims despoiled.

All told, between 1815 and 1848 the United States grew by more than 1.5 million square miles, almost doubling its size from the time of the Louisiana Purchase. It acquired or secured more than twelve hundred miles of coastline along the Pacific Ocean and added twelve new states. Another three joined the Union by the end of the 1850s. Essentially still an eastern nation at the end of the War of 1812, by 1860 nearly 15 percent of the American population lived west of the Mississippi River.

Migrations and Markets, Technology and Urban Development. No matter how many Americans made the decision to move west in the first half of the nineteenth century, national population density inexorably increased nonetheless, because the people of the United States grew immensely more numerous even as they became more restless.

Around 8.5 million people lived in the United States in 1815. That number shot up to more than 23 million by 1850, and another 8 million residents appeared on the U.S. Census rolls by 1860. In part the result of natural reproduction, the stunning population growth of the period also came from a massive wave of European immigration lasting nearly thirty years. Arriving mostly from Ireland, where famine created widespread desperation, and from Germany, where economic shifts pushed many to look elsewhere for opportunity, immigrants fundamentally altered the ethnic and religious makeup of the nation, as well as the composition of its labor force.

Migrations and population increase alike contributed significantly to the spectacular economic growth that the United States experienced in the antebellum era. As American settlers filled out western frontiers, their output of agricultural products skyrocketed. Production of grain, livestock, and other foodstuffs boomed in what is now the Midwest, while in the South, farmers moving into places like Alabama and Mississippi transformed what had only recently been Indian land into the cotton kingdom. By the middle of the 1830s, cotton constituted more than half the value of all goods that America sent overseas, and it maintained that majority nearly uninterrupted until the Civil War.

Cotton production may have made southern plantation owners extraordinarily wealthy, but its impact was devastating for the enslaved laborers who worked their fields. Though the institution of slavery seemed to be struggling in the United States at the turn of the nineteenth century, the expansion of the cotton economy reinvigorated it. By 1820 the slave population sat at 1.5 million, twice what it had been in 1800. It more than doubled again by 1850, at which point the United States had the largest slave population in the world.

As the domestic slave trade that provided southern cotton growers with the bulk of their workforce moved more than a million slaves from east to west in the first half of the nineteenth century, it not only engineered another of the era's important large-scale migrations but also marked the emergence of a market in coerced laborers at the center of a burgeoning integrated national economy. Even though slaves could be bought and sold only in the South, the slave trade drew upon capital investment from outside the slave states, and the cotton that slaves brought out of the ground fed the flourishing northern textile industry. Links in a long chain of finance, commerce, agriculture, and manufacturing that connected a wide range of people and large swaths of the landscape, slavery and the slave trade were thus part and parcel of a broad economic transformation. Some historians have called this economic transformation the "market revolution" because antebellum Americans became increasingly connected to ever-larger economic networks that attenuated and often subsumed the local exchange networks that characterized the colonial and early republican eras.

Enabling the accelerated pace and amplified size of antebellum market development were a more sophisticated banking system, a favorable legal climate, and—especially—technological innovations and infrastructural improvements that made for greater efficiencies in the production and distribution of commodities and consumer items. Building elaborate webs of roads, canals, and railways, and capitalizing on advances ranging from the steam engine and the cotton gin to the steel plow and the mechanical loom, Americans made their country's economy into one of the most dynamic of the age. They also managed to intensify the sense of their own interconnectedness despite their far-flung geography because the breakthroughs of the nineteenth century let them share worlds of both goods and information—first thanks to growing numbers of newspapers moving via the roads and canals of the 1820s and 1830s, and then thanks to telegraph wires running alongside the railroad tracks of the 1840s and 1850s.

Few of these economic changes could be separated from the development of American cities, which served simultaneously as infrastructural hubs, commercial and banking powerhouses, manufacturing and cultural centers, and gathering places for the agricultural products of their surrounding countrysides. They also, consequently, served as population magnets for native-born rural Americans and immigrants alike. The United States remained a predominantly rural nation well into the nineteenth century, but urban growth in the antebellum era was substantial and rapid all the same. The nation's urban population jumped from roughly 6 percent in 1800 to nearly 20 percent by 1860. In 1860 more than forty cities had populations over twenty thousand—whereas just four did in 1800—and more than a dozen cities in 1860 were larger than America's biggest city had been at the turn of the century. New York City's population alone grew from around 60,000 in 1800 to more than 800,000 sixty years later.

The Consequences. The sweeping changes of the antebellum age imbued many white Americans with a great deal of pride and optimism and even with a bit of swagger. In significant ways, however, those changes were also profoundly disconcerting. Extensive population movements disarticulated families and communities across the country. Urban development upended customary household organization and means of making a living, and

the expansion of wage work that accompanied industrialization subverted traditional labor rhythms and worker prerogatives. Economic growth was uneven, crippling depressions periodically wracked the nation, and although markets and information bound Americans together, marketplace values and material disparities also seemed to make society more anonymous, grasping, coarse, and fragmented along lines of social class, race and ethnicity, and politics, as exhibited by the hundreds of riots and other episodes of mob violence that erupted during the era.

Responses to the more troubling elements of American life ranged widely. Evangelical religion flourished as revivalist preachers promised converts moral regeneration and the ability to exert control over their individual lives and improve the world around them. Members of a growing middle class embraced a new set of gendered bourgeois values that they believed steeled men to grapple with the tumultuous public world and encouraged women to make a nurturing and pious domestic sphere as a private shelter from that world. Laborers and artisans began unionizing and striking so that they might retain some power in the workplace and reasonable working conditions.

Many of these responses converged in the astonishing variety of reform societies and movements that appeared in the antebellum era. Inspired both by religious conviction and by a secular faith in progress, reformers looked to eliminate the social evils that came from social and economic change and that marred America's pretensions to greatness. Not unlike the voters engaged by the era's new political parties, reformers who organized themselves into voluntary associations found the trend toward participatory democracy in the United States invigorating and their activities a way to counter the social

ANTEBELLUM ERA · 45

atomism of American life. Even more than the political parties, however, reform movements drew on the energies of men and women alike, as women took advantage of notions about their supposedly moral and pure natures to act publicly in ways that most advocates of those notions never intended.

Antebellum reformers launched assaults on prostitution, alcohol and alcohol abuse, and poverty. They founded new religious sects and utopian communities, and they campaigned for public schools, better conditions in asylums and prisons, and rights for women. Whatever their cause, reformers often met resistance and sometimes outright ridicule. But no reform movement was so divisive or aroused so much hostility as the abolitionist movement to end slavery, whose white and black supporters faced condemnation and the prospect of physical violence in every section of the country as they challenged racial hierarchy and entrenched economic interests alike. Yet as Americans needed to make choices about whether the territory acquired during the Mexican War ought to be opened to slavery, the abolitionist critique took on new meaning. Though the developments of the antebellum era had led Americans everywhere to believe in a democratic, prosperous, and nationally triumphant future, by the end of the 1840s northerners had come to see that future as guaranteed by a free labor system, while southerners had become more invested in a future underwritten by slavery. Only one of those futures could be in the West, a reality that political attempts at compromise could stave off for only so long.

[*See also* Antebellum Reform; Antislavery; Asylums and Mental Illness; Bleeding Kansas; Civil War Era; Communication Networks; Communication Revolution, Modern; Free-Soilers; German Americans; Great Awakenings; Internal Migration, *subentry on* Nineteenth-Century Westward; Irish Americans; Labor Movements; Native American History and Culture, *subentry on* 1800 to 1900; Native American Removal; Prisons and Penitentiaries; Revivals; Riots, Urban; Separate Spheres Ideology; Slave Trades; Stanton, Elizabeth Cady; Strikes and Industrial Conflict; Utopian and Communitarian Movements; *and* Women's Rights Movement, Antebellum Era.]

BIBLIOGRAPHY

Deyle, Steven. *Carry Me Back: The Domestic Slave Trade in American Life*. New York: Oxford University Press, 2005.

Hatch, Nathan O. *The Democratization of American Christianity*. New Haven, Conn.: Yale University Press, 1989.

Haynes, Sam W. *James K. Polk and the Expansionist Impulse*. 3d ed. New York: Pearson Longman, 2006.

Howe, Daniel Walker. *What Hath God Wrought: The Transformation of America, 1815–1848*. New York: Oxford University Press, 2007.

Morrison, Michael A. *Slavery and the American West: The Eclipse of Manifest Destiny and the Coming of the Civil War*. Chapel Hill: University of North Carolina Press, 1997.

Ryan, Mary P. *Cradle of the Middle Class: The Family in Oneida County, New York, 1790–1865*. New York: Cambridge University Press, 1981.

Sellers, Charles. *The Market Revolution: Jacksonian America, 1815–1846*. New York: Oxford University Press, 1991.

Wallace, Anthony F. C. *The Long, Bitter Trail: Andrew Jackson and the Indians*. New York: Hill and Wang, 1993.

Walters, Ronald G. *American Reformers, 1815–1860*. Rev. ed. New York: Hill and Wang, 1997.

Wilentz, Sean. *Chants Democratic: New York City and the Rise of the American Working Class, 1788–1850*. New York: Oxford University Press, 1984.

Joshua D. Rothman

ANTEBELLUM REFORM

Looking back on the antebellum period (1815–1860), the Boston abolitionist Thomas Wentworth Higginson noted the presence of a "Sisterhood of Reforms," which he described as a variety of "social and physiological theories of which one was expected to accept all, if any" (*Cheerful Yesterdays* [Boston: Houghton, Mifflin, 1900], p. 119). Higginson's description of antebellum reform as a "Sisterhood" highlights the influential role that women held in American reform. Reformers relied on gender ideals that described women as the moral core of the family and, by extension, society. Reformers also relied on women's labor in promoting reform. Yet "Sisterhood" implies unity where often division and dissension existed. Many reform organizations were initially segregated by gender. Likewise, reform groups were often established along racial and class lines. In the 1830s, as reform efforts expanded, some reformers challenged the status quo and sought to place reform on a more radical foundation by encouraging equal participation by all reformers regardless of sex, race, or class.

Regardless of individual opinions about gender roles or racial equality, reformers were united in their desire to perfect American society in the nineteenth century. Antebellum reformers sought a thorough, permanent moral transformation of American society. Of the antebellum reform movements, abolitionism was the most prominent and the most extreme, representing a fundamental attack on American culture and politics. Temperance, in contrast, was the largest and most sustained of the antebellum reform movements, while education reform attracted the broadest constituency. Though not always the "Sisterhood" described by Higginson, reform movements'

ideas and strategies developed and changed in dynamic relationship with each other. Competing visions of American reform may have hindered sweeping social change, but such an array of organizations, strategies, and ideas may well have encouraged broader participation by advocates of reform. In the end, antebellum reformers were most successful in placing critical questions about race, class, and gender on the public agenda and encouraging activists and nonactivists alike to come to terms with the meaning of America's revolutionary heritage.

Market Revolution. American reform developed in response to geographic, economic, political, and cultural changes that transformed society in the nineteenth century. The antebellum period witnessed significant changes in the American landscape. In 1815 there were eighteen states; by 1860 there were thirty-three. Likewise, during this same period the United States nearly doubled in area. Despite a declining birthrate, the American population kept pace with territorial expansion. A steady flow of immigrants, primarily from Germany, Ireland, and England, kept population growth high: the growth rate averaged 33 percent per decade in this period. Immigration coincided with the most intense period of urbanization in American history when the country's urban population increased fivefold, growing from 7 to 18 percent of the American population. For reform-minded men and women, immigration and urbanization were evidence that America was changing rapidly, often in troubling ways.

Immigration, urbanization, and territorial expansion were also driven by and contributed to the development of the "market revolution," a term used by historians to describe the dramatic shift in the American economy as manufacturing replaced agriculture as the primary economic foundation. Industrial capitalism revolutionized the workplace as the relationship between employer and employee was replaced by an impersonal relationship that often pitted the interests of employer and employee against each other. Labor became simply a commodity available for negotiation. As a result, industrialization created distinctions between the working and the middle classes and gave rise to the creation of urban working and middle classes. The two classes had different experiences of the dramatic changes of the antebellum period: working-class men and women experienced greater economic instability, while the middle class enjoyed an increase in leisure time.

Working-class men and women struggled to survive in the market economy. Dependent on cash wages, workers lacked the resources to survive economic downturns that were part of the capitalist boom-and-bust cycle. Antebellum reformers sought not only to relieve the suffering of the working class, but also, through education, temperance, and other reforms, to aid them in becoming virtuous citizens. Often those reformers were members of the newly developed middle class, who used their increased leisure time to participate in reform movements.

Among the middle class, industrialization influenced the development of new gender ideals. In the antebellum period, the distinction between the female-led home and the male-dominated workplace influenced the development of new ideas about gender and society that historians have called the "ideology of separate spheres." According to this ideology, men and women were endowed by God and nature with opposite but complementary traits. Men occupied the public realm of economic and political activity, while women occupied the private realm of the home and family. The ideology of separate spheres was based on the idea that men earned enough money to support their nonlaboring wives and children at home. Thus separate spheres was not an accurate description of enslaved, immigrant, working-class, and female-headed families, in which by force or necessity all members were required to make an economic contribution to the household. Even the middle class, whose members were the greatest supporters of the ideology of separate spheres, was not always able to live up to such ideals. Still, these new gender ideals constituted a powerful set of prescriptions in antebellum America, to which many men and women aspired and against which all men and women were assessed and measured.

Inspired by the renewed religious fervor of the period and influenced by its social dislocations, men and women formed associations to improve the morals of individuals and society. The vast array of antebellum reform movements reflected the broad changes underway in American society. Antislavery, temperance, women's rights, nonresistance (or peace), and education, labor, moral, and penal reform movements all developed in this period. Some of the more radical movements drew strong protests from opponents, while others, such as education reform, relied on a wide range of supporters.

Education Reform. Literacy was essential to all other reform movements as activists worked to inform Americans of the many social evils present in antebellum society. In the antebellum period, reformers called for tax-supported schools. Public education, activists believed, would mitigate the problems of an expanded male suffrage, a growing immigrant population, and economic instability. The Whig reformer Horace Mann claimed that public schools were a way for

Americans to "free ourselves from the low-minded and the vicious; not by their expatriation, but by their elevation" (Ronald G. Walters, *American Reformers, 1815–1860*, p. 209) An educated public, according to Mann and his fellow reformer Calvin Stowe, was essential to the proper functioning of democratic institutions and processes. State-supported schools would provide an established standard of education, instill self-discipline, and teach civic virtue. Thus fundamentally reformers believed that public schools would create responsible citizens and informed voters and would render the unruly, uneducated, and dangerous classes trustworthy. Of the "Sisterhood of Reforms," education brought together the most diverse group of supporters—people who held out hope that human character could be shaped by a rational system of education.

Prior to the establishment of public schools, education was a private, voluntary matter. In the early nineteenth century, Sunday schools, for example, were opened in larger cities such as New York and Philadelphia. These privately funded schools were open only on Sundays, when the factories were closed, and offered a basic education in reading, writing, arithmetic, and religion. By 1827, Sunday schools provided basic education to two hundred thousand American children. In contrast, the children of the elite were educated in private academies or were taught at home by tutors. Despite these early attempts, teaching quality was uneven and student attendance sporadic. Education reformers sought a state-supported school system that would rationalize both teacher training and student education.

In Massachusetts, Horace Mann led the fight for public schools. In 1837 the Massachusetts state legislature established a board of education and appointed Mann its first secretary. Supported by a government sympathetic to state-supported schools, Mann used this post to promote his agenda of education reform. Mann convinced taxpayers that it was in their best interest to support public schools, arguing that the wealthy had a responsibility to support public education. Businessmen, he argued, would benefit from public education through the creation of an industrious, disciplined workforce that would contribute to the state's economic prosperity. And to the working class, Mann promoted public education as the great equalizer, providing the children of the working class with the skills and knowledge necessary for upward mobility. Mann outlined a plan whereby public schools would be organized according to a statewide system funded by state and local taxes, governed by an elected school board, staffed by trained teachers, and free of church control. Massachusetts led the way in a series of education reforms: first public high school (1821), first teacher-training school (1839), and first compulsory school attendance law (1852). The Massachusetts example spread to other states. In the South, however, white families continued to rely on private schools, and slave literacy remained illegal.

Women's education took on particular importance in the antebellum period as activists emphasized women's moral role within the family. Catharine Beecher connected the public-school movement to women's education, while the feminist leaders Elizabeth Cady Stanton and Emma Willard argued for women's educational equality as part of a larger program of women's rights. Teaching, according to Beecher, provided women with a career path and gave them an opportunity to shape the morals of future generations. During the 1820s and 1830s the education pioneers Willard, Beecher, and Mary Lyon founded several notable seminaries for girls. The primary function of these schools was to train girls in the proper fulfillment of their maternal roles and, by preparing them to become teachers, more broadly to enable them to exercise their moral guardianship. By claiming that women could meet the highest intellectual standards while also serving as the moral protectors of the family and society, education reformers simultaneously reinforced and challenged traditional gender roles.

Temperance. Temperance was the largest and most sustained of the nineteenth-century reform movements. It is estimated that between 1790 and 1830, alcohol consumption nearly doubled, increasing from five to ten gallons per year per drinking-age individual. Northern evangelicals, concerned about the rise in consumption, established temperance organizations beginning in the 1820s. Reformers linked intemperance to a variety of social evils including poverty, crime, family violence, and poor parenting, as well as poor physical health. Temperance reform focused on self-discipline, particularly male self-discipline, as reformers described women as the victims of male drunkenness.

The American Temperance Society (ATS) was established in Boston by evangelical reformers in 1826. By 1829 nearly one thousand local societies had been established throughout the North, with a combined membership of one hundred thousand men and women. By the mid-1830s the ATS boasted that one million Americans—one in nine adults—had signed an abstinence pledge. The ATS benefited from its evangelical origins. Temperance societies in this period resembled Bible and tract societies and reiterated evangelicals' claims that salvation and self-discipline were intimately linked. And like the revivals of the Second Great Awakening, women were the primary supporters, while men filled leadership roles.

Temperance reformers used lectures, pamphlets, and rallies to persuade men and women to pledge abstinence from alcohol. Temperance rhetoric emphasized the effects of alcohol abuse on the family, particularly on wives and children. Such writings accorded with accepted cultural ideals that husbands and fathers should be the protectors of women. As the legal writer Henry Folsom Page wrote in 1850, intemperance "blunted" men's morals and rendered them unable to fulfill their "relations" as spouse, father, and citizen. As a result, the wife of the drunkard was forced to share the marriage bed with a stranger. In the 1840s and 1850s, writers of sentimental fiction dramatized personal and familial struggles with alcohol abuse. Of these fictional works, T. S. Arthur's *Ten Nights in a Bar-Room* (1854) sold four hundred thousand copies, making it one of the best-selling books of the nineteenth century. *Ten Nights* underscored the damage done to the middle-class family as a result of liquor consumption. Arthur, playing on middle-class gender ideals, portrayed victimized womanhood. In *Ten Nights*, female moral suasion proved helpless against the male demon rum.

In the 1830s increasing numbers of working-class men, worried about the effects of alcohol on job performance, joined temperance societies and signed pledges. By 1835 more than five thousand temperance societies had been established throughout the United States. In 1840, formerly inebriated working-class men in Baltimore founded the Washington Society. Unlike earlier temperance societies, which had focused on preventing intemperance, the Washingtonians reached out to the drunkard. Through tales of personal tragedy, Washingtonians urged audiences to avoid the temptations of alcohol and to provide compassion and support to the degraded drunkard. By 1841, with the establishment of local societies throughout New England, the Washingtonians claimed nearly two hundred thousand members.

In 1841, northern women organized Martha Washington Societies as auxiliaries to the male groups. Like the Washingtonians, the Martha Washington Societies spread rapidly, particularly in the Northeast and Midwest. By 1842, New York City had forty societies and six thousand members. The Martha Washington Societies brought a decidedly female cast to temperance reform by focusing on practical assistance, as well as on mutual support. Women held fairs and bazaars to raise money for the temperance movement and to provide both financial assistance and also clothing and food to the families of drunkards. The Martha Washington Societies were distinct from many other women's reform groups of the antebellum period. First, though a cross-class group, the societies were dominated by working-class women. Second, the Martha Washington Societies reached out to female drunkards, providing vital assistance to reform these "fallen sisters." Finally, taking women reformers out of their usual domestic sphere and into a more public role, women who worked with the Martha Washington Societies assumed leadership of their organizations and visited at their homes those individuals and families affected by intemperance.

Women's participation in the temperance movement was not, however, without controversy. For example, at the World's Temperance Convention in New York City in 1853, on the platform the Reverend Antoinette Brown presented her credentials as a delegate and attempted to speak to the audience. Brown was hissed and shouted down by the crowd. Women did not dominate the movement until 1874 with the establishment of the Woman's Christian Temperance Union.

Despite these controversies, temperance reformers were successful. By the 1840s, reformers had significantly reduced the consumption of alcohol. By the 1850s, many states either limited or prohibited the sale of alcohol and allowed drunkenness as grounds for divorce.

Moral Reform.   Originally published in England in 1791, Susanna Rowson's *Charlotte Temple* became the first best-selling novel in the United States, selling nearly fifty thousand copies by 1812. *Charlotte Temple* recounted the classic story of seduced and abandoned womanhood, highlighting the perils of the new market economy for women, especially the young, single woman who found herself alone in the city without friends or family to support her. At the end of the novel, Charlotte is penniless, unmarried, and lifeless, with a newborn daughter at her side. In the antebellum period, Charlotte's alleged gravesite in the cemetery of Trinity Church in New York City became a popular tourist attraction. Charlotte Temple challenged the traditional ideal of virtuous womanhood. For male reformers, Charlotte personified the "fallen woman."

Initially, moral reform societies were organized by male merchants, philanthropists, and clergymen and reflected their benevolent origins. Merchant reformers such as the brothers Lewis and Arthur Tappan worried that their young male laborers, who had moved to the city from rural areas, were particularly vulnerable to the wiles of prostitutes. One strategy adopted by early moral reformers urged prostitutes to repent, promising moral and economic support to them after their redemption. The Magdalen Society of Philadelphia, for example, founded in 1800, pledged to "restor[e] to the paths of virtue those unhappy females who in unguarded hours have been robbed of their innocence." The society's Magdalen Home, established in 1808, provided a refuge to women who applied for assistance. Women who were granted admission to the home agreed to a series of conditions including regular Bible reading and no obscene language. Women were not allowed to leave the home without the permission of the visiting committee and were forbidden from discussing with their housemates the circumstances that had led them to seek refuge. Lessons in domestic skills such as sewing and yarn making aimed at helping reformed women find work as domestics. Pregnant, diseased, or African American women were not admitted to the home. African Americans were also not allowed membership in the society.

By the 1820s the Magdalen Society, along with many other moral reform groups, began to encourage greater participation by women in the work of reform. In 1831, John McDowell, an evangelical who had been converted by Charles Grandison Finney, issued a report on prostitution in New York City. McDowell's call to the "virtuous women" of the city to aid their "fallen sisters" resonated with female reformers. The New York Female Moral Reform Society was organized in 1834. The American Female Moral Reform Society organized soon after, boasting more than five hundred local chapters by 1840. The society also published a periodical, the *Advocate of Moral Reform*. Initially, following McDowell's example, activists sought to save prostitutes by getting them to renounce sin and accept Christ; however, reformers quickly realized that doing so overlooked the male customers of prostitutes. Drawing on evangelical ideas about female sexual purity, many moral reformers eventually placed blame for "fallen women" and female prostitution on men rather than on women. According to the reformers' characterizations, women lacked sexual desire, whereas men were controlled by their sexuality. Thus dominant man used his power to seduce defenseless woman, leaving her "ruined" and outcast from society. In the pages of the *Advocate of Moral Reform*, such a man was described as "The Destroyer."

Female moral reformers engaged in bold and unfeminine acts such as visiting prostitutes, publishing the names of their male clients, and campaigning for antiseduction laws. When male reformers suggested that men were better suited to the indelicate work of reforming prostitutes, female reformers replied that only women could truly understand the problem.

The New York Female Moral Reform Society used the tactics of earlier organizations, while simultaneously broadening the focus of their reform work, developing over time an overtly antimale tone. In addition to establishing houses of refuge and giving reformed prostitutes moral and economic support, reformers hoped to eradicate vice by attacking it where it resided, in the brothels. Reformers launched a national campaign to eliminate obscene publications. Moreover, reformers encouraged mothers to educate their sons and daughters to the dangers of vice. Since mothers spent more time with their children than fathers did, moral reformers urged women to oversee the sexual education of their sons. In doing so, mothers would deepen the ties already existing between mother and son and encourage the son to reject traditional masculine values in favor of feminine morality. Thus overall, by transforming women from perpetrators of seduction into victims of male licentiousness, female moral reformers effectively reversed the traditional double standard of morality.

Prison Reform. Prison reformers focused on reform of the individual rather than on physical punishment, incarceration, or execution, and they called for the establishment of programs that would emphasize instruction and personal discipline. Realizing that the mentally ill and children fared poorly when incarcerated with the general prison population, reformers also worked to establish separate, publicly funded institutions for juveniles and the insane.

In the 1820s, in New York at Auburn and Ossining (Sing Sing) and in Pennsylvania at Pittsburgh and Philadelphia, state governments implemented new prison systems that isolated prisoners from one another and from the outside world. In New York, provisions were made for some interaction among prisoners, while the Pennsylvania institutions kept prisoners in solitary confinement. The New York and Pennsylvania systems were based on reformers' belief that environment rather than an individual's character flaws had led to sinful behavior. Removing the individual from society and from the conditions that had produced the crime would provide criminals with an opportunity to reflect on their sins, to repent, and to learn the self-discipline necessary for reformation. Reformers established educational programs, prison libraries, and Sunday-school programs for prisoners.

In the early 1840s, while teaching a prisoners' Sunday school, the reformer Dorothea Dix had an opportunity to observe the effect of imprisonment on the mentally ill. Over an eighteen-month period, Dix surveyed jails, prisons, and almshouses in Massachusetts and then presented her findings in the form of a memorial to the state legislature in 1843. The legislature approved appropriation of funds to provide better care for the mentally ill. Like prisons, mental hospitals provided regimented activities and treatment in an attempt to teach morality, discipline, cleanliness, and thrift.

Prison reformers also established institutions specifically for juvenile offenders. The New York House of Refuge, which opened in 1825, was established by members of the Society for the Prevention of Pauperism and the Society for the Reformation of Juvenile Delinquents, as well as the state and federal governments. Similar houses were built in Boston in 1826, in Philadelphia in 1828, and, by the late 1850s, in New Orleans, Chicago, and Providence, Rhode Island. Most of these were publicly supported, but like the New York House of Refuge, many continued to rely on financial support from individuals and groups.

Some houses of refuge and reform schools used solitary confinement and corporal punishment, while others relied on more humanitarian measures. Regardless of the means, the emphasis was on instilling self-discipline and encouraging a moral, upright lifestyle. Juvenile inmates received conventional schooling and training in domestic skills, and they were often given an opportunity to work as an apprentice to learn a trade.

Labor Reform. The rise of industrial capitalism in the antebellum period revolutionized the workplace, changing both the methods of production and the relationships between individuals and groups. Prior to the development of the factory system, skilled artisans working alongside their helpers manufactured goods in home-based workshops. Urbanization and advances in transportation increased consumer demand for manufactured goods, prompting artisans to develop more efficient means of production. For example, shoe manufacturers "put out" various stages of shoemaking to less-skilled laborers, both saving time and money and increasing production. Other industries such as textile production relied on specialized and less-skilled jobs that could be completed by inexpensive laborers, generally women and children, working in factories. For manufacturers, the emphasis was on increasing production and reducing costs.

The adversarial relationship that developed between employer and employee during the market revolution led to a series of sporadic labor strikes in the 1820s and early 1830s. Labor activists established workingmen's organizations in this period to fight for a variety of reforms: free public schools, lien laws (to recover wages from employers who declared bankruptcy), abolition of imprisonment for debt, and the ten-hour workday. Though the organizations floundered in the early 1830s, wages rose by 1837 and the ten-hour workday became more common. With the Panic of 1837, however, wages fell, reforms languished, and the remaining workingmen's associations collapsed. Labor reform gained strength again in the 1840s as the economy rebounded.

Women were also active in labor reform. In 1836, mill hands in Lowell, Massachusetts, organized the Factory Girls' Association. Other textile workers throughout New England followed suit and established local organizations committed to promoting working women's interests. In the 1840s, women workers joined with men in the labor movement in agitating for the ten-hour day. Female Lowell workers testified before the Massachusetts legislature about the poor working conditions in the mills. Though it did not lead to any reforms, this event signaled the development of a class and gender consciousness among working-class women, who realized that they shared common struggles and interests. In the 1820s, as women started to work in textile mills, many female workers proclaimed an allegiance to the ideals of true womanhood and defended their respectability as "ladies," even as they ventured away from the confines of the family. The protests of the 1830s and 1840s signaled a shift in women's activism as they questioned the limits of women's sphere and joined other antebellum reformers in claiming a broader role for women in speaking and acting in public life.

Abolitionism. Abolitionism was the most prominent and probably the most controversial of the reform movements that emerged in the 1820s and 1830s. In the late eighteenth century, antislavery societies were generally established by white elite males, usually members of the Society of Friends, or the Quakers. Early abolitionists fought for the abolition of the international slave trade and the gradual abolition of slavery.

When gradual abolition failed in the wake of the abolition of the international slave trade, abolitionists organized the American Colonization Society (ACS) in 1816. Members of the ACS hoped to establish an American colony in Africa for freed slaves and free blacks. Opponents of abolition worried about the presence of a large population of free blacks in the United States; thus proponents of the ACS believed that slaveholders were more likely to emancipate their slaves if those same slaves immigrated to Africa after emancipation. Clearly racist and antiblack in intent, members of the ACS believed that blacks and whites could not live together and that blacks would be assured of their rights only if they were resettled into a colony established specifically for them. The ACS was most successful in ways that members had not expected: the radical abolitionist movement, associated with William Lloyd Garrison, developed out of opposition to colonization.

The 1831 publication of the first issue of Garrison's newspaper the *Liberator* is often pointed to as the inaugural moment in the antebellum abolition movement. Garrison and his supporters established a new, radical abolitionist movement that called for an immediate end to slavery and equal civil rights for blacks. Slavery was a sin that prevented blacks from exercising their innate free will to make good choices; therefore, slavery had to be abolished without delay. Abolitionists also pointed out that slavery corrupted the slaveholder by sanctioning brute force, lust, and hatred of an entire group of people. To fight slavery, abolitionists formed the New England Anti-Slavery Society in 1832. In 1833, Garrison helped form the American Anti-Slavery Society (AASS), the first such national organization. By 1840, abolitionists had formed more than fifteen hundred local organizations.

The abolitionist movement of the 1830s drew from a broad base of support that included women, blacks, and white men of all classes. The evangelical middle class of New England, upstate New York, and the Old Northwest (particularly Ohio) provided the movement's primary constituency, however. Garrison dominated the New England group, while Arthur and Lewis Tappan dominated the New York group and James G. Birney, Elizur Wright, and Theodore Dwight Weld dominated antislavery activity in Ohio. American activists also sought support from British abolitionists who had been successful in gaining parliamentary passage of an emancipation act in 1833. Unlike other reform movements, such as those related to temperance and education, abolitionism constituted a relatively small part of the overall reform movement and occupied the margins of American political and social life. Abolitionism, unlike temperance and education, represented a fundamental attack on American politics and culture.

In the mid-1830s, abolitionists launched two campaigns to convert proslavery supporters to abolition. First, in 1835 abolitionists initiated a postal campaign targeting ministers, politicians, and newspaper editors throughout the South, inundating them with thousands of pieces of abolitionist literature. If slaveholders could be convinced of the hostility of world opinion, abolitionists believed,

then slaveholders would realize the futility of the fight against abolitionism. Rather than peaceful conversion, the abolitionists instead witnessed the outbreak of violence throughout the South as southerners and slaveholders searched incoming mail to confiscate and destroy any abolitionist literature. Also in 1835, abolitionists launched a national antislavery petition campaign. Abolitionists had already petitioned for an end to slavery in Washington, D.C., and an end to the interstate slave trade. By May 1838 the American Anti-Slavery Society reported that it had sent more than 415,000 petitions to Congress. However, no congressional action was taken on the antislavery petitions. The gag rule, implemented in 1836, tabled all antislavery petitions without further discussion.

Antiabolitionist mobs were not limited to the South in the 1830s. In 1835 the British abolitionist George Thompson, making a lecture tour through the United States, was met by mobs everywhere he went. Later that year in Boston, antiabolitionist mobs looking for Thompson found William Lloyd Garrison instead and dragged him through the city streets. In November 1837, Elijah P. Lovejoy, a printer in Alton, Illinois, was murdered by an angry mob after he refused to back down from his antislavery stance. The following spring, antiabolitionist mobs destroyed the newly constructed Pennsylvania Hall in Philadelphia, disrupting several meetings, including those of the second Anti-Slavery Convention of American Women and the Requited Labor Convention. Throughout the North and the South, antiabolitionist mobs destroyed property and threatened the lives of reformers.

Women responded in large numbers to the call for immediate abolition of slavery. Abolitionism drew on evangelical ideas of the Second Great Awakening, and abolitionists called on women's innate morality to support the fight against the sin of slavery. Petitioning was one of the most popular antislavery strategies for women, who found signing petitions a safe and effective way of voicing their support for the abolitionist cause. Women also boycotted slave-labor products such as cotton and sugar. Significantly, women participated in local, state, and national organizations and formed antislavery societies that served as auxiliaries to larger, male-dominated organizations. The Boston Female Anti-Slavery Society (BFASS) and the Philadelphia Female Anti-Slavery Society (PFASS) were both established in 1833. The BFASS included prominent women such as Helen Garrison and the author Lydia Maria Child, while the PFASS counted among its members the Quaker activist Lucretia Mott. Both groups organized antislavery fairs to raise funds for the cause, circulated petitions, and aided in the creation and distribution of antislavery literature. Both groups departed from traditional patterns of female organizing, however, by recruiting working-class women and black women.

By the mid-1830s, many women sought a more public role in the fight against slavery. Of particular prominence were Angelina and Sarah Grimké, sisters and members of a well-known South Carolina slaveholding family. Hired by Garrison in 1836 as lecturers for the American Anti-Slavery Society, the sisters were powerful spokespersons for the cause because of their family background. Their popularity grew, and soon the two sisters were attracting mixed-gender audiences, shocking the general northern public. In 1837 the Congregational clergy rebuked the sisters, claiming that when women like the Grimké sisters assumed the public role of men, they risked shame and dishonor.

In May 1840 the debate over women's role in the abolitionist movement irreparably divided American abolitionists when Abby Kelley was nominated to the business committee of the American Anti-Slavery Society. The conservative abolitionist Lewis Tappan worried that the continued linkage of women's rights and abolitionism would taint the abolitionist cause. After Kelley's nomination, Tappan and three hundred supporters—including the entire executive committee—left the American Anti-Slavery Society meeting and soon formed the American and Foreign Anti-Slavery Society (AFASS). Garrison assumed leadership of the AASS, which maintained a broad reform platform including women's rights; Garrison also continued to recruit abolitionists regardless of religious, social, or political views. The AFASS under the leadership of Tappan, however, maintained a more orthodox platform: in part out of fear that radical movements such as women's rights might alienate many would-be supporters, the AFASS preferred not to mix abolitionism with these movements.

In June 1840, both groups sent delegates to London to the first World's Anti-Slavery Convention, organized by members of the British and Foreign Anti-Slavery Society. In doing so, the American abolitionists moved their disagreements to an international stage. Not surprisingly, the members of the American Anti-Slavery Society selected several women delegates, while the American and Foreign Anti-Slavery Society selected only men. When the conservative British abolitionists refused to recognize the female delegates of the AASS, divisions among and between British and American abolitionists deepened and pushed the question of women's rights onto the international political agenda.

Women's Rights. The exclusion of women delegates from the London convention in 1840 had a decided impact on the events that led to the first women's rights convention, held in Seneca Falls, New York, eight years later; however, other developments also influenced the debate about women's rights and gender equality. Well before the 1848 convention, reformers had agitated for improved economic and legal rights for women, whose vulnerable economic status had only worsened with the market revolution. Prior to 1828, wealthy New Yorkers could protect the property rights of their wives and daughters through trusts administered by the equity courts. But in 1828 the law was revised and the courts were abolished, along with protection for married women's property rights. Despite this setback, support for married women's property rights continued to grow throughout the 1830s, driven in part by the boom-and-bust nature of the market economy. After the Panic of 1837, federal and state governments passed a series of laws to protect the assets of debtors. In 1839, Mississippi passed the first married women's property act, protecting a woman's real and personal property from the debts of her husband. In 1848, New York passed similar legislation. Though important for women's economic status, these laws did little to protect women's earnings during marriage and did not address women's subordinate position in marriage.

Elizabeth Cady Stanton believed that the passage of the married women's property act in New York created a favorable environment for a women's rights convention. As she later noted in the *History of Woman Suffrage*, "discussions in the constitutional convention and the Legislature, heralded by the press to every school district, culminated at last in a woman's rights convention." Stanton and her husband, Henry, had traveled to London in 1840 for the World's Anti-Slavery Convention. While in London, Stanton met the Quaker abolitionist and reformer Lucretia Mott. In July 1848 a tea party hosted by the Quaker

Jane Hunt at her home in Waterloo, New York, near Seneca Falls, brought Stanton and Mott together again. Stanton, Mott, Mott's sister Martha Wright, and the Quaker Mary Ann M'Clintock decided to "do and dare anything," as Stanton later recalled. Just ten days later, on 19 and 20 July, three hundred men and women gathered in Seneca Falls for the first women's rights convention. Delegates wrote the Declaration of Sentiments, which was modeled after the Declaration of Independence and a similar document written by abolitionists in 1833 at the founding of the American Anti-Slavery Society. In the declaration, delegates outlined women's civil and political grievances, including the failure of men to grant women the elective franchise; legal discrimination against women, especially married women; women's rights in relation to work, education, and participation in the church; the sexual double standard; and the exclusion of women from the public sphere. The Declaration of Sentiments was a comprehensive critique of women's social role in the antebellum period, though the document did not address whether these rights were intended for all women regardless of race. Sixty-eight women signed the document, and thirty-two men signed a separate document, representing a compromise that allowed women to make their own demands yet still give men a voice on the issue.

Reaction to the convention and the Declaration of Sentiments was mixed. Some critics worried that the declaration was a reversal of gender roles, while others denounced the convention altogether and branded the reformers as "erratic, addle-pated comeouters." Though the declaration was a touchstone for many supporters of women's rights, others retreated from the movement in the face of public criticism and ridicule. Still, through a series of meetings and conventions, reformers kept the question of women's rights on the public agenda throughout the 1850s. Reformers continued to assert the need for women's full citizenship rights, including control of wages, property and legal rights, educational and employment opportunities, suffrage, and the right to define goals and ambitions outside women's traditional sphere.

Legacy. The social, economic, political, and cultural changes of the antebellum period fundamentally altered how men and women lived and worked, ultimately transforming their ideas about the individual, the family, and society. New ideas about gender and religion influenced these ideas and ascribed particular roles to men and women. Reformers worked to address the challenges of a rapidly changing society, though divisions over religion, politics, and gender often hampered their efforts. In seeking to define appropriate standards for education, individual behavior, political and civil rights, and human oppression, reformers challenged old ways of thinking and established an enduring tradition of activism.

[*See also* Alcohol and Alcohol Abuse; Antebellum Era; Antislavery; Asylums and Mental Illness; Beecher, Catharine; Beecher, Henry Ward; Colonization Movement, African; Dix, Dorothea; Douglass, Frederick; Education; Free-Soilers; Garrison, William Lloyd; Great Awakenings; Grimké, Sarah and Angelina; Hospitals and Dispensaries; Labor Movements; Mott, Lucretia; Prisons and Penitentiaries; Separate Spheres Ideology; Sexual Reform and Morality; Slavery, *subentry on* Nineteenth Century; Stanton, Elizabeth Cady; Underground Railroad; Utopian and Communitarian Movements; Weld, Theodore Dwight; Woman Suffrage Movement; Women's Rights Movement, Antebellum Era; *and* Working-Class Life and Society.]

BIBLIOGRAPHY

Bacon, Margaret Hope. *Valiant Friend: The Life of Lucretia Mott.* New York: Walker and Company, 1980.

Boylan, Anne M. *The Origins of Women's Activism: New York and Boston, 1797–1840.* Chapel Hill: University of North Carolina Press, 2002.

Burin, Eric. *Slavery and the Peculiar Solution: A History of the American Colonization Society.* Gainesville: University Press of Florida, 2005.

Cott, Nancy F., ed. *No Small Courage: A History of Women in the United States.* New York: Oxford University Press, 2000.

Dorsey, Bruce. *Reforming Men and Women: Gender in the Antebellum City.* Ithaca, N.Y.: Cornell University Press, 2002.

Douglas, Ann. *The Feminization of American Culture.* New York: Alfred A. Knopf, 1977.

Ginzberg, Lori D. *Women and the Work of Benevolence: Morality, Politics, and Class in the Nineteenth-Century United States.* New Haven, Conn.: Yale University Press, 1990.

Hewitt, Nancy A. *Women's Activism and Social Change: Rochester, New York, 1822–1872.* Ithaca, N.Y.: Cornell University Press, 1984.

Howe, Daniel Walker. *What Hath God Wrought: The Transformation of America, 1815–1848.* New York: Oxford University Press, 2007.

Isenberg, Nancy. *Sex and Citizenship in Antebellum America.* Chapel Hill: University of North Carolina Press, 1998.

Jeffrey, Julie Roy. *The Great Silent Army of Abolitionism: Ordinary Women in the Antislavery Movement.* Chapel Hill: University of North Carolina Press, 1998.

Johnson, Paul E. *A Shopkeeper's Millennium: Society and Revivals in Rochester, New York, 1815–1837.* New York: Hill and Wang, 1978.

Kessler-Harris, Alice. *Out to Work: A History of Wage-Earning Women in the United States.* New York: Oxford University Press, 1982.

Lutz, Alma. *Crusade for Freedom: Women in the Antislavery Movement*. Boston: Beacon Press, 1968.

Martin, Scott C. *Devil of the Domestic Sphere: Temperance, Gender, and Middle-Class Ideology, 1800–1860*. DeKalb: Northern Illinois University Press, 2008.

Melder, Keith E. *Beginnings of Sisterhood: The American Woman's Rights Movement, 1800–1850*. New York: Schocken Books, 1977.

Penney, Sherry H., and James D. Livingston. *A Very Dangerous Woman: Martha Wright and Women's Rights*. Amherst: University of Massachusetts Press, 2004.

Salerno, Beth A. *Sister Societies: Women's Antislavery Organizations in Antebellum America*. DeKalb: Northern Illinois University Press, 2005.

Sellers, Charles. *The Market Revolution: Jacksonian America, 1815–1846*. New York: Oxford University Press, 1991.

Stokes, Melvin, and Stephen Conway, eds. *The Market Revolution in America: Social, Political, and Religious Expressions, 1800–1880*. Charlottesville: University Press of Virginia, 1996.

Walters, Ronald G. *American Reformers, 1815–1860*. New York: Hill and Wang, 1978.

Wellman, Judith. *The Road to Seneca Falls: Elizabeth Cady Stanton and the First Woman's Rights Convention*. Urbana: University of Illinois Press, 2004.

Welter, Barbara J. "The Cult of True Womanhood, 1820–1860." *American Quarterly* 18 (Summer 1966): 151–174.

Yellin, Jean Fagan, and John C. Van Horne, eds. *The Abolitionist Sisterhood: Women's Political Culture in Antebellum America*. Ithaca, N.Y.: Cornell University Press, 1994.

Julie Holcomb

ANTHONY, SUSAN B.

(1820–1906), women's rights activist. Born in Adams, Massachusetts, Susan Brownell Anthony was influenced by her father's Quakerism, as well as his independence in marrying Lucy Read, a Baptist. When his business failed in 1837, Susan became a teacher. She never married and was a lifelong believer in the importance of self-support for women. In 1851 she met Elizabeth Cady Stanton and became a passionate subscriber to Stanton's women's rights ideas. The partnership of Stanton and Anthony sustained American feminism for the next half a century. Starting in 1854 they focused on the denial of basic economic rights to married women. For six years, Anthony collected petitions to the New York state legislature, which in 1860 passed its comprehensive Married Women's Property Act. Simultaneously, she worked for the American Anti-Slavery Society, viewing women's rights and abolitionist sentiments as closely related. In 1863 she and Stanton collected nearly half a million women's signatures petitioning Congress to abolish slavery.

After the Civil War, following the lead of the antislavery movement, Stanton and Anthony concentrated on equal citizenship and political rights for women. They tried but failed to convince Congress to include women in the Fourteenth and Fifteenth Amendments. Now committed to a focus on political equality and on the Constitution as the source of such rights, they formed the National Woman Suffrage Association in 1869, precipitating a split with Lucy Stone and other women's rights activists who were not willing to break with longtime abolitionist and Republican Party allies. For the next half a decade, Stanton and Anthony advanced the argument that the Fourteenth Amendment included women when it bestowed federal citizenship on "all persons born or naturalized in the United States." Because the vote was, they contended, a fundamental right of citizenship, woman suffrage was already constitutional. Accordingly, in November 1872, Anthony performed the most famous act of her life: she convinced election officials to allow her to vote for president. For this the U.S. District Court found her guilty of illegal voting and fined her $100, which she refused to pay. Three years later, in 1875, the U.S. Supreme Court ruled against the suffragists' line of argument.

From this point on, Anthony realized the necessity of a separate woman suffrage amendment and dedicated herself to that goal. In 1876 she presented a militant women's Declaration of Rights at the Fourth of July ceremonies held at the Centennial Exposition in Philadelphia. In 1880 she began to compile and publish the multivolume *History of Woman Suffrage*, an act of historical consciousness unequaled in American reform. In 1890 she oversaw the unification of the suffrage movement, split since 1869, and the election of Stanton as the first president of the National American Woman Suffrage Association. In 1892, Anthony succeeded Stanton as president. Throughout the 1890s, despite advancing age, Anthony traveled to California, Kansas, South Dakota, and Colorado to work for state suffrage referenda, and she traveled to England and France to organize suffragists internationally. She retired in 1900. By the time the Nineteenth Amendment passed in 1920, no name was more identified with woman suffrage than that of Susan B. Anthony.

[*See also* Antislavery; Feminism; Stanton, Elizabeth Cady; *and* Woman Suffrage Movement.]

BIBLIOGRAPHY

Barry, Kathleen. *Susan B. Anthony: A Biography of a Singular Feminist.* New York: New York University Press, 1988.

Sherr, Lynn. *Failure Is Impossible: Susan B. Anthony in Her Own Words.* New York: Times Books, 1995.

Ellen C. DuBois

ANTIABORTION MOVEMENT

The origins of the antiabortion movement have been attributed to activities by Catholics, Evangelicals, and political conservatives, but the movement can also be said to have tied into a larger tradition of American social activism through massive demonstrations against the war in Vietnam, particularly one at the Washington Memorial in November 1969. Protests like that at the Lincoln Memorial in 1972 around abortion rights, organized by the National Youth Pro-Life Coalition, were modeled on those of the antiwar movement and capitalized on tie-ins to the abolition of slavery and protests against the Holocaust that focused on the sense of victimhood shared by slaves, concentration-camp inmates, and the fetus in the womb.

After the Supreme Court decision in *Roe v. Wade* in 1973 provided women with the right to abortions, large-scale demonstrations became annual events and inspired activism of a much less benign nature, ranging from trespass and vandalism to arson and bombings against abortion clinics. Since the late 1970s, picketing has remained the most common activity directed against clinics, averaging some nine thousand a year, but significant harassment and stalking of abortion providers has also occurred: one estimate in the late 1990s puts the number of murders at eight and attempted murders at seventeen. One of the most disturbing developments in the antiabortion movement has been the fluidity of its interface with white supremacists, patriot groups, and volunteer militias, facilitating progress from protests to violence and allowing for the sharing of personnel and material resources among the groups. Convergence along these lines has occurred among such groups as the anti-Semitic Posse Comitatus, the U.S. Taxpayers Party,

Missionaries to the Preborn, and the Oklahoma Constitutional Militia, as well as the American Coalition of Life Activists. This last group hosted as the Christian Gallery website called the "Nuremberg Files"—a site that promoted the assassination of abortion providers by listing their home and work addresses, Social Security numbers, and automobile license numbers, along with other personal data, and maintained a running toll of those targeted, wounded, and murdered.

The violence associated with the antiabortion movement has tended to overshadow less dramatic activity on the legal front, largely at the state level, which has been very effective in limiting access to abortion so long as such laws fall outside what the Supreme Court justice Sandra Day O'Connor has termed an "undue burden," the present standard for what is considered an unconstitutional obstacle to a woman's accessing an abortion (see both O'Connor's dissent in *City of Akron v. Akron Center for Reproductive Health*, 1983, and also the triauthored plurality with Justices Anthony Kennedy and David Souter in *Planned Parenthood of Southeastern Pennsylvania v. Casey*, 1992). Crafting antiabortion legislation at both the state and the federal levels has become a centerpiece of the right wing of the Republican Party, which has made the antiabortion issue a critical part of its political strategy. Within the goals of establishing a right to life for the fetus and ensuring its legal protection, antiabortion legislation has been successful in establishing such constraints on a woman's right to an abortion as the twenty-four-hour waiting period, parental notification and consent for minors, preabortion counseling for the pregnant woman, and preclusion of government Medicaid funds for abortions. The 2003 Partial-Birth Abortion Ban Act, which has no exemption to protect women's health, was upheld by the Supreme Court in *Gonzales v. Carhart* (2007). In the second decade of the twenty-first century, antiabortion legal strategy has moved toward more states legislating requirements that women undergo ultrasound imaging before an abortion. Antiabortion advocates have on occasion cooperated with advocates for abortion rights on increasing health-care funding for children and on promoting sex education to prevent pregnancies, without giving up the ultimate goal of overturning *Roe v. Wade* by advocating the nomination of conservative Supreme Court justices to create an antiabortion majority.

The most recent reports of abortion attitudes suggest that women's attitudes in 2009 still tend to be more pro-abortion than those of men, both black and white men, although white women and white men tend overall to have more liberal attitudes toward abortion; their attitudes have tended to converge over time only to diverge again. Black women, by contrast, have tended to have more liberal attitudes than black men over time, although their attitudes appear to be converging. Race differences, in any case, vary by region. Older people hold more positive attitudes toward abortion than younger people do. Church attendance influences abortion attitudes (away from abortion), as does education (toward abortion) and political party (Democrats toward, Republicans away from abortion). At the same time, marital status no longer is a predictor of abortion attitudes. Women tend to be split by social class in their attitudes toward abortion, even within pro-abortion groups, depending upon whether a woman supports traditional authority or resists it. Antiabortion groups, nevertheless, tend to construct for themselves an alternative culture that resists government influence; in that sense, lower-class women who support abortion rights are more identified with the attitudes of antiabortion groups than with other members of abortion-rights groups. Moreover, many black working-class women regard themselves as outsiders and are critical of upper-class white women with whom they might otherwise share pro-abortion views. Middle-class pro-abortion women are themselves conflicted, but along other lines: they uphold an abstract right to abortion as it relates to others but personally question it for themselves.

Despite these differences between and within pro- and antiabortion groups, certain perspectives are shared, including a preference for responsible sexual behavior, racial justice, and identification with the role of mother. Both abortion-rights and antiabortion groups value community, but with a different sense of community; in the same way, each side values individual rights, but privileges different individual rights. Finally, it is clear that abortion-rights groups are characterized by much greater heterogeneity than are antiabortion groups. Thus the two sides are not unavoidably opposed; their profiles reveal considerably more complexity and overlap than might be expected, which accounts for the variety of splinter groups that emerge on both sides.

[*See also* **Abortion; Birth Control and Family Planning; Conservative Movement; Law and Society; Militia Movement, Modern; Pregnancy; Reproductive Rights Movement;** *and* **Sexual Reform and Morality.**]

BIBLIOGRAPHY

Carter, J. Scott, Shannon K. Carter, and Jamie Dodge. "Trends in Abortion Attitudes by Race and Gender: A Reassessment over a Four-Decade Period." *Journal of Sociological Research* 1, no. 1 (2009): 1–17. An updating presentation of relevant statistical data related to abortion attitudes.

Hughes, Richard L. "Burning Birth Certificates and Atomic Tupperware Parties: Creating the Antiabortion Movement in the Shadow of the Vietnam War." *Historian* 68, no. 3 (2006): 541–558. An informative course-correction on the history of the antiabortion movement and its influences.

Vitiello, Michael. "The Nuremberg Files: Testing the Outer Limits of the First Amendment." *Ohio State Law Journal* 61 (2000): 1175–1246. A study of an important legal case treating an antiabortion website that sponsored violence.

"What's Next for the Anti-Abortion Movement?" *Talk of the Nation*, National Public Radio, 15 January 2009. http://www.npr.org/templates/transcript/transcript.php?storyId=99409402. Transcript of a thoughtful, updating discussion with the chief counsel for the American Center for Law and Justice, the founder of the antiabortion group Operation Rescue, and a theologian.

Linda Myrsiades

ANTI-CATHOLICISM

Anti-Catholicism has been a constant yet shifting phenomenon in colonial British American and United States history. After King Henry VIII's break with Rome in 1534, Catholicism was outlawed in England and hundreds of Catholics, including prominent figures such as Thomas More and Bishop John Fisher, were executed for refusing to repudiate the spiritual authority of the pope. Catholics were barred from participating in all government, military, and legal positions, and they faced other forms of official discrimination and persecution into the nineteenth century. In colonial British America, similar legislation was adopted by almost all colonial governments. Catholicism was more commonly derogated as "popery" and Catholics as "papists." In Maryland, initially founded by and governed by Catholics, religious toleration was extended to both Catholics and Protestants for the first time in the English-speaking world, though by the 1690s the leadership was overthrown and strict anti-Catholic laws were adopted. In both Britain and its colonies, Catholicism was viewed as a false religion, the pope as Antichrist, and Catholics as potential traitors.

In the eighteenth century, amid near-constant warfare with Catholic France and Spain and internal disunity, colonial British antipopery was used to solidify national identity. It was most pronounced in areas where the Catholic population was smallest, such as New England, where the Catholic population was one-tenth of 1 percent. Antipopery was expressed in colonial law, literature, history, and theology, as well as in popular festivals. "Pope's Day," on which an effigy of the pope was carried through the streets on a noose before being publicly burned, was celebrated annually in New England. *The French Convert* (first published in London, 1696 and Boston, 1708), an anti-Catholic novel, went through almost fifty editions in England and America by the end of the nineteenth century. In 1750, Judge Paul Dudley of Massachusetts endowed a series of lectures at Harvard College, one of which was dedicated to "exposing the Idolatry of the Romish church." Although significant progress in toleration was achieved after the Revolution, restrictions on full Catholic participation in civic life were adopted in the constitutions of New Hampshire, Massachusetts, Connecticut, New Jersey, North Carolina, South Carolina, and Georgia. In Connecticut, Catholics were not allowed to purchase land, and in North Carolina they were barred from holding state office until 1835.

The massive waves of Irish and Germans arriving in the United States in the early decades of the nineteenth century inspired a violent resurgence of anti-Catholicism. Though directed at immigrants, its rhetoric retained a theological and political character.

This resurgent anti-Catholicism became the core ingredient in the American Nativist Movement. Like English, Scottish, Welsh, and Irish Protestants, many Anglo-Americans considered popery a subversive culture as well as an alien creed. They were convinced that Catholics, submissive to papal authority and beset by superstition, could never be loyal or productive citizens. Before 1820, with Catholics few in number, nativist worries were more fantasy than reality. After that date, massive Irish immigration provided a large, visible enemy and intensified fears and anxieties about the future of American institutions and values. This situation inspired vicious anti-Catholic propaganda with pornographic overtones, such as Maria Monk's *Awful Disclosures* (1836), triggered attacks on Catholic neighborhoods and churches, increased demands for limitations on immigration and more rigid qualifications for citizenship, and in the 1850s produced the American (Know-Nothing) Party with an anti-Catholic agenda.

Reflecting economic conditions, nativism waxed and waned during the nineteenth and twentieth centuries. Inspired by social Darwinism, it took on racist and anti-Semitic dimensions, but anti-Catholicism remained a key ingredient. Immigration brought large numbers of Catholics from Italy and eastern Europe into urban America; Irish Americans gained control of a rapidly expanding Catholic Church with a large institutional structure, including parochial schools; and Catholic immigrants won political domination in many cities, as well as leadership in labor movements. All this frightened nativists. The religious factor in American prejudice was particularly noticeable in rural areas and small towns. But even in more sophisticated environments such as business, the professions, and academia, Catholics as well as Jews often faced either exclusion or quotas.

In the late nineteenth and early twentieth centuries, the American Protective Association, the Guardians of Liberty, the American Minute Men, the Covenanters, the Knights of Luther, and especially the revived Ku Klux Klan all appealed to anti-Catholic bigotry. The Klan mobilized against the Catholic presidential candidates Alfred E. Smith in 1928 and John F. Kennedy in 1960.

Conditions improved as the twentieth century moved along. The favorable presentation of priests in 1930s and 1940s movies, Catholic patriotism during World War II, economic and social mobility after the war, growing religious tolerance, and the popularity of John F. Kennedy all helped to diminish anti-Catholicism and open doors of opportunity to its former victims. In the late 1960s academics were the last important segment of the population to abandon their prejudice.

Although most Catholics felt comfortable in the United States by century's end, some still complained that they experienced more media criticism and ridicule than other racial or religious minorities did. What remained of anti-Catholicism was often directed at the church's official condemnation of contraception and abortion.

[*See also* **Antiabortion Movement; Anti-Semitism; Immigration; Irish Americans; Italian Americans; Ku Klux Klan, Second; Labor Movements; Militia Movement, Modern; Racism;** *and* **Religion.**]

BIBLIOGRAPHY

Billington, Ray Allen. *The Protestant Crusade, 1800–1860*. New York: Macmillan, 1938.

Cogliano, Francis D. *No King, No Popery: Anti-Catholicism in Revolutionary New England*. Westport, Conn.: Greenwood Press, 1995.

Higham, John. *Strangers in the Land: Patterns of American Nativism, 1860–1925*. New Brunswick, N.J.: Rutgers University Press, 1955.

McGreevy, John T. *Catholicism and American Freedom: A History*. New York: W. W. Norton and Company, 2003.

Lawrence J. McCaffrey; revised by
Michael S. Carter

ANTI-CHILD-LABOR MOVEMENT

Children had always worked alongside adults. But in the late nineteenth century, reformers argued that individuals under the age of fourteen needed special protections from labor that harmed their health or inhibited their ability to attend school. Focusing on industrial wage-work and street trades, the anti-child-labor movement largely ignored the work of children, many of them African American and Hispanic, on family farms and in commercial agriculture.

The first laws regulating child labor passed in 1842. Massachusetts restricted the employment of children under twelve years of age to ten hours a day, six days a week, and Connecticut did the same for youngsters under fourteen. By 1900 most states had passed laws requiring school attendance, but they had done little to restrict children's employment. From 1870 to 1910 the proportion of wage-earning children rose from approximately 14 percent of all Americans aged ten through fourteen to 20 percent.

The General Federation of Women's Clubs and the National Consumers League used boycotts to demand safer and healthier workplaces, as well as to demand an end to child labor. The 1902 anthracite coal strike drew attention to the circumstances of breaker boys. In 1903, Mary "Mother" Jones led what was called the March of the Children from Philadelphia to New York City to highlight abuses in the textile and garment industries. The next year, anti-child-labor organizations in Alabama and New York City formed the National Child Labor Committee (NCLC) for a national propaganda campaign to end child labor. By 1914 thirty-six states prohibited the employment of workers under the age of fourteen in factories and mines. However, loopholes, inconsistencies, and lax enforcement made evasion common.

Buoyed by the creation of the U.S. Children's Bureau in 1912, the NCLC focused on gaining a federal anti-child-labor law. Reformers celebrated passage of the 1916 Keating-Owen Act that used federal authority to regulate interstate commerce to ban employment of children less than fourteen years of age and restricted the employment of fourteen- through seventeen-year-olds. But the U.S. Supreme Court declared the law an overreach of federal interstate commerce authority (*Hammer v. Dagenhart*, 1918). Congress responded by passing a very similar second law, but it met the same fate (*Bailey v. Drexel Furniture Company*, 1922). The passage of a constitutional amendment in 1923 that relied on the same child labor restrictions seemed to be the way to satisfy the court's objections, but strong opposition by business groups, newspaper editors, and the American Catholic Church meant the new effort lagged over the next decade without the needed ratification by the states.

By 1930, 2 million children aged ten through fourteen still worked for wages. High unemployment among adults in the Great Depression led many to call for the removal of young workers, even older adolescents, from the job market. Further, more Americans believed that a high school education was essential for future job security. In response, Congress included federal child-labor regulations in the 1938 Fair Labor Standards Act. This seminal legislation did not protect all young workers, but it remains the foundation of anti-child-labor regulation in the United States. The law also serves as a model for international policies set forth by the United Nations in the 1959 Declaration of the Rights of the Child and the 1989 Convention on the Rights of the Child. In the early twenty-first century the anti-child-labor movement lobbies on behalf of young workers throughout the world.

[*See also* **Child Workers; Feminist Reforms in the Progressive Era, Maternal; Law and Society; New Deal Social Reforms;** *and* **Progressive Era.**]

BIBLIOGRAPHY

Hindman, Hugh D. *Child Labor: An American History*. Armonk, N.Y.: M. E. Sharpe, 2002.
Sallee, Shelley. *The Whiteness of Child Labor Reform in the New South*. Athens, Ga.: University of Georgia Press, 2004.

Kriste Lindenmeyer

ANTILYNCHING MOVEMENT

Protest against mob murder has held central importance in African Americans' struggle for justice in the United States. Other marginal groups, like immigrants and radicals, have occasionally been subject to vigilantism, but the lethal attacks directed against African Americans were particularly systematic, intense, and well-documented. Indeed, the mythic and ideological function of ritual murder combined with its destructive and terroristic power to make lynching a central feature of racial politics in the late nineteenth and early twentieth centuries. The best statistics available indicate that between 1882 and 1930, 4,761 persons were lynched in the

United States, 71 percent of whom were black.

Ida B. Wells-Barnett (1862–1931) is the most significant antilynching activist in U.S. history. Born in Mississippi, during the 1890s she lived in Memphis, Tennessee, where she witnessed—and criticized—the consolidation of the stereotypic lynching scenario: murder of a black man as punishment for the rape of a white woman. In newspaper articles and speeches, Wells-Barnett described how this kind of rape represented, to white southerners, an inversion of sexual and racial hierarchies. She pointed out that this lynching-for-rape scenario relied on stereotypes of African Americans as uncontrollable, unteachable beasts and of white women as passive, weak, and vulnerable. Mob murder, often abetted by the media, ran roughshod over the rape charge, which was rarely subject to court procedures. Ida B. Wells-Barnett was the first person to tally these outrages, analyze the figures, and inaugurate what became nearly three decades of agitation to make lynching a crime.

The arguments from pamphlets that Wells-Barnett wrote in the 1890s were quickly adopted by the African American press, educators, and social reformers, especially women organized through the National Association of Colored Women (NACW). Of her many sociological insights, two stand out. First was her statistical finding that though in the press the rape charge against black men was ubiquitous, less than 30 percent of reported lynchings involved even the charge of rape, much less its proof in a court of law. This finding laid bare the slanderous nature of the charge and its use as a cover to justify oppression of any black person who moved out of a subordinated economic, political, or social role. The second insight was Wells-Barnett's perception that the sexual double standard and the control of women's

bodies, black and white, underlay the fear and excess of the mob. That is, white men's sexual predation of black women and their need to control white women's physical movement and sexual choice-making produced guilt and anxieties that had no language at the time, and instead found outlet in violent mob behavior. The loss of control over previously dependent and submissive sectors of southern society underlay the fury of white men across class.

Wells-Barnett's insights about racism were adopted by her readers, but her tactics proved controversial for shaping a protest movement to end lynching. She advocated exposé, education, economic and political pressure (boycotts and voting), and the active support of white allies, both in the United States and in England, to sway public opinion against lynching. The leading black educator and political boss of her day, Booker T. Washington, opposed lynching, but he also opposed active confrontation with racists—something that Wells-Barnet deemed essential. Leaders with a more activist agenda were generally based in the North, and their social and professional networks did not include Wells-Barnett. Though she was present at the founding of the National Association for the Advancement of Colored People (NAACP) in New York City in 1909, she was marginalized from the group's effort to promote federal antilynching legislation, notably the Dyer Antilynching Bill that was introduced in 1919 and went down to defeat in the U.S. Senate in 1922.

Wells-Barnett was more effective at the local level, specifically in Chicago, where she relocated in 1895. Activists there successfully pressed for the Illinois Anti-mob-violence Act of 1905, which required the removal of law enforcement officials who failed to protect inmates in their custody. The consolidation of a legislative agenda at the state and especially federal level was a hallmark of the mature antilynching movement, tied directly to suffrage and voting rights for African Americans. This approach stands in sharp contrast to the stance against white male excess taken by white women such as Rebecca Latimer Felton of Georgia or, later, Jessie Daniel Ames of Texas. Wells-Barnett and the NAACP framed lynching as a national problem needing a legislative—especially federal—solution. In this effort they made important if embattled gains. Propagandistic and educational efforts around Dyer—especially those put forward by the Anti-Lynching Crusaders (an arm of the NACW) during the 1920s—as well as the failed Wagner-Costigian Act (1934), raised consciousness within the United States and beyond. In 1935 the NAACP mounted An Art Commentary on Lynching, a photography exhibit that documented the grotesque cruelty of mob murder and the role of white women and children in mobs. During the 1930s the Scottsboro case did much to delegitimize the stereotype of black male as natural rapist of white woman. Billie Holiday's rendition of "Strange Fruit," first performed in 1939, offered a haunting indictment of lynching, reaching listeners by means of live performance, and, later, recordings.

Ida B. Wells-Barnett lived to see major shifts in the nature of racial violence and the policing of the color line. The first shift concerned the structure and dynamics of urban racism, through spatial segregation enforced by both acts of physical violence and institutions like the real estate industry and police. The second general shift involved the penal system's slow but steady absorption of the work of maintaining the color line. Wells-Barnett understood that by World War I, policing regularized the racial boundary keeping and stigmatization that lynching rhetoric, images, and mob behavior had accomplished in the previous century. As a probation officer and prisoner's rights advocate in Chicago, Ida B. Wells-Barnett had a finger on the pulse of this critical domain of ongoing racial inequity. Her multisided attack on white supremacy through education, advocacy, economic pressure, and electoral and legislative efforts constitutes a signal accomplishment in the long civil rights movement in the United States.

[*See also* **Law and Society** *and* **Racism.**]

BIBLIOGRAPHY

Brundage, W. Fitzhugh, ed. *Under Sentence of Death: Lynching in the South*. Chapel Hill: University of North Carolina Press, 1997.

Feimster, Crystal. *Southern Horrors: Women and the Politics of Rape and Lynching*. Cambridge, Mass.: Harvard University Press, 2009.

Goodman, James. *Stories of Scottsboro*. New York: Pantheon, 1994.

Hall, Jacquelyn Dowd. *Revolt Against Chivalry: Jessie Daniel Ames and the Women's Campaign Against Lynching*. New York: Columbia University Press, 1979.

Schechter, Patricia A. *Ida B. Wells-Barnett and American Reform, 1880–1930*. Chapel Hill: University of North Carolina Press, 2001.

Patricia A. Schechter

ANTI-SALOON LEAGUE

The Anti-Saloon League (ASL) was an innovative, controversial lobbying group that spearheaded campaigns for local and state bans on beverage alcohol, campaigns that culminated in 1920 in the implementation of national Prohibition. First organized in Ohio in 1893, the ASL quickly established state affiliates through much of the nation. Staffed by Protestant ministers and attorneys, the ASL dedicated itself to a practical, politicized form of dry activism. It ignored other reform causes to focus solely on the fight against liquor. Instead of attempting to save individual drinkers, the ASL attacked the retail and manufacturing outlets of the liquor industry, and instead of challenging the established parties after the fashion of the Prohibition Party, the ASL targeted individual lawmakers and pressed them to support specific pieces of antiliquor legislation proposed or endorsed by the league. The ASL did not demand immediate prohibition, but engaged the drink industry where it was weakest, building dry territory at the precinct, township, and county level until there was sufficient sentiment to push for state liquor bans and then national prohibition. Drawing on Progressive Era themes of corporate regulation, health reform, and the application of state power in the public interest, ASL activists contrasted the neighborhood-destroying presence of saloons with the order, prosperity, and community well-being of dry enclaves.

Led by the hard-charging Ohio attorney Wayne Wheeler, the ASL built a power base through Protestant churches and its own publishing enterprise, the American Issue Publishing Company. Conducting annual field days in churches, league agents raised money, explained legislation, and organized voters. League representatives emphasized that dry voters should support politicians who would vote for dry laws even if the office seekers were otherwise objectionable. Since most American women could not vote before 1920, the ASL promoted masculine activism. It cooperated with the Woman's Christian Temperance Union (WCTU). Nevertheless, in some states tension over dry leadership and tactics endured between the league and WCTU branches. Critics argued that the ASL was a fanatical, disruptive organization that damaged party cohesion and sowed religious and ethnic discord. Although some Catholics and liturgical Protestants held league posts, suspicion and hostility characterized the relationship between ASL Evangelicals and members of the other Christian confessions, especially Catholics. Immigrant groups considered the ASL a nativist, repressive group intent on curbing freedom and family autonomy.

In 1913, after state prohibition had reached its limits in the Midwest, South, and interior West, the ASL pushed for national prohibition. Concentrated dry pressure and wartime concerns overcame congressional opposition, and the Eighteenth Amendment to the Constitution was passed in 1917, quickly ratified in 1919, and implemented under the tough standards of the Volstead Act in 1920. ASL leaders split over enforcement policy. Wheeler demanded strict law enforcement. Ernest H. Cherrington, director of ASL publications, instead argued for an education strategy to persuade Prohibition's opponents to embrace the reform voluntarily. Declaring that it was not a detective agency, the ASL refused any direct enforcement role, relying instead on mostly unwilling public authorities. As Prohibition collapsed, the league's influence dissipated. With repeal in 1933 by means of the Twenty-First Amendment, the ASL became moribund.

[*See also* **Alcohol and Alcohol Abuse; Public Health;** *and* **Taverns and Bars.**]

BIBLIOGRAPHY

Kerr, K. Austin. *Organized for Prohibition: A New History of the Anti-Saloon League.* New Haven, Conn.: Yale University Press, 1985. The best detailed history of the Anti-Saloon League.

Pegram, Thomas R. *Battling Demon Rum: The Struggle for a Dry America, 1800–1933.* Chicago: Ivan R. Dee, 1998. A short history that places the Anti-Saloon League within the context of American temperance reform.

Thomas R. Pegram

ANTI-SEMITISM

Anti-Semitism in the social history of the United States has been a fringe ideology. Nonetheless, from colonial times to the twenty-first century, anti-Semitism has sprung from three consistent sources: Christian beliefs, economic fears, and xenophobia. The creation of the modern state of Israel was a more recent trigger for anti-Semitic beliefs.

Colonial Era through 1920. From 1654 to 1881, although Jews generally represented less than 1 percent of the population, Christian beliefs and suspicion of Jewish business practices led to occasional bursts of anti-Semitism. The first Jewish settlers in New Amsterdam (later New York City), Dutch immigrants from Recife, Brazil, had to petition the Dutch government to allow them to remain there over objections from Peter Stuyvesant, the colony's governor. After the Revolution, New Hampshire and North Carolina forbade Jews from holding office from statehood through the end of the Civil War.

As Jews migrated from the German-speaking lands of central Europe and entered the American economy as peddlers, Jews became symbols of modern commerce, and anti-Semitism flared as a result. Although some successful Jewish entrepreneurs were given high rankings by credit agencies, struggling Jewish merchants were accused of arson, theft, and fraud. During the Civil War, both the Confederate and the Union governments suspected Jews of disloyalty. The Straus family was driven out of their hometown of Talbotton, Georgia, accused of being Northern agents, and General Ulysses S. Grant issued an order barring Jewish merchants from having any contact with Union forces. Although Grant's order was revoked, lingering suspicion of even the most successful Jews led the Grand Union Hotel in Saratoga Springs, New York, to bar the banker Joseph Seligman from vacationing there in 1877, even though his family and other prominent Jews had previously done so. Resorts, country clubs, and fraternities around the country began to follow suit.

The wave of Jewish migration from eastern and central Europe at the turn of the twentieth century brought more Jews to the United States. Poverty and lack of English literacy among Jewish immigrants, coupled with stereotypes of Jews in popular culture and Christianity, prompted greater anti-Semitism. Anti-Semitism flourished in Populist writings, in which Jews represented the evils of capitalism and of urbanization more generally. Some Progressives used social-scientific reasoning to attribute such "racial" characteristics to Jews as sharp dealing, clannishness, and intensity. As vaudeville and film became more popular, so-called Jew comics with false noses, wigs, and beards performed on American stages, reinforcing old ethnic stereotypes. Fears of Jewish radicalism, especially in the wake of Russian Jews' praise for the end of the czarist system, added to the rising anti-Semitic climate of the early twentieth century.

1920–1948. The interwar years saw anti-Semitism become respectable in the United States, even though the actions taken against Jews paled in comparison to the horrors of Europe in the same period. The most prominent anti-Semite was Henry Ford, whose four-volume compilation *The International Jew*, published between 1920 and 1922, sold millions of copies at Ford dealerships around the world. Ford's writings, mostly ghostwritten by his public-relations agent, claimed that Jews had debased traditional American culture through movies and popular music, had instigated the recent world war, and had plotted to loot the world in order to control it.

For "proof" of the last of these assertions, Ford reprinted the *Protocols of the Elders of Zion*, a notorious forgery first printed in Russia around 1905.

Less overt forms of anti-Semitism occurred in education, where selective colleges set out to reduce the percentage of Jews in their student bodies. Through the 1920s, elite institutions and state universities feared that their Protestant character would end if Jewish attendance was not limited. The resultant quota policies prompted many Jews to travel far from home to attend college.

Religious and economic anti-Semitism inspired a small, fragmented proto-fascist movement to take root during the 1930s. Led by the broadcasters and clergymen Charles Coughlin and Gerald L. K. Smith, traditional Christian anti-Semitism was grafted onto economic resentments triggered by the Great Depression. Pro-Nazi movements like the Silver Shirts and the German American Bund attracted occasional media and law enforcement attention, but they wielded little influence on American culture. At the same time, a form of unspoken anti-Semitism can be inferred from Congress's refusal to amend immigration-restriction laws of the 1920s to accommodate Jewish refugees from the Holocaust. Even after the war ended, a poll found that 58 percent of Americans believed that "Jews have too much power in the United States."

Since 1948. The defeat of fascism and the rise of the civil rights movement made the anti-Semitic rhetoric of the 1930s disrespectable. Occasional anti-Semitic statements appeared in publications by far-right political organizations, but after Israel's victory and seizure of Jordanian, Egyptian, and Syrian territory in the Six-Day War of 1967, anti-Semitic sentiments became more visible. Groups on the American left equated the Palestinian struggle with the student, antiwar, and Black Power movements, and they called Zionism a racist ideology.

Anti-Semitism on the political right continued in the person of President Richard M. Nixon, whose tape-recorded statements denigrated even his close advisers of Jewish background, like Henry Kissinger. Anti-Semitic violence flared up in the 1980s when groups like the Posse Comitatus and other antigovernment groups placed individual Jews and Jewish groups at the heart of a conspiracy to run the globe. Members of the sect known as Christian Identity, begun by disciples of Gerald L. K. Smith, assassinated a Jewish talk-radio host who had mocked them on his program.

Anti-Semitism continued to occur along these lines in the twenty-first century. Israeli actions toward Palestinians have resulted in anti-Israel sentiments, which are occasionally directed toward Israel's American Jewish supporters. The Jewish background of many neoconservative politicians and strategists has also attracted occasional anti-Semitic comments from the political left.

By contrast, the twenty-first-century American right tended reflexively to support Israeli politicians, though some conservative political figures saw sexually explicit and transgressive popular culture as part of a Jewish plot. Hearkening back to Henry Ford's arguments, "the Jews who run Hollywood" were seen as responsible for promiscuity in films, music, and television.

[*See also* **Conservative Movement; Jewish Americans; Militia Movement, Modern; Nativist Movement; Race and Ethnicity;** *and* **Racism.**]

BIBLIOGRAPHY

Barkun, Michael. *Religion and the Racist Right: The Origins of the Christian Identity Movement.* Chapel Hill: University of North Carolina Press, 1994.

Cohen, Naomi W. *Jews in Christian America: The Pursuit of Religious Equality.* New York: Oxford University Press, 1992.

Dinnerstein, Leonard. *Antisemitism in America.* New York: Oxford University Press, 1994.

Singerman, Robert. *Antisemitic Propaganda: An Annotated Bibliography and Research Guide.* New York: Garland, 1982.

Jonathan Z. S. Pollack

ANTISLAVERY

The American antislavery crusade was a multifaceted, long-term social-reform movement that persisted from the mid-eighteenth century through the Emancipation Proclamation, issued 1 January 1863. Over the years, the movement evolved from religious protest and colonization efforts to political organization, abolitionism, violent protest, and, finally, emancipation. Antislavery also evolved from being a local and regional concern to being organized on a national level. It was linked to other reform issues, and the American crusade exhibited influences from British and other European sources. The objects of antislavery evolved from ridding the United States of slavery (and persons of color), to creating a perfect moral society, to creating new political expressions to achieve social changes.

Beginnings of Antislavery Agitation. Antislavery originated as a moral and religious issue. Various Protestant denominations— Mennonites and Amish, Presbyterians, Congregationalists, Methodists, Baptists, and the Society of Friends (Quakers)—all contributed, with Quakers the early leaders. The eighteenth-century Quakers George Keith, John Woolman, and Anthony Benezet each attacked slavery on the basis of moral principle: namely, the equality of all persons before

God. In the middle colonies and with strong support from the Friends meetings, a bondwoman from New Jersey who escaped into Philadelphia, Dinah Nevil, sued for her emancipation and caused the founding in 1775 of the world's first antislavery organization, the Pennsylvania Society for the Relief of Free Negroes Unlawfully Held in Bondage, later known as the Pennsylvania Abolition Society.

In the South, Presbyterians like Samuel Davies canvassed Virginia and urged teaching slaves to read, inviting them to join churches and assume their full humanity. In New England, James Manning—as part of the oldest Baptist congregation in the United States and as a founder and president of Brown University—joined Moses Brown's local antislavery organization in Providence, Rhode Island, and as a result lost the support of leading merchants. Congregationalists formed societies and held lectures across New England from 1820 onward. Jonathan Blanchard, Leonard Woods, Jonathan Edwards Jr., and Moses Stuart, all exponents of the New Divinity at Yale and Andover, laid a solid theological foundation for antislavery. Through sermons that were widely reproduced in the United States, John Wesley in England weighed in as an opponent to slavery in the British Empire, and George Whitefield's concern for persons of color and Indians had wide influence both in Britain and in the American colonies, through which he toured as a preacher.

By the second decade of the nineteenth century, religious activists had formed antislavery societies that held public meetings and distributed literature to raise consciousness about the moral issues involved. Regional antislavery associations meeting in conjunction with conferences, associations, and presbyteries provided opportunities for church folk to receive information about slavery and contribute to efforts to end its practice.

The Colonization Movement. An early effort to achieve the progressive elimination of slavery was the African colonization movement. As a "gradualist" compromise between the moral issue of human bondage and the racial prejudices of white society, national leaders like Bushrod Washington, Thomas Jefferson, James Monroe, and Henry Clay advocated manumitting (freeing) slaves and returning them to Africa, with the costs—including compensation to the owners—to be paid from a combination of public and private funds. The American Colonization Society, established in 1816, founded Monrovia (later Liberia) on the West African coast in 1822 as a colony for freed slaves. By 1860, some twelve thousand African Americans had emigrated to Africa.

The colonization movement stirred hostility, however, from southerners opposed to manumission, from those who disapproved spending public monies on the project, and from persons truly interested in the slaves' well-being, who saw repatriation to Africa as simply a further injustice to persons of color. The emigration of blacks to Africa seemed not to solve the moral problems facing a young democratic nation, and in general the colonization movement implied that America was destined to be white and Anglo-Saxon.

Religious Fervor Shapes a Social Crusade. By the late 1820s, rising public indignation in the North and northwestern frontiers, called by some "ultraism," strengthened antislavery sentiments. Local societies began to appear, particularly in New England, New York, and the Western Reserve in Ohio, three regions bound by a Calvinistic moral conscience. In Boston and Framingham, Massachusetts, those opposing slavery gathered in homes, organized conferences, and held fairs and bazaars to raise money for the cause. Women were drawn to antislavery because of its obvious implications for a more gender-inclusive society. Some clergymen like Theodore Parker and Parker Pillsbury married local abolitionists, and persons with different outlooks mingled freely in antislavery circles, such as William M. Chace (a bachelor), John Greenleaf Whittier and Maria Weston Chapman, or Henry I. Bowditch and Julia Ward Howe.

A significant regional step was taken in 1831–1832 with the formation of the New England Anti-Slavery Society, which became a model for other regions and states. In 1833 antislavery leaders including Joshua Leavitt and Lewis and Arthur Tappan in New York City, William Lloyd Garrison of Boston, and Theodore Dwight Weld and Elizur Wright Jr. of Ohio took the next step and founded a national organization, the American Anti-Slavery Society (AAS). By 1840 there were more than thirteen hundred local and regional societies of varying temperaments, enrolling a quarter of a million members in the antislavery cause.

Garrison, regarded by some as a fanatic and by others as even an incendiary, brought to the cause a sense of urgency, a genuine threat to slaveholders, and an uncompromising periodical, the *Liberator*, founded in 1831. Less vituperous than Garrison but nonetheless effective, Joshua Leavitt was appointed editor of the New York Association of Gentlemen's *Evangelist* in 1830; a postmillennialist, he urged churches to create a grassroots campaign of reform. Meanwhile the organizational genius of Garrison created a system whereby paid AAS agents fanned out across the North to lecture, debate, distribute tracts, sell newspaper subscriptions, and assist free blacks and fugitive slaves wherever possible. Through the AAS and local and regional organizations and churches, the antislavery leadership combined careful planning and organization with the zeal of an evangelical religious crusade. In the 1830s the socioeconomic makeup of antislavery in the Northeast included skilled workers and proprietors and managers.

A new group identifiable among antislavery advocates across the country was women. Among the most effective AAS lecturers were the Grimké sisters of South Carolina, Sarah and Angelina, who had embraced Quakerism and moved north. In 1839 the Grimkés and Weld (whom Angelina had married) published *American Slavery as It Is*, a powerful documentary record of brutal abuses. Studies of women in the abolitionist movement have demonstrated the variety and caliber of female writers, lecturers, and advocates in the cause, women such as Anna Elizabeth Dickinson, a Radical Republican playwright from Philadelphia; Mary Berkeley Blackford, a Virginia writer and organizer; Antoinette Brown Blackwell of Henrietta, New York, near Rochester, the first ordained woman in the United States; and Lydia Maria Child, a women's and Indian rights activist from Massachusetts whose 1833 book *An Appeal in Favor of That Class of Americans Called Africans* was the first book by a white person to advocate emancipation.

The religious dimension of antislavery continued to find expression powerfully in the ministry of the Charles Grandison Finney and at two Ohio schools: Lane Theological Seminary in Cincinnati (1829) and Oberlin College (1833). Lane, a Presbyterian school, was located near a large population of free blacks. Its faculty and students included many antislavery firebrands, and a series of public lyceum debates soon gave Lane such a reputation as a hotbed of activism that in 1834 the trustees forbade further discussion of the matter. Fifty-one Lane students, called "the Rebels," withdrew and enrolled at Oberlin, an antislavery center where Finney was

professor of theology. Through various forms of ministry and activism, Oberlin students and faculty infused the antislavery cause with new energy and momentum, making the college one of the movement's major leadership resources. Hillsdale College in Michigan, behind President Ransom Dunn, became a Freewill Baptist center of abolitionism.

The Turn to Politics. Events like the murder of the abolitionist editor Elijah P. Lovejoy by a proslavery mob in Alton, Illinois, in 1837 shook the sensibilities of many Americans. Lovejoy became the martyr of the antislavery cause. In 1840, Theodore Dwight Weld, the Tappan brothers, and other antislavery leaders turned to political organization. They were encouraged by the British Parliament's abolition of slavery throughout the British Empire in 1833. Correspondence with members of Parliament and visiting representatives of British churches and reform societies propelled the American effort. The recent history of strikes, insurrections, and revolts by slaves on the island of Jamaica, plus moral support from black preachers and missionaries, linked American reformers, both in the North and in the South, and British Chartist reformers in a hemispheric moral struggle.

The formation in 1840 of the Liberty Party, also known as the Human Rights Party, was a significant political step. The party nominated James G. Birney, a slaveholder-turned-abolitionist, for president. In part a reaction against Garrison, who was displaying increasingly radical and anarchist tendencies, the Liberty Party stressed natural rights and political action. In 1840, too, these same individuals founded the American and Foreign Anti-Slavery Society, which challenged Garrison for leadership of the movement. (The issue of women's rights and equality, which Garrison supported and more conservative antislavery leaders opposed, figured in this split as well.) Although Birney received only about seven thousand votes, his candidacy brought national attention to the antislavery cause—and sharpened the proslavery defenses of southern whites. Running for president again in 1844, Birney received a bit more than sixty-two thousand votes. Studies have shown that the Liberty Party also suffered from regional competing factions, notably the Cincinnati clique in Ohio and the Liberty Leaguers in New York; it was unable to develop an expanding strategy.

Congress's defeat in 1846 of the Wilmot Proviso—a resolution to bar slavery in any territories other than Texas acquired in the Mexican War—coupled with the failure of either national party to take an unequivocal stand against slavery, further energized the effort to oppose slavery at the ballot box. In 1848 the Free-Soil Party took up the antislavery banner, nominating the former president Martin Van Buren on a platform opposed to the expansion of slavery into the territories; the party's positions were summed up in the slogan "Free Soil, Free Speech, Free Labor, and Free Men." The real strength of Free-Soil lay with Congressman Joshua Giddings and Salmon P. Chase in Ohio's Western Reserve, and a coalition that Chase urged forward, composed of former "Barnburners" and "Hunkers" in New York State and Conscience Whigs in Massachusetts. Giddings, the Tappans, and Weld frequently met to review strategies and plot a congressional course at Mrs. Ann Sprigg's boardinghouse on First Street in Washington, D.C., considered the birthplace of national political abolitionism. Although candidate Van Buren came in third behind the Whig Party candidate Zachary Taylor (who won) and the Democrat Lewis Cass of Michigan, he did garner nearly three hundred thousand votes. The Free-Soil Party's lasting contribution was consciousness raising and serving as a bridge to the future. Within a few years, many Free-Soil voters joined the new Republican Party, a coalition of antislavery enthusiasts, religious leaders, and former Whigs. Meanwhile, "abolition" had become the cry of the more ardent antislavery advocates and so-called action men. Radical activity ensued.

Abolitionists flooded the South with inflammatory pamphlets. Free northern blacks and escaped slaves like Frederick Douglass, William Wells Brown, and William and Ellen Craft played an important role in the movement. Douglass became a major abolitionist spokesman, particularly with the publication of his *Narrative of the Life of Frederick Douglass, an American Slave* (1845). Abolitionists organized and operated the so-called Underground Railroad, a complex network of antislavery households that spirited runaway slaves to the North and the West, the Caribbean, and Canada. Newspapers printed heart-wrenching stories of heroic figures like Harriet Tubman, raising popular consciousness. The growing literary output of the antislavery movement—including sermons, tracts, broadsides, travel and slave narratives, poetry, and novels—constituted the first multiracial literature in American culture.

The 1850 Fugitive Slave Act, a victory for slaveholders, heightened abolitionist fervor and directly inspired the most famous of all antislavery works, Harriet Beecher Stowe's 1852 novel *Uncle Tom's Cabin*. The Kansas-Nebraska Act (1854) and the Supreme Court's Dred Scott decision (*Dred Scott v. Sandford*, 1857), representing further victories for the so-called Slave Power, added fuel to the abolitionist cause. As a region, the North came to new life in opposing slavery. Most radical of all were the ultraists like John Brown, who were prepared to wage armed conflict to achieve their objectives. Brown's career of antislavery violence, first in Kansas and then at Harpers Ferry, Virginia (now West Virginia), in 1859, won the support of Douglass and other prominent abolitionist leaders. Politically, the new Republican Party evolved as a coherent, sectional antislavery coalition. Within two years of Brown's raid at Harpers Ferry, the Civil War, which finally ended slavery in America, was underway.

Assessment. From its inception, the antislavery movement benefited greatly both from the evangelical energies unleashed in the Second Great Awakening and from the many voluntary associations generated within the Protestant community. This multifaceted, essentially Protestant renewal phenomenon strove to "sanctify" or perfect society according to biblical principles that called for upright personal and family life, a high moral standard for communities, and repudiation of evil habits and social maladies. Antislavery work was awash in religious rhetoric, symbols, and vocabulary. There was an implicit assumption in pulpit discourse of the period 1820–1860 that the Kingdom of God on earth could be achieved. The principal communication of these values came through public sermons and lectures and through widely distributed tracts and religious journalism. At the same time, however, antislavery produced irreparable damage to the fabric of American Protestantism by creating long-term sectional divisions in each of the major denominations. Mission boards refused to appoint slaveholders, and educational and benevolent efforts suffered deeply from lost support on both sides of the moral issue.

The brokenness of the mainline churches over slavery and antislavery in the 1840s presaged the political breakup of the nation two decades later. With roots in the election of 1848, political antislavery in the 1850s focused first on limiting slavery's territorial expansion and later on the total abolition of slavery, reflecting a major change in the character of the movement. Countless political leaders and supporters had roots in the evangelical missionary and revivalist traditions, and many also participated in other reform arenas, from anti-Masonry and Adventism to the temperance and women's rights movements. Such leading national women's rights advocates as Lucretia Mott, the Grimké sisters, and Elizabeth Cady Stanton received their start in the antislavery movement.

Overall, antislavery was the first great human rights crusade in American history. A sustained campaign lasting more than a century, it not only helped bring about the emancipation of the slaves, but also inspired a long tradition of social reform.

[*See also* **African Americans; Antebellum Era; Antebellum Reform; Beecher, Henry Ward; Benezet, Anthony; Bleeding Kansas; Child, Lydia Maria; Civil War Era; Clergy; Colonization Movement, African; Douglass, Frederick; Emancipation of Slaves; Finney, Charles Grandison; Free Communities of Color; Free-Soilers; Garrison, William Lloyd; Great Awakenings; Grimké, Sarah and Angelina; Revivals; Slavery; Stanton, Elizabeth Cady; Tubman, Harriet; Underground Railroad; Union Leagues; Voluntary Associations; Weld, Theodore Dwight; West, The;** *and* **Women's Rights Movement, Antebellum Era.**]

BIBLIOGRAPHY

Abzug, Robert H. *Passionate Liberator: Theodore Dwight Weld and the Dilemma of Reform.* New York: Oxford University Press, 1980.

Blight, David W., ed. *Passages to Freedom: The Underground Railroad in History and Memory.* Washington, D.C.: Smithsonian Books with the National Underground Railroad Freedom Center, 2004.

Cumber, John T. *From Abolition to Rights for All: The Making of a Reform Community in the Nineteenth*

Century. Philadelphia: University of Pennsylvania Press, 2008.

Friedman, Lawrence J. *Gregarious Saints: Self and Community in American Abolitionism, 1830–1870.* Cambridge, U.K.: Cambridge University Press, 1982.

Kraditor, Aileen S. *Means and Ends in American Abolitionism: Garrison and His Critics on Strategy and Tactics, 1834–1850.* New York: Pantheon, 1969.

Magdol, Edward. *The Antislavery Rank and File: A Social Profile of the Abolitionists' Constituency.* New York: Greenwood Press, 1986.

Mitchell, Thomas G. *Anti-slavery Politics in Antebellum and Civil War America.* Westport, Conn.: Praeger, 2007.

Pierson, Michael D. *Free Hearts and Free Homes: Gender and American Antislavery Politics.* Chapel Hill: University of North Carolina Press, 2003.

Rayback, Joseph G. *Free Soil: The Election of 1848.* Lexington: University Press of Kentucky, 1970.

Staudenraus, P. J. *The African Colonization Movement, 1816–1865.* New York: Columbia University Press, 1961.

Strong, Douglas M. *Perfectionist Politics: Abolitionism and the Religious Tension of American Democracy.* Syracuse: Syracuse University Press, 1999.

Walters, Ronald G. *The Antislavery Appeal: American Abolitionism after 1830.* Baltimore: Johns Hopkins University Press, 1976.

Wyatt-Brown, Bertram. *Lewis Tappan and the Evangelical War against Slavery.* Cleveland, Ohio: Press of Case Western Reserve University, 1969.

William H. Brackney

APPALACHIA

Geographically, Appalachia includes the mountains and valleys of states eastward from the Ohio River to the Piedmont and northward from Georgia to Maine. Appalachia most often refers to the more populated areas of the southern Allegheny, Blue Ridge, Appalachian, Ozark, and Great Smoky Mountains, a land inhabited by a people with a distinct history, memory, and culture.

Appalachian settlement constituted part of the fourth great migration wave from Europe to America, that from about 1717 to 1775. More than 60 percent of the settlers came from England's borderlands region surrounding the Irish Sea: the Scottish Lowlands, northern Ireland, and the six northern counties of England. The numbers averaged 5,000 per year, or about 285,000 total. Largely Presbyterians at first, many were converted to more evangelical forms of Christianity by Methodist and Baptist missionaries. From the Palatinate of southwestern Germany about a hundred thousand German Protestants— Lutherans, Quakers, Moravians, Calvinists, Dunkers, and Mennonites and Amish—came to British America in a series of waves that began in 1683 and continued until the Revolutionary War. The number who settled in Appalachia is unknown, but at the first federal census in 1790, they constituted only 5 percent of the population of the Carolinas, Georgia, Tennessee, and Kentucky, compared to 90 percent who were English, Irish, or Lowland Scots.

Demographically, one of Appalachia's most arresting features has been the fertility rate. Beginning in the nineteenth century and continuing for roughly a hundred and fifty years, the birthrate of Appalachia exceeded the national average. If the reasons are unclear, the consequences are obvious. In a region of narrow valleys, steep mountainsides, and rocky ridges, continuous population growth and practices of partible inheritance over time produced overpopulation, land scarcity, and rural poverty. Consequently, throughout its history, mobility has been another distinctive feature of Appalachian life. The need to find supplementary work to preserve the family in a kinship-based society has been called the "stable ideal." Such conditions also bred a patriarchal family structure with strong male authority over women and children in the household.

Poverty and isolation, often mistakenly associated with Appalachia's entire history, actually arose in distinct periods of its development. Between 1850 and 1900, as turnpikes and railroads diverted traffic around Appalachia, the region grew isolated. Overpopulation led to increasing landlessness. Sectionalism and the Civil War exacerbated these conditions, giving rise to xenophobia and a more introverted society.

Simultaneously, beginning in the 1880s, local-color writers began to paint literary pictures of a "strange land and a peculiar people." The "hillbilly" genre they created persisted into the twenty-first century as the source of misunderstandings and caricatures of regional history and culture. More than eight hundred movies, from the early nickelodeon one-reelers to late twentieth-century films like *Deliverance*, *Thelma and Louise*, and *Raising Arizona*, depicted hillbillies as cultural "others." Other twentieth-century writers and folklorists such as Altina Waller, Durwood Dunn, and David Whisnant provided correctives to these distorted images, however.

Between the 1890s and the 1930s, migration to nearby rural industries such as quarrying, coal mining, lumbering, and iron making provided some respite from chronic rural poverty. In Appalachia's version of the New South, local and state governments, legislatures, and politicians transformed themselves into propagandists for the region and invented tax-incentive schemes to encourage industrial development. Outside capital flowed into the region and, together with inside help from a small, commercially minded urban elite of lawyers, bankers, and merchants, stimulated rapid urban and industrial growth. With the coming of alternative fuels in the 1920s and the Great Depression of the 1930s,

the boom decades ended. Racial segregation—as seen, for example, in Coe Ridge, Kentucky, and Piedmont, West Virginia—and higher rates of lynching than in the non-Appalachian South during these years shattered the illusion of racial harmony in the region.

Between 1940 and 1970, New Deal programs, the World War II draft, and out-migration brought more contact with other Americans. Many fled to the so-called Appalachian ghettos in Baltimore, Cleveland, Dayton, Cincinnati, Chicago, and Detroit. The 1960 U.S. Census revealed a regional population decrease for the first time since the area was settled by Europeans. John F. Kennedy focused attention on poverty in Appalachia in his 1960 campaign for the Democratic Party's presidential nomination, as did Michael Harrington in *The Other America* (1962). The 1970s saw a reversal, demographically and economically, as out-migrants returned, young people chose to remain, and many older Americans decided to retire in Appalachia.

[*See also* **Cumberland Gap; Hatfield-McCoy Feud; Internal Migration; Poverty;** *and* **Rural Life and Society.**]

BIBLIOGRAPHY

Eller, Ronald D. *Miners, Millhands, and Mountaineers: Industrialization of the Appalachian South, 1880–1930.* Knoxville: University of Tennessee Press, 1982.

Fischer, David Hackett. *Albion's Seed: Four British Folkways in America.* New York: Oxford University Press, 1989.

Gates, Henry Louis, Jr. *Colored People: A Memoir.* New York: Alfred A. Knopf, 1994.

Shapiro, Henry D. *Appalachia on Our Mind: The Southern Mountains and Mountaineers in the American Consciousness, 1870–1920.* Chapel Hill: University of North Carolina Press, 1978.

Shifflett, Crandall A. *Coal Towns: Life, Work, and Culture in Company Towns of Southern Appalachia,*

1880–1960. Knoxville: University of Tennessee Press, 1991.

Waller, Altina L. *Feud: Hatfields, McCoys, and Social Change in Appalachia, 1860–1900*. Chapel Hill: University of North Carolina Press, 1988.

Crandall Shifflett

ASIAN AMERICAN MOVEMENT

A self-identified Asian American movement emerged in the late 1960s and 1970s as a response to racial discrimination against and exclusion of Chinese, Filipino, Japanese, Korean, and other Asian communities in the United States. Anti-Asian attitudes existed long before the 1960s. The Chinese Exclusion Act became law in 1882, the Immigration Act of 1924 excluded most other Asians, and the 1934 Tydings-McDuffie Act excluded Filipinos. Asians already living in America faced violence and legal restrictions, such as when they tried to purchase real estate or marry white people. They also faced segregated education, housing, and employment, and they suffered economic exploitation as sources of cheap labor. Although various Asian ethnic groups earlier voiced their opposition to such discrimination, it was only in the late 1960s, inspired by the African American civil rights and Black Power movements, that there developed a sense of common oppression as a racial group, primarily among students and other youth.

The new movement asserted that the myth of the successful "model minority" pitted Asians against other minorities and that Asians were injured by white supremacy and societal inequities in the same ways that other people of color were. Just as African Americans rejected their designation as "Negroes" and asserted that they were "black and proud," Asian Americans rejected being labeled "Orientals," considering that a pejorative term that signified their marginalization by the dominant white society, and instead regarded themselves with pride as "Asian Americans." One of the first assertions of this identity was introduced during the 1968 Third World Strikes at the University of California, Berkeley and San Francisco State College, when Asian students united as the Asian American Political Alliance, joining with other so-called Third World black, Chicano, and Native American groups in what they called the Third World Liberation Front.

Asian American activists viewed antiracist struggle as linked to the anticolonial movements for national liberation and freedom that were then raging in what was known as the Third World: Latin America, Africa, and Asia. Most of the activists in the late 1960s and early 1970s were not recent immigrants but either had been born in the United States or immigrated as children; the sense of being "American" and yet denied rights was strong. Many of the college students were among the first wave to be admitted as a result of equal-opportunity programs, and the movement was initially based on campuses. When protests against the U.S. war in Vietnam grew, the fact that the war was being waged against an Asian population made a strong impact—particularly the racial aspects of the war, such as calling the Vietnamese "gooks." Self-identified Asian American contingents took their places in anti–Vietnam War demonstrations. In addition to the Vietnamese resistance to the United States, the Chinese revolution and its Communist leader Mao Tse-tung (Mao Ze-dong) were another source of inspiration.

At the same time, Asian Americans joined members of other Third World communities to demand ethnic studies programs and departments in colleges in order to include histories and cultures of minorities, subjects that were previously missing in higher education. Students demanded a "relevant" education, which meant that learning and serving their communities were integrally linked. Asian Americans formed coalitions to "serve the people," joining with their elders to protect Chinatowns, Little Tokyos, Manilatowns, and other Asian urban enclaves from evictions, urban renewal, or other forms of destruction in such cities as Boston, Honolulu, Los Angeles, New York, Philadelphia, San Francisco, and Seattle. Most Asians were restricted to employment in the low end of the agricultural, service, and manufacturing sectors of the economy, and the newly emerging movement also demanded equal-employment policies and affirmative action programs, and it supported labor organizing among farmworkers, sweatshop garment workers, and others.

As the movement thrived, a dynamic developed between organizing on a pan-Asian basis and organizing with a focus on each ethnic community. At the same time, activists became increasingly radicalized, with many creating new Marxist-oriented and Maoist political groups, while others formed community organizations to provide services or to oppose discrimination. Cultural groups and individual artists emerged in visual arts, media, theater, music, and literature.

The Asian American community became increasingly more complex with the arrival of growing numbers of immigrants. The reform of immigration laws in 1965 did away with the national-origins quota system, giving preference to skilled workers and professionals, as well as to family reunification, increasing the numbers of new immigrants. By 1980 the majority of Asian Americans were foreign-born, except for the Japanese, with burgeoning Filipino and Chinese communities, along with refugees from Southeast Asia and growing

Indian, Pakistani, and other South Asian communities. Data from the 2010 U.S. Census showed that the Indian American population had surged, making Indian Americans the third-largest Asian group closely behind the Filipinos. The class and cultural dynamics of the different communities began to change, particularly with an expanding middle class.

As each ethnic group became more diverse, the movement of the 1960s and 1970s began to change. The different ethnic groups continued to oppose racial discrimination and violence, as well as to assert political influence and transnational solidarity. The pan-Asian approach continued through coalitions and networks for electoral politics and for professional and business activities. At the same time, each of the diverse ethnic groups took on issues within its own specific community, such as immigration rights and concern with the affairs of the home country. Yet the groups also united with other Asian, African American, Latino, and other minority groups to oppose racial discrimination and demand social justice and equal rights.

[*See also* **Affirmative Action; Asian Americans; California; Immigrants' Rights Movement; Race and Ethnicity; Racism; San Francisco; Seventies, The; Sixties, The;** *and* **Transnational Identity.**]

BIBLIOGRAPHY

Habal, Estella. *San Francisco's International Hotel: Mobilizing the Filipino American Community in the Anti-Eviction Movement.* Philadelphia: Temple University Press, 2007.

Liu, Michael, Kim Geron, and Tracy Lai. *The Snake Dance of Asian American Activism: Community, Vision, and Power.* Lanham, Md.: Lexington Books, 2008.

Maeda, Daryl J. *Chains of Babylon: The Rise of Asian America*. Minneapolis: University of Minnesota Press, 2009.

Estella Habal

ASIAN AMERICANS

The extending reach of European but primarily American empires shaped patterns of migration from Asia and Pacific islands to the Americas, and the numbers of migrants increased with the uneven emergence of Asian nation-states in the late nineteenth century. The Spanish galleon trade from about 1565 to 1815 first systematized mobility and commerce across the Pacific, creating contacts that continued with the Yankee clippers of the late eighteenth century through 1869. The subsequent U.S. imperial expansion in the Pacific, including the annexation of Hawai'i and the Philippines, China's precipitous decline and troubled quest for modernity, the rise of the modern Japanese state, World War II, decolonization, the Korean War, the Cold War, and the Vietnam War all influenced which Asian groups came to the U.S., their numbers, and their treatment once in the U.S. Most came as laborers, but many also came as merchants, family dependents, refugees, skilled artisans and workers, students, sailors, and other seekers of opportunity. Hawaiian and Caribbean plantations required tens of thousands of workers, as did developing industries and agriculture in the American West. An Asian diaspora scattered throughout the Americas in response to shifts in the fastest-growing areas of the world's economy and encountered, often on unequal terms, counterparts in Australia, the Caribbean, and South Africa, among other places.

Asiatic Exclusion.   In the mid-nineteenth century the California gold rush and pressing needs for labor in railroad construction, mining, and agriculture mobilized successive influxes of Chinese and later Japanese, Koreans, Indians, and Filipinos. Perceptions of Asians as essentially "inassimilable foreigners" inflamed resentments and fears of the so-called yellow peril among many white, working-class people. Declines in the U.S. economy aggravated concerns about unfair job competition, contributing to volatile yet organized movements demanding the exclusion of Asians—Chinese in 1882 through the Chinese Exclusion Act and other laws, Japanese and Koreans in 1907 with the gentlemen's agreement, natives of the Asiatic Barred Zone designated in a 1917 immigration act as extending from eastern Asia to the Middle East, and all "aliens ineligible to citizenship" with the 1924 Immigration Act. This legal category stemmed from the 1790 Nationality Act, which reserved naturalization for "free white persons" and severely limited the rights of immigrant Asians until the 1952 McCarran-Walter Act ended racial restrictions concerning citizenship rights. As U.S. nationals, Filipinos were the last Asian group to face restricted entry; the 1934 Tydings-McDuffie Act promised the Philippines eventual independence from the United States but also restricted the number of Filipino immigrants.

The terms of exclusion varied according to U.S. relations with the Asian countries. Around the turn of the twentieth century, weak China faced the most openly racist restrictions, while colonized Korea and India had no recourse to diplomatic negotiations. In contrast, the emerging world power Japan negotiated a treaty with more benign terms that permitted family reunification, particularly the migration of wives, and integrated schools for Japanese American children. Despite these relative advantages, Japanese in California and other western states were targeted with laws restricting the rights of "aliens ineligible to citizenship" to own or lease farmland. The failure of court challenges to these and other discriminatory laws, along with generally hostile conditions, diminished the immigration of Asians, as did the Great Depression of the 1930s and World War II. Asian Americans occupied primarily hard-won, labor-intensive economic niches in small service businesses such as restaurants, laundries, boardinghouses and hotels, migratory labor, gardening, and domestic service.

Until the 1960s, men greatly outnumbered women in all Asian American communities as a result of immigration restrictions, limited economic options, and antagonism to the possibility of permanent settlement. For example, the few women who did immigrate to America—less than 10 percent of the roughly one hundred thousand Chinese immigrants—were harassed through legislation and were stereotyped as prostitutes and slaves. Japanese American men, however, could bring so-called picture brides, and consequently the Japanese American community had the best gender balance and, with the emergence of American-born generations, the largest numbers. Male Chinese and Filipino laborers faced more difficulties bringing wives to the United States and lived in almost exclusively male social worlds. Up through World War II, even educated Asian Americans with birthright U.S. citizenship confronted the same racialized restrictions as did their immigrant forebears.

Treatment during and after World War II.
World War II provided the most dramatic example of the United States' hypocritical treatment of Asian Americans. Even as the United States valorized China and the Philippines as wartime allies, it forcibly interned more than 110,000 Japanese Americans, of whom two-thirds were native-born U.S. citizens, based on assertions of national-security needs. Despite discrimination, Filipino Americans, Chinese Americans, and Japanese Americans participated in military service in large numbers. The wholly Japanese American 442d Regimental Combat Team drew upon both Hawaiians and mainlanders—many of whose families were interned—and attained a record for valor that remains unmatched.

After the war, veterans' benefits helped many Asian Americans gain education, employment, and rights that they were previously denied. The War Brides Act of 1945 and its 1947 amendment enabled many couples to reunite in the United States, and for the first time, more Asian women than men immigrated, ameliorating gender imbalances and turning bachelor communities into family societies. The postwar period generally brought rising prosperity and civil rights gains. Reflecting U.S. foreign-policy considerations, Congress repealed the Chinese Exclusion Act in 1943 to support its alliance with China, and the 1952 McCarran-Walter Act removed the 1924 ban on Asian immigration. During the Cold War, piecemeal refugee acts and increased outreach to international students brought new waves of better-educated, professional classes of immigrants; their notable successes and greater integration laid the foundations for late twentieth-century stereotypes of Asians as "model minorities."

The 1965 Immigration Act consolidated the transformation of Asian immigrants from bachelor laborers to professionals and entrepreneurs through a preference system that favored family reunification and people with certain education levels and skills. Native-born Asian Americans combined with many new Asian immigrants to produce one of the fastest-growing segments of the U.S. population. By the 1970s, many migrants from the Philippines, Taiwan, Korea, India, and other

Asian nations with newly gained entry rights migrated to the United States, often in family units and frequently to work in high-tech industries where they joined a growing number of second- and third-generation Chinese and Japanese Americans in white-collar jobs that had previously barred Asians. By the 1980s the two most numerous groups of immigrants from Asia were South Koreans and Filipinos. Their paths to the United States paralleled that of migrants from Pacific islands with U.S. military bases, such as Samoa, Okinawa, and Guam. Since 1965 the Asian-Pacific American population has become nearly 70 percent foreign-born, and in 2008 it stood at more than 15,281,000, or just over 5 percent of the total population.

Alongside the educated and highly skilled arrived Asian immigrants who were less well prepared. After the Vietnam War, tens of thousands of refugees who had been identified with the U.S. cause came to the United States from South Vietnam, Cambodia, and Laos. Although they had aligned with the United States military, in America many had difficulty finding work. Perhaps worst off were the Hmong, people from nomadic hill tribes recruited by the Central Intelligence Agency to fight the North Vietnamese. Accustomed to a village economy and culture, they were ill-equipped for life in urban industrial North America. Some have become trapped in welfare, while others have found their way back to farming. Asian Americans without English-language skills or acceptably credentialed scientific, technical, and business skills have experienced limited job options and under-employment. Despite the celebrated successes of "model minority" achievers, by the early twenty-first century many Asian Americans remained locked into historic dead-end economic niches such as family-run restaurants and other small businesses, unskilled textile factory work, and care-giving labor.

[*See also* **Angel Island Immigration Station; Asian American Movement; California; Chinese Americans; Demography; Deportations and Repatriations; Filipino Americans; Hmong Americans; Immigration; Indian (Asian) Americans; Japanese Americans; Japanese Americans, Incarceration of; Korean Americans; Multiracial and Multiethnic Americans; Native Hawaiians and Pacific Islanders; Race and Ethnicity; Racism; Transnational Identity;** *and* **Vietnamese Americans.**]

BIBLIOGRAPHY

Chan, Sucheng. *Asian Americans: An Interpretive History*. Boston: Twayne, 1991.

Lai, Eric, and Dennis Arguelles, eds. *The New Face of Asian Pacific America: Numbers, Diversity, and Change in the 21st Century*. San Francisco: AsianWeek, with UCLA's Asian American Studies Center Press, 2003.

Ngai, Mae M. *Impossible Subjects: Illegal Aliens and the Making of Modern America*. Princeton, N.J.: Princeton University Press, 2004.

Okihiro, Gary Y. *Margins and Mainstreams: Asian Americans in American History and Culture*. Seattle: University of Washington Press, 1994.

Takaki, Ronald. *Strangers from a Different Shore*. Boston: Little, Brown, 1989.

Madeline Hsu

ASSIMILATION

"Assimilation" refers to processes that lead to greater homogeneity in a society. The term commonly describes the weakening of ethnic ties, cultures, and identities among members of an immigrant ethnic group, who in turn forge links to, and adopt the identities and cultural traits of, the larger society or its dominant ethnic group. Assimilation can also describe cases in which members of different, nondominant ethnic groups find common ground. Understanding assimilation requires knowledge of what an individual or group is assimilating to.

Americans have discussed assimilation in terms of three main stances toward immigrants. "Anglo-conformity" was the assumption that newcomers and their children would adopt the culture of the nation's self-defined "Anglo-Saxon core." The "melting pot" stance—the term is from the title of a popular 1908 play by Israel Zangwill—foresaw a mixing of peoples that would produce a new American culture. From the eighteenth century on, the third stance, "cultural pluralism," foresaw immigrant groups retaining their separate social worlds within a common political framework. This approach has nineteenth-century antecedents, but intellectuals such as Randolph Bourne and Horace Kallen, a German Jewish immigrant who later taught philosophy at the New School for Social Research in New York City, articulated it most fully in the 1910s. Significantly, until the mid-twentieth century, most European American proponents of these stances envisioned no role for non-Europeans. Most scholarly theories of assimilation likewise have historically had European newcomers as their main reference point; this has hampered understanding of how non-European immigrants have or have not assimilated.

The first sustained scholarly treatment of assimilation came from University of Chicago sociologists who developed a set of influential concepts in the early twentieth century. One cast migration as a process involving the "disorganization" of peasant communities and their members' journeys to the more individualized world of the city. Another concept broke social interaction into stages running from competition to assimilation. The concept of "ecological succession" depicted immigrant city-dwellers as moving from

ethnic "colonies" through new districts, until they became absorbed into a hazily defined "American" population.

When immigration history became a professional subfield beginning in the 1920s, its practitioners made assimilation a central theme. They also adopted Chicago concepts. The historian Oscar Handlin's *The Uprooted* (1951), for example, described European immigrants as dislocated peasants who Americanized by becoming individuals. But scholars also began to define more clearly assimilation's social setting. Marcus Lee Hansen, arguing that third-generation immigrants showed renewed interest in their heritage, suggested in 1937 that ethnic identity might reemerge. Ruby Jo Reeves Kennedy proposed in 1944 that assimilation was occurring along religious lines, within a "triple-melting-pot" structure. Writing in 1956, Will Herberg saw these Protestant, Catholic, and Jewish melting pots as stemming from the third generation's discovery of religion as a permissible version of ethnic identity. The sociologist Milton Gordon's *Assimilation in American Life* (1964) found cultural assimilation to the "core subsociety" of white, middle-class Protestants, but not structural assimilation into its institutions. The result was a society centered on the core but retaining religious subdivisions, unassimilated racial groups, and some European ethnic "vestiges."

The 1960s saw a rejection of assimilation theory and a stress on the persistence of ethnic groups. This approach, presaged by Gordon, was heralded by Nathan Glazer and Daniel Patrick Moynihan's *Beyond the Melting Pot* (1963) and Rudolph J. Vecoli's 1964 critique of Handlin's *The Uprooted*. The decade's turbulent politics fueled the shift, underlining the discrimination historically suffered by non-Europeans and encouraging a European American "ethnic revival." Beginning in the early 1980s, however, historians cautiously revisited assimilation. Some depicted a pluralistic America with room for assimilative processes between ethnic groups. Others examined how European ethnics claimed a common "white" identity, how second-generation Mexican and Japanese immigrants underwent a measure of acculturation even as they contended with racism, and how 1930s unionism brought greater unity to an ethnically divided working class. By the end of the century, assimilation had reemerged as an acknowledged factor in ethnic history.

[*See also* **Americanization Movement; Immigration; Labor Movements; Multiracial and Multiethnic Americans; Nativist Movement; Race and Ethnicity;** *and* **Religion.**]

BIBLIOGRAPHY

Abramson, Harold J. "Assimilation and Pluralism." In *Harvard Encyclopedia of American Ethnic Groups,* edited by Stephan Thernstrom, pp. 150–160. Cambridge, Mass.: Belknap Press of Harvard University Press, 1980.

Gleason, Philip. *Speaking of Diversity: Language and Ethnicity in Twentieth-Century America.* Baltimore: Johns Hopkins University Press, 1992.

Gordon, Milton M. *Assimilation in American Life: The Role of Race, Religion, and National Origins.* New York: Oxford University Press, 1964.

Kazal, Russell A. "Revisiting Assimilation: The Rise, Fall, and Reappraisal of a Concept in American Ethnic History." *American Historical Review* 100 (April 1995): 437–471.

Morawska, Ewa. "In Defense of the Assimilation Model." *Journal of American Ethnic History* 13 (Winter 1994): 76–87.

Sánchez, George J. *Becoming Mexican American: Ethnicity, Culture, and Identity in Chicano Los Angeles, 1900–1945.* New York: Oxford University Press, 1993.

Russell A. Kazal

ASYLUMS AND MENTAL ILLNESS

Asylums, or hospitals specifically built to care for the mentally ill, first appeared in the United States in the early 1800s. Their construction marked the end of a more diverse, fluid approach to caring for people with serious mental illness. Colonial Americans were no strangers to such disorders. The first European missionaries observed that Native Americans recognized such ailments and had special rituals to treat them. The English colonists and enslaved Africans arriving in the late 1600s brought their own traditions of explaining and treating mental illness. Families generally cared for their deranged relatives at home. If violent or friendless, lunatics might be sent to local jails, almshouses, or (in large colonial cities) hospitals, where they were confined rather than treated.

As the numbers of mentally ill patients confined in hospitals and almshouses increased, so, too, did medical interest in their treatment, evident in the career of Benjamin Rush. As an attending physician at the Pennsylvania Hospital from 1783 until his death in 1813, the Edinburgh-trained Rush experimented with more aggressive forms of treatment, such as placing patients in a "tranquilizing chair" to calm them and shaming them into more reasonable behavior. In 1812, Rush reported his results in *Observations and Inquiries upon the Diseases of the Mind,* the first American treatise on mental illness.

A New Institution. The same evangelical zeal and Enlightenment optimism evident in Rush's work gave rise to a new institution dedicated to curing the mentally ill, called variously a "retreat" or "asylum." The York Retreat, founded in York, England, in 1796 by the Society of Friends, exemplified the new approach. Known as moral treatment, the approach relied on an ordered regimen and a kindly paternalism to effect cures. In the United States, the first asylum modeled on the York Retreat opened at Frankford, Pennsylvania, now part of Philadelphia, in 1813, and similar institutions soon followed in other states. Inspired by reports of spectacular cure rates, the Massachusetts General, New York, and Pennsylvania Hospitals spun off separate asylum branches, while reformers such as Dorothea Dix convinced state legislators to erect public asylums, starting with the Worcester State Hospital in Massachusetts, opened in 1833. By 1880 there were 139 mental hospitals in the United States, and almost every state had one public asylum in operation.

The rapid expansion of mental hospitals created a new medical specialty. In 1844 the heads of thirteen mental hospitals met in Philadelphia to form the Association of Medical Superintendents of American Institutions for the Insane (AMSAII), the first national medical association in the United States. (The American Medical Association was founded in 1847.) Through its annual meetings and publication of the *American Journal of Insanity*, the AMSAII—renamed the American Psychiatric Association in 1921—dominated early asylum medicine. Following its guidelines for hospital design and management, which were written by the AMSAII member Thomas Story Kirkbride, many nineteenth-century asylums were built according to what became known as the Kirkbride plan.

The new asylums did not fulfill their early promoters' curative claims. Though some patients did indeed recover, others did not, hardly surprisingly given that many probably suffered from organic brain syndromes that no amount of moral treatment could reverse. The advocates of the asylum argued that with

even modest cure rates, mental hospitals represented a vast improvement over almshouses and jails. But public officials began to look for cheaper means to accommodate the growing population of the chronically ill. After the Civil War, the Kirkbride-style hospital lost favor in comparison to larger institutions such as New York State's Willard Asylum, opened in Ovid in 1869, built explicitly for incurable patients who were expected to work to support themselves. More pessimistic medical theories that equated mental illness with chronic, degenerative diseases of the brain reinforced the trend toward custodial care. Although private asylums continued to offer affluent patients a more optimistic message, public mental hospitals remained largely custodial in their goals from the late 1800s until the 1930s.

New Approaches. In the Progressive Era, new approaches to mental illness developed outside the traditional mental hospital, in research institutes and psychiatric clinics attached to general hospitals. There a younger generation of medical specialists combined psychoanalysis with neuroscience into an approach known as dynamic psychiatry. The mental hygiene movement, begun by the former patient Clifford Beers, reinforced the emphasis on prevention through better child-rearing methods and mental-health education.

Dynamic psychiatry had little to offer the traditional mental hospital, which grew even more isolated as a medical institution in the early twentieth century. But in the 1930s, new shock treatments that used insulin, metrazole, and electricity showed promise in treating schizophrenia and other conditions; between 1935 and 1941, an estimated seventy-five thousand patients underwent some form of shock treatment. Then came psychosurgery, which severed fibers connecting the brain's hemispheres; between 1936 and 1951, more than eighteen thousand such operations were performed in the United States. During World War II, successful use of psychodynamic methods to treat combat-related mental disorders led to a renewed interest in both individual therapy and milieu therapy, an updated form of moral treatment.

As part of a postwar commitment to improving the nation's health care, Congress in 1946 established the National Institute of Mental Health to fund basic research and guide policy reform. In the early 1950s, new drugs such as thorazine, reserpine, and iproniazid, which reduced the worst symptoms of schizophrenia and depression, increased optimism that, at long last, the mental hospital could return to its curative mission.

In this optimistic spirit, Congress in 1955 authorized creation of the Joint Commission on Mental Illness and Health to explore new ways to meet the nation's mental-health needs. Its final report, issued in 1960, placed great emphasis on expanding community-based care. The Joint Commission's recommendations were enacted in the Community Mental Health Centers Act of 1963, which sought to create a less stigmatizing, affordable alternative to the traditional mental hospital.

New sensitivities to civil rights contributed to the shift toward community-based care. In the late 1950s, the psychiatrists Thomas Szasz and R. D. Laing produced radical critiques of the mental hospital as an oppressive institution, while legal reformers began to challenge the legitimacy of involuntary commitment. Inspired by 1960s social movements, former patients began to organize, creating a network of activist groups calling for a liberation movement among mental patients. Patient advocates called for a community-based care overseen by patients themselves, a vision outlined in Judi Chamberlin's 1978 landmark book *On Our Own: Patient-Controlled Alternatives to the Mental Health System.*

Many of the new community mental-health centers focused primarily on people suffering from emotional distress, not serious mental illness. Meanwhile, states eager to cut costs accelerated discharge rates from mental hospitals without expanding their support for community-based programs. Patient populations plunged precipitously, from 475,000 in 1965 to 119,000 in 1986. Without strong community programs in place, many patients ended up homeless or in jail.

Though often referred to as "deinstitutionalization," the downsizing of state hospitals might better be described as a "transinstitutionalization." Changes in Medicare and Social Security disability funding in the 1970s and 1980s resulted in the moving of some patients to nursing homes or short-term residency hotels. Although many state hospitals did close, inpatient psychiatric care in hospitals remained heavily used, albeit for much shorter periods of time. For many poor Americans suffering from mental illness, the prison has replaced the mental hospital as the most likely destination. In 2006 the Bureau of Justice Statistics reported that half of all prison inmates reported symptoms of mental illness, for which they received no treatment.

[*See also* Dix, Dorothea; Health and Fitness; Homelessness and Vagrancy; Hospitals and Dispensaries; Prisons and Penitentiaries; Public Health; *and* Rush, Benjamin.]

BIBLIOGRAPHY

Gamwell, Lynn, and Nancy Tomes. *Madness in America: Cultural and Medical Perceptions of Mental Illness before 1914.* Ithaca, N.Y.: Cornell University Press, 1995.

Grob, Gerald N. *The Mad among Us: A History of the Care of America's Mentally Ill.* New York: Free Press, 1994.

Pressman, Jack D. *Last Resort: Psychosurgery and the Limits of Medicine.* New York: Cambridge University Press, 1998.

Reiss, Benjamin. *Theaters of Madness: Insane Asylums and Nineteenth-Century American Culture.* Chicago: University of Chicago Press, 2008.

Yanni, Carla. *The Architecture of Madness: Insane Asylums in the United States.* Minneapolis: University of Minnesota Press, 2007.

Nancy Tomes

ATLANTA

Established in 1836 as a regional railroad hub, "Terminus" (briefly, "Marthasville") was incorporated as the city of Atlanta in 1847. As late as 1860, its population stood at just 9,554. The Civil War Union general William T. Sherman brought this municipality to national attention in 1864. The Atlanta that Sherman's Army of the Tennessee occupied on 2 September 1864 had served as the nerve center of the Confederacy, but the smoldering city that he evacuated on 15 November was a burned-out ruin. It did not remain so for long.

On 21 December 1886, the Atlanta *Constitution* editor Henry Grady, addressing the New England Society of New York, singled out General Sherman and assured him that he was "considered an able man in our parts, though some people think he is a kind of careless man about fire, and that from the ashes he left us in 1864 we have raised a brave and beautiful city." In 1881, 1887, and 1895, Atlanta boosters promoted their city's rebirth with a series of international expositions; during the 1920s and again in the 1960s, its commercial leadership launched "Forward Atlanta" campaigns to attract new businesses to the city. These manifestations of the "Atlanta spirit," together with the city's development as a transportation center—first rail, then air and automotive—meant growth and expansion, resulting in population bursts from 37,409 in 1880 to more than 200,000 in 1920 and nearly 500,000 in 1970. By the early 1990s, when Atlanta was advertising its internationality and was successfully advancing itself as host city for the 1996 Summer Olympics, the municipality served as the focal point for a metropolitan region of more than 3 million inhabitants.

As the transportation and communications center for the Southeast, Atlanta by the late twentieth century provided regional offices for most major American corporations and was also corporate headquarters for Coca-Cola, Delta Airlines, and the Turner Broadcasting division of Time Warner. Its major research universities included Emory, Georgia State, the Georgia Institute of Technology, and the four-member Atlanta University Center Consortium, the world's largest concentration of historically black institutions of higher learning.

Through the late nineteenth and early twentieth centuries, Atlanta promoted itself ceaselessly, some said shamelessly, as the capital of a new—albeit segregated—South. Booker T. Washington's apparent acceptance of this "separate but equal" doctrine in his address at the 1895 Cotton States and International Exposition came to be called the "Atlanta Compromise." But many black Atlantans—from Washington's contemporary W. E. B. Du Bois to the Reverend Martin Luther King Jr.—rejected this policy of accommodation, challenged it in the courts and in the streets, and eventually overturned racial segregation. Their long struggle earned for Atlanta the title of Civil Rights Capital.

As the civil rights movement unfolded, Atlanta presented itself to the nation as the "city too busy to hate." Unlike other southern cities, its leadership preached and practiced controlled change. Atlanta could embrace relatively progressive racial policies because, as the political scientist Clarence N. Stone demonstrated in *Regime Politics: Governing Atlanta, 1946–1988* (1989), a tight coalition of business leaders and government officials assumed leadership during the 1940s, expanded its base during the 1960s and 1970s, and survived into the post–civil rights era. Maintaining its regional leadership in the face of increasing competition from other New South cities loomed as Atlanta's challenge for the twenty-first century.

[*See also* Civil Rights Movement; King, Martin Luther, Jr.; South, The; *and* Sunbelt.]

BIBLIOGRAPHY

Bayor, Ronald H. *Race and the Shaping of Twentieth-Century Atlanta*. Chapel Hill: University of North Carolina Press, 1996.

Roth, Darlene R., and Andy Ambrose. *Metropolitan Frontiers: A Short History of Atlanta*. Atlanta: Longstreet Press, 1996.

Dana F. White

ATLANTIC WORLD

The westward expansion of European empires between 1500 and 1820 profoundly altered the lives of those inhabiting the four continents bordering the Atlantic Ocean. Those around the Atlantic were brought together by migration and commerce, and adaptation and creolization—the process by which new cultural forms arose from the mixture of preexisting ones—defined their social experiences. Although migrants from Europe and their descendents dominated the political and economic history of Atlantic colonies, the overwhelming majority of people who settled in the Americas were unfree. Of the 11 million people who traveled to the New World between 1500 and 1820, 8.5 million were enslaved Africans.

Initial Settlement. The densities of indigenous populations, Europeans' economic goals, and the demographics of migrant groups combined to determine the social history of each region in the Atlantic. In Mesoamerica, for example, the Spanish found large native populations whom they could compel to work for them. Under what scholars call the encomienda system, small numbers of Spaniards grew rich off indigenous populations who labored in their mines and on their agricultural estates. Officially free, indigenous workers nevertheless had few rights and limited access to political power, and they were compelled to learn Spanish and convert to Catholicism. Together with epidemic diseases, encomiendas destroyed many pre-Columbian cultures, reorienting them around new communities of blended Indian, African, and European peoples.

Where local populations were insufficient to meet labor needs, colonizers used the forced migration of unfree (mostly African) laborers to populate their settlements. Though the Spanish supplemented their indigenous labor force with slaves, they did not at first depend on African slavery—unlike colonists in Portuguese Brazil. Because of disease and royal opposition to Indian slavery, the Portuguese colonists could not depend on indigenous labor. By 1600, Brazil was already dominated by sugar cultivation and populated by fifteen thousand African slaves. In the next half century, planters imported two hundred thousand slaves to plant and process sugarcane. After 1650 similar slave-centered plantations became the basic unit of European colonization.

Plantation Societies.

Running in a continuum from the Chesapeake to Brazil, plantation societies were defined by export-oriented agriculture and enslaved labor. Like Brazil, the sugar islands of the British and French West Indies had the most stratified societies. Here small numbers of elites living on large plantations dominated society; for instance, the top 7 percent of landowners controlled 54 percent of Barbados's wealth in 1680. The majority of the population of the British and French Caribbean—about 85 percent by 1700—was enslaved. A form of economic and labor organization almost unknown in Europe, the plantation system created societies that looked dramatically different from those in Europe and Africa. With most of the population unfree, with population growth dependent on immigration, and with almost unprecedented mixtures of cultures—for instance, slaves arriving in Barbados in the eighteenth century spoke at least four major languages—daily life in plantation societies was unstable and difficult.

Where slavery was less prevalent, as in New England, societies more closely resembled those in Europe. Yet even though English political and religious traditions, nuclear farming families, and European customs dominated this region, relative isolation and the presence of many European and Native American cultures made communities different from the towns that their residents had left behind. More typical of the rest of the Atlantic world was the situation in the Chesapeake. At first a roughly egalitarian society of small farmers and white indentured servants, by the 1680s the colonies of Virginia and Maryland developed into hierarchical plantation societies centered on African slavery.

With most workers unable to marry or migrate freely, the region contrasted sharply with rural life in Britain. For whites, however, cheap and abundant land in mainland North America meant that more had access to property ownership—and the benefits it brought—than in Britain. As different as these colonies looked from Europe, social mores often remained similar. Even those behaviors that seem discordant (such as higher rates of pre-marital pregnancy and lower rates of church attendance) were more the result of circumstances (unbalanced sex ratios and less access to clergy) than of different social norms.

Adaptation and Creolization.

As was the case in the Chesapeake, all migrants to the Americas faced the difficult task of adapting their Old World traditions to the new environments, demographics, and complex mix of peoples they found in the Americas. For English colonists in backcountry Pennsylvania this meant learning to live alongside Indians, Germans, and the Scotch-Irish; for French fur trappers in Quebec it meant forming alliances with the Iroquois and Huron. But for no group was this more demanding than for enslaved Africans. Forcibly removed from their own communities and carried thousands of miles to the Americas, by necessity slaves had to reinvent and reshape their societies. Conditioned by the circumstances in which they were held—whether one field hand among several hundred on a cane plantation, or the only enslaved worker of an urban blacksmith—most Africans had social experiences that were defined by their own efforts to build familial and community networks. Most significantly in North America, where the climate and labor regime allowed the enslaved population to be self-replicating, but also to some degree everywhere they lived, enslaved Africans rejected their masters' efforts at deracination and carved out distinctive social worlds for themselves. Enslaved Africans created independent communities that were distinguished by the blending of many African traditions with those of Europeans and Amerindians, and ultimately these communities formed a basis from which to resist slavery. Sometimes this resistance was violent, as was the case for the Jamaican Maroons—fugitive African slaves living in the highlands of central Jamaica—who clashed with British planters, and for the slaves in Saint-Domingue who revolted in the 1790s. More often, however, the persistence and reblending of African cultures enabled slaves to resist by giving them agency over the most basic of human traits—what they ate, how they worshipped, and how they structured their families.

These processes of adaptation and recombination defined the social experience of the Atlantic and varied everywhere depending on the particular ingredients that intersected in each national enclave. Yet binding the Atlantic together was the circulation of enslaved Africans. These people, and the plantation economies they made possible, unified the Atlantic world for four centuries.

[*See also* **Caribbean; Colonial Era; Columbian Exchange; Exploration, Conquest, and Settlement in North America; Maroon Societies; Slavery;** *and* **Slave Trades.**]

BIBLIOGRAPHY

Elliott, J. H. *Empires of the Atlantic World: Britain and Spain in America, 1492–1830.* New Haven, Conn.: Yale University Press, 2006. A comparative history of the development of the Spanish and British empires.

Greene, Jack P. *Pursuits of Happiness: The Social Development of Early Modern British Colonies and the Formation of American Culture.* Chapel Hill: University of North Carolina Press, 1988. The best overview of scholarship on the social history of the British American colonies.

Greene, Jack P., and Philip D. Morgan, eds. *Atlantic History: A Critical Appraisal.* Oxford and New York: Oxford University Press, 2009. A collection of essays offering a thematic and geographic overview of the newest scholarship in Atlantic history.

Kulikoff, Allan. *Tobacco and Slaves: The Development of Southern Cultures in the Chesapeake, 1680–1800.* Chapel Hill: University of North Carolina Press, 1986.

Voyages: The Trans-Atlantic Slave Trade Database. http://www.slavevoyages.org. Provides detailed information of some thirty-five thousand slave voyages.

Walvin, James. *Making the Black Atlantic: Britain and the African Diaspora.* London and New York: Cassell, 2000. An accessible introduction to the concept of the "black Atlantic."

Christian J. Koot

AUTOMATION AND COMPUTERIZATION

Automation and computerization are related but distinct concepts that have their origin in production engineering but are applied to many forms of economic, social, and political activity. Both automation and computerization are used in efforts to reduce the costs of labor and to make institutions more responsive to market forces. Both have substantially altered the labor force and changed the way that organizations make decisions.

Automation. Traditionally, automation is a three-stage activity in which a process is created to produce goods with as little human intervention as possible. In the first stage, the human labor in a production process is analyzed and the entire process is broken into a collection of individual steps. In the second stage, the human labor in some or all those steps is replaced with machine labor. In the third stage, another machine is used to coordinate or control all the steps in the process.

The first stage of automation was identified by Adam Smith in the first chapter of his *Wealth of Nations* (1776). Smith described the process of making pins, dividing it into the steps of straightening wire, cutting wire into short segments, sharpening one end of the segment, and so forth. The "important business of making a pin is, in this manner, divided into about eighteen distinct operations," he explained.

Smith also noted the second stage of automation, the extent to which "labour is facilitated and abridged by the application of proper machinery." In Smith's time, most of the "proper machinery" was hand-controlled and hence did not automate a production process. Perhaps the best example of an eighteenth-century automatic machine was Jesse Ramsden's circular dividing engine of about 1775, which engraved regular markings on a circular piece of metal. Later automatic machines include Joseph-Marie Jacquard's loom of 1801 and Thomas Blanchard's duplicating lathe of about 1822.

The third stage of automation, which involves moving from automatic machinery to automatic processes, was described by Charles Babbage in his book *On the Economy of Machinery and Manufactures* (1832). After reviewing Smith's analysis of pin making, Babbage described how each step of the process could be controlled by a single mechanism. This mechanism is "highly ingenious in point of contrivance," he wrote, "and, in respect to its economical principles, will furnish a strong and interesting contrast with the manufacture of pins by the human hand."

Few products are as simple as pins, and hence few products were produced by truly automated processes in the nineteenth century. Still, the new products of that era were produced by increasingly sophisticated divisions of labor, more complicated machines, and a few devices that could control certain aspects of production. The invention of the bicycle, which was first mass-produced in the 1880s, marked an important moment in the process of automation, according to the historian David Hounsell. The workers were able to use a variety of automatic machines to manufacture bicycle parts, but they were unable to solve a fundamental problem of automation: the final assembly of complex goods.

The problem of final assembly was solved by the American automobile manufacturer Henry Ford. Ford developed an assembly process that relied heavily on human labor but coordinated the work with an automated conveyor system or assembly line. This system carried partially assembled automobiles past workers, each of whom added one part to the final product. "When we call the new system 'automatic' or 'mechanical,'" explained the twentieth-century management consultant Peter Drucker, "we do not mean that the machines have become automatic or mechanical. What has become automatic and mechanical is the worker" (Peter Drucker, *The Future of Industrial Man* [London: Heinneman, 1943], p. 71).

Scientific Management. At the start of the twentieth century, Ford was one of many engineers who was thinking about how to incorporate human labor into a tightly controlled manufacturing process. The most prominent of these other engineers was Frederick Winslow Taylor. Taylor and his followers promoted a technique that they called "scientific management." This technique focused on the first two stages of automation: the division of labor and the application of proper tools. Taylor claimed that scientific management identified the "one right way" for doing any kind of job.

More than any other engineer, Taylor laid the foundation for the third stage of automation by restricting the freedom and judgment of the worker. In scientific management, the workers did the labor but the engineers controlled the manufacturing process. Taylor argued that such an approach would create "an almost equal division of work and responsibility between management and workmen" (Frederick Winslow Taylor, *Principles of Scientific Management* [New York: Harpers Brothers, 2d ed., 1915], p. 37).

Critics of Taylor have argued that scientific management has never created an equal partnership but has undermined the position of the worker. Writing eighty years after Taylor, Harry Braverman argued that such techniques created deskilled jobs, "labor from which all conceptual elements have been removed and along with them most of the skill, knowledge and understanding of the production process" (Harry Braverman, *Labor and Monopoly Capital* [New York: Monthly Review Press, 1974], p. 319).

Computerization. Strictly defined, computerization is a specialized form of automation that developed after the introduction of the stored-program computer in 1946. In this specialized form, computers can operate either as automatic tools that perform one step of a production process or as control devices that manage the entire production process.

Because of their ability to manipulate symbols, computers found applications in jobs that had previously been considered the domain of skilled human workers. Beginning in 1952, they replaced employees who managed information. They handled such tasks as bookkeeping, inventory tracking, scheduling, and typesetting. The introduction of the microprocessor in the early 1970s allowed computers to be placed in small, portable objects that could move beyond the offices and plants that had traditionally housed computing equipment. The expansion of digital communications in the 1980s and 1990s allowed computers to coordinate the activities of organizations that were dispersed across a large geographic area.

Because of their versatility, computers could be simultaneously an automatic tool and an element of a large system that controlled production. A single machine could do bookkeeping tasks, analyze production figures, and prepare a production plan for the organization.

Computerization has tended to restrict the actions of certain kinds of workers and strengthen the position of those who design and implement the production system. However, computerization has also tended to elevate a third class of workers, a class made up of people who understand the production system and know how to interpret the information that comes from computers. Peter Drucker has dubbed them "knowledge workers."

The effects of computerization can be seen in as simple an organization as a restaurant wait staff. Traditionally restaurants had a uniform and undifferentiated staff of waiters who dealt with customers. This staff would consist of a single manager and a group of people, equal in status and pay, who handled all the interactions with the customers: greeting them at the table, taking the order, getting the order properly filled by the kitchen, delivering food, reconciling the bill, and clearing the dishes.

Wait staffs were computerized by the introduction of order-management software. By keeping track of the food ordered by each table and the bill incurred by each table, this software reduced waiters' work to a series of simple tasks that included delivering the proper food to a table and clearing the plates when the diners were done with their meal. These tasks could be done by people with far less skill than the traditional waiter, hence they were assigned to low-wage workers who did not even get the title "waiter" but were called something like "food runner."

The new system still needed a staff of knowledge workers, however: employees to interact with customers, operate the system, manage the food runners, and make judgments about specific events. These employees retained the title "waiter" and were paid more than the food runners were, because they were responsible for a larger number of customers and had greater authority. In a pattern repeated in organization after organization, this new division of labor created a few positions that required sophisticated skills and a much larger number of positions that were directed by others through computer technology and hence required fewer skills.

Computerization has changed not only production but also organizational management. As computers and computer software moved into every part of company operations, some managerial tasks turned into routine activities that could be handled by less skilled employees, while other, newly created tasks required skilled employees who could make refined decisions from large amounts of data.

The use of both computerization and automation expanded widely during the second half of the twentieth century. They tended to increase the productivity of workers but also had the effect of regimenting labor, disciplining management, and favoring individuals who have the skill and understanding to make judgments about large, complicated systems. Both have been blamed for the decline in the number of manufacturing jobs, as well as of some white-collar jobs.

Impact of Automation and Computerization.
Many writers have made the claim that automation and computerization will end unskilled labor. Human "labor is being systematically eliminated from the 'production process,'" wrote the journalist Jeremy Rifkin in 1995. "Within less than a century, 'mass' work in the market sector is likely to be phased out in virtually all of the industrialized nations of the world."

Although both automation and computerization have certainly altered the labor market by increasing the demand for certain types of workers and decreasing the demand for others, they have not entirely eliminated manual or unskilled labor. Instead, both automation and computerization have reshaped the nature of labor by disciplining it with machinery, computer systems and software, and detailed production plans. In 1776, Adam Smith noted that this replacement is controlled by the demand for the good or service being produced. Goods or services with large markets are more likely to have more sophisticated divisions of labor and hence are easier to computerize or automate.

However, the extent of automation and computerization is also dependent upon the cost of the three stages of automation: the cost of analyzing a production process, developing tools to perform the steps of the process, and creating a procedure that automatically controls the process. In some cases the cost of producing machines and control proves to be more than the cost of simply moving the work to a lower-cost labor market. In other cases the analysis of the labor process reveals that tasks are involved that are difficult to adapt to a computer or a machine, such as tasks that require human judgment, compromises based on broad knowledge of the process, and an understanding of all the interested parties involved.

Rather than bring an end to mass labor, automation and computerization have produced a dynamic and unstable labor market. Automation has created large demands for certain skills in one year and made those same skills obsolete a decade later. Computerization has spread that same phenomenon to workers who process information and make decisions about organizations.

[*See also* **Communication Networks; Communication Revolution, Modern; Deindustrialization; Electricity and Electrification;** *and* **Work.**]

BIBLIOGRAPHY

Braverman, Harry. *Labor and Monopoly Capital: The Degradation of Work in the Twentieth Century.* New York: Monthly Review Press, 1974.

Cortada, James W. *The Digital Hand: How Computers Changed the Work of American Manufacturing, Transportation, and Retail Industries.* Oxford: Oxford University Press, 2004.

Cortada, James W. *The Digital Hand, Volume 2: How Computers Changed the Work of American Financial, Telecommunications, Media, and Entertainment Industries.* Oxford: Oxford University Press, 2006.

Cortada, James W. *The Digital Hand, Volume 3: How Computers Changed the Work of American Public Sector Industries.* Oxford: Oxford University Press, 2008.

Drucker, Peter F. *The New Society: The Anatomy of the Industrial Order.* New York: Harper, 1950.

Hounshell, David A. *From the American System to Mass Production, 1800–1932: The Development of Manufacturing Technology in the United States.* Baltimore: Johns Hopkins University Press, 1984.

Kanigel, Robert. *The One Best Way: Frederick Winslow Taylor and the Enigma of Efficiency.* New York; Viking, 1997.

Levy, Frank, and Richard J. Murnane. *The New Division of Labor: How Computers Are Creating the Next Job Market.* New York: Russell Sage Foundation, 2004.

Rifkin, Jeremy. *The End of Work: The Decline of the Global Labor Force and the Dawn of the Post-Market Era.* New York: G. P. Putnam's Sons, 1995.

David Alan Grier

AUTOMOBILES

Although automobiles first appeared on American streets as early as the 1880s, the enormous cultural significance of the private car began with mass production and was almost entirely a product of the twentieth century: only about 8,000 automobiles were registered in the United States in 1900, compared with about 225 million by 2000. Indeed, in its early decades the automobile garnered significant public resistance; the so-called devil wagon was frequently characterized in the popular press as a dangerous plaything of the irresponsible rich. These connotations began to fade as the application of assembly-line techniques of production made cars available to a wider audience. By the time Henry Ford introduced his iconic Model T in 1908—which eventually had a price of less than $300—the automobile had begun a series of profound transformations of American daily life.

The Automobile and Small-Town America.

Perhaps most immediate were the automobile's effects on rural America. Here the Model T, which dominated the market through the 1910s—and 65 percent of Ford dealerships were located in rural areas as late as 1930—demonstrated its usefulness in a variety of ways. Indeed, some of these applications had nothing to do with the automobile's ostensible function, for the car's internal combustion engine and transmission could be fairly easily adapted to power a range of farm implements, from mechanical threshers to water pumps. In addition, its rugged design suited the vehicle for use as a rudimentary tractor in agricultural fields. It could even serve as an electrical generator for those far from the nascent grids of the early twentieth century. Thus the automobile functioned not merely as a means of transportation for rural

Americans, but as the first widely available and relatively affordable replacement for muscular labor.

Yet its ability to transcend rural isolation might be its most profound legacy for the majority of Americans who lived outside urban areas in the first decades of the century. The car provided farmers expanded opportunities to find markets for selling their produce and for purchasing necessary manufactured goods, reducing dependence upon the railroad monopolies for these functions and solidifying the small-town ideal of the local "Main Street" as the core of rural community life.

For farm women in particular, the automobile provided a way to expand their social sphere, affording relatively autonomous connections to church, market, and school. As a means of entry into the public realm, the automobile seemed to many to be as potentially revolutionary as suffrage. As one car-industry observer put it in 1927, "there are millions of women drivers where there were only hundreds a few years ago. . . . Every time a woman learns to drive—and thousands do every year—it is a threat at yesterday's order of things" (quoted in Scharff, p. 117). At the same time, the family car also eroded the bonds that held family members together in rural America, gradually allowing the substitution of commercialized and individualized activities in town for shared, home-based pursuits. Ultimately, moreover, the automobile undermined the cohesion of farm communities themselves. As one observer wrote in 1926, "before the days of the automobile mere propinquity made neighbors more or less intimate. Today the automobile enables farmers to pick their associates much as do people in cities" (Williams, p. 154).

As Michael Berger observed, "this new mobility effectively doubled the farm family's range of social activities, from six or seven miles with horse and buggy to nine to twelve miles with the motor car" (p. 63). Initially these cosmopolitan effects of the automobile were greatly hindered by early twentieth-century America's inadequate road network; rural roads generally connected farms only to local railheads or river ports, and rarely to larger metropolitan centers. The utility of the automobile was greatly expanded, then, by the concerted efforts—originated during the cycling boom of the late nineteenth century, but soon taken over by the automobile industry—to "get America out of the mud," as the slogan of the so-called good roads movement put it. Road-building projects, generally carried out on the local level, gradually connected town to town, county to county, across rural America, culminating in a series of improved—although rarely fully paved—long-distance roads by the early 1920s.

Perhaps most famous of these early long-distance arteries were the Lincoln Highway, the nation's first transcontinental road—formally dedicated in 1913 and often dubbed the Main Street across America—and U.S. Highway 66, which achieved lasting fame during the Depression as a conduit of mass exodus from the Dust Bowl. These highways engendered a broader physical mobility throughout small-town and rural America: the family automobile could potentially now be a ready means to personal migrations large and small. The same road that brought the farm family into town might also take its members to a very different life across the continent. With these highways came, by the 1930s, the development of chains of restaurants, motor hotels, and an array of other establishments catering to motorists and thus providing necessary roadside services, but at the same time betokening an increasing homogenization of cultural and regional variation.

The Automobile and the City. As wide-ranging as the effects of the automobile were upon rural life, equally profound was the concomitant transformation of American cities. Early twentieth-century city planners exerted great efforts to accommodate the motorcar into the existing infrastructure of the metropolis, where electric trolleys, delivery wagons, pedestrians, and horses had long vied for limited street space. By 1920, conflicts over traffic priority led to political clashes in cities such as Los Angeles, where a business-hours downtown parking ban for cars, intended to protect streetcar service from the increasing competition from private automobile traffic, was quickly overturned amid public protests. The rise of widespread automotive commuting in southern California during the 1920s —automobile ownership there exceeded that of any other American metropolis even by 1915—enabled a new model of American urbanism that became nationally widespread in the coming decades. In Los Angeles, the decentralization of commerce and recreation and the emergence of alternative commercial "strips" along major roadways, accompanied by a sprawling infrastructure of low-density housing, speeded the decline of the existing interurban rail transit system and led to a novel, and frequently disorienting, urban topography.

Soon, even planners in older cities with existing infrastructures for heavy transit sought to find ways to incorporate the automobile into established street grids, often at the expense of entrenched ethnic and immigrant neighborhoods. In so doing, planners prioritized traffic flow and urban legibility over the communal and sociable uses of streets, which had previously often functioned more as playgrounds than as traffic conduits. Thus valuable urban public space was effectively given over to the automobile and its often middle-class drivers. The reconstruction of Chicago's Wacker Drive as a multilevel urban highway, completed in 1926, demonstrated how reconstructing the street grid to make room for the private automobile could justify extensive urban renewal and slum clearance efforts.

Road-construction projects altered the relationships between cities and their peripheries as well. Main-line suburbs, which had begun to emerge in the nineteenth century, often along railroad routes, offered secluded and spacious habitation for a relatively well-to-do minority, sheltering a growing managerial class from the increasingly rough edges of the ethnically diverse industrial cities of the era. Road-building projects in the first half of the twentieth century were overwhelmingly dedicated to easing the commuting travails of these wealthy suburbanites and providing leisure drives for recreational purposes. Thus although the democratization of car ownership accelerated throughout the 1920s—by 1929, almost 27 million automobiles were registered in the country, or approximately one for every five Americans—pressure for urban road "improvements" still often originated in elite circles. Starting in the late 1920s and continuing for several decades, New York's powerful planner Robert Moses laid out an elaborate system of publicly funded automotive parkways that facilitated that elite transportation by excluding the urban carless majority from suburban amenities— for instance, by deliberately constructing parkway overpasses too low to allow bus access for transit-dependent New Yorkers.

Although car ownership actually declined slightly during the Great Depression, not recovering its 1929 levels until 1936, and remained stagnant through World War II because of supply shortages, these years effectively solidified the cultural dominance of the automobile in American life, highlighted by Hollywood cinema's romanticization of automotive travel, which associated the "open road" with individual freedom, escape, and leisure.

During World War II, the spread of automobility briefly slackened, as gasoline and rubber rationing, along with a larger culture of sacrifice and solidarity, led citizens to renewed dependence on public transit. Yet this brief renaissance proved to be the zenith of communal transportation in the twentieth century: the wear and tear and deferred maintenance of that period meant that many transit infrastructures required extensive renewal after the end of the war. Instead, these systems were largely abandoned as America's institutional and cultural commitment to the personal automobile deepened in the postwar period and as concerted public policy sought to reshape the American urban landscape in the style of the low-density, automobile-dependent Los Angeles model that had first emerged three decades earlier.

The Interstate and the Suburb. Seeking to boost the postwar manufacturing sector, the federal government worked to reduce consumers' anxious reluctance, born of the years of privation, about profligate spending by promoting the mass ownership of two items previously restricted to a minority of the population: the suburban home and the private automobile. Starting in 1956, the federal government began investments that eventually totaled $129 billion (almost half a trillion dollars in real terms) to construct the Interstate and Defense Highway System. Heavily promoted by President Dwight D. Eisenhower's secretary of defense Charles Erwin Wilson, who had previously spent twelve years as the president of General Motors, the interstate system connected the majority of the contiguous United States with limited-access highways. This network of freeways altered the landscape of the country, greatly promoting the culture of automobility during the Cold War.

Although the interstates were originally intended largely to bypass existing American cities, by the 1960s the roads instead frequently justified large-scale federally funded urban renewal and slum clearance projects. Many traditional neighborhoods were bulldozed or divided as new highways cut directly through the existing metropolitan fabric. Meanwhile, in rural areas, the homogenization and standardization of retail commerce greatly intensified, and local communities found their tourist traffic drawn away by the mass-marketed chains of hotels and fast-food restaurants clustered at the exits of the limited-access freeways; economic decline in the bypassed towns often resulted. Similar hardship struck railroad networks, which found their lucrative freight businesses usurped by the rise of long-distance trucking on the new highways; at the same time, in combination with the spread of subsidized air travel, the popularity of the highways led to the cessation of private long-distance rail passenger service by the end of the 1960s. But the most profound effects of the interstate system manifested themselves in the spaces between city and country.

As traditional urban centers began to decline for lack of inward investment after World War II, white residents took advantage of generous mortgage subsidies through the Veterans Administration and the Federal Housing Administration (FHA) and moved to new suburban residential communities built on former farmland, such as the iconic Levittown on Long Island, New York. Residents of these racially homogeneous developments— because of FHA lending policies and racially restrictive deed covenants, Levittown had virtually no African American residents from 1947 through the late 1960s—found their new homes to be architecturally adapted to automobility, fronted by attached garages between house and street. With lifestyles effectively subsidized by federal highway funds, which greatly reduced the infrastructural costs of their long commutes, and federal mortgage guarantees, which often made it cheaper to own than to rent, these new suburbanites outfitted their new homes with a range of manufactured consumer products, such as domestic appliances, purchased at the new peripheral suburban shopping malls that began to replace urban business districts. Ironically, these new malls, accessible only by automobile and surrounded by acres of free parking, drew shoppers by simulating the public, pedestrian street life that had been displaced from urban cores half a century earlier by the rise of automobile traffic.

The Culture of the Automobile.

The most substantial of new suburban consumer goods was the automobile itself, without which shops and work in these new communities were practically inaccessible. Following the lead of the General Motors chief Alfred Sloan, whose marketing philosophy of "a car for every purse and purpose" caused GM to surpass Ford in sales by the late 1920s, automobiles defined mid-twentieth-century consumer style, emphasizing trends in ornamentation—such as tail fins and other aeronautically inspired but nonfunctional elements, heavily promoted in mass-media advertising—over technological innovation and refinement. Yet automotive style could also be shaped by subcultural identity. Starting in the 1950s, car customizers labored to transform their "jalopies" into individualized works of artistic expression or signs of group identity. Likewise, for adolescents, many of whom claimed their right to the public spaces of their communities by collectively "cruising" their streets, access to an automobile often enabled both personal autonomy and social interaction, providing a realm for self-expression and sexual experimentation away from the supervision of adult chaperones. Meanwhile, the broader ideologies that associated the automobile and the "road trip" with personal autonomy and adventure were further circulated through advertising and popular media in the postwar era: film, literature, and song all emphasized the "romance of the road."

As a consequence of this cultural enthusiasm, along with generous direct and indirect subsidies, between 1945 and 1965 the number of automobiles on American roads tripled, to more than 90 million. Combined with a system of planned obsolescence, this dependence on the automobile guaranteed considerable profits for the so-called Big Three American manufacturers, GM, Ford, and Chrysler; their oligopoly guaranteed them, cumulatively, 94 percent of the market. Despite a campaign of ruthless corporate resistance to unionization during the 1920s and 1930s—resistance that provoked a series of decisive sit-down strikes in Flint, Michigan, and elsewhere during the Depression—by 1945 the Big Three and the United Auto Workers set a routine of annual bargaining that suppressed labor dissent in exchange for generous pay and benefits, or what one union leader termed a "civilized relationship." As a result, from the end of World War II through the 1970s, low-skill, high-wage automobile manufacturing jobs exemplified for many workers the route to the American dream.

Yet by the time of the oil shocks of the early 1970s, this culture of complacent consensus had started to unravel as the industry began to lose market share to foreign competition. In the subsequent decades, as the internal combustion automobile came under attack for inefficiency, pollution, and the mounting pressures of traffic, Americans increasingly migrated back to higher-density urban areas and revived abandoned public-transit systems, even as the formerly homogeneous suburbs became more ethnically and economically diverse. Indeed, the budgetary and foreign-policy implications of an economy premised so heavily on the consumption of imported oil has come in recent years to shadow Americans' enthusiasm for the automobile. Yet despite a steady decline in per capita car ownership since the late 1980s, the private car continues to play an important role in defining contemporary American cultural identities, from the suburban "soccer moms" whose days are consumed in ferrying children around in large SUVs to the teenagers for whom acquiring a driver's license remains a rite of passage.

[*See also* Cities and Suburbs; Consumption; Everyday Life; Route 66; Slums; Tourism and Travel; *and* Urban Renewal.]

BIBLIOGRAPHY

Axelrod, Jeremiah B. C. *Inventing Autopia: Dreams and Visions of the Modern Metropolis in Jazz Age Los Angeles*. Berkeley: University of California Press, 2009.

Berger, Michael L. *The Devil Wagon in God's Country: The Automobile and Social Change in Rural America, 1893–1929*. Hamden, Conn.: Archon, 1979.

Caro, Robert. *The Power Broker: Robert Moses and the Fall of New York*. New York: Alfred A. Knopf, 1974.

Flink, James J. *The Automobile Age*. Cambridge, Mass.: MIT Press, 1988.

Jackson, Kenneth T. *Crabgrass Frontier: The Suburbanization of the United States*. New York: Oxford University Press, 1985.

Lewis, David L., and Laurence Goldstein, eds. *The Automobile and American Culture*. Ann Arbor: University of Michigan Press, 1983.

Mills, Katie. *The Road Story and the Rebel: Moving through Film, Fiction, and Television*. Carbondale: Southern Illinois University Press, 2006.

Patton, Phil. *Open Road: A Celebration of the American Highway*. New York: Simon and Schuster, 1986.

Scharff, Virginia. *Taking the Wheel: Women and the Coming of the Motor Age*. New York: Free Press, 1991.

Williams, James M. *The Expansion of Rural Life: The Social Psychology of Rural Development*. New York: Alfred A. Knopf, 1926.

Jeremiah B. C. Axelrod

B

BACON'S REBELLION

Beginning with vigilante actions by frontier residents who opposed Governor William Berkeley's Indian policy, the 1676 Virginia uprising known as Bacon's Rebellion quickly escalated into a struggle that left Berkeley disgraced and the colony tightly in the grip of the Stuart monarchs. The leader of the uprising, the twenty-nine-year-old Nathaniel Bacon, a wellborn English immigrant with substantial property holdings and close ties to Berkeley, mobilized disgruntled frontier planters, small property holders, white servants, and African slaves against both Indians and the governor.

Although granted a council seat by Berkeley, Bacon shared his wealthy neighbors' conviction that the governor's policies left them vulnerable to Indian attack and excluded from the Indian fur trade. The large planters' discontents, worsened by falling tobacco prices, might have remained confined to name-calling, lawsuits, and duels had not the small property holders also decried Berkeley's alleged failure to protect them from Indians. Under Bacon's leadership, a frontier force disobeyed Berkeley's orders and in April 1676 brutally attacked a nearby settlement of peaceful Susquehannock Indians.

Under challenge, Berkeley called the first election in fifteen years. Bacon won election to the House of Burgesses, Virginia's upper house, but was arrested when he tried to take his seat. Soon released and commissioned by Berkeley to fight Indians, he rallied a force of some thirteen hundred men for more attacks that killed hundreds of Indians along the Potomac and Rappahannock Rivers. When Berkeley reversed himself and declared

Bacon a traitor, Bacon's army marched on Jamestown, the capital, which they burned on 19 September. As Berkeley raised his own force, the conflict became colonywide, with combatants gutting their opponents' houses and seizing their property.

Bacon's followers complained of overtaxation, political exclusion, religious persecution, and economic restrictions. A handful of influential white women supported Bacon's cause, as did many servants and some four hundred slaves who, promised their freedom by the rebels, were the last to surrender to Berkeley's troops. With Bacon's death from dysentery on 26 October and the arrival of a royal commission to investigate the rebellion, the uprising dissipated, leaving Virginia under tighter royal control and in the grip of a conservative reaction that restricted both the public influence of white women and the de facto freedom of enslaved people. Although scholars continue to debate the significance of this short-lived rebellion, there is agreement that this upheaval came just as Virginia fully embraced slavery. Thus the political wounds left by Bacon's Rebellion may have been partially healed, inadvertently or intentionally, by the racial imperatives of slavery.

[*See also* Colonial Era; Native American History and Culture, *subentry on* 1500 to 1800; *and* Slavery.]

BIBLIOGRAPHY

Morgan, Edmund S. *American Slavery, American Freedom: The Ordeal of Colonial Virginia.* New York: W. W. Norton and Company, 1975.
Washburn, Wilcomb. *The Governor and the Rebel: A History of Bacon's Rebellion in Virginia.* Chapel Hill: University of North Carolina Press for the Institute of Early American History and Culture, Williamsburg, Va., 1957.

Kathleen M. Brown

BAKER, ELLA

(1903–1986), civil rights activist. Born in Norfolk, Virginia, in 1903 and raised in North Carolina, Ella Baker came from a background of relative advantage for a black southern daughter. She had the benefit of a college education—she attended Shaw University in Raleigh—at a time when many blacks and whites did not finish high school. In many ways she epitomized W. E. B. Du Bois's Talented Tenth, that group of black intellectuals whom Du Bois believed would rise up from the masses of black Americans to lead their people to freedom. Yet despite her advantages, Baker chose not to separate herself from the so-called masses. Throughout her career as an activist she fought to empower ordinary people to challenge the circumstances that oppressed them; moreover, she confronted the leaders—white and black, and primarily male—who would have others look to them as some hero to solve their problems. She stepped outside the constrictions of conventional ladylike behavior to challenge authority in all its guises, and in doing so she passed to a new generation of activists an organizing tradition that valued ordinary people and their abilities to change their own lives.

In choosing to work on a grassroots level, Baker deliberately eschewed the limelight. She recognized the value of organizing beyond the restrictive gaze of public, especially white, attention. In short, she used her invisibility to accomplish social change. Baker's invisibility served two purposes: not only did she encourage the people she worked with to use their own invisibility as a shield against the white public and its authority, but she also tried to work behind the scenes within that invisible community, so that the people she worked with empowered themselves rather than looking to her for leadership. It is now well known that Baker launched the Student Nonviolent Coordinating Committee (SNCC) at a Southern Christian Leadership Conference meeting at Shaw University in 1960. Less well known is precisely what Baker imparted to those student activists at their three-day meeting in Raleigh and in the years that followed. Baker herself never articulated her views in a list or manifesto, but she passed on a philosophy of leadership and organizing gleaned from her own forty years of experience as an organizer in both the North and the South. The principles she passed on include identifying with the needs of the people with whom one is working, recognizing the value of discussions among people with different viewpoints, and recognizing the usefulness of small groups. Additionally, Baker believed that the relationships between organizers and those they served were crucial, especially across race, class, and gender lines. Baker insisted on the development of local leadership and on resisting traditional, hierarchical leadership styles that are competitive, authoritarian, and charismatic. And finally, Baker recognized the plodding, unglamorous, often unrewarded nature of organizing and the value and strength of southern folk culture.

Taken together, Baker's principles can be seen as the foundation of a new method for social change, and they can also be seen as the basis for much of the success of the Civil Rights Movement. The nature of that success must be understood precisely: it was not just in the passage of civil rights legislation, although the Civil Rights Act (1964) outlawed segregation and the Voting Rights Act of 1965 made possible thousands of new black voters who dramatically changed the political leadership of the South. Rather, the success of the civil rights movement exists most poignantly and effectively in the thousands of new leaders who were created, leaders working in their own communities to cast off oppression and improve their own lives. Baker passed away in 1986.

[*See also* **African Americans; Community Organizing; Desegregation;** *and* **South, The.**]

BIBLIOGRAPHY

Grant, Joanne. *Ella Baker: Freedom Bound.* New York: Wiley, 1998.

Payne, Charles M. *I've Got the Light of Freedom: The Organizing Tradition and the Mississippi Freedom Struggle.* Berkeley: University of California, 2007. Includes a new preface; originally published in 1995.

Ransby, Barbara. *Ella Baker and the Black Freedom Movement: A Radical Democratic Vision.* Chapel Hill: University of North Carolina, 2003.

Susan M. Glisson

BARS

See **Taverns and Bars.**

BEECHER, CATHARINE

(1800–1878), educator and promoter of women's roles in the home. Catharine Beecher helped to establish the nineteenth century's ideology of domesticity that characterized women as the intellectual and moral center of the home. At the same time, she was instrumental in creating opportunities for women outside the home, working tirelessly to incorporate women into the educational system as students and as teachers.

Catharine Esther Beecher was born in East Hampton, New York, on 6 September 1800, the eldest child of the prominent clergyman Lyman Beecher and his wife, Roxana (née Foote) Beecher. She received more education than many girls of her time did, and she sought as much additional education as she could obtain. Like most women of her class, she was expected to marry, and she became engaged to Alexander Fisher. The death of her fiancé, in 1823, was coupled with a crisis of faith and rejection of her father's Calvinism. Nevertheless, after Fisher's death her father helped Catharine establish a school in Hartford, Connecticut, where she began to formulate her educational theories, especially her hopes of offering women educational opportunities equal to those of men. Later, with her family she moved to Cincinnati, where in 1833 she opened the Western Female Institute.

At the same time, although she herself never married nor owned a home, Catharine Beecher highly valued women's roles as wives and mothers. Her views differed from those of the women's rights activists with whom she debated in the 1850s. Though she shared their belief in the natural intelligence and moral power of women, she did not agree that women should exercise their powers independently or equally. Instead, she argued that women should function within a hierarchy that gave men power outside the home and women explicit dominion within the home, as teachers of their children and moral guides for their husbands. Beecher's beliefs led her to oppose women's suffrage, a position that she reiterated in her 1872 volume, *Woman's Profession as Mother and Educator, with Views in Opposition to Woman Suffrage.*

She also held conservative views on abolition and race relations. Like other members of her family, she opposed slavery but also opposed immediate abolition in the United States. Her hope was that slavery would somehow die out gradually, and that African Americans would leave the United States and move to Africa. Her publications on these issues brought her into conflict with other U.S. intellectuals, but they did not decrease her influence in the areas of domesticity and education.

Catharine Beecher's focus on women's lives included a deep concern about women's health. She was dismayed by the heavy clothing and corsets that were the fashion of her time, and encouraged women to exercise and to pay attention to diet and other aspects of health. She wrote a number of books on home management, including the *Treatise on Domestic Economy for the Use of Young Ladies at Home and at School*, which was extremely popular as a textbook and for home use, with fifteen editions published between 1841 and 1856. Later, with her sister Harriet (the author of *Uncle Tom's Cabin*), she revised this volume into *The American Woman's Home, or Principles of Domestic Science* (1869). The book, which included recipes and information on all aspects of housekeeping including gardening and how to manage servants, was an immediate and long-standing best seller.

[*See also* **African American Emigration; Antebellum Reform; Beecher, Henry Ward; Beecher, Lyman; Education; Separate Spheres Ideology; Woman Suffrage Movement;** *and* **Women's Rights Movement, Antebellum Era.**]

BIBLIOGRAPHY

Beecher, Catharine Esther, and Harriet Beecher Stowe. *The American Woman's Home.* Edited by Nicole Tonkovich. New Brunswick, N.J.: Rutgers University Press, 2002. Tonkovich's introduction provides a clear, concise context for the work.

Sklar, Kathryn Kish. *Catharine Beecher: A Study in American Domesticity.* New Haven, Conn.: Yale University Press, 1973. A detailed and sympathetic portrait.

White, Barbara A. *The Beecher Sisters*. New Haven, Conn.: Yale University Press, 2003. Provides rich documentation on Catharine Beecher's life and her relationships with her family, especially her sisters Harriet Beecher Stowe and Isabella Beecher Hooker.

JoAnn Elisabeth Castagna

BEECHER, HENRY WARD

(1813–1887), clergyman and social reformer. Henry Ward Beecher, the ninth of twelve children, was born in 1813 into the family of Lyman Beecher, a leader of the Second Great Awakening. After growing up in Litchfield, Connecticut, he graduated from Amherst College in 1834, followed his father west to attend Lane Seminary in Cincinnati, and accepted his first pastorate in 1837. Two years later, at a new position in Indianapolis, he delivered a series of talks, subsequently published as *Lectures to Young Men on Various Important Subjects* (1844), on the dangers posed by gambling and prostitution. This book caught the attention of the Plymouth Congregational Church in Brooklyn, New York, which issued a call to him in 1847. For nearly four decades thereafter, Beecher held his thirty-two hundred parishioners spellbound and used his access to New York publishers to develop a national reputation as a preacher and social reformer.

In 1850 he turned his attention to the plight of slaves and free blacks. Although more moderate in his antislavery views than, for instance, William Lloyd Garrison, Beecher had a flair for dramatizing problems. He held a mock slavery auction to raise funds for the abolitionist cause—which helped inspire his sister, Harriet Beecher Stowe, to write her pathbreaking novel *Uncle Tom's Cabin* (1852).

Beecher's antislavery activities intensified in the 1850s when he edited the *Independent*, a widely circulated religious newspaper. He also lectured on the lyceum circuit on temperance and moral character. After the passage in 1854 of the Kansas-Nebraska Act—which allowed the settlers of those new territories to decide for themselves whether to allow slavery—Beecher joined the newly formed Republican Party and advocated sending Sharps rifles, popularly known as "Beecher's Bibles," to the free-soil settlers in Kansas. Although he did not hesitate to criticize northern racist discrimination against free blacks, Indians, and Mexicans, Beecher, like his sister Harriet, supported the colonization of blacks in Africa. He campaigned for Abraham Lincoln and in the 1860s lectured in England during the Civil War to strengthen English support for the North.

After the war, Beecher was drawn into the debate within women's rights circles over the right to vote. In 1869 he initially supported radical feminists such as Elizabeth Cady Stanton who argued that women deserved the vote before blacks and campaigned for laws to make divorce easier. Later that year, he was elected president of the American Woman Suffrage Association, an organization that avoided the divorce controversy and focused on voting rights. In the 1870s, accused of adultery with a parishioner, Beecher barely survived two trials: one exonerated him and one was canceled by a hung jury. Nevertheless, his national reputation persisted.

Within Protestantism, Beecher became an advocate for liberal Christian theology. A gifted speaker whose sermons sparkled with thoughtful comments and powerful visual imagery, Beecher emphasized a gospel of love and the power of personality to improve the world. Through his *Yale Lectures on Preaching* (1871–1873) and his editorship of the *Christian Union* (later called the *Outlook*), he helped redefine mainline American Protestantism by supporting Darwinian ideas. When he died in 1887, he was widely mourned as the best-known preacher in America.

[*See also* **Antebellum Reform; Bleeding Kansas; Clergy; Colonization Movement, African; Free-Soilers; Great Awakenings; Religion;** *and* **Woman Suffrage Movement.**]

BIBLIOGRAPHY

Applegate, Debby. *The Most Famous Man in America: The Biography of Henry Ward Beecher*. New York: Doubleday, 2006.
Dorrien, Gary. *The Making of American Liberal Theology: Imagining Progressive Religion, 1805–1900*. Louisville, Ky.: Westminster John Knox Press, 2001.

Clifford E. Clark

BEECHER, LYMAN

(1775–1863), Presbyterian clergyman and reformer. Lyman Beecher was born on 12 October 1775 in New Haven, Connecticut, to David Beecher and Esther Lyman Beecher. Beecher's forebears arrived in New England in 1638; the Lymans came later from Scotland and settled in Middletown, Connecticut. Lyman Beecher spent his formative years among his mother's relatives. In 1793 he entered Yale College, graduating in 1797. From 1797 to 1798, Beecher studied divinity with Timothy Dwight, a grandson of Jonathan Edwards and the president of Yale. In 1799, Beecher was ordained and accepted a call to the Presbyterian church of East Hampton, Long Island.

On 19 September 1799, Beecher married Roxana Foote. An energetic pastor and popular preacher, Beecher moved to Litchfield, Connecticut, in 1810 to become minister of the Congregational church there, a position he held until 1826. Several prolonged revivals solidified his growing reputation for energetic godliness. His moderate Calvinism left ample room for human agency, and his eschatology fueled his conviction that preaching the Gospel would bring about a Christian America. In 1817, the year after his wife, Roxana, died of tuberculosis, Beecher married Harriet Porter, member of a prominent Maine family. In 1826 he accepted a call to the Hanover Street Church in Boston's North End, a place from which he declared that he would do battle with Unitarianism. Beecher ably marshaled Boston's Trinitarian minority, and at the same time he encouraged a new generation of reformers with high hopes for the nation's future. Hanover Street Church came to be noted for its music as well as its preaching: Beecher hired the young musician Lowell Mason, who revived congregational singing, promoted adult and children's choirs, and introduced new tunes and lyrics.

A leader in the revivals that collectively came to be known as the Second Great Awakening, Beecher took a prominent role in the voluntary associations that mobilized Americans for religious and social causes. Convinced that the nation's future would be decided in the West, he shared a Protestant anxiety with immigration trends and the growth of the Catholic population, and his passion for Protestant cultural dominance shaped his famous 1834 sermon, distributed widely in pamphlet form, *A Plea for the West*. By then Beecher had accepted a call to the presidency of the newly founded Lane Seminary in Cincinnati, Ohio (1833–1850), and the pastorate of Cincinnati's Second Presbyterian Church (1833–1843).

Beecher's blend of revivalist and conservative instincts created difficulties that drew him into controversies. In 1834, Lane Seminary's future was jeopardized when a vocal minority followed the fiery abolitionist Theodore Dwight Weld from Lane Seminary to Oberlin College. In 1835, conservative Presbyterians brought Beecher to trial on heresy charges. Beecher offended rigid Calvinists by affirming human ability to respond to the Gospel, and his warm evangelical instincts prioritized shared Christian faith above denominational distinctions. Beecher was vindicated, but the trial was a step along the path to denominational schism. In the summer of 1835, Harriet Beecher died, and Lyman Beecher married Lydia Beals Johnson.

Beecher spent the last years of his life, 1851–1863, in semiretirement in Boston and New York. He died on 10 January 1863 at his home in Brooklyn Heights and was buried at his request in Grove Street Cemetery in New Haven beside his cherished friend, the Congregational theologian Nathaniel William Taylor. His wife, Lydia, survived him, as did eleven of his thirteen sons and daughters: all seven sons were ordained clergymen, including the famous reformer Henry Ward Beecher, and three of the four daughters were notable public figures, including the educator Catharine Beecher and the author of *Uncle Tom's Cabin*, Harriet Beecher Stowe.

[*See also* **Antebellum Reform; Beecher, Catharine; Beecher, Henry Ward; Clergy; Great Awakenings; Nativist Movement; Religion; Revivals; Voluntary Associations,** *subentry on* **British Colonies and Early Republic;** *and* **Weld, Theodore Dwight.**]

BIBLIOGRAPHY

Beecher, Lyman. *Autobiography, Correspondence, etc., of Lyman Beecher, D.D.* Edited by Charles Beecher. 2 vols. New York: Harper & Bros., 1864–1865.

Harding, Vincent. *A Certain Magnificence: Lyman Beecher and the Transformation of American Protestantism, 1775–1863.* New York: Carlson, 1991.

Snyder, Stephen H. *Lyman Beecher and His Children: The Transformation of a Religious Tradition.* New York: Carlson, 1991.

Edith Blumhofer

BENEZET, ANTHONY

(1713–1784), abolitionist and educator. Anthony Benezet was born to the Huguenots Jean and Judith Benezet on 31 January 1713 in Saint-Quentin, France. Persecuted by the Catholic regime, the Benezets left France and eventually settled in Philadelphia in 1731. In 1735, Benezet was naturalized as a British citizen, and in May 1736 he married Joyce Marriot, a Quaker; he had become a Quaker himself some years earlier. In 1742 he took charge of the Friends' English School in Philadelphia and became one of the first to educate Quaker girls. In 1750 he began to teach young black children in his home. Some years later he founded the School for Black People, also known as the African Free School. Students included Absalom Jones, the first priest of African descent in the Episcopal Church, and James Forten, the prominent sailmaker. Richard Allen, the founder of the African Methodist Episcopal Church, also greatly appreciated Benezet's work. Unlike many of his fellow contemporaries who were against the slave trade, Benezet went further, actively fighting to end slavery and proclaiming the complete equality of Africans.

Benezet applied Quaker principles in forming his position on free and enslaved Africans, including beliefs in equality before God and nonviolence. Critical of excessive material acquisition, he linked Europeans with the love of wealth and argued that prior to the slave trade, Africans had lived in relative peace and freedom, with an abundance of the necessities of life. He asserted that the slave trade morally corrupted Europeans, as well as some Africans, who became their accomplices. Benezet's most important works are *A Short Account of That Part of Africa Inhabited by the Negroes* (1762) and *Some Historical Account of Guinea* (1771), which appeared in Philadelphia, London, Paris, Ireland, Germany, and Scotland. Seven other of his pamphlets dealt exclusively with slavery. His publications powerfully influenced other antislavery activists, including Olaudah Equiano.

Benezet closely collaborated with the Quaker leader John Woolman. Benezet wrote hundreds of letters to religious leaders such as George Whitefield and John Wesley and to secular leaders such as Benjamin Franklin and Patrick Henry. Wesley's *Thoughts upon Slavery* (1774) is based almost entirely on Benezet's *Some Historical Account of Guinea*. The correspondence between Benezet and the British abolitionist Granville Sharp proved to be a key link in the transnational fight against slavery and the slave trade. Benezet's descriptions of Africa proved to be so central that William Wilberforce quoted Benezet at length in the great 1792 parliamentary debates on ending the slave trade.

In 1775, Benezet and others called for the establishment of the Society for the Relief of Free Negroes Unlawfully Held in Bondage. This was one of the first abolitionist societies dedicated to ending slavery and the slave trade. In 1784, a few months before his death, the society was re-formed as the Pennsylvania Society for Promoting the Abolition of Slavery and for the Relief of Free Negroes Unlawfully Held in Bondage, and Benezet's friend Benjamin Franklin took the helm in 1787. Members included Benjamin Rush and Tom Paine. That year, 1787, Allen and Jones

formed the Free African Society: meeting first in Allen's home and later at Benezet's school for Africans, it was founded as a nondenominational service organization to aid Philadelphia's population of free blacks. The society kept records of black Philadelphians, provided funeral services, and assisted widows, orphans, and others in need.

The French Revolution leader Jacques-Pierre Brissot wrote of Benezet's funeral procession in 1784, "What author, what great man, will ever be followed to his grave by four hundred Negroes. . . . Where is the man in all of Europe, of whatever rank or birth, who is equal to Benezet. . . . Who was more useful to society, to mankind?" (Jacques-Pierre Brissot, *Letter addressed to the Marquis*, Paris, July 1, 1786).

[*See also* Colonial Era; Free Communities of Color; *and* Slavery, *subentry on* Colonial and Revolutionary Era.]

BIBLIOGRAPHY

Jackson, Maurice. *Let This Voice Be Heard: Anthony Benezet, Father of Atlantic Abolitionism*. Philadelphia: University of Pennsylvania Press, 2009.

Maurice Jackson

BETHUNE, MARY McLEOD

(1875–1955), school founder, government administrator, and leader of African American women. Born in Mayesville, South Carolina, and educated at a Presbyterian school in North Carolina and at Chicago's Moody Bible Institute, Bethune in 1904 founded the Daytona Normal and Industrial Institute for girls in Florida; she was its president until 1942. Merged with the Cookman Institute in 1923, it was subsequently known as

Bethune-Cookman College—the only extant historically black college founded by a black woman. In 1935, Bethune founded the National Council of Negro Women, which united the major black women's organizations, including the National Association of Colored Women, of which she had been president from 1924 to 1928. She was also active in several interracial civil rights organizations.

Bethune's service from 1936 to 1943 on the advisory committee of the New Deal's National Youth Administration extended her influence, particularly after she became director of its Negro Affairs Division in 1939. Her access to the White House and her alliance with First Lady Eleanor Roosevelt facilitated her efforts to bring more black men and women into New Deal agencies and to combat racial discrimination in federal social-welfare programs. Organizing the blacks in New Deal agencies into the Federal Council of Negro Affairs in 1936, she initiated two government-sponsored National Negro Conferences (1937 and 1939), which delineated the plight of African Americans and offered policy recommendations. In 1949, Bethune retired to Daytona Beach to live with her son, Albert, born in 1899 during her marriage (1898–1909) to Albertus Bethune.

[See also African Americans; Education; National Association of Colored Women; National Council of Negro Women; and New Deal Social Reforms.]

BIBLIOGRAPHY

Ross, B. Joyce. "Mary McLeod Bethune and the National Youth Administration: A Case Study of Power Relationships in the Black Cabinet of Franklin D. Roosevelt." *Journal of Negro History* 60 (January 1975): 1–28.
Smith, Elaine M. "Mary McLeod Bethune and the National Youth Administration." In *Clio Was a Woman: Studies in the History of American Women*, edited by Mabel E. Deutrich and Virginia C. Purdy, pp. 149–177. Washington, D.C.: Howard University Press, 1980.

Paula Giddings

BIRTH CONTROL AND FAMILY PLANNING

Margaret Sanger first referred to contraception as "birth control" in 1914 in efforts to ignite a movement to overturn laws prohibiting the sale and distribution of contraceptives in the United States. By the twenty-first century the term was a common colloquialism for the collection of methods used before, during, after, or independent of sexual activity to prevent conception. "Family planning," a term that arose in the 1930s as the birth control movement matured into a public-health movement, situates birth control in a normative script about its proper practice. According to the family-planning script, married couples should avoid having children until they can afford to support them, and then they should space pregnancies to maintain the wife's health and the family's economic well-being.

The rationale for family planning grew out of fractious cultural debates about sexual morality, women's health, individual rights, and social responsibility that permeated the entire history of contraceptive distribution and use in America. Behind the public debate, individual practices have taken place in a context sharply contoured by a person's gender, age, race, economic standing, marital status, and religion. In general, however, white middle-class married women and men enjoyed the most access to voluntary family planning, and they experienced the greatest social pressure to have large families. Low-income families, women of color, and immigrants have had the least access and have been subject to the greatest public regulation of their fertility.

Early Contraceptive Methods. Some of the earliest contraceptive methods included prolonged breast-feeding, coitus interruptus (commonly called "withdrawal"), and periodic marital abstinence. In the colonial period, women viewed prolonged breast-feeding as a means of spacing their pregnancies and protecting their health. Men understood withdrawal as a responsibility, and they referred to its practice by colloquialisms such as "minding his pullbacks." Couples also relied on periodic abstinence as they sought to balance their desire for both intimacy and limited childbearing. Yet as the ideal of romantic love took hold in the nineteenth century, abstinence caused increased marital discord. It was also an uncertain technique. Human physiology was not well understood. Physicians and moral philosophers alike offered contradictory advice about women's so-called fertile period. As commerce in patent medicines grew, douching potions and equipment, herbal vaginal suppositories, condoms, and other barrier methods became increasingly available through pharmacies and mail-order catalogs. Many women received advice from female family members and midwives who cared for them in pregnancy and birth. The medical profession also offered options. For instance, the water cure recommended several cold-water douches per day, as well as douches before and after intercourse, to maintain health. Following that advice, douches displaced withdrawal as the primary preventive among the middle classes. In addition, commercial production of rubber after 1860 reduced the cost of condoms, making them a more popular choice. These methods provided a measure of control to free women. Enslaved women, however, were subject to the will of owners, who manipulated slave marriages and rewarded high fertility with less work, more food, and promises not to sell women; owners also engaged in direct sexual exploitation and forced breeding. Enslaved women resisted sexual exploitation, and slaveholders complained that women used preventives. Still, enslaved women were less successful at avoiding pregnancy than free white women were.

When preventives failed, women often relied on abortion, which was legally and commercially available until the mid-nineteenth century. The distinction between avoiding pregnancy and inducing abortion was much less clearly marked in an era before the existence of definitive medical tests for pregnancy. Cessation of menstruation could be a sign of many things; women's perception of fetal movement in the womb, called "quickening," proved the existence of a pregnancy. Actions taken before quickening could easily be construed as restoring health by "bringing on blocked menses." Between 1860 and 1880, after states passed laws prohibiting abortion, women continued to rely on it as a backup, despite the increased risks. Whatever the method, the birthrates of white middle-class Americans declined greatly by 1900.

Arguments for and against Contraception. Protection of women's lives and health provided the main argument for preventive measures. Childbirth represented the "vale of death" for women; even middle-class women knew of family members or friends who had died from complications of pregnancy or birth. Thus the ability to control when, and if, they became pregnant promised to give women greater control over their lives. The goal of protecting women's lives and health also served as a persuasive counterbalance to moral and religious concerns about separating sexual pleasure and procreation. Although there was wide social and religious support for "natural" preventive measures, "artificial" preventives that explicitly avoided the so-called natural consequences of sex were seen as more problematic in the private lives of women and men and in public discourse. Reflecting the private moral ambivalence about preventive measures, women generally did not use them until after the birth of a first child. Women's efforts to control fertility, and their frustrations in this regard, increased as they experienced more pregnancies. Public concerns focused on the threat that commercial contraceptives posed to public morality. The fear was that public distribution of sexually explicit materials, including information and devices related to contraception, would corrupt young people, undermine women's purity, and arouse the passions of lesser men. In 1873, Congress included contraceptive information and devices among the obscene materials whose distribution and sale it prohibited in the Comstock Law. By 1885, twenty-four states had passed similar laws.

Despite these laws, a black market in contraceptives of uncertain safety and effectiveness thrived. Euphemistic language exploiting the long-standing gray area between health and contraceptive practice became a staple of advertising for patent medicines. Thus in the twentieth century, douching agents were sold as feminine hygiene products. Alongside the black market, social anxiety about birthrates among groups considered "undesirable" led to the first legally sanctioned contraceptive technique, surgical sterilization. Beginning in 1907, Indiana and other states enacted laws requiring the compulsory sterilization of the mentally and physically handicapped. Such bigoted judgments about what was called "fitness" quickly extended to include the young, the poor, immigrants, and racial minorities. During the 1920s, California judges sent sexually active young women to state hospitals, where they would be sterilized; young men

were often sterilized while in juvenile detention. Across the nation, during the 1950s and 1960s, poor women of color who depended on government-supported health care were deemed irresponsible for becoming parents and were often sterilized without their knowledge and consent. Such practices continued a pattern that dates back to slavery of denying reproductive autonomy to women of color. Women's health advocates exposed these injustices, and the federal government issued guidelines prohibiting the most egregious practices in 1974.

Establishing the Individual Right to Contraception. The twentieth-century birth control movement represented the first sustained effort to establish the individual right to contraception. In Brooklyn, New York City, in 1916, Margaret Sanger opened the first birth control clinic in the United States. In subsequent years, clinics opened in many more cities, and by 1942 these had blossomed into nationwide network of clinics sponsored by the Planned Parenthood Federation of America. Relying on family-planning rhetoric, these physician-run clinics operated in a legal gray area, prescribing contraception for health reasons. Although most people still obtained contraception in the marketplace, birth control clinics played an important role in developing many modern contraceptives, including spermicides, diaphragms, intrauterine devices (IUDs), and, especially, the pill. In 1953, Sanger persuaded a wealthy friend and supporter, Katharine McCormick, to underwrite Dr. Gregory Pincus's research on the biochemistry of ovulation. In 1960, after an investment of more than $2 million, the first birth control pill hit the market, promising near 100 percent effectiveness; women rushed to obtain prescriptions. Five years later, the Supreme Court ruled in *Griswold v. Connecticut* that the use of contraceptives was a matter of marital privacy. In *Eisenstadt v. Baird* in 1972, the Court extended the right to single persons. Despite these changes, opposition to "artificial" contraception continued into the twenty-first century, especially within conservative religious groups. The Catholic Church, for instance, continued to allow only periodic abstinence, the "rhythm method."

New contraceptive options in the twenty-first century emphasized long-acting female methods, including hormones delivered in intrauterine and vaginal devices and injections such as Depo-Provera. Sterilization, however, continued to be the leading form of birth control in the United States. Moreover, long-standing moral debates have continued to shape the context of the distribution and use of contraceptives. Thus controversy surrounded the Food and Drug Administration's approval in 2006 of over-the-counter sales of a postcoital contraceptive called "emergency contraception." Its name carries with it the continuing view that family planning should occur prior to sexual activity. Nonetheless, many social and religious conservatives oppose easy access to it, reflecting continued anxieties about the sexual and reproductive autonomy of young unmarried women. In 1996, such concerns led to a ban on information related to contraceptives in government-funded sex-education programs. Reminiscent of the Comstock Law, abstinence-only legislation assumes that exposure to knowledge about contraceptives undercuts chastity.

At the same time, anxieties about the reproductive practices of the poor and of racial minorities have continued as well. Based on the widely held fallacy that teen pregnancy causes poverty, in 1990 some hailed the first long-acting hormonal contraceptive, Norplant, as a means of containing welfare costs and solving inner-city social problems. While restricting public funding for education related to contraceptives, state governments subsidized the distribution of Norplant to poor women through Medicaid. Reminiscent of earlier efforts to sterilize poor women of color, many Norplant users complained that they were pressured into using it, were not fully informed about its side effects, and were denied when they requested its removal. Thus although in the twenty-first century there are more choices for birth control and family planning, age, gender, ethnicity, and economic standing still fundamentally influence the options to which an American has access.

[*See also* **Abortion; Antiabortion Movement; Family; Planned Parenthood; Pregnancy; Reproductive Rights Movement; Sanger, Margaret; Sex Education; Sexual Reform and Morality; Slaves and Childbirth; Stanton, Elizabeth Cady;** *and* **Sterilization.**]

BIBLIOGRAPHY

Brodie, Janet Farrell. *Contraception and Abortion in Nineteenth-Century America*. Ithaca, N.Y.: Cornell University Press, 1994.

Gordon, Linda. *The Moral Property of Women: A History of Birth Control Politics in America*. 3d ed. Urbana: University of Illinois Press, 2002.

McCann, Carole. *Birth Control Politics in the United States, 1916–1945*. Ithaca, N.Y.: Cornell University Press, 1994.

Roberts, Dorothy. *Killing the Black Body: Race, Reproduction, and the Meaning of Liberty*. New York: Pantheon Books, 1997.

Schoen, Johanna. *Choice and Coercion: Birth Control, Sterilization, and Abortion in Public Health and Welfare*. Chapel Hill: University of North Carolina Press, 2005.

Tone, Andrea. *Devices and Desires: A History of Contraceptives in America*. New York: Hill and Wang, 2001.

Carole R. McCann

BLACK NATIONALISM

Black nationalism is an ideology that holds that people of African descent should exercise control over the politics and resources in the communities in which they are a majority. Reflecting the beliefs of such early black nationalists as Paul Cuffe (1759–1817), Martin Delany (1812–1885), and Marcus Garvey (1887–1940), over time the concept has included calls not only for black self-determination, but also for armed self-defense, black capitalism, a return to Africa, and a black cultural aesthetic to instill unity and pride among black people.

In the 1960s and 1970s black nationalism was closely identified with the Black Power movement and was reflected both in a variety of social, political, and cultural movements related to Black Power, such as the Black Arts Movement, and also through a variety of groups including the Revolutionary Action Movement, the Republic of New Africa, the Nation of Islam, and for a time the Black Panther Party for Self-Defense, which adopted and espoused the principles of Black Power.

Perhaps most identified with the Nation of Islam and its fiery spokesmen Malcolm X, who helped to popularize the Nation's nationalist approach, in the early 1960s black-nationalist thought also received a boost from the independence of a significant number of African states from colonial rule. Especially influential was Kwame Nkrumah, the leader of the West African nation of Ghana, who became a celebrated symbol of black liberation and unity across the black diaspora.

In the late 1960s a number of scholars, including Theodore Draper, Robert Allen, and Harold Cruse, sought to explain black nationalism's origins and influence. Some, including Draper, citing the traditional definition of "nationalism," were critical of the term and instead had approaches that were more cultural in orientation. As Draper conceptualized the problem in a 1970 article in the *New York Review of Books*, "real nationalism is based on the relationship of a people to a land." "The historic inability of black nationalists in America to solve the land problem," he proposed, encouraged the development of what he termed "quasi-nationalism," resulting in "substitutes for sovereignty, such as separate, autonomous, all-black Black Studies programs and departments." Draper's observations echoed the concerns of the founding director of Cornell University's Africana Studies and Research Center, James Turner, whom Draper quoted as writing that "without control over land, resources and production, there can be no self-determination for a people."

In spite of Draper's critique, black-nationalist thought continued to flourish in the United States. In lieu of state building, for example, black nationalists in the 1960s and 1970s began to develop alternative philosophies that encapsulated the core concepts of black unity without the emphasis on a return to an African homeland, although this was still a central theme. In travels throughout the world as an emissary for the Black Panther Party, Eldridge Cleaver, for instance, spoke in terms of a black autonomy that would give African Americans the power to engage in diplomatic relations with other nation-states. Meanwhile the Republic of New Africa demanded the forfeiture of five states from the United States: they hoped that these could become the nucleus of a new black nation. In his 1969 *Black Manifesto*, James Forman, the former leader of the Student Nonviolent Coordinating Committee, likewise demanded reparations from white Christian churches and Jewish synagogues that would allow African Americans to gain greater political autonomy.

This diversity in thought and action often inspired conflict between black-nationalist organizations—which, aided by government efforts at repression, undercut the organizations' influence. The Black Panther Party, for example, was involved in a significant rivalry with Maulana Karenga's US Organization (or Organization Us) over the control of the black studies program at the University of California, Los Angeles. The conflict turned deadly in January 1969 when two Panther members were shot and killed by members of US. The Federal Bureau of Investigation was later found to have worked clandestinely to increase tension between the two organizations.

Like other ideologies, black nationalism could also be fairly criticized for replicating sexist structures that sought to limit and control the role of women in the black liberation movement. Inspired in part by the racism they encountered in the women's movement and the sexism that was part of the civil rights and Black Power movements, black feminists sought to set their own agenda: an agenda that was also heavily influenced by black-nationalist thought, but took away the emphasis on black masculinity.

Developing an independent black political agenda and privileging the unique contours of black culture, cultural-nationalist organizations such as Maulana Karenga's influential US Organization, along with the Black Arts Movement, which featured prominent black artists like the poet Amiri Baraka, not only promoted black unity but also helped to define a new black cultural aesthetic in literature and the visual and performing arts. In the process, black-nationalist thought has had a continuing impact on American art and culture even in the twenty-first century.

[See also African American Emigration; African Americans; Black Panthers; Civil Rights Movement; Delany, Martin; National Black Feminist Organization; and Universal Negro Improvement Association.]

BIBLIOGRAPHY

Brown, Scot. Fighting for US: Maulana Karenga, the US Organization, and Black Cultural Nationalism. New York: New York University Press, 2003.

Draper, Theodore H. "Exchange on Black Nationalism." New York Review of Books, 3 December 1970.

Draper, Theodore H. The Rediscovery of Black Nationalism. New York: Viking Press, 1970.

Joseph, Peniel. Waiting 'til the Midnight Hour: A Narrative History of Black Power in America. New York: Henry Holt, 2006.

Shelby, Tommie. "Two Conceptions of Black Nationalism: Martin Delany on the Meaning of Black Political Solidarity." Political Theory 31, no. 5 (2003): 664–692.

Van Deburg, William L., ed. Modern Black Nationalism: From Marcus Garvey to Louis Farrakhan. New York: New York University Press, 1997.

Williams, Yohuru. Black Politics, White Power: Civil Rights, Black Power, and the Black Panthers in New Haven. Saint James, N.Y.: Brandywine Press, 2000.

Yohuru R. Williams

BLACK PANTHERS

Founded in Oakland, California, in 1966 by Huey P. Newton and Bobby Seale, the Black Panther Party for Self-Defense soon became the best-known revolutionary, nationalist organization of the Black Power era. Rejecting the civil rights movement's integrationist goals and nonviolence, Panthers advocated self-help, community control, and armed defense against police brutality. The party's youthful, urban constituency organized citizens' patrols in black neighborhoods, wore paramilitary uniforms featuring black berets and leather jackets, and operated health clinics, food pantries, "liberation schools," and children's breakfast programs. Newton's 1967 imprisonment after his conviction (later reversed) for killing a policeman spurred a nationwide "Free Huey" campaign.

Addressing African Americans' specific problems, party leaders freely modified classical Marxism-Leninism, moving from a black-nationalist stance to revolutionary socialism to intercommunalism. In this revolutionary vision, a Black Power vanguard would overcome the tyrannies of race and class, lead the masses in seizing the means of production, and redistribute wealth, technology, and political power. To this end, the Panthers forged alliances with nonblack leftists and established trade-union caucuses.

Black Panther militancy frightened white America and many black moderates. The Federal Bureau of Investigation (FBI) and local police targeted the Panthers in a campaign against what they considered black-nationalist hate groups. A joint FBI-police raid in Chicago in 1969 left dead both the head of the Illinois Black Panthers, Fred Hampton, and an associate, Mark Clark. Other Black Panthers died in police shootouts, and many were imprisoned. Bobby Seale was among the "Chicago Eight" radicals tried for conspiracy in 1969. The party's minister of information, Eldridge Cleaver, fled the United States to Cuba and then to Algiers. Bitter internal division and ideological disputes with other nationalist groups further weakened the party. Fading by 1972, the Panthers nevertheless inspired later activists by proving that class consciousness and the concept of black self-rule need not be mutually exclusive.

[*See also* **African Americans; Black Nationalism;** *and* **Sixties, The.**]

BIBLIOGRAPHY

Newton, Huey P. *To Die for the People.* New York: Random House, 1972.

Seale, Bobby. *Seize the Time: The Story of the Black Panther Party and Huey P. Newton.* New York: Random House, 1970.

Van Deburg, William L. *New Day in Babylon: The Black Power Movement and American Culture, 1965–1975.* Chicago: University of Chicago Press, 1992.

William L. Van Deburg

BLEEDING KANSAS

In the spring of 1854, Samuel and Margaret Wood packed their bags in Ohio and set off for Kansas Territory, hoping to use the doctrine of popular sovereignty to make Kansas a free state. Like thousands of other so-called free-state migrants, the Woods moved to Kansas after passage of the Kansas-Nebraska Act, which opened the region west of Missouri to white settlement and allowed local settlers to determine whether slavery would be legal there. The Woods and their like-minded neighbors from New England and the upper Midwest locked horns with proslavery settlers from Missouri, Kentucky, and the upper South, as elections for territorial representatives descended into armed conflict and bloody reprisals.

Although this conflict got its name "Bleeding Kansas" from events like the 1856 sack of Lawrence, when a group of proslavery settlers ransacked the "abolitionist den" of Lawrence, the first blood spilled in Kansas was Indian, when thousands of Native Americans arrived in Kansas and clashed with the resident Osage, Kaw, and Pawnee tribes. Some tribes split over the slavery question, while others asserted their allegiance to one particular side.

The Delaware wrote letters to Washington, D.C., protesting the abrogation of the Missouri Compromise and joined antislavery settlers by resisting the 1850 Fugitive Slave Act, while the Shawnee, many of whom resided on a Methodist mission that owned dozens of black slaves, supported their Missouri neighbors and retrieved runaway slaves who sought freedom across the border. These runaways, along with the few hundred slaves who migrated with their southern owners, made it very difficult for the institution of slavery to be planted in the Kansas soil. Together with local white abolitionists, many of whom were women, slaves resisted their enslavement, and many slaves seized the opportunity to flee on the expanding tracks of the Underground Railroad.

Free-state women wrote about their experiences with the "suffering slaves" and demonized the Missouri "Border Ruffians," arguing that they forced slavery on a reluctant people. By sharing their letters with politicians like Charles Sumner and newspapers like the *New York Tribune*, they publicized the trials of free-state settlers and elicited donations of essential foodstuffs, clothing, and arms, like the Sharps rifles nicknamed "Beecher's Bibles" after the activist and preacher Henry Ward Beecher, who helped raise money for them. Local settlers connected with representatives of the Kansas National Committee, who canvassed large cities like Boston and Chicago and secured monetary donations and additional migrants to support the free-state cause. Missouri settlers made similar efforts to colonize the region with proslavery men, holding emigration meetings in small towns in Georgia and Alabama to raise parties of settlers. They also formed squatters associations that discouraged antislavery settlement and protected slavery by passing strict slave codes that included penalties for not only rebellious blacks but also rebellious whites. In the end, however, the free-state settlers more effectively transmitted their antislavery zeal into action, and a free Kansas entered the Union in 1861. The nation soon followed Kansas's lead and came to blows over the slavery question, but like Kansas, it emerged as a free nation.

[*See also* **Antebellum Era; Antislavery; Civil War Era; Free-Soilers; Internal Migration,** *subentry on* **Nineteenth-Century Westward; Middle West, The;** *and* **Slavery,** *subentries on* **African Americans by Native Americans** *and* **Nineteenth Century.**]

BIBLIOGRAPHY

Etcheson, Nicole. *Bleeding Kansas: Contested Liberty in the Civil War Era.* Lawrence: University Press of Kansas, 2004. The best political history of Bleeding Kansas.

Oertel, Kristen Tegtmeier. *Bleeding Borders: Race, Gender, and Violence in Pre–Civil War Kansas.* Baton Rouge: Louisiana State University Press, 2009. A social and cultural history of Bleeding Kansas.

Kristen Tegtmeier Oertel

B'NAI B'RITH

The oldest Jewish fraternal organization in the United States, B'nai B'rith—Hebrew for "Sons of the Covenant"—was established by German Jewish immigrants in New York City on 13 October 1843. According to the preamble of their first constitution, the twelve founders, led by Henry Jones, adopted the "mission of uniting Israelites" against an increasingly fragmented Jewish communal landscape that lacked any overarching rabbinic or organizational leadership. Separation of church and state in America meant that religious beliefs were a matter of personal choice.

As a result, Jews created and sustained institutions of their choosing, and in doing so, they mimicked American rather than Jewish patterns of communal affiliation.

Though Jewish organizational affiliation followed American patterns in form, its content differed markedly. B'nai B'rith fused the structure of American fraternal organizations such as the Masons and the Odd Fellows in terms of their hierarchical organization, ceremonial rites, and regalia with Jewish history and symbols. German remained the official language until English was adopted in 1855, but officers received Hebrew titles. Membership was restricted to men until 1909 when the first chapter of B'nai B'rith Women was founded in San Francisco.

In addition to bringing a measure of unity to the Jewish community, B'nai B'rith aimed to provide social solidarity and economic security for immigrants living in a potentially precarious world. Membership ensured immigrants a slate of services, including survivor benefits for widows and orphans, money to educate children, and funeral benefits. As the organization spread across the country, membership linked lodge members who worked as small merchants into a growing network of business contacts and fraternal connections as they traveled to unfamiliar cities. B'nai B'rith also offered a range of social, recreational, and educational benefits. Committed to "developing and elevating the mental and moral character" of Jews and "supporting science and the arts," the organization sponsored lectures and opened the Maimonides Library Association in the early 1850s to provide cultural enrichment to German Jewish immigrants.

By the mid-1860s the increasing affluence of German Jewish immigrants undermined the value of the order's economic and cultural benefits. As many members moved into the American middle class, B'nai B'rith turned to philanthropy as the main vehicle through which it would achieve a fresh set of universalist goals, reflected in a new constitutional preamble concerned with "the highest interests of humanity." Though remaining committed to mutual aid, B'nai B'rith expanded its philanthropic activities to reach the wider community by opening hospitals, old-age homes, and orphanages and by providing relief to Jews overseas. At the same time, the B'nai B'rith became the spokesman for and defender of Jewish rights at home and abroad. A tradition of diplomatic intercession on behalf of Jews and in defense of Jewish rights peaked in 1913 with the establishment of the Anti-Defamation League of B'nai B'rith, which sought to fight prejudice and discrimination against Jews. In the 1920s, concern for the anti-Semitism faced by Jewish youth motivated B'nai B'rith to create Hillel, a Jewish student organization on college campuses, and a network of youth groups under the auspices of the B'nai B'rith Youth Organization. In the late 1990s and early 2000s, the B'nai B'rith Women, the Anti-Defamation League, Hillel, and the B'nai B'rith Youth Organization became independent organizations.

[*See also* **Fraternal Organizations; German Americans;** *and* **Jewish Americans.**]

BIBLIOGRAPHY

Cohen, Naomi W. *Encounter with Emancipation: The German Jews in the United States, 1830–1914.* Philadelphia: Jewish Publication Society of America, 1984.

Grusd, Edward E. *B'nai B'rith: The Story of a Covenant.* New York: Appleton-Century, 1966.

Kuzmack, Linda Gordon. "B'nai B'rith Women." In *Jewish Women in America: An Historical Encyclopedia,* edited by Paula E. Hyman and Deborah Dash Moore. New York: Routledge, 1997.

Moore, Deborah Dash. *B'nai B'rith and the Challenge of Ethnic Leadership.* Albany: State University of New York Press, 1981.

Schappes, Morris U. *A Documentary History of the Jews in the United States, 1654–1875.* New York: Citadel Press, 1950.

Katherine Rosenblatt

BOARDING SCHOOLS, NATIVE AMERICAN

See **Native American Boarding Schools.**

BONUS ARMY

In 1932, with the nation mired in the Great Depression, thousands of unemployed World War I veterans traveled to Washington, D.C., to petition Congress for the immediate payment of thousand-dollar bonuses that 1924 legislation had promised to pay them in 1945. Styling themselves the "Bonus Expeditionary Force"—a takeoff on the American Expeditionary Forces of 1918—these protestors, many with their families, set up camp in vacant federal buildings and in shacks on the Anacostia Flats a few miles from the Capitol.

The House approved the so-called Bonus Bill, but in June the Senate decisively rejected it. Yet many members of the Bonus Army stayed in Washington. In July, the administration of Herbert Hoover ordered the veterans' eviction from the federal buildings. During this operation, police gunfire killed one veteran. Hoover sent in troops under the command of General Douglas MacArthur to restore calm. Exceeding his orders, MacArthur employed his forces, complete with a machine-gun squadron and several tanks, to drive the veterans out of the District of Columbia entirely. Using tear gas and bayonets, the troops cleared the petitioners and their families from their makeshift homes, which were then burned.

The spectacle of U.S. troops forcibly driving from the nation's capital peaceful, unarmed citizens who were themselves veterans illustrated the gap that had opened by the end of Hoover's presidency between the government and Great Depression victims. MacArthur insisted that the "mob" was "animated by the essence of revolution" and was bent on taking over the government. In fact, the rout of the nonresisting Bonus Army demonstrated that government officials in 1932 were more fearful of a revolution than the unemployed were interested in fomenting one.

[*See also* **Great Depression Era; Military Personnel,** *subentry on* **World War I;** *and* **Veterans' Rights Movement.**]

BIBLIOGRAPHY

Daniels, Roger. *The Bonus March: An Episode of the Great Depression.* Westport, Conn.: Greenwood Press, 1971.

Lisio, Donald J. *The President and Protest: Hoover, MacArthur, and the Bonus Riot.* 2d ed. New York: Fordham University Press, 1994.

Robert S. McElvaine

BORDERLANDS

The historiography of early American frontiers and borderlands is littered with contested models, for scholars have long struggled to impose definitional order on places that lacked obvious geographic or cultural borders. Some have emphasized time (the frontier as a moving, temporary zone), while others have emphasized space (the borderlands as places of hybrid continuities). Constructs have also depended on perspective, for one person's "frontier" is another's "backcountry," and the borderlands marked both the greatest extent of colonialism and its overstretched limits. Recent scholarship leans toward an understanding of early American borderlands as spaces of cultural, linguistic, and sexual encounter that were superficially shaped by broader power-politics but were highly responsive to localized forces—as sites of accommodation rather than exclusion. Within the borderlands themselves, patterns of interaction were fluid, and there was more elasticity in practices of trade, diplomacy, and sexual relations than could be expected among long-established societies. These interactions also profoundly influenced ideas and practices outside the borderlands, including conceptions about race. Indeed, American self-identity itself—both among settler groups and among indigenous peoples—was in large part a function of the lessons of the borderlands.

All borderlands exhibited distinctive characteristics based partly on geographic and environmental parameters and partly on the demographic characteristics of the peoples that they encompassed. Notable borderlands included the Pays d'en Haut (Great Lakes), the lower Missouri valley, the northeastern region between New England and the Canadian Maritimes, the Southeast (especially Florida and Louisiana), and the greater Rio Grande basin. Some patterns, notably of captivity and conversion, varied starkly, but a key defining feature of borderlands regions, and one that frequently drew the attention of commentators, was the high degree of social intercourse and intermixture. Explaining this phenomenon comparatively has opened up new fields of inquiry, as scholars have focused on how gender, the family, and sexuality either sustained peaceable borderlands or disrupted them. Indian women in particular were central to the networks of kin and commerce that

proliferated in the borderlands. Where feasible, they were co-optive, making creative adaptations to Catholicism and agriculturalism and often acting as critical cultural brokers.

The Great Lakes country became a larger borderland in the seventeenth century, when preexisting Amerindian geopolitics cross-fertilized with Europeans' appetite for the extensive peltry of the region. In and amid the many wars that followed, in which allegiances changed rapidly, many groups were dislocated, relocated, or creatively absorbed into multiethnic communities, and such patterns were accelerated by the profound impact of waves of disease that tore through Native American populations. For the small numbers of French settlers (*habitants*) in the region, who were overwhelmingly male, vulnerability was more demographic than biological. The traders and missionaries of New France, in turn, were heavily dependent on goodwill in order to harvest furs and souls. An uneasy equilibrium, formed out of these counterweighing vulnerabilities, encouraged the mobile residents of these borderlands to adapt to one another, allowing symbiotic exchange to shape the pattern of Indian-European relations to a greater extent than elsewhere. Pressed by aggressive competitors, particularly the Iroquois and English to the southeast and later the Sioux to the west, the French and their Great Lakes trading partners recognized the utility of cementing their relationships. Both peoples, in effect, manifested a high degree of cultural deference and commercial reciprocity that was choreographed inside the French trading posts (which spread down through the Mississippi valley in the eighteenth century) but played out on a wider stage through *métissage* (biological and cultural intermarriage).

The northern peripheries of Spanish America reached across from the modern border zone between the United States and Mexico into Louisiana and, by the late eighteenth century, into the Florida peninsula and northward up the Mississippi. The "Southwest" or "Spanish borderlands," labeled so to differentiate them from the loaded Anglocentric model of Frederick Jackson Turner's "frontier," were the prototype for North American borderlands. From the sixteenth through the nineteenth century the Spanish borderlands presented a robust challenge to expansionistic ambitions: time and again the European powers discovered the limits of their authority, as in the Pueblo Revolt of 1680, the expansion of the Comanches, and the persistence of a "native ground" in the Arkansas River valley. Native communities, for their part, were inexorably permeated by European goods, diseases, and missionaries, and they found themselves repeatedly confronting displaced or opportunistic Indian neighbors. The innumerable squabbles over military, territorial, and cultural sovereignty in these borderlands—epitomized in the relations among Pueblo peoples, Hispanic New Mexicans, and the nomads of the southwestern Great Plains—generated not just frequent raiding but also complex improvisations and adaptations, and accentuated the importance of trust, kinship, and interpersonal networks of exchange. Bloodlines, languages, and traditions intersected: creole and mestizo (mixed-race) identities proliferated, while Catholic sacramental practices and traditional native ceremonies awkwardly coexisted. Here, as elsewhere in the borderlands, ethnocentrism often proved an ineffective force—until the nineteenth-century hegemony of the United States unleashed it, with transformative effects.

[*See also* **Assimilation; Exploration, Conquest, and Settlement in North America; Frontier, The; Internal Migration; Multiracial and Multiethnic Americans; Native American Removal; Race and Ethnicity; Rural Life and Society; Southwest, The;** *and* **West, The.**]

BIBLIOGRAPHY

Adelman, Jeremy, and Stephen Aron. "From Borderlands to Borders: Empires, Nation-States, and the Peoples in between in North American History." *American Historical Review* 104, no. 3 (1999): 814–841.

Barr, Juliana. *Peace Came in the Form of a Woman: Indians and Spaniards in the Texas Borderlands.* Chapel Hill: University of North Carolina Press, 2007.

DuVal, Kathleen. *The Native Ground: Indians and Colonists in the Heart of the Continent.* Philadelphia: University of Pennsylvania Press, 2006.

Nobles, Gregory H. *American Frontiers: Cultural Encounters and Continental Conquest.* New York: Hill & Wang, 1997.

Ben Marsh

BRACERO PROGRAM

On 4 August 1942, Mexico and the United States entered into the binational agreements framing the Emergency Farm Labor Program, more commonly known as the bracero program. The Mexican and U.S. governments introduced this temporary contract-labor program as an emergency wartime program. Both countries promoted the contracting of male Mexican braceros, or laborers, to work in the United States for one to six months at a time as a binational act of friendship in a time of war. Recruited to satisfy alleged labor shortages in the United States caused by World War II, braceros emerged as an invaluable source of labor in the cotton, fruit, vegetable, and railroad industries. Both countries expanded and continued the bracero program until 31 December 1964.

The Mexican president Manuel Ávila Camacho recruited Mexican men from Mexico's northwestern region most aggressively. The prevalence of underemployed Mexican men experienced in the harvesting of crops, as well as their nearness to transportation systems into the United States, made this region and its residents especially appropriate for the bracero program. Mexican women were not contracted into the bracero program. Both governments feared that once in the United States, Mexican couples or single women and men laboring near each other would work as a family or enter into extended-family arrangements that would inspire them to settle permanently in the United States.

Upon being recruited, prospective braceros were encouraged to focus their attention on the program's potential to transform them into modern citizens. Without adequate protections or resources, prospective braceros were nevertheless expected to move effortlessly into and out of the bracero program. They were urged to labor in the United States, earn U.S. wages, and learn U.S. agricultural and railroad maintenance methods and skills that would move the nation forward.

Securing a bracero contract was an ordeal for everyone. Prospective braceros had to obtain the authorization of the Mexican government, separate from their families, and accept expensive loans to finance their journeys to various selection centers within Mexico. Once prospective braceros arrived at these centers, Mexican officials screened and transported them to U.S. processing centers. Then U.S. officials interrogated and inspected the men, and if they were accepted, U.S. employers and officials contracted them. They were then transported to their U.S. employment sites. These procedures did not familiarize braceros with the program's conditions and terms. An exploitative situation was created by the braceros' thus entering into a contract without understanding their obligations.

In 1951 the U.S. Congress passed Public Law 78 to streamline the bracero program and, at the urging of the Mexican government, provide the braceros some nominal protections. The law prohibited contracting braceros to replace American workers or depress Americans' wages; guaranteed braceros transportation, housing, food, and repatriation; set the prevailing wage at fifty cents an hour; and exempted braceros from U.S. military service. In practice, however, the law did little to protect braceros from exploitation. Throughout the United States braceros were paid a prevailing wage of forty cents an hour to work a day or night shift: this was sixty cents lower than the wages earned by American workers. They were denied fair health insurance, housing, meals, and transportation to and from their workplace; they faced discrimination and were not allowed to interact in public venues with whites and other U.S. residents and workers or share their grievances with government representatives. These violations were the result of U.S. employers' implementing the program at their discretion, with little government oversight.

The bracero program intensified the alienation of individuals of Mexican descent. Expressing their concerns often resulted in braceros' immediate repatriation to Mexico. Such conditions motivated them to remain in the United States as undocumented Mexican immigrants to earn enough U.S. wages either to return to Mexico or to settle in the United States at their discretion. Indeed, braceros and other recently arrived Mexican immigrants intensified undocumented Mexican immigration and settlement in the United States. They became pejoratively identified and treated as "wetbacks," and they labored for increasingly lower wages. Additionally, their undocumented entry and settlement fueled existing tensions among and between individuals of Mexican descent and helped paved the way for what the U.S. Immigration and Naturalization Service called "Operation Wetback." Throughout the summer of 1954, this campaign by border-patrol agents did not distinguish between Mexicans legally in the United States and undocumented Mexican immigrants. It exposed individuals of Mexican descent to harassment and resulted in the deportation of an estimated 230,000 undocumented Mexican immigrants.

Mexican Americans protested the bracero program and the presence of undocumented Mexicans. The National Agricultural Workers Union, a predominantly Mexican American union, organized in favor of robust enforcement of the border between the United States and Mexico and termination of the bracero program. The scholar and activist Ernesto Galarza emerged as a leading voice against the program's conditions and terms. By the program's end an estimated 5.2 million braceros had been contracted, and even into the twenty-first century an uncalculated number continued to protest their right to owed wages and savings.

[*See also* **Deportations and Repatriations; Immigration; Labor Movements; Mexican American Civil Rights Movement; Mexican Americans; Racism; Southwest, The;** *and* **World War II, Home Front.**]

BIBLIOGRAPHY

Galarza, Ernesto. *Strangers in Our Fields.* Washington, D.C.: Joint United States–Mexico Trade Union Committee, 1956.

Gonzalez, Gilbert G. *Guest Workers or Colonized Labor? Mexican Labor Migration to the United States.* Boulder, Colo.: Paradigm, 2006.

Ngai, Mae M. *Impossible Subjects: Illegal Aliens and the Making of Modern America.* Princeton, N.J.: Princeton University Press, 2004.

Ana Elizabeth Rosas

BRITISH AMERICANS

British Americans—including the English, Scots, Welsh, and Scotch-Irish—began to settle North America permanently in 1607. They dominated immigration in the colonial era, bringing with them the English language and Protestant Christianity, as well as the legal system and political, cultural, and economic values that shaped the nation. Arriving from distinct parts of Britain and settling in distinct parts of America, they laid the foundations of America's regional cultures. By 1776, with about half the white population consisting of English immigrants and their descendents, America was overwhelmingly a British world. Through the twentieth century, Britons continued to constitute a substantial though diminishing share of immigrants.

Between 1820 and 1930, at least 5 million Britons, including Canadians of British origins, permanently settled in the United States. These immigrants were "invisible" in the sense that they blended into the dominant culture and society more readily than other immigrant groups did. Generally they did not form ethnic settlements, nor were they seen as foreigners. In the antebellum era, many Britons came seeking farmland and helped push the frontier westward; by the 1880s, more settled in cities. Throughout the nineteenth century, British Americans loomed large in literature and the arts, in banking and finance, and in the industrialization process, especially in the textile industry, the iron and steel industry, mining, railroads, and engineering. In the twentieth century, though spread across the economic spectrum, British Americans figured prominently in the skilled and professional ranks, continuing to blend in with American society and to contribute to its development. Despite the nation's growing ethnic diversity, British Americans dominated national politics, the judiciary, and higher education well into the twentieth century.

[*See also* **Immigration.**]

BIBLIOGRAPHY

Erickson, Charlotte. *Invisible Immigrants: The Adaptation of English and Scottish Immigrants in*

Nineteenth-Century America. London: Weidenfeld and Nicolson, 1972.

Fischer, David Hackett. *Albion's Seed: Four British Folkways in America.* New York: Oxford University Press, 1989.

William E. Van Vugt

BROWN BERETS

Founded in East Los Angeles, California, in January 1968, the Brown Berets was a Chicana and Chicano self-defense organization that was formed and led by the youth activist David Sanchez with militant members of the local group Young Chicanos for Community Action (formerly Young Citizens for Community Action). Primarily composed of working-class and low-income barrio youth, both male and female, Brown Beret chapters sprouted across the nation, mostly in urban areas: chapters ranged from Seattle, Washington, and Pueblo, Colorado, to Chicago and San Antonio, Texas, with smaller chapters appearing in such places as, Yakima, Washington; Kalamazoo, Michigan; and Oxnard, California. Though the Brown Berets' national headquarters was established by the original East Los Angeles organization, upon expansion, Brown Beret chapters operated disparately throughout the nation and were in existence roughly from 1968 until 1981. In 1994 a new chapter in Watsonville, California, initiated a resurgence of the organization. Since then, active chapters have existed with varying rates of consistency throughout the United States.

Ideologically, some early Beret chapters ranged from cultural-nationalist to those having Marxist or socialist leanings, while others merely acted to support already-established organizations of the Chicano movement—such as the Crusade for Justice, the Raza Unida Party, the Alianza Federal de Mercedes, and the United Farm Workers—and non-Chicano organizations such as the Black Panther Party and the American Indian Movement. The Berets would work with each of these on an issue-by-issue basis. Specific Brown Beret initiatives revolved around an initial ten-point platform that spoke to piecemeal civil rights and labor rights reforms such as the right to quality and relevant education, the need for jobs training and voting reforms, the right to bear arms, and the need for better representation of Mexican Americans on juries and in all aspects of law enforcement—sought as a way to alleviate police abuse. Additionally, Berets participated in establishing community-based health clinics in East Los Angeles, Chicago, and Seattle and initiated programs for free meals and food, modeled after those begun by the Black Panther Party. Berets also began other community-service initiatives such as toy and clothing drives, house-painting services, parks cleanups, and waste-disposal services in underserved barrios, as well as programs to help low-income farmworkers.

With respect to organizational hierarchy, most Beret chapters operated in a top-down quasi-military fashion, with leadership positions mostly held by men. An important exception was the East Los Angeles officer Gloria Arellanes, who was responsible for the East Los Angeles Free Clinic and for maintaining the Berets' *La Causa* newspaper. But subsequently she, along with other men and women members, left the organization because of the patriarchal structure of the leadership.

Most notably, the original Beret chapter played a fundamental role in organizing both the East Los Angeles High School walkouts of 1968—during which participants rallied against poor conditions and racist treatment and advocated for Chicano teachers to be hired and for Chicano studies courses to be taught—and the 1970 National Chicano Moratorium against the Vietnam War. Both events brought about multiple arrests of Beret members, police harassment, and constant law-enforcement surveillance, including by the Federal Bureau of Investigation's Counter Intelligence Program (COINTELPRO); this surveillance persisted throughout the organization's existence. However, these developments did not deter similar pro-education and antiwar demonstrations led by Beret chapters throughout the United States.

[*See also* **Chicano Movement; Mexican American Civil Rights Movement;** *and* **War Resisters.**]

BIBLIOGRAPHY

Chávez, Ernesto. *"Mi Raza Primero!" (My People First!): Nationalism, Identity, and Insurgency in the Chicano Movement in Los Angeles, 1966–1978.* Berkeley: University of California Press, 2002.

Espinoza, Dionne. "'Revolutionary Sisters': Women's Solidarity and Collective Identification among Chicana Brown Berets in East Los Angeles, 1967–1970." *Aztlán* 26, no. 1 (Spring 2001): 17–58.

Valdes, Dionicio Nodin. *Barrios Nortenos: St. Paul and Midwestern Mexican Communities in the Twentieth Century.* Austin: University of Texas Press, 2000.

Milo M. Alvarez

BROWNSVILLE INCIDENT

In the summer of 1906, despite local white protest, the U.S. Army garrisoned Fort Brown in Brownsville, Texas, with three companies of the Twenty-Fifth Infantry, a regiment whose enlisted personnel were all African American. Racial tension became intense. Around midnight on 13 August 1906, eight to ten men marched through the town's streets firing their rifles. They killed one man, wounded another, and thoroughly terrified the townspeople. White Texans concluded that the raiding party came from the fort. After several investigations,

the army reached the same conclusion. President Theodore Roosevelt authorized the army to present the soldiers with an ultimatum: the guilty men in the regiment must come forward, or all would suffer punishment. No one responded, and all 156 men were discharged. Booker T. Washington tried but failed to change Roosevelt's mind. In 1909, Congress authorized an army court of inquiry into the claims of the discharged soldiers. Eventually, fourteen were readmitted into the service. In 1972 the army changed the discharges to honorable, and Congress authorized a payment to the one living survivor.

The controversy can be viewed from several perspectives. At the time, many whites accepted the notion that African Americans would naturally attack whites and join in a conspiracy of silence, while most blacks deemed the lack of due process typical of white justice. Though some of the African American soldiers probably were guilty of the shooting, a different standard of justice clearly prevailed for African Americans; all were presumed guilty and had to prove their innocence. Booker T. Washington's inability to achieve justice despite his long-established policy of racial acquiescence became clear. Southern whites continued for many years to cite the Brownsville incident to reinforce their fear of armed African Americans taking justice into their own hands.

[*See also* **African Americans; Jim Crow Era;** *and* **Racism.**]

BIBLIOGRAPHY

Christian, Garna L. *Black Soldiers in Jim Crow Texas, 1899–1917.* College Station: Texas A&M University Press, 1995.

Fletcher, Marvin E. *The Black Soldier and Officer in the United States Army, 1891–1917.* Columbia: University of Missouri Press, 1974.

Marvin E. Fletcher

BUFFALO SOLDIERS

Soldiers who served in U.S. Army regiments set aside for black enlisted men in 1866, just after the Civil War, are now widely known as buffalo soldiers. Black servicemen have continuously participated in the regular military forces of the United States since then. Their inclusion, albeit on a segregated basis, was considered a step toward full participation in society, and their presence in and contributions to the military became matters of interest and pride to black civilians.

These regiments, the Ninth and Tenth Cavalry and Twenty-Fourth and Twenty-Fifth Infantry, served mainly west of the Mississippi River, in campaigns against Indians. They constituted about 12 percent of the combat force and participated in a proportionate number of skirmishes and battles. Sixty-one died as a result of combat, thirty-seven in the Apache wars of 1877–1881. Eighteen received the Medal of Honor, eight for actions against Apaches. As combat operations declined in the 1880s and 1890s, the buffalo soldiers and the rest of the army became more involved in quelling civil disturbances ranging from cattle wars to industrial disputes.

At the turn of the twentieth century, buffalo soldiers fought in Cuba against Spain (1898), including in the charge up San Juan Hill for which Theodore Roosevelt and the Rough Riders gained fame, and in the Philippines against Filipino revolutionaries demanding independence (1898–1902). The regiments were with rare exception staffed by white officers, and all four remained active until President Harry S. Truman ordered the desegregation of the army in 1948.

Although the name "buffalo soldiers" dates from the period of the Indian wars, it is sometimes applied to all black veterans of the segregated army. It is generally supposed that Indians of the Great Plains, either Comanche or Cheyenne, first used the name to describe the Tenth Cavalry, and the best guesses are that the name reflected a perceived resemblance between the brown skin and nappy hair of some of the men and the color and texture of the fur of the bison. The earliest published uses of the name appeared in the 1870s. In his pathbreaking 1967 book *The Buffalo Soldiers*, William Leckie claimed that because the buffalo was essential to these tribes the name was probably a sign of respect and that the soldiers accepted it as such. This has not been proved, and the origins and significance of the name remain obscure. There is no evidence to indicate that the soldiers themselves used or referred to "buffalo soldiers," so claims concerning their views of the usage also remain unproved. The Tenth Cavalry adopted the buffalo as a central element of its unit crest, but not until 1911.

General awareness of the participation of black soldiers in the westward movement dates from the Civil Rights Movement of the 1960s. General Colin Powell's tenure as the chairman of the Joint Chiefs of Staff (1989–1993) and his central involvement in creating a monument to the buffalo soldiers at Fort Leavenworth, Kansas, in 1992 marked the emergence of the buffalo soldier as a prominent figure in American popular culture.

[*See also* **African Americans; Desegregation; Military Personnel;** *and* **Segregation, Racial.**]

BIBLIOGRAPHY

Dobak, William A., and Thomas D. Phillips. *The Black Regulars, 1866–1898*. Norman: University of Oklahoma Press, 2001.

Leckie, William H. *The Buffalo Soldiers: A Narrative of the Negro Cavalry in the West*. Norman: University of Oklahoma Press, 1967.

Phillips, Tom. "Sobriquet: A Chronological Commentary on the Name 'Buffalo Soldier.' " *Journal* of America's Military Past 113 (Spring/Summer 2010): 5–30.

Schubert, Frank N. *Black Valor: Buffalo Soldiers and the Medal of Honor, 1870–1898.* Wilmington, Del.: Scholarly Resources, 1997.

Schubert, Frank N., ed. *Voices of the Buffalo Soldier: Records, Reports, and Recollections of Military Life and Service in the West.* Albuquerque: University of New Mexico Press, 2003.

Frank N. Schubert

BURNED-OVER DISTRICT

The central and western part of the state of New York earned the label "Burned-Over District" for the frequency and intensity of its religious revivals and reform activity in the first half of the nineteenth century. The region is often defined to include western Vermont as well.

In his memoirs the revivalist Charles Grandison Finney (1792–1875) used the term "burnt district" to describe an area resistant to his revival because of an earlier, inauthentic revival. The mid-twentieth-century historians Alice Felt Tyler and Whitney Cross instead used the term to describe the successive waves of revival and reform in the area. Scholarship in the 1970s and 1980s produced specific studies of reform and religion in the area, some of which challenged Cross's idea that the area was unique in the intensity of its revivals.

Stretching from Albany to Lake Erie, bisected by the Erie Canal, and filled with natural lakes, the Burned-Over District experienced rapid economic development from 1790 to 1860. A series of treaties between New York and the Iroquois opened the region to settlement by 1800. The 1825 opening of the Erie Canal allowed goods, people, and ideas to flow in and out of the region. Manufacturing cities, notably Rochester and Syracuse, developed along the route of the canal. Protestant revivalists like Finney toured the area frequently.

New religious groups found fertile soil in the district. Mother Ann Lee shaped the Shaker movement from her home in Watervliet, near Albany, until her death in 1784. The Shaker community of Sodus Bay, located on the shore of Lake Ontario between Rochester and Syracuse, opened in 1826, and a decade later it moved to Groveland in the Finger Lakes region. The Universal Friend Jemima Wilkinson chose a site between Lake Keuka and Lake Seneca for her community in 1790. Joseph Smith was in Palmyra, an Erie Canal town, when in 1827 he discovered the golden tablets that are foundational for Mormons, and in the 1840s William Miller found many converts to millennialism in the region. When the world did not end as predicted in 1844, followers regrouped to form Seventh-Day Adventism. The so-called spirit rappings of the Fox sisters, also living along the Erie Canal, helped create a spiritualist movement.

Many reformers saw the Burned-Over District as an attractive place to experiment with sexual and economic roles. The "complex marriage" practiced by the Oneida Community under its founder John Humphrey Noyes eventually resulted in prosecution and the conversion of the community to a joint-stock company. The district also housed small Fourierist phalansteries, in which property was held in common.

The Rochester area was home to important abolitionists including Frederick Douglass and Harriet Tubman. A visit by the Quaker abolitionist Lucretia Mott to Waterloo, between Cayuga and Seneca Lakes, reunited her with Elizabeth Cady Stanton, a resident of nearby Seneca Falls. The Seneca Falls Convention, a national women's rights convention held on 19 and 20 July 1848, resulted. The next year, Amelia Bloomer began publishing the *Lily*, a temperance and women's rights newspaper, from her Seneca Falls home.

By the end of the nineteenth century, transportation and settlement patterns had changed, muting social experimentation in the district.

[*See also* **Antebellum Reform; Finney, Charles Grandison; Great Awakenings; Itinerant Preachers; Lee, Ann; Religion; Revivals; Smith, Joseph; Stanton, Elizabeth Cady; Utopian and Communitarian Movements; Women and Religious Institutions;** *and* **Women's Rights Movement, Antebellum Era.**]

BIBLIOGRAPHY

Cross, Whitney. *The Burned-Over District: The Social and Intellectual History of Enthusiastic Religion in Western New York, 1800–1850.* Ithaca, N.Y.: Cornell University Press, 1950.

Finney, Charles G. *The Original Memoirs of Charles G. Finney.* Edited by Garth M. Rosell and Richard A. G. Dupuis. New ed. Grand Rapids, Mich.: Zondervan, 2002. Finney's memoirs were first published in 1876.

Folts, James D. "The Fanatic and the Prophetess: Religious Perfectionism in Western New York, 1835–1839." *New York History* 72 (1991): 357–387.

Hewitt, Nancy A. *Women's Activism and Social Change: Rochester, New York, 1822–1872.* Ithaca, N.Y.: Cornell University Press, 1984.

Martin, John H. "Saints, Sinners, and Reformers: The Burned-Over District Re-Visited." *The Crooked Lake Review,* Fall 2005. http://www.crookedlakereview.com/books/saints_sinners.

McMillen, Sally G. *Seneca Falls and the Origins of the Women's Rights Movement.* New York: Oxford University Press, 2008.

Pritchard, Linda K. "The Burned-Over District Reconsidered: A Portent of Evolving Religious Pluralism in the United States." *Social Science History* 8, no. 3 (1984): 243–265.

Tyler, Alice Felt. *Freedom's Ferment: Phases of American Social History from the Colonial Period to the Outbreak of the Civil War.* Minneapolis: University of Minnesota Press, 1944

Joan R. Gundersen

C

CAJUN (ACADIAN) AMERICANS

An American ethnic group, the Cajuns descend from eighteenth-century exiles from Acadia and other ethnic groups with whom these exiles and their descendants intermarried in southern Louisiana. Cajuns today number more than five hundred thousand, and despite the long-standing stereotype of Cajuns as poor, ignorant rustics, they now occupy every social class and work in virtually every field of human endeavor.

The Cajuns' French and Catholic ancestors, the Acadians, hailed from Acadia ("Acadie" in French), which roughly comprised present-day Nova Scotia, New Brunswick, and Prince Edward Island. Both the French and the British governments regarded Acadia as strategically

important. As a result the colony passed repeatedly between the rival empires until Britain permanently captured Acadia in 1710. Nearly half a century later the British used the Acadians' refusal to swear unconditional allegiance to the English crown as a pretext for expulsion. Troops rounded up Acadian men, women, and children, herded them onto overcrowded vessels, and dispersed them throughout the Western Hemisphere.

Between 1764 and 1788 about three thousand Acadian exiles made their way to Spanish-held Louisiana. Colonial administrators settled them on the semitropical frontier as a bulwark against British and later U.S. expansion. A few Acadians became affluent planters by embracing the South's slave economy. Most, however, labored as subsistence farmers or worked in folk occupations, such as fishing, trapping, and boatbuilding. The Acadians also intermarried with other ethnic groups in southern Louisiana, including French, Spanish, and German Creoles. It was this process of ethnic interaction that transformed the Acadians, as well as those with whom they intermarried, into a new people—the Cajuns.

Cajuns remained relatively isolated from mainstream American culture well into the twentieth century. They underwent some minor Americanization prior to World War II—for example, educators began to punish Cajun schoolchildren around 1920 for speaking French instead of English—but it was the war that sparked the group's rapid and widespread Americanization. Although many Cajuns had never before left home, thousands became U.S. soldiers during the conflict and served around the globe alongside English-speaking troops.

After the war Cajuns spoke English as their primary and often sole language, increased their educational attainment, and embraced the American dream by using new disposable incomes (often generated by the booming southern Louisiana oil industry) to cast off their ancestors' poverty. In the mid- to late 1960s, however, Cajuns emulated other American minorities by embracing a newfound sense of ethnic pride and empowerment. In 1968, for example, they created the Council for the Development of French in Louisiana (CODOFIL), which sought and continues to seek to preserve and promote Cajun culture by integrating French education in public schools.

Once denigrated by outsiders as backward, Cajun culture became fashionable during the 1980s when mainstream Americans "discovered" Cajun food and music. This trend resulted in a deluge of faux Cajun cuisine, not to mention inaccurate and often unflattering portrayals of Cajuns in movies and on television. Yet the same period gave rise to a new respect for Cajuns. Historians, folklorists, and anthropologists legitimized the serious study of Cajun culture, while the federal government recognized the Cajun people as a bona fide ethnic group, a view backed up by geneticists who discovered a telltale Cajun genotype.

[*See also* **Americanization Movement; Assimilation; Multiracial and Multiethnic Americans;** *and* **Race and Ethnicity.**]

BIBLIOGRAPHY

Ancelet, Barry Jean, Jay D. Edwards, and Glen Pitre. *Cajun Country.* Jackson, Miss.: University Press of Mississippi, 1991. An overview of Cajun folk practices; includes chapters on Cajun folk music, folk architecture, and folk medicine, among other related topics.

Faragher, John Mack. *A Great and Noble Scheme: The Tragic Story of the Expulsion of the French Acadians from Their American Homeland.* New York: W. W. Norton and Company, 2005. Presents new findings on the settlement of Acadia and the circumstances of the brutal expulsion.

Shane K. Bernard

CALIFORNIA

With a population of nearly 40 million people living in about 160,000 square miles of territory, California is the nation's most populous state and the third largest in area. The state displays enormous variety in climate and landscape features, from the Mojave Desert in a vast geologic basin in the southeast corner—one of the hottest and driest places on earth—to the Sierra Nevada mountain range cutting through the central two-thirds of the state, to a Pacific coastline that is more than one thousand miles long. California's natural diversity is matched by its intricate human history. The complexity of human experience in what is now California has long drawn the sustained attention of scholars interested in social history.

Eurasian Paleoindians slowly dispersed throughout the region between twelve thousand and thirty thousand years ago, likely crossing into North America over the Bering land bridge (now mostly underwater) during the Pleistocene Ice Age. Debates over the timing, size, origin, and genetic legacies of this migration continue; some scholars believe that seagoing migrants may have arrived earlier than land-bridge travelers. Once in what is now California, Eurasian peoples established complex and highly divergent communities with well over one hundred different languages, differing hunter-gatherer cultures, and various patterns of social organization. Scholars believe that precontact population density in what is now the United States was highest in California.

The Portuguese explorer Juan Rodriguez Cabrillo sailed alongside the southern California coast for the Spanish crown in the mid-sixteenth century. The Englishman Sir Francis Drake may have landed north of present-day San Francisco in 1579. The Franciscan missionary Junípero Serra's string of nearly two dozen missions along the Pacific coast, meant to Catholicize California natives, started with the founding of Mission San Diego in 1769; the mission era, though brief, was of great significance and continues to attract the interest of social historians. With Mexican independence in 1821, California became a possession of Mexico. The Mexican government secularized the missions in the 1830s, theoretically freeing native Californians from coerced attachment to the missions. The cultural, economic, political, and social transitions of the Mexican period are of importance to social historians.

Americans began coming overland to northern California in larger numbers by the early 1840s. Some joined the community surrounding Swiss migrant John Sutter's ranching, farming, and lumber enterprise on the American River in the Sacramento valley. By the mid-1840s, Americans clashed with the dominant ranching class of people of Mexican or Spanish descent, the "Californios." The 1846 Bear Flag Revolt of some of these Americans and their Mexican allies saw the brief establishment of an unrecognized republic in California. The Mexican-American War of 1846–1848 soon followed, with a few scattered clashes in California. The defeat of Mexico resulted in the treaty of Guadalupe Hidalgo, which transferred California and much of the rest of the Southwest to the United States.

Gold Rush and Its Impact. No episode in California history has been the subject of more historical scrutiny than the gold rush. Gold was discovered in January 1848 in John Sutter's millrace by James Marshall, a migrant from the East Coast. The serendipitous event brought the world's attention to California—along with hundreds of thousands of people from across the world. Within a year, miners and merchants, young and old, men (mostly) and women (few) raced as quickly as they could to California, many stopping briefly in the instant city of San Francisco before roaring off to gold country in the northern Sierra Nevada mountains. The gold rush made California known the world over, but the heady days had a downside, including a skewed sex ratio (ten men to every woman in the earliest years of the rush), discriminatory laws regarding foreigners and people of color, and spasmodic violence, rampant loneliness, disease, and death. Nonetheless, the gold rush hastened California's entry into the Union as the thirty-first state in 1850.

With gold and people came urbanization and railroads. California's Central Pacific Railroad, begun in 1863, made a transcontinental linkage in 1869. Nearly all the railroad labor was done by tens of thousands of Chinese immigrants. California's first tourist boom consisted of wealthy visitors eager for California sights and sunshine; tourism continues to be a critical facet of the state's economy. The expanding citrus and real estate economies of the late nineteenth century lured settlers to southern California and provided a capital base for urban and industrial growth. Indeed, the social history of California's transition from its pastoral past to industrial agriculture to urbanized manufacturing reads like a primer of such transitions across the history of the nation. By the 1920s, southern California's oil and film industries had become integral to the economic life of the state.

California has a dark past with regard to discriminatory law and custom. The Foreign Miner's Tax, enacted in the gold rush era, was accompanied by violence toward ethnic groups, particularly Chinese, Mexicans, and Native Americans. Chinese exclusion laws, enacted at the federal level in the 1880s, owed their existence to actions initiated by the California congressional delegation, prompted in turn by decades of discrimination at the grassroots level. The state's 1913 Alien Land Act prohibited noncitizens from owning agricultural land. The Great Depression only exacerbated these tendencies. The novelist John Steinbeck explored the miserable conditions of Central Valley migrant farmworkers in *The Grapes of Wrath* (1939). In and around Los Angeles, hundreds of Mexican and Mexican American workers, most working at low-wage agricultural or industrial jobs, faced forced repatriation to Mexico. African Americans faced discriminatory hiring and labor practices, and statewide restrictive real estate covenants blocked, through both tradition and law, nonwhites from home ownership or residence in many neighborhoods. Wartime California brought further discrimination; most glaring was the internment of more than a hundred thousand Japanese and Japanese Americans, most of whom were native-born American citizens. Mexican Americans and African American men and boys faced the infamous zoot-suit riots in 1940s Los Angeles.

War and Postwar Clout. The state's continuing economic clout dates from growth and diversification undergone during and just after World War II. Relatively small industries before the war, like aircraft manufacturing, exploded into giant economic sectors during the 1940s. The social history of such organizations, from the shop floor to the executive suite, remains generally understudied. An exception is careful studies of the Rosie the Riveter phenomenon: the social history of American women in the wartime workforce is largely understood through reference to California and California women. Less understood is the postwar migration to the far West by servicemen and their families, a demographic expansion that made California subdivisions synonymous with Cold War working- and middle-class prosperity. Soon to be the epicenter of postwar American leisure, Disneyland was founded in 1955 in Anaheim, not far from Los Angeles.

Social historians chart an increasingly conservative electorate in postwar California. Alienated by the countercultural and anti–Vietnam War movements of the 1960s and 1970s, these voters furthered the careers of the Californians Richard M. Nixon and Ronald Reagan. Nixon lost the gubernatorial race in 1962 but ascended to the presidency in 1968. Reagan, a migrant from the Midwest, served two terms as California governor starting in the late 1960s and then two as U.S. president starting in 1980.

The history of late twentieth-century California often tacks toward crisis. The 1965 Watts riots in Los Angeles stunned the nation and foreshadowed similar upheavals across inner-city America. In 1992, after white Los Angeles police officers were acquitted of charges stemming from the beating of a black man named Rodney King, entire neighborhoods of the city and county erupted in spasmodic violence and destruction. Shortly thereafter, world attention was again focused on Los Angeles when the retired professional football player O. J. Simpson, an African American, faced criminal and civil trials for the murder of his former wife and her friend, both of whom were white. Such moments suggest that at the levels of jurisprudence, law enforcement, and everyday life, California acts as a national barometer of potentially explosive issues related to American race relations. The state continues to exhibit time-worn patterns of divisive and controversial legislation. Propositions in the 1990s regarding immigration and affirmative action have become touchstones of support and opposition across the nation; so, too, with the state's topsy-turvy history of acknowledging or blocking the right of same-sex people to marry. California continues to attract millions of tourists and migrants each year.

[*See also* Alcatraz Island, Occupation of (1969); Angel Island Immigration Station; Asian Americans; Chavez, Cesar; Chicano Movement; Chinese Americans; Counterculture; Demography; Disney Amusement Parks; Environmentalism; Franciscans; Gold Rushes; Huerta, Dolores; Internal Migration; Japanese Americans; Los Angeles; Mexican Americans; Migrant Camps, Depression Era; Missions, in America; Riots, Race; Riots, Urban; San Francisco; Southwest, The; Tourism and Travel; West, The; *and* World War II, Home Front.]

BIBLIOGRAPHY

Flamming, Douglas. *Bound for Freedom: Black Los Angeles in Jim Crow America.* Berkeley: University of California Press, 2005.

Gluck, Sherna Berger. *Rosie the Riveter Revisited: Women, the War, and Social Change.* Boston: Twayne, 1987.

Hackel, Steven W. *Children of Coyote, Missionaries of Saint Francis: Indian-Spanish Relations in Colonial California, 1769–1850.* Chapel Hill: University of North Carolina Press, 2005.

HoSang, Daniel Martinez. *Racial Propositions: Ballot Initiatives and the Making of Postwar California.* Berkeley: University of California Press, 2010.

Pubols, Louise. *The Father of All: The de la Guerra Family, Power, and Patriarchy in Mexican California.* Berkeley: University of California Press, 2009.

Rohrbough, Malcolm J. *Days of Gold: The California Gold Rush and the American Nation.* Berkeley: University of California Press, 1997.

Sánchez, George J. *Becoming Mexican American: Ethnicity, Culture, and Identity in Chicano Los Angeles, 1900–1945.* New York: Oxford University Press, 1993.

Starr, Kevin. *Americans and the California Dream, 1850–1915.* New York: Oxford University Press, 1973.

William Deverell

CAPTIVITY NARRATIVES, NATIVE AMERICAN

An archetypal genre recounting an innocent's descent into, and redemption from, an alien world, Native American captivity narratives were uniquely both a product and a representation of the American historical experience. Emerging from real conflicts between indigenous peoples and encroaching Euro-Americans, these narratives also served ideological and political needs. Tropes of captivity already figure in some sixteenth- and seventeenth-century European reports of exploration and discovery, John Smith's recollection of his rescue by Pocahontas among them, but a fully formed, distinctive literary type emerged only in 1682 with the publication of Mary Rowlandson's extremely popular *The Sovereignty and Goodness of God*. A Massachusetts minister's wife, Rowlandson had spent three months among Algonquians during King Philip's War (1675–1676), a conflict that both palsied New England's expansion for a generation and devastated the local tribes. During the next two centuries, Native American captivity narratives gained such regard that many editions have disappeared because they were literally read to pieces.

Captivity narratives ran the gamut from fact to fiction, but the plot remained consistent: the protagonist is ripped from family and friends, is initiated into native society, and becomes ineffably changed. Most returned to their original homes when they could, but a few preferred to "go native," becoming—as did Mary Jemison in James Seaver's exposition of 1824—fully transculturated. Captured by Shawnees at her family's farm in Pennsylvania during the Seven Years' War in 1758, when she was fifteen, Jemison spent most of her long life among the Senecas in New York State, marrying twice, bearing eight children, and rejecting all suggestions of repatriation. Some accounts portrayed Native Americans as kindly people who adopted hostages into their families or as moral paragons who showed up American society's sins, but most depicted them as ignorant, barbaric and devilish, or, at worst, subhumans deserving extirpation.

The captivity narratives' messages changed more than their plots. Self-consciously religious, most of the early tracts exemplified God's providence and believers' faith. Eighteenth-century examples tended toward propaganda in which natives served first as cruel proxies for French or British foes, then as epitomes of evil in their own right. Tendencies toward both sensationalism and sentimentality climaxed in the nineteenth century. Eastern audiences idealized natives as noble relics of a national past now sadly expiring, but westerners, still living under the tomahawk's chop, saw only bloody threats and linked the Native Americans' extermination to America's Manifest Destiny. The genre declined as the 1800s ebbed, its imagery no longer resonant in an urbanizing culture seemingly devoid of aborigines. It did enjoy an afterlife in American popular culture, however, as in Alan Le May's novel *The Searchers* (1954), cinematized by John Ford in 1956 with John Wayne starring as a rancher who searches for his niece, kidnapped by Comanches.

Cogent generalizations about the narratives' authorship are deeply problematic because the issues surrounding their composition and authenticity are so often vexed. That Rowlandson penned her story is unquestionable, but as writers adopted novelistic forms and readers' appetite for gripping tales grew, a host of wholly or partly fictionalized chronicles entered the market. Determining authentic from fictive, fabricated, or romanticized treatments is difficult; for instance, some scholars accept John Dunn Hunter's writings about Plains tribes as wholly credible, while others question whether Hunter really lived and consider the works a hoax. Moreover, a text may be multivocal even if attributed to a single, unimpeachable source; unable to write, Jemison dictated her story to Seaver, who inserted his own perspectives and persona into the published book.

The narratives' highly stereotyped representations of Native Americans reflect Euro-American attitudes toward natives more accurately than they portray frontier life, although; read carefully, they can reveal valuable ethnographic information. They are significant in American literary history as one of the first bodies of writing to feature women, sometimes as authors, most usually as subjects. Focused, as one critic has remarked, on a "domestic drama" of abduction that foregrounds female sentiments and actions, captivity narratives developed a version of America's "rise to greatness" in which women played a major role.

[*See also* Adoption; Colonial Era; Exploration, Conquest, and Settlement in North America; *and* Native American History and Culture, *subentries on* 1500 to 1800 *and* 1800 to 1900.]

BIBLIOGRAPHY

Derounian-Stodola, Kathryn Zabelle, and James Arthur Levernier. *The Indian Captivity Narrative, 1550–1900*. New York: Twayne, 1993.

Namias, June. *White Captives: Gender and Ethnicity on the American Frontier*. Chapel Hill: University of North Carolina Press, 1993.

Sayre, Gordon M., ed. *American Captivity Narratives: Selected Narratives with Introduction*. Boston: Houghton Mifflin, 2000.

Strong, Pauline Turner. "Transforming Outsiders: Captivity, Adoption, and Slavery Reconsidered." In *A Companion to American Indian History*, edited by Philip J. Deloria and Neal Salisbury, pp. 339–356. Malden, Mass.: Blackwell, 2002.

Charles L. Cohen

CARIBBEAN

The archipelago of the Caribbean Sea and several coastal nations in the western Atlantic world are linked culturally through a shared history of economic and social domination by British, French, Spanish, Dutch, and Danish powers. Questions of slavery, emancipation, independence, and migration have sustained uneasy social bonds between the Caribbean and first the British North American colonies and then the United States for some four hundred years. English settlers and enslaved Africans from Barbados were among the first settlers of South Carolina in 1670, the English settlers using their decades of experience in lucrative staple-crop production through human enslavement. Caribbean and North American slave societies emerged with a high ratio of Africans to Europeans, with mixed-race people occupying varied legal status. Most notable was Prince Hall (1738?–1807), born in Barbados and enslaved in Boston, who was refused acceptance within white American Freemasonry after his manumission in 1770. Within a decade Hall established African Freemasonry as a social structure that still bears his name.

During the age of Atlantic revolution that witnessed American and Uruguayan declarations of independence in 1776 and 1825, respectively, the Caribbean staged only one successful revolution. In 1791 a slave and religious leader named Boukman (d. 1791) in the French colony Saint-Domingue inspired enslaved Africans to revolt against slaveholders. The island's white and mulatto war refugees brought the openness of Caribbean interracial relationships to the streets of North American cities, where transracial intercourse remained prevalent but private. The revolutionary leader Toussaint Louverture (c. 1743–1803) secured universal emancipation, and the island was declared independent under its Arawak name "Haiti" in 1804. The Haitian revolution sparked a short-lived emigration movement among Africans from the United States to Haiti and inspired black slave rebellions across the Caribbean and the United States in the early nineteenth century. Britain and France abolished slavery throughout their colonies in 1834 and 1848, respectively. Caribbean emancipation intensified the U.S. slavery debate, with the lack of avenging violence emboldening abolitionists and the economic failure of the system of nonslave labor strengthening proslavery arguments. In 1863, Dutch colonies and the United States abolished slavery.

Postemancipation migrations from the Caribbean pushed the number of U.S. residents of Caribbean derivation to more than three hundred thousand by the 1920s, just as the Great Migration brought millions of rural African Americans to northern cities. These increased numbers of black people sought greater inclusion in American society. The Jamaican Marcus Garvey (1887–1940) and his Universal Negro Improvement Association (UNIA) linked struggles for black equality across the Atlantic. The Harlem Renaissance of the 1920s and 1930s, fueled in part by the writings of Hubert Harrison (1883–1927), who was born in the Danish West Indies, and the Jamaican American poet Claude McKay (1889–1948), redefined black art and culture within American society around the same time that Martinique's Aimé Césaire (1913–2008) pioneered *négritude* as a literary rebuttal to white racism. Shared ideas about equality gave way to the American Civil Rights Movement and Caribbean independence in the 1960s. Post-1965 changes to U.S. immigration laws encouraged millions of Caribbean immigrants to pursue impressive educational and economic strides within the United States. Some historians and sociologists point to Caribbean social advances beyond those of African Americans as a breach in the twentieth century's earlier diaspora unity.

[*See also* **African American Emigration; African Americans; Atlantic World; Cuban Americans; Dominican Republic Americans; Emancipation of Slaves; Haitian Americans; Immigration; Internal Migration,** *subentry on* **African Americans; Maroon Societies; Masonic Order; Puerto Rican Americans; Slave Rebellions; Slavery,** *subentry on* **Colonial and Revolutionary Era; Slave Trades;** *and* **West Indian Americans.**]

BIBLIOGRAPHY

James, Winston. "Explaining Afro-Caribbean Social Mobility in the United States: Beyond the Sowell Thesis." *Comparative Studies in Society and History* 44 (2002): 218–262.

Moya Pons, Frank. *History of the Caribbean: Plantations, Trade, and War in the Atlantic World.* Princeton, N.J.: Markus Wiener, 2007.

Ronald Angelo Johnson

CARMICHAEL, STOKELY

(1941–1998), civil rights activist. Stokely Standiford Churchill Carmichael was born on 29 June 1941 in Port of Spain, Trinidad, to Adolphus and Mabel Charles Carmichael. By 1952 the Carmichael family, which now included Stokely and his four sisters, moved to the Bronx, New York. In 1956, Carmichael enrolled at the prestigious Bronx High School of Science, one of New York's best public schools. As a teenager he participated in radical study groups and, under the tutelage of Bayard Rustin, the nation's leading black social democrat, helped organize garment workers. He imbibed black history and culture through visits to Harlem to see relatives and listen to street speakers along the neighborhood's famous 125th Street corridor.

In 1960, Carmichael enrolled at Howard University in Washington, D.C., where he joined the Nonviolent Action Group (NAG), a campus affiliate of the Student Nonviolent Coordinating Committee (SNCC). Perhaps the most important grassroots organization of the civil rights era, SNCC was born in the wake of that year's nationwide sit-in movement. At Howard, Carmichael organized protests and sit-ins in Baltimore and Washington, and in 1961 he participated in the Freedom Rides. It was as a rider that he endured his first arrest, in Jackson, Mississippi, after which he spent more than a month at the infamous Parchman prison.

After graduating from Howard in 1964, Carmichael turned to full-time organizing and became project director for the Second Congressional District, in Lowndes County, Alabama, during the voter-registration campaign known as Freedom Summer. After the Mississippi Freedom Democratic Party's failure to unseat the state's all-white delegates at the Democratic National Convention in Atlantic City, New Jersey, in 1964, Carmichael vowed to organize independent political parties. In 1965–1966, Carmichael and SNCC workers helped to organize a third political party for blacks in Lowndes County; it came to be known by its symbol: the black panther.

On 16 June 1966, Carmichael, now chairman of SNCC, unleashed the slogan "Black Power" during the Meredith March against Fear in Mississippi, the last great march of the civil rights era. Black Power caused instant controversy, and Martin Luther King Jr., who considered Carmichael a friend, distanced himself from the slogan. Over the next two and a half years, Carmichael became Black Power's most visible face, and he took over Malcolm X's role as King's public counterpoint. Carmichael defined Black Power as a movement for social, political, economic, and cultural determination, a message that he spread around the world through hundreds of speeches, television interviews, and a bestselling book.

His high profile triggered intense surveillance from various federal and international intelligence agencies, including the Federal Bureau of Investigation. By 1969, Carmichael moved to Conakry, Guinea, with his new wife, Miriam Makeba, to begin a new life as a Pan-African revolutionary.

By 1979, Carmichael was the leader of the All African Peoples Revolutionary Party and had changed his name to Kwame Ture, in honor of his two African mentors: Kwame Nkrumah, the president of Ghana and Ahmed Sékou Touré, the president of Guinea and one of the world's best-known Pan-Africanists. During the course of his almost thirty years in Africa, Carmichael frequently returned to the United States for fund-raising tours. In 1996 he was diagnosed with terminal prostate cancer; he died two years later, on 15 November 1998, in Conakry.

[*See also* **Black Nationalism; Black Panthers; Civil Rights Movement;** *and* **Student Nonviolent Coordinating Committee.**]

BIBLIOGRAPHY

Carmichael, Stokely, and Charles V. Hamilton. *Black Power: The Politics of Liberation in America.* New York: Random House, 1967.

Carmichael, Stokely, with Ekwueme Michael Thelwell. *Ready for Revolution: The Life and Struggle of Stokely Carmichael (Kwame Ture).* New York: Scribner, 2003.

Joseph, Peniel E. *Waiting 'til the Midnight Hour: A Narrative History of Black Power in America.* New York: Henry Holt, 2006.

Peniel E. Joseph

CATT, CARRIE CHAPMAN

(1859–1947), woman suffrage leader. Born in Wisconsin and reared mostly in Iowa,

Catt by the early 1880s was already a widely traveled suffragist. By the late 1880s, recognized as a tireless campaigner, keen strategist, and skilled political tactician, she was a major figure in the National American Woman Suffrage Association (NAWSA). Succeeding Susan B. Anthony as the head of NAWSA, she served from 1900 to 1904 and again in 1915–1920, a period that brought victory in New York State in 1917 and final ratification of the Nineteenth Amendment (granting woman suffrage) in 1920. A single-minded, disciplined leader who considered herself a political realist, Catt employed whatever strategies she believed necessary, including placating white racists in the South. While supporting U.S. involvement in World War I, she always kept the suffrage goal paramount.

In 1919–1920, Catt helped launch the League of Women Voters, to enable newly enfranchised women to exert real political influence. She envisioned the league as a nonpartisan organization that would promote a different politics from the partisan struggle she had come to detest. Catt became active in the international peace movement before and after World War I, but world peace proved a more elusive goal than woman suffrage.

Catt was twice widowed; the 1905 death of her second husband, a successful civil engineer, left her financially independent. In her later years she cultivated close personal relationships with many women. Childless, she nurtured friendships as she had earlier honed her skills at devising the political strategies that made women's suffrage a reality.

[*See also* **Woman Suffrage Movement.**]

BIBLIOGRAPHY

Fowler, Robert Booth. *Carrie Catt: Feminist Politician.* Boston: Northeastern University Press, 1986.

Robert Booth Fowler

CENTRAL AMERICAN AMERICANS

Despite its linguistic awkwardness, "Central American American" is an increasingly accepted term for both Central American–born people living in the United States and those born in the United States who claim Central American ancestry as a result of family ties. Maya Chinchilla's 1999 poem about "life on the hyphen," about feeling a connection to "over there" while living "over here"—that is, in the U.S. diaspora—has played an important role in popularizing the term.

Makeup. As a social group, Central American Americans are as diverse as the Central American region itself, defined here as Guatemala, El Salvador, Honduras, Belize, Nicaragua, Costa Rica, and Panama. They include both immigrants and those born in the United States; both those with "legal" or "authorized" status (permanent residents, citizens, people granted temporary protected or refugee status, and so on) and those who are "undocumented" or "unauthorized"; both those who live in crowded rented apartments and those who own their own homes; and both those who are better educated and earn a comfortable income (Nicaraguans and Costa Ricans, for example) and those who have less education and disproportionately populate the ranks of the working poor.

Central American Americans are also diverse in terms of their racial or ethnic backgrounds, including people whose background is European, indigenous (Mayan, Garifuna, Miskito, and so on), African, mestizo, and mulatto, as well as a multitude of racial or ethnic mixtures. Important minority racial or ethnic Central American American subgroups that struggle to preserve their traditional cultures and languages in the face of discrimination and pressures to assimilate include the indigenous Mayans who come from highland villages of Guatemala and settle primarily in Los Angeles, Houston, Florida, and North Carolina and the Garifuna (descendants of Carib, Arawak, and West African people) who come from the Caribbean coasts of Belize, Guatemala, Nicaragua, and Honduras and settle primarily in New York City, Los Angeles, and Miami.

Salvadorans and Guatemalans are the largest national-origin groups among Central American Americans, constituting 62 percent of the total. After Mexicans and Puerto Ricans, Salvadorans are the third-largest U.S. Hispanic group (1,736,221, or 3.6 percent of the total), and Guatemalans are the sixth-largest such group (1,077,412, or 2.2 percent of the total), just below Dominicans. Hondurans, one of the most rapidly growing so-called new Latino groups, are the only other U.S. Central American–origin group of any significant size (624,533).

Catholicism remains the predominant religious affiliation of most Central American Americans, but since the later twentieth century, Protestant evangelical and Pentecostal groups have won many converts. Other denominations and religious traditions such as Mayan, Mormon, Jehovah's Witness, Seventh-Day Adventist, and Baptist have also gained adherents.

Though some regional clusters of Central Americans have been in the United States for generations—for example, Salvadorans in San Francisco, Guatemalans in Los Angeles, and Hondurans in New Orleans—the majority in each national subgroup are relative newcomers. More Hondurans (69 percent), Guatemalans (68 percent), and Salvadorans (63 percent) are foreign-born than is true in the overall Hispanic population (37 percent), and more of the Central American foreign-born are recent arrivals, with 78 percent of

Hondurans, 73 percent of Guatemalans, and 62 percent of Salvadorans having arrived in 1990 or later, compared to 23 percent of the overall Hispanic population.

Push and Pull. Since the 1980s the conditions pushing Central American emigrants out of their home countries and pulling them to the United States have also varied widely. Some, particularly Guatemalans, Salvadorans, and Nicaraguans, fled war and political upheavals in the late 1970s and 1980s—the Sandinista revolution and the Contra War in Nicaragua and the armed insurgencies in Guatemala and El Salvador prior to the peace accords in the early 1990s—some fled the devastation of earthquakes, hurricanes, and other environmental disasters, and some chose to migrate as a way to improve their economic opportunities or out of a desire to reunify with family members. On average, Central American–born migrants to the United States are better-educated, healthier, and younger than their nonmigrant counterparts are, and they are younger than the overall U.S. Hispanic population.

In contrast to Mexicans, women constituted more than half of the immigrants from each of the seven Central American countries prior to 1980. Among those who came in the five-year period before the 1980 U.S. Census (1975–1980), women from Panama (59.9 percent), Nicaragua (58.3 percent), and Honduras (58.4 percent) constituted the largest proportions of their national groups. At the time of the 1990 U.S. Census, Panamanian, Honduran, Costa Rican, and Belizean women were still half or more of their respective immigrant populations. By the 2000 U.S. Census, the absolute numbers of women immigrating were still high, but the upsurge in male migration from Guatemala, Honduras, and El Salvador meant that the proportion of women had dropped to 36.3 percent for Guatemala and 44.0 percent for El Salvador and Nicaragua.

The dominance of women in Central American immigration flows prior to the 1980s was caused by a combination of U.S. demand for their labor and factors in Central America that increased the pool of available and willing female workers. Female migrants from Central America helped to fill a growing demand for nannies, housekeepers, and eldercare workers (especially as live-ins), as well as a demand for workers in building maintenance and food service in the expanding economies of global cities such as Los Angeles. In certain regions of the United States, higher-educated women from Nicaragua and Costa Rica helped to fill a demand for Spanish-speaking office workers and professionals, or in the global cities they expanded the rapidly growing ranks of immigrant entrepreneurs that complement the growth of the industrial and financial sectors. An increasing need in Central America for married women with children to contribute economically to household incomes, combined with the difficulty of earning good wages because of gender discrimination, increased the pool of women workers available for migration in the 1960s, 1970s, and 1980s.

Central American Americans have challenges and issues similar to those of other immigrant, ethnic, and working- or middle-class groups: expanding educational and economic opportunity, getting credit for home mortgages and businesses, keeping their neighborhoods secure, and so on. But the future is cloudy for a very large number of immigrant Central Americans who desire to legalize their status and eventually become citizens but who are blocked under the late twentieth and early twenty-first-century patchwork of contradictory and outdated U.S. immigration policies. Not only do the undocumented immigrants themselves suffer from these policies, but their citizen children and other family members suffer, too. Communities with a large number of undocumented residents also suffer from a lack of full civic engagement by residents who may have deep roots but lack a path to legalization. The passage of a pragmatic, comprehensive reform of U.S. immigration policies would have a significant positive effect on the well-being of the Central American American community and on its ability to contribute to the future of the United States.

[See also Caribbean; Demography; Immigration; Race and Ethnicity; and Transnational Identity.]

BIBLIOGRAPHY

Chinchilla, Maya. "Central American American." *La Revista*, University of California, Santa Cruz, 1999.

Dockterman, Daniel. *Hispanics in the United States: Country of Origin Profiles*. Pew Hispanic Center Report. Washington, D.C.: Pew Hispanic Center of the Pew Charitable Trusts, 26 May 2011.

Fix, Michael, and Wendy Zimmermann. "All under One Roof: Mixed-Status Families in an Era of Reform." International Migration Review 35, no. 2 (2001): 397–419.

Fry, Richard. "Gender and Migration." Pew Hispanic Center Report, 5 July 2006. http://pewhispanic.org/files/reports/64.pdf.

Suro, Roberto. "Counting the 'Other Hispanics': How Many Colombians, Dominicans, Ecuadorians, Guatemalans, Salvadorans Are There in the United States?" Pew Hispanic Center Study, 9 May 2002. http://pewhispanic.org/files/reports/8.pdf.

Terrazas, Aaron. "Central American Immigrants in the United States." Migration Information Source, January 2011. http://www.migrationinformation.org/usfocus/display.cfm?ID=821.

Norma Stoltz Chinchilla

CENTRAL AND EASTERN EUROPEAN AMERICANS

Central and eastern Europeans in the United States make up dozens of different ethnic groups, each with a unique history and experience that cannot be easily generalized. Although the largest waves of immigrants came during the years 1880 to 1924, eastern and central Europeans were present in America since colonial times and continue to come to America in the twenty-first century.

Eastern and central Europe is a highly diverse region. The majority of the immigrants to America have been Slavs: Poles, Czechs, Slovaks, Sorbs (Wends), Ukrainians, Russians, Belarusians, Carpatho-Rusyns, Croatians, Slovenes, Serbs, Bosnians, Macedonians, and Bulgarians. In addition are Balts (Latvians and Lithuanians), Magyars (Hungarians), Estonians, Romanians, and Albanians. Minorities include ethnic Germans, Jews, and Romanies (Gypsies), Armenians, Vlachs, Tatars, and Karaites. This tally does not even begin to account for local and regional identities and religious minorities, like Old Believers or Mariavites. By the early twenty-first century the largest of these groups in America were the Poles (9 million), Jews (5 to 6 million), and Hungarians (1 to 2 million).

First Communities. Scattered individuals began arriving in North America as early as the 1600s. Longer and more permanent migrations to the Americas originated on the western edges of eastern Europe. Czechs, Sorbs, and Poles followed Germans to the New World in the 1850s. Significant economic emigration from eastern Europe began in the 1870s and 1880s. Although settler migrants with families predominated in the earliest stages, a different pattern emerged by the 1880s and 1890s

as ever more massive waves of people left eastern Europe. The new immigrants traveled individually, pursuing short-term goals of making as much money as possible to bolster the family economic situation. Return migration was common.

In the United States, communities of eastern European immigrants first emerged in midwestern agricultural areas and around extractive industries. Changes in industrial practice raised the demand for unskilled and semiskilled labor, so that between 1890 and 1914, eastern Europeans, especially those from Austria-Hungary and Russia, came into the United States in unprecedented numbers, dominating the immigrant flow and contributing to the largest per capita influx yet recorded in U.S. history. In 1870, for example, there were fifty thousand Poles in the United States. By 1880 that number had grown to half a million, by 1890 it had doubled to a million, by 1900 it had doubled again, and by 1910 it was 3 million. The entry of so many eastern European immigrants into the nation's industrial life put them at the forefront of struggles over worker's rights. Eastern European immigrants received the lowest pay and the most dangerous jobs. Accidents were common and often fatal. Pay cuts and mass firings struck at the basis of immigrants' goals and economic strategies. Thus eastern European immigrants engaged in a series of intense labor struggles from the 1880s to the 1930s. Most were conducted with little support from established unions. By the 1930s, eastern Europeans were a dominant presence in many heavy industries. Their mass movement of the 1930s, which was harnessed by the leadership of such new unions as the Congress of Industrial Organizations, the United Mine Workers of America, and the United Auto Workers, brought major changes in the treatment of all workers.

This result was not achieved easily, and eastern Europeans were often victims of bloody reprisals by police and company thugs. The attack on striking canal workers in Lamont, Illinois, in 1893 and the attack on striking coal miners in Lattimer, Pennsylvania, in 1897 were the most notable of these tragedies. Support for violence against eastern Europeans was common. During a strike by Polish workers at an oil refinery in Bayonne, New Jersey, in 1915, a company executive said: "Get me 250 husky men who can swing clubs. . . . I want them to march up East Twenty-second street through the guts of Polacks" (James S. Pula, *The Polish Americans: An Ethnic Community* [New York: Twayne, 1995], p. 51). Such sentiments were supported by America's Progressive elite, which saw eastern and southern European immigrants as culturally and racially inferior. In an 1891 article titled "Immigration and Degradation," the president of the Massachusetts Institute of Technology, Francis Amasa Walker, described eastern Europeans as miserable, corrupt, abject, and worthless, "representing the utterest failures of civilization, the worst defeats in the struggle for existence, the lowest degradation of human nature" (*Forum* 11 [1891]: 644).

While the mainstream society looked down on the eastern Europeans, these immigrants were developing their own intense community and cultural life. Immigrant newspapers flourished. Some were ephemeral, but others became well-established: the Polish-language daily *Ameryka-echo* of Toledo, Ohio, for example, achieved a national circulation of more than one hundred thousand. Several newspapers founded in the 1880s or 1890s continued to publish in the twenty-first century. Immigrant publishing houses also flourished, producing reprints of classics and works by immigrant authors in inexpensive paperbound formats. By the 1920s eastern European Americans had begun record companies, film

and theater companies, and radio stations. Nearly every local community, school, fraternal lodge, parish, congregation, or political party sponsored amateur productions. Similar vitality was found in music, art, and architecture. The Czech composer Antonín Dvořák found a welcoming climate among his immigrant compatriots when he visited the United States, where he wrote his symphony titled *From the New World* (1893).

Immigrant community life arose within the confines of urban neighborhoods and rural enclaves. The center of such communities was almost always a parish church. Although they performed a vital religious function, they were also community social halls, social-service agencies, and cultural centers.

Twentieth Century and Beyond. After 1924, when the United States enacted restrictions on immigration from eastern Europe, a cultural change took hold. The creation of new nations in Europe—Poland, Czechoslovakia, Yugoslavia, the Baltic states—meant independent homelands. Despite some initial enthusiasm for return migration, most immigrants decided to stay in America. The interwar years brought new cultural forms to eastern European ethnic communities as ethnic media adapted to new technology and styles. Second-generation young people embraced the new styles and movements of the Jazz Age and in so doing helped introduce new cultural forms to the mainstream. At the same time, they actively participated in the creation and recreation of unique, hybrid ethnic cultures that combined elements of the cultures of both America and the old country.

Significant new immigration from the region did not occur until after World War II. The destruction of the war, the Holocaust and other genocides, the huge number of displaced persons, and the Soviet takeover of the region impelled the United States to admit many refugees and other displaced persons. Large numbers of Jews, Poles, Ukrainians, and others arrived in the late 1940s and early 1950s. Following the 1956 Hungarian revolution, some sixty thousand Hungarian refugees were admitted. After the lifting of immigration restrictions in 1965, growing numbers of eastern European immigrants came to America. Some came under the auspices of reuniting families; others fled political repression. After the imposition of martial law in Poland in 1981, more than thirty-four thousand Polish refugees were admitted. By the end of the 1980s, as Communist rule decayed and then collapsed, more and more eastern Europeans arrived. Cities such as New York, Chicago, Detroit, Los Angeles, and San Francisco have seen the largest influxes. In the early twenty-first century, Poles continued to be the largest of these groups, along with Russians and Ukrainians. Since the 1990s conflicts in the Balkans, increasing numbers of Bosnians, Croatians, and Albanians have immigrated.

Since the early twentieth century, academic and media pundits have frequently predicted the demise of many eastern European American ethnic communities. Yet this has failed to occur. Although the nature and meaning of eastern European ethnicity has changed significantly since the first immigrants arrived in America, these diverse communities continue to be a vital component of a multicultural nation.

[*See also* **Immigration; Jewish Americans; Labor Movements;** *and* **Race and Ethnicity.**]

BIBLIOGRAPHY

Bukowczyk, John J. *A History of the Polish Americans.* Rev. ed. New Brunswick, N.J.: Transaction, 2008.

Kuropas, Myron B. *Ukrainian Americans: Roots and Aspirations, 1884–1954.* Toronto: University of Toronto Press, 1991.

Pula, James S. *Polish Americans: An Ethnic Community.* New York: Twayne, 1995.

Radzilowski. John. *The Eagle and the Cross: A History of the Polish Roman Catholic Union of America, 1873–2000.* Boulder, Colo.: East European Monographs, 2003.

John Radzilowski

CHARITY ORGANIZATION MOVEMENT

The charity organization movement was a late nineteenth-century philanthropic reform that sought to bring rich and poor together even as the forces of immigration, industrialization, and urbanization drove them apart. Beginning in England in 1869, the movement quickly crossed the Atlantic and established a beachhead in numerous American cities with the formation of local charity organization societies. The practitioners of charity organization tack led poverty by making charity more professional, efficient, and "scientific," while retaining the humanitarian basis by recruiting "friendly visitors." These trained charity workers, usually female, pioneered the case method of social work. The methods of scientific charity—organization, coordination, and investigation—brought private resources to bear upon the lives of the urban poor. With its network of local societies, the charity organization movement soon established influential journals, participated actively in the National Conference of Charities and Corrections, and in 1898 established the first professional training school for social work: the New York School of Philanthropy. These elements provided the basis for twentieth-century approaches to poverty and dependency.

The American charity organization movement drew ideological nourishment from many sources, including English poor-law reform, Puritan ideology, social Darwinism, and liberal Christian philanthropy as embodied in the Social Gospel. According to the movement's leaders, the aim of charity was not primarily to assuage suffering but rather to uplift and transform the recipients into productive and independent members of society. As the movement progressed, women played an important role as leaders and workers. In the 1880s and 1890s, Josephine Shaw Lowell (1843–1905) of New York and Annie Adams Fields (1834–1915) of Boston moved their organizations from repressive measures to more positive programs stressing environmental conditions. After the devastating depression of 1893–1896, a new generation of leaders such as Edward T. Devine (1867–1948) of New York and Mary Richmond (1861–1928) of Baltimore promoted innovations that ensured the continued influence of charity organization ideas and practices in the twentieth century.

Charity organization had numerous critics, including ministers and settlement-house workers who chastised it for being all head and no heart. Historians who view the movement as little more than a handmaiden to industrial capitalism, however, ignore its role in initiating such reforms as tenement-house regulation and tuberculosis-prevention programs. Charity organization's greatest legacy was in facilitating the move from volunteerism to professional social work. The movement outlived its usefulness by the 1920s, as government agencies took over many of its most successful programs. The Great Depression of the 1930s brought a massive federal presence in areas previously dominated by private charities.

[*See also* **Gilded Age; Philanthropy; Poverty; Progressive Era; Settlement Houses; Social Work;** *and* **Welfare.**]

BIBLIOGRAPHY

Katz, Michael B. *In the Shadow of the Poorhouse: A Social History of Welfare in America.* New York: Basic Books, 1986.

Watson, Frank Dekker. *The Charity Organization Movement in the United States: A Study in American Philanthropy.* New York: Macmillan, 1922.

Waugh, Joan. *Unsentimental Reformer: The Life of Josephine Shaw Lowell.* Cambridge, Mass.: Harvard University Press, 1997.

Joan Waugh

CHAUTAUQUA MOVEMENT

The Chautauqua movement occupies an important niche in American social and cultural history. Chautauqua's cofounder, a southern-born Methodist Episcopal minister (and later bishop) named John Heyl Vincent, began his career as a hellfire-and-brimstone preacher on the Methodist circuit in the 1850s. In 1873, Vincent, then living in Chicago, joined forces with Lewis Miller, a wealthy manufacturer of farm implements from Akron, Ohio, to find suitable headquarters for a national training center for Sunday-school teachers. They settled on Fair Point, a Methodist camp meeting on the shores of Chautauqua Lake in far western New York State. The following year, Vincent and Miller opened Fair Point's doors to both serious students and fun-seeking vacationers, thus transforming it into a semipublic, ecumenical institute and vacation retreat.

By the 1880s, Chautauqua had evolved into a national movement. Its eight-week summer program combined Bible study with classes in science, history, literature, and the arts. Through correspondence courses, journals like the *Chautauquan*, and especially reading circles, Chautauqua's influence spread far beyond its campus boundaries. In 1878, Vincent inaugurated the Chautauqua Literary and Scientific Circle (CLSC). By century's end, 264,000 people—at least three-quarters of them women—had enrolled in the CLSC. Students completing the four-year reading program received official (if symbolic) diplomas. Many CLSC women worked to establish independent Chautauqua assemblies in their own communities. By 1900, nearly one hundred towns, mainly in the Midwest, held assemblies on grounds patterned after those of the original Chautauqua.

Chautauqua's relevance in national cultural and political life peaked in the Progressive Era. Speakers espousing laws for compulsory education, environmental sanitation, and improved factory safety found a receptive audience at Chautauqua assemblies. William Jennings Bryan was the movement's star orator. The New Dealer Rexford Tugwell, whose mother was an avid Chautauquan, said: "Even a mild sort of socialism was given a hearing in the literature going out to the Reading Circles." By the early 1900s the Chautauqua movement—originally founded for sacred purposes—had reinvented itself along secular lines.

However, the Chautauqua movement soon fell victim to its own success. It struggled to compete with imitators, such as the mobile "tent" Chautauquas, or circuits, that debuted in 1904. Circuit Chautauquas brought edifying fare to thousands of communities across the nation. Competition from the circuits forced independent assemblies to hire lecture bureaus to handle their programming, hastening their decline. Educational fare gave way to sentimental plays, inspirational speakers, and "animal and bird educators"—that is, pet tricks.

By the 1920s, Chautauqua's model of self-culture was indistinguishable from that provided by the other purveyors of democratic citizenship and middle-brow culture, including museums, free libraries, book-of-the-month clubs, university extension divisions, and municipally sponsored lectures. The rise of commercial radio, movies, amusement parks, and automobiles signaled the end of the circuits' popularity as a tourist destination. The last tent show folded in 1933. Nevertheless, in the twenty-first century the original "mother Chautauqua" in western New York was more popular than ever and continued to offer an edifying vacation for those who could afford its steep lodging costs and gate fees.

[*See also* **Education; Learned Societies; Libraries; Progressive Era;** *and* **Tourism and Travel.**]

BIBLIOGRAPHY

Canning, Charlotte M. *The Most American Thing in America: Circuit Chautauqua as Performance.* Iowa City: University of Iowa Press, 2005.

Halgren Kilde, Jeanne. "The 'Predominance of the Feminine' at Chautauqua: Rethinking the Gender-Space Relationship in Victorian America." *Signs* 24, no. 2 (Winter 1999): 449–486.

Rieser, Andrew C. *The Chautauqua Moment: Protestants, Progressives, and the Culture of Modern Liberalism.* New York: Columbia University Press, 2003.

Trachtenberg, Alan. "'We Study the Word and Works of God': Chautauqua and the Sacralization of American Culture." *Henry Ford Museum and Greenfield Village Herald* 13, no. 2 (1984): 3–11.

Andrew C. Rieser

CHAVEZ, CESAR

(1927–1993), labor activist and founder and president of the United Farm Workers of America. Chavez spent his early childhood on his grandfather's homestead near Yuma, Arizona. After losing the farm in the late

1930s, the Chavez family joined California's migratory farm-labor force. Following military service, Chavez in 1945 resumed work as a farm laborer in California. After marrying in 1948, Chavez and his family relocated to San Jose's notorious barrio known as Sal Si Puedes (literally, "get out if you can"). Becoming involved in Mexican American political and social action, Chavez established the National Farm Workers Association in Delano, California, in 1962; it was rechristened the United Farm Workers Organizing Committee in 1966 and the United Farm Workers of America (UFW) in 1972. His new union gained prominence in 1965 when, together with a union of Filipino farmworkers backed by the AFL-CIO, it embarked on a campaign to organize growers of table grapes in California. The five-year campaign became a cause célèbre in the United States and abroad, bringing Chavez to national and international prominence.

Chavez's approach to worker activism sought social and racial justice and employed not only strikes and boycotts but also mass marches, fasts, and nonviolent civil disobedience. He won a fiercely dedicated following of young Chicano and Anglo organizers and the support of Hollywood celebrities, political luminaries, and social reformers. Unprecedented union victories against leading wineries and table-grape producers caused antiunion employers, in collusion with the Teamsters, to block Chavez's further advance. In response, Chavez turned to political action. In 1975, with the help of a sympathetic liberal governor, Chavez won passage of the California Agricultural Labor Relations Act, which granted the state's farmworkers the organizing rights long denied them under federal law. By the late 1970s the UFW's membership approached fifty thousand. By the early 1980s, however, employer opposition, surplus labor, and internal dissension diluted

most of the UFW's earlier gains. Increasingly insular and eccentric, Chavez invested the UFW's dwindling resources in ineffectual boycotts and direct-mail fund-raising efforts. He nevertheless ranks as the most influential Mexican American leader of his generation and arguably the most important in the nation's history.

[*See also* California; Community Organizing; Huerta, Dolores; Labor Movements; Mexican American Civil Rights Movement; Mexican Americans; Strikes and Industrial Conflict; *and* United Farm Workers of America.]

BIBLIOGRAPHY

Griswold del Castillo, Richard, and Richard A. Garcia. *César Chávez: A Triumph of Spirit.* Norman: University of Oklahoma Press, 1995.
Levy, Jacques E. *Cesar Chavez: Autobiography of La Causa.* New York: W. W. Norton and Company, 1975.

Cletus Daniel

CHICAGO

Founded in 1833 on Lake Michigan's swampy shores, Chicago rebounded from a devastating 1871 fire to reach more than a million residents by 1890. It was for decades the nation's second-largest metropolis (now third, behind New York City and Los Angeles). Long a railroad hub, Chicago boasts one of the world's busier airports, O'Hare International. For much of the late twentieth century, it hosted the world's (formerly) tallest structure, the Sears (since 2009, Willis) Tower. Chicago also developed an extensive park system along the Lake Michigan waterfront and throughout its neighborhoods.

Historically a meatpacking and heavy-industry powerhouse, late nineteenth-century Chicago was, as Carl Sandburg put it, "hog butcher for the world," a major manufacturing and printing center, and home to the retailing giants Sears, Roebuck and Montgomery Ward. The early social elite—men such as the meatpacker Philip Armour, the retailer Marshall Field, the hotelier and retailer Potter Palmer, and the industrialist George Pullman—inhabited a far different world from that of the immigrants portrayed in William Stead's *If Christ Came to* Chicago (1894) and Upton Sinclair's *The Jungle* (1906). Gilded Age Chicago was a hotbed of unionism and radical activism, epitomized by the Haymarket affair (1886) and the Pullman strike (1894). The Progressive Era reformer John Dewey and the revivalist Dwight L. Moody also shaped Chicago's culture, while Jane Addams established a new settlement house model; her Hull-House pioneered the link between academic research and social activism.

Generations of immigrants did the city's work: first Irish, Germans, Italians, Poles, and others from eastern Europe, and later, Mexicans, Puerto Ricans, and Asians. From the Reconstruction Era on, thousands of African Americans also migrated to Chicago. Each new group found its own patch of the city and tried to protect it. The Irish, Italians, and Poles built independent Catholic parishes and a completely separate school system, and violence often marked interactions between various ethnic and racial groups. A 1919 race riot, started at a swimming beach, echoed again in the racial unrest of the mid-1960s when living conditions for African Americans languished behind those of other groups. The lawlessness of the gangster Al Capone during Prohibition epitomized the contrast between Chicago's neighborhood life and the sometimes violent intrusion of larger social and political realities. So did, later, the raw violence of the 1968 Democratic National Convention, which displayed local social tensions on national television.

All the migrant and immigrant groups helped define the self-contained character of the city's neighborhoods, each with its distinctive ethnic, religious, and cultural institutions. Most neighborhoods had commercial cores at streetcar intersections, with ornate movie theaters and abundant local commerce. After 1900, Chicago's neighborhoods boasted a distinctive look: brick bungalows and flats, and large masonry courtyard apartments. Midcentury white flight to the suburbs paralleled a post-1950s surge in the minority population, as misconceived efforts at urban renewal produced high-rise (and often high-crime) housing projects such as the now-demolished Robert Taylor Homes and Cabrini-Green.

Known for brash politics, Chicago produced one of the nation's most durable political machines, extending through the mayoralties of the Republican William Hale "Big Bill" Thompson (1915–1923, 1928–1932) and the Democrats Anton Cermak (1931–1933) and Richard J. Daley (1955–1976). In 1983, Harold Washington (1922–1987) became the city's first black mayor. Facing widespread industrial decline, Richard M. Daley (mayor 1989–2011) helmed Chicago's transformation to a service economy, and he also championed a series of "green" projects, epitomized by the lakefront Millennium Park.

Chicago has a broad and diverse cultural scene. Its musical culture extends from jazz and blues clubs to the Chicago Symphony and the Lyric Opera. The Art Institute leads a broad array of cultural institutions. Chicago produced such diverse writers as Theodore Dreiser, Sherwood Anderson, Harriet Monroe, Richard Wright, Saul Bellow, and Studs Terkel. Professional baseball, football, and basketball teams vie for Chicagoans' loyalty. Like other major cities, Chicago lost population after 1960, only to start growing again by 2000, and also to become younger. In the twenty-first century Chicago mirrors America's diversity, with whites, blacks, and Hispanics each making up a quarter of the city's population. "Chicagoland"—the larger metropolitan area beyond the city limits—has also grown dramatically, with seven Illinois counties spreading toward Wisconsin and Indiana.

[*See also* Chicago Fire; Cities and Suburbs; Housing, Public; Immigration; Riots, Race; Riots, Urban; Slums; Strikes and Industrial Conflict; *and* Urban Renewal.]

BIBLIOGRAPHY

Clavel, Pierre. *Activists in City Hall: The Progressive Response to the Reagan Era in Boston and Chicago*. Ithaca, N.Y.: Cornell University Press, 2010.

Cronon, William. *Nature's Metropolis: Chicago and the Great West*. New York: W. W. Norton and Company, 1991.

Pacyga, Dominic A. *Chicago: A Biography*. Chicago: University of Chicago Press, 2009.

Venkatesh, Sudhir Alladi. *Gang Leader for a Day: A Rogue Sociologist Takes to the Streets*. New York: Penguin, 2008.

Wilson, William Julius. *When Work Disappears: The World of the New Urban Poor*. New York: Alfred A. Knopf, 1996.

Judith A. Martin

CHICAGO FIRE

The Chicago fire of 8–10 October 1871 is perhaps the most famous urban disaster in American history. Its exact cause is unknown, notwithstanding the legend that it was started by Mrs. Catherine O'Leary's cow kicking over a lantern. Whatever the conflagration's origin, the combination of a long drought, high winds, a delay in the alarm system, and an overmatched fire department assured catastrophe for the new metropolis, which was constructed almost entirely of wood. The flames destroyed a third of the city, including the entire commercial downtown and the homes of about 100,000 of Chicago's 334,000 residents. The fire claimed remarkably few lives (estimates range in the low hundreds), however, and it spared most of Chicago's factories and railroad facilities.

Striking a city that seemed to embody the spirit of modernity in the United States, the disaster drew worldwide attention and led to a massive outpouring of charity. No less impressive than Chicago's destruction was the astonishing rapidity with which it was rebuilt, a testimony not only to the grit and energy of its citizens but also to the young city's strategic location between the industrial East and the agricultural West, which made it a major center of communications, transportation, manufacturing, and trade. The heroic story of Chicago's triumphant resurrection from the ashes, endlessly retold, overlooks many social divisions accentuated by the whole experience, but the city's recovery does reveal the resilience of the individual spirit and the force of urbanization in nineteenth-century America.

[*See also* Chicago *and* Cities and Suburbs.]

BIBLIOGRAPHY

Sawislak, Karen. *Smoldering City: Chicagoans and the Great Fire, 1871–1874*. Chicago: University of Chicago Press, 1995.

Smith, Carl. *Urban Disorder and the Shape of Belief: The Great Chicago Fire, the Haymarket Bomb, and the Model Town of Pullman*. 2d ed. Chicago: University of Chicago Press, 2007.

Carl Smith

CHICANO MOVEMENT

The Chicano movement emerged both as a reaction to the long-standing political, economic, and social status of Mexican Americans and as a proactive crusade for social change during the Vietnam era. Although there is no agreement among historians regarding the exact beginning and end of the Chicano movement, most believe that it occurred between 1966 and 1978. Emerging predominantly in the Southwest, *el movimiento*, as activists referred to it, was unified not by a single agenda, but by a shift in consciousness and political strategy among Mexican Americans. The adoption of a new political philosophy, Chicanismo, and a new identity, Chicano or Chicana, exemplified this new awareness.

At its core, Chicanismo was driven by Chicano cultural nationalism and represented a new political ideology that rejected the perceived assimilationist endeavors of the previous Mexican American generation. Instead Chicanismo called for ethnic pride based on a Mexican, not American, heritage and sought to challenge mainstream institutions. Chicanismo embraced and celebrated the indigenous pre-Columbian roots of Mexican Americans, extolled a collective identity among them, sought new methods of political expression including boycotts and walkouts, and viewed this group as a potential nation, based on the concept of the Chicano homeland, Aztlán.

The inhabitants of this potential Chicano nation were both young and old, both seasoned activists and political neophytes. Whereas in prior eras, ethnic Mexican political activism had been largely labor-oriented, composed of workers and their allies, this movement was made up of a large percentage of youth, both high school and college students.

Although referred to as one entity, the Chicano movement was in fact a constellation of political and social activity unified by a belief in Chicanismo. Activists shared the identity and took on a variety of issues within their communities. In 1968, high school students in East Los Angeles organized a walkout of five campuses to protest their inferior educational conditions. A year later La Raza Unida Party (LRUP), a Chicano third party, emerged in Texas and attempted to use the ballot box to empower Chicanos. La Raza Unida Party waged a variety of political campaigns in Texas and eventually organized in California. The Golden State was also the breeding ground for the Chicano Moratorium Committee, which organized an August 1970 demonstration, the largest Mexican American protest against the Vietnam War.

In addition to these activities, various political networks emerged, bolstered by a burgeoning of community and college-campus newspapers, as well as conferences that addressed a variety of issues, including immigration, feminism, and electoral politics. Movement newspapers included *El Grito del Norte* (Northern Call), published in New Mexico; *La Raza*, published in California; and *La Raza Nueva*, published in Texas. Conferences became important spaces for movement activists to rally together, debate issues, and develop strategies and platforms. Through both newspapers and conferences, Chicanos and Chicanas also addressed a range of national and international issues, such as the relationship between the Chicano movement and other social movements of the period, the war in Vietnam, and issues in Cuba and Puerto Rico.

Although seemingly united around ethnic and racial lines, several tensions arose among Chicano movement activists. During the course of the insurgency, notions of class and race came into conflict. Disagreements over issues of gender and sexuality also fissured the movement. One of the best-known manifestations of these gendered dynamics occurred at the 1969 Chicano Youth Liberation Conference sponsored by the Crusade for Justice, an activist group based in Denver, Colorado. At this gathering, the spokesperson for the women's workshop dismissed women's liberation, declaring that it was not something that Chicanas needed. Over the next decade, women in the Chicano movement addressed issues related to gender and feminism in a variety of forums, crafting a Chicana feminism that spoke to their lived experience and creating their own organizations. In terms of sexuality, the ideology of Chicanismo was grounded in a belief in collectivism based on a nuclear-family model. This model did not easily accept homosexuality. But by the late 1970s and early 1980s, gay and lesbian Chicanos and Chicanas opened the avenues for a more inclusive Chicanismo.

Inner tensions within the movement existed in tandem with tensions brought forth by law enforcement. Both local and national law-enforcement agencies routinely surveilled, infiltrated, and caused disruptions in various organizations of the Chicano movement. Many Chicano activists were also arrested, charged, and convicted for a variety of criminal offenses stemming from their actions in the movement.

In addition to drawing attention to political issues, the Chicano movement also engendered a cultural renaissance, based on ethnic pride. Although this renaissance encompassed a wide variety of media, the visual arts and poetry were predominant. Cultural production became the vessel through which Chicanas and Chicanos affirmed their ethnic pride and heritage, while simultaneously urging political action. Major movement poets included Lorna Dee Cervantes, Alurista,

Bernice Zamora, and Ricardo Salinas. In art, one of the primary forms of expression was muralism. Artists in the movement employed indigenous iconography and depicted sources both of struggle and of pride for Chicanos and Chicanas. Notable muralists of the period include the collectives Los Four, ASCO, and Mujeres Muralistas and the individuals Judith Baca and Barbara Carrasco.

Through grassroots and political organizing, a newfound ethnic pride, and a more militant outlook and strategies, the Chicano movement of the late 1960s and 1970s addressed and attempted to change Mexican Americans' lack of political representation in electoral politics, educational inequalities, stagnant socioeconomic position, discrimination, and the inequalities perceived in relation to the Vietnam War. Ultimately the Chicano movement did not permanently change the status of ethnic Mexicans in the United States. Instead it represented a pivotal shift in Mexican American history, garnering this group newfound pride and recognition from mainstream society.

[*See also* **Brown Berets; California; Immigration; Mexican American Civil Rights Movement; Mexican Americans; Race and Ethnicity;** *and* **War Resisters.**]

BIBLIOGRAPHY

Chávez, Ernesto. *"¡Mi Raza Primero!"* (*My People First!*): *Nationalism, Identity, and Insurgency in the Chicano Movement in Los Angeles, 1966–1978.* Berkeley: University of California Press, 2002.

García, Alma M. *Chicana Feminist Thought: The Basic Historical Writings.* New York: Routledge, 1997.

Mariscal, George. *Brown-Eyed Children of the Sun: Lessons from the Chicano Movement, 1965–1975.* Albuquerque: University of New Mexico Press, 2005.

Oropeza, Lorena. *¡Raza Sí! ¡Guerra No! Chicano Protest and Patriotism during the Viet Nam*

War Era. Berkeley: University of California Press, 2005.

Rodríguez, Richard T. *Next of Kin: The Family in Chicana/o Cultural Politics*. Durham, N.C.: Duke University Press, 2009.

Marisela R. Chávez

CHILD, LYDIA MARIA

(1802–1880), antebellum reformer. Lydia Maria Francis, born in Medford, Massachusetts, in 1802, had an early life marked by considerable emotional strain: she had to deal with the death of her mother and was denied the educational opportunities afforded her elder brother, Convers. At seventeen years old she began working as a teacher, but beginning in 1824 when she published *Hobomok: A Tale of Early Times*, she quickly established a reputation as a prolific and eclectic author. Her writings included publications for children, and from 1826 to 1834 she edited the *Juvenile Miscellany*. In 1829 she published *The Frugal Housewife*, a major contribution to the cult of domesticity that sought to channel women's domestic labors toward the national good. Following her marriage in 1828 to the often impecunious Boston lawyer and reformer David Lee Child, she was drawn to the reform movements that characterized the antebellum era. No issue was more divisive than that of slavery, and influenced partly by William Lloyd Garrison, Lydia Maria Child embraced the abolitionist cause. Unlike some of her female colleagues, Child eschewed public speaking, preferring instead to use her experience and reputation as a writer to denounce slavery. In 1833 she published *An Appeal in Favor of That Class of Americans Called Africans*, which detailed starkly the horrors of slavery in the South, including the contentious matter of miscegenation.

Despite her determination to ensure women's right to participate equally alongside men in the antislavery movement, and notwithstanding her growing awareness of the civil and cultural constraints that served to limit opportunities for American women, Child regarded slavery as a more immediate issue than women's rights. In 1839 she was elected to serve on the executive committee of the American Anti-Slavery Society, and in 1841 she began a two-year term as coeditor of the society's weekly newspaper, the *National Anti-Slavery Standard*. Although the paper was nominally coedited by Child and her husband, it was widely understood that David was an editor in name only. Unimpressed by some of the more radical antigovernment views expressed by Garrisonian abolitionists and frustrated by the internecine conflicts within abolitionist organizations, during the mid-1840s Child retreated from the public crusade against slavery. But she continued to write and publish on a diverse range of subjects, and the apparent ascendency of the slaveholders during the 1850s, culminating with the execution of John Brown in 1859, impelled Child to rejoin the crusade.

During 1860–1861, Child assisted a former slave, Harriet Jacobs, in writing and publishing *Incidents in the Life of a Slave Girl*. The January 1861 publication of Jacobs's book, with its explicit rendering of the abuses inflicted on slave women, galvanized Northern antislavery opinion at a crucial moment in the sectional crisis. During and after the Civil War, Child worked to assist former slaves; as ever, she valued education and envisaged that her *Freedmen's Book* would help former slaves acquire the literacy necessary to help them participate as equals in American society. Child also had a long interest in the rights of Native Americans, and in 1868 she published *An Appeal for the Indians*. Although she believed that the issue of

African American suffrage was more pressing, Child's continuing concern for women's rights drew her toward the postbellum suffrage movement. In 1878, led by her enduring interest in the connections among religion, reform, and the future of the republic, she published *Aspirations of the World*, a collection of writings from various religions. Finally achieving financial security late in life, during the 1870s Child donated to a host of causes she deemed worthy of support. Lydia Maria Child died in 1880.

[*See also* **Antebellum Era; Antebellum Reform; Antislavery; Woman Suffrage Movement;** *and* **Women's Rights Movement, Antebellum Era.**]

BIBLIOGRAPHY

Baer, Helene G. *The Heart Is like Heaven: The Life of Lydia Maria Child*. Philadelphia: University of Pennsylvania Press, 1964.

Karcher, Carolyn L. *The First Woman in the Republic: A Cultural Biography of Lydia Maria Child*. Durham, N.C.: Duke University Press, 1994.

Karcher, Carolyn L., ed. *A Lydia Maria Child Reader*. Durham, N.C.: Duke University Press, 1997.

Chris Dixon

CHILDREN'S BUREAU, U.S.

Beginning in the first decade of the twentieth century, Progressive activists such as Florence Kelley, Lillian Wald, and Jane Addams, all involved in the National Child Labor Committee, led the call for creation of a federal bureau to advocate on behalf of the nation's youngest citizens. After nine years of lobbying and with the support of the 1909 White House conference on children, on 9 April 1912, President William Howard Taft signed legislation establishing the U.S. Children's Bureau within the Department of Labor and Commerce. The agency transferred to the new Department of Labor in 1913. Taft named Julia C. Lathrop, a former resident of Addams's Hull-House, the bureau's first chief, thereby making her the first woman to head a federal U.S. government agency.

With a meager budget of $25,640, the U.S. Children's Bureau began investigating and reporting "on all matters pertaining to the welfare of children and child life among all classes of our people." Because of its fragile beginning, at least initially the bureau sought to avoid the most controversial issues of the time, such as child labor. Instead, Lathrop skillfully chose to study why so many more babies died in the United States than in other modern nations. The bureau concluded that in addition to inadequate sanitation and a lack of access to high-quality and affordable medical care, poverty was an important factor contributing to America's high infant death rate. The bureau's early infant-mortality studies were among the first conducted in the United States and led to the passage and implementation of the Sheppard-Towner Maternity and Infancy Protection Act of 1921. Sheppard-Towner was a popular education and diagnostic program operated as a federal-state. By the mid-1920s, however, the American Medical Association, the American Catholic Church, and political conservatives, along with private insurance companies, led strong opposition to the program, calling it "socialized medicine" run by laywomen; as a result, funding for the act ended in 1929.

The U.S. Children's Bureau's second chief, Grace Abbott, faced similar fights. But under the direction of Katharine F. Lenroot in the 1930s, the Children's Bureau reached the height of its influence. For example, Lenroot,

Abbott, and the bureau physician Martha May Eliot—who in 1951 became the agency's chief—wrote the sections of the 1935 Social Security Act related to children's welfare, sections that established the Aid to Dependent Children program, provided for aid to handicapped children, and set up an infant and maternal health-care program for pregnant women and young children living in poverty. In addition, the New Deal's 1938 Fair Labor Standards Act included the first successful ban on the most exploitative forms of child labor and federal regulations for the employment of adolescents from ages fourteen to seventeen.

The expansion of the U.S. Children's Bureau during the administration of Franklin D. Roosevelt was only temporary. In 1946 the reorganization of federal agencies by the administration of Harry S. Truman reduced the Children's Bureau to a clearinghouse for information about the nation's youngest citizens. Unlike the elderly, by the end of 1946 children and adolescents no longer had a single federal agency to lobby, investigate, and administer programs on their behalf.

[*See also* **Anti-child-labor Movement; Child Workers; Feminist Reforms in the Progressive Era, Maternal; New Deal Social Reforms; Progressive Era;** *and* **Welfare.**]

BIBLIOGRAPHY

Ladd-Taylor, Molly. *Mother-Work: Women, Child Welfare, and the State, 1890–1930.* Urbana: University of Illinois Press, 1994.

Lindenmeyer, Kriste. *"A Right to Childhood": The U.S. Children's Bureau and Child Welfare, 1912–46.* Urbana: University of Illinois Press, 1997.

Muncy, Robyn. *Creating a Female Dominion in American Reform, 1890–1935.* New York: Oxford University Press, 1991.

Kriste Lindenmeyer

CHILD WORKERS

Most American children have been workers; only recently has this status been exchanged for that of student. From the eighteenth to the twentieth century, the family farm provided the principal setting for child labor. There were exceptions: slave children began to work for masters in their early teens; indentured servants labored for those who held their contract; and in urban middle-class and wealthy households, children might not work at all. On the farm, boys' tasks mirrored those of adult males, while girls generally carried out domestic chores under the direction of their mothers. From this female work emerged an occupational path into paid household service off the farm, an important niche for teenage girls. As in other agricultural societies, the use of children as workers was considered normal and contributed to the successful operation of farms.

However, the appearance of child industrial workers in the late nineteenth century provoked sharp reaction among members of the American middle class, who insisted that their children attend school. Though rarely critical of child farmworkers, reformers rejected industrial labor, in which, it was assumed, bosses were crueler than parents. For working-class parents—often immigrants recently arrived from agricultural societies—children's work remained conventional and school imposed a steep opportunity cost. They wanted children to contribute to family economies as they always had. Indeed, though urban settings increasingly made children costly rather than profitable, the initial response of working-class families was to encourage their children to enter the labor force and to add their wages to family income. This strategy could be successful, enabling parents to move from barely sustaining budgets when children were very young to having considerable surpluses when the children began to work.

The strategy worked in part both because schooling was not necessary for jobs in the industrial sector and because boys in their teens could earn relatively high wages. Males conventionally began work at age fourteen; child-labor laws usually set that age as appropriate for wage labor. Moreover, there is substantial evidence that many children wanted to work, greatly preferring the factory floor to the schoolroom. Surprisingly, considering the attention given them, very few children thirteen and younger worked during the industrial era. Data from the U.S. Census between 1880 and 1920—which capture industrial workers but miss many children working on family farms—indicate that near 60 percent of boys age fourteen and over were gainfully employed in 1880, compared with only 25 percent of those from ages ten to thirteen. The rate fell precipitously over the next forty years, with only 6 percent of the younger boys reporting gainful employment in 1920. Girls were even less likely to work. In 1880 only 8 percent of those aged ten to thirteen had gainful employment, and that fell to 3 percent in 1920; meanwhile, among girls from ages fourteen to seventeen, rates stayed steady at just over 20 percent. Industrial work was therefore always rare among children less than fourteen years of age.

Reformers also claimed that ethno-cultural deficiencies led certain groups to exploit their children. There was some justice in this assertion: many immigrants had come from agricultural societies in which child labor was common, and at first, extending the practice to industrial employment seemed normal. Certain ethnic groups were slightly more likely to have children working. Still, even in those groups singled out for criticism, child labor was rare. In 1880, although Italian American girls from ages fourteen to seventeen had relatively high rates, only 4 percent of their younger sisters worked. What stands out in the period is not an ethnic distinction but a racial one. Black children, even very young black children, were at great risk. In 1910, 43 percent of black boys from ages ten to thirteen reported gainful labor, as did a third of black girls this age. These rates fell over time but remained substantially higher than those of children of other races. Economic pressures also mattered: children whose household was headed by a female were more likely to work, as were those whose head was illiterate or had a low-status occupation. Work settings influenced the likelihood of labor. For younger children, farms and rural places led to greater likelihood of work, and urban places a lower one; for the older children, urban rather than rural places provided opportunities.

By 1930 a precipitous decline in child labor was evident, and by 1950 the practice was nonexistent among the very young. Higher male incomes, technological change favoring adult workers, and increased cultural opposition to child labor—more than any legal restrictions—influenced this trend, as did the disappearance of the family farm, the classic setting for children as workers. School emerged as the normal place for children, one where they are bent over books rather than over the plow and the lathe.

[See also **Anti-child-labor Movement; Children's Bureau, U.S.; Education; Rural Life and Society; Work;** and **Working-Class Life and Society.**]

BIBLIOGRAPHY

Gratton, Brian, and Jon Moen. "Immigration, Culture, and Child Labor in the United States, 1880–1920." *Journal of Interdisciplinary History* 34 (2004): 355–391.

Hindman, Hugh D. *Child Labor: An American History*. Armonk, N.Y.: M. E. Sharpe, 2002.

Macleod, David I. *The Age of the Child: Children in America, 1890–1920*. New York: Twayne, 1998.

Nasaw, David. *Children of the City: At Work and At Play*. Garden City, N.Y.: Anchor Press/ Doubleday, 1985.

Brian Gratton and Jon R. Moen

CHINATOWNS

The social history of Chinatowns in urban America reflects the wider impacts of shifting global dynamics. From 1882 to 1943 when the Chinese Exclusion Act was in force, Chinatowns were frozen in the status of "bachelor societies" of immigrant workers denied rights of naturalized citizenship, property ownership, and legal representation. The relaxation of U.S. immigration restrictions after World War II and the growth of free trade policies from the 1960s onward fed the expansion of Chinatowns into family-centered communities and dynamic motors of trade and investment in the new global economy. The exclusion period is mainly a story of Chinatowns in West Coast cities such as Sacramento, San Francisco, and Los Angeles. New York City's Chinatown and suburban Chinatowns such as the so-called ethnoburb in the San Gabriel valley of southern California have emerged since World War II.

Chinese labor on the West Coast in the era of the Gold Rushes and Manifest Destiny made up for the relative lack of African and European labor sources. Initially welcomed in mining and railroad work, Chinese immigrants subsequently faced racist violence and victimization both on the frontier and in cities, such as during the so-called Chinese massacre of 1871 in Los Angeles that left seventeen dead. The movement toward Chinese exclusion in federal immigration law was stoked by regional nativist political reprisals from organized labor and white-supremacist groups such as the Workingmen's Party of California and the Native Sons of the Golden West in San Francisco. Urban Chinatowns emerged as a refuge for Chinese immigrants, a place where they could be sheltered from violence and prejudice and could promote the ethnic community. Chinese immigrants began to specialize in socially undesirable occupational niches such as vegetable peddling and laundry work. In Los Angeles they were relegated to a mixed-race area near the old City Plaza dubbed "Calle de los Negroes." In San Francisco the Six Companies, later called the Chinese Consolidated Benevolent Association, emerged in the 1880s as the headquarters of a consortium of the main merchant, clan, and district associations to foster immigrant adjustment, business life, and self-governance. New York had a Chinatown, too, consisting like the others of mainly male sojourners who labored in America as resident aliens without naturalization rights.

During the exclusion years, tourism emerged as a source of livelihood for Chinese immigrant businesses such as restaurants and curio shops and as a form of cultural diplomacy. The world's fairs of the turn of the century offered an urban context for the exhibition of global ethno-cultural life as representations of American empire. With lures of exotic and forbidden sights, regional guidebooks and operators offered "slumming" tours of urban enclaves such as the New York and San Francisco Chinatowns. White artists such as the photographer Arnold Genthe doctored and retouched their images to "Orientalize" the Western view of Chinatown. In the 1930s and 1940s when U.S. relations with China were improved in joint response to the expansionist threat of Japan, Chinese Americans in Los Angeles built upon the new market for the consumption of Chinese food and culture with touristic redevelopment projects, including China City and New Chinatown in 1938.

Immigration acts in 1952 and 1965 extended the right of naturalized citizenship to Chinese immigrants, widened immigration quotas, and added manpower and family-reunification incentives. The removal of protectionist immigration barriers and the addition of incentives to immigrant and foreign direct investment marked the mobility of new labor and capital flows into the Chinatowns of America. New York's Chinatown grew particularly rapidly from the 1960s onward, with the growth of a Chinatown garment production zone and a foreign investment and banking center. Outer-borough Chinatowns in Queens and Brooklyn have emerged to accommodate the residential and commercial expansion and congestion at the downtown core. The patronage of the old traditional associations is making way for the brokerage of new community and political leadership. The Chinatown in Los Angeles has experienced similar expansion, and in the 1970s a new suburban Chinatown, or "ethnoburb," began to develop in Monterey Park, in the San Gabriel valley. In the 1980s an English-only nativist and slow-growth movement emerged in response to the rapid growth of Chinese-language signs and redevelopment, but it gave way to new Chinese American political and economic leadership. The ethnoburb eventually spread to neighboring cities throughout the San Gabriel valley.

Tourism plays a continuing role in the life of American Chinatowns, which increasingly contend with contemporary urban dynamics such as redevelopmental gentrification. New York's Chinatown marks the experience of a community devastated by the terrorist attacks of 11 September 2001, with tourism also a linchpin of the plan for recovery.

[*See also* Angel Island Immigration Station; Asian Americans; California; Chinese Americans; Cities and Suburbs; Immigration; Slums; *and* Tourism and Travel.]

BIBLIOGRAPHY

Li, Wei. *Ethnoburb: The New Ethnic Community in Urban America*. Honolulu: University of Hawai'i Press, 2009.

Lin, Jan. *Reconstructing Chinatown: Ethnic Enclave, Global Change*. Minneapolis: University of Minnesota Press, 1998.

Pfaelzer, Jean. *Driven Out: The Forgotten War against Chinese Americans*. New York: Random House, 2007.

Jan Lin

CHINESE AMERICANS

Chinese Americans constitute the largest Asian American ethnic group. Totaling 3,796,796 in 2010, they accounted for 22.4 percent of the Asian American population. They are also a predominantly immigrant community and are notable for their highly diversified settlement patterns and extensive participation in transnational activities.

Origins and Settlement Patterns. Chinese began to settle in the United States in significant numbers during the Gold Rush years. There were 325 Chinese in San Francisco in 1849. Three years later, the number grew to 20,026. By 1880, the Chinese population in the United States had reached 105,465. The vast majority of the Chinese immigrants originated from the Pearl River Delta region in Guangdong (Canton) Province in South China. Social turmoil and economic hardships caused by the Opium War (1839–1842), the Taiping Rebellion (1850–1864), civil strife between local people and migrants (the Kejia, or Hakka, people), and heavy taxation by the Manchu regime were some of the major factors that pushed the Cantonese to California. Meanwhile, economic development and labor shortages on the West Coast, especially during the construction of the Transcontinental Railroad (1865–1869), also pulled Cantonese to America, which was known as the "Gold Mountain" among the Chinese.

The Chinese American population declined drastically, however, after Congress passed the Chinese Exclusion Act in 1882. The exclusionary policies and racial discrimination severely constrained opportunities for Chinese living in America. It was not until after Congress repealed all the Chinese exclusion laws in 1943 that the Chinese American population grew again in substantial numbers. The historical immigration reform of 1965 led to a dramatic increase in the numbers of Chinese in the United States. More immigrants have arrived since Congress granted China (the People's Republic of China, or PRC), Taiwan, and Hong Kong separate immigration quotas in 1979.

For these reasons, except for a short span of twenty years—between 1940 and 1960—immigrants have always outnumbered the native-born in the Chinese American community. In 2010, about two-thirds of all Chinese Americans had been born overseas; 80 percent of immigrants since 1980 have come from the Chinese world—from countries and regions in Asia that are populated by the Chinese. If children born to immigrant parents are included, then by 2010 almost 90 percent of Chinese Americans were of the first or second generation. They include virtually all the most prominent Chinese Americans—people such as Secretary of Labor Elaine Chao, the writer Maxine Hong Kingston, the film director Ang Lee, the cellist Yo-Yo Ma, the architect I. M. Pei,

Chancellor of the University of California, Berkeley, Chang-Lin Tien, and the eight Chinese American Nobel laureates in science.

Chinese Americans are also a highly diversified community in terms of their origins in the Chinese world and their settlement patterns in the United States. Until the late 1940s, nearly 80 percent of the Chinese in America were Cantonese speakers, but by 2010, Cantonese speakers accounted for only around 8 percent of the immigrants. Others have come from all over the Chinese world, especially from China (the PRC). Although PRC immigrants did not arrive until after President Richard M. Nixon's historic 1972 visit to Beijing that normalized relations between the United States and China, they have become the largest subgroup in the Chinese American community: by 2010, they constituted more than 60 percent of all the overseas-born Chinese in the United States.

Socioeconomic Structure. Socioeconomically, Chinese Americans are divided into two distinct groups: the "uptown" and the "downtown." The uptown are professionals who reside in suburban cities and are well-integrated into mainstream society; the downtown are predominantly working-class immigrants struggling to survive in isolated urban Chinatowns. On the one hand, many new immigrants are highly skilled in terms of training and education. Statistics show that between 1950 and the mid-1980s, nearly a hundred and fifty thousand students from Taiwan came to America for education and advanced training; most of them stayed in the United States after graduation. The years after 1980 also saw approximately six hundred thousand students and scholars from China studying in American institutions of higher learning. The vast majority of them eventually settled in the United States, including more than eighty thousand who adjusted their status under President George H. W. Bush's Executive Order 12711, issued on 11 April 1990, and the Chinese Student Protection Act passed subsequently by Congress in 1992.

The arrival of so many student immigrants has deeply affected Chinese America. With their strong educational credentials, they have adapted well to the mainstream job market and society, thus being primed for career success to an extent unimaginable among earlier Chinese immigrants. They have produced, for example, a disproportionately large number of America's top scientists and scholars.

On the other hand, immigration laws, such as those allowing family reunion and those offering protection or asylum for refugees, have brought to the United States large numbers of non-English-speaking, uneducated immigrants from the Chinese world. Illegal immigration, especially from Fujian Province in South China, has also had an impact on Chinese America. With few readily transferable skills and limited resources, these immigrants have often been trapped in poverty-stricken urban ghettos. Caught in a world of gangs, drugs, prostitution, and poverty, the downtown Chinese have lives that differ dramatically from those of their uptown counterparts.

For example, although Chinese Americans are "overrepresented" in managerial and professional occupations, they are also heavily concentrated in low-paid manual and unskilled service work. As a result, although Chinese Americans' median household income in 2010 was higher than that of the overall U.S. population, more Chinese than non-Hispanic whites lived in poverty: 9 percent versus 8.1 percent. This is especially true of PRC immigrants. A study in 2000 revealed that 30 percent of the families in New York City's Chinatown, which has the largest presence of PRC immigrants in America, lived below the poverty level.

Similarly, 2010 statistics indicated that about 60 percent of Chinese Americans had a bachelor's degree or higher, double the rate of the overall U.S. population. However, the percentage of Chinese Americans who had not completed high school was also larger than that of the rest of the population, 18.7 percent versus 15.4 percent. In fact, whereas only 3.7 percent of American-born Chinese had not completed high school, a stunning 25.6 percent of PRC immigrants had not done so. Such a bimodal socioeconomic structure explains why there exists a striking and widening gap between the uptown and downtown Chinese in almost every aspect of American life. In reality, an illiterate villager or an illegal immigrant from China and a computer scientist from Taiwan or a U.S.-born Chinese medical doctor may feel that they share little in their experience in America.

More significantly, the vast differences in their socioeconomic status have turned Chinese Americans into groups with separate political interests. Whereas the uptown Chinese may feel embittered about the "glass ceiling" phenomenon that inhibits their career advancement, their downtown counterparts, locked in dead-end jobs with little chance to move upward, are more concerned for their immediate survival. Thus Chinese Americans often have conflicting views on a wide range of issues in American politics, from changes in health-care regulations to welfare reforms to affirmative action programs.

Transnational Networks. Because their community is constantly replenished with newcomers, it is not surprising that Chinese Americans stand out for their extensive involvement in transnational activities. The strong community network developed by

PRC immigrants with China is a case in point. Their arrival in the United States has coincided with China's opening up to the outside world after the 1976 death of Mao Zedong, and they have been influenced by the powerful trends of globalization—the massive economic, technological, political, and sociocultural changes that have occurred throughout the world in recent decades. As such, two parallel and interconnected developments have profoundly and critically changed the makeup and dynamics of the transnational linkages of Chinese America. One is the tremendous increase in trade, finance, and other business activities between China and the United States, which has spun a rich and complex web of networking between Chinese Americans and their family members and friends across the Pacific. Another is the reverse flow of large numbers of Chinese Americans, both immigrants and those born in the United States, who return to their ancestral land to work or start businesses or are hired by U.S. companies to manage local offices in China. One early twenty-first-century study has revealed, for instance, that among those who ran foreign businesses in Beijing, more than half were Chinese transnational migrants, including many Chinese Americans. In fact, virtually all the Internet companies in China, including China's most popular search engine, "Baidu," were founded by Chinese Americans.

Those Chinese who have maintained their involvement in both American and Chinese societies have carried with them a network of connections that enhances the flow of capital, cultural ideas, entrepreneurial talent, and professional activities across the Pacific. Thus, the years since 1980 have seen the emergence of many new types of transnational community organizations in Chinese America. Established by recent Chinese immigrants, these nongovernmental organizations include various kinds of transnational hometown associations, professional organizations, and academic societies. The Wenzhou Association California, the USTC (University of Science and Technology of China) Alumni Foundation, and the Overseas Young Chinese Forum are a few outstanding examples. Though largely unknown to the general public, these transnational community organizations enjoy enormous popularity among Chinese Americans, especially recent immigrants, because they provide social stability for new arrivals in a strange land and because they have contributed, in one way or another, to the social, economic, and cultural development of Chinese America.

That Chinese in America have strengthened rather than weakened ties with their ancestral land during the migration process constitutes a remarkable divergence from the traditional assimilation model. Exerting a profound influence on Chinese America, these transnational migrants represent new and emerging trends in immigrant life in the age of globalization and demonstrate a distinctive complexity that existing immigration theories are unable to explain fully.

Finally, it is worth mentioning that by 2010, there was a large presence of U.S. citizens, 67.2 percent, in Chinese America. Although they are new arrivals, the majority of Chinese immigrants, 60.9 percent, have been naturalized. Chinese Americans' growing voting power will lead to their becoming an important political force in American life. This is particularly true in southern California, which has surpassed New York City and San Francisco to become the home of the largest Chinese community in America.

[*See also* **Angel Island Immigration Station; Asian American Movement; Asian Americans; California; Chinatowns; Immigration;**

New York City; San Francisco; *and* Transnational Identity.]

BIBLIOGRAPHY

Asian American Studies Program, University of Maryland, College Park. "Preview: A New Profile of Chinese Americans in a New Century." 2011. Available through http://www.aast.umd.edu/newprofile_chinese_americans.html.

Kwong, Peter, and Dušanka Miščević. *Chinese America: The Untold Story of America's Oldest New Community*. New York: New Press, 2005.

Lai, Him Mark. *Cong Huaqiao dao Huaren* [From Overseas Chinese to Chinese Americans]. Hong Kong: Joint Press, 1992.

U.S. Census Bureau. S0201. "Selected Population Profile in the United States, Population Groups: Chinese alone or in any Combination," 2011.

Waters, Mary C., and Reed Ueda, eds. *The New Americans: A Guide to Immigration since 1965*. Cambridge: Harvard University Press, 2007.

Yin, Xiao-huang. *Chinese American Literature since the 1850s*. Urbana: University of Illinois Press, 2000.

Yin, Xiao-huang. "Diverse and Transnational: Chinese (PRC) Immigrants in the United States." *Journal of Chinese Overseas* 3, no. 1 (May 2007): 122–145.

Zhao, Xiaojian. *The New Chinese America: Class, Economy, and Social Hierarchy*. New Brunswick, N.J.: Rutgers University Press, 2010.

Xiao-huang Yin

CIRCUSES

The circus's roots as an American popular amusement can be traced back to 1793 when the Scottish equestrian John Bill Ricketts and his troupe put on an exhibition in Philadelphia. In the decades that followed, circus impresarios staged their shows in theaters or wooden buildings located in cities and large towns, and they expanded the entertainment content of their shows by including wild animals, clowns, and acrobats, along with riding. But it was the 1825 invention of a portable canvas tent, which allowed showmen to stage their shows not only in established communities but also in the American backcountry, that fully transformed circus performances into social—rather than mere entertainment—events.

To be sure, nineteenth-century Americans of all classes and colors turned out on what was billed as "Circus Day" in order to witness the incredible attractions and exotic beasts that showmen displayed inside their tents. Yet people also came out to take up their roles in the wider social drama that took place in the fields, alleys, and streets of the community where the circus had raised its enclosures. Circus-hungry people arrived in town early in order to see show trains unload, to seize prime locations from which to watch the spectacle of the free morning street parade, to listen to the entreaties of the sideshow barkers on the show lot, and to experience the press of the crowd, all before they ever set foot under canvas.

After purchasing tickets, customers typically first entered the sideshow or menagerie tents to observe human "spectacles" or rare animals. Unlike during theater or vaudeville performances, at circuses people of all ages, races, classes, and genders pressed together and moved freely from exhibit to exhibit inside the open spaces within these enclosures. Only when witnessing the circus performance proper under the "Big Top" did customers find themselves separated by class and segregated by color. All in all, these factors helped the circus capture the imagination of turn-of-the-century Americans and made it the nation's leading popular entertainment.

By the early twentieth century, circuses faced a number of pressures that acted to erode their popular appeal. These included increasingly intense competition from emerging diversions such as film, professional sports, and radio broadcasts. At the same time, the ever-growing number of automobiles limited the ability of circuses to shut a town down and block auto traffic with lengthy parades. Likewise, the growth of American towns and cities made it increasingly difficult for showmen to find large open fields in which to erect their tents. Accordingly, by the mid-twentieth century, circuses had largely eliminated their parades and had begun performing inside sports arenas or other permanent enclosures, developments that fundamentally transformed the social nature of the circus experience and effectively led to the end of Circus Day as a holiday. As a result, by the early twenty-first century, circus attendance largely placed customers in the position of being spectators of an entertainment rather than participants in a social event.

[*See also* **Amusement Parks and Theme Parks; Everyday Life; Holidays and Festivals;** *and* **Leisure.**]

BIBLIOGRAPHY

Barnum, P. T. *Struggles and Triumphs, or Forty Years' Recollections of P. T. Barnum.* Hartford, Conn.: J. B. Burr, 1869. A valuable portrait of the mind of America's greatest circus showman.

Davis, Janet M. *The Circus Age: Culture and Society under the American Big Top.* Chapel Hill: University of North Carolina Press, 2002. Stresses the cultural implications of the turn-of-the-century American circus.

Renoff, Gregory J. *The Big Tent: The Traveling Circus in Georgia, 1820–1930.* Athens, Ga.: University of Georgia Press, 2008. Emphasizes the social aspects of circus performances in a representative southern state.

Gregory J. Renoff

CITIES AND SUBURBS

The United States long has been a metropolitan nation. Since 1920 the majority of Americans have lived in urban places, and cities have been the sites and the catalysts of major social, political, and economic transformations over four centuries of American history. America's urban age also has been a suburban one. Suburbs have been an important feature of the American urban landscape since the middle of the nineteenth century. The concurrent growth of cities and suburbs resulted not only from economic and technological transformations, but also from cultural responses to America's ethnic and racial diversity and public policy choices, particularly since 1945, that subsidized suburban development. Though the last two hundred years of human history have witnessed unprecedented rates of urbanization around the globe, the United States has been distinctive in its high degree of urban decentralization and in the functional and social segregation within the urban built environment.

Precolonial and Colonial Patterns. Cities and other fixed settlements served as hubs of economic and political power for indigenous North American societies many centuries before European contact. One of these cities was Cahokia, established around 700 CE by the Indians of the Late Woodland culture in what is now East Saint Louis, Illinois. At its height around 1100 CE, Cahokia was a city of between ten and twenty thousand, with another thirty thousand people living in fifty miles of surrounding hinterland. Cahokia's political and trade networks extended across a territory from the modern Dakotas to New York, south to Florida, and southwest to Mexico. Other urban places with broad trade and political networks included the pueblo villages of the Anasazi people of the Southwest. By the time the first Europeans arrived in the early sixteenth century, these cultures had been superseded by societies that rarely built permanent settlements, instead moving across their territory in traveling bands and living in small, seasonal villages.

Forts, trading posts, missions, and towns were outposts of empire from which European societies gained control of North America between the sixteenth and eighteenth centuries. Spanish rulers made the building of towns and cities the central part of their imperial project. Spain's Laws of the Indies (1573) dictated precise standards for urban planning and development, establishing a network of colonial cities throughout the Americas that are strikingly similar to each other in both their layout and their architecture. This urbanization was not so pronounced in North America, but the Spanish missions and trading posts established there—particularly in what became the state of California—were the core settlements around which large metropolitan areas later developed.

French, Dutch, and English interests established port cities along the eastern and southern coasts of North America beginning in the seventeenth century. Some were founded to establish territorial dominance and profit from lucrative trade between the Americas and Europe, such as New Amsterdam (later New York City), a small, fortified settlement founded by Dutch traders in 1624. Religious freedom was another reason to establish urban places. English Puritans founded Boston in 1630 under the leadership of John Winthrop, who urged his followers to build their city along Christian principles, saying "we must consider that we shall be as a city upon a hill." Several decades later, William Penn, an English Quaker and proprietor of Pennsylvania, established the city of Philadelphia as another

haven from religious persecution. Penn's background as a country gentleman influenced his plan for Philadelphia, which sought to distinguish itself from the crowded and chaotic cities of Europe by featuring a uniform street grid, ample lot sizes, and parks and gardens. The blend of the urban and the rural in this "greene country towne," as Penn called it, was a seminal influence on American urban and suburban planning.

From the eighteenth century onward, gridded streets also became a consistent and defining characteristic of North American urban places: European colonizers sought to impose some regularity and "civilization" on an unfamiliar and dangerous landscape. Fortified port cities like New Orleans (founded by France) and Charleston, South Carolina (founded by England), and missions and pueblos like Los Angeles (founded by Spain) all laid out street grids in advance of settlement, a pattern that was repeated many times over in the nineteenth century as American settlement advanced westward.

Urban Life and Commerce. Preindustrial cities in North America remained small compared to those of the rest of the world. By 1790 only 5 percent of the U.S. population lived in settlements of twenty-five hundred or more; the largest city, Philadelphia, had a population of about forty thousand. In contrast, the world's largest city in 1800, Beijing, was home to more than a million people; London, the second largest, had 860,000. Despite their small size, American cities had a significant influence upon the political and economic life of the thirteen colonies and the new nation. Deepwater port cities along the Atlantic coast—Boston, New York, Philadelphia, and Charleston—became hubs of international trade and the centers of regional economies. Their orientation was commercial: their chief activity was moving raw materials from the American hinterland onto Atlantic-crossing ships. These ships, in turn, brought manufactured and finished goods back from England and the rest of Europe. Such mercantile cities adhered to preindustrial rhythms of work and rest, and their streets became the stages for political action and public celebration.

Cities played pivotal roles in the American Revolution. Urban newspapers galvanized patriotic sentiment and built support for the revolutionary cause. Urban coffeehouses, wharves, and public squares became sites where news of politics and war was shared and where crowds rallied in support of each side. Cities were the sites of political conventions and military mobilizations, and they were theaters of war.

Density and Disease. The cities of the late eighteenth and early nineteenth centuries were densely populated "walking" cities where people of many classes, races, and professions lived in proximity to one another. Both artisans and merchants lived above their storefronts or next to their warehouses, so home and work were often in the same place. Social differences were expressed through clothing and comportment rather than through opulent residences.

The density and lack of water and sewage infrastructure in early American cities led to regular outbreaks of disease. In the hot and humid summer months on the Atlantic coast, many thousands fell ill and often died from cholera, typhoid, and malaria. A yellow fever epidemic in Philadelphia in 1793 killed five thousand of the city's forty-five thousand residents. Urban epidemics such as these continued in American cities throughout the nineteenth century and prompted the construction of citywide water and sewer systems.

Public health also served as a catalyst for early suburbanization: beginning in the mid-1700s,

affluent citizens chose to escape heat, crowds, and disease by building villas on the lightly populated outskirts of cities. Suburban spaces of this period were characterized more by poverty than by wealth, however, and they were mixed-use rather than exclusively residential. The urban fringes of cities like Boston, New York, and Philadelphia during this period were sites of polluting activities and marginalized populations whose presence was shunned elsewhere in the city.

Early American leaders had conflicting opinions about the role of cities in American life. The nation's founders came from an affluent landowning class; many, like the Virginia plantation owner Thomas Jefferson, argued that an urban manufacturing economy was a threat to democracy and antithetical to the American character. "Mobs of great cities," Jefferson wrote, "add just so much to the support of pure government, as sores do to the strength of the human body." Jefferson's views encapsulated a persistent anti-urbanism in American culture and politics that became amplified as the United States became more diverse, more industrial, and more urban in the nineteenth century.

Antebellum Industrial Cities and Suburbs.
Jefferson died in 1826, and before the end of his lifetime the United States was already becoming a major manufacturing economy. Cities were the hubs of industrial growth and the sources of capital. Manufacturing vastly expanded the size of metropolitan areas and increased their social and economic importance. In the Antebellum Era, this urbanization and industrialization occurred nearly entirely in northern states, while the slaveholding South became increasingly attached to large-scale, labor-intensive agricultural production. Major public and private infrastructure projects of the early nineteenth century fueled industrial growth in the North,

as well as establishing thriving regional networks of cities.

Early industrial production between the 1790s and 1840s encouraged the development of new urban centers, as well as that of towns on the metropolitan periphery of long-established cities. In New England towns like Lowell, Massachusetts, Boston-based investors and entrepreneurs established large water-powered textile mills that drew upon an underemployed rural workforce of young women and girls to create the nation's first large-scale manufacturing enterprises. In doing so, these mills expanded the economic reach of cities like Boston and Providence and mapped out roadways and railways that later served as paths for suburban development. Industrialization fueled the development of the urban West, too, as the growth of manufacturing cities like Pittsburgh and Chicago shifted the economic activity of the nation westward from the Atlantic coast.

The Role of Transportation. New transportation technologies and infrastructure fueled America's Industrial Revolution and vastly enlarged its cities. Steamboat technology opened up the Mississippi River and Ohio River to long-distance trade and led to the rapid growth of river-port towns like Cincinnati in Ohio, Saint Louis in Missouri, and Louisville in Kentucky during the first decades of the nineteenth century. Steamboats shrank the distance between these inland cities and the port of New Orleans, allowing producers and merchants to move their goods to international markets much more quickly.

The greatest infrastructure triumph of the antebellum era was the construction in New York State of the Erie Canal. Opened in 1825, the canal created a navigable water route between the Atlantic and the Great Lakes, opening up a vast western hinterland to trade and settlement. Trade flowing down the Erie

Canal encouraged the growth of a chain of prosperous towns along the canal's length, and it made New York City, located at the canal's Atlantic end, the undisputed financial and commercial capital of the United States. Within a few years of the canal's opening, New York had surpassed Philadelphia as the largest city in the country.

As cities grew, their dense and diverse streetscapes began to spread outward and become separated by type of activity, as well as by social class and race and ethnicity. The introduction of horse-drawn public transportation (the omnibus, the horse car) gave urbanites the ability to travel greater distances in shorter periods of time, encouraging the development of larger, less dense urban neighborhoods.

An emergent middle class of business owners, managers, and professionals moved to more spacious, well-appointed houses located at some distance from their places of work. In New York City, the development of elite residential districts pushed urbanization north from the crowded tip of Lower Manhattan. The establishment by the 1830s of regular ferry service to Brooklyn encouraged its development as a middle-class residential area—making Brooklyn the United States' first commuter suburb.

Social Structure. The large-scale global migrations prompted by the Industrial Revolution brought new immigrant populations to American cities in the first half of the nineteenth century. Immigrants of this period came chiefly from northern Europe, with the largest cohorts coming from Germany and Ireland. A steady stream of Irish immigrants grew in magnitude after Ireland's potato famine of the 1830s and 1840s: whereas in 1830, fewer than 3,000 Irish immigrated to the United States, by 1850 this number had increased to 164,000. Large cities were the destinations for the vast majority of these new arrivals. Poor, uneducated, and subject to virulent ethnic and religious discrimination and violence, Irish immigrants had few choices over where they could live and work, and they found themselves crowded into slums and working in particularly dangerous and dirty jobs. African American urbanites, whose numbers in many American cities remained comparatively small, faced similar discrimination in housing and in the workplace, and they often lived in the same slum areas. Over time, the Irish increased their economic status and political power, while African Americans remained segregated and economically marginalized.

Industrialization transformed employment for urban residents of all classes. The preindustrial model of artisanal or small-shop production gave way to larger-scale manufacturing involving a waged workforce. The factories where this manufacturing occurred developed in and around cities, drawing on urban areas' large pools of labor and of capital investment. As Americans began to produce and sell in mass quantities goods that previously had been made by hand, clusters of specialized manufacturers emerged in different cities. New York City became the center of garment and shoe manufacturing; Pittsburgh, the Iron City, became a hub of steel production.

Gender roles became more clearly delineated in the early industrial city. An emerging cultural ethos of middle-class respectability defined the workplace as a male domain and the home and family as a female one. Popular culture celebrated women's roles as wives, mothers, and managers of the household. More middle-class families began to employ domestic workers drawn from the burgeoning populations of immigrants and racial minorities. The early nineteenth-century upsurge in evangelical Christianity and the growing

populations of immigrant poor led to widespread charitable activities—many of them having a strong moralistic and missionary bent—in the urban slums.

Working-class and poor city residents did not have the luxury of separate domestic and productive spheres, and both men and women lived more of their lives in public. Working people of both genders participated in the manufacturing economy, both on the factory floor and by performing piecework or outwork at home. Unionization was limited in the antebellum era, and most working people earned meager wages, had few benefits, and labored long hours. Unlike the irregular working rhythms of life on the farm or in the mercantile city, the workday now became standardized and regularized. The character of urban recreation and community activities changed as a result, with the coffeehouse culture, parades, and street celebrations of an earlier era giving way to various after-work amusements, from theater to baseball games, and to a more informal street culture in neighborhoods and public areas of the city.

The Industrial Metropolis of the Late Nineteenth and Early Twentieth Centuries.

As America's industrial economy expanded in the second half of the nineteenth century, American cities expanded along with it. Revolutions in transportation and communication spurred both industrialization and urbanization of unprecedented speed and scale. Across the continent, railroads stimulated urban growth both by the wealth they created and by the networks of new towns and cities that were created along the lines as the railroads pushed west. Within metropolitan regions, railroads and streetcar systems vastly expanded the size of cities and suburbs. Occurring at the same time that huge numbers of new migrants and immigrants were arriving in cities and that economic polarization between rich and poor was increasing, rail-stimulated suburbanization furthered the physical distance between people of different classes, races, and ethnicities.

The arrival of the railroad was an economic boon to existing cities and towns along the main lines, and railroad companies further boosted urbanization—particularly in the far West—by founding new towns to promote settlement and trade. As had occurred throughout American history, towns and cities were the spearheads of settlement on the frontier and served critical economic and cultural functions throughout the western expansion of the nineteenth century.

By connecting manufacturing cities with a vast rural hinterland abundant in timber, ore, grain, and cattle, the railroad enabled the rapid rise of western metropolises and fueled the growth of new industries. Chicago, strategically located between the grazing lands of the Great Plains and one day away by rail from the cities of the East, became a major meatpacking center after the advent of refrigerated railcars. Farther west, cities like Denver, San Francisco, Los Angeles, and Seattle grew in size and influence through wealth created by mining, timber, and oil; rail connected these and other major cities and further encouraged the migration of people and manufacturing.

Railroad and Streetcar Suburbs.

In and around the cities, rail networks had become vital channels for suburban expansion and spurred the private development of carefully planned elite residential areas. The first planned community in the United States was Llewellyn Park, established in 1857 in the New Jersey suburbs of New York City, which featured extensive landscaping and curvilinear roadways that presented a dramatic contrast to the grid pattern of city streets. Inspired by the romantic movement and playing upon deep-rooted cultural ideas about the desirability of a certain kind of country life, many planned suburbs with similar landscape and architectural features appeared in the decades following, including Bronxville, also near New York City; Riverside, near Chicago; and Brookline, near Boston. Despite their reputation as havens for the rich, these suburbs also had working-class people who worked as domestic servants or in other service jobs.

By the 1880s, electric streetcars had replaced horse-driven omnibuses in most major American cities. The urban grid extended farther outward along the car lines as private developers built new residential neighborhoods for the white-collar workers of the expanding professional middle class. The streetcar suburbs of the late nineteenth century encouraged the decentralization of the urban middle class and increased the separation of the feminine world of home and the masculine world of work.

Mass Immigration.

The decentralization of the urban middle class occurred in a context of extraordinary population growth in American cities. Much of this growth was the result of foreign immigration, which transformed the ethnic and religious makeup of the United States and ultimately made it a majority-urban nation. Pulled by the promise of factory jobs in a rapidly expanding American industrial complex and pushed by economic hardship and political turmoil at home, 28 million immigrants arrived in America between 1860 and 1920. Unlike earlier waves of immigration, many were from southern and eastern Europe and were Catholic and Jewish rather than Protestant. Cities were both where immigrants first arrived and also often where they stayed. By 1910, 40 percent of the people in New York City—nearly 2 million—were foreign-born.

Because of poverty and ethnic and family ties, foreign immigrants clustered together in crowded urban neighborhoods. These ethnic enclaves were home to a rich assortment of vibrant neighborhood institutions, from churches and schools to foreign-language newspapers and community banks. Earning meager wages and forced to live in substandard housing, immigrants relied on family members and a neighborhood-based network of fellow countrymen for economic and social support in their new country. Native-born Americans—including those from so-called old-stock immigrant groups like the Irish and Germans—viewed new arrivals as economic competitors and possible political subversives. Perceived large numbers of politically militant socialists and anarchists among the new immigrant communities worried the middle-class urban establishment. High-profile acts of violence by individuals from immigrant backgrounds, like the 1901 assassination of President William McKinley by Leon Czolgosz, a Michigan-born child of immigrants from central Europe, validated these fears in some Americans' minds. Yet the increasing numbers of immigrants became increasingly powerful voting blocs in American cities, and they were critical to the sustained electoral success of urban political machines like New York's Tammany Hall.

City Life and Architecture. The industrial city became home to a variety of new kinds of entertainment and means of communication. Professional sports like baseball became hugely popular urban pastimes; affordable tickets and game times that accommodated the rhythms of the factory and the office catered to the budget and schedule of the workingman. Live entertainment like vaudeville and musical theater drew large crowds of people of both genders and most classes, and touring companies brought a shared culture to large cities as they moved the same shows from place to place. Amusement parks like New York's Coney Island provided cheap and novel entertainment to people during their hours off. Department stores offered urbanites an extraordinary range of goods under one roof, and they became a favored destination for both middle-class housewives and also working single women with their own money to spend. Newspapers and magazines proliferated in number and in size of circulation. Muckraking journalists used the pages of these publications to expose the excesses of corporate capitalism and the economic inequities of the industrial city.

The city was moving up as well as out. Technological advances in steel-frame construction allowed for multistory buildings. The introduction of elevators allowed these structures to soar even higher. Chicago was home to many of the first skyscrapers, with architects like Louis Sullivan and Daniel Burnham defining a particular type of building design that became known as the Chicago school. By the end of the nineteenth century the large American metropolis had taken on a form that it adhered to for the next half a century: a dense downtown of high-rise office buildings, transit and transportation networks radiating out from the central core, working-class and poor neighborhoods ringing downtown, and wealthier residential areas on the metropolitan periphery.

Progressive Reform. The vast increase in the size and diversity of urban populations during the industrial age spurred a significant uptick in urban reform initiatives designed to make cities and their poorer residents more healthful, efficient, and orderly. As in an earlier era, reformers of the Progressive Era were chiefly native-born, middle-class Protestants. But whereas churches or charities were the main vehicles of reform during the antebellum period, by the late nineteenth century local governments or professionalized social-service institutions tended to take the lead in reform. Women remained active participants in social reform. Female-led institutions like the settlement houses gave some educated, middle-class women opportunities for public engagement and provided an entry point for careers in politics, government, and academia. New immigrants were major targets of reformers, who hoped to improve the material conditions of the foreign-born, as well as to Americanize them.

In politics, reformers pushed for a permanent and nonpartisan professional class of civil servants to replace patronage-driven cronyism. The era also saw the emergence of professional city planning and civil engineering, as urban leaders embarked on ambitious infrastructure and urban-planning projects to bring order and efficiency to chaotic urban spaces. City governments began to finance and provide an increasing number of services, from water and sewer systems to road and bridge systems, civic centers, and parks. The 1893 World's Columbian Exposition in Chicago had a seminal influence on these planning schemes. The fair's centerpiece was the White City, a place of neoclassical buildings and grand public promenades that inspired the City Beautiful planning movement, which led to the creation of similar spaces in Washington D.C., Philadelphia, San Francisco, and Los Angeles, among others.

The Early Automobile Age. By 1920, half the U.S. population lived in urbanized areas. Ambitious city-planning schemes, robust infrastructure development, a proliferation of entertainment and cultural attractions, and booming new urban industries made the 1920s the apex of the American urban age. Yet the widespread adaptation of the automobile during the decade propelled a decentralization of urban people, industries, and culture that presaged the mass suburbanization to come. In 1900, approximately 8,000 cars were on American roads; by 1920 the number had become 6 million, and by 1929 it was 29 million.

Immigration Restriction and Black Migration. An isolationist mood after World War I and continued fears about socialist and communist policies among immigrant groups contributed to severe restrictions on immigration in the early 1920s. Ethnic enclaves in cities continued to thrive, but the slowdown in the number of foreign arrivals helped set in motion a gradual weakening of older ethnic and linguistic ties and a geographic dispersal of European immigrant families. Widespread unionization created new connections and identities among and across immigrant groups and, over time, contributed to their assimilation into a mainstream "white" American culture.

The demographics of American cities changed as the result of the mass migration of African Americans from the rural South during and after World War I. Known as the First Great Migration, this movement gave cities like New York, Philadelphia, and Chicago significant African American populations, spurring the establishment of a robust set of urban black community institutions, religious bodies, and political groups. Increased Mexican immigration to California and the Southwest after the Mexican Revolution of 1910 and through the interwar period further changed the racial and ethnic mix of cities like Los Angeles.

Urban Culture and Industry. Cities remained the centers of entertainment and culture, including the newest form of mass entertainment, Hollywood movies. Movie attendance soared from 50 million a week in 1920 to 90 million in 1927. By the end of the decade, about 75 percent of the American population was attending movies every week. The expansion of the film industry helped propel the expansion of Los Angeles, a metropolis already made rich on oil and railroads. Joining Los Angeles as another hub of industrial energy and wealth was Detroit, home to the nation's major automakers.

Known as the industry of industries because of its size and economic impact, Detroit's auto manufacturing economy shaped a city that was a dynamic urban model of modernity and automobility. Assembly-line manufacturing required factories with a great deal of floor space, leading companies like Ford and General Motors to set up large plants in outer areas of the city or its suburbs. With their smokestacks and working-class housing, the industrial suburbs created around Detroit were a change from the wealthy residential suburbs of an earlier era.

Like Los Angeles and other metropolises that grew large during the streetcar age, Detroit was a horizontal city that radiated out in a low-density fashion along major trolley lines. As car ownership increased, Detroit became one of the first to adapt and expand this horizontal structure to car traffic, featuring long, straight avenues that allowed workers to commute easily between home and factory. A low-density landscape allowed cities like Los Angeles and Detroit to provide workers of nearly all incomes with the opportunity to live in detached, single-family homes.

Automotive Suburbs. The interwar period also saw the creation of a number of suburban planned communities designed to incorporate and accommodate the automobile. The Country Club District of Kansas City, Missouri, and the Palos Verdes Estates south of Los Angeles are two notable examples of high-end suburbs designed with the car in mind. In addition to the usual array of suburban residential amenities, these developments featured shopping plazas whose convenience and abundant parking made them precursors to the postwar shopping mall.

Other developers put forth suburban models that attempted to minimize the visibility of the car. Inspired by the British planner Ebenezer Howard's idea of a so-called garden city that blended industrial and residential development in a landscaped setting of curved roads and greenbelts, influential planners like Lewis Mumford and Clarence Stein encouraged the development of towns like Radburn, New Jersey, which placed garages at the backs of houses and shared green space in the front. The federally sponsored greenbelt towns of the New Deal were similarly inspired by garden-city ideas. Though early garden cities featured homes for people of different incomes and were meant to have areas with multiple land uses, over time these design principles encouraged exclusively residential and demographically homogeneous suburban settings.

The Great Depression and the New Deal. The Great Depression was economically devastating for American cities. At the Depression's height, Chicago and Detroit had close to 50 percent unemployment; in Toledo, Ohio, it hit 80 percent. Vast shantytowns of displaced workers—labeled "Hoovervilles"—sprang up in the shadows of American downtowns. Homeownership plummeted and the number of foreclosures rose, slowing the suburban housing boom and resulting in little new construction in or around cities between 1929 and 1945.

The mobilization of public resources in response to this economic crisis funded a series of infrastructure projects in cities, suburbs, and adjacent rural areas that created a foundation for vast suburban expansion after World War II. New Deal programs such as the Civil Works Administration and the Civilian Conservation Corps built roads, bridges, and parks in cities and around the urban periphery. In New York City, federal funds fueled the already expansive public works projects spearheaded by the New York State official Robert Moses. The limited-access parkways that Moses built on Long Island and in the Hudson River valley became models for later freeways and encouraged the decentralization of people and industry.

Far beyond the cities, too, 1930s federal infrastructure investment provided another critical ingredient for the mass suburbanization of later decades. Hydroelectric dams like the Hoover Dam, completed in 1935, provided the water and electricity that allowed southwest cities like Las Vegas and Phoenix, as well as urban and suburban southern California, to survive and thrive. The Rural Electrification Administration and the Tennessee Valley Authority performed a similar function in the South, providing electricity and capital to rural areas that in the postwar period morphed into suburbs and exurbs.

The New Deal also generated the first interventions by the U.S. government into the housing market. Seeking to spur mortgage lending and increase homeownership, the federal Home Owners' Loan Corporation and the Federal Housing Administration provided loan guarantees. Yet federal agencies also contributed to the widespread adaptation by banks of a rating system that graded neighborhoods according to their racial and ethnic composition. This contributed to a scarcity of mortgage and other investment capital in minority neighborhoods, whose designation as "red" under these classifications led to the practice's being called "redlining." The federal government also established its first public housing programs during this period. The earliest projects were low-rise, garden apartments targeted to working-class families.

The Era of Mass Suburbanization and the Rise of the Sunbelt.

Visions of a suburbanized, car-dependent future began to emerge before the beginning of World War II. The 1939 New York World's Fair featured a General Motors–sponsored exhibition called "Futurama" that presented a model metropolis of the future. The city center featured high-rise superblock buildings, and ten-lane highways led to verdant suburbs. This was the modern city rebuilt and remade to accommodate the car. After the end of World War II, this landscape of highways, rebuilt urban neighborhoods, and residential subdivisions became ubiquitous throughout metropolitan America.

Wartime Industry and Sunbelt Migration.

The regional economic and demographic shifts set in motion by World War II assisted in this transformation. White workers left the North and the Middle West for war work in the factories and shipyards of the Pacific West. Both whites and blacks left the rural South to escape economic depression and racial discrimination. This period marked the beginning of the Second Great Migration of African Americans to the urban North and West; the black population of large cities continued to increase well into the civil rights era. The balance of people and jobs in the United States moved from what became known as the Rustbelt of the industrial Northeast and Midwest to the Sunbelt of the South and West. Between 1940 and 1950 alone, the population of the seventeen western states grew by 8 million people, or 31 percent. Much of this growth was urban.

The new urban geography of World War II solidified during the Cold War, when hubs of war industry continued to be major sites of defense-related research, development, and manufacturing. San Francisco's Bay Area, Los Angeles, and Seattle were among those metropolitan areas that benefited the most from heavy defense investment. The Cold War also triggered new federal investment in university-based research, which spurred development of high-tech industry clusters near Boston (home to Harvard and the Massachusetts Institute of Technology) and San Francisco (near Stanford and the University of California, Berkeley).

Mass Suburbs. Though American cities had long exhibited a pattern of decentralization and suburbanization, several factors present in the postwar period prompted suburbanization of an unprecedented scale and scope. One critical factor was technology. Wartime production had given American industry the capability to mass-produce construction materials and build homes cheaply and quickly. The widespread introduction of air-conditioning made regions of the South and Southwest appealing as year-round destinations for both residents and industry.

Another important factor was demographics. America was a nation of young families. Two-thirds of Americans in 1950 were married. Between 1946 and 1964, 79 million babies were born. Immigration restrictions had resulted in a nation that was more culturally homogenous; the shared experience of wartime combat and life on the home front further propelled the development of a common American identity.

Public policy was a third, and most decisive, factor. The Serviceman's Readjustment Act of 1944, also known as the GI Bill, provided 8 million returning veterans with college tuition and subsidies for home mortgages.

The numbers of Americans with college degrees skyrocketed in this period, creating an educated class of workers with the credentials to perform the white-collar service jobs of the emerging postindustrial economy. Mortgage subsidies, combined with the mass development of inexpensive suburban housing, put the purchase of a single-family home within the reach of millions of returning veterans and their families.

The vast majority of these homes were in suburbs, developed by mass home-builders like Arthur Levitt, whose Levittowns in New York and New Jersey epitomized the new suburbia. These developments also were almost entirely white. Levitt, like many other developers, went to some lengths to keep minority home-buyers out of his subdivisions. Black families who attempted to buy homes in white neighborhoods in city and suburb often were met with violent reprisals. In a nation where home buying was closely connected with economic opportunity and political identity, white homeowners fiercely fought the arrival of neighbors whose presence might lower property values.

Slum Clearance, Public Housing, and Highways. The housing market got a further federal boost with the Housing Act of 1949, which expanded loan guarantees for housing and provided municipalities with millions of dollars in matching funds to clear slum neighborhoods and build public housing. Cities throughout the nation used these monies to clear "blighted" and "obsolete" neighborhoods of older, mixed-use structures, replacing them with large, modernist developments. Though intended to improve the availability and quality of low-income housing, these projects often demolished poorer areas without immediately providing adequate replacement housing. Because many of the areas targeted for urban renewal were home to racial minorities, this urban renewal program came to be labeled "Negro removal" by some of its critics.

Public housing of the postwar period proved to be a similarly inadequate response to urban poverty. Though there are public-housing success stories from this period, large high-rise housing projects quickly became bleak and crime-ridden symbols of failed federal policy. As early as the 1960s, these projects began to be torn down and replaced with lower-rise, mixed-income housing developments.

Interstate highways were another federal policy that had a profound effect on cities and suburbs. By the time that Dwight D. Eisenhower signed the Interstate Highway Act into law in 1956, many major cities had plans underway for elaborate networks of limited-access highways and arterial road-ways. Federal highway policy created a 90 percent match to local funds for roadway construction, spurring these projects forward. While many urban freeways were built, others were blocked by strong and sustained resistance by residents of neighborhoods in their path. These so-called freeway revolts continued through the 1960s and early 1970s, by which time expansive freeway networks had fallen out of favor with urban leaders and planners.

White Flight and Urban Crisis. Education was another decisive factor in the reshuffling of people around the American metropolis. Throughout the country, school desegregation prompted many white parents to move their children into private academies or leave the cities for all-white suburban school districts. By the late 1960s, many districts had resorted to court-ordered busing programs to ensure racial balance in urban schools, prompting further flight of white middle-class families to suburban districts.

As people and jobs moved out of cities, new forms of community emerged in suburban areas. Shopping malls functioned not only as centers of consumption but as community gathering places, hosting celebrations and events that in an earlier era might have taken place in a town hall or public park. Churchgoing increased in this suburban age, and new suburbs seeded the growth of evangelical Protestant megachurches, particularly in the South and Sunbelt. A suburban generation of stay-at-home housewives led to a dynamic set of formal and informal women's associations in the suburbs, and women were at the forefront of grassroots political movements on both the right and the left ends of the political spectrum.

Poor minorities were left behind in this rising tide of metropolitan affluence, and continued discrimination and lack of economic opportunity led to explosions of violence in American cities over several years in the late 1960s. Beginning with several days of civil disorders in Los Angeles's Watts neighborhood in 1965, riots in subsequent summers in cities like Detroit, Newark, and Washington, D.C., cost hundreds of lives and millions of dollars. It took decades for the neighborhoods where riots occurred to be fully rebuilt, and the broadcast of these events on network television created for white suburbanites indelible images of urban crime.

The 1970s continued this period of urban crisis. Deindustrialization, high energy prices, the rise of foreign competition, and cuts in defense spending ended a quarter of a century of American economic expansion. Shrinking tax rolls and rising social-service costs had devastating effects on municipal governments. New York City nearly declared bankruptcy in 1975. Crime rates in major cities escalated, aided by a television news industry that gave exhaustive coverage to violent crimes, particularly those committed by minorities. Municipalities of all sizes found their incomes shrinking as a result of voter revolts against high property taxes, starting with California's Proposition 13 in 1978. But this period also saw the emergence of fresh urban leadership, with blacks and Hispanics occupying mayor's offices and city council chambers.

The Information Age Metropolis. The last decades of the twentieth century witnessed both the economic and cultural resurgence of many central cities and an even further expansion of suburbs. The United States continued to become more intensely metropolitan, and after 1980 the majority of its population lived in suburbs. Yet these suburbs were highly diverse, and older patterns of wealth and poverty were beginning to change. As development took off even higher densities spread out farther into the countryside, the distinctions among city, suburb, and rural area became blurred.

The decline of American manufacturing and the rise of a postindustrial economy of knowledge work and low-skilled service jobs prompted a new metropolitan geography of work and leisure. Suburbs became dotted with office parks and research parks; major clusters of technology and telecommunications companies were chiefly suburban in location. In retailing, big-box retailers joined shopping malls on the metropolitan outskirts. An imbalance between where jobs were located and where people could afford to buy or rent homes led to long commutes for many workers. Both commute distance and traffic congestion increased measurably in many American cities during the 1990s.

Meanwhile, economic and demographic change helped central cities bounce back from the crises of the 1970s and 1980s. Historic preservation and restoration of older neighborhoods in cities like New York, Washington D.C., and Chicago turned these neighborhoods into desirable residential and commercial districts, but this preservation and restoration also drove up real estate prices and displaced poor and minority residents. Urban revival and gentrification made central cities into tourist destinations and entertainment hubs for suburban residents, and popular culture again began to portray cities like New York as exciting playgrounds for the young and affluent. Yet some of the great cities of the industrial age continued to struggle with chronic poverty and unemployment. Detroit became the most extreme example of a city in decline, and by the early twenty-first century some of its abandoned urban spaces were being converted into parks and farmland.

Immigration once again changed the character of the American metropolis. The lifting of restrictive quotas in 1965 allowed for giant new flows of immigrants, particularly from Asia and Latin America. These new groups of immigrants built dynamic ethnic enclaves in older urban neighborhoods, driving economic revitalization and population growth. Yet as many, if not more, of these immigrants chose to settle in suburbs, profoundly changing suburban demographics and culture from Seattle and Los Angeles to Detroit and Atlanta.

By the early twenty-first century, immigration, technology, culture, and trade linked American cities and suburbs to one another and to cities around the world. Though throughout its history the American metropolis has been a product of global flows and systems, its fortunes and its futures had become connected to those of the rest of the world like never before.

[*See also* **Americanization Movement; Amusement Parks and Theme Parks; Central and Eastern European Americans;**

Chinatowns; Coffeehouses and Coffee; Demography; Electricity and Electrification; Exploration, Conquest, and Settlement in North America; German Americans; Great Depression Era; Immigration; Internal Migration; Irish Americans; Jewish Americans; Lowell Textile Mills; Missions, in America; New Deal Social Reforms; Riots, Urban; Segregation, Racial; Separate Spheres Ideology; Tourism and Travel; *and* Working-Class Life and Society.]

BIBLIOGRAPHY

Barth, Gunther P. *City People: The Rise of Modern City Culture in Nineteenth-Century America.* New York: Oxford University Press, 1980.

Bodnar, John. *The Transplanted: A History of Immigrants in Urban America.* Bloomington: Indiana University Press, 1987.

Boyer, Paul S. *Urban Masses and Moral Order in America, 1820–1920.* Cambridge, Mass.: Harvard University Press, 1978.

Cronon, William. *Nature's Metropolis: Chicago and the Great West.* New York: W. W. Norton and Company, 1991.

Erickson, David J. *The Housing Policy Revolution: Networks and Neighborhoods.* Washington, D.C.: Urban Institute Press, 2009.

Jackson, Kenneth T. *Crabgrass Frontier: The Suburbanization of the United States.* New York: Oxford University Press, 1985.

Kruse, Kevin M. *White Flight: Atlanta and the Making of Modern Conservatism.* Princeton, N.J.: Princeton University Press, 2005.

May, Elaine Tyler. *Homeward Bound: American Families in the Cold War Era.* New York: Basic Books, 1988.

McGirr, Lisa. *Suburban Warriors: The Origins of the New American Right.* Princeton, N.J.: Princeton University Press, 2001.

O'Mara, Margaret Pugh. *Cities of Knowledge: Cold War Science and the Search for the Next Silicon Valley.* Princeton, N.J.: Princeton University Press, 2005.

Sugrue, Thomas J. *Origins of the Urban Crisis: Race and Inequality in Postwar Detroit.* Princeton, N.J.: Princeton University Press, 1996.

Teaford, Jon C. *The Unheralded Triumph: City Government in America, 1870–1900.* Baltimore: Johns Hopkins University Press, 1984.

Warner, Sam Bass. *The Private City: Philadelphia in Three Periods of Its Growth.* 2d ed. Philadelphia: University of Pennsylvania Press, 1987.

Margaret Pugh O'Mara

CIVIL RIGHTS ACT (1964)

The Civil Rights Act of 1964 is regarded as the postwar civil rights movement's most significant victory. Its passage culminated a hundred years of efforts after the Civil War to enshrine equality in American society. In addition to improving the lives of millions of African Americans, it set a precedent for affirmative action laws. And because the act was the result of grassroots activism, its passage validated continued civil rights efforts among a variety of U.S. ethnic minorities and women.

The civil rights movement, spurred by the Supreme Court's decision to strike down educational segregation in *Brown v. Board of Education* in 1954, put increasing pressure on the executive and legislative branches to back the fight against racial discrimination in American life. Civil rights acts passed in 1957 and 1960 during the Republican administration of Dwight D. Eisenhower had little force. During the first years of his presidency, the Democrat John F. Kennedy limited his support for civil rights because of the need to satisfy his party's large southern wing. In 1963, however, direct-action protests against segregation in Birmingham, Alabama, led by the Southern Christian Leadership Conference and the Reverend Martin Luther King Jr., forced the government's hand. As the nation watched via television news footage and photojournalism, the Birmingham police commissioner Eugene "Bull" Connor ordered the use of fire hoses and attack dogs against nonviolent protesters, including children. Soon religious and labor groups joined civil rights organizations in lobbying the president and Congress. After attempts to mediate the crisis in Alabama, the president and his advisers concluded that without strong federal action, the protests would spread. Some Birmingham blacks had already responded to white terrorism with violence in kind, and the administration sensed that it would be held responsible in the 1964 election. In a nationally televised speech on 11 June 1963, Kennedy finally called for new legislation.

The administration sent its bill to the House Judiciary Committee, chaired by Emanuel Celler, a Democrat from New York, with William McCulloch, a Republican from Ohio, the ranking minority member. Celler and McCulloch developed the language, with McCulloch's input crucial to satisfy the administration's insistence on a bipartisan bill. The bill remained in subcommittee in August 1963 when civil rights leaders led the March on Washington. In his first address to Congress, made just days after Kennedy's assassination in November 1963, President Lyndon B. Johnson portrayed the bill in part as a tribute to his fallen predecessor, but not until late January 1964 could Celler bring the bill to the House floor. Among many proposed amendments designed to weaken or kill the bill that were introduced during the nine-day House debate, the Virginia Democrat Howard Smith's offered to prohibit employment discrimination based on sex. It passed, and what began as a joke on behalf of segregationists turned into a weapon in the fight against sex discrimination.

The bill then survived a three-month filibuster in the Senate. Johnson lent important support throughout the process, working back channels and bringing his extensive legislative experience to bear. With cloture finally imposed on 10 June 1964, and after consideration of 104 amendments, on 22 June the bill passed the Senate by a vote of 73 to 27. The House accepted the Senate version on 2 July, and Johnson signed the bill into law later that day.

The Civil Rights Act of 1964 had a sweeping impact on American society because it fundamentally interpreted the Fourteenth Amendment's equal protection clause as a federal bulwark against race and sex discrimination. The act had its greatest impact in making discrimination in interstate transportation, schools, workplaces, and "public accommodations"—hotels, restaurants, and other public places—illegal. The act attempted to protect voter registration, strengthening the federal commitment to the Fifteenth Amendment. However, by supporting a standard of education—namely, completion of the sixth grade—rather than eliminating the idea of voting qualifications, the act did little to increase registration in the South and made the 1965 Voting Rights Act necessary. The act did eventually lead to the elimination of separate school districts based on race, and its impact on actual integration of schools meant that most southern black children attended desegregated schools by 1970.

In addition, the Civil Rights Act established the Equal Employment Opportunity Commission to enforce the act's ban on workplace discrimination based on race, color, religion, sex, or national origin. The act banned discrimination in labor unions, as well as separate locals based on race. The provision against sex discrimination gave legal backing to women's activism for equality. Members of the President's Commission on Status of Women, appointed in 1961, founded the National Organization for Women in 1966 in part to insist on enforcement of the clause against sex discrimination. Finally, the Civil Rights Act influenced the character of Johnson's Great Society measures of the 1960s and all government initiatives beyond. In an era of expanded federal presence in American society, the bill prohibited discrimination in federally funded programs and benefits.

[*See also* Affirmative Action; African Americans; Civil Rights Movement; Desegregation; Great Society Reform Programs; Law and Society; March on Washington; National Organization for Women; *and* Segregation, Racial.]

BIBLIOGRAPHY

Branch, Taylor. *Parting the Waters: America in the King Years, 1954–63.* New York: Simon & Schuster, 1988.

Branch, Taylor. *Pillar of Fire: America in the King Years, 1963–65.* New York: Simon & Schuster, 1998. *Parting the Waters and Pillar of Fire,* the first two volumes of Branch's King biography, provide a nearly day-by-day narrative of the civil rights movement, including the Birmingham protests and the responses by the Kennedy and Johnson administrations.

Evans, Sara. *Personal Politics: The Roots of Women's Liberation in the Civil Rights Movement and the New Left.* New York: Alfred A. Knopf, 1979. A classic study of Second Wave feminism of the 1960s and 1970s, with special attention devoted to the activities of NOW.

Grofman, Bernard, ed. *Legacies of the 1964 Civil Rights Act.* Charlottesville: University Press of Virginia, 2000. Essays on the act's impact.

Loevy, Robert D. *To End All Segregation: The Politics of the Passage of the Civil Rights Act of 1964.* Lanham, Md.: University Press of America, 1990. Provides a close focus on the act's legislative history.

Patterson, James T. *Grand Expectations: The United States, 1945–1974.* New York: Oxford University Press, 1996. Situates the civil rights movement

and the act in the context of U.S. foreign and domestic policy and traces the movement's triumphs, along with the backlash of the later 1960s and 1970s.

Benjamin Cawthra

CIVIL RIGHTS MOVEMENT

Encompassing three centuries of daily struggle for freedom in the face of white supremacy, the U.S. civil rights movement is best understood in this broad context of the Revolutionary era through the twentieth century. The movement culminating in the organized protests and civil rights legislation of the 1950s and 1960s drew upon the experiences of rebel fugitive slaves, Maroon communities, black and white abolitionists, and free blacks who battled second-class citizenship. During the eighteenth century, the egalitarian rhetoric of the American, the French, and especially the Haitian revolutions, as well as the religious doctrines of the Black Freedom Church and the Quakers (Society of Friends), produced a nascent antislavery movement. The outlawing of American involvement in the international slave trade in 1808 and the creation of the American Colonization Society in 1816 anticipated the abolitionist movement that arose in the 1820s and 1830s. Abolitionist activity, in turn, focused attention on civil rights, especially in northern cities where free-black communities, sustained by strong, independent black churches, sheltered fugitive slaves, nurtured abolitionist leaders such as Frederick Douglass and Sojourner Truth, created independent educational and political institutions, and advocated for equality.

Nineteenth-Century Background.
By the 1840s several elements of the post–World

War II civil rights movement fell into place: armed self-defense in the face of racial terrorism, some interracial cooperation and conflict, patterns of community-organized protest, the political mobilization of black religious institutions, the creation of regional and national civil rights organizations, and the use of divergent tactics in the North and the South. The Fugitive Slave Act of 1850 intensified civil rights activism, as did the 1857 Dred Scott decision (*Dred Scott v. Sandford*) and John Brown's 1859 raid on Harpers Ferry.

For most of the Civil War (1861–1865) abolitionists failed in their efforts to center the war effort on the destruction of slavery. Though the administration of Abraham Lincoln eventually acknowledged that the war for the Union was also a war of emancipation, it showed no interest in promoting equal black citizenship or curtailing political white supremacy. Nevertheless, blacks' service in the Union army, the Emancipation Proclamation (1863), and Radical Republicans' proposals for a postwar reconstruction of the South ultimately resulted in the Thirteenth Amendment, abolishing slavery, in 1865. Its concrete meaning remained undefined and, for many freedpeople, unrealized. Consequently, some Republican leaders drafted the Fourteenth Amendment, ratified in 1868, to strengthen equal protection and due process, and encouraged Congress to enact additional civil rights acts in 1870, 1871, and 1875.

Nonetheless, white Republicans' most egregious betrayal of African Americans occurred in the contested election of 1876: in exchange for the presidency, Republicans pulled all federal troops out of the South and allowed white supremacists legally to terrorize any blacks who advocated equality over the next ninety years in the region. In 1883 the Supreme Court codified this treachery, declaring the 1875 Civil Rights Act unconstitutional. The generation of white politicians who had ended slavery passed from the scene without honestly addressing the underlying structures, laws, and habits of white supremacy or massive racial inequality.

During the 1890s, black participation in the Populist revolt briefly revived the civil rights cause, but the demise of the Populist Party left African Americans with bleak prospects for social, economic, or political equality. In the North, African American communities were too small to influence a political culture focused on immigrants, not native blacks. In the Jim Crow South, home to the vast majority of African Americans, terror inhibited challenges to the racial status quo. A few scattered civil rights protests occurred, including several boycotts of segregated streetcars, but most southern blacks were forced to live with disenfranchisement, debt peonage, and a rigid system of racial segregation reinforced by the "separate but equal" doctrine of the 1896 Supreme Court decision in *Plessy v. Ferguson.*

Before World War II. In the early twentieth century Booker T. Washington's accommodationist philosophy dominated discussions of racial progress. But as white-supremacist violence mounted, an alternative philosophy rooted in racial pride and earlier protest traditions reemerged. In New York City in early 1909, following notably bloody race riots in Wilmington, North Carolina, in 1898, in Atlanta in 1906, and in Springfield, Illinois, in 1908, African American and liberal white intellectuals founded the National Association for the Advancement of Colored People (NAACP) to promote equal civil rights. In 1910 a second group, also based in New York City and more focused on urban amelioration, formed the National Urban League (NUL). Although several decades passed before these organizations became fully effective, they provided an embryonic organizational base for the modern civil rights movement. The NAACP proved especially influential, primarily through the activities of W. E. B. Du Bois, the outspoken editor of the NAACP's magazine *The Crisis*, and James Weldon Johnson, the NAACP's first black executive secretary. Though the formal organizational center of the civil rights struggle remained in the North, grassroots southern movements for equality grew, especially among youth NAACP groups, railroad porters and other black union members, and black business owners.

During the 1920s the civil rights cause diversified its philosophies and tactics, led most visibly by the black nationalist Marcus Garvey, writers and artists of the Harlem Renaissance, Socialist and Communist politicians, and black labor leaders such as A. Philip Randolph. Black workers in the South fused locally based traditions, ideologies, and strategies of resistance with the Pan-African agenda of Garvey's Universal Negro Improvement Association to create a dynamic and multifaceted movement. The struggle now set the stage for a future national movement during the Great Depression decade of the 1930s. President Franklin Delano Roosevelt's political dependence on white southern Democrats and his single-minded focus on the economic crisis meant that he paid scant attention to racial discrimination. But the New Deal's social-justice orientation offered a measure of hope to civil rights activists, who for the first time since Reconstruction regarded the federal government as a potential ally. The 1936 election marked the first time that a majority of African Americans, 71 percent, voted for the Democrats instead of the party of Lincoln. The NAACP devoted almost all of its scanty resources to judicial and legislative reform. While Charles Hamilton Houston, Thurgood Marshall, Oliver Hill, and other NAACP attorneys attacked the legal structure of racial segregation, the executive secretary Walter White campaigned for federal antilynching legislation.

The 1940s proved a pivotal decade. Threatening a mass march on Washington in 1941, A. Philip Randolph forced Roosevelt to create the Fair Employment Practices Committee (FEPC), empowered to combat racial discrimination in wartime employment. Black servicemen and industrial workers proved critical to the war effort; Randolph and others promoted the Double V campaign, which called for victory against fascism abroad and against racism at home. The campaign yielded mixed results. The armed forces remained rigidly segregated throughout the war, and interracial violence erupted in Detroit and other northern cities.

Still, the war produced a generation of black servicemen who had traveled outside the South and put their lives on the line for a democracy that they expected to participate in upon their return. These African American servicemen quietly and steadfastly asserted their citizenship by registering to vote and insisting on equal access to taxpayer-supported institutions like libraries and parks. This generation's sea change in attitude led to a wide array of challenges to white supremacy: sit-ins, economic boycotts, and protest marches. The emergence of direct action as a significant component of the civil rights struggle dates to the war years. The NAACP's Youth Councils and the Communist Party USA fostered some direct action, but more important was the Congress of Racial Equality (CORE), an interracial organization of northern pacifists, labor activists, and left-wing intellectuals founded in 1942.

The 1950s. Civil rights activism intensified in the immediate postwar era, spurred by black veterans, the U.S. government's propaganda discrediting Nazi racial theories, the Pan-African liberation movements of the 1940s, a shift in racial attitudes among intellectuals—some influenced by Gunnar Myrdal's 1944 study of American race relations *An American Dilemma*—and *Smith v. Allwright*, a 1944 Supreme Court decision outlawing all-white primaries. Jackie Robinson broke the color line in major-league baseball, CORE's Journey of Reconciliation through the upper South challenged segregation in interstate buses, the Supreme Court issued a series of encouraging rulings, and President Harry S. Truman desegregated the armed services and convened a presidential commission on civil rights. The NAACP, meanwhile, expanded its legal assault on Jim Crow, culminating in the 1954 *Brown v. Board of Education* school desegregation decision.

Legal backsliding and white politicians' demagoguery, however, soon slowed the pace of the civil rights revolution to a crawl. In a 1955 follow-up to the *Brown* decision, the Supreme Court's hazy timetable allowed white school districts to desegregate "with all deliberate speed." For some districts, this meant that desegregation still had not arrived by the 1970s; others remained more segregated in the twenty-first century than they were in 1954. Meanwhile segregationist White Citizens' Councils spread across the South, revoking mortgages and keeping business loans and jobs from any blacks who challenged Jim Crow.

In this context, in 1955, Emmett Till, a fourteen-year-old from Chicago, was visiting family in Money, Mississippi, for the summer. He either talked to a white woman or looked her directly in the eye. The woman's husband and brother-in-law tortured and subsequently beat to death the eighth-grade boy. Till's mother, Mamie Till Bradley, asked Pullman porters to sneak her son's body out of the state under cover of darkness. She then held an open-casket funeral for her son in Chicago,

inviting the world press, so that the world could "see what they did to my baby." An all-white jury found the two men accused of the murder not guilty. Till's murder mobilized an entire generation of civil rights activists— people in his age-group of baby boomers, nearly every one of whom could recall fifty years later when and where they were upon hearing about Till's murder.

Four months later, in December 1955, a well-organized activist network mobilized behind an act of courage to galvanize the entire black community of Montgomery, Alabama. The arrest of Rosa Parks, a seamstress and NAACP activist who violated a local segregation ordinance by refusing to move to the back of a city bus, sparked a thirteen-month bus boycott that attracted international attention. Led by E. D. Nixon of the local NAACP, Jo Ann Gibson Robinson of the faculty of Alabama State College, and a twenty-six-year-old minister who was new to town, the Reverend Martin Luther King Jr., the Montgomery Improvement Association (MIA) illuminated the political power of a southern black community united by a Gandhian strategy of nonviolent resistance. A testing ground for differing theories of social change, Montgomery's bus boycott made vivid the economic and moral vulnerability of segregation, the inability of even moderate segregationists to compromise, the stout resolution of many southern blacks, and the importance of politically mobilizing the black church.

In 1957 the movement seemed to gain momentum, with King organizing southern black ministers together under the Southern Christian Leadership Conference (SCLC), President Dwight D. Eisenhower's use of federal troops to desegregate Little Rock's Central High School, and the passage of the first federal civil rights law since Reconstruction. It is important to note even at this early stage the variety of tactics that civil rights activists employed. For instance, it was at this time, not in the late 1960s, that Robert F. Williams, the local NAACP leader in Monroe, North Carolina, set up the Black Armed Guard to defend Monroe's black residents from Ku Klux Klan night riders. His insistence on every American's right to self-defense reminded civil rights activists in 1958 that arms had always been just as important to the civil rights struggle as nonviolence, challenging the national NAACP and Dr. King to reexamine their reliance on legal challenges and nonviolent tactics.

But the later 1950s proved disappointing: the pace of school desegregation slowed, the lack of enforcement power of the 1957 Civil Rights Act became apparent, and the NAACP suspended Robert Williams. Cold War politics dominated American public life, frustrating efforts to refocus national attention on civil rights. Meanwhile, outside the limelight, a pivotal civil rights organizer began to kick into high gear. In the late 1950s the longtime activist Ella Baker, a leader of the SCLC, intensified her emphasis on community-based voter registration in black communities throughout the South. Using the slow, patient work of recruiting people to register through what were called "citizenship schools," staffed by education pioneers like Septima Clark, Annelle Ponder, and Dorothy Cotton, such key efforts, which were largely invisible to the outside world, literally made possible the next decade's passage of the Voting Rights Act.

The 1960s. Then in February 1960, four black college freshmen staged an impromptu sit-in at a segregated Woolworth's lunch counter in Greensboro, North Carolina. The movement soon spread to more than a hundred southern cities and prompted the founding of the Student Nonviolent Coordinating Committee (SNCC). Although many NAACP

and SCLC leaders were wary of SNCC's confrontational style, King's endorsement and the wise counsel of Ella Baker helped sustain the new organization. A young Methodist minister who had just returned from studying Gandhian tactics in India, James Lawson, trained those in SNCC how to wield the "nonviolent anvil." Soon thousands of college and high school students across the South—most but not all African American—refused to obey Jim Crow at every juncture, simply by acting as if they were free and equal citizens.

In 1961, CORE sponsored the first Freedom Ride—modeled after the 1947 Journey of Reconciliation—from Washington, D.C., all the way to New Orleans, in order to test a recent Supreme Court decision prohibiting segregation on interstate buses. Whites firebombed the buses in Anniston and Birmingham, Alabama. CORE called off the ride out of fear for the lives of their activists. The youth of SNCC vowed to complete the journey: "if they stop us with violence, the movement is dead," SNCC's Diane Nash declared. Activists from across the nation joined the ride, each group confronting state officials and other white supremacists in Alabama and Mississippi. Dr. King nicknamed SNCC "the storm troopers of the South," opening free space previously untouched by the movement. The administration of John F. Kennedy, deep in preparations for an upcoming Soviet summit in Vienna, only begrudgingly intervened, and that to forestall international embarrassment. However, rather than enforce federal law, Attorney General Robert Kennedy betrayed the riders by making a deal with Mississippi's governor: in exchange for assurance of the riders' safe passage into Mississippi, Kennedy would not intervene in the riders' imprisonment in that state's infamous Parchman prison. At Parchman, Kennedy left riders to be tortured with impunity: they were hung from prison bars by their arms, beaten with wire brushes, and burned with cattle prods.

Rather than leading to an expression of regret to the riders, however, the Freedom Ride crisis only deepened the Kennedy administration's fears of an uncontrolled mass movement that undermined U.S. claims of being the greatest beacon of freedom in a world divided between unfree Communism and free democracy. The Kennedy brothers urged civil rights leaders to redirect their efforts from highly publicized direct-action sit-ins and Freedom Rides toward the voter-registration campaigns quietly generated by Ella Baker, Septima Clark, and others. Activists, including King, decided to pursue both strategies: voter-registration efforts and direct action such as sit-ins, pray-ins, wade-ins, and Freedom Rides. Surprising the Kennedys, voter registration provoked as much if not more violence than direct actions like sit-ins. Together, all these actions provided a dramatic focus for media coverage and recruited thousands more to the movement.

Local Organizing and National Notice.
Across the South's Black Belt between 1957 and 1963, thousands of local people began to organize voter-registration drives, citizenship schools, political campaigns, and economic cooperatives. From this rich grassroots activity nurtured by intellectuals like Fannie Lou Hamer, Amzie Moore, and Victoria Gray Adams, the South's political landscape was forever altered: day laborers, domestics, and sharecroppers gained literacy, then began to advocate on the city and county levels for civic goals like paved streets, black sheriffs, and equal allotment of agricultural subsidies and school buses. Such prosaic activities were largely invisible when compared to the energizing drama of the sit-ins and Freedom Rides, but they nonetheless led to a whole-sale transformation of the Democratic Party

with the formation of the Mississippi Freedom Democratic Party (MFDP) in 1964, as well as to the national political discourse on Black Power through the Lowndes County (Alabama) Freedom Organization in 1965.

Despite the astounding long-term achievements of this quiet, persistent organizing at the base of society, this kind of civil rights activity was still largely invisible to those outside the movement in the early 1960s. What was visible to most news outlets was, for instance, the "action" appearing in Albany, Georgia, in late 1961 and 1962—action that was interpreted as showing that the black community had a new commitment to mass action of a type that was assertive and defiant. White power pushed back: local officials, warned by a complicit Federal Bureau of Investigation, figured out how to confound the SCLC's strategy of intentionally filling the jails with protesters. In addition, persistent tensions among the SCLC, SNCC, and local activists eventually convinced King to abandon the Albany campaign. Still, the community's commitment continued, providing a huge breakthrough example for black communities around the South. Later in 1962, James Meredith's attempt to desegregate the University of Mississippi caused a wide-scale riot by white supremacists. The Kennedy administration sent in U.S. marshals, military police, an army battalion, the Mississippi Army National Guard, and the U.S. Border Patrol to allow Meredith entrance to the University of Mississippi—and more than 160 of them were wounded.

Intervention by the Federal Government.
White-supremacist opposition reached a fever pitch in 1963: this year saw the murder of the Mississippi NAACP leader Medgar Evers, the Alabama governor George Wallace's demagogic "stand in the schoolhouse door" to prevent integration, the Birmingham commissioner

of public safety Eugene "Bull" Connor's use of attack dogs and fire hoses against SCLC-sponsored demonstrations, and the murder of four black girls in a Birmingham church bombing. To the rest of the country, such violence indicated that, indeed, the federal government needed to intervene on the side of the civil rights movement. The movement's rising power was confirmed by a successful mass march on Washington in August and the Kennedy administration's long-awaited endorsement of a comprehensive civil rights bill. Following President Kennedy's assassination in November, Lyndon B. Johnson used his legislative skills and the image of a martyred president to push through a civil rights act that for the first time since 1875 used federal law-enforcement powers to ban state-supported racial discrimination in all public accommodations.

Though the 1964 Civil Rights Act proved a milestone in the movement's history, King and other leaders continued to demand black enfranchisement. Freedom Summer, a 1964 voter-registration campaign in Mississippi, brought hundreds of college students and other volunteers to see firsthand the results of political exclusion. Freedom Summer also revealed the depths of opposition to the movement: by the end of June, three civil rights workers had been murdered. By the end of the summer, twelve more were murdered, more than one thousand workers and locals were arrested, and thirty-seven churches were bombed or burned. As a young SNCC staffer, Jane Stembridge, wrote: "America, we have paid a high price for your attention." In August 1964, even the national Democrats betrayed the movement: at the Democratic National Convention, Johnson refused to seat the Mississippi Freedom Democratic Party (MFDP), acceding to the state's all-white delegation. That December, Malcolm X, recently estranged from the Nation of Islam, invited the

MFDP activist Fannie Lou Hamer to speak in Harlem. She concisely pointed out that in both the North and the South, "the Thirteenth, Fourteenth, and Fifteenth Amendments to the U.S. Constitution haven't done anything for us yet." Malcolm X formed the Organization of Afro-American Unity (OAAU) to bring northern and southern strategies to the same table, an agenda that was cut short by his assassination in February 1965. After activists slogged through the spring of 1965 in Alabama, however, including the Selma-to-Montgomery march of March 1965, Congress approved the Voting Rights Act of 1965. Finally the federal government would enforce equal access to the franchise nationwide.

Disillusionment of the Late 1960s. The exhilaration of having two major pieces of civil rights legislation passed within a year did not last. Among African Americans, the protracted struggle for legal equality raised expectations that people might experience day-to-day lived equality; ongoing white resistance led quickly to frustration and exacerbated tensions within the movement. The limitations of the civil rights revolution became glaringly clear from 1964 through 1967 when the media focus shifted northward to cities such as Chicago and Detroit, where poverty, unequal access to quality education, and de facto segregation bred despair, economic apartheid, and rage. Indeed, it became increasingly clear that northern de facto segregation was strongly supported by government structures that dated back to the Progressive and New Deal eras. Young people thus responded enthusiastically to the SNCC chairman Stokely Carmichael's call for "black power for black people" in June 1966 during the Meredith March against Fear. James Meredith, after integrating Ole Miss, decided four years later to march from Memphis to

Jackson to encourage black Mississippians to register and vote.

A year earlier, in Lowndes County, Alabama, Carmichael had begun a voter-registration drive: though the county's population was 80 percent African American, African Americans constituted not even 1 percent of the electorate. During this time Carmichael and others decided to form a third party, the Lowndes County Freedom Organization, whose symbol was a black panther. This immediately resonated with Huey Newton and Bobby Seale, two young law students with southern roots living in Oakland, California. By October 1966 they had founded the Black Panther Party to educate their community about each person's civil rights when confronting police brutality and murder.

Thus baby boomers' expectations for equality crashed against the resistance of older generations holding institutional power in the late 1960s; as a result many youth found the politics of self-determination, racial pride, Black Power, or black nationalism increasingly attractive. This was more than rhetoric or identity politics; indeed, in many urban areas one could find the same kind of community-based organizing that powered the southern movement. Before such organizing could make a significant impact, a series of urban uprisings in 1965–1968 exacerbated racial polarization and white backlash. The movement's commitment to nonviolence seemed inadequate to challenge economic inequality or politically mobilized white supremacy. Fearing this change, many moderate whites' liberalism dissipated in the face of a call by white Republicans for a politics of law and order. Over the subsequent two decades, whites defected en masse to the Republican Party.

Sacred Ground: The Contested Legacy of the Civil Rights Movement. By 1968, the year of King's assassination and the public's growing preoccupation with the Vietnam War, the classic phase of the civil rights movement was over, leaving its fragmented remnants to struggle over such issues as urban renewal, affirmative action, court-ordered busing, economic inequality, and de facto segregation. They did so, however, in the political and cultural context of the so-called rights revolution—an ever-expanding struggle by a wide variety of groups seeking civic equality. Over the subsequent fifty years, feminists, Latinos, Asian Americans, gays and lesbians, older Americans, abortion opponents, persons with disabilities, and other groups drew upon the organizing strategies, symbolism, and rhetoric of the black-led civil rights movement.

This legacy continues to pulse through American culture in the twenty-first century. Civil rights workers cleared new spaces through their slow, patient grassroots work: they learned how to act as full citizens and helped bring forth that same knowledge within tens of thousands of others. The vision they carved out provided a dream of a more profoundly democratic body politic. The practical and ideological successes of the American civil rights movement provided a model for subsequent freedom struggles not only within the United States but internationally: in Czechoslovakia, China, South Africa, and Iran, among others. Still, this vision has been—at best—unevenly adopted by the wider culture, both domestically and abroad. As Ella Baker once noted, the struggle continues: "Until the killing of black men, black mothers' sons, is as important as the killing of white men, white mothers' sons, we who believe in freedom cannot rest" (Waldo E. Martin and Patricia Sullivan, eds., *Civil Rights in the United States.* Vol. 1 [New York: Macmillan, 2000], p. 58).

[See also Affirmative Action; African Americans; Antilynching Movement; Atlanta; Baker, Ella; Black Nationalism; Black Panthers; Carmichael, Stokely; Civil Rights Act (1964); Community Organizing; Congress of Racial Equality; Desegregation; Education; Fifties, The; King, Martin Luther, Jr.; Law and Society; Lynching; Malcolm X; March on Washington; National Association for the Advancement of Colored People; National Urban League; Parks, Rosa; Poverty; Racism; Riots, Race; Riots, Urban; Segregation, Racial; Sixties, The; Slums; South, The; and Student Nonviolent Coordinating Committee.]

BIBLIOGRAPHY

Austin, Curtis J. *Up against the Wall: Violence in the Making and Unmaking of the Black Panther Party*. Fayetteville: University of Arkansas Press, 2006.

Branch, Taylor. *Parting the Waters: America in the King Years, 1954–63*. New York: Simon and Schuster, 1988.

Carmichael, Stokely, with Ekwueme Michael Thelwell. *Ready for Revolution: The Life and Struggles of Stokely Carmichael (Kwame Ture)*. New York: Scribner, 2003.

Carson, Clayborne. *In Struggle: SNCC and the Black Awakening of the 1960s*. Cambridge, Mass.: Harvard University Press, 1981.

Chafe, William H. *Civilities and Civil Rights: Greensboro, North Carolina, and the Black Struggle for Freedom*. New York: Oxford University Press, 1980.

Crosby, Emilye, ed. *Civil Rights History from the Ground Up: Local Struggles, A National Movement*. Athens, Ga.: University of Georgia Press, 2011.

Dittmer, John. *Local People: The Struggle for Civil Rights in Mississippi*. Urbana: University of Illinois Press, 1994.

Dudziak, Mary L. *Cold War Civil Rights: Race and the Image of American Democracy*. Princeton, N.J.: Princeton University Press, 2000.

Evans, Sara M. *Personal Politics: The Roots of Women's Liberation in the Civil Rights Movement and the New Left*. New York: Alfred A. Knopf, 1979.

Franklin, John Hope. *From Slavery to Freedom: A History of American Negroes*. New York: Alfred A. Knopf, 1947.

Harding, Vincent. *There Is a River: The Black Struggle for Freedom in America*. New York: Harcourt Brace Jovanovich, 1981.

Harold, Claudrena N. *The Rise and Fall of the Garvey Movement in the Urban South, 1918–1942*. New York: Routledge, 2007.

Hogan, Wesley. *Many Minds, One Heart: SNCC and the Dream for a New America*. Chapel Hill: University of North Carolina Press, 2007.

Holsaert, Faith, ed. *Hands on the Freedom Plow: Personal Accounts by Women in SNCC*. Urbana: University of Illinois Press, 2010.

Jeffries, Hasan Kwame. *Bloody Lowndes: Civil Rights and Black Power in Alabama's Black Belt*. New York: New York University Press, 2009.

Joseph, Peniel E., ed. *The Black Power Movement: Rethinking the Civil Rights–Black Power Era*. New York: Routledge, 2006.

Kluger, Richard. *Simple Justice: The History of "Brown v. Board of Education" and Black America's Struggle for Equality*. New York: Alfred A. Knopf, 1975.

Lewis, John, with Michael D'Orso. *Walking with the Wind: A Memoir of the Movement*. New York: Simon and Schuster, 1998.

Louis, Debbie. *And We Are Not Saved: A History of the Movement as People*. Garden City, N.Y.: Doubleday, 1970.

Malcolm X, with Alex Haley. *The Autobiography of Malcolm X*. New York: Grove Press, 1965.

Payne, Charles M. *I've Got the Light of Freedom: The Organizing Tradition and the Mississippi Freedom Struggle*. Berkeley: University of California Press, 1995.

Raines, Howell, ed. *My Soul Is Rested: Movement Days in the Deep South Remembered*. New York: Putnam, 1977.

Robnett, Belinda. *How Long, How Long? African-American Women in the Struggle for Civil Rights*. New York: Oxford University Press, 1997.

Theoharis, Jeanne, and Komozi Woodard, eds. *Freedom North: Black Freedom Struggles outside the South, 1940–1980*. New York: Palgrave Macmillan, 2003.

Theoharis, Jeanne, and Komozi Woodard, eds. *Groundwork: Local Black Freedom Movements in America*. New York: New York University Press, 2005.

Tyson, Timothy B. *Radio Free Dixie: Robert F. Williams and the Roots of Black Power*. Chapel Hill: University of North Carolina Press, 1999.

Walker, Alice. *Meridian*. New York: Harcourt Brace Jovanovich, 1976.

Woodward, C. Vann. *The Strange Career of Jim Crow*. 3d ed. New York: Oxford University Press, 1974.

Wesley Hogan

CIVIL WAR ERA

The development of a textile-based industrial economy in early nineteenth-century New England required the production of short-staple cotton picked on vast southern plantations by African American slaves. The interdependent economic systems in the North and South generated enormous wealth for both industrialists and planters. However, it relied upon an exploitative wage-labor system in the expanding northern industrial belt and a racially defined system of chattel slavery across the plantation South. As these two economic and social systems developed, political, religious, and intellectual leaders in each section advanced more coherent ideological defenses of their own systems of labor and social organization. Basic questions concerning gender relations in the household, the meaning of freedom and citizenship in the republic, the settlement of the West, and the cultural construction of racial and ethnic identities hung in the balance of this increasingly antagonistic sectional divide. It did not become a true crisis, however, until the treaty of Guadalupe Hidalgo settled the Mexican War in 1848 and transferred half of Mexico's land to the United States.

Growing Crisis. Initially, the so-called Compromise of 1850—which admitted California to the Union as a free state, while granting the South the strong new federal Fugitive Slave Act—appeared sufficient to answer the nation's post–Mexican War sectional crisis. Politicians in the Democratic and Whig Parties turned their attention to other social matters, including immigration and temperance. Burgeoning numbers of Irish Catholics escaping famine in Ireland altered the calculus of mass politics in cities across the country. And large-scale economic crisis in Germany forced millions of small farmers and skilled tradesmen to migrate to the cities and farms of the Midwest. At the same time, American family farms began to consolidate as commercial institutions, with large numbers of rural Americans beginning life anew in growing industrial cities like Chicago, Cincinnati, and Baltimore. Native Protestant and immigrant Catholic populations clashed in these cities over Sabbatarian laws, the right to drink alcohol, and the legality of immigrant voting. Anti-immigrant Know-Nothing organizations and Catholic parishes fought—sometimes with riots, as in Baltimore and Louisville, Kentucky—over basic questions of American cultural identity.

Just as immigrants and native-born Americans wrestled over the contours of American life and culture, women made an unprecedented challenge to the traditional male prerogatives of citizenship. During New England's Industrial Revolution of the 1820s, separate gendered spheres emerged among the middle class, where women were expected to perform the duties commensurate with the "cult of true womanhood." Part of this domestic-oriented vision was republican motherhood, or the responsibility to raise virtuous sons for the new American republic. Young women received classical educations at prestigious schools like the Emma Willard Academy in Troy, New York, and Mount Holyoke Seminary in South Hadley, Massachusetts. But a generation later the graduates of these schools insisted that young women should train for their own participation in American civic life. The culminating moment for this new feminism came at Seneca Falls, New York, in 1848, where the Declaration of Sentiments authored by Elizabeth Cady Stanton and Susan B. Anthony spelled out demands for women's equality. Northern working-class women made similar demands in the 1850s, especially through direct labor action at factories like those in Lowell, Massachusetts. By the time of the Civil War, women in the North had attained leadership positions and experience in various national charitable and civil rights organizations. This experience proved critical to the Union war effort as women led sanitary commissions, hospitals, and organizations for supporting soldiers.

For women in the South, the traditional household framework persisted up to the Civil War. Plantation mistresses directed the social and domestic affairs within the household, including management of the domestic slave population. Slave women, forbidden from prioritizing familial duties to their own children, served in the fields and kitchens alongside slave men. Though yeoman women modeled their households after those of the planter class as best they could, poorer white women performed farm tasks alongside their husbands, sons, and daughters. Unlike in the North, women in the South had not developed large-scale public charitable organizations and thus during the Civil War were faced with the far more daunting task of assuming traditionally male agricultural roles.

For African Americans in the 1850s, the federal Fugitive Slave Act tightened restrictions on free blacks in the North, even as high cotton prices forced slaves in the South to work at a more fevered pace than ever before. The internal slave trade, which funneled slaves from the tobacco and hemp farms of Virginia and Kentucky to the cotton plantations of the Deep South, grew in intensity. The rice fields of South Carolina's Lowcountry employed armies of slaves using the task system of organization, but the real growth lay in the gang-labor-based cotton-plantation system stretching from South Carolina to Texas. Persistent fears of slave insurrection, culminating with John Brown's raid at Harpers Ferry, Virginia (now West Virginia), in 1859, encouraged white southerners to clamp down even harder on free blacks and runaway slaves. The slave system was as strong and profitable as ever in 1860 on the eve of the Civil War, and southern planters insisted that the region's future was permanently and inextricably bound to the "peculiar institution."

In 1854 the briefly dormant sectional crisis reemerged with the plan proposed by the Illinois Senator Stephen Douglas to organize the Kansas and Nebraska Territories under a new principle known as popular sovereignty. The immigration and temperance debates of the early 1850s gave way to the far more explosive question of slavery's expansion in the Kansas and Nebraska Territories. The events making up the conflict called "Bleeding Kansas," the Dred Scott Supreme Court decision (*Dred Scott v. Sandford*, 1857), and high-profile battles in Congress between abolitionists and southern "fire-eaters" signaled the end of national political unity. Major religious denominations—including especially the Methodists, Baptists, and Presbyterians—split along sectional lines over the Bible's justification of slavery. When the Republican nominee Abraham Lincoln won the presidency in 1860, Cotton Belt political leaders began the process of seceding from the Union and creating their own Confederate States of America. Months of failed negotiations led to war at Fort Sumter in April 1861 and to four upper South states' joining the Confederacy. The Civil War was on.

War. The two most important social effects of the Civil War were the total mobilization of Northern and Southern society for war and the emancipation of 4 million African American slaves. At the beginning of the war, the Union army numbered fewer than ten thousand men; the Confederacy had to create an army from scratch, mostly by reorganizing Southern militias once used to prevent slave insurrection and Indian attack. By the end of 1861 each army enrolled several hundred thousand men—most of them farmers who joined up for what they thought would be short terms filled with adventure and camaraderie. Companies and regiments formed based on existing social networks such as local militias, ethnic organizations, and even schools.

By spring 1862, Northern and Southern society came to grips with what was to become a long and bloody war. Facing manpower shortages, the Confederacy issued its first Conscription Act in 1862, with the Union passing its own in 1863. Resistance to the draft proved intense and occasionally destabilizing. In the South, so-called home guards chased deserters and draft evaders into the Appalachian Mountains. And Northern cities exploded in violence as resisters burned draft offices and attacked such symbols of the Union war effort as recruiting stations and African American orphanages. The worst was the New York City draft riot of July 1863, which required returning soldiers from Gettysburg to squelch.

Just as men did, women mobilized immediately for war. Northern women formed the United States Christian Commission, various sanitary commissions, and well-organized battlefield hospitals wherever the army went. They held Union Ladies' Aid Society meetings at which they organized to sew uniforms and provide material and moral support for local men sent off to war. After 1862, many abolitionist women began to establish schools and hospitals for freed slaves—especially in the South Carolina Sea Islands. Women also took on industrial jobs formerly performed by men.

In the South, white women mobilized for war by assuming the responsibilities of plantation management formerly held by male overseers. Like their Northern counterparts, they offered moral and material support for Confederate soldiers through public celebrations and uniform-sewing organizations. Poorer white women agitated for—and occasionally rioted against—Confederate food-distribution centers, especially as rampant inflation made basic necessities unaffordable. The overall effect of the Civil War was arguably more consequential for Southern women than for Northern women because there had been virtually no official, public interaction between the state and Southern women before the war.

The total mobilization of Northern and Southern society had enormous economic consequences. For the North, massive increases in military production meant a tremendous boost in industrial production and trade. After a brief scare in late 1861 associated with the Trent affair—when two Confederate diplomats to Britain and France were intercepted at sea—the Union's economy boomed. Some of these economic gains were limited, however, by inflation caused by the issuance of non-specie greenback currency.

The Southern economy initially thrived as well, though Confederate plans to embargo cotton in hopes of forcing British and French recognition limited output a bit. However, the extended war proved disastrous for the Southern economy for a few reasons. First, the Confederate government issued paper currency without the financial mechanisms in place to insure the debt. The result was a catastrophic inflationary spiral that made basic foodstuffs unaffordable for most Southern households. Second, the physical damage to the Southern infrastructure—railroads, cities, turnpikes, and farmsteads—proved too devastating for the Southern economy. But the most drastic effect on the Southern economy—and on Southern life as a whole—was the immediate emancipation of 4 million African American slaves. The liquidation of billions of dollars in chattel property, combined with the loss of productive labor on the plantations, left the Southern economy in a state of total and complete disarray.

Emancipation of Slaves. In fact, it was the emancipation of African American slaves that proved to be the most important social consequence of the Civil War. As the Union army penetrated into the Confederate heartland, slaves ran away en masse from their owners and presented themselves for service—and hopes of freedom—to Union lines. As early as May 1861, General Benjamin F. Butler responded to the flood of runaway slaves by declaring them "contraband of war," or legally seized property. By August 1861 the First Confiscation Act codified this new policy, allowing the Union army to press into service any slave who reached Union lines and could demonstrate that he or she had been performing military work for the Confederacy. This limited approach merely created confusion among the Union officer corps, however. And as the army pushed farther into the Deep South, the number of runaway slaves in Union lines swelled. Congressional policy was still quite limited in

spring 1862, agreeing to eliminate slavery in the District of Columbia but failing to offer compensated emancipation to the border states. By July, however, pressure from runaway slaves, army officers, and more radical elements in Congress resulted in the passage of the Second Confiscation Act. This act freed any slave who reached Union lines, regardless of his or her prior occupation. It signaled a dramatic change in Union policy. On 22 September 1862, shortly after the bloody battle of Antietam, President Lincoln issued the preliminary Emancipation Proclamation, which pledged freedom to any slave in any state or portion thereof still in rebellion on 1 January 1863. Issuance of the full proclamation on New Year's Day formally altered Union policy into a war of emancipation, even though it did little in and of itself to free the slaves.

The most important factor in the emancipation of slaves after this point was the enlistment of nearly two hundred thousand African Americans in the Union army and navy. This proved to be the deciding factor in the border states and states of the upper South—which had been exempted from the Emancipation Proclamation—and it lent critical manpower support to the Union army in the final years of war. Perhaps most important, it offered blacks a path to eventual legal equality: after the war, having served alongside whites in defense of the U.S. government, black men could make a claim to the same rights and responsibilities of citizenship that whites enjoyed. Indeed, President Lincoln offered support for black suffrage in his final public address before his assassination in April 1865.

The Civil War, itself a result of deepening social divisions between the North and South, resulted in a social revolution that altered the nature of American identity forever. It was a political crisis—as all wars are—but it was directly bound up in internal social conflicts in ways that no other American war has ever been. The Union victory secured industrial, wage-labor capitalism, a robust federal government, and a Constitution that—on paper at least—recognized equality under law. It took another century, however, for the last goal to be realized.

[*See also* Antebellum Era; Antebellum Reform; Antislavery; Bleeding Kansas; Draft Riots, Civil War; Emancipation of Slaves; Free-Soilers; Military Personnel, *subentries on* Civil War *and* Civil War, African Americans; Reconstruction Era; Sanitary Commission, U.S.; Slavery, *subentry on* Nineteenth Century; South, The; *and* Union Leagues.]

BIBLIOGRAPHY

Bensel, Richard Franklin. *Yankee Leviathan: The Origins of Central State Authority in America, 1859–1877.* Cambridge, U.K.: Cambridge University Press, 1990.

Berlin, Ira. *Slaves No More: Three Essays on Emancipation and the Civil War.* Cambridge, U.K.: Cambridge University Press, 1992.

DuBois, Ellen Carol. *Feminism and Suffrage: The Emergence of an Independent Women's Movement in America, 1848–1869.* Ithaca, N.Y.: Cornell University Press, 1978.

Faust, Drew Gilpin. *Mothers of Invention: Women of the Slaveholding South in the American Civil War.* Chapel Hill: University of North Carolina Press, 1996.

Foner, Eric. *The Fiery Trial: Abraham Lincoln and American Slavery.* New York: W. W. Norton and Company, 2010.

Foner, Eric. *Free Soil, Free Labor, Free Men: The Ideology of the Republican Party before the Civil War.* New York: Oxford University Press, 1970.

McCurry, Stephanie. *Confederate Reckoning: Power and Politics in the Civil War South.* Cambridge, Mass.: Harvard University Press, 2010.

McCurry, Stephanie. *Masters of Small Worlds: Yeoman Households, Gender Relations, and the Political Culture of the Antebellum South Carolina Low Country.* New York: Oxford University Press, 1995.

McPherson, James M. *Battle Cry of Freedom: The Civil War Era.* New York: Oxford University Press, 1988.

Potter, David M. *The Impending Crisis, 1848–1861.* Completed and edited by Don E. Fehrenbacher. New York: Harper & Row, 1976.

Aaron Astor

CLERGY

The history of the clergy in North America begins with the colonial ventures of the Spanish and French in the fifteenth and sixteenth centuries. Spanish conquests led to the establishment of missions in Saint Augustine, Florida, in 1565, and New Mexico beginning in 1598. The Spanish Catholic clergy hoped to both convert and "civilize" the native peoples. Though they were often insensitive toward native cultures, they were not simply tools of the crown: some also argued against excessive brutality and exploitation of native labor. Meanwhile, French Récollets, or Recollects, and Jesuits labored among native tribes in Canada and the Great Lakes region. They founded settled missions and lived among hunting parties to effect conversions, writing about their experiences in *The Jesuit Relations*, reports published annually in Paris.

The colonial era British clergy, including Anglicans in Virginia, Catholics in Maryland, and Puritans in the Northeast, focused on Anglo settlers. Although they established some praying towns and small-scale mission efforts for local native populations, the clergy, like the settlers, largely preferred a model of separation and supported violent efforts to put down native opposition, as in King Philip's War of 1675–1676. Clergy in the southern British colonies ministered to a widely dispersed population, covering parishes that sometimes stretched for miles on end. New England's population was more concentrated, especially in major towns like Boston and New Haven. Because schooling opportunities were minimal for ordinary people, the colonial clergy's education lent them authority to teach the laity's children, care for their sick, and preside over births, marriages, and funerals.

Early Tensions. The eighteenth-century revivals that some scholars have termed the Great Awakening created tensions among the colonial clergy in British North America. Supporters encouraged emotional conversions among laypeople and encouraged lay exhorters, including women and African Americans. Others viewed the revivals as excessively enthusiastic promotions of short-lived piety that undermined the authority of educated clergy. Meanwhile, the established clergy (Congregationalists in the North, Anglicans in the South) continued to receive state-mandated support from the people, leading nonconformists (Baptists and Quakers in the Northeast, Presbyterians in the South) to agitate for "no taxation without representation" before that phrase became the rallying cry of the American revolutionaries.

During the Revolution, many clergy supported the patriots' cause, interpreting events in a millennialist framework. After the war, the separation of church and state caused the previously disestablished clergy to rejoice and those who had formerly received state support to worry. Yet most ministers soon found that the new voluntaristic atmosphere aided in denomination building, as lay members were more likely to join a denomination out of conviction than force. Modifying their

theology to include more volition than predestination, by the mid-nineteenth century the evangelical clergy had refined revivals to an art, publishing handbooks for each other on the best ways to produce conversions in varying circumstances. They also sought to reform antebellum society through benevolent organizations with aims like promoting temperance, encouraging Sabbatarianism, and outlawing prostitution and gambling.

The separation of church and state also created fertile ground for the success of populist ministers. African Americans in independent churches like the African Methodist Episcopal Church, as well as a number of women in denominations like the Campbellite Christians and Millerites, also claimed expanding opportunities to preach. The populists argued that, using common sense, anyone could interpret the Scriptures and that preaching did not require intensive theological training, which was unavailable to the general public. Their success, however, spurred the populists toward the establishment of their own colleges and seminaries in an effort to compete with the older and wealthier denominations.

The major denominations split over the slavery issue in the antebellum era. By and large, the clergy became cheerleaders for their respective causes during the Civil War itself. Chaplains on both sides spurred camp revivals among soldiers whose thoughts turned to death on the verge of battle. After emancipation, educated African American ministers from northern churches sometimes clashed with powerful preachers who had been slaves and whose emotional and vernacular styles seemed, to the educated ministers, to bespeak a backward style.

Meanwhile, challenges to evangelical clerical authority came from Darwinism, biblical higher criticism, mass immigration of Jews and Catholics, and the difficulties of city life in an industrializing nation. Liberal clergy maintained that the Bible could be read historically and contextually and by focusing on the practical application of the gospel to social woes. By contrast, conservative clergy reaffirmed the fundamentals of their faith, including the inerrancy of the Bible, the divinity of Jesus, and the primary necessity of conversion. For their part, the Holiness-Pentecostal clergy, who gained prominence in the early twentieth century, stressed the importance of baptism by the Holy Spirit, which they believed could manifest itself in glossolalia (speaking in tongues) and divine healing. Jewish and Catholic religious leaders ministered to the economic and social needs of immigrants, while facing their own divisions between reformers who wanted to Americanize traditional practices and those who opposed such innovations.

Despite their differences, many ministers actively supported American military efforts in the Philippines, Cuba, and World Wars I and II. Serving alongside soldiers as chaplains helped the clergy to gain renewed respect from the American public. Serving alongside clergy of other faiths also helped ease public tensions among Protestant, Catholic, and Jewish religious leaders in the 1940s and 1950s.

Renewed Tensions. The Civil Rights Movement again exacerbated tensions both among the clergy and between the clergy and laity. Many religious leaders—both black and white, and regardless of denomination or creed—supported efforts to end racial segregation. But some white clergy in the South had to work behind the scenes because of a vocal minority of clerical critics and widespread white lay opposition to the clergy's involvement in seemingly secular affairs. Still, other clergy, particularly black religious leaders, saw the civil rights movement itself as a religious movement aimed at finally ending the unholy practices of racial segregation and violence.

The rise of the Black Power movement in the late 1960s alienated some ministers who had supported earlier nonviolent efforts at achieving reform. Vietnam created further divisions: many mainline liberal clergy opposed the war, while conservatives decried this opposition, suggesting that they had no competence to judge issues of national security. The issue of women's ordination was also divisive.

These fissures have translated into divergent political allegiances that have persisted into the twenty-first century. Fundamentalist and conservative clergy tend to vote Republican and sometimes encourage their parishioners to do the same, seeing that party as the bulwark of traditional family values. Yet they also serve as critics when party platforms do not match their visions. Liberal mainline ministers tend to vote Democrat and to support progressive social causes, though they grapple with the issue of gay and lesbian ordination. Catholic clergy are split between more conservative and more liberal factions; the most pressing issue they have faced in the late twentieth and early twenty-first centuries is whether the priesthood should remain celibate, especially in the wake of sexual-abuse scandals.

Despite continuing divisions, the clergy remain an important part of twenty-first-century American society, interacting in the daily lives of their parishioners as they visit the sick, preside over births and deaths, and interpret current events by their opposition to or championship of various social and political causes.

[*See also* **Franciscans; Itinerant Preachers; Missions, Foreign; Missions, in America; Religion; Roman Catholic Orders in Early America, Female; Voluntary Associations,** *subentry on* British Colonies and Early Republic; *and* Women and Religious Institutions.]

BIBLIOGRAPHY

Brekus, Catherine. *Strangers and Pilgrims: Female Preaching in America, 1740–1845.* Chapel Hill: University of North Carolina Press, 1998. The definitive account of the opportunities and obstructions facing women preachers in America.

Carpenter, Joel A. *Revive Us Again: The Reawakening of American Fundamentalism.* New York: Oxford University Press, 1997. Examines fundamentalism after the Scopes Trial, including the rise of clerical superstars like Billy Graham.

Carwardine, Richard J. *Evangelicals and Politics in Antebellum America.* New Haven, Conn.: Yale University Press, 1993. Details the clergy's various political allegiances in antebellum America, differentiating by denomination and region.

Hatch, Nathan O. *The Democratization of American Christianity.* New Haven, Conn.: Yale University Press, 1989. Looks at the rise of populist denominations in the early republic, focusing on charismatic religious leaders like Lorenzo Dow.

Holifield, E. Brooks. *God's Ambassadors: A History of the Christian Clergy in America.* Grand Rapids, Mich.: William B. Eerdmans, 2007. The best overview covering the colonial era to the twenty-first century, Protestants as well as Catholics.

Sutton, Matthew Avery. *Aimee Semple McPherson and the Resurrection of Christian America.* Cambridge, Mass.: Harvard University Press, 2007. A fascinating portrayal of Aimee Semple McPherson, one of the most famous and controversial Pentecostal preachers of the early twentieth century.

Kathryn Gin

CLOTHING

Despite a renaissance in the field of material-culture studies, textiles remain a neglected subject of historical inquiry. But since the late twentieth century a growing number of scholars have turned to clothing as a rich source through which to interpret the major changes in American life over its history. The heterogeneous mix of cultures in America resulted in a wide array of dress styles. From the plain suits of Pennsylvania Quakers to the colorful head wraps of enslaved African American women, from blue jeans to bandanas, dress has been used to create, strengthen, and challenge cultural and national identities. A nexus of the personal and the political, garments possess the unique capacity to symbolize protest and articulate alternative political visions.

Early American Clothing.　During the colonial period, English, French, and Spanish settlers appropriated many aspects of the dress of the native peoples around them. These Europeans quickly adopted moccasins, deerskin hunting shirts, and leggings as more practical frontier wear. Derived from plant, animal, and other materials indigenous to the local geography, the clothing of Indian groups in North America varied widely but shared common elements such as the use of tanned animal skins, furs, body paint, and jewelry made of metals, shells, or bone. Both sexes wore moccasins and hair jewelry, as well as brightly colored woolen blankets and furs as outerwear. Like Europeans, Indians altered their dress in response to intercultural contact and trade. Brightly colored Spanish cloth and English waistcoats were favorites of Indian society during this period, accelerating natives' dependence on European trade goods. Yet Indians asserted their own ethnic and individual identities by adapting European garments to their own use, decorating cloth shirts, hats, and coats with beadwork, embroidery, and fringe, style elements that were gradually assumed by the broader society and ultimately became viewed as distinctly American. Even when faced with dwindling populations and forced relocation to reservations at the end of the nineteenth century, many native peoples steadfastly maintained indigenous hairstyles: long and beaded for men, braided for women.

Up until the Civil War, clothing reflected the social role of its wearer. Male and female laborers wore looser versions of mainstream fashions, made of coarser materials, which allowed greater freedom of movement. Most women wore cotton or woolen dresses with petticoats, corsets of various materials, and some sort of head covering, such as a cap or straw bonnet. Male laborers were distinguished by loose trousers, short jackets or shirts, and felt hats—all in distinct contrast to the dark, fitted three-piece suits of the business classes.

With industrialization and the introduction of I. M. Singer's home sewing machine in 1856, the price of cloth decreased dramatically and enabled ordinary people to afford fashionable garments without the expense and aid of a seamstress or tailor. Inexpensive men's ready-to-wear clothes produced in metropolitan sweatshops permitted newly arrived immigrants, free African Americans, and the working class to appropriate a middle-class appearance. This prompted a backlash among elites and conservative critics, who responded to the democratization of fashion by accelerating seasonal fashion change and proliferating new ensembles for every occasion.

The mounting differences between mass-manufactured clothing and custom creations by European couturiers expressed the glaring social inequality of the Gilded Age. Yet waves of young immigrants and workers seized the opportunity to participate in a shared culture of youthful modernism. Their labor and earnings created a mass market for American-made goods. Though dominant fashion trends in this period idealized an ornamental female body, featuring skin-tight sleeves, restrictive corsets, and ballooning skirts and bustles, the increasing numbers of women involved in education, reform, and wage labor challenged such restrictions by adopting the Gibson girl ensemble of the 1890s, which jettisoned the bustle in favor of simple flared skirts, men's collars, and shirtwaist blouses.

Twentieth Century. Clothing in the early twentieth century provided a powerful mechanism for both men and women to make political statements and express new freedoms. World War I peace activists and Progressive Era reformers contested capitalism and war through a romantic embrace of artist smocks, peasant blouses, sandals, and loose trousers. Prosperity, youth culture, and women's entrance into college led to the revolutionary adoption of short skirts, loose dresses, and bobbed hair, culminating in the flapper look of the 1920s. Jazz music influenced the introduction of the drape-shaped suit and even shorter hemlines—to show off new dance styles—and created interest in African styles.

The Depression and World War II introduced a somber mood, while government rationing and sanctions led to a new surge in American-based design. Athletic styles introduced in New York and California economized cloth and reflected a casual, sporting look that has become the hallmark of American style. Wartime led to the appearance of a unified culture, yet marginalized African, Italian, and Mexican Americans expressed their discontent by adopting ostentatious suits that featured long coats, wide and padded shoulders, and tightly cuffed trousers. These suits, called "zoot suits," flouted government restrictions on wool and symbolized a subversive subculture, leading to violent confrontations between zoot-suiters and servicemen in Los Angeles and other cities in 1943.

Peace and the Cold War reintroduced gender hierarchy and conformity in clothing, with a reversion in the 1950s to full skirts and dresses for women and, for men, short, cropped hair and suits of gray flannel. Young members of a Beat counterculture inspired by bebop and jazz challenged these social conventions by donning black clothing, casual T-shirts, and blue jeans. Jeans had been manufactured by Levi Strauss & Co. of San Francisco since the mid-nineteenth century, but James Dean's denim-clad performance in *Rebel without a Cause* (1955) and the Beats brought them into the mainstream, where they remain the single most important piece of American clothing.

By the 1960s, fashion reflected a fractured and politicized culture such that no style could claim cultural dominance. Each year featured new and competing motifs that reinforced the turbulent times. The space race introduced silver, plastic, and futuristic themes. Youth protested the Vietnam War by donning the hippie look: long hair, peasant skirts with loose blouses, faded jeans, natural fibers, and ethnic prints. African American men contending for civil rights staged sit-ins and protests in sober dark suits and narrow ties, using dress to symbolize the basic respectability they were seeking from white society.

Yet by the 1970s, political conflict and economic recession had taken their toll, and men and women were focused on employment and security. Polyester suits, in bright colors and featuring wide collars, were worn by both sexes. As the recession wore on, however, the 1980s returned to more formal suits: dark, single- and double-breasted suits for men and conservative skirts for women. Women adopted male tailored shirts and softer versions of neckties to ease their entrance into traditional male occupations. By this time and continuing into the twenty-first century, fashion sought to encourage individual self-expression rather than conformity to any one style. Designers and manufacturers began to introduce clothing changes seasonally, and brands have become important expressions of personal style. Clothing remains a richly expressive source for scholars, its meanings intimately revelatory of the historical moment and milieu of its creation.

[*See also* **Consumption; Everyday Life; Gender;** *and* **Transvestism.**]

BIBLIOGRAPHY

Cunningham, Patricia A. *Reforming Women's Fashion, 1850–1920: Politics, Health, and Art.* Kent, Ohio: Kent State University Press, 2003.

De Marly, Diana. *Dress in North America.* Vol. 1: *The New World, 1492–1800.* New York: Holmes & Meier, 1990.

Stamper, Anita, and Jill Condra. *Clothing through American History: The Civil War through the Gilded Age, 1861–1899.* Santa Barbara, Calif.: Greenwood, 2011.

Wass, Ann Buermann, and Michelle Webb Frandrich. *Clothing through American History: The Federal Era through Antebellum, 1786–1860.* Santa Barbara, Calif.: Greenwood, 2010.

Welters, Linda, and Patricia A. Cunningham, eds. *Twentieth-Century American Fashion.* Oxford: Berg, 2005.

White, Shane, and Graham White. *Stylin': African American Expressive Culture from Its Beginnings to the Zoot Suit.* Ithaca, N.Y.: Cornell University Press, 1998.

Linzy Brekke-Aloise

COFFEEHOUSES AND COFFEE

Coffee was commercially traded in Yemen by the mid-1400s but remained within the Arab world until Syrian traders introduced it to Mecca, Cairo, and Istanbul in the sixteenth century. From there, coffee drinking spread to western Europe: the first coffeehouses appeared in Italy, France, and England by the early 1600s and had spread across the Atlantic to North America by the 1680s.

These establishments quickly distinguished themselves from taverns and bars, pubs, and inns. Though almost all early modern public houses provided food and drink, and many also offered lodging and stabling, coffeehouses positioned themselves as business institutions by hosting currency-exchange days and auctions, subscribing to multiple newspapers, and hosting early maritime-insurance endeavors. In this sense, coffeehouses became a principal feature of urban social and mercantile life, taking their place midway between taverns for all classes and gentleman's clubs for the well-heeled. Some early coffeehouses even banned the sale of alcohol, gambling, and swearing, although these restrictions did not last long. The space itself reflected coffeehouses' business orientation. A common room, with a caged bar often set against one wall for alcohol sales, usually filled the ground floor. Small circular or rectangular tables accommodated two to eight patrons each, while broadsides and advertisements covered the walls. Many proprietors kept city directories of local institutions and vendors, further proof of coffeehouses' economic orientation.

Coffeehouses also distinguished themselves from other seventeenth- and eighteenth-century public houses by catering almost exclusively to men, although women often worked in, and sometimes owned, these businesses. Both enslaved workers and indentured servants also appeared in a variety of coffeehouse capacities, as barkeepers, cooks, and wait staff. If gender was a clear dividing line in coffeehouses' clientele, class was less so. Most required a small admission fee, but rather than being meant as a fiscal barrier, such charges were used to offset the cost of the periodicals and newspapers that members could freely peruse. Indeed, because of the exchange of ideas and opinions, coffeehouses became known as "penny universities," a term that was first invented for London establishments but that applied equally well to their American counterparts. But if coffeehouses were sites of social, cultural, and political exchange in early America, they also served practical needs. Investors in particular economic ventures, especially merchants and early maritime insurers, often held office hours in their favorite coffeehouses, while nearby businesspeople of all sorts— from music teachers to blacksmiths—publicized their location in terms of proximity to specific haunts.

North American colonies initially modeled their coffeehouses after popular European establishments, although they assumed more regionally distinct characteristics as the eighteenth century progressed. Coffeehouses could be found in all major port cities, as well as in many provincial and rural towns, though their buildings varied in size depending on when and where they were built. Samuel Carpenter opened Philadelphia's first coffeehouse in 1683, for example, which measured just over seven hundred square feet, but by 1785 the proprietors of the Merchants Coffee House in the same city advertised a building twice as large, with second-floor club rooms that could be used as offices or combined into a grand ballroom for large social events.

Colonial proprietors may have initially tried to mimic coffeehouses in metropolitan centers, but they as enthusiastically hosted events that facilitated American independence. Throughout the thirteen American colonies during the 1760s and 1770s, coffeehouses frequently served as sites for public protest. They hosted demonstrations against the Stamp Act (1765), posted political broadsides, and held meetings both of committees of correspondence, formed to encourage intercolonial communication and mobilization against British parliamentary policy, and also of committees of compliance, charged with overseeing imports during colonial embargos. Thus coffeehouses continued the tradition of fostering political and economic debate, as well as serving as centers for the dissemination of public information.

In the first half of the nineteenth century, coffeehouses became less associated with business activities as more of their former economic functions became discrete industries, such as banking, insurance, and postal services. By the late nineteenth century, some served as salons for the urban intellectual elite, philanthropic societies, or literary associations. In the late twentieth century, coffeehouses reemerged as powerful social hubs for all classes. Though the focus of most modern coffeehouses remains food and beverage service, many also offer newspapers, Internet access, and book and music clubs. And so twenty-first-century coffeehouses continued to play a central role in the circulation of information in American society.

[*See also* **Cities and Suburbs; Colonial Era; Everyday Life;** *and* **Revolution and Constitution Era.**]

BIBLIOGRAPHY

Cowan, Brian. *The Social Life of Coffee: The Emergence of the British Coffeehouse.* New Haven, Conn.: Yale University Press, 2005. Uses the themes of curiosity, commerce, and civil society to track Britain's coffee habits from discovery abroad to widespread absorption into the domestic diet.

Craig, Michelle L. "Grounds for Debate? The Place of the Caribbean Provisions Trade in Philadelphia's Prerevolutionary Economy." *Pennsylvania Magazine of History and Biography* 128, no. 2 (April 2004): 149–177. Uses coffee to trace the importance of West Indian commodities in North American trade prior to the American Revolution, as well as to argue for the increasing politicization of such goods during colonial boycott efforts in the 1760s and 1770s.

Ellis, Markman, ed. *Eighteenth-Century Coffee-House Culture.* 4 vols. London: Pickering & Chatto, 2006. Reprints many, exclusively English, primary sources; the volumes focus on coffeehouses as represented in literature (volumes 1 and 2), drama (volume 3), and medical and history writing (volume 4).

Hattox, Ralph S. *Coffee and Coffeehouses: The Origins of a Beverage in the Medieval Near East.* Seattle: University of Washington Press, 1985. A social history of coffeehouse culture in the Middle East; explores when and how coffee arrived in the region, as well as its medical, religious, and social acceptance.

Pendergrast, Mark. *Uncommon Grounds: The History of Coffee and How It Transformed Our World.* Rev. ed. New York: Basic Books, 2010. A popular rather than academic history that covers coffee's history from its early African origins and transplantation to European plantations in the East and West Indies to its rise in Latin America and mass consumption in North American culture. Most of the volume focuses on the United States and the twentieth century.

Michelle Craig McDonald

COLONIAL ERA

Perceptions of the "colonial era of the United States" are often Anglocentric and teleological. The most usual periodization—from 1607 to either 1763 or 1775—enshrines an English (after the union of England and Scotland in 1707, British) frame of reference: the first permanent settlement at Jamestown, the Treaty of Paris that secured British hegemony over eastern North America, and the outbreak of the Revolutionary War. This perspective is defensible, since the polities that coalesced into the United States had all been provinces of the British Empire, but it should be contextualized within the larger transatlantic narrative of imperial competition in the Western Hemisphere, which involved not only the North and South American landmasses but also Europe, Africa, and the Caribbean islands. Moreover, restricting the story to only components of the American republic-to-be implies that its formation was preordained, whereas in the mid-eighteenth century the "thirteen colonies" that became the United States were not collectively distinguishable from Britain's other imperial jurisdictions, and their future collective identity was in no way predictable. The colonial period should be understood on its own terms and not as the preface to a national historical narrative.

Interpretations of the era have changed markedly, and, as in other fields, social history has become more prominent. At the beginning of the twentieth century, scholars operating with a "scientific" methodology that celebrated the "objective" parsing of data dismissed as nationalist apologetics the claims of nineteenth-century historians that the colonies were nascent states built by refugees from a tyrannical homeland and argued that Britain had ruled the colonies benignly. Intellectual historians gained ascendance at midcentury, proposing both that attention to the writings of educated elites could also divine underlying social realities and that the declension of New England Puritanism was paradigmatic for understanding American history in general. The next generation, influenced by social-scientific theory, statistical techniques, contemporary popular movements, and access to computer technology, sought to write history "from the bottom up," reconstructing the mundane doings of individuals, families, and communities. In the process, they debunked the idea of New England's typicality and pushed social

history to the forefront. Though their propensity for portraying the colonies as a congeries of "small places" has been superseded, social historians have joined others to conceptualize an "Atlantic world" in which narratives of Britain's empire interlock with those of its imperial rivals. Twenty-first-century historians know far more about colonial Anglo-America than did their predecessors a century ago, but greater knowledge has lessened confidence that a single comprehensive synthesis is possible.

Imperial Contexts. Spain conquered more of the Western Hemisphere and held more of its territory longer than did any European rival. Its blueprints for colonization developed during the *Reconquista*, the centuries-long campaign to unify the kingdom and expel the Moors, which bestowed on the conquistadores and their descendants the techniques and mindset for subduing, exploiting and then assimilating indigenes. The crown and the Catholic Church worked in concert—if not always harmoniously—to create the political and ecclesiastical order conducive to fulfilling this design. The king delegated authority to a hierarchy of regional and local officials, while the church deployed brigades of missionaries to convert the Indians. Built next to the natives' pueblos or as compounds surrounded by their fields and protected by soldiers, missions became a central means for securing Indian labor. In the dense populations of Mexico and Peru—New Spain alone held 2.5 to 3 million people in 1750, more than did mainland Anglo-America—Spanish colonial society took on an urban, multiracial cast and produced piles of bullion, but Spain occupied the Borderlands primarily to secure the empire's northern frontiers and protect the Caribbean seaways through which the treasure fleets passed. Florida anchored chains of missions that filtered along the Atlantic coast and into the interior, serving tens of thousands of natives, but fewer than two thousand Europeans resided there. New Mexico consisted of missions and small Hispanic settlements that incorporated the Pueblo peoples as laborers, acolytes, and sometimes kin, in the eighteenth century enduring endemic raids by more nomadic tribes. The northern Borderlands never prospered, and the failure to plant settlers thick on the ground ultimately advantaged the aggressive expansionism of the far more populous United States in the nineteenth century.

Expelled from South America by Portugal and from Florida by Spain, France penetrated deep into North America via a series of liquid highways: the Saint Lawrence River, the Great Lakes, and the Mississippi River. The pursuit of beaver by voyageurs and of souls by Jesuit missionaries eventuated in a discontinuously settled arc of towns, trading posts, and hamlets that produced furs for export and food for subsistence but, unlike the French West Indian sugar plantations, did not enrich the metropole. Indeed, by the eighteenth century, the crown—which divided its provincial authority between governors-general and intendants (civil officials), who ruled with unelected councils—willingly subsidized New France to counteract British occupation of the mid–North Atlantic littoral. Restrained by a relative lack of religious conflict—the small Protestant minority, when expelled in 1685, generally remained in Europe—and the peasantry's ties to the land, immigration was meager and heavily male, factors that together suppressed New France's population growth. New France contained twenty-five hundred Europeans in 1663 and only seventy-five thousand a century later, but because the colony and its native neighbors, neither able to dominate the other, developed habits of commercial and military

cooperation, New France exercised power greater than its numbers and desultory economic performance would suggest. For two-thirds of the eighteenth century, New France and Louisiana threatened their British and Spanish adversaries.

Controlling perhaps 80 percent of Europe's merchant marine during the earlier seventeenth century and technologically capable of reclaiming land from the sea, thereby easing population pressure, the Dutch scattered colonies across the world to increase commerce rather than to amass territory. New Netherland—the West India Company's holdings along the Hudson and Delaware Rivers—typified this pattern. Conceived as a corporate outpost staffed by employees and run by directors-general without elected councils, the colony struggled to attract migrants—it never held as many as nine thousand denizens—and never paid the anticipated dividends, though the company maintained it for strategic reasons. The Dutch traded with the Five Nations of the Iroquois and established peaceful relations with the Hudson Valley Algonquians, but relations soured in the 1640s and 1650s as a liberalized land policy stimulated a modest immigration that stressed Indian holdings. Though fellow Protestants, the English regarded the Dutch as major impediments to their own commercial aspirations, fighting three wars with them between 1652 and 1674, during the second of which they captured New Netherland and reorganized it as New York.

The Colonies Founded. England could not contemplate colonization until two major conditions had been met: the resolution of long-standing agitations over the dynastic succession and the character of the national church afforded the requisite internal stability, and the emergence of an outward-looking merchant class supplied the necessary capital.

The English occupied the mainland between roughly latitudes 32° and 45° north, an expanse between New France and the Spanish Borderlands whose fertile soils and temperate climate proved capable of sustaining high agricultural productivity. North America attracted the English crown as a forward base from which to attack Spain's possessions, and the Church of England fitfully heeded biblical imperatives to proselytize the heathen. But private, not public, parties underwrote English ventures, and personal motives for migration—obtaining land, worshipping God as conscience dictated, or both—predominated. Between 1600 and 1640, some eighty thousand people left England for the Chesapeake, New England, and the West Indies, staking the English to a long-term demographic advantage over their competitors, European and native alike.

Anglo-American colonies were molded by their continuing encounter with the Eastern Woodland aborigines, scores of different peoples whose villages typically contained a few hundred members. Individual bands were extremely autonomous, and supertribal entities like the Five Nations exceptional. Indians' interactions with the English were not uniformly hostile. Natives showed colonists how to survive in the wilderness and exchanged furs for textiles, pots, guns, and alcohol; occasionally they slept with European lovers or worshipped the Christian god. Inexorably, however, relations worsened as the Indians—their numbers ravaged by catastrophic epidemics—defended their lands and cultural integrity. For most of the seventeenth century, conflicts involved only particular colonies and bands, but as English claims collided with those of France and Spain, Indians were drawn into imperial wars, although their own objectives always dictated how, when, and with whom they fought. The native impact on colonial life was immense:

as producers and consumers, they expanded markets; as healers, farmers, and hunters, they offered specialized knowledge; as allies to reward or as enemies to placate, they engendered political debate; as darkly imagined presences, they embodied a putative savagery against which Europeans could pronounce their own civility; and as woodland warriors, they contributed to the militarization of colonial society, in which virtually all adults, men and many women, could handle a gun.

Colonial societies did not necessarily cohere easily, as the Chesapeake proved. In early modern England, social standing underwrote political authority. Absent the means of policing their subjects by direct force, elites elicited respect by flourishing their wealth, lineage, and Protestant faith. In seventeenth-century Virginia, however, few could assume the requisite lineaments of status. De facto leadership fell to planters who had clawed their way to the top of the tobacco economy but lacked gentility. Migration patterns that left the so-called Old Dominion with a surplus of young, single men combined with endemic disease to inhibit family formation and retard the alchemy by which the transmission of riches across generations turned fortune into lineage—i.e., into a status sanctified by wealth that had been inherited, not earned. Doubts about the legitimacy of the colony's headmen, discontent over restricted access to land, and fury about the government's Indian policy precipitated Bacon's Rebellion (1675–1676), the largest, most violent uprising against a colonial governor until the American Revolution. Meanwhile, religion underwrote unrest in Maryland, where a Protestant majority continually challenged the Catholic proprietor's prerogatives.

Theology and demography organized New England more readily. Perceiving what they called God's "controversy with England" in a host of ecclesiastical, moral, social, economic, and political upsets, Puritans flocked to the "American strand" intent upon creating a godly society anchored in the collaboration of church and state as separate but coordinated agencies to uphold religious orthodoxy and moral behavior. The character of the so-called Great Migration facilitated realizing these ambitions. Placing a premium on household governance, which included deputizing wives to instruct and discipline children and servants, Puritans arrived in fully formed families or even congregations, which from the outset allowed for population growth by natural increase. The speedy erection of political and religious institutions, a demographic regime that facilitated family formation, an economy that allowed most households a competence, and a shared ethical system enabled New England to achieve political and social stability more quickly than did the Chesapeake.

The second round of colonization began after the Restoration of the monarchy in 1660 and took place under the crown's watchful eye. With mercantile companies no longer inclined to wager large sums for uncertain returns, leadership passed to prominent nobles and gentry on whom the king bestowed generous proprietary grants. Such gifts provided a cheap way for the sovereign to liquidate his substantial political debts while extending his nation's claims. Charles II transferred New York to his brother, who in turn devolved part of his holding—which became New Jersey—onto others. Grandiose schemes of social engineering propelled two other proprietorships. William Penn devised Pennsylvania as simultaneously a sanctuary for the Society of Friends (Quakers) and a commercial center. To attract an ideal balance of large and small property holders, the lords of Carolina schemed to introduce a hereditary nobility to govern a society of small freeholders. Neither experiment worked as planned, though both prospered—in part because each attracted settlers by promising liberty of conscience, a pledge that Pennsylvania carried out most consistently.

Imperial policy aimed to benefit the British metropolis principally and its subordinate provinces secondarily. The crown attempted to regulate the colonies' economies and to standardize political forms, while the colonists, fearful that closer imperial oversight would curtail their trade and liberties, sought to hold officials at arm's length. When the Glorious Revolution (1688–1689) deposed James II, rebellions in Massachusetts and New York overthrew the Dominion of New England, which had combined all of the colonies north of New Jersey into a single administrative entity, while a simultaneous revolt in Maryland replaced the Catholic proprietorship with a government of Protestants. Yet by 1700, England's policies had largely taken hold. Trade flowed substantially according to the Navigation Acts, with little damage to merchants' pocketbooks. Meanwhile, self-sustaining population growth—which abetted family formation, orderly transfers of wealth within kinship networks, and the solidification of elites—grounded a stable imperial polity in which royal governors ruled most colonies but representative assemblies were ubiquitous.

Consolidation and Expansion. Fueled by explosive demographic and territorial increases, between 1700 and 1775 the mainland colonies achieved levels of economic growth high for preindustrial societies. Enjoying ample harvests, adequate supplies of fuel, and a favorable disease environment, colonial populations multiplied at nearly the maximum possible rate of natural increase, their numbers augmented through the immigration of perhaps a quarter of a million

Europeans fleeing poverty, war, and religious persecution. The slave trade brought a roughly equal number of Africans. Rising densities in some coastal areas reduced the size of land-holdings, cutting family income, but the availability of western lands limited crowding overall. By the Revolution, the leading edge of internal migration was poised to spill across the Appalachians.

Because land throughout the colonial era was usually more plentiful than labor, and because freemen preferred to own (or rent) a homestead rather than hire themselves out, planters looking for larger workforces came to rely on two systems of bondage. The first, pioneered during early seventeenth-century Virginia's tobacco boom, featured indentured male and female servants, who deeded their sweat in return for passage to the colonies. Servants contracted for only a limited numbers of years, however, necessitating constant replacement, and when competition from both English and a multiplying number of other colonial labor markets cut supplies and drove up prices, masters turned to importing African slaves, who could be held in perpetuity. The English first fully exploited slavery on Barbados, where by 1660 planters had transformed forests into cane fields and built lucrative sugar refineries. The conversion to slave labor did not occur blithely, for the English regarded Africans as brutish, heathen, and ignorant outlanders, attitudes that helped rationalize enslaving them but made assimilation problematic. Nevertheless, the profitability of harnessing a permanent labor force won out. Between 1685 and 1720 the southern mainland colonies converted to slavery, and as early as 1708, South Carolina had a black majority. Slaves toiled in every mainland colony, 80 percent of them in the South. Meanwhile, constructing gang labor as the domain of a degraded racial class drove white female servants from the fields, though

everywhere women of every status contributed to the prosperity of family farms by producing household goods and creating local exchange networks.

Regional patterns of crop production and exports intensified. The South specialized in agricultural staples cultivated mainly by slaves: tobacco from the Chesapeake, rice from the Carolina and Georgia tidewater, and indigo from the Carolina piedmont. Mid-Atlantic farmers marketed wheat and livestock. With horticulture constrained by rocky soils and shorter growing seasons, New Englanders exported fish and whale products along with livestock, as well as rum. Valued as reexports or military necessities, southern commodities fell under British control, and the Navigation Acts mandated shipping them to the metropolis. Northern goods were considered less vital and were hence less regulated. Webs of commerce traversed the Atlantic and the Caribbean. With their increasing amounts of disposable income, colonial households eagerly sought the array of consumer items that began to pour in from British manufactories by midcentury, importing textiles, ceramics, metal goods, and books. Carried by traders along a slowly exfoliating series of roads, these goods reached purchasers hundreds of miles from the coast.

As wealth accumulated, social-class structures became more articulated, most markedly after midcentury, with the greatest stratification occurring in coastal and riverine areas linked to transatlantic markets. Slaves constituted the lowest social rank, their manumission virtually impossible. In the South they frequently lived in gangs of twenty or more; in the North they more often worked as individuals who staffed the elite's townhouses. Perhaps one in five Euro-Americans lived at or near subsistence, but the majority resided in yeoman or artisan families that earned a competent livelihood. Upper-class planters and merchants held more than half the total value of property. Aspiring to the status and power of the British gentry, they purchased metropolitan luxuries and manuals of gentility to distinguish themselves from the lower orders both materially and morally. Eighteenth-century American society increasingly resembled Britain's, but with significant differences: mobility was greater, property holding was more widespread, and—elite pretensions notwithstanding—the patronage networks that governed social advancement in Britain were virtually nonexistent. The population was also more ethnically and racially heterogeneous. By 1775, 20 percent of the colonies' 2.5 million people were African-born or African American, and half of the Euro-Americans south of New England were not ethnically English.

The religious structure differed markedly from Britain's as well, most notably in its denominational diversity and the Church of England's failure to achieve exclusive status. Pluralism diluted the power of religious establishments, facilitated the growth of religious liberty, and, combined with settlers' tendency to move beyond clerical oversight, exploded the presumption that everyone in a vicinity had to (or would) join a particular faith. In the face of voluntary church membership, ministers recruited congregants through the newly developing mechanism of the revival, the most spectacular of which—the Great Awakening of 1739 to 1745—featured George Whitefield preaching to mass audiences gathered by the same publicity techniques that merchants were using to expand commercial markets. The Awakening's immediate impact can be exaggerated—rates of conversion soon declined to previous levels—but the process of organizing new churches with believers who had experienced a spiritual new birth became the centerpiece of nineteenth-century American evangelicalism.

The conditions of colonial society sponsored a politically active citizenry. Widespread property-holding allowed most white adult males—certainly a far greater percentage than in Britain—to meet suffrage requirements, and relatively unrestrictive religious tests barred few from voting or holding office. Convinced that their property gave them a stake in political decisions and quick to voice opinions shaped by weekly newspapers and gossip, householders regarded their legislators as agents for promoting local interests. Though barred from formal involvement, women participated out-of-doors, their power to influence political decision-making and domestic consumption habits becoming more visible as resistance to Britain intensified.

Instructed by engaged constituents and claiming that provincial assemblies were miniature Houses of Commons, representatives repeatedly faced off against the governor and his council. Legislative battles frequently involved allocating military expenses, since between 1689 and 1763 the colonies participated in four worldwide struggles for empire between Britain, France, and Spain. These struggles inextricably implicated native peoples, who chose sides based on assessments of their own self-interest. The first two confrontations—King William's War (1689–1697) and Queen Anne's War (1702–1713)—had little long-term impact except for the communities disrupted, mainly in New England, and the individuals killed. The second pair, however—King George's War (1739–1748) and the French and Indian War (1754–1763)—eventuated in Britain's making good its claims to the Ohio valley, expelling France from the North American mainland, and limiting the opportunities for the Woodlands peoples to play one empire against the other for their own advantage.

Assessment. By 1763, characteristic patterns distinguished colonial regions from each other. New England's town meetings, Congregational establishment, and ethnocentrism earned it a reputation for egalitarianism, moralism, and xenophobia. The mid-Atlantic colonies remained the most ethnically and religiously heterogeneous, their diverse interest groups forcing the appearance of long-term partisan political blocs in Pennsylvania and New York earlier than elsewhere. In the South monoculture, slave labor, and guaranteed British markets supported the largest population, the highest per capita income, and the wealthiest, most powerful mainland elite. Everywhere families moved into the interior, less a distinctive cultural enclave than a transient zone in which migrants, having outstripped organized institutions and thrust themselves upon native tribes, concocted out of custom and exigency societies temporarily less hierarchical and more violent than coastal communities.

At the same time, certain similarities appeared everywhere. Habits of enterprise had erected transatlantic commercial networks that yielded one of the world's highest standards of living. The European state-church system failed to materialize, the Reformed Protestant tradition colored worship, and although denominations competed for power and place, they united in identifying Britain as the champion of true religion over against Catholic superstition and tyranny. Jealous of their English rights—even as, and perhaps because, they denied those rights to slaves—citizens regarded their representative assemblies as bulwarks against monarchical prerogatives and protectors of their liberties. Triumph over France fired colonists' pride in the empire and themselves.

None of these conditions made the American Revolution inevitable. Some historians have argued that the prevalence of ecclesiastical schisms, class conflicts, and sectional antagonisms amounted to a social crisis that propelled rebellion, but confrontations were ordinarily resolved without resort to violence, and in any case how or why such tensions might have been displaced onto British authorities is not clear. The colonial era's legacy was an architecture of finite contingencies, framed by the elaborated cultural rules of Britain and adorned by those of northwest Europe, from which the future of Anglo-America would emerge. In creating the United States, the American Revolution actualized one possibility out of many.

[*See also* **Atlantic World; Bacon's Rebellion; British Americans; Captivity Narratives, Native American; Caribbean; Coffeehouses and Coffee; Demography; Exploration, Conquest, and Settlement in North America; Franciscans; Great Awakenings; Health and Healing, Eighteenth and Nineteenth Centuries; Impressment; Internal Migration** *subentry on* **Colonial Era; Itinerant Preachers; Jamestown; Jesuits; Leisler's Rebellion; Letters and Letter Writing; Loyalists; Maroon Societies; Militias, Early American; Missions, in America; Native American History and Culture,** *subentry on* **1500 to 1800; New England; New York City; Paxton Boys; Philadelphia; Pirates; Plymouth; Praying Towns; Pueblo Revolt; Puritan Great Migration; Redemptioners; Regulator Movement; Roman Catholic Orders in Early America, Female; Salem Witchcraft; Slavery; Slave Trades;** *and* **Voluntary Associations,** *subentry on* **British Colonies and Early Republic.**]

BIBLIOGRAPHY

Bailyn, Bernard. *The Peopling of British North America: An Introduction.* New York: Alfred A. Knopf, 1986.

Beeman, Richard R. *The Varieties of Political Experience in Eighteenth-Century America*. Philadelphia: University of Pennsylvania Press, 2004.

Breen, T. H. *The Marketplace of Revolution: How Consumer Politics Shaped American Independence*. Oxford: Oxford University Press, 2004.

Butler, Jon. *Becoming America: The Revolution before 1776*. Cambridge, Mass.: Harvard University Press, 2000.

Elliott, J. H. *Empires of the Atlantic World: Britain and Spain in America, 1492–1830*. New Haven, Conn.: Yale University Press, 2006.

Fischer, David Hackett. *Albion's Seed: Four British Folkways in America*. New York: Oxford University Press, 1989.

Games, Alison. *Migration and the Origins of the English Atlantic World*. Cambridge, Mass.: Harvard University Press, 1999.

Greer, Allan. *The People of New France*. Toronto: University of Toronto Press, 1997.

Hornsby, Stephen J. *British Atlantic, American Frontier: Spaces of Power in Early Modern British America*. Hanover, N.H.: University Press of New England, 2005.

Morgan, Edmund S. *American Slavery, American Freedom: The Ordeal of Colonial Virginia*. New York: W. W. Norton and Company, 1975.

Pestana, Carla Gardina. *Protestant Empire: Religion and the Making of the British Atlantic World*. Philadelphia: University of Pennsylvania Press, 2009.

Richter, Daniel K. *Facing East from Indian Country: A Native History of Early America*. Cambridge, Mass.: Harvard University Press, 2001.

Taylor, Alan. *American Colonies*. New York: Viking, 2001.

Charles L. Cohen

COLONIZATION MOVEMENT, AFRICAN

The notion of removing black people from America first surfaced in the early 1700s. By the revolutionary era, colonization proposals of this sort circulated on a regular basis. These projects came to naught, largely because doubts about their humanitarianism, feasibility, and efficacy undermined them in the North, while proslavery antipathy stymied them in the South. In 1816, however, an eclectic mix of northern reformers, southern modernizers, Jeffersonian southerners, and proslavery advocates established the American Colonization Society (ACS). Though some ACS members hoped to strengthen slavery by removing free blacks only, others championed the relocation of all black Americans, free and slave alike. With the federal government's assistance, the ACS founded the colony of Liberia in 1822. Government policy makers and ACS officials continued to shape the colonization movement's course, but so did countless ordinary individuals. Indeed, whereas the movement's leaders envisioned colonization as a pacific enterprise, the clashing ideas and actions of ACS agents, black emigrants, and others often made the venture complex and contentious.

This was true from the start. When ACS leaders selected men to be their agents in Liberia, they usually chose northern evangelicals, who believed that colonization would Christianize and "civilize" Africans, redeem "degraded" black Americans, and showcase their own religious devotion. The agents repeatedly quarreled with free black emigrants from the South, who constituted a majority of settlers during the movement's early years. Skilled, literate, and entrepreneurial, these emigrants compelled the ACS to relinquish some power and authority over colonial affairs. Such settlers came to dominate Liberia, revealing that for them colonization was not just an avenue by which to escape oppression in America but an opportunity to build a world of their own.

By the mid-1830s, more and more slaveholders were liberating their bondpeople on the condition that they move to Liberia. These emancipators often expressed misgivings about slavery's viability and morality, but they were not antislavery radicals. Rather, they expected that the prospect of freedom in Africa would elicit obedience and sedulousness from bondpeople. Their slaves, however, did not mindlessly follow the bait of liberty. Instead, they haggled over the terms of manumission, sought reliable intelligence from Liberia, and tried to ensure that emigration was a familial endeavor. Slaves did not always get what they wanted, but they drove the hardest bargain they could.

The tug-and-pull between slaveholders and bondpeople rendered ACS manumissions socially expansive enterprises. For example, because slaves demanded trustworthy reports from Liberia, the ACS needed to circulate previous emigrants' letters, accommodate so-called investigative parties, and ride circuit with settler boosters who came back to America to tout the colony's virtues. Likewise, slaves' desire to emigrate with their kin meant that colonizationists had to effect "conjunctive manumissions"—that is, instances in which two or more slaveholders liberated members of one black family. Like pebbles dropped in water, ACS manumissions rippled outward, affecting all in their wake.

The size and location of ACS operations determined white southerners' response to them. A relatively large emancipatory endeavor could provoke indignation, especially if it occurred in the lower South. A small manumission in an urban area or in the border areas of the South was less likely to incur white southerners' wrath. In either case, ACS supporters faced the difficult task of trumpeting their exploits without outraging white southerners.

ACS activities had equally profound effects in the North. Most black northerners denounced the ACS, and their vociferousness prompted some white reformers to forsake colonization and embrace abolitionism. Among those white northerners who remained committed to colonization, some vainly hoped that the region's black population would move to Liberia, but others focused their energies on facilitating ACS manumissions in the South. Financing and showcasing these emancipatory enterprises made them feel that colonization was an interregional program that secured real antislavery results, especially in comparison to what they regarded as the abolitionists' inflammatory, counterproductive sectionalism.

By these means, approximately sixteen thousand black Americans emigrated to Liberia. Once there, the settlers endured horrific mortality rates and unremitting poverty, but they also enjoyed freedoms and opportunities denied to them in America. Their reports from Liberia shaped manumitters' thoughts about colonization, informed black Americans' decisions concerning emigration, and provided both pro- and anticolonizationists with proof for their positions. In this sense, the colonization movement was truly a transatlantic phenomenon.

Ultimately colonization failed to solve America's problems concerning slavery and race. The sixteen thousand black Americans who moved to Liberia represented a tiny fraction of the nation's African American population. But when one considers how ACS operations reverberated throughout the Atlantic world, the relatively minuscule numbers belie the enterprise's import.

[*See also* **African American Emigration; African Americans; Antebellum Era; Antislavery; Emancipation of Slaves; Free Communities of Color; Liberia, Colonization of;** *and* **Slavery,** *subentry on* **Nineteenth Century.**]

BIBLIOGRAPHY

Burin, Eric. *Slavery and the Peculiar Solution: A History of the American Colonization Society*. Gainesville: University Press of Florida, 2005. Examines various participants in ACS manumissions.

Shick, Tom W. *Behold the Promised Land: A History of Afro-American Settler Society in Nineteenth-Century Liberia*. Baltimore: Johns Hopkins University Press, 1980. Shows how settler ideals were challenged by African circumstances.

Staudenraus, P. J. *The African Colonization Movement, 1816–1865*. New York: Columbia University Press, 1961. Places colonization within the era's larger reform culture.

Eric Burin

COLUMBIAN EXCHANGE

Separated from Europe and Africa for millions of years, and separated from Asia for more than ten thousand years, the Americas acquired a distinct assemblage of plants and animals. Old and New World humans developed their own ways of life, featuring distinct crops, domesticated animals, and diseases. When Christopher Columbus and other European explorers established contacts between these great landmasses, they triggered an exchange of life-forms that had massive consequences for humans and the biosphere. Weeds, animals, crops, and microbes demonstrate this unprecedented exchange.

The Old World had more species of weeds, that is, plants equipped to spread swiftly on disturbed soils, because it was much larger in area and because it had more species of grazing animals, to whose teeth and hooves Eurasian and African grasses and herbs had been obliged to adapt. Many of these weeds followed colonizers to the Americas. As a result, many of the most aggressive weeds now in the Americas, especially in the temperate zones, have European origins: dandelions, crabgrass, wild oats, sow thistle, kudzu, tumbleweed, plantain, cheat grass, and many others. Only a few weeds—amaranth and Canadian water weed, for example—went the other way and established themselves east of the Atlantic.

The Eastern and Western Hemispheres also exchanged many animal species. Black and brown rats, for instance, traveled to America, and gray squirrels and muskrats made it to Eurasia. The movement of domesticated animals was largely from Old World to New. Amerindians had had less success as animal domesticators than their European counterparts had, likely because they had fewer potentially domesticable animals to work with. Their livestock—llamas, guinea pigs, turkeys, and dogs—included none that were ridden, pulled heavy loads, or supplied large quantities of meat and milk for human consumption. The domesticated animals of Eurasia and Africa, in contrast, included horses, cattle, sheep, goats, pigs, donkeys, and chickens. These offered a major source of nourishment, leather, fiber, fertilizer, and power. With their introduction into the Americas after 1492, these domesticated animals facilitated European colonization and transformed the lives of many Amerindians.

The exchange of crops was more balanced. Prior to 1492, New and Old World populations cultivated entirely different plants. Cotton was the only significant crop grown on both sides of the Atlantic. The most important Native American cultivars were maize, white potatoes, sweet potatoes, and manioc (or cassava). By the late twentieth century these crops had spread worldwide and accounted for roughly one-third of global food production. Meanwhile, a longer list of Eurasian and African crops (as would be expected given the relative land areas) also traveled: wheat, barley, rice, sugarcane, oats, rye, soybeans, bananas, carrots, cabbage, oranges, and many others. These transformed the agricultural landscape of the Americas.

The situation with diseases is more complicated and more tragic. Although pre-Columbian Amerindians certainly suffered a host of endemic bacterial, viral, and helminthic infections, they had few distinctive pathogens. Chagas' disease provides one example, but it never spread beyond the Americas. Syphilis might provide another, but its history remains controversial. Many historians now believe that Europeans acquired syphilis from Amerindians during Columbus's first voyage. Skeletal evidence for the presence of syphilis in pre-Columbian America is strong; no similarly definitive evidence exists in Europe. But this does not prove the point. It is possible that the dramatic appearance of syphilis in Italy and then the rest of Europe after 1493 is entirely coincidental.

There is little doubt, in contrast, about the impact of Old World pathogens. Eurasian and African populations had lived, for millennia, in close contact with domesticated animals and rats. These became a source of many human diseases. To make matters worse, the sanitary conditions of Old World farms and cities facilitated the propagation of waterborne infections. Intensive trade across long distances allowed the wide diffusion of microbes. As a result, Old World populations suffered an appalling burden of virulent pathogens, including smallpox, measles, chicken pox, bubonic plague, malaria, yellow fever, diphtheria, and influenza. When Europeans and Africans crossed the Atlantic, many of these pathogens followed. The result of this aspect of the Columbian Exchange was catastrophic: Old World pathogens devastated Amerindians, reducing many populations by more than 90 percent.

Although the magnitude of the mortality is clear, debate persists about the causes of the susceptibility of Amerindian populations. Some scholars have argued that Old World populations, long exposed to these pathogens, had evolved inherited resistance to them. New World populations, without this selective pressure, remained vulnerable. There is, however, no evidence that Old World populations actually possess special resistance to smallpox, influenza, or the other dire viral pathogens. Other scholars have argued that the chaos triggered by European colonization, especially displacement, enslavement, malnutrition, and demoralization, weakened Amerindians and left them susceptible to Old World pathogens. Whatever the causes of the mortality, the decimation of Amerindians facilitated the movement of Europeans and Africans across the Atlantic Ocean.

The impacts of the Columbian Exchange continue into the twenty-first century. The exchange of cultivated plants and livestock increased food production on both sides of the Atlantic (and Pacific), making possible the enormous growth of human populations. Potatoes, for instance, enabled farmers in northern Europe to extract more nourishment from the soil than ever before. Hundreds of millions of Chinese depend on maize, sweet potatoes, and even the peanut. Africans grow maize, peanuts, and, especially, manioc. The Americas, in turn, produce and export wheat, rice, beef, chicken, and many other Old World foods. Not all crops have been so beneficent. If projections hold true, tobacco, taken from the Americas throughout the world, will kill a billion people over the next century. The full significance of the Columbian Exchange, so dramatic over the past five hundred years, continues to unfold.

[*See also* **Atlantic World; Disease; Exploration, Conquest, and Settlement in North America;** *and* **Native American History** and Culture, *subentries on* Migration and Pre-Columbian Era, Distribution of Major Groups circa 1500, *and* 1500 to 1800.]

BIBLIOGRAPHY

Crosby, Alfred W. *The Columbian Exchange: Biological and Cultural Consequences of 1492.* Westport, Conn.: Greenwood, 1972.

Crosby, Alfred W. *Ecological Imperialism: The Biological Expansion of Europe, 900–1900.* Cambridge, U.K.: Cambridge University Press, 1986.

Denevan, William M., ed. *The Native Population of the Americas in 1492.* 2d ed. Madison: University of Wisconsin Press, 1992.

Diamond, Jared. *Guns, Germs, and Steel: The Fates of Human Societies.* New York: W. W. Norton and Company, 1997.

Jones, David S. "Virgin Soils Revisited." *William and Mary Quarterly,* 3d ser., 60, no. 4 (2003): 703–742.

Kelton, Paul. *Epidemics and Enslavement: Biological Catastrophe in the Native Southeast, 1492–1715.* Lincoln: University of Nebraska Press, 2007.

Thornton, Russell. *American Indian Holocaust and Survival: A Population History since 1492.* Norman: University of Oklahoma Press, 1987.

Alfred W. Crosby; revised and updated by David S. Jones

COMMUNICATION NETWORKS

America's communication networks reflect both the nation's insatiable desire for access to timely news and information and its deep aversion to government interference with information transfer. Unlike many European governments in the eighteenth and nineteenth centuries, the United States government neither imposed access restrictions on the nation's evolving communication networks, nor censored information transmitted across these networks. This approach to network access and information transfer influenced the growth of communication networks accessible to any American with the necessary financial means.

Colonial and Republican Postal System.

The postal system represented the earliest attempt by Americans to create a systematized network for communicating across the ever-expanding width and breadth of the young nation. During the nineteenth century, the United States Post Office annihilated time and space by connecting the western and southern frontiers to the seats of political and economic power in the East. In the 1770s the Continental Congress founded a rudimentary postal system modeled after the British colonial system, but during the Revolutionary era, poor management limited the effectiveness of the new service. Postal routes failed to keep pace with westward expansion, and the system required large federal subsidies to maintain basic service.

Three years after Americans ratified the federal Constitution, Congress set about reforming the American postal system through the Post Office Act of 1792. The act granted Congress the power to designate new postal routes. Over the next thirty years, Congress created more than two thousand new routes to link every corner of the expanding nation. The Post Office Act also forbade postal officials from opening private mail and ensured that the constitutional protection of free speech would extend to the mail system. Most significantly, the act permitted newspapers to be mailed at a nominal rate, which facilitated the free flow of timely news and information from metropole to periphery, in effect creating a national information market. Newspapers made up the bulk of mail deliveries until the mid-nineteenth century: high postage rates for letters, along with a requirement that all postage fees be paid in currency, dissuaded most Americans from using the mail. Letter-writing merchants, ministers, and wealthy farmers constituted the majority of postal customers, and members of Congress sent out a steady stream of correspondence to their constituents at government expense.

The Post Office and Social Change.

Throughout the nineteenth century, the postal system reflected the changing political and social landscape of the United States. Beginning in 1829, Andrew Jackson and his successors sought to reorient the postal service as a tool for political patronage, and many competent local postmasters found themselves purged to make room for party loyalists. The postal service also faced challenges from social reformers during this era. Twice during the first half of the nineteenth century, Sabbatarians organized unsuccessful campaigns to persuade Congress to suspend mail transport and close post offices on Sundays. Beginning in the mid-1830s, abolitionists used the postal system to flood the South with antislavery pamphlets. The campaign infuriated slave owners and prompted Postmaster General Amos Kendall and other postal officials to devise an informal plan to isolate and block abolitionist literature from reaching the South. The unofficial censorship system remained in place until the Civil War.

Postal reform acts in 1845 and 1851 reduced postage rates for letters dramatically and allowed customers to prepay for postage through the use of stamps. By midcentury these reforms had transformed the postal system into a tool for mass communication and the primary medium for long-distance personal correspondence in the United States. Despite the development of faster, but more expensive, communication technologies such as the electrical telegraph and the telephone, until the early twentieth century a significant majority of Americans continued to depend on the Post Office for time-sensitive, long-distance communications.

The Telegraph.

Samuel F. B. Morse's successful demonstration in May 1844 of long-distance telegraphy ushered in the era of electrical communication in the United States. Morse believed that the telegraph should complement the existing mail system and conceived of a national network built and operated by private firms acting under the direct oversight of the Post Office Department. Morse and his partners lobbied Congress to purchase the patent rights to the new technology in order to secure federal control over the nascent system, but after Congress failed to act, Morse reluctantly began to license his patent to private entrepreneurs in 1845.

Alternative telegraph technologies, including the House and Bain systems, emerged in the late 1840s and challenged the dominance of the Morse patent. Competition among patent holders led to a dramatic expansion in the number of telegraph firms chartered in the United States during the early 1850s. By mid-decade, telegraph lines connected East Coast cities with communities along the Mississippi valley and the Gulf Coast, and planning was underway to lay a transatlantic cable from Newfoundland to the west coast of Ireland. The high message rates charged by telegraph firms during the nineteenth century precluded personal use by most Americans. Journalists, merchants, and financial speculators, who recognized the competitive advantage that rapid telegraph service offered over the slower postal service, provided the bulk of business for telegraph firms until the early twentieth century. Industry mergers before and during the Civil War eventually led the Western Union Telegraph Company to emerge as the nation's dominant telegraph firm by 1866, but the mergers also made possible the dramatic expansion and consolidation of national commercial markets during this era.

As telegraph networks expanded across the nation during the second half of the nineteenth century, labor shortages encouraged Western Union and smaller firms to hire female operators to staff telegraph offices. Operator jobs offered women adequate wages and were perceived as socially acceptable by the public. Many young women retired as operators after marriage, but a few worked in the industry for their entire careers and rose to managerial and senior technical positions. For both women and men, the telegraph profession provided a means for upward social mobility. Telegraph operators formed part of an expanding lower middle class. Many came from working-class backgrounds, but their proficiency in mastering the complex and arcane details of Morse telegraphy elevated them to the status of skilled, white-collar workers. Operators of both genders participated actively in the bourgeoning labor movement of the late nineteenth century. In 1883 the Brotherhood of Telegraphers, an affiliate of the Knights of Labor, engaged in a monthlong, nationwide strike against Western Union and a number of smaller commercial telegraph firms. Striking telegraphers demanded greater pay, equal wages for male and female telegraphers, and other reforms. Western Union withstood the labor challenge, but operators retained a significant degree of labor militancy in the decades that followed.

During the first decade of the twentieth century, in response to federal regulatory pressures and a brief acquisition by the American Telephone and Telegraph Company (AT&T), Western Union began to provide facilities for individual consumers. Low prices and convenience became the hallmarks of Western Union service throughout the century. Declining demand for telegraph service in the face of competition from long-distance telephone, fax, and electronic-mail applications eventually led to the demise of Western Union's telegraphic message services in 2006.

The Telephone. In 1875 the investor Gardiner G. Hubbard hired his future son-in-law Alexander Graham Bell to develop a multiplex telegraph instrument to sell to either Western Union or one of its rivals. As an outgrowth of his research, Bell developed a process for transmitting human speech electrically and later constructed a simple telephone device. When Western Union failed to purchase the rights to Bell's invention, Hubbard decided to commercialize the new technology himself. In 1879 a group of Boston investors licensed the Bell patents from Hubbard and formed American Bell, which became a subsidiary of AT&T in 1899. Prior to the mid-1890s, telephone promoters primarily marketed the new communication technology as a business tool that would enable professionals such as merchants, lawyers, and doctors to dispense with personal messengers and speak directly with other telephone subscribers. Initially, local Bell operating companies charged subscribers high flat rates for service, but soon they discovered that flat rates encouraged intensive use of the telephone and permitted subscribers to engage in casual conversations that tied up the network. In response, many operating companies attempted to implement measured service: this generated heated objections from telephone users, who feared that the new fee structure would increase telephone bills and prevent them from using the telephone for social communication. Subscriber boycotts in numerous cities delayed the implementation of measured service for many business users until the 1910s.

The telephone's shift from an elite business tool to a mass medium of communication began around 1900. Bell's telephone patents expired in 1894, and by 1900 a flood of independent telephone companies had entered the American telephone market and had begun to challenge the dominant position enjoyed by AT&T and the local Bell operating companies. AT&T offered business subscribers access to its medium- and long-distance intercity toll network, but independents offered competitive, fixed-rate service to business and nonbusiness subscribers and access to advanced technologies such as automatic-dial telephones. Angus Hibbard, general manager of the Bell affiliate Chicago Telephone, experimented with coin-box public telephones for casual users and introduced a variety of measured, local service options for home and business subscribers, including party lines and pay-as-you-go. Soon, Bell managers in other cities adopted these service innovations, making it increasingly difficult for independents to compete against regional Bell operating companies. The growth of low-cost, local telephone service during the first decade of the twentieth century dramatically expanded the pool of potential telephone users to include middle- and lower-class men and women.

The popularization of the telephone encouraged AT&T executives to begin developing a national communication system encompassing both telephone and telegraph services, but in 1913 antimonopoly officials within the administration of Woodrow Wilson forced AT&T to divest its non-telephone holdings and provide independents with access to its long-distance telephone network. The settlement ended AT&T's drive to dominate the American communication market, but it implicitly endorsed AT&T's goal of serving as a universal provider of high-quality local and long-distance telephone service for the American public. Despite the firm's focus on serving a national market, only business subscribers and affluent Americans could afford routinely to use long-distance services. Until the late 1970s, most American continued to use letters and telegrams for long-distance, time-sensitive communication.

Wireless Communication and the Internet. Experiments with wireless telegraphy and telephony during the first two decades of the twentieth century had little direct impact on America's communication networks. AT&T maintained an interest in radiotelephone technologies, but it also viewed the new technology as a potential threat to its national wired telephone network. During the 1920s the company added a few short-distance radiotelephone links to its network in order to provide telephone service to subscribers in isolated locations that could not be reached by wires. Using microwave radio technologies developed for World War II, AT&T began constructing a long-distance wireless telephone network shortly after the war. During the 1950s, AT&T moved the bulk of its long-distance telephone service to the new wireless network because it offered greater capacity and lower operating costs compared to the older wired network.

Low-cost microwave radio also introduced competition to the national, long-distance telephone market. In 1963 a group of midwestern entrepreneurs formed Microwave Communications, Incorporated (MCI) to sell microwave radio equipment and operate a microwave radio network for long-haul truckers between Chicago and Saint Louis. MCI executives later realized that their microwave system could be integrated into the local phone networks in both cities, creating a de facto long-distance, interstate telephone system. MCI, Sprint, and other low-cost, long-distance carriers began challenging AT&T's near monopoly over the domestic long-distance market in the 1970s. The growing financial and legal conflict eventually led to renewed scrutiny of AT&T by the Justice Department: the result was the 1984 breakup of the company into a long-distance division and independent regional operating companies. Competition in the long-distance telephone market dramatically lowered rates for consumers by the late 1980s and led to a marked decline in the use of letters and telegrams for routine long-distance communication in the United States.

Approval by the Federal Communications Commission (FCC) of analogue cellular telephone standards in 1982, along with the 1984 AT&T divestiture, provided the impetus for the dramatic expansion of wireless telephone networks in the United States during the 1980s and 1990s. In the early 1970s, engineers at Bell Labs had developed computer software that enabled mobile radiotelephones to shift seamlessly from one transmission and reception tower to the next, but early commercialization of cellular telephone service had taken place outside the United States. Following regulatory approval of cellular telephone standards and the reemergence of competition in the local and long-distance markets in the early 1980s, cellular telephone manufacturers and service providers raced to construct larger and more reliable cellular telephone networks across the United States. By the end of the 1980s, more than a million cell-phone handsets were in use throughout the nation, and over the next twenty years the number increased more than three-hundred-fold.

Cellular telephony provided Americans with mobile access to timely news and information, but the popularization of the Internet in the 1990s and early 2000s dramatically altered how Americans accessed information and communicated with each other. Based on computer networking technologies developed jointly by the federal government and American research universities during the Cold War era, the Internet provided access to electronic mail, instant messaging, and other computer-based communication platforms that challenged the primacy of older and more established methods of business and personal communication. Like earlier networks, the Internet was open and accessible to nearly all Americans, and users vigorously resisted legislative efforts to regulate or restrict online content. Although the Internet supplanted older communication networks, it embodied the same social and political values that Americans had embedded into communication networks dating back to the early years of the republic. Consequently the Internet should be recognized as a lineal descendant of the post office, telegraph, and telephone networks that shaped the growth and development of the nation during the nineteenth and twentieth centuries.

[*See also* **Automation and Computerization; Communication Revolution, Modern; Electricity and Electrification;** *and* **Letters and Letter Writing.**]

BIBLIOGRAPHY

Blondheim, Menahem. *News over the Wires: The Telegraph and the Flow of Public Information in America, 1844–1897*. Cambridge, Mass.: Harvard University Press, 1994. A detailed study of the relationship between the telegraph industry and the American press during the nineteenth century.

Cantelon, Philip L. *The History of MCI: The Early Years, 1968–1988*. Dallas, Tex.: Heritage Press, 1993. An in-depth corporate history of the creation and expansion of MCI; remains the most detailed and authoritative history of the early independent microwave communications industry in the United States.

Coe, Lewis. *The Telephone and Its Several Inventors: A History*. Jefferson, N.C.: McFarland and

Company, 1995. A general history of the technological development of the telephone and its impact on American society during the nineteenth and twentieth centuries.

Fischer, Claude S. *America Calling: A Social History of the Telephone to 1940.* Berkeley: University of California Press, 1992. Focuses on the impact of the telephone on American society, making comparisons between the impact of the telephone and the impact of the automobile on American ideas about distance, community, and connectivity.

Gabler, Edwin. *The American Telegrapher: A Social History, 1860–1900.* New Brunswick, N.J.: Rutgers University Press, 1988. Provides a detailed study of the 1883 telegrapher strike and examines the social and cultural background of commercial telegraphers in the United States.

Headrick, Daniel R. *When Information Came of Age: Technologies of Knowledge in the Age of Reason and Revolution, 1700–1850.* Oxford: Oxford University Press, 2000. A comparative study of methods of organizing, storing, displaying, and transmitting information in western Europe and the United States during the eighteenth and nineteenth centuries.

Jepsen, Thomas C. *My Sisters Telegraphic: Women in the Telegraph Office, 1846–1950.* Athens, Ohio: Ohio University Press, 2000. A detailed social and cultural study of American female telegraphers during the nineteenth and twentieth centuries.

John, Richard R. *Network Nation: Inventing American Telecommunications.* Cambridge, Mass.: Harvard University Press, 2010. A definitive and groundbreaking study of the development of telegraph and telephone networks in the United States and the role of local, state, and federal politics and regulation in shaping these networks during the nineteenth and early twentieth centuries.

John, Richard R. *Spreading the News: The American Postal System from Franklin to Morse.* Cambridge, Mass.: Harvard University Press, 1995. An authoritative political-economic history of the United States Post Office Department during the early republic and the antebellum period.

Klemens, Guy. *The Cellphone: The History and Technology of the Gadget That Changed the World.* Jefferson, N.C.: McFarland and Company, 2010. A popular history of the development of cellular telephone technologies and the cell phone's impact on world society.

Temin, Peter and Louis Galambos. *The Fall of the Bell System: A Study in Prices and Politics.* Cambridge: Cambridge University Press, 1987. Important study of the role of public policy and corporate decision making in the 1984 AT&T divestiture.

Thompson, Robert Luther. *Wiring a Continent: The History of the Telegraph Industry in the United States, 1832–1866.* Princeton, N.J.: Princeton University Press, 1947. A dated but authoritative history of the telegraph industry in the United States prior to the formation of the Western Union.

Benjamin Schwantes

COMMUNICATION REVOLUTION, MODERN

The term "communication revolution" is widely used to refer to the interlaced socioeconomic, political, and technological changes associated with the extremely rapid expansion of digital data processing and telecommunications during the late twentieth and early twenty-first centuries. This revolution appears to be deeper and moving much more rapidly than previous social revolutions associated with communication technology, such as the introduction of movable type, the telegraph, or television.

Technologies central to modern communication revolutions are generally labeled "information and communication technologies," or ICTs. These include computers and high-speed telecommunication infrastructure, of course. But other digital technologies are also integrally involved in such revolutions. Examples include human–computer interfaces other than keyboards, such as video, audio, touch, and emerging human-nerve–computer links; "intelligent" objects such as buildings, roadways, billboards, weapon systems, and power grids; geographic information systems linked to global positioning satellites; digital-sensor-based inspection and social surveillance systems; and financial-trading, clearing, and business intelligence systems.

Statistics about the growth and impact of the Internet and related technologies are staggering. By 2010 there were about a billion World Wide Web (WWW) sites that were theoretically capable of reaching a global audience, for example, and total traffic on the Internet increased more than 40,000 percent between 1990 and 2010. The network router manufacturer Cisco Systems predicted that Internet traffic would more than quadruple by 2014. At the same time, other sectors of contemporary society—such as the publishing trades, network television, the U.S. advertising industry, retailers, and even the Internet itself—are in the midst of major, structural changes whose outcome remains uncertain.

Communication Revolutions. These ongoing communication revolutions are often experienced most deeply in spheres of life that might seem to be separate from the simple use of media such as the WWW, mobile computing, or cellular telephones. For example, many observers point out that current communication technologies have radically altered aspects of the distance and time that otherwise separate people, societies, and cultures. Among other effects, the evaporation of some costs associated with communicating over long distances provided a necessary prerequisite for outsourcing or off-shoring entire industries in order to reduce costs or gain access to markets. That in turn created or destroyed communities surrounding the displaced industries, thereby transforming the lives and customs of uncounted people in both economically developed and economically developing countries. Roughly similar transformative effects stemming from greatly accelerated digital data processing and telecommunications can be readily observed in other economic relationships, politics, military affairs, research, and education, as well as in the structure and content of media enterprises.

Popular literature about "the" communication revolution generally places its origin in the United States and views the emergence of a commercialized version of the Internet in the mid-1990s as its most important catalyst. This argument emphasizes the United States' role during this period as the primary innovator in digital communications, the central crossroads for global telecommunication traffic, the leading mass-media hub, and the singular global superpower.

Yet that argument must be balanced by the realization that modern communication revolutions are a much broader, global phenomenon. A number of countries have outstripped the United States in various aspects of digital media uptake and in access to broadband telecommunications. For example, in 2011, Internet penetration per capita was higher in South Korea, Japan, Australia, and several European countries than it was in the United States. That same year, Internet penetration per capita in China was roughly half of what it was in the United States, yet China's giant population made it by far the largest Internet user in the world, with an annual Internet-usage growth rate more than ten times higher than that in the United States. Perhaps most tellingly, the sweeping adoption of digital cellular telephones and short-message service (SMS) throughout much of Africa and Asia demonstrated that contemporary communication revolutions have had the largest impact on day-to-day life in societies where the Internet as such had previously played a relatively marginal role.

Digital Divides. In the early twenty-first century, public access to sophisticated digital technologies is growing very rapidly worldwide. The International Telecommunication Union (ITU) reported 5.3 billion cellular telephone subscriptions worldwide in 2010, with a solid majority—3.8 billion subscriptions—in developing economies. Some 15.8 percent of households in developing economies were reported to have Internet access in the home in 2010, compared to 65.6 percent in developed economies. (The ITU is a United Nations agency, and its statistics are based on reports by member governments.) However, significant divides exist between the so-called information rich and those who are impoverished. The specific dimensions of these divides are often debated, in part because different measures are used to support contrasting political and ethical conclusions.

Nevertheless, digital divides are clearly rooted in the entrenched disparities between developed and developing economies, as well as in the deep splits between rich and poor within most countries. These divides are compounded by factors including inadequate access to education and to economic opportunity in general; discrimination based on gender, ethnicity, social rank or caste, disability, or similar factors; the relatively high "entry cost" of Internet use in remote areas; and the difficulty and expense of creating relevant Internet content in local languages. Exclusion from ICTs and digital communications often intensifies existing structural violence and disenfranchisement of the poor. For many, the brutality of poverty grows sharper as job opportunities, medical care, and government services move online. Ameliorative programs such as distribution of computers to schools have in some circumstances accentuated the relative disadvantage of poor children by introducing a new stigma of information poverty into cultures where it had not previously existed.

Social Organization and Communication Revolutions. The driving forces of modern communication revolutions are found in the complex interactions of human agency, social institutions, and the mediating technologies that people employ in the communicative processes that underpin society. It is through mediated communicative processes that people reshape societies; technology alone does not create effects. The distinction is important. It means that a central issue for understanding communication revolutions is to understand how societies decide to use available technologies.

The pioneering media scientist Harold Innis argued that the characteristics of the media that people use have always subtly shaped human social structures and worldviews. Take broadcast television, for example. Its key business and technological characteristics since its introduction in the mid-twentieth century have mostly depended on broad, capital intensive, one-way distribution of professionally produced media content to passive, largely undifferentiated audiences. This model of public communication and information exchange was in turn embedded in government and legal structures. Taken together with other media such as daily newspapers and radio, these media provided the basis for an "industrial information economy" characteristic of the second half of the twentieth century that shaped both national political conversations and also many aspects of social relationships, especially in consumer societies.

Analysts generally agree that this pattern has been challenged by emergence of a "network society" whose key features were said to have become clear by the mid-1990s. Manuel Castell's influential 1996 book *Rise of the*

Network Society announced a "new social morphology of our societies . . . [that] substantially modifies the operations and outcomes in processes of production, experience, power, and culture." (p. 469) The rise of multiple cable channels, the twenty-four-hour Cable News Network (CNN), and transnational broadcasting was said to have ended the dominance of network television in the United States. The one-way transmission pattern of TV broadcasting was predicted to be rapidly supplanted by the individualized, multidirectional, computer-mediated communication characteristic of the mid-1990s' computer bulletin boards and of "a unique blending of military strategy, big science cooperation, and counter cultural innovation." (p. 351)

This version of communication revolution was said to have established a global capitalist society, though without a capitalist class: a society in which diffusion of networked information technologies had increased employment, thus ending mass unemployment for the foreseeable future, and in which labor had lost its collective identity and become increasingly individualized and diffuse.

Contesting Communication Revolutions.

The dominant interpretation among social scientists and many other observers at the end of the first decade of the twenty-first century remained that communication revolutions offer opportunities for positive or negative outcomes for various social groups. Greater benefits are often assumed to accrue to those who participate most thoroughly in use of digital tools and entertainment. All other things being equal, each new human generation is widely expected to benefit more from communication revolutions than its predecessor did.

But the evidence supporting that popular prediction is thin and difficult to test.

The argument that ICTs virtually guarantee long-term social progress has been repeatedly called into question, including by many ICT advocates. By the second decade of the twenty-first century a more subtle consensus had begun to emerge that took fuller account of the dystopian potential of the technologies, as well as of the continuing strength of existing power structures from the industrial era. Jonathan Zittrain, for example, has argued that the relative success of the Internet between 1990 and about 2005 has encouraged technological and business developments that threaten to "curtail further innovation and to facilitate invasive forms of surveillance and control . . . allowing [communication web] regulators to alter basic freedoms that previously needed no theoretical or practical defense." Evgeny Mozorov, Siva Vaidhyanathan, and others have examined in-depth the trends toward Internet oligopolies, surveillance, and persecution, in both democratic and authoritarian societies. Robert McChesney has argued that the changes associated with modern digital communications continue an enduring struggle over the control and content of communication systems.

In the twenty-first century, surveillance and knowledge-management technologies devised for network management or for Internet advertising are quickly adopted by both democratic and authoritarian governments, as well as by multinational corporations. Simulaneously, protesters engaged in the well known Arab spring of 2011 and similar movements took up cell phones and some web-based tools in an effort to spread news of their struggle. Digital ICTs increasingly "define the workplace and produce ever more complex regimes of surveillance and control," according to Jonathan Burston (http://conferences.fims.uwo.ca/DigitalLabour/default.aspx. Digital Labour: Workers, Authors, Citizens). "At the same time, new possibilities for agency and new spaces for collectivity are borne" from digital innovation.

[*See also* **Automation and Computerization; Communication Networks; Deindustrialization; Radio;** *and* **Television.**]

BIBLIOGRAPHY

Benkler, Yochai. *The Wealth of Networks: How Social Production Transforms Markets and Freedom.* New Haven, Conn.: Yale University Press, 2006. An analysis of sociopolitical outcomes associated with the technological characteristics of digital media and the Internet.

Castells, Manuel. *The Rise of the Network Society, The Information Age: Economy, Society and Culture,* Vol. 1. Cambridge, Mass.: Blackwell, 1996.

Ekine, Sokari, ed. *SMS Uprising: Mobile Phone Activism in Africa.* Cape Town, South Africa: Pambazuka, 2010.

Innis, Harold. *Empire and Communications.* Oxford: Clarendon Press, 1950.

International Telecommunications Union. "ITU Statistics: Mobile Cellular Subscriptions, by Level of Development." 2011. http://www.itu.int/ict/statistics.

McChesney, Robert W. *Communication Revolution: Critical Junctures and the Future of Media.* New York: New Press, 2007. A critical study of media and communication studies during contemporary media shifts.

Morozov, Evgeny. *The Net Delusion: The Dark Side of Internet Freedom.* New York: Public Affairs, 2011. An analysis of net surveillance and public apathy, particularly in emerging democracies and authoritarian states.

Vaidhyanathan, Siva. *The Googlization of Everything (and Why We Should Worry).* Berkeley: University of California Press, 2011.

Zittrain, Jonathan. *The Future of the Internet and How to Stop It.* New Haven, Conn.: Yale University Press, 2008. A sophisticated study that examines the social outcomes associated with the technological characteristics of communication media.

Christopher Simpson

COMMUNITY ORGANIZING

For most people the history of community organizing in the United States begins with Saul Alinsky's efforts in the Back of the Yards neighborhood of Chicago in 1938 and Alinsky's subsequent codification of community organizing in his *Reveille for Radicals* (1946) and, later, *Rules for Radicals* (1971). Responding to the Great Depression and the threat of global fascism and emboldened by contemporaneous radical organizing efforts such as those of the Congress of Industrial Organizations and the Unemployed Councils, Alinsky promoted a form of union organizing in the community. Relying on the power of an organizer who could help identify grassroots leaders and mobilize members, these so-called people's organizations, grounded in the democratic participation of neighborhood residents, combated the injustices of economic and political elites. In the 1950s Alinsky's community organizing fell on hard times, as anti-Communist attacks undermined all liberal and leftist social change.

In the 1960s the rebirth of progressive activism in the civil rights movements revived not only Alinsky's effort and reputation but also the use of community-organizing strategies and tactics. His strategies and techniques to "let the people decide" were evident both in the black struggle for equality, in organizations such as the Student Nonviolent Coordinating Committee (SNCC; later called the Student National Coordinating Committee), and on the white New Left in Students for a Democratic Society (SDS). The SDS's Port Huron Statement called for "participatory democracy" in order to create a more just and equitable society.

As inner cities erupted in unorganized rebellions in the late 1960s, Alinsky's method grew in popularity. In the 1970s antiwar activists discovered with the end of the Vietnam War that their efforts had few ties to working people, that they were a youth movement without a grassroots base. Their "discovery" of community organizing resulted in the proliferation of thousands of efforts across the nation, a veritable "backyard revolution" of groups trying to fulfill the aspirations and resolve the major inequities exposed by the movements of the day. Building on the community-based, "new social movement" forms of organizing started in the 1960s and improved upon by the women's movement in the 1970s and gay and lesbian organizing in the 1980s, community organizing continued to grow as a form of social activism that was an alternative to class-oriented, factory-based models. Since the 1980s, however, the reassertion and concentration of corporate power and the deconcentration of forms of resistance have resulted in an ongoing growth at the local level of community-based organizations, albeit for the most part without the conflict and radical orientation of prior community-organizing efforts. ACORN (Association of Community Organizations for Reform Now) was one exception. Begun in 1970, ACORN united local affiliates in a powerful national organization that focused on issues of economic injustice and, increasingly in 2004 and 2008, on voter-registration campaigns. ACORN's success attracted the wrath of the right, still smarting from the election of Barack Obama; the right's concentrated attack destroyed the organization, then nearly forty years old.

The history of community organizing is, however, broader and more diverse than simply the Alinsky strand, notwithstanding its centrality. Community organizing preceded Alinsky in, for example, the local struggles of African Americans prior to 1930 and the community-based efforts of nascent social workers in the settlement houses of the early twentieth century. Moreover, there are many forms of community organizing, from community building, development, and planning to social action, and there are many approaches to grassroots social action, including those of Fred Ross, Cesar Chavez, and Paulo Freire, not just Alinsky's. Ross worked for Alinsky, but whereas Alinsky's approach could be described as based on religious congregations, Ross developed an approach based more on going door-to-door and meeting at people's houses. Chavez used Ross's model to organize the United Farm Workers of America. Freire, a Brazilian, exported a critical theory of education and confronting oppression, adopted and modified in the United States that emphasized participation, reflection, dialogue, and capacity building.

In addition, organizations vary in their focus: goals include building relationships and a sense of community, making economic improvements, delivering services, and challenging the powers that be. Critically, community organizing is a strategic technique that spans efforts from left to right; it is not inherently liberal or progressive, as demonstrated by the deep history of exclusionary neighborhood-improvement or property associations and reactionary efforts from the White Citizens' Councils of the 1950s to the Christian Coalition of the 1990s. At its best, community organizing is a significant form of engaging in American public life—especially so in early twenty-first-century America, where labor unions and political parties are weak, the public sector remains suspect, and voluntary efforts are expected to address the social problems created by a largely unbridled global capitalist economy.

[*See also* **Gay and Lesbian Rights Movement; Labor Movements; Living-Wage Movement;** *and* **War Resisters.**]

BIBLIOGRAPHY

Atlas, John. *Seeds of Change: The Story of ACORN, America's Most Controversial Antipoverty Community Organizing Group.* Nashville, Tenn.: Vanderbilt University Press, 2010.

DeFilippis, James, Robert Fisher, and Eric Shragge. *Contesting Community: The Limits and Potential of Local Organizing.* New Brunswick, N.J.: Rutgers University Press, 2010.

Fisher, Robert. *Let the People Decide: Neighborhood Organizing in America.* New York: Twayne, 1994.

Horwitt, Sanford D. *Let Them Call Me Rebel: Saul Alinsky, His Life and Legacy.* New York: Alfred A. Knopf, 1989.

Shaw, Randy. *Beyond the Fields: Cesar Chavez, the UFW, and the Struggle for Justice in the 21st Century.* Berkeley: University of California Press, 2008.

Robert Fisher

CONGRESS OF RACIAL EQUALITY

The Congress of Racial Equality (CORE), one of the most important national organizations of the post–World War II African American freedom movements, was founded by an interracial group of pacifists in 1942. Committed to nonviolent direct action and interracial activism, CORE first launched protests against racial segregation in public accommodations in the North. In 1947, CORE activists undertook the Journey of Reconciliation, riding buses into the South to test a recent U.S. Supreme Court decision outlawing segregation in interstate travel facilities. Although mob violence stopped the trip in Chapel Hill, North Carolina, the project served as a model for CORE's 1961 Freedom Rides.

Initially a mostly white organization in the Northeast and Midwest, CORE expanded into the South after the Montgomery bus boycott of 1955–1956. The charismatic leadership of James Farmer, appointed national director in 1961, and increased media attention surrounding the Freedom Rides enabled CORE to launch a wide range of campaigns in the South during the 1960s. The experience of CORE organizers, the influence of southern blacks, and the impact of black nationalists like Robert F. Williams and Malcolm X led to a growing radicalization. In 1966, under the leadership of Floyd McKissick, CORE endorsed the "Black Power" slogan and the following year deleted the term "multi-racial" from its constitution, forcing whites from the organization. In 1968 the new national director Roy Innis promoted black separatism and black capitalism. Although CORE had lost most of its national influence and vitality by the end of the 1960s, for nearly three decades it had played an influential role in the struggle to topple America's formal racial caste system and to create a new black sense of self.

[*See also* African Americans; Black Nationalism; Civil Rights Movement; Desegregation; Segregation, Racial; *and* Sixties, The.]

BIBLIOGRAPHY

Bell, Inge Powell. *CORE and the Strategy of Nonviolence.* New York: Random House, 1968.

Farmer, James. *Lay Bare the Heart: An Autobiography of the Civil Rights Movement.* New York: Arbor House, 1985.

Meier, August, and Elliott Rudwick. *CORE: A Study in the Civil Rights Movement, 1942–1968.* Urbana: University of Illinois Press, 1975.

Van Deburg, William L. *New Day in Babylon: The Black Power Movement and American Culture, 1965–1975.* Chicago: University of Chicago Press, 1992.

Simon Wendt

CONSERVATION MOVEMENT

Conservationists first gained notice during the late nineteenth century in response to the second phase of the Industrial Revolution. Urbanization, coupled with rapidly increasing production that threatened natural resources and blackened cities with smokestack soot, moved some middle- and upper-class European Americans to reassess the relationship of humans with nature. The result was sweeping legislation that sought to remold the natural world in the conservationist vision. Although the nature parks set aside through conservation efforts remain wildly popular, historians examining the early years of the conservation movement have raised challenging, if not disturbing, questions regarding both whom nature was being protected for and whom it was being protected from. From its earliest days the conservation movement faced charges that, despite their good intentions, its proponents too often acted callously toward working people, the poor, and people of color.

The intellectual origins of conservation are located in both the romantic movement of the early nineteenth century and a pioneering book published near the end of the Civil War. Romantic writers and artists, rejecting the emphasis on science and reason that since the Enlightenment had grown to dominate modern thought, instead sought larger truths through a direct, emotional relationship with nature. Their works were joined by George Perkins Marsh's seminal *Man and Nature, or Physical Geography as Modified by Human Action* (1864), the first book to warn of the disaster that might come unless greater care were given to the environment. Marsh believed that humans were "disturbing agents," and he warned that environmental catastrophe would prove the ruin of American civilization unless proper steps were taken to conserve resources and the environment. This was an attitude that inspired not only conservation but also the suspicion and distrust of those who made a living from the land.

Various conservationists, in the spirit of the romantics, sought to preserve natural spaces deemed especially aesthetically pleasing. Chief among them was John Muir (1838–1914). Although he was born in Scotland and grew up in Wisconsin, it was in California's forests and mountains that Muir found his spiritual home. He was instrumental in the creation of Yosemite National Park in 1890. To ensure continued appreciation and protection of the area, two years later he and others founded the influential Sierra Club "to explore, enjoy, and render accessible the mountain regions of the Pacific Coast" and "to enlist the support and cooperation of the people and government in preserving the forests and other natural features of the Sierra Nevada." By "the people" the club was referring only to other whites—not the American Indians who had called the area home.

Other early conservationists took a different tack and, in keeping with the ethos of the Progressive movement, sought not so much to preserve pristine nature as to ensure the efficient use and management of natural resources for growing cities and industry. The leading voice of this so-called utilitarian conservation ethic was Gifford Pinchot, who trained in forestry at Yale and was appointed by President Theodore Roosevelt in 1905 to be the first head of the U.S. Forest Service. Muir and Pinchot clashed over the proposed building of a dam on the Tuolumne River in the Hetch Hetchy valley in Yosemite National Park to create a reservoir that would supply water for San Francisco: Muir fought to preserve the space unaltered, but Pinchot argued that San Francisco's need for water was paramount. After years of controversy, the dam was finally built beginning in 1913, but the tensions between preservation and utilitarian conservation remained, as did troubling issues of race and class.

Both preservation and utilitarian conservation were dominated by politically and culturally powerful middle- and upper-class European Americans, whose emergent views on the proper relationship between humans and the environment were privileged above all others. The result often was legislation that favored the sporting and recreation desires of urban and rural elites and the resource needs of corporations over the living and working needs of Native Americans and poor whites who depended on the land for their livelihoods. Muir's beloved Yosemite National Park, for example, eventually forced the removal of Yosemite Indians who had long called the area home but whose presence ran counter to the romantic conservation ideal of unpeopled wilderness. Other parks, such as the Adirondacks in New York, forced the removal of European Americans who depended on subsistence hunting and fishing, supplemented by the sale of timber, to make a living. What occurred at Yosemite and the Adirondacks was repeated in the creation of many other parks and wilderness areas, whose construction at the urging of elites often came at the expense of Native Americans and poor whites.

Conservation grew in cultural and political significance during the twentieth century, and the tension between utilitarians and preservationists has persisted into the twenty-first century. Following World War II the conservation movement's focus expanded into what came to be termed "environmentalism." The advent of the atomic bomb, with the accompanying realization that humans now possessed the ability to destroy all life, forced a radical transformation in the way Americans viewed their world and their relationship to the earth and moved some to ponder other ways that humans might be destroying the planet. Issues like population and pollution came to the fore, and best-selling books in the late 1940s, including Fairfield Osborn's *Our Plundered Planet*, William Vogt's *Road to Survival*, and Aldo Leopold's *A Sand County Almanac*, all warned of the apocalyptic doom that might result unless humans began striving for ecological balance in their relationship with the earth.

[*See also* **Environmentalism** *and* **Progressive Era.**]

BIBLIOGRAPHY

Fox, Stephen. *John Muir and His Legacy: The American Conservation Movement.* Boston: Little, Brown, 1981.

Hays, Samuel P. *Conservation and the Gospel of Efficiency: The Progressive Conservation Movement, 1890–1920.* Cambridge, Mass.: Harvard University Press, 1959.

Jacoby, Karl. *Crimes against Nature: Squatters, Poachers, Thieves, and the Hidden History of American Conservation.* Berkeley: University of California Press, 2001.

Leopold, Aldo. *A Sand County Almanac.* New York: Oxford University Press, 1949.

Osborn, Fairfield. *Our Plundered Planet.* Boston: Little, Brown, 1948.

Spence, Mark David. *Dispossessing the Wilderness: Indian Removal and the Making of the National Parks.* New York: Oxford University Press, 1999.

Vogt, William. *Road to Survival.* New York: William Sloane, 1948.

White, Richard. "'Are You an Environmentalist or Do You Work For a Living?': Work and Nature." In *Uncommon Ground: Rethinking the Human Place in Nature,* edited by William Cronon. New York: W. W. Norton and Company, 1996.

Worster, Donald. *Nature's Economy: A History of Ecological Ideas.* 2d ed. Cambridge, U.K.: Cambridge University Press, 1994.

Thomas P. Jundt

CONSERVATIVE MOVEMENT

Though the modern conservative movement began in earnest following World War II, its social dimension developed much later. Traditionalist thinkers of the 1940s and 1950s, such as Richard Weaver and Russell Kirk, lamented a declining civilization but avoided specific policy recommendations. Through the era of Dwight D. Eisenhower, the intellectual right organized in opposition to both domestic and international Communism, but even as it regarded the nuclear family and organized religion as deterrents to further spread of the Red Menace, social issues were not a priority.

During the 1970s the New Right developed as a response to the sociopolitical changes of the previous decade. Opinion leaders recast political and civil rights as part of a zero-sum game in which a gain for one group was viewed as a loss for another. Conservatives used an emotionally charged rhetoric to mount spirited defenses of traditional family and gender roles and portray increased welfare spending as unwise and counterproductive. By 1980 the New Right had become a force in the Republican Party, and since the election that year of Ronald Reagan it has used social issues to energize voters and dominate the party.

Race. Conservatives had a mostly negative opinion of the Civil Rights Movement. The *National Review*, the flagship journal of the right, endorsed grassroots protests such as the Montgomery bus boycott of 1955 but saw judicial decisions, including 1954's *Brown v. Board of Education*, and civil rights legislation as unconstitutional expansions of federal power. The Arizona senator Barry Goldwater, the 1964 Republican nominee for president, cited this strict constructionist idea in his vote against the Civil Rights Act (1964). This vote and the backing of the extreme anti-Communist John Birch Society defined Goldwater on the campaign trail.

As Lyndon B. Johnson implemented his Great Society Reform Programs and anti-Communism lost its political saliency, conservatives developed a palpable sense of frustration over what they deemed as federal encroachments on their personal freedoms. Urban unrest in places like Los Angeles's Watts section, Cleveland, and Detroit convinced many that the government was stripping away tax revenue from productive Americans and redistributing it to ungrateful minority groups. A growing welfare rights movement portrayed the poor as victims and found some support in Congress among liberal Democrats, fueling a white backlash among blue-collar voters in the North and Midwest. In the 1968 presidential election, both the Republican candidate Richard Nixon and the independent candidate George Wallace tapped into this alienation. Whereas Wallace came across as a radical, Nixon won the presidency using a color-blind rhetoric that underscored the fears of middle America without being overtly racist.

In office, Nixon's record on race relations was inconsistent. In its 1971 decision in *Swann v. Charlotte-Mecklenburg Board of Education*, the U.S. Supreme Court determined that busing was an acceptable remedy to racial imbalances in public schools. The ruling kicked off a firestorm of controversy in many cities around the country. Parents and politicians combined conceptions of localism, citizenship, and private property to argue that elite officeholders and opinion leaders had restricted their right to send their children to neighborhood schools. Nixon stoked the busing issue to rally what he called the "silent majority" against liberal bureaucrats and "activist judges" who if left unchecked, he claimed, would continue to take away the rights of average Americans.

On the other hand, the Nixon administration also implemented a program requiring federal construction contractors to hire a specific number of minority employees. As the concept of affirmative action became more widespread in government employment and educational admissions, conservatives took aim at what they regarded as reverse discrimination. The New Right could claim a partial victory in the 1978 decision by the Supreme Court in *Regents of the University of California v. Bakke*, in which the Court ruled by a 5 to 4 margin that although race could be considered in higher-education admissions, it could not be the sole consideration. During the Reagan administration, politicians and the courts chipped away at affirmative action programs.

As the discrimination question remained unsettled, welfare lost its efficacy as a political issue. President Reagan, continuing the race-blind rhetoric of his predecessors, often used the term "welfare queens" as a proxy for individuals who allegedly shirked responsibility and gamed the system to the detriment of the taxpayer. In 1994, following strong Republican gains in Congress, the Democratic president Bill Clinton pivoted to the right and supported welfare reform. The resulting legislation, passed in 1996, ended the long-standing Aid to Families with Dependent Children program and replaced it with the more restrictive Temporary Assistance for Needy Families. The new program required able-bodied heads of households to find employment in two years and set a maximum lifetime limit of five years of assistance. Though many on the left expressed outrage at the time, by 2004 the act had significantly reduced the welfare rolls and largely depoliticized the issue.

Immigration. Though immigration restriction has a long history of controversy in the United States, its postwar context did not develop until the 1965 Hart-Celler Immigration Act removed quotas on immigrants from certain countries and allowed immigrants to enter the country for the purpose of family unification. As the number of immigrants increased in the 1970s and 1980s, anti-immigration groups made scattered arguments against population growth, but their influence was too weak to prevent Congress from passing an amnesty measure for illegal immigrants in 1986. As the influx of immigrants from Asia, Latin America, and the Caribbean continued into the 1990s, activists zeroed in on the impact of Hispanics on American society and infused their arguments with a more racial tone. The television pundit Patrick Buchanan ran in the 1992 Republican primary on an anti-immigration, pro-enforcement platform, and many of his supporters came out in favor of so-called Americanization programs.

By 2000 the issue remained contested among conservatives, with immigration opponents becoming more militant and extreme. In 2005 the controversial Minuteman Project began patrolling the border between the United States and Mexico, and in 2010 Arizona passed a measure to enable police to identify and arrest illegal immigrants. Both developments stemmed from the idea that the federal government was too lax on immigration and supported the rights of the immigrant over those of the citizen.

Gender. The 1970s also saw a growing defense of traditional family and gender relations under the umbrella of what was called "family values." In March 1972, Congress passed the Equal Rights Amendment (ERA), a succinct measure outlawing discrimination based on sex. The longtime Republican activist Phyllis Schlafly tapped into a grassroots network of conservative women to form Stop

Taking Our Privileges ERA (STOP ERA). Schlafly argued that the ERA and the so-called feminist agenda would redefine the American family and take away a woman's right to be a homemaker and mother. Though by the deadline in 1979 thirty-five of the necessary thirty-eight states had ratified the ERA, Schlafly and her associates successfully helped rally to prevent the ERA from ever becoming law.

Part of Schlafly's success can be attributed to the reaction to the Supreme Court's 1973 decision in *Roe v. Wade*. *Roe* outlawed state restrictions on abortions and contributed to the idea that the nuclear family was under attack. Numerous religious groups opposed abortion. The Catholic Church formed the National Right to Life Committee, the most visible antiabortion lobbying and activist group, on the heels of the *Roe* decision. Well into the twenty-first century, abortion remained one of the most divisive issues in American politics, with the pro-choice and pro-life movements sparring over issues such as parental notification, federal funding of family-planning organizations, and embryonic stem-cell research. *Roe* has also become a litmus test for judicial nominees, a testament to the contested nature of abortion in American life.

Religion. The growth of evangelical Protestantism in the 1970s also contributed to the reconceptualization of rights among social conservatives. Though the restriction of religious practice in public schools began with the Supreme Court's 1962 decision in *Engel v. Vitale*, which struck down New York's state-mandated teacher's prayer, political mobilization of the so-called religious right began in earnest in the late 1970s. In 1978 the Internal Revenue Service issued guidelines to review and revoke the tax-exempt status of private schools, many with church affiliations,

ostensibly created as havens from desegregated education. Evangelicals led by the Reverend Jerry Falwell, pastor of the Thomas Road Baptist Church in Lynchburg, Virginia, sent more than one hundred thousand letters of complaint to the IRS and pressured it to drop its program the following year. With the help of the direct-mail pioneer Richard Viguerie, Falwell tapped into this feeling of persecution to create the Moral Majority, an activist organization that encouraged Evangelicals to stand up for their interpretation of biblical values by supporting conservative policies and politicians. The Moral Majority and other organizations of the so-called New Christian Right threw their support behind Reagan during the 1980 election. Reagan, in turn, embraced social causes during the 1980 campaign and as president frequently spoke to groups like the National Association of Evangelicals.

Through the end of the twentieth century the New Christian Right advanced its family-values agenda against what it saw as threats to the nuclear family. Out-of-wedlock mothers came under frequent criticism, as did homosexuality. Social conservatives strongly opposed the Gay and Lesbian Rights Movement, with the former beauty queen Anita Bryant firing the first salvo against Miami's civil rights ordinance in 1976. Many religious groups saw the emerging AIDS epidemic of the 1980s as a moral crisis, not a health one.

In the 1990s President Clinton accepted some parts of the family-values agenda, including the 1996 Defense of Marriage Act, which defined marriage as a union between a man and a woman and ensured that no state would be legally obligated to recognize a homosexual marriage licensed in another state. From there the battle moved to the states, where social conservatives countered state court decisions allowing gay marriage in Massachusetts, Vermont, and Iowa with numerous ballot initiatives. The passage in 2008 of California's Proposition 8, which prohibited gay marriage, marked the continued strength of social conservatives at the start of the administration of Barack Obama.

[*See also* Americanization Movement; Antiabortion Movement; Community Organizing; Desegregation; Law and Society; Militia Movement, Modern; Nativist Movement; *and* Racism.]

BIBLIOGRAPHY

Crespino, Joseph. "Civil Rights and the Religious Right." In *Rightward Bound: Making America Conservative in the 1970s*, edited by Bruce J. Schulman and Julian E. Zelizer, pp. 90–105. Cambridge, Mass.: Harvard University Press, 2008. A nice, brief piece on the importance of the private-school controversy in mobilizing the New Christian Right.

Critchlow, Donald T. *The Conservative Ascendancy: How the GOP Right Made Political History.* Cambridge, Mass.: Harvard University Press, 2007. The most instructive survey on political conservatism since World War II.

Critchlow, Donald T. *Phyllis Schlafly and Grassroots Conservatism: A Woman's Crusade.* Princeton, N.J.: Princeton University Press, 2005. A well-researched biography of the key opponent of the ERA.

Davies, Gareth. *From Opportunity to Entitlement: The Transformation and Decline of Great Society Liberalism.* Lawrence: University of Kansas Press, 1996. A case study on the changing politics of welfare reform in the late 1960s.

Formisano, Ronald. *Boston against Busing: Race, Class, and Ethnicity in the 1960s and 1970s.* Chapel Hill: University of North Carolina Press, 1991. A classic work on grassroots agitation around busing and white flight.

Lassiter, Matthew D. "Inventing Family Values." In *Rightward Bound: Making America Conservative in the 1970s*, edited by Bruce J. Schulman and Julian E. Zelizer, pp. 13–28. Cambridge, Mass.: Harvard University Press, 2008. Explores how the New Christian Right used social issues to obscure class inequalities in the 1970s.

Lassiter, Matthew D. *Silent Majority: Suburban Politics in the Sunbelt South.* Princeton, N.J.: Princeton University Press, 2006. Approaches the busing controversy from a suburban context to explore the importance of homeowner and taxpayer identities in the New Right.

Patterson, James T. *Restless Giant: The United States from Watergate to "Bush v. Gore."* New York: Oxford University Press, 2005. The best single-volume history on the political and cultural changes of the late twentieth century.

Rodgers, Daniel T. *Age of Fracture.* Cambridge, Mass.: Belknap Press of Harvard University Press, 2011. A concise summation of American intellectual history in the last third of the twentieth century.

Michael Bowen

CONSUMER MOVEMENT

The modern consumer movement—organizations promoting the economic interests of consumers—arose during the Progressive Era. Citizens concerned about unsafe products and business monopolies used journalistic exposés, "white lists" of approved stores, and lobbying to press for government action. The first enduring consumer organization, the National Consumers League, was formed at the turn of the twentieth century. Led by Florence Kelley, the league pressured for both worker and consumer protections. The consumer protections included passage of three landmark consumer laws: the Meat Inspection Act (1906), the Pure Food and Drug Act (1906), and the Federal Trade Commission Act (1914). The movement built on an older tradition of consumer activism in which consumer boycotts were used in pursuit of political independence for the U.S. colonies, abolition of slavery, humane working conditions, and other social goals.

A second wave of the consumer movement arose during the 1920s and 1930s when the Industrial Revolution spread from the factory to the American home. Technological progress brought branded products, typically produced by companies whose factories were hundreds or even thousands of miles away from the point of purchase. These packaged products were often difficult for shoppers to evaluate. The resulting "impenetrable ignorance," a term used by Stuart Chase and Frederick J. Schlink in *Your Money's Worth: A Study in the Waste of the Consumer's Dollar* (1927), gave rise in 1936 to the Consumers Union, whose magazine *Consumer Reports* provides consumers with objective information based on rigorous product testing. By the twenty-first century the Consumers Union could boast more than 7 million subscriptions and had spawned similar magazines in numerous countries.

The consumer movement's third wave and heyday took place during the 1960s and 1970s, a time of heightened social activism in general. The consumer movement had the support of President John F. Kennedy, who in 1962 urged Congress to recognize the consumer's right to be safe, be informed, have meaningful marketplace choices, and be heard by government bodies in the formulation of consumer policy. The movement also had a celebrity in the person of a young lawyer, Ralph Nader. His book *Unsafe at Any Speed: The Designed-In Dangers of the American Automobile* (1965) detailed safety hazards plaguing the U.S. auto industry and the Corvair, produced by General Motors, in particular. Using $425,000 won in an invasion-of-privacy suit against General Motors in 1970, Nader founded numerous consumer groups, led by Nader's Raiders, that pursued legal challenges to unsafe products and demanded greater government protection for consumers. The formation in 1968 of the

Consumer Federation of America as an umbrella organization for the movement and the formation in 1972 of the Consumer Product Safety Commission attested to the movement's success but also to its reformist bent. The movement spoke in terms of correcting market imperfections and protecting vulnerable consumers. It did not pose a fundamental threat to everyday business practices, let alone capitalism. When the movement sought the ambitious goal of establishing a consumer protection agency within the federal government, the business community mobilized to defeat it in the late 1970s.

The early twenty-first century saw a revival of the consumer movement, spurred by concerns regarding financial and medical privacy, as well as by mortgage lending practices. New organizations (e.g., the Electronic Privacy Information Center, the Center for Responsible Lending) and new federal legislation (e.g., the Fair and Accurate Credit Transactions Act of 2003, the Credit Card Accountability, Responsibility, and Disclosure Act of 2009) are products of this latest wave of movement activity. The movement's most notable feat, however, was creating the Consumer Financial Protection Agency, with broad powers to regulate credit transactions, including mortgages. The successful campaign to establish the agency illustrated the consumer movement's continued relevance.

[*See also* **Consumption**.]

BIBLIOGRAPHY

Cohen, Lizabeth. *A Consumers' Republic: The Politics of Mass Consumption in Postwar America.* New York: Alfred A. Knopf, 2003.

Glickman, Lawrence B. *Buying Power: A History of Consumer Activism in America.* Chicago: University of Chicago Press, 2009.

Hilton, Michael. *Prosperity for All: Consumer Activism in an Era of Globalization*. Ithaca, N.Y.: Cornell University Press, 2009.

Mayer, Robert N. *The Consumer Movement: Guardians of the Marketplace*. Boston: Twayne, 1989.
                                    Robert N. Mayer

CONSUMPTION

From the vantage point of the twenty-first century, in which advertisements, logos, and commercials bombard us daily, it seems difficult to believe that until the 1980s scholars paid little attention to the history of consumer culture. Critiques of materialism and the corroding effects of wealth are at least as old as the Bible, but historical analysis of the ways in which past societies acquired goods and services and the significance attached to these endeavors is surprisingly recent. Focus on production rather than consumption, on supply rather than demand, and on states rather than shoppers contributed to this lacuna. In the United States, a nation whose very political identity was forged through opposition to the taxation of consumer goods, the field of consumer studies has grown slowly but significantly. Monographs and synthetic works produced since the 1990s have brought to light the myriad ways in which consumerism has transformed American life: European settlers' pursuit of civility and refinement, contributing to what might be called a "consumer revolution" in the eighteenth century; the influence of new trade goods on native societies and cultures; the increasing value placed on leisure and domestic comfort; and the emergence of department stores, advertising, and commercial credit, culminating by the twentieth century in a culture of mass consumption. Though broad themes have become clear, scholars continue to debate the timing, extent, and implications of the process by which American definitions of freedom and an abundant material life became closely intertwined.

Consuming in Early America. Consumer desire for exotic goods and comestibles fueled European exploration to the New World. After stumbling upon the Caribbean, explorers began exporting spices, foodstuffs, timber, and metals that quickly changed the diet, political economy, and lifestyle of Europeans. A host of nation-states rushed to settle the Americas in order to secure access to its trade wealth. These colonists began exchanging manufactured objects like guns, knives, kettles, and cloth for indigenous goods such as cacao, tobacco, corn, and animal pelts. European trade goods eased Indians' labor and enhanced their personal appearance and status, but they also introduced so-called imaginary wants into Indian society that had not previously existed. This unleashed competitive hunting practices that decimated the beaver, deer, and fox populations and contributed to intertribal warfare, which, with the advent of flintlock guns, was also becoming more deadly. Alcohol and debt further decimated Indian communities, driving more chiefs to sell land to pay for consumer commodities and thus creating a destructive cycle of dependence and dislocation that ruined many native lives. In response, some tribes launched purifying movements—notably in 1763 and then again in 1810—that advocated a return to indigenous ways and a total rejection of the white man's goods.

European settlers benefited from the easy access to fertile land that trade and declines in the Indian population made possible. Some groups in North America, like the French and the Dutch, initially focused more on exporting raw goods than on settlement, and their villages remained small and rudimentary. The English and Spanish, by contrast, sent missionaries and families to establish permanent residence, and they constructed sturdy houses, churches, and towns to exhibit the superiority of European civilization. Spanish Catholics beautified missions and cathedrals with dazzling painted murals and ornate silver chalices and communion vessels. Spanish settlers of rank spent their wealth on fine brocade cloth, lace, and chocolate.

English Puritans embellished their material lives more slowly, believing that worldly things distracted from the proper worship of God. In English, the word "consume" meant to "devour, waste, spend" and had a strongly negative connotation. Puritans legalized their disapproval of materialism by enacting sumptuary laws, which prohibited the construction and use of expensive garments. Other Protestant groups, notably the Quakers, were even more severe, excommunicating members who did not scrupulously follow the doctrine of plainness and simplicity in all aspects of life. Quakers dressed in dark, sober colors and eschewed ornamentation; some even forbade the use of toys among children. Yet many Quakers were successful merchants, and over time their material lives began to differ very little from those of their non-Quaker neighbors. Nevertheless, Quakers remained uniquely ethical consumers, refusing to sell alcohol to Native Americans or to buy the products of slave labor such as cotton and sugar.

Throughout the colonial period, consumer activity remained structurally constrained because of a lack of cash, poor transportation networks, and the vast distances between rural villages and seaport towns. Farmers and their families often bartered with one another and with local dry-goods dealers for the things that they could not produce themselves. They reinvested profits in land, tools, labor, and other productive enterprises rather than in consumer items.

Eighteenth-Century "Consumer Revolution"?

Over the course of the eighteenth century, several key economic, demographic, and cultural changes disrupted older colonial consumption patterns and contributed to an unprecedented rise in consumer demand. Commercial success, accompanied by long intervals of peace, ushered in a period of prosperity for Britain and its mainland colonies. Innovations in production and distribution combined with more aggressive marketing tactics to lower prices and enlarge the quantity and choice of goods available in the marketplace. Using the proceeds of agricultural surplus and the easy availability of store credit, the exploding number of colonists—the population doubled approximately every twenty-five years—bought up the increasing array of manufactured goods on offer. In fact, by midcentury, consumption of imported goods grew even faster than the population did.

The decline of the power of religious institutions and the increasing importance placed on comfort and civility facilitated a positive embrace of consumerism. Rising literacy rates and the importation of metropolitan courtesy books and magazines introduced people to fashion and the genteel world of European elites. The ideals of polite society began to permeate the rural hinterland and influenced even ordinary artisans to seek out better food, warmer and softer clothing, and new household goods such as forks, spoons, beds, and chairs in order to make life more "respectable." As the requirements of material life expanded, women began to play an increasingly important role as household consumers, devoting more time to studying and selecting merchandise. By the last third of the eighteenth century, colonial Americans were proud to have transformed their country from a rough frontier outpost to a civilized state.

The new variety of material objects that knit disparate colonists together in a shared consumer marketplace made them both key to the British economy and heavily indebted to British creditors. When Britain tried to increase tax revenues on popular consumer items, the colonists protested by organizing boycotts of imported goods—the nation's first real collective political act. When the boycotts failed to restore local autonomy, the colonists revolted, deciding that they would be better off managing their own economic and political affairs. Thus some scholars have argued that consumer politics played a more critical role in the American Revolution than has often been recognized, highlighting the centrality of consumption to American identity. In the wake of victory, however, newly independent Americans faced an economy in shambles and almost no capacity to manufacture domestically the things that they needed. It remained unclear whether the republic would long survive without the ability to provide the fundamental material goods that its citizens had come to desire.

Industrialization and the New Republic of Goods.

The Revolution and the War of 1812 made Americans realize that to be truly independent, they had to bolster manufacturing and reorient consumer demand toward domestic products. Politicians created a national bank and enacted protective tariffs to support economic growth. The government also sponsored the construction of railroads, canals, roads, and turnpikes to improve transportation, resulting in major construction projects such as the Erie Canal in upstate New York, which opened in 1825. This waterway made New York City a central commercial hub, connecting the Eastern Seaboard with the Great Lakes, and created a surge in settlement and trade in the western interior. Advances in transportation eased the movement of people and goods and lowered its cost. The waves of families moving west in search of new opportunity needed wagons, cloth, shoes, tableware, and furniture. They expanded the market for American entrepreneurs who were busy applying new technologies of steam and waterpower to improve their manufacturing practices. The result was a massive growth in industrial production to meet the demands of a striving population.

Antebellum Americans across the social spectrum sought consumer goods to ease the burden of daily life and attain a measure of respectability. As domestic slavery expanded, enslaved African Americans worked after dusk and on Sundays to hunt, trap, and till garden plots to earn cash and credit at local stores to augment the meager allotments provided by owners. Skilled and free blacks, especially in urban areas, were able to acquire fine cloth, metal watches, and wool shawls, as well as better food, from the proceeds of their labor.

Young people, including women, quit family farms and domestic employment in order to earn cash wages in seaport cities and new manufacturing centers. Mill girls, white-collar clerks, and urban laborers expressed their freedom and independence through consumer goods and leisure activities. They spent their earnings on fashionable clothing, travel, and entertainment. Eating in ice-cream parlors, riding on a steamship, and acquiring dresses like those featured in *Godey's Lady's Book* (1830–1878), America's first fashion magazine, a new generation associated participation in consumer culture with democracy and social progress. They continued to value hard work and saw material objects as symbols of personal and national civility.

The dramatic expansion of consumerism in the nineteenth century had negative consequences as well. Rapid industrialization, urbanization, and population growth caused deforestation, water and air pollution, and the destruction of the buffalo and bison. The stress placed on living a refined life divided communities and drove many into debt. The availability of inexpensive status goods blurred social distinctions and confused the visual hierarchy of public life. Middle-class families anxiously accelerated their household consumption in order to solidify their social status and create a sanctuary away from capitalist work routines. Elaborate domestic interiors filled with pianos, carpets, and books became symbols of Christian morality and the civilized family. Yet keeping up with fashion and learning about new goods was work, and by 1850 an entire genre of etiquette books and style manuals had emerged to assist uneasy consumers. Some felt so overwhelmed by the materialistic tenor and competitive pace of American life that they tried to escape it altogether; romantic transcendentalists like Henry David Thoreau retreated to the New England woods, while others moved to separatist religious settlements like those of the Shakers, whose members gave up their worldly goods in a bid for spiritual unity and social equality.

The Civil War and Reconstruction destroyed the socioeconomic system of the South and slowed commercial developments in the North as both sides suffered from the effects of prolonged conflict. Many thought that the Union victory demonstrated the superiority of the North's industry over the South's agriculture; indeed, the North's ability to meet the material needs of both the military and the civilian population was critical to its success. With its labor force freed and its infrastructure in ruins, the South began to rebuild itself along a northern model, improving transportation networks and expanding its capacity to produce manufactured goods. Though planters could not reinstitute slavery, they did exploit African Americans' longing for independence by enticing them into tenant farming. By renting lodgings and land to former bondmen and offering easy credit for supplies until harvest time, whites created a system of debt peonage that differed very little from slavery.

Gilded and Progressive Age Consumption and the Rise of the Department Store. With peace, the nation focused anew on industrial development and westward expansion. Government initiatives resulted in the completion in 1869 of the transcontinental railroad, connecting the Pacific and Atlantic coasts together for the first time, and the development of the telegraph and telephone. The potential for nationwide communication and transportation facilitated the development of large corporations like Standard Oil and Coca-Cola, which were intent on capturing larger segments of a rapidly expanding market. Gilded Age merchants pitched their wares through innovative mail-order catalogs such as the one pioneered by Sears, Roebuck in 1888. Consumers, especially in rural areas, marveled at the wide variety of items offered at fixed prices and became loyal Sears customers. Catalogs, in conjunction with newspaper advertisements, billboards, and chromolithographed posters, flooded the marketplace with information about goods. Commodities were increasingly associated not with a merchant but with trademarks or brand names, which sought to imbue objects with human qualities like sex appeal and dependability to earn the allegiance of buyers. People bought things, no longer simply to feel warmer or to ease the burden or labor, but to express their personality and modernity.

New department stores built to resemble European palaces—some a full city block long—awed patrons with the size and scope of their merchandise. Marshall Field's in Chicago, opened in 1852, and Macy's in New York, opened in 1858, offered a wide range of personal and household items, each featured in its own department, at a variety of price points. Department stores changed the way customers, increasingly women, shopped; rather than patronizing several specialty shops, people could find everything they needed in one place. Department stores competed fiercely to attract customers, employing lavish window displays, fashionable interiors, and novel amenities. Department stores became destinations in their own right as shopping became a refined cultural pursuit.

Waves of impoverished immigrants poured into gateway cities, lured by a vision of America as a land of prosperity and material abundance. They found work in precisely those industries of mass production that made consumer goods available to a large swath of American society. Pushed into crowded tenements, they toiled in sweatshops, coal mines, and steel factories in hopes of materially improving their lives. Well-meaning activists and journalists deplored the relative poverty of these newcomers, but the immigrants themselves often marveled at how quickly they had been able to raise their standard of living since leaving Europe. Eager to enjoy a modern lifestyle, immigrants thronged dance halls and movie theaters, bought new clothing, furniture, and automobiles on the installment plan, and measured the success of their assimilation by their ability to acquire contemporary luxuries.

But the same capitalistic logic that drove manufacturers to standardize production and boost worker efficiency in order to lower prices also led to wage cuts and deteriorating working conditions. Poverty shamed and alienated farmers and industrial workers who could not share in the rituals of consumption. It was in part to secure what many viewed as their rights as consumers that many of these groups embraced socialism, labor unions, and agrarian Granger movements to challenge monopolistic corporations and laissez-faire government. Progressive activists like Florence Kelley and Upton Sinclair joined their cause. Sinclair shocked middle-class consumers with *The Jungle*, his 1906 novel of fraud, corruption, and unsanitary conditions in the nation's meat industry. Pressured by President Theodore Roosevelt, Congress passed the Pure Food and Drug Act in 1906, which outlawed adulterated food and unsafe medicine and forced companies to label their products accurately. The law led to the creation of the federal Food and Drug Administration in 1927. Kelley worked tirelessly to eradicate sweatshops, unsafe working conditions, and child labor. She became the first secretary general of the National Consumers League (NCL), founded in 1899, a nonprofit organization that advocates on behalf of consumers and workers. Linking the working conditions of laborers to the products they made, the NCL pioneered the use of the "White Label" to identify goods produced under fair conditions.

As the world recovered from World War I, the United States experienced exceptional prosperity that inaugurated a new era of decadence and consumer freedom. Refinements in assembly-line organization lowered the prices on automobiles, appliances, and other goods, making them more affordable for middle-class consumers. The $500 Model T, or Tin Lizzie, produced from 1908 to 1927 by Henry Ford's Ford Motor Company expanded people's ability to travel, increasing commercialized leisure and tourism. The organization of radio technology in the early 1920s extended the reach of brand advertisers, who sponsored radio broadcasts that reached millions of listeners. Inspired by radio, cinema, and travel, young men and women experimented with sexual freedom and independence. Women bobbed their hair and rouged their lips in a liberating display of so-called New Womanhood; in so doing they dramatically expanded the market for beauty products and services. Men bought cars and liquor in record quantities (despite the ratification of the Eighteenth Amendment, prohibiting alcohol, in 1919), investing the proceeds of financial speculation on sporting events and entertainment. These activities laid the foundations of a mass consumer culture, one in which individuals pursued self-discovery and personal fulfillment through an "empire of things."

The era of conspicuous consumption—a term coined by the sociologist Thorstein Veblen in 1899 to describe the frenzied obsession with proving one's status through consumer goods—came to a screeching halt with the stock-market crash of 1929 and the ensuing Depression. Many interpreted the economic deprivations of the Great Depression not only as a market correction but also as a moral rebuke of the nation's materialistic culture. The Depression challenged American's faith in the free-enterprise system and an economy of boundless prosperity.

World War II and Mass Consumption.

Massive government spending, new regulations on business—including the right of workers to strike—and America's entrance into World War II pulled the United States out of economic decline. Patriotic consumers rationed goods and cultivated victory gardens to help the nation marshal its resources in support of the war. Women went to work in heavy industry as manufacturers shifted production from domestic goods to military supplies like tanks, airplanes, and ammunition. With Allied success came a postwar population surge as citizens turned to establishing families. With the Servicemen's Readjustment Act of 1944 (the GI Bill), the government sponsored the growth of private homeownership through low-interest and zero-down-payment loans for veterans, resulting in a substantial increase in single-family housing construction and suburban development. The expansion of residential enclaves far beyond city centers had profound ramifications on consumer culture, the built environment, and civic life more broadly. Sprawling subdevelopments lacked public transportation, making cars a necessity. The mass adoption of automobiles created a concomitant need for new transportation networks and interstate highways to link suburbs with cities. Shopping centers, grocery stores, and other commercial services migrated from urban downtowns to meet the needs of suburban residents.

The physical structure of suburban dwellings—usually with three bedrooms, a formal living room, and front and back lawns—required an array of new consumer commodities such as lawn mowers, swing sets, furniture, and appliances. Single and married women continued to join the workforce in droves, entering white- and so-called pink-collar service industries in order to secure and enhance a middle-class life. Some married women left the workforce after the war to assume the role of housewife. The housewife's primary job was to consume, aided and abetted by the introduction of credit cards in 1958. Though she also cooked, cleaned, and raised children, shopping constituted a major component of her daily routine. During this time of the Cold War the American family's material bounty was used as a foil for the deprivations of Communist Europe. Amid affluence, many postwar Americans felt lonely and adrift. Racially, economically, and aesthetically homogenous, suburbs bred social conformity and isolation.

Racial discrimination in housing and lending left African Americans and Hispanics out of the American dream of homeownership. This exclusion was further exacerbated by the postwar decline in urban centers that resulted from suburbanization, segregation, and white flight. In the 1960s these minority groups drew on their power as consumers to contend for civil rights, using boycotts, sit-ins, picketing, and selective buying to highlight their lack of basic freedoms. These freedoms included the right to enjoy consumer and leisure pastimes that whites took for granted: the right to shop, eat, lodge, ride, and swim without restriction. Operation Breadbasket, part of Martin Luther King Jr.'s Southern Christian Leadership Conference, used the threat of boycotts to pressure white businesses, such as the A&P supermarket chain in 1967, to hire blacks and otherwise reinvest in the black neighborhoods where they were located. The successes of African American activism only reinforced the significance of consumer politics in American life.

The Consumer Movement, E-Commerce, and Anticonsumerism.

The optimism in the future that buoyed mass consumption during the 1950s fell apart amid the political turmoil and unrest of the 1960s and 1970s. Sales executives had to retool their approach to a deeply divided society. A professional class of advertisers drew on new techniques of market segmentation, using psychology, demographic research, and sampling to divide consumers and target products to specific subgroups. Instead of expressing personality through objects, brands became proxies for individual and group identity.

Writers and social activists questioned the manipulative tactics used by advertisers to induce desire for their products. A growing consumer movement claimed that corporations sought profit at the expense of safety, gave false information about goods, and persecuted those who tried to expose them. On 15 March 1962, President John F. Kennedy proposed what he called the Consumer Bill of Rights to protect consumers against faulty products and deceptive advertising. Ralph Nader pushed for even deeper reforms, and he exposed dangerous practices at the General Motors Corporation in his 1965 best seller, *Unsafe at Any Speed*. Over the next two decades, Nader's Raiders, as many consumer-protection advocates were called, helped win the passage of numerous pieces of protective legislation.

Environmentalists of the period began raising concerns about pesticides, pollution, and the effects of consumption on the natural world. Factories producing durable goods and farms spraying pesticides to increase crop yields spread toxins deadly to humans and animals. The economic recession and oil crisis of the 1970s further stressed the importance of energy conservation, reuse, and recycling and seemed to inaugurate a new era of ethical consumption. Buyers began to demand smaller, more fuel-efficient cars, and patronizing thrift stores and second-hand shops became chic. As the economy rebounded, however, consumers returned to their former hedonism. The 1980s glorified luxury and excess, with cable television broadcasting the opulent lives of the wealthy (interspersed heavily with commercials) twenty-four hours a day.

The advent of the Internet and the World Wide Web only exacerbated the trend toward the total commercialization of American culture. Subject to little government regulation, pop-up advertisements and spam began to inundate personal email, websites, and search engines. E-commerce websites allow consumers to purchase an endless array of goods and services at the click of a button, shifting the location of consumption from physical locations to cyberspace. The resulting sense of consumer saturation and psychic exhaustion has produced a backlash against consumption itself. In the late 1990s, eco-activists, opponents of globalization, and locavores—people committed to purchasing locally sourced foodstuffs and commodities—coalesced into an anticonsumer movement advocating for an end to the addictive cycle of material acquisition. Only by radically reducing one's consumption of goods and resources and reengaging with the local community, organizations like Adbusters and the Compact argue, can citizens avert environmental disaster and reclaim their civic autonomy.

Over the course of their history, Americans steadfastly sought to overcome a Puritan heritage critical of materialism in order to advance a capitalist economy and a democratic political system. Free people and free markets went hand in hand. In the first decades of the twenty-first century, amid a global economic downturn, home foreclosures, and skyrocketing rates of personal indebtedness, citizens were finally coming to terms with a material pursuit of happiness that had not delivered the spiritual and social fulfillment that they sought.

[*See also* **Automobiles; Consumer Movement; Environmentalism; Leisure;** *and* **Social Class.**]

BIBLIOGRAPHY

Breen, T. H. *The Marketplace of Revolution: How Consumer Politics Shaped American Independence.* New York: Oxford University Press, 2004.

Bushman, Richard L. *The Refinement of America: Persons, Houses, Cities.* New York: Alfred A. Knopf, 1992.

Carson, Cary, Ronald Hoffman, and Peter J. Albert. *Of Consuming Interests: The Style of Life in the Eighteenth Century.* Charlottesville: University Press of Virginia for the United States Capitol Historical Society, 1994.

Cohen, Lizabeth. *A Consumer's Republic: The Politics of Mass Consumption in Postwar America.* New York: Alfred A. Knopf, 2003.

Glickman, Lawrence B., ed. *Consumer Society in American History: A Reader.* Ithaca, N.Y.: Cornell University Press, 1999.

Hyman, Louis. *Debtor Nation: The History of America in Red Ink.* Princeton, N.J.: Princeton University Press, 2011.

Lears, T. J. Jackson. *Fables of Abundance: A Cultural History of Advertising in America.* New York: Basic Books, 1994.

Schor, Juliet B., and Douglas B. Holt, eds. *The Consumer Society Reader.* New York: New Press, 2000.

Strasser, Susan. *Satisfaction Guaranteed: The Making of the American Mass Market.* New York: Pantheon Books, 1989.

Linzy Brekke-Aloise

COUNTERCULTURE

To think of the counterculture as a single entity adhering to shared practice and ideology would be a mistake. Instead, the term "counterculture" is generally applied to a wide range of largely white, largely youth-led oppositional "movements" (again the term must be applied loosely) that imagined themselves as operating either against or outside the confines of mainstream American society. Although the American roots of the counterculture run deep and can be found in areas as diverse as transcendentalism, the Beat generation, the rock and roll of the 1950s, the Civil Rights Movement, and the folk music revival, the counterculture, as such, effectively existed between the mid-1960s and the early 1970s.

Though the counterculture was oppositional in form, its existence depended upon the postwar economic boom that created unprecedented affluence for millions of Americans in the 1950s and 1960s. Its numbers were drawn from the baby boomers, at a time when there were many more teenage and twenty-something citizens than ever before. Sheer weight of numbers inevitably generated a raised profile for young people and had a major effect in persuading corporate America to invest in youth culture in the 1950s. At a time when moral panic over juvenile delinquency was at a peak, movies such as *The Wild One* (1953), *Rebel without a Cause* (1955), and *Blackboard Jungle* (1955), as well as the emergence of figures such as Elvis Presley, demonstrated that big business was willing to upset the mainstream in the pursuit of the youth dollar. By the height of the counterculture a decade later, this process had accelerated to the point that every major record label had to have at least one hip band on its roster, and Hollywood produced a string of countercultural movies including *Bonnie and Clyde* (1967) and *Easy Rider* (1969).

The large numbers of students brought together on new university campuses became eager adherents to causes and movements that they might have missed if they were still living in the suburban America created by their parents' generation. Though the majority of these students had little serious interest in political revolution and were generally more interested in rock music and drugs than in listening to New Left and other radical speakers, the participation of so many young people in certain patterns of behavior—dress, hairstyle, relative sexual freedom, and so forth—did create the impression of cultural, if not political, revolution. At the Human Be-In held in San Francisco's Golden Gate Park on Saturday, 14 January 1967, for example,

the crowd was largely indifferent to what the future Yippie figurehead Jerry Rubin had to say and preferred to drop acid and listen to San Francisco rock bands and to poets such as Allen Ginsberg and Gary Snyder. The impact of such change was increased by the media coverage of the often heavy-handed response of police, politicians, and conservative commentators, who as a result of class or generational differences saw an irreconcilable chasm between their own efforts to live the American dream and a community raised in privileged economic circumstances but appearing to be disillusioned with materialism.

Key Figures. The heart of the counterculture was indubitably in San Francisco and the Bay Area. San Francisco already had a reputation as a more liberal and tolerant place than other major conurbations and was an obvious destination for cultural dissidents. Here, events including Ken Kesey's series of parties called the Acid Tests promised new possibilities for communal existence through a combination of music, light shows, and films experienced under the influence of LSD. Bands like the Grateful Dead (who performed at many of the Acid Tests), Jefferson Airplane, and Big Brother and the Holding Company were popular enough to suggest that a new social order was possible, even if that order did depend upon the post-scarcity culture created by American affluence and global hegemony. The prime example of the possibilities afforded by the national prosperity was the San Francisco–based collective called the Diggers, whose "free" project included the Free Frame of Reference, a store providing free clothing and other items, while also offering a free medical center and distributing free acid, housing, and legal services.

The Diggers' form of street theater provided a wider and more lasting legacy for the counterculture through the establishment of inseparable ties between artistic and political practice, a combination that was later imitated most famously by the Yippies. The Yippies were created as an East Coast equivalent to the Diggers, but they adopted a fundamentally different agenda. Whereas the Diggers functioned within and sought to extend the countercultural community, the Yippies were more concerned with taking their "guerrilla theater" into the heart of American capitalism, usually alerting the press in advance and seeking as much publicity as possible. The Yippies' activities included a plan to levitate the Pentagon, smoke-ins, and pie throwing, and they reached their zenith at the 1968 Democratic National Convention in Chicago. Although there was never any chance—or even intention—that they would accomplish any of the extreme actions that they promised, the threat was enough in itself to raise the sense of the event as spectacle and to ensure that when police (perhaps deliberately provoked by the Yippies) clubbed demonstrators in the city's streets, a mass television audience was watching.

Demise and Legacy. For a number of reasons the demise of the counterculture was—certainly with the benefit of hindsight—predictable. In part the counterculture was a victim of its own success: even by 1967, San Francisco's Haight-Ashbury neighborhood had been overrun with often emotionally traumatized teenagers and with people happy to exploit them. The commercial success of top bands, such as the Rolling Stones and Crosby, Stills, and Nash, also led to a widening gulf between artists and their audiences and to the increasing incorporation of rock music by big business. Meanwhile Bob Dylan—whose transformation from protest singer to rock icon perhaps exemplifies the countercultural practice of the 1960s—had

largely gone underground after his motorcycle accident in 1966. Although the effort to highlight the contrast between the "three days of peace and music" of the Woodstock festival and the violence precipitated by the Hells Angels who acted as "security" when the Rolling Stones headlined at Altamont in December 1969 has become clichéd and is not entirely accurate, that contrast has become an effective symbol of the implosion of much of the counterculture at the end of the 1960s. Altamont was indicative of a more general turn to violence in America at the end of the 1960s, a turn that—although it was embraced by elements such as the Weather Underground and Charles Manson's "Family"—prompted many other groups and individuals to distance themselves from what could be perceived as the counterculture's rejection of the "peace and love" mantra. The shift from more social drugs, such as marijuana and LSD, toward heroin and cocaine undermined the collectivism that united participants in happenings and other drug-related events. In addition, by the early 1970s America's actions in the Vietnam War, which had been a principal focus of countercultural political activism, were also being attacked by mainstream politicians and commentators, with a consequent dilution of the association of counterculture and protest.

Nevertheless the counterculture has left significant legacies: it was integral to the maturation of environmentalism in the 1970s and beyond, and it played a significant role in the emergence of feminism and the Gay and Lesbian Rights Movement. The arrival of members of the countercultural generation on university faculties, especially in the humanities, also led to significant paradigm shifts, including the rise of multiculturalist syllabi, an enthusiasm for the kinds of postmodern playfulness that had (at least in part) been initiated by countercultural authors including Richard Brautigan and Thomas Pynchon, and the so-called canon wars of the 1980s and 1990s. The influence of the counterculture on popular culture has also been immense: by the late 1960s the advertising industry was rushing to reject traditional forms and embrace the colorful styles of countercultural artists; once-dissident music swiftly became incorporated and was used to sell clothing, cars, and almost every other element of the American dream; and many leading figures from 1960s artistic and political radicalism have become mainstream politicians. Though in part this demonstrates that the counterculture effected lasting changes, it is probably more indicative of the ease with which the counterculture—or many of its leading players—was susceptible to the overtures of hegemonic culture.

[*See also* Drugs, Illicit; Sixties, The; *and* War Resisters.]

BIBLIOGRAPHY

Braunstein, Peter, and Michael William Doyle, eds. *Imagine Nation: The American Counterculture of the 1960s and '70s.* London: Routledge, 2002. An edited collection of essays engaging with a wide range of countercultural material.

Echols, Alice. *Shaky Ground: The '60s and Its Aftershocks.* New York: Columbia University Press, 2002. An important and original reappraisal that pays particular attention to women's roles in the counterculture.

Frank, Thomas. *The Conquest of Cool: Business Culture, Counterculture, and the Rise of Hip Consumerism.* Chicago: University of Chicago Press, 1997. An invaluable study of the ways in which the counterculture was appropriated by, but also helped to reshape, consumer culture.

Gair, Christopher. *The American Counterculture.* Edinburgh: Edinburgh University Press, 2007. An interdisciplinary approach, with chapters focusing on literature, music, painting, and film.

Gitlin, Todd. *The Sixties: Years of Hope, Days of Rage.* New York: Bantam, 1987. An indispensable history of the New Left, written by a participant in the events described.

Roszak, Theodore. *The Making of a Counter Culture: Reflections on the Technocratic Society and Its Youthful Opposition.* Berkeley: University Of California Press, 1995. A pioneering study of the counterculture, first published in 1969.

Christopher Gair

COURTSHIP AND DATING

Colonial Americans generally cared more about the suitability of their marriage partners than about love, which they expected to develop after marriage. As a result, couples courted publicly and received aid and advice from families and neighbors. Premarital pregnancy rates were low during the seventeenth and early eighteenth centuries, and premarital sexual relations, even if pregnancy did not result, produced strong social and even legal pressures for marriage. Toward the end of the colonial era, however, the ideal of romantic love gained wide currency. Many families allowed "bundling"—the controversial practice of letting courting couples spend an evening in bed together fully clothed, sometimes with a board placed between them. In the same period, the number of couples producing children before eight and a half months of marriage rose to nearly 30 percent.

By the early nineteenth century, couples began to consider romantic love prerequisite for marriage and based their unions on companionship. The era's fiction frequently drew on love themes, while articles, essays, and public orations stressed mutual respect, reciprocity, and romance as ingredients of good marriages. Young courting couples chose their own partners, and their letters focused on romance rather than on the practical matters that had dominated the correspondence of earlier generations. As romanticism developed, so did a new "separate spheres" ideology, which held that a woman's proper sphere of influence was in the home, and a man's in the public realm. As men and women increasingly occupied separate spheres, romance and candor became the strongest links between people living in different worlds.

As families and neighbors lost influence over couples, genteel standards of propriety came to guide courting behavior. Particularly after the Civil War, an elaborate system of rules governing courting emerged. On a woman's invitation, men conducted formal "calls" to her home, during which couples might converse, read aloud, play parlor games, or give a piano recital. Parents gave their children privacy to court alone, often removing themselves from the parlor, trusting that decorum would prevent improper behavior. As the century progressed, however, new opportunities for interacting outside the home emerged. College enrollments rose, and students developed their own rules governing relationships. More women entered the workforce, particularly as schoolteachers. And especially in urban areas, new public diversions like dance halls, amusement parks, theaters, and parks enticed courting couples away from the safety of their parlors.

World War I accelerated the disintegration of etiquette based on the ideology of separate spheres, but popular magazines and advice columns quickly outlined new rules to replace the old. By 1925, traditional courtship had fallen out of fashion. Instead, young couples began to go on "dates," which differed significantly from courting: they cost money, focused less on long-term commitment, took place in public, and were initiated and paid for by men. Standards of sexual morality also changed, and the terms "necking" and "petting"—the former referring to kisses and caresses above the neck, the latter to the same below it—entered public discussion, giving names to previously unspoken private activities. In some circles, young people dated widely, rather than with one exclusive partner, because status hinged on being seen regularly with different desirable dates. During this period, for example, people considered dancing all evening with one partner a social failure: the "belle of the ball" was the young woman who danced with more partners than anyone else.

After World War II, "going steady"—two people dating exclusively—partially replaced the competitive system of the interwar years. For one man to cut in on another at a dance, once considered flattering to the young woman, came to be deemed rude. A profusion of articles, columns, and even marriage classes defined the new dating etiquette: boys "protected" girls, exercising control by opening car doors, ordering in restaurants, and taking responsibility for asking girls for dates, while girls behaved submissively to help their dates feel like men. Americans began marrying younger and more often than at any point in the century, and married couples had more children.

In the late 1960s and early 1970s, however, the sexual revolution—a revolution more in customs than in actual sexual behavior—turned this whole system on its head. Few of the carefully elaborated rules of the 1940s and 1950s still held. Couples still dated—some going steady—but women began to ask men on dates, many men stopped automatically reaching for the check, and living together became a widely accepted step toward marriage. The social norms governing sexuality fractured, with no unifying set of rules filling the void. "Singles" clubs and bars proliferated, and people of all ages sought congenial partners through dating services, the "personals" sections of magazines and newspapers, and Internet sites. Couples conducted courting on their own terms, as both men and women assumed more individual responsibility and initiative in finding a mate than at any previous time, while also exercising greater freedom in the process.

[*See also* **Adolescence; Amusement Parks and Theme Parks; Dance Halls; Family; Life Stages; Marriage and Divorce; Separate Spheres Ideology;** *and* **Sexual Reform and Morality.**]

BIBLIOGRAPHY

Bailey, Beth L. *From Front Porch to Back Seat: Courtship in Twentieth-Century America.* Baltimore: Johns Hopkins University Press, 1988.

Lystra, Karen. *Searching the Heart: Women, Men, and Romantic Love in Nineteenth-Century America.* New York: Oxford University Press, 1989.

Peiss, Kathy. *Cheap Amusements: Working Women and Leisure in Turn-of-the-Century New York.* Philadelphia: Temple University Press, 1986.

Rothman, Ellen K. *Hands and Hearts: A History of Courtship in America.* New York: Basic Books, 1984.

Turner, E. S. *A History of Courting.* New York: Dutton, 1954.

Christopher W. Wells

COWBOYS

The American cowboy descended from the Spanish and Mexican vaquero, who evolved in New Spain after the arrival of cattle in the Western Hemisphere. As cattle ranching spread northward into California and Texas, Americans adopted the tools and techniques of the vaquero. Texas cowboys watched over cattle, branded them, and rounded them up before herding them to markets first in New Orleans and by the 1850s northward to Missouri and beyond. As railroads pushed westward following the Civil War and the demand for beef increased in the East, Texas cowboys began to drive cattle herds north to railheads in Kansas and later Nebraska. By the late 1870s, cowboys, including many of African American and Hispanic descent, were found in cattle-raising regions throughout the West. After the invention of barbed wire and the fencing of ranches, the cowboy became a hired man on horseback, repairing fences, doctoring cattle, and participating in cattle-branding roundups. By 1900 the golden age of the American cowboy was over.

Compared to his counterpart south of the Rio Grande, the American cowboy played a regional and relatively short-lived role. Yet he found his place in the history and mythology of the West, celebrated for fairness, justice, and courage, as exemplified by the hero of Owen Wister's enduring novel *The Virginian* (1902). Dime novels, folk songs, motion pictures, television series, and the fashion and advertising industries all helped to create the mythic version of the American cowboy that survives today.

[*See also* **Southwest, The,** *and* **West, The.**]

BIBLIOGRAPHY

Dary, David. *Cowboy Culture: A Saga of Five Centuries.* New York: Alfred A. Knopf, 1981.

David Dary

CRACK COCAINE

Crack is a smokable form of cocaine that first appeared in 1984 in impoverished neighborhoods in New York City, Los Angeles, and Miami. Produced by cooking a mixture of powder cocaine (cocaine hydrochloride), water, and baking soda in a microwave, crack was typically sold in tiny vials costing $5 to $20. Crack was not a new drug: its active ingredient is entirely cocaine. Nor was it a new way of using cocaine: freebase cocaine had been smoked since the 1970s. Rather, it was a marketing innovation. It repackaged an expensive, upscale commodity (powder cocaine) into small, inexpensive units (crack) that were sold by and to mainly working-class individuals.

The marketing innovation succeeded for several reasons. First, a workforce of unemployed young people was available to take jobs in the new inner-city business of crack preparation and sales. Second, from 1986 to 1992 a frenzy of media stories about the risks of crack use effectively advertised the drug by describing an intense high and reporting incorrectly that crack's use was spreading rapidly from cities to suburbs. Third, crack offered an extremely intense but very brief intoxication. Smoking crack is a strong, even harsh, way to use cocaine, but some people, especially those who could afford little else, were willing to try it.

Contrary to widespread claims of media, politicians, and law enforcement, most people who tried crack did *not* find it appealing and have *not* continued using it. Daily or routine crack use takes a severe toll on users' bodies and disrupts their social functioning. The drug has been used heavily mainly by the poorest, most marginalized people in American society—and only by a small minority of even this population, chiefly the same population that has used heroin regularly. Because crack's heavy use is so disruptive and unsatisfying, crack never became a popular or widely used drug in either the United States or anywhere else in the world.

Crack's most harmful and lasting effects have been legal, economic, and social. U.S. government health surveys have consistently found that whites use powder and crack cocaine at the same rates as or at higher rates than blacks do, and that drug use is found in all American communities. But drug policing is concentrated in low-income urban neighborhoods, and African Americans have been arrested and imprisoned for all drug offenses at much higher rates than whites have.

Beginning in 1986 the United States enacted and strongly enforced laws against crack that were the most punitive that it ever adopted for low-level drug offenses. But the intense policing, many arrests, and long sentences did not significantly reduce crack's availability or use. Instead they created more job openings in the crack business, which drew in yet more impoverished young people, many of whom also eventually received long prison sentences for crack possession. This legal, judicial, and law-enforcement war on crack was a major cause of the largest imprisonment wave in American history, with the prison population nearly tripling from 1986 to 2006.

For many years, prominent reform and philanthropic organizations sought to reform crack law and enforcement policies, pointing out their racial bias and harmful effects and calling attention to reputable medical and scientific findings that crack is no more addictive than powder cocaine. In 2010, Congress passed the Fair Sentencing Act, which reduced the sentencing disparity of crack to powder cocaine from 100 to 1 down to 18 to 1. This reduced but by no means eliminated the racial disparities and harmful social consequences of the still well-funded war on crack.

[*See also* Drugs, Illicit; Law and Society; Slums; *and* War on Drugs.]

BIBLIOGRAPHY

Porter, Nicole D., and Valerie Wright. "Cracked Justice." The Sentencing Project, March 2001. http://sentencingproject.org/doc/publications/dp_CrackedJusticeMar2011.pdf.

Reeves, Jimmie L., and Richard Campbell. *Cracked Coverage: Television News, the Anti-Cocaine Crusade, and the Reagan Legacy.* Durham, N.C.: Duke University Press, 1994.

Reinarman, Craig, and Harry G. Levine. *Crack in America: Demon Drugs and Social Justice.* Berkeley: University of California, 1997.

Reinarman, Craig, and Harry G. Levine. "Crack in the Rearview Mirror: Deconstructing Drug War Mythology." *Social Justice* 31 (2004) 182–199.

Harry G. Levine and Craig Reinarman

CUBAN AMERICANS

Politically, economically, and culturally, Cuban Americans occupy a unique place in American society. Compared to the overall Latino population in the United States, Cuban Americans are more likely to have college or graduate degrees. Their median household income is higher, and they are more likely to own their own homes. Statistically, Cuban Americans are also older than members of other Latino groups. All these features are tied to the processes that have shaped Cuban migration since the early twentieth century.

Located just ninety-eight miles from the coast of Florida, the island of Cuba is one of the United States' closest neighbors. Throughout the period of Spanish colonial rule, Cuban dissidents like José Martí (1853–1895) found shelter in the United States and used their temporary home as a launchpad for revolution. During the Ten Years' War (1868–1878) between Cuban nationals and the Spanish military, scores of Cuban cigar manufacturers also fled the island, reestablishing their businesses on the U.S. mainland and recruiting many workers to follow. Together these migrants helped to create thriving, transnational communities in Florida, New York, and New Jersey.

Cold War Migrations. The largest numbers of Cuban migrants, however, have come to the United States since the early 1960s. In the immediate years following Fidel Castro's socialist revolution in 1959, an estimated quarter of a million Cubans fled Cuba for the United States. The first to leave were primarily members of the former government and its close supporters. But as the new government moved farther left, confiscating private property, closing Catholic schools and churches, and working to build national economic and political independence from U.S. interests, more Cubans began to leave the island. Executives from American multinational corporations and many well-established professionals also left Cuba for the United States during this period. Another more than fourteen thousand were children, sent out of Cuba by their parents, who feared for their future and were aided by the Catholic Church and the U.S. Central Intelligence Agency through a program called Operation Pedro Pan. This first major wave of Cuban out-migration continued until 1962 when the United States imposed a blockade on the island after U.S. spy planes found Soviet missile sites there.

Coming at the height of the Cold War, a time when U.S. foreign policy was sharply binary and fervently anti-Communist, Cuban immigrants were afforded special immigration status as political refugees and also became a critical force within American agencies related to national security and foreign policy. Worried that Cuba's socialist transformation would set off a domino effect within the Western Hemisphere, threatening

U.S. political and economic hegemony across Latin America, the U.S. government began to aid Cuban refugees directly: the goal was to create a "unified Cuban government in exile" and to train and equip its members to overthrow Castro's government (Peter Wyden, *The Bay of Pigs: The Untold Story* [New York: Simon and Schuster, 1979], p. 25). The United States also actively encouraged Cuban emigration through official propaganda, transportation programs, and financial and material aid, believing that the mass exodus of prominent Cubans would provide the most vivid evidence to the world that communism was a failure. As the U.S. congressman Walter Judd famously claimed in 1959, "Every refugee who comes out is a vote for our society and a vote against their society."

The second major wave of Cuban outmigration began in 1965 when Fidel Castro opened the door to any Cubans who had family residing in the United States. President Lyndon B. Johnson facilitated this movement, instituting the Freedom Flights, a program offering low-cost flights to the United States. This program continued until 1973. During this time another three hundred thousand Cubans arrived in the United States: some traveled directly to the United States, while others arrived indirectly, traveling first to countries like Spain and Mexico.

Many of these first arrivals were forced to leave Cuba without any material possessions. Because of their special immigration status as political refugees, Cubans enjoyed some advantages over other immigrants, including federal assistance in relocating, finding housing, and being placed in jobs or retraining programs. Licensing requirements, language barriers, and discrimination in hiring, however, limited most Cubans' ability to resume the professional occupations that they had had in Cuba. Physicians became taxi drivers, industrialists became gas-station attendants, and professional women became maids.

Despite attempts by the U.S. federal government to disperse Cuban refugees across the country—it was thought that this would speed their assimilation and ultimately benefit them socially and economically—many Cubans chose to concentrate themselves into distinct ethnic communities. Two of the largest Cuban American communities developed in Miami, Florida, and Union City, New Jersey. Applying skills brought over from Cuba and taking advantage of the growing size of these ethnic communities, these first- and second-wave migrants grew up new businesses, dispensed character loans to fellow countrymen and countrywomen, and slowly created the thriving Cuban American cultural and political centers that these cities came to enjoy.

In 1980, another 125,000 Cubans entered the United States. Most arrived within a narrow six-month span between April and September in a dramatic boat lift from the Cuban port of Mariel. Unlike earlier migrants, who had been largely of the upper and middle classes, migrants from this third wave were more heavily of the working class. Seeking to discredit these new arrivals to the United States and angered over ongoing U.S. efforts to support Cuban emigration, Castro also opened the nation's jails, sending a large group of prisoners and mentally ill individuals to the United States.

After the Cold War. When the Soviet Union collapsed in 1991, Cuba's economy suffered deeply, shrinking by almost half over three years. Riots broke out in Havana, and for a brief period between 1993 and 1995, Castro again allowed exit to any Cubans who wished to leave, marking the fourth major wave of Cuban emigration. Those who did leave left quickly, often using anything that would carry them. Floating aboard truck tires, lashing pieces of wood into makeshift rafts, and overcrowding fishing boats, tens of thousands of *balseros*, or "raft people," left Cuba, trying to make their way to Florida's shores.

In 1995 the Cuban government agreed to issue regular visas to Cubans who wanted to leave the island for the United States, capping the number at twenty thousand a year. These policies have remained intact into the twenty-first century. Whether these policies would remain in place following a political transition in Cuba is uncertain, however, and remains a major concern to U.S. policy makers.

Between 12 and 15 percent of the population of Cuba left for the United States over the course of these four major waves of immigration. According to estimates by the U.S. Census Bureau, in 2010 nearly 1.8 million people of Cuban birth or Cuban ancestry were living in the United States, making up 3.5 percent of the nation's Latino population. More than two-thirds of Cubans (990,000 people) lived in Florida. New Jersey had the next-highest concentration (81,000), followed by New York (78,000), California (74,000), and Texas (34,000).

[*See also* Caribbean; Immigration; *and* Miami.]

BIBLIOGRAPHY

Behar, Ruth, and Lucía M. Suárez, eds. *The Portable Island: Cubans at Home in the World.* New York: Palgrave Macmillan, 2008.

Cristina García, María. *Havana, USA: Cuban Exiles and Cuban Americans in South Florida, 1959–1994.* Berkeley: University of California Press, 1997.

Pedraza, Silvia. *Political Disaffection in Cuba's Revolution and Exodus.* New York: Cambridge University Press, 2007.

Melanie Shell-Weiss

CUMBERLAND GAP

The Cumberland Gap was one of the most important geographic features of the early United States. Located near the junction of Tennessee, Virginia, and Kentucky, the Cumberland Gap pierced the Appalachian Mountains to provide a natural entry point into Kentucky and Tennessee. About twelve miles long, the Cumberland Gap helped connect three highly productive agricultural regions: Virginia's Shenandoah Valley, Kentucky's bluegrass region, and Tennessee's Nashville basin. Each of these areas became highly productive agricultural regions filled with farms and plantations. The Cumberland Gap acted as a strategic gateway between these regions and helped speed white settlement of the trans-Appalachian West.

Well before white settlement, herds of bison, deer, and elk used the Cumberland Gap to migrate from Kentucky to the salt licks around Roanoke, Virginia, and the grasslands of the Shenandoah Valley. The Cherokees, the Iroquois, and other Native Americans also traveled extensively through the pass; the Cumberland Gap made it easier for hunting groups, war parties, and trading missions to travel through the Appalachian Mountains. The Iroquois in particular used the Cumberland Gap to contest Kentucky hunting grounds, thus exerting diplomatic and military power far beyond their New York base. Indeed, the name "Kentucky" is thought to be Iroquois in origin, meaning "land of tomorrow."

In 1750, Dr. Thomas Walker, working for a Virginia land company, was the first white explorer to discover the Cumberland Gap. Though Walker never made it as far the bluegrass region or the Nashville basin, a steady trickle of hunters and explorers spread the word of these highly productive hunting grounds. In 1775 the Transylvania Land Company purchased Kentucky lands from the Cherokees and the Iroquois. Although the Virginia legislature eventually invalidated the purchase, the company hired Daniel Boone—a frequent explorer and hunter in the Kentucky region—to lead a construction and surveying party that ultimately marked the Wilderness Road extending from Virginia through the Cumberland Gap to central Kentucky. Settlers often took the Great Wagon Road extending along the Shenandoah Valley before taking the Wilderness Road into Kentucky.

Tenacious opposition from Native Americans—especially from Shawnee war parties based in Ohio—and the upheaval of the American Revolution slowed white settlement. After the United States achieved independence, white settlers moved into Kentucky and Tennessee at a dramatic rate. By 1790 the population of Kentucky had already grown to 73,677; by 1810 it stood at 406,511. The population of Tennessee was 35,691 in 1790, and it had grown to 261,727 by 1810. Though there are no firm statistics on how many migrants traveled through the Cumberland Gap, historians have estimated that two to three hundred thousand did so. Travelers' accounts suggest that the Cumberland Gap was the most popular route to reach Kentucky and Tennessee. Settlers might have taken the Ohio River to Kentucky, but the mountainous terrain of western Pennsylvania and Virginia, as well as the threat of Indian attack,

made such a journey particularly difficult. Livestock, manufactured goods, and mail often traveled through the Cumberland Gap as well. The advent of steamboats and the construction of more direct routes through the Appalachians eventually lessened the importance of the Cumberland Gap. By 1820 the Pittsburgh Pike and the National Road each provided a more direct connection between eastern localities and the Ohio River, which lessened the strategic significance of the Cumberland Gap.

In the popular imagination, the Cumberland Gap is often associated with hardy pioneers and farm families passing through the rugged mountains. In his famous 1893 essay "The Significance of the Frontier in American History," the historian Frederick Jackson Turner reflected the nostalgic romance surrounding the Cumberland Gap: "Stand at Cumberland Gap and watch the procession of civilization, marching single file—the buffalo following the trail to the salt springs, the Indian, the fur-trader and hunter, the cattle-raiser, the pioneer farmer—and the frontier has passed by." What Jackson ignored is that a good many slaves accompanied the "pioneer farmer." In 1810, Kentucky and Tennessee contained a combined total of more than 125,000 slaves. The Cumberland Gap—located at the intersection of three slave states—helped ensure the spread of slavery and plantation agriculture in the U.S. West. Indeed, the gap helped spread southern influence throughout the Ohio River valley. During the Civil War, residents of southern Ohio, Indiana, and Illinois often opposed using force to stop Confederate secession.

[*See also* **Appalachia; Frontier, The; Internal Migration,** *subentries on* **Colonial Era** *and* **Nineteenth-Century Westward;**

Middle West, The; Rural Life and Society; *and* West, The.]

BIBLIOGRAPHY

Aron, Stephen. *How the West Was Lost: The Transformation of Kentucky from Daniel Boone to Henry Clay*. Baltimore: Johns Hopkins University Press, 1996.

Faragher, John Mack. *Daniel Boone: The Life and Legend of an American Pioneer*. New York: Holt, 1992.

John Majewski

D

DANCE HALLS

Though dancing has long been a popular pastime for Americans, the dance hall was most influential during the period from the 1890s to the end of the first half of the twentieth century. Before the rise of the commercial hall, dancing revolved around family weddings, christenings, neighborhood gatherings, and other church functions, or community organizations raised money by sponsoring a dance at a multipurpose neighborhood hall or the back room of a saloon. By the 1910s the craze for dancing was so significant that entrepreneurs began building metropolitan halls or ballrooms specifically for dancing. The best-known example is the lavish dance palace, which made its first appearance in New York City in 1911 and which could accommodate as many as three thousand patrons. By the mid-1920s similar palaces appeared in other large cities across the country.

The dance hall's rise reflected larger economic and social changes. Urban populations grew significantly after the Civil War with the influx of millions of southern and eastern European immigrants and as rural-to-urban migration kept pace with an expanding industrial base. Though conflict characterized the industrial workplace, these changing economic opportunities afforded factory and office workers the time for leisure needed for an occasional outing and the wherewithal to afford it—an especially significant change for women, whose economic futures were often bleak. Live-in domestic service was one of the principal sources of employment for young, single, white women before the industrial expansion of the post–Civil War era. Domestic service paid poorly and severely restricted women's leisure time.

The dance hall was also popular because it promoted a peer culture in which men and women could escape their parents' prying eyes and experiment with alcohol and cigarettes, as well as engage in intimate relations. Men and women were often seen holding hands at dance halls, and the balcony became a particularly notorious place for couples to meet. New dance styles also encouraged a physicality unfamiliar to most contemporaries. The traditional waltz was waning with the rise of spieling and pivoting, dances in which couples tightly embrace and spin across the floor. Other popular dances allowed America's youth to bend their knees, swivel their hips, and celebrate an improvisational style that was more sexually expressive than the waltz's precise steps and formal positions.

Women's search for autonomy was more complicated than it was for their male counterparts. With lower wages than men's and working-class parents who frequently laid claim to their pay envelopes and insisted on regulating their daughters' personal lives, women struggled to take advantage of commercial leisure and to pay for it. Their male partners were willing to treat them to a night out but often expected their dates to reciprocate with at least a good-night kiss, if not other forms of intimate contact. The potential problems surrounding treating compelled some women to slip away unexpectedly during the break between dances or to require a female friend to serve as a chaperone. All of them struggled to balance the dance hall's excitement and promise of autonomy with the realities of their workaday lives and their family and community's ideas about relationships and courtship and dating.

[*See also* Cities and Suburbs; Domestic Workers; Everyday Life; Women Workers; *and* Working-Class Life and Society.]

BIBLIOGRAPHY

McBee, Randy D. *Dance Hall Days: Intimacy and Leisure among Working-Class Immigrants in the United States*. New York: New York University Press, 2000. One of the more in-depth studies of dance halls that also considers working-class men's experiences.

Nasaw, David. *Going Out: The Rise and Fall of Public Amusements*. New York: Basic Books, 1993. One of the general studies of leisure that also explores how different types of amusement changed after World War II.

Peiss, Kathy. *Cheap Amusements: Working Women and Leisure in Turn-of-the-Century New York*. Philadelphia: Temple University Press, 1986. The earliest general overview of working women's leisure; has become the standard work that other scholars rely upon to understand the rise of commercial leisure.

Randy D. McBee

DAUGHTERS OF THE AMERICAN REVOLUTION

The Daughters of the American Revolution (DAR) is the largest patriotic hereditary women's organization in the United States. Founded in 1890 in Washington, D.C., in response to the refusal of the Sons of the American Revolution to admit women, the DAR accepts as members only women who can prove lineal descent from Americans who contributed actively to the cause of the American Revolution. It promotes patriotism and the preservation of U.S. history through commemoration and education. White Americans' increasing interest in genealogy around 1900, coupled with the organization's relative exclusivity, made the DAR extremely popular. By the early 1920s the organization boasted a membership of almost 140,000. By the early twenty-first century the DAR claimed to have 168,000 members in three thousand chapters across the United States.

Throughout its history, the DAR's membership has consisted primarily of white, often college-educated, middle-class women who belonged overwhelmingly to Protestant denominations. It has always accepted Catholics and Jews but excluded Mormons (until the 1940s) and African Americans (until the 1980s). Most of its members were also active in other women's organizations. Prior to World War I, these organizations included both liberal and conservative groups such as the General Federation of Women's Clubs and the United Daughters of the Confederacy. But by the early 1920s there was an increasing overlap in membership between the DAR and right-wing groups such as the American Legion Auxiliary, the Woman Patriots, and, later, the John Birch Society.

This development was primarily a result of the organization's ideological shift after World War I. In its early years, the DAR supported many campaigns associated with the Progressive Era, including settlement houses, the Anti-child-labor Movement, and the Americanization Movement. In the wake of World War I, however, the organization became increasingly conservative, supporting military preparedness, restrictive immigration legislation, and antiradicalism. Prior to the 1940s, despite the DAR's interest in current affairs, many local chapters focused on commemorative activities. Among other things, they issued publications and raised funds for monuments that called attention to the history of the American Revolution, westward expansion, and Native Americans. While stressing the contributions of women to this history, the DAR upheld traditional gender roles,

regarding women merely as men's helpmates. This belief was also reflected in the organization's continuous opposition to women's rights activism. After 1945, the DAR's activities shifted away from commemoration and focused instead on instilling patriotism in American children and warning the American public about the danger of communism and international organizations. As early as the 1920s the DAR warned of the potentially detrimental effect of socialism and the League of Nations on the United States. The DAR rejected the New Deal, considering it inspired by communism, and remained fervently anticommunist throughout the Cold War. It continues to oppose the membership of the United States in the United Nations, which its leaders believe undermines the nation's sovereignty.

In the twenty-first century, the DAR is remembered primarily for barring the black singer Marian Anderson from its Constitution Hall in Washington, D.C., in 1939. Its opposition to the Civil Rights Movement in the 1960s cemented its image as a racist organization. Beginning in the 1970s, the DAR sought to change this image by admitting African American members and calling attention to the contributions of black patriots to the American Revolution. These attempts have, however, done little to stop the DAR's diminishing public significance.

[*See also* **Conservative Movement; Jim Crow Era;** *and* **Women's Club Movement.**]

BIBLIOGRAPHY

Arsenault, Raymond. *The Sound of Freedom: Marian Anderson, the Lincoln Memorial, and the Concert That Awakened America.* New York: Bloomsbury Press, 2009. A historical study that focuses on the controversy over the DAR's decision to bar

Marian Anderson from singing in Constitution Hall.

Morgan, Francesca. *Women and Patriotism in Jim Crow America*. Chapel Hill: University of North Carolina Press, 2005. A meticulously researched comparative study that examines the DAR's gendered nationalism vis-à-vis other patriotic women's organizations prior to 1945.

Simon Wendt

DAUGHTERS OF THE CONFEDERACY

See **United Daughters of the Confederacy.**

DEATH AND DYING

Starting in the 1980s, social historians began to trace the history of death in America, a subject once considered outside the realm of historical analysis. Their contributions rescued the subject from oversimplification and clichés, including the stereotype—reinforced by such books as Jessica Mitford's *The American Way of Death* (1963)—of Americans as a death-denying people, too optimistic, energetic, or youth-obsessed to accept its finality. Instead, this new scholarship established critical phases in the history of death and demonstrated the links between this history and broader themes in the nation's development.

The Colonial and Antebellum Eras.
Although Americans experienced death in very different ways over the course of two hundred years—pioneering families did not respond to death on the nineteenth-century frontier in the same ways that immigrant families responded in early twentieth-century urban ghettos—two distinct stages mark the history of death in America. In the first stage,

death was a religious and communal event, part of a shared experience. In the second, death was a medical event, isolated and hidden behind institutional walls. The experience in antebellum New England under the influence of evangelical Christianity well represents the first stage. The experience of death in the modern, scientifically based, twentieth-century hospital captures the second.

Many of the precepts of Puritanism survived well into the nineteenth century, particularly in New England, and these precepts, even in modified form, framed the society's fundamental encounter with death and dying. Religious doctrine established the definition of the good death: one that was fully and consciously prepared for. The bad death, as the injunction in the Anglican Book of Common Prayer declared, was the unexpected and quick death: "From sudden death, good Lord deliver us." No document better expresses the need for preparation than Cotton Mather's 1710 treatise addressed to pregnant women, *Elizabeth in Her Holy Retirement*. Its essential message is that the pregnant woman should prepare herself for her death. This was not only because of the actual risks involved, but also because preparation for death was so vital a task that any occasion, and especially one as fundamental as childbirth, was made to serve this purpose. Indeed, well into the nineteenth century, textbooks for young children carried such exhortations as: "Look in the graveyard and you shall see, Children buried there shorter than thee."

Early nineteenth-century physicians as well as clergymen shared this outlook. Thus, one noted Boston physician advised a patient suffering from tuberculosis that it was time for her to prepare for death, not to combat it through more visits to doctors. "Submit and be content," he counseled. Such medical reliance upon the influence of religion persisted through much of the nineteenth century.

"In serious illness," a leading medical text-book instructed doctors, "you can very properly prepare the way for the introduction of the clergy. We are physicians of the physical body, the temporary life. They are the physicians of the soul, the eternal life. Never belittle anything that your patients earnestly believe."

Death in antebellum New England was a communal event. The dying person called in neighbors, made formal farewells, distributed personal effects, and selected those who would watch over his or her final hours. In this same spirit, the actual moment of death was critically important. The dying person was to pass over "without struggle." This constituted the most telling sign that salvation and a heavenly reunion could be anticipated. Thus the religious-communal death, with the two features very much interconnected, was the central feature in premodern America. Death was not hidden, and death was not the enemy. It was the testing ground of faith, to be witnessed by family and a wide circle of friends.

From the Civil War to the End of the Twentieth Century.

The transition to a second and very different encounter with death came in the Civil War, because death in war contradicted all the inherited religious and social definitions of the good death. Soldiers died alone on the battlefield, violently, often without witnesses, or in military hospitals, far from family and friends. The enormous effort made by both the Union and the Confederate armies to locate the bodies of dead soldiers and transport them home—an effort that gave rise to the practice of embalming—testifies to just how radically death in war violated prevailing beliefs and conventions.

However atypical the war experience was, it became the prototype of the modern experience of death, that is, death in the hospital. This institution took death out of the home, away from the family, and gave it over to strangers. Why did hospitals over the course of the twentieth century assume a monopoly over death? Part of the reason was their growing ability to treat illness; because their therapeutic efforts were not always successful, the patient under care sometimes turned into the dying patient. Some of the hospital's centrality also reflected the facts of urban life, including smaller apartments, scattered families, and weakened community relationships. Whatever the cause, the results were unequivocal. The hospital sequestered death and rendered it nearly invisible, not only from the community and friends, but from family as well.

William Osler of the Johns Hopkins University Medical School, a giant of early twentieth-century clinical medicine, was highly critical of the change. "The tender mother, the loving wife, the devoted sister, the faithful friend and the old servant all are gone," Osler observed; "Now you [health-care professionals] reign supreme and have added to every illness a domestic complication of which our fathers knew nothing. You have upturned an inalienable right in displacing those who I have just mentioned. You are intruders, innovators and usurpers." Osler's critique remained equally valid in the post–World War II period. Studying death in public hospitals in the 1960s, the sociologist David Sudnow found that institutional routines enforced the separation of dying patients from their social support network. "While patients in critical conditions technically have the right to round the clock visitors," he noted, "nurses strove to separate relatives from those patients about to die. They urged family members to go home or insisted that they wait outside in the corridors, not in the patient's room. Why? If a relative was present then it was necessary for someone from the staff to be present to demonstrate continuing concern which was inefficient as well as futile." And what was true for nurses was still more true for physicians.

Although by the closing decades of the twentieth century the demographics of death had changed in many ways—men living, on average, well into their seventies, and women living almost to their eighties—the most central social development related to death in these years was the broad-based effort to recapture death from the hospital and the health-care professional. The rise of hospices, the emergence of advance directives and living wills, and even the movement for physician-assisted suicide all represent a rebellion against the prevailing system. The goal now was to facilitate death at home among family and friends and give decision making about death to the patient. By the twenty-first century, neither religion nor organized medicine commanded the authority they once had, and many Americans appeared determined to seize control over the process of dying, even if biology ultimately placed that goal beyond reach.

[*See also* **Demography; Disease; Health and Fitness; Health and Healing, Eighteenth and Nineteenth Centuries; Hospitals and Dispensaries; Life Expectancy; Life Stages; Medicine, Popular and Non-Western; Religion;** *and* **Suicide.**]

BIBLIOGRAPHY

Ariès, Philippe. *The Hour of Our Death*. Translated by Helen Weaver. New York: Alfred A. Knopf, 1981.

Elias, Norbert. *The Loneliness of the Dying*. Translated by Edmund Jephcott. Oxford: Blackwell, 1985.

Laderman, Gary. *The Sacred Remains: American Attitudes toward Death, 1799–1883*. New Haven, Conn.: Yale University Press, 1996.

Richardson, Ruth. *Death, Dissection, and the Destitute*. 2d ed. Chicago: University of Chicago Press, 2000.

Stannard, David E. *The Puritan Way of Death: A Study in Religion, Culture, and Social Change*. New York: Oxford University Press, 1977.

Sudnow, David. *Passing On: the Social Organization of Dying*. Englewood Cliffs, N.J.: Prentice-Hall, 1967.

David J. Rothman

DEFERENCE

"Deference" is a term used to delineate the sociopolitical characteristics of early British America. The concept was first introduced in the nineteenth century to describe English society. In the mid-twentieth century, historians of early America borrowed the idea in an attempt to reconcile an apparent paradox: the political systems of the colonies and early United States granted broad franchise and enjoyed popular consent, even while consolidating power in the hands of a small socioeconomic elite. Proponents of the concept of deference note that despite having a political process that was much more inclusive than that of any contemporaneous Western society, American voters repeatedly elected a relatively narrow cadre of wealthy gentlemen to lead. Scholars argue that seventeenth- and eighteenth-century Americans believed in a social order that vested greater social and political power in the hands of wealthy men. Early Americans believed that property ownership conveyed upon elites superior claims to economic independence, social refinement, emotional self-control, and intellectual aptitude—in short, the qualities for good governance. Substantial wealth, it was believed, moreover, gave elites an expanded stake in the well-being of the community: they would be most likely to govern well and in the best interests of the public good. Critically, deference entailed reciprocal social obligations. Elites expected political and social precedence; in return they owed service including holding public office, protecting community liberties and privileges, and performing certain obligations, notably "treating" constituents to alcohol on election days. Some historians stress this reciprocal, even negotiated quality of deference, whereas others insist that elites dominated deferential relationships.

Historians identify the demise of deference as a gradual process occurring from the American Revolution to the election of Andrew Jackson in 1828. As the western states entered the Union, they awarded universal suffrage, which encouraged the eastern states eventually to do the same. Eliminating property requirements from voting qualifications, in tandem with the rise of print media and the advent of popular political parties, broke down older political traditions. Increasingly Americans embraced egalitarianism and rejected the idea that a certain class of men ought to rule.

However, many scholars dispute the degree to which deference meaningfully describes early American society or government. Some object to the geographic sweep of deference, arguing that it cannot be universally applied to diverse social, economic, and political structures from Massachusetts to Virginia to Barbados. Deference may have analytic power when studying local variations, but it cannot describe all of early America.

Others have argued that deference was an ideal held by elites but never the reality. Compared to England's, America's social hierarchy remained truncated, with neither a true aristocracy at the top, nor a white landless, laboring mass at the bottom. The bulk of white Americans inhabited what in England would have been the middle strata of society. Provincial elites lacked the wealth and patronage

to set themselves apart from their neighbors; meanwhile farmers' widespread access to land and the high wages commanded by artisans gave most white American men a degree of economic—and, therefore, social and political—independence. Moreover, geographic mobility combined with religious and ethnic diversity to create an increasingly heterogeneous population with many competing loyalties, not easily swayed by deference. Wealth may have given some men privileged access to political power, but it did not, these historians argue, elicit a deferential mentality from the less wealthy. Some historians go further, insisting that an emerging class consciousness among "the lower sorts" led to positive group identification vis-à-vis the gentry and outright rejection of elite pretensions. Others point to the consumer revolution, which made more widely available the material trappings of gentility, confounding outward markers of social status and leading to an increasing identification with an all-embracing "middling" status.

The concept of deference was first introduced to explain white men's political behaviors by plotting their status along a socioeconomic axis. As a result, discussions of deference largely avoid direct engagement with racial or gender hierarchies, though these, too, produced unequal access to political, social, and economic power. Despite its general limitations to the formal public world dominated by white men, however, the concept of deference —or its rejection—provides one mechanism for framing socioeconomic class in preindustrial America, linking class to civic engagement and political transformation in the Revolutionary and early national period.

[*See also* **Colonial Era; Democratic-Republican Clubs; Early Republic Era; Revolution and Constitution Era; Social Class;** *and* **Wealth.**]

BIBLIOGRAPHY

Beeman, Richard R. *The Varieties of Political Experience in Eighteenth-Century America*. Philadelphia: University of Pennsylvania Press, 2004.

Wood, Gordon S. *The Radicalism of the American Revolution*. New York: Alfred A. Knopf, 1991.

Zuckerman, Michael. "Authority in Early America: The Decay of Deference on the Provincial Periphery." *Early American Studies* 1, no. 2 (Fall 2003): 1–29.

Jessica Choppin Roney

DEINDUSTRIALIZATION

Deindustrialization is one of the most important economic changes in recent American history. In 1950, for example, half of the American workforce was employed in the manufacturing sector, but by 2006 just 10.4 percent was. Since the onset of the global financial crisis, moreover, the pace of job loss has accelerated, and in the decade from 2000 to 2010 alone the United States lost 5.5 million manufacturing jobs. Once a problem associated only with the Rust Belt states of the Northeast and Midwest, deindustrialization has spread to affect other parts of the country, including the South, which has been hit by a wave of closures in the textile, tobacco, paper, and furniture industries. Between 2001 and 2004 more than 20 percent of the national drop in manufacturing employment occurred in the South, with almost every southern state suffering a double-digit decline in industrial employment.

The social consequences of deindustrialization have been extensive. In the 1980s and early 1990s, pioneering work on the northern steel and auto industries showed that job loss affected employees deeply because most of them identified heavily with their work. Manufacturing workers generally started work straight after high school, and attracted by the good pay and benefits available, they expected to stay in their jobs for life. Because of their long tenure in their jobs, workers built up strong bonds with their coworkers. As the anthropologist Kathryn Marie Dudley summarized in her book on displaced autoworkers in Kenosha, Wisconsin: "The loss of an industrial job can be so devastating. Friendships built up over twenty years on the shopfloor gradually fade away, and with them the sense of community that gives us all a meaningful place in the world" (Kathryn Marie Dudley, *The End of the Line: Lost Jobs, new Lives in Postindustrial America* [Chicago: University of Chicago Press, 1994], p. xi).

Scholars who have studied other industries have reached similar conclusions. When plants closed, workers felt angry, betrayed, and worthless, and they struggled to adjust. Many suffered long periods of joblessness or underemployment. Scholars have also linked long-term unemployment with increased levels of alcoholism, family violence, and crime. As the sociologists Richard Sennett and Jonathan Cobb have noted, losing a job is so traumatic because "the source of social legitimacy in capitalist society comes primarily from what a person produces" (Richard Sennett and Jonathan Cobb, *The Hidden Injuries of Class* [New York: Alfred A. Knopf, 1972], pp. 267–268). Many workers affected by deindustrialization have even likened the experience of losing their jobs to bereavement. Both southern and northern workers have experienced these emotions. Because they relied heavily on industrial jobs and experienced discrimination in rehiring, racial minorities, women, and older workers have been particularly hard-hit by deindustrialization.

Deindustrialization has also had broader social costs. Unable to keep up their mortgage payments, many displaced workers have lost their homes, and communities affected by deindustrialization usually suffer from declining house prices. The loss of tax revenues from industrial plants also undermines the provision of vital social services, with schools, hospitals, and public amenities all hit. At the same time, property taxes and utility bills rise, making these communities less attractive to live in. Affected communities indeed suffer from out-migration and depopulation. Once home to the most famous steel mill in the world, Homestead, Pennsylvania, had a population of more than twenty thousand in 1940, but this had fallen to four thousand by the early 1990s. Other classic postindustrial communities such as Youngstown, Ohio, and Detroit, Michigan, have also suffered from depopulation. Additional social costs of deindustrialization can include significant soil and water pollution and increased demand among the population for higher education and retraining. Desperate for new jobs, some former industrial communities have even welcomed public and private prisons.

Conservative commentators and many economists have long claimed that displaced industrial workers can easily shift to jobs in growing areas of the economy, particularly the retail and service sectors. Such a shift is, however, complicated by the strong sense of identity that manufacturing workers derived from their jobs. Pay and benefit levels are also generally higher in the manufacturing sector than they are in the retail or service sectors. Because manufacturing jobs are more likely to come with health-care benefits, deindustrialization is also an important contributor to the nation's growing health crisis. In 1993, for example, data from the Department of Labor's Bureau of Labor Statistics showed that about half the workers in private service industries received health insurance that was at least partially paid by their employer, whereas in manufacturing four-fifths of workers received health insurance from their employer. As manufacturing declined, the number of Americans without health insurance rose steadily, even when workers were gaining new jobs in service industries. In 2008 a report by the Urban Institute calculated that every time the unemployment rate rose by one percentage point, another 1.1 million people became uninsured.

It is very difficult for communities to fight back. Because deindustrialization shatters bonds among workers, it is hard to mobilize them once the workplace that brought them together has disappeared. Also, for many years deindustrialization was seen as a matter of losing jobs in "dinosaur" industries, and few politicians seemed to care. In the early twenty-first century, however, as job losses have spread outside the Rust Belt and even to high-tech industries, national political leaders have started to respond to growing economic anxiety among their constituents.

[*See also* **Automation and Computerization; Labor Movements; Lowell Textile Mills; Social Class; Unemployment, Social Impact of;** *and* **Working-Class Life and Society.**]

BIBLIOGRAPHY

Bamberger, Bill, and Cathy N. Davidson. *Closing: The Life and Death of an American Factory.* New York: W. W. Norton and Company, 1998. A richly illustrated work on a southern plant closing.

Bluestone, Barry, and Bennett Harrison. *The Deindustrialization of America: Plant Closings, Community Abandonment, and the Dismantling of Basic Industry.* New York: Basic Books, 1982. A pathbreaking work responsible for publicizing the term "deindustrialization," which the authors define as "a widespread, systematic disinvestment in the nation's basic productive capacity" (p. 4).

Cowie, Jefferson, and Joseph Heathcott, eds. *Beyond the Ruins: The Meanings of Deindustrialization.*

Ithaca, N.Y.: ILR Press, 2003. Wide-ranging essays illustrate how writing on deindustrialization has evolved since the 1980s.

Dudley, Kathryn Marie. *The End of the Line: Lost Jobs, New Lives in Postindustrial America.* Chicago: University of Chicago Press, 1994. Explores the impact of the 1988 closure of a large Chrysler plant in Kenosha, Wisconsin.

Timothy J. Minchin

DELANY, MARTIN

(1812–1885), African American political philosopher, activist, physician, newspaper editor, and convention organizer. Born free on 6 May 1812, Martin Robison Delany was an influential black leader, and he was also the first black field officer in the American military.

Delany spent his childhood in Charles Town, Virginia (now West Virginia). Seeking to further his education, he went to Pittsburgh in 1831. He quickly established himself as a leader among educated young people in the black community, organizing literary and reform groups and serving as secretary for an organization that helped fugitive slaves escape north and thwart slave catchers. By the beginning of the next decade Delany was active throughout the state, helping to organize the State Convention of Colored Freemen of Pennsylvania in 1841. His work as a writer, publisher, and editor in the 1840s began a career in print that established Delany as one of the most important African American nationalist thinkers of the nineteenth century. He founded the first African American newspaper in Pittsburgh, the *Mystery*, in September 1843. After meeting the African American abolitionist Frederick Douglass in 1847, Delany left the *Mystery* to coedit the *North Star* with Douglass in December of that year. Although the partnership with Douglass lasted only two years, ending in 1849, it was the start of a long relationship, and at times rivalry, between the two.

Delany is best known for his work in the 1850s, a decade that began with the Compromise of 1850's Fugitive Slave Act and his own dismissal from Harvard Medical School after white students petitioned to rid all blacks from the school. He became convinced that the most promising political and economic future for African Americans might be somewhere other than the United States. In 1852 he wrote *The Condition, Elevation, Emigration, and Destiny of the Colored People of the United States, Politically Considered*, in which he denounced the denial of citizenship to African Americans and called for U.S. blacks to consider emigrating to Central or South America. He organized the National Emigration Convention, held in Cleveland, Ohio, in August 1854, and developed his hemispheric perspective on blacks in America in his serialized novel *Blake*, published in the *Anglo-African Magazine* in 1859 and then in the *Weekly Anglo-African* in 1862. The novel, which imagines a black revolution throughout the Americas, was published around the time that Delany was traveling to West Africa to explore the possibility of establishing an African American community in the Niger region.

After serving as an officer during the Civil War, Delany helped administer the Freedmen's Bureau in the South Carolina Sea Islands from 1865 to 1868. Afterward he remained in South Carolina, continuing to work to protect the interests of freed slaves, serving as a judge, and even running as a candidate for lieutenant governor in 1874. In 1877, disillusioned by the erosion of what little freedom had been gained by African Americans after the war, he turned his attention back to emigrationist projects, which ultimately never fully succeeded. Martin Delany retired to his home in Ohio in 1884, where he died on 24 January 1885.

[*See also* **African Americans; Colonization Movement, African; Free Communities of Color; Military Personnel,** *subentry on* **Civil War, African Americans; Reconstruction Era;** *and* **Slavery,** *subentry on* **Nineteenth Century.**]

BIBLIOGRAPHY

Levine, Robert S. *Martin Delany, Frederick Douglass, and the Politics of Representative Identity.* Chapel Hill: University of North Carolina Press, 1997.

Eric Curry

DEMOCRATIC-REPUBLICAN CLUBS

The first Democratic-Republican clubs formed in 1793, an expression of the transatlantic republican idealism attending the French Revolution, as well as the fear and dismay with which many Americans regarded the policies of the administration of George Washington. Self-consciously imitating the style and substance of local organizations formed during the American and French Revolutions, these societies greatly alarmed many early Americans, especially members of the nascent Federalist Party, who believed that such "self-created" societies represented a seditious threat to the legitimacy of duly elected representatives.

The clubs were located throughout the United States: in urban centers and hamlets, in coastal areas and the trans-Appalachian backcountry, and in the northern, middle, and southern states. The precise number of societies is unclear; estimates range from forty-two to more than a hundred. The size of the societies also varied substantially; a few claimed several hundred members, while many others numbered only a dozen or so.

The societies brought together disparate groups of Americans: merchants and planters, lawyers and government officials, and workingmen and farmers, as well as professionals, common laborers, middling politicians, and landed elites. The clubs formed dense communication networks through committees of correspondence and a system of intervisitation.

The societies expressed the republican fervor unleashed by the creation of the French Republic, an event they believed to be a continuation of America's own revolution. Thus the clubs celebrated French victories on the battlefield, advocated an official American alliance with France, feted the French ambassador Edmond Charles Genet, and, in the case of a club in Charleston, South Carolina, actually applied—successfully—for membership into the French Jacobin Society.

This same republican ebullience also led the societies to protest energetically numerous policies of the nascent Federalist Party: the Proclamation of Neutrality, the appointment of John Jay as emissary to Great Britain, and, most significantly, Alexander Hamilton's financial program. In vastly strengthening the power and influence of the central government, Hamilton's program awakened traditional fears of a distant, unaccountable, and corrupt ruling class.

Federalists, meanwhile, were horrified by the clubs and the democratic spirit they expressed. After attacking the societies relentlessly for well over a year, Federalist critics were able to use the Whiskey Rebellion of 1794 as leverage to link domestic insurrection both with the clubs of western Pennsylvania and, by association, with all the Democratic-Republican clubs. President Washington, himself extremely contemptuous of the clubs, publicly branded them as "self-created." Although the societies earnestly defended their right to associate and criticize the actions of the government, their number soon began to dwindle, and by the latter 1790s they had completely disappeared.

By organizing open discussions of public policy and encouraging ordinary people to criticize local and national leaders, the societies forced for the first time a discussion of the place and limits of legitimate political opposition in a republican society. In their brief career the societies challenged received notions of a deferential electorate and at once radically challenged elite command of the public sphere and ensured that it would be far more contentious than ever before.

[*See also* **Early Republic Era** *and* **Voluntary Associations,** *subentry* **British Colonies and Early Republic.**]

BIBLIOGRAPHY

Cotlar, Seth. "Reading the Foreign News, Imagining an American Public Sphere: Radical and Conservative Visions of 'the Public' in Mid-1790s Newspapers." In *Periodical Literature in Eighteenth-Century America*, edited by Mark L. Kamrath and Sharon M. Harris, pp. 307–338. Knoxville: University of Tennessee Press, 2005.

Schoenbachler, Matthew G. "Republicanism in the Age of Democratic Revolution: The Democratic-Republican Societies of the 1790s." *Journal of the Early Republic* 18, no. 2 (1998): 237–261.

Matthew Schoenbachler

DEMOGRAPHY

Demography examines the sources and consequences of population increases or decreases. This, in turn, involves assessing the rates of birth, death, and geographic movement—that is, fertility, mortality, and migration.

Historically, American demography fits into a three-stage progression characteristic of societies that now have low birth- and death rates. Convenient labels for these three stages are "Malthusian-frontier," "neo-Malthusian," and "post-Malthusian." (The term "Malthusian" comes from the name Thomas Robert Malthus, a pioneering English theorist of demography.) Originating in the theory of demographic transition, this periodization scheme locates, between two periods of relative stability, a turbulent transitional period during which a demographic pattern of roughly balanced high birth- and death rates gives way to one of roughly balanced low birth- and death rates.

Demographic Transition. Although theorists of demographic transition once portrayed the decline in fertility as a response to a reduction in mortality, by the twenty-first century this theory had come to be seen as a useful description, or first approximation, of historical experience rather than as a guide to cause and effect or a detailed blueprint that adequately captures all the features of the demographic history of the United States or of any other society. In comparative terms, the most distinctive feature of American demographic history is the extremely rapid increase in the number of people of European and African origins, from 250,000 in 1700 to 300 million in 2010—a thousandfold increase. Over these same three hundred years, the population of Europe increased only fivefold.

The human impact of this demographic transition is profound. Before 1800—during the traditional, or pretransitional, period of high fertility—the average woman who survived to age fifty had seven children; in the 1990s she had two children. The high fertility of the traditional period produced a very young aggregate population. About half of the pre-1800 population was under age sixteen;

by the 1990s this median age was thirty-three years. Only one in forty Americans in 1800 was over age sixty-five, compared to one in eight at the end of the twentieth century.

Mortality rates have changed dramatically as well. Until about the 1870s, the average life expectancy in the United States was around forty-five years, compared to seventy-six years in the 1990s. The impact of mortality decline is somewhat misleading if portrayed in terms of averages, however, since relatively few individuals actually die at the average age at death. Instead, infants and young children once died at radically higher rates than they do today, pulling the average down. In the pre-1870s period, about one in six infants died before his or her first birthday, and one in four died before age five. In the 1990s, less than 2 percent of American infants died before their fifth birthday. Instead of infectious diseases that took a heavy toll on the young, the major killers at the end of the twentieth century were chronic diseases related to aging, especially cardiovascular disease and cancer, which together accounted for nearly two-thirds of all deaths.

Three elements characterize the demography of the earliest stage of American population history: (1) an extremely high rate of overall growth that, despite a substantial contribution from immigration, was mostly caused by natural increase—the difference between birth- and death rates; (2) high fertility caused by markedly younger marriage ages for women than in western Europe; and (3) mortality that was high compared to that of the late twentieth century, but was moderate compared to contemporary death rates in Europe.

The term "Malthusian-frontier" summarizes the larger economic and cultural context of this demographic regime of rapid natural increase in early America. Writing in 1798, Malthus linked mortality rates and marriage age to the tenuous but ultimately equilibrating relationship between population size and food supply. Because Malthus lived at a time when sustained growth of economic productivity was nearly inconceivable, long-term population growth seemed impossible. Demographic expansion, he theorized, would ultimately be halted by what he called the "positive check" of higher mortality caused by famine and malnutrition.

Malthus, however, viewed eighteenth-century America as an exception to his general rule that resource constraints would limit population growth. America's seemingly boundless frontier and low population density meant that land was cheap and labor expensive. Because couples could acquire land relatively easily, they could, Malthus reasoned (as had Benjamin Franklin half a century earlier), marry earlier than their counterparts in Europe. This relaxation of what Malthus called the "preventive check" of late marriage spurred American population growth.

Over the course of the nineteenth century, couples married later and, more significantly, began to practice family limitation. Fertility fell by 50 percent, even though few couples apparently made use of contraceptive devices. These nineteenth-century trends can be attributed in part to the declining availability of agricultural land as the frontier moved toward closure. Urbanization also played a role in this large-scale demographic transition. Before 1800, during the "Malthusian-frontier" period, only one in twenty Americans lived in a town or city. Since 1970, with the process of urbanization nearly complete, about three-fourths of Americans have lived in places with populations of more than twenty-five hundred. Though large numbers of foreigners arrived in the United States from 1840 to 1920, in no decade did immigration account for more than one-third of the total population growth. High (though declining) rates of natural increase continued as a distinctive feature of American demographic history during this transitional stage.

The third stage of American demographic history, the closing decades of the twentieth century, was characterized by the increasing irrelevance of marriage, demographically speaking. The wide gap between fertility rates of married and unmarried women shrank dramatically in this period. By the 1990s, further, Americans were marrying later than at any time in the nation's history.

African Americans and Native Americans. The three-stage framework fits the historical experience of African Americans also. As with the population as a whole, rapid rates of aggregate growth characterized the early historical demography of the American black population, especially in the era of slavery. Of the 10 to 11 million Africans brought to the New World in the slave trade, some 600,000 to 650,000 were imported into the area that became the United States. During the nineteenth century, annual natural increase among American slaves was more than 2 percent, only slightly less than the rate for the white population. Compared to slaves in other regions of the Americas, the enslaved population in the United States had both higher fertility and lower mortality. Since emancipation, blacks and whites have experienced the same trends in mortality and fertility, although both rates have been consistently higher for blacks. The black-white difference in life expectancy at birth was six years in 1990 compared to eight years in 1900.

Prior to the twentieth century, the Native American population experienced a radically different demographic trajectory from that of European and African Americans. Instead of rapidly increasing, the numbers of Indians declined precipitously, a demographic catastrophe owing largely to extremely high death rates from diseases of European origin—in particular smallpox, typhus, and measles. Having no previous experience with these diseases, whole populations were nearly wiped out by epidemics. Estimates of the numbers of Indians in North America before European contact are varied and disputed. One estimate places the number at more than 5 million in the coterminous U.S. area in 1492. By 1800 the Indian population was about 600,000. It reached its nadir of 250,000 in the 1890s. The Indian population rebounded after 1900, however, reaching nearly 1.9 million in the 1990 census.

Discussion. The public discussion of population-related issues over the course of American history has typically reflected these broad trends. During the colonial era, Americans exulted in, and British officials worried about, the colonies' exploding population. Central to nineteenth-century demographic thinking were the relationships among land availability, population, and the social order. Thomas Jefferson and James Madison believed that territorial expansion would sustain the egalitarian economic basis of republican political institutions. During the antebellum era, both southern and northern writers tied the eventual extinction of slavery to a limitation of its territorial expansion into cheap lands. At century's end, the historian Frederick Jackson Turner saw the closing of the frontier as the end of an epoch in American history.

Differential fertility among various groups attracted considerable comment during the period of transition to lower birthrates. Native-born New Englanders, the vanguard group in the control of fertility within marriage, were thought to be on a path toward "race suicide." By the twenty-first century, population questions often intertwined with value debates over such issues as abortion, women's status, and intergenerational equity.

Even in the third stage of relative demographic stability, important changes still occurred. The baby boom of the post–World War II era, peaking in 1957, nearly doubled total fertility rates. A "baby bust" of equal magnitude then surprised the experts. These fluctuations gave rise to the prospect of the nation's having too few people of working age to fund the retirement of the baby boomers beginning in the second decade of the twenty-first century. A new wave of immigration, principally from Latin America and Asia, was another important development of the late twentieth century that had demographic implications.

Despite these changes, by the late twentieth century, fertility fluctuated narrowly around replacement levels, mortality was declining at a markedly lower pace than in the three-quarters of a century after 1800, urbanization had nearly ended, and Americans had become less residentially and geographically mobile. With only 3 percent of the workforce engaged in agriculture, it was obvious that the long-term shift from farm to city was over. By the early twenty-first century, demographic phenomena were much more stable than they had been during the previous century and a half.

[*See also* African Americans; Birth Control and Family Planning; Death and Dying; Disease; Immigration; Internal Migration; Life Expectancy; Life Stages; Marriage and Divorce; *and* Native American History and Culture.]

BIBLIOGRAPHY

Anderton, Douglas L., Richard E. Barrett, and Donald J. Bogue. *The Population of the United States*. 3d. ed. New York: Free Press, 1997.

Haines, Michael R. "The Population of the United States, 1790–1920." In *The Cambridge Economic History of the United States*, edited by Stanley L. Engerman and Robert E. Gallman, vol. 2, *The Long Nineteenth Century*, pp. 143–205. Cambridge, U.K.: Cambridge University Press, 2000.

Livi-Bacci, Massimo. *A Concise History of World Population*. 4th ed. Malden, Mass.: Blackwell, 2007.

Preston, Samuel H., and Michael R. Haines. *Fatal Years: Child Mortality in Late Nineteenth-Century America*. Princeton, N.J.: Princeton University Press, 1991.

Wells, Robert V. *Revolutions in Americans' Lives: A Demographic Perspective on the History of Americans, Their Families, and Their Society*. Westport, Conn.: Greenwood Press, 1982.

Daniel Scott Smith

DEPORTATIONS AND REPATRIATIONS

Deportation, or removal, is the process by which a noncitizen may be expelled from a country for violations of immigration law. In the United States deportation is a highly structured, bureaucratized process that applies to any "alien," a legal term meaning "any person not a citizen or national of the United States." Deportation may apply both to noncitizens who have entered the United States legally and also to others. U.S. deportation law has two basic forms, reflecting distinct goals: extended border control and post-entry social control. Extended border control seeks to remove those noncitizens who have evaded the rules that govern legal entry. Post-entry social control regulates those who have been legally admitted but who then engage in any of various prohibited behaviors. An array of fast-track mechanisms also exists, such as expedited removal, administrative removal, and reinstatement of removal.

Indeed, much of the evolution of deportation law in the late twentieth and early twenty-first centuries has involved what is termed "deformalization," in which procedural rights are severely restricted. Harsh substantive changes to the U.S. deportation system, implemented in 1996, have resulted in the deportation of millions of noncitizens—many undocumented but also hundreds of thousands with legal immigration status. Many are barred from ever returning.

Historically, deportation has evolved as a rather anomalous legal process. Its direct roots may be traced back to colonial and state practices regulating the movement of the poor and to processes for the transportation and banishment of criminals. Deportation's modern form—controlled by the federal government—developed from late nineteenth-century laws regulating the admission of Chinese laborers. Legal challenges to these race-based laws resulted in Supreme Court decisions recognizing "plenary" government power, largely insulated from many constitutional norms. The Supreme Court held in 1893 that deportation, though it may be harsh, is not constitutional "punishment" or a criminal process. As a result, deportees do not have the right to jury trial, the right to counsel if unable to afford one, the right to bail (even in the twenty-first century, thousands are put in mandatory detention every day), the right to have illegally seized evidence suppressed (unless the police conduct was widespread or egregious), the right against ex post facto (retroactive) laws, or a clear right against selective prosecution that is inspired by one's nationality, political opinions, or other characteristics.

Deportation has long been recognized as a powerful, flexible enforcement tool that has been wielded by the national government against various groups in the service of many different agendas. Implicating much more than border control, it is essentially a fulcrum upon which majoritarian power has been brought to bear against discrete, marginalized segments of society.

The deportation system that exists in the twenty-first century is the result of years of incremental and reactive growth. Following the legal acceptance of the exclusion and removal of Chinese workers, deportation developed during an early twentieth-century war on crime that was aimed at various drug and "morals" offenses. It was also a powerful tool of ideological social control, deployed during the 1919–1920 "Palmer Raids" against anarchists, Bolsheviks, and other dissidents. Its ideological functions were used widely during the Cold War McCarthy era.

In the early twentieth century, deportation also began to be increasingly focused on Mexican noncitizens, newly conceptualized as "illegal aliens," who continued to be recruited by U.S. employers following deep historical labor patterns. Massive repatriations took place during the 1930s, and with a major, militaristic deportation initiative in the 1950s, called "Operation Wetback," the Immigration and Naturalization Service claimed to have solved the problem of illegal Mexican immigration. Since then, of course, the patterns of undocumented labor migration have continued, and by around 2010 the United States had a population of at least some 12 million undocumented noncitizens, mostly from Mexico and Latin America. An array of deportation mechanisms have been deployed against these workers and their families, including large workplace raids during the administration of George W. Bush and various controversial state and local enforcement initiatives such as those of Arizona. Deportation of the post-entry social control type was a central component of the Bush administration's war on terror in the aftermath of the terrorist attacks of 11 September 2001.

The administration of Barack Obama has focused on deporting so-called criminal aliens, a population that may include long-term legal permanent residents who have spouses and children who are U.S. citizens. Such deportations may be based on serious crimes, but many thousands have also been deported for such minor offenses as simple drug possession.

[*See also* **Aliens during Wartime; Angel Island Immigration Station; Borderlands; Bracero Program; Ellis Island; Immigration;** *and* **Japanese Americans, Incarceration of.**]

BIBLIOGRAPHY

Kanstroom, Daniel. *Deportation Nation: Outsiders in American History.* Cambridge, Mass.: Harvard University Press, 2007.
Ngai, Mae M. *Impossible Subjects: Illegal Aliens and the Making of Modern America.* Princeton, N.J.: Princeton University Press, 2004.

Daniel Kanstroom

DESEGREGATION

Desegregation was both a legal goal of the civil rights movement and a process by which segregation in schools, public accommodations, housing, and employment would be eliminated. The freedom movement achieved the goal by the 1960s. The complications of a multiracial society with a long history of white supremacy and privilege meant that the process of desegregation continues.

Desegregation as a goal derived from the Civil War era. Although African Americans were no longer enslaved, during Reconstruction they suffered violence and economic subordination. Initial black efforts to create their own institutions served the community's needs, but the onset of legal segregation meant that separation from white society ensured compromised citizenship and limited opportunity. By the 1890s, southern states had not only been "redeemed"—controlled by whites—but laws restricting voting, movement, legal testimony against whites, education, and housing opportunities proscribed African American lives in a legal web known as "Jim Crow." The Supreme Court's 1896 *Plessy v. Ferguson* decision validated the notion of "separate but equal," bolstering segregation laws for sixty years.

Desegregation proved an ideological fault line within black leadership at century's end, personified in the conflict between Booker T. Washington, an accommodationist, and W. E. B. Du Bois, who favored unconditional racial equality. Along with antilynching and voting rights, desegregation became a major goal of civil rights organizations. Founded in 1909 by Du Bois and others, the National Association for the Advancement of Colored People (NAACP) pursued its agenda through field reporting, lobbying, and legal test cases. Key 1930s victories include the Maryland Appeals Court decision in *Murray v. Pearson*, argued by Thurgood Marshall, and the Supreme Court decision in Missouri *ex rel. Gaines v. Canada*, argued by Charles Houston. These decisions on behalf of professional-school students led to the formation of the NAACP Legal Defense Fund in 1939. In the postwar years the fund played a crucial role in attacking segregation.

Efforts to desegregate the military, housing, education, and public accommodations dominated postwar civil rights efforts. Minorities who had fought for democracy demanded equality on the home front, and activists argued that segregation compromised the U.S. image as leader of the "free world." Providing important precedents for federal involvement in desegregation, in 1946 the Democratic president Harry S. Truman, bucking the southern wing of his party, commissioned an important study of U.S. civil rights—published in 1947 as *To Secure These Rights*—and in 1948 he ordered the desegregation of the military.

Fair housing also became an important battleground. Local cases such as *Doss v. Bernal* (1943) in Orange County, California, prepared the way for the 1948 *Shelley v. Kraemer* Supreme Court victory rendering restrictive housing covenants unenforceable. The court system held firm against segregation, with the Supreme Court in *Mulkey v. Reitman* (1967) invalidating California's Proposition 14, which had overturned a state fair-housing law.

Educational desegregation also gained traction. Another California case, *Mendez v. Westminster* (1947), led to desegregation in state schools as ordered by Earl Warren, then the governor of California and later the chief justice of the Supreme Court. *Mendez* set an important precedent for the NAACP's greatest legal victory, *Brown v. Board of Education*, a case argued by Marshall and decided by the Warren-led U.S. Supreme Court in 1954. *Brown* urged desegregation of schools "with all deliberate speed," and it took further civil rights legislation to enforce the decision. But *Brown* had struck down the notion of "separate but equal," a ruling with wider implications. The 1957 crisis at Central High School in Little Rock, Arkansas, provided the decade's most dramatic effort to make educational desegregation a reality. Only under the protection of federal troops were the so-called Little Rock Nine able to attend school.

Public accommodations provided perhaps the most iconic moments in the desegregation fight. In the late 1940s the Congress of Racial Equality (CORE) led local protests against segregated restaurants. In 1955, black citizens pursued a bus boycott in Montgomery, Alabama, that sparked the creation of the Southern Christian Leadership Conference (SCLC), led by the Reverend Martin Luther King Jr. Another new organization, the Student Nonviolent Coordinating Committee (SNCC), held sit-ins at lunch counters in the late 1950s and early 1960s. Perhaps most dramatic were SNCC's interracial 1961 Freedom Rides on buses and trains through the South to test the federal ban on segregation in interstate travel. SCLC-led protests in Birmingham, Alabama, and pressure created by the March on Washington in 1963 led to the 1964 Civil Rights Act banning segregation in public accommodations, school districts, and labor unions.

The act did not end all segregation. Various factors, including white flight from urban school districts and ongoing steering practices in real estate, made desegregation as a process continue into the twenty-first century. The elimination of de jure segregation in the South did not disturb de facto segregation elsewhere. Efforts to bus minority students to white-majority schools, for example, led to violent protests by whites in Boston and other cities in the 1970s. At the same time, desegregation came with costs for minorities, including black professionals' loss of jobs, the decline of black-owned businesses, and the plight of impoverished and formerly segregated neighborhoods.

[*See also* **Affirmative Action; African Americans; Civil Rights Act (1964); Civil Rights Movement; Education; Law and Society; Military Personnel,** *subentry on* **Modern Wars; Segregation, Racial; Slums;** *and* **South, The.**]

BIBLIOGRAPHY

Anderson, James D. *The Education of Blacks in the South, 1860–1935*. Chapel Hill: University of

North Carolina Press, 1988. Traces the development of "colored" education, revealing various models that grew during the Jim Crow era.

Brilliant, Mark. *The Color of America Has Changed: How Racial Diversity Shaped Civil Rights Reform in California, 1941–1978.* New York: Oxford University Press, 2010. California's racial diversity puts it at the forefront of civil rights change in this study.

Carson, Clayborne. *In Struggle: SNCC and the Black Awakening of the 1960s.* Cambridge, Mass.: Harvard University Press, 1981. A classic account of the Student Nonviolent Coordinating Committee's activities and ideological evolution.

Klarman, Michael J. *From Jim Crow to Civil Rights: The Supreme Court and the Struggle for Racial Equality.* New York: Oxford University Press, 2004. The definitive account of the Supreme Court's central role in the history of segregation's rise and fall.

Kluger, Richard. *Simple Justice: The History of "Brown v. Board of Education" and Black America's Struggle for Equality.* Rev. ed. New York: Alfred A. Knopf, 2004. Still perhaps the most detailed account of the *Brown* decision, though the full implications of the decision continue to be debated.

Litwack, Leon F. *Trouble in Mind: Black Southerners in the Age of Jim Crow.* New York: Alfred A. Knopf, 1998. A comprehensive treatment of the Jim Crow world of the South after Reconstruction.

Sugrue, Thomas J. *Sweet Land of Liberty: The Forgotten Struggle for Civil Rights in the North.* New York: Random House, 2008. Situates the freedom movement in the North, paying special attention to individuals and organizations grappling with de facto segregation in the cities.

Benjamin Cawthra

DISABILITY RIGHTS MOVEMENT

The U.S. disability rights movement seeks to extend the full exercise of citizenship, democracy, and self-determination to people with disabilities. The activist movement focuses on legal efforts to forbid discrimination in employment, education, access, and public transportation, as well as on institutional transformations that better enable the self-determination of those with disabilities. Like the movements for women's rights, lesbian, gay, bisexual, and transgender rights, the environment, and racial freedom, the disability rights movement began to coalesce into one movement in the 1970s, but its previously disparate elements were active decades earlier. Organized activist groups of disabled veterans, parents, blind people, deaf people, and other groups of people with disabilities had sought to shape their own lives for decades previous.

The disability rights movement also argues that disability is not simply a medical, bodily grounded condition. Indeed, it has sometimes directly challenged medical authority to define disability. Using the work of intellectual theorists such as Erving Goffman, Jacobus tenBroek, and Irving Kenneth Zola, activists have argued that disability is also a social condition of discrimination and unmerited stigma. Such discrimination and stigma needlessly harms and restricts the lives of those with disabilities and results in economic disparities, social isolation, and oppression.

People with disabilities have always sought to shape and determine their own lives. For example, veterans disabled by the Revolutionary War sought compensation and employment. Nineteenth-century deaf citizens actively lobbied for education and employment, as well as for their own organizations led by deaf people. In the early twentieth century, blind adults sought to create their own advocacy institutions, resisting the paternalistic authority of others to determine their lives. As early as 1935, the League of the Physically Handicapped, likely the first cross-disability organization, engaged in public protests over discrimination against people with disabilities by the Works Progress Administration (WPA) and in housing. Their activism resulted in, among other things, the opening of fifteen hundred WPA jobs to people with disabilities.

Just as the World War II experiences of African American, Latino, and American Indian soldiers and their communities propelled racial-freedom movements forward, so did World War II drive the contemporary disability rights movement. Conscientious objectors to the war, compelled into alternative service at institutions for those with psychiatric and intellectual disabilities, were shocked by the institutions' brutal conditions. The public spotlight that they brought to these conditions provided the initial impetus for the deinstitutionalization that occurred in the 1970s and 1980s. Disabled veterans demanded employment, and like previous generations of veterans, they propelled further changes in rehabilitation programs so that they could live more independent lives. Unlike members of previous generations, however, many late twentieth-century disabled veterans were able to draw on emerging civil rights ideologies to argue that employment, access, education, and housing were civil rights issues—not simply questions of charity.

A vital part of the broader movement for disability rights has been the independent living movement. Grounded in several decades of prior activism, the movement became most particularly active in the counterculture activism on the campus of the University of California, Berkeley, in the 1960s and 1970s. In 1962, the same academic year in which African American James Meredith matriculated at the University of Mississippi after suing for access and racial integration, polio survivor Edward Roberts sued the University of California for access

and integration. Roberts's suit was successful, but Berkeley required Roberts to live in the infirmary rather than in the dormitory. The third floor of the infirmary soon became the emotional and activist center of the Rolling Quads, a disability pride and activist group with Roberts at the center. The group sought barrier-free access to the community and the university.

Battling paternalistic assumptions about disability, Roberts and others across the nation organized independent living centers. Along with activists such as Corbett O'Toole at Berkeley and Carr Massi in New York City, in the 1960s, 1970s, and 1980s independent living activists sought both the removal of the architectural and transportation barriers that made civic participation almost impossible for people with disabilities and also institutional supports and accommodations that would enable people with disabilities to live independently, manage their own lives, and make their own decisions. They also sought to remove work disincentives. In 1988 the historian Paul Longmore, for example, protested restrictive Social Security policies that, by denying nearly all benefits to disabled individuals who had employment, thus discouraged employment. Longmore burned his newly published first book in front of the Los Angeles Federal Building to protest that the book's royalties—in no way enough to live on—had rendered him ineligible for any Social Security benefits.

The contemporaneous landmark court decisions that expanded civil rights for many population groups, the growing advocacy and discontent of people with disabilities and their allies, and a series of legislative victories expanded the scope and successes of the disability rights movement. People with disabilities increasingly thought of themselves as experiencing a shared oppression—regardless of variations in their physical, mental, or cognitive disabilities, and regardless of their race, class, sexual, and gender differences. The growing cross-disability community both made possible and was a result of the increasingly confident disability rights movement.

The Americans with Disabilities Act (ADA) of 1990, which forbids employment, access, housing, and educational discrimination against people with disabilities, is the best-known civil rights legislation for those with disabilities, but it is not the only one. The ADA builds on legislation such as the Architectural Barriers Act of 1968, the Rehabilitation Act of 1973—of which Section 504 requires that any organization receiving federal funds make accommodation for those with disabilities—and the Individuals with Disabilities Education Act of 1975. The ADA and its consequences, as well as those of other disability rights legislation, have been consistently tested and confirmed in the courts and denied in practice. Only the constant vigilance and activism of disabled people have maintained the expansion of civil rights that the disability rights movement made possible.

[*See also* **Americans Disabled for Accessible Public Transport; Asylums and Mental Illness;** *and* **Veterans' Rights Movement.**]

BIBLIOGRAPHY

Fleischer, Doris Zames, and Frieda Zames. *The Disability Rights Movement: From Charity to Confrontation*. Philadelphia: Temple University Press, 2001.

Kornbluh, Felicia. "Disability, Antiprofessionalism, and Civil Rights: The National Federation of the Blind and the 'Right to Organize' in the 1950s." *Journal of American History* 97, no. 4 (2011): 1023–1047.

Longmore, Paul K., and David Goldberger. "The League of the Physically Handicapped and the Great Depression: A Case Study in the New Disability History." *Journal of American History* 87, no. 3 (2000): 888–922.

Taylor, Steven J. *Acts of Conscience: World War II, Mental Institutions, and Religious Objectors*. Syracuse, N.Y.: Syracuse University Press, 2009.

Kim E. Nielsen

DISEASE

Americans have a naive belief that the conquest of disease is a realistic goal. Some have faith in the curative powers of new medical therapies, while others suggest that environmental and behavioral changes can eliminate many diseases. Implicit in these views is the faith that disease is unnatural and that human beings have it within their power to control completely their own destiny. Disease is often perceived as the enemy of humanity, and only a war can result in its banishment.

Such beliefs reflect a fundamental misunderstanding of the biological world. "It is seldom recognized," wrote the distinguished biologist René Dubos in 1961, "that each type of society has diseases peculiar to itself—indeed, that each civilization creates its own diseases. (71)" Conceding that methods of control can be developed for any given pathological state, he nevertheless insisted that "disease will change its manifestations according to social circumstances." Nowhere are his generalizations better illustrated than in the changing morbidity and mortality patterns in the United States from the distant past to the present.

The Encounter of Native Americans and Europeans.

Prior to the arrival of Europeans in the Americas, the indigenous population and the environment in which they lived differed in important ways from those of other continents. The indigenous people either had crossed from Asia to Alaska on a land bridge produced by a lowering of the seas during the last Ice Age or else had arrived by sea. Whatever their origins, they developed in cultural, physical, and biological isolation from the rest of humanity. Indeed, many of the pathogens responsible for infectious diseases that took a heavy toll in Asia, Europe, and Africa probably did not survive the migration through the harsh climate of Siberia and Alaska. Peoples of the Americas were thus isolated from many of the endemic and epidemic diseases that were characteristic elsewhere. Moreover, their isolation made them genetically homogenous, since they did not come into contact with other diverse populations.

For these and other reasons, pre-Columbian America had a unique disease environment. The diseases that took a heavy toll on other continents—malaria, bubonic plague, smallpox, and other infectious diseases associated with childhood—were largely unknown. Nevertheless, some diseases—tuberculosis and infections associated with the cocci group of bacteria—were common. The greatest threat to health in the Americas, however, included accidents, wildlife diseases associated with hunting and gathering, warfare, and sporadic famines. The relative absence of domesticated livestock minimized zoonotic (animal-transmitted) diseases, and low population density and the absence of commercial contacts among tribes reduced the threat of epidemic and infectious diseases. To be sure, life was harsh, and life expectancy at birth for Amerindians was generally in the low thirties, even though the causes of morbidity and mortality differed from those of much of the rest of the world.

The Europeans' movement throughout the world that began in the fifteenth century had dramatic health consequences. Commercial contacts made possible the dissemination of pathogens that led to devastating epidemics.

For the native people of the Americas the contact with Europeans had a catastrophic impact. The introduction of new infectious pathogens from other continents into a population lacking immunological defenses against them led to extraordinarily high mortality rates. Genetic homogeneity may have also enhanced the Amerindians' vulnerability. Having no experiences with such new diseases as smallpox, Amerindians often responded by engaging in practices that proved counterproductive; custom, tradition, and religion all failed to provide any guide to caring practices.

Consequently the Amerindian population suffered a precipitous decline in the period following the first contacts with Europeans. Smallpox in particular had the greatest impact. In the century following the arrival of the Spanish in Peru, the native population virtually disappeared. The importance of other infectious diseases—including measles, respiratory infections, and gastrointestinal disorders—was probably magnified among people under stress from smallpox. High mortality rates, periodic famines, and the social dislocations that accompanied these crises also reduced fertility to such low levels that recovery was impossible. On the eve of colonization the indigenous population of the future contiguous United States was between 2 and 12 million. By 1800 it had fallen to about 600,000, and by the end of the nineteenth century it had reached a nadir of 248,000. To native peoples the arrival of foreign settlers and entrepreneurs proved a catastrophe of immense proportions.

Health in Colonial America. The individuals who migrated to America encountered a quite different environment. Western Europe's climate is oceanic in character; seasonal fluctuations are relatively small. Eastern North America, by contrast, has a continental climate with far greater temperature extremes. Summers are warmer and more humid, winters colder, and precipitation unpredictable. Early settlers mistakenly assumed that because the latitude and longitude were similar to Europe's, their surroundings would match that of their homeland. Unprepared for their new environment, they had to undergo a process of "seasoning," which meant a physical adjustment to their new environment.

Nowhere were the difficulties of adjustment more evident than in the settlement of Virginia. Within nine months only 38 of the 104 colonists who settled Jamestown were alive. Dysentery and typhoid fever were the most likely causes of high mortality. Both were spread by a polluted water supply. A fall in river discharges during the summer left stagnant and brackish pools of water, which were contaminated by salt, sediment, and fecal matter. Since the settlers drew their water from either the river or shallow wells, they were susceptible to a variety of intestinal disorders. Indeed, the colony of Virginia remained a deathtrap for much of the seventeenth century. Between 1607 and 1699, some 50,000 to 100,000 people migrated to the colony, yet its population in 1699 was only 63,000. The situations in the Chesapeake region in Maryland and the Carolinas were similar, even though in these regions malaria proved the greatest threat to life. Indeed, the greater resistance of African Americans to the ravages of such tropical diseases as malaria contributed to the growth of slavery in the South.

The experiences of those who settled in New England and the Middle Atlantic regions proved quite different. The Pilgrims who relocated to Plymouth, Massachusetts, in 1620 arrived late in the autumn. The rigors of the long journey across the Atlantic, an inadequate diet, and the need to focus on the construction of dwellings weakened the settlers and rendered them susceptible to respiratory diseases, probably influenza. Adult mortality reached 58 percent in the early months of settlement. Once the initial phases of settlement had passed, the colony prospered. Its location on high ground, an uncontaminated water supply, and a varied diet created optimum health conditions.

The major settlement of Massachusetts began in 1628. Salem, Charlestown, and Boston experienced high mortality rates, though not for the same reasons. At Salem lack of planning and poor housing led both to such nutritional disorders as scurvy and to respiratory disorders, whereas a contaminated water supply at Charlestown was responsible for high mortality. Nevertheless, once the residents of Massachusetts had adjusted to their new environment by constructing adequate housing, ensuring a sufficient and nutritious food supply, and developing safe sources of water, health indicators rose dramatically. Life expectancy at birth was much higher in the region than in England and Europe. Nevertheless seaports—because of higher population density and trade that sometimes brought infectious pathogens—suffered proportionately more than rural towns did. In Andover, Massachusetts—a town that was relatively isolated—the average age of death for first-generation people was 72 for men and 71 for women. The health advantages of New England were generally matched in the Middle Atlantic region.

After 1700 there were major changes in the disease ecology of the American colonies. Population growth and economic development each had a profound influence on morbidity and mortality rates. Acute infectious diseases continued to remain the major threats to health. Their patterns, however, assumed new forms in response to environmental changes. Rising population density, expansion of internal and external trade and commerce, new forms of agriculture, and landscape transformations all combined to alter the complex relationships that existed between pathogens and human hosts.

Throughout the eighteenth century there was an increase in mortality from infectious diseases, particularly among infants and children residing in larger towns and urban port areas. Boston, New York, Philadelphia, and Charleston, South Carolina—the most important colonial ports—had contacts both with each other and with the Caribbean, Europe, and Africa. Their populations included many people who had not acquired immunity to bacterial and viral pathogens. The history of smallpox is illustrative. Between 1721 and 1792, for example, Boston experienced seven epidemics. The first was the most devastating. In a population of 10,670, there were 6,006 reported cases and 850 deaths. Given patterns of trade and commerce, smallpox tended to spread to other areas. Because of the more dispersed population and agricultural rather than commercial economy, in the Chesapeake and the South smallpox was less significant. Nor was smallpox the only imported disease. Yellow fever also struck seaboard areas in all the colonies. During the Philadelphia epidemic of 1793, about half of the 51,000 residents fled. Of those who remained, between 9 and 12 percent perished.

Periodic epidemics of smallpox and yellow fever tended to overshadow other endemic and epidemic diseases that played far more significant roles. Mortality from measles among children, for example, equaled modern death rates for cardiovascular diseases and cancer. A diphtheria epidemic that began in 1735 in Kingston, New Hampshire, killed more than a third of the town's children. In the following five years the epidemic spread to several adjacent colonies. Perhaps the greatest threat to life, however, came from

endemic disorders such as dysentery, which took a heavy toll particularly among infants and children. In the South malaria remained a major health hazard.

During the eighteenth century an overall increase in mortality occurred. In New England there was a 5 to 10 percent loss of population during infrequent epidemic years and an average loss of about 2 percent in other years. In the Middle Atlantic colonies, aggregate mortality was marginally higher. In both regions, port cities like Boston and Philadelphia had the highest rates because of the introduction of epidemic infectious diseases from abroad. The demographic pattern in the South, by contrast, differed in fundamental respects from that of all other British mainland colonies. Mortality rates exceeded even those in Europe. Indeed, without a constant inflow of immigrants to replenish a population devastated by extraordinary death rates, not only would the southern colonies have failed to develop economically, but the very survival of the society would have become questionable.

Threats to Health in Expanding America. In the nineteenth century, America underwent fundamental social, economic, and technological changes. The construction of canals and railroads hastened the creation of a national market economy that transcended local boundaries. Changes in the production of goods and services, the emergence of new occupations, and the creation of novel industries began to alter the lives of Americans in fundamental ways.

Urban Areas. The acceleration in economic activity was accompanied by an increase in the size and number of urban areas. However beneficial urbanization was to economic development in the long run, it magnified the risks from infectious diseases.

Urban growth for much of the nineteenth century, moreover, tended to be somewhat haphazard. Although they created police and firefighting departments and paved streets, municipal governments tended to ignore threats to the health of inhabitants.

Providing inhabitants with safe and widely accessible water supplies and removing wastes presented authorities with their greatest challenges. At the beginning of the nineteenth century, residents drew their water from local sources such as wells and neighboring streams. Local water supplies, however, proved inadequate to the needs of a burgeoning population. The lack of water to flush streets or fight fires created additional problems. Moreover, human and other organic wastes, as well as wastewater, were generally drained into cesspools and privy vaults adjacent to homes. Such drainage systems became sources of biological contamination.

Cognizant of the need to supply densely populated areas with pure water, cities began to construct public systems that brought water from rivers and reservoirs outside their border. Nevertheless, population growth and rising per capita water usage—partly accelerated by indoor sinks and toilets—overloaded the already inadequate means of water and waste disposal. The common practice of dumping organic and industrial wastes into rivers from which water was drawn only enhanced the spread of pathogens responsible for many infectious diseases.

Prevailing systems of water and waste disposal were not alone in magnifying threats to health. In the nineteenth century, urban transportation was based on the horse; the result was that city streets were covered with manure that turned into cesspools during periods of precipitation and attracted huge swarms of insects. Street paving only exacerbated the problem, since the manure was ground into fine dust by wheels. Municipal codes,

moreover, were silent on housing standards, and many residential buildings were constructed without regard to the health of inhabitants. No provisions were made for drainage or ventilation. The accumulation of organic wastes on adjacent streets led inhabitants to keep windows shut, preventing the circulation of fresh air indoors and thus facilitating the dissemination of infectious organisms. Crowding within households only increased health risks. In a classic description of sanitary and housing conditions among working-class and poor residents in New York City in 1845, Dr. John H. Griscom noted that such terrible living conditions led to "much sickness and many premature deaths"; one-fourth of those born died before their fifth birthday, and one-half died before their twentieth.

Cities also provided ideal environments for epidemics such as cholera, yellow fever, and smallpox. However spectacular, these epidemics did not have a major impact on population growth and mortality rates. Between 1800 and 1859, yellow fever resulted in perhaps 55,000 deaths, or an average of slightly more than 900 per year. Much the same was true for cholera deaths during the three epidemics between 1832 and 1866.

By contrast, endemic infectious diseases flourished in densely populated and unhygienic environments and took a far heavier toll in urban areas than periodic epidemics did, even though the epidemics created far greater fear among inhabitants. Tuberculosis was among the most significant and affected a largely adult population. An infectious disease caused by the *Mycobacterium tuberculosis*, it is particularly responsive to environmental factors, including crowded and poorly ventilated housing and unhygienic working conditions. Perhaps 23 percent of all deaths in New York City in 1804 were caused by tuberculosis and other pulmonary disorders. Data from Boston, Philadelphia, and

Baltimore suggest a similar pattern. Likewise, typhus—a disease caused by *Rickettsia prowazekii* and transmitted to human hosts by a body louse—flourished among poor residents living in crowded housing and lacking facilities to bathe or wash clothes.

Urban environments were also conducive to the spread of a variety of other infectious diseases. Respiratory disorders, diphtheria and croup, measles, whooping cough, and scarlet fever all added to the health burden of residents. Diarrheal diseases took an especially heavy toll among infants and young children. Whatever the specific etiology, the typical mode of communication was by water or food that had been contaminated by inappropriate hygiene or spoilage, as well as by bacterial transmission by insects.

To demonstrate that infectious diseases were the major element in urban mortality is not to suggest that other disorders were absent. Chronic degenerative and long-duration diseases were present, including cancer and cardiovascular-renal diseases. Their incidence and prevalence, however, were low, if only because high mortality rates among the young meant that older people constituted a relatively small percentage of the total population.

The burden of disease had profound consequences for urban populations during the first half of the nineteenth century. Infants and children in cities were far more vulnerable than their rural counterparts. Of 4,866 deaths in Baltimore in 1860, 1,227 were of infants and 2,616 were of children younger than ten years old. Mortality rates, however, were not equal. New York and New Orleans had higher mortality rates than Boston, Baltimore, and Philadelphia. Both grew at a much faster rate, thus exacerbating those features of urban life that increased health risks. Both were gateways to the interior; their ports received more transients and ships from other regions of the world, which made it difficult to prevent the entry of infectious pathogens. That environmental conditions facilitated the transmission of infectious diseases is true. But equally if not more important was the fact that there was little understanding that mortality from enteric disorders, particularly among infants and children, could be limited by preventive measures to minimize contamination of water, milk, and food and to ensure rehydration during acute episodes.

The South and Rural Areas. With its warm and moist climate and the importation of certain African diseases, notably falciparum malaria (the form with the highest mortality), hookworm, and filariasis, the South presented a quite different epidemiological environment. By the mid-nineteenth century, mortality rates of southern whites resembled those in other regions. The morbidity and mortality experiences of slaves, however, were quite different. The death rate on the Middle Passage from Africa and during the first year was excessive. Even after adjusting to a new environment, African slaves faced formidable health problems. Both Africans and whites suffered from the same diseases, but the conditions under which slaves lived magnified the significance of many diseases. Overcrowding, lack of ventilation, damp earthen floors, and poor sanitary conditions facilitated the transmission of respiratory and gastrointestinal diseases. Slave infants weighed less than their white counterparts. Their mortality during the first year of life was about 350 per 1,000; between the ages of one and four it was 201. The figures for the white antebellum population, by contrast, were 179 and 93.

Despite economic development, for much of the nineteenth century the United States remained a predominantly rural nation. In 1800, 94 percent of the population lived in rural areas; on the eve of the Civil War the comparable figure was 80 percent. In general, rural residents enjoyed somewhat better health than their urban counterparts did. Low population density tended to inhibit the dissemination of many infectious pathogens. Yet the benefits of residing outside cities were only relative; mortality rates were on an upward trend in the early nineteenth century and affected all segments of the population.

The Frontier. The urban-rural dichotomy, as a matter of fact, was less of a sharp break and more of a continuum with gradations that diminished over time. The westward movement of people over the Appalachian Mountains after the War of 1812, for example, created novel risks largely unknown to urban dwellers. The long journey was arduous; families had to travel over difficult terrain, endure harsh climatic conditions, and live with a marginal food supply until they reached their final destination. Moreover, the areas into which they moved lacked the amenities of more mature communities. The process of migration and settlement, the adjustment to new surroundings, and the environmental transformation that followed often resulted in higher morbidity and mortality than those found in older rural areas. Ecological changes also created conditions that fostered the appearance of new diseases previously absent.

The medical problems faced by those who traversed the two overland trails to Oregon and California were typical. Between 1851 and 1866 perhaps 350,000 people took the southern route to California. On average the trip covered two thousand miles and took four and a half months to complete. Gastrointestinal illnesses, including typhoid fever and cholera, were common and debilitating, as were Colorado tick fever, malaria, and scurvy.

Even those who migrated to the Middle West—a shorter journey—faced new health conditions as a result of the transformation of both the natural environment and the ecology of disease. Before settlement of the upper Mississippi valley (Illinois, Missouri, Iowa, Wisconsin, and Minnesota), for example, malaria—a disease that requires the presence of infected people and susceptible people, as well as of the *Anopheles* mosquito—was unknown. Between 1820 and 1870 the disease peaked and then disappeared.

What elements shaped the odd appearance and disappearance of a disease that was unknown in pre-Columbian America? Of key importance was the movement of people from areas in which malaria was endemic and of susceptible people from malaria-free regions, as well as the presence of the *Anopheles* mosquito. The Midwest was always an ideal breeding ground for mosquitoes, largely because pools of stagnant water were created both by overflow from streams and rivers from melting snows and also by the prairies' poor drainage. The initial stages of settlement were along waterways because the absence of roads made waterways the basic means of transportation, especially after the introduction of steamboats. Such areas were ideal breeding grounds for mosquitoes. Moreover, many of the early settlers constructed log cabins with no or one window (glass was a luxury on the frontier) or mud huts and sod houses for shelter. These shelters' dark, damp, and warm environment was favored by insects, facilitating the spread of malaria from infected to susceptible people. Thus population movements, settlement in poorly drained areas, and housing combined to make malaria one of the most important diseases in the Middle West.

Just as environmental conditions fostered conditions conducive to the spread of malaria, so later changes contributed to its disappearance. After 1850, railroad construction shifted people away from waterways and lowlands, thus reducing their nearness to the stagnant water that provided breeding grounds for insects. The improvement of housing was also significant; new structures were dry, were better sealed, and included more windows and screens. The introduction of cattle breeding played a role as well, since mosquitoes would rather feed off cattle than off human beings. Thus after 1870 malaria all but disappeared.

Although many believed in the superiority of rural living, the frontier environment was hardly a health utopia. Contaminated water supplies and crude sanitation created an environment in which a variety of infectious diseases could flourish. Typhoid fever and other enteric disorders were common. There were few regional differences in infant mortality, but losses among one- to four-year-old children were higher on the frontier. Mortality was also highest in larger families. More subtle in shaping health patterns was the sex imbalance that existed in many frontier areas. Young unmarried men—who were more prone to violent and antisocial behavior, were much less likely to eat nutritious food or pay attention to personal hygiene, and worked in mines and construction—frequently succumbed to infectious diseases and accidents. Their behavior and excessive use of alcohol had a devastating effect on their health and longevity. Areas with a more balanced sex ratio had far better health outcomes; family life generally restrained male behavior.

Young men who served in the army during the nineteenth century faced many of the same risks to health and life as those in civilian life. The infectious diseases that accompanied the westward movement were present among soldiers assigned to frontier posts. The exigencies of war exacerbated conditions that led to high mortality. During the War of 1812, the 1846–1848 war with Mexico, and the Civil War, the number of deaths from infectious diseases far exceeded the number of battlefield deaths. In the Civil War, for example, about 67,000 Union soldiers were killed in battle and 43,000 died of wounds, yet 225,000 died from disease. The conditions of military life—camp crowding and poor sanitation—created ideal conditions for the spread of infectious diseases. Moreover, new recruits lacked the discipline and experience of regular troops, and hence proved more vulnerable to disease.

Rising Levels of Mortality.

Despite rapid population and economic growth, rising wages, and territorial expansion, both life expectancy and height declined during the first two-thirds of the nineteenth century. Mortality rates rose in the antebellum decades, and life expectation—even among adults—declined. One scholar has estimated that the life expectancy for a twenty-year-old man fell from 46.4 in 1800–1809 to 40.8 in 1850–1859; the comparable figures for women were 47.9 and 39.5. Thus economic and industrial development were in their early stages accompanied by rising levels of mortality.

The creation of a national transportation network increased both internal migration and interregional trade, and thus contributed to the movement of infectious pathogens from urban to rural areas where more susceptible people resided. Movement into new areas also promoted environmental changes that sometimes had adverse health consequences.

By midcentury, economic and industrial changes were also in the process of transforming the workplace in ways that sometimes had adverse consequences for many workers. The rise of new industries and technologies magnified older, and created novel, occupational risks. These took a variety of forms. The most important were dusty environments, unsafe machinery, the use of toxic substances, and crowded workplaces that enhanced the spread of infectious diseases.

During the latter half of the nineteenth century the burgeoning industrial economy's need for energy led to the rise of the coal industry. By 1850 surface mining was inadequate to meet the growing need for coal. Underground mining quickly became the norm. The dusty environment, the presence of methane gas, and the smoke and carbon dioxide from powder charges all combined to make underground mining one of the most dangerous occupations in the nation. Coal worker's pneumoconiosis (CWP) resulted from the constant inhalation of coal dust and led to high mortality rates. Accidents added to the health burden of miners. Dust diseases were also found in textile mills, lead mines, and various other industrial sites. By the early twentieth century, tenement workshops and factories were producing clothing and other consumer goods. Crowding and inadequate ventilation were common, thus enhancing risks from dust and infectious diseases.

Stopping the Spread of Infection. Beginning in the late nineteenth century the United States, as well as England and many European nations, experienced what has become known as the second epidemiological (or health) transition. The first such transition, which occurred perhaps ten thousand or more years ago, involved the development of agriculture, which created a stable food supply. The result was a more sedentary population that increased in both size and density. Population growth in turn heightened the potential for epidemic and endemic diseases, which require a host that permits the survival of invading pathogens. During the second epidemiological transition, by contrast, infectious diseases began to decline as the major cause of mortality. This unparalleled transformation had a profound impact

on American society, for it altered the structure of the population. In the nineteenth century the population was relatively young. In 1850 and 1900 the median ages were 18.9 and 22.9, respectively. In 1850 only 4 percent of people were sixty years old or over; by 2008 the figure was 17 percent, or 51.7 million out of a total population of 304 million. As infectious diseases began to decline as the major cause of mortality, they were replaced by chronic long-term and degenerative diseases.

The Examples of Smallpox, Yellow Fever, Malaria, and Polio. By the end of the nineteenth century, some of the endemic and epidemic infectious diseases had become less common or almost completely disappeared. Although Robert Koch did not identify the cholera vibrio until 1883, the earlier epidemiological work of John Snow provided persuasive evidence that the disease was transmitted by contaminated water. The demonstration that public health interventions could prevent the spread of cholera all but eliminated its threat.

The disappearance of smallpox, yellow fever, and malaria came about for other reasons. In the case of smallpox vaccination, isolation and surveillance played a role. Equally significant was the fact that *Variola major*, a lethal virus that had predominated since the seventeenth century, was replaced by *Variola minor*, which had a far lower mortality rate. As late as 1930 there were thirty thousand cases, but the mortality rate was only 0.3 percent, and by midcentury the disease had disappeared altogether.

The disappearance of yellow fever reflected a process shaped less by conscious design than by serendipity. Quarantines, an emphasis on sanitary reform, street paving, and sanitary sewers decreased the number of stagnant water pools, thus depriving mosquitoes of breeding places. The decline in frequency of the disease in Cuba diminished the threat of its import, as did an apparent decline in the virulence of the virus. By the time of the last outbreak in 1905, a better understanding of etiology and the introduction of more effective mosquito-suppression measures led to yellow fever's disappearance.

The disappearance of malaria followed a somewhat slower course. In the 1930s malaria still persisted in southern regions. In the Mississippi delta region, agricultural workers lived adjacent to the fields, where stagnant ponds remained after the receding of river floods in the spring. Although drainage projects and the use of insecticides were common after 1900, they did not play a major role in malaria's disappearance. More important was the movement of people from the countryside to towns and cities, a result of large-scale farming and mechanization; this movement away from the stagnant ponds and their mosquitoes sharply decreased the transmission of the plasmodium. By 1940 the disease had disappeared.

The decline in mortality from infectious diseases, however, was not on a linear gradient. Social and economic change could both reduce and enhance the virulence of infectious diseases. In urban areas, for example, sewage was dumped into the very rivers that served as a source of water. As a result, mortality from some waterborne infections did not decline until the introduction of filtration systems. On the other hand, improvement of sanitation, hygiene, and housing could actually magnify diseases hitherto innocuous. The appearance of the paralytic form of poliomyelitis is one such example. Poliomyelitis is a common enteric disease. In the nineteenth century most children had contracted the disease by the time they were three or four years old. At that age the symptoms included a low fever, headache, and sore throat. The production of antibodies

inhibited the virus's spread, and recovery occurred within two or three days. The result was lasting immunity.

The later in life an individual is exposed to the disease, however, the greater the chance that the virus will reach the spinal cord and brain, where it is devastating. Middle- and upper-class children raised in relatively clean households did not have early exposure and thus did not acquire immunity. Therefore, when they were older, they had far higher rates of the paralytic form of the disease than did people who as children had lived in poor and crowded neighborhoods, been exposed, and acquired immunity. Polio, in other words, was a disease whose impact was magnified by cleanliness. Franklin Delano Roosevelt is a prime example. Raised in privileged surroundings, he was exposed as an adult, developed the paralytic form, and could never again walk unaided.

Shifts. Despite epidemiological shifts, infectious diseases still accounted for 56 percent of total mortality in 1900. The highest death rates were among infants and children; the major killers were gastrointestinal and respiratory diseases, as well as diseases associated with childhood, such as measles, scarlet fever, diphtheria, and whooping cough. By World War II these diseases, though still prevalent, were insignificant causes of mortality. In 1950, heart disease, cancer, and stroke accounted for slightly more than 60 percent of total mortality.

What was the cause, or causes, of this massive shift in morbidity and mortality patterns? Most scholars agree that medical interventions played a relatively minor role. Prior to 1940 the primary function of medicine was the diagnosis of disease. With the exception of surgical procedures, antitoxins (e.g., for diphtheria), smallpox immunization, and drugs such as digitalis and insulin, physicians had few effective therapies to deal with infections. Antibiotic therapy was not widely used until the 1940s, and the development of vaccines for many viral diseases lay in the future. Yet by 1940 infectious diseases had ceased to be a major element in mortality patterns. Indeed, after 1945 the widespread use of antibiotic therapy fostered a belief that infectious diseases—historically the major elements in mortality—would no longer play so decisive a role in either morbidity or mortality.

It is far easier to describe than to explain the decline in mortality from infectious diseases. Many scholars have attributed it to economic growth and a rising standard of living. The difficulty with such global explanations is that they are not based on empirical data that shed light on the precise mechanisms responsible for the mortality decline for specific diseases. Some have pointed to dietary improvements as the most important factor. Yet the relationship between diet—excluding severe malnutrition, which rarely existed in the United States—and most infectious diseases is tenuous at best. Moreover, economic growth involves more than increased living standards; it also involves rising levels of literacy, education, and a variety of other complex social changes. Some of these changes and their interactions—including housing arrangements, population density, water and food purity, personal hygiene, individual behavioral patterns, and public-health interventions—may have had a more direct influence on mortality levels. Although the importance of economic development in the reduction of mortality is generally recognized, no consensus exists on the precise role of specific factors.

Mortality from specific infectious diseases often declined in specific ways. In the case of tuberculosis, mortality began to fall well before overt efforts were made to contain the disease. Improved diets and a reduction in exposure thanks to better housing and the construction of sanatoriums may account for growing resistance to the disease, but the evidence for them is inconclusive. The fall in infant mortality from diarrheal diseases probably followed changes in baby-feeding practices, improvement in the milk supply (pasteurization), and the efforts by public-health authorities to sensitize parents to more effective means of care and prevention. Greater attention to sick children may explain why measles (which often led to respiratory complications) declined as a cause of mortality even while incidence remained high. Mortality from scarlet and rheumatic fever, by contrast, probably declined because of changes in the virulence of the bacteria and a fall in household population density.

Chronic Diseases. To emphasize the importance of infectious diseases as the major cause of mortality before 1900 is not to imply that long-duration or chronic diseases were unimportant. The fact of the matter was that high death rates among the young tended to overshadow the presence of chronic illnesses and disabilities among both young and older adults. Moreover, the changes that transformed American society magnified older, and created novel, occupational dangers. Dusty environments, unsafe machinery, the use of toxic substances, high rates of industrial accidents, and crowded workplaces magnified occupational diseases that often led to severe disabilities as well as death.

The mortality decline among infants and children that began in the late nineteenth century meant that more Americans survived to old age. The longer individuals survived, the more likely they were to die from cancer or from cardiovascular or pulmonary diseases. At the end of the twentieth century these diseases accounted for more than two-thirds of total mortality.

Focus on Risk Factors. To explain the etiology of long-duration or chronic diseases is also not an easy task. Since the later twentieth century the emphasis has been on the role of risk factors in disease etiology, which in turn leads to the belief that a major role for medicine is to prevent disease by modifying the risks responsible for the disease. Thus the management of risk, in addition to the treatment of disease, has become a major theme in medical practice. Such a function, of course, places considerable responsibility for disease upon individual behavior. Efforts to demonstrate the importance of risk factors in disease etiology, however, have been fraught with pitfalls. Many of the epidemiological studies attempting to identify risk factors for a variety of other diseases suffer from methodological shortcomings. The examples of coronary heart disease (CHD) and cancer—the two major causes of mortality in the twenty-first century—are illustrative.

Between 1900 and 1920 the death rate from CHD remained more or less stable. About 1920 an upward trend commenced and continued unabated for thirty years. The rise was especially concentrated among young males in their thirties and forties. This increase was international in scope and occurred in more than two dozen countries among people with quite different lifestyles. Somewhere in the 1950s mortality rates began to fall. Between 1950 and 2006, age-specific mortality rates for all heart diseases fell from 587 per 100,000 to 200, and CHD became largely a disease of the very old.

What explains this pattern? In 1944, Paul Dudley White—perhaps the nation's most famous cardiologist—expressed puzzlement. "Why should the robust and apparently most masculine young males be particularly prone to this disease?" he wrote in his authoritative *Heart Disease* (482). A decade later Ancel Keys developed the thesis that dietary fat raised serum cholesterol and led to atherosclerosis. At about the same time the Framingham Heart Study—a community study in Massachusetts that began in 1948 and tracked three generations of residents—seemed to indicate that hypertension, obesity, smoking, and a family history of heart disease played crucial roles in CHD. A variety of other studies reached similar conclusions.

Although immensely popular, the emphasis on risk factors as major elements in the etiology of CHD is not entirely persuasive. Why did CHD mortality rise among younger males in their thirties and forties between the 1920s and 1950s, particularly since many of the alleged risk factors were unimportant until the late twentieth century? Why did mortality increase during the Great Depression of the 1930s and World War II when rich diets and sedentary lifestyles were uncommon? To be sure, cigarette smoking became prominent in the 1920s, but its health effects did not appear until several decades later. Moreover, CHD mortality began to decline sometime in the 1950s, well before the emphasis on risk factors to promote behavioral change and the introduction of statins to lower cholesterol and other medications could have had any effect. Claims that medical interventions and behavioral modifications explain the decline in CHD mortality after 1980 ignore that the decline began more than two decades earlier. Comparative data from other countries fail to substantiate the claim that risk factors—notably high-fat diets—explain CHD mortality.

Like CHD, cancer presents similar enigmas. Oddly enough, despite decades of research and the introduction of a variety of therapies, cancer mortality rates have not fluctuated radically since 1950, although the mix of cancers has changed. In 1950 the death rate was 194 per 100,000; in 2006 the comparable figure was 181. What is clear is that mortality rates for cancer increase with age. Between twenty-five and thirty-four the mortality rate is 11 per 100,000, whereas between sixty-five and seventy-four it is 841.

Speculation about cancer etiology has involved a myriad of competing theories. Heredity, microbes, viruses, irritations, occupation, diet, toxins, behavior, environment, and stress were all advanced at one time or another as causes of cancer. That smoking and exposure to a relatively small number of chemicals and radiation can cause cancer seems clear. These examples fostered the emergence of an explanatory model that emphasized an environmental and behavioral etiology for virtually all cancers. This model rested on epidemiological research that relied on cohort analysis and observational studies. In such studies, investigators monitor disease rates and lifestyle factors (e.g., diet, physical activity) and then infer conclusions about the relation between them. Thus they identify risk factors—such as noting that high fat diets are associated with, and so perhaps lead to, cardiovascular disease. The problem is that risk factors are associations. At best, cohort analysis and observational studies can generate hypotheses; they can say nothing about causation. Indeed, the etiology of most common cancers (breast, colon, prostate) is unknown, even though research has shown that genetic changes (e.g., impairment of tumor-suppression genes) play a major role. Epidemiological studies, however valuable, are often limited by methodological inadequacies and often fail to shed light on pathological mechanisms.

Cancer, cardiovascular-renal disease, diabetes, mental illnesses, and other long-duration illnesses, many of which are associated with age, are also accompanied by high rates of disability. Not all disabilities, to be sure, result from illnesses; developmental and injury-related disabilities are not necessarily the consequence of disease. But many pathologies—including osteoarthritis, cancer, heart disease, diabetes, and Alzheimer's disease—increase the risk of disability. Indeed, in 1990 the Institute of Medicine estimated that 35 million Americans, or one in seven, had a physical or mental impairment that hampered their daily activities, and perhaps 9 million were unable to work, attend school, or maintain a household.

Disease despite Antibiotics. The development after 1945 of antibiotic therapy and vaccines to prevent various diseases fostered a belief that infectious diseases might cause transient discomforts but would never again become major threats to health or life. This belief, however, rested on a shaky foundation. Faith in antibiotic therapy failed to take into account the evolution of resistant strains. In recent decades, for example, multidrug-resistant strains of the tubercle bacillus emerged. Consequently, infectious diseases continued to play a significant direct role in morbidity and perhaps an equally important if indirect role in mortality.

The example of HIV/AIDS, which appeared in 1981, is instructive. A retrovirus—human immunodeficiency virus (HIV-1)—compromises T cells, a critical component of the immune system, which renders the individual susceptible to a host of opportunistic infections and diseases that often prove fatal. HIV is transmitted in a variety of ways, including sexual contact, contaminated needles used by intravenous drug users, blood transfusions, and blood from a pregnant mother to her fetus. By 1996 there were about half a million reported cases and 340,000 deaths.

Influenza, sexually transmitted diseases, and hospital-acquired infections are other examples of diseases that, under certain conditions, can have high mortality rates. Human factors often play a role in the dissemination of infectious pathogens. Crowding, the increased density of susceptible hosts, the domestication of animals, the intermingling and rapid movement of populations, and changing behavioral norms all play roles in shaping the pattern of infectious diseases.

The Future. Since the late twentieth century, interest groups whose purpose is to conquer or prevent specific diseases have received a great deal of publicity and have even played significant roles in the allocation of federal biomedical research funds. Nevertheless, the historical record offers little to sustain the belief that the "conquest" of disease is a realistic possibility. Most contemporary diseases, as David Weatherall has noted, do not have a single cause; they have "complex and multiple pathologies that reflect the effects of both nature and nurture together with the damage that our tissues sustain as we age." Human systems are complex and interactive, and they involve large numbers of genes; there are multiple routes to a given disease (312–316).

What, then, can we expect in the future? A wise answer to this question was given by George H. Bigelow and Herbert L. Lombard in an important study of chronic disease written in 1933. "Is it not that we would have, after a span of years passed in reasonable serenity, a reduction to a minimum of the span of crippling and terminal illness, and then a humane departure, which can certainly be faced with more assurance than could an irrevocable guarantee of immortality here.... [The goal is not to] entirely eliminate disease and death but ... delay them and make them more humane" (2).

[*See also* Alcohol and Alcohol Abuse; Asylums and Mental Illness; Atlantic World; Columbian Exchange; Death and Dying; Demography; Everyday Life; Health and Fitness; Health and Healing, Eighteenth and Nineteenth Centuries; Hospitals and Dispensaries; Internal Migration; Life Expectancy; Medicine, Popular and Non-Western; Oregon Trail; Sanitary Commission, U.S.; *and* Santa Fe Trail.]

BIBLIOGRAPHY

Ackerknecht, Erwin H. *Malaria in the Upper Mississippi Valley, 1760–1900.* Baltimore: Johns Hopkins University Press, 1945.

Aronowitz, Robert A. *Making Sense of Illness: Science, Society, and Disease.* New York: Cambridge University Press, 1998.

Bigelow, George H., and Herbert L. Lombard. *Cancer and Other Chronic Diseases in Massachusetts.* Boston: Houghton Mifflin, 1933.

Brandt, Allan M. *No Magic Bullet: A Social History of Venereal Disease in the United States since 1880.* Expanded ed. New York: Oxford University Press, 1987.

Crosby, Alfred W., Jr. *The Columbian Exchange: Biological and Cultural Consequences of 1492.* Westport, Conn.: Greenwood, 1972.

Dubos, René. *The Dreams of Reason: Science and Utopias.* New York: Columbia University Press, 1961.

Duffy, John. *Epidemics in Colonial America.* Baton Rouge: Louisiana State University Press, 1953.

Feinstein, Alvin R. "Scientific Standards in Epidemiologic Studies of the Menace of Daily Life." *Science* 242, no. 4883 (1988): 1257–1263.

Griscom, John H. *The Sanitary Condition of the Laboring Population of New York.* New York: Harper and Brothers, 1845.

Grob, Gerald N. *The Deadly Truth: A History of Disease in America.* Cambridge, Mass.: Harvard University Press, 2002.

Grob, Gerald N., and Allan V. Horwitz. *Diagnosis, Therapy, and Evidence: Conundrums in Modern American Medicine.* New Brunswick, N.J.: Rutgers University Press, 2010.

Humphreys, Margaret. *Malaria, Poverty, Race, and Public Health in the United States.* Baltimore: Johns Hopkins University Press, 2001.

Kraut, Alan M. *Silent Travelers: Germs, Genes, and the "Immigrant Menace."* New York: Basic Books, 1994.

Kunitz, Stephen J. "Mortality Change in America, 1620–1920." *Human Biology* 56 (1984): 559–582.

Maulitz, Russell C., ed. *Unnatural Causes: The Three Leading Killer Diseases in America.* New Brunswick, N.J.: Rutgers University Press, 1988.

McKinlay, John B., and Sonja M. McKinlay. "The Questionable Contribution of Medical Measures to the Decline of Mortality in the United States in the Twentieth Century." *Milbank Memorial Fund Quarterly* 55 (1977): 405–428.

Meckel, Richard A. *Save the Babies: American Public Health Reform and the Prevention of Infant Mortality,* 1850–1929. Baltimore: Johns Hopkins University Press, 1990.

Mukherjee, Siddhartha. *The Emperor of All Maladies: A Biography of Cancer.* New York: Scribner, 2010.

Oshinsky, David M. *Polio: An American Story.* New York: Oxford University Press, 2005.

Pickard, Madge E., and R. Carlyle Buley. *The Midwest Pioneer: His Ills, Cures, and Doctors.* Crawfordsville, Ind.: R. E. Banta, 1945.

Preston, Samuel H., and Michael R. Haines. *Fatal Years: Child Mortality in Late Nineteenth Century America.* Princeton, N.J.: Princeton University Press, 1991.

Rosenberg, Charles E. *Our Present Complaint: American Medicine, Then and Now.* Baltimore: Johns Hopkins University Press, 2007.

Rosner, David, ed. *Hives of Sickness: Public Health and Epidemics in New York City.* New Brunswick, N.J.: Rutgers University Press, 1995.

Rothstein, William G. *Public Health and the Risk Factor: A History of an Uneven Medical Revolution.* Rochester, N.Y.: University of Rochester Press, 2003.

Savitt, Todd L. *Medicine and Slavery: The Diseases and Health Care of Blacks in Antebellum Virginia.* Urbana: University of Illinois Press, 1978.

Stallones, Reuel A. "The Rise and Fall of Ischemic Heart Disease." *Scientific American* 243 (1980): 53–59.

Tarr, Joel A. *The Search for the Ultimate Sink: Urban Pollution in Historical Perspective.* Akron, Ohio: University of Akron Press, 1996.

Wailoo, Keith. *How Cancer Crossed the Color Line.* New York: Oxford University Press, 2011.

Weatherall, David J. *Science and the Quiet Art: The Role of Medical Research in Health Care.* New York: W. W. Norton and Company, 1995.

Gerald N. Grob

DISNEY AMUSEMENT PARKS

Opened to the public in the summer of 1955 amid former orange groves in Anaheim, California, about twenty-five miles south of Los Angeles, Disneyland Park almost immediately became an icon of American Cold War culture. Inspired by urban amusement parks such as Brooklyn's Coney Island, seasonal county fairs, and international expositions, this new venue marketed itself as a "theme park," organizing its attractions in thematically consistent spaces arranged around mythical subjects.

Geared explicitly toward the normative white middle-class families that dominated the culture of the era, Disneyland substituted culturally hegemonic narratives and a controlled environment for the chaotic midway attractions, carnivalesque transgressions of decorum, and heterosocial sexual play that characterized previous amusement parks. Indeed, Disneyland's enormous cultural appeal during the postwar period can be attributed to the extent to which its attractions mirrored dominant ideologies and reinforced conventional, even reactionary, visions of society. For instance, entering the park through Main Street USA, the visitor thus was immediately immersed in a nostalgic fantasy of small-town Americana that was sharply at odds even in 1955 with the increasingly diverse surrounding metropolis of Los Angeles. Adventureland concatenated an array of Western Orientalist impressions of Africa, Asia, and Latin America, presenting familiar colonialist oppositions between "civilization" and darkly exciting "savagery" through such attractions as the Jungle Cruise boat ride. Frontierland did the same for the American West, inspired by Disney's own fabulously successful and highly fictionalized "Davy Crockett" series that had aired nationally on Disneyland's televisual counterpart, also originally called *Disneyland*.

The interconnection of fantasy narrative and physical space, simulation and real, inspired a generation of social theorists to take Disneyland as a prime example of what Umberto Eco termed the "hyperreal" aspects of mass-mediated American culture. Disneyland also impressed city planners and architects by the way in which the theme park embeds emotional cues and stories into the layout and design of its emblematic "lands," all legibly arrayed around a central hub marked by a visually arresting central architectural icon, such as Sleeping Beauty's Castle.

Disneyland soon drew visitors from around the world, and by the early twenty-first century more than 600 million were estimated to have visited since its opening. Inspired by that success, Walt Disney World in central Florida opened for business in 1971; eventually it became the most visited vacation destination in the world. Disney theme parks in Tokyo (1983), Paris (1992), and Hong Kong (2005) followed, with a Shanghai venue scheduled to open in 2016. The ability of the Disney Corporation to translate and adapt quintessentially American ideologies and narratives into different cultural contexts distinguishes these theme parks as exemplary case studies in globalization, just as the parks themselves exemplify the interconnections in contemporary society between popular ideological narratives, corporate mass media, recreational tourism, mass-marketed commodity consumption, and the tightly controlled privatization of architectural space.

[*See also* **Amusement Parks and Theme Parks; Consumption; Leisure;** *and* **Tourism and Travel.**]

BIBLIOGRAPHY

Eco, Umberto. *Travels in Hyper Reality: Essays.* Translated by William Weaver. San Diego, Calif.: Harcourt Brace Jovanovich, 1986. The essay "Travels in Hyper Reality" was published in 1975.

Kasson, John F. *Amusing the Million: Coney Island at the Turn of the Century.* New York: Hill and Wang, 1978.

Marling, Karal Ann. "Disneyland, 1955: Just Take the Santa Ana Freeway to the American Dream." *American Art* 5, nos. 1–2 (Winter–Spring 1991): 169–207.

Jeremiah B. C. Axelrod

DIX, DOROTHEA

(1802–1887), social reformer. Dorothea Lynde Dix, born in Hampden, Maine, on 4 April 1802, became a successful teacher and author but as a devout Unitarian felt unfulfilled until she embarked upon the mission that made her famous. In 1841, Samuel Gridley Howe, a reform-minded member of the Massachusetts legislature, urged her to investigate the condition of the indigent insane in that state. Dix did so zealously and then wrote an impassioned memorial in which she described pens, jails, and poorhouses where deranged inmates endured beatings, filth, and cold. When the legislature subsequently voted to enlarge the state insane asylum at Worcester, Dix had found her calling.

For the rest of her active life, Dix had no permanent home. She traveled tirelessly, gathering evidence, writing memorials, and lobbying state legislatures to establish new asylums or expand existing ones. Although the impact of her efforts cannot be measured precisely, it appears indisputable that Dix did more than anyone else to make the funding of mental hospitals the single greatest social-welfare expenditure of American states in the nineteenth century. In 1848, Dix extended her campaign to the federal government, seeking to have the revenue from millions of acres of the public lands dedicated to the support of the state asylums. Her bill was passed in Congress but was vetoed by President Franklin Pierce in 1854.

Dix was active in other causes, especially prison reform and the funding of schools for children with disabilities. She was, however, antipathetic toward the two greatest reform movements of her age: Antislavery and the Woman Suffrage Movement. Steering clear of abolitionism permitted Dix to carry her campaign for insanity reform into the southern states. Shunning women's rights and portraying herself as a paragon of feminine benevolence and self-sacrifice gave her leverage over conservative male politicians. Yet her stances were not merely expedient. She genuinely believed that God intended women to remain within their separate domestic sphere, and she regarded African Americans as belonging to an inferior childlike race for whom a life in bondage was no tribulation.

Dix's later years were troubled. At the outbreak of the Civil War, she volunteered her unpaid services as superintendent of women nurses for the Union army. When the war morphed into a titanic struggle that almost nobody had foreseen, she was overwhelmed by an administrative task for which she was entirely unsuited. After the war she resumed campaigning on behalf of her beloved hospitals, but by then it was becoming evident that cures for insanity were far more elusive than either medical experts or Dix had earlier believed. Consequently, many hospitals had become badly overcrowded, and some of them afforded conditions only marginally better than those of the prisons and poorhouses

that had so horrified Dix at the start of her crusade. She carried on undaunted until 1881, when illness and debility ended her travels. Dix retired into modest rooms that had been set aside for her use in the New Jersey state mental hospital at Trenton. Physically frail but mentally sound to the end, she died there on 17 July 1887.

[*See also* **Antebellum Reform; Asylums and Mental Illness; Prisons and Penitentiaries;** *and* **Public Health.**]

BIBLIOGRAPHY

Brown, Thomas J. *Dorothea Dix: New England Reformer.* Cambridge, Mass.: Harvard University Press, 1998. A factual and balanced portrait.

Gollaher, David. *Voice for the Mad: The Life of Dorothea Dix.* New York: Free Press, 1995. Although necessarily speculative, Gollaher's psychodynamic analysis is both fascinating and plausible.

Tiffany, Francis. *Life of Dorothea Lynde Dix.* Boston: Houghton, Mifflin and Company, 1890. The earliest of many hagiographies.

David L. Lightner

DOMESTIC WORKERS

Since the colonial era, domestic labor has been a significant contributor to economic production and development in America. Though domestic labor encompasses a wide range of market and nonmarket activities, this article will focus on three major productive elements: household manufactures for home consumption; industrial outwork, a form of wage labor conducted in the home; and independent production within the home for sale in wider commodity markets.

From Rural Areas to Urban. Household manufactures for home consumption prevailed as a system of domestic labor in rural areas prior to the era of industrialization. With the emergence of mechanized textile, shoe, and garment production after 1830, household manufactures declined steadily. With the growth of the factory system in the nineteenth century, initially concentrated in New England and the mid-Atlantic states, household manufactures declined in those regions, while remaining substantial in the South and Middle West. The rapid expansion of commercial markets for items previously produced within the home substantially reduced household manufacturing across the United States. American families after World War II rarely produced goods at home for their own consumption.

Independent production within the home for sale in broader markets declined at the same time. Such independent production was more commonly concentrated in cities than in rural areas. In the first half of the nineteenth century, independent male weavers or shoemakers often worked in their own homes, drawing upon the unpaid labor of family members for certain steps in the production process. Women dressmakers and laundry workers also brought work home and commonly sold their services to a varied clientele. Technological developments and the steady commodification of goods and services undermined independent production within the home. Increasingly individuals who performed such work at home were displaced by wageworkers employed in urban factories and shops that took advantage of machinery or economies of scale to undersell homeworkers.

Industrial outwork, by contrast, has had a much longer and more significant history. For almost 150 years, a substantial share of industrial wage-work was performed in workers' homes. From the emergence of the first factories in the 1790s until the passage of the Fair Labor Standards Act in 1938, employers found it economical to distribute work to be performed outside factories or workshops. Rural and urban residents alike were drawn into a system of dispersed contracting out, earning wages for domestic labor performed with raw materials owned by their employers and producing goods for sale in distant markets.

Industrial outwork flourished initially in rural communities: wives and daughters in farming families supplemented farm income by laboring for textile mills, storekeepers, or middlemen who distributed raw materials throughout the countryside and sold the finished cloth, hats, and shoes in widely dispersed markets. The first water-powered cotton spinning mills typically expanded production by putting out yarn to be woven by members of farming families. Handloom weaving on an outwork basis grew significantly in New England in the early nineteenth century, but it declined after the mid-1820s with the adoption of the power loom. Farm women turned to braided straw hats and palm-leaf hats as an outwork occupation, and by 1837 more than fifty thousand women and children were employed on a part-time basis in Massachusetts alone. At about the same time, farm women also worked at binding and stitching shoe uppers. By midcentury a decentralized hybrid system had developed: much of shoe binding was done by women in their own homes, while male artisans working in small urban shops did the shoemaking itself. Domestic labor in boot and shoe manufacturing declined sharply after the Civil War with the fuller mechanization of shoemaking and the adoption of steam power in urban factories.

In the Gilded Age the garment industry became the leading employer of homeworkers. In Boston, for instance, clothing manufacturers put cut goods into rural communities;

by 1870, Boston employers paid some $2 million in wages to a workforce of about fifty thousand New England farm women. By then, however, urban homework in the garment industry dwarfed its rural cousin. In Boston, New York City, and Philadelphia, home employment in the needle trades came to be known as the "sweating" system, as women and children in urban immigrant families earned meager wages from employers whose exploitative practices led them to be known as "sweaters." By the early twentieth century, the impoverishment of immigrant families and the squalid conditions within which they worked and lived attracted the concern of Progressive Era reformers, who lobbied to outlaw tenement-house production and child labor in manufacturing.

Regulation and Deregulation. Whereas in the antebellum era, rural outwork had been a part-time occupation for members of farming families, its later urban counterpart was full-time and highly exploitative, depending on a system of underpaid subcontracting that forced workers to put in long hours during peak seasons simply to survive. The low wages and long hours of homeworkers, in turn, undermined wages and employment in factories and workshops. State and local efforts to regulate or outlaw homework were typically stymied by court rulings: the U.S. Supreme Court's decision in *Lochner v. New York* (1905), for example, protected workers' putative right to "freedom of contract" under the Fourteenth Amendment. Only when Congress enacted the Fair Labor Standards Act in the New Deal era did industrial outwork become largely unprofitable. Afterward, the federal government's enforcement of wage and hours regulations on homeworkers and the outright ban of homework in a number of industries sharply limited these practices.

Industrial outwork, though exploitative, has nonetheless had a certain appeal for individuals and families that have sought to work within its bounds. In an economic system in which the wages of male household heads were—and often still are—insufficient to support a family, outwork permitted the employment of children and married women to supplement family income. Homework has also permitted women homemakers to combine housekeeping, cooking, and child rearing with wage-earning activities. Homework has had a certain logic for urban immigrant families in the United States since the early twentieth century, but it has been a logic based on the inadequacy of state regulation of wages and hours of labor.

At the end of the twentieth century industrial outwork made a comeback with the growth of an underground, largely immigrant economy in the garment trades of New York, Los Angeles, and other large cities. In the 1980s the administration of Ronald Reagan rescinded the laws against homework in several industries and cut back on regulatory enforcement. These steps, coupled with the growth of telecommuting among white-collar clerical workers, led to a resurgence of homework. Whether this form of domestic labor will see continued growth depends on future technological changes and legal struggles. Homework, then, is an issue that refuses to go away.

[*See also* **Child Workers; Cities and Suburbs; Clothing; Immigration; New Deal Social Reforms; Poverty; Women Workers; Work;** *and* **Working-Class Life and Society.**]

BIBLIOGRAPHY

Boris, Eileen. *Home to Work: Motherhood and the Politics of Industrial Homework in the United States.* Cambridge, U.K.: Cambridge University Press, 1994.

Boris, Eileen, and Cynthia R. Daniels, eds. *Homework: Historical and Contemporary Perspectives on Paid Labor at Home.* Urbana: University of Illinois Press, 1989.

Dublin, Thomas. "Rural Putting-Out Work in Early Nineteenth-Century New England: Women and the Transition to Capitalism in the Countryside." *New England Quarterly* 64 (1991): 531–573.

Dublin, Thomas. *Transforming Women's Work: New England Lives in the Industrial Revolution.* Ithaca, N.Y.: Cornell University Press, 1994.

Nobles, Gregory. "Merchant Middlemen in the Outwork Network of Rural New England." In *Merchant Credit and Labour Strategies in Historical Perspective*, edited by Rosemary E. Ommer, pp. 333–347. Fredericton, New Brunswick: Acadiensis Press, 1990.

Tryon, Rolla Milton. *Household Manufactures in the United States, 1640–1860: A Study in Industrial History.* Chicago: University of Chicago Press, 1917.

Thomas Dublin

DOMINICAN REPUBLIC AMERICANS

Large movements of Dominicans to the United States can be traced back to 1892. More than five thousand Dominicans traveled to New York City through Ellis Island from 1892 to 1924. Many of these early immigrants settled in various neighborhoods of New York City, including Harlem and Washington Heights. A major influx of Dominican immigrants occurred after the country's 1965 revolution, the subsequent U.S. invasion and occupation, and the ascendance of Joaquín Balaguer to the presidency of the Dominican Republic in 1966.

Under the tutelage of the United States, Balaguer transformed Dominican society by facilitating the penetration of massive foreign capital and emphasizing industrial production. Balaguer also took political control of the country by eliminating opposition, undermining civil liberties, and allowing political assassinations. His economic model failed to generate enough jobs to absorb the increasing working-age population, however; salaries remained low, while the prices of basic goods skyrocketed. Though birth control was openly imposed to control population growth, the emigration of thousands of Dominicans was a tacit solution to avoid potential social unrest and keep social order.

Dominican migration to the United States has been dominated by women: between 52 and 54 percent of Dominican immigrants in any given year are women. Prior to 1980, most migrants settled in New York City, but by 2008 less than half of all Dominicans in the United States lived in New York City. By the twenty-first century, New Jersey, Florida, Massachusetts, Pennsylvania, and Rhode Island were all home to large Dominican communities.

In the past, reflecting the numerical dominance of those born in the Dominican Republic, studies of Dominicans focused exclusively on analyzing immigrants. But this has changed. By the early twenty-first century, U.S.-born Dominicans accounted for the largest part of Dominican population growth. From 2000 to 2007, U.S.-born Dominicans represented more than three-quarters of the Dominican population increase. The rapidly growing second generation has been transforming the Dominican Americans, forcing scholars to rethink the stereotype that portrays Dominicans as immigrants who continue with one foot in the United States and the other in the Dominican Republic.

A large portion of U.S. Dominicans live below the poverty line, a reflection of Dominican Americans' low annual household income and high levels of unemployment. In 2008, Dominican per capita income in New York was $15,516, below that of Hispanics, which was $16,799 for the same year. Despite such distressing economic indicators, Dominicans have been achieving educational levels higher than those of other Latino subgroups; a middle class and elite class has also been forming at unprecedented rates. In 2008, a relatively high percentage of U.S.-born Dominicans had obtained at least a college degree: a higher percentage than of Puerto Rican Americans, Mexican Americans, or other U.S.-born Latinos. Whereas in 1970, 7 in 10 Dominicans twenty-five years of age or older did not have a high school diploma, by 2008 this proportion had declined to less than 4 in 10. Similarly, teachers, judges, elected officials, high-ranking members of government, and entrepreneurs, particularly owners of various supermarkets chains that generate approximately $3 billion per year, have emerged from the community, creating a complex Dominican social landscape in the United States.

[*See also* Caribbean; Immigration; *and* Transnational Identity.]

BIBLIOGRAPHY

Hernandez, Ramona. *The Mobility of Workers under Advanced Capitalism: Dominican Migration to the United States.* New York: Columbia University Press, 2002.

Hernandez, Ramona, and Anthony Stevens-Acevedo. "Dominican Immigrants." In *Multicultural America: An Encyclopedia of the Newest Americans,* edited by Ronald H. Bayor. 4 vols. Santa Barbara, Calif.: Greenwood, 2011.

Moya Pons, Frank. *Manual de historia dominicana.* 9th ed. Santo Domingo, Dominican Republic: Caribbean, 1992.

Ramona Hernandez

DOUGLASS, FREDERICK

(1818–1895), writer, orator, and crusader for social justice. Frederick Douglass, the most important black leader of the nineteenth century, was the preeminent figure in the movement to end American slavery.

Born on Maryland's Eastern Shore to a slave woman and a white man (probably his master), Frederick Augustus Washington Bailey passed a formative period of his childhood serving a woman who began, illegally, teaching him how to read. His literacy provided him both the tools necessary to escape slavery—which he accomplished at twenty—and his chosen surname, which he took from a British epic poem. Living in eastern Massachusetts, in 1841 he joined William Lloyd Garrison's American Anti-Slavery Society and became a powerful public speaker, agitating for emancipation and women's rights.

Douglass chronicled his early life, escape, and entry into abolitionism in the *Narrative of the Life of Frederick Douglass, an American Slave* (1845), which remains among the finest works of American autobiography. Through both eloquent testimony of slavery's cruelties and piercing analysis of its social toxicity, the *Narrative* established Douglass's formidable intellect, transcending the role of embodied victimhood that white abolitionists initially encouraged him to perform. By making Douglass's then-disputed personal history verifiable, however, its publication also exposed him to legal recapture, occasioning his departure for England. After two years, British supporters raised the money to purchase his freedom. He returned to the United States a free man and moved to Rochester, New York, where he started his own newspaper, the *North Star*. His newspaper writings, decades of oratory unmatched for rhetorical brilliance, and two subsequent autobiographies—*My Bondage and My Freedom* (1855) and the *Life and Times of Frederick Douglass* (1881)—have made him a giant of American letters.

Douglass worked closely with the Garrisonians in the early 1840s, but his move to Rochester indicated growing estrangement.

Though he never ceased to acknowledge Garrison's inspiration, Douglass had come to resent his mentor's racial condescension (all too common among white abolitionists) and dogmatic leadership. Moreover, as the question of slavery's western expansion increasingly dominated public debate in the 1850s, Douglass saw promise in electoral politics, an arena that Garrison stubbornly shunned. When Douglass joined the abolitionist Gerrit Smith's Liberty Party and declared in print that the Constitution was fundamentally antislavery—thereby repudiating one of Garrison's central tenets, the Constitution's proslavery nature—he completed his break with the elder antislavery leader.

Douglass also began a pattern of pragmatism: taking up the most effective weapons to battle slavery and racism, even if wielding them meant compromising on principle. Foreseeing his Liberty Party's failure in the 1856 presidential election, Douglass endorsed the Republican John C. Frémont in June; despite advising John Brown against the 1859 Harpers Ferry raid, he gave aid to the enterprise; and, losing hope amid increasingly vitriolic racism just before war broke out, he reversed a decades-long opposition to colonization schemes, endorsing African American emigration to Haiti and even planning his own trip there. When war erupted, however, Douglass disavowed emigration again.

Having struggled to reconcile millennialist visions for emancipation and racial equality with the stark reality of American bigotry, Douglass greeted the Civil War as a biblical reckoning. Abraham Lincoln consequently infuriated Douglass by advocating, well into the war, colonization schemes and the necessity of racial separation. Lincoln's 1862 address to a delegation of black leaders, in which he denied the possibility of racial equality and blamed the war on the presence of blacks in America, earned him a bitter rebuke from Douglass as "a genuine representative of American prejudice and Negro hatred."

Nevertheless, Douglass remained a steadfast Republican. He threw himself into Union propaganda, recruited black soldiers, and insisted that the war be understood as a quest to vanquish slavery, a view that Lincoln vindicated by issuing the Emancipation Proclamation on 1 January 1863. Douglass subsequently met with the president twice in the White House to advise him on matters of war and politics. Despite their differences, Douglass found himself "well satisfied with the man."

In the 1870s Douglass's joy in emancipation and Union victory veered into disappointment as tenacious white supremacy derailed Reconstruction and began systematically denying freedmen their rights. Nevertheless, through speeches and writings he continued to fight for racial and women's equality. He attacked Jim Crow, lynching, and the insidious "lost cause" narrative of the Civil War as a dispute over states' rights. A Republican until his death, Douglass served as U.S. marshal (1877–1881) and recorder of deeds (1881–1886) of Washington, D.C., and as a U.S. representative in Haiti (1889–1891).

On 20 February 1895, Douglass died in Washington. As one newspaper put it the following day, he died "in an epoch which he did more than any other man to create."

[See also **Antebellum Era; Antislavery; Civil War Era; Emancipation of Slaves; Reconstruction Era; Slavery,** *subentry on* **Nineteenth Century;** *and* **Women's Rights Movement, Antebellum Era.**]

BIBLIOGRAPHY

Blight, David W. *Frederick Douglass' Civil War: Keeping Faith in Jubilee.* Baton Rouge: Louisiana State University Press, 1989.

Douglass, Frederick. *Autobiographies*. Edited by Henry Louis Gates. New York: Library of America, 1994. Includes the *Narrative of the Life of Frederick Douglass, an American Slave, My Bondage and My Freedom,* and the *Life and Times of Frederick Douglass.*

Stauffer, John. *The Black Hearts of Men: Radical Abolitionists and the Transformation of Race.* Cambridge, Mass.: Harvard University Press, 2001.

David N. Huyssen

DRAFT RIOTS, CIVIL WAR

By late 1862, as Civil War casualties mounted in costly military campaigns, the patriotic fervor that had inspired many men in the North to enlist was waning. The Emancipation Proclamation further eroded support for the war in some quarters. Accordingly, in March 1863, Congress passed the Conscription Act to draft men into military service. Racial animosity, dissatisfaction with the administration of Abraham Lincoln, and labor unrest all helped fuel opposition to the draft. Most odious to many was the commutation clause, which enabled a draftee to avoid service by hiring a substitute or paying a $300 fee. Draft resistance erupted across the Middle West but was concentrated in Ohio, Indiana, and Iowa. New England resistance was centered mainly in Boston, Vermont, and New Hampshire. Violent opposition also broke out in the Pennsylvania coal regions.

The most serious outburst arose in July 1863 in New York City, where Irish American immigrants bitterly resented the draft and feared job competition from free blacks. Violence erupted on 13 July and continued for four days, as mobs attacked draft offices, public buildings, the homes of city officials and Republican Party leaders, and African Americans. Many blacks were lynched, and an African American orphanage was destroyed. The rioting ended only after Lincoln dispatched to the city Union troops from General George Meade's army, which was pursuing the Confederates after the battle of Gettysburg. Overall, the violence claimed at least 105 lives.

The draft riots had several aftereffects. Draft resistance continued, but on a lesser scale after the New York City riot. In 1864, Congress repealed the commutation clause. Federal authorities vigorously enforced later drafts, employing sufficient military force to quell any resistance. In politics, Tammany Hall, the Democratic Party's New York City machine, arose from the ashes of the riots by balancing the interests of immigrants and workers with those of the conservative elite.

[*See also* **Civil War Era; Military Personnel,** *subentry on* **Civil War; Riots, Urban;** *and* **War Resisters.**]

BIBLIOGRAPHY

Bernstein, Iver. *The New York City Draft Riots: Their Significance for American Society and Politics in the Age of the Civil War.* New York: Oxford University Press, 1990.

Cook, Adrian. *The Armies of the Streets: The New York City Draft Riots of 1863.* Lexington: University Press of Kentucky, 1974.

Jonathan M. Berkey

DRUGS, ILLICIT

In the beginning there were no illicit drugs. From the seventeenth through the early nineteenth centuries, narcotics were simply part of medical practice. A few patients—and doctors—exhibited symptoms of opium addiction, but they were never numerous and posed no threat to the social order. The main problems were overdose and adulteration.

Imported from the Middle East, opium often contained sand, fruit pulp, flour, beeswax, lead, and the like. Indeed, the first national drug law, enacted in 1848, was intended to bar adulterated foreign drugs, not drugs per se.

In the later nineteenth century, narcotic addiction took on a more visible and sinister aspect. Morphine, the principal alkaloid of opium, came into wide use with the spread of hypodermic medication in the 1860s and 1870s. Morphine injected hypodermically was more addictive than opium taken orally. By the mid-1890s, perhaps as many as 220,000 Americans were addicted to morphine or another medicinal opiate. Contrary to legend, most addicts were not Civil War veterans, but rather ailing women introduced to morphine by physicians or through patent medicines, which often contained narcotics and alcohol.

Habitual opium smokers, mostly Chinese laborers and members of the white underworld, were less common, numbering at most ninety thousand by the mid-1890s. Regarded far less sympathetically than medical addicts, they inspired restrictive local and state legislation, typically designed to outlaw public opium dens. The possibility of sexual relations between white women and Chinese men in the dens stirred fears, though in fact Chinese smokers usually kept to themselves.

Nonmedical cocaine use inspired similar sexual anxieties. Like morphine, cocaine began its career as a promising new alkaloid drug. In the mid-1880s Parke, Davis, its leading U.S. manufacturer, promoted cocaine for a range of illnesses, from hay fever to alcoholism. Cocaine's outstanding therapeutic property, the local anesthesia first noted in 1884, helped to revolutionize surgery and dentistry. But overdose cases soon appeared in the medical literature. So, as early as 1886, warnings of addiction resulting from medical treatment began to emerge.

In the 1890s the popular press chronicled the growing use of cocaine in the underworld, where prostitutes, pimps, and gamblers added cocaine to their repertoire of cigarettes, alcohol, and opium. In 1900, half the prostitutes jailed in Fort Worth, Texas, were said to be cocaine addicts. By then cocaine was sufficiently cheap that ordinary laborers, including African Americans working on southern plantations and construction sites, could afford occasional use. A racially charged folklore sprang up, linking African American cocaine use to violent rampages and "increased and perverted" sexual desires.

Early Legislation. Alarmed city councils and state legislatures passed laws restricting cocaine's purchase to those holding a prescription from a licensed physician—a provision increasingly applied to opiates as well. But economic and competitive considerations tempted physicians, particularly older and marginal practitioners, to continue to prescribe liberally. Conscientious pharmacists criticized such practices and found catering to addicts distasteful. But they knew that spurned customers would take their lucrative business to rival druggists or, if necessary, to street dealers, middlemen who resold drugs acquired from unscrupulous pharmacists or manufacturers. Their customers included teenage boys in slums and vice districts who snorted "decks" of cocaine and heroin, a powerful derivative of morphine. Opium smokers also enjoyed a ready supply, courtesy of smugglers and illegal manufacturers who dodged the heavy customs duty. The cliché that the 1914 Harrison Narcotic Act created the black market and the drug subcultures of twentieth-century America is a political myth. Illegal sales, smuggling, and underworld use flourished decades before 1914. Drug abuse and trafficking spawned legislation, not the other way around.

The catalyst for national legislation, however, was the diplomatic situation in East Asia. American missionaries had long deplored the British opium trade in China. In 1905, they helped secure a policy of suppressing opium smoking in the Philippines, which had become a U.S. possession. In 1906, the Episcopal missionary bishop serving in the Philippines, Charles Henry Brent, asked for President Theodore Roosevelt's help in setting up an international opium conference, which finally convened in Shanghai in February 1909. But while the U.S. government was calling for suppression of the Asian opium traffic, it continued to tolerate (and tax) opium smoking at home. To refute charges of hypocrisy, Roosevelt's secretary of state, Elihu Root, persuaded Congress to prohibit imports of opium prepared for smoking. This legislation, signed into law a week after the opening of the 1909 Shanghai conference, represented the first nationwide ban on a particular type of drug. In this sense, smoking opium was America's first "illicit drug."

The next major piece of legislation, the 1914 Harrison Narcotic Act, required dealers in opiates and cocaine to register, pay a nominal tax, and keep accurate records of their transactions. Unregistered dealers faced prosecution. Thus narcotic distribution would be confined to legitimate medical channels and made a matter of public record.

The Harrison Act skirted a key issue: whether registered doctors and pharmacists could legally maintain a supply of drugs for those who were addicted. In 1919, the U.S. Supreme Court, in its 5 to 4 decision in *Webb et al. v. United States*, ruled that they could not. The federal antimaintenance policy, for which *Webb* provided the key precedent, had lasting implications, particularly after the Treasury Department quickly closed more than thirty experimental municipal clinics designed to provide a legal supply of drugs for addicts. The closures forced the addicts into the black market.

Patterns of Illicit Trafficking and Use.

In the 1920s, street drugs, mostly diverted from surplus European manufactures, were still relatively pure. However, international agreements in 1925 and 1931 made the large-scale diversion of legally manufactured drugs more difficult. Smuggled and adulterated heroin became the mainstay of the black market, which centered on New York City, home to approximately half the nation's non-medical narcotic addicts. In 1924, Congress effectively outlawed heroin, which, like smoking opium, was associated with vice and crime.

The Bureau of Narcotics, under the direction of Harry J. Anslinger from 1930 to 1962, vigorously suppressed the illicit drug traffic. Anslinger wanted traffickers behind bars and addicts either behind bars or in institutions like the federal prison hospitals in Lexington, Kentucky, and Fort Worth, Texas. Anslinger also worked to increase the scope and penalties of drug laws. He played a key role in the passage of the 1937 Marijuana Tax Act, which added a national ban to state and local legislation. Practically unknown before 1910, marijuana smoking was introduced by Mexican immigrant laborers and by Caribbean and South American sailors visiting New Orleans. By the 1930s it had spread to New York, Chicago, and other cities. Popular among jazz musicians and urban hipsters, marijuana offered a cheap high, fifteen cents for a "reefer" in a Harlem "tea pad." At first, Anslinger and other authorities condemned marijuana for inciting wild violence. Later they emphasized its role as a stepping-stone drug. More than half of young heroin addicts had started with marijuana, Anslinger testified in 1951. When they had become bored with marijuana, they had begun injecting the stronger heroin.

Though most young addicts had indeed smoked marijuana, the most important precursors of heroin addiction were social and geographic. The typical postwar addict was a young man living in a ghetto or barrio near a heroin-trafficking area in New York, Chicago, Los Angeles, or another large industrial city. He had come from a single-parent family, dropped out of high school, and had poor job prospects and few conventional aspirations. He aspired instead to a hipster lifestyle centered on jazz, drugs, and "hustling"—criminal activity that accelerated the flight from cities of longtime residents and businesses, feeding a lethal cycle of isolation, poverty, and depopulation. "Heroin," as the historian Eric Schneider put it, "was a city-killing drug" (Eric C. Schneider, *Smack: Heroin and the American City* [Philadelphia: University of Pennsylvania Press, 2008], p. ix). Increasingly it was also an African American drug. The older white and Chinese narcotic addicts, who had been addicted before World War II, were either burning out or dying off. In the early 1930s, only one of every four Detroit addicts known to officials was African American. By 1951, four out of five were.

Concern over the post–World War II resurgence of heroin trafficking and addiction prompted Congress to enact the 1951 Boggs Act and the 1956 Narcotic Control Act, which provided progressively stiffer mandatory sentences, all the way up to the death penalty for selling heroin to minors. States followed suit. Texas made marijuana possession punishable by life imprisonment. The prison-mindedness of drug policy provoked a reaction among those who viewed addiction as a public health problem. In 1958, a joint committee of the American Bar Association and the American Medical Association criticized the police approach and suggested the possibility of a controlled legal supply. In the 1960s, two physicians, Vincent Dole and Marie Nyswander, showed that heroin addicts could be maintained indefinitely on oral methadone, a synthetic narcotic. Their work challenged both the antimaintenance policy and the reigning explanation of addiction, which held that addicts suffered from defective, often psychopathic, personalities. For Dole and Nyswander, addicts were more or less normal people whose drug use triggered a permanent metabolic change. They needed narcotics just as a diabetic needed insulin. Methadone maintenance satisfied that need and kept the addicts out of the illicit market.

Methadone maintenance proved to be a cost-effective treatment for narcotic addiction. Methadone patient rolls expanded rapidly during the heroin epidemic of the late 1960s and early 1970s, when the country had an estimated half a million narcotic addicts. After 1974, however, methadone's star faded, owing to more onerous federal regulations, local resistance to clinics, and methadone's therapeutic irrelevance to marijuana, cocaine, lysergic acid diethylamide (LSD), and other drugs popular in the youthful counterculture.

The efflorescence of that counterculture and the rapid spread of illicit drug use among middle-class youth had no precedent in American history. Critics blamed lax parental discipline, a commercialized ethos of self-gratification, antiwar protest, and proselytizing gurus like the poet Allen Ginsberg, the novelist Ken Kesey, and the onetime Harvard psychologist Timothy Leary, whose psychedelic gospel attracted widespread media attention. Public-health experts noted the growing consumption of alcohol and tobacco, which served as social and pharmacological "gateways" to illicit drug use; the military buildup in drug-rich Vietnam; new sources of illicit supply from Asia and Latin America; and the entry of tens of millions of baby boomers into their teens and twenties, the prime drug-experimenting years. (This wave of "susceptibles" also helps explain why youthful drug use increased throughout the world in the 1960s and 1970s, the postwar baby boom being a global phenomenon.) Complicating matters further, amphetamine, a stimulant introduced in the mid-1930s, had spread outside medical circles by way of soldiers, athletes, long-haul truckers, cramming students, bohemians, and even prisoners who cracked open Benzedrine inhalers. By the 1960s, diverted amphetamines ("uppers"), as well as barbiturates and tranquilizers ("downers"), had become part of a complex and fast-growing recreational drug scene.

The War on Drugs. Worried by military and youthful drug use, and pledged to reduce crime, the administration of Richard M. Nixon (1969–1974) launched a multifront war on drugs. Federal agents stepped up international enforcement efforts, with some notable successes in Turkey and France. In 1971, the White House created the Special Action Office for Drug Abuse Prevention, which became the foundation for the National Institute on Drug Abuse. The administration funded methadone and other new treatment approaches, including therapeutic communities modeled on California's Synanon Foundation. All told, federal antidrug spending increased from $80 million in 1969 to $730 million in 1973. Legislatively, the 1970 Controlled Substances Act rationalized six decades of piecemeal statutes and court decisions. The law sorted drugs into five schedules, depending on their potential for abuse and their therapeutic value. Schedule I drugs, including heroin, marijuana, LSD, peyote, and other hallucinogens, were illicit in that the sense that they were off-limits to everyone, including physicians. Drugs in Schedules II through V could be used therapeutically, but with varying restrictions.

The farther down the schedule, the less onerous the restrictions.

The emergence of new patterns of abuse prompted later changes in the list, such as the addition of the amphetamine-based hallucinogen MDMA, also known as Ecstasy, to Schedule I in 1985. Congress also enacted significant punitive amendments in 1986 and 1988, in the midst of a crack epidemic and a renewed, bipartisan drug war. Crack was a cheap, smokable form of cocaine that spread rapidly in inner cities in the mid-1980s, adding an exclamation point to a sustained, fifteen-year increase in national cocaine consumption. Like heroin, crack was associated with rapid addiction, prostituion, sexual degradation, and violence. Though the 1986 and 1988 legislation increased penalties generally, crack offenders received the stiffest sentences. Possessing just five grams of crack with intention to distribute brought a mandatory minimum sentence of five years, the same penalty prescribed for five hundred grams of powder cocaine. Federal penitentiaries began filling with crack dealers, virtually all of whom were African American or Latino. Congress partially rectified the disparity in the 2010 Fair Sentencing Act, but crack dealers continued to receive stiffer sentences than those caught with equivalent amounts of powder cocaine.

Reaction against the War on Drugs. As in the 1950s, the punitive turn provoked a reaction. Libertarians proposed "controlled legalization"—a regulated adult market in psychoactive drugs—as an alternative to the drug war. Liberals and public-health advocates espoused harm-reduction measures, notably needle-exchange programs, which spread during the 1990s despite a ban on federal funding. Drug courts, which diverted nonviolent drug offenders into mandatory treatment, also became more common. Even so, federal policy remained basically unchanged during the administration of Bill Clinton (1993–2001). Clinton knew that liberalization invited attacks both from Republicans allied with moral conservatives and from worried parents who wanted the government to lock up dealers, clean out the schools, warn kids about drugs, and shun anything that smacked of toleration.

Whatever its political advantages, the war on drugs failed to diminish the supply of illicit drugs. Prices fell and potency rose even as prosecutions mounted. Drugs poured into the country, notably from Mexico, where rival drug cartels battled one another as well as police and military officials who were not themselves complicit in the traffic. Domestic marijuana and methamphetamine production also expanded, particularly in remote and impoverished rural areas. By 2006, marijuana was reportedly the most valuable cash crop in the United States. That same year eleven thousand Americans lost their lives through accidental overdoses with opiate analgesics—up from four thousand in 2001. OxyContin (oxycodone), a long-acting synthetic opiate, was only the most notorious of the potent analgesics and tranquilizers diverted into the black market.

Law enforcement had some deterrent effect. But could such deterrence be achieved at less cost, particularly in view of successful European experiments with harm reduction and decriminalization? Marijuana, the drug that generated the most arrests but that also benefited cancer and AIDS patients battling nausea and appetite loss, became the reform lightning rod. In 1996, voters in California and Arizona passed initiatives that allowed physicians to authorize patients to smoke marijuana. Despite conservative insistence that medical marijuana was a stalking horse for legalization, fifteen states and the District of Columbia enacted similar measures by the end of 2010. The growing dissensus over

marijuana's status as a Schedule I drug represented a breach in drug-war solidarity and a rare instance of states openly defying federal policy. In other respects, though, little had changed since the 1980s. In the early twenty-first century, illicit drug use continued to be defined, suppressed, and managed principally by criminal statutes and law enforcement.

[*See also* **Alcohol and Alcohol Abuse; Conservative Movement; Crack Cocaine; Gambling; Hospitals and Dispensaries; Juvenile Delinquency; Organized Crime; Prisons and Penitentiaries; Progressive Era; Prohibition; Sexual Reform and Morality;** *and* **Sixties, The.**]

BIBLIOGRAPHY

Burnham, John C. *Bad Habits: Drinking, Smoking, Taking Drugs, Gambling, Sexual Misbehavior, and Swearing in American History.* New York: New York University Press, 1993. Describes the vice "constellation" that includes illicit drug use.

Courtwright, David T. *Dark Paradise: A History of Opiate Addiction in America.* Expanded ed. Cambridge, Mass.: Harvard University Press, 2001.

Courtwright, David, Herman Joseph, and Don Des Jarlais. *Addicts Who Survived: An Oral History of Narcotic Use in America, 1923–1965.* Knoxville: University of Tennessee Press, 1989.

Jonnes, Jill. *Hep-Cats, Narcs, and Pipe Dreams: A History of America's Romance with Illegal Drugs.* New York: Scribner, 1996.

MacCoun, Robert J., and Peter Reuter. *Drug War Heresies: Learning from Other Vices, Times, and Places.* Cambridge, U.K.: Cambridge University Press, 2001. Provides historical and international perspectives on American drug policies.

Massing, Michael. *The Fix.* New York: Simon & Schuster, 1998. Recounts the late twentieth-century drug wars.

Musto, David F. *The American Disease: Origins of Narcotic Control.* 3d ed. New York: Oxford University Press, 1999. A policy-oriented study that is especially strong on the early twentieth century.

Rasmussen, Nicolas. *On Speed: The Many Lives of Amphetamine.* New York: New York University Press, 2008.

Schneider, Eric C. *Smack: Heroin and the American City.* Philadelphia: University of Pennsylvania Press, 2008.

Spillane, Joseph. *Cocaine: From Medical Marvel to Modern Menace in the United States,* 1884–1920. Baltimore: Johns Hopkins University Press, 2000.

David T. Courtwright

DUST BOWL

"Dust Bowl" is the name applied to the high plains of Texas, Oklahoma, New Mexico, Colorado, and Kansas during the later 1930s as immense dust storms blew across the region, darkening the sky and depositing soil hundreds of miles to the east. At its peak the Dust Bowl covered nearly 100 million acres, with similar conditions extending northward into Canada. In 1938, the worst year for erosion, farmers lost an estimated 850 million tons of topsoil.

Severe wind erosion led to a precipitous drop in farm income, impaired health, and caused widespread damage to houses and machinery. Those conditions, combined with national economic depression, turned many people into refugees; in the worst-hit counties, one-third to one-half of the population left, many migrating to California. For those who stayed, bankruptcies were common in both town and country.

The causes of this environmental catastrophe are disputed. Some historians see the farmers as innocent victims of drought; others argue that agricultural practices were heavily to blame. During World War I and the 1920s, wheat farming expanded rapidly into the windy, drought-prone plains. Native grasses that had evolved a high degree of climatic resilience abruptly disappeared under the plow. For a while crops were abundant and profits high, but then began a record-breaking drought that withered the fields and left them bare.

Severe but short-lived droughts recurred in the decades after the 1930s, but none had the impact of the Dust Bowl years, leading many observers to conclude that farmer ingenuity and improved technology had made another disaster impossible. In truth, although a constant flow of federal dollars, along with irrigation from deep aquifers, managed to stave off a repeat catastrophe, the future of the region remains volatile and uncertain.

[*See also* **Automobiles; Great Depression Era; Internal Migration,** *subentry on* **Twentieth Century and Beyond; Migrant Camps, Depression Era;** *and* **Rural Life and Society.**]

BIBLIOGRAPHY

Hurt, R. Douglas. *The Dust Bowl: An Agricultural and Social History.* Chicago: Nelson-Hall, 1981.

Worster, Donald. *Dust Bowl: The Southern Plains in the 1930s.* New York: Oxford University Press, 1979.

Donald Worster

E

EARLY REPUBLIC ERA

The American Revolution, with its universalist appeals to human liberty and radical assertions of basic equality among all men, unleashed forces capable of producing sweeping change. As war with the British wound down in 1783, negotiating the precise meaning of liberty and equality within a diverse population became central to social, political, and economic developments at the local, state, and national levels. The terms of basic governance exposed a series of ideological rifts between various sectors of the American population who possessed very different understandings of what the goals and precise meaning of the Revolution had been. Debtors and creditors, the "middling" and the "better" sorts, masters and slaves, settlers and Indians: each group of people struggled to shape events to suit their own ambitions both during and in the immediate aftermath of the conflict. The debate over the Constitution encapsulated that struggle.

The Constitution. By and large, the Constitution's creators—and defenders—were nationalists. That is, they hoped to concentrate governing power in the hands of a federal apparatus and at the expense of individual state legislatures. Their motivations for eliminating the Articles of Confederation in 1787 were twofold. The first objections were structural and procedural: the Congress set up by the Articles lacked the power to tax and could not amend the Articles without unanimous consent among the individual states. The second objection to the Articles was what critics considered to be the overly democratic tendencies among legislatures governing the respective states. In the aftermath of the Revolution, watchwords such as "freedom," "liberty," and "equality" had inspired the creation of constitutions and electoral reforms at the state level that brought previously disenfranchised classes of men into politics. State legislatures increasingly filled not with gentlemen, but rather with farmers, artisans, mechanics, and other ordinary persons who pursued legislation that benefited poorer debtors, not the wealthier gentry.

These were threatening developments, and the nationalist faction's fears of popular radicalization crystallized in 1786 with a rebellion among common farmers in western Massachusetts led by a Continental army veteran named Daniel Shays. He and his followers, like many poorer farmers in the nation, suffered immensely during the economic dislocation following the American Revolution. They responded by arming themselves and barricading courthouses to prevent land seizures. Though a Massachusetts state militia eventually dispersed the rebels, some individuals saw the uprising as a dangerous precedent that indicated the subversive potential of an empowered class of common people. These alarmed individuals' mission was to create the framework for a national government that would limit those democratic dangers by curtailing popular political participation and concentrating authority at the federal level.

Federalists, as supporters of the Constitution came to be known, won ratification for the new national government in large part by hurrying the process before an Anti-Federalist opposition could mobilize effective resistance.

It is doubtful that a majority of the country's citizens at the time ever openly supported the Constitution. Anti-Federalists complained that the new government was by design aristocratic, monarchical, and counterrevolutionary in nature, that it concentrated power in the hands of the few at the expense of the many, and that the undersized House of Representatives was the only popularly elected component. When the first government under the new Constitution met in New York City in 1789, however, most of the nation's citizenry proved willing to give the new framework a try, in large part because of the widespread public confidence in President George Washington.

That fragile consensus quickly evaporated in 1790 when debate began regarding Treasury Secretary Alexander Hamilton's proposed national economic program. Designed to address the financial disarray created by the Revolutionary War, Hamilton's plan had the new federal government assume the entire nation's debt, including that of individual states. The new government, now armed with the power to tax, would impose a series of tariffs, customs duties, and excise levies, all designed to pay interest on that newly assumed debt. And with the creation of the federally chartered Bank of the United States, the national government would possess a repository for its funds, a source of loans, and a mint for currency.

These maneuvers quickly aroused opposition. Given that the Constitution granted no expressed authority to the federal government for the creation of a national bank, Thomas Jefferson, James Madison, and their allies believed that Hamilton and his fellow Federalists advocated a blatantly unconstitutional program. And, in a more general sense, they feared the concentration of power at the national level. Opposition that organized against Federalist centralization deemed themselves "Republicans": defenders of the interests of ordinary people against the tyranny of would-be aristocrats.

Problems of the West.

Some of the most strident resistance to the new Federalist-dominated constitutional order came along the frontier. The Whiskey Rebellion of the early 1790s, during which disgruntled Pennsylvania taxpayers took up arms against the Hamiltonian financial plan's liquor levies, pointed to the chronic disorder that plagued the trans-Appalachian West. Part of the problem was the multiple, competing claims to authority in the region. Indians occupied the land, the British and Spanish sought to check American expansion, and private land speculators such as those making up the Ohio Company claimed to own vast tracts that they would sell to settlers, while white squatters defied all by pouring through mountain passes and clearing the land.

Initially the national government attempted to legislate its way out of the problem of the West. The Land Ordinance of 1785 and the Northwest Ordinance of 1787 sought to manage the distribution of trans-Appalachian real estate by dividing the territory into 640-acre square-shaped plots that would be sold to settlers and speculators. Yet the ideal of methodical, federally managed westward expansion remained illusory. The vast majority of settlers in the region, after all, were squatters seeking so-called free land. But in moving westward they discovered, not vacant space, but rather a series of Indian confederations totaling around one hundred thousand people.

Trans-Appalachian Native Americans were hardly the primitive peoples that white settlers self-servingly represented them as. They practiced a mixed economy of farming and hunting and were often congregated in densely populated villages. Native Americans, because they did not cultivate—that is, use—the land they occupied in any way that was familiar to western observers, and because they had allied with the hated British during the Revolution, were seen by ethnocentric settlers as expendable enemies. Here lay the seeds from which Manifest Destiny later grew: the energy and enterprise of white men would allegedly make productive what had been left to waste in the hands of savages. Meanwhile, the nominal policy of the federal government was to encourage civilization and assimilation within Indian communities—to make proper farmers out of savage natives.

Later politicians waxed eloquent about divinely guided Anglo-American conquest along the frontier, but only numbers made white dominance inevitable. By 1788 the average number of people floating down the Ohio River on flatboats each month was greater than the region's entire population of Shawnee Indians. A young, rapidly expanding population flooded into the West and clashed with the land's Indian occupants. Cycles of retributive violence between Native Americans and settlers escalated further when the federal government dispatched sizable armies into the Ohio River valley. Meant to pacify Indians, American forces in 1790 and again in 1791 were instead annihilated by a native confederation under the leadership of the Miami chief Little Turtle and the Shawnee chief Blue Jacket. At enormous expense to the new, cash-strapped government, a third expedition, mounted by General Anthony Wayne, did defeat Indians in the Old Northwest, forcing land cessions in the 1795 Treaty of Greenville. That agreement tacitly acknowledged natives as a sovereign military force that would compel the respect, resources, and attention of the federal government for many years to come.

Slavery.

Variations on a similar theme of aggressive territorial expansion appeared in the Old Southwest. Yet unlike the Old Northwest, where slavery had been banned by the Northwest Ordinance, bound labor fueled the American push into Indian, Spanish, and French held land throughout the Gulf South. Though slaves on the eve of the Revolution made up fully a fifth of the nation's population—and in some parts of the South, a majority—many people into the 1780s predicted the institution's eventual demise. All states north of the Mason–Dixon Line had, by 1800, enacted gradual emancipation laws that would eventually abolish slavery within their borders. Meanwhile in southern states manumissions—a master's voluntary emancipation of his slaves—were on the rise.

Events into the 1790s and early 1800s, however, retrenched slavery in the South. Part of that story was economic. Eli Whitney's invention of the cotton gin (short for "engine") in the early 1790s made the production of short-staple cotton much less labor-intensive and thus far more profitable. Southern planters dedicated more and more acreage to that enormously lucrative crop, and so began King Cotton's long reign in the region. Yet slavery's strengthening into the nineteenth century is also a political story. The outbreak of a massive slave rebellion in 1791 in the French Caribbean colony of Saint-Domingue generated widespread fears of the appearance of similar racial violence in the United States. In response, southern slaveholders and states began to curtail manumissions, opting instead to tighten the laws and regulations governing enslaved peoples. A more rigid racial ideology—fueled by Enlightenment-era "scientific" theories on the biologically immutable inferiority of African peoples—increasingly emphasized that slavery was the only proper condition for black individuals.

Armed with the twin verities of profit and prejudice, white Americans flooded into the Gulf South, dragging their slaves with them. Cotton production became the most lucrative enterprise in the country, fueling much of the era's economic growth. In securing those lands, the federal government was instrumental. Thomas Jefferson, elected president in 1800, was a particularly zealous expansionist and pursued territorial aggrandizement as fundamental to protecting the nation's survival. The Louisiana Purchase of 1803 was emblematic of that instinct. It doubled the size of the nation, but its real legacy was to secure for the United States both the vital cotton port of New Orleans and rich soils in which to grow even more of that crop. No single act did more to expand the institution of slavery than the Louisiana Purchase. Jefferson may have celebrated the yeoman farmer, but he entrenched the plantation owner.

Yet making the land safe for slavery meant clearing it of Native American inhabitants, and here again the federal government proved instrumental. By 1811, powerful Indian coalitions began to oppose further American intrusion onto their lands. At the battle of Horseshoe Bend in 1814, Andrew Jackson defeated a Creek force and then, in the Treaty of Fort Jackson, forced the Creeks to cede vast tracts of prime cotton-growing land. Meanwhile, at the 1813 battle of the Thames along the northern frontier, William Henry Harrison's army defeated a northwestern pan-Indian alliance assembled by the brilliant Shawnee leader Tecumseh. These battles were part of the larger War of 1812 against the British, which among their Indian allies was an unmitigated catastrophe. Wartime losses and the absence of Native American leaders at the peacemaking table spelled disaster for further resistance to white encroachment east of the Mississippi River. When the Creek leader Red Eagle wept at the end of the war that "my people are no more," he spoke to a much larger truth.

Common Ground and Economic Growth.

In one sense, the disappearance of slavery in northern states and its rampant spread throughout the South seemed to distinguish the two regions. Sectional divergence found political expression in 1819 when a body of northern congressmen led an effort to abolish slavery in Missouri when that territory sought admission to the Union as a slave state. Fiery debate eventually led to the so-called Missouri Compromise of 1820, which maintained a sectional balance of power by admitting Maine as a free state alongside a proslavery Missouri, but the controversy foreshadowed future conflict over the ultimate disposition, slave or free, of western territory.

Yet for all the professions of sectional difference, common ground remained. Rampant racism surely united the nation: northern blacks might have been free, but they were subject to segregation and discrimination and were attacked regularly by bigoted mobs. One observer, Alexis de Tocqueville, noted that "race prejudice seems stronger in those states that have abolished slavery than in those where it still exists." Indeed, the shared national sentiment of racism kept a lid on abolitionist agitation in the North; most there loathed the idea of a million freed slaves pouring out of the South and "tainting" northern communities with the presence of an "inferior" race. Enslavement in other ways encouraged sectional interdependence; slavery and the slave economy's productions tied each region together. Burgeoning northern mills spun southern cotton and clothed its slaves. Northern and western farms fed captive laborers farther south. New York and Philadelphia banks financed plantations, built railroads essential to export, and insured valuable human property.

All of that activity points toward the growth in the early republic of a vast market internal to the nation that knit the Union closer together and changed the economic lives of Americans. Increasingly, farmers and artisans shifted away from subsistence production and oriented themselves toward the pursuit of profit within domestic and international markets. Household and agricultural labor was reorganized, specialized, and geared toward the demands of specific and increasingly distant marketplaces. In towns and cities, workshops and factories grew to accommodate increased demand. Urbanization amplified as workers moved in to find employment, thus enlarging the market for rural produce in burgeoning cities. A system wherein craftsmen painstakingly trained apprentices in a trade was supplanted by impersonal wage labor; masters were replaced by employers, and apprentices became employees who were not taught a skill but merely sold their labor. Workers and bosses no longer lived together, but rather apart, in separate quarters of stratified cities. Relations between employers and employees became more antagonistic, and strikes became a common occurrence. It was a process best exemplified by the growth of the New England textile industry. The largest of these industrial facilities, Massachusetts's Lowell mills, was by the standards of the time a massive operation that employed thousands—mostly women and children on eighty-hour weeks—turning southern cotton into cloth. The Lowell system pointed to America's industrial future. By 1820, in a nation previously dedicated entirely to agriculture, well over a quarter of the New England and mid-Atlantic labor force was working in small factories.

The rapid economic growth and increasingly frantic pace of social change it entailed became instrumental to the early republic's politics, with many debating the extent to which federal and state governments should help to promote development. By the early 1820s, individuals styling themselves "National Republicans" began to advocate for the intervention of the federal government in the country's economy. Individuals such as Henry Clay, John Quincy Adams, and Daniel Webster championed what came to be known as the American system: a federally managed program of tariffs to protect national industry from foreign competition, activist banking to spur enterprise through loans, and government spending on internal improvements. In building roads, bridges, canals, and other infrastructure, National Republicans hoped to speed economic growth by facilitating rural and urban access to markets. Opposed to these developments were old-line Democratic-Republicans (by 1828 known as the Democratic Party), who fastened onto New York's Martin Van Buren and the western military hero Andrew Jackson. Democrats denied that the federal government possessed the explicit constitutional authority to regulate the economy. And, more significantly, men such as Jackson were suspicious of the manner in which market capitalism seemed to produce inequalities in wealth, status, and power between working people and what was often referred to as the "moneyed elite." If the government fostered economic growth, it could serve only to benefit capitalists at the expense of the common man. Southerners, meanwhile, remained suspicious of federal activism for other reasons. Federal power of any kind might ultimately threaten the security of slave property.

Although national bills for harbors and rivers began to dredge, dam, and improve the country's waterborne transit networks and bills for roads built overland routes, true innovation more often took place at the state and local level. New York State's ambitious Erie Canal, opened in 1825, extended from the Hudson River west to Lake Erie and provided upstate farmers with access to markets in New York City and beyond. Widely celebrated as one of the era's engineering marvels, the canal spurred explosive economic growth along its entire route. Other states and localities followed suit, hoping to encourage similar success. Canals, turnpikes, and roads mushroomed across the North. Developing steam technology such as the railroad and Robert Fulton's steamboat shrank distances by shortening travel times. All this innovation connected previously distant peoples and, in John C. Calhoun's phrase, helped "bind the republic together."

Religion and Revivals. Yet in a period of such astonishingly increased mobility, many other observers concluded that American society had become unglued. People were in perpetual, dizzying motion. They moved in endless search for opportunity: from east to west, from farm to city, along bustling rivers and canals. An effusion of religious activity, reformism, and voluntary associations sprung up during the early republic to give direction to itinerant Americans. The detached might find meaning in evangelical revivals or concerted efforts at social improvement. The Second Great Awakening, the collective name given to a series of Christian religious revivals, occurred alongside the tide of economic transformation. No surprise, then, that the largest of these revivals took place in regions characterized by the greatest degree of fluidity and transience. Mass religious enthusiasm in Cane Ridge, Kentucky, along the rapidly growing frontier regions of the West, and in upstate New York, amid the flux created by the Erie Canal, were particularly indicative of larger trends toward revivalism. Indeed, Charles Grandison Finney and other evangelical preachers spread so much religious enthusiasm upon the latter region that it became known as the Burned-Over District.

In churches, dislocated people found the fellowship and stability that their rapidly changing world otherwise conspired against. Americans in the early republic became a "nation of joiners": membership at temperance societies, debate clubs, lyceums, antislavery organizations, and all manner of voluntary associations skyrocketed. This was particularly true for many women, who tended disproportionately to fill both the pews in houses of worship and the membership rolls of most organizations. Economic transformation led to the rise of a middle class whose higher standard of living allowed for the creation of new behavioral ethics. The household and workplace were increasingly considered separate spheres, with women now idealized as the sole and proper guardians of the domestic realm. Marriages became companionate, and children less economic units than objects of affection. A so-called cult of domesticity stressed the nurturing role that women would play in this arrangement as mothers and caregivers, and many women extended their special dispensation toward moral guardianship to claim an active role for themselves in perfecting the ills of society more broadly. Later pushes toward the inclusion of women in American politics, such as the 1848 Seneca Falls Convention, were rooted in the experience of middle-class women organizing themselves within churches, temperance societies, and antislavery associations.

Looking Forward. When Andrew Jackson was inaugurated as president in 1829, he presided over a rapidly transformed and still transforming nation. The population had grown dramatically, more than twice the rate of any contemporary European nation. Americans had spread themselves over half a continent at an astonishing pace. New York's population had quadrupled, Kentucky's had multiplied eight times, and Ohio, a virtual wilderness in 1790, had grown to become larger than most of the original colonies. In three decades the nation had swelled to territorial and demographic heights that three centuries of colonial development had been unable to achieve. The Democratic Party's rise to power, meanwhile, revealed larger trends. Its 1828 candidate, the victorious Andrew Jackson, championed the common man but was actually one of the wealthiest people in America. His sprawling Tennessee plantation, the Hermitage, was built with cotton profits, was situated atop Indian land, and was made productive by gangs of enslaved laborers marched in from the Atlantic coast. All this speaks to the emerging economic and social realities of the early republic.

Yet Americans such as Andrew Jackson looked forward, not backward. They tended not to lament the costs, but rather to celebrate the blessings, of territorial empire. "Philanthropy," Jackson asserted in 1830, "could not wish to see this continent restored to the conditions in which it was found by our forefathers." Considering the history of the era, this western warrior turned plantation owner could only ask "what good man would prefer a country covered with forests and ranged by a few thousand savages to our extensive Republic, studded with cities, towns, and prosperous farms, embellished with all the improvements art can devise or industry execute, occupied by more than 12,000,000 happy people, and filled with all the blessings of liberty, civilization, and religion?" A question that Jackson confidently dismissed in 1830, as though it answered itself, by the twenty-first century remained more elusive.

[*See also* **Appalachia; Burned-Over District; Cumberland Gap; Democratic-Republican Clubs; Frontier, The; Great Awakenings; Internal Migration,** *subentry* on Nineteenth-Century Westward; Lewis and Clark Expedition; Lowell Textile Mills; Middle West, The; Militias, Early American; Native American History and Culture, *subentry on* 1500 to 1800; Native American Land Use; Revivals; Revolution and Constitution Era; Shays's Rebellion; Slavery; Slave Trades; Society of the Cincinnati; Steamboats; Voluntary Associations, *subentry on* British Colonies and Early Republic; *and* Whiskey Rebellion.]

BIBLIOGRAPHY

Aron, Stephen. *How the West Was Lost: The Transformation of Kentucky from Daniel Boone to Henry Clay.* Baltimore: Johns Hopkins University Press, 1996.

Dorsey, Bruce. *Reforming Men and Women: Gender in the Antebellum City.* Ithaca, N.Y.: Cornell University Press, 2002.

Dowd, Gregory Evans. *A Spirited Resistance: The North American Indian Struggle for Unity, 1745–1815.* Baltimore: Johns Hopkins University Press, 1992.

Holton, Woody. *Unruly Americans and the Origins of the Constitution.* New York: Hill and Wang, 2007.

Johnson, Paul E. *The Early American Republic, 1789–1829.* New York: Oxford University Press, 2007.

Kennedy, Roger G. *Mr. Jefferson's Lost Cause: Land, Farmers, Slavery, and the Louisiana Purchase.* New York: Oxford University Press, 2003.

Richter, Daniel K. *Facing East from Indian Country: A Native History of Early America.* Cambridge, Mass.: Harvard University Press, 2001.

Rockman, Seth. *Scraping By: Wage Labor, Slavery, and Survival in Early Baltimore.* Baltimore: Johns Hopkins University Press, 2009.

Rothman, Adam. *Slave Country: American Expansion and the Origins of the Deep South.* Cambridge, Mass.: Harvard University Press, 2005.

Sellers, Charles. *The Market Revolution: Jacksonian America, 1815–1846.* New York: Oxford University Press, 1991.

Sheriff, Carol. *The Artificial River: The Erie Canal and the Paradox of Progress, 1817–1862.* New York: Hill and Wang, 1996.

Silver, Peter. *Our Savage Neighbors: How Indian War Transformed Early America.* New York: W. W. Norton and Company, 2008.

Stansell, Christine. *City of Women: Sex and Class in New York, 1789–1860.* New York: Alfred A. Knopf, 1986.

Waldstreicher, David. *In the Midst of Perpetual Fetes: The Making of American Nationalism, 1776–1820.* Chapel Hill: University of North Carolina Press for the Omohundro Institute of Early American History and Culture, Williamsburg, Va., 1997.

Wilentz, Sean. *Chants Democratic: New York City and the Rise of the American Working Class, 1788–1850.* New York: Oxford University Press, 1984.

Wood, Gordon S. *The Creation of the American Republic, 1776–1787.* Chapel Hill: University of North Carolina Press, 1969.

Wood, Gordon S. *Empire of Liberty: A History of the Early Republic, 1789–1815.* New York: Oxford University Press, 2009.

Brian Rouleau

EDUCATION

Traditional education in England centered on the household, buttressed by formal relationships and institutions. The home, the church, the great manor house, and schools inculcated basic moral and religious instruction, provided apprenticeship in trades, or offered steady integration into the rhythms of farming and husbandry, handicrafts and household management. A minority received instruction in reading; an even smaller number learned to write. Formal education was patriarchal—preparation for later gendered roles in adult life in a feudal society. Because society was hierarchical and some modes of production were highly specialized, so, too, was education. Schools proliferated for a variety of specific purposes, from writing to accounting to singing, though most usually offered basic reading skills for religious purposes. Latin grammar schools, many of which were endowed free schools, offered advanced education in classical languages for a small percentage of boys, in preparation for college, commerce, or service to a wealthy man or household. A handful of colleges and the Inns of Court capped the hierarchy of educational institutions.

Unlike the European model, Native American education was thoroughly noninstitutional, built into the fabric of everyday life and ceremonial experiences. American Indian societies used extended families and communities to inculcate tribal culture in youth. Children learned to be economically productive within gendered spheres. Tribal life was usually patriarchal, though aristocratic women might sometimes assume leadership roles within a tribe, just as men might help with women's work. All learned the stories describing the religion and history of the tribe and had deep respect for oral tradition; there was no written language. Despite European claims to the contrary, Indian societies were, though weakly hierarchical, socially complex, and they were well adapted to available natural resources. After contact, European diseases exacted huge tolls on Indian populations, a catastrophe that, exacerbated by war, led some tribes on the borderlands to accept aspects of European education as a survival strategy.

Colonial Education. From the beginning, English colonization plans in North America rested on a utopian educational idealism. Colonial planners imagined Indians flocking to English settlements to trade for goods and to receive instruction in civilization and Christianity. In practice, Indians and Europeans typically rejected each other's societies, though some did cross the cultural divide in both directions—more often Europeans crossing in the direction of the Indian.

James Axtell argues that Indians were more successful at enculturation of outsiders than the English were because the English did not bring Indians into their homes, but rather engaged them through other institutions and imagined Indians as social or racial inferiors. Thousands of Europeans joined Indian tribes in the colonial era, most as captives who chose to stay.

When European colonial leaders attempted to enact formal Indian educational programs, their traditional institutions—the household, the church, and the school—proved ill suited to the task they had set themselves: namely, to civilize. The only major exception occurred in New England from the 1650s to 1675, when a movement of Christian conversion and acculturation of "praying Indians" attracted approximately twenty-five hundred people, or a fifth of the New England Indians, until its collapse in the aftermath of King Philip's War. By the mid-eighteenth century, missionaries had opened several unsuccessful schools and colleges for Indians, including Dartmouth College. Outside Virginia and New England, limited Christian missionary activity sponsored by international groups such as the Jesuits, the Moravians, and the Society for the Propagation of the Gospel in Foreign Parts usually constituted the only systematic attempts at European education for Indians.

Among Europeans, regional settlement patterns, religious affiliations, and colonial policies determined who acquired an education and how. Formal colonial education focused on religious instruction, which for the vast Protestant majority included the ability to read sacred texts—especially, for Puritans, the Bible—and, increasingly, the ability to write. Apprenticeships for vocational training included provisions for formal education. For book learning, beginning students used a primer, either in the form of a small bound book or a hornbook containing the alphabet, basic letter combinations, and the Lord's Prayer. From there, children would move to prayer books and Bibles, as well as chapbooks and, by the mid-eighteenth century, a variety of schoolbooks, fables, fairy tales, courtesy and advice books, and more. Greater supply of print material increased demand for literacy instruction.

New England. The New England colonies developed a strong tradition of community support and regulation. Not only did a high proportion of immigrants already know how to read and write, but their highly intellectual form of Protestantism demanded that every individual man, woman, and child have a personal understanding of religion. Moreover, the Congregational model, in which each congregation ran its own affairs, encouraged communal responsibility for moral behavior, including the education of youth. Massachusetts, Connecticut, New Haven, and Plymouth, as well as New York and Pennsylvania, required individual households either to take direct responsibility for the education of all their children and servants or to have them taken away and placed elsewhere.

Moreover, by the mid-seventeenth century, Massachusetts, Connecticut, and New Haven required entire towns that reached a certain size to provide both basic English schools for teaching reading and (increasingly) writing and also advanced Latin schools to prepare boys for college. Some towns simply ignored the school requirement altogether, finding it easier to pay the fine for noncompliance. Over time, however, this two-tiered model gave way to a ubiquitous New England town school that offered a combination of English and Latin. These schools were intended for boys only, and in practice only between 4 and 6 percent of them allowed girls. The New England colonies also made provisions for the training of home-grown leaders. The Massachusetts Bay Colony, for example, founded Harvard College in 1636, six years before the first law regulating mass education. After decades of failed attempts, Yale followed in 1701. For parents of young children of both sexes, women ran so-called dame schools within the home. As a result of these cultural, religious, and regulatory factors, the white inhabitants of colonial New England were among the most literate people in the world.

Middle Atlantic. In the middle-Atlantic colonies, ethnic and religious diversity led to a more entrepreneurial approach to formal education, resulting in a variety of local patterns of educational supply and demand and a far smaller role for government at the local or colony level. As the British empire absorbed former Swedish and Dutch colonies, as well as hosting communities of English Catholics and Quakers, German speakers, and Huguenots (to name a few), education took on special importance as a means of preserving cultural identity in a multicultural society. For some groups, notably Anglicans, education was a private matter, while for others, such as Presbyterians, Baptists, Catholics and Jews, a large enough population would support a community school. Quaker schools were conspicuously tolerant, open to girls as well as boys and to blacks and Indians as well as whites. As in New England, education could be gained in the home from parents or a tutor, in a dame or town school, in a grammar school or academy, or at the handful of denominational colleges that formed in the mid-eighteenth century, including the future Princeton University (College of New Jersey, 1746), University of Pennsylvania (Academy of Philadelphia, 1751), Columbia University in New York City (King's College, 1754), and

Rutgers University in New Jersey (Queen's College, 1766).

Chesapeake and Southern Colonies. In the Chesapeake and southern colonies, settlement patterns, the educational background of immigrants, and religious and political traditions resulted in an intensification of private and family responsibility for formal education. In the early decades of Virginia, for example, high rates of mortality, low rates of female (or whole-family) immigration, low population density, and a short-term focus on land speculation and development made the establishment and staffing of established Anglican churches difficult, let alone the creation (or requirement) of schools. Viewed in terms of its religious and economic significance, formal education outside large population centers lacked the same popular demand and colonial-level imperative to supply that were seen in other regions, especially New England. A child's opportunity to get an education rested on what his or her parents could impart, pay for, or organize, or in rare cases what the parents could receive as a form of charity.

Southern patterns of education reinforced the class-based ordering of society and resulted in lower rates of literacy than elsewhere. Wealthy families tended to use tutors for their own children, sent them to England for advanced education, or sent them to the South's only colonial college, William and Mary (established in 1693). Education for this class emphasized refinement and social status as much as reading, writing, and numeracy. For backcountry yeomen farmers in the middle and lower levels of society, low population density made the home the only plausible place for children to learn the three R's, and backcountry culture rejected the cosmopolitan orientation of formal learning.

In places where the population density was high enough, parents in southern colonies might organize a pay school in an uncultivated field, known as an "old field school." In some places, missionaries operated primary schools. In concentrated population centers, such as Charleston, Richmond, or Baltimore, teachers opened private-venture schools. Endowed free schools—of which there were a dozen or so in the colonial era—charity schools, and denominational academies offered an education beyond the elementary level. Outside schooling, apprenticeship might also offer an opportunity for a formal education (Virginia law required it), though the provisions for education within a given apprenticeship varied.

Enslaved People. Because of the paucity of sources, scholars debate the character of education among and for enslaved people. Very few newcomers would have been able to read, or even have lived previously in a literate culture. The degree to which enslaved people in the colonies could acquire a European-style education varied by region; New Englanders, for instance, were much more likely to educate enslaved people as they would their servants. In the metropolitan centers of the middle colonies, African Americans might acquire a formal education in special charity schools, from missionaries, or on an individual basis. In the South, enslaved people working in houses or those in metropolitan areas might be able to learn to read for religious or practical purposes; those working in plantation fields were unlikely to do so. South Carolina in 1740 and Georgia in 1755 banned writing instruction for slaves, but not reading instruction. Mixed (slave and free) families could also share education.

Revolution and Antebellum Era, 1789–1860. The American Revolution transformed political ideology, law, and government at all levels. Of equal consequence for education, however, were broad, transnational revolutions in industrial production, transportation, and communication: with these revolutions came an intensification of immigration from Europe, westward settlement within North America, and changing slave economics in the South. All these social factors altered the institutional organization of formal education and its content.

Republicanism. The broad political ideology of republicanism contained the notion that mass virtue and intelligence were necessary components of a republic, whether conceived at the federal, state, or local level. Among other things, republicanism also meant limited government, religious freedom, personal autonomy, and opportunity. Though deployed as an argument against slavery, republican ideology commonly commingled with white supremacy as well. As the historian Hilary Moss has shown, both whites and blacks could invoke claims of republican liberty in their advocacy for or against school integration, and whites sometimes used such claims in their resistance to there being any black schooling at all in their vicinity. For promoters of female education, republican motherhood provided a rationale for girls' education, because women were future mothers of republican boys. Significantly, republicanism shifted the dominant discourse of childhood education: instead of focusing on education's primarily religious purposes, the discourse focused on its primarily political and social ones.

Federal and State Involvement. Republican ideology resulted in a variety of state and federal initiatives to encourage mass education. These laws varied in significance for ordinary people, however. In the Northwest Territory, Congress set aside one square mile for every thirty-six to support a school, but the provision generally failed because land—in such abundance—could not generate enough rent. Provisions for education that were written into federal treaties with Indian nations usually failed. On the other hand, a state lottery in New York and the sale of Western Reserve lands in Connecticut created sizable funds for support of local schooling. In southern states, the class-based tradition of education as a private matter endured, despite the provision, by most states, for the creation of special funds for the instruction of paupers and for state colleges for elites. Across the United States there was no one dominant pattern for organizing formal education until after the Civil War.

District Schools. In New England, the ubiquitous colonial town schools developed into secular school districts, often still taught by ministers within the district lines of parishes, with a strong religious orientation. In areas of new settlement, particularly in the North, many communities organized local schools through private subscription and through the collection of tuition, called a "rate bill," with varying levels of assistance from state and local government. Attendance in district schools was high, though sporadic.

Charity Schools. Although the Revolution closed off the British imperial charity-school effort, specific American denominations and the Roman Catholic Church continued to support schools for the poor, especially the urban poor. In competition with these, urban elites formed voluntary, nonsectarian school societies—usually pan-Protestant in religious orientation—to provide education for the poor. The most popular charity-school model, the monitorial school, provided a cheap means of offering education to the masses. At these schools, large groups of children would sit at benches, their place on the bench determined by their ability; gradually they made their way up to the position of monitor, in which they would monitor the progress of a bench. Frequent testing and sorting, rote memorization, and repressive discipline kept the students moving forward. The schools were usually nonsectarian, racially segregated, relatively inexpensive, and widely appealing to school reformers in antebellum era cities until their decline in the face of criticism for their low standards and harsh methods. Remarking on its international popularity, Carl Kaestle has called the monitorial school movement the most successful reform movement of its day in the Western world.

Academies. By the early national period, private academies became the most common form of higher schooling in the United States, especially in the South. What distinguished academies from ordinary venture schools, Kim Tolley has shown, was not the curriculum (which was just as broad and often practical), nor a devotion to Enlightenment principles, but the perceived need of other entities—churches, local and state governments, and parents—to put schools on more permanent footing by incorporating them, seeking funding beyond tuition, and installing a board of trustees. Academies were increasingly nondenominational, served girls and young women as well as boys, served blacks as well as whites, and often functioned as institutions for teacher training. Hilary Moss has shown that, paradoxically, some antebellum northern white communities violently opposed the creation of black academies or seminaries, while in the slave city of Baltimore, whites openly tolerated

black schools, knowing that racial caste was secure.

Life in Schools. The typical early nineteenth-century schoolhouse in America was rural, had one room, and catered to children of mixed ages and, increasingly, both genders. The teacher's role was to maintain discipline and hear recitations from students based on memorized portions of text. School enrollment followed the rhythms of the farm, with a winter session for all children—especially older ones—and a summer session for younger children; in the summer, those who were able to work, did. The curriculum depended on the textbooks brought by the children, which were sometimes, especially early in the century, nothing more than a Bible. American-made schoolbooks containing a republican nationalism emerged slowly. Noah Webster was by far the most successful American textbook author, fashioning a unique American language and identity with his *American Dictionary of the English Language* (1828) and *Speller* (first edition 1783), which sold 1.5 million copies by 1801 and a staggering 20 million by 1829. These and other schoolbooks increasingly replaced traditional Calvinistic religious content with pan-Protestant, patriotic, and moralistic readings, as well as basic arithmetic. By the late nineteenth century, pressure from non-Protestants led publishers to be more inclusive, though racism and sexism persisted into the late twentieth century.

Women. From 1780 to 1840, American women saw a revolution in education: more girls and women attended schools, and more women were the teachers working in them. The number of institutions of higher learning for women, such as academies and seminaries, exploded in the early decades of the republic, offering women a rigorous academic curriculum, including advanced science and math, and opportunities for employment and community leadership after graduation as teachers, writers, and organizers in the expanding educational marketplace. At the same time, promoters of women's higher learning were careful to frame women's education as being specific to the traditional woman's sphere. Coeducation for girls at the primary-school level was a rurally based, bottom-up reform movement that happened on a school-by-school, district-by-district basis during the first half of the nineteenth century across all regions of the United States. Whether in single-sex or coeducational schools, girls aged five to nineteen lagged behind boys in school enrollment for their region by approximately 6 percent in 1850. Meanwhile women entered the teaching force, though unevenly: by the 1850s in the Northeast, a large majority of teachers were women, but twenty years later in the South, men still accounted for two-thirds of the teaching force.

The Common-School Reform Movement.

From the 1830s to the Civil War, the common-school movement was the first broad-based, transregional reform effort in the nineteenth-century United States to focus on mass education for all students, not just the urban poor. The movement targeted the organizational features of schooling: who ran schools, how they were paid for, and who could attend. The common-school "system" was a method of organizing nonsectarian, district-based elementary schooling, run by elected trustees, paid for (in part, at least) through property tax within the district, and, in theory, open to all children within the district, girls as well as boys, though racial integration was highly contested, and local majorities could be hostile to religious minorities.

Regionally, the movement originated and was strongest in the rural Northeast—which had already developed district schools—was weakest in the South, and was uneven in the Middle West. The principle of nonsectarianism among Protestants emerged for practical reasons: rural communities could support a single common school but might be home to people of various faiths. Common-school reform was popular because promoters promised solutions to the problems caused by the market revolution without challenging the underlying economic system, including the racial caste system necessary to support the slave economy.

Despite state involvement, common schools were deeply local institutions. Nancy Beadie has shown that communities supported common schooling as a way to build local social capital; in the context of the market revolution, the proliferation of permanent and public schools created the bridging capital necessary for the rise of the liberal state with universal white male suffrage. Moreover, schools developed human capital compatible with the increasingly market-oriented, wage economy: reading, writing, mathematical computation, and the habits of delayed gratification, regular schedules, and acceptance of authority. At the same time, common schools reflected local cultures and tastes. The constant churn of population in the early nineteenth century led to frequent revision of school-district boundaries, which in turn could result in minority majorities. The religious affiliation of school trustees and teachers, the opening exercises, and even the language of instruction reflected local preference, even as participation in the ubiquitous curriculum of common-school textbooks encouraged a common national identity.

Slave Communities.

Institutional education was closed to the one in ten Americans enslaved in the South by 1860. Despite limited evidence, the historian Thomas Webber has shown that communities of enslaved people developed formal and complex systems of cultural transmission and resistance to oppression within the plantation system, including both the co-optation of Christianity as a tool for empowerment and liberation and also clandestine efforts to acquire literacy.

Consolidation and Reform, 1865–1900.

The late nineteenth century saw the consolidation of public education in all regions of the United States, leading to greater bureaucratization, state regulation, and multiple reform efforts. The public school—indeed, more broadly, the school in general—became the nearly universal educative institution in American society, with the age-graded school becoming the standard model by which all schooling was judged. This movement brought challenges and opportunities to groups that did not fit neatly into the secular, capitalist, and Anglo-Protestant model of the public school.

Reconstruction. The Civil War caused major disruptions in education, but it was the Reconstruction Era that profoundly reshaped education by changing the relationship between the federal government and the states and by requiring a radical reorganization of mass education in the South. Working with private northern philanthropists, the federal government insisted on schooling for freedpeople. As a condition for readmission to the union, Congress required southern states, and all subsequent new states, to include in their constitutions provisions for universal public education.

During Reconstruction, freedmen's schools were not triumphs of democracy so much as contested gateways to civic identity and power. Freedpeople sought literacy in order to read the Bible—an act of subversion of white authority and an affirmation of community identity—to negotiate business deals and engage in commerce, and to claim an equal share of their human inheritance and civic identity. Ronald Butchart has found that one-third of all teachers in Reconstruction black schools were themselves African American—such teachers outnumbered northern whites who came south to teach—and they usually did not receive assistance from the Freedmen's Bureau but instead operated private-venture schools. The dominant class of white planters challenged these efforts. Moreover, paternalistic northern mission societies and many teachers—half of whom were southern whites—imagined African American children to be incapable of benefiting from a high-quality education; rather they were considered destined to be peasants.

After Reconstruction, African Americans led the southern struggle at the local and state levels to create and maintain public schools, resulting in more formal educational opportunity for both blacks and whites. In the Jim Crow era, southern leaders erected barriers to black civic and economic equality through legal and extralegal means, including creating separate and unequally funded public schools. Within a generation this educational system managed to include people of color and poor whites without seriously upsetting the racial and social order of southern or American society.

Catholic Schools. In the North, expansion of public schooling heightened tensions with various minority groups, especially members of the Roman Catholic Church and smaller non-Anglo-Protestant denominations, such as Lutherans. In the popular press, at the pulpit, and in politics, the relationship between public schools and patriotism flared in the 1870s and again, more briefly, in the 1890s, resulting in a spate of state laws and constitutional amendments forbidding public funding for sectarian schools. Although some Catholic leaders initially endorsed common schools, the American Catholic hierarchy took an increasingly hard line against public education, where children might face ethnic or religious persecution, learn Protestant values, fraternize with non-Catholics, or learn to question church authority. Protestant public-school promoters countered with anti-Catholic screeds of their own, questioning the compatibility of the Catholic Church with American political and social values.

At the local level, however, school districts often brokered compromises between the two positions. At the same time, the American Roman Catholic hierarchy built a nationwide system of parish schools in every major city in the United States. Lay enthusiasm for parish schools varied by city and ethnic group. Nationally, more Catholic children attended public schools than nonpublic ones. By 1900 slightly more than 90 percent of children in schools were in public schools, and 90 percent of children not in a public school were in a Catholic school.

Indian Education.

In the first half of the nineteenth century, American Indian nations paid the cost of Manifest Destiny, but they did not do so as passive victims or in culturally static ways. Federal Indian policy encouraged formal education to fully acculturate and civilize Indian children, initially through mission schools and then increasingly through a federal educational bureaucracy that included the Commissioner of Indian Affairs (a position created in 1832) and a system of schools offering manual training (1839). In the decades after the Civil War, the federal government embarked on what it saw as the ultimate solution to the so-called Indian problem: the end of armed conflict and a full educational assault on native culture. Seen by its promoters as a humanitarian effort, this educational program created a national network of reservation day and boarding schools and special off-reservation boarding schools; compulsory attendance laws began in 1891. The conditions in the schools—especially the boarding schools—were harsh, with an emphasis on manual labor, obedience, and cultural cleansing through physical and emotional punishment.

Indian parents and children often resisted federal public schools, which they rightly saw as attempts to annihilate their culture and community. Many sought ways to preserve their culture while learning knowledge and skills that would be of use. A few even embraced acculturation. Indian schooling did not meet its aims of bringing prosperity to the reservations or wiping out tribal cultures, but ironically the off-reservation schools nurtured a pan-Indian consciousness that paved the way for the Red Power movement later in the twentieth century.

Latino Southwest.

For Latinos of the Southwest and California, conquest by Texas and the United States resulted in new schooling patterns that challenged a traditional Catholic system. Protestant missionaries opened competing schools to convert children, while state governments created systems of public schools. In Texas, the white-supremacist legislature banned Spanish-language instruction. In New Mexico, on the other hand, the public system absorbed the Catholic to form hybrid bilingual and bicultural schools in which many nuns and priests remained in teaching positions and local communities forged compromises between the secular, civic aims of public schooling and the religious, ethnocentric aims of the church.

By the 1880s public schooling became the dominant form of mass education in the Southwest.

Expanding the Range. As public-school systems became the countrywide norm, educationists and outside groups enacted significant reforms to expand their scope. Public high schools, begun in a few cities in the common-school era, rose in popularity as selective extensions of lower public schools in places with enough demand and density, displacing and often absorbing nondenominational academies. At the other end of the age spectrum, the kindergarten movement, a German innovation focused on the perceived needs of children too young for elementary school, began initially in private schools in Saint Louis and Boston in the 1850s and spread to public schools during the 1870s and 1880s. By 1911–1912 a survey by the U.S. Bureau of Education found that well over half of American school systems had kindergartens.

Colleges and Universities. The number of American colleges grew from 18 to 450 in the nineteenth century, including public schools and private schools, schools for African Americans and schools for whites, schools for men and schools for women, and schools sponsored by multiple religious denominations, as well as a few that integrated all comers. Even the idea of college expanded in the late nineteenth century, with the founding of research universities including Cornell (1865) and Johns Hopkins (1876). By the turn of the twentieth century the university topped the American educational system, while the four-year liberal arts college had become the mainstay of American higher education. Though college attendance was by no means typical in nineteenth-century America, the role of colleges in the educational system in training leaders and teachers, in broadening knowledge, and in influencing popular culture grew increasingly significant.

Twentieth Century into the Twenty-First. Over the course of the twentieth century, mass schooling in the United States outstripped the world at all levels in terms of enrollment, scope, and funding, until the final decades of the century, which saw a modest decline. The actual organization and experience of schooling at the classroom level remained stable throughout the century, despite the major reform periods that swept over mass education during the Progressive Era, the Civil Rights Movement, and the corporatist resurgence that began during the 1980s. Of these, only the civil rights era can be characterized as a coordinated series of mass movements: the others were led by diverse interests, the most successful being intellectual elites and corporate capitalists. All these reforms took place within the context of an ever-expanding American empire, one that attracted tens of millions of workers to the United States and continued to push American political and economic control beyond North America. Finally, the twentieth century saw the rise of new suppliers of formal education outside schools: corporate, for-profit mass media (radio and television) and the Internet.

Progressive Era. Historians of education view Progressive Era school reforms as a group of separate reform efforts united mainly in the negative: as responses to the interrelated problems and opportunities of industrialism, urbanism, immigration, and modernity. The best known of these reform efforts was the attempt to make teaching methods more child-friendly, pragmatic, and democratic. This pedagogical Progressive movement began in the late nineteenth century but came to be associated with John Dewey. Despite much public attention, these reforms made only moderate impact, at best, on how teachers taught outside kindergarten and early elementary school. On the other hand, administrative Progressives, led by business elites and university faculty, engineered an extremely successful reorganization of the organizational and curricular aspects of public schools, shrinking school boards and professionalizing school administration, enforcing long-neglected laws related to compulsory education, consolidating rural school districts, expanding vocational education, and, aided by intelligence testing, organizing curricular tracks to prepare students for their future roles in society. These reformers felt that their crowning achievement was the comprehensive public high school.

As the industrial economy attracted millions of immigrants from southern and eastern Europe, American public schools began programs to Americanize immigrants—the children through regular classes and the adults through evening schools—emphasizing patriotism and English-language instruction. American empire-building abroad resulted in another form of Americanization. Colonial leaders in the Philippines built a comprehensive, American-style system of public schools on the model of the administrative Progressives, with an emphasis on low-skill industrial education; this mirrored similar programs in Liberia, in the Jim Crow South, and on American Indian reservations. People in each context resisted or appropriated these forms of education, depending on the individuals and the context.

Civil Rights Movement, 1940–1980.

In the early twentieth century, Jim Crow laws in southern states continued to require separate schools for black and white children.

Western states maintained a patchwork of segregationist, or even exclusionary, policies regarding Latinos and Asian Americans. De facto segregation was common in northern states, where state-encouraged residential segregation and biased ability-tracking within schools often kept black and white children apart. Although the Supreme Court ruled in *Brown v. Board of Education* (1954) that segregating students by race—by law in southern states and through racist housing policies in many northern states—was unconstitutional, state and local governments ignored or resisted the ruling for more than a decade. Meanwhile the National Association for the Advancement of Colored People (NAACP) and a variety of other national organizations mobilized resistance against segregation in court, in the media, through public protest, and at the polls. These actions led to the Civil Rights Act (1964), which also included antidiscrimination protections for women and minorities. The years from 1964 to 1974 were the most intense period of forced desegregation of public schools across the United States. Desegregation usually occurred on white terms, however, and resulted in the widespread dismissal of African American administrators and, to a lesser degree, African American teachers as black schools closed down and black children went to formerly white schools. In northern cities, desegregation plans usually involved redrawing district boundaries and busing students out of their local neighborhoods.

Beginning in the 1960s, other groups such as women, Latinos, American Indians, Asian Americans, and advocates for children with disabilities built on the African American rights movement, winning legal decisions, protective legislation, and local policy changes regarding discrimination and joining efforts to edit offensive curriculum materials. Teachers, who had begun unionizing in resistance to reforms by the administrative Progressives, organized and successfully pressed most state legislatures to grant them collective bargaining rights, starting with Wisconsin in 1959. Although a majority of teachers did not belong to a union until the 1960s, by 2011, approximately 3.2 million teachers belonged to the National Education Association and another 1.5 million to the American Federation of Teachers.

Era of Contrapuntal Reform, 1980–2010s.

Reforms from 1980 through 2010 pulled mass education in several directions at once. Racial integration peaked during the 1980s and then began to decline, rapidly. The integration of students with disabilities into regular classrooms, in contrast, increased during the same period, as did the steady removal of overtly racist and sexist content in curriculum materials. The conservative political resurgence of the 1980s fueled what were called "back to basics" curriculum changes at the high school level. By the 2000s, state curriculum standards and federally mandated tests had led to widespread teaching reforms that emphasized literacy, math, and test preparation and dramatically reduced instruction at the elementary level in the arts, science, and social studies. Starting in the 1990s, many states moved toward deregulation in school organization, including limited experiments with public vouchers for private schools and public charter schools. The fastest-growing movement in mass education, however, was not a particular kind of school at all, but rather homeschooling, usually for religious reasons: in 2007, an estimated 1.5 million children, or 2.9 percent of the school-age population, were being homeschooled.

Higher Education.

World War II and the Cold War marked a major turning point for American higher education, both in terms of major federal investment in military training and technological research and also—because of the Servicemen's Readjustment Act, or GI Bill, and subsequent federal student-loan programs—in terms of a massive expansion in enrollment. Community and other two-year colleges, begun in the late nineteenth century as gateways to four-year institutions, have enjoyed rapid growth since the 1960s, accounting for roughly one-third of all college enrollments in 2010.

The civil rights movement resulted in a slow process of desegregation across all sectors of higher education, and affirmative action policies led to increases in the number of women and minorities in student bodies, faculty, and staff. By the 1990s colleges and universities had reformed curricula and campus life to include new courses, new departments, new facilities, and new regulations intended to eliminate white supremacy and Eurocentrism. The Internet provided a new venue for teaching and learning at the end of the twentieth century, and the birth of online universities, most notably the University of Phoenix, heralded a major new movement in American education.

Despite fundamental changes to the social organization of information in America, the utopian promise of formal education as the panacea to social problems remained as strong at the start of the twenty-first century as it was in colonial times. Public schooling in particular served as a convenient scapegoat for explaining underlying inequalities and abuses of power—even as, paradoxically, it remained a powerful, if underused, force for combating them.

[*See also* **American Indian Movement; Americanization Movement; Anti-Catholicism; Asian American Movement; Child Workers; Clergy; Columbian Exchange; Disability Rights Movement; Disease; Everyday**

Life; Feminism; Labor Movements; Mexican American Civil Rights Movement; Missions, in America; Native American Boarding Schools; Praying Towns; Segregation, Racial; Separate Spheres Ideology; Slave Families and Communities; *and* Slave Resistance.]

BIBLIOGRAPHY

Altenbaugh, Richard J. *The American People and Their Education: A Social History.* Upper Saddle River, N.J.: Merrill Prentice Hall, 2003.

Anderson, James D. *The Education of Blacks in the South, 1860–1935.* Chapel Hill: University of North Carolina Press, 1988.

Axtell, James. *The Invasion Within: The Contest of Cultures in Colonial America.* New York: Oxford University Press, 1985.

Beadie, Nancy. *Education and the Creation of Capital in the Early American Republic.* Cambridge, U.K., and New York: Cambridge University Press, 2010.

Butchart, Ronald E. *Schooling the Freed People: Teaching, Learning, and the Struggle for Black Freedom, 1861–1876.* Chapel Hill: University of North Carolina Press, 2010.

Cuban, Larry. *How Teachers Taught: Constancy and Change in American Classrooms, 1890–1990.* 2d ed. New York: Teachers College Press, 1993.

Geiger, Roger L., ed. *The American College in the Nineteenth Century.* Nashville, Tenn.: Vanderbilt University Press, 2000.

Kaestle, Carl F. "Public Education in the Old Northwest: 'Necessary to Good Government and the Happiness of Mankind.'" *Indiana Magazine of History* 84, no. 1 (March 1988): 60–74.

Mirel, Jeffrey E. *Patriotic Pluralism: Americanization Education and European Immigrants.* Cambridge, Mass.: Harvard University Press, 2010.

Monaghan, E. Jennifer. *Learning to Read and Write in Colonial America.* Amherst: University of Massachusetts Press, 2005.

Moreno, José F., ed. *The Elusive Quest for Equality: 150 Years of Chicano/Chicana Education.*
Cambridge, Mass.: Harvard Educational Review, 1999.

Moss, Hilary J. *Schooling Citizens: The Struggle for African American Education in Antebellum America.* Chicago: University of Chicago, 2009.

Nash, Margaret A. *Women's Education in the United States, 1780–1840.* New York: Palgrave Macmillan, 2005.

Orme, Nicholas. *Medieval Schools: From Roman Britain to Renaissance England.* New Haven, Conn.: Yale University Press, 2006.

Reese, William J. *America's Public Schools: From the Common School to "No Child Left Behind."* Updated ed. Baltimore: Johns Hopkins University Press, 2011.

Szasz, Margaret Connell. *Indian Education in the American Colonies, 1607–1783.* Albuquerque: University of New Mexico Press, 1988.

Tolley, Kim. "The Rise of the Academies: Continuity or Change?" *History of Education Quarterly* 41, no. 2 (Summer 2001): 225–239.

Tyack, David, and Elisabeth Hansot. *Learning Together: A History of Coeducation in American Schools.* New Haven, Conn.: Yale University Press, 1990.

Urban, Wayne J., and Jennings L. Wagoner Jr. *American Education: A History.* 4th ed. New York: Routledge, 2009.

Webber, Thomas L. *Deep Like the Rivers: Education in the Slave Quarter Community, 1831–1865.* New York: W. W. Norton, 1978.

Benjamin Justice

EDWARDS, JONATHAN

(1703–1758), pastor, theologian, and philosopher who helped shape early American society through his writings and prominence in the first Great Awakening. After completing his education at Yale College in 1722, Edwards served brief stints as a temporary minister before undertaking a long-term position in Northampton, Massachusetts. This post allowed Edwards to emerge as a thinker and revival personality. His unpopular stances in heated controversies, however, ultimately led to his dismissal, after which he accepted a pastorate in Stockbridge, Massachusetts, focusing on missionary work to Mahican, Mohawk, and other American Indians. Then, just after assuming the presidency of what is now Princeton University, Edwards died as a result of complications from his smallpox inoculation.

During the Great Awakening, colonial America witnessed an organic refashioning of piety. Lay ministry flourished and worshippers experimented with spontaneous meeting times in fields, barns, and other unconventional spaces. Initially, Edwards was an avid supporter of the awakening and his *Faithful Narrative* (1738) on a previous revival became a widespread template for rejuvenating congregations. Furthermore, Edwards never ceased to insist that the movement was a work of God and he applauded several of its developments: its emphasis on scriptural authority, its openness to itinerant ministry, its tendency to increase Christian charity, and its ability to enhance relations between clergy and laity as well as unity among the faithful. His support was not unmitigated, however, for he also took exception to the movement's opposite tendencies toward church schism and the breakdown of ecclesiastical accountability.

A number of social tensions contributed to these problems. For one, revival strained age-group relations, dividing the church along generational lines. Land in the area was quickly becoming scarce, making the future for young people in the largely agrarian society uncertain. Those affected found themselves trapped in protracted adolescence and often responded to their financial inability to marry and start families by frequenting taverns and flouting sexual conventions. As an adult only just beyond this age-group,

Edwards sympathized and regularly exhorted young people to spend their time in more spiritually productive ways. In his view, as opposed to the prevailing sentiment, age had no inherent advantage when it came to spiritual wisdom and if young people reformed, they could have much to teach others. When the youth proved especially responsive to Edwards's exhortations, however, older congregants were suspicious, even antagonistic. Still, in reference to those whose faith endured, it was difficult to deny the power of Edwards's perspective. Consequently his commitment to the spiritual potential of young people did much to shape later views on the piety of youths.

A second social tension contributing to unrest in the Awakening involved gender relations. Male identity was previously located in farm and family, but as it became increasingly difficult to begin independent domestic life, men resisted this traditional model. Premarital pregnancy and denial of paternal responsibility escalated. For his part, Edwards took the controversial position that men needed to accept the consequences of their actions in this regard. This perspective accorded with his high regard for women overall, though the point should not be overstated; his views on women were rooted in an orthodox Christian morality rather than a progressive social agenda, as evinced by his simultaneous insistence on the matrimony of expectant couples.

Edwards is regularly praised for his theological creativity and philosophical acumen and many scholars have, accordingly, emphasized the contribution of his intellectual gifts to American and Western religious thought. It is nevertheless important to note that he was also a pastor who cared about the spiritual and moral development of his people, a care that shaped the way he chose to use those gifts.

[*See also* Clergy; Colonial Era; Great Awakenings; Itinerant Preachers; Religion; *and* Revivals.]

BIBLIOGRAPHY

Chamberlain, Ava. "Edwards and Social Issues." In *The Cambridge Companion to Jonathan Edwards*, edited by Stephen J. Stein, pp. 325–344. Cambridge, U.K.: Cambridge University Press, 2007. A lucid and concise study of Edwards in connection with issues of age and class conflict, changing gender relations, and African slavery.

Minkema, Kenneth P. "Old Age and Religion in the Writings and Life of Jonathan Edwards." *Church History* 70, no. 4 (December 2001): 674–704. The best treatment on the subject, singularly helpful in illuminating the ways in which Edwards dealt with the intergenerational tensions of his day.

Tracy, Patricia J. *Jonathan Edwards, Pastor: Religion and Society in Eighteenth-Century Northampton.* New York: Hill and Wang, 1980. A landmark work that is still influential; seminal for examining Edwards through the lens of social, rather than intellectual, history and for approaching him primarily as pastor rather than philosopher or theologian.

Bryan McCarthy

ELECTRICITY AND ELECTRIFICATION

Electricity—so named by the Englishman William Gilbert around 1600—was known since ancient times in the form of static electricity, which can be induced by rubbing amber, for example. From the seventeenth century onward, such scientists as Robert Boyle, Henry Cavendish, Alessandro Volta, G. S. Ohm, and the American Benjamin Franklin added to electrical knowledge. Franklin, whose *Experiments and Observations on Electricity* (1751–1753) won international attention, is best remembered for his 1752 experiment with a kite and a key in a thunderstorm, which demonstrated that lightning is an electrical discharge. By the early nineteenth century, Michael Faraday and other scientists were developing techniques of generating electricity. Working independently of Faraday, the American Joseph Henry began research on electromagnetism in 1827. Henry constructed an electromagnetic motor in 1829 and later discovered electrical induction, crucial to generating power, and demonstrated the oscillatory nature of electrical discharges.

Practical applications came slowly and piecemeal, long before anyone conceived of electrification as a universalizing process. Most early electrical technologies, including fire-alarm systems, railway signaling, burglar alarms, doorbells, servant-calling systems, and the telephone, were modifications of the telegraph, first demonstrated in 1838. These devices relied on batteries to supply a modest direct current. A much more powerful current was needed for practical lighting, heating, electroplating, and electric motors. Such applications developed only after about 1875 when improved generators and dynamos became available. After 1878, arc lighting, a powerful but crude form of illumination, drew crowds to demonstrations in city centers and expositions. Large cities quickly adopted lights for streets and public places such as theaters and department stores. Once Thomas Edison's firm installed incandescent lighting systems across the country, beginning in New York City in 1881, however, most indoor sites and street-lighting companies chose his technology. Edison and his assistants developed not only a practical incandescent lightbulb (1879), but also the now familiar system of wiring, wall switches, sockets, meters, insulated transmission lines, and central power plants. Edison designed this distribution system to compete with gaslight on price, while offering brighter and safer illumination. Rapidly adopted by the wealthy for fashionable indoor venues, including theaters, clubs, expensive homes, and the New York Stock Exchange, electric lighting became a prestigious and sought-after form of illumination.

Initially electrical technology had a separate energy source, as well as different financial backers. Lighting utilities, factories, and streetcar lines maintained their own power plants and delivery systems, with no uniform standards for wiring or current. The private systems installed by hotels, skyscrapers, and large private homes in the 1880s were incompatible with one another, but they did have the advantage of not requiring overhead wires—which soon became so numerous in the major cities as to constitute a public nuisance—or costly underground conduits. This pattern of development merely continued the earlier piecemeal commercialization of electricity.

Commercial Development and Standardization.

The electrical industry was the most dynamic sector of the economy between 1875 and 1900, growing into a $200-million-a-year industry with the backing of farsighted investors like J. P. Morgan, who financed Edison's work. Once commercial development began, a flurry of mergers reduced the field from fifteen competitors in 1885 to only General Electric and Westinghouse in 1892. Railroads, once America's largest corporations, were now a mature industry, in contrast to the rapidly expanding electric traction companies, local utilities, and equipment manufacturers that collectively exemplified the spread of managerial capitalism (as opposed to partnerships and family firms). From its inception, the electrical industry also relied heavily on scientific research and development, a fact formalized when General Electric founded the first corporate research laboratory in 1900.

Electric trolleys, eagerly sought by burgeoning cities to replace dirty, slow horsecars, became practical after 1887 when Frank Sprague's new motor proved itself in hilly Richmond, Virginia. By 1890, two hundred cities had ordered similar systems. By 1902, $2 billion had been invested in electric railways, and a typical urban family of four spent about $50 a year on fares. Electric trams were faster and cleaner than horsecars. They greatly expanded urban housing districts, and the lines soon expanded into the rural hinterland. They improved mobility for women and older children, who no longer needed a horse-drawn vehicle to visit town or the new (and heavily electrified) amusement parks built at the ends of the urban lines, starting in the early 1890s.

Electricity spread into factories with equal speed, starting with lighting in textile and flour mills. From a worker's point of view, incandescent lighting improved visibility and reduced pollution and the danger of fire, but it also made possible round-the-clock shifts. Furthermore, as electric motors and cranes provided more horsepower for production, they brought radical changes in the construction and layout of factories, most strikingly in Henry Ford's assembly line (1913), an innovation partly anticipated by Edison's experiments with automating iron mining in the 1890s. The assembly line was literally impossible in any complex industry before electricity freed machines from fixed, steam-driven overhead drive shafts.

As electrical systems spread throughout the industrial, commercial, and residential worlds, utilities improved the technologies for generating power and achieved economies of scale. They began to sell current and service so cheaply that the myriad small plants could no longer compete. Samuel Insull left Thomas Edison's employ in 1892 to head Chicago's Commonwealth Edison and remained a leading figure in utility development until 1929. Insull early grasped the importance of consolidating power production and maximizing consumption. Insull convinced traction companies and factories to abandon their power plants and to purchase electricity from him. Through astute marketing he created one of the world's largest electrical utilities. As others copied his methods, holding companies created regional power companies and linked the many local systems into a national power grid. Private companies proved more agile in the consolidation process, for they possessed readier access to capital and had fewer jurisdictional problems than government-run utilities did, and by the 1920s they owned all but a fraction of national generating capacity.

Between the 1880s and the 1940s the spread of electrification, first in cities and towns and then in rural areas, provided a major economic stimulus and transformed everyday life. An array of electric appliances—from fans, irons, and mixers to vacuum cleaners, refrigerators, and washing machines—eased labor for middle-class housewives. Domestic servants largely disappeared, men did less housework, and women were saddled with more responsibilities. For example, men and boys had typically been responsible for beating rugs and helping with spring cleaning, but after the vacuum cleaner became common, this work fell almost exclusively to mothers and daughters. Another different form of electric power, the storage battery, enhanced the manufacture and use of new technologies, including both the automotive and aviation industries. Electricity was also crucial to the new mass media—radio, films, and recordings—as well as to night

baseball, introduced in Cincinnati, Ohio, in 1935.

During the Depression of the 1930s, the federal government promoted public utilities, in part to create a yardstick to measure the price and performance of private power companies. The government built a system of dams on the Tennessee River—administered by the Tennessee Valley Authority (TVA), which sold power to rural cooperatives—as well as systems of dams on the Colorado and Columbia Rivers. Because private power had generally ignored farmers, only 10 percent of whom had electricity as late as 1935, President Franklin D. Roosevelt in 1935 established the Rural Electrification Administration (REA) to bring power to this neglected sector of the nation. Rural electrification spread comparatively slowly in the South and Middle West, where customers were widely dispersed, but more rapidly in the arid West, where farmers wanted electric pumps for irrigation, and in areas served by interurban trolleys. The REA and the TVA organized cooperatives and made available loans and technical expertise. By 1945, thanks to the New Deal, most of America was electrified. Electricity had important military applications as well, playing a crucial role in World War II and the Cold War era, for example, in the development of radar, rocketry, and the mainframe computers essential to ballistic missiles and space technology.

Changes beyond the Functional. Electric lighting dominated public spaces and changed the culture in ways that went far beyond the functional. American cities became the most intensively lighted in the world, not least because of the spread of electric advertising. Spurred by the marketing campaigns of Westinghouse, General Electric, and the utilities, the illuminated skyline became a source of civic pride. Even small cities aspired to emulate New York City's "Great White Way," where millions of flashing bulbs in Times Square and the theater district created a scintillating artificial environment. Nightlife expanded as hundreds of brightly lit amusement parks emerged as early as the 1890s, followed by stadiums and other outdoor venues.

As early as 1903, American cities were far more brightly lit than their European counterparts: Chicago, New York, and Boston had three to five times as many electric lights per inhabitant as Paris, London, and Berlin. This indicated more than prosperity and wealth. Levels and methods of lighting varied from culture to culture, and what was considered dramatic and necessary in the United States often seemed a violation of tradition elsewhere. Many European communities continued throughout the twentieth century to resist electric signs and spectacular advertising displays. At the 1994 Winter Olympics in Lillehammer, Norway, for example, the city council refused corporate sponsors the right to erect illuminated signs.

Once American families acquired electrical lighting, they had less reason to cluster at night around the hearth, giving rise to a pattern of dispersed privacy. With power available at the flick of a switch, consumers ceased to associate lighting with physical work such as hauling wood and ashes or cleaning lamps. Electricity also extended the range of usable space. Domestic activity after sunset was no longer confined to the hearth and the range of the kerosene lamp. In commerce, immense department stores, office buildings, and eventually malls could be built with adequate illumination far from any natural light source.

In industry, the flexibility of electrical power permitted the rearrangement of the work flow, and the expansion of the electrical grid made it possible to locate a factory virtually anywhere, without regard for proximity to coal supplies or water power. Further, because not only factories but also shops, homes, and businesses could spring up wherever the grid reached, electrification facilitated urban deconcentration. By the 1930s this trend was being assisted by the development of air-conditioning and climate control, and later it was assisted by computers and the electrical transmission of information.

But if electrification homogenized space, delivering light, power, climate control, and information to any site, it also facilitated the concentration of people in cities. Indeed, night satellite photographs of the United States reveal the location of thousands of cities as intense blobs of light. Electricity, a scientific curiosity in 1800 and still a novelty for the rich in 1880, had become indispensable by the mid-twentieth century and beyond. Domestic consumption increased faster than industrial uses did. The typical family of 2010 used as much electricity in a month as their grandparents had during an entire year in 1940. Families acquired more electrical devices, notably televisions, computers, and clothes dryers. As houses grew larger and air-conditioning became the norm, peak electrical demand shifted from night to day and from winter to summer. After the 1980s, power outages, once largely caused by storms and malfunctions, became common on hot afternoons because demand exceeded supply. For all its advantages, electricity also proved inseparable from blackouts, air pollution, and global warming.

[*See also* **Automation and Computerization; Cities and Suburbs; Communication Networks; Everyday Life; Gilded Age; New Deal Social Reforms; Progressive Era; Rural Life and Society;** *and* **Twenties, The.**]

BIBLIOGRAPHY

Hughes, Thomas P. *Networks of Power: Electrification in Western Society, 1880–1930.* Baltimore: Johns Hopkins University Press, 1983.

Nye, David E. *Electrifying America: Social Meanings of a New Technology, 1880–1940.* Cambridge, Mass.: MIT Press, 1990.

Nye, David E. *When the Lights Went Out: A History of Blackouts in America.* Cambridge, Mass.: MIT Press, 2010.

Platt, Harold L. *The Electric City: Energy and the Growth of the Chicago Area, 1880–1930.* Chicago: University of Chicago Press, 1991.

Rose, Mark H. *Cities of Light and Heat: Domesticating Gas and Electricity in Urban America.* University Park: Pennsylvania State University Press, 1995.

Tobey, Ronald C. *Technology as Freedom: The New Deal and the Electrical Modernization of the American Home.* Berkeley: University of California Press, 1996.

David E. Nye

ELLIS ISLAND

Ellis Island served as the entry point for millions of immigrants to the United States. Situated in Upper New York Bay, the island has had various names, including Gibbet Island, recalling its history as an execution site where pirates were hanged as late as the 1850s. The present name comes from Samuel Ellis, a butcher who owned the island in the 1780s. New York City ceded ownership to the state in 1794, which transferred it to the federal government in 1808. The city, however, retained jurisdiction for legal and tax purposes. In 1834, Congress divided jurisdiction over Ellis Island between New York and New Jersey, although the U.S. Supreme Court did not resolve competing claims until 1998.

Enlarged to some twenty-seven acres, Ellis Island opened as an immigration facility on 1 January 1892 in the wake of the 1891 immigration law, replacing the earlier embarkation point at Manhattan's Castle Garden. Some 446,000 immigrants arrived the first year. Although wealthier passengers continued to be processed dockside, third-class or steerage passengers were taken to Ellis Island. Over the years the increased volume of these immigrants led to increased concerns over social hygiene and public health, the worry that poor immigrants might become wards of the state, and fears over the political risks of foreign anarchists. With the 12 million who followed came overcrowding, deterioration, and public-health problems. Ellis Island also housed a hospital for immigrants detained for medical reasons. During the first decade of the twentieth century, the peak years of operation, a surge of immigrants arrived from southern and eastern Europe, although significant numbers also arrived from the Ottoman Empire and the Caribbean. Three-quarters of immigrants passed through Ellis, and for the 2 percent denied entry, Ellis became the "Island of Tears." Nevertheless, even this control regime failed to allay concerns. The quota laws of 1921 and 1924, which limited immigration on the basis of national origins, brought a sharp decline in activity. During World War II, Ellis Island was an enemy-alien detention facility. The immigration center briefly reopened after the war, but it closed permanently in 1954 and was declared surplus property in 1955. In 1965, the same year that immigration reform removed quotas, President Lyndon Johnson declared that the island would be administered by the National Park Service as part of the Statue of Liberty National Monument.

A surge of interest in ethnic history and genealogy in the 1970s led to the reopening of the decaying site to visitors in 1976. Coinciding with the restoration of the

Statue of Liberty, a well-publicized private fund-raising campaign began in 1982 and led to the renovation of the Great Hall as the focal point of the Ellis Island Immigration Museum, which opened to the public in 1990. Restoration work on other buildings continued into the twenty-first century. Meanwhile the success of the museum at Ellis Island has led to other immigration museums including the Angel Island Immigration Station in California and foreign immigration stations in Buenos Aires, Hamburg, and Paris. As a monument to the special—though hardly unique—role of immigration in America, Ellis Island represents an era before immigrant control became a consular matter, one to be handled abroad before immigrants are allowed to arrive at international arrivals centers, airports, and border crossings.

[*See also* **Aliens during Wartime; Caribbean; Central and Eastern European Americans; Deportations and Repatriations; Immigration;** *and* **Jewish Americans.**]

BIBLIOGRAPHY

Benton, Barbara. *Ellis Island, A Pictorial History.* New York: Facts on File, 1985.

Green, Nancy L. "History at Large: A French Ellis Island? Museums, Memory, and History in France and the United States." *History Workshop Journal* 63 (Spring 2007): 239–253.

Pitkin, Thomas M. *Keepers of the Gate: A History of Ellis Island.* New York: New York University Press, 1975.

Leo Hershkowitz;
updated by Kenneth A. Scherzer

EMANCIPATION OF SLAVES

Slavery came to the British North American colonies slowly and haphazardly. The first blacks who arrived in 1619 were treated as indentured servants, and some became free. As late as the 1670s courts in Virginia held that some blacks had come into the colony as servants and thus were free at the completion of their indenture. By this time, however, newly imported Africans were coming into the colony as slaves. From its creation South Carolina had slavery, and by 1739 it was two-thirds black. By this time slavery could be found in every colony; it had emerged as a major source of labor in Virginia, Maryland, and the Carolinas, and it was beginning to have the same status in Georgia. Slavery was also an important part of the economy in New York, New Jersey, and parts of Pennsylvania. Less important in New England, slavery was hardly uncommon there. Wherever slavery was found, some masters manumitted their slaves, and slaves always sought freedom. Not surprisingly, the nature of slavery and the number of slaves in a particular area affected the possibility of manumission and often its legality.

Colonial and Revolutionary Eras. From the emergence of slavery there was a tension between bondage and freedom that was accentuated by English traditions of liberty. The British who first came to America had no experience with slavery and were culturally hostile to the institution. Indeed, the earliest British settlers and traders in the New World saw themselves as liberators who would save Indians and blacks from Spanish oppression. By the end of the seventeenth century, however, a culture of slavery had emerged, supported by the legal system, the Anglican Church, and local legislatures. By 1700, slaves were valuable, prized possessions, especially in the South. They were also increasingly important to the southern production of tobacco, forest products, indigo, and rice. Few masters had any qualms about owning slaves, and even fewer were willing to forgo their value by manumitting them. In 1691, Virginia, the largest colony and the one with the most slaves, prohibited manumission unless the slaves were transported out of the colony. Pre-Revolutionary South Carolina allowed manumission, but the practice was most used to free slave mistresses and their mixed-race children. In 1790 the first U.S. Census found eighteen hundred free blacks in the state. Maryland had about the same number of free blacks in 1755, 80 percent of whom were of mixed ancestry, suggesting that they were slave children manumitted by their white fathers.

However, not all settlers in British North America accepted the emerging slave system. In 1688, Mennonites in Pennsylvania issued the English world's first protest against slavery, and within half a century almost all Quakers and other Pietists opposed the institution. In 1700, Judge Samuel Sewall in Massachusetts published *The Selling of Joseph*, which was the first extensive condemnation of slavery in the New World. In the 1740s and 1750s the writings and lobbying of the Quaker abolitionists Anthony Benezet and John Woolman convinced many of their coreligionists of the immorality of slavery. In 1758 the Philadelphia Yearly Meeting urged all Quakers to free their slaves. Other Quaker meetings followed this lead, and by the eve of the Revolution almost all northern Quakers had manumitted their slaves or were trying to do so. Some early Baptists opposed slavery, as did John Wesley, who initially required that anyone joining his Methodist Church manumit his or her slaves. In the southern colonies, legal restrictions on manumission limited Quaker manumissions.

By the eve of the Revolution, there were about fifty thousand slaves in the North, with nearly a third of them in New York. By this time there was a significant free-black population as well. Some of these blacks gained their freedom through manumissions; others were fugitives. Some were the children of white women and black men, which was more common in New England than elsewhere. One famous example was the Reverend Lemuel Haynes. His mother was white and his father black. He later married a white woman. Most of the free blacks lived in urban centers, such as New York, Philadelphia, and Boston, and many free-black men were mariners. As early as 1709, Rhode Island tried to control interactions between slaves and free people (both black and white), understanding that such relationships led to escapes and in other ways undermined slavery. In the 1740s New York officials complained about slaves mixing with whites and free blacks in taverns and other public places. The discovery of a slave plot in 1741 led to trials of whites and slaves in New York: sixteen blacks and four whites were hanged, and another thirteen blacks were burned at the stake. This event illustrated the danger of slave revolts, even in the North, but the involvement of both blacks and whites in the plot also suggests the instability of slavery in the large seaport towns of the North. Many scholars doubt that the plot ever existed. Whether the plot was real or not, northerners were clearly concerned about slavery, interracial cooperation, and free blacks. However, the northern colonies did little to stop private manumissions, which often resulted from the religious convictions of Quakers, Methodists, Baptists, and Puritans and their theological descendants (Congregationalists and Unitarians).

As the Americans moved toward the Revolution, slaves in New England sought their freedom. In 1773 and 1774, slaves in Massachusetts petitioned Governor Thomas Hutchinson for their freedom, and when the Revolution began, they turned to the new government for help, arguing that if the

Americans were entitled to their liberty, so were the slaves in America. Although unsuccessful, these petitions set the stage for emancipation later.

The Revolution undermined slavery throughout the nation. In Virginia, Lord Dunmore offered freedom to any slaves who would serve in the British army. At least eight hundred slaves answered his call before he was forced to take refuge on a ship off the coast. At the end of the war, about eight thousand blacks left America with the departing British army. Most ended up as free people in Canada, Britain, the West Indies, or West Africa. A few evacuated with the Hessians and moved to Germany. Some were also reenslaved in the Caribbean. In the South, thousands of other slaves simply used the turmoil of the war to escape their bondage; mostly they moved to the few cities in the region or to the North.

Of the southern states, only Maryland authorized the enlistment of slaves—who gained their freedom through their service. Virginia allowed some free blacks to fight, and a few masters manumitted their slaves for this purpose, but there was no general movement of masters to manumit their slaves so that they could then fight in the army. James Madison proposed a regiment of slaves— who would become free—led by white officers, but the state had no interest in such plans. When Lord Cornwallis was ravaging Virginia, Governor Thomas Jefferson complained that the British had taken some of his slaves, but Jefferson opposed enlisting slaves to help stop the British.

The North. In the North, thousands of slaves enlisted in the army. Many free blacks were already in the colonial militias when the war began, and free blacks fought at Bunker Hill. Hundreds more blacks soon joined them as New England masters manumitted their slaves so that they could join the patriot cause. More than half the soldiers in the First Rhode Island were recently manumitted slaves, and by the end of the conflict this heavily integrated regiment was one of General George Washington's most reliable. While northern black men marched off to fight Britain, on the home front whites and blacks rejected human bondage. In 1778 the town meetings in Massachusetts rejected a proposed state constitution, in part because it did not end slavery. John Adams then drafted a new document: it began with the clear statement, "All men are born free and equal." The new constitution was ratified in 1780. In 1781 a Massachusetts slave named Quock Walker left his master, Nathaniel Jennison, to work for wages. The disgruntled Jennison was prosecuted after he seized Walker and beat him. A series of cases involving Walker led to the state's highest court's declaring in 1783 that slavery was no longer legal in the Bay State. By that time a jury in western Massachusetts had reached the same conclusion in the case of Elizabeth Freeman, known as Mumbet. In 1783, New Hampshire adopted a similar clause in its constitution, and by 1800 the Census reported no slaves in that state. Meanwhile, in 1780 Pennsylvania passed a gradual-abolition act, strengthened in 1788, that provided that the children of all slave women would be born free, subject to an indenture until they were adults. Such gradual-abolition laws were an attempt to balance the property interest that masters had in slaves with the liberty interest of the slaves themselves. After the laws' passage many masters began to free their slaves, reflecting the North's growing opposition to slavery. In Pennsylvania the slave population went from about 10,000 at the beginning of the Revolution to less than 4,000 by 1790; by 1800 it was less than 2,000. In 1784, Connecticut and Rhode Island passed similar laws for gradual abolition, as did New York in 1799 and New Jersey in 1804.

The effects of these laws and constitutional provisions, along with the wartime manumissions, were palpable. In 1775 there were about 14,000 slaves in New England. Twenty-five years later there were just 1,339 slaves, and by 1810 there were fewer than 500. In 1840 the Census found 23 aging slaves in all of New England. In 1817, New York accelerated its abolition process by decreeing that all slaves in the state would be emancipated on 4 July 1827.

Free blacks in all of these states faced varying amounts of discrimination, but clearly the North provided them with opportunities unknown in the South. Some states would not admit blacks to the bar, but otherwise no professions or skilled trades were formally closed to them. Education—although often segregated and inferior—was legal and available. There were no restrictions on what property blacks could own. They could vote in Massachusetts, New Hampshire, New York, Pennsylvania, and Vermont, the fourteenth state. Before 1850 a few blacks held public office in the North, and some became doctors and lawyers and attended colleges. The black population in New England grew from 17,000, including about 3,900 slaves, in 1790 to 24,700, all of whom were free, in 1860. In the middle Atlantic the growth was more impressive, from 50,000 blacks, including 36,000 slaves, in 1790 to more than 131,000 free blacks in 1860. Much of this growth came from the arrival of fugitive slaves. Free blacks created their own churches, schools, social organizations, and self-help groups. Out of these communities emerged two major black institutions that have continued into the twenty-first century. The Prince Hall Masons, named for a black Revolutionary War hero, began as an independent Masonic lodge in Boston in the 1770s and became a separate organization in 1791. In 1787 the Philadelphia blacks Richard Allen and Absalom Jones, fed up with discrimination and segregation in white churches, founded the Free African Society, which later evolved into the African Methodist Episcopal (AME) Church. Both the AME Church and the Prince Hall Masons became national institutions in the nineteenth century.

The Northwest Ordinance of 1787 banned slavery in what is today Ohio, Indiana, Illinois, Michigan, and Wisconsin. At the time, however, there were already a significant number of slaves in Indiana and Illinois. The ordinance did not act as an emancipation proclamation, and slaveholders, mostly of French origin, tenaciously held on to their human property. In *State v. LaSalle* (1820) the Indiana Supreme Court ruled that the slave woman Polly was entitled to her freedom under the state's constitution of 1816. However, there is some evidence that she and other blacks were held in bondage into the 1830s. Illinois ended slavery in its 1818 constitution, but public pressure undermined any implementation of the provision for those already held in bondage, and as late as the 1840s, blacks were held in slavery or long-term servitude in the state. Indiana and Illinois, along with Ohio until 1849, also had enormously restrictive laws on black migration, requiring that blacks entering the state prove their freedom, register with local authorities, and find sureties to guarantee their support and good behavior. These states prohibited blacks from testifying against whites, voting, or attending public schools. The registration laws were mostly unenforced, and southern blacks—both fugitives and those recently manumitted—moved to the lower Midwest throughout the antebellum period. Thus Ohio's black population, for instance, grew from only 198 in 1800 to more than 25,000 in 1850. In Ohio these blacks found jobs, bought property, created churches, and sent their children to school. At statehood in 1818, Illinois had about 1,300 blacks, two-thirds of whom were slaves. Despite that state's discriminatory laws, in 1850 Illinois had more than 5,400 free blacks.

By 1850 the North had free-black communities spread from Maine to Iowa. Former slaves had died, succeeded by freeborn blacks who struggled against discrimination, joined antislavery societies, helped fugitives through the Underground Railroad, and, where possible, voted and participated in politics. They sent their children to school wherever possible—and both literacy and school attendance among northern free blacks exceeded those of the whites in a number of southern states. Some emancipated slaves and freeborn blacks attended northern colleges. Though most were laborers, sailors, farmers, and domestic workers, many were skilled craftsmen, and a few became doctors, lawyers, dentists, and teachers. Though many were poor, a significant number owned land. Northern black communities were constantly augmented by manumitted slaves from the South—people like John Mercer Langston, whose white Virginia father freed him and sent him to Ohio, where in the 1850s he became a lawyer and an elected public official, while his brother Charles became a schoolteacher. Fugitive slaves—most famously Frederick Douglass—added to the growth and leadership of these communities. The free states also liberated slaves whose masters brought them north on business or pleasure. Transit accounted for relatively few slaves' gaining their freedom, but the northern court decisions on this issue showed that northerners, whatever their views of free blacks, were unwilling to tolerate any slavery in their communities, even if this led to a growing population of free blacks and strained sectional relations. A number of southern states complained about these decisions when justifying secession.

The South. Though the Revolution destroyed slavery in the North, it had a very different effect on the South. Before the war, most of the slaves brought to the mainland had come from British traders. At the beginning of the Revolution, as part of their economic boycott of British merchants, all of the American states had prohibited the African slave trade. About eight thousand slaves, mostly from the South, evacuated with the British. This loss, combined with slaves who ran away during the war, meant that after the war southern masters were desperate to regain enough slaves to profitably operate their farms and plantations and expand into new lands to the west. After the war, slave prices were high, and demand was strong. This did not bode well for any kind of emancipation scheme. In 1782, Virginia allowed masters to privately manumit adult slaves without the newly freed people's having to leave the state. Thousands of masters took advantage of this law, and the state's population of free blacks grew from about 2,000 in 1780 to more than 30,000 by 1810. In 1806 the manumission law was repealed, though until 1852 Virginia sporadically allowed some in-state manumission on a case-by-case basis or by special legislation. By 1830 in-state manumissions were rare, and for the next three decades births accounted for virtually all the growth of the free-black population in the state. Virginia's 1852 constitution prohibited in-state manumission and required the enslavement of any newly freed black who remained in the state more than twelve months; the constitution also authorized the legislature to pass laws to expel all free blacks from the state.

There are a few examples of dramatic and important private manumissions. In the

1790s Robert "King" Carter manumitted more than 450 slaves, convinced that he must do so as a Christian. George Washington freed all his slaves in his will, which was written to disinherit any heir who challenged the manumission clause. While serving as James Madison's private secretary during the War of 1812, Thomas Jefferson's neighbor Edward Coles decided to free his slaves, but by the time the war was over, it was virtually impossible to do this and keep the slaves in the state. Thus he took all his slaves to Illinois, bought six thousand acres of land there, and freed them. Jefferson, on the other hand, freed only three slaves during his life and only a few more at his death, leaving hundreds to be auctioned off. All those freed were either the brothers of his slave mistress Sally Hemings or the children he had with her. He did not manumit Sally.

From 1790 to 1860 numerous, less famous southern masters tried to free their slaves in their wills. Early on, southern legislatures and courts were sympathetic to these masters. When the Quakers John Pleasants and his son Jonathan died during the Revolution, they directed their executor Robert Pleasants (John's son) to free their slaves if and when the laws of Virginia allowed this to be done without the slaves' having to leave the state. The 1782 law allowed this, but Robert was not able to act on the wills until the 1790s. In 1799, Virginia's highest court upheld both wills, even though technically they may have violated the rule against perpetuities, which prohibited tying up property through estates for indefinite periods of time. In order to free these slaves—numbering more than one hundred—Robert had to sue many of his relatives, who did not share his Quaker faith or his antislavery principles.

When Herbert Elder died in Petersburg, Virginia, in 1826, his will provided that all his slaves be examined and given the choice of either remaining in Virginia as slaves or going to Liberia as free people. In 1833, Virginia's highest court upheld this will, over the protests of heirs who wanted the slaves themselves. However, in 1858 the Virginia court rejected an almost identical will, saying that slaves could not be asked to make any legal decisions, including the decision of whether they wanted to remain as slaves or go to Liberia. Other states had a similar jurisprudence. Alabama allowed manumission by will until 1834, but the courts would not approve manumissions after that date, even if the testator had died before the new law was passed and the will had been probated. In *Mitchell v. Wells* (1859), Mississippi's highest court ruled that a slave was not free under Mississippi law even though her master (who was also her father) had taken her to Ohio and formally manumitted her under the laws of that state.

By the eve of the Civil War, most of the states that ultimately joined the Confederacy had either banned in-state manumission or made it extraordinarily difficult. Manumission was possible in Kentucky and Missouri, but it was uncommon. In 1850, Kentucky had 10,011 free blacks, and a decade later there were only 10,684. Manumission was at a standstill there, and free blacks were moving out. Even though Kentucky continued to export slaves to the Deep South, its slave population was still growing from births. Missouri had an even smaller number and percentage of free blacks. Only in Maryland and Delaware was manumission common. Maryland had only 8,000 free blacks and 103,000 slaves in 1790. The state's slave population peaked in 1810 at 112,000 and then slowly declined through out-of-state sales and manumissions. By 1860, Maryland had 87,000 slaves and 84,000 free blacks. In Delaware the changes were more dramatic. In 1790 the state had about 3,900 free blacks and about 8,900 slaves. By 1860 it had just under 20,000 free blacks but only 1,800 slaves.

Wherever they lived in the South, recently manumitted slaves, like other free blacks, faced far greater obstacles than their counterparts in the North did. In some parts of the North, free blacks were not allowed to attend public schools; in most of the South it was illegal to teach a free black to read and write. Northern blacks like Richard Allen started their own churches to escape the racism of white-dominated churches; in many parts of the South, free blacks were not allowed to worship without some white person present to monitor what they were saying and talking about. Blacks in the North faced discrimination in courts, and the few black lawyers struggled to find clients; in the South, free blacks could never testify for or against whites, and no blacks could be lawyers—or for that matter doctors, dentists, gunsmiths, printers, typesetters, or pharmacists. Only a few northern colleges admitted blacks, but none in the South did.

In some slave states, free blacks had to have white guardians, and all the slave states limited the kind of property they might own, as well as their mobility. Most of all, free blacks in the South were in constant jeopardy of losing their freedom if they went into debt or were convicted of some crimes. Free blacks who married slaves—and many did—were indirectly subjected to the will of their spouse's master, and their marriage could be destroyed by sale or even by the refusal of a master to allow the slave to see his or her spouse. Because almost all southern states prohibited the in-migration of free blacks, if the master of a slave spouse moved, the free black probably could not follow. If a free-black male married a slave, his children would be slaves, owned by his wife's master. All these unions were, of course, marriages in name only; the law did not recognize the right of a slave to be legally married.

In 1832, in the wake of Nat Turner's rebellion, the Virginia House of Delegates debated a proposal to gradually end slavery. The measure would have disrupted the system, and had it been adopted, many decades would have been needed before bondage was ended. The proposals were never passed in the House of Delegates and were not even considered by the state senate. This was the only time before the Civil War that any legislature of a slave state even debated emancipation. In the next thirty years, attitudes toward slavery hardened. Indeed, by 1860 the slave South was debating whether it should reenslave all its free blacks. Arkansas passed a law requiring all free blacks to leave the state by 1862. At this time Charleston, South Carolina, had a substantial community of mixed-race people, many of whom were reasonably well-off. But on the eve of the Civil War they felt enormous pressure. Nearly a thousand left the city, fearful that they would be reenslaved. South Carolina officials, fearful that these people might use their knowledge of the city and its port against it, would not let some of them leave.

Civil War. Thus in 1860, freedom was far from the horizon of southern slaves, and bondage loomed over the horizon for the quarter of a million or so free blacks who lived in the South. All this changed after 12 April 1861 when the war began. Under the Constitution the national government had no power to interfere with slavery in the states, and in his first inaugural address President Abraham Lincoln reiterated this. When the war began, Lincoln assured the four loyal slave states, as well as northern conservatives, that the war was not about emancipation: it was being fought only to preserve the Union. But the slaves knew better. In May

1861 three slaves owned by the Confederate colonel Charles K. Mallory escaped to Fort Monroe, Virginia, which was under the command of the U.S. Army general Benjamin F. Butler. A day later, a Confederate major, under a flag of truce and citing the Fugitive Slave Law, demanded the return of the slaves. Acting as Mallory's agent, this Confederate officer argued that Butler had a constitutional obligation to return the slaves. Butler, a successful Massachusetts lawyer before the war, had devoted some thought to the issue. He responded that "the fugitive slave act did not affect a foreign country, which Virginia claimed to be[,] and she must reckon it one of the infelicities of her position that in so far at least she was taken at her word." Butler then offered to return the slaves to Colonel Mallory if he would come to Fort Monroe and "take the oath of allegiance to the Constitution of the United States." Until Mallory took such an oath, however, his slaves were contrabands of war and could not be returned.

By the end of the summer the army had adopted Butler's notion of contrabands, and army commanders were authorized to give sanctuary to any Confederate-owned slaves who escaped to their lines. In the summer of 1862, Congress prohibited officers from returning fugitives. A few months before that, Congress freed all the slaves in the District of Columbia through compensated emancipation and ended slavery in the territories without compensation. Meanwhile tens of thousands of slaves escaped to army lines, where they were employed as cooks, teamsters, burial crews, nurses, and laborers of all kinds. Though not technically soldiers, they were usually dressed in U.S. Army uniforms and often went into battle to support the troops. In September, Lincoln issued the preliminary Emancipation Proclamation and ordered the immediate enlistment of black troops. Ultimately more than two hundred thousand blacks served in the U.S. army and navy, most of whom were slaves when the war began.

After the announcement of the final Emancipation Proclamation on 1 January 1863, the war to preserve the Union became a war for freedom. As the armies marched deeper into the South, slaves ran from their owners and to their liberators. Masters across the South who believed that their slaves were happy and content woke up shocked to discover that all their "people" had fled to freedom. Hundreds of thousands gained their freedom this way, but the majority of slaves were emancipated by the Confederate surrender, which brought the Emancipation Proclamation to those parts of the South untouched by U.S. Army contact. In January 1865, Congress sent the Thirteenth Amendment to the states for ratification. When adopted in December of that year, slavery was forever abolished in the United States.

The newly freed people were universally poor and mostly illiterate. Many had never handled money, much less worked in a cash economy. They were eager for education and to work for wages. They lined up before army chaplains and at courthouses to take vows and to register their slave unions as legal, valid marriages. Many traveled enormous distances to find spouses, children, and parents from whom they had been separated by sale and forced migration. Most of all, they savored their liberty. Their future would be grimmer than any might have imagined, but it was always better than the slave past they left behind.

[*See also* **African American Emigration; African Americans; Antislavery; Civil War Era; Colonization Movement, African; Free Communities of Color; Law and Society; Maroon Societies; Military Personnel,** subentry on Civil War, African Americans; Reconstruction Era; Slave Families and Communities; Slaveholders; Slave Rebellions; Slave Resistance; Slavery; and Underground Railroad.]

BIBLIOGRAPHY

Berlin, Ira. *Slaves without Masters: The Free Negro in the Antebellum South.* New York: Pantheon, 1974.

Breen, T. H., and Stephen Innes. *"Myne Owne Ground": Race and Freedom on Virginia's Eastern Shore, 1640–1676.* New York: Oxford University Press, 1980.

Finkelman, Paul. *An Imperfect Union: Slavery, Federalism, and Comity.* Chapel Hill: University of North Carolina Press, 1981.

Finkelman, Paul. "Lincoln, Emancipation, and the Limits of Constitutional Change." *Supreme Court Review* 2008 (2009): 349–387.

Finkelman, Paul. *Slavery and the Founders: Race and Liberty in the Age of Jefferson.* 2d ed. Armonk, N Y: M. E. Sharpe, 2001.

Franklin, John Hope. *The Free Negro in North Carolina, 1790–1860.* Chapel Hill: University of North Carolina Press, 1943.

Horton, James Oliver, and Lois E. Horton. *In Hope of Liberty: Culture, Community, and Protest among Northern Free Blacks, 1700–1860.* New York: Oxford University Press, 1997.

Johnson, Michael P., and James L. Roark. *Black Masters: A Free Family of Color in the Old South.* New York: W. W. Norton and Company, 1984.

Jones, Bernie D. *Fathers of Conscience: Mixed-Race Inheritance in the Antebellum South.* Athens, Ga.: University of Georgia Press, 2009.

Levy, Andrew. *The First Emancipator: The Forgotten Story of Robert Carter, the Founding Father Who Freed His Slaves.* New York: Random House, 2005.

Morris, Thomas D. *Southern Slavery and the Law, 1619–1860.* Chapel Hill: University of North Carolina Press, 1996.

Nash, Gary B., and Jean R. Soderlund. *Freedom by Degrees: Emancipation in Pennsylvania and Its Aftermath.* New York: Oxford University Press, 1991.

Schafer, Judith Kelleher. *Becoming Free, Remaining Free: Manumission and Enslavement in New Orleans, 1846–1862.* Baton Rouge: Louisiana State University Press, 2003.

White, Shane. *Somewhat More Independent: The End of Slavery in New York City, 1770–1810.* Athens, Ga.: University of Georgia Press, 1991.

Wiencek, Henry. *An Imperfect God: George Washington, His Slaves, and the Creation of America.* New York: Farrar, Straus and Giroux, 2003.

Zilversmit, Arthur. *The First Emancipation: The Abolition of Slavery in the North.* Chicago: University of Chicago Press, 1967.

Paul Finkelman

ENVIRONMENTALISM

Although its roots go back much earlier, the social movement known as environmentalism first appeared in the 1960s. It soon became one of the most successful movements in modern history, with a national and global impact on health, land use, politics, economics, technology, design, and personal values. When the twentieth century ended, that impact seemed likely to endure, yet how truly profound it would be remained unclear. As it grew the movement came to mean different things to different groups, though at its core it remained an effort to improve human relationships with the other-than-human world.

Roots of Environmental and Ecological Awareness. In the early twentieth century, the word "environmentalism" referred mainly to the effects of external social influences (as opposed to genetic endowment) on the individual. But after World War II, "environment" increasingly came to mean the natural world surrounding people, including flora, fauna, climate, water, and soil—the entire ecosphere. At the same time, that natural world began to seem highly vulnerable to human activity; it was no longer an all-powerful Mother Earth providing boundless nourishment for her children but an endangered source of life. That sense of vulnerability inspired a social and political reform movement. Environmentalists called for a more responsible relationship between human beings and nature. Human survival was at stake, they argued, as was the stability and integrity of the whole fabric of life on the planet.

More and more citizens sensed that the human-natural world umbilical link was itself under attack, and that defending it required a radically new way of thinking. The environment, they insisted, had to be seen holistically. For them, nature was not a realm set above and apart from human beings, like another country that one visits from time to time, but instead was a vast, intricate community interacting all around us, a system of connections and interchanges to which all belong. Human beings, they concluded, cannot move away from that community, nor ignore it with impunity, even in the midst of the largest metropolis.

A defining work in the emergence of environmentalism was Rachel Carson's *Silent Spring* (1962), which warned of the wholesale contamination of the environment by chemical pesticides such as dichlorodiphenyltrichloroethane (DDT). Like many others of her generation, Carson was shaken by the fear of all-out nuclear war and worried that radioactive fallout from weapons testing was polluting food chains even in the remotest parts of the planet. In 1967 a group of scientists and lawyers founded the Environmental Defense Fund: arguing that pesticides were a threat to the health of both human beings and natural ecosystems, the fund sought to get them banned by the courts. The National Environmental Policy Act (1969) required

the preparation of an "environmental assessment" and an "environmental impact statement" for any federally funded project that might cause damage to the earth. On 2 December 1970, following a proposal by President Richard M. Nixon, a new federal regulatory agency, the Environmental Protection Agency, was established. Meanwhile the 1963 Limited Nuclear Test Ban Treaty, a ban on DDT use in the United States, and the passage of many new laws, including the 1960 Clean Water Act and the 1963 Clean Air Act, all sprang from a growing conviction that the human-natural world relationship was more essential than Americans had generally realized, and that what happened to one side of the relationship inevitably affected what happened to the other.

Capping a decade of ferment, environmentalists in 1970 declared the first Earth Day, an event to celebrate human-natural world interdependence. An estimated 20 million people, most of them North Americans and most under the age of thirty, participated, far outnumbering student demonstrations for the civil rights movement or for an end to the Vietnam War. The event became an annual, and eventually a truly international, ritual—an unprecedented global celebration of the Earth. More substantially, almost all nations passed laws similar to those enacted in the United States, and several nations surpassed the United States in cleaning up their rivers and air, recycling their wastes, reducing toxic emissions, improving energy efficiency, and preserving critical habitats for biodiversity.

Background Strands of Environmentalism. Within the United States, environmentalism was an amalgamation of several older strands of intellectual and political consciousness. Among them were nineteenth-century transcendentalism and the romantic movement. Rachel Carson acknowledged her indebtedness to such figures as Henry David Thoreau (1817–1862) and John Muir (1838–1914), both of whom had celebrated American nature in its wilder state and sought to recover a direct personal relationship with the nonhuman. Both looked for ways of getting outside the confines of civilization now and then and into primeval woods or mountains. Painters and poets had encouraged people to seek the sublime in nature, alone or in small groups, in such awe-inspiring landscapes as Yellowstone, Yosemite, and the Grand Canyon. Carson herself, a marine biologist with the U.S. Fish and Wildlife Service, was passionate about the sea; she found her wilderness in tidal pools along the Maine coast.

But by the 1960s, in a highly urbanized nation of more than 200 million people, with a far denser web of artifice obscuring the natural order, this kind of romantic quest had become increasingly difficult to satisfy by solitary, private excursions. Environmentalism, though inspired by romantic yearnings for contact with nature, could not be simply an individual act of reverence for nature or withdrawal from modernity; it must be a public project pursued collectively in the courtroom, the legislative chamber, and the corporate headquarters. Organization and lobbying were required to win passage of the 1964 Wilderness Act, which over the next three decades protected 105 million acres and stood as one of the great successes of the American environmental movement.

A second strand was the Progressive Era conservation movement, which gained momentum in the early twentieth century under the leadership both of Gifford Pinchot, chief forester during Theodore Roosevelt's presidency, and of Roosevelt himself. That movement supported the preservation of national parks and wildlife refuges, but more characteristically it set up a national forest system based on sustained-yield management principles and called for protecting the nation's soils and minerals from over-rapid development. The core ideal was "wise use." For Pinchot and his allies, that ideal required the federal government to be permanently in charge of managing land and overseeing national economic development. American society could not endure, they felt, without a secure, continuing permanent supply of natural resources. Unregulated private exploitation, they feared, threatened the nation's long-term security. The post-1960 environmental movement shared that same concern about stopping waste and inefficiency and safeguarding resources for the future, but it went further, calling for an overhaul of the entire modern industrial way of life to fit consumption patterns to the limits of the land.

A third source of modern environmentalism was a public-health movement working for cleaner, safer factories and urban neighborhoods. By the mid-nineteenth century, physicians and other professionals in Europe and North America were agitating for better sanitation to prevent devastating outbreaks of cholera and typhoid fever. The early targets had been water supplies contaminated by human waste, slaughterhouse offal, and garbage. As coal replaced wood as the nation's chief energy source after 1870, public-health concerns broadened to include air pollution, though clear medical evidence of the effects of such combustion on lungs and other body tissues was slow in coming. The urban environmentalist Alice Hamilton—a medical doctor, social worker at Jane Addams's Hull-House in Chicago, and professor of industrial hygiene at Harvard University—pioneered in investigating the poisons that infected workplaces and tenement dwellings. Reformers found life in the modern city particularly degraded and unwholesome, but they soon extended their efforts into rural areas, including Indian reservations and sharecroppers' cabins, wherever poor people disproportionately bore the costs of progress. Not until Rachel Carson, however, did public-health reformers generally begin to realize that the human body is a part of nature, too, and that its pollution by dangerous substances is one with the pollution of the earth.

A pivotal event in environmental health concern occurred in 1978 when a blue-collar community in Niagara Falls, New York, discovered that a dump of twenty thousand tons of toxic wastes was leaking into their homes and causing health problems. Hooker Chemical Company had buried those wastes in the old Love Canal, covered them with dirt, and sold the site to the school board and real estate developers. Those who had moved there suffered a huge number of miscarriages, birth defects, and urinary-tract diseases. The federal government was forced to move more than two hundred families out of the area, demolishing their houses and closing a school. But that remedy came only after people organized a vigorous protest movement, launching a new "environmental justice" crusade of national significance. Such grassroots activism to protect health, though part of modern environmentalism, seldom lasted beyond the immediate threat or raised broader issues of consumption, health, and planetary stability.

Development of the Concept of Human Ecology. More comprehensively, the emergence of environmentalism owed much to a relatively obscure group of natural scientists in such fields as ecology, geology, climatology, epidemiology, and oceanography who first perceived the environment as an interactive physical system connecting human beings and the rest of nature. Visualizing that system on a global scale, many of them dramatically transcended the national

perspective of the Progressive conservationists or the localized concerns of urban health reformers. Their basic theories often came from abroad as well: from the Russian geologist V. I. Vernadsky, originator of the concept of the biosphere; from French and German geographers, who had long debated the question of nature as a limiting factor on human activity; and from a succession of English naturalists, including Charles Darwin, Charles Elton, and Arthur Tansley, who suggested the idea of the ecosystem. A key American figure in this emerging body of scientific thought was Aldo Leopold, a University of Wisconsin wildlife expert, who introduced many readers to the science of ecology through his *Sand County Almanac* (1949).

By the 1950s these scientific ideas had come together in a new integrative and interdisciplinary view that united the natural and social sciences, a view that might be called "human ecology." Avoiding the extremes of environmental determinism, which had tried to reduce cultures to their physical conditions, and of a technological optimism that was blind to all environmental limits, the new view insisted that human life must be lived within natural constraints, both physical and moral. Those constraints appeared in the form of delicately balanced earth systems, all of them increasingly vulnerable to human disturbance.

The concept of human ecology emerged on many fronts in the late 1940s and 1950s. The anthropologists Betty Meggers and Julian Steward—one working in Amazonia, the other in the American Southwest—laid the foundations for the field of cultural ecology. The historian James Malin argued for an ecological approach and applied it in his own studies of the relations of plants, animals, soils, climate, and human populations on the Great Plains. Among geographers, Carl Sauer produced influential essays and books exploring the effects of European colonialism on New World peoples and landscapes. Several of these scholars and others from diverse disciplines gathered in Princeton, New Jersey, in 1955 for a symposium on the deteriorating state of the human-nature relationship. The resulting publication, *Man's Role in Changing the Face of the Earth* (1956), dedicated to the nineteenth-century American conservationist George Perkins Marsh, played a major role in preparing the deeper intellectual ground for the environmental movement.

Among the symposium participants was Paul B. Sears, a botanist who chaired the conservation program at Yale University. In his short but prophetic paper "The Processes of Environmental Change by Man," included in *Man's Role*, Sears reviewed the global impact of human population growth, the intensification of agricultural land use, and water and air pollution in industrial areas, noting that the United States, with less than a tenth of the world's population, was consuming more than half of its mineral production. Neither Sears nor the other conference-goers called themselves "environmentalists," but their concern over the growing effect of human beings on global ecology helped give environmentalism a set of defining ideas and theories. In 1972 when environmentalists from many countries assembled in Stockholm, Sweden, to resurvey the global situation, they drew on the perspective worked out by these pioneering human ecologists. By the later 1990s, that same perspective had become widely popularized in the United States, and ecology—however shallow or profound—was part of the daily language of masses of people worldwide.

Growing Urgency and Backlash: Post-1960 Developments.

What the environmentalist movement added to these fertile new ideas of human ecology was a growing sense of urgency, bordering at times on apocalyptic fear. By the 1960s, activists warned of an environmental "crisis." Rachel Carson's nightmare of a future springtime when no birds would sing, because all were dead from manmade poisons, introduced a tone of anxiety that was missing from the writings of Thoreau, Pinchot, Hamilton, Leopold, or Sears. Following Carson, another anxious biologist, Paul Ehrlich, warned in *The Population Bomb* (1968) of a demographic hazard that "keeps ticking," ready to explode. In *The Closing Circle: Nature, Man, and Technology* (1971), the Washington University biologist Barry Commoner alerted the country to the death of Lake Erie from pollutants and the death of people from radioactivity, smog, and groundwater contamination. Commoner explained that he had first been alerted to the environmental crisis by the activities of the Atomic Energy Commission (predecessor of the Nuclear Regulatory Commission), which during the 1950s had exposed Americans and others to deadly strontium 90 through nuclear-weapons testing and then failed to let the public know the full consequences of that exposure. The urgent need, in his view, was for an awakened public, led by informed scientists, to force the government and corporate America to develop technologies that were less life-threatening. The specter haunting each of these environmentalists was nothing less than death—the death of birds, of ecosystems, of nature itself, and, because of our dependence on nature, the death of human beings as well.

Only slightly less apocalyptic were those environmentalists who by the 1970s called for a reevaluation of the purposes and consequences of economic development. In their view, an economy that was expanding geometrically, using ever more energy, land, minerals, and water, must eventually encounter the limits of the earth's resources. In 1972 a team of computer scientists published the book *The Limits to Growth*, which sought to understand how a complex set of five global trends—"accelerating industrialization, rapid population growth, widespread malnutrition, depletion of nonrenewable resources, and a deteriorating environment"— might interact with each other in nonlinear ways to overrun the carrying capacity of the earth. The book made a huge impact; it sold millions of copies and was translated into thirty-seven languages, making it by far the most influential environmental work of the modern era.

The environment, scientists insisted, must be seen as more than a storehouse of commodities to be ransacked and consumed. Here the new environmentalism challenged attitudes deeply engrained in economists, business leaders, politicians, and the public about the virtues of economic growth, attitudes underlying the modern economic system and indeed the whole materialistic ethos of contemporary culture. Although the popular response to this challenge was difficult to gauge, polls did show a growing tilt toward environmentalist views in all the industrial countries and a greater public willingness, at least in affluent societies, to make economic sacrifices to reduce pollution, preserve species, and consume less energy.

During the 1980s, as American politics turned conservative, a rising chorus of antienvironmentalists, led by President Ronald Reagan and Secretary of the Interior James Watt, insisted that the environment was neither fragile nor a real constraint on human ambition. The antienvironmental backlash continued during the presidency of George W. Bush (2001–2009). Closely linked to corporate interests and energy companies, the Bush administration sought to roll back environmental regulations, promoted logging in

national forests and oil drilling in the Arctic National Wildlife Refuge, and dropped investigations of more than 140 refineries and industrial sites suspected of violations of the Clean Air Act. The administration also withdrew from negotiations over the final terms of the 1997 Kyoto Protocol, an effort sponsored by the United Nations to reduce emissions contributing to global warming. Environmentalists responded by renewing their sense of mission and increasing their numbers.

The Sierra Club and other environmental organizations vigorously protested this retreat from a well-established bipartisan commitment to environmental protection. They countered opposition by seeking alliances with other groups demanding cultural change: with feminists, some of whom insisted that women were more attuned to ecological interdependencies than men were; with ethical radicals, who wanted to extend rights to animals, trees, and the rest of nature; and with social-justice advocates at home and abroad, who demanded protection for the poor from the environmental damage and toxic dumping by the rich. Above all, environmentalists tried to temper their gloomier tendencies with a more hopeful, and more politically acceptable, emphasis on creating a new "green future" in which environmentally sensitive cities, economies, and technologies would all be made harmonious with the tangled web of life.

[*See also* **Conservation Movement; Conservative Movement; Consumption; Deindustrialization; Feminism; Law and Society; Progressive Era; Public Health;** *and* **Seventies, The.**]

BIBLIOGRAPHY

Blum, Elizabeth D. *Love Canal Revisited: Race, Class, and Gender in Environmental Activism.* Lawrence: University Press of Kansas, 2008.

Fox, Stephen. *John Muir and His Legacy: The American Conservation Movement.* Boston: Little, Brown, 1981.

Gottlieb, Robert. *Forcing the Spring: The Transformation of the American Environmental Movement.* Washington, D.C.: Island Press, 1993.

Hays, Samuel P., with Barbara D. Hays. *Beauty, Health, and Permanence: Environmental Politics in the United States, 1955–1985.* Cambridge, U.K.: Cambridge University Press, 1987.

Kempton, Willett, James S. Boster, and Jennifer A. Hartley. *Environmental Values in American Culture.* Cambridge, Mass.: MIT Press, 1995.

Paehlke, Robert C. *Environmentalism and the Future of Progressive Politics.* New Haven, Conn.: Yale University Press, 1989.

Rothman, Hal K. *The Greening of a Nation? Environmentalism in the United States since 1945.* Fort Worth, Tex.: Harcourt Brace College, 1998.

Sale, Kirkpatrick. *The Green Revolution: The American Environmental Movement, 1962–1992.* New York: Hill and Wang, 1993.

Taylor, Bob Pepperman. *Our Limits Transgressed: Environmental Political Thought in America.* Lawrence: University Press of Kansas, 1992.

Worster, Donald. *Nature's Economy: A History of Ecological Ideas.* 2d ed. Cambridge, U.K.: Cambridge University Press, 1994.

Donald Worster; updated by Paul S. Boyer

EQUIANO, OLAUDAH

(1745?–1797), author of an autobiography about his life as a slave and antislavery activist. Olaudah Equiano, also known as Gustavus Vassa, virtually single-handedly founded the genre of the African American slave narrative when he published the story of his life. *The Interesting Narrative of the Life of Olaudah Equiano, or Gustavus Vassa, the African: Written by Himself,* published in London in March 1789, established many of the structural conventions used in nineteenth-century slave narratives.

Equiano's *Interesting Narrative* is a spiritual autobiography, captivity narrative, travel book, adventure tale, slavery narrative, economic treatise, apologia, and argument against the transatlantic slave trade and slavery. Equiano tells us that he was born into an Igbo ruling-class family in 1745 in what is now southeastern Nigeria, and that he was kidnapped and enslaved at around the age of eleven by fellow Africans. He writes that he was then sold to Europeans, who forced him to endure the transatlantic Middle Passage from Africa to the West Indies. Within a few weeks, he says, he was brought to Virginia. Recent biographical discoveries cast doubt on Equiano's story of his birth and early years. Baptismal and naval records say that he was born in South Carolina sometime between 1745 and 1747. If these records are accurate, Equiano must have invented his African birth, as well as his much-quoted account of the Middle Passage on a slave ship. The truth about the place and date of his birth may never be known.

A planter in Virginia sold him to Michael Henry Pascal, an officer in the British Royal Navy. Pascal renamed him Gustavus Vassa, which remained his legal name for the rest of his life. Pascal brought Equiano to London in 1754, and for the next eight years he saw military action with Pascal during the Seven Years' War. Pascal shocked Equiano at the end of the war in 1762 when he refused to grant him his freedom, instead selling him into the horrors of West Indian slavery. Always a clever businessman, Equiano was able to save enough money to buy his own freedom in 1766.

As a free man Equiano went on voyages of commerce, adventure, and discovery to North America, the West Indies, the Mediterranean, the Middle East, and the Arctic. His travels enabled him to observe and comment on types of involuntary servitude known during the eighteenth century, including galley slaves in Italy and Christians enslaved by Muslim Turks. After Equiano returned to London from his voyage toward the North Pole in 1773, he converted to Methodism. He became an outspoken opponent of the transatlantic slave trade during the 1780s, first in letters and book reviews in London newspapers and then in his autobiography. Equiano was a remarkably successful businessman. He never sold the copyright to his book, which he saw through nine editions, keeping all the profits himself. Unauthorized editions of the *Interesting Narrative* were also reprinted during his lifetime in Russia, Holland, Germany, and New York City. Equiano married an Englishwoman in 1792, with whom he had two daughters. One of his daughters survived to inherit the sizable estate he left at his death on 31 March 1797.

[*See also* **Slavery, subentry on Colonial and Revolutionary Era,** *and* **Slave Trades, subentry on An Overview.**]

BIBLIOGRAPHY

Carretta, Vincent. *Equiano, the African: Biography of a Self-Made Man.* Athens, Ga.: University of Georgia Press, 2005.
Equiano, Olaudah. *The Interesting Narrative and Other Writings.* Edited by Vincent Carretta. Rev. ed. New York: Penguin, 2003.

Vincent Carretta

ESKIMOS

In 1867 the United States purchased the Alaska Territory from Russia. The Territory had three major groups of Eskimos—the Iñuit, the Yupiit, and the Yupiget—living mainly along the northern, central, and southwestern coastal areas. In the twenty-first century, Alaska's Eskimos are distinguished by unique tribal histories and cultures that reflect deep ties to indigenous homelands. First languages of the Eskimo-Aleut family (Central Yup'ik, Siberian Yupik, and Iñupiaq) and dialectical variants further distinguish individual tribes.

Migrations of pre-Eskimo peoples into Alaska probably occurred circa 6500 BCE or before. Most evidence of Alaskan Eskimo presence, however, is based on archaeological remains of settlements dating from circa 1 BCE to 1200 CE or later. These remains, found in many regions, suggest critical cultural and socioeconomic patterns that persist in the twenty-first century. On Sivuqaq (Saint Lawrence Island), home to the Yupiget, for example, remains of household objects, tools, and semi-underground dwellings of stone, sod, and whalebone abound that date from 100 CE to 1200 CE and document the island's history of marine mammal hunting. On the Seward Peninsula, the village of Wales (*Kiŋigin*), once one of the largest whaling settlements on the Bering Sea coast, dates to 800 CE. Iñupiaq coastal societies featured "community" houses (*qaġzriq or kasġi*) where men discussed hunting, boys received instruction, and tribal celebrations were held. Nearby, women and children lived in small houses (*iġġluq*). In all Eskimo settlements, men conducted warfare, hunted, trapped, butchered animals, made tools, and built boats. Women reared children; made skin clothing, footwear, and boat covers; prepared and stored foods; and gathered greens, roots and berries. Men taught boys and women taught girls the essential skills, traditions, and histories that their particular sex would need.

The network of extended family, lineages, and, where present, clans was and is central to Eskimo social life. Among the Central Yup'ik of the Yukon-Kuskokwim delta and the

Yupiget of Saint Lawrence Island, there were named clans, and family ties were traced through patrilineal descent. In many cases male hunting crews still reflect clan membership. In most tribes, a male bias prevailed. That bias and strong extended kin ties remain ubiquitous features of rural communities and urban diasporas alike in the twenty-first century. Social organization, hunting, and ceremonial life were intertwined. At the center was respect for animals and plants that made survival possible. Animals (and humans) possessed named spirits that returned when treated respectfully. The spirits of harvested whales and polar bears were extraordinarily powerful and required extensive rituals, and successful hunters were highly esteemed. In the twenty-first century, hunting families participate fully in the cash economy, but they also rely on older socioeconomic patterns including subsistence hunting, fishing, birding, and gathering, and urban relatives welcome gifts of "real" food from village kin. Store-bought foods are known pejoratively as "white man's food."

Christian conversion and the adoption of English were at the heart of the educational mission in Alaska. Sheldon Jackson, the first General Agent of Education in the Alaska Territory (1885–1907), recruited husband-wife teams to staff village schools. Their task was to exemplify a Christian lifeway, to teach English, and to encourage participation in a cash economy. The model was the farmer-citizen of the 1880s and early 1900s. By the 1950s many residents had become Christian. In southwest Alaska the Russian Orthodox Church, present since the late 1700s, dominated. Farther north, Jackson, a Presbyterian minister, insisted on the Christian credentials of the teachers he hired.

Although twenty-first-century Eskimo communities adhere to older spiritual beliefs including respect for animals, they also hold strong Christian beliefs. Marriage, once a socioeconomic event, exemplifies the mix of old and new traditions. For example, until the 1940s, family elders arranged marriages that reinforced political and economic ties. On Saint Lawrence Island, marriages were initiated after an intended groom's extended family presented gifts to the bride's family. Soon after, the groom commenced hunting and performing chores for the bride's family. Several years later, the bride's family signaled approval of the groom and hosted a "return" gift ceremony. The couple then joined the groom's family. These traditions continue, although the groom's service lasts only twelve months. Once the groom's service and gift exchanges are completed, the couple appears before a local magistrate to legalize their union, followed eventually by a church marriage.

At the onset of the twenty-first century, there were approximately 130 federally recognized Eskimo tribes. In 2000 the U.S. Census Bureau reported 54,761 persons of Eskimo descent in Alaska, of which 25 percent still spoke their Native language. Tribal members lived in regional cities or town centers such as Anchorage, Nome, Kotzebue, and Bethel, as well as in remote homeland villages. Twenty-first-century Eskimo land ownership was established through the Alaska Native Claims Settlement Act of 1971. Native-owned lands represent but a small percentage of the large land bases that tribes occupied prior to Russian and then American conquest.

[*See also* **Assimilation; Missions, in America;** *and* **Native American History and Culture.**]

BIBLIOGRAPHY

Burch, Ernest S., Jr. *Social Life in Northwest Alaska: The Structure of Iñupiaq Eskimo Nations.*

Fairbanks: University of Alaska Press, 2006. Probably the most thorough examination of northern Iñupiaq social life.

Fitzhugh, William W., Julie Hollowell, and Aron L. Crowell, eds. *Gifts from the Ancestors: Ancient Ivories of Bering Strait*. Princeton, N.J.: Princeton University Art Museum; New Haven, Conn.: Yale University Press, 2009. A catalog to accompany an exhibit of the same name, this volume includes essays by contemporary Native and non-Native Arctic scholars and Native artists . A related website is at http://artmuseum.prince ton.edu/gifts.

Jolles, Carol Zane, with Elinor Mikghaq Oozeva. *Faith, Food, and Family in a Yupik Whaling Community*. Seattle: University of Washington Press, 2002. One of the few volumes to examine the integrated relationships of contemporary Christian belief and traditional Siberian Eskimo life. Focuses on the village of Gambell, Saint Lawrence Island.

Lee, Molly, and Gregory A. Reinhardt. *Eskimo Architecture: Dwelling and Structure in the Early Historic Period*. Fairbanks: University of Alaska Press, 2003. Examines Eskimo housing and other village structures; filled with excellent, detailed drawings and descriptions.

Carol Zane Jolles

EVERYDAY LIFE

"The life of any community," wrote the pioneer historical ethnographer Francis Underwood in 1893, "is made up of infinite details." It may be, then, that the task of creating a comprehensive summary of the subject of everyday life over the course of American history is truly impossible, lost in an immense tangle of communities, ethnicities, decades, and generations—New England towns in the 1660s, slave quarters in the Carolina Sea Islands in the 1830s, Irish neighborhoods in Chicago in the 1930s, the barrios of Los Angeles in the twenty-first century. Only an encyclopedia devoted to everyday life alone could provide even a condensed survey of all these microclimates of ordinary life; they are not literally innumerable, but they are multifarious beyond schematic or narrative presentation.

Voices have disdained the subject itself. The great intellectual historian Perry Miller famously despised the study of everyday life as the antiquarian study of chairs and bathtubs, irrelevant to serious concerns; to focus on the details of ordinary experience, he argued, is to subvert the master narratives of the society, the polity, and the mind. But if it is true that as our quotidian circumstances alter, so does our experience, it might be argued that to study everyday life is to pose the question, "What is it like to be another?" Studying the commonplaces of life is one way of attacking the mystery of time. When visitors come to historic sites and old houses, they often perform a calculus of gain and loss—crackling hearth fire versus silent cooktop, bright skies and unpolluted streams versus staggering childhood mortality. They are not wrong to do so. In one sense, the study of everyday life is an attempt to explore experiential difference, the otherness of the past, without completely losing commensurability.

Accounts of everyday life have always been most effective as a way of describing and evoking the specificity, the otherness, of a particular place, a particular group (or intertwined groups) of people, at a particular time. Not surprisingly, the study of everyday life has almost always seemed more potent and been practiced more often when it deals with the deeper past, with the shock of the old—with the strangeness that has undoubtedly drawn many scholars to the study of more distant eras.

Any study of everyday life runs the risk of becoming "Whig history"—a cheerful catalog of increasing comfort, ease, speed, convenience, and safety. It runs the risk, too, of antiquarianism, the piling up of curious details for their own sake. But lacking its materials completely, there would be considerably less context for the exercise of historical imagination, the attempt to reach empathically over time.

By the early twenty-first century, Americans could look back on nearly four centuries of transformation and material improvement in the conditions of life—however the costs and consequences might be counted. The technologies that shape, enfold, and soften our everyday lives have become steadily more powerful. Our dwellings, our appearance and clothing, our possessions, the way we treat our bodies—all these have changed. Most of the changes have occurred in rough synchrony with broader patterns of social and cultural history. Many of the changes have been unalloyed good things, at least from our current perspective. Still, many voices have been raised to assail our current comforts on the grounds of energy costs, pollution, and greed in the face global inequality: the comforts are unsustainable, the voices argue, and we need to return to some version of the lifeways of the past.

Because power, possessions, and access to technologies have always been distributed unequally among the American people, some aspects of everyday life have changed very unevenly. Perhaps the most extreme example is that of domestic sanitation. As late as 1940, a majority of rural Americans—and a vast majority of African Americans—still used chamber pots and privies, living within a sanitary regime that would have been familiar to George Washington or Thomas Jefferson; meanwhile almost all their urban counterparts had long had bathrooms and flush toilets.

The pattern of most of these changes has followed a narrative of democratization, of diffusion from the top down. Much of the impetus for America's eighteenth- and early nineteenth-century "refinements" in ordinary life, for example, ultimately came from the changing ways of the English upper classes, transferred by means of the examples set by their American cousins. Modes of life once available to, or only valued by, the few have become commonplaces. As goods have become less expensive and as new technologies have appeared, luxuries have become amenities, and amenities have become necessities. This is not to valorize that process but rather, within the limits of a large-scale account, simply to describe it. It is at the level of the everyday microclimate that individual agency and adaptation, even resistance, might be seen—perhaps calling for a new history of everyday life.

The literature on everyday life is exceedingly scattered and fragmented: multifarious in its potential sources, yet fairly scarce in its interpretations. Rather than historiographic debates, for the most part what exists is a variety of different examples; it is not easy to generalize about a subject matter of "infinite details."

To write most summarily would be to identify a sequence of landscapes of everyday experience. First, a world of candles, oxcarts, and exceedingly slow travel persisted from the founding of colonial societies to late in the eighteenth century. This gave way, after 1790, to a world of oil lamps, stagecoaches, and post offices. That world in turn was replaced by a Victorian world of railroad travel, telegraph lines, and gaslight, to be succeeded toward the end of the nineteenth century by a world of electric lights, telephones, radio, and automobiles. Air travel, television, and electronic technology followed, and then the digital revolution. Across these centuries the number and variety of goods, experiences, and entertainments available have grown almost beyond count. By the twenty-first century, much of everyday life was becoming digital, even virtual, as a growing number of Americans spent much of their waking lives connected to personal technologies of information, communication, and entertainment.

But to begin to understand this process beyond so reductive a summary, it is necessary to return to the "infinite details": of house and household, personal appearance, domestic sanitation, and quotidian experience.

House, Household, Landscape.

It might be useful to begin in a small place, at a time not quite halfway in this long history: the town of Sturbridge in central Massachusetts in 1775, a year that might also be thought of as marking a point of transition between early America and the society of the United States that was soon to be.

Captain Parker's House.

Edward Parry, a younger son of an aristocratic English family, came to America in 1772 as an Admiralty mast agent, surveying New England forests to find timber for building the Royal Navy's ships. When the Revolution erupted in the spring of 1775, Parry found himself an enemy alien, and in July he was seized by men who considered him a British spy. They brought him to Boston, where the Massachusetts legislature decreed that he be interned safely in the interior; Parry was sent to Sturbridge with the man who would be both his host and his jailer, Captain Timothy Parker, the town's state representative. This incident would be an inconsiderable footnote in the history of the Revolution and of no relevance to this article except for one thing: Parry kept a diary, and in his boredom and isolation he made a secret record, now in the Lilly Library of Indiana University, of his nearly yearlong stay in Captain Parker's house.

Whether in England or America, individuals of Parry's class rarely bothered to notice in any detail the lifeways or domestic arrangements of those below them. But these were unusual circumstances, and Parry took several pages of his journal to create a rare "thick description"—hostile, but closely observed—of life in an American household. Parry's judgments reflected his elite status, that is, his life in London where he had had his own quarters, personal servants, and barriers between himself and the infrastructure of domestic life. "I stayed in the representatives house, which was a very miserable one," Parry wrote; "here let me attempt to describe it."

At the front of the house was "the bed Room of the Representative his wife and five small children, in which we breakfasted, dined and supped." Next to it was "the other Room the other side of the chimney," which "had some squares painted with Spanish brown and Oker on the floor and had a clock in it and a small corner Cupboard this was called the best Room." To the rear were "a kitchin ten feet wide" spanning most of the width of the house and "a small bed Room of 10 feet by 7." Above was "a loft or garret without any divisions."

Parry drew no floor plan of the house, but it can be reconstructed from his description. With "two rooms each side of the chimney," the house had one of New England's commonest architectural forms: a dwelling with one and a half stories, a center chimney, four rooms downstairs, and above these an unfinished space under the eaves was reached by a narrow staircase.

Captain Parker's Family.

The house that Parry entered held a large "family." It comprised Captain Parker and his wife, five young children, two hired girls, and two "Men servants and labourers." There was also "a Negro man," a slave; Parry noted that he received "many a drubbing." His emancipation would not come until after the war.

In the "bed Room," Parry observed, Timothy and Hannah Parker slept surrounded by their children's beds, presided at all the household's meals, and entertained ordinary visitors. The "best Room" was almost always empty of people, opened "only on extraordinary occasions, when the Minister of the Parish or some other person of consequence visited."

The serving men and women slept in the unfinished garret, a steeply sloping space where the roofing nails pushed through the walls and glittered with ice in the winter. At most there was a blanket hung across its center to separate the sexes. Parry himself was the only member of the household who slept alone. Despite the tumult of the Revolution he seems, as a gentleman, to have been treated with exceptional deference.

Everywhere in the dwelling, Parry saw, space was made for food storage, laundry, dairying, and textile production as these activities overflowed from the kitchen. The "best Room," except on the rare occasions of its ceremonial use, was used "to store Milk pans, baked apples and rough dry cloaths." While spinning wheels whirred alongside the cooking hearth, the loom thumped "in the loft or garret over my head."

His own "little Room" was crowded with "all the Stockings of the Family not in use," hanging on lines along with "sundry Peticoats, Gowns, Female shoes"; on the other side of his bed hung "the industry of the Family being all the Skains of Yarn, & linnen for the next weaving." In one corner of the room was a decorous chest with "the Sheets and Spare linnen belonging to Madam the Representative's wife." But in another corner sat "an Indigo dye Pot filled with Chamber lye"—the concentrated urine from the household's chamber pots, used in cleaning raw wool and dyeing yarn. Its ammoniac reek was "a constant perfume."

Parry took hundreds of meals with the family. They ate salt pork, sometimes lamb, and freshly killed fowl, "but all was boiled in one pot, together with Cabbage, Turnips, Potatoes, Carrots, Parsnips," and the food was brought to the table "upon one dish."

The "Negro man" was given his meal first, eating alone in the kitchen. Next the children were fed, "to prevent their cryings." Then the rest of the household sat down to eat around the table, pushing aside the beds and bedsteads to make room. Timothy and Hannah Parker were at the head, with Parry at the captain's right, followed by the laborers, probably in order of age. The women sat to Hannah's left. Before breakfast and after supper, Parry was asked to read a chapter of the Bible. Captain Parker's subsequent prayers he found maddeningly incoherent.

The family drank hard cider poured from an encrusted, sticky pewter pot. The tablecloth, Parry thought, was perhaps "washed every week." The knives and forks they ate with looked "black and dirty—never Scoured, seldom whetted, and sometimes washed."

Most difficult for Parry was the surrender of what he regarded as his personal space. "Capt Parker," he wrote, "requested me to suffer such persons as occasionally came into his house to partake of my bed." The worst instance of this "aggravating circumstance" was the arrival of a man whose itinerant status and menial trade made him seem virtually untouchable to Parry, "a Journeyman Shoemaker who made shoes for the Family."

Old Ways. What is to be made of Parry's diary for understanding everyday life in America? Parry's account leads in more than one direction. First, he describes much that was very nearly universal in early American life, from 1607 up through at least 1800.

The sheer density of life in the Parker household strikes a modern reader as it struck Parry. Most houses were far smaller than they are in the twenty-first century, and most families were far larger; domestic life was crowded. Work and domestic space interpenetrated. Parents and children more often than not slept in the same room (in the smallest houses, of course, there was only one room); parental beds were often "hung" or curtained, but in any case sexual intercourse took place within earshot, as did the use of chamber pots.

Households very often contained men, women, and children from outside the nuclear family: they were there to work, their presence usually determined by the age and sex of the family's children. Beds, whether feather mattresses or piles of straw covered by ticking, were considerably fewer than people in American houses; the same-sex sharing of beds that so offended Parry had always been the norm for unmarried people. Immersed in the routines of agriculture, and without running water, men and women were necessarily casual about smells. The odors of cheese and souring milk, beer and cider, tobacco and dried apples, and dinner boiling or frying on the hearth were mixed with the stench of sweat, manure, dye cauldrons, and uncovered chamber pots.

New Ways. On the other hand, if the Parker house is positioned in the stream of time, more might be learned than Parry thought he was telling. Within their means and circumstances, the Parkers were striving, however imperceptibly to Parry, to achieve his vision of domestic order.

In some important ways the Parker house pointed to change, even modernization. Built around 1760, it was generally symmetrical in its fenestration and organization of space, differentiating it from the more organic and asymmetric forms of earlier dwellings. Just as important, it had a small central entryway controlling access to the other rooms, a threshold space between outside and inside. Most earlier houses were socially open: visitors could simply open a front door and plunge directly into the family's life. Only a single door, that anyone could open, separated house from roadside, family from community. Houses like Parker's were socially closed. Their entryways marked a separation between the outside world and the life of the household—however crowded and lacking in privacy the house might otherwise be for its members. The family could compose itself to meet its guests and could determine how guests should be received. This expectation of physical separation between visitors and family members became the norm of domestic respectability, in apartments as well as houses, until the advent of far more informal designs in the mid-twentieth century.

"Miserable" as the house seemed to Parry, with four rooms and a garret it was larger and better than the considerable majority of American dwellings. Most of what is known about the overall housing landscape of early America comes from the direct tax of 1798, whose schedules reveal an enormous number of very small houses of one or two rooms, valued at a third or less of houses like Parker's. At least two-fifths of the population lived in such dwellings, which had no entryways and usually no more than three windows. They formed the massive base of an American housing pyramid at whose apex stood a relative handful of Georgian and Federal mansions. Many of the houses in Sturbridge, as elsewhere, were dwellings that Parry would have refused to enter, let alone stay in.

The situation of Parker's enslaved laboring man—not only beaten, but separated from the rest of the household at mealtimes and sleeping rough in the kitchen—reaches to another reality. Most northern and some southern slaves lived like this, in the marginal spaces of white households, often with only a few rags in place of a straw pallet. The rest lived in the cabins and shacks of the slave quarters—the only houses not counted in 1798. These were and continued to be America's poorest and most crowded habitations, with scanty bedding and without tables, chairs, or chests. Even after Emancipation, the housing of African Americans in the South echoed the living conditions of early America.

Some of what Parry saw signified changes that foreshadowed the future. The "best Room," consecrated to important social occasions and domestic display even while sleeping spaces were crowded, was the Victorian parlor in embryo: all that was needed was for its casual storage functions to be swept away. The tall clock would have been both rare and expensive in the countryside. As a costly piece of furniture it signaled the Parkers' economic status to their visitors; ticking away in the best room, and periodically needing to be wound, it can also be understood as the emblem of a dawning consciousness of time. The cupboard, with its display of the family's best ceramics, followed a tradition that went back to the beginnings of American settlement and that, in somewhat fossilized form, continues in most twenty-first-century American households.

The Parker family's possessions that Parry noted—the clothing and textiles hanging on hooks and lines and packed in cupboards and chests, beds, bedsteads and hangings, cooking equipment and cutlery, boxes and baskets, a handful of books—indicate increasing abundance. Archaeological studies of domestic sites and the analysis of probate inventories reveal that such households were on a long upward curve of material acquisition. Since the time of first settlement, over the

generations American families had gradually increased the number and value of their material goods. In 1775 the Parker family had enough chairs—eight at least, and perhaps a dozen—for all the adults to sit down at dinner. This represented a major material advance, for it would have been a great rarity in a rural household in 1700. And although Parry criticized the family's mealtime practices and insufficiently clean utensils, these, too, reflected an emerging abundance: the individual plates, knives, and forks for each diner were a decisive break with ordinary Anglo-Americans' earlier tradition of eating together out of a common dish.

Newer Ways. The curve of material acquisition continued upward, of course, as it has in many ways up to the twenty-first century. Americans in the nineteenth and twentieth centuries built and lived in an enormous variety of houses, abandoning the ancient practices of timber framing for balloon-frame construction after 1840, turning from traditional housing vernaculars to plans and pattern books, using an immense range of building materials, and creating a bewildering number of housing forms. Within all this complexity emerge at least three clear patterns of change affecting daily life.

One of these was the increasing importance of comfort. As a distinct category of domestic concern, comfort became highly visible in the early nineteenth century; the drive for comfort dealt not with decorum and signals of status but with physical ease. Newton Hubbard, who grew up within sight of the Parker house a generation later, would write to his grandchildren in 1895 how comfort had come to his family's home, as it had to millions of others: they had abandoned textile production and moved agricultural work and storage elsewhere, making the "front and pleasantest parts of the house" their everyday living spaces. American families created domestic comfort through cushioned furniture, carpets, and drapery and window blinds, through stoves that would heat rooms more evenly and provide warmth to previously frigid bedchambers, and through an increasing abundance of domestic ceramics, textiles, and lighting devices. The accumulation of things conspicuously devoted to material ease reached its peak in the remarkable ordered clutter of Victorian homes of the late nineteenth century. The look of most homes has become sparer over time, with more and more invested in the technologies of entertainment, but a huge industry devoted to household furnishings continues a nearly two-hundred-year campaign for comfort.

Another change was the expansion of physical privacy. Beginning at the very end of the eighteenth century, American households, because of both a declining birthrate and changing patterns of co-residence, have steadily become smaller. Homes have become, on the average, much larger. A few detailed studies of housing density from 1798 to 1800 give figures of 80 to 150 square feet per person; the United States Census housing survey for 2000, in contrast, reported an average of 1,200 square feet per person, and most American dwellings have more rooms than people. The old norm of sharing beds was long ago abandoned, and that of sharing rooms is likewise increasingly uncommon. In many households, family members carry out most of their daily activities in separate spaces.

Over the same long span of time has come the transformation of American homes into ever more elaborated "machines for living." The technologies of heating, sanitation, and food preparation reached a mechanical apex in the late nineteenth century with stoves, gas light, plumbing, and hand-operated devices.

They were transformed in their turn by electrification and its accompanying central heating, lighting, and powered appliances. At each stage of development, technologies have increasingly separated household members from the physical effort and unpleasantness that once went into sustaining everyday routines. Virtually all twenty-first-century American homes, from city tenements and trailer parks to "McMansions," share this infrastructure, if often not much else.

Domestic Landscapes. Parry did not say so in his diary, but no doubt he stepped gingerly around the outside of the Parker house. The domestic landscape of the ordinary American farm had hardly changed at all over two centuries. The front door of every farmhouse was "barricadoed," wrote a reformer, by a "mingled mass of chip and dirt." Chickens roosted on the windowsills, and pigs rooted around the doorsteps. The farmyard itself was "an inlaid pavement of bones and broken bottles." This description is borne out by the archaeological record; the landscape of domestic detritus was the norm for most American families. Into the early nineteenth century, housewives tossed broken dishes and glasses out the most convenient door or window, and they threw bones and food scraps into the yard to be picked over by domestic animals. Unfenced spaces were trampled and bare or sprouted straggling uncut weeds.

This, too, was transformed as a more orderly vision of the domestic landscape was gradually realized. By the time that Walt Whitman wrote "When Lilacs Last in the Dooryard Bloom'd" in 1865, many American families had fenced front yards with grass and ornamental plantings, and—so archaeology reveals—they had given up the casual, broadcast disposal of their trash around the house. This shift has endured for a century and a half, a widely embraced norm of domestic respectability. The lush green lawn with manicured plantings, emerging around 1920, has shaped the look of American suburbs, even in places where irrigation is necessary for grass to grow at all—and it has spawned a large industry producing lawnmowers, weed killers, and grass seed.

Appearances. Nothing provides so visceral a sense of time's passage as the historical record of clothing and bodily appearance. The look of faces and everyday attire provides an almost physical sense of periodization, changing in ways sometimes ephemeral but often clearly reflective of broader changes in society.

Bodies. American bodies have not always looked the same. Careful studies of military records have revealed that Americans in the seventeenth century were shorter by several inches than they are today. Thanks to generations of better nutrition, however, by the 1770s they had become considerably taller than Europeans, averaging five feet eight inches or so for men. In the nineteenth century, rural Americans remained relatively tall, but city populations, because rapid urban growth and immigration led to poorer nourishment overall, were a bit shorter. Americans grew taller still in the twentieth century: by the twenty-first century, men's average height was about five feet ten or eleven inches. Men and women also surely became heavier, although that is harder to measure. These changes, at least in part, account for the generally smaller size of early clothing that has survived.

Sexual maturity came later as well. Girls' average age at the onset of puberty (menarche) was between fifteen and fourteen in the mid-nineteenth century, so that twelve- and thirteen-year-olds, as well as many fourteen-year-olds, were still truly children. Since then the average age of menarche has decreased steadily, to just over twelve by the twenty-first century.

A large proportion of American adults, perhaps through most of the nineteenth century, had at least some badly rotted teeth, a source of chronic pain and foul breath whose only cure was extraction. Americans' noted and long-standing predilection for sugar was often given as the reason. Early portrait sitters kept their mouths firmly shut, but satirical prints often showed men and women with missing teeth. As the practice of brushing the teeth became more widespread and improved regimens of care—including anesthesia for extractions—appeared, dental health and appearance improved. The gleaming, white-toothed American smile became an icon in the twentieth century.

From Scarcity to Abundance. In early America, clothing was scarce and valuable, because both woolen and linen cloth and leather footwear were difficult and time-consuming to produce. In the seventeenth century their power as signifiers of rank was so great that some colonial governments sought to prohibit those "of mean conditions" from wearing the lace, gold buttons, and "great boots" of their betters, although only a few could have afforded such sartorial impudence. Over the course of the eighteenth century, individual wardrobes grew larger, but most women would not have had more than two or three gowns, and most men would not have had more than a coat and two pairs of breeches. An individual's clothing usually constituted a significant fraction of his or her total wealth: a man's suit of fine broadcloth, for example, would have been the purchase of a lifetime, to be cherished and carefully kept. Ordinary men and women often worked their fields and gardens in bare feet. The poorest were defined by the stained and tattered garb that they stood in, most often all that they owned.

This world of scarcity, in which every petticoat, shirt, shift, and pair of boots was precious, was undone in the early nineteenth century. The Industrial Revolution in textiles and the emerging mass production of shoes created an unprecedented abundance; an observer in 1840 recounted how the new technologies had already "greatly cheapened and multiplied almost every species of clothing worn." By 1860 the substantial majority of American households had given up their laboriously produced linens and woolens for factory-made cotton and woolen cloth. Ordinary people's wardrobes expanded greatly in size, and the sight of shoeless farm families or even slaves became rare. The state of Americans' personal hygiene depended not only on how often they bathed, but on how often they could wash their shirts and shifts, the garments that lay closest to their skins. Cheaper cotton fabrics meant far more underclothes, neatly dovetailing with the growing acceptance of bathing.

The ascendancy of machine-made and machine-printed textiles provided entry for millions of Americans, primarily women, to a world of fashion once confined to the elite. The expansion of the web of commerce and communications gave them access to a great variety of fabrics, colors, and trimmings, as well as access to information, only a few weeks late, about the most recent styles. The introduction of the sewing machine and of readymade clothing drove a continuing explosion of abundance: the first made home sewing far more efficient, while the second began to take the construction of clothing out of the home altogether. In the long run, mass production and the appeal of the shopping experience have triumphed. Clothing has become an immense category of consumer goods, most of them astonishingly cheap by the standards of earlier times, whose selection and acquisition has become an absorbing concern to many millions of women and some men—an American national pastime.

The Look of Clothes. Just around 1800 came the most sudden and dramatic of all changes in the look of men's clothes in America. Shared with their counterparts in Great Britain and western Europe, this change of shape and silhouette has never been reversed. In the space of a decade or so, knee breeches, long, broad-tailed coats, and cocked or broad-brimmed hats gave way to pantaloons, "short, snug, close-fitting" coats, and tall hats with narrow brims. By 1815 the only adherents to traditional garb were elderly men, who as Joseph B. Felt wrote in *Customs of New England* in 1852, "became objects of curiosity, almost derision, to the boys in the street." The new styles were in reality an embellished version of the working costume of sailors and laborers. As the United States began its transition into the market and industrial revolutions, its men donned working dress.

Since that time, coat, trousers, and shirt, accompanied by waistcoat (vest) and necktie, have constituted the paradigm for male attire, though it was gradually simplified with the disappearance of vests and formal headgear outside ceremonial garb. Only in the late twentieth century did the paradigm finally begin to come apart as a new informality emerged in the workplace. Coats and ties, abandoned by manual workers late in the nineteenth century, have since 1990 or so been disappearing from offices, schools, and universities, though they remain in law, finance, and politics.

The styles of women's clothing in America have had a far less linear history, defined by cultural pushes and pulls—sexual tension over the presentation of women's bodies, contests over the control of women's physical activity, the use of female dress to convey fine gradations of taste and status, a fashion economy of tastemakers and dressmakers whose livelihood depends on constant change. Above the rhythm of seemingly countless changes in cut, length, and decoration, some points of change can be identified that align with broader social patterns. In between the covered-up gowns of the eighteenth century and most of the nineteenth came the Grecian style of 1790–1820, which fit the figure much more closely and exposed far more of the arms and upper body. The style not only expressed the new nation's broader fascination with the classical past but also, by displaying the figures of the young at the expense of the middle-aged and elderly, foreshadowed American society's growing exaltation of youth.

In the 1890s, shirtwaists and skirts appeared as the costume for the young women who were coming in to work in offices and stores, and bloomers, scorned in the 1850s, were now worn as part of the campaign for women's greater freedom of movement, on bicycles and elsewhere. The corsetless flapper fashions of the 1920s signified a time of expanding sexual freedom, just as the miniskirts, fishnet hose, and rejection of brassieres of the 1960s signified another. Twenty-first-century America exhibits a truly astonishing variety of styles, from the low-cut, midriff-baring, and thigh-high fashions of pop-music stars to the headscarves and burkas of recent Muslim immigrants.

The Look of Faces. American men have alternated between sharply different regimes of facial hair. Beards were common, if not quite universal, for most of the seventeenth century. After 1690, beards fell out of fashion, and they remained so for more than a

century. Facial hair began to return around 1820 when young elite men, "dandies," experimented with moustaches and even with full beards, much to the dismay and anger of the majority who for many years had identified shaving with Christianity and civilization. They sometimes offered violence to the unshaven, having literally forgotten the faces of their society's founders. However, by 1850 the beard had triumphed, again becoming Christian, civilized, and nearly universal; the Civil War was fought by bearded patriarchs.

The closely shaven face returned at the end of the nineteenth century, leading to seven decades of beardless countenances with an occasional small moustache. In the late 1960s beards made their third appearance, this time as emblems of an exceptionally vehement youthful defiance.

There have been two major inflection points of social significance for men's hairstyles. Long hair for men was often scorned as sybaritic in the seventeenth century, but the general fashion in the eighteenth century was for men to display their hair abundantly, either in the wigs that many gentlemen wore or in the long flowing locks, often tied back with a satin ribbon or eel-skin queue, adopted by others. But long hair went out of fashion as part of the republican transformation of clothing and manners in the 1790s, vanishing along with knee breeches and buckled shoes. Long-haired older men looked uncomfortably at their sons with their closely shorn "brush heads," some versions of which copied the look of classical Roman statuary. Hair, along with beards, returned in the 1960s, again as a sign of rebellion; this time, long-haired sons faced down their crew-cut fathers and teachers, as well as a host of angry barbers. Since the 1980s both haircuts and facial hair have become part of an increasingly informal and pluralistic regime of personal appearance. A sizable minority of men, from professional ballplayers to professors, wear beards, and virtually every option from shaved heads to long locks can be seen.

The Long March to Cleanliness.

At the end of the eighteenth century, Americans began a long process of cleaning and polishing their bodies and separating themselves from the body's wastes. At that time the sanitary infrastructure of household life was still what it had been for centuries in America and Europe. Ultimately the changes in the practice of bodily cleanliness and in the disposal of urine and excrement were linked, culminating in the recognizably modern bathroom of the late nineteenth century, but they proceeded separately and very unevenly.

The Body's Wastes.

Neither the chamber pot nor the privy was completely universal. Some of the poorest households, in the slave quarters and elsewhere, had not "even a pot to piss in," as the traditional expression went; however, by 1800, the growing availability and cheapness of ceramics had made this rare. The privy was most often a stand-alone miniature house constructed over a pit that held the waste; it represented an investment in time and materials that was not trivial—one that a significant minority of households could not or would not make, as archaeological investigations attest. These Americans simply went to the closest available patch of woods or brush. Most privies were small, with simply a seat or two opening onto the pit. But they could be far more elaborate. The so-called necessary houses of wealthy homes often had elegant architectural details, separate sections for each sex, and numerous seats, some sized for children. The privies of Thomas Jefferson's Monticello displayed innovative design; those of Charles Carroll Jr.'s Homewood estate in Baltimore were truly palatial. Still,

their design inevitably meant that family members carried out in each other's presence what are now considered the most private of functions.

Traditionally, privies were hard to miss, sited with what came to seem an all-too-obvious functionality. Indeed, they had often been built, as an early critique claimed, "within the territory of a hog yard, that the swine may root and ruminate and devour the nastiness thereof." Many farm households seeking refinement responded architecturally, disguising their privies at the end of a connected ell of workshops and storage sheds.

In 1829 the emerging technologies of water supply and sanitation made their dramatic appearance in America when the new Tremont House hotel in Boston opened with a basement suite of eight bathtubs and water closets. Replicated many millions of times, this was a template that presaged the eventual end of the world of privy and chamber pot. But the actual adoption of indoor plumbing was gradual, halting, and extremely uneven, because for a long time it was both expensive and experimental. After 1830 an expanding number of prosperous households in and around American cities built their own water supplies and constructed water closets. By the 1850s, domestic plumbing had moved beyond the Eastern Seaboard to the Midwest; the small city of Indianapolis, for example, saw its first plumber in 1853 and had one house with a full bathroom in 1858. Although these earliest adventures in the new sanitation were facilities for the elite, they were not always safe or effective. Pipes broke, connections failed, foul gases did not vent to the outside, sewage invaded houses. American plumbers had to learn their new trade through trial and error. Plumbing remained solely a sign of elite status until the 1880s.

The building of urban waterworks beginning in the 1830s, along with continuing technical improvements in waste disposal, created the conditions for the arrival of plumbing on a grand scale: urban sewer systems were constructed, and sanitary codes were elaborated and enforced. By 1900, these massive public works had transformed this most fundamental aspect of everyday life for millions of urban Americans, allowing the tearing down of innumerable privies and the filling up of their waste pits. Even within the cities the reach of waterworks was far from universal, of course, often leaving the poorest sections, the cheapest tenements, unplumbed. Plumbing became an emblem of middle-class respectability and working-class aspiration. For households with plumbing, the experiential distance from earlier generations was vast: the new bathrooms, with their "perennial supply of hot water and cold" and "beautiful white tubs" and water closets, made of the new impervious vitreous china, were far from the old stench and spatter of wastes. In the following decades, city building and health codes ensured the expansion of plumbing to the urban poor.

The new sanitation came much more slowly to the vast American countryside. Water and sewage systems arrived in small towns and mill villages only gradually, because first an expensive infrastructure of wells, pumps, and septic systems had to be built house by house. As late as 1940, one-third of all American households lacked a flush toilet; that proportion was more than 80 percent in Mississippi, the poorest state and one of the most rural. By the turn of the twenty-first century, only a tiny portion—less than half of 1 percent—of American dwellings lacked indoor plumbing. A curiosity in 1830, a luxury in 1860, and an amenity in 1900, plumbing has finally become a necessity for decent living.

The Body's Surfaces. By the modern understanding of the word, until near the end of the eighteenth century, almost no Americans bathed. The universal practice was to wash hands, face, and neck while fully clothed, using a basin in the kitchen or adjacent ell. Only those who did not meet this standard—whose hands and faces were clearly smudged or greasy—were beyond the pale. But in the 1790s, upper-class Americans, following the lead of the English elite, began to bathe completely: they went to their bedchambers, undressed, and scrubbed themselves down with cold water. No new technology was required, only a washstand, a basin, and a closed door. The new practice seems to have been inspired in part by a belief that keeping the body clean was good for health, but it may have owed more to a revulsion from bodily smells and a growing sense of a connection between refinement of the mind and lack of grease and grime on the body's surface.

Bathing—and the notions that it embodied—diffused downward in the social order and from city to village to countryside. Domestic advice books in the 1830s extolled its virtues to middle-class families. Advice books in the 1860s and later assumed that bathing was universal among such people and sought instead to convert farm and working urban families. Bathing practices themselves changed, too, from the chilly rigor of the years before 1840; reflecting the power of the new notions of bodily comfort, Americans increasingly bathed with hot water and used the newly available galvanized metal tubs in which they could stand or sit. Bathing made its way to farms and rural county seats, to industrial villages, and into the tenements; the great majority of Americans were thoroughly washing themselves, at least weekly, long before the advent of universal indoor plumbing. The modern American regimen of cleanliness requires one shower a day at the very least, and most people react with great repugnance to any deficiencies in public sanitation.

Smells. The triumph of flush toilets and daily bathing or showering means that twenty-first-century people do not smell each other very much, and the other smells of daily life have changed as well. Dominating the olfactory environment of early America were the odors not only of chamber pots and privy pits, but of sweat and manure, wood smoke, horses and horse tackle, tallow candles, and wet wool. In the nineteenth century came the new smells of coal smoke, whale-oil lamps, the heated iron and lampblack of cookstoves and parlor stoves, and the the acrid tang of illuminating gas in city households and kerosene in the countryside. Electricity, as it became the universal source of household light and made central heating possible, erased most of these smells. In the twenty-first century, most Americans spend a good deal of their time in offices, schools, and shopping malls, breathing processed air, sometimes with specific artificial scents added to soothe, motivate, or entice. Away from farms and forests, the defining outdoor smells of the twentieth and early twenty-first centuries register the triumph of the automobile: gasoline, motor oil, asphalt, and exhaust fumes.

Dimensions of Everyday Experience. So far this account has concerned itself with houses, comfort, clothing, and bodies. But there are other crucial dimensions of change: the everyday experiences of light, sound, speed, and time.

Light. Seen from space at night, in a view unimaginable until only recently, the United States glows with a shining lacework of electric illumination, produced by the street lamps and building lights of cities and suburbs, airports and highways. This web of light covers the great bulk of the nation's territory, revealing that only the most thinly populated sections are truly dark. In 1700 such a view would have shown the entire continent dark, except perhaps for a wildfire or a tiny pinpoint of light from an urban conflagration; in 1800 the view would have been only feebly brighter. Then the night sky and its bright stars arched over the world. By the twenty-first century it had been virtually abolished in many parts of America by city lights.

The stars were bright, but the visual world within houses and workshops lit only by candles and firelight was dim. During the day, workers moved their tasks if they could from window to window, following the sun. Readers perused books and newspapers close to the hearth. The elderly and others with visual limitations struggled to see.

In the early nineteenth century an accelerating increase in illumination began, a brightening of the world. For an increasing number of households, firelight and candles gave way to whale-oil lamps; Captain Ahab and his crew, like other whalemen, undertook their dangerous, quasi-heroic butchery to keep American parlors well-illuminated. By the 1850s, urban gas-lighting systems were expanding to light hundreds of thousands of city houses and to contest with outdoor darkness. After 1860, kerosene became the light source for most of rural America. Each of these iterations was welcomed as vastly brighter than the one before.

Of course, by far the greatest share of this brightening of the everyday world is thanks to the lightbulb and the system of electrical power generation and distribution that made it possible. An elderly man in 1895 delighted in "the new and beautiful light" of the electric lamps of the city of New York, then by far the brightest place in America. He contrasted it with the "dreary dimness" of the oil lamps of earlier days, though in his youth, of course, these had been hailed as dazzlingly bright. The total output of electric light has increased vastly, almost unrecognizably, since then. Over the long run of time from the seventeenth century, the average number of "candlepowers" per American household has increased perhaps a thousandfold. Since the early twentieth century the recommended light levels for offices, homes, and public spaces have continued to increase. What seemed bright to the lighting engineers of 1910 is unacceptably dim to their successors today.

The night can still be a repository of our fears, but it is no longer truly a separate realm from day. Once, what happened at night outside the house was thought of as covert, immoral, or criminal. By the twenty-first century, late-night shopping and socializing until two in the morning had become commonplace. Night shifts in public-safety, factory, and transportation work have long existed, but the proliferation of twenty-four-hour stores and call centers, and the habits of the city of Las Vegas, suggest a determination to abolish the night completely.

Sounds. The everyday world was once much quieter. The auditory surround of early America consisted of the sounds of livestock and horses' hooves, the creaking and rolling of carts and wagons, the bells of meetinghouses and churches. Apart from the use of ear trumpets or the sounding board suspended over pulpits, nothing could be amplified. Each of the trades had its characteristic noises—ringing hammers at the blacksmith's forge, saws and planes, rumbling mill wheels and water rushing into sluiceways. The loudest places were water-powered trip-hammers for forging iron or up-and-down sawmills with their insistent thumping. It has been suggestively argued that in this quieter world, voices—of preachers, magistrates, and storytellers, church singers and tavern fiddlers—counted more heavily, and had greater symbolic import, in people's lives than they have since.

Urbanization and industrialization created an increasing din. Growing cities gave rise to multitudes of horses pulling heavy, iron-tired freight wagons and omnibuses on hard-paved streets; later came clanging trolley cars. Voices filled the crowded streets and came from every doorway. By the 1840s the cries of city newsboys on the street accompanied the calls of peddlers. As workshops mechanized and grew greatly in scale, so did the noise they made. The machines that replaced men and women were astonishingly noisy. The "appliances and accompaniments of civilization," wrote the neurologist George M. Beard in his 1881 work *American Nervousness*, made sounds that are "unrythmical, unmelodious": they were the sounds of "manufactures, locomotion, travel."

The new technologies transformed sound as well as production and travel. The whir of the spinning wheel and the thump of the loom might soothe a child—but the noise of their mechanical equivalent, of thousands of spindles or shuttles in motion at the same time, was deafening. This auditory onslaught worsened as factories grew in size. New operatives emerged from textile factories with, as one recalled in 1841, "the noise of the mill in my ears, as of crickets, frogs, and jew's-harps, all mingled together in strange discord." Relatively quiet waterpower gave way to hissing, whistling steam engines running metal components at high velocity, the creaking of the stagecoach to iron wheels clacking over iron rails. The clangor of steel mills, the animal bellowing of stockyards and packing plants, the underground explosions of coal mining—all these became part of the American soundscape. The balance of sound changed even on the farm, as quiet hand-tools were replaced by horse-drawn machines and then by far noisier steam- and gasoline-powered ones. As decibels were added to the environment, a growing number of American workers had their hearing damaged.

Through the later years of the twentieth century, many features of this soundscape were abated or insulated away as so-called noise pollution became a public-health concern. Machines have been made quieter, but all people are still immersed in their sounds. Train whistles are sometimes heard, but they are now the stuff of folksongs; since the 1920s, the true background music of life in America has been the roar of automobile traffic. Indoors is heard the hum of air-conditioning and the beeping of ubiquitous digital devices.

Time and Speed.   People in early America did not complain much about the slowness and sheer physical difficulty of their travel and communications; knowing no other way, they simply endured travel's rigors and unpredictability, and the paucity of news. No American could travel faster on land than he or she could ride a horse, and except for semaphore systems across short distances, information was bound by the same constraints; it was firmly embodied. Travel beyond the farm or village was, in almost all cases, immensely effortful, and Americans steeled themselves for long journeys. The ability to ride and manage a horse was a valued skill of ordinary life. Clocks were expensive and rare, individual watches far more so—and indeed, few occasions required knowing time with any accuracy.

After 1790 came accelerating change in the times and technology of travel, with Americans each decade remarking on the newfound velocity of stage lines and improved roads, on the great proliferation of wagons and carriages and of steamboats and canals.

Before 1830, travel was still bounded by the limits of animal power, but then the railroad locomotive broke the equine speed barrier, at first doubling the speed of horse-drawn travel and eventually surpassing it tenfold. People were at first astonished at the increase in speed, but soon they took it for granted, and medical opinion abandoned earlier warnings about the deleterious effects on the body of rapid motion. Still, horsemanship continued to be a crucial everyday skill: the railroad could bring goods and people to the station, but horse-drawn conveyances were needed to get them to their final destinations.

As the pace of travel increased after 1800, clocks, now mass-produced, multiplied in American households, and thousands of Americans began to wear watches. These were symbols both of prosperity and of an increasing consciousness of time, geared to stagecoach schedules and a new need for punctuality.

The nineteenth century's great expansion of the industrial workforce transformed time in another way. Factory bells called workers—most of them accustomed to time only as measured by the sun and the seasonal rhythms of the farm—into an environment of precisely structured hours and close confinement. In other parts of the economy, offices, stores, and even many small workshops increasingly adopted clock-driven schedules. Farmers and ranchers did not—with the striking exception of southern plantation owners, many of whom were, by the 1830s, imposing the discipline of clock time on field hands, drivers, and overseers. One of the benefits of emancipation for many freedmen may have been the ability to return to seasonally modulated sun time.

In the late 1840s the electric telegraph achieved the first disembodiment of information, separating it from the constraints of human travel and transmitting it at a speed that seemed nearly instantaneous; by 1881, the world defined by telegraphy, railroad networks, precisely kept time, and daily newspapers seemed speeded up almost beyond comprehension. In his *American Nervousness* of that year, Beard claimed that the increasing pace of life was causing great stress. The telegraph and the daily press—with their constant flow of information about epidemics and disasters, crimes and scandals, the rapid fluctuations of prices and business conditions—had saturated businessmen with anxiety. Now that clocks were in the great majority of American homes and millions of men and women owned watches, these instruments had come to "compel us to be on time, and excite the habit of looking to see the exact moment." There once had been "a wider margin" of time for everything, when "men judged of the time by probabilities, by looking at the sun." But the new systems of transport ran on precise timetables. Earlier generations had had "incomparably fewer experiences wherein a delay of a few moments might destroy the hopes of a lifetime."

That acceleration has continued. The driver's license has replaced the skills of horsemanship; although air travel is much faster, airline schedules and delays create far more anxiety than railroad timetables ever did. The telegraph has given way to the telephone, electricity to electronics—the cell phone, the Internet, the smartphone, the social network, and an ever-proliferating array of digital devices. By the twenty-first century an increasing number of workers found themselves tethered to their jobs night and day by the invisible bonds of email and text, and more and more adolescents and young adults spent much of their waking lives completely immersed in the digital technologies of communication. It seemed that much of everyday life might soon be enacted in the virtual world.

[*See also* **Automation and Computerization; Automobiles; Cities and Suburbs; Clothing; Communication Networks; Consumption; Electricity and Electrification; Leisure; Public Health; Rural Life and Society; Work;** *and* **Working-Class Life and Society.**]

BIBLIOGRAPHY

Blassingame, John W. *The Slave Community: Plantation Life in the Antebellum South.* Rev. ed. New York: Oxford University Press, 1979. Still the most comprehensive and insightful study of community, family, and ordinary life under plantation slavery.

Bushman, Richard L. *The Refinement of America: Persons, Houses, Cities.* New York: Alfred A. Knopf, 1992. A wide-ranging interpretation of how Americans transformed their bodies and their environments in the years between 1750 and 1850.

Deetz, James. *In Small Things Forgotten: The Archaeology of Early American Life.* Rev. ed. New York: Anchor, 1996. An ambitious and highly readable interpretation both of how everyday life was and of how it then began to be transformed.

Demos, John. *Entertaining Satan: Witchcraft and the Culture of Early New England.* Rev. ed. New York: Oxford University Press, 2004. Demos is a historian unrivaled in his ability to unravel the experiences, complexities, and subtleties of life in the far landscape of early America.

Demos, John. *A Little Commonwealth: Family Life in Plymouth Colony.* New York: Oxford University Press, 1970.

Faragher, John Mack. *Women and Men on the Overland Trail.* New Haven, Conn.: Yale University Press, 1979. A comprehensive, pathbreaking account of the experience of the women, men, and children on America's great and transformative westward migration.

Green, Harvey. *The Uncertainty of Everyday Life, 1915–1945.* New York: HarperCollins, 1992. Concentrates on the everyday anxieties of modernity.

Grier, Katherine C. *Culture and Comfort: Parlor Making and Middle-Class Identity, 1850–1930.* Washington, D.C.: Smithsonian Institution Press, 1997. Based on a close reading of a wide variety of documentary sources and material culture, a study of the most value-laden of American domestic spaces.

Hawke, David Freeman. *Everyday Life in Early America.* New York: Harper & Row, 1988. A relatively brief survey.

Hutchins, Catherine E., ed. *Everyday Life in the Early Republic.* Winterthur, Del.: Henry Francis du Pont Winterthur Museum, 1994. Brings together a dozen essays on the themes of everyday life, including domestic consumption, rural and urban homes and landscapes, domestic rituals, and visual culture.

Ierley, Merritt. *The Comforts of Home: The American House and the Evolution of Modern Convenience.* New York: Clarkson Potter, 1999. A concise and useful account of the development of American domestic technologies.

Isaac, Rhys. *The Transformation of Virginia, 1740–1790.* Chapel Hill: University of North Carolina Press for the Institute of Early American History and Culture, Williamsburg, Va., 1982. Reading every scrap of documentation and material culture with ethnographic care, an extraordinarily vivid piece of historical ethnographic "thick description" of Virginia society.

Larkin, Jack. *The Reshaping of Everyday Life, 1790–1840.* New York: Harper & Row, 1988. Deals with the impacts of the market and industrial revolutions and the coming of reform and refinement.

Larkin, Jack. *Where We Lived: Discovering the Places We Once Called Home—the American Home from 1775 to 1840.* Newtown, Conn.: Taunton Press and the National Trust for Historic Preservation, 2006. A study of American houses, from mansions to one-room cabins, in the context of the everyday lives of those who lived in them.

Rath, Richard Cullen. *How Early America Sounded.* Ithaca, N.Y.: Cornell University Press, 2003. A striking, pioneering account of the early American soundscape; argues for the existence of a deeply significant aural culture.

Schlereth, Thomas J. *Victorian America: Transformations in Everyday Life, 1876–1915.* New York: HarperCollins, 1991. An encyclopedic vision of Victorian America, focused on the immense elaboration of material culture.

Sutherland, Daniel E. *The Expansion of Everyday Life, 1860–1876.* New York: Perennial Library, 1989. Deals with the complexities of ordinary life during a time of civil war and political upheaval.

Ulrich, Laurel Thatcher. *A Midwife's Tale: The Life of Martha Ballard, Based on Her Diary, 1785–1812.* New York: Alfred A. Knopf, 1990. A profound, detailed, and evocative study of an ordinary woman's life in the contexts of family, marriage, household routines, work, childbirth, and healing.

Underwood, Francis H. *Quabbin: The Story of a Small Town with Outlooks upon Puritan Life.* Boston: Lee and Shepard, 1893. Still a masterpiece, a remarkably insightful account of everyday life in a rural New England town, 1820–1880.

Wolf, Stephanie Grauman. *As Various as Their Land: The Everyday Lives of Eighteenth-Century Americans.* New York: HarperCollins, 1993. Engages the great cultural and regional diversity of American life and the emergence of consumerism.

Jack Larkin

EXPLORATION, CONQUEST, AND SETTLEMENT IN NORTH AMERICA

According to American myth, the first explorer to arrive in North America was Christopher Columbus. That statement is as false as it is common. Columbus's initial expedition came thousands of years after the first humans explored North America after crossing a land bridge that once connected modern western Asia and Alaska. Columbus was not even the first European to see the Western Hemisphere, a feat accomplished by Norse sailors sometime around the turn of the first Christian millennium. Still, Columbus's actions mattered. The Europeans who followed him displaced countless native communities and paved a way for the eventual migration of millions of Old World peoples, primarily from Europe and Africa, to the territory that became the United States.

The First American Explorers. The story of exploration, conquest, and settlement must begin with the ancient Americans. An unknown number crossed the Bering Strait and then broke into smaller groups. Some traveled across the northern portions of the continent and soon became the masters of the Arctic. The descendants of these earliest explorers are the modern-day Inuit, as well as other Arctic and Subarctic peoples, including Crees and Alaska natives. They lived too far north to practice farming, so their populations never became very large. The peoples who migrated the farthest east developed into groups including the Beothuks and Micmacs who were present when Norse explorers arrived.

Other ancient explorers spread out across the Americas. Over time these groups separated and spawned many different indigenous nations. They adapted to a wide range of environments, stretching from the semi-arid deserts of the Southwest, which became home to Puebloan and Apachean peoples, to the more fertile vales of the Mississippi valley. Those who settled along the Mississippi obtained maize (*Zea mays*), usually called "corn" in the modern United States, from indigenous people in Mexico. Maize cultivation provided large supplies of food, so those who could grow the crop tended to have larger populations than those who lived in places where the growing season was too short or the climate too cold. Mississippian maize cultivators built their largest settlement at Cahokia (in modern East Saint Louis, Illinois), where thousands of indigenous Americans gathered centuries before Columbus set sail across the Atlantic.

Devastating droughts eventually led these people to abandon Cahokia. Presumably after another period of active exploration, some of these people migrated to more promising regions and created the native cultures that Europeans encountered when they arrived on the mainland in the generation after 1492.

There are no written records of these early explorations and the settlements they produced. But the absence of records should not relegate these natives into a primordial era called "prehistory." As many archaeologists, anthropologists, and historians have painstakingly revealed, the peoples who lived in North America during the European age of discovery inhabited communities that had been shaped by specific historical processes and continued to evolve. The dynamism evident in these societies was crucial for their interactions with Europeans who sailed westward across the Atlantic. Indeed, the historian James Axtell has referred to the period as the "age of mutual discovery," a phrase suggesting that acts such as exploration and conquest should be understood from the perspective of peoples on each side of the cultural divide.

Early European Explorers. The earliest encounters between Europeans and Americans took place in southern Greenland and the modern Maritime Provinces of Canada. The Norse who sailed across the ocean did so in a series of shorter-distance migrations that took them first to Iceland, then to Greenland, and eventually to North America. Possibly as early as the year 1000 the Norse established a settlement at L'Anse aux Meadows in Newfoundland. By then the Norse had realized that they could send dried fish from the North Atlantic to markets across Europe.

But though only small numbers of Norse reached North America, tensions between them and natives still erupted. The Norse called the people they met *skraelings* (wretches), and violence erupted from the earliest moment of contact. These tensions likely discouraged many Norse from launching expeditions that would reach North America. Instead, the Norse became increasingly concerned about threats to their own society, notably the arrival in 1349 of the most virulent form of bubonic plague ever to reach Europe. The so-called Black Death killed approximately one-third of all Europeans and brought an end to any hopes that the Norse would use their base in Newfoundland to launch explorations of the interior of the North American continent.

By the sixteenth century, non-Norse Europeans, notably from Brittany, Normandy, the Basque Country, and the west of England, began to sail ever farther into the Atlantic. In many ways these were explorers, too, though they set off not to discover new lands but instead to meet the market for dried and salted fish that the Norse had abandoned. Some of these fishing crews likely reached North America, but there are no extant records.

When the fishing fleets sailed west across the Atlantic, other Europeans were more interested about opportunities in the opposite direction. Ever since antiquity, silks and spices from East and Southeast Asia had come west to the Mediterranean, thereby enhancing the range of foods, medicines, and clothing that Europeans could enjoy. But these products reached western Europe after a long and arduous journey along the ancient Silk Road, an overland route over thousands of miles of rough roads and with periodic threats from raiders. Because goods moved from one trader to another, the trade was also expensive: each time a parcel changed hands, its price increased. By the late fifteenth century, some Europeans came to realize that it

would be better if cinnamon, cloves, nutmeg, and peppers from the Spice Islands of the southwest Pacific could come to Europe on ships, thereby reducing the costs and possibly the risks as well.

Spices from the East Indies improved the taste of food—as did sugar, which Europeans had begun to import during the Crusades—but the passion for them came from widely held perceptions of their medicinal properties. Cinnamon could be used to calm an upset stomach and had benefits for the brain, liver, and lungs. Cloves could quell nausea. Mace could be boiled to ease heartburn or colic. Pharmacists who mixed sugar with peppers, mace, and pomegranate made a powder to cure black jaundice, a deadly condition caused by contact with rat urine. Nutmeg cleared up urinary-tract infections and eradicated headaches; taken properly it could eliminate ringworms, improve one's memory, bring sleep to an insomniac, and halt internal bleeding. Pepper could break a fever and reduce tumors, ease the symptoms of gout, and, if mixed with onions, soothe sciatica. One herbalist in the sixteenth century identified sixty-three possible medicinal uses for peppers alone.

Columbus traveled across Europe seeking financial support to find a quick route to the Spice Islands. The same commercial desires drove the Portuguese nobleman Vasco da Gama southward, around Africa, through the Indian Ocean, and into the Pacific on a voyage launched from Lisbon on 8 July 1497. His small flotilla reached India in May 1498. In subsequent years the Portuguese explorer Diego Lopes de Sequeira extended European knowledge of the Indian Ocean when he sailed farther eastward, landing at Sumatra in August 1509 and then moving to Malacca in 1511, thereby establishing Portuguese control over the spice trade for much of the next century.

Columbus.   But it was Columbus who had the greatest effect on the Western Hemisphere, though no one could have known this in advance. Columbus went westward with the belief that it would be quicker to reach the East Indies by sailing directly across the Atlantic. His calculations proved wrong, but it was perhaps the most auspicious error in the history of European exploration. Reports about what he saw on his four voyages spread across Europe, translated from one language into another in books emanating from printing presses—themselves relatively new innovations—across the continent.

The first report from Columbus, the so-called Barcelona Letter of 1493, set the tone for much of the European exploration of the Americas that followed in the sixteenth century. Columbus had "discovered a great many islands inhabited by people without number," he wrote to Ferdinand of Aragon and Isabella of Castile, the monarchs who had funded his venture, informing them that he had taken possession of these lands in their name, erected a royal flag to mark his claim, and faced no opposition from the islands' denizens. He proceeded to list the names he had provided for the islands, even though he acknowledged that the locals had other names for them.

Columbus filled much of the rest of the report with details that he thought would be of interest to his sponsors. He praised the rich soil of Hispaniola, which was ideal for both crops and pasturage and thus could support any new towns the Spanish wanted to build. He spoke of the island's natural harbors and extensive rivers, claiming that gold flowed in them. He reported that he found abundant spices and mines producing gold, as well as other mines on the island he named "Juana." He also described the people he met, noting that they were naked, had no inclination to attack the newcomers, and were so generous that they tended to give their possessions to the Europeans if they asked for them. Columbus reported that he kidnapped some of the locals so that he could teach them Spanish and hence have them provide information about events in the Indies. He also added that he had "not found any monstrous men in these islands, as many had thought"— a reference to the monsters that ancient authorities claimed could be found at the edges of the world.

This report became a model for the accounts that virtually every other explorer offered when an expedition entered a region previously unknown to Europeans. Columbus presumed that he could lay claim to the islands because he believed that the Europeans came from a superior culture, marked in particular by the fact that they were Christians. (The Protestant Reformation had not yet divided Christendom, so there was then no distinction between Protestants and Catholics.) He offered a description of a place that no European had described earlier, and he identified its particular virtues—a docile population, fertile lands, the availability of natural resources ranging from spices to gold. His depictions of the native Tainos anticipated many European depictions of indigenous Americans, which typically used external symbols related to clothing (or its absence) as a marker of civilization. By adding that he had taken some of the locals so that he could teach them to speak his own language, he acknowledged a larger truth: the natives were capable of learning European ways and hence could come to accept both the lessons of the church and the rule of distant monarchs. The earliest picture of the encounter, created by a European artist who read Columbus's report, emphasized the bashful countenance of the nude natives in contrast to the clothed Europeans who arrived on technologically sophisticated vessels.

In the years that followed, Columbus returned to the Indies three more times, but never with the same kind of success as on his first voyage. By the time he returned to Spain in November 1504, he had become a target of hostilities from all sides, including both indigenous peoples, who accused him of brutality and of enslaving them, and Spanish authorities, who believed that he had exceeded the authority he had gained as the "Admiral of the Ocean Sea." He also faced skepticism about what, exactly, he had found. Until his death in 1506 he believed that he had reached the East Indies, his original goal, though a growing chorus of scholars, who had received other reports from the Americas, eventually convinced European mapmakers that the Western Hemisphere needed to be added to any new maps of the world.

European Explorers and Conquerors. News about Columbus's ventures spread throughout Europe, with wide-ranging consequences. In 1493, Pope Alexander VI, himself Spanish-born, issued the bull *Inter caetera* (also known as the bull of donation), which gave to Spain a claim to any lands lying more than 100 leagues (about 300 miles) west of the Azores. But that papal decree threatened lands already claimed by the Portuguese, claims that had been affirmed by Pope Sixtus IV's bull *Aeterni regis* in 1481 and gave to the Portuguese ownership of lands discovered south of the Canary Islands. To resolve likely conflicts, the Spanish and Portuguese agreed in advance to divide any newly discovered parts of the world: the Spanish would have the western portion, and the Portuguese would have the eastern portion. A year later, in 1494, the monarchs of the two Iberian powers agreed to the terms of the Treaty of Tordesillas, which divided up any newly discovered lands along a line 370 leagues (about 1,100 miles) west of the Cape Verde Islands.

In 1492, Amerigo Vespucci, a Florentine banker, poet, and onetime Medici ambassador to France, took up residence in Seville and became involved in supplying ships for long-distance voyages. In 1499, he sailed to South America, then went back to Europe and crossed the Atlantic again in 1501 with the support of the Portuguese crown, this time reaching the site of modern Rio de Janeiro. He, like Columbus, described what he saw, and his small book, the *Mundus Novus* (New World), circulated across Europe, as did his name, which eventually became the basis for calling the Western Hemisphere "America." More important, his voyage confirmed Portuguese claims to a substantial portion of the Western Hemisphere east of the line established by the treaty of 1494.

In 1497, a Venetian known to the English as John Cabot, in the company of his son Sebastian, departed from Bristol into the northwest Atlantic. He returned to England later that year with three indigenous Americans, likely Inuit, who were at first unintelligible to the English and clad in furs. A few years later one local observer noted that the visitors had learned to speak English and dress like Englishmen, another signal of the possibility of converting Native Americans to European mores. In 1498 the elder Cabot set off again for the same region, but he never returned, thereby reminding the English of the potentially high cost of such explorations. A decade later, in 1508, Sebastian led a mission for what he hoped would be the Northwest Passage, the channel that Europeans believed connected the Atlantic to the South Sea (the Pacific Ocean). He returned to Bristol the following year and eventually became a cartographer, using his skills for both the English and the Spanish despite the animosity between the two monarchies.

In the aftermath of these late fifteenth- and early sixteenth-century explorations of the

Americas, other Europeans became fascinated by the opportunities they perceived there. The Spanish were the most consistent and aggressive, supporting military invasions to take control of Mexico in the late 1510s, under the command of Hernán Cortés, and of Peru in the 1530s, under the command of Francisco Pizarro. Spaniards also began to explore land that eventually became part of the United States. Among these were Juan Ponce de León, who landed near modern Saint Augustine on the east coast of Florida in 1513, and Hernando de Soto, who led an epic journey from Cuba into the interior of the Southeast from 1539 to 1541, providing Europeans with their first sustained views of the modern states of Georgia, Alabama, Mississippi, Louisiana, and eastern Texas. In 1540 a conquistador named Francisco Vásquez de Coronado led his troops northward from Mexico and into the Southwest on a fool's quest for the fabled city of Cibola, rumored to be a land of gold and jewels. He made it as far as Kansas before he realized that the city, if it existed, was not going to be found on his journey.

When the Spanish moved into an area, they quickly sought to bring it into their burgeoning empire. To do so they often resorted to violent tactics, evident in campaigns in the West Indies and especially in Mexico and Peru. During the siege of Tenochtitlán (modern Mexico City), Cortés's conquistadores treated the locals savagely, a feature of the conquest chronicled by both indigenous and Spanish observers. Among those who witnessed Spanish military violence was a Dominican friar named Bartolomé de Las Casas, who published the book known in English as *A Short Account of the Destruction of the Indies* in Seville in 1552. The book, which included gruesome descriptions of atrocities bordering on genocide—and likely exaggerated the actual violence that the conquistadores perpetrated on Americans—spawned the so-called black legend of the Spanish conquest. Las Casas, for his part, did not advocate abandoning the conquest of the Americas but instead argued that it should be done with peaceful means.

Other Spaniards did not exactly follow his suggestions. When Spanish conquistadores moved northward from Mexico into the modern Southwest, they read a document known as *El Requerimiento*, or the Requirement, to the Indians they met. The text, which the Spanish had developed in Europe in the early sixteenth century, instructed those listening to it to accept the authority of the Spanish monarchy. If they did so, the soldiers would allow them to remain on their lands and receive (what the Spaniards saw as) the benefits of Christianity, though they would need to pay tribute. If they refused, they risked assault. Considering that the document existed only in Spanish, one can only imagine what natives listening to it thought. Nonetheless, the performance of the Requirement revealed the close connection between exploration and conquest—in this instance supported by theological doctrine.

While the Spanish tried to solidify their hold on northern New Spain, the Breton sea captain Jacques Cartier set off to sea toward what he hoped would be the Northwest Passage. Like the Cabots, he never found it. But he did enter the mouth of the Saint Lawrence River and followed it into an interior populated by Iroquoian peoples. Reports of his journeys soon circulated in Europe as well, including details about the native peoples of Hochelaga (modern Montreal) and Stadacona (near modern Quebec City). Cartier's journeys gave the French a claim, recognized by other Europeans, to the Saint Lawrence valley, the eventual center of New France, though the arrival in 1608 of Samuel de Champlain proved more effective at asserting France's ownership.

Unlike the Spanish, the French never migrated in large numbers to Canada. Indeed, the three major groups of French migrants who arrived consisted of men: fur traders, who often married into indigenous families; soldiers, who guarded scattered colonial outposts but were never sufficient in number to mount an actual conquest of New France; and missionaries, especially Jesuits, who often lived among Indians and tried to colonize them through persuasion rather than military force. As a result, native peoples in New France had perhaps greater power over early French colonial settlements than they had in other areas. After all, they decided both whether to establish profitable relations with the newcomers and whether they would allow missionaries to live among them.

The Columbian Exchange. European journeys into the interior of North America provided Europeans with knowledge about natural resources and local populations, but the consequences for the indigenous peoples were substantial. Explorers unwittingly carried Old World diseases, notably the pathogens that caused smallpox, measles, influenza, and chicken pox. Scholars remain divided about how these viruses managed to cross the Atlantic Ocean, but whatever the mode of transmission, the effects were almost unimaginable. Between the time of Columbus's first voyage and 1800, the indigenous population of the Americas declined by approximately 90 percent. Contemporaries believed that the high death toll reflected divine punishment against the Indians, but in fact the explanation for the demographic catastrophe was more mundane. These diseases were always circulating in Europe, which made them endemic, and typically children got them and survived, building up some immunity. But the diseases were unknown in the Americas, and so no one had any immunity to them.

In these circumstances, Old World childhood diseases became raging epidemics in the Americas, sometimes known as "virgin-soil epidemics." Modern scholars have suggested that viruses alone did not kill indigenous Americans. Instead, the high death rates from these illnesses resulted from stresses on indigenous bodies, stresses produced by (among other things) conquistadores and, later, land-hungry European settlers, many of whom brought Old World livestock—cows, pigs, sheep, and horses. The newcomers often let these animals browse for themselves, and the creatures feasted on maize and other crops planted by Indians. Under these circumstances, the immune systems of native peoples were weakened, including by famine, hence explaining the astronomic mortality rates.

The historian Alfred Crosby labeled the transatlantic movement of biota the "Columbian Exchange." In his theory, the movement of Old World diseases, insects, livestock, plants, and pathogens across the ocean provided new opportunities for each of these species. Some of the migrants, such as the honeybee and the peach, were benign or even advantageous; others—notably smallpox—acted as brutally as the conquistadores did. But the exchange of biota went in both directions. Europeans reaped profits at home when they brought back potatoes, tomatoes, tobacco (widely believed to cure an enormous range of human ailments), and other plants once indigenous to the Western Hemisphere.

The Early Anglo-American Experience. Despite the early voyages of the Cabots, the English proved to be reluctant explorers and even more laggard conquerors. Until the 1558 accession of Queen Elizabeth I, a daughter of Henry VIII and an eager promoter of the expansion of English power in Ireland, few in England showed any public interest in North America. That situation began to change in the 1570s when the queen began to support long-distance exploration and conquest. Among those who traveled abroad was Sir Humphrey Gilbert, a brutal military commander during the Elizabethan conquest of Ireland: he once ordered his soldiers to decapitate the native Irish dead and to set up "a lane of heddes" (as the chronicler of the expedition called it) intended to terrorize any survivors. In 1576, Gilbert argued that the English should launch missions into the Northwest Passage. If they succeeded, they would be able to command much of the spice trade and also provide employment opportunities for young Englishmen, many of whom had resorted to crime to support themselves, and were hanged when convicted.

Gilbert died when his ship went down on his return from Newfoundland in 1583, but Richard Hakluyt the Younger, a trained minister eager to promote the English colonization of North America, soon picked up the argument. By 1580, Hakluyt had read about Cartier's travels to Canada, which he arranged to have translated and published. Soon after, he began to edit his own books, each filled with details about why the English should launch colonizing missions and about the likely success they would find if they did so. His efforts brought him to the attention of Sir Francis Walsingham, one of the queen's closest advisers, who sent Hakluyt to Paris to gather information on the continent about North America. While there he formulated a plan that circulated among the queen's advisers and laid out in detail the reasons why the English should immediately launch colonizing efforts in eastern North America, among other places.

Hakluyt never traveled to North America, but he nonetheless managed to crystallize the argument for English exploration and colonization. In addition to finding the Northwest Passage and hence enriching the nation, English colonists in North America would be able to spread Protestant Christianity and thereby halt the spread of Roman Catholicism advocated then by French and Spanish missionaries. Hakluyt, like others in England, had absorbed the critique written by Las Casas—an English-language edition was published in London in 1583—and so infused his arguments with anti-Iberian sentiments.

The English launched their first serious colonization effort in the mid-1580s in Roanoke, along the modern Outer Banks of North Carolina. Eventually, for reasons that remain a mystery, the colonists there disappeared, but the English did not give up. They managed to establish a permanent settlement on the American mainland when they set up Jamestown in Virginia in 1607. Earlier explorations of the coasts of Newfoundland and Maine did not lead to the formation of colonies. Unlike their earlier efforts, the English poured resources into Virginia, especially migrants, who were necessary to replace colonists who kept dying from diseases, notably typhoid fever and dysentery caused by bacteria in polluted water supplies. Most of those migrants were men, which for much of the century created a gender imbalance that inhibited the formation of colonial families. The vast majority—including virtually all of the relatively small number of women—arrived as indentured servants who owed years of their labor to pay off the cost of their transatlantic journey.

The English hoped that their settlement of the mainland would be peaceful, but that dream proved elusive. Tensions between the English settlers and Powhatans in early Virginia exploded in 1622 when the natives, under a headman named Opechancanough, launched a raid against the newcomers, who, to the Indians, had overstepped their bounds. The natives killed 347 colonists on a single day, which prompted the English to launch a series of brutal reprisals that took hundreds of Powhatan lives. Tensions flared in the region again in 1644, prompted by Opechancanough—then rumored to be one hundred years old—who sought to limit expansion of English settlements. In 1676 a colonial uprising known as Bacon's Rebellion also took a devastating toll on natives.

In New England, where the English established Plymouth in 1620 and Massachusetts Bay in 1630, tensions also divided natives from newcomers. Unlike the colonization of the Chesapeake, the English migration to New England had an almost balanced sex ratio and relatively few indentured servants, which allowed for the maintenance of stable families and contributed to an enormous increase in the colonial population even after the flow of migrants dwindled to a trickle in the early 1640s (as a result of the English Civil War). But even before population growth put pressure on indigenous peoples, tensions had begun to fester in the region. The Pilgrims of Plymouth and the Puritans of Massachusetts each needed the fur trade to help pay off the debts of their travel across the Atlantic, which meant that they had to maintain peaceful relations with indigenous hunters. The Indians, for their part, were keen to establish and maintain the trade because the English offered manufactured goods never before seen in the region. But mutual suspicion percolated in native towns and colonial villages, prompting the English to make an alliance with the Narragansetts against the Pequots. In 1637 the English and their native allies launched one particularly violent assault against a Pequot town on the Mystic River, setting it ablaze and shooting at those fleeing the fire. Governor William Bradford of

Plymouth believed that approximately four hundred Indians died that night in an action that he understood, using the logic common to the Puritans, to be the unfolding of a divine plan. Violence abated for a time but then spiked again in the mid-1670s when Metacom's, or King Philip's, War killed hundreds of Indians and colonists.

The European Conquest of North America. The English were not the only Europeans to cross the Atlantic looking for new opportunities. In 1609 the Dutch East India Company, hoping (like the English) to find a water route to the Pacific, sponsored a mission led by the English sea captain Henry Hudson to sail through the Northeast Passage, which European cartographers claimed ran along the northern edges of Russia. Unable to get through the ice, Hudson and his crew decided to search for the Northwest Passage instead. After cruising along the Atlantic coast of North America, Hudson entered into modern New York Bay and up the river that now bears his name. When he got as far as modern Albany he realized that he had not found the route to the Pacific, so he turned home, though not before a violent encounter with the local Munsees. Hudson returned to North America the following year on an English expedition bound for the Northwest Passage. He made it as far as Hudson Bay in northern Canada, but his crew mutinied and left him for dead in June 1611.

Though Hudson never went back to the Netherlands, the Dutch used his venture to establish a claim to the lands he had seen. In 1624, New Netherland, with its capital New Amsterdam (later New York City), became part of the Dutch Republic. In 1638, Scandinavian migrants launched their own colony, called New Sweden, along the shores of Delaware Bay. Led by Peter Minuit, who had earlier worked for the Dutch West

India Company and been governor of New Netherland, a group of Swedes and Finns probably numbering no more than several hundred settled near modern Wilmington, Delaware. But the enterprise proved short-lived, and the Dutch absorbed the colony in 1655. The Danes, too, joined the colonizing business when they established themselves on Saint John, Saint Thomas, and Saint Croix, a cluster of islands known in the mid-seventeenth century as the Virgin Islands in the Leeward Islands. The Danes retained ownership until the United States purchased the islands from Denmark in 1916.

By the mid-seventeenth century, Europeans had laid claim to virtually all of North America, but the situation was far from static. Three Anglo-Dutch wars led to shifting claims for the territory that had been first in the control of Munsees and other Algonquian speakers in the early seventeenth century, then in the control of the Dutch, and after 1664 claimed by the English, who renamed the region New York. Though the English claimed territory lying to the west, it remained under the control of the Iroquois until the American Revolution. Indigenous peoples retained control of much of the Southeast as well, and they did so until the age of removal in the 1830s. They were not alone in having control. Farther west, native peoples often controlled the pace and location of Euro-American settlement—or stopped it entirely. Long before the arrival of Europeans, local groups in the Southwest had figured out how to survive despite the difficulties posed by the environment. As they understood it, they thrived because of the good relations that they had with the gods. Spanish colonization undermined many indigenous communities, an action that threatened indigenous mastery of the region. In 1680, divine forces speaking through kachinas (deified ancestral spirits) commanded Pueblos to rise up against the newcomers. Their revolt, which targeted settlers and clerics, drove the Spanish out of New Mexico for a decade.

After the American Revolution, the newly named United States revived the tradition of exploration and conquest of earlier European colonizers. In 1803, President Thomas Jefferson authorized the Corps of Discovery under the command of Meriwether Lewis and William Clark to chart a path to the Pacific. They succeeded in part because they found native allies along the way, a reminder of the continuing authority of Indians in much of North America. The Comanches, for example, had earlier taken advantage of the arrival of Old World horses to become an equestrian power, dominating much of the middle of the continent until well into the eighteenth century. Later the Sioux—Lakota, Dakota, and Nakota—who had also mastered the equestrian arts, controlled the northern Great Plains, at least until Euro-Americans destroyed the vast bison herds that were vital to their economy. Eventually the federal government sent troops into the West to force surviving Indians onto reservations, a final signal that European exploration had led to conquest, forced emigration for natives, and eventual settlement by Euro-Americans.

[*See also* **Alaska; Atlantic World; Borderlands; Caribbean; Colonial Era; Columbian Exchange; Disease; Frontier, The; Internal Migration,** *subentry on* **Colonial Era; Jamestown; Lewis and Clark Expedition; Missions, in America; Mississippi River; Native American History and Culture,** *subentries on* **Migration and Pre-Columbian Era, Distribution of Major Groups circa 1500,** *and* **1500 to 1800; Native American Land Use; New England; Plymouth; Pueblo Revolt; Puritan Great Migration; Southwest, The;** *and* **West, The.**]

BIBLIOGRAPHY

Anderson, Virginia DeJohn. *Creatures of Empire: How Domestic Animals Transformed Early America*. New York: Oxford University Press, 2004. A fascinating study of how animals, especially those brought from Europe, played a leading role in the conquest and colonization of eastern North America.

Axtell, James. "Europeans, Indians, and the Age of Discovery." *American Historical Review* 92, no. 3 (1987): 621–632.

Chaplin, Joyce E. *Subject Matter: Technology, the Body, and Science on the Anglo-American Frontier, 1500–1676*. Cambridge, Mass.: Harvard University Press, 2001. A thorough study of the evolving interactions between technology and people in eastern North America, with particular emphasis on efforts to understand indigenous bodies.

Crosby, Alfred W., Jr. *Ecological Imperialism: The Biological Expansion of Europe, 900–1900*. Cambridge, U.K.: Cambridge University Press, 1986. Crosby coined the term "Columbian Exchange" in 1972 in a book with that name, but this book sets his theory into a broader historical context and includes material on Norse explorations.

Elliott, J. H. *The Old World and the New, 1492–1650*. Cambridge, U.K.: Cambridge University Press, 1970. A series of pioneering essays tracing how early modern explorations and discoveries in the Americas altered life in Europe.

Grafton, Anthony, with April Shelford and Nancy Siraisi. *New Worlds, Ancient Texts: The Power of Tradition and the Shock of Discovery*. Cambridge, Mass.: Harvard University Press, 1992. A lavishly illustrated account depicting how Europeans, particularly scholars, wrestled with findings from the Western Hemisphere, which often challenged age-old beliefs.

Gutiérrez, Ramón A. *When Jesus Came, the Corn Mothers Went Away: Marriage, Sexuality, and Power in New Mexico, 1500–1846*. Stanford, Calif.: Stanford University Press, 1991. A powerful in-depth study of colonization in the Southwest, with extraordinary materials on encounters between Pueblos and Spaniards.

Hämäläinen, Pekka. *The Comanche Empire*. New Haven, Conn.: Yale University Press, 2008. The most thorough account of the most powerful indigenous American population in the eighteenth century.

Jones, David S. "Virgin Soils Revisited." *William and Mary Quarterly*, 3d ser., 60, no. 4 (2003): 703–742. A historian of medicine's reevaluation of why Old World diseases were so lethal in the Americas, drawing from clinical advances in epidemiology that have been made as a result of research on HIV and AIDS.

Konstam, Angus. *Historical Atlas of Exploration, 1492–1600*. New York: Checkmark Books, 2000. A useful guide to the most famous explorers of the early modern age.

Kupperman, Karen Ordahl. *Indians and English: Facing Off in Early America*. Ithaca, N.Y.: Cornell University Press, 2000. A sustained analysis of the earliest encounters between the English and indigenous peoples in eastern North America.

Las Casas, Bartolomé de. *A Short Account of the Destruction of the Indies* (1552). Edited and translated by Nigel Griffin. London: Penguin, 1992. The most powerful European critique of European conquest in the Americas.

Mancall, Peter C. *Fatal Journey: The Final Expedition of Henry Hudson—A Tale of Mutiny and Murder in the Arctic*. New York: Basic Books, 2009. An account of the English explorer Hudson, who also worked for the Dutch, whose crew abandoned him in James Bay in 1611.

Mancall, Peter C. *Hakluyt's Promise: An Elizabethan's Obsession for an English America*. New Haven, Conn.: Yale University Press, 2007. An analysis of the life and work of Richard Hakluyt the Younger, the most avid and important promoter of the English colonization of North America, who eventually believed that the Spice Islands held more potential.

Mancall, Peter C., ed. *Travel Narratives from the Age of Discovery: An Anthology*. New York: Oxford University Press, 2006. A large collection of travel accounts, putting explorations in the Americas into a global context.

Merrell, James H. *The Indians' New World: Catawbas and Their Neighbors from European Contact through the Era of Removal*. Chapel Hill: University of North Carolina Press for the Institute of Early American History and Culture, Williamsburg, Va., 1989. The most perceptive account of the changes in any region of the North American mainland that were produced by the arrival of Europeans and of the efforts of indigenous Americans to adapt to constantly changing circumstances.

Richter, Daniel K. *Before the Revolution: America's Ancient Pasts*. Cambridge, Mass.: Harvard University Press, 2011. A monumental study of the encounter between European and American civilizations, from medieval times to the late eighteenth century.

Richter, Daniel K. *Facing East from Indian Country: A Native History of Early America*. Cambridge, Mass.: Harvard University Press, 2001. European exploration and colonization from the perspective of Native Americans.

Salisbury, Neal. "The Indians' Old World: Native Americans and the Coming of Europeans." *William and Mary Quarterly*, 3d ser., 53, no. 3 (1996): 435–458. An excellent essay focused on the dynamism of pre-1492 North American societies.

Taylor, Alan. *American Colonies*. New York: Viking, 2001. The most balanced overview of the formation of European colonies across the Americas, including the far West.

Peter C. Mancall

F

FAMILY

The history of the American family is ongoing. Before the 1970s only antiquarians, museum exhibitors, and fiction writers speculated about what past families were like. Traditional historians analyzed wars and international relations, politics, large-scale economic changes, various kinds of elites, leaders, and workers: all mostly men. Biographers scrutinized family backgrounds, but their individualistic accounts defied generalization. Consequently, until the so-called new social history emerged, historians interested in families borrowed conceptual frameworks from anthropology, demography, and sociology.

The Cambridge Group for the History of Population and Social Structure, founded at the University of Cambridge, England, in 1964, began the turn to family history; its interdisciplinary scholarship described families as social institutions that are shaped by biological and psychological variables interacting with socioeconomic change. Methodologies focused on the effects of change on family formation over several centuries. Scholars identified long-term components of modernization, tracking changes in family organization, household composition, kin relationships, and the productive roles of members. Families could be nuclear or extended, their size usually linked to various survival strategies adopted when adjusting to shifting socioeconomic, environmental, and political forces. The Cambridge Group was especially interested in how families in western Europe and North America responded to the transition from agriculture to industrialization. Though this scholarship opened new perspectives on family history, only when historians of women posed different kinds of questions did social history begin to focus on experience, emotional life, and the role of culture and ideology.

Women's History, Gender History, Family History.

Historians of women also began contributing to the new social history in the 1970s. Leftist political activism in the 1960s led social historians to rethink methodology, subject matter, and periodization. They also wrote histories of those called "the inarticulate": groups whose experiences had been neglected. This drew the historians to the reciprocal interaction of economic life and the cultural formations of those they studied, such as might be found among sailors, street mobs, peasants, artisans, and new industrial workers. What individual and collective assumptions shaped activities and experience at crucial moments of historical change?

Demographic changes in the profession contributed to engagements with new subject matter: historians who were women and people of color vitally shaped the study of the family. Whereas renewed interest in the working class led some to reevaluate women's participation in factory work, others turned increasingly to private life. They found women in spaces that traditional historians had assumed to be male. For example, scholars studying the colonial era revisited women's work in the preindustrial family in order to understand the evolution of gender roles in the American colonies. In the North and the nonslaveholding South, the majority of people were subsistence farmers. As in England, men dominated agricultural production, especially after the invention of the plow, but all family members were flexible workers, because the seasonal constraints of planting and harvesting required all hands. In the family economy, women contributed primarily to household production: spinning, cooking, weaving, tending gardens, tending domestic animals, and transforming staples into consumable products. Family members made their own clothing, and during the long winter, boys and men might take their place at the loom. Middle children cared for weaned infants; more mature daughters aided their mothers or became hired-out helps to neighbors. In the eighteenth century, New England women acted as "deputy husbands" for absent spouses. In preindustrial society, women were as crucial as men to family economic survival: "a man without a wife is a fool," as the peasant aphorism put it.

Treating women as historical actors made a difference: within a decade, social history's landscape had changed. Women's historians also analyzed cultural formations. The historian Carroll Smith-Rosenberg insisted in an agenda-setting address to the Berkshire Conference of Women Historians in 1974 that writing about women required new categories of analysis. She agreed that women's presence was crucial to "household, the family, the bed, the nursery, and kinship systems." But how were historians to understand the psychodynamics that transpired in these private spaces? Women's historians were among the first social historians to highlight *experience*, thereby refocusing the agenda of family history on the interactions among cultural, economic, and political change.

Setting aside presuppositions about the family as "natural," these historians examined how individuals and groups created a language and ideology of family life within a particular temporal context. How did meaning and behavior interact with social and economic obligation to influence changing notions of family that redefined masculinity, femininity, parenting, childhood, and marriage relations? What role did competing understandings of class, race, ethnicity, and gender play? How did people experience familial roles? Building on anthropological and sociological insights, scholars explored what Raymond Williams in his 1977 work *Marxism and Literature* (Oxford: Oxford University Press) called "structures of feeling." Turning to culture enabled family historians to clarify how both dominant and alternative families interacted with economies, social change, and "foundationalist" assumptions about gender difference, helping scholars to historicize such notions as "public" and "private."

These developments coincided with the discipline's turn in the 1980s toward cultural history. Several so-called new cultural histories of that time enabled the rapid expansion of family history. When Joan Wallach Scott published *Gender and the Politics of History* (New York: Columbia University Press) in 1988, many scholars were acting on Smith-Rosenberg's challenge to rethink the relationship between families and society— or between what Second Wave feminists called "the personal" and "the political."

By the end of the 1980s, historians of the American family had adopted anthropologists' loose, functionalist definition of "family," forged in the 1970s when that field grappled with the question of whether or not the family was a universal institution. Here the family was defined as an institution performing at least three categories of responsibility. The first two were often interconnected: biological reproduction, resulting in genealogical relations or kinship relations or both, and social reproduction, both ensuring that workers returned to the workplace fed, rested, and willing and also raising children to become conforming and productive members of their communities. But the third category of responsibility intrigued historians

most: families facilitated the creation of power, status, and inequality, often through participating in social and economic exchange. Scholars historicized "the family," deconstructing its presumption of timelessness and universality, while exposing various multiple claims and interests that always ran through it. Families performed their tasks variously at specific moments in the American past. In studying families as fundamental units of social organization, differences of geographic location, race, class, and culture mattered. Finally, the new work raised questions about culture: more than simply a social formation, the family was a discursive entity that shaped and reflected a society's ideals. How did cultural understandings of the ideal family change over time, and what were the stakes for society at large? Research on English and European families in North America in the seventeenth and eighteenth centuries delivered answers.

Early in the sixteenth century, migrants from emerging European nation-states mounted geographically far-reaching imperialist projects. By the seventeenth century, colonists established settlements in regions that had long been inhabited by native peoples with a diversity of tribal and family structures. Colonial historians scrutinized how English settlers and westward-moving Americans interacted with these groups, whose radically different social economies and family patterns shaped Americans' understanding of themselves. Mutual encounters— sometimes peaceful, more often brutally violent—affected both civilizations.

North American Indian Societies. Indian societies were as ancient as European ones, boasting a variety of social formations. Artifacts of an advanced urban culture built by mound builders circa 1000–1500 have surfaced in southwest Illinois; cliff dwellers, assumed to be ancestors of the Pueblos, farmed in semipermanent horticultural villages, and built their communal housing into canyon walls to protect themselves from marauders in the Southwest. Traversing various regions were seminomadic hunter-gatherer groups whose economies, family organizations, housing, and migration patterns differed according to available resources. Continentally dispersed from the Arctic coast to the tip of Florida were 10 to 12 million indigenous inhabitants in roughly six hundred societies speaking countless languages. Even Europeans' earliest contacts brought radical change: catastrophic pandemics from the transmission of Old World diseases against which North Americans had no immunity. By 1700, even as the settlers first arrived, the decimation of native populations and the remaking of economies, societies, and social institutions was well under way.

Native kinship groups consisted of blood relatives and fictive kin. Some societies were matrilineal, others patrilineal. Kin groups monitored duties and rights, promoted circulation of people and resources, determined selection of marriage partners, and managed individuals' participation in polities. Conducive to informal sharing and reciprocity in production, such responsibilities mitigated economic inequality and accumulation of wealth. Though certainly present, hierarchies rested on gift-giving practices that measured rank by degree of generosity to others. By being "obliged to give to the mob," one Dutch missionary observed, chiefs were often "the poorest." Despite their impressive differences, all native societies confounded European expectations in three ways: none based production on private ownership of property or land; none engaged in a distributive market; and absent a territorial state, none participated in larger political, judicial, or administrative systems.

After the 1970s the history of Native Americans expanded rapidly in tandem with gender and family history, complicating the ledger of gains and losses resulting from the clashes between European and indigenous societies. Conflicting notions of family organization, masculinity and femininity, property rights, and work regimes often generated crucial misunderstandings that eventually led to conflict. According to Kathleen Brown's pioneering work, English settlement in North America opened up a "gender frontier" in which contested notions of family organization shaped the meeting of cultures. For Brown, gender defines not only understandings of sexual difference, but also the social roles that give those differences meaning in daily life. Gender discourses are the prescriptive languages of proper behavior that inscribe both individuals and groups into a given social and political order. Though always historically specific, these languages are often understood to be ordained by nature or the divine.

On first arriving in the Chesapeake in 1607, the Virginia Company encountered natives on the coastal plain whose sex roles, sexuality, social organization, and economy differed profoundly from their own. Among the cultures belonging to the Powhatan confederacy in Virginia, women were the agriculturalists. They earned respect for producing the needed staples consumed by the people of the coastal plain: corn, peas, beans, and squash. Women's association with agriculture was also spiritual: it symbolized life giving, sexuality, and reproduction. They were important in tribal decisions. As warriors and hunters, men had roles that complemented those of women. Indians highly valued meat; whole villages accompanied the men on the winter hunt, provisioning them while taking pride in their fishing, hunting, and fighting skills. To the English, Indian men appeared lazy and henpecked; even their appearance—they lacked the facial hair worn by mature English males—fed suspicions of feminization. Unwillingness to tame the wilderness, tolerance of women's control over farming, indifference to private property—all gave the English proof of inferior manliness.

When Jamestown was established, England was in the final throes of transitioning from feudalism to capitalism. The flexible gender arrangements of medieval society were already being dislodged, along with reciprocity between peasants and aristocracy. Once hunting and fishing defined the leisure of the rich, peasant access became restricted. As a robust patriarchal private-property regime gradually replaced the manorial system, relations between men and women became extraordinarily contentious. Pamphlet wars between the sexes generated mutually vicious denunciations. Advice books proliferated, detailing the proper behavior of the "goodwife," whose subordination became a crucial measure of English claims to civilization. Men dominated agriculture, confining women to domestic production. Indeed, the unstable gender discourses then plaguing English society had greater salience than discourses about race did. Though late sixteenth-century coastal explorations of Africa generated interest, quotidian encounters with Africans in England came later. Only after a century of colonial settlement did early impressions mature into a hardened racial system of social distinction, power, and legal exploitation.

The colonies were the crucible for English encounters with difference. New patriarchal discourses colored settlers' impressions of natives, along with individuals' understanding of the colonial project itself. The reigning image of proper English families bolstered England's national identity during these centuries of nation building. English familial,

economic, and social structures were believed to be divinely ordained. English intolerance increased as successive engagements with African and North American indigenous cultures became more exploitative. Indians also believed that their social and gender customs were "natural," thus creating on both sides a conundrum that authorized violent competition for land and resources. These fraught encounters effected changes in gender relations in both cultures, with warfare exacerbating male dominance. Eventually English military superiority over natives, disruption of livelihoods, and disease radically reduced indigenous populations in the region from fourteen thousand inhabitants in 1607 to about three thousand a century later. By then, gender regimes in the American colonies were becoming intertwined with the racialized system of slave labor that eventually became the hallmark of the southern economy.

Colonial Families, Slavery, and the Construction of Race.

Kathleen Brown's analysis of English engagement with indigenous peoples becomes paradigmatic for the later history of race relations, too. Gender and race worked together. English gender ideology mixed with an unanticipated system of slavery to fashion a particular set of patriarchal family relations that shaped southern politics, social structure, and power relations for centuries to come.

Indentured servants could not satisfy the South's voracious need for labor. The English copied their rivals, Spain and Portugal, who were importing Africans to South America and the Caribbean. In Virginia, slavery developed gradually, but by the 1670s Africans' legal status deteriorated. Colonial laws curtailed the freedoms of black men and women, but the restrictions on women reveal best how gender and race overlapped as social categories.

Gender molded colonial culture, politics, and class relations by differentiating black slavery from white servitude. It supplied social assumptions and legal rationales for bondage, and it shaped the idealized family form adopted by gentry families. Specifically, free, indentured, and slave men and women initially worked together, but from the start, black women experienced no concessions to their womanhood. Their labor was always associated with men's. White female indentured servants were soon removed from the fields; black women remained. Their labor was taxed similarly to male laborers', even if they were married to free black men. Black women's status deteriorated in other ways, too: for instance, they were punished more harshly than female indentured servants were. New laws restricted interactions between black and white workers, barring interracial relationships. In a reversal of English law, the children of a slave mother inherited her bondage, no matter the father's race or status.

The staple-producing slave economy gave rise to three kinds of families: those of planter elites and lesser slaveholders, those of yeoman farmers, and those of African American slaves. Laws codified slavery by the eighteenth century, but in piecemeal fashion— not just in the South, but also in New England, New York, and Pennsylvania. Most southern whites, roughly three-quarters of them, were nonslaveholding artisans or yeomen. Like their northern counterparts they eked out a subsistence living, a minority managing a modest surplus for the market. Of slaveholders at the top of the South's governing hierarchy, 88 percent owned twenty slaves or fewer, while some of the wealthiest held several plantations with hundreds of slaves.

The "civilized," Christian, white, male-dominated family remained the prescriptive ideal in the English colonies. In Virginia, though Anglo-American women were privileged by their whiteness, male elites gained authority at the expense of women's earlier public roles. As the exercise of power migrated from community to courtroom, plantation patriarchs increasingly regulated sexuality, marriage, and female public speech.

Overwhelmingly smallholders, slaveholding families departed from the class hierarchies emerging in the North. Southern race hierarchy bound all white men together, from subsistence yeoman farmers and artisans to backcountry hardscrabble croppers. By 1776, planter elites had shaped a political order of white male solidarity that required lavishly patronizing their social inferiors, who rarely relinquished the dream of becoming slaveholders. A calendar of male homosocial performances intended to cement white racial solidarity pervaded the year, including cockfights, militia musters, horse races, gambling, and election-day drinking bashes. Dependent women, children, old people, and slaves, an audience relegated to the sidelines, stood watching.

The institution of slavery lurks at the heart of American democracy as an original sin, fashioning perceptions of human difference into an ideology of American family life that has remained raced, gendered, and classed. American values drew their discursive power from the assumed inferiority of imagined opposites, successive categories of negative "others": first Indians and Africans; later Irish, Chinese, and Mexicans; and finally millions of southern and eastern Europeans, joined by even later migrants who flocked to the United States to work in steel mills, coal mines, oil refineries, garment factories, meatpacking plants, and the postindustrial service industries of a flourishing twentieth-century capitalist economy. Some eventually adopted familial norms of the white majority. Others, hampered by economic inequality, always a tonic for the fiction of "race" difference, remained outside the circle of "we."

The Mexican War of 1846–1848, with its popular cry of "manifest destiny," illustrates the malleability of racial assumptions derived from colonial racial regimes. The Spanish settled outposts in New Mexico as early as the seventeenth century; they encountered the Pueblo Indians, whose agricultural matriarchal society presumed the convergence of sexuality and the sacred. Though Franciscans attempted to convert members of this highly erotic culture to Christianity, success was limited: some priests lamented that mission settlements were filled with friars' children. When Mexico won its independence from Spain in 1821, Americans' perceptions of Mexican society came rapidly into play. New Mexico had become a multiethnic Hispanic society already experiencing market penetration and the beginnings of capitalism. Peopled by natives, Africans, Mexican Indians, Europeans, and mixed-race children, New Mexico had a location and resources that proved strategic to American westward expansion. When the two nations went to war over land, race differences justified Americans' entitlement to the territory. Anti-Catholicism, already being inspired by the immigration of the Irish, was folded into additional claims that Mexican society was feudalistic and based on peonage. New Mexico's extensive race mixing aroused Americans' worst fears, and dime novels circulated these themes in American popular culture.

Black Families, 1607 to 1920: From Slavery to Debt Peonage.

Slavery gathered together individuals from African societies that differed linguistically, religiously, and socioeconomically. Families were necessarily created anew. Governed by planters' whim and the vagaries of the plantation economy itself (cotton, tobacco, rice), relationships and familial structures among slaves varied widely. Some masters refused permission to marry; others forced particular marriages for breeding purposes. Women were prey to the prurience or violence of overseers, masters, and their sons. Even when permitted families, slave men lacked the privileges of the patriarchal norm: fathers and husbands were helpless to protect wives and children. Members of families belonging to different masters found themselves separated for long periods.

Life within an oppressive system required adaptation. Three strategies survived into emancipation. First, a more egalitarian family structure gave women power in the slave community. Second, fictive kin relationships were common: "going for sisters," "going for brothers," or calling adult slaves "auntie" and "uncle" broadened responsibilities for parenting, comforting, and feeding children. Through these networks of care, slave communities coped with the system's imposed fluidity of human relations. Finally, slave religion, a syncretic form of African practice and Protestant Christianity, cemented families and communities. Especially salient was the privileging of music for purposes of worship; music was one of the few forms of expression that was not suppressed.

Many families survived regardless. After 1865, former slaves scoured the South searching for lost family members. Even when not legal, long-term commitments led husbands and wives to reaffirm their married status in law. To the missionary Frederick Ayers, black husbands and fathers reconstituted their families as a powerful symbol of masculine independence: "The idea of 'freedom' . . . of calling their wives . . . children, and little hut their own" sustained "their spirits" (Tera W. Hunter, *To 'Joy My Freedom: Southern Black Women's Lives and Labors after the Civil War* [Cambridge, Mass.: Harvard University Press, 1997] p. 37). Hopes would be shattered, however, by the failure of Reconstruction.

Radical Reconstruction, from 1865 to 1877, promised land redistribution, equal access to public education, economic opportunities, and black political participation, including the vote. For the large majority of freedpeople, little materialized. When the federal government withdrew troops from the South in 1877, neither safety nor hard-won political gains were guaranteed. Sharecropping ensnared the large majority of black families, many poor white families, and even Mexican American families in Texas. Most African Americans in the South became family farmers who rented primitive cabins on small plots of land owned by whites. Working together, much preferable to slavery's gang labor, each family produced its own food, along with cotton or tobacco as a cash crop. Everything needed was provided by landowners on credit against income from the yearly harvest. Sharecroppers were plagued by debt; states passed laws banning blacks from moving until debt-free. Many skilled black workers left the South, but sharecroppers had little choice. At least black families gained some privacy and community. For access to cash, husbands sometimes sought seasonal employment on the levees or in the city, while wives and older daughters worked in nearby towns and cities as maids, washerwomen, or live-in servants, sometimes outearning their husbands. By 1900, 86 percent of black people worked on farms or in service, and racial hierarchies defined the South's labor market.

By 1900, three phenomena structured the social, cultural, political, and psychic contexts in which black and white families now made their lives. One was the surge in racial violence. The worst spectacle of such violence, lynching, claimed almost five thousand African Americans lives between 1882–1930. Lynchers invoked the purity of white homes and womanhood, using the myth of the black rapist to license mutilation and terror. Old photographs and postcards testify that collective white violence became popular entertainment for family outings. Second, following the final defeat and removal of native peoples to western reservations, these same years saw a more aggressive U.S. imperialism overseas, culminating in the 1898 Spanish-American War. In response to a new series of encounters with entirely new groups of external others—encounters that were unsettling, exoticized, and often extremely violent—the concept of the family was again reworked: missionaries, doctors, nurses, businessmen, and anthropologists, as well as soldiers and government agents, sought to shape what they thought were proper family forms. The mass immigration from southern and eastern Europe, the third phenomenon of these years, drew much of the same ideological attention. But if European immigrants were exploited as cheap labor and considered inferior, they were not put into the same category as African Americans, Indians, the Chinese, or the colonized people of American protectorates. States and welfare agencies sponsored Americanization programs to reshape immigrant family values. "Race science" and eugenics justified these efforts. Northern Europeans were assumed to head an elaborate hierarchy, and new immigrants were lower. But social scientists still singled out black family life, insisting that "the Negro has little home conscience or love of home" and was as "destitute of morals" as "lower animals" (Herbert Gutman, *The Black Family in Slavery and Freedom 1750–1925* [New York: Pantheon Books, 1976] pp. 458–459).

Despite the failure of Reconstruction, emancipated slaves and northern blacks collaborated on community-building projects that yielded a small middle class, building national church groups, schools, teacher-training institutions, and colleges in the South to prepare black professionals and entrepreneurs for leadership roles. Families educated their children for productive adulthood, while sharing whites' norms of respectability. Only in their greater gender equality did black marriages differ: because black men of all classes earned less than white men did, their wives were often kept in the workforce, thus preserving the role flexibility originating in slavery. Middle-class black activism expanded exponentially through the first part of the twentieth century: the black poor was targeted for "racial uplift," and middle-class blacks participated in national Progressive reform movements, including for temperance and women's suffrage, as well as in women's reading and other club associations and clubs for self-improvement. Northern leaders able to speak out without violent retaliation led national antilynching and antidiscrimination campaigns. Eventually southern black families began to move north, sometimes together at once, sometimes in parts over time. Called the Great Migration, this systematic resistance of last resort occurred between 1880 and 1970.

White Families in the North. While racialized families experienced violence, cultural and economic dispossession, and marginalization, whites in New England and the middle colonies created patriarchal, household subsistence families, and the nation-state treated these as the units of taxation, conscription, and social control. Puritanism acknowledged women's spiritual equality through "the priesthood of all believers," but men achieved full adulthood only as property-owning patriarchs exercising moral authority over wives and children of their own. Court records in colonial Massachusetts reveal strict enforcement of gender roles. When Anne Hutchinson voiced a dissenting doctrinal interpretation in 1638, she was convicted of sedition. The Massachusetts governor John Winthrop summarized her transgression thus: "You have stept out of your place, you have rather bine a Husband than a Wife, a preacher than a Hearer; and a Magistrate than a Subject."

In addition to subsistence farming, the colonial economy generated enormous wealth for English investors, southern slaveholders, landowning squires in the middle colonies, and merchants and captains involved in transatlantic trade. These networks supported growing commercial centers of industry. With land the primary form of capital, aspiring families continually violated Indian land treaties. After independence the government removed Native American tribes from desired land. Justifications rested on difference: Indians' failure to adopt American familial and economic systems. The fates of Massachusetts "praying" Indians—late seventeenth-century converts to Christianity—and the Cherokees in the South—members of the so-called Five Civilized Tribes who adopted the patriarchal household family form and become farmers—reveal the actual intent: all Indians would be forcibly removed and dispersed as settlers and speculators pushed ever farther west.

Available land produced a boom in agriculture in the first half of the nineteenth century, hastening a market economy. Better-off families produced for regional markets; poorer, subsistence families that previously survived on seasonal winter "outwork"—taking in piecework in shoemaking or textiles—gradually entered the factories. Steam engines freed industry from the need for rural waterpower, enabling factories to relocate to cities and their outskirts. By midcentury, 41 percent of the national labor force toiled outside agriculture, and one in five Americans lived in cities of twenty-five hundred people or more. Urban hubs varied between one hundred thousand and five hundred thousand inhabitants. Industrialization sharpened the separation of middling from worker families. Classical republicanism presumed a family background of wealth, education, and status enabling the attributes of virtuous leadership, but artisans in the cities developed a more egalitarian interpretation of republicanism. Both groups presumed that propertied personhood anchored the respectability of male-headed families. Republican thinkers in the Revolutionary period defined masculine virtue as the capacity to subordinate one's private interests to the public good, a quality vital for the citizens of a successful republic.

Constituting roughly 20 percent of the population by the end of the nineteenth century, middle-class families were successful farmers and urban dwellers. They included ministers, lawyers, doctors, bankers, bureaucrats, business tycoons, traders, industrial and factory managers, shopkeepers, teachers, governesses, and clerks. The developing capitalist economy measured success by a man's ability to support his family and keep his wife and daughters out of the workforce. Middle-class wives managed servants but also, with daughters' help, engaged in domestic production. Men increasingly derived their identity from their work. The ideology of the male breadwinner authorized self-interest, competition, and aggression as necessary to achievement, a contrast to the Revolutionary ideal of masculine virtue. Middle-class respectability, what historians call an "ideology of domesticity," functioned as a way of explaining status that presumed other sets of social relations, such as race, class, and gender. Crucial to middle-class self-understanding was an imaginary gap between the public world of politics and business and the "home," now sentimentalized as a yearned-for place of refuge. The more competitive and self-interested the

capitalist world became, the more "virtue" became identified with women, who were now charged with preserving the old moral virtues. As repositories of respectability, virtuous women were sexually pure and distanced themselves from competition and striving. By the end of the nineteenth century, the capitalist elite became an object of emulation. Inspired by this new "breadwinner" family ideology, working-class men also claimed property in their own labor, an argument that won them the vote and justified their unrealized demands for what was labeled a "family wage."

The nineteenth-century middle-class family evinced a powerful ambivalence toward the capitalist materialism and exploitation inherent in its labor relations. Domesticity understood mother love, nurturing, and selflessness to be timeless female qualities. Mothers supplanted fathers as the primary child-rearers: the ideology of republican motherhood obligated them to raise responsible citizens. Meanwhile, capitalist culture increasingly offered middle-class men outlets for manly aggression, independence, and adventure.

The ideology of domesticity galvanized a wide range of nineteenth-century female moral-reform movements, from abolitionism to health reform, temperance, antiprostitution, and suffrage. The post-Revolutionary decades witnessed what Mary Kelley in the study of antebellum elite women's education, *Learning to Stand and Speak* has called "gendered republicanism," a cluster of ideas linked to the progress of female education. During the period from 1790 to 1860, elite, middle-class, and some black women attended academies and seminaries in roughly the same numbers as men, studying curricula similar to those of their male counterparts. Their reading and literary societies fashioned notions of female virtue and civic responsibility that engaged them in uplift projects among the urban poor, for example, whose numbers, enhanced by Irish immigration, grew rapidly by the end of the century. By regenerating the moral character of husbands, children, and the nation, women would stabilize both the family and society. By the early twentieth century, reforming women generated a full-fledged critique of capitalist industrialization when they joined the Progressive movement and fought for suffrage. Wives also gained legally in this century, winning the right to their own property and labor, the right to divorce under certain conditions, and custody of young children.

Consumer Culture and the Emergence of the Modern Family.

By 1900 the United States led the world in industrial manufacturing. Huge corporate hierarchies managed the economy, restructuring traditional economic institutions. American families adjusted to these changes according to class. A merchandizing revolution, the appearance of new entertainment spaces, and growth in advertising created a culture of consumption. By the early twentieth century, vast emporiums known as department stores transformed urban landscapes. Cities' crowded downtown commercial districts offered a profusion of goods. For nine to ten hours a day, increasing numbers of native and immigrant working-class daughters worked at factories or, standing at the sales counters of department stores, served white middle-class women. A vibrant commercial aesthetic captivated crowds and promoted desire for goods. Women became family purchasing agents, their daily routines taking them beyond their homes. Riding streetcars to financial districts, they paid bills and allocated expenditures. Respectability, already encompassing scientific child-rearing and attention to morality, now included the tasteful adornment of homes.

Whereas earlier in the nineteenth century, middle-class men might lunch with their families, now they remained at work all day. Financial success measured men's attractiveness for marriage. Wives domesticated husbands' manners: no more hats indoors or feet on the furniture. Needing time to become established, men married older than women did. Withdrawing from social clubs and philanthropic committees, the earlier sites of male sociality, they relaxed at home, reading newspapers or playing with children. The parlor was the space of family-centeredness. Consumer choices in domestic furnishings— the carpet, the sofa, the piano—became markers of class.

Working-class women of the turn of the twentieth century had their own canons of domesticity: though lacking space for a parlor, better-paid worker families often purchased a piano, an icon of respectability. Wives shared husbands' desire to keep women out of the workforce. They fed their families, cleaned, shopped, kept a cow, grew vegetables, and monitored younger children. Tenements lacked electricity or running water. When the wage economy developed, "work" became synonymous with the payment of "wages," obscuring the onerous household tasks inherent in the new gendered division of labor. The arduous, time-consuming, backbreaking social reproduction wives performed enabled family workers to return to the factories every morning but became hidden. Low wages, combined with a belief that family survival demanded contributions from all members, brought many immigrant daughters and even some wives "out to work." Had workingmen allied with female workers, most of whom were single, employers might not have been able to hire women at half pay, thereby ignoring male demands for a "family wage" that could keep women and children at home. But the breadwinner family also gave workingmen their own version of patriarchy.

American Families in the Twentieth Century.

American families experienced four crucial twentieth-century transformations: changing sexualities in public and private life that led to shifting definitions of marriage; the continued development of adolescence and young adulthood; the construction of a social-welfare state; and the increase of married women in the workforce. In each case, shifts in the economy, material needs, and consumerism provide the backdrop.

Changing Sexualities in Public and Private Life.

Across the classes, cultures of consumption changed attitudes toward leisure, abundance, and mass entertainment. Nineteenth-century traditions of hard work and self-denial eroded gradually, no less among the Protestant majority than among second-generation immigrants. By the 1920s, all classes of immigrant, ethnic, black, and white adolescents dated, participating in a burgeoning entertainment culture of dance halls, movie palaces, bars, amusement parks, outdoor concerts, and sports. They learned about sexuality from the erotics of motion pictures, from which immigrant girls also discovered ways to become American. Girls repaid boys with a variety of sexual favors. College culture developed its own conventions, and automobiles allowed privacy to the more privileged.

In these years doctors and other professionals, women, reformers, bohemians, and working people all engaged in remaking sexualities. The final stages of the movement for women's suffrage brought thousands onto city streets claiming both citizenship and new subjectivities. Between 1870 and 1920, nearly half of female college graduates, black and white, rejected marriage; others married later and had fewer children. Twentieth-century corporate expansion increased demand for literate workers as stenographers, typists, and secretaries; independent career women created new lifestyles. They lived together as roommates, served as residential faculty in girls' schools, and founded settlement houses to live communally as social workers in poor neighborhoods. Moving beyond the family, they claimed a place for women in the public sphere. Some lived alone, created alternative friendship circles, or lived as lesbians.

By the 1920s, members of middle-class families began looking inward: cultivating the self, love, intimacy, and psychological development. The previous century anticipated these changes, as courting couples gradually acknowledged romance, companionship, and emotions. But although Victorians accepted legitimate sexual expression in validating feelings, they feared the erotic; sex for its own sake reduced humans to animals. Linking female sexual affection to maternal desire, women were to monitor husbands' sexual appetites and teach children the values of purity and self-control. By 1920 the profession of marriage counseling emerged, made up of doctors, psychologists, and social workers with relaxed attitudes toward sexuality and birth control. In the late 1930s Alfred Kinsey began the scientific study of human sexuality, and medical discourse on homosexuality entered public conversation. Fifty years earlier, valuing love's spirituality over its physical embodiment, Victorians had tolerated homosocial romantic friendships in both sexes, sometimes coexisting alongside marriages. At that time, a professionalizing medical profession had only just begun to study homosexual attraction, but by 1920 doctors defined homosexuality as a disease. That demonizing now worked in tandem with a fierce support for the heterosexual norm as represented by companionate marriage. Neither counseling nor the new availability of sex manuals could give wives who managed to embrace their sexual feelings equality with men. Nevertheless, if women's autonomy failed to advance, companionate families became the new ideal. Democratizing familial relations also encouraged more demonstrative interactions among parents and children, husbands and wives.

Childhood, Youth, Adolescence. Class determined childhood experience. For many families, children remained working hands and insurance against old age. Older children cared for younger ones, prepared meals, tended animals, helped with housework, earned wages. "Childhood" and "adolescence" were nineteenth-century middle-class inventions, enabled by the appearance of what Viviana Zelizer in her book, *Pricing the Priceless Child: The Changing Social Value of Children* labels the "economically worthless child." The size of the average American family declined from seven to three children well before the legalization of dependable birth control. Parents treated childhood as a special life stage, sentimentalizing family relations. Middle-class families defined childhood by education, fantasy, and play; both girls and boys responded, especially once they were of high school age. Girls invented private languages of introspection, kept diaries, and corresponded enthusiastically. By the twentieth century, such attention to feelings and intimacy shifted the marriage relationship, while high school education helped girls and society rethink the narrowness of expectations for women. Early twentieth-century psychologists, sociologists, welfare workers, and physicians, among them many first-generation women college graduates, mobilized new expertise to claim the child for scientific study. So-called scientific mothering declared child rearing a learned, not a natural, skill, and the Parent-Teacher Association translated the new expertise for unsure parents.

Advertisers targeted children's consumer identities in new magazines geared to youth. Marketers familiarized middle-class young people with brand-name products, including bicycles, typewriters, soaps, cereals, and toys, teaching them the desire for goods. By 1920, experts described children as more worldly and self-reliant. The sociologists Robert and Helen Lynd found parent-child relationships less hierarchical and more affectionate, citing both the power of children's peers and the consumer market for this transformation.

Working-class children's economic value was enhanced by industrialization, so changes in childhood came more slowly: they carried adult responsibilities well into the 1940s. In, *The Way We Never Were*, Stephanie Coontz reminds us that for every protected wife and child, "there was an Irish or German scrub girl, a Welsh boy mining coal . . . a black girl doing the family laundry, a black mother and child picking cotton" to be made into garments, and "a Jewish or Italian daughter in a sweatshop making 'ladies' dresses or artificial flowers" for middle-class consumption. In 1900 one in six children, sometimes as young as six or seven, worked for wages. Progressives fought with employers and even working-class parents, who believed that hard work taught children self-discipline and familial duty. But campaigns for an anti-child-labor amendment and laws for compulsory education failed; only the declining early twentieth-century demand for unskilled labor removed children from industrial work.

If childhood experience in all classes converged by the 1960s, even in the twenty-first century class remains the primary determinant of adult success. Between the 1920s and the 1950s, young people developed their own cultures. Dating and commercial amusements weakened parental authority. During the 1930s the New Deal initiated relief and training programs for teenagers to prevent them from competing with adult breadwinners for jobs. Success in keeping teenagers in high school engendered a peer culture that was targeted by marketers. World War II's labor shortage brought more teenagers into the workforce, while relaxing adult authority. Iconic images from the 1940s show middle-class teenage bobby-soxers dancing to big bands and swooning over Frank Sinatra, alongside black, Latino, and white "hipsters" associated with jazz culture. By the 1950s teenagers were a source of cultural anxiety. Suburban white parents saw a threat in their children's fascination with race and working-class rock and roll, while through music, clothing, and film, the teenage culture industry was actively creating and encouraging this fascination. Young people's critiques of suburban "conformity" carried over into the 1960s.

University expansion at midcentury exemplified the prosperity shaping the experiences of the baby boomers. Those years produced political realignments and social fissures inaugurated by young people, eventually generating political and social backlash in the 1980s. Families watched the black freedom struggle from their living rooms, making racial discrimination impossible to ignore. Radical student movements in the 1960s coincided, not only with Second Wave feminism, but with the awakening of minority youth to their experiences of discrimination, resulting in civil rights campaigns among Latino, Native American, and Asian youth. These campaigns addressed the unfinished business of a nation whose families had always been raced, gendered, and classed. As the music, stylistics, and transgressive lifestyles of the counterculture challenged "respectable" family values, the availability of the birth control pill helped undermine the old rules barring sex before marriage. The children of the 1960s smoked marijuana, took LSD, and experimented with new forms of sexuality, while back-to-nature and cooperative commune movements reconsidered middle-class child rearing and even medicalized childbirth.

The Family, the Economy, and the State.

The American Revolution rejected the divine right of kings and replaced absolute husbandly power with republican wifely "consent." But families were patriarchal: as citizens deferred to elected leaders, so a wife accepted her spouse's authority. Men owned their wives' property and labor. In return, they were expected to support their families. American law reinforced the gendered division of labor, regulating marriage, divorce, separation, child custody, and sexuality. Christianity held sway over family governance, too: American law made divorce extremely difficult and enforced monogamy. The 1862 Morrill Anti-Bigamy Act, targeting Mormons and select native tribes, prohibited polygamy. Chinese immigrants, linked to forced labor and prostitution, were also marked by familial nonconformity. In 1887 the Dawes Act dismantled a variety of Indian tribal arrangements and communal property regimes, allotting plots of land to individual Indians and thus trying to have Indians assimilate to white ideas of property and family. After emancipation, the Freedman's Bureau urged former slaves to marry, though many states passed laws banning black-white unions. By 1873, Congress regulated not only marriage but also the sexual behavior of unmarried citizens: the Comstock Act of that year declared literature and devices related to birth control "obscene," criminalizing their distribution through the mails. From the 1860s, laws made abortion and contraception extremely difficult to obtain.

Federal and state governments also intervened positively on behalf male breadwinners and their families, while deliberately limiting the equal access of women and racial minorities. The 1907 Expatriation Act declared that women assumed the citizenship of their husbands; citizen women forfeited their citizenship if they married unnaturalized foreigners. Before its 1922 repeal, the law muddied the legal status of thousands of American-born women. In 1935 the New Deal's Social Security Act was intentionally gendered and raced. The law underscored women's dependency and the gendered division of labor. Married and single men received entitlements by virtue of their breadwinner role, even at a time when 24 percent of wives were in the workforce. As one congressional advocate explained, according to Alice Kessler-Harris's study of the 1935 Social Security Act, *In Pursuit of Equity*, "All I ask for an American father" is that his wage be enough to keep his wife "at home" to "bring up her family." Meanwhile, to avoid offending southern congressmen, Social Security also excluded occupations largely populated by black workers. Most entitlements went to industrial workers assumed to be male heads of families. Excluded were nearly half of all workers—including 60 percent of women workers and 85 percent of African Americans. In the 1940s, the GI Bill (Servicemen's Readjustment Act, 1944) delivered welfare to returning soldiers in the form of free college tuition or vocational programs, ignoring the contributions of those too old or too young to fight, as well as the majority of women who had worked on the home front. In the realm of sexual and marital privacy, two noteworthy Supreme Court decisions ratified the companionate family: *Griswold v. Connecticut* (1965) protected a married couple's use of contraceptives, and the more controversial *Loving v. Virginia* (1967) declared race-based restrictions on marriage unconstitutional.

Post–World War II ideology of family life became intimately linked with suburban space. Americans' romance with living close to nature began in the nineteenth century among intellectuals and reformers. By the 1920s, architects had developed several suburban spaces offering attractive single-family dwellings in child-friendly, natural settings. Select middle-class, white Protestant families chose to escape from crowded, politically contentious, and racially and class-diverse cities. Until the 1940s, however, suburbs were bedroom communities, close enough to the city for shopping or family outings.

Through tax incentives and other means, post–World War II government partnered with contractors and real estate developers to build federal and state highways and suburban infrastructures. With small down payments, lower interest rates for longer-term mortgages, and tax discounts exclusively for homeowners, families purchased mass-produced homes. Veterans received low-cost mortgages from the GI Bill, though gays were denied benefits. Racial discrimination limited opportunities for others, but substantial numbers of immigrant and white working-class families reached the suburbs and as a result experienced social mobility. To challenge discrimination, blacks and other families of color were obliged to take lengthy legal action through the courts.

Ancillary purchases required by homeowners stimulated the economy. Third-party universal credit cards appeared, easing the purchase of essential household appliances and furnishings and thus generating a manufacturing boom. Eighty percent of new homes were located in suburbs, obliging families to purchase automobiles. By 1960, with 62 percent of Americans homeowners—compared to only 44 percent in 1940—suburbanites outnumbered urban and rural residents. The government's privileging of suburban development starved the cities, where the poor, the elderly, and the racially marked were abandoned to declining neighborhoods and schools, the loss of jobs, poverty, and crime.

Suburban family life symbolized a congeries of democratic values, touted by Vice President Richard Nixon at the height of the Cold War during a talk with the Soviet premier Nikita Khrushchev at the 1959 American National Exhibition in Moscow. The exhibition featured a display of American consumer goods, including a full-scale suburban ranch-style house with a model kitchen. Khrushchev boasted of Soviet women's productive work, while Nixon praised Americans' familial privacy, self-sufficiency, and the breadwinner companionate family and its gendered division of labor.

Threats to the Breadwinner Family: Married Women's Work, Deindustrialization, and Rise of the Service Economy.

Even as Nixon equated the American breadwinner family with democracy, the economic and cultural supports for this still-cherished family form were eroding. According to research by the Brookings Institution, by the early twenty-first century the traditional American family had broken apart. In 2011, only 48 percent of cohabiting couples in the United States were married. Only 20 percent of these couples had children, compared to 43 percent in 1950. Despite the New Deal welfare state's attempts to back the breadwinner family with unemployment insurance, and post World War II tax benefits for married couples, nothing has stemmed the tide of married women's entry into the workforce since 1960. Many economists consider this the most significant change for American families in the twentieth century. What has happened?

One explanation is the combination of economic growth and suburban living. A postwar manufacturing boom made home appliances widely affordable, reducing wives' domestic labor. By the 1960s, 90 percent of families had hot and cold running water, refrigerators, and gas or electric stoves; 50 percent owned automatic washing machines. In 1950 only 21 percent of married women worked; a decade later, older married women with diminished domestic responsibilities were seeking jobs. Neither pursuing careers nor dissatisfied with familial roles, they aimed to supplement household income, now stretched by homeowning, college education for children, family vacations, an automobile, and available consumer goods. After two decades of economic depression and war, these years also witnessed the sentimentalization of family togetherness and child rearing, making married women's work the focus of much social anxiety. But after 1960, wives' employment increased 10 percent per decade, especially once President John F. Kennedy's Commission on the Status of Women recommended the abrogation of Progressive Era policies limiting women's paid work, and the 1963 Equal Pay Act prohibited sex-based discrimination in pay, mandating equal pay for equal work. By the twenty-first century, women could not be excluded from certain jobs, nor were they legally required to remain home during pregnancy or after giving birth. Successive cohorts, including college-educated female professionals seeking careers, still did more household labor than their husbands, and they compromised with their position as "secondary" earners, especially if they had children. Though they could purchase more domestic goods and services, working wives and mothers consistently experienced the exhaustion of the "double day" and sometimes resented husbands' lackluster participation in domestic chores. In the 1960s these were an incitement to feminism. If only a minority of feminists rejected marriage per se, most deplored traditional marriage with its male prerogatives. By the twenty-first century, women who put their careers first might marry, but many had children much later or not at all.

Since 1950, men have also been rethinking their breadwinner role. As the market provided substitutes for female domestic labor, younger men's felt obligation to support families waned. Changes in law and custom followed: pregnancy no longer dictates a rush to marry, and single mothers often keep their babies. The law recognizes relationships between parents and children born outside wedlock, and past punishment and shaming of unmarried mothers has declined: even some high schools accommodate these mothers. By the twenty-first century, marriage implied love and companionship. Diminished economic necessity has meant that increasingly couples live together long-term but marry only to have children (perhaps). But knowing how to deal with this new kind of intimacy has proved difficult. By the 1970s, divorce rates rose rapidly at all educational and age levels. Child-rearing and household divisions of labor produce tensions, even in so-called egalitarian households with two working parents. The decline of the traditional breadwinner family prompted lawyers to press no-fault divorce in the 1970s, allowing either party to seek divorce without having to state a cause. Because many working wives curtailed careers or delayed workforce entry when children were young, men have retained a strong advantage in division-of-property agreements, though in some states feminist legal scholars have secured guidelines taking working wives' lopsided involvement in domestic labor into account.

An economic transformation and a severe recession in the 1970s and 1980s precipitated these changes. Transition to a service economy resulted in a sharp decline in the number of manufacturing jobs, which combined with severe inflation to batter American families and shift American politics. Faced with global economic competition, industry relocated to developing countries with cheaper labor. Men's wages stagnated. Because black men were first to experience the downturn, their wives had already turned to wage work: 60 percent by 1970. A decade later, white wives caught up. Men's difficulties led to tension among couples, fueling higher divorce and separation rates. Increasingly, high school educated men, black and white, saw family as a burden, not an asset.

Despite changing family cultures, a significant portion of the middle and working classes resisted wives' wage work out of a strong conviction that the gendered division of labor defined family life. Many were Catholics or southern evangelicals, and their self-respect presumed separation of home and work, a presumption reinforced by their faith. In 1970, more than 45 percent of female high school graduates were mothers in their early twenties, compared to 14 percent of female college graduates. But suddenly the recession meant that husbands' wages were insufficient: against strong desires, recession obligated many women to work. Eventually these housewives mobilized: the anti–Equal Rights Amendment League of Housewives claimed that full-time wives and mothers had rights "through laws" that obligated husbands to provide support. While thousands picketed state capitols, feminists argued that the Equal Rights Amendment, passed in 1972 by both houses of Congress, would guarantee women equal opportunity and economic security.

The previous year, 1971, President Richard Nixon unexpectedly vetoed a bill that would have provided government support for universal child care, regardless of whether the working mother was married or single.

Backed by labor, civil rights groups, educational associations, and feminists, the measure would have strengthened the welfare state by demonstrating, as under the New Deal, that "welfare" helped all citizens adjust to economic changes, not just the poor.

Time magazine opposed the veto, hoping that the "bold day-care plan" would generate "a great national debate" in the world's most prosperous nation over a "useful new social service." But radical defenders of free-market capitalism within the Republican Party were joining with those sectors of the middle and working classes most deeply threatened by the loss of their traditional material and familial lives: they blamed too much government for their economic woes. The resulting coalition also embraced an evangelical wing of religious fundamentalists, many entering politics for the first time, who believed that the domestic family was divinely ordained.

The Decline of Democracy: Whither Twenty-First-Century Families?

Since the presidency of Ronald Reagan, the New Deal welfare state has been dismantled. During the twentieth century's first half, federal programs reduced the poverty rate from 20 percent in the late 1920s to 12 percent by early 1970s. Yet since 1980, most willingness to assist women's work or the families of the poor has disappeared. Though many European countries provide myriad supports for women's work outside the home regardless of class, including high-quality affordable day care and paid maternity leave (sometimes paternity leave, too), a weak American welfare state, combined with antigovernment bias and still greater contention over "family values," has blocked such legislation. A coalition of religious conservatives and defenders of the free market have reinstated the federal government as custodian of family morality: laws limit access to abortion and contraception

and reduce government supports for poor families—who are often judged to be poor, not because of devastating shifts in the economy, but because they do not work hard enough. Two measures reveal these views, each passed in 1996 during the presidency of Bill Clinton. The antigay Defense of Marriage Act defined marriage as a union between a man and a woman, though by the second decade of the twenty-first century several states recognized same-sex marriage, and polls showed that a majority of Americans supported it. The Personal Responsibility and Work Opportunity Reconciliation Act reduced government aid to poor families, many headed by single mothers, placing a lifetime cap on aid. Adding insult to injury, its opening language claimed marriage to be the "foundation of society" and in the best interests of children.

Though evangelical political leaders have revived religion as a force in politics, they have not halted the changes in family life linked to shifts in the economy. From 1950 to the late 1970s, social-welfare programs originating in the New Deal yielded the greatest equality the United States has ever enjoyed, radically reducing the gap between rich and poor. By the early twenty-first century, government tax breaks for homeowners were four times as high as housing subsidies for the poorest 20 percent of Americans. That women and minorities are overrepresented among the poor testifies that unequal opportunity leads to unequal citizenship.

Between the years 1984 and 2003, though the U.S. gross domestic product increased by 77 percent, there was no equivalent increase in the number of better-paying jobs available for the majority of Americans. The very rich saw a jump of 181 percent in their earnings, while middle-class Americans gained 23 percent. As for the working poor, Lyndon B. Johnson's War on Poverty was the last government effort to improve their lives; they have lost much ground since the 1970s. Families with children under the age of eighteen account for more than half of the 41 percent increase in the number of poor people from 1979 to 1990. The poverty rate for children is double the rate for any other age-group: by the early twenty-first century the average age of the poorest Americans was eight years old. The United States has the highest wealth gap of any industrial country except Brazil. With the bottom 50 percent of Americans holding less than 1 percent of the nation's wealth, the gap between rich and poor in American society in the early twenty-first century is close to what it was a century before.

Assessment.   If the character and experience of families have changed radically since the early 1980s, how are these changes to be explained? How should social and economic changes be weighed against cultural changes not specifically linked to families—cultural changes such as voracious consumption, with its individualistic messages to nurture the self; the erosion of civic commitment; and the weakening of urban neighborhoods through suburbanization and the geographic mobility required by the postindustrial job market? How much should a just democratic polity commit to the next generation?

American politicians love to cull the American past for support when defending policies in the present. Given the ambiguities and multivalence of language, and especially of political rhetoric, historians are deeply skeptical of this habit. But if such an exercise were to be performed, one interpretation of "republicanism" proposed in the 1970s by some historians of the American Revolution might be recuperated. These historians characterized the struggle as a fight between two contenders: the party of virtue and the party of commerce. Whereas "commerce" might be identified with the commitment to the unfettered free market, "virtue" might be understood as civic commitment. Embracing the rewards of private property is not enough: virtue also demands the maintenance of equality of opportunity, the setting aside of individual interests on behalf of the collective public good. Given what American families face in the early twenty-first century, perhaps virtue should once more be given its chance.

[*See also* **Adolescence; Child Workers; Courtship and Dating; Demography; Everyday Life; Feminism; Gay and Lesbian Love and Relationships; Gender; Leisure; Life Stages; Marriage and Divorce; Rural Life and Society; Separate Spheres Ideology; Sexual Reform and Morality; Slave Families and Communities; Slaveholders; Welfare; Women Workers;** *and* **Working-Class Life and Society.**]

BIBLIOGRAPHY

Brown, Kathleen M. *Good Wives, Nasty Wenches, and Anxious Patriarchs: Gender, Race, and Power in Colonial Virginia*. Chapel Hill: University of North Carolina Press for the Institute of Early American History and Culture, Williamsburg, Va., 1996.

Cobble, Dorothy Sue. *The Other Women's Movement: Workplace Justice and Social Rights in Modern America*. Princeton, N.J.: Princeton University Press, 2004.

Coontz, Stephanie. *The Social Origins of Private Life: A History of American Families, 1600–1900*. New York: Verso, 1988.

Coontz, Stephanie. *The Way We Never Were: American Families and the Nostalgia Trap*. New York: Basic Books, 1992.

Cott, Nancy F. *Public Vows: A History of Marriage and the Nation*. Cambridge, Mass.: Harvard University Press, 2000.

Gordon, Linda. *Heroes of Their Own Lives: The Politics and History of Family Violence, Boston, 1880–1960*. New York: Viking, 1988.

Hsu, Madeline Yuan-yin. *Dreaming of Gold, Dreaming of Home: Transnationalism and Migration between the United States and South China, 1882–1943.* Stanford, Calif.: Stanford University Press, 2000.

Jones, Jacqueline. *Labor of Love, Labor of Sorrow: Black Women, Work, and the Family from Slavery to the Present.* Rev. ed. New York: Basic Books, 2010.

Kessler-Harris, Alice. *In Pursuit of Equity: Women, Men, and the Quest for Economic Citizenship in 20th-Century America.* New York: Oxford University Press, 2001.

May, Elaine Tyler. *Homeward Bound: American Families in the Cold War Era.* Rev. ed. New York: Basic Books, 2008.

Miles, Tiya. *Ties That Bind: The Story of an Afro-Cherokee Family in Slavery and Freedom.* Berkeley: University of California Press, 2005.

Mintz, Steven. *Huck's Raft: A History of American Childhood.* Cambridge, Mass.: Belknap Press of Harvard University Press, 2004.

Naples, Nancy A. *Grassroots Warriors: Activist Mothering, Community Work, and the War on Poverty.* New York: Routledge, 1998.

Newman, Louise Michele. *White Women's Rights: The Racial Origins of Feminism in the United States.* New York: Oxford University Press, 1999.

Rosenzweig, Roy. *Eight Hours for What We Will: Workers and Leisure in an Industrial City, 1870–1920.* Cambridge, U.K.: Cambridge University Press, 1983.

Rotundo, E. Anthony. *American Manhood: Transformations in Masculinity from the Revolution to the Modern Era.* New York: Basic Books, 1993.

Schoen, Johanna. *Choice and Coercion: Birth Control, Sterilization, and Abortion in Public Health and Welfare.* Chapel Hill: University of North Carolina Press, 2005.

Stern, Alexandra Minna. *Eugenic Nation: Faults and Frontiers of Better Breeding in Modern America.* Berkeley: University of California Press, 2005.

Stevenson, Brenda E. *Life in Black and White: Family and Community in the Slave South.* New York: Oxford University Press, 1996.

Thistle, Susan. *From Marriage to the Market: The Transformation of Women's Lives and Work.* Berkeley: University of California Press, 2006.

Wilcox, W. Bradford, and Andrew J. Cherlin. "The Marginalization of Marriage in Middle America." Brookings Institute Center on Children and Families. CCF Brief no. 46, August 2011. http://www.brookings.edu/papers/2011/0810_strengthen_marriage_wilcox_cherlin.aspx.

Regina Morantz-Sanchez

FAMILY PLANNING

See Birth Control and Family Planning.

FATHER DIVINE'S PEACE MISSION MOVEMENT

Father Major Jealous Divine was an African American who was probably born George Baker in Maryland in 1879. By the 1920s Divine was preaching a politicized, millenarian version of New Thought, a faith that emphasized the power of thought to mold reality. In the 1930s his followers, then numbering thirty to fifty thousand people, proclaimed him God and formed the Peace Mission movement. Because the majority of Divinites were African American women, the Peace Mission can be seen as a black women's social movement.

Divine taught followers to reject their human nature and live in heavenly transcendence. Believing that "thoughts are things," or that words had creative power, Divinites took angelic names, such as Glorious Illumination, to mark and manifest their new angelic state. Similarly, Divinites used the greeting "peace" instead of "hello" in order to avoid speaking of and so creating hell. Divinites also embraced celibacy to symbolize their distance from their former selves. Finally, Divinites rejected racial difference and, to an extent, sexual difference. They refused to use words that referred to race, thereby hoping to destroy racism, racial segregation, and discrimination. Divine encouraged women to perform traditionally male jobs, and some female Divinites adopted male angelic names, such as Joshua Love.

Divine's ritual practice was centered in the three-story Harlem, New York City, commune, known as the Peace Mission, where he lived with his wife, Peninnah (also spelled Peninniah or Pinninnah), and his interracial, mixed-gender staff. There Divine offered free, multicourse banquets to thousands of people in the midst of a severe economic depression. Divine's followers soon opened numerous Peace Mission "extensions" or "heavens." By the mid-1930s these communes—low-priced residential hotels, or cooperative businesses (mostly restaurants, food stores, or dressmaking and clothing stores), run by smiling, white-clad Divinites—were a feature of many black urban communities. Divinites also ran the Promised Land, nearly seven hundred communal farms on more than two thousand acres of land in upstate New York.

The Peace Mission peaked in 1936 when Divinites registered to vote en masse and created what they called the "Righteous Government Platform." Among the planks were calls for idle plants to be turned over to workers, for free universal education, and for abolishing the term "hello" in favor of "Peace." Divinites also began challenging segregation by entering restaurants in racially mixed groups. That year, perhaps in response to this perceived political threat, government harassment of Peace Mission businesses increased. The movement experienced a spate of exposés, defections, and sex scandals—all fairly typical of millennial movements, which tend to attract rebellious or unstable individuals and are thus prone to splits and fissures.

In 1942, Divine moved to Philadelphia in order to avoid paying fines on a suit brought by a former follower. Peninnah died in 1943. In 1946, Divine married Mother Divine, formerly Edna Rose Ritchings. In 1953 he and Mother Divine moved to a private estate in Gladwyne, Pennsylvania. By then, as the economy recovered and as racial injustices that had provoked Peace Mission members to reject mainstream life were addressed by the Civil Rights Movement, Divine's following dramatically diminished. Divine died in 1965. Well into the twenty-first century, Mother Divine continued to lead the remnants of the Peace Mission movement.

[*See also* **African Americans; Great Depression Era; Religion; Revivals;** *and* **Utopian and Communitarian Movements.**]

BIBLIOGRAPHY

Satter, Beryl. "Marcus Garvey, Father Divine, and the Gender Politics of Race Difference and Race Neutrality." *American Quarterly* 48, no. 1 (March 1996): 43–76. A gender analysis of the Peace Mission movement.

Watts, Jill. *God, Harlem, U.S.A.: The Father Divine Story.* Berkeley: University of California Press, 1992. A thorough but uncritical history of Father Divine.

Weisbrot, Robert. *Father Divine and the Struggle for Racial Equality.* Urbana: University of Illinois Press, 1983. A study emphasizing Divine's racial politics.

Beryl E. Satter

FEMINISM

Feminism is the belief that women and men should be valued equally in social, political, and economic life and that because they are not, organized action is necessary to bring this about. Since the mid-nineteenth century, self-identified "feminist" activism in the United States arose most often out of democratic movements geared toward the achievement of universal male suffrage and racial and class equality. Historians of the United States have found the "wave" metaphor useful for describing the "ebbs and flows" of feminist activism, as well as its persistent presence in American life.

First Wave Feminism. The first wave of sustained women's activism in the United States was inaugurated in 1848 at the nation's first women's rights convention, held in Seneca Falls, New York. Organized by the abolitionists Elizabeth Cady Stanton and Lucretia Mott, the Seneca Falls Convention attracted three hundred participants and led to the creation of the Declaration of Sentiments, a document modeled after the Declaration of Independence that called for the equal treatment of men and women under the law. Although the movement that began at Seneca Falls emphasized women's suffrage as a primary goal, a diverse group of antebellum women's activists agitated for a variety of other reforms, including increased educational opportunities, credit and property rights for married women, and an end to the double standard governing the sexual conduct of women and men. The struggle launched in 1848 to win American women the right to vote encountered a number of obstacles. Nineteenth-century women's activists faced fierce opposition from the mainstream media and a majority of Americans, who feared that female political participation was unnatural and would lead to the disintegration of familial order and domestic life. After the Civil War, ideological and strategic divisions within the women's movement also created obstacles. The question of whether or not to pursue suffrage for both women and newly emancipated slaves created a schism within the movement that stalled progress toward women's suffrage for years.

During the first decades of the twentieth century, new leadership and new strategies—large, public parades and the formation of partnerships with labor, antilynching, and other reform organizations—helped galvanize the suffrage effort. At the same time, a broader, self-identified "feminist" movement that was less explicitly geared toward suffrage also began to take shape. Influenced by socialist critiques of the sexual division of labor and a burgeoning radicalism associated with Progressive art and politics, women like Charlotte Perkins Gilman, Crystal Eastman, and the anarchist Emma Goldman called for a cultural revolution that would lead to increased independence and self-determination for American women. In contrast to suffrage activists, who focused primarily on electoral politics, these feminist "New Women" pursued a diverse range of causes—from sexual, economic, and reproductive freedom to international peace. By the close of World War I, both feminism and the suffrage movement had achieved high visibility and growing public support. The Nineteenth Amendment to the United States Constitution was ratified in 1920, securing the right to vote for American women and signaling the end of a struggle that had lasted more than seventy years.

Midcentury Women's Activism. The period between 1920 and 1960 is sometimes referred to as the "doldrums" because of a perceived lack of feminist activism during that time. Despite this perception, a number of women and men continued to organize for women's rights and social advancement throughout the period. After the passage of the Nineteenth Amendment, suffrage organizations like the National Woman's Party shifted their attention to passage of the Equal Rights Amendment, which declares that "Equality of rights under the law shall not be denied or abridged by the United States or by any State on account of sex." Less-conservative feminist groups that had been formed during the 1910s and 1920s also remained active and gained new participants through activism based in voluntary associations and in established leftist organizations. The 1930s and 1940s witnessed a continued rise in women's participation in wage labor, a development that inspired an upsurge in labor activism and increased efforts to secure protective laws for women in industry. The New Deal also led to new opportunities for women in policy-making positions, particularly in connection with the Women's Bureau of the U.S. Labor Department, the first federal agency devoted to improving the welfare of wage-earning women.

The onset of World War II and the entrance of millions of women into professions traditionally held by men unleashed profound and lasting changes in American life and workplaces. Rosie the Riveter, a stylized image of a war worker flexing her muscles and proclaiming "We Can Do It!" was first introduced by the federal government on a poster designed to encourage female participation in wartime mobilization. This image ultimately became a feminist icon—a symbol of women's strength and patriotic service—though some feminists noted later that Rosie's feminine appearance and pale skin offered an unrealistic vision of women war workers as primarily white and middle class.

Second Wave Feminism.

The postwar era was a watershed moment for feminist activism in the United States. The 1953 publication in English of the French feminist Simone de Beauvoir's *The Second Sex* (1949) offered a philosophically grounded critique of gender inequality that was read widely by college-educated American women. The civil rights movement in the southern United

States served as another catalyst for feminist activism, attracting the participation of thousands of women, black and white, who fought valiantly for the social and political advancement of black Americans. Although a handful of women, including Ella Baker, held leadership positions in civil rights groups, an emphasis on traditional gender roles in parts of the movement led to criticisms from some female members, who called for a heightened focus on gender inequality alongside racial discrimination. The publication in 1963 of Betty Friedan's book *The Feminine Mystique* offered yet another enticement for women to organize in the name of feminist goals. Capturing the frustrations of many educated, middle-class American women who had been confined to domestic life, Friedan urged her readers to seek careers outside the home and to pursue personal fulfillment in the public sphere. Though Friedan's text was criticized for its failure to respond to the struggles of low-income women and women of color, it quickly became a best seller and is often credited with launching the second wave of American feminism.

The antiwar and student movements of the 1960s, like the antislavery and civil rights movements that preceded them, attracted the participation of large numbers of female activists. Widespread sexism and a paucity of leadership opportunities for women within New Left groups such as the male-led Students for a Democratic Society, however, helped underscore for many female activists the necessity of women's social and political advancement. As a result, the late 1960s and 1970s witnessed a flowering of feminist activism. Liberal feminists, led by Betty Friedan's National Organization for Women (NOW), formed in 1966, agitated for political and legislative change, particularly in the realms of education, paid labor, and reproductive rights. The efforts of NOW and other liberal-feminist groups proved highly effective and led to landmark decisions in the courts—including the U.S. Supreme Court's 1973 decision in *Roe v. Wade*, which secured women's right to abortion—and legislation such as Title IX of the Education Amendments of 1972, which secured equal access to educational resources. At the same time, a group of younger women, radicalized by the contemporaneous New Left movements, became participants in what came to be known as women's liberation. Advocates of "women's lib" called for a widespread cultural transformation that touched on nearly every aspect of American life—from workplace interactions and the division of household labor to conventional beauty standards and the portrayal of women in popular culture.

Second Wave feminists developed a diverse set of strategies for combating "sexism," a word that they popularized, and for improving the position of American women. The journalist Gloria Steinem, the founder of *Ms.* magazine, became an influential advocate for women in media and founded a number of feminist organizations, including the Women's Action Alliance and the Women's Media Center. Radical feminists, some of whom called for the creation of gender-segregated, "women's only" spaces, encouraged the celebration of femininity and a renewed appreciation of women's work and culture. Unlike their liberal-feminist counterparts, who sought equality with men within existing institutional frameworks, radical feminists emphasized the differences between the sexes and sought to remake the world in a more "feminine" light.

Feminists also pursued a number of grassroots projects, including efforts to expand women's access to health care, combat rape and domestic violence, and create venues for female sexual, spiritual, and artistic expression. The formation of so-called consciousness-raising groups became one of the primary grassroots strategies developed by feminists during the 1960s and 1970s. Across the country, thousands of women gathered informally to share with each other their personal struggles, escape isolation, and make connections between individual hardship and larger, structural forces. The resulting formulation, "the personal is political," became a mantra of Second Wave feminism and served as a rallying cry for women to unite against systematic, patriarchal oppression.

Backlash and Internal Divisions. The conservative turn in American politics during the 1980s struck a powerful blow to feminist activism and fueled an increasingly negative public perception of feminism—a development termed "backlash" by the journalist Susan Faludi. Long-standing divisions within the women's movement exacerbated this trend, leading to a splintering of feminist groups that culminated in a series of highly publicized battles over the proposed Equal Rights Amendment to the Constitution, over the role of lesbianism and separatism within the movement, and over attempts by some feminists to ban all forms of pornography. At the same time, women of color and low-income women—long excluded and ostracized by many white and middle-class feminists—criticized Second Wave organizations for inadvertently (and, on some rare occasions, intentionally) perpetuating racism, classism, and homophobia. By the 1990s, backlash and a growing emphasis within feminist thought on the differences between women, rather than on their shared experiences, served as evidence for some commentators that Second Wave feminism had ended.

Third Wave Feminism. Though many Second Wave organizations remained active and influential, at the turn of the twenty first century the participation of a new generation of American women in politics and the changing goals and strategies of feminist activism led some to suggest that a third wave of American feminism was under way. Defined more by its differences from previous movements than by any coherent political vision, Third Wave feminism is considered more demographically diverse, more accepting of racial and sexual minorities, and more affiliated with popular culture than earlier feminist waves were.

The creation of women's studies programs in universities across the nation during the 1980s and 1990s served as a catalyst for Third Wave feminism and led to the development of new fields of feminist theory and scholarship. During this era, psychoanalytic, postcolonial, and poststructural feminists criticized the perceived "essentialism" of First and Second Wave activists, arguing that the category "women" was socially constructed, not rooted in natural or biological reality. This theoretical approach, though not accepted by all Third Wave activists, played an important role in shaping feminist thought at the beginning of the twenty-first century. Engagement with popular culture became another hallmark of Third Wave feminism. Media icons like the pop singer Madonna served as important symbols of freedom for this new generation of American women, who identified female sexual expression, self-empowerment, and the fluidity of identity as central elements of feminist action.

During the first decades of the twenty-first century, feminism has remained a vital and active element of American life. Economic inequality, racial discrimination, and the denial of rights to lesbian, gay, and transgender individuals serve as important sites of activism for an increasingly diverse set of feminists in the United States. Globalization and migration have also become major areas of concern for American feminists, who, in partnership with international women's organizations, continue the struggle to improve the lives of women in the United States and around the world.

[*See also* Antebellum Reform; Conservative Movement; Friedan, Betty; Men's Movement; Mott, Lucretia; National Black Feminist Organization; National Organization for Women; Sixties, The; Stanton, Elizabeth Cady; Steinem, Gloria; Woman Suffrage Movement; Women's Rights Movement, Antebellum Era; *and* Women Workers.]

BIBLIOGRAPHY

Cott, Nancy. *The Grounding of Modern Feminism.* New Haven, Conn.: Yale University Press, 1987. A study of feminism in the United States during the early twentieth century, with a focus on the period following the suffrage movement.

Evans, Sara. *Tidal Wave: How Women Changed America at Century's End.* New York: Free Press, 2003. A broad overview of the women's movement from the 1960s onward that makes connections between Second Wave and Third Wave feminism.

Flexner, Eleanor, and Ellen Fitzpatrick. *Century of Struggle: The Woman's Rights Movement in the United States.* Enlarged ed. Cambridge, Mass.: Harvard University Press, 1996. A classic study of First Wave feminism and the suffrage movement, first published by Flexner in 1959.

Freedman, Estelle B. *No Turning Back: The History of Feminism and the Future of Women.* New York: Ballantine Books, 2002. A comprehensive history of feminism and women's activism, written from a global perspective.

Moraga, Cherríe, and Gloria Anzaldúa, eds. *This Bridge Called My Back: Writings by Radical Women of Color.* Watertown, Mass.: Persephone Press, 1981. One of the earliest anthologies of work by feminists of color, this collection was influential for its critique of the racial politics of Second Wave feminism.

Schneir, Miriam, ed. *Feminism in Our Time: The Essential Writings, World War II to the Present*. New York: Vintage Books, 1994. A source anthology of influential Second Wave feminist writings notable for its breadth and depth.

Walker, Rebecca, ed. *To Be Real: Telling the Truth and Changing the Face of Feminism*. New York: Anchor Books, 1995. A collection of essays written by Third Wave feminists.

Caley Horan

FEMINIST REFORMS IN THE PROGRESSIVE ERA, MATERNAL

The term "maternal feminism" describes the social outlook of Progressive Era feminist reformers who based their ideals on archetypal notions of motherhood. As feminists, these reformers advocated the goals of the contemporary women's movement, such as woman suffrage and access for women to higher education and careers. But as women who idealized motherhood they promoted a larger social vision of a government more active in caring for its citizens. They were especially concerned about women and girls, whose sexual vulnerability and potential for motherhood seemed to require unique protections. They also paid special attention to the physical and moral safety of children. In general they favored almost any government intervention that, in their view, enhanced family welfare. Such intervention might range from legislating controls on the consumption of alcoholic beverages to advocating more rigorous building standards for tenement houses and more protections for industrial workers, including minimum wages and maximum hours, compensation for job-related injuries, and government-sponsored unemployment and health insurance.

Maternal Feminists in Action. Maternal feminists used a variety of means to promote

their vision. Some acted alone, but most worked through their single-sex voluntary associations. These groups educated their members about current issues and built supportive networks, many of which came to include men as well as women, for collective action. Local networks that expanded to other cities and pursued especially popular reforms often founded statewide and even national federations.

Some maternal feminist networks became powerful engines for reform. At the turn of the twentieth century, the largest was the Woman's Christian Temperance Union (WCTU). Women had participated in movements against alcohol since the early 1800s, but after the Civil War they became movement leaders. A spontaneous "women's crusade" against the liquor trade, which arose in the Midwest in December 1873, spread rapidly across the country and soon formed a national organization. By 1900 the WCTU claimed a membership of some two hundred thousand, making it the largest women's organization of its time and temperance the most popular cause of Progressive Era maternal feminists.

As articulated by one of its early and most persuasive presidents, Frances Willard, the WCTU's plan was to "do everything" to foster the security of home and family. Thus it went beyond just urging laws to prohibit the manufacture, importation, sale, and consumption of alcohol. It also promoted political, economic, and social reforms. These included woman suffrage, an eight-hour workday, equal pay for equal work, the right of workers to form labor unions, laws to guarantee the purity of commercially prepared food and drugs, kindergartens (at the time not part of public education systems), cash allowances to widowed or abandoned mothers with young children ("mothers' pensions"), higher penalties for the seduction and rape of women and girls, and an end to prostitution. In the view of these temperance workers, a state reconfigured as an agent of family welfare could, and should, accomplish all these goals.

In addition to the WCTU, many of the era's women's clubs also urged government to act on behalf of family welfare. The first women's clubs were founded after the Civil War, primarily by middle-class white and African American women, who met in separate venues but with similar goals: self-improvement, intellectual stimulation, and sociability. Over time, as members shared their knowledge of cultural topics, the clubs began to turn their attention to social and economic problems and to put civic, social, and political plans for reform into action. Some clubs concerned themselves with girls' education, others with the founding of town libraries, clubs, and vacation homes for working girls, homes for unwed mothers, and public playgrounds. Yet others lent support to political action, such as advocacy of tenement-house reform, pure food and drug regulations, and laws to protect wageworkers, especially women and children.

The leaders of the Progressive Era settlement-house movement, such as Jane Addams, Edith Abbott, Lillian Wald, and Florence Kelley, also promoted maternal feminist reforms. Settlements began to appear in the 1880s when middle-class activists "settled" into impoverished urban neighborhoods to lend assistance to the poor. These activists set up programs that they thought would be helpful, such as nurseries for the children of working parents, supervised playgrounds that got older children off the streets, kindergartens, cafeterias providing cheap dinners for working families, health clinics, visiting-nurse services, bathing facilities (lacking in most homes in poor neighborhoods), and cooperative apartments for single working women.

By 1897 the number of settlements in American cities had grown to 74; by 1910, there were more than 400, with many providing similar forms of aid to their neighborhoods.

Frustrated by the limits of their own resources, settlement leaders eventually turned to the state for more help. They sought laws to make tenements more safe and sanitary. They insisted that poor neighborhoods receive pure supplies of water and milk, decent sewage and garbage-collection systems, and controls on air pollution. To counteract the exposure of youth to such vices as gambling, liquor, and prostitution, they lobbied for government licensing of commercial amusements and public funding for more parks and playgrounds. In some cities they persuaded local governments to take over services that settlements had been providing, such as health clinics, kindergartens, and supervised playgrounds. Finally, they supported Progressive Era movements for the municipal ownership of public transportation and utilities essential to the maintenance of a decent quality of life.

In acting as "spearheads for reform," in the historian Allen Davis's famous phrase, settlement workers did not act alone. They initiated or joined alliances, coalitions, and clearinghouses of other reform-minded groups. Some of these groups were of secular origin, such as the National Consumers League, the General Federation of Women's Clubs, the National Association of Colored Women, the Women's Trade Union League, the National Congress of Mothers, and organizations of both male and female professionals and philanthropists. Other groups were identified with a particular religious group, such as the National Council of Jewish Women and the Young Men's and Young Women's Christian Associations (YMCA and YWCA). Coalitions sent representatives to lobby state and federal officials on maternal feminist agendas.

Some Results of Maternal Feminist Reform Campaigns.

Maternal feminist reformers achieved a number of victories. Especially notable were the establishment of mothers' pensions, laws forbidding child labor, and agencies for female and child welfare. They also won passage in 1921 of the Sheppard-Towner Maternity and Infancy Protection Act.

Mothers' Pensions. Along with temperance, "child saving," as it was then called, held a high place on Progressive Era maternal feminist agendas. Mothers' pensions were an early result of this child-saving impulse. Variously called "mothers' aid" or "widows' pensions," such aid was supposed to help mothers who had lost a male breadwinner keep their young children out of orphanages, foster care, or the workforce. Giving pensions to mother-only families was not widely accepted until the first White House Conference on the Care of Dependent Children, called by President Theodore Roosevelt and held early in 1909, which endorsed the more economical option of home over institutionalized care for children. Illinois became the first state to authorize mothers' pensions. By 1919 thirty-nine states had done likewise, administering allowances through county or town governments. Levels of aid, as well as the requirements for receiving it, varied widely, with some administrative entities more generous than others. Because mothers' pensions never added up to a full subsidy, mothers still had to work and were expected to do so. The Aid to Dependent Children provision of the New Deal's Social Security Act of 1935 largely replaced mothers' pensions.

Anti-child-labor Laws. The child-saving impulse of maternal feminism led directly to a movement to end child labor. In the laboring classes, the work of children had always supplemented household incomes. Even though a child's income might be small, impoverished families often depended on it to stay alive. The consequences for children, however, could be permanent damage to their physical and mental developments.

Organizations opposed to child labor joined together in 1904 to form the National Child Labor Committee (NCLC) to press for federal legislation. Social-settlement workers and reformers, including Florence Kelley, Robert Hunter, and Lillian Wald, along with the religious leaders Felix Adler and Alexander Jeffrey McKelway, led the committee's work. By the mid-1910s many states prohibited children under the age of fourteen from working in factories and mines, but these state laws were poorly enforced. When the U.S. Supreme Court invalidated federal anti-child-labor laws passed by Congress, the NCLC organized a campaign for a constitutional amendment, a resolution which passed Congress in 1924 but was never ratified. The passage of the Fair Labor Standards Act of 1938 largely ended official tolerance of child labor in the United States, although the practice continues in poor communities.

Federal Agencies for Female and Child Welfare. Maternal feminists were behind the establishment of two federal agencies concerned with family welfare. The Children's Bureau was the first government agency in the world to concern itself solely with documenting the social and economic conditions of childhood. The impulse behind its founding came, once again, from settlement workers, primarily Kelley and Wald, who believed that a government that collected information about crop damage should also investigate its "child crop." After a nine-year campaign, they persuaded President Theodore Roosevelt to approve the idea, and in 1912 Roosevelt's successor, William Howard Taft, signed a law establishing the U.S. Children's Bureau. Julia Lathrop, a former resident of Chicago's Hull-House settlement, served as its first chief. In addition to starting a birth registration system that could track infant mortality and enforce school attendance, the bureau allied itself with the NCLC to press for anti-child-labor bills. It also worked for such labor reforms as unemployment and health insurance, minimum-wage and maximum-hour statutes, mothers' pensions, and juvenile justice codes.

The Women's Bureau, the second agency advocated by maternal feminists, collected information concerning women's wage work. It was modeled on the Women in Industry Service, founded in the U.S. Department of Labor during World War I to standardize wages, hours, and working conditions for the women who took jobs previously held by the men drafted into military service. In 1920, women's organizations successfully urged Congress to make this agency permanent. After becoming its director, Mary Anderson, founder of the Chicago Women's Trade Union League, guided the Women's Bureau in its support of labor legislation that protected women workers. Assuming that women's primary role was motherhood, Anderson and her colleagues took the position that working conditions should never threaten the health of mothers or potential mothers. As a result, the bureau lobbied against the National Woman's Party's proposed Equal Rights Amendment, which it feared would overturn special protections then in place for female industrial workers.

The Sheppard-Towner Maternity and Infancy Protection Act, 1921.

After national woman suffrage in 1920, maternal feminists' first major goal was to win federal funding for centers where women too poor to afford prenatal and early childhood care could learn how to take better care of themselves and their babies. One motivation behind this goal was the nation's high rate of maternal and infant mortality; another, and the one that ultimately convinced Congress to approve the idea, was the high rate of draft-board rejections during World War I of American youths in poor physical condition. Working together, the Children's and the Women's Bureaus convinced two federal legislators, Senator Morris Sheppard of Texas and Representative Horace Mann Towner of Iowa, to propose a bill for matching grants to states to fund maternal and infant-care centers. The Sheppard-Towner Maternity and Infancy Protection Act passed in 1921, after which activists had to convince state legislators to accept the federal money and approve the matching funds. Many state legislators resisted, calling the act "socialistic"; the American Medical Association also criticized the program as an unwarranted government intrusion into private affairs. Congress ended its funding in 1929. Still, Sheppard-Towner set an important legislative precedent for the child and family welfare legislation of the Great Depression era.

Ongoing Controversies.

Progressive Era maternal feminist reforms aroused considerable controversy. Opponents of an enlarged government role in providing social services argued that private philanthropy was sufficient to care for the needy. Other opponents included taxpayers asked to foot the bill for social-welfare initiatives. Even those people whom the reforms were supposed to help sometimes opposed them. Laws against child labor, for example, could mean privation for families lacking any other source of income. Laws protecting women in the workplace sounded good in the abstract, until they led to women being barred from lucrative jobs deemed "too dangerous" for their personal welfare.

Citizens also opposed maternal feminist reforms because, in agreeing to receive certain kinds of protections, they also had to accept some controls over their behavior. The requirements of administering mothers' pensions, for example, led to the imposition of rules and regulations that women raising families alone came to detest. And although the most famous maternal feminist reform of all, Prohibition, which became law in 1919 with the Eighteenth Amendment to the U.S. Constitution, cut down the incidence of alcoholism so harmful to family life, wide swaths of the population both hated and flagrantly violated the law. Even some of its original maternal feminist supporters despised the national hypocrisy that the amendment had brought about and ended up demanding its repeal.

In 1909 the social reformer Belle Moskowitz expressed the essence of the maternal feminist vision by calling for a "general motherhood of the commonwealth." Debates over whether government should function in such a parental fashion—in later times derided as "the nanny state"—are ongoing. Questions as to whether government can still afford to do so have dominated discussions since the later twentieth century. Some reforms originally inspired by Progressive Era maternal feminists, however, have become so entrenched that most Americans now consider them entitlements of citizenship. The reforms may endure, although financial exigency may always threaten their stability.

[See also Addams, Jane; Alcohol and Alcohol Abuse; Anti-child-labor Movement; Charity Organization Movement; Children's Bureau, U.S.; Consumer Movement; Kelley, Florence; Progressive Era; Prohibition; Settlement Houses; Welfare; Willard, Frances; Woman's Christian Temperance Union; Woman Suffrage Movement; and Women's Club Movement.]

BIBLIOGRAPHY

Bordin, Ruth. *Woman and Temperance: The Quest for Power and Liberty, 1873–1900.* Philadelphia: Temple University Press, 1981. An interpretation of the WCTU's reform program.

Davis, Allen F. *Spearheads for Reform: The Social Settlements and the Progressive Movement, 1890–1914.* New York: Oxford University Press, 1967. The essential introduction to this topic.

Goodwin, Joanne L. *Gender and the Politics of Welfare Reform: Mothers' Pensions in Chicago, 1911–1929.* Chicago: University of Chicago Press, 1997. Focuses on the interplay of sex, race, and class in the provision of mothers' pensions.

Laughlin, Kathleen A. *Women's Work and Public Policy: A History of the Women's Bureau, U.S. Department of Labor, 1945–1970.* Boston: Northeastern University Press, 2000.

Lemons, J. Stanley. "The Sheppard-Towner Act: Progressivism in the 1920s." *Journal of American History* 55 (1969): 776–786.

Muncy, Robyn. *Creating a Female Dominion in American Reform, 1890–1935.* New York: Oxford University Press, 1991. Focuses on the role of maternal feminist reforms to both the Progressive Era and the New Deal.

Perry, Elisabeth Israels. "'The General Motherhood of the Commonwealth': Dance Hall Reform in the Progressive Era." *American Quarterly* 37 (1985): 719–733. Describes Belle Moskowitz's campaign for controls on commercial recreation as a quintessential maternal feminist reform.

Trattner, Walter I. *Crusade for the Children: A History of the National Child Labor Committee and Child Labor Reform in America.* Chicago: Quadrangle Books, 1970.

Elisabeth Israels Perry

FESTIVALS

See Holidays and Festivals.

FIFTIES, THE

Most popular and historical accounts of the 1950s emphasize prosperity, especially in contrast with the sharp economic dislocations of the Great Depression and the social uncertainties of wartime. The newly prosperous world of everyday life in the 1950s was actually the end product of sweeping social and economic changes set in motion in the late 1930s and through the war years. Income redistribution began during the war when redistributive tax policies instituted in the late 1930s and full wartime employment led to more equitable distribution of an increasing national income. The share of the richest 5 percent declined from nearly 24 percent to nearly 17 percent between 1941 and 1945. Because the United States came out of the war with expanded industrial capacity, between 1946 and 1960 the national measure of productivity doubled, and average annual earnings, adjusted for inflation, rose by more than one-third.

The combination of New Deal safety-net measures and war spending brought many families out of poverty. Public transfer payments began to make a difference. By 1951, three-fourths of American workers and their survivors were part of the Social Security system, and by 1960, nearly 6 million were receiving Social Security checks. Hard-fought battles for union recognition and collective-bargaining agreements resulted in discretionary income for some working families for the first time. Unions represented more than a third of the nonagricultural workforce by the mid-1950s, and industry standards for labor agreements included provisions for job security and cost-of-living increases.

The Postwar Family Experiment. Less constrained by economic insecurity, many men and women turned to private family lives for personal fulfillment. They rushed to marry and have children. By 1943, marriage, birth, and divorce rates began a marked rise. Families formed at a frantic pace and followed similar sequencing. Rather than being bound by dependence on parents and kin, young men and women married at younger ages: by the end of the 1940s, the age of marriage fell to a hundred-year low. Rather than delaying child rearing, the women in these couples got pregnant soon after they tied the knot, and they had more children, producing the cohort known as the baby boom. After 1946 the divorce rate stabilized at prewar levels, and high birthrates and relatively low divorce rates persisted until the late 1950s. More people than ever before were married and living in families, and fewer women remained childless in the 1950s than in any other decade since the late nineteenth century.

On the face of it, this widespread and accelerated family formation was made possible by, and in turn supported, a socially valorized family wage system that consisted of male breadwinners and female dependents. In these years, social and cultural norms insistently associated maturity and personal happiness with heterosexual marriage, child rearing, and the domestic consumption that marked and facilitated these. However, despite the dominance of the image of the celebrated postwar family in its glory days, exceptions to the new prosperity, cracks in the family wage system, and alternatives to it were present, if less visible in the public record.

The presumption that family incomes depended on male breadwinners was always less true of black and working-class families, and it was entirely untrue of women supporting themselves and any children on their own. In 1950 when an all-time high of 60 percent of children were born into families consisting of a male breadwinner and a female homemaker, an increasing number of white women found themselves needing to work. For the first time in U.S. history, more than half of working women were married, and married women's workforce participation increased more in the 1950s than in any other previous decade. By 1960, mothers were the fastest-growing component of the workforce, even though the persistent significant gendered wage differential relegated women's paychecks to 60 percent of what men earned.

Although the proportion of black mothers who worked was higher than that of white mothers, at least in part because black fathers faced discriminatory hiring practices and were much more likely to find themselves unemployed, black women's wages declined relative to those paid to white women in this period. Between 1950 and 1960, of women who had never married or who were divorced, widowed, or abandoned, more whites than blacks were trying to make it on their own, and white women found more opportunities for work outside domestic service. By the late 1950s the increasing workforce participation of mothers began to unsettle household rhythms and social policies that depended on men's paid and women's unpaid labor. By 1960, median family income was 30 percent higher in purchasing power than it was in 1950, and families newly reliant on mothers' wages began to experiment with the kinds of adjustments that had been improvised by black and working-class families when mothers had to work outside the home.

An Expanding Public Sphere. The intensified presence of government in daily life during wartime continued through the 1950s. Various kinds of public spending reshaped opportunities. Forty percent of young men were eligible for veteran's benefits under the generous GI Bill (Servicemen's Readjustment Act, 1944), supported in part by progressive federal taxes that taxed the wealthiest individuals at 87 percent and resulted in corporations' paying nearly a quarter of the federal income taxes collected during the decade. The GI Bill underwrote the postwar expansion of higher education: by 1947–1948 it was subsidizing half of all male college students, with the added consequence of significantly enlarging the gap between the numbers of male and female college graduates. Public-works spending at all levels of government increased, as did new public construction of schools and sewers. Federal grants-in-aid paid for welfare, public works, and public housing.

By the end of World War II the federal workforce had quadrupled. Cold War–inflamed political tensions justified continuing high levels of federal spending and created an extensive peacetime national-security system. The formulation of a federal-level anti-Communist loyalty program beginning in 1947 meant that some 20 percent of the labor force was vulnerable to loyalty investigations as a condition of their employment: the more than 12 million workers employed by the government and those whose employment depended on government contracts, workers ranging from federal bureaucrats and state and local public employees to public-school and university teachers to workers in defense industries. Charges of disloyalty could be based on membership in a wide range of civil rights, civil liberties, peace, and labor organizations, and investigations threatened the government employment of accused "homosexuals and other moral perverts."

Public spending on highways and on new single-family housing construction reorganized the relationships between cities and between downtowns and outlying areas, encouraging expenditures on private automobile use and homeownership. It profoundly accelerated racially segregated suburbanization.

The resulting decentralization of industry and the remade commercial landscape of shopping centers ravaged older neighborhoods and downtowns and divided racial opportunities. The federal government paid 90 percent of the cost of the new high-speed interstate highway system; over the decade the share of passenger miles carried by public buses and subways dropped precipitously. Federal housing and veterans' programs reorganized home financing, underwriting low down payments and long-term mortgages for new construction in racially homogenous areas outside central cities. By 1960, one-third of Americans lived in suburbs, nearly two-thirds of Americans had become homeowners, and suburban shopping centers occupied as much land as central business districts.

Desegregation and Resegregation.

The migration of rural southern blacks to cities and the migration of whites to suburbs reshaped urban life in the 1950s. By 1960, more than half of black people, but only one-third of white people, lived in central cities. Black urban migration fostered a commitment to channeling increased voting strength into demands for equal rights. The membership of the National Association for the Advancement of Colored People (NAACP) increased from 50,000 in 1940 to 500,000 by 1946, and NAACP legal campaigns to expand voting rights and appeal inferior and ill-funded black schools resulted in the Supreme Court's *Brown v. Board of Education* decision dismantling the legal doctrine of "separate but equal." The 1955–1956 bus boycott in Montgomery, Alabama, marked a new stage of more assertive collective grass-roots protest, spearheaded by local activists from the labor movement, the women's political caucus, and the black church and supported by the working-class black people who carried the burden of staying off the buses.

In contrast, suburban areas were 95 percent white, and most of the few black suburbanites were likely to live in all-black areas on the outskirts of cities, where they were likely to be poorer and have less schooling available to them than urban blacks had. The discriminatory practice of redlining—the term comes from the use of red ink to mark areas where banks refused to invest—left residents in black and racially mixed urban neighborhoods both without access to loans from the Federal Housing Administration (FHA) and also more vulnerable to having their neighborhoods designated as blighted areas. New York City's Chinatown and Los Angeles's Japantown changed character when postwar citizenship status and family formation encouraged residents to disperse into a wider range of neighborhoods. Formal and informal mechanisms of housing segregation meant that increasing postwar migration from Mexico and Puerto Rico consolidated urban barrios in many cities, including New York, Chicago, Los Angeles, and El Paso, Texas. Working-class areas near central business districts were often targeted for urban-renewal programs that provided for new construction of offices, high-income apartments, and university expansion; two-thirds of city dwellers evicted by urban renewal were black or Latino. Public-housing projects were generally planned, situated, and constructed in such a way as to serve all white residents in white neighborhoods or all black residents in black neighborhoods without challenging established racial boundaries. The growth of suburbs considerably expanded both white homeownership and the stakes in maintaining the racial exclusion on which property values were dependent.

Cultural Consensus and Dissonance.

Even though political rhetoric, print advertising, magazine articles, some best sellers, and most of the situation comedies delivering audiences for the new commercial entertainment medium of television were all dominated by the ideal norm of white middle-class heterosexual couples raising children in suburbs, alternative cultural frameworks, sexual possibilities, and dissenting visions were also present. Increased policing of the boundaries of the "normal" simultaneously exposed these boundaries' fragility. Even as European immigrant cultures receded, foreign-language newspapers and radio broadcasts folded, and Ellis Island was deserted and readied for sale as surplus property by 1955, extended families, informal kinship, and public sociability persisted, maintaining ethnic and racial working-class neighborhoods as distinct from white middle-class suburban living. In the same years during which membership in churches and synagogues grew substantially and the president and Congress added "under God" to the Pledge of Allegiance and "In God We Trust" to the currency, the circulation of the wholesome *Life* magazine began to decline and both hit Broadway plays and successful Hollywood films dramatized sexual passion, homoerotic tensions, alienation, and rebellion.

Teenagers as a distinct group became more publicly visible after the appearance in 1944 of *Seventeen* magazine and the emergence in the early 1950s of a youth audience for music popularized as "rock and roll," and the 1955–1956 congressional hearings on juvenile delinquency announced them to be a significant consumer market, a subculture, and a challenge to authority. Varied musical performance styles coexisted: the popular crooners Rosemary Clooney and Eddie Fisher, the country singers Johnny Cash and Patsy Cline, and the rhythm-and-blues singers Fats Domino and Little Richard all produced chart-topping hits between 1954 and 1957. A vision of pleasure-focused heterosexual masculinity independent of the commitments of being a breadwinner, husband, and father circulated in the pages of Hugh Hefner's *Playboy*, a magazine that helped move male-only publications from under to over the counter with its first issue in 1953. Grace Metalious's 1956 instant best-seller *Peyton Place* repositioned the family as a potential locus of transgressive sexuality. And despite anti-Communist suspicion of dissent, anti-intellectualism, and compulsory heterosexuality, Beat poets, artists, and writers, gender nonconformists, interracial couples, and homosexual men and women found each other, often in cities' downtown neighborhoods adjacent to less-respectable commercial sex districts, occupying spaces that their presence then recast as bohemian.

[*See also* **Civil Rights Movement; Desegregation; Family; Juvenile Delinquency; Kinsey Reports; Marriage and Divorce; Music,** *subentry on* **Popular Music; Television; Urban Renewal;** *and* **Women Workers.**]

BIBLIOGRAPHY

Agnew, Jean-Christophe, and Roy Rosenzweig, eds. *A Companion to Post-1945 America.* Malden, Mass.: Blackwell, 2002.

Coontz, Stephanie. *The Way We Never Were: American Families and the Nostalgia Trap.* New York: Basic Books, 1992.

Coontz, Stephanie. *The Way We Really Are: Coming to Terms with America's Changing Families.* New York: Basic Books, 1997.

Creadick, Anna G. *Perfectly Average: The Pursuit of Normality in Postwar America.* Amherst: University of Massachusetts Press, 2010.

D'Emilio, John, and Estelle B. Freedman. *Intimate Matters: A History of Sexuality in America.* 2d ed. Chicago: University of Chicago Press, 1997.

May, Elaine Tyler. *Homeward Bound: American Families in the Cold War Era.* New York: Basic Books, 1988.

Patterson, James T. *Grand Expectations: The United States, 1945–1974.* New York: Oxford University Press, 1996.

Polenberg, Richard. *One Nation Divisible: Class, Race, and Ethnicity in the United States since 1938.* New York: Viking, 1980.

Smith, Judith E. *Visions of Belonging: Family Stories, Popular Culture, and Postwar Democracy, 1940–1960.* New York: Columbia University Press, 2004.

Solinger, Rickie. *Wake Up Little Susie: Single Pregnancy and Race before "Roe v. Wade."* New York: Routledge, 1992.

Judith E. Smith

FILIPINO AMERICANS

According to a 2010 report by the Migration Policy Institute, the United States is home to about 1.7 million Filipino immigrants. In addition, 1.4 million native-born U.S. citizens claim Filipino ancestry. Early twenty-first-century demographics indicate that Filipino immigrants are better educated than the immigrant population overall, and that Filipino immigrants account for a large share of immigrants in the western states of Hawai'i, Alaska, Nevada, and California. The Immigration and Nationality Act of 1965 ushered in these demographic changes. In place of the previous quota system based on immigrants' national origins, the act set up a system that allocated about twenty thousand visas to each country. Filipinos took advantage of the act's preference system, which favored skilled labor and family reunification. However, this upwardly mobile image obscures the historical existence of a multigenerational and socioeconomically diverse Filipino American community.

Located southeast of China and northeast of Indonesia, the Philippines is an archipelago of more than seven thousand islands.

Filipino American history must begin with the histories of Spanish and U.S. colonialism in the archipelago. Filipino nationalists declared independence from Spain on 12 June 1898, but the beginnings of Asia's first republic coincided with the Spanish-American War. After the U.S. defeat of Spain, American colonizers replaced Spanish ones. U.S. colonial projects of racial uplift and economic exploitation shaped early twentieth-century Filipino migrations to Hawai'i and the U.S. mainland. Beginning in 1903 the U.S. colonial government sponsored an elite group of Filipino students called *pensionados* to study in the United States, with the majority returning to the Philippines to assume leadership positions in U.S.-established institutions there. The recruitment by the Hawaiian Sugar Planters' Association between 1906 and 1934 of approximately 119,000 Filipino laborers known as *sakadas* constituted the first mass migration. Overpopulation and land scarcity in the archipelago's Ilocos region motivated men and some women to migrate overseas, as did the promise of socioeconomic opportunity publicized by American teachers and returned *pensionados*. *Sakadas* encountered backbreaking labor and poor living conditions, however, and resisted their dehumanization through labor strikes in 1924, 1937, and 1946.

After the 1924 Immigration Act virtually banned Asian immigration, American agribusiness turned to the Philippines as a source for inexpensive labor because Filipinos were able to enter the United States as U.S. nationals. Between 1920 and 1929, 37,600 predominantly male migrants from the Philippines arrived on the U.S. mainland. In California, examples of the racial discrimination and violence against Filipinos during this time include both the passage of antimiscegenation laws that prohibited marriage between Filipinos and whites and also race riots against

Filipino men's patronage of taxi dance halls. The Great Depression exacerbated anti-Filipino hostility and culminated in 1934 in the passage of the Tydings-McDuffie Act, which provided for gradual independence of the Philippines but also restricted the number of Filipino immigrants to fifty per year. Nevertheless, World War II created new opportunities for employment and U.S. citizenship, and Filipino American men enlisted in the First and Second Filipino Infantry Regiments to liberate the Philippines from Japanese occupation.

After the passage of the new immigration legislation in 1965, the number of Filipino immigrants rose dramatically, making them the country's second-largest immigrant group (Mexicans make up the largest group). The increase in the number of female immigrants from the Philippines balanced the sex ratio in Filipino American communities. Since the 1960s the Philippines has sent the most professional immigrants to the United States. In addition to the aggressive recruitment of their labor by U.S. health-care institutions, Philippine political instability under the dictatorship of Ferdinand Marcos motivated Filipino professionals to work abroad. Since the second half of the twentieth century the Philippines has been a major sending country of foreign-trained nurses and physicians to the United States. They have alleviated shortages in the number of health workers, especially in public, inner-city hospitals, but they have also faced various obstacles, such as obtaining licensure and encountering accent and language discrimination in the U.S. workplace.

The Philippines is also the leading source of foreign-born U.S. military personnel. As a result of the U.S. Navy's long-standing recruitment of Filipino nationals, by 1970 there were more Filipinos in the U.S. Navy than in the Philippine navy, and Filipino American communities can be found near naval bases throughout the United States. A major challenge of Filipino American enlistees has been occupational advancement within the U.S. Navy, where most of them work as stewards and in clerical positions. Finally, the vast majority of Filipinos immigrate to the United States through the immigration law's preference for family reunification. As a result, it would be more accurate to characterize new Filipino immigration as having a dual nature in which working-class as well as middle-class Filipinos have immigrated in large numbers.

[*See also* Angel Island Immigration Station *and* Immigration.]

BIBLIOGRAPHY

Bulosan, Carlos. *America Is in the Heart: A Personal History*. New York: Harcourt, Brace and Company, 1946. A seminal work that captures the collective experiences of Filipino American laborers and labor organizers in California and the Pacific Northwest during the 1930s.

Choy, Catherine Ceniza. *Empire of Care: Nursing and Migration in Filipino American History*. Durham, N.C.: Duke University Press, 2003. In the context of U.S. colonial education in the archipelago, explores how and why the Philippines became the leading sending country of professional nurses to the United States.

España-Maram, Linda. *Creating Masculinity in Los Angeles's Little Manila: Working-Class Filipinos and Popular Culture, 1920s–1950s*. New York: Columbia University Press, 2006. Documents the role of gambling, boxing, taxi dance halls, and clothing in the forging of the identity of the early twentieth-century young, masculine Filipino American.

Espiritu, Augusto Fauni. *Five Faces of Exile: The Nation and Filipino American Intellectuals*. Stanford, Calif.: Stanford University Press, 2005. A history of U.S. colonialism in the Philippines through the perspectives and experiences of the diplomat Carlos P. Romulo, the poet José

García Villa, and the writers N. V. M. Gonzalez, Bienvenido Santos, and Carlos Bulosan.

Fujita-Rony, Dorothy B. *American Workers, Colonial Power: Philippine Seattle and the Transpacific West, 1919–1941*. Berkeley: University of California Press, 2003. Examines how transpacific trade, militarism, and colonial education transformed Seattle into a colonial metropolis for Filipinos in the United States.

Posadas, Barbara M. *The Filipino Americans*. Westport, Conn.: Greenwood Press, 1999. A reference work that provides an overview of Filipinos in the United States before and after 1965.

Catherine Ceniza Choy

FILM

From the opening of the first nickelodeon— a name that combined the cost of admission, a nickel, with the Greek word for theater—in 1905, movies did more than simply entertain. They represented a new means of communication for a new century, one that bypassed traditional authorities and spoke directly to millions of Americans. Unlike most newspapers, movies reached a mass audience that cut across class, ethnicity, gender, race, religion, age, geography, and political affiliation.

Early movie theaters were boisterous social centers where people went to meet their friends, gossip, flirt, discuss politics, and watch films. By 1914, every American town with a population of more than five thousand had at least one movie theater; six years later, 50 million Americans flocked to one of the nation's fifteen thousand theaters or to one of the twenty-two thousand churches, union halls, schools, or voluntary associations that screened movies. By 1930, weekly admission figures reached 90 million people. One of the few amusements that financially strapped families could afford, the new medium proved especially popular with immigrants and working people. Contemporary writers referred to the movies as the "academy of the working man," the "poor man's amusement," and a medium built upon the "nickels of the working class."

Emerging in the midst of the Progressive Era, a time of unbridled optimism when many Americans believed that they could solve the ills of society, filmmakers entered into national debates over the problems of the age. Between 1905 and April 1917, directors such as Edwin Porter, D. W. Griffith, Lois Weber, and Oscar Apfel made social-problem films that visualized a broad range of controversial issues. Porter's *The Kleptomaniac* (1905) critiqued a justice system that forgave a thieving wealthy woman but sent a poor mother to prison for stealing a loaf of bread to feed her starving children. Before he made the brilliant but racist *The Birth of a Nation* (1915), D. W. Griffith directed a slew of social-problem films that depicted the exploitation of sweatshop laborers (*The Song of the Shirt*, 1908), the evils of monopoly capital (*A Corner in Wheat*, 1909), the misguided efforts of middle-class reformers (*Simple Charity*, 1910), and a corrupt legal system that practiced one law for the rich and another for the poor (*One Is Business, the Other Crime*, 1912).

None of these productions rivaled the popularity of Charlie Chaplin's films. No one in power was spared from the Tramp's sharp cinematic barbs. He attacked authority figures up and down the class scale: from the follies of the extremely wealthy in *The Count* (1916) and *The Rink* (1916) to the pretensions of the upwardly mobile middle-class in *Work* (1915) and *The Floorwalker* (1916) to the foibles of the working class in *Dough and Dynamite* (1914).

Ignored by mainstream filmmakers and excluded from or forced to sit in segregated sections of white movie theaters, African Americans attended "colored" theaters where they watched silent "race films" made by black filmmakers such as George and Noble Johnson (*Realization of a Negro's Ambition*, 1916) and Oscar Micheaux (*Within Our Gates*, 1920; *Symbol of the Unconquered*, 1920; and *Body and Soul*, 1925). Asian and Mexican immigrants also encountered racism on the screen and in theaters, so they often preferred to watch movies at ethnic-owned houses such as Los Angeles's Bankoku-za and Toyo-za theaters or at local houses that welcomed people of color, such as Chicago's Olympia Theater.

The outbreak of World War I precipitated dramatic changes in the evolution of the American movie industry, the content of its films, and the composition of its audiences. In 1914 the United States produced approximately half the world's movies; by 1919, with European film production in shambles, that figure rose to 90 percent. Taking advantage of Europe's tragedy, the American movie industry assumed its modern identity as "Hollywood" in the 1920s. The geographically scattered array of small and medium producers, distributors, and exhibitors of early years was supplanted by an increasingly oligarchic, vertically integrated studio system centered in Los Angeles and financed by some of the largest industrial and financial institutions in the nation. Movies were now a multimillion-dollar industry, and as in other industries, the most successful studios increased their profits by securing greater control over the market. By the end of the 1920s, the eight major studios controlled more than 90 percent of the films shown in the United States.

The postwar era witnessed a dramatic shift in the composition of audiences as studios and exhibitors looked to increase profits by attracting a broader array of middle-class and wealthy Americans. To that end, they erected exotic movie palaces and produced lavish films aimed at turning moviegoing into an experience that both transcended and reshaped traditional class boundaries. Earlier social-problem films that emphasized class conflict were superseded by extravagant productions—such as *Saturday Night* (1922) and *Orchids and Ermine* (1927)—that blurred class distinctions, hailed the virtues of class harmony, and focused on the good-natured and often romantic interactions between the classes. Films about class conflict, racism, sexism, and exploitation did not disappear from the screen during the 1920s, but they grew fewer in number and rarely appeared in the studio-owned first-run theaters that gave movies their greatest visibility and profits.

The Talkies Arrive. The coming of "talking pictures," or "talkies," in 1927 signaled a new era in American film. The Great Depression and the high cost of wiring theaters for sound drove many smaller studios and independent groups out of business and strengthened the power of the eight dominant studios. Audiences sought relief from hard times by attending movie theaters in unprecedented numbers. In 1936, for example, 88 million people flocked to the movies each week—a figure that greatly exceeded the 45.6 million votes cast in the presidential election that year, for instance.

During the 1930s and 1940s, an era that film scholars refer to as the golden age of Hollywood, Warner Brothers and Metro-Goldwyn-Mayer (MGM) dominated box-office returns by offering audiences two different types of films. Allying with Franklin D. Roosevelt and the New Deal, Warner Brothers produced scores of social-problem films dealing with domestic ills caused by the Great Depression—films such as *Little Caesar* (1931), *I Am a Fugitive from a Chain*

Gang (1932), and *Wild Boys of the Road* (1933). By the mid-1930s, Warner Bros. also made films that alerted the nation to the dangers posed by Fascism and Nazism—films such as *Black Legion* (1937) and *Confessions of a Nazi Spy* (1939).

MGM's cinematic ideology proved a stark contrast to the progressive features coming out of the Warner studio. Whereas Warner Bros. exposed audiences to what was wrong in American life—poverty, corruption, lack of opportunity—MGM turned out lavish films, such as *Grand Hotel* (1932), *The Barretts of Wimpole Street* (1934), and *Marie Antoinette* (1938), that offered Depression-era audiences an antidote to hopelessness and despair. MGM's most successful series— the Hardy Family films made between 1937 and 1943—created an updated Victorian world in which anything was possible so long as one adhered to family, country, and God. Success was a matter of individual effort, not collective action. The family, not the state, was the only institution that one needed to turn to for help in hard times. Although in the twenty-first century these may seem like old-fashioned values, at the time MGM went against the tide of the New Deal's more collectivist vision of increased reliance on the government. Indeed, films such as *Judge Hardy's Children* (1938) offered oblique attacks on federally owned corporations such as the Tennessee Valley Authority.

Once the United States entered World War II in December 1941, studios produced films promoting national unity, patriotism, and the heroic struggles of the American men and women fighting abroad. After the war, the rabidly anti-Communist House Un-American Activities Committee (HUAC) quickly forgot Hollywood's vital contribution to the "good war" and launched a series of investigations that linked earlier anti-Fascist films with Communist efforts to undermine democracy.

Movie-industry personnel who helped the war effort by making films heralding cooperation with America's Russian allies—*Mission to Moscow* (1943), *The North Star* (1943), and *Song of Russia* (1944)—were accused of being Communists or fellow travelers who aided them. Known as the Hollywood Ten, the ten writers, directors, and producers who refused to answer HUAC's questions were sent to prison for contempt of Congress. In order to prove their loyalty, studios turned out a series of anti-Communist films: *The Red Menace* (1949), *I Married a Communist* (1949), *Walk East on Beacon* (1952), and *Big Jim McLain* (1952). They all proved box-office disasters.

Despite Hollywood's conservative turn, filmmakers managed to grapple with an array of social issues ranging from the difficulties of postwar readjustment (*The Best Years of Our Lives*, 1946) to the problems of anti-Semitism (*Gentleman's Agreement*, 1947) to the persistence of racial discrimination (*No Way Out*, 1950) to the growing problem of juvenile delinquency (*Blackboard Jungle*, 1955).

The Hollywood studio system dominated the world market until the late 1940s and early 1950s, when challenges from television and a Supreme Court decision ordering the separation of production and exhibition wings weakened its oligarchic control of the industry. Following a peak box-office year in 1946, movie attendance steadily declined until 1958, when box-office receipts stabilized at one-half the 1945–1948 average. Movie-industry leaders tried to increase attendance by building drive-ins aimed at younger audiences and by turning out films that explored the disparities between the promises and the problems faced by millions of people living in President Dwight D. Eisenhower's America. The story told by *Rebel without a Cause* (1955) of discontent and death amid suburban prosperity challenged dominant ideas about family, sexuality, gender roles, and the meaning of success.

The New Hollywood.

By the mid-1960s, the older men who ran the major studios had lost touch with a young audience being politicized by urban violence, an increasingly militant civil rights movement, an unpopular war in Vietnam, and a burgeoning women's movement. Unable to attract teenagers and twenty-somethings with old-fashioned fare featuring the likes of Doris Day and Rock Hudson, a new generation of industry leaders revived Hollywood by releasing of a series of edgy films—*Bonnie and Clyde* (1967), *The Graduate* (1967), *The Wild Bunch* (1969), *Midnight Cowboy* (1969), and *Easy Rider* (1969)—that brought baby boomers back into movie theaters. The elimination in 1968 of the Production Code Administration—the movie industry's self-censorship body, created in 1934—gave filmmakers freedom to deal with previously forbidden subjects.

The success of the civil rights movement, especially after Martin Luther King Jr.'s 1963 March on Washington and the passage of the Civil Rights Act in 1964, prompted a number of liberal integrationist films, many of them starring the black actor Sidney Poitier: *To Sir, with Love* (1967), *In the Heat of the Night* (1967), and *Guess Who's Coming to Dinner?* (1967). Militant African Americans, however, felt little connection to Poitier's saintly image or to liberal calls for patience.

Fed up with the way they were being portrayed on the screen, independent black filmmakers—and, later, studios eager to duplicate their box-office success—created a new genre known as blaxploitation films. The first movies since silent-era "race films" to be aimed specifically at African American audiences, *Sweet Sweetback's Baadassss Song* (1971), *Shaft* (1972), *Superfly* (1972), *Cleopatra Jones* (1973), and *Foxy Brown* (1974) revealed an urban world filled with drugs, money, violence, and black resistance rarely seen in mainstream films. Popular at the box office with young audiences, blaxploitation films generated debate and concern among critics and community leaders, black and white, who deplored plots that stressed individual indulgence rather than collective action.

Willing to deal with urban violence, Hollywood proved reluctant to deal with the war in Vietnam. The first major film related to Vietnam, John Wayne's *The Green Berets* (1968), which offered a staunch defense of American involvement in Vietnam, did not appear until well into the war. Only after the war ended in April 1975 did studios release a spate of antiwar films—*The Deer Hunter* (1978), *Coming Home* (1978), *Apocalypse Now* (1979)—that questioned America's involvement in the long-standing conflict. However, as the New Right rose to power in the 1980s, films like *Red Dawn* (1984), *Missing in Action* (1984), and *Rambo: First Blood Part II* (1985) helped restore American confidence in the military and generate public support for military actions taken by Presidents Ronald Reagan and George H. W. Bush. Reagan's fervid anti-Communism also sparked a new wave of Cold War films that once again portrayed the Soviet Union as America's enemy, among them *The Hunt for Red October* (1990) and *Crimson Tide* (1995).

Hollywood proved far more liberal when it came to domestic issues. The social and political activism of the 1970s and 1980s inspired films—*The Front* (1976), *The China Syndrome* (1979), *Norma Rae* (1979), *Reds* (1981), *Silkwood* (1983), and *Matewan* (1987)—that attacked Red-baiters, warned against the dangers of nuclear power, and offered positive visions of unions, labor organizers, and radicals.

Battles between left and right concerning the proper roles of men and women were also fought out on and off the screen. Influenced by the women's movement of the 1960s, feminist films of the 1970s—*Alice Doesn't Live Here Anymore* (1974), *The Turning Point* (1977), *An Unmarried Woman* (1978)—showed men and women struggling to see each other as fully developed people rather than living narrowly defined traditional gender roles. For women, this meant being able to choose whatever career or relationship they wanted: single, married, divorced, parent, or childless. The 1980s, however, witnessed a conservative backlash that called for a return to more traditional gender roles, for men as well as for women. Films like *Fatal Attraction* (1987) and *The War of the Roses* (1989) showed how straying outside conventional gender roles and behavior threatened marriage, family, and happiness. The "you can't have it all" message that permeated these films called for Americans to return to the more narrowly proscribed and allegedly happier gender roles and family lifestyles associated with the 1950s.

The nastiness and cynicism that marked American politics during the 1990s and 2000s also made its way onto the screen. Hollywood responded with a series of films that offered disparaging views of electoral life: *Bob Roberts* (1992), *Wag the Dog* (1997), *Primary Colors* (1998), and especially *Bulworth* (1998). Directed and written by, as well as starring, Warren Beatty, *Bulworth* skewered the hypocrisy of the Democratic Party and the unwillingness of African American voters to hold politicians to their promises. This climate of skepticism helped the producer-director-writer-star Michael Moore take the documentary from the margins to the center of American film with three surprising box-office hits, *Bowling for Columbine* (2002), *Fahrenheit 9/11* (2004), and *Sicko* (2007).

Fahrenheit 9/11 returned $222.4 million by January 2005, making it the most commercially successful documentary.

Post-9/11 Cinema. 11 September 2001 marked a turning point in American history. Yet fears of terrorism made it to the screen well before the destruction of the World Trade Towers. *Navy Seals* (1990), *True Lies* (1994), and *Executive Decision* (1996) all featured threats by nefarious Middle Eastern forces, while *The Siege* (1998) showed Islamic terrorists plotting an attack on New York City. Unlike their handling of the war in Vietnam, Hollywood studios did not wait a decade before dealing with conflicts in Afghanistan and Iraq. But with studios hesitant to venture too far in front of public opinion, films such as *Home of the Brave* (2006), *In the Valley of Elah* (2007), and *Stop-Loss* (2008) focused on the difficulties faced by American troops rather than on the government and military leaders who mishandled the war; only *Green Zone* (2010), a political film in the guise of an action-adventure movie, placed the blame for the botched war in Iraq on the administration of George W. Bush.

The late twentieth-century globalization of Hollywood and changes in technology have altered both the content of films and the ways in which people watch them. Studios no longer consider Americans their main audience. In 1993, American movies generated $13 billion in revenue, $8 billion of which came from outside the United States. In July 2011, for instance, the top ten grossing films made more money in foreign sales than in domestic box office. The growing dependence on foreign markets encouraged studios to produce blockbuster action films that contained little dialogue and could be easily understood by non-English-speaking audiences throughout the world. Domestic box-office receipts suffered as greater numbers of

Americans chose to watch films at home—first in the form of videotapes, then DVDs and DVRs, and then by downloading or streaming film on their computers. These changes, in turn, have privatized the exhibition experience and eliminated the public interactions and audience exchanges—both good and bad—that characterized American moviegoing for more than a hundred years.

[*See also* Everyday Life; Leisure; *and* Television.]

BIBLIOGRAPHY

Bogle, Donald. *Bright Boulevards, Bold Dreams: The Story of Black Hollywood.* New York: One World Ballantine Books, 2005.

Brownlow, Kevin. *Behind the Mask of Innocence, Sex, Violence, Prejudice, Crime: Films of Social Conscience in the Silent Era.* Berkeley: University of California Press, 1992.

Butsch, Richard. *The Making of American Audiences: From Stage to Television, 1750–1990.* New York: Cambridge University Press, 2000.

Ceplair, Larry, and Steven Englund. *The Inquisition in Hollywood: Politics in the Film Community, 1930–1960.* Garden City, N.Y.: Anchor Press/Doubleday, 1980.

May, Lary. *The Big Tomorrow: Hollywood and the Politics of the American Way.* Chicago: University of Chicago Press, 2000.

McDonald, Paul, and Janet Wasko, eds. *The Contemporary Hollywood Film Industry.* Malden, Mass.: Blackwell, 2008.

Quart, Leonard, and Albert Auster. *American Film and Society since 1945.* 3d ed. Westport, Conn.: Praeger, 2002.

Ryan, Michael, and Douglas Kellner. *Camera Politica: The Politics and Ideology of Contemporary Hollywood Film.* Bloomington: Indiana University Press, 1988.

Schatz, Thomas. *The Genius of the System: Hollywood Filmmaking in the Studio Era.* New York: Pantheon, 1988.

Sklar, Robert. *Movie-Made America: A Cultural History of American Movies.* Rev. ed. New York: Vintage Books, 1994.

Steven J. Ross

FINNEY, CHARLES GRANDISON

(1792–1875), revivalist, reformer, and educator. Born in Connecticut and reared in western New York, Charles Grandison Finney became a schoolteacher and apprentice lawyer. In 1821, while practicing law in Adams, New York, Finney experienced a religious conversion. He received Presbyterian ordination in 1824 and became a missionary in the Lake Ontario region. In 1825 he began a seven-year series of revivals in Oneida County, New York, that brought him national fame and enabled him to develop new evangelistic techniques. With the exception of George Whitefield, earlier evangelists had usually worked within individual churches. Finney pioneered citywide campaigns supported by numerous committees for publicity, prayer, and so forth. After conducting revivals in Philadelphia, New York City, Boston, and elsewhere, he preached in Rochester, New York, for six months in 1830–1831, ushering in the great revival of 1831–1832. Eschewing emotionalism, Finney ministered especially to the professional classes, which responded in great numbers to his dignified meetings. Many of the techniques he pioneered became standard in mass evangelism. Theologically he was a New School Calvinist and placed particular emphasis on sanctification, or perfectionism.

In 1832, Finney became pastor of the Second Presbyterian Church in New York City, moving in 1835 to the Broadway Tabernacle, where he remained until 1837. His series of lectures on revivals, published in 1835, enjoyed a wide influence. In 1835 he also became professor of theology at Oberlin College in Ohio, dividing his time for many years thereafter between Oberlin and evangelistic campaigns across the North. Finney was president of Oberlin from 1851 to 1866. Active in numerous reform movements of the day, especially antislavery, he inspired many to embrace these causes.

[See also Antebellum Reform; Antislavery; Burned-Over District; Clergy; Great Awakenings; Itinerant Preachers; Missions, in America; Religion; Revivals; and Whitefield, George.]

BIBLIOGRAPHY

Hambrick-Stowe, Charles E. *Charles G. Finney and the Spirit of American Evangelicalism.* Grand Rapids, Mich.: Eerdmans, 1996.

Hardman, Keith J. *Charles G. Finney, 1792–1875: Revivalist and Reformer.* Syracuse, N.Y.: Syracuse University Press, 1987.

Rosell, Garth A., and Richard A. G. Dupuis, eds. *Memoirs of Charles G. Finney: The Complete Restored Text.* Grand Rapids, Mich.: Academie Books, 1989.

Keith J. Hardman

FITZHUGH, GEORGE

(1806–1881), author of controversial proslavery writing. George Fitzhugh's withering critique of so-called free society established him as antebellum America's most controversial proslavery ideologue. Though he hoped that his assault on nineteenth-century "progress" might deflect attention from the slave South's plantation regime, his writings of the 1850s and early 1860s served mainly to gain him unparalleled notoriety.

Fitzhugh had reached a level of middle-age respectability when he transformed himself from a Port Royal, Virginia, lawyer into a reactionary polemicist extraordinaire. Two slim pamphlets—*Slavery Justified, by a Southerner* (1850) and *What Is to Be Done with the Free Negroes?* (1851)—departed in several respects from those defenses of human bondage already systematized by southern politicians and clergymen. The pamphlets displayed an unrelenting hostility to modern equality and liberty as (unwelcome) new developments. In crafting his cosmopolitan frame of reference, Fitzhugh drew freely from the more conservative British quarterlies. A seminal influence was the British writer Thomas Carlyle, who was in these years pairing his stark disillusionment with black freedom in Jamaica with an attack on the political and social radicalism that had flourished during the European revolutions of 1848.

Fitzhugh's most original contribution lay in his appropriation of views expressed by American and French socialists. In 1854 he compiled a book-length study titled *Sociology for the South, or The Failure of Free Society* that extensively cited reformers' criticisms of unfettered markets and liberal political democracy. Marshaling these criticisms as evidence of free society's failure, Fitzhugh praised the comparative stability and happiness of slave society. In laying out the case for a counteroffensive against antislavery activism, Fitzhugh explained how "the South can lose nothing, and may gain, by the discussion" because "she has, up to this time, been condemned without a hearing."

In *Cannibals All! or Slaves without Masters* (1857), Fitzhugh urged wageworkers of the North toward a greater consciousness of their own exploitation. Yet far from gaining converts among the white working classes, his increasingly outrageous appeals were skillfully co-opted by the emerging free-soil

Republican Party, which was intent on publicizing southern hostility to manual laborers both slave and free. Most notably, Abraham Lincoln drew from Fitzhugh's editorials in the *Richmond Enquirer* when drafting his influential "House Divided" address of 1858.

In the late 1850s Fitzhugh wrote dozens of articles for *De Bow's Review* of New Orleans. Once war began, these increasingly praised the Confederate States of America for their embrace of counterrevolutionary militarism. With Union victory, Fitzhugh's reactionary advocacy tapered off, and he spent the last decade of his life in relative obscurity.

[*See also* Antebellum Era; Emancipation of Slaves; Slavery, *subentry on* Nineteenth Century; *and* South, The.]

BIBLIOGRAPHY

Bonner, Robert. "Proslavery Extremism Goes to War: The Counterrevolutionary Confederacy and Reactionary Militarism." *Modern Intellectual History* 6 (2009): 261–285.

O'Brien, Michael. *Conjectures of Order: Intellectual Life and the American South, 1810–1860.* Chapel Hill: University of North Carolina Press, 2004.

Robert E. Bonner

FORTEN, JAMES

(1766–1842), free black abolitionist and businessman. James Forten was born in Philadelphia to a free black couple, Thomas Forten and Margaret Waymouth. Thomas was a sailmaker, and James learned the elements of the sail-making trade in the sail loft of Robert Bridges, the white man who employed his father. He also received two years of formal education at the Quaker-sponsored African School founded by Anthony Benezet.

The Revolution had a profound impact on James Forten's life. He was committed to independence, and as a teenager he served on an American privateer. He was captured by the British on his second cruise in 1781 and was offered various inducements to switch sides, but he refused, insisting that he would not under any circumstances betray the American cause. His refusal resulted in many months of incarceration on a British prison ship.

At the end of the war Forten returned to Philadelphia. After a stint as a merchant seaman, he took up his father's trade and sought employment in the Bridges sail loft. A close bond developed between Robert Bridges and James Forten, and in 1798, when Bridges retired, he arranged for Forten to take over the sail loft. Forten managed to retain most of Bridges's customers, and his skill and attention to detail gained him many more customers. He proved a shrewd businessman, investing his profits in real estate and making loans at interest. His rise to prominence and prosperity was remarkable for an African American man in a city and a state where slavery, although declining in importance, was still accepted by the majority of whites.

Legally free and financially secure, Forten threw himself into the campaign to end slavery and racial discrimination. His *Letters from a Man of Colour* (1813), written to protest a move in the state legislature to curb the rights of black Pennsylvanians, was and remains an eloquent statement of his belief that the Revolution had been fought to achieve freedom for all Americans.

During the 1810s Forten espoused the idea of African resettlement. He and his friend, the New England shipowner Paul Cuffe, a man of African and Native American parentage, joined British reformers in promoting emigration to Sierra Leone. They hoped that slave owners could be persuaded to liberate their slaves if they knew that the slaves could be sent to a distant shore once they were free. The formation of the American Colonization Society (ACS) in 1817 led to a change in Forten's attitude. Pronouncements by some ACS members made him fear that the society's agenda was actually the forced removal from the United States of free people of color and the bolstering of the institution of slavery. From 1817 on, he became one of the ACS's harshest critics.

For the rest of his life James Forten battled for the rights of people of African descent in the United States. He helped fund William Lloyd Garrison's newspaper the *Liberator*, served as an officer of the American Anti-Slavery Society, founded and presided over the American Moral Reform Society (1835–1841), and continued to advocate for the creation of an America that was truly inclusive.

[*See also* **African American Emigration; African Americans; Colonization Movement, African; Free Communities of Color; Revolution and Constitution Era;** *and* **Slavery**, *subentries on* **Colonial and Revolutionary Era** *and* **Nineteenth Century.**]

BIBLIOGRAPHY

Winch, Julie. *A Gentleman of Color: The Life of James Forten*. New York: Oxford University Press, 2002.

Julie Winch

4-H CLUB MOVEMENT

In 1914 the Cooperative Extension Service of the U.S. Department of Agriculture established its Rural Youth Division by bringing together a number of independent clubs for farm boys and girls under the direction of country agricultural agents. The term "4-H" (Head, Heart, Hands, and Health), popularized by Extension Agent Gertrude Warren, became the clubs' official name in 1919. The 4-H clubs, which proved highly popular, served as a useful vehicle for training young people in advanced farming and home economics techniques often resisted by their parents.

In the 1920s a Chicago-based private organization, the National 4-H Service Committee, solicited contributions from corporate donors to underwrite 4-H prizes and established rules for participation in 4-H projects and county-fair competitions emphasizing animal husbandry, crop production, and home economics. In 1948 the Cooperative Extension Service established a second private organization, the National 4-H Foundation, in Washington, D.C., primarily to underwrite international exchanges of farm youth, an activity that the 4-H Service Committee proved reluctant to sponsor. The two organizations sustained an uneasy working relationship until 1976 when they merged into the single National 4-H Council.

In the 1960s, as the farm population continued its long decline, 4-H added to its list of sponsored projects a number of hobby activities designed to appeal to small-town and urban youth. Although 4-H continued to promote traditional farm-related programs, it placed considerable emphasis on leadership training and community-development projects. In the twenty-first century, 4-H has continued to rank among the nation's largest youth organizations, and the only one that is federally sponsored.

[*See also* **Rural Life and Society.**]

BIBLIOGRAPHY

Wessel, Thomas, and Marilyn Wessel. *4-H, an American Idea, 1900–1980: A History of 4-H.* Chevy Chase, Md.: National 4-H Council, 1982.

Thomas Wessel and Marilyn Wessel

FRANCISCANS

The term "Franciscan" indicates a diverse range of people inspired by the life and writings of the Italian mystic Francis of Assisi (1181–1226), including friars, nuns, brothers, sisters, and lay women and -men. Although various groups of Protestant Franciscans have emerged since the nineteenth century, this article is confined to Roman Catholic groups of Franciscans.

Franciscans consist of many and varied groups responding to the immediate needs in front of them and maintaining an independence that they identify with the inspiration of the Holy Spirit. Their variety prevents easy generalization about their organizational structures. Because of internal differences by the mid-sixteenth century, the one group of friars founded directly by Francis, often called the "first order," had been divided by two popes into three bodies: the Order of Friars Minor, the Order of Friars Minor Conventual, and the Order of Friars Minor Capuchin. Franciscan Third Order Regular women's congregations arose locally in Europe to deal with immediate ministerial needs. Their resistance to amalgamation continued in the United States as congregations came to work among same-language immigrants. The Franciscan Third Order Regular congregations founded in the United States generally pursued specific ministries, often initiated by charismatic women who saw and responded to needs for teachers, medical care, or social work.

History in America. The friars first came to the Americas on the second voyage of Christopher Columbus in 1493. Friar Marcos de Niza's travels through the southwestern United States in 1539 led a few years later to the expedition of Francisco Vásquez de Coronado, which included several friars. Friars established missions in Florida (1573), New Mexico (1598), Maryland (1672), Michigan (1701), Texas (1716), Louisiana (1720 and 1722), and California (1769). These colonial friars were inspired "to go among the Saracens and other nonbelievers," as Francis of Assisi wrote, in order to share the gospel of Jesus Christ. With the exception of English Franciscans in Maryland, the friars also served the nationalist political purposes of their royal Spanish and French sponsors. They brought agricultural, architectural, engineering, and medical advancements along with religious and social ideas. Inevitably their work brought drastic changes to long-existent Native American cultures. North of the Rio Grande, Franciscan influence lasted the longest in New Mexico—from 1598 to the 1840s—and there the Native American cultures proved most resilient when later challenged by Anglo-American society. Political developments ended colonial-era Franciscan missions in the United States by the 1840s, with the exception of Santa Barbara, California.

Less scholarship has focused on Franciscans in the United States since 1840 than on the early Franciscan missions. Most histories of Franciscans in the United States attempt to tell the story of one of the more than one hundred individual provinces of Franciscan friars, monasteries of nuns, or congregations of Third Order Regular Franciscans that emerged between 1840 and 2000. In 1846 the first European immigrant group of Franciscans arrived, following a few solitary friars who came in the late eighteenth century, including the Irish-born Michael Egan, the first bishop of Philadelphia, and the Irish-born Charles Whelan, the first resident Catholic priest in New York City. Through the 1840s and 1850s, in response to bishops' requests for ministers for their immigrant flocks, groups of friars came to the dioceses of Cincinnati, Ohio; Galveston, Texas; Buffalo, New York; and Alton, Illinois. Two Swiss diocesan priests came to Milwaukee, Wisconsin, in 1857 on their own initiative and founded a Franciscan community. In Buffalo, Italian friars taught Irish immigrant seminarians. Elsewhere the first nineteenth-century friars engaged in parochial ministry among German-speaking immigrants.

Two groups of Poor Clares, or Franciscan nuns of an order cofounded by Francis with Clare of Assisi (1194/5–1253), came to the United States in the 1870s. Other men and women—initially called Tertiaries or Third Order Franciscans and, after Vatican II, called Secular Franciscans—have been part of the Franciscan movement since the thirteenth century, though living as individuals in the world. A Secular Franciscan fraternity in Santa Fe, New Mexico, claims to date from 1610, and after 1900, Secular Franciscans were found throughout the country. Some Tertiaries in early modern Europe began living a common life and undertaking common ministries, emerging as a new form of apostolic Franciscan religious life known as the Third Order Regular. Third Order Regular brothers from Ireland founded Saint Francis College in Pennsylvania in 1847. The first Third Order Regular sisters arrived in 1849 and began work in schools, orphanages, and hospitals in Wisconsin. By World War I more than fifty different congregations of Franciscan women, some with a thousand members, worked in various apostolates among German, Irish, Italian, Polish, and eventually Slovak, Czech, Lithuanian, and Croatian

immigrants. The work done by many Franciscan congregations, like that of the friars, evolved over time as immigrants assimilated, conditions changed, and new needs were recognized and met. The Poor Clare nuns remain cloistered and dedicated to a contemplative life of prayer.

Assessment. Colonial Franciscan activity was more extensive than that of any other Christian missionary effort in the United States, but it was also entangled in the controversies of colonialism itself. U.S. Franciscan history began as immigrant history, rooted in the immigrant groups to which Franciscans belonged. Early U.S. Franciscans often dealt with misunderstanding and persecution that resulted from American nativist Anti-Catholicism, the lack of understanding of their religious charism, and nationalist rivalries within the Catholic Church. The hard work of Franciscans, often in ministries new to them in the United States, contributed greatly to the advancement of their ethnic communities and to the other groups with whom they worked. Franciscan community life reflected the society around it—for instance, with numerical growth during the baby boom followed by a collapse in membership numbers during the antiestablishment 1960s and 1970s, and an aging membership in an aging U.S. population since the 1980s.

Even as the groups with whom they originally identified assimilated into mainstream culture and prospered, Franciscans continued to focus much of their attention on the materially poor and marginalized. The Franciscan charism has consistently inspired the formation of new groups, the renewal of existing ones, and innovations in the ministries that Franciscans undertook. The varied contributions of thousands of Franciscans are woven into the history of America across four centuries and through countless class-rooms, pulpits, hospitals, parishes, missions, stories, and even names, including San Francisco, Los Angeles, and San Diego in California and San Antonio in Texas.

[*See also* Assimilation; Clergy; Exploration, Conquest, and Settlement in North America; Jesuits; Missions, in America; Religion; *and* Roman Catholic Orders in Early America, Female.]

BIBLIOGRAPHY

Bargellini, Clara, and Michael K. Komanecky, eds. *The Arts of the Missions of Northern New Spain, 1600–1821.* Mexico City, Mexico: Antiguo Colegio de San Ildefonso, 2009. The catalog of a breakthrough art exhibition exploring the Franciscan and Jesuit missions of the borderlands between the United States and Mexico; includes seven major background essays.

Iriarte de Aspurz, Lazaro. *Franciscan History: The Three Orders of St. Francis of Assisi.* Translated by Patricia Ross. Chicago: Franciscan Herald Press, 1982. The fullest history of the Franciscan movement available, but heavily concentrated on the First Order.

Monti, Dominic V. *Francis and His Brothers: A Popular History of the Franciscan Friars.* Cincinnati, Ohio: St. Anthony Messenger Press, 2009. A short history that has little on the United States but provides a concise background for understanding the Franciscans.

Schwaller, John F., ed. *Francis in the Americas: Essays on the Franciscan Family in North and South America.* Berkeley, Calif.: Academy of American Franciscan History, 2005. Twelve of twenty essays represent recent scholarship on Franciscans in North America from the colonial era to the 1950s.

Slowick, Margaret A. *The Franciscan Third Order Regular in the United States: Origins, Early Years, and Recent Developments.* Tiffin, Ohio: Sisters of St. Francis of Tiffin, Ohio, 1999. The only

compendium describing the ninety-four Franciscan Third Order Regular congregations in the United States.

Jack Clark Robinson

FRATERNAL ORGANIZATIONS

Fraternal organizations—voluntary associations organized around secret rituals and seeking to create close, familial ties among their members—enjoyed enormous popularity in nineteenth-century America. Freemasonry, the earliest and largest of these organizations, provided the model for many of them. Imported from England about 1730, the Masonic Order grew rapidly after the Revolutionary War but faced a massive, organized Anti-Masonic movement in the 1820s and 1830s. Masonry's temporary decline allowed other fraternal organizations to take root. The popularity of the Odd Fellows, another English import, grew dramatically after the 1830s. Following the Masonic model of using regalia, initiation rituals, and symbolism to encourage fraternal bonding, mutual aid, and universal brotherhood, the Odd Fellows by the end of the century rivaled the earlier society in popularity. Many other national orders, including the Knights of Pythias, the Improved Order of Red Men, and the Benevolent and Protective Order of Elks, also developed in the mid-nineteenth century.

Typically claiming mythic origins and sponsoring convivial eating and drinking, moral training, mutual aid (sometimes including, but almost always going beyond, formal insurance), and networking (both business and political), the fraternal order became a primary form of social organization in the late nineteenth and early twentieth centuries. The form was increasingly used for specific purposes: labor organization, as in the Knights of Labor and the Granger movement; politics, as in the Grand Army of the Republic and the Ku Klux Klan; mutual insurance, as in the Modern Woodmen of the World; college life, as in the Greek-letter fraternities; and ethnic solidarity, as in the B'nai B'rith, the Ancient Order of Hibernians, and many other organizations. The Knights of Columbus, founded in 1882, provided fraternal fellowship for Roman Catholic men. African Americans, excluded by almost universal racial discrimination, formed their own groups, including Prince Hall Freemasonry. The Elks removed their formal whites-only restrictions only after a series of court battles in the 1970s. Women more often belonged to the ladies' auxiliaries of national orders; the Odd Fellows formed one of the first such orders, the Daughters of Rebekah, in 1851. By 1900, probably more than 20 percent of all adult men, though many fewer women, belonged to a fraternal group.

The popularity of these orders declined later in the century, undermined by the welfare state, the decline of single-sex sociability, and the broadened horizons offered by the automobile, radio, and (later) television. In the 1920s a number of popular service organizations such as the Rotary appropriated fraternalism's ability to encourage business contacts and public benevolence but stripped away its elaborate symbolism and rituals. The economic and social upheavals of the Great Depression dealt a more direct blow. Nearly all the orders lost substantial membership during the 1930s—and most never recovered. The size of the Odd Fellowship, for example, dropped by some 3 million members, nearly 90 percent of its total, in the sixty years after 1915. Although Freemasonry gained ground in the 1940s and 1950s, it and other fraternal orders subsequently declined markedly.

[*See also* **B'nai B'rith; Granger Movement; Knights of Columbus; Ku Klux Klan, First; Ku Klux Klan, Second; Labor Movements; Learned Societies; Masonic Order; Sororities and Fraternities, College; Voluntary Associations;** *and* **Women's Club Movement.**]

BIBLIOGRAPHY

Carnes, Mark C. *Secret Ritual and Manhood in Victorian America.* New Haven, Conn.: Yale University Press, 1989.

Clawson, Mary Ann. *Constructing Brotherhood: Class, Gender, and Fraternalism.* Princeton, N.J.: Princeton University Press, 1989.

Steven C. Bullock

FREE COMMUNITIES OF COLOR

Free African Americans shaped the development of the United States from the colonial period through the Civil War. The composition and character of their communities changed meaningfully over time and included significant regional variation. Free African American communities in the North played memorable roles in the founding of the United States, the abolition of slavery, and the pursuit of black citizenship rights. So, too, did their lesser-known counterparts in the southern United States.

Early Roles. In early colonial North America, the line between slavery and freedom was relatively fluid. In the midst of rapid colonial development, control of labor dominated planters' concerns, but little distinction was yet made among European, Native American, and African laborers. With ancestral roots that spanned Europe, Africa, and the Caribbean, blending diverse linguistic and cultural skills, so-called Atlantic Creoles worked as sailors, translators, merchants, and servants from New Netherlands to Virginia. Many escaped bondage and gained a significant foothold in the colonial social hierarchy prior to the development of racial slavery. Thus Anthony Johnson, for example, who was sold to the English in 1621 at Jamestown, later farmed independently, obtained 250 acres of land, held slaves, and thrived as a successful plantation owner in Virginia.

As plantation slavery expanded in the late seventeenth century, however, new ideas about race were codified in law, and free African Americans were increasingly constrained by colonial restrictions that barred them from voting, holding office, and testifying against white colonists. As fear of slave revolts escalated, free African Americans were perceived as a threat to the stability of enslaved labor. Though some free African Americans continued to hold property and travel freely, they were often taxed more heavily and punished more severely than white colonists and slaves were. Legislators systematically limited access to freedom: they denied slaveholders the right to free their slaves (manumission) and denied enslaved people the right to buy their freedom (self-purchase). As a result, for most of the eighteenth century, the free-black population declined and was increasingly limited to the "mulatto" children of indentured women and enslaved men.

The population of free African Americans expanded dramatically, however, in the wake of the American Revolution. The sudden upheaval and egalitarian rhetoric of the revolutionary era stirred many enslaved African Americans to strike out for freedom. Across the northern and southern colonies, some enlisted with British or colonial militia on the uneasy promise of freedom; some were manumitted or purchased their freedom from their masters; many more fled as fugitives during and after the war, exploiting political exigencies to take refuge in growing towns and cities, among indigenous peoples, or in neighboring Spanish and French territories.

Offering relative anonymity and distance from the plantation regime, cities from Boston to Charleston attracted large numbers of free African Americans at the turn of the nineteenth century. At the same time, Maroon communities—organized enclaves of runaway slaves and multiracial "outlaws"—proliferated on the periphery of colonial settlement, especially in the woods, swamps, and bayous of the lower South. Beginning in the 1790s, the Haitian revolution drove thousands of black refugees from the Caribbean to cities throughout the United States. Most important, the abolition of slavery in the North spurred the rapid growth of free-black communities in Boston, Philadelphia, and other northern cities. By 1820, one hundred thousand free African Americans lived in the North, and more than one hundred thousand lived in the upper South—more than 10 percent of the black population of this region. Though the population of free people of color in the lower South was relatively small, it nevertheless nearly tripled between 1790 and 1810.

In the nineteenth century, free African Americans became increasingly central to local and regional economies in both the North and the South, performing a wide variety of artisanal and service work, including barbering, cooking, nursing, laundering, and shoemaking, as well as factory work. At the same time, they faced mounting racial discrimination, especially in the North where their numbers were largest. In cities like Philadelphia, free African Americans celebrated the construction of their own churches, schools, and fraternal societies, even as they faced growing segregation, disenfranchisement, and brutal competition with white immigrant workers for service and factory jobs. In the upper South, although most free African Americans remained relatively poor and without property, a few joined a small but growing leadership class, building local institutions and demanding their rights as citizens with much of the same fervor as their northern counterparts. New forms of cultural expression and entertainment, such as black literary societies and vaudeville, emerged in cities like Baltimore that had burgeoning free-black populations.

Slaves versus Free African Americans.

In the North, many free African Americans protected southern migrants and fugitives in a joint movement for abolition; many prominent northern abolitionists, such as Sojourner Truth and Frederick Douglass, were themselves former slaves. Similarly, in the upper South, many free African Americans maintained close ties with enslaved men and women, with whom they continued to live, form families, work, and worship. By contrast, free people of color in the lower South allied more frequently with the white slaveholding class, often relying on their former owners or other white patrons to obtain a degree of economic and physical security; they were not, however, considered equal, and their political participation was markedly limited. Unlike their counterparts in the North, most free people of color in the lower South did not publicly protest the expansion of slavery; in fact, some became slaveholders themselves. By the early nineteenth century, nearly one-third of free-black families in Charleston owned slaves; though many of these purchased family members to ensure their freedom, others sought economic gain.

As cotton and slavery expanded into the lower Mississippi valley, free people of color took refuge in port cities like Mobile. In the long-established, cosmopolitan port of New Orleans, a small but significant minority of Afro-Creoles created during this period what the historian Caryn Cossé Bell has described as "one of the most assertive, prosperous, well-educated, and cohesive free black societies in nineteenth-century North America" (p. 6). Though some free people of color spoke out boldly on behalf of the enslaved, others cultivated their own elite institutions and manifested their distance from plantation slavery.

The gulf between the free and the enslaved expanded during the antebellum period, as thousands more African Americans secured their freedom, especially in the North, while millions of enslaved men and women were forced deeper into the expanding southern plantation regime. The mere presence of free men and women of color continued to highlight the glaring contradictions of racial slavery; many legislators thus continued to restrict their place in southern society and, as evidenced by the 1850 Fugitive Slave Act, across the growing nation. Following the Civil War, many of these well-established restrictions were hurriedly imposed upon all southern African Americans, affirming the historian Ira Berlin's assertion that "freedom—not slavery—was the taproot of postwar Southern race relations" (*Slaves without Masters,* p. xiv). Indeed, although the history of free people of color may appear to be "the study of exceptions," their experiences powerfully reveal the meaning of slavery and freedom in the United States (*Slaves without Masters,* p. xvii).

[*See also* **African Americans; Antislavery; Caribbean; Emancipation of Slaves; Maroon Societies; Slavery;** *and* **Voluntary Associations,** *subentry on* **African American.**]

BIBLIOGRAPHY

Bell, Caryn Cossé. *Revolution, Romanticism, and the Afro-Creole Protest Tradition in Louisiana, 1718–1868.* Baton Rouge: Louisiana State University Press, 1997.

Berlin, Ira. *Generations of Captivity: A History of African-American Slaves.* Cambridge, Mass.: Belknap Press of Harvard University Press, 2003.

Berlin, Ira. *Slaves without Masters: The Free Negro in the Antebellum South.* New York: Pantheon, 1974.

Franklin, John Hope. *The Free Negro in North Carolina, 1790–1860.* Chapel Hill: University of North Carolina Press, 1943.

Horton, James Oliver. *Free People of Color: Inside the African American Community.* Washington, D.C.: Smithsonian Institution Press, 1993.

Johnson, Michael P., and James L. Roark. *Black Masters: A Free Family of Color in the Old South.* New York: W. W. Norton and Company, 1984.

Landers, Jane G. *Atlantic Creoles in the Age of Revolutions.* Cambridge, Mass.: Harvard University Press, 2010.

Kendra Taira Field

FREEDMEN'S BUREAU

To assist the adjustment of newly freed slaves in the post–Civil War South, Congress in March 1865 established the Bureau of Refugees, Freedmen, and Abandoned Lands under the leadership of General Oliver Otis Howard and the auspices of the War Department. Given an initial life of one year, the agency provided food, clothing, fuel, and medical treatment to destitute and dislocated freedpeople and white refugees. It was also supposed to parcel out abandoned and confiscated lands in forty-acre plots to freedmen, but President Andrew Johnson, a staunch critic of the agency, undercut this effort by restoring most of the available land to its former white owners. Local agents of the

bureau thus spent much time mediating labor contracts and disputes between the freedmen and intransigent white employers and attempting to secure economic and civil justice for the freedmen—even as they slipped into a debilitating sharecropping system.

More positive was the bureau's work with northern philanthropic groups to establish some three thousand freedpeople's schools by 1869. In July 1866, over Johnson's veto, Congress renewed the bureau for two years, and personnel reached a high of nine hundred, but as the former Confederate states rejoined the Union, Congress limited the agency's work to education and bounty payments to African American soldiers. Sharply reduced in personnel by 1869, the Freedmen's Bureau ceased operations in June 1872. Overall the bureau provided invaluable relief and educational aid for the 3.9 million former slaves, but its initial promise was limited by inadequate funding and manpower, excessively paternalistic leadership, and deeply embedded racial antagonisms.

[*See also* **African Americans; Education; Emancipation of Slaves;** *and* **Reconstruction Era.**]

BIBLIOGRAPHY

Bentley, George R. *A History of the Freedmen's Bureau.* Philadelphia: University of Pennsylvania Press, 1955.

McFeely, William S. *Yankee Stepfather: General O. O. Howard and the Freedmen.* New Haven, Conn.: Yale University Press, 1968.

Terry L. Seip

FREE-SOILERS

Free-Soilers opposed the extension of slavery into the American West on the argument that the perpetuation of the American republic rested on the morally and economically superior system of individuals controlling their own destiny by the free use of their own labor. The political slogan "Free Soil, Free Speech, Free Labor, and Free Men" stemmed from a greater social movement, as a rising generation of Americans steeped in the evangelical fervor of the Second Great Awakening came to espouse moral objections to the institution of slavery.

Evangelical Protestants made up the majority of the northern antislavery vanguard. They fused the evangelical piety that captivated so many Americans in the early republic with opposition to slavery—all in a concerted effort to stem the growth of slavery, halt its extension to America's territorial acquisitions, and assert northern social and political power against the South. Critical divisions emerged, however, between radical abolitionists who demanded the immediate abolition of slavery and advocated for some semblance of racial equality and moderate antislavery proponents who sought the gradual demise of the peculiar institution but did not support equal rights for African Americans. Nonetheless, radicals and moderates alike increasingly viewed the free North as a section distinct from the slave South, believing that southern leaders composed a cabal—the so-called Slave Power—dedicated to the extension and perpetuation of slavery. The persistence of slavery in the South and its abolition in the North caused social divisions between northerners and southerners.

By the early 1840s, however, the abolition movement found itself hopelessly divided between immediate and gradual abolitionists, between the advocates and the opponents of racial equality. The Free-Soil movement emerged as an alternative to radical abolitionism. Whereas abolitionists sought to end slavery throughout the Union, Free-Soilers focused on halting the extension of slavery to the western territories. Citizens of the United States had long seen westward expansion as a uniquely American panacea for the problems of a rapidly expanding populace, but the extension of slavery to the West threatened the ability of poorer white men to seek upward social and economic mobility on new land. In sum, free-soil activists came to believe that slavery—and the right of one man to own another's labor—threatened the virtues of the Jeffersonian agrarian republic. The presence of slaves and free blacks laboring in field and factory meant lost opportunities for free white men seeking work.

The Free-Soil outlook on preserving and expanding socioeconomic opportunities for white men called not only for preventing the extension of slavery and keeping slaves out of the West, but also for preventing free blacks from moving to the territories. Free-Soilers saw slaves and free blacks alike as unwanted competition for the free white laborer. This racist dimension—by present-day standards—of the Free-Soil movement has attracted the attention of scholars who contrast it with the more radical pronouncements of militant abolitionists who called for racial equality. Indeed, the Free-Soil platform best represented the views of antislavery northerners who opposed slavery but could not countenance the idea of racial equality.

The Free-Soil movement burgeoned with the debates in the 1840s and 1850s over territorial expansion. The nation's assumption of the Mexican Cession in 1848, which Free-Soilers viewed as a southern plot to expand the slave domain, led to renewed calls for halting the extension of slavery. The Kansas-Nebraska Act of 1854, however, marks the high point of Free-Soilism, the point when the social movement fused with political action that transformed the republic.

The infamous law potentially opened to slavery a territory that had been declared free soil in the Missouri Compromise. The uproar over popular sovereignty reignited the Free-Soil movement and gave renewed voice to its demands for free territory where white Americans could immigrate and control their own destiny, free from competition with slavery and the presence of the free black.

Though the abolitionist movement may have had greater social significance for the American conflict over slavery, the Free-Soil movement and its socioeconomic premises ultimately translated more effectively into political action. Free-Soilers successfully extended their social beliefs to a platform that northerners ultimately came to embrace. Political parties—namely the Republicans—had impressive successes, albeit with disastrous consequences for the Union. Passage of the Homestead Act of 1862 serves as a fitting coda to the Free-Soil movement; in securing free land for Americans, President Abraham Lincoln and the Republican Congress embraced the Free-Soilers' call for socioeconomic opportunity in the West.

[*See also* **Antebellum Era; Bleeding Kansas; Civil War Era; Great Awakenings; Internal Migration,** *subentry on* **Nineteenth-Century Westward; Middle West, The; Racism;** *and* **Slaveholders.**]

BIBLIOGRAPHY

Filler, Louis. *The Crusade against Slavery, 1830–1860.* New York: Harper, 1960.

Foner, Eric. *Free Soil, Free Labor, Free Men: The Ideology of the Republican Party before the Civil War.* 2d ed. New York: Oxford University Press, 1995.

Walters, Ronald G. *The Antislavery Appeal: American Abolitionism after 1830.* Baltimore: Johns Hopkins University Press, 1976.

Christopher Childers

FRIEDAN, BETTY

(1921–2006), a leader in the modern American feminist movement and the author of the influential book *The Feminine Mystique.* Born Bettye (later Betty) Goldstein in Peoria, Illinois, on 4 February 1921, Friedan attended Smith College, where she wrote for and edited the college newspaper, studied psychology, and developed a passionate commitment to left-wing and progressive politics. After graduating summa cum laude in 1942, she enrolled as a PhD student in the psychology department at the University of California at Berkeley.

After a year, Friedan left graduate school, moved to New York, and began working as a labor journalist. She worked for the Federated Press, a left-wing news service, between 1943 and 1946 and for the *UE News,* the paper of the United Electrical, Radio & Machine Workers union, between 1943 and 1952. She reported on strikes, union politics, international affairs, racial discrimination, and the role of women in the workforce and the world. While at the *UE News,* she also witnessed the damage dealt by McCarthyism to social movements, particularly liberal and leftist feminism.

In 1947 she married Carl Friedan, with whom she had three children. Betty Friedan continued to work for the *UE News* after her first child was born in 1948, but she was fired during her second pregnancy in 1952. For the next decade, Friedan participated in community activism, wrote freelance magazine articles, underwent psychoanalysis, raised her children, and conducted research for *The Feminine Mystique.* She and Carl divorced in 1969.

The Feminine Mystique was published in 1963. In it, Friedan skillfully weaves a resonant cultural critique, drawing on her readings of history, psychology, sociology, contemporary journalism, education, and popular culture. *The Feminine Mystique* presents a scathing indictment of full-time domesticity and the culture that promotes it. Friedan argues that marriage and motherhood alone offer a poor substitute for fulfilling, meaningful work. The absence of a larger sense of purpose, she contends, leads to feelings of emptiness, boredom, and despair among housewives. Friedan excoriates neo-Freudian psychology, women's magazines, advertisers, and "sex-directed" educators, all of whom, she argues, present full-time homemaking as the only normal goal for women. She calls for women to pursue intellectually rigorous work, insisting that this will make them better wives, mothers, and citizens.

Friedan carefully tailored the book to avoid the anti-Communist attacks that had undone Popular Front feminism in the 1940s and 1950s. Issues of class and race are almost entirely absent from *The Feminine Mystique*. She presents herself as a typical housewife who questioned the ideology of domesticity only when she saw her own discontent mirrored in the responses of her Smith classmates to a survey she conducted.

The Feminine Mystique sold millions of copies in its first few years and turned Friedan into a household name. In 1966, at a meeting of the state Commissions on the Status of Women, Friedan and a small number of like-minded women founded the National Organization for Women. Elected its first president, Friedan served until 1970, cementing her role as a leader in the bourgeoning feminist movement. In the early 1970s Friedan became controversial even within feminist circles. She attacked as dangerous the growing visibility of lesbians within the movement, and to radicals she seemed the embodiment of the limitations of white, liberal feminism. By the mid-1970s Friedan was no longer at the center of the feminism, but she remained one of its most prominent symbols for the rest of her life. She died on 4 February 2006.

[*See also* **Antiabortion Movement; Family; Gender; Marriage and Divorce; Separate Spheres Ideology; Sexual Reform and Morality; Sixties, The;** *and* **Women Workers.**]

BIBLIOGRAPHY

Coontz, Stephanie. *A Strange Stirring: The Feminine Mystique and American Women at the Dawn of the 1960s.* New York: Basic Books, 2011.

Horowitz, Daniel. *Betty Friedan and the Making of "The Feminine Mystique": The American Left, the Cold War, and Modern Feminism.* Amherst: University of Massachusetts Press, 1998.

Elizabeth Singer More

FRONTIER, THE

The word "frontier" has multiple meanings and connotations. In Europe the term has long denoted a boundary dividing two countries. In the United States the term "frontier" had, by 1900, come to signify the boundary between the settled and the unsettled part of the nation, and the idea of the frontier was central to the belief that America's history was exceptional. Frederick Jackson Turner legitimized this use of the word in American academic thought in his 1893 paper "The Significance of the Frontier in American History," delivered to the American Historical Association in Chicago. This paper, which arguably became the most significant ever written about American history, defined the frontier as an area of free land whose "continuous recession," along with "the advance of American settlement westward," explained the development of social, political, and economic life in the United States of America.

Turner's frontier thesis dominated American historiography for much of the twentieth century. Beginning in the 1980s, social historians argued against it as Eurocentric and misogynist because it omitted women entirely and treated Native Americans only as barriers to settlement. These historians—who make up what is called the "new western history" movement—argued that the West was a place, not a process, and applied the methods and philosophies of social history to its investigation. Around the turn of the twenty-first century, historians returned their attention to the global and local processes that shaped the conquest of the American continent, and they argued convincingly that new western history's initial rejection of the idea of a frontier limited its ability fully to contextualize American expansion. Many now define frontiers as zones of cultural interaction and boundary crossing whose internal dynamics influence and are influenced by global processes such as capitalism and imperialism. Social history is central to these inquiries.

Frontiers in Colonial America. Both Spanish and French colonization severely disrupted native communities, yet the need for native labor resulted in the development of frontiers of inclusion, places where Indians, Europeans, and Africans intermingled. Scholarship on these frontiers of 1600–1700 demonstrates how cross-cultural connection triggered a domino effect that could shape the course of continental history. Examples include the Métis—mixed-blood people who developed their own dialects from French and Native American languages—who moved in the 1670s from French-Canadian settlements along the Saint Lawrence into modern-day Minnesota and spurred the expansion of the French empire

into the Spanish Mississippi River valley. The inclusive nature of social life in French and Spanish America includes many such examples of cross-cultural contact reshaping relations among empires.

Life on the British frontier was more exclusive—and rife with conflicts. With high birthrates and with indentured servants widely available, the British colonists had little use for Indians' labor and so pushed them to the periphery of colonial society rather than incorporating them within it. From their first attempt at Roanoke (1585), the British aimed to settle and create European-style societies. As British populations grew in the first two centuries through immigration (mostly German and Scotch-Irish) and natural increase, colonists clamored for more lands and moved ever westward. With each new settlement, they further infuriated Indian people who saw each move as a provocation to war. War did indeed erupt between Britons and Indians, most notably Virginia's Bacon's Rebellion (1676) and New England's King Philip's War (1675–1676).

The mid-Atlantic colonies of the late 1600s initially told a less violent story of Indian-European contact. William Penn insisted on limiting settlement until fair treaty agreements had been reached in his colony of Pennsylvania, and throughout this region cultural interaction and accommodation created a unique backcountry culture that combined elements from European and Indian societies. In the middle of the eighteenth century, though, the relations between Indians and whites began to shift toward a more exclusive model in these frontier areas, with native peoples losing more land and leverage with each so-called pen-and-ink fraud the British colonists committed.

The loss of territory resulting from these breaches of trust contributed to the decline of the playoff system whereby Indians and

Europeans triangulated their alliances in order to gain advantages over their rivals. This practice had long been central to North American Indians' strategy for maintaining autonomy from the European powers. The French and Indian War (also known as the Seven Years' War, 1754–1763), the American Revolution, and the War of 1812 gradually eliminated this strategy from the frontiers of North America, forever changing the dynamics of interaction between Europeans and Indians.

The United States and the Frontier. When the thirteen colonies achieved their independence, they inherited 230 million acres of land partially settled by Euro-Americans but outside the boundaries of the states. This was a massive frontier inhabited by a diverse group of Indians and a new nation, each believing their claim more legitimate. The American government forced the major tribes into new treaties ceding large parts of their homelands. Even Indians who fought alongside the Americans against the British, like the Passamaquoddy Indians of New England, were forced to make large land concessions. This practically guaranteed the continuation of bloody warfare in areas where Americans continued to push their way onto Indian homelands. Squatters were encouraged by the federal government's efforts to explore and survey newly acquired territories, most famously by the expeditions of Meriwether Lewis and William Clark (1804–1806) and Zebulon Pike (1806–1807) and by the Corps of Topographical Engineers. Thousands of individual settlers sought better land, climate, or economic future in the West during the nineteenth century, and by midcentury their movement resulted in the incorporation of the Old Northwest, the Mississippi valley, Texas, the Oregon Country, and California. After the Civil War, another round of settlers set their sights on the Great Plains and the Southwest.

Andrew Jackson's Indian Removal Act (1830), which led to the Cherokee Trail of Tears, provides an example of the government's enabling settlers to take over Indian land. The Cherokees' attempts at assimilation through a constitution, written language, and participation in the capitalist slave economy did little to protect them from being targeted by this law, which empowered the president to move all eastern Indians west of the Mississippi. Despite Supreme Court decisions in *Cherokee Nation v. Georgia* (1831) and *Worcester v. Georgia* (1832) that affirmed the integrity of the Cherokee nation, Jackson refused to use federal power to stop Georgians from illegally occupying Cherokee territory. He ordered the Cherokee removed. Most refused. In the spring of 1838, troops rounded up the remaining Cherokees and brutally marched them over a thousand miles to their new territory along the Arkansas River. Subsequently the federal government moved the other so-called civilized tribes— Creeks, Choctaws, Chickasaws, and Seminoles—west. Removal was not only a story of a federal policy, but also a story both of the grassroots movements of Euro-American squatters on Cherokee land and of native resistance.

At midcentury, Manifest Destiny ideologues who believed that Anglo-Saxon Americans were destined to expand across the North American continent converged with American interests in the northern provinces of Mexico, and war was declared on 13 May 1846. The causes and outcomes of the war were deeply affected by conflict and raids among powerful mounted Indian tribes of northern Mexico, yet the United States was victorious. In the February 1848 treaty of Guadalupe Hidalgo, Mexico surrendered what became the entire southwestern United States. Many Americans resisted incorporating this territory and its inhabitants, whom they considered a mongrel race. Thus the war resulted in the incorporation of a massive frontier zone into the United States.

Almost simultaneously, on 24 January 1848, gold was discovered at Sutter's Mill in California. The resulting gold rush created a new and extremely diverse international frontier where American social norms were challenged. Indians and Mexican Americans, who had lived in California longer than any of the miners, lost out in the state constitution of 1850. Indian peoples of California were overrun, and California courts failed to uphold Mexican land titles, as they were legally required to do. By 1850 the United States contained a vast and diverse frontier stretching to the Pacific Ocean. The expansion of transit (most notably the transcontinental railroad completed in 1869), economy, and communication (like the 1861 telegraph joining Kansas City to Sacramento) helped unify the continental nation, but national identity required more than technology, and communities throughout this zone remained fractured and divided.

Indian policy had been focused on reservations since the 1850s. In 1887 the government changed tactics to allotment—formalized in the Dawes Severalty Act of that year—and broke up reservation land to distribute to individuals; excess land was sold to private buyers. Indians across the West responded with an explosion of spiritual energy. Most noteworthy was the Ghost Dance movement led by the Paiute Wovoka. In 1889 the Sioux on Pine Ridge reservation began to practice the dance widely. Alarmed whites called for the army's protection. The Seventh Cavalry—famously defeated at the Battle of Little Bighorn in 1876—caught up to Ghost Dancers on Wounded Knee Creek and opened fire, killing 146 Sioux, including

44 women and 18 children. The massacre is widely accepted as the end of the Plains Indian wars that had raged since the 1860s. With armed resistance at an end and the vast majority of the continent formally ceded to whites, by 1890 the era of physical struggle over land with Native Americans had drawn to a close.

But does it follow that the frontier was now closed? Many scholars say no. Some point to the frontier-like quality of life in the West's many cities. Others, like the Chicana feminist scholar Gloria Anzaldúa, define a frontier as a place not only of conflict, but also of intimate contact. She argues that wherever two or more cultures or classes come into contact, they constitute "borderland cultures" from which the syncretic, multilayered, and infinitely complex social fabric of the United States continues to emerge.

[*See also* **Antebellum Era; Borderlands; Exploration, Conquest, and Settlement in North America; Gold Rushes; Internal Migration,** *subentries on* **Colonial Era** *and* **Nineteenth-Century Westward; Lewis and Clark Expedition; Multiracial and Multiethnic Americans; Native American History and Culture; Native American Removal** *and* **Wounded Knee Tragedy.**]

BIBLIOGRAPHY

Anzaldúa, Gloria. *Borderlands: The New Mestiza = La Frontera.* 3d ed. San Francisco: Aunt Lute Books, 2007. This interdisciplinary volume lays the foundations of borderlands studies.

Brooks, James. *Captives and Cousins: Slavery, Kinship, and Community in the Southwest Borderlands.* Chapel Hill: University of North Carolina Press for the Omohundro Institute of Early American History and Culture, Williamsburg, Va., 2002.

Demonstrates the complexities of the Spanish inclusive frontier.

DeLay, Brian. *War of a Thousand Deserts: Indian Raids and the U.S.-Mexican War*. New Haven, Conn.: Yale University Press, 2008. A groundbreaking work on the centrality of Indian raids to the Mexican War.

Hine, Robert V., and John Mack Faragher. *The American West: A New Interpretive History*. New Haven, Conn.: Yale University Press, 2000. The best synthesis of the American West, concentrating on the frontier as a zone of cross-cultural contact.

Johnson, Susan Lee. *Roaring Camp: The Social World of the California Gold Rush*. New York: W. W. Norton and Company, 2000. The best work on social life in the gold camps.

Klein, Kerwin Lee. "Reclaiming the 'F' Word, or Being and Becoming Postwestern." *Pacific Historical Review* 65, no. 2 (May 1996): 179–215. This seminal article provides a detailed genealogy of scholarship on the frontier. See also: Klein's *Frontiers of Historical Imagination: Narrating the European Conquest of Native America, 1890–1990* (Berkeley: University of California Press, 1997) for an expansion of the argument.

Spear, Jennifer M. "Colonial Intimacies: Legislating Sex in French Louisiana." *William and Mary Quarterly*, 3d ser., 60, no. 1 (January 2003): 75–98. A useful and well-researched article on metropolitan attempts to regulate the intimate lives of frontier dwellers to meet imperial goals.

Usner, Daniel H., Jr. *Indians, Settlers, and Slaves in a Frontier Exchange Economy: The Lower Mississippi Valley before 1783*. Chapel Hill: North Carolina Press for Institute of Early American History and Culture, Williamsburg, Va., 1992. An informative treatment of the local construction of frontier economies.

MacKenzie K. L. Moore

G

GALVESTON HURRICANE AND FLOOD

The Galveston hurricane and flood was by far the deadliest natural disaster in United States history. On Saturday, 8 September 1900, a powerful hurricane battered Galveston, Texas, and the surrounding countryside with winds of 120 miles per hour and a storm surge (a wall of water, similar to a tidal wave) that briefly submerged the entire city. This inundation caused most of the estimated six thousand deaths in Galveston, a city of thirty-seven thousand on Galveston Island, a barrier island in the Gulf of Mexico. The hurricane took another four to six thousand lives in the surrounding rural areas of the island and on the Texas mainland.

After the storm, Galveston's business and professional elites coalesced to undertake three major projects to restore confidence in the city's safety and viability. First, capitalizing on general postdisaster civic-mindedness and emergency-induced cooperation from the city's strong maritime labor unions, they created a new city charter that gave Galveston the nation's first commission system of municipal government. In subsequent years the commission system, along with the city-manager system, spread to hundreds of medium-size cities, becoming a major part of Progressive Era urban reform. To mitigate the city's vulnerability to future hurricanes, the new city government also undertook two ambitious engineering projects, building a massive, seventeen-foot-high seawall to protect Galveston's southern gulf front from storm surges and, using sand and silt dredged from Galveston Bay, raising by several feet many of the city's low-lying sections. Galveston was rebuilt but never again approached the prominence it had enjoyed in the Texas economy of the nineteenth century. Nevertheless, all three projects won national praise and soon became symbols of the country's Progressive Era romance with efficiency, bureaucracy, technology, and engineering.

[*See also* **Houston; Hurricane Katrina; Johnstown Flood;** *and* **Progressive Era.**]

BIBLIOGRAPHY

Erikson, Kai. *A New Species of Trouble: Explorations in Disaster, Trauma, and Community.* New York: W. W. Norton and Company, 1994.

Rice, Bradley Robert. *Progressive Cities: The Commission Government Movement in America, 1901– 1920.* Austin: University of Texas Press, 1977.

Stephen Kretzmann

GAMBLING

The lure of gambling has existed since the founding of Jamestown. Throughout American history, gambling has provided a popular form of leisure activity for members of all social classes, as well as a convenient means of raising funds for churches and governments. Questions of its moral worth sparked conflicts between professional gambling interests and their opponents. Consequently, a profound ambivalence about the social utility of gambling has pervaded the public discourse.

Gambling in colonial America was most prominent in the Tidewater region, where slave owners engaged in quarter-horse racing and high-stakes card and dice games. In all colonies, games of chance routinely occurred in local taverns, and local governments and churches operated lotteries to finance major projects. By the early nineteenth century the first oval tracks had opened, and the sport had extended into the new West, where leading citizens such as Andrew Jackson owned thoroughbred horses and wagered enthusiastically on the outcome of races.

A thriving gambling culture developed on the frontier after the War of 1812, especially in the lower Mississippi valley, where cardsharps practiced their profession on riverboats and in riverfront saloons, most noticeably in Natchez and Vicksburg in Mississippi and in New Orleans. The quintessential American game of poker originated in this environment. By rewarding skill and calculated risk taking, poker displaced such popular European games as faro and three-card monte. Gambling flourished on the mining frontiers of California, Nevada, and Colorado, where mining stocks provided a speculative atmosphere that encouraged gambling. The boom city of San Francisco during the 1850s was awash in gambling clubs.

By the eve of the Civil War, professional gambling operations existed in major cities, offering both posh casinos for affluent men and shabby gambling dens with low-end games for immigrant workers. Professional gamblers and their syndicates, protected by local political machines, thrived in growing urban markets. Syndicates derived a steady stream of profits by offering a form of lottery called "policy," in which bettors selected three random numbers in hopes of hitting a big payday against high odds. By the 1920s, numbers rackets became pronounced in African American neighborhoods. Syndicates also promoted lucrative offtrack wagering on horse races, along with betting pools on professional baseball. Syndicate gambling took on a structured business model that emulated those of legitimate companies.

Antigambling Reform and Regulation.

These developments naturally produced a backlash in the form of a strong antigambling reform movement. Reformers, often tied to middle-class Protestant churches, repeatedly clashed with machine politicians and gambling interests. Although they won temporary victories, through the twentieth century they steadily lost ground to the rising power of organized gambling. The antigambling movement crested during the Progressive Era of the early twentieth century: many states, including New York, abolished betting on horse races, and the number of operating racetracks in the United States declined to just twenty-five in 1910. In response to political pressure, local law enforcement waged a highly publicized crusade against gambling syndicates. The pervasive influence of gambling, however, was driven home to the American people when it was revealed that eight members of the Chicago White Sox baseball team had conspired with gamblers to throw the 1919 World Series.

In the 1920s, with the Progressive reform impulse waning, state political leaders discovered that the new pari-mutuel betting system could provide substantial revenue for state governments. Several states, including Illinois, California, and New York, authorized the opening of racetracks. Illegal offtrack betting parlors became popular in large cities, receiving up-to-the-minute racing results via telegraph wire services. Gambling syndicates also expanded the realm of sports betting in the form of parlay cards offering action on college and professional football.

The devastating impact of the Great Depression of the 1930s contributed to the spread of gambling. Although such games of chance were illegal in most states, churches and local organizations such as the American Legion or the Elks Club raised funds with weekly bingo games. The most dramatic change in public policy occurred in the state of Nevada, where gambling had become deeply imbedded during a succession of mining booms. In 1931 the state legislature voted to legalize full-scale casino gambling. Small casinos in Las Vegas and Reno were opened, and a building boom produced luxurious hotel-casinos in the decades following the war. Between 1945 and 1980, Nevada enjoyed a near monopoly on legalized gambling. Following World War II, organized-crime leaders insinuated themselves into control of most Nevada casino operations, and the iconic Las Vegas Strip became a national curiosity and tourist destination. Las Vegas was transformed from a dusty railroad town of 8,000 in 1940 to a booming metropolis of 2 million in 2010.

Las Vegas thrived despite a renewed antigambling campaign spearheaded by Senator Estes Kefauver of Tennessee, who conducted a series of televised hearings into the criminal enterprises of the Mafia in 1950–1951. His sensational hearings produced the first federal antigambling laws that sought to cripple organized crime by squashing money laundering, interstate gambling operations, sports wagering, and ultimately Nevada's casinos. Kefauver focused much of the attention he paid to interstate gambling operations on illegal horse parlors and their wire services, but his committee overlooked a dramatic change in sports betting: the introduction of the point-spread system by urban sports bookies during the 1940s had stimulated a surge in betting on college and professional basketball and football. In the wake of the Kefauver hearings, the state of Nevada strengthened regulation of its primary industry, and during the 1970s legitimate corporations gained control of Nevada's casinos.

Gaming. The spectacular growth of Nevada's so-called gaming industry sparked other states to get in on the action. In 1963, New Hampshire established a state lottery, and within twenty years, thirty-seven state governments and the District of Columbia sponsored lotteries, thereby undercutting moral arguments against gambling. In 1976, New Jersey voters approved casino gambling for Atlantic City, and within a decade fourteen other states had licensed casinos. In 1988, after a series of federal court decisions had greatly expanded the sovereignty of Native American tribes in a way that permitted them to sponsor gambling, President Ronald Reagan signed into law the Indian Gaming Regulatory Act that provided rules for the further development of Indian gambling. By 2000, more than two hundred tribes permitted gaming on their lands, and the Foxwoods Resort Casino in Connecticut had become one of the largest in the world. During the 1990s, popular Internet gambling sites began appearing on the World Wide Web, featuring sports betting and simulated casino games that created major challenges for the American gaming industry and its regulators. By 2010, only the states of Utah and Hawai'i did not offer some form of legalized gambling.

The rapid spread of gambling across American society prompted social conservatives to seek to slow the trend. In response, Congress established the National Gambling Impact Study Commission in 1996, but any hope that a rollback would occur was scuttled by strong resistance from city and state officials who had come to depend upon gaming taxes and feared the loss of casino jobs. The best that the commission could do was warn about compulsive gambling. By 2010, total legal gambling in the United States generated an estimated $100 billion in revenues, and 60 percent of the American people gambled in a legal venue at least once a year.

Gambling had become part of everyday American life.

[*See also* **Las Vegas; Leisure; Native American History and Culture,** *subentry on* **Since 1950; Organized Crime;** *and* **Taverns and Bars.**]

BIBLIOGRAPHY

Chafetz, Henry. *Play the Devil: A History of Gambling in the United States from 1492 to 1955.* New York: C. N. Potter, 1960.

Davies, Richard O., and Richard G. Abram. *Betting the Line: Sports Wagering in American Life.* Columbus: Ohio State University Press, 2001.

Fabian, Ann. *Card Sharps, Dream Books, and Bucket Shops: Gambling in 19th-Century America.* Ithaca, N.Y.: Cornell University Press, 1990.

Findlay, John. *People of Chance: Gambling in American Society from Jamestown to Las Vegas.* New York: Oxford University Press, 1986.

Haller, Mark H. "The Changing Structure of American Gambling in the Twentieth Century." *Journal of Social Issues* 35, no. 3 (1979): 87–114.

Schwartz, David G. *Roll the Bones: The History of Gambling.* New York: Gotham Books, 2006.

Richard O. Davies

GARRISON, WILLIAM LLOYD

(1805–1879), abolitionist, advocate of women's suffrage, and pacifist. William Lloyd Garrison was a principal early leader in the movement to end American slavery.

Born the younger son of an alcoholic sailor and an itinerant domestic servant in Newburyport, Massachusetts, on 12 December 1805, Garrison clawed his way out of poverty through a potent combination of ambition and moral perfectionism. He apprenticed himself to a printer at fourteen and took jobs at several northeastern newspapers before landing at Benjamin Lundy's *Genius of Universal Emancipation* in Baltimore. The religious revivals of the 1820s deeply influenced Garrison's early abolitionist thought; under Lundy he became an immediatist, demanding instant and total emancipation. Garrison's jailing in 1830—he failed to pay a fine for libeling a slave trader in Lundy's paper—further inflamed his radicalism. After the abolitionist philanthropists Arthur and Lewis Tappan bailed him out, they helped him start his own newspaper, the *Liberator*, whose first issue appeared on 1 January 1831.

Both as the *Liberator*'s editor and as a founding leader of the American Anti-Slavery Society (AASS), Garrison directed the ideological and intellectual currents of U.S. abolitionism through the 1830s, creating alliances with British abolitionists and focusing on his passions: immediate abolition through moral suasion, moral perfectionism, racial equality, pacifism, anticlericalism, disunionism, and women's rights and equality. He appealed directly to the American people's religious conscience, scorning as hypocrites all Christians who supported anything less than immediatism and denouncing both electoral politics and most organized religion as bearing slavery's indelible stain.

Garrison's zealotry attracted violence and political repression. A Boston mob nearly lynched him in 1835, and Congress suppressed House debate over AASS-organized antislavery petitions with a gag rule from 1836 to 1844. Such hostility, however, transformed into publicity and sympathy for abolitionism. The gag rule particularly backfired, confirming abolitionists' warnings of the so-called Slave Power in Congress amid debates over slavery's western expansion.

Garrison's uncompromising moral vision, exemplified by his 1844 assertion that the Constitution was "a covenant with death, and an agreement with hell," exacerbated the nation's divisions and helped move slavery decisively to the center of national politics. It also, however, marginalized him within the abolitionist movement. Longtime allies viewed Garrison's disunionism and disavowal of politics as increasingly impractical. Many also rejected his endorsement of women's equality. Dissenters on women's rights split from the AASS in 1840 to found the American and Foreign Anti-Slavery Society. Others, Frederick Douglass among them, broke with Garrison to pursue political strategies through the Liberty and Free-Soil Parties. Although Garrison remained a lightning rod in slavery debates, his direct influence waned in the 1840s and 1850s.

When the Civil War came, Garrison finally relinquished his pacifism, supporting both Abraham Lincoln and the Union. His pragmatism, however, was short-lived. Splitting again from antislavery contemporaries who continued to struggle for black suffrage and equal rights long after the war, Garrison declared his mission accomplished with the adoption of the Thirteenth Amendment in 1865 and resigned from the AASS. He spent his final years with family and died in 1879.

[*See also* **Antebellum Era; Antislavery; Civil War Era; Emancipation of Slaves; Free-Soilers; Slavery,** *subentry on* **Nineteenth Century;** *and* **Women's Rights Movement, Antebellum Era.**]

BIBLIOGRAPHY

Blight, David W. *Frederick Douglass' Civil War: Keeping Faith in Jubilee.* Baton Rouge: Louisiana State University Press, 1989.

Mayer, Henry. *All on Fire: William Lloyd Garrison and the Abolition of Slavery.* New York: St. Martins, 1998.

Stewart, James Brewer, ed. *William Lloyd Garrison at Two Hundred: History, Legacy, and Memory.* New Haven, Conn.: Yale University Press, 2008.

David N. Huyssen

GAY AND LESBIAN COMMUNITIES

In the United States, gay and lesbian communities have existed in two senses: as imagined communities of people who think of themselves as members of a distinct social group and as geographically situated communities in which people associate and congregate. In both senses, communities based on same-sex sex, love, and intimacy first formed in the nineteenth century. They developed in scale and complexity and changed in scope and character in the first half of the twentieth century. In the second half of the twentieth century, gay and lesbian communities inspired political movements that campaigned for sexual freedom and equality.

Early Developments. Before the United States was established in the late eighteenth century, Native Americans, European Americans, African Americans, Asian Americans, and Native Hawaiians and Pacific Islanders experienced same-sex sex, love, and intimacy in the territories later claimed by the United States. They did not, however, think of Americans who engaged in same-sex sex as members of either an imagined or a geographic community. Same-sex sex was understood in behavioral terms—as an act that anyone might commit rather than as an orientation or preference of a distinct social group. Euro-American authorities generally condemned same-sex sex as sinful and criminal in the context of their more general opposition to nonmarital sex. Many ordinary people similarly expressed hostility toward same-sex sex, but there is evidence of tolerance and acceptance in some ethnic, linguistic, national, racial, and religious communities.

In the eighteenth century, knowledge about communities of people who engaged in same-sex sex in European cities such as London, Paris, and Amsterdam circulated in the Atlantic world. Philadelphians, for example, learned about European "sodomites" and "mollies" as they traveled across the Atlantic, imported books published in Europe, and read newspaper accounts of people arrested for engaging in same-sex sex. These accounts often focused on feminine men attracted to masculine men or older men attracted to male youth, so their presumptions do not correspond precisely to the more inclusive conceptions of homosexuality that developed later. Nevertheless, the accounts signal an emergent conception of a community defined in part by interest in same-sex sex, though such communities do not appear to have existed in American cities.

The first accounts that hint at the possible existence of such communities in the United States appeared in the mid-nineteenth century, when New Yorkers began to refer to the "sodomites" in their midst. Discussing recent media attacks on European immigrants bent on seducing young American men, one newspaper declared in the 1840s: "Already do the beastly Sodomites of Gotham quake. They feel their brute souls quiver with fear" (*The Whip*, 5 February 1842, p. 2). The sodomites—depicted as biologically male though sometimes characterized as feminine—were described in terms suggesting that they were a group of like-minded individuals with similar sexual proclivities and shared urban territories.

From the 1870s through the 1930s. By the 1870s, 1880s, and 1890s, there were significant communities of U.S. men and women who viewed their same-sex desires, loves, and intimacies as important aspects of their lives. These communities were commonly believed to be geographically situated in large cities such as Boston, Chicago, New York City, Philadelphia, San Francisco, and Washington, D.C., but they were also imagined and experienced in ways that extended beyond major population centers. Large-scale urbanization, immigration, and industrialization contributed to the emergence of these communities, in part because they created more possibilities for individuals to live beyond the constraints of traditional family economies and gender roles. As these communities were noticed by a variety of social observers—and especially by scientific experts, sensational journalists, antivice reformers, and legal professionals—they were publicized in ways that contributed to their growth, development, and transformation. This, in turn, led to increased policing by hostile social, cultural, and political authorities, who continued to view homosexuality as immoral, unnatural, and undesirable.

Men and women interested in same-sex sex, love, and intimacy congregated in specific geographic locations both inside and outside U.S. cities. Popular residential neighborhoods, often featuring housing options that appealed to independent individuals and same-sex pairs, included the Near North Side and South Side in Chicago; the Bowery, Greenwich Village, Harlem, and Times Square in New York; and the Barbary Coast, Tenderloin, and North Beach in San Francisco. Specific bars, bathhouses, cafés, clubs, parks, restaurants, theaters, and toilets developed reputations for attracting people interested in making same-sex sexual connections. Performance venues that featured female and male impersonators and vacation destinations such as Fire Island, New York, and Provincetown, Massachusetts, also proved popular. Large cities featured hundreds of sites where people interested in same-sex sex, love, and intimacy might find one another, but smaller towns and cities had such sites as well.

Many of these spaces were predominantly or exclusively male, which in part reflected the gendering of private and public space in the United States. Women interested in same-sex sex, love, and intimacy congregated, too, and often were more successful at avoiding negative public attention. In many contexts, people with same-sex and cross-sex sexual interests socialized together, but in others they did not. Many of these sites reproduced the patterns of social class segregation, gender segregation, and racial segregation that were pervasive in U.S. society, but others were less exclusive. Everyone who visited these spaces was vulnerable to legal and extralegal repression by police authorities and hostile outsiders.

Two relationship patterns seem to have been particularly common in these communities or were more routinely noticed by outsiders. In one, a more feminine partner paired off with a more masculine one. In the other, an older partner paired off with a younger one. There were also contexts in which partners crossed boundaries of race and class, though racism and class divisions often made this less likely.

The language used by community insiders and outsiders, often highly localized and changing over time, reflected and produced complex understandings of same-sex sex. In many contexts, same-sex desire was understood to be linked to gender inversion, so that feminine male "fairies," "pansies," and "inverts" were seen as invariably attracted to "normal" men or to masculine male "husbands," "trade," or "wolves." In other contexts, older "wolves" or "jockers" were typically paired with younger "lambs" or "punks." Feminine men and masculine women—called "studs," "dykes," and "bulldaggers"—were commonly seen as deviant, while their partners might be seen as "normal" men who enjoyed sex with feminized bodies or "normal" women who responded to sexualized masculinity. Over time, "homosexuality," a term that originated in medical discourse, came to be associated with anyone who practiced same-sex sex, regardless of their gender presentation, though homosexuality never lost its cultural associations with gender inversion. The term "homosexuality," understood by many insiders as part of a discourse that constructed homosexuality as a pathological disease, was not as popular as vernacular terms such as "queer" and "gay," which were favored by community insiders. More women called themselves "gay" than "lesbian" during this period.

By the 1920s and 1930s there were large, diverse, and complex gay and lesbian communities in all regions of the United States. These communities were imagined in ways that extended well beyond regional and national borders. Gay and lesbian communities resisted the oppression they faced with tactics that included physical self-defense, verbal communication, artistic expression, and collective action. Various sexological reformers, political anarchists, and exceptional individuals challenged antihomosexual persecution, but unlike in Europe, there were no organized gay and lesbian political movements in the late nineteenth and early twentieth centuries. This changed in the post–World War II era.

From the 1940s through the 1960s.
Mass mobilization during World War II, which disrupted traditional social structures, contributed to the growth of gay and lesbian communities during and after the war. In the 1940s and 1930s, however, the U.S. federal government persecuted gay and lesbian communities in new ways, which encouraged the policing of homosexuality in other sectors of society. New antihomosexual policies and practices were implemented at the federal level in the military, the civil service, the immigration system, and various government programs, and these in turn encouraged similar actions at the state and local levels and in the private sector. Gay and lesbian communities responded in multiple ways as they experienced significant growth in all regions of the country during the 1940s, 1950s, and 1960s.

In the middle decades of the twentieth century, New York and San Francisco earned reputations as the gay and lesbian capitals of the United States, but every large U.S. city had residential enclaves, commercial establishments (especially bars and restaurants), and public territories (especially parks and beaches) that were popular with gay men and lesbians. On a smaller scale, gay and lesbian communities also existed in smaller towns and cities, including Boise, Idaho; Buffalo, New York; Jackson, Mississippi; Portland, Oregon; and Salt Lake City, Utah. Gay men typically had more success in claiming public space, but lesbian "butch-fem" cultures were well-established in many locations. Gay men and lesbians formed sports teams, motorcycle clubs, veterans' organizations, religious denominations, interracial clubs, clubs for specific racial groups, and other social organizations. Many of these continued to replicate patterns of class, gender, and racial segregation in U.S. society, though some of this began to break down in the context of the civil rights movement and the women's movement.

References to the gay and lesbian "community" became increasingly common in the 1950s and 1960s, but the notion remained a contested one. Many people who engaged in same-sex sex did not see themselves as members of a distinct sexual community. For some, this was because they also engaged in cross-sex sex and did not believe that references to the gay and lesbian "community" were useful in comprehending the complex behavioral realities of their lives. For others, people who engaged in same-sex sex could not be classified as a community because they did not share enough in common to merit classification as such, especially in the context of racial, class, religious, gender, and other forms of diversity. Notwithstanding these objections, by the mid-twentieth century the gay and lesbian community functioned in ways that were similar to other social and cultural communities. The community had distinct economic, cultural, linguistic, and territorial features; there were principles and practices that distinguished between insiders and outsiders; and there were meaningful forms of collective consciousness and group solidarity.

Beginning in the 1950s and 1960s the gay and lesbian community also featured another common element of twentieth-century social and cultural communities in the United States: a political movement that attempted to defend and promote community interests. "Homophile" groups such as the Daughters of Bilitis, the Janus Society, the Mattachine Society, and the Society for Individual Rights featured diverse political orientations that ranged from respectable Cold War liberalism to radical sexual liberationism. Movement organizations attempted to mobilize and politicize the gay and lesbian community while challenging antihomosexual oppression. Relationships between the movement and the community were complex. Just as the vast majority of people who engaged in same-sex did not think of themselves as members of the gay and lesbian community, the vast majority of gay men and lesbians did not participate in the movement. In part this was because of apathy, lack of interest, and fear, but many community members did not participate in the movement because they did not see their aspirations reflected in the agendas and achievements of gay and lesbian activism.

From the Stonewall Riots of 1969 to the Twenty-First Century. The gay and lesbian community changed after New York City's Stonewall Riots of 1969, when thousands fought back on the streets of Greenwich Village after a police raid on a gay bar. After Stonewall, the radical gay liberation and lesbian feminist movements encouraged everyone to come out as gay or lesbian and support the revolutionary transformation of society, while the more mainstream gay and lesbian rights movement promoted political reform. In 1973 the American Psychiatric Association declassified homosexuality as a mental illness, and over the next several decades most states decriminalized private homosexual acts by consenting adults. The number of gay and lesbian social, cultural, occupational, political, professional, and religious groups exploded in the 1970s, 1980s, and 1990s. There was also significant growth in the number of commercial establishments that were popular with gay men and lesbians and the range of organizations that addressed specific constituencies, including people of color, people with disabilities, the old and the young, bisexuals, sadomasochists, and parents. Gay and lesbian neighborhoods expanded in cities that had long featured visible gay and lesbian enclaves, and they emerged in other locations as well.

Notwithstanding these changes, the gay and lesbian community has faced many challenges in the decades after Stonewall. Although some forms of police harassment and social violence have declined, they remain significant problems, especially for young people, people of color, and people who violate gender norms. The U.S. Supreme Court overturned state sodomy laws in 2003, but various forms of antihomosexual discrimination remain legal in most U.S. jurisdictions, and heterosexuals continue to enjoy countless special rights and privileges in U.S. society. The rise of the Christian Right and the New Right, both of which express strong opposition to homosexuality, has resulted in significant setbacks for the gay and lesbian movement. The HIV/AIDS epidemic, first identified in the 1980s, has had devastating effects on gay men (and especially gay men of color), and many blame those devastating effects on the antihomosexual prejudices of government policy makers, medical experts, public-health officials, and private drug companies. The community has also continued to be challenged by internal dynamics of sexism and racism, economic exploitation and inequality, discrimination against people with disabilities, and hostility to transgenderism. Though in some respects the gay and lesbian community of the twenty-first century is better described as a gay, lesbian, bisexual, transexual, intersexual, and two-spirit community, in other respects there continue to be conflicts and divisions among these intersecting and overlapping constituencies.

In the early 1990s, radical "queer" critics of gay and lesbian politics began to challenge the community in new ways. Many queer activists and queer theorists questioned what they perceived as the increasingly normative nature and conservative politics of the gay and lesbian community. In part they objected to the mainstream gay and lesbian movement's emphasis on securing marriage and parenting rights, which queer advocates saw as normalizing the radical agenda of sexual liberation. They also revisited long-standing debates about whether the notion of a gay and lesbian community was useful in addressing the complex realities of same-sex desires, acts, identities, and movements, which do not always line up in expected ways—as in the case of people who engage in same-sex sex but do not identify as gay or lesbian. Some activists and theorists were interested in developing a "queer" community that would incorporate diverse sexual dissidents, including nonnormative straights and excluding normative homosexuals, while others wanted to do away entirely with the notion of gender and sexual communities. Despite their efforts, so long as there are large numbers of U.S. Americans who regard their same-sex sexual interests as important aspects of their lives, and so long as they continue to act collectively in socially meaningful, culturally visible, and politically significant ways, the United States will continue to have something that can be called a gay and lesbian community.

[*See also* **Conservative Movement; Feminism; Gay and Lesbian Love and Relationships; Gay and Lesbian Rights Movement; Law and Society; Marriage and Divorce; Sexual Reform and Morality;** *and* **Transgendered Persons and Communities.**]

BIBLIOGRAPHY

Boag, Peter. *Same-Sex Affairs: Constructing and Controlling Homosexuality in the Pacific Northwest.* Berkeley: University of California Press, 2003.

Boyd, Nan Alamilla. *Wide Open Town: A History of Queer San Francisco to 1965.* Berkeley: University of California Press, 2003.

Chauncey, George. *Gay New York: Gender, Urban Culture, and the Making of the Gay Male World, 1890–1940.* New York: Basic Books, 1994.

D'Emilio, John. *Sexual Politics, Sexual Communities: The Making of a Homosexual Minority in the United States, 1940–1970.* Chicago: University of Chicago Press, 1983.

Faderman, Lillian, and Stuart Timmons. *Gay L.A.: A History of Sexual Outlaws, Power Politics, and Lipstick Lesbians*. New York: Basic Books, 2006.

Howard, John. *Men Like That: A Southern Queer History*. Chicago: University of Chicago Press, 1999.

Hurewitz, Daniel. *Bohemian Los Angeles and the Making of Modern Politics*. Berkeley: University of California Press, 2007.

Johnson, David K. *Lavender Scare: The Cold War Persecution of Gays and Lesbians in the Federal Government*. Chicago: University of Chicago Press, 2004.

Kennedy, Elizabeth Lapovsky, and Madeline D. Davis. *Boots of Leather, Slippers of Gold: The History of a Lesbian Community*. New York: Routledge, 1993.

Krahulik, Karen Christel. *Provincetown: From Pilgrim Landing to Gay Resort*. New York: New York University Press, 2005.

Meeker, Martin. *Contacts Desired: Gay and Lesbian Communications and Community, 1940s–1970s*. Chicago. University of Chicago Press, 2006.

Newton, Esther. *Cherry Grove, Fire Island: Sixty Years in America's First Gay and Lesbian Town*. Boston: Beacon, 1993.

Rupp, Leila J. *A Desired Past: A Short History of Same-Sex Love in America*. Chicago: University of Chicago Press, 1999.

Stein, Marc. *City of Sisterly and Brotherly Loves: Lesbian and Gay Philadelphia, 1945–1972*. Chicago: University of Chicago Press, 2000.

Stein, Marc, ed. *Encyclopedia of Lesbian, Gay, Bisexual, and Transgender History in America*. New York: Charles Scribner's Sons, 2004.

Marc Stein

GAY AND LESBIAN LOVE AND RELATIONSHIPS

Historians of sexuality have challenged the long-standing notion of sex as something natural, instinctive, and ahistorical by showing that the feelings, actions, and practices that constitute the "sexual" vary widely across cultures and over time. Histories of same-sex love, intimacy, sex, and friendship offer a powerful testament to the idea that sexualities are constantly moving subjectivities rather than fixed, clearly definable categories of identity. Until the early twenty-first century, much of the scholarship advanced the notion that prior to the Victorian era, sex between people of the same sex did not signal a distinct identity in the same way that the modern category of homosexuality conflates desire and practice with being. The rigidity and periodization of both ideas have been challenged by important research. It remains to be seen, however, whether enough evidence can be found to completely upend the "acts" versus "identity" organizing principle as a way of understanding how people viewed sex between people of the same sex before and after the late nineteenth century.

Early America. Any reflection on same-sex intimacy necessarily raises questions about gender, and this is especially the case when considering the earliest records of Native American cross-gender people. Historical interpretations of those most commonly referred to as "berdache" vary dramatically, from men who were forced to cross-dress as women and serve in the denigrated capacity of another man's household servant and sexual submissive to men who embodied both masculine and feminine energies and whose tribes recognized them as spiritual leaders, precisely because of their embodiment of ambiguous gender roles. Most records of berdache referred to biological males or hermaphrodites. But Native American tribes had complex gender systems that recognized more than two genders, and it was not uncommon for biological females to live as men, too, and take female partners. European missionaries were uncomfortable and critical of the ways in which Native American women expressed themselves, describing overt nudity, physical expressiveness, and sexual aggression as representative of their barbarism—and of their propensity for sin, including sexual intimacies with each other.

From the earliest Puritan settlements in New England, British colonists were aware of and concerned about sex between men, largely because they believed that those who engaged in sodomy were not only morally and spiritually weak but also likely to lure others into the practice. "Sodomy" was any sexual act other than procreative sex between a man and a woman, but women were rarely charged with it. Because sodomy was regarded as a sin, however, with proper penitence a person could be forgiven for its commission and reinstated to a respected standing in society. Despite severe legal codes for sodomy—it was punishable by death throughout the colonial period—social attitudes were far more lax, particularly in the mid-Atlantic and the South, areas beyond the reach of Puritan religious influence. Evidence of women in relationships with other women is once again found through records of gender deviance. Throughout the eighteenth century, newspaper accounts of "female husbands" described women who lived as men and "married" other women. Most of these accounts, unlike the more prominent narratives of "female soldiers" and "female marines," avoided discussion of sexual intimacy and focused on the social relationships between the two.

Like Native American women, African American women under slavery were categorized by European men as being excessively lascivious and seductive—probably to justify the rampant sexual abuse meted out by their own hands. Whereas sex between white masters and black women certainly played a vital, violent role within the plantation culture, historians continue to search for evidence of same-sex intimacies within slave communities. In the mid-nineteenth century, however, African American women engaged in intimate, loving, and likely sexual relationships with other women. These "romantic friendships" were first documented through the letters of middle- and upper-class white women in the Victorian period, women who socialized in a world of "separate spheres" from their husbands. The question of whether or not these women engaged sexually with each other is largely unanswerable, only further advancing the long-standing notion that whatever it is that two women can do together physically, it does not constitute "sex." In the later twentieth century, meanwhile, scholars of male same-sex relationships began using this framework to expand the field for the study of men beyond public culture and court records to incorporate the significance of male intimacy and friendship that was so prevalent in the personal writings from the late eighteenth and early nineteenth centuries.

Progressive Era. The Progressive Era marks the most significant period in the shaping of the meaning of same-sex sexual relationships. During this era the scientific study of human sexuality was introduced, primarily in Europe but also in the United States—and certainly with far-reaching consequences. In the early decades of the field, attraction to people of the same-sex was thought to be a result of gender inversion, as researchers looked for physical causes of sexual behavior. Havelock Ellis later advanced the notion that sexual desire and object choice were a distinct aspect of identity, not a behavior resulting from moral weakness. Though the findings of sexologists largely signaled that those engaging in same-sex sexual intimacies were deviant and pathological, such research publicly documented a relatively high incidence of same-sex sex, paving the way for the future creation of a community and political movement by and for those marked as homosexual. A handful of gay men who were friends and comrades in the struggle for workers' rights challenged some of the findings and educated people about the larger social structures that served to marginalize and stigmatize gay people.

The early twentieth century was marked by a shift in social expectations and possibilities for young people who migrated to cities in massive numbers for work as part of the Industrial Revolution. Freed from the watchful eyes of family members and the cultural norms of churches and small communities, sexual intimacies with others of the same-sex were more available and relationships were tenable. Men who did not claim a gay identity engaged in sex with other men as penetrators, or "tops." This practice crossed race and class and was most widely noted in northern cities. An intimate relationship between two women who lived together was called a "Boston marriage" and reflected a trend among educated women to reject the subservience and dependency of marriage to a man. Some of these women defined their relationship as sexual.

Mid-Twentieth Century and Beyond.

Opportunities for sexual intimacies with others of the same sex abound for both men and women in single-sex environments, and such environments proliferated during the massive enlistment in the military and the Army Nurse Corps during World Wars I and II. Following the wars, a public gay community and culture flourished, even though homosexuality was still classified as a psychological disorder and sodomy was a punishable crime. Working-class gay and lesbian cultures thrived in cities of all sizes throughout the 1950s. Relationships between women during this period embraced opposing gender roles, often described as "butch" and "femme."

Such roles were shaped in varying degrees on an individual basis by both desire and necessity but reflected a larger social and economic reality that policed and enforced a rigid gender binary both at work and on the streets. Some women navigated this by dressing and passing as men, while others embraced the conventional femininity expected of all women. In larger cities, subcultures of gay men flourished, creating opportunities for both single-sex and integrated social and political community building. African American gay male culture thrived in cities with large African American communities, and integration of these African American gay communities with the white gay community varied greatly by location.

The transgender community led the fight against police brutality of gender and sexual deviants in 1966 at Compton's Cafeteria in San Francisco. The transgender and cross-dressing patrons were frequently harassed and arrested under anti-cross-dressing laws in part because their gender transgression challenged efforts to regulate same-sex sexuality. In this respect, as in earlier accounts of berdache and female husbands, the history of same-sex relationships also requires an exploration of gender roles and defiance. The counterculture of the 1960s had a tremendous impact on sexual practices, particularly among young people. The women's liberation movement challenged female subservience in its many forms and inspired women to embrace their own sexual needs and desire. Women-only spaces and communities flourished across the country, in rural and urban areas alike. Some women argued that lesbianism was a logical conclusion to feminist theories that located men as the source of individual and structural oppression, leading feminists to identify as political lesbians. For gay men the 1970s marked a decade of sexual liberation and a vibrant public sexual culture—one that soon come crashing to a halt with the AIDS crisis in the 1980s.

The activist movement from the 1970s through 2010 made tremendous strides in a short period of time, dramatically shifting both the legal and the popular perception of same-sex relationships. The 2003 Supreme Court ruling in *Lawrence v. Texas* finally overturned antisodomy laws across the country; such laws had routinely been used to punish and stigmatize gay people engaging in consensual sexual activity and had served as justification for the denial of employment, housing, custody, and adoption rights. By the mid-1990s the national movement for lesbian, gay, bisexual, and transgender (LGBT) rights had come into its own and was increasingly divided into two camps. More radical social-justice activists viewed the gay rights movement as one of liberation, intimately linked to movements for women's liberation, transgender equality, and racial and economic justice. The other camp advocated a conciliatory, assimilationist approach to activism, advancing the notion that gay people simply want the same rights that straight people have. This part of the movement dedicated most of its resources to advancing relationship-recognition legislation in the form of domestic partnership, civil unions, and same-sex marriages and was the face of the national movement into the twenty-first century.

[*See also* **Courtship and Dating; Gay and Lesbian Communities; Gay and Lesbian Rights Movement; Gender; Marriage and Divorce; Sexual Reform and Morality; Transgendered Persons and Communities;** *and* Transvestism.]

BIBLIOGRAPHY

D'Emilio, John. *Sexual Politics, Sexual Communities. The Making of a Homosexual Minority in the United States, 1940–1970.* Chicago: University of Chicago Press, 1983.

Duberman, Martin Bauml, Martha Vicinus, and George Chauncey Jr., eds. *Hidden from History: Reclaiming the Gay and Lesbian Past.* New York: NAL Books, 1989.

Enke, Anne. *Finding the Movement: Sexuality, Contested Space, and Feminist Activism.* Durham, N.C.: Duke University Press, 2007.

Foster, Thomas, ed. *Long before Stonewall: Histories of Same-Sex Sexuality in Early America.* New York: New York University Press, 2007.

Kennedy, Elizabeth Lapovsky, and Madeline D. Davis. *Boots of Leather, Slippers of Gold: The History of a Lesbian Community.* New York: Routledge, 1993.

Rupp, Leila J. *A Desired Past: A Short History of Same-Sex Love in America.* Chicago: University of Chicago Press, 1999.

Stein, Marc. *City of Sisterly and Brotherly Loves: Lesbian and Gay Philadelphia, 1945–1972.* Chicago: University of Chicago Press, 2000.

Stryker, Susan. *Transgender History.* Berkeley, Calif.: Seal, 2008.

Jennifer Manion

GAY AND LESBIAN RIGHTS MOVEMENT

The movement to protect the civil rights of lesbian, gay, bisexual, and transgender (LGBT) people emerged in the wake of World War II. Thousands of men and women who had thrived in the military's same-sex worlds began to understand their sexual activities as central to their identities. They settled in the nation's cities, constructing dynamic social lives woven from private parties, select bars and restaurants, and, for men, certain parks and bathhouses. Though these subcultures were not new, they expanded dramatically and became increasingly segregated along lines of race and gender. With that expansion, however, came much greater political and legal condemnation: federal, state, and local governments began to prohibit homosexuals from working within the civil service, the military instituted an elaborate homosexual-exclusion process, and local police forces began regularly to raid bars and arrest their patrons, vigorously enforcing old laws criminalizing homosexual conduct and cross-dressing. Participating in same-sex subcultures could thus be both exhilarating and dangerous, a resistance to societal rules that could have life-altering consequences and that led some individuals, though hardly all, to forge a sense of shared identity and community. The movement, initially focused on civil rights for gays and lesbians, was born from that combination of subcultural expansion and repression.

Birth of Political Activism. The first explicitly political phase of that movement started in Los Angeles in 1950 when several homosexually active men, mostly former Communist and Progressive activists called together by Harry Hay, founded the Mattachine Society. Though Mattachine can be said to have an American predecessor in the German-inspired Society for Human Rights that operated in Chicago for a few months in the 1920s, Mattachine's founders established a new framework for addressing lesbian and gay rights. Drawing on leftist ideas about oppressed minorities and a new cultural emphasis on psychology and self-expression, they created a network of discussion groups in which men and women shared their experiences and constructed a common identity as a social minority. Mattachine—whose membership peaked in the thousands, with groups meeting across southern California and as far east as Chicago and New York City—was soon joined by other organizations, including the lesbian-focused Daughters of Bilitis, founded in San Francisco in

1955 by Del Martin and Phyllis Lyon. Members of this handful of small organizations around the country began to refer to themselves as "homophiles."

Homophile activists were typically white and middle class, not deeply involved in the bar scene, and integrationist in their goals: the homophile leadership steadily encouraged homosexuals to conform to social standards. Nevertheless, over two decades, they helped to fashion what can be considered a gay culture, publishing newsletters and creating social forums. They offered guidance about dealing with the police and prosecution. And they pursued fairly subdued politics, trying to build relationships with legal, religious, and medical leaders in the hope that these leaders might in turn convince society that homosexuals were otherwise normal. In one early achievement, activists won a U.S. Supreme Court decision declaring that their publications were not obscene and could be sent through the mail.

During the 1960s, gay rights activism became more public. Inspired by the other public protests that were occurring in American society, homophile activists staged small picket lines in front of several government offices in Washington, D.C., including the White House, and at Philadelphia's Independence Hall to protest federal discrimination. Less explicitly organized bar patrons also took to the streets in several cities in the late 1960s to protest police harassment. In San Francisco, police were publicly criticized for their raid of a 1965 New Year's party, and the following year, a local café was the scene of a fight between the police and street queens and transgender people. Most famously, in the early hours of 28 June 1969, at New York's Stonewall Inn, patrons refused to disperse after a police raid and instead fought back; street rioting ensued for several days.

The Stonewall riots in particular are seen as marking the emergence of a second phase of gay rights activism, one that was much more aggressive and visible and that was identified as "gay liberation." Gay liberation brought thousands more into the movement: compared to the fifty homophile organizations that existed in 1969, there were eight hundred gay-liberation groups in 1973, and thousands by 1979. Following the leads of the Black Power movement and the counterculture, gay liberationists demanded "gay power" and insisted that homosexuals "come out of the closet" by announcing their homosexuality to friends, families, and colleagues. Younger and often less socially established than their homophile predecessors, gay liberationists forcibly resisted sanctions against homosexuality. Joining groups like the Gay Activists Alliance and the Gay Liberation Front, activists around the country interrupted city council meetings and psychiatric conferences, staged sit-ins at magazine offices and the headquarters of political campaigns, and marched through the nation's streets. Their actions yielded social and political changes. The American Psychiatric Association removed homosexuality from its disease list, countless editorial policies were modified, and Congress considered antidiscrimination legislation. In fact, by 1976, seventeen states had repealed their laws criminalizing homosexual activity, and thirty-six cities had passed antidiscrimination laws. And within the movement, often in reaction to its own sexism, strong lesbian-centered organizations developed as well.

Conservative Backlash and AIDS Crisis.

These political achievements produced a sharp backlash. In 1977 the singer and former beauty queen Anita Bryant led a successful campaign in Florida to overturn Dade County's new nondiscrimination law, and other cities followed suit. The following year, a California state senator proposed an initiative to ban homosexuals from teaching in the state's public schools. Although the proposition was defeated, the leading opponent of it, an openly gay San Francisco city supervisor named Harvey Milk, was assassinated shortly after the vote. These backlash actions drew a new conservative constituency into the fold of gay activism and pushed the movement toward more traditional political actions. Lobbying groups established a gay presence in government, working to elect openly gay politicians and forging formal relationships with various administrations.

Much of the energy that might have augmented those efforts in the 1980s was instead devoted to fighting HIV and AIDS. As the disease spread among gay men in the early 1980s and the federal government largely failed to respond, gay men and lesbians around the country formed their own social-service organizations to support and advocate for the sick and dying. Organizations like Gay Men's Health Crisis in New York City and AIDS Project Los Angeles set up hotlines and buddy systems and developed safe-sex guidelines to offer some direction in the midst of a devastating epidemic.

Beyond the physical suffering, community members also felt besieged by governmental indifference: in 1986 the Supreme Court affirmed the continued criminalization of homosexual behavior; President Ronald Reagan made no national statements about AIDS until 1987, more than six years into the epidemic; and only in that year did the Food and Drug Administration (FDA) finally approve its first drug to fight HIV. Dismayed by these attitudes, activists launched a campaign of aggressive demonstrations. Led largely by the AIDS Coalition to Unleash Power (ACT UP), demonstrators staged sit-ins at Wall Street, the FDA, and pharmaceutical corporations, and they garnered enough media and governmental attention to yield improved care. That fight brought greater political influence to LGBT communities and also galvanized a new cohort of self-identified "queer" activists. Indeed, in the 1992 presidential campaign, Bill Clinton actively sought the support of LGBT voters, becoming the first presidential candidate to do so.

Policy Debates and Cultural Shift. Perhaps because of that political attention, the 1990s proved contentious as questions related to gay rights were debated and resisted in the political mainstream. Clinton, who as a candidate had promised voters that he would repeal the military's ban on gay and lesbian soldiers, initiated a congressional debate in 1993 that ultimately reaffirmed the ban under the name "Don't Ask, Don't Tell." That policy, promoted as more lenient to LGBT soldiers, actually led to an increase in the number of men and women pushed out of the service.

Same-sex marriage also moved center stage in the 1990s, driven there by couples around the country who sued for the right to marry. In 1991, three same-sex Hawaiian couples sued their state after being denied marriage licenses, and two years later the state supreme court deemed the denial unconstitutional. That decision—which did not, ultimately, lead to marriage equality in Hawai'i—nonetheless set off a wave of political activity as most states scrambled to define marriage as exclusively heterosexual and to assert their right not to recognize same-sex marriages performed elsewhere. Clinton and the U.S. Congress codified that right in the Defense of Marriage Act (DOMA) in 1996. Despite DOMA, a few states began to offer limited recognition of same-sex relationships, and in 2000 Vermont became the first state to license what are called "civil unions" as the same-sex equivalent to marriage.

The tenor of these debates shifted in 2003 when the U.S. Supreme Court, in *Lawrence v. Texas*, struck down all laws criminalizing homosexual sex between consenting adults. As Justice Anthony Kennedy wrote in a decision that was heralded as the *Brown v. Board of Education* for the LGBT rights movement, LGBT individuals "are entitled to respect for their private lives. The State cannot demean their existence or control their destiny by making their private sexual conduct a crime." Building on that decision, which implied that all discrimination on the basis of sexual orientation was intolerable, the supreme court of Massachusetts deemed it unconstitutional to deny marriage licenses to same-sex couples. In the spring of 2004, that state officially began to allow same-sex couples to wed. As several municipalities, including San Francisco and New Paltz, New York, also began issuing marriage licenses, controversy erupted: President George W. Bush declared his support for a federal constitutional amendment banning same-sex marriage nationwide, and conservatives in several states put similar proposals on their ballots. Nonetheless, by the summer of 2011, five other states and Washington, D.C., had followed Massachusetts's example and allowed same-sex marriages, eight more offered or were about to offer options like civil unions with rights equivalent to marriage, and another handful extended some limited benefits to same-sex couples.

The *Lawrence* decision also paved the way for a reevaluation of the ban on military service. Especially after the country became involved in war in Iraq in 2003—forcing many servicemen and servicewomen on extended tours of duty even as gay servicemen and servicewomen were discharged—the "Don't Ask, Don't Tell" policy came under increasing scrutiny. In December 2010, Congress repealed the ban, and when

President Barack Obama signed the legislation, he declared, "We are not a nation that says 'Don't ask, don't tell.' . . . We are a nation that believes all men and women are created equal."

Not insignificantly, these policy shifts, both about same-sex marriage and about military service, have been buttressed by a steady increase in pop-culture representation of LGBT individuals across the 1990s and 2000s. Many high-profile individual performers—such as Rosie O'Donnell, George Michael, and Ellen DeGeneres—came out publicly, and LGBT characters became regular features of mainstream films and television. *Will & Grace*, a sitcom in which two of the four main characters were gay men, was a top-ratings hit on NBC from 1998 until 2006, and the cable channels Showtime and Bravo featured more explicit LGBT dramas. Mainstream Hollywood films increasingly featured gay characters in both supporting and lead roles, as in *Philadelphia* (1993), *The Birdcage* (1996), and *Brokeback Mountain* (2005). In fact, in 2010, the openly lesbian political commentator Rachel Maddow was one of the country's top TV news anchors, gay characters were prominently featured on the TV programs *Glee* and *Modern Family*, and one of the Oscar-nominated films of the year, *The Kids Are All Right*, focused on a two-mom family. That cultural shift was reflected by opinion polls, too, which in 2010 showed that the majority of Americans viewed gay and lesbian relationships as morally acceptable, with greater support coming from younger Americans.

Transgender Movement. Beyond marriage and the military, the other major development since the 1990s has been the emergence of a self-identified "transgender" movement within the larger LGBT movement. The term "transgender" took hold as a broad label in the 1990s for individuals who, whether through dress, self-naming, surgery, or some other sense of identity, resisted dominant gender categories. In truth, transgender activists had been developing support networks and organizations since the 1950s—when early support groups focused on male cross-dressers—and during the 1960s and 1970s, transgender activists played crucial roles in the public actions of gay liberation, including the Stonewall riots. During the 1990s, however, inspired by the writing of Leslie Feinberg, transgender activists began to organize as a distinct faction under the wider umbrella of queer politics. Galvanized in part by the killings of transgender individuals like Brandon Teena, these activists brought both legislative and media attention to the violence and discrimination that transgender individuals face. Indeed, as the wider movement worked to pass hate-crimes legislation that protected LGBT individuals—particularly after the slaying of the Wyoming college student Matthew Shepard—transgender activists increasingly drew attention to the widespread violence faced by people because of their gender expression. The alliance between the wider movement and the transgender faction was not always smooth: the New York State LGBT lobby group was roundly criticized for its support of a 2003 hate-crimes law that excluded transgender people. But when President Obama signed expanded federal hate-crimes legislation in October 2009, the new law addressed both sexual orientation and gender identity.

Despite the many gains since the 1990s, the goals for twenty-first-century LGBT activists remain numerous. Activists emphasize the need for antidiscrimination laws regarding employment and housing, as well as greater protection for LGBT families and young people, whose experiences of bullying and rates of suicide remain shockingly high. The work of this movement continues.

[*See also* **Conservative Movement; Gay and Lesbian Communities; Gay and Lesbian Love and Relationships; Gender; Law and Society; New York City; San Francisco; Sexual Reform and Morality; Sixties, The; Stonewall Riots; Transgendered Persons and Communities;** *and* **Transvestism.**]

BIBLIOGRAPHY

Chauncey, George. *Why Marriage? The History Shaping Today's Debate over Gay Equality.* New York: Basic Books, 2004.

Clendinen, Dudley, and Adam Nagourney. *Out for Good: The Struggle to Build a Gay Rights Movement in America.* New York: Simon & Schuster, 1999.

D'Emilio, John. *Sexual Politics, Sexual Communities: The Making of a Homosexual Minority in the United States, 1940–1970.* 2d ed. Chicago: University of Chicago Press, 1998.

Gould, Deborah B. *Moving Politics: Emotion and ACT UP's Fight against AIDS.* Chicago: University of Chicago Press, 2009.

Hurewitz, Daniel. *Bohemian Los Angeles and the Making of Modern Politics.* Berkeley: University of California Press, 2007.

Marcus, Eric. *Making Gay History: The Half Century Fight for Lesbian and Gay Equal Rights.* New York: Harper Collins, 2002.

Stryker, Susan. *Transgender History.* Berkeley: Seal Press, 2008.

Daniel Hurewitz

GENDER

To paraphrase the historian Joan Wallach Scott, "gender" is most usefully understood as an analytical category of historical thought. Although usage in this way dates only from the mid-1980s, it has largely displaced the analytical category from which it developed: the social history of women. The concept of gender brings together the many ways in which the distinctions between male and female operate in history. Put simply, it focuses on the history of the concepts of masculinity and femininity rather than on the history of men and women. Together with the categories of race and social class, gender forms the modern conceptual triad for analyzing the structures and workings of power and inequality in American society.

"Gender" has two long-standing meanings: an element of grammar and a colloquial, polite equivalent for "sex." With the revival of feminist thinking in the 1970s, "gender" became a term for distinguishing biological sexual differences from the historically variable and socially imposed meanings attached to those differences. This distinction underscored that the biological differences between the sexes did not have inherent, inescapable meanings for people's lives. The proliferation of this usage in subsequent decades was a measure of the spread of the feminist claim that sex roles are socially imposed and largely arbitrary, and that they can and should be changed.

By the mid-1980s when the concept of gender became increasingly common among historians, the first wave of modern historical writings about women was almost two decades old. Inspired by the 1960s burgeoning of social history, this scholarship had focused on the lives of people long ignored by historians. The proliferation of scholarship on women's experience concentrated on those very activities with which women were identified and which therefore had long been considered historically insignificant: family, domesticity, kinship, emotion, private life. The dominant framework for women's social history initially reflected the nineteenth-century ideology of separate sexual spheres and the monumental divide that this ideology created between men's and women's lives; the historian's job was to investigate the women's side of the divide.

By the mid-1980s, however, historians began to realize that the social-historical information they were gathering on women needed to be supplemented with answers to other kinds of questions: how and why distinctions between men and women developed, operated, and changed in history; how and where men (as well as women) were positioned on the sexual divide; how women's experience was shaped by the wide range of women's class and racial backgrounds; and how discoveries about women could be made to change understandings of the core of U.S. history, rather than remain in a scholarly ghetto. The neglect of the ideological sources and functions of the separate spheres model of women's history, historians concluded, had led to a superficial and too-literal description of social life and sexual difference.

These concerns resulted in the replacement of the category of women's history with that of the history of gender. This new focus has been producing scholarship that addresses historical topics left relatively untouched by the women's social-historical scholarship. Work, citizenship, even military service, all historical areas associated with men, are being examined for the ways in which they assumed and helped to shape the historic divide between the sexes. Historians are asking whether anything that women workers did was ever really considered "skilled labor," or whether the meaning of the term shifted depending on where women were located in the wage-labor force. Gender-conscious studies on citizenship in the Revolution and constitution eras examine how the exclusion of women shaped the self-understanding of American republicans and their faith in their own civic virtue.

Scholarship organized around the concept of gender rather than that of women has also proved better able to address the relations of racial power. For example, historians of the South in the decades after Reconstruction, adopting an analytic approach informed by the new emphasis on gender, have traced how postbellum upheavals in power relations between the races, as well as the efforts of former slaves to realize their freedom and to re-create their communities, led to dramatic shifts in the relations between men and women and to tremendous conflicts over sexuality, culminating in the lynching epidemic late of the nineteenth century.

[*See also* **Feminism; Race and Ethnicity; Separate Spheres Ideology; Social Class;** *and* **Women Workers.**]

BIBLIOGRAPHY

Baron, Ava, ed. *Work Engendered: Toward a New History of American Labor.* Ithaca, N.Y.: Cornell University Press, 1991.

Bederman, Gail. *Manliness and Civilization: A Cultural History of Gender and Race in the United States, 1880–1917.* Chicago: University of Chicago Press, 1995.

Kerber, Linda K., Nancy F. Cott, Robert Gross, Lynn Hunt, Carroll Smith-Rosenberg, and Christine M. Stansell. "Beyond Roles, Beyond Spheres: Thinking about Gender in the Early Republic." *William and Mary Quarterly*, 3d ser., 46 (July 1989): 565–585.

Rubin, Gayle. "The Traffic in Women: Notes on the 'Political Economy' of Sex." In *Toward an Anthropology of Women*, edited by Rayna R. Reiter, pp. 157–210. New York: Monthly Review Press, 1975.

Scott, Joan Wallach. *Gender and the Politics of History.* Rev. ed. New York: Columbia University Press, 1999.

Ellen Carol DuBois

GENERAL FEDERATION OF WOMEN'S CLUBS

Founded in 1890 at the initiative of the journalist Jane Cunningham Croly, the General Federation of Women's Clubs brought together local women's clubs in a national organization. By 1890 there was a proliferation of women's clubs across the United States. Most prominent among them were the New England Woman's Club and Sorosis in New York City, both established in 1868. Croly was herself the founder of Sorosis, which, like the New England club, was in its early years primarily devoted to the study of literature and culture. During an era in which even upper-class women generally had limited educational opportunities, the clubs provided means for, in the clubs' words, women's "self-improvement." Most club meetings consisted of members reading papers on particular topics of study, thus allowing women to practice public speaking. Increasingly, many clubs began to discuss social problems such as poverty and engage in direct activism, generally at the local level. The change in focus was controversial, but by the General Federation's founding the shift toward social issues in the Women's Club Movement was already well under way.

A diverse array of clubs joined the federation, including mothers' clubs, literary clubs, and travel clubs, as well as clubs more concerned with civic improvement. Soon state and regional federations formed that used the General Federation's model and then eventually joined the national federation. Every two years the General Federation held a national convention in a different city, to which member clubs sent representatives. Conventions provided opportunities for clubwomen to communicate, exchange ideas, and publicize local accomplishments. The biennial conventions also revealed internal tensions, including the ongoing tension between civic-minded clubwomen and those more interested in cultural pursuits. Most contentious, however, was the long-standing controversy about the status of black clubwomen. Although Boston's New Era Club, a black women's club established by Josephine St. Pierre Ruffin in 1894, was admitted into the General Federation in 1900, at the time of its admittance General Federation officers did not know that the New Era Club was a black women's club. When Ruffin's attempt to attend the 1900 convention as a representative of the New Era Club was thwarted, controversy ensued. The matter was not settled until 1902 when the national federation reached a compromise that left matters of club membership in the hands of state and regional federations.

The turn toward civic action continued throughout the period from 1900 to 1920. Animated by the principle of "municipal housekeeping," or the idea that women ought to transfer their skills as mothers and housekeepers to the public sphere, affiliated clubs embarked on a variety of projects that included conservation, establishment of public libraries, city beautification, reforms of the education system, and reforms of government policies related to American Indians. In some states, clubs were actively involved in the struggle for women's suffrage. After the Nineteenth Amendment was ratified in 1920, membership in the General Federation began to decline, and like many organizations nationwide, the federation drifted in a more conservative direction. No longer did clubwomen look to the government as an answer to social problems; instead clubwomen focused on private philanthropy. During the Cold War period, this conservatism was especially apparent. Despite reduced prominence and visibility, the General Federation survived to the twenty-first century.

[*See also* **Conservative Movement; Feminist Reforms in the Progressive Era, Maternal; Fraternal Organizations; Progressive Era; Separate Spheres Ideology;** *and* **Woman Suffrage Movement.**]

BIBLIOGRAPHY

Blair, Karen J. *The Clubwoman as Feminist: True Womanhood Redefined, 1868–1914.* New York: Holmes & Meier, 1980. A strong overview of the early women's club movement in relation to ideas about womanhood.

Meltzer, Paige. "'The Pulse and Conscience of America': The General Federation and Women's Citizenship, 1945–1960." *Frontiers* 30, no. 3 (2009): 52–76. Documents the conservative turn of the Federation in the 1920s and especially after World War II.

Scott, Anne Firor. *Natural Allies: Women's Associations in American History.* Urbana and Chicago: University of Illinois Press, 1991. Places the General Federation of Women's Clubs within a larger historical context of women's associations.

Sarah Kapit

GERMAN AMERICANS

Nearly 6 million Germans immigrated to America between 1830 and 1930, making them the country's largest ethnic group and by far the largest language minority. At the peak in 1900, German immigrants and their children constituted 10.5 percent of the U.S. population. Despite a substantial German presence in colonial America, especially in Pennsylvania, there was little institutional continuity into the nineteenth century. German immigration was second only to Irish in the 1830s and 1840s, then took the lead, making up more than one-third of the total in the 1850s and 1860s and more than

27 percent in the 1870s and 1880s. Half or more of the migrants came as families, with women constituting a sizable 40 percent. Most Germans came motivated by economic hardship and—notwithstanding some religious and a few secular colonization groups—without formal organization. Refugees from the failed revolutions of 1830 and 1848 and from Prussian persecution of Catholics and socialists in the 1870s and 1880s emigrated as well.

Though predominantly of rural origins, German Americans were more heavily urbanized than the contemporaneous populations of either Germany or the United States. Prominent in mid-Atlantic cities, they dominated the ethnic population of the urban and rural Midwest. The 1980 U.S. Census's ancestry data revealed a solid block of sixteen states stretching from Pennsylvania and Maryland to Colorado and Montana (along with Alaska) in which Germans made up the largest ethnic element.

Widely distributed across the occupational spectrum, Germans were most heavily represented in skilled artisanal and industrial trades. Active as unionists and labor radicals, they formed a large contingent of the socialist movement. They dominated American brewing, were prominent in the entire food and drink sector, and often rose to prominence in more specialized branches of manufacturing. Their proportion in agriculture, initially below the national average, increased across generations. Census figures suggest relatively low rates of labor-force participation for German women but overlook much work done on farms and in family businesses. Although occupational diversity suggests successful acculturation, in fact this diversity allowed Germans to obtain everything they needed within their ethnic community.

Because of Germany's belated national unification (1871) and immigrants' religious, regional, and socioeconomic diversity, German Americans rarely united behind one political party, giving them a reputation for political impotence. Indeed, no other German immigrant approached the prominence of the diplomat, Republican senator, and cabinet member Carl Schurz (1829–1906). However, German Americans were nearly as successful as Irish Americans in winning election as big-city mayors, and they used politics effectively to defend their culture. Resisting nativist movements, Prohibition, and blue laws, they promoted their language in both the public and private arenas. In the late nineteenth century, Catholics and Lutherans—the two largest German confessional groups—built up substantial networks of parochial schools, which operated largely in their native tongue. Public elementary schools in several dozen cities and towns also offered German instruction and in some instances truly bilingual education. An unofficial, incomplete survey taken around 1900 recorded 550,000 pupils studying German at the elementary level, 42 percent of them in public schools, 35 percent in Catholic schools, and 16 percent in Lutheran schools. The German-language press reinforced these efforts at cultural preservation. At its peak in 1894, with ninety-seven daily newspapers among eight hundred total publications, the German-language press's combined circulation equaled half the German-born population.

The intolerance engendered by World War I markedly accelerated the decline in German American culture initiated by falling immigration in the 1890s. The language was banned from schools and many areas of public life, and the number of German periodicals fell by half. Neither the 130,000 refugees from Nazi Germany nor some half a million postwar immigrants effected an appreciable revival.

[*See also* **Aliens during Wartime; Assimilation; Immigration; Race and Ethnicity; Redemptioners;** *and* **World War I, Home Front.**]

BIBLIOGRAPHY

Conzen, Kathleen Neils. *Immigrant Milwaukee, 1836–1860: Accommodation and Community in a Frontier City.* Cambridge, Mass.: Harvard University Press, 1976.

Kamphoefner, Walter D., Wolfgang Helbich, and Ulrike Sommer, eds. *News from the Land of Freedom: German Immigrants Write Home.* Translated by Susan Carter Vogel. Ithaca, N.Y.: Cornell University Press, 1991.

Keil, Hartmut, and John B. Jentz, eds. *German Workers in Industrial Chicago: A Documentary History of Working-Class Culture from 1850 to World War I.* Urbana: University of Illinois Press, 1988.

Luebke, Frederick C. *Bonds of Loyalty: German-Americans and World War I.* DeKalb: Northern Illinois University Press, 1974.

Pickle, Linda Schelbitzki. *Contented among Strangers: Rural German-Speaking Women and Their Families in the Nineteenth-Century Midwest.* Urbana: University of Illinois Press, 1996.

Rippley, La Vern J. *The German-Americans.* Boston: Twayne, 1976.

Walter D. Kamphoefner

GHOST DANCE

With the conclusion of the Civil War in 1865, the United States recommitted itself to solving the so-called Indian Problem. Rather than returning to its failed antebellum policies of armed conflict and removal, however, the federal government chose instead to follow the counsel of an influential group of eastern philanthropists who called themselves the Friends of the Indians and promoted the dual processes of civilization and Christianization.

This radical shift in federal Indian relations called for negotiating treaties with yet-autonomous Great Plains and western tribes that would commit them to settling on reservations, adopting the customs of the Euro-American majority, and abandoning their own religions for Christianity.

Although viewed by its white supporters as an instrument of cultural and religious progress, the policy of civilization and Christianization was initially rebuffed by most Indians, who had no desire to forsake their sovereignty and traditional lifeways. Ironically, because of this resistance, backers of the new, supposedly humanitarian policy felt compelled to call upon the army to force recalcitrant tribes onto their new homelands. Even after this coerced relocation, however, reservation agents found that most of their charges still refused to submit to the government's program of assimilation. To add to agents' frustrations, episodes of epidemics, droughts, and starvation seemed only to harden the Indians' opposition to the government's agenda. The Indians longed instead for a return to the relative prosperity of pre-reservation days when they were free to practice their own customs and pray to their own gods.

For the Northern Paiutes of Nevada's Walker River reservation, a message that promised a return to better days arrived in the late 1860s through the visions of one of their shamans, Wodziwob. According to Wodziwob, the spirits had advised that if Northern Paiutes performed a series of rituals, the world would be returned to a condition before their contact with whites. Most important, their dead ancestors would be resurrected and join the living in the remade world. At the center of this ritual complex was the "Ghost Dance," a traditional Northern Paiute round dance to which new elements had been added to transform it from a social to a sacred performance. Wodziwob's

movement was short-lived because it failed to effect the changes that Wodziwob had prophesized.

Yet continuing poor conditions on the reservations made the circumstances ripe for a new movement under a different leader, a Northern Paiute prophet named Wovoka (Jack Wilson), who revived the Ghost Dance in 1887. In common with Wodziwob's Ghost Dance, Wovoka's movement was inspired by visions in which he was instructed to inform his people that their suffering would soon be ended by the dawning of a new world that was free of whites and in which they would live forever in a traditional Paiute fashion alongside their resurrected ancestors. Also like before, adherents would be required to dance this new world into existence by performing the Ghost Dance. The main difference between the two movements lay in Wovoka's incorporation of many apocalyptic elements of Christianity, including Jesus's role in ushering in the remade world.

Once again, news of the Northern Paiute's Ghost Dance spread rapidly to other Indian tribes, this time including Great Plains peoples, many of whom sent delegates via railroad to assess Wovoka's credibility. Among these visitors were the Lakotas Short Bull and Kicking Bear, who accepted Wovoka's message of peace and regeneration as valid and carried it back to their home reservations of Rosebud and Pine Ridge in South Dakota. With or without Wovoka's encouragement, by the time they had left Nevada, both Lakotas identified him as Jesus.

As was the case with all other tribes, Lakotas did not accept Wovoka's Ghost Dance without adapting it and adding elements to it that were consistent with their own cosmologies. Among the most notable of the innovations were Ghost Dance shirts and dresses that practitioners believed had the power to protect those who wore them from the bullets of hostile whites. Though some historians argue that these garments illustrate the Lakotas' transformation of Wovoka's movement from peaceful to aggressive, the evidence suggests that these and other Lakota additions and changes were defensive, not offensive, in nature.

Whatever the Lakota Ghost Dancers' intentions, however, as their numbers swelled, homesteaders living near the Pine Ridge and Rosebud reservations feared that the ceremony was a prelude to an Indian war. Responding to their concern, the army sent soldiers to both reservations to monitor the situation. On 28 December 1890, troops of the Seventh Cavalry intercepted a large body of Chief Big Foot's Lakota as they were on their way to join a large contingent of Ghost Dancers in Pine Ridge's Badlands. After escorting their captives to a site near Wounded Knee Creek, the soldiers forced them to make camp. Tragedy ensued the following morning when the army opened fire on the Lakota camp, killing approximately a hundred and fifty men, women, and children in what has come to be known as the Wounded Knee Tragedy (1890) or Massacre of Wounded Knee.

The carnage at Wounded Knee Creek brought an abrupt end to Wovoka's movement. However, though rarely performed today, the Ghost Dance remains for many American Indians a potent symbol of the federal government's unjust treatment of native peoples.

[See also Native American History and Culture, *subentry on* 1800 to 1900; Native American Removal; Religion; *and* West, The.]

BIBLIOGRAPHY

Andersson, Rani-Henik. *The Lakota Ghost Dance of 1890.* Lincoln: University of Nebraska Press, 2008. The best modern treatment of the Ghost Dance, focusing on the Lakotas' version of the ceremony and the events leading to the tragic events at Wounded Knee.

Hittman, Michael. *Wovoka and the Ghost Dance.* Edited by Don Lynch. Expanded ed. Lincoln: University of Nebraska Press, 1998. An excellent history of the Northern Paiute origins of the nineteenth-century Ghost Dance that examines both Wodziwob's and Wovoka's movements.

Mooney, James. *The Ghost Dance Religion and the Sioux Outbreak of 1890.* Introduction by Raymond J. DeMallie. Lincoln: University of Nebraska Press, 1991. First published in 1896; still the best study of the Ghost Dance, valuable particularly for the way it places the 1890 Ghost Dance movement in historical context.

Harvey Markowitz

G. I. BILL

See Servicemen's Readjustment Act.

GILDED AGE

The term "Gilded Age" is popular with historians and the public to describe the decades between the Reconstruction Era and the Progressive Era. The term derives from the title of a novel published in 1873 by Mark Twain and Charles Dudley Warner. Contemporaries appreciated this satire of the era's politics and business, but they rarely used "Gilded Age" as a name for their times. It was popularized after World War I by cultural critics because it conveyed their view that the country had taken a shallow and materialistic turn in the late 1800s. Historians have off and on debated abandoning the label as melodramatic and misleading. Experts generally discuss the Gilded Age as demarcated by two depressions—1873–1878 and 1893–1897—that dramatized the upheaval accompanying huge social and economic changes. The United States can be thought of as experiencing, all at one time, forces of expansion, incorporation, and transformation.

Expansion. In 1867 the United States purchased Alaska and admitted Nebraska as the thirty-seventh state. In 1898 the United States, now forty-five states, annexed Hawai'i, Puerto Rico, Guam, and the Philippines. Americans settled more land between 1870 and 1900 than they had in the 260 years preceding, though much of this was sparse ranchland in the West. In 1890 the Census Bureau highlighted this geographic expansion by announcing that it could no longer identify the frontier of settlement.

The country's population expanded from 40 million in 1870 to 76 million in 1900. Immigrants accounted for about one-third of this increase. Throughout the period, between 13 and 15 percent of the population was foreign-born. More than a fifth of native-born Americans had at least one immigrant parent. Around 90 percent of these people came from Europe; most of the rest crossed from Canada. Until the Mexican Revolution of the 1910s, Hispanic migration remained minimal; conflict across the Southwest between Anglo-American settlers and the pre-existing Mexican population did not entice newcomers. Less than 2 percent of migrants came from China, with even fewer before 1900 from Japan. More than 90 percent of the 107,500 Chinese in the 1890 U.S. Census lived in the West, more than two-thirds in California. About 95 percent of Chinese migrants were men, and they endured meager conditions in the hope of saving to return home. Western states were the focus of the anti-Chinese agitation that led to the Chinese Exclusion Act of 1882.

The most important immigration trend in the Gilded Age was a shift from northern and western Europe to the Mediterranean lands and eastern Europe. In the 1870s around 70 percent of immigrants came from Germany, Ireland, Great Britain, and Scandinavia, while around 6.5 percent came from Italy, Polish regions of Germany, and the Austro-Hungarian and Russian empires. By the 1890s around 40 percent came from northern and western Europe, while more than 50 percent came from southern and eastern Europe. This influx of people from supposedly strange and backward lands invigorated the anti-immigrant sentiment known as nativism, hitherto targeted mainly at Irish Catholics or, in the West, Asians.

A million immigrants worked on farms by the 1890s, but immigration meant the most to industry and cities. At century's end, more than a third of workers in oil refining, coal mining, textiles, and meatpacking were foreign-born, as were around two-thirds of copper and iron miners and makers of ready-made clothing. Immigrants and their children accounted for 50 to 80 percent of the population of every major city except Baltimore, New Orleans, and Washington, D.C., places with ties to the slower-growing South and with large populations of African Americans competing for similar jobs. Until the Great Migration of the 1910s–1920s, the black population of New York City and Chicago was only around 2 percent of the total, and that of Philadelphia was under 6 percent. Even so, in the 1890s alone, 185,000 blacks left the South, mainly for cities in the Northeast and the Middle West; African Americans also migrated to southern cities such as Atlanta and Memphis.

Between 1870 and 1900 the United States went from producing around 70,000 tons of steel per year to producing more than 12 million tons, about half the world's supply.

The country went from producing almost no oil in the 1850s to producing 64 million barrels per year by 1900. Such new industries obscured the extent to which the era's industrialization involved mechanized processing of traditional products: raw materials and agricultural goods. Meatpacking plants and farm-machinery factories in Chicago, mechanized flour mills in Minneapolis, huge copper smelting plants in El Paso, Texas, and Butte, Montana, large-scale logging enterprises in the Northwest, cotton mills in New England and the Carolinas—these explained how the United States came to outproduce Britain, France, and Germany combined by 1900. Big business stimulated small business, too. Cities such as Philadelphia and Newark, New Jersey, featured networks of medium and small firms making tools, furniture, jewelry, and other specialized products.

By 1900 the value of industrial production was nearly three times that of agriculture, which in 1865 had still accounted for the largest share of the American economy. And this reversal occurred despite agricultural innovations and the opening of new lands, which together caused agricultural production and exports to soar. Farm exports exploded in other countries as well, however, deflating commodity prices and saddling farmers with debt even as they became more efficient. This situation catalyzed the agrarian protests that became known as the Populist Movement.

The expansion of industry entailed the growth of cities. Transit innovations, especially the electric trolley, introduced in Richmond, Virginia, in 1887, facilitated intracity movement, even as railroads and steamboats moved ever more goods and people between cities. Cities expanded outward as their populations burgeoned. As they expanded in area, cities segmented into warehouse, industrial, and residential districts, themselves increasingly segregated by social class and race and ethnicity. Old city centers became central business districts, where corporate headquarters, professional offices, retail, entertainment, and government all concentrated. Around 30 million Americans lived in cities and towns by 1900, nearly equivalent to the entire population in 1860. The urban percentage of the population doubled from around 20 percent in 1860 to around 40 percent in 1900. In 1860 the country had 9 cities with a population of more than one hundred thousand—the traditional threshold for a large city—and by 1900 it had 38 such cities. New York, Chicago, and Philadelphia each had a million people by the end of the century. By the late 1800s, cities could seem large beyond comprehension and their social relations hopelessly anonymous and tense.

Incorporation. Expansion was accompanied by the incorporation of dispersed places and activities into systems and organizations. One expression of this trend was the proliferation of the business corporation, an organizational form suited for administering complex, far-flung enterprises. The railroads served as models for this form. By their nature, railroads needed to coordinate thousands of people doing hundreds of different jobs spread out over more than hundreds or thousands of miles. The practical challenges involved in operating railroads coherently even affected people's perceptions of space and time. For example, to simplify scheduling, railroads in the 1880s persuaded Americans to divide the country into time zones. Hitherto, each town set its clocks by the sun, which meant even such nearby cities as Boston and Hartford differed by a few minutes, a formula for chaos in an age of railroads.

In a geographic sense, railroads incorporated the country. They also pervaded literature, art, and music because they were the lifeline of rural areas and the rationale for cities. Two dozen lines met at Chicago alone. Cities surrendered prime locations for stations, tracks, and freight yards; tracks bisected even the Mall in Washington. National and state governments provided railroad companies with loosely supervised land grants and other subsidies. In eight years after the Civil War, railroad mileage doubled to seventy thousand miles. Despite the Panic of 1873, precipitated by bankruptcy of the Northern Pacific Railway, mileage doubled again in the next fifteen years and reached more than two hundred thousand miles by the century's end. Starting in 1869, when the Central Pacific met the Union Pacific in the Utah desert, transcontinental lines knit the Far West into the country. Regional networks meant that by 1900 nearly everyone in the East and Midwest and most people in the South had access to a railroad.

Popular resentment of this indispensible but often arrogant business came to the fore during the Great Railroad Strike of 1877, when locals joined workers in ransacking rail yards and equipment in Pittsburgh, Baltimore, and elsewhere. Throughout the period, railroads and related businesses became the focus of fierce labor disputes, culminating in the nationwide Pullman strike of 1894. Deadly clashes such as the Haymarket affair in Chicago in 1886 and the Homestead strike in Homestead, near Pittsburgh, in 1892 reinforced fears that as it industrialized, the country would descend into intractable class conflict. The Knights of Labor (founded in 1869) and the American Federation of Labor (founded in 1886) offered alternative models of unionization to workers, who like farmers sought forms of collective action to offset the power of corporations.

Transportation and communications put pressure on groups seeking a measure of isolation. Transcontinental railroads brought buffalo hunters to the West and carried hides to eastern tanneries. Between 1865 and the early 1880s the bison population plummeted from an estimated 13 million to several hundred, ending what remained of the Plains Indians' self-sufficiency. The United States Army and the Bureau of Indian Affairs pressured Native Americans onto reservations, where in theory they were to learn to live as settled, modern people. This policy, along with constant clashes with settlers, fueled the last phase of the centuries-long Indian wars, culminating in the Wounded Knee Tragedy (1890). To Americanize Indians, officials suppressed tribal institutions, religions, and customs, and established immersion-style boarding schools for young people. Under the Dawes Allotment Act of 1887, the government divided tribal lands into individual farms, a reform that backfired, magnifying the poverty and disarray of Native American peoples.

After the collapse of Reconstruction in the mid-1870s, proponents of a "New South" argued for adopting northern methods and ideas, but this time under control of southern elites. This approach achieved much in terms of establishing schools and other public services, industrializing and urbanizing portions of the region, and upgrading its agriculture. But the South depended on northern investment for railroads, factories, mines, lumber operations, and textile mills. Southern cities and industries grew less fast than those elsewhere and not fast enough to combat the region's poverty and lack of capital.

Amid such economic troubles, the third of the southern population that was African American had little opportunity to expand the rights and opportunities they had gained during Reconstruction. Freed slaves had hoped to build lives as independent farmers, but by 1900, more than 75 percent of southern black farmers worked as tenants or sharecroppers.

White landowners manipulated prices and interest rates to trap black sharecroppers in chronic debt. Southern white farmers also struggled amid stagnant cotton prices and a cycle of debt, which accounts for the fervor and anger of the southern wing of the Populist movement. With prospects bleak on the land, blacks sought opportunities in towns, lumber camps, and coal mines throughout the South. Mobile, self-reliant young blacks evoked the worst racist fears of southern whites. Sanctioned by favorable federal court rulings, southern state legislatures and city councils segregated blacks in transit, parks, and other public places, while employing stratagems to disenfranchise black men, despite the Fifteenth Amendment (1870). Custom and ritual reinforced such laws, vividly so in the gruesome ritual of lynching. This mixture of formal and extralegal oppression that characterized what is known as the Jim Crow era failed to stem efforts by southern blacks to improve their circumstances. Southern blacks vastly increased their literacy rates and established networks of schools, businesses, and organizations.

Transformation. New technologies and products transformed the feel of everyday life. People adopted readymade clothing, Coca-Cola, Gillette safety razors, Ivory soap—goods whose mundaneness brought home the novelty of a society of mass consumption. The Eastman Kodak camera and the Edison phonograph changed the sights and sounds of middle-class life. At the 1876 Centennial Exposition in Philadelphia or the 1893 Columbian Exposition in Chicago, people were fascinated by telephones and electricity.

Department stores and chain stores made new products available to town dwellers, while mail-order catalogs brought consumer goods to rural people. New methods of organization and public relations lay behind popular leisure and entertainment trends such as professional baseball and vaudeville. Middle-class readers encountered trends in the humanities and sciences and much else through mass-circulation magazines, whose pages were also filled with display advertising, another innovation. Every large city had numerous daily newspapers, often in several languages. Ranging in tone from intellectual to sensationalist, these intricate businesses brought new management techniques together with the latest communications and printing technologies.

Evangelists such as Dwight Moody and movements such as the Social Gospel illustrated ways that American Protestantism sought to address urban conditions. Despite prejudice, Catholicism and Judaism became more established and struggled with how far to Americanize their institutions and rituals. The most enduring religious division arose over how to respond to the theory of Darwinian evolution and other transformations in social and natural science. Modernists argued for accommodating new discoveries and ideas, while traditionalists laid the groundwork for the fundamentalist movements of the twentieth century. Americans' enthusiasm for science had a basis in experience. Effective treatments were not yet available for tuberculosis and other endemic diseases. But antisepsis and anesthesia made surgery viable for conditions from appendicitis to breast cancer. Indoor plumbing, water filtration, and sewerage dramatically decreased the incidence of typhoid or cholera, even though people were only beginning to understand the germ theory of disease.

The education required of the so-called new middle class of managers, office workers, technicians, and professionals explains the spread of high schools, from which still only about 6.5 percent of Americans had graduated in 1900. College remained a privilege, with about 22,200 men and 5,200 women earning bachelor's degrees in 1900—but the figure for men was nearly three times that of 1870, and the figure for women was nearly four times that of 1870. Johns Hopkins University, founded in 1876, and the University of Chicago, founded in 1890, drew upon German precedents to create model research universities producing PhDs in natural and social science. The 1862 Morrill Act subsidized state efforts to build public universities, devoted to agriculture and engineering, among other fields. New professional organizations took on the task of raising standards and inculcating professionalism in members. The Chautauqua Movement was one of many programs that encouraged people to pursue education throughout their lives. Libraries, museums, and orchestras became standard cultural institutions in major cities.

By the 1870s the number of women in high school frequently exceeded that of men. Women's colleges such as Wellesley and Bryn Mawr provided intense educations to upper-middle-class women excluded from private male universities. Most state universities were coeducational from the start. The percentage of women employed outside the home increased from 15 percent in 1870 to 21 percent in 1900, but most of these women were young and single. The presumption remained strong that when possible, married women should devote themselves to the household and family. Gradual changes in notions of intimacy and marriage nonetheless appeared in rising divorce rates and falling fertility rates. Poorer women, especially immigrants and African Americans, worked in industry or as domestic workers, while young women from more prosperous families gained skills to work as typists, stenographers, switchboard operators, store clerks, and such.

Nearly three-fourths of teachers were women. Nursing, librarianship, and social work also had reputations as women's professions. Women who sought to enter law or medicine encountered considerable resistance. When possible, women involved themselves with reform groups such as the Woman's Christian Temperance Union or those that were part of the Woman Suffrage Movement. At the local level, women's volunteer organizations concentrated on civic and social reform, education, and public health.

Most Americans welcomed the material and technological developments of the Gilded Age, but they disputed how this apparent progress was organized and shared. Two severe depressions, repeated violent clashes between business and labor movements, profound rural discontent, and widespread misgivings over corporate power made clear that the country had unleashed industrial capitalism but had as yet little ability to channel the organizational and technological innovations associated with the new industrialism to public ends. The Progressive reformers of the early twentieth century often defined themselves against what they perceived as the confusion and drift of the late 1800s, but virtually every idea and program tried during the Progressive Era originated in the manifold, fascinating efforts of the Gilded Age to understand the urban, industrial society that was taking shape with immense speed and force. Perhaps the bitterest legacy of the Gilded Age was the abandonment of the Civil War–era vision—never deeply held to begin with—of a society less stratified by race. By 1900 a set of rationalizations for racial oppression—some backed by pseudosciences such as eugenics—had emerged that could be extended from traditional targets such as blacks and Asians to many groups. Thus although Americans began to confront the problems of political economy that came to the fore during the Gilded Age, they ran away from its racial dilemmas.

[*See also* Anti-Catholicism; Asian Americans; Automation and Computerization; Central and Eastern European Americans; Cities and Suburbs; Communication Networks; Demography; Electricity and Electrification; German Americans; Internal Migration, *subentry on* African Americans; Irish Americans; Labor Movements; Native American Boarding Schools; Native American Removal; Nativist Movement; Racism; Scandinavian Americans; Segregation, Racial; Strikes and Industrial Conflict; *and* Women's Club Movement.]

BIBLIOGRAPHY

Ayers, Edward L. *The Promise of the New South: Life after Reconstruction.* New York: Oxford University Press, 1992.

Calhoun, Charles W., ed. *The Gilded Age: Perspectives on the Origins of Modern America.* 2d ed. Lanham, Md.: Rowman & Littlefield, 2007.

Cotkin, George. *Reluctant Modernism: American Thought and Culture, 1880–1900.* Boston: Twayne, 1992.

Edwards, Rebecca. *New Spirits: Americans in the "Gilded Age," 1865–1905.* 2d ed. New York: Oxford University Press, 2011.

Edwards, Rebecca, Richard R. John, and Richard Bensel. "Forum: Should We Abolish the 'Gilded Age'?" *Journal of the Gilded Age and Progressive Era* 8 (2009): 461–485.

Meinig, D. W. *The Shaping of America.* Vol. 3: *Transcontinental America, 1850–1915.* New Haven, Conn.: Yale University Press, 1998.

Menand, Louis. *The Metaphysical Club: A Story of Ideas in America.* New York: Farrar, Straus & Giroux, 2001.

Postel, Charles. *The Populist Vision.* New York: Oxford University Press, 2007.

Schlereth, Thomas J. *Victorian America: Transformations in Everyday Life, 1876–1915.* New York: HarperCollins, 1991.

Schneirov, Richard, with responses by James L. Huston and Rebecca Edwards. "Thoughts on Periodizing the Gilded Age: Capital Accumulation, Society, and Politics, 1873–1898." *Journal of the Gilded Age and Progressive Era* 5 (2006): 189–240.

Alan Lessoff

GOLD RUSHES

The nineteenth century was the great era of North American gold rushes. Beginning in North Carolina in 1799, gold rushes were initially a southern phenomenon, centered along the eastern piedmont of the Appalachians. A rush in the lands of the Cherokee nation contributed to the forced removal of Cherokees in the 1830s.

The western rushes began in 1848—just as the United States acquired California from Mexico—with a gold discovery in the foothills of the Sierra Nevada, and they shared characteristics with those in the South. They dispossessed native peoples, focused on placers (surface gold deposits), and attracted disproportionately male and stunningly diverse populations. California's was the most male of the rushes, though native women were present in the diggings, and Miwok women, for example, took up mining in order to supplement older subsistence strategies. The rush drew gold seekers from around the world, especially from Mexico, Chile, the United States, China, and several European nations. California also set a pattern for future rushes in that Anglo-Americans, sometimes aided by the state, fought to control the placers. As Anglo women began to arrive, they, too, inaugurated a pattern common in later rushes by campaigning against such public amusements as dance halls and brothels, which often employed Mexican, Chilean, French, and Chinese women.

These patterns were repeated during gold rushes in Nevada and Colorado in the late 1850s; in Montana, Idaho, and Arizona in the 1860s; and in Dakota Territory in the 1870s. By the 1880s the emphasis in western mining was shifting to the underground, hard-rock mining of gold, silver, and copper, which required heavy capital investment, industrial processes, and large numbers of wageworkers. Not until the 1890s, however, did hard-rock miners outnumber placer miners in the West. And the 1890s saw new placer rushes following a series of discoveries in Alaska Territory and Canada's Yukon Territory.

The western rushes coincided with industrialization and class formation in the United States and with an era of North Atlantic global economic dominance. For many in industrializing nations and in countries ruled by colonial powers, the rushes seemed to provide opportunities outside the economic and geopolitical bounds that circumscribed their lives. That so many people from so many different places descended on the placers and contended with one another over access to gold, and that Anglo-American men often succeeded in limiting access for so many others, demonstrates that gold rushes were no sideshow; they were part of the main event of nineteenth-century history. Even Anglo men, however, try as they might to impose themselves as the rightful claimants of North American gold, could not extract from the hills the promise they sought: at most, a fortune; at least, an escape from a lifetime of wage labor. For most participants, gold rushes never lived up to the hopes they inspired.

[See also Alaska; California; Chinese Americans; Internal Migration, subentry on Nineteenth-Century Westward; Social Class; and West, The.]

BIBLIOGRAPHY

Blodgett, Peter J. Land of Golden Dreams: California in the Gold Rush Decade, 1848–1858. San Marino, Calif.: Huntington Library, 1999.

Paul, Rodman Wilson, and Elliott West. Mining Frontiers of the Far West, 1848–1880. Rev. ed. Albuquerque: University of New Mexico Press, 2001.

Williams, David. The Georgia Gold Rush: Twenty-Niners, Cherokees, and Gold Fever. Columbia: University of South Carolina Press, 1992.

Susan Lee Johnson

GRAHAM, BILLY

(1918-), the most important and influential American evangelist of the second half of the twentieth century. William Franklin "Billy" Graham Jr. was born in Charlotte, North Carolina, on 7 November 1918. Beginning in 1939 after his ordination as a Southern Baptist minister and continuing until 2005, he preached a born-again message in 185 countries to live audiences totaling some 200 million people. During this long and impressive career, he became the face and embodiment of evangelical Christianity for countless Americans.

Graham's singular career was typical, however, of both American Protestant and Evangelical history. The global reach of his ministry recalled the historic Baptist connections between Britain and America and the work of Baptist missionaries who evangelized around the world. His peripatetic ministry also recalled the gritty circuit riders of the eighteenth and early nineteenth centuries and such figures as Dwight Moody (1837–1899) and Billy Sunday (1862–1935). Graham even showed an affinity for the Puritan theology of Jonathan Edwards when he preached a variation of Edwards's 1741 sermon "Sinners in the Hands of an Angry God" at his Los Angeles crusade in 1949.

Graham identified Moody as the model for his evangelism. Graham, like Moody before him, created an evangelical empire through the formation of the Billy Graham Evangelistic Association (BGEA) in Minneapolis, Minnesota, in 1950. The BGEA handled the logistics and financials of his crusade ministry and assisted Graham with his many media ventures, including his radio program *Hour of Decision* (from 1950), his syndicated newspaper column titled "My Answer" (from 1952), *Decision* magazine (from 1960), the Billy Graham Evangelistic Film Ministry (from 1952), and his dozens of best-selling books, beginning with *Peace with God* (1953) and ending with *The Journey* (2006).

Graham's connections to the past and the unmatched reach of his evangelism established him as both the most familiar and the most remote figure of recent American Protestantism. Born-again messages of Christianity had been a commonplace among Evangelicals for two centuries, and Graham's distribution of this type of message through modern technologies only added to its familiarity. Indeed, Graham entered the homes of his constituents through television, radio, and print and acted as a private, if physically absent, confessor who addressed their most intimate concerns, worries, and sins. At the same time, the large stadiums and the media of print, radio, and television insulated Graham from his audience. Unlike most ministers, Graham faced a different congregation each time he preached, and he had no sustained contact with everyday Evangelicals. Graham's admirers often revered him like a saint, placing him above critical discourse

and separating him further from their Christian lives. In this way, Graham's age-old message, his electronic evangelism, and his iconic Christian status contributed to both the privatization of faith and the ever-presence of faith in the public sphere.

Both Graham's message and his highly organized method led his critics—Reinhold Niebuhr among them—to argue that he neglected the social issues of his day. Graham argued instead that those who had experienced a personal transformation through Jesus Christ best effected changes to society. Still, early in his career, when confronted with the injustice of American racial segregation, Graham protested against such discrimination by desegregating all of his crusades following the *Brown v. Board of Education* decision in 1954, by renouncing segregation in *Life* magazine in 1956, and by inviting Dr. Martin Luther King Jr. to lead a prayer at his New York City crusade in 1957.

After Graham's resistance to segregation in the 1950s, his social ministry deepened and broadened. By 1974, Graham formalized his commitment to an evangelical social gospel when he signed the Lausanne covenant at the 1974 International Congress on World Evangelization at Lausanne, Switzerland. The covenant privileges evangelism and yet calls Evangelicals to sociopolitical involvement as a matter of Christian duty. Following Lausanne, Graham redoubled his efforts in combating discrimination, worldwide poverty, and, later, the AIDS epidemic. Still, Graham was ultimately a social moderate who stressed above all else the need for individuals to come to Christ and advocated for gradual change in social relations.

[*See also* **Clergy; Itinerant Preachers; National Association of Evangelicals;** *and* **Religion.**]

BIBLIOGRAPHY

Finstuen, Andrew. *Original Sin and Everyday Protestants: The Theology of Reinhold Niebuhr, Billy Graham, and Paul Tillich in an Age of Anxiety.* Chapel Hill: University of North Carolina Press, 2009.

Martin, William. *A Prophet with Honor: The Billy Graham Story.* New York: William Morrow and Company, 1991.

Miller, Steven P. *Billy Graham and the Rise of the Republican South.* Philadelphia: University of Pennsylvania Press, 2009.

Andrew Finstuen

GRANGER MOVEMENT

The Granger movement was the first stage of the agrarian crusade of the late nineteenth century in which farmers voiced their dissatisfaction with deteriorating economic conditions and agriculture's declining status in a rapidly industrializing nation. The Patrons of Husbandry, or the Grange, was founded in 1867 in Washington, D.C., by Oliver Hudson Kelley (1826–1913). A Minnesota farmer who became a government clerk, Kelley believed that a rural social organization modeled on the Masonic Order but admitting women to full membership could improve the intellectual life of farmers and overcome rural isolation. As secretary of the group, Kelley set out to form local Granges. He enjoyed little success at first, but beginning in 1869 the Grange grew rapidly. At its peak in the mid-1870s, with a network of county and state organizations, the national Grange claimed 775,000 members in twenty thousand local groups.

Although Kelley initially viewed the Grange as primarily a social organization, the order discovered other interests as it grew in strength. Its social role remained, especially at the local level, but the Grange also became an educational agency. Granges devoted a portion of each meeting to debate and discussion, thereby encouraging the members to read and to think about contemporary issues. Granges interested themselves in the one-room country schools, seeking to make the instruction more relevant to pupils' lives, and in the land-grant colleges, which they considered to be their institutions. The Patrons of Husbandry embraced economic cooperation as one way to improve farmers' economic condition, especially by reducing the role of middlemen. Members formed farmer-owned stores, elevators, and creameries, launched mutual insurance companies, and in a few instances established factories to manufacture farm machinery. Most of these enterprises failed because of inadequate capital and management, but they presaged the successful farm cooperatives of the twentieth century.

Although officially the Grange was nonpartisan, discontented farmers organized by the Grange often turned to political action. Railroad abuses especially concerned them, and in the four states of the upper Mississippi valley they successfully campaigned for the so-called Granger laws that sought to bring railroads under public control. These laws, in turn, laid the groundwork for the Interstate Commerce Act of 1887. By then, however, the Grange had lost most of its membership and influence, though the organization remained a voice of agriculture and a social institution for farmers in the northeastern states.

[*See also* **Fraternal Organizations; Populist Movement;** *and* **Rural Life and Society.**]

BIBLIOGRAPHY

Nordin, D. Sven. *Rich Harvest: A History of the Grange, 1867–1900.* Jackson: University Press of Mississippi, 1974.

Woods, Thomas A. *Knights of the Plow: Oliver H. Kelley and the Origins of the Grange in Republican Ideology.* Ames: Iowa State University Press, 1991.

Roy V. Scott

GREAT AWAKENINGS

The two major religious "awakenings"—the First Great Awakening of the mid-eighteenth century and the Second Great Awakening of the early nineteenth century—are important events in the social evolution of colonial British America and the United States. Both arose from popular, democratic impulses reacting against elite control, and both laid the foundations of modern American Christianity.

First Great Awakening. The First Great Awakening began in the early 1730s when Christians on both sides of the Atlantic sought a deeper religious experience. In response to the increased religious sensibility among their congregants, a circle of New England clergymen led by Jonathan Edwards of Massachusetts urged their colleagues to abandon the ornate preaching style then prevailing in New England and instead to use simpler language and metaphors that would be more easily understood by their audiences. They found likeminded brethren among middle-colony Presbyterians such as William Tennent Sr. and his sons Gilbert and William Jr., who established what became known as the Log College in Neshaminy, Pennsylvania, to train ministers who preached a more conservative form of Protestant Calvinist Christianity. These "New Lights" railed against ministers who, they felt, embraced the perquisites of clerical authority and endorsed pernicious liberal theologies. Antirevivalist opponents, dubbed "Old Lights," saw what they considered a dangerous enthusiasm being spread among the laity by irresponsible, informally educated, and heterodox preachers. The differences between New Lights and Old Lights gradually sundered churches throughout the colonies and formally split the Presbyterian Church in 1741. New denominations arose out of the religious ferment.

Context. The First Great Awakening arose from a number of factors. One was the growth of evidentialism, rationalist "natural" religion that sought to reconcile reason with revelation by harnessing advancing scientific discoveries to prove the truths of Christianity. A parallel spread of formalism in organized Christian practice disparaged emotive expression, as well as buttressing the power and influence of the clergy. A third factor was Pietism, a phenomenon that began in German lands. Pietism emphasized a strong emotional aspect to one's personal relationship with God and was influenced by popular religious beliefs that stretched back deep into Europe's and America's pasts, beliefs related to magic, folk medicine, astrology, and occult practices. A tradition of revivalism brought by Scottish and Scotch-Irish settlers in the early eighteenth century likewise laid the foundation for American evangelicalism.

Demographic, economic, and political trends also contributed to the Awakening. In the seventeenth century, religion had helped stabilize colonial society, but by the early eighteenth century it seemed less essential to Americans' lives. The two decades or so preceding the First Great Awakening witnessed the rapid social, economic, and political maturation of British America. The population grew through immigration and natural increase and became more ethnically, culturally, and religiously diverse. Economic expansion and rising wealth improved the standard of living for many and fostered the steady

Anglicization of colonial American societies in the eighteenth century. Provincial politics became steadily more democratic, which led to democratization in the churches. Ordinary churchgoers became alienated as a more professionalized clergy bolstered its authority by forging closer ties with the most influential church members. As the American colonies grew more prosperous, clergymen and government officials alike complained about widespread religious indifference among the laity. Popular piety had declined noticeably, as evidenced by declining church attendance and the persistent belief in "pagan" folk religion among the colonists. These trends encouraged a growing conviction among some clergymen that a return to fundamental theological principles, as well as the revival of "vital piety," were necessary.

Lower- and middle-class churchgoers increasingly bristled at the power and influence of the elites, who controlled the churches as much as they did town, county, and provincial politics. Radical New Light rhetoric inspired antiauthoritarianism among ordinary people. Women in particular challenged boundaries and redefined authority. At a time when female church membership and attendance already outpaced that of men, the First Great Awakening opened new doors to female religious expression. By 1700, women had come to constitute the vast majority of church members. Consequently it was women who were among the first and most ardent respondents to revivalism. The Awakening's moderate anti-intellectualism also gave women—who were barred from seeking an advanced education—an opportunity to assert their authority in a male-dominated realm.

Another issue involved the "enthusiasm" of New Light worship. Old Light critics frequently complained about the shouting, singing, weeping, and gesticulations that characterized New Light services, arguing that these indicated exploitation of women's supposed emotional weakness, whereas revivalists generally applauded male and female enthusiasm as evidence of what they called "heart religion."

Shift to the Southern Colonies.

Although revivalism in New England and the middle colonies had waned by the outbreak of the French and Indian War in 1754, echoes of it reverberated throughout the southern colonies, particularly in the backcountry. Starting in the 1750s, itinerant Baptist and Presbyterian ministers had been winning souls away from the Anglican Church, especially among the poor and middle-class populations of Virginia and the Carolinas. Moreover, in a culture widely regarded as profligate, Baptists offered a sense of community. Presbyterians were especially successful in ministering to the widely scattered communities of mainly Scotch-Irish settlers in the Virginia and Carolina backcountry.

Slaveholders generally rejected attempts to convert slaves: they feared that slaves' conversion and the literacy that often attended conversion would undermine the slave system. Such notions changed in the middle of the eighteenth century when New Light Presbyterians and Baptists began to proselytize heavily among free-black and slave communities, which in turn prompted the Anglican Church also to missionize more aggressively to them, largely through the Anglican Society for the Propagation of the Gospel in Foreign Parts. Previously alienated from the religion of their oppressors, slaves and free blacks were now drawn to the same heart religion that other Americans were. As evangelical Christianity moved southward, slaves discovered a refreshing egalitarianism and confirmation that the enthusiastic Christianity they had developed in secret could have public legitimacy. Slave preachers emerged to offer messages of hope and comfort, and some of them gained enough esteem from their white counterparts that they preached to white audiences as well as to mixed gatherings. Though this was only the beginning of African American Christianization, it is the Awakening's greatest legacy, because it gave slaves and free blacks tools for demanding recognition of their humanity, as well as for demanding their liberation.

Second Great Awakening.

The American Revolution grew out of the same forces that gave rise to the First Great Awakening and accelerated its democratizing trends. Inspired by the egalitarianism of the Revolution, Americans challenged old notions of deference to authority based on rank, birth, wealth, and education in society and politics. Similarly, they recast American Christianity on populist lines. In a way that echoed the years following the Reformation, ordinary people were empowered to interpret Christian doctrine, thus eroding the authority of clergymen and theologians. Paradoxically, the new religious movements of the Revolutionary era—for instance, Baptists, Methodists, Mormons, Disciples of Christ—centered on charismatic figures who wielded great authority. Religious demagoguery justified itself in the name of revolutionary egalitarianism and the common people; it was hoped that this democratic impulse in religion would lead to an eventual coming together of all American Christians into one harmonious body. Against the vocal concerns of prominent theologians, evangelical itinerants urged people to read the Scriptures for themselves and decide for themselves what it meant to be a Christian: no formal education was necessary, they preached, to understand divine truth. Backcountry evangelicalism challenged the prerogative of a natural elite to speak for the people,

arguing that Christianity must be antiauthoritarian and individualistic. The future of American Christianity lay with these backcountry men and women: the Second Great Awakening began on the Kentucky frontier in the 1790s.

Context. Just as the First Great Awakening developed in the midst of an unprecedented economic expansion, so also did the Second Great Awakening attend a major market revolution, that of the 1820s and 1830s.

The period saw the advent of a much larger middle and professional class, a class in which white male breadwinners working outside the home were expected to be married to women who created clean, harmonious, and pious households as refuges for their husbands from the "vexations and embarrassments of business" (Russell J. Reising, *Loose Ends: Closure and Crisis in the American Social Text* [Durham, N. C.: Duke University Press, 1996], p. 260). Housewifery became a solemn duty expected of women, one that developed into what scholars have called the "cult of domesticity" and the "cult of true womanhood." Women continued to constitute the majority of church members, with only approximately 10 percent of membership rolls being single men or all-male households. The evangelicalism of the Second Great Awakening, with its attendant social-reform movements, also gave women opportunities to assert a measure of independence and authority previously unavailable to them. Though they were barred from ministerial ordination, some evangelical women nevertheless preached to large audiences in the camp meetings and even some churches. Charles Grandison Finney encouraged women to testify and even preach at his spectacular revivals—Elizabeth Cady Stanton was one of his converts—and women also emerged as religious authors and theologians, publishing works in the many denominational and sectarian magazines of the period. Women joined and sometimes led social-reform movements, particularly the abolitionist and temperance movements, often with the blessing of male religious authorities; their participation in these movements spawned a women's rights movement based on a belief that women's current status was little better than that of slaves.

Response to Attacks.   Attempts by older and well-established religious institutions to bridle revivalism during both Awakenings were interpreted by radical evangelicals as naked elitism, and the new sects and denominations that arose maintained their central authority primarily by refusing to enforce any sort of orthodoxy—which resulted in further sectarianism. Evangelical women and African Americans perceived attacks upon revivalism as an effort by conservative forces to maintain white male authority and power, thus feeding the rising tide of abolitionism and sparking a sustained women's rights movement.

The social conflict of the years following the Revolution and during Thomas Jefferson's presidency (1801–1809) led to the religious ferment of the Second Great Awakening, sundering old ways of understanding Christianity and creating still more division, rather than forging American national unity. Individuals, fired with individualistic zeal against wealth, rank, learning, and clerical authority, set out to found new churches and even new denominations to serve their needs. The old Puritan emphasis on literacy that resulted in one of the most literate nations on earth facilitated the profusion of print material in the early national period. New religious journals and newspapers used plain logic and simple language, as did the preachers in sermons, eschewing the old formats of exposition and argument that were redolent with elitist formalism unsuited to a simple,

democratic, republican people. Also, the old hymns were either discarded or modified to suit a more popular audience as folk songs, reels, jigs, and original tunes were set to a simplified poetry usually free of complicated doctrine and filled with folksy imagery and everyday experience. This was especially effective for African Americans, who readily adopted and adapted the new hymnal style to create an entirely new Christian musical culture.

Formalization and Respectability.   The radical populism unleashed in the early years of the 1800s gave way gradually to centripetal forces toward formalization and respectability in the immediate antebellum years. The second-generation leadership of the Methodists, Baptists, and Disciples of Christ began to criticize self-trained itinerant ministers, as well as the evangelical revivalism typical of the outdoor camp meetings that had become ubiquitous before the Civil War. By the time of Reconstruction, camp meetings had lost their centrality except on the frontier, individualist interpretations of doctrine were discredited in favor of formal college instruction and settled theology, and rustic simplicity surrendered to gentility.

The charismatic revivalism of the Second Great Awakening also inspired an optimistic millennialism that in turn led to the foundation of various movements for social reform—movements for the abolition of slavery, women's rights, temperance, and standardized universal education, among others—as well as a flurry of communitarian experiments. However, what had once been considered an extraordinary phenomenon had by the twentieth century become a defining feature of Christianity in the United States.

[***See also*** **Antebellum Era; Antebellum Reform; Burned-Over District; Clergy; Edwards, Jonathan; Itinerant Preachers;**

New England; Religion; Revivals; Utopian and Communitarian Movements; *and* Women and Religious Institutions.]

BIBLIOGRAPHY

Bonomi, Patricia U. *Under the Cope of Heaven: Religion, Society, and Politics in Colonial America.* Rev. ed. New York: Oxford University Press, 2003.

Bushman, Richard L., ed. *The Great Awakening: Documents on the Revival of Religion, 1740–1745.* New York: Atheneum for the Institute of Early American History and Culture, Williamsburg, Va., 1969.

Butler, Jon. *Awash in a Sea of Faith: Christianizing the American People.* Cambridge, Mass.: Harvard University Press, 1990.

Butler, Jon. "Enthusiasm Described and Decried: The Great Awakening as Interpretive Fiction." *Journal of American History* 69, no. 2 (1982): 305–325.

Goen, C. C. *Revivalism and Separatism in New England, 1740–1800.* New Haven, Conn.: Yale University Press, 1962.

Hatch, Nathan O. *The Democratization of American Christianity.* New Haven, Conn.: Yale University Press, 1989.

Kidd, Thomas S. *The Great Awakening: The Roots of Evangelical Christianity in Colonial America.* New Haven, Conn.: Yale University Press, 2007.

Lambert, Frank. *Inventing the "Great Awakening."* Princeton, N.J.: Princeton University Press, 1999.

Westerkamp, Marilyn J. *Women and Religion in Early America, 1600–1850: The Puritan and Evangelical Traditions.* London: Routledge, 1999.

John Howard Smith

GREAT DEPRESSION ERA

An era defined by unprecedented economic hardship and government intervention, the Great Depression began with the collapse of the United States economy in 1929. Soon a global economic crisis, the Depression did not fully end in the United States until the economy rose to meet military demand during World War II. Americans experienced several notable low points during the Great Depression. In 1932, unemployment peaked near 25 percent, and the Dow Jones Industrial Average fell to almost one-tenth its 1929 value. And on Black Sunday, 14 April 1935, dust storms swept the country and carried topsoil from the Great Plains as far east as the Atlantic. But single events fail to capture the worst of the Great Depression. For years Americans saw their lives torn apart by the broken economy. Faced with job losses, decreased wages, failed savings, and faltering sources of support, Americans of all class backgrounds struggled to provide basic food and shelter for themselves and their families.

Political Context. Herbert Hoover and Franklin D. Roosevelt both served as president during the Great Depression. Hoover, who was president from 1929 to 1933, made the first attempts to manage the impending economic disaster. A strong believer in laissez-faire capitalism, he was reluctant to use the federal government to intervene in the economy or to provide aid directly to the American people. Largely as a result of this policy, Hoover is believed to have done too little to combat the economic forces at work against the country. The election of Franklin D. Roosevelt in 1932 signaled a drastic change in course. Promising to aid the "forgotten man"—those working-class people who had been most affected by the Depression—Roosevelt aimed to reinvigorate the economy, stabilize agriculture, regulate the financial industry, and create reasonable working conditions for Americans. Roosevelt famously said that his programs constituted "bold, persistent experimentation." He was also the first national executive to implement the policies of the British economist John Maynard Keynes, who supported an active and influential federal government in response to economic dysfunction.

Under Roosevelt's guidance, the federal government took an interventionist role in both the economy and American life. This change, and the legislation supporting it, came to be known as the New Deal. Congress passed an impressive fifteen major bills during Roosevelt's first one hundred days as president. This watershed sweep of legislation was followed by the passage of a second set of bills in 1935. New Deal programs redefined the scope of American government. They laid the foundation for what became the American welfare state—a move that lastingly changed the relationship both of the federal government to the citizens and of the citizens to the federal government.

Urban America. Urban areas quickly felt the effects of the Depression. During the 1920s the cities had come to define American social and cultural life. These so-called Roaring Twenties ushered in the era of automobiles and introduced Americans to the future staples of their social lives—the radio and the moving picture show. Combined with abundant employment opportunities and growing infrastructure, these new diversions made cities attractive places to live. But in the early years of the Depression, most cities fell into a downward spiral that they were unable to escape. As the economy weakened, consumer confidence and purchases followed suit. Companies struggled to maintain profits, and they responded to decreased demand with cuts to both production and workforce. As more workers lost their jobs, found their income reduced, and generally lost faith in the economy, they became unwilling and unable to spend their money.

This lack of spending kept demand low, which in turn left industry unable to recover lost profits and workers unable to recover lost wages and jobs.

The situation worsened for all Americans when the banking system collapsed. As wages fell, Americans became unable to pay their loans and service their debts. Fearing for their savings, many customers made runs on their banks. Others stayed away from banks entirely. Numerous banks were forced into insolvency. President Roosevelt felt the situation serious enough to call a bank holiday in March 1933, closing all the country's banks until their solvency could be confirmed.

Perhaps the most visible urban symbols of the economic collapse were the shantytowns that sprang up in and around metropolitan areas. Known as "Hoovervilles" after the president whose inadequate responses seemed to deepen the Depression, these camps were populated by displaced and homeless men and women. In 1932, nearly twenty thousand veterans of World War I marched to Washington, D.C., to demand early payment of a war bonus owed by Congress. Known as the Bonus Army, these men and women made shelters out of whatever materials they could find. The veterans pleaded their case to no avail. Their camp met a disastrous end when President Hoover ordered the U.S. Army, led by General Douglas MacArthur, to disperse the inhabitants by force.

Responding to the Crisis. Many Americans began to see the government as a legitimate source of aid. Although some at first resisted the idea of government handouts, they eventually found themselves with no-where else to turn. Traditional sources of aid—family, friends, religious and fraternal organizations—all proved unable to meet the substantial needs of suffering Americans. Federal work programs helped to ease the handout stigma by providing a way to earn assistance. Chief among these programs were the Works Progress Administration (WPA) and the Civilian Conservation Corps (CCC). The WPA, launched in 1935, enlisted almost one-third of those out of jobs in public works projects across the country. The CCC, launched in 1933, provided 2 million young men with work fortifying environmental infrastructure.

Elderly Americans turned to the government for aid as well. The California physician Dr. Francis Townsend played an important role in advancing this cause. Townsend proposed that the government pay Americans who were at least sixty years old and retired $200 per month, provided that the recipients spent the money within thirty days and on American goods. The Townsend Movement enjoyed considerable national support, despite criticisms that its benefits could not be funded. Responding in its own way to the needs of America's elderly citizens, and pressured in part by Townsend and his followers, Congress passed the Social Security Act in 1935.

Mass-production workers looked to improve their lives through unionization. Early attempts at representation among the members of the struggling working class included company unions and Communist unemployed councils. But the passage in 1935 of the National Labor Relations Act helped lay the legal groundwork for independent labor unionization. This act benefited workers by protecting their right to collective bargaining and by establishing the National Labor Relations Board to oversee their relationship with employers. Many employers resisted union recognition. But with legal backing, workers were adamant that unions could bring them a higher and more stable quality of life. The growth of the Congress of Industrial Organizations (CIO) was pivotal in the formation of mass-production unions. The CIO helped organize industrial

workers and included both white and black Americans.

Not all unionization went smoothly. Worker militancy and owner resistance varied from city to city and from plant to plant. A big union breakthrough came in Flint, Michigan, in 1937, when a volatile sit-down strike threatened to heighten tensions among company, workers, and law enforcement, but the strike ultimately ended with the important recognition of the United Automobile Workers union. Another clash occurred in 1934 with the Teamsters' strike in Minneapolis, Minnesota, where local business owners, the police, and the National Guard quelled potential violence.

Other Americans advocated for change through the political process. For example, the writer Upton Sinclair's End Poverty in California (EPIC) movement supported the election of Democratic candidates in California. Sinclair, who proposed the creation of cooperative work programs for the unemployed, received the Democratic nomination for governor in 1934. Portrayed by the Republicans as a Communist who would attract the nation's down-and-out by the score, he received more than eight hundred thousand votes but lost the election.

Rural America. Rural Americans began the Great Depression already behind their urban counterparts. They had fared well during World War I, when agricultural demand surged in order to meet the needs of the armies fighting in Europe. But by 1925 prices for cotton, corn, and wheat had dropped significantly. Throughout the 1920s the agrarian way of life still captivated the American imagination. People thought great opportunity awaited them on the farm. Companies offered free train rides to the Great Plains and boasted— often deceitfully—about infrastructure and farming conditions.

Rural America fell into its own cyclical pattern of economic decline. Farmers struggled to adjust when World War I ended and the demand for their products declined. Many had taken on large debts in order to buy farm equipment, seed, and land. Though the price of their goods fell, the money required to operate their farms did not. Their only way to make more money was to plant more crops. With the help of technology like the tractor, this proved to be an easy task. But production only created more surplus, driving prices down further and doing nothing to help farmers.

Throughout the 1920s, bank failures and farm foreclosures were already common. After 1929, however, the economic problems in rural America deepened considerably. Foreclosures were so frequent that rural farmers banded together to fight them. Organizing themselves at property auctions (sometimes called "penny auctions"), they would allow bids no higher than ten cents—and would then give the property back to its original owner. In some cases farmers even resorted to physically threatening those responsible for carrying out the foreclosures, or any investors coming to the auction to place meaningful bids.

To make matters worse during the 1930s, the American Great Plains was also the site of the worst ecological disaster in American history. Affecting land in six states, and indelibly captured in photographs by Dorothea Lange, Arthur Rothstein, and others, the Dust Bowl literally blew farmers off the land and crushed their agrarian dreams. Driven by the prospect of financial gain, farmers had spent decades plowing up as much of the Great Plains as they could. Blinded by their ambition, and tricked by a few years of abnormally abundant rainfall, they laid waste to the prairies. But a severe drought began in 1930 and lasted for nearly a decade. The drought, searing heat, and punishing winds proved to be a ruinous combination. Winds picked crumbling topsoil off the ground and carried it in murderous storms. The clouds generated by the Dust Bowl were so thick that animals suffocated when left outside. Static electricity built in the air to the point that car engines died and people avoided touching each other for fear that they would be knocked down. Black Sunday, 14 April 1935, became the most infamous day of the Dust Bowl. So much dirt was torn from the Great Plains that it rained down in New York City and Washington, D.C., and was even found collecting on ships three hundred miles out in the Atlantic Ocean.

Despite all their efforts to remain on the land, many farmers, both tenants and owners, had no choice but to leave. Fleeing the Great Plains in hopes of finding opportunity elsewhere, these migrants—often called "Okies" because so many came from Oklahoma—discovered that there was no prosperous place to go. Arriving in California, they found themselves turned away or denied work. Their suffering went largely unnoticed until John Steinbeck chronicled their plight in his 1939 novel *The Grapes of Wrath*.

Although he could not make it rain, President Roosevelt did not sit by while America's agriculture failed. He introduced a system of centralized planning that aimed to rescue rural areas and stabilize the agricultural markets in the future. The landmark legislation was the Agricultural Adjustment Act (AAA) of 1933. In an effort to drive down supply, the AAA created a program of "domestic allotment" that worked by paying farmers to reduce cultivated land and livestock. In the spring of 1932, farmers approved the program by large majorities. But some remained skeptical, especially when ordered to kill newborn livestock and plow under crops in the field. Although the Supreme Court declared the AAA unconstitutional in 1936, it set a lasting precedent in American agriculture. Similar laws were soon passed to take its place. The government has been heavily invested in farming ever since.

The government also used works programs to improve the quality of life in rural areas. The disparity between rural and urban homes was displayed nowhere better than in the lack of rural electrification. Programs like the Tennessee Valley Authority (TVA) began to close this gap. The TVA, begun in 1933, was a novel program that built dams and brought electricity to rural areas. Expanding on its successful model, Roosevelt established the Rural Electrification Administration (REA) in 1935 in an attempt to bring electricity to rural areas nationwide. By 1939 the number of rural households with electricity had increased by 400 percent; efforts to bring electricity to all Americans continued until the early 1950s.

Women and Minorities. In this time before the Civil Rights Movement, African Americans faced both de jure and de facto racism. For example, workplace racism was rampant. Some white bosses fired their black workers and replaced them with unemployed whites. Many New Deal programs gave priority hiring to white applicants. Even the AAA's benefits could be racially manipulated. In the South, where the vast majority of African Americans worked as sharecroppers on white-owned farms, often former plantations, little if any of the AAA benefits went to them. Instead, landowners either kept the funds for themselves or actually evicted the sharecroppers so that less would be grown on their land and the AAA payment would thus be increased. An eviction of thirty-four sharecroppers from a plantation brought about the creation of the Southern Tenant Farmers' Union (STFU) in Poinsett County, Arkansas, the first race and gender integrated farmers' alliance in the South. With help from local socialist organizers, the STFU worked across the cotton-growing states to keep tenant farmers on their land. Members faced fierce resistance from whites in their communities.

Important steps were taken toward racial equality during the Great Depression. African Americans found representation in unions, which put them on an equal footing with their white coworkers. Although few blacks came to national prominence in the political arena, President Roosevelt relied on a group of African American advisers, known as the "Black Cabinet," when deciding racial issues. The Black Cabinet contained one woman, the respected educator Mary McLeod Bethune. In an event during 1939, the black singer Marian Anderson was prohibited from singing in Constitution Hall by its owners, the Daughters of the American Revolution. First Lady Eleanor Roosevelt worked with Secretary of the Interior Harold Ickes to arrange for Anderson to sing at the Lincoln Memorial instead—which she did on Easter Sunday, to a crowd of seventy-five thousand.

Other people of color faced similar challenges during the Great Depression. Mexican Americans faced deportation or coerced "voluntary" repatriation, as well as widespread workplace discrimination. Japanese Americans experienced extensive discrimination, and an estimated 22 percent of the immigrant population returned to Japan in the 1930s. Filipino Americans saw the passage of laws that banned them from marrying whites, excluded them from federal aid, and offered to pay for their passage back to the Philippines. Many survived by establishing strong ethnic communities and organizations. In California, for example, Mexican and Filipino laborers organized together to improve working conditions in the Central Valley's agricultural fields.

The Great Depression brought dramatic changes to the lives of the indigenous people of the United States. Under the leadership of John Collier, the so-called Indian New Deal revoked and revised scores of laws and policies that had stripped Native Americans of their lands and tribal customs. The allotment of land was halted, indigenous arts and crafts were protected, the practice of religious traditions was legalized, and tribal government was strengthened. Not all Native Americans agreed with the Indian New Deal; many believed that only self-determination would truly empower Native American men and women. However, for the first time in three centuries, Indian mortality rates began to improve and traditions began to be revived.

Women of all racial and ethnic backgrounds found themselves bearing increased responsibility in both rural and urban households during the Great Depression. Mothers were forced to make do with whatever scant resources they could find. Rural and urban women, for example, went back to growing their families' food and canning fruit and vegetables for the winter. The economic downturn affected women in other ways as well. When women tried to find employment, for example, they often faced discrimination in the workplace and in New Deal agencies. It was assumed that married women needed jobs less than others did because their husbands would be the family breadwinners. But this model of the male patriarch often failed in the Great Depression. Many men, who defined themselves by their jobs and by their ability to provide for a family, felt emasculated and detached by unemployment. It was not uncommon for husbands to lose interest in their families and to disappear for weeks or months at a time. Young men, likewise, felt it was impossible to marry or begin a family with prospects for employment so poor.

[*See also* Appalachia; Electricity and Electrification; Homelessness and Vagrancy; Internal Migration, *subentry on* Twentieth Century and Beyond; Labor Movements; Migrant Camps, Depression Era; New Deal Social Reforms; Poverty; Rural Life and Society; Southern Tenant Farmers' Union and National Farm Labor Union; Strikes and Industrial Conflict; Unemployment, Social Impact of; Women Workers; Work; *and* Working-Class Life and Society.]

BIBLIOGRAPHY

Cohen, Lizabeth. *Making a New Deal: Industrial Workers in Chicago, 1919–1939.* 2d ed. Cambridge, U.K., and New York: Cambridge University Press, 2008.

Egan, Timothy. *The Worst Hard Time: The Untold Story of Those Who Survived the Great American Dust Bowl.* New York: Houghton Mifflin, 2006.

Katz, William Loren. *The New Freedom to the New Deal, 1913–1939.* Austin, Tex.: Raintree Steck-Vaughn, 1993.

Nishi, Dennis, ed. *The Great Depression.* San Diego, Calif.: Greenhaven Press, 2001.

Rauchway, Eric. *The Great Depression and the New Deal: A Very Short Introduction.* New York: Oxford University Press, 2008.

Stock, Catherine McNicol. *Main Street in Crisis: The Old Middle Class on the Northern Plains.* Chapel Hill: University of North Carolina Press, 1992.

Catherine McNicol Stock and Brian F. Irving

GREAT MIGRATION, AFRICAN-AMERICAN

See Internal Migration: African Americans.

GREAT SOCIETY REFORM PROGRAMS

In his 1964 State of the Union address, President Lyndon B. Johnson announced an "unconditional war on poverty"—an idea conceived by the late president John F. Kennedy—that became the major focus of his Great Society. Two pieces of legislation, the Civil Rights Act (1964) and the Voting Rights Act (1965), were monumental gains for the African American community. Other historic achievements included the creation of Medicare and Medicaid, as well as legislation and new administrative priorities in the areas of education, primary health care, public housing, immigration, transportation safety, and the environment.

The immense amount of attention given the nation's poor by the Johnson administration cannot be attributed to a conventional stimulus for social change such as a rising public demand, lobbying, interest groups, or war. Vast improvements in agricultural productivity—in part the result of extensive mechanization that accelerated in the 1940s—displaced millions of rural workers, who migrated to the cities in search of factory employment. Although poverty in the United States was an old problem, urban migrations north by a large portion of the country's least privileged, the rising civil rights movement that demanded the nation's attention to the problem of inequality, and increased interest by intellectuals in the growing fields of social science combined to create an unusual impetus for the Great Society antipoverty programs.

The Economic Opportunity Act of 1964 created federally operated antipoverty programs through the newly created Office of Economic Opportunity. The Office of Economic Opportunity directly operated the Community Action Program, the Job Corps, and Volunteers in Service to America (VISTA), while a number of programs were delegated to other federal agencies. Under the Community Action Program, federal funds were combined with local funds to encourage initiatives in areas such as education, health service, employment and housing, and community organization. Community organizing activities, largely by giving the poor considerable discretion over programs and strategies, were intended to develop reform constituencies within individual communities. However, the poor's control of organizing often led to confrontations with existing political and social leadership. In reaction, in 1967 the U.S. Congress passed the Green Amendment to the Economic Opportunity Act, ending independent organizing by giving local governments control of the community-action agencies.

In addition to organizing activities, the Community Action Program initiated a wide variety of programs. Upward Bound was operated by academic institutions in partnership with the Office of Economic Opportunity to encourage low-income high school students to attend college. The Legal Services Program provided legal representation, research, education, and advocacy in legal matters and the law. Foster Grandparents trained people who were at least sixty years old and had low incomes to work as foster parents. Grants made to public and private nonprofit organizations provided for the needs of seasonally employed agricultural workers and their families in areas such as education and day care. Under Project Head Start, preschool-age children from low-income families were given social services, medical and dental examinations, and learning experiences aimed at having them start school on an equal footing with children from better-off families. Health Service Centers were started in low-income neighborhoods in an effort to provide for more accessible medical, dental, and diagnostic services.

Programs from the Office of Economic Opportunity that were delegated to other federal departments included the Neighborhood

Youth Corps, Special Impact, Operation Mainstream, and New Careers, all of which were administered by the Bureau of Work Programs within the Department of Labor; the Work Study and Adult Basic Education programs, which were administered by the Department of Education; Work Experience, which was administered by the Welfare Administration; Rural Loans, which was administered by the Farmers Home Administration of the Department of Agriculture; and Small Business Loans, which was administered by the Small Business Administration.

The answer to the question of whether the war on poverty was won or lost remains ideological. It is not clear whether the large apparent drop in the poverty rate, from 18 percent of the population in 1964 to 11 percent in 1973, was a result of Great Society initiatives, a buoyant economy, both, neither, or some other factor. Liberals argue that there were direct as well as indirect contributions to a substantial reduction in poverty and that the war was one worth fighting, if for no reason other than for placing poverty on the public agenda. Conservatives contend that the antipoverty programs were moral hazards that actually increased poverty and dependency by relieving individuals of responsibility for their own welfare. That the Great Society's antipoverty programs, notably the direct service programs, were largely ineffective in achieving their goals may even suggest that rather than strategic attempts to address social problems, programs such as the war on poverty—like many public policies in an open society—more often are totems of popular preferences or the product of mass consensus.

[*See also* **Internal Migration,** *subentries on* **Twentieth Century and Beyond** *and* **African Americans; New Deal Social Reforms; Sixties, The; Social Class;** *and* **Welfare.**]

BIBLIOGRAPHY

Epstein, William. *Democracy without Decency: Good Citizenship and the War on Poverty.* University Park: Pennsylvania State University Press, 2010.

Haveman, Robert H., ed. *A Decade of Federal Antipoverty Programs: Achievements, Failures, and Lessons.* New York: Academic Press, 1977.

Marris, Peter, and Martin Rein. *Dilemmas of Social Reform: Poverty and Community Action in the United States.* New York: Atherton Press, 1967.

Murray, Charles. *Losing Ground: American Social Policy, 1950–1980.* New York: Basic Books, 1984.

Patterson, James T. *America's Struggle against Poverty in the Twentieth Century.* Cambridge, Mass.: Harvard University Press, 2000.

Salina I. Offergeld

GRIMKÉ, SARAH AND ANGELINA

(1792–1873) and (1805–1879), reformers. Born into the antebellum aristocracy of Charleston, South Carolina, the sisters Sarah and Angelina Grimké both had household slaves in their youth. After a spiritual and moral transformation as young adults, however, both became active in the antislavery crusade and other reforms.

Sarah, visiting Philadelphia in 1819, was drawn to the Quakers' moral-reform interests. Moving to Philadelphia, she joined the Society of Friends; Angelina followed in 1829. Engaging in local benevolent activity, the sisters emerged as antislavery activists with two 1836 tracts: Sarah's *Epistle to the Clergy of the Southern States* and Angelina's *Appeal to the Christian Women of the South.* The latter was banned in the South and led to threats of imprisonment in South Carolina. Angelina, recruited by William Lloyd

Garrison, lectured and wrote for the American Anti-Slavery Society in 1836–1838. In *Reply to an Essay on Slavery and Abolition* (1838), she denounced gradualism and called for immediate abolition.

When Massachusetts Congregational ministers disapproved of their public lectures in 1837, the Grimkés responded forcefully. In *Appeal to the Women of the Nominally Free States* (1837), Angelina argued that women shared with men the nation's moral guilt over slavery. Sarah's *Letters on the Equality of the Sexes and the Condition of Women* appeared in 1838. Along with antislavery and women's rights, they also embraced the temperance and peace movements.

The sisters stopped lecturing after Angelina's marriage to the abolitionist leader Theodore Dwight Weld in 1838, but they continued to circulate antislavery petitions, and Angelina collaborated with Weld on an influential documentary collection, *American Slavery as It Is* (1839). Angelina's extensive correspondence with Weld comments insightfully on the economics of slavery and the political realities of abolition and offers shrewd observations on politicians and antislavery leaders. Sarah's correspondence, too, with family members, antislavery associates, and leaders in reform and religion, including the evangelist Charles Grandison Finney, illuminates her moral and religious views.

After years in Belleville and Perth Amboy, New Jersey, where they operated a school, Angelina and Theodore Weld, with Sarah, moved to West Newton, Massachusetts, in 1863. There for several years they were associated with a school conducted by the physical-culture advocate Dioclesian Lewis.

[*See also* **Antebellum Era; Antebellum Reform; Antislavery; Weld, Theodore Dwight;** *and* **Women's Rights Movement, Antebellum Era.**]

BIBLIOGRAPHY

Ceplair, Larry, ed. *The Public Years of Sarah and Angelina Grimké: Selected Writings, 1835–1839.* New York: Columbia University Press, 1989.

Lerner, Gerda. *The Grimké Sisters from South Carolina: Pioneers for Women's Rights and Abolition.* Rev. ed. Chapel Hill: University of North Carolina Press, 2004.

William H. Brackney

GUNS

The gun holds a central, yet contentious, place in American society. No other consumer product has generated such passionate debate, largely because no other modern consumer product is both entrenched in the founding history and mythology of the United States and yet also involved in tens of thousands of deaths a year. Most Americans consider firearm ownership to be an essential right: 91 percent of gun owners and 63 percent of people who do not own guns believe that the Constitution's Second Amendment guarantees an individual the right to own firearms. Thus attempts to regulate or restrict gun sales have been countered by the fear that such laws would violate fundamental liberties. Such thinking is rooted in historical concerns, and most Americans cite a fear of tyranny to justify their opposition to gun control. During the 2010 election campaign for a U.S. Senate seat in Nevada, the Republican candidate Sharron Angle claimed that if "Congress keeps going the way it is, people are really looking toward those Second Amendment remedies," adding that the Founding Fathers "put that Second Amendment in there for a good reason and that was for the people to protect themselves against a tyrannical government."

History. The history of guns and gun culture has been clouded by misrepresentation. Consider Thomas Jefferson's admission in a 19 June 1796 letter to George Washington that "one loves to possess arms." This popular quotation, used to support individual gun ownership, returns more than a hundred thousand hits in a Google search and appears on the website of the National Rifle Association's Institute for Legislative Action, in anti-left paraphernalia, and in published pro-gun scholarship in law journals. The problem is that Jefferson was not talking about actual guns at all, as the context of the quotation reveals. Instead, Jefferson was looking for some political, not actual, ammunition against Alexander Hamilton and Henry Knox: he was asking Washington for a copy of their correspondence with the president on French policy. "Tho I do not know that it will ever be of the least importance to me," he wrote, "yet one loves to possess arms, tho they hope never to have occasion for them. They possess my paper in my own handwriting. It is just I should possess theirs."

Although Jefferson was not involved in writing the Constitution or the Bill of Rights, it is accurate to say that he and many other Founders supported the natural right to self-defense and that guns played a key role in that defense, particularly on the Frontier. The historical question of exactly how many Americans owned guns is difficult to answer because records are often inconsistent and incomplete. If we can extrapolate from local studies, then a majority of American adults owned guns in the colonial era. Gloria Main's study of six counties in Maryland from 1650 to 1720 found that an average of 76 percent of young fathers owned arms of some sort (usually a gun). In general, wealthy men were more likely to own a gun than poorer men were, and southerners were more likely to own guns than northerners were.

Concern that there was a relationship between guns and interpersonal violence emerged in the Early Republic Era. The early 1800s saw the passage of America's first laws regulating the concealed carrying of weapons, partly in response to the proliferation of inexpensive and mass-produced handguns before the Civil War. These laws were different from colonial regulations of gunpowder, initially establishing time and place restrictions but eventually criminalizing the sale and possession of certain types of weapons. At the same time, several states revised existing or drafted new state constitutions to support explicitly an individual's right to bear arms for self-defense, an ideology echoed by abolitionists and eventually radical Republicans seeking to protect blacks from violence. Connecticut ratified its first constitution in 1818 with the guarantee that "every citizen has a right to bear arms in defense of himself and the state," a much different formulation than neighboring Massachusetts's assertion in its 1780 constitution that "the people have a right to keep and to bear arms for the common defence."

Modern Attitudes. Although the gun industry flourished at times throughout the 1800s, the guns manufactured then have little impact on modern gun numbers because 80 percent of all private guns today were acquired after 1974. Although Americans own more guns than do the people of any other western nation—about 230 million as of 2010—gun ownership decreased during the late twentieth and early twenty-first centuries. According to Gallup, the percentage of Americans who keep some kind of firearm in their home has declined from 1960 (49 percent) to 2010 (39 percent), and about 22 percent of all U.S. households have a handgun in them. At the same time, the number of people who think that handguns should be restricted to the police has decreased from 60 percent in 1959 to 29 percent in 2010, and support for stricter gun laws has waned since the 1990s. That being said, only about 12 percent of Americans think that existing gun laws should be made less strict.

Democrats initiated the major pieces of federal gun-control legislation in the twentieth century, namely the National Firearms Act (1934), the Gun Control Act (1968), the Brady Handgun Violence Prevention Act (1993), the Federal Assault Weapons Ban (1994), and the Gun-Free School Zones Act (1995). Political affiliation, however, does not necessarily dictate one's stance on the great gun debate: in 1987, major gun-control legislation (the original Brady bill) was defeated in part by opposition from Speaker of the House Tom Foley, a Democrat. Still, Democrats have been largely unsuccessful in attracting pro-gun voters despite (or perhaps because of) tactics like those seen in the 2008 presidential election when the American Federation of Labor and Congress of Industrial Organizations (AFL-CIO) sent out mailers proclaiming that Barack Obama would protect the "Second Amendment right of an individual to bear arms." Certainly Obama's endorsement from the now-defunct American Hunters and Shooters Association was no match for the National Rifle Association's unequivocal condemnation of his campaign.

With the debate over guns and violence far from resolved, and with the Supreme Court's break from precedent to affirm that the Second Amendment protects an individual's right to bear arms (*District of Columbia v. Heller*, 2008), it is certain that the gun will continue to play a crucial role in United States history.

[*See also* Homicide; Law and Society; Militia Movement, Modern; *and* Militias, Early American.]

BIBLIOGRAPHY

Cornell, Saul. *A Well-Regulated Militia: The Founding Fathers and the Origins of Gun Control in America.* Oxford: Oxford University Press, 2006.

Lott, John R., Jr. *More Guns, Less Crime: Understanding Crime and Gun-Control Laws.* Chicago: University of Chicago Press, 1998.

Main, Gloria L. *Tobacco Colony: Life in Early Maryland, 1650–1720.* Princeton, N.J.: Princeton University Press, 1982.

McDowell, Earl E. *America's Great Gun Game, Gun Ownership vs. Americans' Safety: An Outline of the Need for Increased Federal Gun Legislation.* New York: iUniverse, 2007.

Spitzer, Robert J. *The Politics of Gun Control.* 4th ed. Washington, D.C.: CQ Press, 2008.

Nathan Kozuskanich

H

HAITIAN AMERICANS

Haitian immigration to the United States began in 1791 when Haitians seeking refuge from the violence of the Haitian revolution began to settle in American cities along the East Coast and in New Orleans. Another phase of Haitian immigration was stimulated by the American occupation of Haiti from 1915 to 1934. In 1957 the rise of François "Papa Doc" Duvalier initiated a third phase of Haitian immigration to the United States. The first to flee Haiti under Duvalier were politically connected and wealthy Haitians, the most immediate targets of the new president. In the early 1960s, students and professionals left the country, soon followed by members of the urban working class, with the vast majority going to New York City.

Haitian immigrants who settled in the United States relied on family and social networks to locate housing and employment. In New York the largest Haitian community concentrated in Brooklyn; the majority of employed Haitians found work in manufacturing and service positions. Opposition to the Duvalier dictatorship shaped the politics and culture of the New York Haitian community, which by the late 1970s numbered at least a quarter of a million. Through the collapse of the Duvalier dictatorship in 1986 and beyond, Haitians in the United States have remained invested in the politics of their homeland.

In 1972, Haitians initiated a new phase of migration to south Florida, many making the dangerous journey by boat. These so-called boat people were, like earlier migrants, escaping political violence in Haiti. However, those traveling to south Florida throughout the 1970s and early 1980s were also displaced by a new economic model implemented by François Duvalier's son and successor, Jean-Claude "Baby Doc" Duvalier, who, with U.S. assistance, sought to transform Haiti into an exporter of both agriculture and manufactured goods. A massive increase in migration to south Florida from 1979 to 1981, which included large numbers of Haitian peasants, brought the population of south Florida's Haitian community, centered in the northeastern Miami neighborhood of Little Haiti, to an estimated eighty thousand.

Boston, Washington, D.C., Chicago, and other American cities have also attracted substantial Haitian populations. Across the United States, Haitians have had to contend with anti-Haitian discrimination; stigmatization as disease carriers has done particular damage. From the early 1980s Haitian Americans mounted major campaigns against government policies that highlighted their community's association with AIDS. In addition, police violence has been a serious problem for Haitians, as highlighted by two cases in New York City: the police beating and forced sodomy of Abner Louima in 1997 and the police shooting of Patrick Dorismond in 2000.

United States immigration policy, which historically has classified Haitians as ineligible for political asylum, also creates hardship for Haitians in the United States. Campaigns against the imprisonment and deportation of undocumented Haitians have been central to Haitian American history; notable successes include the passage of the Haitian Refugee Immigration Fairness Act of 1998 and the granting of temporary protected status for Haitians already in the United States on 12 January 2010, the day that Port-au-Prince was struck by an earthquake with a magnitude of 7.0.

[*See also* **Caribbean** *and* **Racism.**]

BIBLIOGRAPHY

Laguerre, Michel S. *American Odyssey: Haitians in New York City*. Ithaca, N.Y.: Cornell University Press, 1984. The fullest introduction to Haitian immigrants in New York City from 1957 to the early 1980s.

Stepick, Alex. *Pride against Prejudice: Haitians in the United States*. Boston: Allyn and Bacon, 1998. One of the only book-length works to focus on the south Florida Haitian community within the larger context of Haitian immigration.

Zéphir, Flore. *The Haitian Americans*. Westport, Conn.: Greenwood Press, 2004.

Carl Lindskoog

HATFIELD-McCOY FEUD

The most famous feud in American history occurred in the mountains of southern West Virginia and northeastern Kentucky between 1878 and 1890. Legend attributes the feud to lingering Civil War hostilities and a dispute over the ownership of a hog, but the evidence suggests that rapid economic and cultural change shaped the conflict.

Anderson "Devil Anse" Hatfield (1839–1921) and Randolph "Old Ranel" McCoy (1825–1913) first became entangled in a court case over land and logging rights in 1872. However, most writers claim that the feud actually began with a legal dispute over a hog in 1878. From there things became worse. On Election Day in 1882, three of McCoy's sons killed one of Hatfield's brothers, and Hatfield fought back by ritually executing the three McCoy youths. No further incidents or press coverage occurred, however, until nearly six years later. By that time, the discovery of coal had brought the Norfolk and Western Railroad through Hatfield land, increasing its value. Almost overnight, state politicians became obsessed with economic development in the mountains. In this volatile context, a relative of Randolph McCoy's, a lawyer named Perry Cline, in 1887 persuaded the Kentucky governor Simon Buckner to authorize a posse to cross into West Virginia and arrest the Hatfields. The Kentucky posse fought several battles with a Hatfield group calling themselves "regulators," during which several individuals on both sides were killed. Finally, on New Year's morning in 1888, a small group of Hatfield supporters—but not Devil Anse himself—crossed the Tug River and trudged up the mountain to the McCoy cabin, which they set on fire, killing two of Randolph McCoy's children. The rest of the family fled to Pikeville, Kentucky, never to return to their mountain home.

Meanwhile, the West Virginia governor E. Willis Wilson, claiming that Buckner had violated extradition procedures, took the case to the Supreme Court, which upheld Kentucky's right to try the Hatfields. Of the eight Hatfields convicted, seven spent time in prison and one was hanged. Devil Anse, however, died peacefully of old age. In contrast to legends suggesting that hundreds were killed over a period of a hundred years, the death toll was actually a dozen within as many years. Press sensationalism obscured the fact that economic development and modernization, not primitive mountain culture, had exacerbated the violence.

[*See also* **Appalachia.**]

BIBLIOGRAPHY

Jones, Virgil Carrington. *The Hatfields and the McCoys*. Chapel Hill: University of North Carolina Press, 1948.

Rice, Otis K. *The Hatfields and the McCoys*. Lexington: University Press of Kentucky, 1978.

Waller, Altina L. *Feud: Hatfields, McCoys, and Social Change in Appalachia, 1860–1900*. Chapel Hill: University of North Carolina Press, 1988.

Altina Waller

HAWAI'I

The archipelago of the Hawaiian Islands was settled by 400 CE, with a possible second migration from Tahiti around 1100. Four separate island kingdoms—Hawai'i, Maui, O'ahu, and Kaua'i—developed, and at Captain James Cook's arrival in 1778, they were in a state of civil war. Kamehameha of Hawai'i Island conquered most of the islands by the mid-1790s, and the islands were unified by 1810.

In 1819, Kamehameha's death and the breaking of the *kapu* (traditional law) system paved the way for drastic change. Boston missionaries arrived in 1820, bringing Protestant Christianity and printing presses to promote literacy in both Hawaiian and English. A constitutional monarchy started in 1840, and a Western land-tenure system began in 1848. Because of their lack of immunity to new diseases, native Hawaiians died in large numbers; by 1872 the native population was at a low of 56,897, representing a drop of 75 to 95 percent of the precontact population.

The islands' strategic location and ports tied Hawai'i's economy to a global market for goods and labor—first with the sandalwood, fur, and whaling trades and later with the California gold rush that spurred the export of foodstuffs to North America. Native Hawaiian sailors—listed as "Kanakas" or "Sandwich Islanders" in records—often settled in the Pacific Northwest and West Coast upon completion of their journeys. It was the cultivation of sugarcane, however, that transformed the geographic, social, and political landscape of Hawai'i from the mid-nineteenth century onward. Contract laborers were recruited from China, Portugal, and Japan; by the early twentieth century they also came from the Philippines, Korea, and Puerto Rico.

Despite their small number, residents of American descent increased in power throughout the nineteenth century, with sugar planters and merchants promoting closer ties to the United States during King David Kalā-kaua's reign (1874–1891). When a reciprocity treaty with the United States was renewed in 1887, it granted the United States exclusive rights to Pearl Harbor in exchange for the continued duty-free export of sugar. In an 1893 coup assisted by the presence of U.S. Marines, Americans overthrew Queen Lili'uokalani, establishing first a provisional government and later the Republic of Hawaii (1894–1898) when they could not garner enough support for annexation by an internationally recognized treaty. In 1898 the Spanish-American War and President William McKinley brought use of a joint resolution of Congress to annex Hawai'i as a territory of the United States.

World War II was a watershed time for the islands, with the bombing of Pearl Harbor in 1941, martial law for the territory until 1944, and increased attention on the islands' significance in the Pacific. Unlike those in the continental United States, Japanese in Hawai'i—making up one-third of the population and vital to the labor force—were not interned in large numbers. Many Nisei (second-generation) males volunteered for military service in the highly decorated 442d Regimental Combat Team. Returning veterans were some of the first Asians to enter politics with the revitalization of the Democratic Party in the postwar years. The International Longshore and Warehouse Union was successful in organizing plantation and other laborers in class-based, interracial strike activities, notably in the great sugar strike of 1946. With the backing of labor unions, the Democratic Party has largely dominated the state's politics since.

After Hawai'i was admitted into the United States as the fiftieth state, in 1959, tourism and federal and military spending replaced agriculture as the primary sectors of the economy. By 1967 a million tourists visited the islands yearly; by 1988 this number was more than 6 million. Data from the 2010 U.S. Census show a population of 1.3 million, with native Hawaiians accounting for about 20 percent. No ethnic group constitutes a majority, but when grouped together, Asians, native Hawaiians and Pacific islanders make up more than 70 percent of the population.

An ongoing renaissance of native Hawaiian culture began in the 1970s, with the revitalization of the Hawaiian language, voyaging practices, and traditional chant, hula, and song. By the 1990s, charter schools with a focus on Hawaiian language had emerged, and in 1993 President Bill Clinton signed the Apology Resolution recognizing the U.S. role in the overthrow of the kingdom a century before. The native Hawaiian sovereignty movement has developed, with political positions ranging from working toward nation-within-a-nation status to outright independence. Because no treaty of annexation was ever signed, many groups contend that Hawai'i's inherent sovereignty is still intact.

[*See also* **Asian Americans; Japanese Americans; Native Hawaiians and Pacific Islanders; Tourism and Travel;** *and* **World War II, Home Front.**]

BIBLIOGRAPHY

Coffman, Tom. *Nation Within: The History of the American Occupation of Hawai'i.* Rev. ed. Kihei, Hawai'i: Koa Books, 2009.

Jung, Moon-Kie. *Reworking Race: The Making of Hawaii's Interracial Labor Movement*. New York: Columbia University Press, 2006.

McGregor, Davianna Pōmaikaʻi. *Nā Kuaʻāina: Living Hawaiian Culture*. Honolulu: University of Hawaiʻi Press, 2007.

John P. Rosa

HAYNES, LEMUEL

(1753–1833) Revolutionary militiaman and Congregational minister. Lemuel Haynes was among Jonathan Edwards's last defenders, the New Divinity ministers, who centered theology on a predestining God who through providential benevolence and divine design overrules sin and evil. Theologically conservative, the New Divinity became in some hands politically revolutionary and even abolitionist. Haynes's sermon *Universal Salvation* (1805), a conservative critique of liberal ("Arminian") religion, was one of the most reprinted American sermons of the nineteenth century. Twentieth-century research, utilizing documents written in the 1770s but not widely known in Haynes's lifetime, revealed that Haynes—a mixed-race man who was never enslaved but rather was indentured as an infant to a white man—criticized the slave trade and slavery. Haynes elucidates a number of important characteristics of the Revolutionary years and the early republic: the nature of the relations between whites and blacks in New England, the role of the frontier in northern Christianity, and a sense among the black population that the persistence of the slave trade and slavery betrayed the American Revolution.

In Haynes's New England, slavery was under attack from several angles—petitions, court decisions, legislative actions, and one state constitution, Vermont's, that declared slavery illegal. Port cities like Boston, Newport and Providence in Rhode Island, and New Haven in Connecticut contained a large minority of poor or working-class African Americans, some free, some enslaved. Haynes himself was born in West Hartford, Connecticut. The black population in New England depended on whites for education, employment, and church membership. At best, whites thought of themselves as "benevolent" or "charitable" to blacks. Though some individuals, like Haynes, benefited from such benevolence, white New Englanders at large marginalized blacks through segregation and harassment. Moreover, colonization—plans for expatriating black people from North America, an idea first broached in the eighteenth century—remained desirable even to later nineteenth-century New Englanders like Harriet Beecher Stowe. Haynes, who preached in New England and New York from 1780 to the end of his life, argued persistently for the inclusion of blacks in American life, not their removal.

Haynes preached in the frontier towns of northern New England, not in the more established port cities. The importance of the frontier in the religion of colonial and early republic New England and New York can hardly be overstated. Conversion and religious revivals were the hallmarks of frontier areas. Splinters of religious traditions—deism, Universalism, Mormonism—multiplied in the frontier areas where Haynes preached. In frontier Vermont (Rutland), then frontier New York (Granville), Haynes led revivals, yet also attacked deism and Universalism. Similarly, the importance of the American Revolution in religion and in race relations can hardly be overstated. Haynes, like many others in the 1770s and 1780s, perceived in the Revolution the possibility that the new nation would terminate the slave trade, slavery, and racial inequality.

In his later writings he argued that white Americans had betrayed their Revolution by allowing slavery and racial inequality not only to exist but also to increase in virulence in the South. The perfidy of white Americans, self-proclaimed heirs to the Revolution, became common coin among the black abolitionists, like David Walker, who emerged around the time of Haynes's death.

[*See also* African Americans; Antislavery; Clergy; Colonial Era; Colonization Movement, African; Early Republic Era; Itinerant Preachers; New England; Religion; *and* Revivals.]

BIBLIOGRAPHY

Brown, Richard D. "'Not Only Extreme Poverty, but the Worst Kind of Orphanage': Lemuel Haynes and the Boundaries of Racial Tolerance on the Yankee Frontier, 1770–1820." *New England Quarterly* 61, no. 4 (December 1988): 502–518.

Roberts, Rita. "Patriotism and Political Criticism: The Evolution of Political Consciousness in the Mind of a Black Revolutionary Soldier." *Eighteenth-Century Studies* 27, no. 4 (Summer 1994): 569–588.

Saillant, John. *Black Puritan, Black Republican: The Life and Thought of Lemuel Haynes, 1753–1833.* New York: Oxford University Press, 2003.

John Saillant

HEALTH AND FITNESS

The pursuit of health has been an integral feature of daily life from colonial times to the present. Amid sickness and other adversities, Americans have always sought advice about physical well-being and taken steps to achieve and maintain this ideal. Common notions of health changed significantly between the seventeenth and twenty-first centuries, as did people's sources of information and their everyday practices.

Early Advice. From the colonial period through the Revolutionary War, most Euro-Americans thought of health holistically, as equilibrium within and among the physical, mental, and spiritual realms of life. They believed that adopting habits of moderation and avoiding excess and vice, especially gluttony and drunkenness, would promote well-being and longevity. Widely available almanacs and advice books proffered suggestions about diet, exercise, sleep, hygiene, and sexual relations, as well as home remedies for common ailments. Toward the end of the eighteenth century, popular imported works included Luigi Cornaro's *Discourses on a Sober and Temperate Life*, George Cheyne's *Essay on Health and Long Life*, S. A. D. Tissot's *Advice to the People in General, with Regard to Their Health*, and William Buchan's *Domestic Medicine*. Emphasizing practical health and do-it-yourself medicine, such literature connected people's daily routines to the Enlightenment's lofty themes of human rationality and control. Advice manuals of the early nineteenth century continued this tradition; enjoying wide popularity among all social groups, imported and homegrown guides contributed to the expectation that the new republic would be uniquely healthy and prosperous.

During the antebellum decades this conviction blossomed into a broad-based health crusade that swept across the Northeast, with ripple effects in the South and the newly settled West. Influenced by the Second Great Awakening, Jacksonian politics, and movements for abolition, temperance, and women's rights, health reformers described health as a personal responsibility and moral imperative and human perfection as a worthy and achievable goal. Sylvester Graham

(1794–1851) preached sexual restraint, vegetarianism, and abstinence from alcohol and tobacco. William Andrus Alcott (1798–1859), a doctor and educator, published widely on popular physiology, nutrition, and physical education. Catharine Beecher (1800–1878) and Dioclesian Lewis (1823–1886) developed systems of calisthenics for use in homes and schools. Other programs of purposive exercise arrived with European immigrants, most notably the gymnastic societies of German settlers, known as "Turnverein." Hydropaths, homeopaths, and botanic healers folded practical health advice into their scathing critiques of orthodox medicine. Celebrating self-reliance, John Gunn's *Domestic Medicine, or Poor Man's Friend* (1830) and other nonsectarian works attracted wide audiences. Specialized literature also appeared, including guides on reproduction and child rearing for parents and texts on popular physiology and health for schoolchildren.

The second half of the nineteenth century brought sober reminders of the fragility of life and health. The Civil War altered American concepts of and responses to death. Urbanization, industrialization, and western expansion exacerbated infectious diseases and other conditions. Disparities in health accompanied an increasingly rigid class structure. The physical demands of work and daily life subjected farmers and ranchers on the Great Plains, miners in the Far West, free blacks in the South, and working-class urban families to hazards unknown among more affluent citizens, who swam at oceanside resorts, played tennis, and rode newfangled bicycles in hopes of relieving the physical and nervous strain that they attributed to America's Gilded Age.

Twentieth-Century Science and Commercialism. During the Progressive Era, concepts of health reflected the cultural values, scientific approaches, and bureaucratic structure of modern industrial society. Doctors depicted the human body as a machine or business whose smooth operation required a well-managed balance between input and output. Exercise physiologists studied the body's efficiency, while anthropometrists measured its size, symmetry, and power—which, in the minds of eugenicists, gave quantitative proof of "racial decline." Outside the laboratory, popular health and fitness combined these social fears with unabashed commerce. John Harvey Kellogg (1852–1943) espoused "biologic living" and the regulation of passions through easy-to-digest food, enemas, and outdoor exercise at his Battle Creek Sanitarium in Michigan. The physical culturist and bodybuilder Bernarr Macfadden (1868–1955) used contests and exhibitions, a publications empire, and his own physique to promote the ideal of muscular, sexualized bodies for men and women alike. Offering a tamer version of femininity, mainstream magazines featured the iconic American Girl and New Woman, whose wholesome forms of recreation embodied white middle-class heterosexuality. Manufacturers of sporting goods and exercise equipment not only cultivated individual consumers, and also found ready markets among public schools, colleges and universities, YMCAs and YWCAs, and other voluntary organizations that sponsored programs in athletics and physical education.

Although informal, independent recreation continued during the 1920s and 1930s, the commodification and institutionalization of health and exercise expanded dramatically. Mass consumer culture convinced many Americans that outward appearance signified true health; beauty, strength, and cleanliness came to symbolize character and status. With sufficient money and motivation, self-conscious Americans could buy products that concealed body odors and rough hands. Meanwhile, "90-pound-weaklings" developed muscle with Charles Atlas's mail-order system, and the flabby became fit at commercial health clubs that began opening in the 1930s.

When strength and security became national watchwords during the 1940s and 1950s, fitness of all types—military, economic, technological, and physical—dominated political discourse and popular culture. Despite scientific debates over the best way to measure and promote fitness, doctors and educators hailed the formation of the President's Council on Youth Fitness in 1956. Labor unions, the Girl Scouts and Boy Scouts, and other private groups organized recreation programs. Television brought exercise into private homes; from 1951 to 1984, the *Jack LaLanne Show* demonstrated calisthenics and weightlifting, leavened with inspirational maxims and advice.

Healthy Lifestyles and Personal Responsibility.

During the 1960s and 1970s, physicians and public health experts redefined health by proclaiming that infectious diseases no longer constituted the country's chief source of sickness and death: instead, the main dangers were heart disease and other chronic degenerative conditions. Average Americans could manage their risks and preserve health, the argument ran, by adopting healthy lifestyles and spurning alcohol, tobacco, and inactivity. Fitness entrepreneurs embraced this ideology to sell stationary bikes, treadmills, and other home equipment. Self-styled exercise gurus quickly joined the cause; Richard Simmons opened a fitness studio in 1974, and Jane Fonda released her first exercise video in 1982. The accomplishments of homegrown Olympic champions, long-distance runners, and professional cyclists also fueled America's so-called fitness boom. In the 1980s, average families and

the U.S. Air Force alike adopted Dr. Kenneth Cooper's "new aerobics," a program of regular, sustained, vigorous exercise. Meanwhile, the New Age counterculture popularized yoga and meditation as equally critical to holistic health.

By the 1990s, experts expressed disappointment with the fitness boom. The surgeon general's landmark 1996 report *Physical Activity and Health* concluded that Americans did not appreciate—nor had science fully confirmed—the value of long bouts of intensive aerobic exercise in staving off cardiovascular disease. In a significant shift, public health officials and sports medicine doctors began "prescribing" moderate "doses" of more diverse types of physical activity to promote broad-based health across an individual's life span. Adopting this new philosophy of health-related exercise, many educational institutions, community centers, and fitness clubs lessened their emphasis on sports skills in favor of instruction for lifetime recreation and physical activity. As the twentieth century closed, the requirements of health seemed to be personal diligence, accessing advice by means of mass media and the Internet, and purchasing the right diet pill, home gym, or health-club membership. This narrow focus on individual responsibility drew criticism from some health advocates and policy makers; people's attitudes about and opportunities for exercise, they insisted, were not private choices alone, but depended also on age, sex, race, ethnicity, class, religion, locale, and the natural and built environments.

The impact of social factors on health practices has drawn the attention of historians as well. Scholarly works in the early twenty-first century have analyzed the attitudes and experiences of specific populations within particular regions and eras (for example, see Fett and Valencius). Older surveys of health and fitness laid an important base of historical understanding by identifying broad trends and mainstream beliefs. General studies written in the 1980s and 1990s demonstrated that American concepts of health are invariably linked to emerging technologies and the market economy. Historians also showed that scientific knowledge and professional viewpoints have always shaped lay concepts and practices of health and, conversely, that popular culture has influenced the work of doctors, public health officials, physical educators, and other experts. Finally, although many health decisions remain private, institutional and governmental directives have increased. Seatbelt use, nutrition labels, and purchases of alcohol and tobacco are subject to legal oversight, and the twenty-first century's so-called obesity epidemic has prompted calls for taxes on junk food.

Despite the growth of external regulation, the premise that health is a personal responsibility has remained strong in American culture. From colonial times to the present, most historians agree, lay citizens and experts alike have viewed health primarily as the result of individual decisions and actions. This enduring outlook has powerful moral overtones; although society has become more secular and scientific, many Americans still regard fitness as the emblem of discipline and righteousness, and ill-health and inactivity as markers of apathy. Although this belief honors the nation's distinctive tenet of individual choice, it also masks the social determinants of health and undercuts collective responsibility for everyone's well-being.

[*See also* **Disease; Everyday Life; Health and Healing, Eighteenth and Nineteenth Centuries; Life Expectancy; Medicine, Popular and Non-Western; Public Health; Sports, Amateur;** *and* **YMCA and YWCA.**]

BIBLIOGRAPHY

Brandt, Allan M., and Paul Rozin, eds. *Morality and Health: Interdisciplinary Perspectives.* New York and London: Routledge, 1997. Raising historical, political, and philosophical issues, this collection of scholarly essays illustrates the interplay between moral values and specific health-related attitudes and behaviors.

Centers for Disease Control and Prevention, National Center for Chronic Disease Prevention and Health Promotion, Division of Nutrition, Physical Activity, and Obesity. http://www.cdc.gov/nccdphp/dnpao. As the federal government's chief online source related to exercise, diet, and health, this site represents public health officials' leading concerns and recommendations.

Fett, Sharla M. *Working Cures: Healing, Health, and Power on Southern Slave Plantations.* Chapel Hill: University of North Carolina Press, 2002. An example of region- and race-specific scholarship examining enslaved blacks' "relational" concept of health and their spiritual, community-based healing practices in the context of racial politics.

Fit: Episodes in the History of the Body. Produced and directed by Laurie Block. 74 minutes. Straight Ahead Pictures, 1991. This film traces American concepts of health and fitness from the late nineteenth to late twentieth centuries, making rich use of original still and moving images.

Green, Harvey. *Fit for America: Health, Fitness, Sport, and American Society.* New York: Pantheon Books, 1986. Drawing on both material culture and written sources, this survey considers how middle-class Americans pursued health and regeneration between 1830 and 1940.

Grover, Kathryn, ed. *Fitness in American Culture: Images of Health, Sport, and the Body, 1830–1940.* Amherst: University of Massachusetts Press; Rochester, N.Y.: Margaret Woodbury Strong Museum, 1989. An eclectic collection of essays that demonstrate how cultural, commercial, and scientific developments intersected with specific aspects of diet, exercise, and sports.

Rosenberg, Charles E., ed. *Right Living: An Anglo-American Tradition of Self-Help Medicine and Hygiene.* Baltimore: Johns Hopkins University

Press, 2003. A collection of scholarly essays on the history of Anglo-American health literature, with particular focus on the colonial period, early nationhood, and the antebellum era.

Valenčius, Conevery Bolton. *The Health of the Country: How American Settlers Understood Themselves and Their Land.* New York: Basic Books, 2002. An example of region-specific scholarship exploring how antebellum settlers of the Missouri and Arkansas territories envisioned health as encompassing the body, the environment, and the nation.

Whorton, James C. *Crusaders for Fitness: The History of American Health Reformers.* Princeton, N.J.: Princeton University Press, 1982. A good starting point for students and scholars alike, this survey of health reform from 1830 to 1920 emphasizes the historical links among religion, science, and popular culture.

Martha H. Verbrugge

HEALTH AND HEALING, EIGHTEENTH AND NINETEENTH CENTURIES

Many people in America during the colonial era adhered to the Greco-Roman humoral theory of disease and treatment. According to humoral theory, an individual's health is determined by the balance of four bodily humors: blood, phlegm, yellow bile, and black bile. Illness results from any humoral imbalance, and treatments reflected attempts to regulate those humors. Common therapies included bloodletting, especially to reduce fevers and pain, vomiting, blistering, purging, and sweating. Medications included cathartics (such as castor oil and mercury compounds), ipecac, cinchona bark, antimony, and camphor, along with opium for pain relief. Infectious diseases were often explained by the concept of contagion —a poisonous substance that had invaded the body—or miasma, a diseased cloud or "bad air" that could arise from rotten smells or effluvia from swamps. In colonies in the American South, for instance, many people believed that exposure to miasma caused infectious epidemics like yellow fever and malaria among English settlers and their European or African servants. Throughout colonial America, inhabitants experienced a period of "seasoning," often lasting at least two years, during which their bodies and humors adjusted to the new environment.

Ideas about health and treatment in the American colonies were closely related to religion and society, and individual health was often linked reflexively to the health of the community. To that end, religious authorities made significant contributions to medical care and public health in early America. The Puritan leader Cotton Mather (1663–1728), for instance, was a vehement supporter of community inoculation to prevent a smallpox epidemic in Boston in 1721, though many Boston physicians opposed the practice because of the risk involved. During the American Revolution and the Early Republic Era, health and medical theory were often intertwined with ideas about morality and civic responsibility. Benjamin Franklin (1706–1790), the gentleman scientist of the Enlightenment, emphasized the direct relationship between healthy politics and healthy bodies, and in 1751 he became a founder of the Pennsylvania Hospital in Philadelphia. Since the most healthful society was viewed as a republican democracy, physicians and other medical practitioners played a significant role in protecting the wellness of American citizens in the young republic.

During the nineteenth century a variety of treatment theories and systems emerged and crystallized. Allopathic ("regular," or "orthodox") practitioners continued to adhere to the humoral theory of illness, and they used treatments that were meant to counteract specific symptoms. Most allopathic practitioners were respected as civic leaders, but some patients and practitioners were becoming concerned about the iatrogenic risks of "heroic" allopathic therapies like purging and bloodletting. The Thomsonian sect, founded by the self-trained herbalist Samuel Thomson (1769–1843) in the early nineteenth century, criticized humoral medicine and heroic applications of purgative remedies. Thomson based his practice on the concept that heat and natural herbal remedies were more effective cures for illness. Homeopathy, a practice that was founded by the physician Samuel Hahnemann (1755–1843) in Germany and arrived in the United States in 1825, argued that remedies should enhance symptoms in the body rather than counteract them but those remedies should be delivered in heavily diluted preparations. The Manhattan practitioner Joel Shew (1816–1855) published his handbook *Hydropathy, or, the Water Cure; Its Principles, Modes of Treatment* in 1844, arguing that water, in various forms and applications, should be the main treatment for a variety of diseases. The eclectic approach to medical practice, founded by Wooster Beach (1794–1868) around 1830, borrowed ideas and therapies from a variety of nineteenth-century treatment systems. Within each treatment system, some practitioners approached therapies more heroically, or with less consideration of risk, and others were more conservative.

Nineteenth-Century Changes in Healing Practices.

Colonial hospitals, the first of which was constructed in Virginia in 1612, were usually populated with chronically ill patients, as well as elderly and indigent inmates. Some colonial port cities, like Boston and Charleston, South Carolina, also established pesthouses or lazarettos to quarantine victims of infectious disease. Such institutions were often more associated with filth, suffering, and depravity than with treatment. Throughout the colonial period and the first half of the nineteenth century, many patients treated themselves and their families for most minor ailments. Domestic medical manuals, published for a lay audience, had become a profitable business by the nineteenth century. James Ewell's *Medical Companion, or Family Physician*, first printed in 1807, and John C. Gunn's *Gunn's Domestic Medicine, or Poor Man's Friend*, first printed in 1830, were popular titles. Slaveholders in the American South also relied on domestic medical manuals to treat illnesses in their human chattel. The rise in sales of proprietary drugs, many based on folk or traditional family remedies, and therapeutics accompanied the rise of newspapers in the 1830s. In more severe cases, particularly during epidemics or if an illness threatened to become chronic or disabling, patients consulted physicians and surgeons. This was also true of slaveholders, who frequently hired physicians on retainer to provide treatment for their slaves so as to prevent epidemics and disabling conditions from compromising their workforce.

In the mid-nineteenth century, several important advances in hospitals and surgical techniques transformed the medical marketplace. The idea of hospitals as healthy environments, based on middle-class, Anglo-American Protestant values, began to emerge and influence therapeutic approaches to inpatient care. Anesthesia, which had appeared in several different forms by the end of the eighteenth century, was first used in a surgical procedure in 1842 when Crawford W. Long (1815–1878) of Georgia used ether for a tumor removal. Theories about germs and disease causation, postulated by European researchers like Louis Pasteur and Robert Koch, began appearing in medical textbooks in the 1880s, and even earlier in the popular press. By the 1870s, antiseptic (Listerian) techniques were used in hospital surgeries, and the first completely antiseptic surgical operation was conducted in Boston in 1879. The popularization of German aseptic techniques—such as using gloves and creating sterile fields—followed in the 1890s and greatly reduced the number of iatrogenic infections in American hospitals.

Medical Practitioners and the Emergence of the Profession.

In colonial America the majority of health-care providers were not academically trained, and there was little distinction between classifications of "physician" and "surgeon," such as there was in England. Most medical treatments were provided by practitioners like ship surgeons, folk healers, bonesetters, midwives, and clergy. By the mid-1700s, however, a more defined allopathic medical profession began to emerge. Some American physicians, like the influential Philadelphia doctor Benjamin Rush (1745–1813), received medical degrees from European universities like those in Paris or Edinburgh. More commonly, practitioners learned their trade through apprenticeships with trained physicians, in addition to studying at American or European colleges and universities. William Shippen Jr. (1736–1808), a Philadelphia physician who had attended the College of New Jersey (now Princeton University) and apprenticed under his father, offered the first formal anatomy course in the American colonies in 1762, and in the same decade he began providing formal courses for midwives. The first formal colonial medical school was founded at the College of Philadelphia by the physician John Morgan in 1765, with lessons in such subjects as botany and materia medica, anatomy, clinical medicine, chemistry, and natural and experimental philosophy. Other medical schools

began to follow, particularly after the American Revolution and the westward expansion of the United States; the first medical school in the West, the Medical College of Ohio, was founded by the physician Daniel Drake in Cincinnati in 1819. The New Orleans School of Medicine, founded in 1856, was the preeminent institution for medical education in the South prior to the Civil War, as well as the first American medical school to emphasize clinical teaching. Practitioners of other treatment systems also began opening schools at this time; for example, Constantine Hering, a German physician in Pennsylvania, established the first American homeopathic college, Allentown Academy, in 1835.

As medical education grew, so did the perceived need for professional regulation. State allopathic medical societies began forming in the early nineteenth century, and the National Medical Convention (forerunner to the American Medical Association) met for the first time in New York in 1846, in part to introduce regulation and reform to American medical education. However, the desire for student enrollment led many medical school administrators to oppose increasing standards for admissions and training. State medical societies also conflicted with medical schools over their authority to issue medical licenses, and many among the American public opposed licensure because it gave "regular" physicians a perceived monopoly on healing practices. The combination of the changing licensure laws and the increased competition among medical schools during this time opened the door for members of underrepresented groups to receive medical degrees and practice as licensed physicians: James McCune Smith (1813–1865) was the first African American to earn a medical degree, in Glasgow, Scotland, in 1837, and Elizabeth Blackwell (1821–1910) was the first American woman to earn a medical degree, at Geneva Medical College in New York in 1849.

After the Civil War, American medical education began to combine an emphasis on clinical instruction with a shift toward medical research at institutions like the Johns Hopkins Medical School, founded in 1893. The American Medical Association also began to recognize medical specialization as new technologies and procedures expanded medical practice.

[*See also* **Asylums and Mental Illness; Education; Everyday Life; Health and Fitness; Hospitals and Dispensaries; Medicine, Popular and Non-Western;** *and* **Midwifery.**]

BIBLIOGRAPHY

Blake, John B. "The Inoculation Controversy in Boston: 1721–1722." *New England Quarterly* 25 (1952): 489–506. An early secondary account of the newspaper and pamphlet war over smallpox inoculation in colonial Boston.

Duffy, John. *From Humors to Medical Science: A History of American Medicine.* 2d ed. Urbana: University of Illinois Press, 1993. An excellent overview of the American medical profession and important trends in medical practice.

Fett, Sharla M. *Working Cures: Healing, Health, and Power on Southern Slave Plantations.* Chapel Hill: University of North Carolina Press, 2002. Exemplary research into healing practices among African American slaves in the nineteenth century.

Morantz-Sanchez, Regina Markell. *Sympathy and Science: Women Physicians in American Medicine.* New York: Oxford University Press, 1985. A significant study of women's entrance and role in the medical profession.

Rosenberg, Charles E. "The Therapeutic Revolution: Medicine, Meaning, and Social Change in Nineteenth-Century America." *The Therapeutic Revolution: Essays in the Social History of American Medicine,* Morris J. Vogel and Charles E. Rosenberg, eds. Philadelphia: University of Pennsylvania Press, 1979, 3–25. An essay explaining the interconnection between therapeutics, the social ritual of healer-patient relationships, and expectations for different types of "cures" from nineteenth-century practitioners.

Ulrich, Laurel Thatcher. *A Midwife's Tale: The Life of Martha Ballard, Based on Her Diary, 1785–1812.* New York: Alfred A. Knopf, 1990. A Pulitzer Prize–winning study of a New England midwife that includes detailed discussions of medical practices and professional changes in the early republic.

Van De Wetering, Maxine. "A Reconsideration of the Inoculation Controversy." *New England Quarterly,* 58 (1985): 46–67. Builds on Blake's earlier argument, but notes that the smallpox inoculation controversy signaled a fundamental shift in American morality as well as public health.

Dea H. Boster

HEMINGS, SALLY

(1773–1835), slave owned by Thomas Jefferson who bore at least seven of his children. Sally Hemings, whose given name was Sarah, was born in 1773 on a Virginia plantation known as the Forest. Her mother was Elizabeth Hemings, an enslaved woman. Her father, an English immigrant, John Wayles, owned the Forest and the Hemings family. Elizabeth and John had six children together: Robert, James, Thenia, Critta, Peter, and Sally, born the year John died. Both Elizabeth and John had other children: seven for Elizabeth and three for John. So, in addition to her six full siblings, Sally Hemings had ten half siblings, some white and some black. When John Wayles died, Hemings and her family came under the ownership of his eldest daughter, Martha, and her husband Thomas Jefferson, then a young lawyer and budding revolutionary. Hemings moved to Jefferson's plantation Monticello when she was two years old, and she spent her early days as a companion to the Jefferson daughters—her half nieces.

When Martha died in 1782, Jefferson sent Hemings with his two youngest daughters, Mary and Lucy, to live with his deceased wife's (and Hemings's) sister Elizabeth Wayles Eppes. Lucy died of whooping cough. Jefferson, then on a diplomatic mission to France, demanded that Mary be sent to him with a mature female enslaved companion who had had smallpox or been inoculated. Instead, in 1787 the fourteen-year-old Hemings accompanied nine-year-old Mary to London and thence to Paris.

Hemings joined her brother James at Jefferson's residence, the Hotel de Langeac. James had been brought to Paris to learn to become a French chef. Early on, Sally Hemings was inoculated for smallpox under the care of the famous Robert Sutton. Like her brother she received wages. Near the end of their stay in Paris, Hemings became pregnant by Jefferson. At first she refused to return to slavery in Virginia. Jefferson persuaded her to go home with him, promising her a good life and freedom for their children. Hemings returned to Monticello in December of 1789. The child she conceived in France died shortly after birth. Over the years she gave birth to six more children, four of whom lived to adulthood: Beverley, a male (b. 1798), Harriet (b. 1801), Madison (1805–1875), and Eston (1808–1852). She spent her life raising her children, acting as a seamstress doing light sewing for the family, and taking care of Jefferson's chambers.

Gossip about Hemings and Jefferson circulated in their neighborhood throughout the 1790s. But in 1802 the journalist James Callender, an enemy of Jefferson's, exposed her life at Monticello in a series of newspaper articles that gained national attention. Hemings was the subject of numerous satirical ballads, some written by John Quincy Adams. Jefferson weathered the storm, and Hemings continued to live at Monticello until Jefferson's death in 1826. Upon that event Hemings moved to nearby Charlottesville to live with her youngest sons, Madison and Eston, who had been freed in Jefferson's will. Her two eldest children had left Monticello in 1822, to live as white people. In an 1830 census Hemings was listed as a free white woman. In an 1833 special census she was listed as black person who had been freed in 1826. She died in Charlottesville in 1835.

[*See also* **Race and Ethnicity; Slave Families and Communities; Slaveholders;** *and* **Slaves and Childbirth.**]

BIBLIOGRAPHY

Gordon-Reed, Annette. *The Hemingses of Monticello: An American Family*. New York: W. W. Norton and Company, 2008.

Stanton, Lucia. *Free Some Day: The African-American Families of Monticello*. Charlottesville, Va.: Thomas Jefferson Foundation, 2000.

Annette Gordon-Reed

HMONG AMERICANS

The Hmong are a people that first entered the United States in 1975 as refugees from Laos. The Vietnam War had led to American military involvement in Laos, and many Hmong under their leader, General Vang Pao, had fought with the United States against the Laotian and Vietnamese Communists. When the United States withdrew from Vietnam and the Communist Pathet Lao seized control of Laos in 1975, the Hmong found themselves in a precarious situation. Fearing persecution, they fled into neighboring Thailand and were placed within refugee camps such as Ban Vinai. In the years that followed, many Hmong were relocated to France, Australia, Canada, and French Guiana, although the greatest number came to the United States. The Hmong in America are usually categorized as belonging to two groups, the White Hmong and the Blue (or Green) Hmong.

To help with the resettlement of the Hmong, volunteer agencies, religious groups, and other organizations worked with the American government. The plan was to disperse the refugees throughout the country to prevent geographic concentration, but the process triggered unease among the Hmong, who were accustomed to close face-to-face relations in their native Laos. As a result, they began a pattern of secondary migration that led to larger concentrations in California, Minnesota, and Wisconsin. In the 1980s, Fresno, California, had the largest population of Hmong, but by the 1990s the population center had moved to the Minneapolis and Saint Paul area of Minnesota. The 2000 U.S. Census, however, showed that the Hmong population of 186,310 had become much more widely distributed, and that they had increasingly moved into other regions, such as the Pacific Northwest and the South.

Traditional life for the Hmong in Laos had been social organization centered on families and clans, belief in shamanism, and subsistence farming. Migration into the United States led to new challenges, as they had to cope with a different culture, a language barrier, and entry into a labor market that valued higher education and specialized training. Hmong communities have struggled with high unemployment, cultural differences with American laws and practices, the rise of youth gangs, intergenerational conflict, the redefinition of roles within the family, and religious conflict stemming from conversion to Christianity. Nevertheless, encouraging signs of educational achievement and social mobility by the younger generation of Hmong have been evident since the later twentieth century. There are also notable examples of Hmong men and women who have been elected to higher political posts in several cities and states.

Even as the Hmong are adapting to life in America, they are also negotiating their transnational ties to Laos. Those who were refugees have mixed feelings about their ancestral homeland. For many years their popular leader, General Vang Pao, had fueled hopes that the Communist government of Laos might be overthrown. The likelihood of that prospect's being realized was diminished by Vang Pao's death in January 2011, which left the Hmong community without a paramount leader to rally them. Many Hmong in the United States are like those in the global Hmong diasporic community that was displaced from Laos. They view Laos as an important cultural link, and traveling to that country has increased.

[*See also* **Asian Americans; Immigration;** *and* **Transnational Identity.**]

BIBLIOGRAPHY

Chan, Sucheng, ed. *Hmong Means Free: Life in Laos and America.* Philadelphia: Temple University Press, 1994. A valuable introduction to the Hmong in Laos and their arrival in the United States; contrary to the title, more recent scholarship indicates that the word "Hmong" does not mean "free people."

Lee, Gary Yia, and Nicholas Tapp. *Culture and Customs of the Hmong.* Santa Barbara, Calif.: Greenwood, 2010. Two anthropologists' helpful guide to Hmong cultural practices and traditions.

Ng, Franklin. "From Laos to America: The Hmong Community in the United States." In *Emerging Voices: Experiences of Underrepresented Asian Americans*, edited by Huping Ling, pp. 17–33. New Brunswick, N.J.: Rutgers University Press, 2008. A succinct account of challenges and changes faced by the Hmong in the United States.

Vang, Chia Youyee. *Hmong America: Reconstructing Community in Diaspora*. Urbana: University of Illinois Press, 2010. A Hmong historian's wide-ranging and thoughtful interpretation of the Hmong experience against the backdrop of the Cold War.

Franklin Ng

HOLIDAYS AND FESTIVALS

Holidays punctuate social life. Extraordinary events, they give shape and meaning to everyday existence. Throughout human history, nations and peoples have marked their calendars with special days to celebrate, commemorate, memorialize, or trace the passage of their lives. Individually and as communities, we set aside times to reflect on the past and future, to rest and renew our bodies and souls, and simply to have fun. We call these extraordinary moments "holidays," a contraction of the term "holy day." Sometimes holidays are literally holy days—the Sabbath, Easter, or Ramadan, for example—but they can also be secular occasions serving local or national political purposes, addressing social needs of communities and individuals, or indulging the whimsies of celebrants. This article can only begin to introduce the complex subject of American holidays and festivals.

Holidays are "times out of time"—moments when time seems to stand still. We put work aside, alter normal activities, assemble in different ways with family, friends, and community, eat special foods, and allow our minds to become more reflective or, often, less practical and more carefree. Holidays cast shadows. As they approach, we anticipate and prepare for them, and in their wake we recover from them, pay their toll, or bask in their afterglow. We can learn much about a people or nation by the holidays they keep. What do they believe, embrace, or revile? What religious faiths or systems of belief predominate, giving meaning and order to their lives? How uniform or diverse are they religiously, culturally, or socially? How rich or poor are they, and how do they invest their lives with value that is not merely monetary but psychic, emotional, or moral? What sorts of bonds unite them, and what differentiates them or pulls them apart? The celebration, commemoration, or observance of holidays and festivals gives us insight into such questions, informing us about the United States and its peoples.

Like most countries, the United States distinguishes between public holidays and religious holidays. Though such a distinction is often sensible and clear, in fact this distinction is a compromise designed to accommodate the complexity of holidays as they function in the real world. In the United States, for example, Christmas (25 December) is a federally authorized public holiday, yet simultaneously it is a Christian religious festival. It is not one or the other but is, rather, both a religious and a public holiday. And while some observe Christmas in a secular if festive fashion, or treat it simply as a day off, others continue to invest it with great religious meaning. In other cases—Saint Valentine's Day (14 February), for example—the religious content has become more tenuous or remote. On Valentine's Day, celebrants do not generally worship—they exchange cards, candy, and loving wishes.

If cycles of holidays or seasonal festivals often seem timeless and conservative, new days and traditions are invented, holidays themselves evolve, and they offer occasions for transgression, reform, or even revolutionary change. American holidays are forces, not merely of tradition, but of innovation. They help Americans both to preserve who they are and to reinvent themselves over time.

The public calendar of the United States has become fuller and more complicated as the country's history has lengthened. And from the beginning, holidays were moments for social and cultural politics. During the early American republic, only two political holidays were widely celebrated: Independence Day (4 July) and George Washington's Birthday (22 February). Both nurtured union and nationalism among American celebrants and symbolized the birth of a new people and polity, and both offered a forum to contest the nature and achievement of national promise: the Fourth of July, for example, as the first American labor day—a time to call for economic democracy—or as a moment to challenge the institution of slavery. As the Civil War approached, both holidays provided tools to mend the distended Union, and both were claimed by North and South. Postbellum America incorporated two additional holidays into the national calendar—Thanksgiving and Memorial Day—that promoted union and reunion. Thanksgiving emphasized the inclusive memory of a more distant time of colonial origins, conceived in terms more social and domestic than political. Memorial Day focused on mourning, on the bravery and loss of both the blue and the gray, and ultimately sought reconciliation through an implicit agreement to forget the issues that had produced the war and that continued to fester—slavery and racism.

In the latter half of the nineteenth century, as life became ever more complex—with unprecedented industrial production, massive urban growth, new immigration, strikes and industrial conflict, new forms of racial discrimination, and the rise of a new commercialized, mass culture—the public calendar of the United States became more crowded and conflicted and less symmetrical. Lincoln's Birthday (12 February), Labor Day, and Columbus Day found their places in the American festive cycle. The new hero Lincoln, paired with Washington, represented both liberation and rebirth and also increased state power. Labor Day recognized the growing power of labor but also sought to institutionalize a moderate working-class Americanism. And Columbus Day became a venue to assert the legitimacy of ethnicity and for the state and civic elites to acknowledge American pluralism—even if some sought to Americanize and contain the pluralism.

In the revolutionary era, newly independent citizens had discovered Christopher Columbus as an American patron saint who offered a past that bypassed Britain. Tercentenary festivals in 1792 helped build a distinctive national identity. But by 1892, Columbus had been transformed into an ethnic champion by non-Anglo, non-Protestant immigrants—first Catholic Irish Americans, then Italian Americans and Hispanics. Columbus Day, like Saint Patrick's Day (17 March), promoted ethnic pride, solidarity, and strength, but the historic Columbus conferred even greater authority as the discoverer of America. By celebrating Columbus, all Americans celebrated the legitimacy of an ethnically hyphenated America. And Columbus Day became a template for subsequent holidays reflecting U.S. diversity, like Cinco de Mayo or the birthday of Martin Luther King Jr.

By the early twentieth century the American calendar had become both denser and lighter: it contained more holidays, but not all were equally weighty or inspired wide participation. Americans increasingly picked their commemorative spots, and they honored them more and more—or seemed to neglect them—through private celebrations or through indulgence in new forms of consumption and leisure. As public holidays commanded more attention from the state—with sponsored programs and parades—ironically they became vernacular in new ways, becoming more recreational, diverse in observance, and commercialized. Holidays could be simultaneously state-sponsored, store-bought, and homemade. And like the newest public holiday in the United States calendar—Martin Luther King's Birthday—they remain public arenas in which American identity, principles, promise, policies, and history might be debated.

[*See also* Religion.]

BIBLIOGRAPHY

Dennis, Matthew. *Red, White, and Blue Letter Days: An American Calendar*. Ithaca, N.Y.: Cornell University Press, 2002. A scholarly but accessible history of American public holidays, from the seventeenth century to the present.

Pleck, Elizabeth H. *Celebrating the Family: Ethnicity, Consumer Culture, and Family Rituals*. Cambridge, Mass.: Harvard University Press, 2000. The best history of American social festivals, centered especially on the family.

Schmidt, Leigh Eric. *Consumer Rites: The Buying and Selling of American Holidays*. Princeton, N.J.: Princeton University Press, 1995. A definitive history of American religious and gift-giving holidays.

Travers, Len, ed. *Encyclopedia of American Holidays and National Days*. 2 vols. Westport, Conn.: Greenwood Press, 2006. A comprehensive collection of essays by the leading scholars of American holidays and festivity.

Matthew Dennis

HOME FRONT

See World War I, Home Front; World War II, Home Front.

HOMELESSNESS AND VAGRANCY

Homelessness first became a national issue in the latter half of the nineteenth century when western railroad construction, crop harvesting, and mining and lumber camps created a huge market for casual, migrant workers. Armies of transient laborers filled seasonal jobs throughout the country, creating the great era of tramps and hoboes: 1870 to 1920. The era faded as widespread mechanization radically changed the labor market. The Depression of the 1930s brought a brief resurgence of homelessness, which again increased in the early 1980s as high unemployment, deinstitutionalization of dysfunctional persons, and a decline in the dollar value of welfare programs all combined with the reduced number of single-room-occupancy (SRO) hotels to put more people on the street or in overnight shelters—perhaps three hundred thousand on a typical night in the mid-1980s, a quarter of them women.

In the colonial era the homeless were the "strolling poor," a mix of itinerant laborers, poor widows and their children, and the disabled. As transiency became tied more closely to the casual labor market in the nineteenth century, the homeless were typically unattached white males in their twenties and thirties, usually native-born or immigrants from the British Isles. The social world of tramping was a robust bachelor subculture anchored in what were known in hobo argot as "main stems," urban areas of cheap lodging houses and saloons. The largest of these, in New York

City, Chicago, and San Francisco, might house forty thousand to fifty thousand transients on a given night. After 1920, homeless men were fewer, older, and less mobile. By the 1950s most Americans associated homelessness with the small groups of "derelicts" in squalid "skid row" districts of major cities.

Transients had simply been "warned out" of colonial-era communities. By the mid-nineteenth century, concerns about the urban poor prompted a debate among charity groups and public officials about "worthy" and "unworthy" indigents, and this informed the largely antagonistic response of communities to the surge of transients after 1870. Homeless men were arrested as vagrants or simply chased out of town. After 1890 the growth of organized charity work, epitomized by the National Conference of Charities and Corrections, fostered explanations of homelessness that incorporated both class-based prejudices and a recognition of the vicissitudes of economic development. Some argued that the free overnight lodgings offered in police stations or mission shelters—the latter an innovation of charitable and religious groups such as the Salvation Army—encouraged tramping. This led to a largely unsuccessful experiment with municipally run lodging houses until about 1930, mostly in the cities of the Middle West and Northeast. As homelessness in the later twentieth century became, to a considerable extent, a by-product of extreme poverty, disability, alcoholism and drug abuse, and the shrinking SRO housing market, efforts to address it focused on government social-welfare programs and on providing permanent, affordable lodging through a combination of private enterprise, public funding, and non-profit organizations.

[*See also* **Asylums and Mental Illness; Charity Organization Movement; Migrant Camps, Depression Era; Poverty; Prisons and Penitentiaries; Slums; Unemployment, Social Impact of;** *and* **Welfare.**]

BIBLIOGRAPHY

Adler, Jeffrey S. "A Historical Analysis of the Law of Vagrancy." *Criminology* 27, no. 2 (1989): 209–229.

Jencks, Christopher. *The Homeless.* Cambridge, Mass.: Harvard University Press, 1994.

Monkkonen, Eric H., ed. *Walking to Work: Tramps in America, 1790–1935.* Lincoln: University of Nebraska Press, 1984.

John C. Schneider

HOMICIDE

At the start of the twenty-first century, the homicide rate of the United States was four times the Canadian rate, six times the Italian rate, and eight times the Irish rate. For at least two centuries, Americans have slaughtered one another at dramatically higher levels than western Europeans have; New York City's homicide rate, for example, has exceeded London's by a factor of fifteen during this period, even though New Yorkers do not commit most other crimes more often than Londoners do.

A number of factors, in combination, have contributed to America's homicidal record. Demographic conditions partially account for this pattern. A land of immigrants, America had a surfeit of men until the 1940s. As a general rule, wherever and whenever young men abound, homicide rates surge, as bachelors jostle and brawl to establish status. Hence America's demographic history helps to explain the rising tide of lethal violence in the South in the seventeenth century, in mining camps on the Frontier, and in mid-nineteenth- and early twentieth-century cities.

Furthermore, the late twentieth-century coming of age of baby boomers produced an increase in the proportion of young people and an explosion of violence.

Racial conflict has also fueled American violence, particularly in the South, which had a high homicide rate in the nineteenth and twentieth centuries. Because slave owners used coercion to control their bondsmen, slaveholding colonies quickly became more murderous; by the mid-eighteenth century, for instance, Virginians committed homicide at almost eight times the rate of New Englanders. Most southern murders, however, occurred within white society, for slavery played an important role in the emergence of an ethic of honor that valorized aggression. Southern whites also killed African Americans, particularly when outside social and political forces threatened the region's racial hierarchy, and southern homicide rose through the nineteenth century, often assuming distinctive forms, such as lynching. Furthermore, as violence against African Americans skyrocketed, homicide within the African American community also increased, and a race-based gap in lethal violence emerged and widened; during the first half of the twentieth century, African Americans died from homicide at a rate ten times the white rate.

Cultural factors have contributed to American homicide as well. High levels of immigration and the resulting imbalance in sex ratios, the social dislocation of industrialization, and the development of gender-, ethnic-, and class-based identities that challenged middle-class norms combined to produce spikes in homicide during the mid-nineteenth century and the early twentieth century, when the homicide rates among Irish Americans and then Italian Americans were particularly high. Yet these surges were short-lived, for the regimen of the factory and the school, along with the gradual adjustment of the newcomers, inculcated restraint and reduced urban murder rates during the late nineteenth century.

Cultural changes transformed the character of lethal violence. At the end of the nineteenth century, as pressures on men to derive fulfillment from family life increased, domestic violence soared; in Chicago, for example, the family homicide rate quadrupled during the final quarter of the century. Moreover, the expansion of a consumer culture triggered an increase in robbery-homicide. As a consequence of these chang-es, by the early twentieth century, homes and streets supplanted working-class taverns and bars as the most violent settings in the nation's cities.

Legal and political factors have also influenced American homicide. For much of early American history, legal institutions were underdeveloped, encouraging Americans to rely on aggressive self-help to resolve disputes. Furthermore, the American criminal justice system has remained decentralized and has granted citizens, particularly white men, enormous discretion in exercising personal autonomy. Nineteenth- and early twentieth-century law enforcers secured convictions in barely a quarter of homicide cases.

The widespread availability of firearms has influenced American violence as well. Until the mid-nineteenth century, few killers relied on guns. By the end of the century, more than half used firearms, and by the late twentieth century nearly three-fourths of American killers shot their victims, giving the United States a firearm homicide rate approximately one hundred times the English rate. Thus Americans were more homicidal than western Europeans even before guns were widely used in murders, though easy access to firearms has surely contributed to America's high homicide rate.

Since the mid-twentieth century, as social and political forces have reduced regional differences and tamped down overt discrimination, many long-standing elements of American homicide have faded. Southern murder rates are still higher, though by a modest margin; the children of immigrants are typically no more violent than old-stock residents; and the gap between the African American homicide rate and the white homicide rate has dropped by half since the early twentieth century. Furthermore, by the early twenty-first century, America's overall pattern of lethal violence, with a decrease during the mid-twentieth century, an increase from the 1960s through the 1980s, and a sharp fall in the 1990s, conformed to trends in other industrialized nations. But despite this convergence, the United States remains horrifically violent, reflecting the enduring effects of America's distinctive demographic, social, political, and institutional history.

[See also Crack Cocaine; Death and Dying; Demography; Hatfield-McCoy Feud; Infanticide; Juvenile Delinquency; Law and Society; Organized Crime; and Police.]

BIBLIOGRAPHY

Adler, Jeffrey S. First in Violence, Deepest in Dirt: Homicide in Chicago, 1875–1920. Cambridge, Mass.: Harvard University Press, 2006.
Lane, Roger. Murder in America: A History. Columbus: Ohio State University Press, 1997.
Roth, Randolph. American Homicide. Cambridge, Mass.: Harvard University Press, 2009.

Jeffrey S. Adler

HOSPITALS AND DISPENSARIES

The first hospitals in America were makeshift: military hospitals during the colonial era and the Revolutionary War, and quarantine and inoculation hospitals during epidemics. By the early nineteenth century, the sick poor were often relegated to almshouses, many of which ultimately became tax-supported municipal hospitals run by local governments. The first permanent institutions for the general care of the sick were organized in northeastern cities in the eighteenth and early nineteenth centuries and included Pennsylvania Hospital in 1751, New York Hospital in 1771, and Massachusetts General Hospital in 1821. These were not intended for the general public; popular opinion regarded medical treatment by strangers in an institution as a last resort, appropriate only for those who had no other choice.

The Nineteenth Century. The number of hospitals increased during the antebellum era, partly in response to growing optimism about the recuperative powers of a regulated moral and physical environment. The new institutions included both general-care hospitals and also a host of specialty hospitals or asylums: mental hospitals, lying-in hospitals usually associated with foundling homes, and hospitals for the care and treatment of the blind. The link between poverty and hospitalization remained strong; whether municipally or privately owned, hospitals were primarily charity institutions.

After the Civil War the number of hospitals increased dramatically, reaching approximately fourteen hundred by 1900. This rapid growth resulted as much from social upheaval as from medical advances. Amid surging immigration and rapid urbanization, local governments, benevolent groups, and churches organized hospitals for the growing ranks of the needy sick. Religious and ethnic groups founded hospitals for religious and cultural reasons. Mullanphy Hospital in Saint Louis, Missouri, the first Roman Catholic hospital in the United States, was founded by the Sisters of Charity in 1828; German Jews in New York City organized Mount Sinai Hospital in 1852. Hospitals mainly cared for the chronically ill, for whom the cultural aspects of daily hospital life were central. Religious hospitals rarely administered distinctive therapeutics, but they did provide a comfortable and familiar environment—and gave visible proof that a denomination was caring for its own. Hospitals were also organized to provide treatment and clinical training for groups excluded or discriminated against elsewhere. Female physicians founded the New York Infirmary for Women and Children (1860) and the New England Hospital for Women and Children (1862). African Americans organized Provident Hospital in Chicago (1891) and Douglass Hospital in Philadelphia (1895). In addition to bed care, many hospitals maintained outpatient facilities, or dispensaries. For the poor, these often represented the only professional medical care available.

By the late nineteenth century, three types of hospitals had evolved: municipal, proprietary, and voluntary. Municipal hospitals, typically larger than the others, were supported by public funds and managed by public authorities; many developed reputations for grim conditions and poor care. For-profit proprietary hospitals, often owned by physicians, relied on patient payments. Voluntary hospitals derived most of their financial support from private philanthropy, supplemented in some cases by public funding. As expanding hospital populations outpaced traditional sources of funding, patients increasingly paid for their hospital stays. Ultimately this helped remove the stigma of hospitalization as a last resort for paupers.

Early Twentieth Century. Hospital growth continued unabated in the early twentieth century, with the number soaring to more than six thousand by the mid-1920s. As the hospital's image as a charity institution faded, hospitals advertised comfortable private rooms to attract patients. Unlike nineteenth-century institutions, which mostly provided chronic care and treatment, these new hospitals typically welcomed the acutely ill, as well as surgical and obstetrical cases. The number of women delivering their babies in hospitals increased, especially after 1914 when the introduction of the sedative scopolamine to induce "twilight sleep" offered the promise of painless childbirth. The professionalization of nursing proved crucial to the emergence of the modern hospital. Hospital nursing schools, which provided a supply of unpaid student nurses to staff wards, became essential components of the hospital economy. Hospital training for medical students also became the rule in this period. Efficiency, professionalization, and standardization came to dominate hospital development. Institutional and professional groups such as the American Hospital Association and the American College of Surgeons worked to modernize all aspects of hospital life, from record keeping to laundry practices. During World War I the military relied on hospitals to provide medical services in Europe, with American hospitals and medical schools sending teams of physicians and nurses to replicate the facilities at home.

By the end of the 1920s, deliveries and abortions, adenoidectomies, appendectomies, tonsillectomies, and the treatment of accident victims accounted for 60 percent of hospital admissions. By 1935, a third of Americans were born in and died in a hospital, but regional and class differences persisted. Rural areas and the South had relatively few hospitals. In an ironic twist, high fees now increasingly excluded hospitals' traditional patients, the poor. Proposals for compulsory national health insurance stirred powerful opposition, but voluntary hospital-insurance plans, such as Blue Cross, flourished. Although hospital lobbyists were unsuccessful in efforts to include federal funding for privately managed hospitals among the New Deal's programs, the 1946 Hill-Burton Act sought to improve hospital care and availability through federal grants to states for hospital construction. The federal government had provided health care for veterans since shortly after the Civil War, when the first soldiers' homes were established for disabled veterans, but World War II spawned a vast new system of veterans' hospitals.

Post–World War II Developments. In the postwar era, hospitals assumed an ever-greater medical and cultural role. The availability of antibiotics improved the safety and sophistication of hospital treatment and stirred optimism about the future promise of medical research. Technological developments expanded hospitals' services and altered their physical organization, creating, for example, intensive-care, coronary, and neurosurgery units. Hospital admissions in 1960 were double those of 1930. Hospitals even played a prominent role in twentieth-century popular culture, as evidenced by a succession of television programs extending over several decades, from *Dr. Kildare, Marcus Welby, M.D.,* and the long-running soap opera *General Hospital* to *St. Elsewhere* and the enormously popular *E.R.*

Hospitals employed huge numbers of workers, skilled and unskilled. Excluded from the gains made by other workers under New Deal labor laws, hospital workers, despite opposition from hospital administrations, began to organize in the 1950s. In 1974, federal prohibitions on striking by hospital workers were lifted.

Financial issues were central to further hospital development. Greater federal involvement in hospital finances resulted from the establishment in 1965 of the Medicare and Medicaid programs, which reimbursed hospitals for the care of the elderly and the poor. In the 1970s and 1980s, as hospital costs climbed, many voluntary hospitals merged in efforts to cut costs, creating regional and national chains. The number of for-profit hospitals rose from 414 in 1977 to 797 in 1997. The turn of the twenty-first century found America's hospitals in a state of flux and financial crisis. As they tried to economize, patient stays were shortened, surgery was more frequently performed on an ambulatory basis, medical testing was contracted out, and recuperating patients were shifted to less-expensive venues. Further, more medical care was delivered outside the hospital: in physicians' offices, patients' residences, nursing homes, and long-term-care facilities. Increasingly, this institution that had developed in the late nineteenth and early twentieth centuries seemed the product of specific historical circumstances, and one that might well evolve in radically different ways. For all their problems, however, America's more than six thousand hospitals, with more than a million beds and 4.4 million staff and employees, remained fundamental to the nation's health-care system and an integral feature of U.S. life.

[*See also* **Asylums and Mental Illness; Death and Dying; Disease; Health and Healing, Eighteenth and Nineteenth Centuries; Midwifery; Orphanages and Orphans; Philanthropy; Public Health;** *and* **Sanitary Commission, U.S.**]

BIBLIOGRAPHY

Dowling, Harry F. *City Hospitals: The Undercare of the Underprivileged.* Cambridge, Mass.: Harvard University Press, 1982.

Gamble, Vanessa Northington. *Making a Place for Ourselves: The Black Hospital Movement, 1920–1945.* New York: Oxford University Press, 1995.

Grob, Gerald N. *Mental Institutions in America: Social Policy to 1875.* New York: Free Press, 1973.

Howell, Joel D. *Technology in the Hospital: Transforming Patient Care in the Early Twentieth Century.* Baltimore: Johns Hopkins University Press, 1995.

Kauffman, Christopher J. *Ministry and Meaning: A Religious History of Catholic Health Care in the United States.* New York: Crossroad, 1995.

Long, Diana Elizabeth, and Janet Golden, eds. *The American General Hospital: Communities and Social Contexts.* Ithaca, N.Y.: Cornell University Press, 1989.

Risse, Guenter B. *Mending Bodies, Saving Souls: A History of Hospitals.* New York: Oxford University Press, 1999.

Rosenberg, Charles E. *The Care of Strangers: The Rise of America's Hospital System.* New York: Basic Books, 1987.

Rosner, David. *A Once Charitable Enterprise: Hospitals and Health Care in Brooklyn and New York, 1885–1915.* Cambridge, U.K.: Cambridge University Press, 1982.

Stevens, Rosemary. *In Sickness and in Wealth: American Hospitals in the Twentieth Century.* New York: Basic Books, 1989.

Vogel, Morris J. *The Invention of the Modern Hospital: Boston, 1870–1930.* Chicago: University of Chicago Press, 1980.

Bernadette McCauley

HOUSING, PUBLIC

Public housing in the United States is more than a series of policies meant to design and manage a collection of frequently vilified low-income neighborhoods in large cities. In terms of social history, it is also a window into evolving attitudes about which of the American poor ought to be served by heavily subsidized housing.

As a term, "public housing" has connoted many different programs, ranging from low-rise neighborhoods erected by the Public Works Administration (PWA) in the 1930s to large postwar projects linked to the urban renewal program. In the United States, conventional public housing has also been distinguished both from project-based housing developed by the private sector and from housing voucher programs in which a housing subsidy travels with the tenant. Also, as both cause and effect of its growing stigma, public housing has served a smaller (and lower-income) proportion of residents in the United States than have "social housing" programs in Europe.

History. As a social phenomenon, public housing began as part of the New Deal Social Reforms, with the PWA and the subsequent prewar United States Housing Authority as a kind of reward mechanism for the upwardly mobile working class. Intended in many cases to replace cleared slums, the earliest public housing rarely had residents from those same razed neighborhoods. Instead, the managers of the new and modern projects actively and carefully selected tenants whose upward mobility had been temporarily waylaid by the Depression. Although slum clearance frequently displaced the poorest of the poor, proponents of public housing preferred to house those with stable jobs and stable family structure, viewing such households as more likely to pay the subsidized rent. Housing authorities sought out chiefly two-parent households with small children, headed by a U.S. citizen. In most cases, both in the North and the South, housing authorities of the 1930s and 1940s constructed racially segregated projects, designated as either Negro or white, depending on broader neighborhood composition.

After 1949, the revival of federal housing legislation paired public-housing construction with other programs aimed at urban redevelopment, a combination known as "urban renewal" following the Housing Act of 1954. In some cases, this edition of the public-housing program served as a relocation resource for those who lost their homes to urban-renewal initiatives. Often, however, these two building programs proceeded on different tracks. If urban renewal produced any new housing at all, this new housing often served those with middle and upper incomes. Housing authorities often seemed surprised by how few of the income-eligible households displaced by federal clearance efforts wished to exercise their ostensible preference to enter public housing. By the mid- to late 1950s, public housing already carried a stigma in many large American cities, both because its designs usually bore little relationship to preferred images of single-family dwellings and because the program as a whole increasingly seemed to be serving nonwhite households. Especially for displaced families of the white working class, other housing options beckoned more benignly, made possible by the burgeoning availability of attractive mortgages from the Federal Housing Administration in many outlying areas. By the 1970s, public housing in nearly all major U.S. cities had turned toward serving the poorest of the poor.

Historiography. The literature on social aspects of public housing has evolved considerably since the mid-twentieth century. Following an initial burst of encouragement and rose-tinted public-relations efforts by housing authorities and others during the 1930s, 1940s, and early 1950s, most accounts of life in the projects turned darker. Books and articles emphasized what they considered to be the decline and fall of public housing in one city after another—variously stressing the inadequacies of site and building design, or the poor performance of management and maintenance systems, or the underlying financial insufficiency of

the public-housing system—and frequently blamed failures on the behavioral problems of dysfunctional residents.

A revisionist literature has emerged since the 1990s, however. Newer writing frequently emphasizes a variety of unexpected successes, and details more "bottom-up" stories of life in the projects. This literature has stressed the collective efficacy of public-housing tenants, often led by low-income black women who initiated rent strikes to protest appalling conditions, and who championed the preservation or redevelopment of their homes in ways that might avoid or forestall displacement. These accounts have acknowledged the many failures of management, maintenance, and design, but instead of blaming the residents for the destructive results, the accounts have explored the coping mechanisms and occasional triumphs of residents who struggled to improve conditions for themselves and their neighbors. And just as poor design and misguided management had contributed to community collapse, these accounts show how better design processes and management systems can markedly improve community life. At the same time, as more books and articles about public-housing development and redevelopment in various American cities have emerged, it has been more possible to identify a broad range of experience, both between cities and among neighborhoods within a single city. Even the titles of important books about public housing in two major American cities tell diametrically opposed tales: Chicago's public housing followed a *Blueprint for Disaster*, according to D. Bradford Hunt, whereas New York City's much larger program is considered by Nicholas Dagen Bloom to have lasted through the twentieth century as *Public Housing That Worked*.

Socially, national and local policy pressures since the early 1990s have pushed public housing back toward earlier rationales, increasingly affecting tenant composition. Under pressure from Congress and internal budgetary strains, housing authorities have sought to restore the reward-system mentality of the earliest decades by establishing work requirements, work preferences, or participation in what are called "family self-sufficiency" programs as a prerequisite for entry into public housing. Housing authorities have also increasingly sought to target households at the top end of income eligibility—that is, the merely poor instead of the extremely poor—and endeavored to regard public-housing residence as a temporary sojourn rather than a permanent condition. In some cities this recalibration has been made possible by the use of mixed-income housing and substantial "vouchering out" of existing residents. Other cities have instead sought to maximize retention of permanently subsidized public housing, recognizing that tens of thousands of households with extremely low incomes remain desperately in search of housing they can afford.

[*See also* Cities and Suburbs; Homelessness and Vagrancy; Migrant Camps, Depression Era; Poverty; Segregation, Racial; Social Class; Welfare; *and* Working-Class Life and Society.]

BIBLIOGRAPHY

Bennett, Larry, Janet L. Smith, and Patricia A. Wright, eds. *Where Are Poor People to Live? Transforming Public Housing Communities.* Armonk, N.Y.: M. E. Sharpe, 2006. Examines the fate of Chicago public-housing residents since serious redevelopment initiatives began in the early 1990s.

Bloom, Nicholas Dagen. *Public Housing That Worked: New York in the Twentieth Century.* Philadelphia: University of Pennsylvania Press, 2008. Sets out a counternarrative to conventional tales of decline, especially notable because New York has the largest public-housing program in the United States.

Feldman, Roberta M., and Susan Stall. *The Dignity of Resistance: Women Residents' Activism in Chicago Public Housing.* Cambridge, U.K.: Cambridge University Press, 2004. Surveys the struggles and setbacks of women leaders in Chicago's Wentworth Gardens housing development.

Hunt, D. Bradford. *Blueprint for Disaster: The Unraveling of Chicago Public Housing.* Chicago: University of Chicago Press, 2009. Offers a multifaceted and definitive account of the rise and fall of the Chicago Housing Authority.

Marcuse, Peter. "Interpreting 'Public Housing' History." *Journal of Architectural and Planning Research* 12, no. 3 (1995): 240–258. Incisively dissects the term "public housing" to reveal the range of quite different programs that have all shared this name.

Vale, Lawrence J. *Reclaiming Public Housing: A Half Century of Struggle in Three Public Neighborhoods.* Cambridge, Mass.: Harvard University Press, 2002. Compares three sagas of the rise, fall, and redevelopment of public housing in Boston, revealing the important roles of residents and their supporters.

Lawrence J. Vale

HOUSTON

Trade filled the minds of the New York State natives John and Augustus Allen when the brothers established Houston in 1836. They envisioned the "great commercial emporium of Texas." They, and others, traded not only with the Alabama-Coushatta Indians camped along the banks of Buffalo Bayou, but also with new residents purchasing the land that the brothers had for sale.

Prior to the Civil War, most of the city's growth came from whites and blacks traveling overland from the southern United States and from European immigrants arriving at the nearby port of Galveston, where they took small craft up the bayou to the city. African Americans were present, mostly as slaves. City law prohibited free blacks from living there permanently.

Following the war, Houston grew steadily as a center for lumber and cotton trading. Migrating southerners joined German immigrants to dominate the city's white population, while a sizable African American minority moved to the city to escape reconstruction era plantations. In 1870 the city was about 60 percent white and 40 percent African American. A proliferation of foundries and railroad shops made Houston a rail center and created a boom in blue-collar jobs. During the latter part of the century, both public schools and private libraries were established with separate facilities for whites and blacks. In the 1890s, Jim Crow era legislation accelerated racial segregation and discrimination.

At the turn of the twentieth century, cotton, banking, and railroads dominated Houston's economy, but as the century turned, so did economic forces in the city. In 1900 a hurricane devastated the port city of Galveston. As a result Houston became and remains Texas's major port. The following year, oil transformed the economy following the strike at Spindletop in east Texas. Enormous crude production necessitated increased transportation and production facilities, and Houston became the oil capital of the world. The new industry and its related support community accelerated growth; between 1900 and 1910 the population nearly doubled. The white community grew at a faster rate than the African American community did. Until the turn of the century, no more than one thousand Hispanics lived in Houston; but then the political upheaval in Mexico and the job market in the city attracted the first of many waves of Hispanic migration.

Through the twentieth century, Houston continued to grow as the energy industry grew; growth spurted further when the city's political clout brought the headquarters of America's space program. Another industry mushroomed when the Texas Medical Center began its ascent, eventually becoming the largest medical community in the world, with more than two hundred thousand direct and indirect employees. Abundant land and low-cost labor kept construction costs among the lowest in the nation, promoting further growth. Styling itself the "Golden Buckle of the Sunbelt," Houston saw its population grow 45 percent in the 1960s and 35 percent in the 1970s. Business leadership maintained control of the city, and laissez-faire economics prohibited both zoning and urban planning. The same leadership resisted demands by black Houstonians for desegregation of public facilities and schools. A series of court suits, often joined by the National Association for the Advancement of Colored People, gradually forced integration of public accommodations. In the late 1960s additional legal action finally forced the city's public schools to begin integration. Throughout the Civil Rights Movement, Houston's two major daily newspapers protected the city's business climate by deemphasizing news of racial progress.

Business owners and middle-income voters maintained politically conservative viewpoints, whereas members of the working class—railroad and industrial workers, for example—have made up most of the liberals. Uncharacteristically for Texas and the South, women and African Americans have been key political leaders. In 1966 voters sent Barbara Jordan to the state senate, making her the first African American to serve there since Reconstruction. Then in 1972 she was elected to the U.S. House of Representatives, making her the first southern black woman ever to serve there. In the 1980s Houston elected its first woman mayor, Kathryn Whitmire. Two decades later, in 2009, voters chose Annise

Parker as the first openly gay mayor of a major U.S. city.

The 1970s energy bubble burst in the early 1980s, but population growth continued. The city's reputation for free-market attitudes and opportunity reached out to America's new waves of immigrants. Most notably, in 1980 the Hispanic population was 18 percent of the total, but ten years later it was 28 percent. By 2000 whites no longer constituted a majority. The 2010 U.S. Census recorded the Hispanic population at 41 percent and revealed that increasing prosperity permitted some Hispanics to move to suburban areas. Other neighborhoods, both in the city center and in outer areas, had become predominantly Middle Eastern or Asian, and Chinese or Vietnamese characters joined English letters on street signs. Voting instructions, long printed in English and Spanish, include Vietnamese. Dozens of mosques, Hindu temples, and Buddhist temples dot the city. Mixed marriages—mixed in both race and religion—are common, and the city's large gay community is well accepted. Diverse and largely tolerant, Houston seems to welcome all groups.

[*See also* Asian Americans; Galveston Hurricane and Flood; Hurricane Katrina; Internal Migration, *subentries on* Nineteenth-Century Westward *and* African Americans; Mexican Americans; Middle Eastern Americans; *and* Vietnamese Americans.]

BIBLIOGRAPHY

Feagin, Joe R. *Free Enterprise City: Houston in Political-Economic Perspective.* New Brunswick, N.J.: Rutgers University Press, 1988. A critical analysis of Houston's growth and its power structure.

Klineberg, Stephen L. "The Changing Face of Houston: Tracking the Economic and Demographic Transformations through 29 Years of Houston Surveys." http://www.has.rice.edu/uploadedFiles/2009_Findings/HAS-2010_(Complete).pdf. The Kinder Institute for Urban Research at Rice University publishes an annual study of Houston's population.

McComb, David G. *Houston: The Bayou City.* Austin: University of Texas Press, 1969. A comprehensive and carefully researched history of Houston.

Patricia Pando and Robert Pando

HUERTA, DOLORES

(b. 1930), labor leader and cofounder of the United Farm Workers of America. Dolores Huerta was born on 10 April 1930 in Dawson, New Mexico. When her parents divorced in 1935, she, her mother, and siblings moved to Stockton, California, in the San Joaquin valley. She led a middle-class life because her mother owned a seventy-room hotel. She finished high school in 1948, and two years later she received a degree and teaching credentials from Stockton Junior College. Growing up, Huerta learned self-reliance, self-sufficiency, and community responsibility from her mother. She had a strong sense of self-esteem: she was a good student, was a Girl Scout, was active in the Catholic Youth Organization, and took dance, piano, and violin lessons. During summers, Huerta worked in the agricultural fields near Stockton, thereby learning firsthand what her friends experienced and making her aware of the problems of poverty and discrimination and the oppressive conditions faced by the farmworkers.

After teaching for a year, Huerta decided to become a labor organizer. In 1955 she was one of the founders of a Stockton affiliate of the Los Angeles–based Community Service Organization (CSO), a Latino civil rights group. Working for the CSO she met Cesar Chavez, then an organizer for the CSO, and

Fred Ross, the CSO's founder. Ross trained Huerta and Chavez in community organizing, Saul Alinsky's theories and methods for organizing ordinary people to protect their community's rights and promote their goals.

In 1962, Huerta and Chavez founded the National Farm Workers Association, which ultimately became the United Farm Workers of America (UFW). From the 1960s through the 1980s, Huerta negotiated contracts, lobbied politicians, walked on picket lines, testified before state and national government committees, and lectured at universities, corporate meetings, churches, labor halls, Chicano conferences, and feminist gatherings. As a lobbyist in Sacramento she advocated for pensions, public assistance, and driver's license exams in Spanish. In 1975 she successfully lobbied for California's Agricultural Labor Relations Act, which gave farmworkers the right to engage in collecting bargaining. As a lobbyist in Washington, D.C., she fought in 1963–1964 to end the Bracero Program, a contract-labor program that the governments of the United States and Mexico had established in 1942 to allow Mexicans to work on the farms and railroads in the Southwest, the Northwest, and the South.

Later in the 1960s Huerta exerted the same energy to reorganize the UFW's headquarters in California's Central Valley, the Forty Acres, into a functional community, with a hospital, a day-care center, a school, a cooperative, a credit union, a gas station, a union hall, and a grocery store, as well as a facility for insurance, employment, and health care. In 1964 she and Chavez also established a newspaper, *El Malcriado*, as the voice of the farmworkers. After Chavez's death in 1993, Huerta continued to work with the UFW, becoming vice president emeritus in the late 1990s. She acted as a roving ambassador for the UFW, lecturing on pesticides, feminist issues, educational problems, and immigration. She also served on the Board of Regents for the University of California and other boards, and in 2003 she established the nonprofit Dolores Huerta Foundation.

The citation that came with an honorary doctorate of laws from Princeton University in 2006 captured her life and work: "Through her insatiable hunger for justice—*La Causa*—and her tireless advocacy, she has devoted her life to creative, compassionate, and committed citizenship."

[*See also* **Chicano Movement; Labor Movements; Mexican American Civil Rights Movement; Mexican Americans; Rural Life and Society;** *and* **Strikes and Industrial Conflict.**]

BIBLIOGRAPHY

García, Mario T., ed. *A Dolores Huerta Reader*. Albuquerque: University of New Mexico Press, 2008.

Griswold del Castillo, Richard, and Richard A. Garcia. *César Chávez: A Triumph of Spirit*. Norman: University of Oklahoma Press, 1995.

Jensen, Joan M. *With These Hands: Women Working on the Land*. New York: McGraw-Hill, 1981.

Levy, Jacques E. *Cesar Chavez: Autobiography of La Causa*. W. W. Norton and Company, 1975.

Richard A. Garcia

HURRICANE KATRINA

Hurricane Katrina arguably is the most culturally significant hurricane in U.S history. Although Katrina was not the most powerful storm ever to hit the country, its aftermath proved more influential than the storm's strength itself. As a result, the memory of Katrina is often a remembrance both of the hurricane itself and of the six-month period immediately following it.

Katrina first made landfall in Florida as a Category 1 hurricane on 25 August 2005. After sweeping through the Gulf of Mexico, it built to a Category 5 and eventually struck the Louisiana and Mississippi coastal region on 29 August. The storm affected Louisiana, Mississippi, Alabama, and Georgia. Newspapers across the country proclaimed it the storm that the Gulf Coast region had always feared; the initial damage to the Gulf Coast was significant, an estimated $81 billion, but not entirely debilitating. The subsequent two major hurricanes, Rita in September and Wilma in October, however, made the damage catastrophic. Extreme flooding, levee failure, and pump shutdowns plagued the city of New Orleans in particular. The loss of life was substantial as federal and local systems of emergency management had delayed response and as hyperexcited media coverage resulted in panic. The reaction to Katrina was heated throughout the country. With the twenty-first century's characteristic twenty-four-hour news media coverage, "Katrina" became an overarching descriptive term for any part of the natural disaster and its aftermath in the Gulf South.

Although Katrina affected the greater Gulf Coast region, its most visible impact was on the New Orleans area, 80 percent of which was under water for three weeks because of massive levee failure. The Federal Emergency Management Association (FEMA) estimates that around 1.2 million Gulf Coast residents were cautioned to evacuate, but it is unknown how many actually did. What is known is that Katrina caused the largest emergency diaspora in U.S. history.

As millions watched Katrina's aftermath unfold live on television, underlying racial and economic problems rose to the forefront of discussion. Poverty levels meant that thousands lacked the financial resources to flee New Orleans; others did not receive adequate aid.

The aftermath was one of the longest-lasting ever caused by a hurricane. Katrina's immediate death toll reached an estimated 1,836, with many more unaccounted for as governmental officials struggled with how to manage an extreme state of disaster. Horrific images of makeshift disaster shelters such as the Superdome football stadium and of a city under marshal law incited widespread rumors of looting, rape, and homicide. The city's demography meant that the group most affected by Katrina was African Americans.

Rebuilding efforts were also turbulent. In the six months following Katrina, New Orleans was an example of chaos, despair, and uncertainty. Mismanagement of federal and local resources by officials brought severe criticism of disaster management systems. The officials criticized included the FEMA director Michael Brown, the U.S. Army Corps of Engineers, the Louisiana governor Kathleen Blanco, the New Orleans mayor Ray Nagin, and President George W. Bush. Nevertheless, with the slow return of residents, universities were reopened by January 2006.

Studies made five years after the storm revealed that New Orleans was still suffering from the effects of Katrina. Although levees may have been rebuilt and an estimated $108 billion in federal spending was allotted within the first year, other issues were yet to be fully addressed. Overall the damage to New Orleans and the Gulf Coast region—both physically and economically—made Katrina the worst hurricane and storm aftermath in U.S. history.

[*See also* **Galveston Hurricane and Flood.**]

BIBLIOGRAPHY

Brinkley, Douglas. *The Great Deluge: Hurricane Katrina, New Orleans, and the Mississippi Gulf Coast.* New York: Morrow, 2006. A best-selling work on storm reaction in the post-Katrina era.

Hartman, Chester, and Gregory D. Squires, eds. *There Is No Such Thing as a Natural Disaster: Race, Class, and Hurricane Katrina.* New York: Routledge, 2006. A compilation of essays by key social scientists on the long-term socio-economic effects of Katrina.

Van Heerden, Ivor, and Mike Bryan. *The Storm: What Went Wrong and Why during Hurricane Katrina—The Inside Story from One Louisiana Scientist.* New York: Viking, 2006.

Elizabeth Skilton

HUTCHINSON, ANNE

(1591–1643), dissident Puritan. Anne Marbury Hutchinson was the central figure in the antinomian controversy of the 1630s, a theological conflict in Puritan New England that raised questions about gender roles, lay interpretation of doctrine, and the limits of clerical authority. "Antinomian" means "opposed to law" and refers to the belief that good works are not necessary for salvation. The controversy arose from Puritan ministers' opposition to Hutchinson's leading religious meetings. The ministers officially charged Hutchinson with heresy, but their ultimate judgment was that she taught women to assume roles reserved for men and so undermined Puritan society.

Hutchinson was born in England in 1591. Her father was an Anglican preacher who provided her with religious instruction from a young age. In 1612 she married William Hutchinson, and the couple became devoted followers of the Puritan preacher John Cotton. Cotton left England for Boston in 1633 because of opposition from Anglican bishops, and in 1634 the Hutchinson family followed their pastor to Massachusetts.

The Hutchinsons quickly became established members of New England society. William was elected to public office, and

Anne served as a midwife in Boston. Anne also began hosting weekly women's meetings to discuss Cotton's sermons. Soon these gatherings attracted more than sixty people, including prominent men like Henry Vane, the colony's governor in 1636. The growth of Hutchinson's meetings troubled Puritan leaders, not only because of their mixed-gender composition but also because she used them to criticize preachers who disagreed with Cotton. Hutchinson praised Cotton's focus on grace and accused others of being "legalists" who preached that believers could gain assurance of salvation through good works. The legalist position was unacceptable to Hutchinson because it implied that humans could influence God's plans.

Hutchinson had many followers within Boston, but she had less support outside the city. She also faced a formidable adversary in John Winthrop, the most powerful politician in the colony, who believed that she was undermining civil order. Hutchinson's opponents first went after Cotton rather than Hutchinson. They interrogated him in the late 1636 and again in early 1637. Cotton survived these inquiries, but in the process he tempered his position and denounced some of Hutchinson's teachings as error.

Deprived of her most prominent supporter, Hutchinson was in a weakened position, and civil and church authorities moved to arraign her. In November 1637 a civil court led by Winthrop banished Hutchinson from Massachusetts as "a woman not fit for our society." During the trial, Hutchinson ably responded to each of her male judges' accusations regarding antinomianism. Only when she claimed that God gave her special revelations did the court declare her guilty. Judge Hugh Peters summarized the verdict when he told Hutchinson, "You have stept out of your place, you have rather bine a Husband than a Wife, a preacher than a Hearer; and a

Magistrate than a Subject." After a winter of house arrest, an ecclesial court excommunicated her in March 1638.

Hutchinson's trials came during her fifteenth pregnancy, and she miscarried as a result of the stress, an event that her opponents interpreted as divine judgment. Soon after, she led her family and several followers to Rhode Island, where she stayed until her husband's death in 1642. From there she moved to New Netherland (modern New York), where she was killed by Lenape Indians in 1643.

More than three centuries after her death, Hutchinson is regarded as a pioneer of women's rights, civil liberties, and religious toleration. Recent scholarship has demonstrated that Hutchinson's theological views were not so far outside mainstream Puritanism as her opponents claimed. Regardless, the legacy of her persecution and perseverance has established her as one of the early forerunners of modern American freedoms.

[*See also* **Clergy; Colonial Era; Puritan Great Migration; Religion;** *and* **Women and Religious Institutions.**]

BIBLIOGRAPHY

Hall, David D., ed. *The Antinomian Controversy, 1636–1638: A Documentary History*. 2d ed. Durham, N.C.: Duke University Press, 1990. A collection of letters, sermons, and trial transcripts written by participants in the antinomian controversy. The fullest published set of primary documents related to Anne Hutchinson.

Lang, Amy Schrager. *Prophetic Woman: Anne Hutchinson and the Problem of Dissent in the Literature of New England*. Berkeley: University of California Press, 1987. Analyzes interpretations of Hutchinson's legacy in New England writings from the seventeenth to nineteenth centuries. Places special emphasis on authors' use of Hutchinson as the archetypal "independent woman," either as a villain or as a hero.

Winship, Michael P. *Making Heretics: Militant Protestantism and Free Grace in Massachusetts, 1636–1641*. Princeton, N.J.: Princeton University Press, 2002. Examines the antinomian controversy, giving special attention to the social milieu of New England in the 1630s and the personal motivations of the primary participants. The most up-to-date historical study of Hutchinson.

Stephen C. Dove

I

IMMIGRANTS' RIGHTS MOVEMENT

Throughout the history of immigration to the United States, migrants have organized for rights. Often migrants have made these efforts in the face of restrictive legislation directed to curb their freedom to come into the country and to bring family members over from their home nations. Anti-immigrant laws, such as those passed in western states in the early twentieth century, have sometimes gone so far as to restrict where immigrants can work and live, whether they can own land, and whom they can marry.

Sometimes immigrants have participated in broader mobilizations around their rights as workers. A large portion of the people involved in the great labor uprisings of the early twentieth century were foreign-born. These struggles have been recorded, but historians have generally not considered them immigrants' rights activities. Still, organization by immigrants around their labor rights has also been a component of the history of immigrants' rights movements.

Mobilizations for immigrants' rights have taken place through the courts as well as in the streets. Chinese Americans, for example, waged a well-coordinated legal effort against the restrictions on the Chinese community during the period of Asian exclusion (1875–1952). During this period, the entry of first Chinese and later all migrants from Asia was prohibited. Only particular classes of migrants, such as students, merchants, and the families of merchants, were allowed to come into the United States.

In the case of *United States v. Wong Kim Ark*, the California-born man Wong Kim Ark traveled to China, only to find himself excluded under the Chinese Exclusion Act (1882) on his return to the United States. Wong's case eventually went to the Supreme Court, which in 1898 decided that because he was born in the United States, he was an American citizen under the Fourteenth Amendment to the Constitution. This victory secured the citizenship of all U.S.-born children of immigrants.

Immigrants' rights mobilizations have sometimes been specific to the particular immigrant communities affected, as with the Chinese legal activity. At other times migrants have worked in coalition with one another. During the 1920s, for example, Catholics from many different ethnic groups worked to oppose restrictive immigration legislation.

Founded in 1935, the American Committee for the Protection of the Foreign Born was originally an offshoot of the American Civil Liberties Union. Based in New York City, the committee focused on defending foreign-born political activists who were targeted for deportation. As they responded to the particular needs of immigrant communities, local chapters became involved with advocacy work. The Los Angeles Committee for the Protection of the Foreign Born organized on behalf of Mexican Americans targeted for deportation under Operation Wetback. The committee also continued to defend other immigrants against deportation proceedings.

Fears about undocumented immigrants have shadowed the history of immigration policy in the United States. After the historic Immigration and Nationality Act of 1965 and the corresponding increase of migration from Asia, Africa, and Latin America, immigration policy has often targeted undocumented immigrant communities as threats to the economy or to national security. These policies, in turn, generate impetus for immigration reform both from these communities and from a broad coalition of religious and humanitarian organizations.

In the 1990s a resurgence of nativism resulted in support for grassroots movements such as that which produced a 1994 California state initiative, Proposition 187, that aimed at restricting undocumented immigrants' access to social services and education. Increasingly, public rhetoric about immigration separated "legal" from "illegal" immigrants, targeting the latter. Such initiatives garnered some popular support; they also resulted in organizing for immigrants' rights by organizations such as the National Network for Immigrant and Refugee Rights (NNIRR) and the Mexican American Legal Defense and Education Fund (MALDEF).

In 2000 the American Federation of Labor and Congress of Industrial Organizations (AFL-CIO) endorsed calls by immigrants' rights groups both for amnesty for undocumented immigrants and also for an end to sanctions against employers who have hired undocumented workers. This landmark reversal in the AFL-CIO's position reflected an increasing awareness by the labor movement of the importance of immigrants as a constituency. It also opened the door for increased collaboration between labor movements and immigrants' rights movements, often through workers' centers, which are community-based centers that offer immigrant workers legal assistance and social services such as classes in English as a second language.

In 2005, Representative James Sensenbrenner, a Republican from Wisconsin, introduced House Resolution 4437, the Border Protection, Antiterrorism, and Illegal Immigration Control Act. This bill would have made undocumented entry a felony offense; it would have criminalized many forms of aid to undocumented migrants, potentially equating humanitarian assistance with human smuggling; and it appropriated money for border enforcement and fence construction. The bill reflected a post-9/11 concern with secure borders, as well as increased pressure to criminalize immigrant communities.

Sensenbrenner's bill had the unintended effect of galvanizing immigrant communities. During the spring of 2006, unprecedented mobilizations took place across the country. Immigrants from different nations have organized together, as in Los Angeles, where the Multi-ethnic Immigrant Worker Organizing Network (MIWON) includes the Koreatown Immigrant Workers Alliance (KIWA), the Coalition for Humane Immigrant Rights of Los Angeles (CHIRLA), the Pilipino Workers' Center (PWC), the Garment Worker Center (GWC), and the Institute of Popular Education of Southern California (IDEPSCA). Muslim American groups have worked in these coalitions to protect their civil liberties, which have been greatly affected by policing by the Department of Homeland Security.

The immigrants' rights movement has sometimes been called the civil rights movement of the twenty-first century. In this movement, immigrants and their allies have and will continue to struggle for democracy.

[*See also* **Aliens during Wartime; Bracero Program; Deportations and Repatriations; Japanese American Citizens League; Japanese Americans, Incarceration of; League of United Latin American Citizens; Mexican American Civil Rights Movement; Nativist Movement; Racism;** *and* **Strikes and Industrial Conflict.**]

BIBLIOGRAPHY

Cho, Eunice Hyunhye. "Beyond the Day without an Immigrant: Immigrant Communities Building a Sustainable Movement." In *Immigrant Rights in the Shadows of Citizenship*, edited by Rachel Ida Buff, pp. 94–121. New York: New York University Press, 2008.

Das Gupta, Monisha. *Unruly Immigrants: Rights, Activism, and Transnational South Asian Politics in the United States.* Durham, N.C.: Duke University Press, 2006.

Romero, Victor C. *Alienated: Immigrant Rights, the Constitution, and Equality in America.* New York: New York University Press, 2005.

Rachel Ida Buff

IMMIGRATION

International migration, as an aspect of the process of globalization, has been taking place on a large scale since 1500. Scholars in the United States usually limit their study to immigration—that is, to entry into the country—and they write national histories of the creation of the American "nation of immigrants." Rarely do they acknowledge those who depart, or compare the United States to the many other nations created through massive immigrations during the past five hundred years. Perhaps this is because the United States is distinctive in featuring immigration so centrally in its national mythology.

Human migration has never been solely an economic phenomenon. Persecution, genocide, war, and famine have also stimulated it. Once migration begins, furthermore, social ties—of family, kinship, friendship, and patronage—can sustain what scholars call "chain migrations" over many decades, as those individuals separated by migration manage to reunite. Similarly, the familiar dichotomy of coerced and free migrations is too simple. In the coerced category, one can distinguish among slaves, exiles, deported convicts, and refugees, while the voluntary category includes colonists, labor migrants, sojourners, adventurers, entrepreneurs, and reuniting friends or families. America has received all of these.

Early Migrations. Although the earliest migrations of settlement—which may have taken place as early as some thirty thousand years ago across the land bridge from Asia—brought the ancestors of the indigenous inhabitants of the Americas (denoted "Indians" by Europeans), neither the descendants of these first or native Americans nor most scholars of the American nation label their arrival as an immigration. How the first Americans migrated from the Arctic regions to occupy almost every corner of North and South America is still little understood. Their migrations nevertheless created a very diverse population that spoke more than twenty-five groups of languages and that lived both as settled cultivators of corn and as more nomadic hunters and gatherers who sometimes incorporated harvesting and cultivation of wild and domesticated crops into their seasonal cycle of moves. Although it is almost impossible to estimate accurately the population in 1500 of the territories that later became the United States, scholars believe that disease and warfare quickly reduced the native population by as much as 90 percent.

Similarly, historians have been reluctant to label as immigrants either the first Europeans or the first Africans who arrived during the period of European colonization of the Americas after 1500. For the early modern European powers, North America, as well as Asia, Africa, Australasia, and South America, became sites of competing imperial ambition and capitalist enterprise. Imperialism required the voluntary and involuntary migrations of labor to exploit resources, to build markets, transportation networks, and other infrastructures, and to operate agricultural, commercial, and industrial establishments.

The Spanish who planted Saint Augustine, Florida, in 1565 and established early settlements in the Southwest came as conquerors and missionaries several decades before the English arrived at Jamestown in 1607. French, Dutch, Swedish and Finnish, and Russian colonizers were eventually incorporated into the British colonies (and then the United States)—again by means of warfare, the conquest of territories from the natives, treaty agreements, or purchase.

Meanwhile, of the 12 million Africans brought in chains to the New World, some 450,000 landed after 1619 in the British mainland colonies (and then the United States). Working alongside them were impoverished Europeans who could afford to travel to British North America only after signing away their liberty under contracts of temporary servitude or indenture. Particularly in the colonies of the South, growing staple crops such as tobacco and indigo required the import of slaves, servants, and also convicts, but by the eighteenth century, African slaves had become the major source of labor.

Because of differing policies regarding proprietors and joint-stock companies, natural resources, and land-distribution systems, other British colonies attracted different mixes of immigrants. Organized migrations of coreligionists—often disliked minorities in their homeland—established the New England colonies, homogeneous communities with a strong Puritan character. By contrast, the Middle Colonies attracted a polyglot, religiously diverse population, sometimes including even Roman Catholics and Jews. Land-hungry German Lutherans and pietists and Scotch-Irish Presbyterians flocked to Pennsylvania, settling the backcountry as far south as Georgia. Although religious motives impelled a minority, most colonists aspired to improve their material conditions. Colonial immigration thus determined long-lasting regional racial, ethnic, and social patterns and conflicts that persisted after the American Revolution.

Far from being a homogeneous Anglo-American population, colonial America was very diverse in culture, language, religion, and race. Of the 3.9 million persons enumerated in the first federal census in 1790 (Indians were not counted), those of English stock constituted only 48 percent; 19 percent were of African ancestry, and another 12 percent were Scots and Scotch-Irish. Germans accounted for 10 percent, with smaller numbers of French, Irish, Welsh, Dutch, and Swedes.

1776–1840. Reflecting this heterogeneity, the Revolutionary War was, in a sense, a civil war, pitting patriots against loyalists, often along ethnic and religious lines. During the war, enslaved laborers of African descent took advantage of moments of military chaos to escape servitude and sometimes found explicit encouragement and refuge with the British. Native Americans, too, shifted alliances toward the British in order to protect their own lands from the rebels. After the war, in the first of a number of emigrations, some eighty thousand loyalists left for Canada and Britain.

Having achieved independence, the leaders of the new republic faced the task of nation building. Lacking deep roots in the soil and ancient ties of blood, they fashioned an American identity from the Enlightenment's doctrine of natural rights; within sharply defined limits, a person became an American by assent, not by descent, creating the grounds for the American "nation of immigrants." Still, the Constitution alluded to immigration only indirectly: it provided that slave importation would not be prohibited prior to 1808, and it gave Congress the power to regulate foreign commerce, thus giving the federal government exclusive jurisdiction over immigration. Authorized by the Constitution to establish

"an uniform rule of naturalization," Congress in 1790 defined the criteria for naturalization as two years' residence (subsequently changed to five years), good character, an oath to support the Constitution, and the renunciation of all foreign allegiances. These liberal requirements enabled millions of immigrants to become American citizens. Equally important, the United States adopted the principle that place of birth, not blood, determined nationality; native-born children of foreign parents were citizens by birthright. The 1790 law, however, also restricted naturalization to "free white person[s]," thus making the racial test of "whiteness" essential to American citizenship. Occasional expulsions or "removals" of American Indians to lands farther west, notably from the American Southeast in the 1830s, reinforced this association of whiteness with citizenship. In 1870, during Reconstruction, Congress extended the privilege of naturalization to "aliens of African nativity and to persons of African descent," and in 1924 it offered citizenship to American Indians. However, court cases explicitly denied Chinese immigrants the ability to naturalize and to gain citizenship until the Immigration and Nationality Act of 1952 finally removed all racial bars to citizenship.

Historians of the United States understand in differing ways the many cycles of U.S. immigration that followed the American Revolution. The United States began counting immigrants only in 1820. Since then, historians have used some combination of changing immigration law and immigrant origins to differentiate one period or "wave" of immigration from another. Again, many refrain from labeling the earliest migrants as migrants. From 1840 until 1890, almost 15 million immigrants arrived in the United States, including more than 4 million Germans, 3 million Irish, 3 million British, and a million Scandinavians. Between 1891 and 1920 an additional 18-plus million—including almost 4 million from Italy, 3.6 million from Austria-Hungary, and 3 million from Russia—immigrated. Then, between 1920 and 1960, immigration fell to only 7.5 million: restrictive U.S. immigration policies, economic depressions, and wars hot and cold explain both the decline and a decided shift toward migrants (mainly Mexicans, Canadians) from the American hemisphere. After 1965 and continuing into the twenty-first century, approximately 29 million immigrants have entered the United States, almost half of them from Central and South America and the Caribbean and a third from Asia. Whereas almost 90 percent of immigrants before 1930 originated in Europe, only 10 percent of post-1965 immigrants were Europeans, suggesting that immigration restriction had introduced a major demographic shift in the American population.

Between 1790 and 1820, as war in Europe again interrupted transatlantic commerce, only a million immigrants arrived. Immigration grew slowly thereafter, surpassing a million only in the decade of the 1840s as canal and railroad projects, mining and lumbering, urban construction, and land settlement in the West created an insatiable demand for labor. Meanwhile, a more than doubling of Europe's population in the nineteenth century and the disruption of traditional livelihoods by the Industrial Revolution displaced millions of peasants and artisans. Not a desire for change, but rather a need to escape radical social and economic transformations, impelled many immigrants. They hoped in America to conserve their customary ways of life. Meanwhile burgeoning transoceanic commerce, resulting in regular and improved shipping (steamboats were introduced by the 1840s), facilitated the migration process. Immigration became an integral part of an Atlantic economy involving the exchange of capital, commodities, and labor.

After 1840, recurring waves of immigration brought roughly 69 million persons to America. The volumes of immigration varied, with peaks and valleys reflecting economic and political conditions in both the United States and the sending countries. Business cycles, famines, persecutions, wars, and migration policies on both ends of the migration process affected the volume and direction of migrations. Mostly voluntary immigrants, the newcomers chose when to leave, how to travel, and where to go. Individual migrants were atypical; families made collective decisions and departed together when they could. Once established, the immigrants called on relatives and friends to join them. Thus international networks linked specific villages in Europe, Asia, and the Americas with settlements in the United States. The lure of America was exerted not only by the advertising of shipping companies, land speculators, and state agencies, but even more by the "America letters" from those who had already come.

1840–1890. During this expansive period, the United States admitted all comers with few restrictions but also began to work out the principles on which persons could be restricted or excluded from entering the country. British immigrants, English-speaking and Protestant, were readily absorbed. Though the Welsh, Scots, and Scotch-Irish immigrants initially organized their own settlements, societies, and churches, they gradually merged into a British American ethnicity, strengthening the emerging definition of the American as white, Anglo-Saxon, and Protestant. Although some established agricultural and utopian colonies, British tradesmen and industrial workers tended to settle in the urban centers of the East. The British often occupied managerial and skilled-labor positions in such emerging industries as mining, steelmaking, and textiles. Experienced in trade unionism, they provided leadership for the emerging American labor movements.

Although Irish Catholic emigration began well before and continued long after the famine years of the 1840s, it was the more than a million fugitives from the so-called Great Hunger who established the negative stereotype of the Irish immigrant as pauperized and disease-ridden. Few of the Irish chose to become farmers, preferring the cities and towns of the East and the Middle West. Some were craftsmen, but most held low-paid, dirty, and often dangerous jobs as railroad and construction laborers, miners, and factory hands. From the 1860s, females, often single young women, predominated among the Irish immigrants. Many worked as domestic servants, textile hands, and seamstresses, sending money back to their families or to bring relatives to America.

Like the British, the Irish figured prominently in establishing trade unions. They also brought modes of resistance that had been used against landlords in Ireland: sabotage and assassination. In the 1870s a group known as the Molly Maguires conducted a campaign of violence against the mining companies in Pennsylvania's anthracite region. The Irish quickly demonstrated talent for American politics; the saloonkeeper became an important agent for mobilizing Irish voters. By 1900, many mayors of northern cities and the majority of their police and firemen were of Irish origin.

Irish immigration made Roman Catholicism a major and controversial force in America. Among the Irish themselves, the Church exerted both political and spiritual leadership. The parish became synonymous with the community, and the priest the acknowledged authority. Irish immigrants had suffered religious as well as economic persecution at the hands of the British, and Catholicism became inextricably intertwined with Irish American ethnicity.

Their Catholicism also subjected the Irish to fierce religious prejudice. The Nativist Movement that culminated in the Know-Nothing Party of the 1850s sought to exclude the Irish from political life and even from the country. The Irish suffered both verbal abuse in Protestant churches and the U.S. Congress and also physical violence on city streets. Anti-Catholicism remained a major theme of American nativism well into the twentieth century.

Objects of bigotry, Irish Americans, ironically, became major antagonists of other racial groups. Competing with urban blacks for jobs, the Irish sought to achieve the privileges of whiteness by venting their hostility toward African Americans. Irish workers also figured prominently in the anti-Chinese movement in California and displayed hostility toward later immigrants from southern and eastern Europe. Nurturing memories of colonial oppression, Irish Americans reserved their deepest hatred for the British. Their support of Irish liberation movements extended from the 1850s to the 1990s. Irish American ethnic nationalism, symbolized by the celebration of Saint Patrick's Day, fused Catholicism, nostalgia for the "auld sod," and bitterness for injuries inflicted by Anglo-Americans.

Ethnic Germans—often espousing provincial identities as Bavarians, Pomeranians, and so forth—constituted the largest group of European immigrants, totaling more than 6 million. Unlike the Irish, religion was not as unifying a force for German immigrants, who included Roman Catholics, Protestants (Lutheran and Reformed), Jews, and freethinkers. German American ethnicity was thus largely invented in the United States, in particular following the creation of the German empire in 1870. More than most immigrant groups, German immigrants came from various ranks of society, with merchants, professionals, artisans, skilled workers, and farmers well represented, along with a cultural elite of intellectuals and artists. Within "Little Germany" neighborhoods in Cincinnati, Saint Louis, Milwaukee, Chicago, and other cities, Germans established clubs, churches, schools, and beer gardens, as well as newspapers, symphony orchestras, choral societies, and literary circles. Unlike members of other immigrant groups, German immigrants were not intimidated by American culture; indeed, many viewed their culture and language as superior to those of the uncouth Americans. Their attitude, plus beer drinking and boisterous singing, particularly on Sundays, antagonized Anglo-Americans. Conflicts over cultural issues such as Sabbatarianism, temperance, and German-language schools long plagued relationships between German Americans and Anglo-Americans.

German immigrants were also denounced as dangerous radicals. Many so-called 48ers—veterans of the 1848 revolutions in Europe—and their turnvereins (cultural and athletic clubs) did indeed profess radical republicanism and atheism. Some espoused Marxist socialism and anarchism. German immigrants established strong labor unions and socialist organizations modeled after those in Germany. The 1886 Haymarket affair in Chicago resulted in the suppression of the German-led anarchist movement and fixed in the minds of many Americans the image of the immigrant radical as a wild-eyed bomb thrower. Recurring "Red Scares" based on such fears became yet another theme of American nativism.

Many German and Scandinavian immigrants shunned urban industrial areas for the rich and affordable farmlands of the Middle West. Arriving in family groups, often coming from the same localities, they settled large contiguous areas. Ethnic maps of rural America resembled patchwork quilts. While they adjusted to new crops, farming methods, agricultural markets, and environmental conditions, their relative isolation enabled them to maintain their cultures and languages over several generations. The church, whether Catholic or Lutheran, played a central role both as community center and as place of worship. But the lure of city lights attracted the youth, and urban migration gradually eroded the demographic base of these German and Scandinavian settlements.

Two other sources of immigration figured significantly in this first period: China and Canada. Although Chinese immigrants numbered only some two hundred thousand, the reaction they elicited influenced U.S. immigration policy for a century. Initially drawn by the gold rush of 1849 Chinese workers in the West provided an important labor supply for building the transcontinental railroad, mining, and agriculture. Sojourners like many Europeans, these predominantly male immigrants came to make money and return home. The objects of vicious stereotypes that depicted them as morally degenerate pagans or servile coolie slaves, they were subjected to riots, lynching, and legal restrictions that were repeatedly enacted by western state governments. After 1875, as a new federal law allowed, immigration agents in the United States tended to view any woman arriving from China as liable to exclusion as a potential prostitute. Supported by many European immigrants and labor unions, the anti-Chinese movement had gained national dimensions, and it culminated in the Chinese Exclusion Act of 1882. Rather than erecting a racial barrier to immigration, this law initially excluded only migrants of the laboring classes of China. But a precedent had been set, and new federal legislation and judicial decisions resulted in the exclusion of all Asians by the 1920s.

Migration from Canada, often slighted in accounts of U.S. immigration history, has been very important, if somewhat invisible, totaling more than 3 million before 1940. Of these, some two-thirds were Anglo-Canadians who quickly blended into the larger American population. However, the other third, the French Canadians, had a distinctive history and influence. In the province of Quebec, a peasantry with large families and few resources increasingly migrated to the mill towns of New England. Because the textile industry employed women and children, this was a family migration. Strong kinship ties, proximity to places of origin, and the French language made the Quebecois resistant to assimilation. The Catholic Church's structure of parishes, parochial schools, and benefit societies represented another powerful cohesive force. For this colonized group subject to Anglo-Protestant domination, Catholicism became, as it did for Irish Catholics, a core element of Franco-American ethnicity.

Although the mid-nineteenth century is often still regarded as an era when the United States chose not to regulate or restrict immigration, in fact the first steps toward immigration restriction and regulation were taken during these years. After 1819, Congress limited the number of immigrants to a fixed relation to trade goods ("tonnage") on Atlantic ships. Beginning already in the 1830s, states attempted to limit the number of poor people admitted by requiring fees of them or the captains of the ships on which they traveled. After 1860 the federal government gained firm control over immigration and began to plan for the erection of immigration stations to replace state-run facilities in port cities. In the 1880s, Congress prohibited the entry of Chinese laborers, immoral persons and anyone traveling under contract to do work in the United States.

1891–1930. The period from 1891 to 1930 witnessed a level of immigration matched only by that of the late twentieth century. In several years the annual total exceeded a million—a very substantial number in a country that numbered only 76 million in 1900. That year, almost 14 percent of the U.S. population was foreign-born; with their American-born children, immigrant families accounted for more than a third of the total population. In the succeeding decades the so-called foreign element grew ever larger and more diverse. Before the 1890s most immigrants came from northern and western Europe; thereafter, eastern and southern Europeans predominated: Italians, eastern European Jews, and Slavs. This shift reflected the movement eastward of European railroads and the rise of industrial and agricultural capitalism. Finns, Slovaks, and Greeks now migrated for reasons similar to those that had earlier uprooted Norwegians, Irish, and Germans: modernization was undermining time-honored forms of work and life. However, owing to improved transportation and differing aspirations, the post-1890s immigrants were much more likely than their predecessors to be temporary sojourners. Like the Chinese, they wanted to earn money and then return home to buy land. For this reason the southern and eastern European immigration was also overwhelmingly male (the Finns were an exception). If they decided to remain, as many did, they sent for wives, brides, and children. The rate of return varied by nationality but often was more than 50 percent. Many immigrants made multiple trips back and forth across the Atlantic. The exceptions were Jews and Armenians fleeing religious and ethnic persecution.

This vast immigration also reflected the labor demands of an expansive, if volatile, American economy. Industrialization and urbanization required workers, skilled and unskilled. Few of the post-1890s immigrants became farmers; they sought out the cities, factory towns, and mining and lumber camps offering immediate wages. With few exceptions, these immigrants bypassed the still largely agrarian South. Southern and eastern European immigrants for the most part entered the labor force as common laborers. Not only did employers consider them less desirable, but the Germans, Irish, and British who had preceded them—as well as old-stock Americans—resisted their entry into the skilled trades and trade unions. Though partly motivated by fear of labor competition, such discrimination also expressed prejudice against southern and eastern European "races" that were not truly "white men" but "black labor."

Although denounced as strikebreakers and wage cutters (which on occasion they were), the southern and eastern Europeans generally proved amenable to labor organization. In their home countries, in fact, many had been involved in socialist and anarchist movements and had participated in strikes and protests. When admitted into unions such as the United Mine Workers or the United Packinghouse Workers, Slavs, Lithuanians, and Hungarians demonstrated strong solidarity. Jews and Italians, excluded from craft unions, formed industrial unions in the clothing and textile industries. Eastern and southern European immigrants were in the forefront of early twentieth-century labor struggles, and they and their children formed the backbone of what became the Congress of Industrial Organizations in the 1930s.

Some eastern European Jews and Italians dispersed throughout the country—the Jews often as peddlers and merchants, the Italians as miners and in agriculture. Most, however, initially concentrated in Manhattan, with the Jews on the Lower East Side and the Italians in East Harlem. Migrants from the shtetls of Poland, Lithuania, and Russia and from the *paesi* of Sicily, Calabria, and Campania, they clustered in tenements with their townspeople. Orthodox Jews eager to observe their religion formed shuls and landsmanshaften and patronized kosher butchers and grocers. A large and important segment of Jewish immigrants, however, was secular and socialist. Active in politics and labor activities, they sponsored bunds, theaters, newspapers, and discussions clubs. Many men and women were tailors and seamstresses, peddlers and small shopkeepers. Entrepreneurial and thirsty for education, the second generation tended to move into business or the professions. These Yiddish-speaking Jews had a difficult relationship with the more established German Jews, who feared a growth of anti-Semitism because of the newcomers' exotic appearance and behavior. Religious, cultural, and political differences, including Zionism, divided Jewish immigrants, old and new, into numerous conflicting camps.

Internal divisions based on regional and local origins plagued the Italians even more. Membership in mutual-benefit societies was often limited to those from the same *paese*, or home village. Family loyalties were intense and exclusive. Although they were nominally Roman Catholics, even their religious piety focused upon the local patron saint, whose annual *festa* was the year's high point. Their alleged religious indifference attracted Protestant proselytizers and the disdain of ardent Irish Catholics. Like the Jews, many Italians were radicals (particularly syndicalists and anarchists) and freethinkers. They were militant, active in the Industrial Workers of the World, and some anarchists resorted to violence. Most Italian immigrants remained unmoved by Italian nationalism. However, patriotic passions aroused by World War I evolved into a sympathy for Fascism that, despite the opposition of an anti-Fascist minority, dominated Italian American communities into the 1930s.

Beginning as unskilled laborers on the railroads and in mines and factories, Italian Americans rarely rose to the level of skilled workers. Exceptions were those with trades such as stonecutters, tailors, and barbers. Others engaged in petty commerce, providing goods and services in the Little Italy neighborhoods. The children normally left school at an early age. The second generation remained largely proletarian, although many moved into the ranks of skilled or unionized blue-collar workers. For Italian Americans, the breakthrough into the middle class was largely a post–World War II phenomenon. One exception was provided by the Italian Americans of the West, where agricultural and fishing enterprises provided a more rapid rise into the middle class.

Among the millions of Slavic immigrants from the German, Russian, and Austro-Hungarian empires, Poles were the most numerous. Largely unschooled peasants, they, too, entered the ranks of unskilled labor. Poles, however, valued by employers for their brawn and reliability, were largely employed in heavy industry: coal mining, meatpacking, steelmaking, and automobile manufacturing. Unlike the Italian and Jewish women who worked in sweatshops and tenements, Polish women more often were employed as domestic workers and factory hands. Densely populated "Poletowns," dotting the industrial heartland from Cleveland to Chicago and south to Pittsburgh, provided an environment in which Polishness prevailed. Dominated by Germans or Russians since Poland's partition in the eighteenth century, Polish immigrants shared the Irish sense of being a colonial people and similarly found a source of identity and resistance in the Catholic Church. Community and parish were congruent, and within both the priest was the accepted leader.

The immigrants' Polish and Catholic identities sometimes clashed, however—resulting, for example, in the formation of rival fraternal organizations, one nationalist, the other religious. Opposition to control by an Irish American Catholic hierarchy gave rise to bitter conflicts and even a schismatic church, the Polish National Catholic Church. World War I catalyzed Polish American nationalism and contributed greatly to Poland's reunification.

Whereas European immigrants entered through Upper New York Bay's Ellis Island after 1892, San Francisco Bay's Angel Island Immigration Station greeted migrants arriving from across the Pacific after 1910, and transnational railroads carried Mexicans across southwestern land borders. Restrictions on the immigration of Chinese laborers in the 1880s encouraged West Coast landowners to seek new sources of agriculture labor, both in Mexico and Hawai'i and from places such as the Philippines (which became a U.S. colony in 1898), Korea (which was colonized by Japan in 1905), and Japan itself. Each new group of arrivals from Asia sparked hostility from white American and European immigrant workers. In 1907, segregation of Japanese children in California schools even sparked an international crisis, causing the United States and Japan to reach an informal gentlemen's agreement under which the Japanese government prohibited further emigration of Japanese laborers, while the United States ended the segregation in California and allowed Japanese laborers already living and working in the United States to bring brides and wives from their home country.

The immigration of the turn of the twentieth century helped to reinforce and transform regional differences in the United States, and it particularly exacerbated differences between, on the one hand, the rural South (where before World War I the majority of African Americans still lived in poverty) and parts of the Midwest (with their earlier immigrant roots) and, on the other hand, the urban Northeast, West, and Southwest. Cities such as New York City or San Francisco now seemed like foreign countries to visitors from the heartland or from the South. The presence of Mexicans marked the Southwest as distinctive, as did the mix of Asian and European immigrants in western cities and agriculture.

The tide of new immigrants evoked anxieties among Anglo-Americans and calls for greater immigration restriction. To the fears of Roman Catholicism and immigrant radicalism was now added the menace of biological pollution. In the late nineteenth century, "scientific" racialism based on eugenics and an assumed hierarchy of races (Nordics being the superior race) became a major tenet of Anglo-American nationalism, justifying imperialism abroad and immigration restriction at home. The influx of southern and eastern Europeans and Asians—people of supposedly inferior racial stock—triggered a nativist campaign against what were called "undesirable and dangerous immigrants."

Both Ellis Island and Angel Island were intended to sift desirable from undesirable immigrants, but demands for new restrictions continued. The Immigration Restriction League, founded in Boston in 1894, and the American Federation of Labor called for even stricter immigration laws, laws that would exclude those who could not read or write: such immigrants were said to constitute "poor material" for naturalization to American citizenship.

World War I intensified the anti-immigrant climate, with demands for "one hundred percent Americanism" and attacks upon "hyphenated Americans." Although this patriotic hysteria focused on German Americans, all foreigners became suspect. Linguistic and other aspects of ethnicity were suppressed or monitored by authorities and vigilante organizations. In this atmosphere the nativist agenda prevailed. Wartime laws against "seditious" organizations, publications, and expressions were aimed particularly at immigrant radicals who opposed the war. Domestic labor strife and Bolshevism abroad further fueled the 1919–1920 Red Scare, leading to the imprisonment of thousands of immigrants and the deportation of hundreds. The eugenic argument loomed especially large in public discussions and congressional debates. The immigration law of 1921 and the 1924 National Origins Act allocated quotas according to the criteria of allegedly superior and inferior races, favoring "Nordics" over "Alpines" and "Mediterraneans" and totally excluding Asians. These statutes sought to protect the genetic character of the American people from foreign contamination.

The debate over immigration involved no less than the issue of what America as a nation was to become. Americans differed on the issue. Countering the xenophobia of the restrictionists, proponents of a liberal immigration policy cited Christian and democratic ideals of universal brotherhood and quoted Emma Lazarus's 1883 sonnet "The New Colossus," engraved on the Statue of Liberty, portraying the United States as an asylum for the oppressed. During much of the nineteenth century, Americans had generally believed that by some alchemy immigrants would be melded into a common national identity. Israel Zangwill's play *The Melting Pot* (1909) provided the metaphor for this ideology of assimilation. However, World War I and its aftermath caused many to question whether the world's "wretched refuse" could be transformed into worthy citizens. Others, including Horace Kallen and Randolph Bourne, had an antithetical vision, espousing what was called "cultural pluralism." But during the 1920s, hard-line Americanizers held the upper hand, and coercive Americanization programs demanded total Anglo conformity. Regardless of their vision of America, many English-speaking citizens were surprised by the unintended consequences of restriction and exclusion, consequences that quickly became obvious over the next thirty years of financial crisis and warfare.

1930–1960. The National Origins Act, passed in 1924 to restrict southern and eastern European immigration and to make permanent the Asian exclusions, did not apply to the Western Hemisphere, and its impact on migration patterns was almost immediate. During the 1930s, 1940s, and 1950s, only 7.5 million immigrants arrived, most after 1945, and the origins of migrants shifted profoundly. World War I, by interrupting transatlantic migration and creating an urgent demand for labor, had stimulated two alternative intracontinental migrations. African Americans from the rural South to the industrial North, and Mexicans from south of the border. Mexicans had long found employment in the agricultural fields and mines of the Southwest, but they now moved farther afield, to work on the railroads and in the packing houses of the Midwest, establishing barrios in cities along the paths of migration. Canadians, too, because their movements were not restricted, again formed a much larger component of immigrants to the United States. Residents of the island of Puerto Rico, which had become a U.S. territory after the war with Spain in 1898, now ventured in growing numbers to New York City, where they began to replace Italian immigrants in East Harlem, a neighborhood that was increasingly associated with and dominated by black people from the South and from the Caribbean islands, including Jamaica, Trinidad, and Barbados.

With the onset of the Depression of the 1930s, and without any real change in U.S. immigration law, the number of immigrants entering and living in the United States dropped, ending more than a century of increasing, if fluctuating, immigration. In some years during the 1930s, thanks to both widespread unemployment and strict enforcement of the quota system, more people left than entered the country. Even Jewish and other refugees desperately seeking asylum from fascist regimes were denied admission, partly because of virulent anti-Semitism. U.S. consuls, who had become responsible for issuing visas, critically reviewed files and deemed almost any adult of working age to be "liable to become a public charge" and thus inadmissible. Such application of the law blocked the road not only to refugees from Europe but also to Mexicans, whose numbers were otherwise not limited by law. Because unemployed foreigners could not, in most states, claim public assistance or unemployment insurance, incentives to naturalization increased, as did rates of naturalization. In some parts of the country, state welfare workers not only denied public assistance to Mexican workers but put them, along with their American-born, citizen children, on trains back to Mexico. Many more Mexican immigrants chose to return to Mexico when they lost their jobs in the United States.

The 1930s brought both heightened ethnic and racial conflict, as organized hate groups mimicked Europe's fascists, and also a blooming of cultural democracy. In literature, the arts, and popular culture, intellectuals and New Deal agencies celebrated American diversity. In *The Native's Return* (1934) and other writings, the Austrian immigrant Louis Adamic popularized the idea that immigrants were as fully American as those whose ancestors had arrived at Plymouth Rock. Adamic's America had room for European immigrants, African Americans, and Mexicans. But congressional supporters of immigration restriction, much like southern supporters of Jim Crow legislation to limit African American opportunities, proved unflagging in their support for the status quo.

The outbreak of World War II further limited traditional sources of immigration and led to a campaign of national unity under the slogan "Americans All." With few exceptions, immigrants and their descendants, along with African Americans, supported the war effort through military service and work in defense industries. Compared to World War I, this war saw less persecution of suspected "enemy aliens"—with one major exception: the confinement of some 112,000 Japanese Americans, including the American-born, in concentration camps, a policy clearly based on racial prejudice. Even as American soldiers liberated the survivors of Adolf Hitler's death camps, revealing the terrible consequences of racial and ethnic hatreds and of American resistance to refugee resettlement, restrictionists in Congress and southern supporters of Jim Crow resisted any proposal for change. Racial prejudice remained the foundation for U.S. immigration and domestic policies. But employers desperately needing labor during a wartime economic boom had also worked their influence in Washington. In 1942 the U.S. and Mexican governments agreed to create a guest-worker program, called the Bracero Program, that recruited young Mexican men to work in U.S. agriculture and railroad construction for a year. When Mexico objected to abuses in the system and withdrew its support, the United States continued to operate the program unilaterally until 1964. By then more than 4 million Mexican men had worked temporarily in the United States, familiarizing themselves and their friends and relatives with the American job market. Thousands of Mexicans began to enter the United States to work without authorization to do so.

With the end of World War II came the Cold War between the United States and the Soviet Union and an upsurge of anti-Communism that influenced American immigration policy for half a century. Some post-1945 efforts were made to resettle millions of European refugees, but Congress, where restrictionists held great power, belatedly admitted only a modest number of these displaced persons. It became a principle of America's Cold War immigration policy to admit only persons fleeing from Communist regimes, while excluding those escaping from sometimes brutal right-wing dictatorships. Thus Hungarians, Czechs, Cubans after Fidel Castro's rise to power, and Jews from the Soviet Union received preferential treatment. Cold War immigration policy also concentrated on deporting, denying visas to, or seizing the passports of persons who allegedly had "subversive" ideas or associations. Paul Robeson, W. E. B. Du Bois, Charlie Chaplin, Bertrand Russell, and many others fell afoul of these policies.

The Immigration and Nationality (McCarran-Walter) Act of 1952 embodied this anti-Communist bias. Although it eliminated the racialist constraints on Asian immigration and naturalization, the law perpetuated the national-origins system for Europeans and created only the tiniest of quotas (one hundred persons annually) for China's immigrants—even after the 1949 Communist revolution there. It also included special provisions for screening out "subversives" and deporting immigrants—even those who had become U.S. citizens—who belonged to suspected Communist organizations.

Throughout the 1950s, naturalized immigrants and their children began to mobilize against the national-origins quotas and on behalf of family and friends still living abroad. Often they demanded the right to sponsor relatives as refugees or for immigration visas.

Though the McCarran-Walter Act made some provisions for family reunification, the racial basis of the quota system continued to anger older immigrants, even as newer immigrants, notably those from Mexico, were pushed toward temporary work visas rather than toward gaining improved access to the visas (now called "green cards") that permitted them to become permanent residents with the option of naturalization.

Since 1960. The 1960s brought many changes in American society, including rejection of the "melting pot" ideal and the affirmation of particularistic identities, initially by African Americans and then by other racial and ethnic groups. This process of ethnicization, a revolt against Anglo-American conformity and dominance, affirmed the survival, despite assimilationist pressures, of cultural memories, forms, and communities stemming from the great migrations of the past. Native Americans, Chicanos, Asian Americans, and groups of people of European descent (labeled "white ethnics") celebrated their distinctive heritages and mobilized politically. Such manifestations of ethnicity among second- and third-generation European Americans, people thought to have been thoroughly assimilated, surprised scholars and policy makers.

After the 1970s the ideology of multiculturalism, celebrating racial and ethnic differences, proved profoundly influential, but it also encountered vigorous opposition from political and religious champions of "traditional values." The resulting culture wars were exacerbated by an explosive growth in immigration in the wake of the Immigration Act of 1965, which radically altered the rules for entry. This law eliminated the national-origins quota system and established preferences favoring relatives of U.S. citizens or of resident aliens, persons with particular skills

and talents, and refugees from Communist countries or the Middle East. It also imposed, for the first time, numerical caps on all countries of the Western Hemisphere. It thus reduced further the number of visas available to migrants from Mexico at almost the same time that Congress eliminated the bracero program. President Lyndon Baines Johnson announced that the days of the "open door" were permanently over, but he predicted no radical changes or increases in U.S. immigration as a result of the new law. Most supporters saw the law positively, as an equivalent to the Civil Rights Act (1964) that ended domestic racial discrimination.

Contrary to predictions, the 1965 act had dramatic consequences. By exempting many close relatives from numerical limits on immigration, the new law soon generated immigration totals far in excess of the 350,000 annual admissions initially set by Congress. So did the tendency of U.S. presidents from both parties, when in pursuit of foreign policy advantages, to allow entry to refugees in excess of congressional limits. More than 4 million newcomers entered the United States in the 1970s, more than 7 million in the 1980s, 10 million in the 1990s, and another 9 million after 2000. Despite increasing totals of authorized immigrants, the numbers entering the United States without authorization, along with those overstaying visas—in both cases with the motive of finding jobs—also increased. By privileging highly skilled immigrants, the 1965 law made it extremely difficult for blue-collar workers to gain a visa—no more than ten thousand were available, worldwide, per year—with the result that the population of foreigners living in the shadows of illegality increased whenever the U.S. economy surged, as it did especially in the years between 1990 and 2008.

Another unexpected consequence of the 1965 law, obvious already in the 1970s, was the reversal of the historical pattern of a predominantly European immigration. The great majority of post-1965 immigrants—more than 80 percent of the total—arrived from Asia and Latin America, with Mexicans, Chinese, Filipinos, and Koreans among the largest contingents. Increasing numbers also arrived from Central America, the Caribbean, the Middle East, and Africa.

The post-1965 immigration shook the American kaleidoscope, producing a dramatic reconfiguration of ethnicities. The range of skin hues expanded (some called it "browning of America"); the country's linguistic, musical, and culinary repertoire grew; and new forms of worship enriched the religious spectrum. The umbrella labels "Hispanic" and "Asian" obscured an extraordinary diversity: Spanish-speaking immigrants included several million each of Puerto Ricans (who are U.S. citizens), Mexicans, and Caribbean islanders, while Chinese, Filipino, Korean, Asian Indian, and Southeast Asian (Vietnamese, Cambodians, Hmong, and Laotians) immigrant groups each totaled a million or more. A less noted influx brought several million Arabic, Persian, and African speakers from Lebanon, Jordan, Syria, Iran, Nigeria, Somalia, and Ethiopia. With perhaps 3 million Muslims and five hundred thousand each of Buddhists and Hindus, the familiar Protestant-Catholic-Jewish triad no longer adequately described the American religious scene.

Although in certain respects these newest immigrants resembled those of past eras, they also displayed striking differences. Rather than being concentrated in the bottom economic stratum, the foreign-born were now conspicuously present at all levels. Many, with education and technical, professional, or business skills, integrated smoothly into upper- and middle-class American life, residing in ethnically diverse suburbs.

But immigrants of rural or working-class backgrounds experienced greater adjustment difficulties and sought security among their own kind. At the bottom of the ethnic-class hierarchy, they competed with disadvantaged native-born Americans for jobs and housing. In fact, the availability of cheap Asian and Hispanic labor resulted in a revival of sweatshops in manufacturing. Since the economy no longer needed armies of workers to build railroads, mine coal, and tend machines, these immigrants often found traditional entry-level industrial jobs unavailable and instead took work in agriculture, construction, and low-wage service positions at hotels and restaurants. In many respects their experience mirrored that of the Europeans who had preceded them. But one difference was especially pronounced: in most groups, male and female migrants were more evenly balanced in numbers than they had been in 1900. Children made up a larger proportion of immigrants, too. Families settled in particular locations, creating new ethnic neighborhoods with specialty food shops, churches, temples, mosques, cultural centers, and publications. Constructing new ethnic identities, they created self-help and political organizations. And as before, ethnic animosities and generational conflicts often made the process of adjustment painful.

Although the cumulative impact of 39 million new immigrants had profound implications for the nation's future, grim forebodings about an "unprecedented immigrant invasion" seemed exaggerated. The *rate* of immigration—the yearly number of immigrants as a percentage of the total population—was 10 per thousand in the 1900s but only 3.5 per thousand in the 1980s. And although the number of foreign-born people reached an all-time high by 2000, they accounted for only 10 percent of the population, as compared with 14.7 percent in 1910. In short, the statistical impact of late twentieth-century immigration was still much smaller than that of the past.

By the early twenty-first century, new immigrants were no longer so densely concentrated in inner cities as they had been in the early twentieth century—on the contrary, many suburbs saw the most rapid growth in foreign-born populations after 2000—but immigrants were more segregated from native-born populations than in the past. A few large states—California, Texas, New York, Florida, and Illinois—were home to well over half of all immigrants. At the same time, southeastern states that in the past rarely attracted immigrants had, by the early twenty-first century, sizable Latin American and Asian populations. New immigration again transformed American regionalism. Florida became both more Cuban and more diverse as Haitians and migrants from Caribbean islands transformed its populations of people of African descent. The huge population of migrants from Mexico and Central America in Los Angeles sometimes seemed to render its other large populations—for example, of Iranians and various groups with roots in Asia—almost invisible. In the Midwest, Chicago acquired a large population of Mexicans, while Minneapolis became home to the largest populations of Somali and Hmong refugees in the nation.

The 1990 U.S. Census underscored the reality of ethnic diversity in America. The 90 percent who responded to a question about ancestry or ethnic origin were classified into 215 ancestry groups. The largest was German, followed by Irish, English, and African American; next came Italian, Mexican, French, Polish, American Indian, Dutch, and Scotch-Irish. Another twenty-one groups accounted for more than a million each, and even many smaller groups had sizable representations: Maltese, Basque, Rom, Wendish,

Paraguayan, Belizean, Guyanese, Yemini, Khmer, and Micronesian, among others. Like glacial terminal moraines, these population groups represented deposits resulting from four centuries of immigration. Adding to these deposits were dozens of more recent immigrants and refugees, the so-called new Americans. Each new group of immigrants had its own story and its own particular characteristics, making pan-ethnic generalizations increasingly difficult by the first decade of the new century.

Still, fears aroused by the newcomers—their skin colors, languages, and cultures, as well as their numbers—spawned a neo-nativist reaction. Though eschewing explicit racialism, advocates of immigration restriction expressed anxiety that the immigrants posed a threat to the homogeneity of the United States. Projecting immigration and birth rates forward, some demographers predicted that the people called "minorities"—persons of American Indian, African, Asian, and Hispanic ancestry—would make up more than half of the American population by 2050 and that the United States would thus cease to be a predominantly white society.

Bilingualism became a lightning rod for nativist anxieties in the 1990s. Some groups, deploring schools' bilingual programs and the use of foreign languages in official documents as threats to the nation's cultural and political integrity, lobbied for a constitutional amendment making English America's official language. Innocent of the country's linguistic history, proponents of this reform asserted that earlier immigrants had speedily and gladly learned and used English and that new immigrants must do likewise. Proponents of bilingualism responded that coerced linguistic conformity violated the rights of non-English speakers and was in any case unnecessary, given the overwhelming dominance of English. The struggle over language, symptomatic of broader ideological and political conflict, seemed sure to continue.

The "illegal immigrant"—who was generally, if unfairly, understood to be a poorly educated, low-wage worker from Mexico—provided a second lightning rod for nativist anxieties. New laws passed by Congress in 1986 and 1996 were ineffective in their attempts to tackle the problem of illegality. In 1986, those who had lived and worked in the United States for years without the necessary papers gained the right to regularize their status, and more than a million and a half people took advantage of the provision. Though Congress also raised the number of visas available, it continued to prefer relatives and highly skilled workers and to limit the number of visas available to less-skilled workers. In an effort to end unauthorized entry and visa overstays, sanctions on employers were introduced, access to public services for foreigners was curtailed, and active programs of detaining and deporting those without legitimate immigration papers grew, especially in the aftermath of the terrorist attacks of 11 September 2001 and the creation of the Department of Homeland Security. Still, evidence suggests that the numbers living in illegality continued to increase, reaching a total of 11 to 12 million prior to the financial crisis of 2008. Most of those living and working in the United States without papers lived in so-called mixed-status families and households, which meant that the detention and deportation of an unauthorized immigrant negatively affected sizable populations of citizens and green-card holders, too.

Despite the neo-nativism, the newcomers generally received a more cordial welcome than Japanese or Greeks did at the turn of the twentieth century. In contrast to earlier eras' laissez-faire attitude, public programs and voluntary agencies provided assistance and social services to newcomers. Further, federal policies and Supreme Court decisions regarding bilingualism, voting rights, and affirmative action legitimized ethnic pluralism. Multiculturalism, a loosely defined movement to make American culture and institutions fully representative of the country's increasing diversity, influenced popular consciousness. Although racism and xenophobia persisted, Americans in the early twenty-first century appeared more accepting and even appreciative of racial and ethnic differences. Still, as negative attention to Muslim immigrants increased with the rise of global terrorism and Islamic fundamentalism, and as the booming economy of the 1990s gave way to a reduced and struggling economy after 2008, calls for greater limits on immigration, fuller enforcement of existing exclusions (including the building of a "wall" to "secure" the U.S. border with Mexico), and harsher treatment of those who entered or worked without authorization to do so suggested that the long history of American nativism also continued.

[*See also* **African Americans; African Immigrants, Recent; Aliens during Wartime; Americanization Movement; Asian Americans; Black Nationalism; British Americans; Cajun (Acadian) Americans; Caribbean; Central American Americans; Central and Eastern European Americans; Chicano Movement; Chinese Americans; Cuban Americans; Demography; Deportations and Repatriations; Dominican Republic Americans; Exploration, Conquest, and Settlement in North America; Filipino Americans; German Americans; Gold Rushes; Haitian Americans; Hmong Americans; Immigrants' Rights Movement; Indian (Asian) Americans; Irish Americans; Italian Americans; Japanese Americans; Japanese Americans, Incarceration of; Jewish Americans; Korean Americans; Letters and Letter Writing;**

Mexican Americans; Middle Eastern Americans; Multiracial and Multiethnic Americans; Native American History and Culture, subentries on Migration and Pre-Columbian Era; and Distribution of Major Groups circa 1500; Native American Removal; Native Hawaiians and Pacific Islanders; Puerto Rican Americans; Puritan Great Migration; Race and Ethnicity; Redemptioners; Scandinavian Americans; Sixties, The; Slavery, subentry on Colonial and Revolutionary Era; Transnational Identity; Vietnamese Americans; and West Indian Americans.]

BIBLIOGRAPHY

Barkan, Elliott Robert. *From All Points: America's Immigrant West, 1870s–1952.* Bloomington: Indiana University Press, 2007.

Gabaccia, Donna. *From the Other Side: Women, Gender, and Immigrant Life in the U.S., 1820–1990.* Bloomington: Indiana University Press, 1994.

Gabaccia, Donna, and Vicki Ruiz, eds. *American Dreaming, Global Realities: Rethinking U.S. Immigration History.* Urbana: University of Illinois Press, 2006.

Higham, John. *Strangers in the Land: Patterns of American Nativism, 1860–1925.* New Brunswick, N.J.: Rutgers University Press, 1955.

Hoerder, Dirk. *Cultures in Contact: World Migrations in the Second Millennium.* Durham, N.C.: Duke University Press, 2001.

Jacobson, Matthew Frye. *Whiteness of a Different Color: European Immigrants and the Alchemy of Race.* Cambridge, Mass.: Harvard University Press, 1998.

Lee, Erika, and Judy Yung. *Angel Island: Immigrant Gateway to America.* New York: Oxford University Press, 2010.

Ngai, Mae M. *Impossible Subjects: Illegal Aliens and the Making of Modern America.* Princeton, N.J.: Princeton University Press, 2004.

Roediger, David. *The Wages of Whiteness: Race and the Making of the American Working Class.* Rev. ed. London: Verso, 2007.

Spickard, Paul. *Almost All Aliens: Immigration, Race, and Colonialism in American History and Identity.* New York: Routledge, 2007.

Waters, Mary C., and Reed Ueda, eds. *The New Americans: A Guide to Immigration since 1965.* Cambridge, Mass.: Harvard University Press, 2007.

Rudolph J. Vecoli; revised
by Donna R. Gabaccia

IMPRESSMENT

During the American colonial era, the British Royal Navy manned its ships in wartime both by enlisting volunteers and by impressing, or forcing, sailors into service. In England the practice dated to the Middle Ages, when select ports had the duty of providing the crown with ships and men in naval campaigns in exchange for special trading privileges. The use of naval press gangs—usually groups of between two and twelve men led by a lieutenant—exploded during the long eighteenth century (1688–1815), when they spread throughout the Atlantic World. Once impressed, a seaman had to serve in the British navy until a particular war ended, he deserted, or he died—whichever came first. Although impressed sailors often likened their condition to slavery, the payment of wages and temporary service in the Royal Navy distinguished impressment from the Atlantic slave trade.

The purpose of impressment in Britain's American colonies was never to raise large numbers of seamen, but rather to compensate for losses caused by death, disease, and desertion in the Western Hemisphere. Despite its limited use, the practice always excited controversy and particularly fierce resistance in North America. Much of the controversy came from confusion over the legality of impressment in the American colonies. In 1707, Parliament passed legislation that banned forced naval service in America and the West Indies except for naval deserters. Known as the "Sixth of Anne," the law did not make clear whether it was meant to remain in effect past the War of the Spanish Succession (which ended in 1714). After sending conflicting signals about the issue, the Royal Navy resumed impressing colonial sailors during Britain's next series of conflicts in the 1740s. In 1746, Parliament omitted North America from a law that banned impressment permanently in the British Caribbean.

Major riots and other forms of violent resistance to impressment occurred in the mainland American colonies in the 1690s, early 1700s, 1740s, 1750s, and 1760s—every decade that Britain was at war in the long eighteenth century before the American Revolution. The so-called Knowles Riot in Boston in November 1747, directed against the recruiting excesses of Admiral Charles Knowles, was the largest disturbance against British imperial authority between the Glorious Revolution of 1688 and the Stamp Act Crisis of 1765. The riot shut down the Massachusetts colonial government for three days and provided the young Samuel Adams with a case study in justified crowd action. In total, impressment was the most consistent cause of crowd violence directed against British imperial officials before the American revolutionary era.

British press gangs further politicized seaport communities during the American imperial crisis, and impressment is listed as one of the grievances against King George III in the Declaration of Independence. After the American Revolution, the Royal Navy continued to remove American citizens from merchant vessels on the high seas on the pretense of searching for British subjects and naval deserters. During the French revolutionary and Napoleonic wars, the British navy impressed an estimated ten thousand American sailors between the years 1793 and 1812. In June 1812 the United States declared war against Britain over the issue of impressment and other depredations suffered in the years following the Revolution. The War of 1812 did not secure a formal agreement against impressment, but it rallied the early United States around the virtues of voluntary citizenship in a republic versus compulsory subjecthood under a monarchy. Britain later converted to a voluntary navy after the war, meaning that American seafarers never again faced the threat of British press gangs.

[*See also* **Revolution and Constitution Era** *and* **Voluntary Associations**, *subentry on* **British Colonies and Early Republic**.]

BIBLIOGRAPHY

Brunsman, Denver. "Subjects vs. Citizens: Impressment and Identity in the Anglo-American Atlantic." *Journal of the Early Republic* 30 (2010): 557–586. Comparison of American responses to impressment in the colonial and early national periods.

Lemisch, Jesse. "Jack Tar in the Streets: Merchant Seamen in the Politics of Revolutionary America." *William and Mary Quarterly*, 3d ser., 25 (1968): 371–407. A pioneering article detailing the role of impressment in the coming of the American Revolution.

Rediker, Marcus. *Between the Devil and the Deep Blue Sea: Merchant Seamen, Pirates, and the Anglo-American Maritime World, 1700-1750.* Cambridge, U.K.: Cambridge University Press, 1987. A classic argument for understanding Atlantic seafarers as an early wage-earning proletariat.

Denver Brunsman

INDIAN (ASIAN) AMERICANS

In 2008 the United States was home to approximately 1.6 million Indian immigrants, making them the third-largest immigrant group in the United States after Mexican Americans and Filipino Americans. Besides those born in India, 2.3 million members of the Indian diaspora lived in the United States, including 455,000 native-born U.S. citizens of Indian ancestry. Between 2007 and 2008 the number of Indian immigrants surpassed the number of Chinese- and Hong Kong–born immigrants for the first time since at least 1960. Indian immigrants are heavily concentrated in California and New Jersey. Nearly half of all Indian immigrants reside in California, New Jersey, New York, and Texas.

As the new so-called model minority in the United States, Asian Indians are thought by majority whites to be hard workers with a good culture that has enabled their greater success relative to other minorities such as African Americans or Latinos. America's earliest encounters with India began in the middle to late 1800s and continue unabated. Popular Orientalism at the turn of the twentieth century exoticized India and Indians as both ghastly and mysterious, exemplifying the East as being the opposite of America and its way of life. This pattern of Orientalizing has continued in twenty-first-century American society: Bollywood, henna, software engineers, yoga, poverty, arranged marriages, snake charmers and elephants, rajahs and maharajahs, gender oppression, an exploitative and casteist society, spices, and saris all continue to be powerful stereotypes that shape American media images of India. Most Americans are unaware of the complex, heterogeneous world and colonial history of India. Part of this new Orientalism is to imagine India and Indian products as indisputably chic. Indian styles have increasingly been appropriated by Western performers. For instance, Madonna used henna and Indian religious iconography in her Ray of Light tour. The success of the 2008 movie *Slumdog Millionaire*, which won multiple Academy Awards, likewise suggested that India was the flavor of the day in early twenty-first-century America.

This more recent commodification of Indian culture in America obscures a history of discrimination. The first Asian Indians who arrived in North America at the beginning of the twentieth century confronted antimiscegenational legal frameworks and social conventions aimed at "protecting" white women from nonwhites. These first immigrants were mostly male Punjabi Sikhs who worked on farms in rural California and married Mexican Americans. In response to the arrival of the Punjabi immigrants, the Japanese and Korean Exclusion League, based in San Francisco, changed its name to the Asiatic Exclusion League. The rise of such anti-Asian forces fostered the first anti–South Asian riots, first in the state of Washington (1907) and then in California (1910). The victims of these riots were overwhelmingly those immigrants who had entered the agricultural labor force or were engaged in lumberyards and railroad construction. The few South Asian professionals and businessmen at this time did not confront similar hostility.

The second phase of Asian Indian immigration to the United States began when the United States revised its policy of discrimination against Asian immigrants in 1965. Over the next twenty-five years, the new policy, designed primarily to attract skilled labor from around the world, resulted in a substantial migration of highly skilled Asian Indians, particularly in the fields of science, engineering, and medicine. For example, between 1966 and 1977, 20,000 scientists with PhDs,

40,000 engineers, and 25,000 doctors came from India alone. At least in the first fifteen years, most of the Indians who arrived were professionals, though subsequently many more have come under provisions for family reunification. The Immigration and Nationality Act Amendments of 1976, the Health Professionals Education Assistance Act of 1976, and the Immigration Act of 1990 erected stringent barriers to immigrants' entry into the labor pool. The immigration of highly educated professionals continued, but at a greatly reduced rate.

Just as the immigration of highly skilled labor steadily decreased, immigration of less educated and economically vulnerable Asian Indians increased. For example, in 1996, of the 65,599 immigrants from South Asia, only 12,315 entered under employer-preference provisions, while 47,091 entered under family-reunification provisions. This third phase of Indian immigration also witnessed an influx of political and economic refugees. Expulsion of Asian Indians from East Africa and dwindling demand for labor in the oil-producing region around the Persian Gulf combined with increased economic transformations and political instability in South Asia to furnish the push factor of this migration. Other than professionals, the third-phase Asian Indian immigrants, at best, occupied working-class jobs: driving taxis and running cheap motels, small neighborhood stores, and marginal gas stations. The stereotype of Asian Indians as "techno-migrants" was blurring in the early twenty-first century, and some have come into the United States illegally to work in low-paid jobs. Asian Indian professionals have been quick to draw boundaries of exclusion against their working-class and sometimes undocumented brethren.

After 9/11, in addition to the black-white binary, the Muslim–non-Muslim binary has become significant in U.S. race politics. Since 9/11, Asian Indians, especially Sikhs, have become more frequent targets of violence and suspicion by the majority, even though they already had encountered the greatest number of hate crimes among Asian Americans in 1998 and 1999. Thus Asian Indians have become vulnerable to contradictory stereotypes: both that of "brown equals terrorist" and that of the "model minority." Both stereotypes have led to the marginalization of Asian Indians in America, and this might be one of the factors why despite their relative success, an increasing number of Indians, including second-generation Asian Indians, have returned to India. The growing Indian economy, emotional attachments to India, and favorable policies by the Indian government have facilitated the return. Many returnees planned to come back to the United States within three to five years of moving to India. Others have extended their stay in India because of the economic downturn in the United States in the late 2000s and did not expect to return to the United States within a stipulated time frame.

[*See also* **Angel Island Immigration Station; Chinese Americans; Race and Ethnicity; Racism;** *and* **Transnational Identity.**]

BIBLIOGRAPHY

Jensen, Joan M. *Passage from India: Asian Indian Immigrants in North America.* New Haven, Conn.: Yale University Press, 1988.

Leonard, Karen Isaksen. *Making Ethnic Choices: California's Punjabi Mexican Americans.* Philadelphia: Temple University Press, 1992.

Maira, Sunaina. *Missing: Youth, Citizenship, and Empire after 9/11.* Durham, N.C.: Duke University Press, 2009.

Maira, Sunaina. "Youth Culture, Citizenship, and Globalization: South Asian Muslim Youth in the

United States after September 11th." *Comparative Studies of South Asia, Africa, and the Middle East* 24, no. 1 (2004): 221–235.

Niyogi, Sanghamitra. "Crafting Identities: Ethnic Incorporation of Two Sub-groups among Asian Indians in the San Francisco Bay Area." PhD diss., University of California, Davis, 2010.

Prashad, Vijay. *The Karma of Brown Folk*. Minneapolis: University of Minnesota Press, 2000.

Terrazas, Aaron, and Cristina Batog. "Indian Immigrants in the United States." Migration Policy Institute, June 2010. http://www.migrationin formation.org/USFocus/display.cfm?ID=785.

Sanghamitra Niyogi

INFANTICIDE

Infanticide—the killing of a child within the first year of life, normally within days of birth—is difficult to document. The victim's body is small and easily concealed, and the murderer is usually the child's mother, often the only person who knows the victim. Thus historians have not reconstructed infanticide rates with nearly the thoroughness with which they have reconstructed the rates of other types of homicide in America, though infanticide rates varied over time and among different populations.

During the colonial era, authorities enforced laws against infanticide rigorously, especially in New England. After the Revolution and during the early and mid-nineteenth century, prosecutions declined, and evidently rates of infanticide reached their highest levels. During this time, higher numbers of unmarried women lived lives of pitiful wage labor in less cohesive, often urbanizing, communities. Also during the Antebellum Era, whatever its basis in reality, the image of the infanticidal slave

mother was a common trope within abolitionist literature and bespoke a more general sympathy for mothers placed in desperate circumstances. Infanticide rates dropped considerably during the 1880s and successive decades, at the same time that Americans established foundling homes and homes for unwed mothers and that contraception became better known and less expensive. Quality of life increased, as did adoption. By the mid-twentieth century, perhaps earlier, infanticide cases became rare.

Typically, infanticidal mothers were poor, young, and unwed, and they lacked family and social networks of support. Frequently these mothers served as domestic workers—an occupation associated with high mobility and high turnover—and were sexually vulnerable. Other infanticidal mothers, however, were married or committed infanticide with help from family members. Some mothers requested help from doctors or midwives in committing infanticide.

Infanticidal mothers acted especially because they knew that they had no means of caring for the child, and often they acted to avoid social shame and sanction from having borne an illegitimate child. Because infanticidal mothers frequently hid their pregnancy, even when a body was discovered it could only infrequently be traced to its mother. As a result historians do not know the relative mixture of other factors associated with infanticide; such factors include immaturity, panic, inebriation, depression, neglect, and mental instability.

Legally, Americans have generally not distinguished infanticide from other forms of homicide. Some historians have argued that American court systems prosecuted infanticide—or the more easily proven charge of concealment of infant death—in an effort to control female sexuality. An infanticide charge was difficult to prosecute, in part because mothers could claim that the child was stillborn, an occurrence that was not uncommon. Absent marks of violence on the body, intent was difficult to discern at a time when infants often died from being rolled upon and smothered. Practically speaking, societal willingness to prosecute infanticide has been highly inconsistent throughout most of American history.

Much work relating to the social history of infanticide remains to be done. Historians need to examine, among other facets, the influence of race, immigration, religion, public policy, and urban and rural life and society, not to mention ideas about mothers and children.

[*See also* **Abortion; Birth Control and Family Planning; Midwifery; Pregnancy;** *and* **Slaves and Childbirth.**]

BIBLIOGRAPHY

Galley, Janet McShane. "Infanticide in the American Imagination, 1860–1920." PhD diss., Temple University, 2007. A wide-ranging study, with excellent bibliography and attention to legal issues.

Green, Elna C. "Infanticide and Infant Abandonment in the New South: Richmond, Virginia, 1865–1915." *Journal of Family History* 24 (1999): 187–211. One of few studies to focus on the American South.

Hoffer, Peter C., and N. E. H. Hull. *Murdering Mothers: Infanticide in England and New England, 1558–1803.* New York: New York University Press, 1981.

Kenneth H. Wheeler

INTERNAL MIGRATION

This entry contains four subentries: Colonial Era; Nineteenth-Century Westward; Twentieth Century and Beyond; *and* African Americans.

COLONIAL ERA

In the colonial period, migration within the British colonies was driven by two primary causes: continued high rates of immigration, both free and unfree, and rapid natural increase. European migrants came to the British colonies for a variety of reasons. For most, the primary motive was economic: migrants sought land and jobs. Others sought to settle with like-minded believers, to seek adventure, or to join family and friends who had already migrated. The migration of these Europeans led to another large-scale migration when these colonists and their descendants began to take part in the African slave trade, creating new streams of forced migration. The arrival of these white and black migrants touched off further waves of movement, as Native Americans chose or were forced to move in response to colonial development.

Seventeenth Century. In the seventeenth century, most migrants to England's overseas colonies came either from Africa or from England itself. English migration was driven in large part by a rapid increase in England's population. Between 1580 and 1640 the population of England rose by 40 percent. As the English endured economic dislocations, many English people, mostly young, single, and male, sought to make their fortunes in the American colonies. Migration within and beyond the first settlements began almost immediately after the arrival of the first colonists. Even in New England, with its generally stable social structures, migrants moved in search of new opportunities. In a study of migrants who left London for New England in 1635, one scholar found that only about one-third remained in the town where they first settled. Others kept moving, whether to nearby towns only a few miles away or to Connecticut, New York, or elsewhere. In the Chesapeake, various demographic factors seemed likely to retard internal mobility. Most migrants to this region arrived as indentured servants, lacking the freedom to move, and the mortality rate was appallingly high. Even so, the continued influx of new settlers led to a growing population and an expansion of settlement. Migrants who first passed through the Chesapeake could later be found in the backcountry, the Carolinas, or Pennsylvania. Migration also took place within the British West Indies, when planters from one island moved to others or to the mainland. Thus, for example, planters from Barbados moved to Jamaica and to the Carolinas.

Slavery. As the English colonies on the mainland and in the West Indies grew, colonists began to participate in the African slave trade, which was already funneling slaves to the Spanish colonies of Latin America. Black majorities soon developed on islands such as Barbados and Jamaica. By 1660 more than twenty-five thousand black people lived on Barbados: they represented three-fourths of the black population in all of British America. High death rates and an unbalanced sex ratio prevented the growth of the slave population through natural increase. Nonetheless, so many Africans were imported that the enslaved population grew rapidly. By 1780, Jamaica held almost a quarter of a million slaves, and they outnumbered whites twelve to one.

As white slaveholders moved, their settlements determined the shape of black migration. When planters from Barbados, for example, moved to Jamaica and the Carolinas, they brought both their slaves and their slave system with them. The same was true when South Carolina farmers moved to Georgia or Florida, or when Virginians moved south and west. Of course, some slaves escaped or joined Maroon communities, but for most, any migration they endured was forced upon them.

Eighteenth Century. In the eighteenth century the patterns of European migration changed and expanded. The largely English strain of the seventeenth century broadened to include hundreds of thousands of Irish, Scots, Scotch-Irish, Dutch, Germans, Swiss, and others. Word-of-mouth and advertising campaigns alike promoted the New World as a land of peace, religious freedom, and inexpensive land. Those who could not afford the trip might still sell themselves or their families into servitude for a set time, as in the well-known example of the German "redemptioners," who contracted with German merchants to enter servitude in exchange for their passage to the New World.

As land that was more desirable—located near the coast or along rivers that provided access to the coast—became unavailable or too expensive, free migrants moved west in search of new opportunities. Germans, for example, pushed westward into Pennsylvania, but they also followed the Great Wagon Road that reached inland all the way from Pennsylvania southward to Georgia. Early waves of immigrants from a particular ethnic group often led to later, larger waves as merchants and promoters assured potential migrants that their compatriots already in America would be able to assist them. As migrants sought to settle among others from their homelands, distinctive ethnic communities formed in the British colonies. Travelers commented on the presence and persistence of Dutch enclaves in New York and of German settlements in Pennsylvania and elsewhere, as well as on the large number of Scotch-Irish communities in the backcountry.

Native Americans. These great migrations of the 1600s and 1700s had consequences for the Indian inhabitants of the British colonies. The Indian population at contact was made up of diverse nations with varying ways of life. The influx of immigrants from Europe and Africa forced Indians into new migrations of their own as they sought to regroup in the wake of disease and warfare and as they moved away—freely or by force—from the rapidly expanding British colonies.

Although some Indians benefited from trade with Europeans and even migrated to acquire goods and control their distribution among other nations, the overall story of postcontact migration is one of disruption and loss. Indians near the coast were among the first to be devastated by epidemic diseases introduced from Europe. The survivors of these diseases sometimes moved inland, forming new communities with others. Other Indians, including the Pequots of New England and the Yamasees of South Carolina, were devastated in colonial wars. Indian captives from these wars were sometimes sold as slaves, either in the mainland colonies or in the West Indies. Survivors often fled farther away from English settlements, incorporating with other groups. Thus, for example, survivors of King Philip's War (1675–1676) moved north into Maine and Canada, joining groups such as the Abenakis that proved willing to adopt the newcomers. Some fifty years later, the Tuscarora Indians fled the Carolinas in the wake of a devastating war with the English. In 1722 they were adopted by

the Iroquois, becoming the last of the Six Nations.

End of the Colonial Period. In the aftermath of the American Revolution, the pace of migration accelerated. The British had attempted to limit colonial expansion into the West with the Proclamation of 1763, which sought to prevent colonial settlement beyond the Appalachian Mountains. As a result of the Revolution, the United States now claimed the lands east of the Mississippi River, and tens of thousands of Americans and new immigrants began to move westward. This migration followed old patterns. As in the past, white settlers sought inexpensive land, expanded the reach of slavery in some regions, and provoked new conflicts with Native Americans.

[*See also* **Appalachia; Colonial Era; Cumberland Gap; Immigration; Maroon Societies; Mississippi River; Redemptioners; Slave Resistance;** *and* **Slave Trades.**]

BIBLIOGRAPHY

Bailyn, Bernard. *The Peopling of British North America.* New York: Alfred A. Knopf, 1986.

Bailyn, Bernard, and Philip D. Morgan, eds. *Strangers within the Realm: Cultural Margins of the First British Empire.* Chapel Hill: University of North Carolina Press for the Institute of Early American History and Culture, Williamsburg, Va., 1991.

Calloway, Colin G. *New Worlds for All: Indians, Europeans, and the Remaking of Early America.* Baltimore: Johns Hopkins University Press, 1997.

Games, Alison. *Migration and the Origins of the English Atlantic World.* Cambridge, Mass.: Harvard University Press, 1999.

Horn, James. "British Diaspora: Emigration from Britain, 1680–1815." In *The Oxford History of the British Empire,* vol. 2: *The Eighteenth Century,* edited by P. J. Marshall, pp. 28–52. New York: Oxford University Press, 1998.

Johnson, Richard R. "Growth and Mastery: British North America, 1690–1748." In *The Oxford History of the British Empire*, vol. 2: *The Eighteenth Century*, edited by P. J. Marshall, pp. 276–299. New York: Oxford University Press, 1998.

Landsman, Ned C. *Crossroads of Empire: The Middle Colonies in British North America*. Baltimore: Johns Hopkins University Press, 2010.

Martha K. Robinson

NINETEENTH-CENTURY WESTWARD

From the first settlers of European origin on the shores of the Atlantic at the opening of the seventeenth century, these adventurers and their children and grandchildren were determinedly expansionist. Most of them, whatever their early station in life, were in search of land. The scarcity of land in Europe and its abundance in British North America laid the foundation for a rising immigration over the first half of the eighteenth century. This population, which reached 1.5 million in 1750, grew to almost 3 million by the opening of the American Revolution. Of this number, some four hundred thousand were slaves of African origin, largely concentrated in the southern colonies. Still, almost everywhere, the numbers of Europeans and Africans were dwarfed by the vast landscape that surrounded them. By 1775, increased tensions with Great Britain over policies of governance and taxation, the looming Appalachian Mountain barrier, and the growing hostility of Indian peoples slowed Europeans' westward expansion.

Up to the Louisiana Purchase. With the close of the Revolution, the attention of many Americans—now citizens of a new, independent nation—turned westward, to the rich lands of the Ohio valley and the Garden of Eden known as Kentucky. From the peace treaty that ended the revolution (1783) to the peace treaty that ended the War of 1812 (1814), this period of westward expansion was dominated by continuing struggles with Indian peoples over the lands between the Appalachians and the Mississippi. The military dimensions of this conflict included early American defeats (1788 and 1789) and eventual victories (1793 and 1811). Parallel to these decisive military engagements was a period of warfare in Kentucky and an ongoing series of diplomatic negotiations between representatives of the new American government and representatives of the Indian peoples west of the mountains. The instrument of these negotiations, the treaty of land cession, became a signature of relations with Indian peoples in this quarter century.

In conjunction with military and diplomatic efforts to promote settlement in the West, the Congress of the United States enacted two important instruments of expansion. The first of these was the Ordinance of 1785, also known as the Land Ordinance. This act established procedures for the administration of the new public domain. In response to the continuing debate over control of lands only loosely identified in colonial charters, those states with western claims ceded them to the nation. This new landed empire became the public domain, and the people's representatives in Congress would pass laws governing their distribution. The ordinance laid out a systematic sequence of steps leading to sale. First the lands would be acquired, with "the utmost good faith," by treaty from Indian peoples; a rectangular survey system would then divide lands into townships six miles square, which in turn would be divided into sections one mile square; finally, these sections would be sold by public auction.

Congress also made provision for a form of government for these new landed settlements by enacting the Ordinance of 1787, also known as the Northwest Ordinance. Under this plan, the lands north and west of the Ohio would be divided into territories, with provisions for their governance, including appointed executive, legislative (later elected), and judicial branches. When the population reached sixty thousand free inhabitants, the territory might petition Congress for admission to the Union as a state, equal to any of the original thirteen states. The ordinance prohibited slavery within the territories of what became the Old Northwest. The provisions of the Northwest Ordinance were later extended to all territories in the West, from Tennessee in the later eighteenth century to Alaska and Hawai'i in the twentieth century.

The first great expansionist landmark of the new American nation was the Louisiana Purchase of 1803. Engineered by Thomas Jefferson with a combination of enthusiasm (a nation of small farmers confirmed) and hesitation (constitutional scruples), this purchase from Napoleon Bonaparte's France almost doubled the size of the new American nation, giving it control of the Mississippi and Missouri river systems and extending its western boundary to the Rocky Mountains.

The center of this new western empire was New Orleans, the site of the confluence of so many strands of peoples and landscape. The Louisiana Purchase forced the new American nation to devise policies to accommodate a new group of European origin. After much negotiation, the terms were set: the French of Louisiana would adopt English, conform to American attitudes toward enslaved peoples, and accept a republican form of government. In exchange, the French retained their local administrative unit, the parish, and kept their own legal system, civil law. Both survive in Louisiana in the twenty-first century.

The War of 1812 had important expansionist dimensions. In the East, this was a war over neutral rights at sea; in the West, it was a war against American Indians. The diplomatic close of the war, the 1814 treaty of Ghent, cleared the way for American expansion as the British government gave up its generation-long struggle to create an Indian barrier state in the West. Henceforth, Indian peoples would face alone the aggressive power of American expansion. In conjunction with the decline of armed Indian resistance, the land system had matured and was now ready to serve the westward migration of tens of thousands.

Cotton Kingdom. The most dramatic feature of the two great westward migrations— 1815–1819 and 1830–1837—was the rise of the cotton kingdom. Driven by high prices for commodities, especially cotton, families surged into the new Southwest in two great waves, and with them came their slaves. These new frontiers, with their new plantations and farms hacked out of the wilderness, were the work of black and white pioneers. A parallel expansion north and west of the Ohio carried American pioneer families to the Mississippi River by 1840. With the collapse of the banking system and commodity prices in 1819, the first great real estate bubble burst. The second burst in 1837. But meanwhile both had spawned a surge of westward expansion.

The national implications of the spread of the institution of slavery in the post–War of 1812 expansion of the cotton kingdom into the Southwest—Mississippi and Alabama were the new states, in 1817 and 1819—were fought out in the national political arena over the admission of Missouri to the Union. The result of these heated debates was the so-called Missouri Compromise of 1820 that admitted Missouri as a slave state and established a line to the west marking a line between slave (to the south) and free (to the north). The outlines of the Missouri Compromise endured for the next generation (1820–1860), during which time westward expansion became increasingly connected to the debate over the expansion of the institution of slavery into the territories.

The physical expansion of the nation continued with both diplomatic and political dimensions. Florida was acquired by treaty from Spain in 1819. The Oregon Country on the distant West Coast was the subject of an 1826 joint-occupation agreement between the United States and Great Britain. The Mexican Republic's policies toward people in northern borderlands offered free land for arriving settler families. Crowds of families of American origin rushed to take advantage of Mexico's generous land grants, and in 1835 they began a revolution for independence. The Republic of Texas lasted from 1836 to 1845 when Texas was annexed to the United States. The following year, the Oregon Treaty with Great Britain made permanent American expansion into the Pacific Northwest.

The culmination of this decade of expansion was the outbreak of war against Mexico, which lasted from 1846 to 1848. Through the 1848 treaty of Guadalupe Hidalgo, the United States acquired the northern third of Mexico, land that became the states of California, Arizona, and New Mexico. This expansion was grounded in the spread of the doctrine of Manifest Destiny, which proclaimed that the United States was destined to expand over the continent of North America. The discovery of gold in California in 1848 led to the rush of Forty-Niners to the far end of the continent, solidifying the new, continental American empire. The political price was another conflict over the expansion of slavery; the solution was a series of laws known as the Compromise of 1850. Under these laws, California was immediately admitted to the Union as a free state, and Utah and New Mexico were organized as territories.

With the attractions of gold and statehood, California became the center of American settlement in the far West.

Prices of Expansion, and Civil War.   This dramatic westward expansion over three generations had its price. A continuing issue was increasingly intense political debate over the spread of the institution of slavery. The political compromises of 1820 and 1850 seemed only temporary interludes in this ongoing conflict. Marching in parallel was the perpetual conflict with Indian peoples over land cessions. A final chapter in this story was the wholesale removal in the 1830s of the great tribal groups of the Southwest— Creeks, Choctaws, Chickasaws, Cherokees, and Seminoles—to Indian Territory (later Oklahoma).

A final dimension of the price paid for westward expansion was the little-known but powerful movement of a slave population. Between 1820 and 1860 the demographic, economic, and political weight of plantation slavery shifted from the upper South and East to the lower South and West. In the course of this period, some one million slaves of African origin from the declining farms and plantations of Virginia, Maryland, and the Carolinas were forcibly moved to the new Southwest of Mississippi, Alabama, Louisiana, and Texas. About half of this migration took place between 1840 and 1860. This was the largest internal migration of any single group in the nineteenth century, and the numbers are the more dramatic when one considers its involuntary nature, for not one of these immigrants moved voluntarily.

The Civil War slowed movement into the West, but it led to legislation that laid the foundations for the great postwar expansions. The first of these laws was the Homestead Act (1862), which offered 160 acres of land free to any citizen (man or woman) or prospective citizen. This law represented the final and decisive movement in the distribution of the public domain from revenue to national resource to be given free to its citizens in pursuit of the national goals. Over the next half a century, the Homestead Act created hundreds of thousands of family farms. Even so, half of those who filed homestead claims never carried through to patenting.

Railroads. Congress also passed a series of acts to promote the transcontinental railroads. The first of these was the Pacific Railway Act (1862), which empowered two corporations, the Union Pacific and the Central Pacific, to construct a continuous railroad along the forty-second parallel. A second act in 1864 doubled the land grants from ten sections per mile to twenty. Lavish federal subsidies included large grants of land, money, and right-of-way. After the completion of the first transcontinental line in 1869, Congress offered huge donations of public lands to three other companies. The Panic of 1873 closed out the first season of frenzied construction. Most of the railroad companies went bankrupt, and construction stopped for four years. These grants, placed on the market by railroads, offered lands to citizens from the eastern half of the nation and to immigrants from Europe. To settle their land grants, the railroads moved thousands of immigrants by rail to distant sites on the Great Plains.

The spread of the railroad system into the West coincided with the final generation of warfare on the Plains. For Indian peoples, the railroad was a thrust into their heartland. The last acts of resistance by Indians (Little Bighorn, 1876) and massacre by soldiers (Wounded Knee, 1890) framed the final acts of Indian opposition.

The emerging range-cattle industry reflected the influence of the railroad. The Great American Desert turned out to be the Great American Grassland. The rise of the industry represented the convergence of range cattle and the railroads. It began with the great trail drives north from Texas to the railheads to Kansas in the 1870s. Then the large-scale grazing industry expanded onto the northern plains. Its expansion opened many opportunities for eastern and European investors. Years of drought were followed by the blizzard of 1886–1887, which devastated the great herds from Texas to Montana. In larger numbers and across a wider landscape, the range-cattle industry found itself with increasing competition in the form of farmers moving west onto the Great Plains.

In addition to agricultural expansion onto the Great Plains, tens of thousands rushed to the new mining sites in the West. Large-scale mining of precious metals began with the California gold rush in 1848, which brought a quarter of a million people to northern California within a decade. Mining rushes expanded out from there: they expanded across the West from Nevada's Comstock Lode to Colorado's silver bonanzas (Leadville and Aspen) to the Dakota Territory's Black Hills (Lead and Deadwood). By the end of the century, mining prospectors—and sometimes producing mines—had reached into the remotest areas of the mountains and the high plateaus of the West.

Americans opened more farmland in the last third of the nineteenth century than in the nation's previous history. This was the generation in which agricultural westward expansion outran the rich prairie lands of Iowa, Minnesota, eastern Nebraska, and eastern Kansas to venture onto the Great Plains. Beyond the ninety-eighth meridian, rainfall dropped to an average of less than twenty inches a year. The cycles of wet and dry years proved hazardous and often catastrophic. Boom years (the wet years of the late 1870s to mid-1880s) were followed by bust (the drought from 1886 to the mid-1890s). In response to these climatic disasters, thousands of farm families left their parched holdings and retreated east. The combination of blizzards and drought, combined with low prices for commodities, led to these reverse migrations of the 1880s and 1890s.

The emigrations of the newly freed slaves out of the South onto the Great Plains were part of this expansion. This pattern began with the close of the Civil War. These "Exodusters," as they were called, left Louisiana and Arkansas for Kansas, eastern Colorado, and Indian Territory. In these new places they established their own independent communities, from which they struggled against the same physical challenges that confronted settlers everywhere on the Great Plains.

The final spasms of expansion onto the Plains played out in the Indian Territory land rushes of 1889 and 1891. Driven by the sense that the century of free, available land was ending, tens of thousands lined up in a race for 160-acre homesteads. From the flawed Indian treaties that opened the land to the confusion and chaos of the events—characterized by those who occupied their tracts early, known as "Sooners"—this last great organized land rush to the West seemed to epitomize the American rush for land. The rumor of the disappearance of land was erroneous, but in 1890 the U.S. Census Bureau reported the disappearance of the continuous frontier line.

Role of Women. Across the cycles of westward expansion—from the first settlements in the trans-Appalachian West to the Great Plains, from the range-cattle industry to the mining camps—women played a central role. Women were active participants in farm families, in which their work patterns ranged from labor in the fields to domestic chores

to childbearing and child rearing. They early organized antislavery societies and temperance associations. As settlement expanded out onto the Plains after the Civil War, they found themselves more isolated in a larger landscape. There they became the important movers in the establishment of schools and churches. In the wide expanses of the West, they sometimes found economic and political advantage. Western states were the first to grant the vote to women, beginning with Wyoming (1890), Colorado (1893), and Utah and Idaho (1896).

The scarcity of women offered them economic opportunities in the services that they could provide. Women established restaurants and boardinghouses in mining camps, beginning in California in 1849 and extending into the gold and silver camps of the West to the Black Hills of Dakota Territory. Some women also took advantage of the Homestead Act to establish their own farms. Across the wide expanse of westward migration during the nineteenth century, the growing numbers of women and children came to represent a benchmark in the maturity of settlement.

With the close of the century, the drought eased, and agricultural prices rebounded. Westward settlement surged in like proportion. The single biggest land boom in the nation's history was 1900–1910. A wet cycle, supplemented by railroad lands on the market, homestead claims, and new varieties of drought-resistant wheat, helped to drive this expansion. Barbed wire, windmills, mechanization, and dry-farming techniques assisted. In the final analysis, none of these technical devices could prevail against the massive climate cycles. This final spasm wrote a close to a century of expansion onto some of the most fertile lands in the world, driven by a national policy of making them available to the citizens (and future citizens) of the republic.

[*See also* Appalachia; Borderlands; California; Cumberland Gap; Frontier, The; Gold Rushes; Immigration; Maroon Societies; Middle West, The; Mississippi River; Native American History and Culture, *subentry on* 1800 to 1900; Native American Removal; Oregon Trail; Rural Life and Society; Santa Fe Trail; Slave Resistance; Slave Trades; Southwest, The; *and* West, The.]

BIBLIOGRAPHY

Aron, Stephen. *American Confluence: The Missouri Frontier from Borderland to Border State.* Bloomington: Indiana University Press, 2006. An important study of the impact of landscape and varied peoples on expansion.

Berlin, Ira. *The Making of African America: The Four Great Migrations.* New York: Viking, 2010. Describes and analyzes the great enforced westward migration of slaves in the first half of the nineteenth century.

Faragher, John Mack. *Women and Men on the Overland Trail.* New Haven, Conn.: Yale University Press, 1979. A pioneer study of the multiple roles of women in the great transcontinental migrations of the 1840s and 1850s.

Hine, Robert V., and John Mack Faragher. *The American West: A New Interpretive History.* New Haven, Conn.: Yale University Press, 2000. An interpretive history of the American West, beginning in the precolonial period.

Moberg, Vilhelm. *Unto a Good Land.* New York: Simon & Schuster, 1954. The second volume of a fictional trilogy of the Swedish settlement of the upper Midwest.

Richter, Conrad. *The Awakening Land.* New York: Alfred A. Knopf, 1966. A fictional trilogy (*The Trees, The Fields, The Town*) of the early settlement of the Ohio valley.

Rohrbough, Malcolm J. *The Trans-Appalachian Frontier: People, Societies, and Institutions, 1775–1850.* 3d ed. Bloomington: Indiana University Press, 2008. The settlement of the middle third of the American nation.

Rothman, Adam. *Slave Country: American Expansion and the Origins of the Deep South.* Cambridge, Mass.: Harvard University Press, 2005. Examines the spread of the cotton kingdom in conjunction with the parallel migration of the slave workforce.

Unruh, John D., Jr. *The Plains Across: The Overland Emigrants and the Trans-Mississippi West, 1840–60.* 1979. Urbana: University of Illinois Press, 1979. The standard account of the transcontinental migrations; complete and detailed.

White, Richard. *"It's Your Misfortune and None of My Own": A History of the American West.* Norman: University of Oklahoma Press, 1991. A wide-ranging interpretive history of the American West.

Malcolm J. Rohrbough

TWENTIETH CENTURY AND BEYOND

Migration is one of the great forces of history. When people move in large numbers, they sometimes rearrange not only their own lives but also the places they leave and the places they settle. Migration can rebalance economies, reorganize politics, transform cultures. Migrations across oceans and borders have continually reshaped the United States. Internal migrations have been at times nearly as significant.

Mobility and Migration. Measuring mobility and identifying historically significant migration patterns is far from simple, especially before the 1940s. Since 1948 the Census Bureau's Current Population Survey (CPS) has provided a yearly estimate of how many Americans change residences and some indications of the dimensions of the move. From 1948 to 1971 the annual relocation rate held steady at 19 to 20 percent, meaning that one-fifth of the population changed residence every year. Other than World War II and probably World War I, this was the high-water era of geographic mobility in the twentieth century. Relocations were less frequent in the early decades of the century and also slowed measurably since the 1970s. From 2006 to 2010, 12 to 13 percent of Americans have moved each year.

Most moves cover short distances and have modest implications. The term "migration" is usually reserved for moves that cross county or state lines. In CPS data, on average 6.5 percent of Americans migrated from one jurisdiction to another each year from 1948 to the 1970s, 3.3 percent of them to a different state. Since 1975 an average of 2.6 percent of Americans has crossed state lines each year.

Although annual mobility rates from earlier periods are not known, birthplace information from the U.S. Census can be used to compare migration across state lines for each decade since 1850. Demographers describe a U-shaped pattern. Migration rates across state lines were very high In the mid-nineteenth century as farmers and slave drivers moved west into the Ohio and Mississippi valleys. Rates declined after the 1870s, then began climbing with the new century, reaching a peak around the 1970s. In 1860, 41 percent of all U.S.-born adults lived outside their state of birth, and in 1900, 32 percent did. That percentage held steady until 1950, then rose to 39 percent by 1980, then retreated slightly to 38 percent by 2007.

Consequential Migrations.

All moves are consequential for the individuals involved, but some migration patterns have broader implications. The twentieth century witnessed a number of consequential migrations that helped reshape culture, politics, or economic structures.

No pattern was more important than the move from farm to city. A nation of farmers became a nation of urbanized workers in the twentieth century, although the trend began much earlier. By 1920 a majority of Americans had moved to areas designated "urban." By 1970 the rural population had shrunk to 27 percent, and only 4 percent still lived on farms. This rural-to-urban migration was more than spatial. It meant a dramatic change in occupation and way of life, a change that has been the focus of generations of social research and social policy. It also meant huge changes in political economy. Farm-belt power drained into the cities along with farm people. The decades of rapid urbanization from the 1920s through the 1960s were also the decades when big cities dominated national political agendas.

Migration to suburbs became consequential in the second half of the twentieth century, with some of the same political-economic dimensions as the urbanization flow. Suburbs were not new, but in the decades after World War II they attracted millions who valued an automobile-centered, nonurban way of life. In 1940, roughly 22 million Americans lived in the suburban areas surrounding major cities. By 1970 the number of suburbanites had tripled and now exceeded the number of major-city residents by 12 million. Race played a role in the postwar rush to suburbs. As black families moved into the major cities, white families moved out. Suburbs also pulled much of the industry and some of the political influence away from big cities. But the millions who made the move from city to suburb experienced some of the transitional challenges that came with migration to cities. In both settings, newcomers negotiated with unfamiliar institutions, people, and patterns of life. The negotiations in turn made both cities and suburbs productive centers of historical change.

Regional Migrations.

Migration also decisively rearranged regions. At the start of the twentieth century, virtually all of the nation's industry and most of the population was concentrated in a bank of northeastern and north-central states stretching no farther west than Illinois and no farther south than Pennsylvania. The redistribution of industry and people has unfolded in several stages.

From 1900 to 1930 the principal industrial states of New York, Pennsylvania, Ohio, Michigan, and Illinois continued to attract more migrants than they lost, drawing farm folk from southern states and the Great Plains region into the factory towns and big cities. A second stream moved west, mostly to California, which attracted more than 3 million migrants in those decades. Florida, too, became a magnet, especially for sun-seeking New Yorkers with money to invest.

Migration slowed dramatically in the 1930s, as it generally does in times of economic stress. The Dust Bowl migration was the much-publicized exception. The three hundred thousand Oklahomans, Texans, and Arkansans who headed to California attracted attention from journalists and policy makers who for a time worried that migration was a public problem rather than a public good.

World War II set off the greatest sequence of human relocation in American history. At least 57 percent of the population changed residence during the war years, 21 percent of them migrating across county or state lines. The military itself is at all times an important source of mobility. Between 1940 and 1945, 16 million Americans were called to service and sent to bases across the country, with family members sometimes trailing behind. Tens of millions more left farms and small towns to take jobs in the defense industries. This often involved long-distance moves and regional redistributions. The older industrial centers were key to the defense buildup, but the federal government also located shipyards and aircraft plants on the Pacific and Gulf coasts. California, Oregon, and Washington gained more than 3 million newcomers during the 1940s. The West was starting to industrialize and populate.

The postwar decades accelerated the population shift to California and the West and continued to drain the South. Between 1940 and 1970 the South lost close to 12 million of its daughters and sons, mostly to the upper Midwest industrial states and the far West. The rate of out-migration was heavier for black southerners than for whites, but whites made up about two-thirds of those leaving. By 1970, 34 percent of southern-born black adults and 19 percent of southern-born whites were living in other regions. Still, some parts of the South were starting to attract migrants. Florida continued to be a magnet, while the coast cities from Virginia to Texas added to the trend that had begun during the war, mostly attracting people from the interior South but also northern businesses and personnel.

The Sunbelt reversal caught demographers by surprise in the 1970s, but in retrospect it is apparent that the urban South had steadily been developing the infrastructure that would bring industries, jobs, and people. The deindustrialization decisions that turned north-central states into the Rust Belt in the 1980s sent millions looking for opportunities elsewhere. The South now became the nation's principal population-importing region, pulling that title away from the West for the first time in American history. The West continued to grow through internal migration, but mostly outside California. After 1988, for the first time since statehood, California began exporting more internal migrants than it took in, sending them mostly to other western states.

These regional shifts were significant on many levels: they had the effect of redistributing political power through congressional redistricting and industrial strength, redistributing racial and ethnic minorities in ways that tended to make regions more alike than ever before, and redistributing religions and other cultural institutions. In the long scheme it is fair to say that migration had a homogenizing effect among the country's various regions: by the end of twentieth century the differences among regions were less pronounced than they had been at the start.

Diversity Redistributed. These broad strokes hide many significant migration experiences, especially those of population groups for whom social interaction and identity development are important. African Americans' Great Migration out of the South was hugely consequential for the big cities in which they settled, for the politics of race and civil rights, and for twentieth-century American cultural development. The history of American music and American religion would not be the same without that internal-migration story.

Latinos are often pictured as an immigrant population even though many have an American pedigree stretching back generations. Latino internal migration has been an important force for the spread of multiracial diversity in the twentieth and twenty-first centuries. Texas plays an important role in this. The center of Mexican American population in the early twentieth century, Texas began losing its Tejano population to California and perhaps more significantly to north-central and northwestern states in the 1920s. The diaspora has continued from that and other southwestern states ever since. As late as 1980, two-thirds of Mexican Americans living in the upper Midwest were U.S.-born migrants or children of migrants not from Mexico but from the American Southwest. Puerto Ricans are also internal migrants. Since World War II, Puerto Ricans have moved readily back and forth between the island commonwealth and New York and other Atlantic states. By 1960, more than a million Puerto Ricans made their homes in the continental United States, by 2000 more than 3 million did, and by 2010 about 4.4 million did.

Migration brought highly significant changes to Indian country. Before World War II, Native Americans lived on or near reservations. The Census does a poor job of tracking Native Americans, but the available statistics suggest that no more than 10 percent of Indians lived in cities in 1940. During the war many left reservations to serve in the military or work in defense plants, and in the decade following, Congress embarked on an explicit program to terminate reservations and relocate native peoples. Even after those policies were overturned in the 1960s, the migration from reservations to cities continued. The 2000 Census found nearly half of self-identified Indians living in metropolitan areas. Migration for native peoples has had many consequences, including the reorganization of Indian identities and politics. In cities like Los Angeles, New York, Phoenix, Chicago, Houston, Anchorage, Alaska, and Tulsa, Oklahoma, members of dozens of tribes have come together to shape pan-Indian communities and new forms of political activism. Urban-based organizations like the American Indian Movement and United Indians of All Tribes led the Red Power movement that changed the tone of Indian country in the 1970s.

Other migration sequences likewise yielded new concentrations and communities. Gays and lesbians have long used migration to come together in cities that offer some measure of tolerance or safety. For much of the twentieth century, New York, Los Angeles, and San Francisco were principal targets of gay migration. Mixed-race couples migrated for similar reasons. Most states banned interracial marriage until the civil rights era, and social intolerance lasted much longer. Lacking such laws, Washington State and a few others became home to disproportionate numbers of mixed-race couples.

Retirees also took advantage of the increased mobility and increased social benefits of the late twentieth century to move in force to particular locations, especially Florida, Arizona, and southern California. By late in the century these areas were also talking about seasonal "snowbird" migrations by elderly northerners wealthy enough to winter in the South.

New Reasons for Moving. As these examples indicate, the twentieth century introduced new patterns of migration: not just new destinations, but also new reasons for moving and some changes in who is likely to move. Young adults have always been the largest cohort of movers and became more so as the twentieth century made college educations and military service more and more common. In earlier centuries, men were more mobile than women, but changes in the job market, new transportation technologies, and cultural shifts helped women become almost as mobile in the second half of the twentieth century. The automobile and the interstate highway system made long-distance migration easier for everyone, but they also reduced one of the key reasons for short-distance moves. With a car it became easier to commute to work, making it less likely that a new job necessitated a new home.

Demographers have wondered whether the century also saw changes in some of the basic motivations for migration. Did noneconomic "lifestyle" considerations become more important reasons for relocating as more Americans became wealthier and as consumerism increased? The Sunbelt surge

since the 1970s encouraged that interpretation, but a set of surveys conducted in the early 1980s left the issue unresolved. Job issues were by far the most common reasons cited for long-distance moves; "amenity" issues like climate were rarely the principal reason for moving, but they did appear more frequently as a secondary factor.

Slowing Down. Since the 1980s, the restless nation has become less so. The rate of moving, both short distances and long, has dropped steadily, and in early twenty-first-century international comparisons, the United States no longer stands alone as the most highly mobile nation. Denmark and Finland have comparable rates, and Canada, Australia, and Great Britain are not far behind. The reasons for the American slowdown are not entirely clear. Is it because of the aging population? Is it because of the housing market, whose ups and downs can make it hard for people to move? Is it because of changes in job markets—that there are fewer fast-growing manufacturing industries, more telecommuting, more dual-job households that keep one partner anchored?

One argument is that migration has become less necessary precisely because of the great migrations of the twentieth century. Regions are more alike now in social, cultural, and also economic dimensions. Metropolitan areas often have reasonably similar economies and occupational distributions, so that opportunities that once required a long-distance move can now be found within commuting distance of home.

What this slowdown means for the nation is even less clear. It certainly has cultural implications. The nation has celebrated geographic mobility since the 1800s, associating migration through space with a variety of signifiers that have helped Americans feel proud and powerful. A nation of pioneers, adventurers, innovators, strivers, and risk takers, a nation in which the freedom to move is thought to be associated with social and economic opportunity—these myths and stories keyed American identity for many generations. And curiously, as migration rates have dipped, so has the volume of discourse about America's being a restless nation. Journalists, politicians, and educators are less likely to celebrate mobility, or even to discuss it. Immigration from other lands attracts attention. Internal migration, so central to American life and identity for the nation's first two centuries, for the moment has become less significant. But perhaps only for the moment.

[*See also* **Automobiles; California; Cities and Suburbs; Demography; Dust Bowl; Migrant Camps, Depression Era; Native American History and Culture,** *subentry on* **Since 1950; Southwest, The; Sunbelt; West, The;** *and* **World War II, Home Front.**]

BIBLIOGRAPHY

Most of the numbers appearing above were calculated from two important databases compiled by the Minnesota Population Center: Steven Ruggles, J. Trent Alexander, Katie Genadek, Ronald Goeken, Matthew B. Schroeder, and Matthew Sobek, *Integrated Public Use Microdata Series: Version 5.0* (Minneapolis: University of Minnesota, 2010), and Miriam King, Steven Ruggles, J. Trent Alexander, Sarah Flood, Katie Genadek, Matthew B. Schroeder, Brandon Trampe, and Rebecca Vick, *Integrated Public Use Microdata Series, Current Population Survey: Version 3.0* (Minneapolis: University of Minnesota, 2010).

Ferrie, Joseph P., ed. "Internal Migration." In *Historical Statistics of the United States*, edited by Susan Carter, Scott Sigmund Gartner, Michael R. Haines, Alan L. Olmstead, Richard Sutch, and Gavin Wright, vol. 1, chapter Ac. Millennial ed. Cambridge, U.K.: Cambridge University Press, 2006.

Gregory, James N. "Paying Attention to Moving Americans: Migration Knowledge in the Age of Internal Migration, 1930s–1970s." In *Migrants and Migration in Modern North America: Cross-Border Lives, Labor Markets, and Politics*, edited by Dirk Hoerder and Nora Faires, pp. 277–296. Durham, N.C.: Duke University Press, 2011.

Gregory, James N. *The Southern Diaspora: How the Great Migrations of Black and White Southerners Transformed America*. Chapel Hill: University of North Carolina Press, 2005.

Hall, Patricia Kelly, and Steven Ruggles. "'Restless in the Midst of Their Prosperity': New Evidence on the Internal Migration of Americans, 1850–2000." *Journal of American History* 91 (December 2004): 829–846.

Jasper, James M. *Restless Nation: Starting Over in America*. Chicago: University of Chicago Press, 2000.

Kuznets, Simon S., and Dorothy Swaine Thomas, eds. *Population Redistribution and Economic Growth: United States, 1870–1950*. 3 vols. Philadelphia: American Philosophical Society, 1957–1964.

Long, Larry. *Migration and Residential Mobility in the United States*. New York: Russell Sage Foundation, 1988.

Molloy, Raven, Christopher L. Smith, Abigail Wozniak. "Internal Migration in the United States." Finance and Economics Discussion Series, Divisions of Research and Statistics and Monetary Affairs, Federal Reserve Board, Washington, D.C. May 2011. Available at http://www.federalreserve.gov/pubsfeds/2011/201130/201130pap.pdf.

Rosenbloom, Joshua L., and William A. Sundstrom. "The Decline and Rise of Interstate Migration in the United States: Evidence from the IPUMS, 1850–1990." *Research in Economic History* 22 (2004): 289–325.

James N. Gregory

AFRICAN AMERICANS

In many ways, African Americans have always been a people on the move. Migration—whether forced or voluntary—has been central to black social, economic, political, and cultural life from the beginnings of slavery to the present day.

The Age of Slavery.

Forced migration brought Africans to the region of the Western Hemisphere that eventually became the United States of America. Historians estimate that the transatlantic slave trade compelled some half a million Africans to migrate there against their will, which constituted only about 6 percent of all Africans who were forcibly transported across the Atlantic Ocean between 1500 and 1870. Throughout the seventeenth century, the social status of the few thousand Africans living in Britain's mainland colonies remained ambiguous, with little distinguishing them from European indentured servants. As the southern colonies began to expand plantation agriculture to meet the increasing world demand for tobacco and rice, planters increasingly preferred African slaves to white indentured servants to fulfill their labor needs. Signaling this shift, Virginia adopted a comprehensive slave code in 1705 that clarified slaves' status as property subject to the will of their masters and that firmly defined the racial basis of slavery in North America. The expansion of plantation agriculture, both in the Chesapeake and in the Carolinas, increased the demand for more African slaves, and American planters imported an estimated three hundred thousand Africans in the eighteenth century. By 1730, South Carolina had become the first mainland colony to have a black majority; by midcentury blacks constituted nearly half of Virginia's population.

Unlike voluntary migrants of other global human migrations, enslaved Africans could not establish migration chains that connected kith and kin. The shock of captivity, the Middle Passage, and enslavement obstructed African migrants' ability to sustain cultural continuity across the Atlantic. Because slave buyers preferred men and teenagers, Africans arrived at the British North American mainland in imbalanced ratios of gender, sex, and age. Believing that Africans who shared a common culture and language might more likely act in concert to resist enslavement, slave traders mixed Africans of different geographic regions, nationalities, religions, and languages, forcing Africans to live in linguistic and ethnic isolation. But by the 1730s, births to slave women began to outnumber the importation of forced migrants from Africa, creating the beginnings of a self-sustaining African American culture, rooted in the common experience of enslavement rather than in the bonds of kinship, ethnicity, language, or religion.

By the early nineteenth century, a transcontinental slave trade emerged that threatened the stability of this emergent African American slave culture. Shortly after the American Revolution, economic changes in the settled South and the nation at large propelled a massive shift in the demographic distribution of African Americans. As slaveholders in the seaboard South converted their farms and plantations from tobacco to cereal crops, they regarded a yearlong labor force of slaves a costly burden. Rather than emancipate their slaves, however, most planters considered them a marketable asset. The abolition of the transatlantic slave trade by Congress in 1808, the opening of the southern interior to white settlement, and the growing market for sugar and cotton created an insatiable demand for slave labor in the West. Not only did the sale of surplus slaves rescue many eastern planters from bankruptcy, but these slaves provided the labor behind the economic development of the antebellum Deep South. An infrastructure of auction blocks, trade routes, warehouses, and slave pens operated by slave traders, merchants, financiers, and insurers connected sellers in places such as Alexandria, Virginia, and Baltimore in the east to buyers in Memphis, New Orleans, and Natchez, Mississippi, in the west. Historians estimate that more than a million slaves were forcibly moved from the older slave states to the interior South between 1790 and 1860, making the internal slave trade the largest forced relocation of people in American history.

Thousands of African Americans resisted their bondage by running away. The profile of the typical runaway remained remarkably consistent throughout the age of slavery. Those who were most likely to run away were young-adult male field hands who were either unmarried or newly married without children. Such men were more willing to defy the authority of masters and overseers. Like voluntary migrants of other human migrations, runaways tended to be young risk takers who had the energy, courage, determination, and resourcefulness to survive a life on the run. Before the 1820s, only a few runaways headed to the North, whereas one in four headed to another southern state to reunite with kith and kin who had been sold; many others went west to the territories beyond the Mississippi River. By the 1840s, only about one in ten escaped to another southern state: many more took advantage of improved transportation and more sophisticated communication networks to make an escape north. Still, most runaways concluded that the anonymity of cities afforded fugitives from slavery the safest haven.

The Age of Emancipation.   During the Civil War, thousands of slaves took advantage of the chaos of war to liberate themselves by seeking refuge with advancing Union armies. By overwhelming Union military bivouacs,

fugitive slaves eventually forced the United States to consider runaways as free people and to adopt emancipation as a war aim. Once the war ended and slavery collapsed, former slaves seized upon the freedom to move, which stood in stark contrast to slavery's long history of forced migrations. Emancipated slaves flocked to the region's cities and towns to seek protection from the pervasive violence of the countryside and work for cash wages, doubling the black population of the South's ten largest cities between 1865 and 1870. Thousands of men and women migrated to the predominantly white communities of the upper Midwest, where they strove to live in dignity as free citizens. Most freedpeople, however, took to the roads on the heels of slavery's demise to reunite with kith and kin that had been scattered by the intercontinental slave trade.

The failure of Reconstruction to initiate land reform, stem political violence, and sustain racial democracy convinced some former slaves to organize migrations out of the region. In the spring of 1879, the migration known as the Kansas Fever Exodus occurred when some six thousand black migrants left Louisiana, Mississippi, and eastern Texas. Fearful of an impending return to slavery and having an expectation of free land, these so-called Exodusters headed to Kansas, where they built black towns. In the 1890s, Bishop Henry McNeal Turner promoted emigration to Liberia as an alternative to life in the Jim Crow South, but despite the appeal of these expeditions to Africa, few southern blacks could or were willing to leave.

Rather than abandon the South, most blacks used mobility to reclaim homes in the region of their birth. Many former slaves abandoned the slave quarters in favor of resettling their families in their own little houses on isolated tenancies scattered across the plantation. In doing so, they forced the collapse of the system of gang labor, one of the hallmarks of slavery, and initiated the transition to sharecropping, a system that, at least initially, promised black agriculturalists economic autonomy. Coincidental with emancipation, the South embarked upon an intensive period of industrialization, and many rural blacks migrated from their farms to the region's growing number of mines, mills, and factories. African Americans entered the wage-labor market only sporadically, with wage-earning objectives oriented toward the acquisition and maintenance of independent rural homes. Blacks' short-term work objectives frustrated industrialists and planters alike, who complained that black mobility undermined their ability to maintain a labor force. As many southern whites feared, black geographic mobility translated into social mobility. By 1910, more than two hundred thousand African Americans, or one-fourth of all southern black farmers, owned part or all of the land that they cultivated. Although modest and often insecure, the property that former slaves accumulated generated strong attachments to particular lands and communities that anchored them to the South.

The Great Black Migrations of the Twentieth Century.

Emancipation thus generated no regional redistribution of the black population in the United States. In 1910 most blacks remained in the South, lived in the state of their birth, and called the countryside rather than the city their home. Mobilization for World War I precipitated a restructuring of the national labor market in the early twentieth century that began to pull millions of blacks out of the South in what became known as the Great Migration. Wartime industrial expansion coincided with a sharp decline in European immigration, creating labor shortages that opened unprecedented employment opportunities for African Americans in the urban North. Between 1915 and 1930, some 1.25 million black southerners relocated to industrial cities such as Chicago, Cleveland, Detroit, New York City, and Pittsburgh. Out-migration tapered off during the Great Depression, but World War II spawned what is known as the Second Great Migration, in which African Americans left the South in greater numbers and at greater rates. Between 1940 and 1970, some 4.5 million blacks migrated out of the South, drawn not only to the industrial North and Midwest but to the cities of the West Coast and their rapidly expanding defense industries. By 1970 the center of African American life had shifted from the rural South to the urban North and West. Whereas only 740,000 African Americans lived outside the South in 1900, more than 10.6 million did so in 1970, constituting 47 percent of all blacks living in the United States. As late as 1940, 14 million African Americans lived on southern farms, but by 1980 fewer than 1.5 million did so, illustrating the extent to which the Great Migration depopulated the rural South.

Historical evidence disputes the enduring stereotype of the typical black migrant as an unsophisticated sharecropper unfit for urban life and industrial employment. Black southerners who relocated were more likely to be young adults of prime working age who had more schooling than those who remained in the South. Although most migrants had been born on southern farms, many had experienced industrial work and urban life in the South before coming north. The Great Migration thus tended to follow a city-to-city rather than a farm-to-factory trajectory. Because of their characteristic self-confidence, determination, and ambition, blacks who left the South had what demographers call a "migrant advantage" that enabled them to sustain stable family lives and achieve modest economic gains in their new homes. The Great Migration also contributed to a brain drain across the black South, as African Americans of talent—lawyers, entrepreneurs, educators, publishers, athletes, novelists, artists, and entertainers—seized professional opportunities in the urban North and West that were unimaginable under Jim Crow, further challenging the image of migrants as ill-prepared for urban life.

Unlike the forced migrants of earlier generations, the black migrants of the twentieth century sustained cultural continuity with the home places that they had left. Once migrants departed, they preserved social bonds with kith and kin in the South through letters and return visits. Demographers have estimated that about one black migrant returned south for every six black southerners who moved north, suggesting a circularity to black migration in the twentieth century. These interregional networks facilitated migration as friends and relatives disseminated practical advice to potential migrants about employment opportunities, living conditions, and the political climate of the North. The northern black press, particularly Robert Abbott's *Chicago Defender*, beckoned southern blacks to move north through optimistic editorials that imagined migration as a panacea for the social and political ills that afflicted African Americans. Migrants worked in concert rather than in isolation to plan and coordinate their moves, giving the migration the characteristics of a grassroots social movement.

Support networks that extended from the urban North down to the far corners of the Deep South eased newcomers' transition to the North. Not only did newcomers rejoin family and friends, but they readily detected the sights, sounds, and smells of the South in the expanding black ghettos of midcentury urban America. Migrants flocked to black-owned restaurants that served barbecue short ribs, macaroni, yams, and grits. Migrants worshiped in unpretentious storefront churches, an institution that was unique to the urban North but that preserved southern folk sensibilities and demonstrative worship styles. An emergent commercial world of popular arts, athletics, motion pictures, street parades, and nightclubs that featured jazz, blues, and swing broadened African American culture. Migrants opened a range of businesses that catered to the emerging black consumer market. Migrant entrepreneurs expanded older media such as newspapers but also launched new ventures, such as black-appeal radio and nationally circulating magazines, that cultivated a national African American cultural and political consciousness. In places such as the automobile plants of Detroit, the packinghouses of Chicago, and the waterfronts along the West Coast, black workers forged a labor-oriented civil rights agenda that combined demands for both political and economic justice. Demographic changes of the Great Migration eventually reshaped urban electoral politics in a way that enabled the election of black legislators and mayors. Black migrants did not merely adjust to urban iving conditions as they found them: rather, through their own creativity, self-determination, and activism they transformed those cities into places that were at once southern and northern, rural and urban, sacred and secular, old and new.

Return Migration since 1970. Despite the creative energy at the heart of black migrant communities, migration failed to deliver American blacks from the poverty, racism, and political subordination that had confined their lives in the South. Residential segregation, employment discrimination, intraracial class conflict, and systemic racial violence confined migrants to all-black ghettos that all too often had become havens of poverty, unemployment, overcrowding, drug addiction, crime, and police brutality. New obstacles in the aftermath of World War II threatened the viability of urban black communities and their institutions. Deindustrialization depleted the manufacturing job base and urban renewal razed black neighborhoods and replaced them with high-rise public housing, contributing to the collapse of the communities that migrants had struggled so hard to build. As economic opportunities in the North and West declined and a more favorable racial and political climate emerged in the South in the wake of the civil rights movement of the 1960s, the distribution of the nation's black population began to shift once again.

As late as the period 1965–1970, the states with the greatest rates of black out-migration were in the South, and the industrial states of the Northeast, the Midwest, and the West continued to attract large numbers of southern blacks. The pattern began to reverse in the 1970s when those industrial states that had attracted black migrants throughout the twentieth century showed net losses in their black population. By the late 1990s the South was the only region in the country that showed net increases in its black population through in-migration, whereas states such as New York, California, and Illinois ranked among those with the greatest losses in black population through out-migration. Return migrants relocated in fast-growing Sunbelt cities such as Atlanta, Dallas, Charlotte in North Carolina, and Orlando in Florida, and they avoided returning to the rural Deep South.

The pursuit of economic opportunity was not the only factor that motivated blacks to return to the South. A reverse chain-migration pulled return migrants to areas of the South that had long been familiar to them through strong family ties. By settling in such homeplaces, return migrants not only cared for aging relatives but also received economic assistance, child care, and other crucial social support that was no longer available in the urban North. As this population shift continues in the twenty-first century, demographers will continue to chart the social, cultural, and political impact of this next phase of black migration in America.

[*See also* **African American Emigration; African Americans; Cities and Suburbs; Demography; Maroon Societies; Slave Resistance; Slavery; Slave Trades; South, The; Sunbelt; Underground Railroad; World War I, Home Front;** *and* **World War II, Home Front.**]

BIBLIOGRAPHY

Berlin, Ira. *The Making of African America: The Four Great Migrations.* New York: Viking, 2010. A scholarly but accessible synthesis of four centuries of African American history centered on the themes of migration and place.

Deyle, Steven. *Carry Me Back: The Domestic Slave Trade in American Life.* New York: Oxford University Press, 2005. Explores the centrality of the domestic slave trade to the broader market revolution of the antebellum United States; argues that local slave sales were as important, if not more important, than long-distance sales, and that even as the slave trade connected buyers and sellers in slaves, it created deepening political conflicts within the South that contributed to the dynamics of secession and civil war.

Franklin, John Hope, and Loren Schweninger. *Runaway Slaves: Rebels on the Plantation.* New York: Oxford University Press, 1999. The most comprehensive study of runaway slaves; draws on an extensive compilation of notices of runaways in newspaper advertisements and petitions to county courts and southern legislatures.

Frey, William H. *The New Great Migration: Black Americans' Return to the South, 1965–2000.* Washington, D.C.: Brookings Institution, 2004. Available at http://www.brookings.edu/~/media/Files/rc/reports/2004/05demographics_frey/20040524_Frey.pdf. A demographic study of migration data from U.S. Censuses; reveals the many patterns of black return migration to the South.

Gregory, James N. *The Southern Diaspora: How the Great Migrations of Black and White Southerners Transformed America.* Chapel Hill: University of North Carolina Press, 2005. An ambitious work that considers the Great Migration as part of a broader out-migration of black and white southerners.

Hahn, Steven. *A Nation under Our Feet: Black Political Struggles in the Rural South from Slavery to the Great Migration.* Cambridge, Mass.: Harvard University Press, 2003. Examines how rural blacks developed a political consciousness over the six decades from the twilight of slavery through the early twentieth century; pays particular attention to theme of mobility in building community in the aftermath of slavery.

Johnson, Daniel M., and Rex R. Campbell. *Black Migration in America: A Social Demographic History.* Durham, N.C.: Duke University Press, 1981. A comprehensive demographic study that provides estimates on the demographics of black migration from the transatlantic slave trade through the 1970s.

Reich, Steven A. "The Great Migration and the Literary Imagination." *Journal of the Historical Society* 9, no. 1 (March 2009): 87–128. Critiques recent social histories of black migration in the twentieth century by revisiting the narratives of black migration written by social-realist novelists in the 1930s and 1940s.

Reich, Steven A., ed. *The Encyclopedia of the Great Black Migration.* 3 vols. Westport, Conn.: Greenwood Press, 2006. A reference work that situates black migration from 1870 through the twentieth century in its broadest social, economic, cultural, and political context.

Schwalm, Leslie A. *Emancipation's Diaspora: Race and Reconstruction in the Upper Midwest.* Chapel Hill: University of North Carolina Press, 2009. Examines the migration of thousands of southern blacks out of the South to Iowa, Minnesota, and Wisconsin during the Civil War and Reconstruction.

Trotter, Joe William, Jr., ed. *The Great Migration in Historical Perspective: New Dimensions of Race, Class, and Gender.* Bloomington: Indiana University Press, 1991. A collection of essays by leading scholars.

Steven A. Reich

IRISH AMERICANS

Irish immigrants and their descendants virtually defined the American conception of "ethnic group." The Irish were the first European people to substantially challenge English cultural dominance in colonial America, to spark significant Anglo-American hostility, to develop a rich array of community institutions, and to demonstrate that ethnicity could have long-lasting social and demographic consequences.

English military operations and land confiscations in Ireland propelled more than ten thousand Irish to the West Indies between the 1640s and the 1660s, with overflow into English North America. Population pressure and English land seizures accelerated emigration in the eighteenth century, with many of the Irish taking advantage of contractual servitude to provide for the Atlantic passage. By 1790, roughly four hundred thousand people of Irish birth or descent lived in the United States, three-quarters of them Roman Catholic. Between 1820 and the mid-1920s, some 4.75 million Irish migrated to the United States, second only to Germans among non-English immigrants. Irish immigration peaked between 1846 and 1851, when the United States received most of the 1.5 million who fled the devastating potato famine. The number of Irish-born immigrants and their children reached an all-time high around 1900 at almost 3.5 million.

Until well into the twentieth century, a strong social and cultural Irish Catholic community existed in America by both choice and necessity. This community, which arose in the United States before the Civil War, owed much to the nature of Irish immigration itself, a calculated movement—even in the famine years—of men and women seeking opportunities superior to those at home. Moreover, this was a chain migration, with relatives, neighbors, and coworkers paving the way for subsequent arrivals, and with families, parishes, and villages reassembling in America.

For much of the nineteenth century, Irish Americans found their social and economic mobility hampered by lack of capital, insufficiency of marketable skills, and outright prejudice. Most avenues of upward mobility—whether politics, the church, or trade—remained focused upon the immigrant subculture and held in the most ambitious youths rather than propelling them outward. One consequence was a highly concentrated population. In 1850, 80 percent of the Irish-born lived in the urban Northeast. In 1860, nearly one-third of the Irish-born lived in just ten American cities, and 40 percent of that number lived in New York City alone. As late as 1920, approximately 90 percent of first-generation Irish Americans lived in urban areas. Not until after World War I did these close-knit Irish neighborhoods begin to erode and disperse.

Irish Americans formed mutual aid societies, fraternal groups, small businesses, Catholic parishes, and political organizations. The last offered protection against—while also provoking periodic assaults by native-born Anglo-American Protestants upon the Irish

Catholics' alleged loyalty, on account of their religion, to a "foreign prince," the pope. Episodes of nativist hostility reinforced Irish Americans' tendency to identify themselves as a people dispossessed—first by the English and subsequently by Anglo-Americans. The Roman Catholic Church provided a source of strength and a path of upward mobility. By 1900, half of the bishops who had served the American church were of Irish birth or descent. Politics, too, served the community. Thousands of Irish Americans earned their wages as policemen, firemen, city laborers, and clerks, while the politicians who secured their places built impressive urban vote-getting machines headed by bosses like New York City's "Honest John" Kelly and by mayors like Boston's James M. Curley and, after World War II, Chicago's Richard J. Daley.

Associated with the Democratic Party from the 1840s, Irish American voters wavered when President Woodrow Wilson showed little enthusiasm for Irish independence but returned to the party to vote for the Catholic presidential candidate Alfred E. Smith in 1928. The New Deal's social-welfare programs, which undercut the social services provided by ethnic politicians, and the erosion of Irish American neighborhoods together weakened pressures for political conformity. A residual ethnic pride emerged, however, in Irish American support for John F. Kennedy in 1960.

As the twentieth century wore on, Irish America slipped into a pan-Catholic culture that was no longer purely ethnic. With the growing secularization of American life, a superficial "Irishness" was embraced as part of the American culture. Saint Patrick's Day, shorn of religious significance, became a national festival, and to claim Ireland as one's ancestral home became both fashionable and, ironically, a badge of assimilation.

[*See also* Anti-Catholicism; Assimilation; Cities and Suburbs; Clergy; Immigration; Knights of Columbus; Nativist Movement; New York City; *and* Race and Ethnicity.]

BIBLIOGRAPHY

Bayor, Ronald H., and Timothy J. Meagher, eds. *The New York Irish*. Baltimore: Johns Hopkins University Press, 1996.

Clark, Dennis. *Erin's Heirs: Irish Bonds of Community*. Lexington: University Press of Kentucky, 1991.

Greeley, Andrew M. *That Most Distressful Nation: The Taming of the American Irish*. Chicago: Quadrangle Books, 1972.

McCaffrey, Lawrence J. *The Irish Diaspora in America*. Bloomington: Indiana University Press, 1976.

Meagher, Timothy J., ed. *From Paddy to Studs: Irish-American Communities in the Turn of the Century Era, 1880 to 1920*. New York: Greenwood, 1986.

Shannon, William V. *The American Irish: A Political and Social Portrait*. 2d ed. Amherst: University of Massachusetts Press, 1989.

Dale T. Knobel

ITALIAN AMERICANS

The U.S. Census Bureau estimated that in 2008 some 17.8 million people of Italian ancestry lived in the United States, of whom the great majority were descended from 5 million Italians who immigrated to the United States after 1890. The high point of the immigration occurred in the first fifteen years of the twentieth century, when some 3.4 million Italians arrived. Predominantly males of working age, peasants, artisans, and laborers, about half remained and sent for wives and families.

This vast migration resulted from fundamental changes in Italian society, including population growth, capitalist innovations that disrupted traditional forms of agriculture and craft production, and burdensome taxes and military conscription imposed by the new Kingdom of Italy. Poverty and illiteracy characterized southern Italy, from which two-thirds of the immigrants originated.

World War I and restrictive immigration legislation in the United States reduced Italian immigration to a trickle: the Immigration Act of 1924 established an annual quota for Italy of 3,845. Following World War II, the family-reunification provision of American immigration policy enabled a modest number of new immigrants to enter the United States. By the 1970s, however, Italy had become a country of immigration rather than emigration.

Though the Italian immigrants included winemakers and fishermen in California, stonecutters in Vermont, cigar makers in Florida, sugarcane workers in Louisiana, and miners in places from Pennsylvania to Utah, more than two-thirds were concentrated in cities along the East Coast from Philadelphia to Boston and west to Chicago. Replacing the Irish, the Italians became the major source of unskilled labor in railroads and construction. Over time, increasing numbers, especially women, found jobs in factories and mills, particularly textiles and clothing manufacturing.

Immigrants who had been labor activists in Italy brought their radical ideologies to America. Italian-born anarchists, socialists, and syndicalists played an important role in such strikes led by the Industrial Workers of the World as those of Lawrence, Massachusetts, in 1912 and Paterson, New Jersey, in 1913. Italian immigrants figured in the leadership and rank-and-file of American Federation of Labor unions and, with their children, of the Congress of Industrial Organizations unions of the 1930s. Initially denounced as strikebreakers, Italians earned a reputation as radicals, a reputation reinforced by the Sacco and Vanzetti case of the 1920s.

The immigrants formed clustered settlements, composed of persons from the same regions and even villages. Here they re-created their cultural patterns and social networks, including banks established by padrones (labor contractors), mutual aid societies providing sickness and death benefits, and the festa of the town's patron saint. Nominally Roman Catholic, many immigrants were anticlerical, and Italian parishes were established with great difficulty. Parents preferred to send their children to free public schools rather than to parochial schools. The second generation became acculturated to American Catholicism, however, and was more devout than the first.

Attached to the particular villages from which they came, the immigrants initially did not identify themselves as "Italians." World War I and the rise of Fascism engendered a nationalist spirit among many, however. Denounced as "dagoes," Italians faced prejudice and discrimination; thus when Benito Mussolini encouraged pride in Italy, many embraced him as a savior. In the 1930s, Fascist propaganda exploited this predisposition. Despite a militant anti-Fascist minority, most Italian Americans initially sympathized with Mussolini's regime.

Slow to naturalize, Italians played a minor role in American politics until after World War II. Fiorello La Guardia, first a congressman and then mayor of New York City, and Vito Marcantonio, a radical congressman from New York City's East Harlem, were exceptions. Following the attack on Pearl Harbor and Italy's declaration of war on the United States, the six hundred thousand Italian immigrants who were still not naturalized became classified as "enemy aliens."

World War II marked a major turning point in Italian American history. Eager to prove their loyalty, Italian Americans served in the U.S. armed forces, purchased bonds, and otherwise supported the war effort. On 12 October 1942, Attorney General Francis Biddle removed the stigma of "enemy alien" from nonnaturalized Italians. In contrast to the mass internment of Japanese Americans, only a few hundred alleged Italian Fascists were placed in concentration camps. The war also accelerated Americanization, as young people left their Little Italy neighborhoods for military service and jobs in war industries.

Following the war, the GI Bill (Servicemen's Readjustment Act) and enlarged education and work opportunities accelerated the social mobility of the second generation—a process reflected in increased migration to the suburbs. The Little Italies also suffered incursions by new migrants, urban renewal, and highway construction. When the so-called black revolution convulsed America's central cities in the 1960s, Italian Americans who sought to defend their turf were accused of a racist backlash. Solidly Democratic since the New Deal era, they increasingly voted Republican in reaction to the cultural conflicts of those years and as an expression of their higher socioeconomic status.

Various indices show Italian Americans' assimilation to the norms of middle-class life. Indeed, by the 1980s, some had attained positions of power and prestige: Mario Cuomo, the New York governor; Lee Iacocca, the head of the Chrysler Corporation; Judge Antonin Scalia of the U.S. Supreme Court; A. Bartlett Giamatti, the president of Yale University; and the filmmaker Martin Scorsese.

Ethnic consciousness not only survived, but even experienced a resurgence in late twentieth-century America. Italian Americans explored their experience through history and the arts, visited archives and cemeteries in Italy, and reestablished ties with long-lost cousins. Old organizations such as the Sons of Italy in America took on new life, while new organizations proliferated. Partially attributable to the general ascendance of the multicultural paradigm, for some this resurgence also offered compensation for the feeling that they were not yet fully accepted as Americans. In the media, for instance, Italian Americans continued to be stereotyped as gangsters and stupid. For others the resurgence was a search for an identity to counter the impersonality of postmodern society.

[*See also* Aliens during Wartime; Anti-Catholicism; Assimilation; Cities and Suburbs; Clergy; Immigration; Nativist Movement; Race and Ethnicity; *and* World War II, Home Front.]

BIBLIOGRAPHY

Alba, Richard D. *Italian Americans: Into the Twilight of Ethnicity.* Englewood Cliffs, N.J.: Prentice-Hall, 1985.

DeConde, Alexander. *Half Bitter, Half Sweet: An Excursion into Italian-American History.* New York: Scribner, 1971.

Eula, Michael J. *Between Peasant and Urban Villager: Italian-Americans of New Jersey and New York, 1880–1980, the Structures of Counter-Discourse.* New York: Lang, 1993.

Mangione, Jerre, and Ben Morreale. *La Storia: Five Centuries of the Italian American Experience.* New York: Harper Collins, 1992.

Vecoli, Rudolph J. "The Italian Diaspora, 1876–1976." In *The Cambridge Survey of World Migration,* edited by Robin Cohen, pp. 114–122. Cambridge, U.K.: Cambridge University Press, 1995.

Vecoli, Rudolph J. "The Search for an Italian American Identity: Continuity and Change." In *Italian Americans: New Perspectives in Italian Immigration and Ethnicity,* edited by Lydio F. Tomasi, pp. 88–112. Staten Island, N.Y.: Center for Migration Studies, 1985.

Rudolph J. Vecoli

ITINERANT PREACHERS

Itinerancy, the practice of preaching from one place to another while never settling down, first came to prominence in America during the First Great Awakening in the person of the British evangelist George Whitefield. Because most clergy remained in one congregation their entire life, itinerancy was a radical innovation. Although most clergy viewed itinerancy with contempt because of its anti-authoritarianism and lack of decorum, its widespread use during the Great Awakening had a significant impact on American evangelicalism. Itinerancy allowed preachers to be free of institutional constraints, opened the way for extemporaneous preaching, and took worship outside the walls of the church to the open fields of the colonies.

It was not until Francis Asbury and the Methodists in the late eighteenth and early nineteenth centuries that itinerancy became a norm in American evangelicalism. Drawing upon his tutelage under John Wesley and his understanding of the apostolic church, Asbury crafted itinerancy into an established institution of early American Methodism. Under Asbury, Methodist itinerant preachers, or circuit riders, never served a single congregation or parish and were generally responsible for a rural circuit that could be as large as two hundred to five hundred miles in circumference. This was a demanding lifestyle. Itinerants lived a life of voluntary poverty; were advised not to marry; faced the elements; confronted hostile, often violent, opponents; and preached nearly every day with very little rest—only a week at most during any given month. Asbury's vision of a mobile and pious network of preachers proved to be key to Methodism's growth in the early republic when most people lived in isolated rural communities outside the slowly emerging urban centers.

Methodist circuit riders not only were suited to the rural nature of the young nation but also were models of its revolutionary ideals. Unlike earlier ministers, such as Jonathan Edwards, itinerant preachers came from ordinary backgrounds, had an average education, and were young. This religious populism was a major factor in the growth of Christianity in the early republic. It offered common people a sense of self-respect and collective self-confidence. The significance of itinerant preachers in this equation was that they preached in the simple language of their audience, revealed the possibilities for social mobility in the new nation, and reflected the charismatic leadership of the early republic. Even though this network of Methodist preachers was highly influential during the early nineteenth century, it began to decline after Asbury's death in 1816.

Charles Grandison Finney gave itinerancy new life in the mid-nineteenth century. Finney's revivals on the western frontier of New York State in the 1820s elevated him to national prominence, a popularity that remained consistent until his death in 1875. Finney caused a stir among many of his fellow ministers for his repudiation of Old School Calvinism and for his lively, exciting meetings, where those concerned about their salvation sat on the anxious seat and where women played an active role. He became widely known for his disdain of the implicit authority of learning, the uselessness of theologically abstract sermons, the muddled complexities of Calvinism, and the elitism of learned ministers. He called for ministers to focus on the needs of their audiences and to deliver their sermons in a straightforward, lively manner in order to avoid the pitfalls of the over-scholarly and pretentious message. Finney was a transitional figure in the early republic, one who brought the democratic styles of early American evangelicalism to respectable churches.

After Finney's death in 1875, the so-called big-tent revivalists were perhaps the most significant inheritors of the itinerant tradition. Prominent big-tent revivalists included Maria Woodworth-Etter, Billy Sunday, and Aimee Semple McPherson. Taking advantage of the rapid improvements in transportation and communication, including radio in the twentieth century, big-tent revivalists took the Gospel to an unprecedented number of people. They continued to express the populist religion of their itinerant predecessors, were key in dismantling Victorian culture, and helped to usher in the consumer revolution of the late nineteenth and early twentieth centuries. By the mid-1920s the big-tent revivalists' popularity began to wane. These traveling preachers continued to have some influence during the mid-twentieth century with the rise of Billy Graham, but urbanization and the advent of radio and television deteriorated the need for itinerant preachers—both because they no longer had to travel to disseminate their message and because followers no longer had to leave their home in order to hear their favorite evangelist.

[*See also* Burned-Over District; Great Awakenings; New England; Religion; Rural Life and Society; *and* Women and Religious Institutions.]

BIBLIOGRAPHY

Stout, Harry S. *The New England Soul: Preaching and Religious Culture in Colonial New England.* New York: Oxford University Press, 1986.

Wigger, John. *American Saint: Francis Asbury and the Methodists.* New York: Oxford University Press, 2009.

Jonathan Root

J

JACOBS, HARRIET

(1813–1897), escaped slave who became an abolitionist and wrote an autobiography. Harriet Ann Jacobs was born in Edenton, North Carolina, in 1813. As a child she lived with her parents and was shielded from the worst aspects of slavery. When she was twelve she unexpectedly became the slave of Dr. James Norcom. He almost immediately began to make sexual demands of her. Jacobs resisted Norcom's demands and determined to control her own life as much as possible. She decided to enter into a liaison with a prominent local lawyer, Samuel Tredwell Sawyer, with whom she had two children and from whom she hoped to receive protection from Norcom. Sawyer was not as helpful as

Jacobs had hoped, and she was frustrated at having no way to attain her freedom. Her dealings with Dr. Norcom became increasingly difficult, and in 1835 Jacobs resolved to flee the plantation to which Norcom had taken her.

After a number of close escapes, Jacobs chose to hide in a tiny attic crawlspace, where she remained almost seven years. In 1842 she made her way to Brooklyn, New York. Jacobs found work in the home of Nathaniel Willis, a noted editor and publisher. While working for Willis, Jacobs made the first of several visits to England. Later she moved to Rochester, New York, where she worked with abolitionists including her brother, John S. Jacobs, and Frederick Douglass. She also lived for a time in Boston. Jacobs formed friendships with a number of African American and white women who, like herself, were passionate abolitionists, including Amy Post. With Post's encouragement, Jacobs began writing her autobiography, but for many years she was not able to find a publisher. Lydia Maria Child, who had significant influence with publishers and the press, offered to help in the editing of the work and was instrumental in getting it published in 1861. Unfortunately, the book was published without the author's name but with the notation "Edited by L. Maria Child" on the title page. Confusion developed, compounded by Jacobs's decision to use a pseudonym, "Linda Brent," within her narrative. Although Jacobs's authorship was recognized in the African American press and among her friends, others assumed that the work was fiction, perhaps written by Child to encourage abolitionist feeling in the early days of the Civil War. It was not until the late twentieth century that Jacobs's authorship was definitively authenticated and the autobiography accepted as fact by historians.

Despite the confusion over its authorship, *Incidents in the Life of a Slave Girl* was well-received and widely read in the United States and in Great Britain during the Civil War and afterward. Both during and after the Civil War, Jacobs worked as an organizer for Quaker organizations and helped to found orphanages, schools, and nursing homes throughout the South. Jacobs died in 1897.

Jacobs's autobiography was one of the first direct expressions of the life of women in slavery by someone who had experienced it. Jacobs's family preserved a large body of writings and letters, a rare source of information on an African American family in the years before and after slavery.

[*See also* **Antebellum Reform; Antislavery; Child, Lydia Maria; Civil War Era;** *and* **Slavery,** *subentry on* **Nineteenth Century.**]

BIBLIOGRAPHY

Yellin, Jean Fagin. *Harriet Jacobs: A Life.* New York: Basic Civitas Books, 2004.

Yellin, Jean Fagin, ed. *The Harriet Jacobs Family Papers.* 2 vols. Chapel Hill: University of North Carolina Press, 2008.

JoAnn Elisabeth Castagna

JAMESTOWN

The first permanent English settlement on the North American continent was established in 1607 up the James River in southeastern Virginia. Like other early modern European imperial ventures, Jamestown was at once thoroughly commercial and deeply religious. Founded and funded by a joint-stock company, privately owned and royally chartered, the settlement was to enrich the kingdom by enriching the individual stockholders. At the same time, indigenous "savages" must be converted to true Christianity: thus in North America, Protestant England would balance or even supplant the rival empire, Roman Catholic Spain.

Most of the several hundred men and boys who settled during Jamestown's first years had no other prospects. Their labor was meant to make the settlement rich; their actual resistance, misery, and frequent death constituted the central problem over which financially invested adventurers, both in London and in Virginia, bitterly wrangled. Captain John Smith—not quite one of the gentlemen—temporarily saved the colony by taking over when it was about to be abandoned. Forced out by 1609, he later published much about Virginia—critique, promotion, and self-promotion—but never himself returned. At other points, collapse was forestalled only by the fortuitous arrival of ships and provisions. Successive charters and policy changes from London attempted to attract new settlers and keep the old ones happier. John Rolfe grew tobacco, setting the course for Virginia's eventual wealth and disgrace. Though slavery did not immediately take root in early Virginia, the first unfree Africans landed in Jamestown in 1619.

Recent scholars of the Virginia Indians have shown impressive resourcefulness. Still, the main source of information about the relations between the settlers and the Indians remains John Smith, and it is difficult to tell exactly what either the English or Powhatan and his people were up to. Clearly Powhatan was a canny leader who thought the English potentially useful. Powhatan's daughter Pocahontas is even more of a puzzle. Her 1614 marriage to John Rolfe (not John Smith) led to some years of peace between her people and his, even though she soon died while on a visit to London. In 1622, Powhatan's successor led a "great assault"—the term, replacing the traditional "massacre" (Helen C. Rountree, *Pocahontas, Powhatan, Opechancanough: Three Indian Lives Changed by Jamestown* [Charlottesville: University of Virginia Press, 2006]). More than a quarter of the English settlers were killed, and the charter of the floundering Virginia Company was soon revoked. Subsequently the English prevailed over the Indians, but Jamestown still failed to thrive. Burned during Bacon's Rebellion in 1676, it never fully recovered.

Jamestown has always stood for more than its on-the-ground realities would suggest. The establishment in 1619 of a representative legislative assembly inspired Jamestown's later grand claims to be "cradle of the republic" and "birthplace of a nation." These "Jamestown before the Mayflower" claims were always aimed straight at New England. Regional passions have mellowed, and scholarship since the later twentieth century has drawn more parallels than distinctions between earliest

Virginia and New England, but the old claim to national priority remains: the survival of Jamestown did secure the English presence in North America and in that sense made the United States of America possible. Every commemoration of the 1607 founding, including the quarto centenary in 2007, has revealed and amplified contemporary passions and anxieties over the meaning of Jamestown and of the nation.

[*See also* Colonial Era; Columbian Exchange; Exploration, Conquest, and Settlement in North America; *and* Plymouth.]

BIBLIOGRAPHY

Appelbaum, Robert, and John Wood Sweet, eds. *Envisioning an English Empire: Jamestown and the Making of the North Atlantic World.* Philadelphia: University of Pennsylvania Press, 2005.

Horn, James. *A Land as God Made It: Jamestown and the Birth of America.* New York: Basic Books, 2005.

Kelso, William M. *Jamestown: The Buried Truth.* Charlottesville: University of Virginia Press, 2006.

Marion C. Nelson

JAPANESE AMERICAN CITIZENS LEAGUE

Established in 1929, the Japanese American Citizens League (JACL) promotes political activism and civil rights advocacy on behalf of Japanese Americans and Japanese immigrants. The founding members were college-educated Nisei—literally "second generation," that is, American-born children of Japanese immigrants—who were highly patriotic toward the United States. West Coast Nisei organized local chapters under the auspices of the national organization. To emphasize the

Americanism of the organization, membership was initially limited to U.S. citizens.

As the Nisei came of age in the 1920s, they faced rampant discrimination in employment and an anti-immigrant sentiment that was institutionalized in various discriminatory state and federal laws. The fledgling organization obtained some success when in 1931 a federal law, the Cable Act of 1922, was amended in a way that enabled Nisei women to retain their U.S. citizenship when they married Asian-born men; at the time, these men were ineligible for citizenship themselves, and under the original law Nisei women lost their citizenship if they married one. Another advocacy effort, to obtain citizenship for Issei—"first generation," that is, Japanese immigrants—veterans of World War I was also successful in the 1930s. Other Japanese immigrants, however, continued to be prohibited from becoming naturalized U.S. citizens.

World War II brought greater visibility and prominence to the JACL, but it was also a very traumatic time for the JACL and all persons of Japanese ancestry. After Japan attacked the United States at Pearl Harbor on 7 December 1941, the Federal Bureau of Investigation (FBI) imprisoned Issei community leaders, and the JACL became the main intermediary between the Japanese American community and the U.S. government. After President Franklin D. Roosevelt signed Executive Order 9066 in February 1942, the military ordered the evacuation from the West Coast and incarceration of all persons of Japanese ancestry. JACL leaders, realizing that evacuation was inevitable, felt it best to comply and thus opposed any type of community dissent or protest. Local chapters helped with an orderly evacuation.

With the West Coast Japanese American population imprisoned in ten internment camps scattered throughout the U.S. interior, the JACL continued to function as the main organization representing community interests, with members playing important leadership roles in camp governance. During this time of uncertainty and chaos, factions within the Japanese American community criticized the JACL for cooperating and collaborating with authorities, and JACL leaders were threatened and physically assaulted. Wanting to prove to the government the loyalty and patriotism of the Nisei, the JACL advocated for the reinstatement of Japanese Americans to selective service; at the start of the war, Nisei had been classified as enemy aliens, ineligible for military service. The JACL's efforts resulted in the formation of the all-Nisei 442nd Regimental Combat Team, a highly decorated military unit that fought in the European theater.

After the war, the JACL successfully helped lobby for the Immigration and Naturalization (McCarran-Walter) Act of 1952, which eliminated race restrictions in U.S. naturalization policy and thus enabled Issei to become U.S. citizens. In the 1970s and 1980s the JACL took a leadership role in the redress and reparations movement, which ultimately led to the Civil Liberties Act of 1988. Thanks to the act, Japanese Americans evacuated and interned during World War II obtained an official apology from the U.S. government and $20,000 each in compensation.

[*See also* **Aliens during Wartime; Immigrants' Rights Movement; Japanese Americans, Incarceration of;** *and* **Race and Ethnicity.**]

BIBLIOGRAPHY

Hosokawa, Bill. *JACL: In Quest of Justice.* New York: William Morrow, 1982. Although this book was commissioned by the JACL, the noted journalist and Japanese American community insider Bill Hosokawa presents a balanced account.

Daniels, Roger. *Asian America: Chinese and Japanese in the United States since 1850.* Seattle: University of Washington Press, 1988.

Susan S. Hasegawa

JAPANESE AMERICANS

Japanese Americans have played an integral role in the formation of the United States for more than one hundred years. During this time, Japanese immigrants and their descendants could be found working in both the industrial and the agricultural sectors. As an ethnic group they endured the deprivation of their most basic civil rights, including the incarceration of 1942. By the early twenty-first century the Japanese American community continued to thrive through youth sports, religious organizations, and civil rights organizations.

Immigration to the Kingdom of Hawai'i and the Continental United States. During the two hundred years of Tokugawa rule (1603–1868), Japan existed as a closed country. In 1868, one hundred and fifty Japanese emigrants were illegally recruited by Hawaiian sugar planters. The relocation of the Japanese eventually failed, and large-scale emigration to the Kingdom of Hawai'i did not begin until the early 1880s when a number of factors coalesced to support the movement. Following the Meiji Restoration in 1868, the Japanese government began levying heavy land taxes on farmers in order to build Japan's industrial infrastructure. Although Japanese went to the cities to find employment, they soon discovered that jobs were scarce and wages were low. The bleak economic conditions facing the Japanese people compelled them to seek their fortunes outside the country.

Beginning in 1885 the Meiji government declared large-scale emigration legal for the first time in two centuries. Between 1885 and 1894, Japanese officials agreed to send thousands of migrants to the Hawaiian Kingdom under labor contracts. Most migrants to Hawai'i came from the southwestern prefectures of Japan. By the end of the contract-labor period in 1894, more than thirty thousand Japanese had migrated to the Hawaiian Kingdom.

In Hawai'i, Japanese migrants were required to work on sugar plantations for a period of three years. Although their monthly wages were greater than what they could earn in Japan, life as a plantation worker was harsh. Seeking to avoid the problems of prostitution, gambling, and alcoholism often existent in bachelor communities, the Hawaiian government actively promoted the immigration of Issei women. ("Issei," literally "first generation," is used to refer to immigrants born in Japan.) They came as wives through the picture-bride system. In addition to caring for their children, women were expected to work in the fields during the day, and in the evenings they took in laundry for pay, cooked, cleaned, and mended. When the contract-labor system was outlawed in 1900 following the annexation of Hawai'i to the United States, thousands of Japanese laborers left the plantations to work in downtown Honolulu. Others went home to Japan or, until the 1907 gentlemen's agreement between the United States and Japan prohibited them from doing so, moved to the West Coast.

Large-scale Japanese emigration to the continental United States did not begin until the early 1890s. In the United States the 1882 Chinese Exclusion Act forced those seeking cheap labor to search for another resource pool. Between 1891 and 1900, roughly twenty-eight thousand emigrants traveled to the

American West Coast directly from Japan. Up until 1910 the Japanese American community on the continent was mostly made up of young men who came to work in lumber mills, coal mines, fish canneries, and railroads. Social life for this young male population revolved around drinking and gambling. The Japanese women who migrated were few in number. Most of the initial female migrants were brought over to work as prostitutes, although some women came independently. Both men and women could be found dispersed in states throughout the West, including California, Washington, Montana, Oregon, and Idaho.

Early Issei Community. In 1900, Issei men and women on the American continent lived in migrant labor camps and followed crops up and down the West Coast. Only a decade later, Japanese were the largest ethnic group among agricultural workers in both California and Hawai'i. By the 1920s they eventually moved into settled positions as owners and managers of farms. As Issei men settled down as farmers, they sent for their wives or arranged for picture brides to join them. By 1911 women made up half of all Japanese migrants to the continental United States. As in the Hawaiian Islands, women had to juggle working beside their husbands in the field and managing their household duties.

Issei in urban areas initially worked as hired laborers and domestic workers. Just as the Issei in rural areas moved into positions of management and ownership, those in urban areas slowly moved into small-scale business. Ironically, discrimination against Japanese by labor unions and employers forced the Issei into a higher status as the owners of small businesses. Los Angeles and Seattle proved to be centers for Issei entrepreneurship, but *Nihonmachis*, or "Japantowns,"

could be found in many cities along the West Coast. The Issei worked together to launch their businesses, often relying on their *kenjinkai*, or network of people from the same prefecture (*ken*), for financial support. For these first-generation immigrants, the *kenjinkai* was the foundation of social organization and shaped business opportunities, marriages, and community.

Japanese Americans also formed and maintained ties around religious institutions. Buddhist temples and Protestant churches brought people together from different prefectures and served as centers of activity and sources of social welfare services. The first Buddhist temples were established in Hawai'i during the 1890s and were followed on the continent in 1898. Many Issei were also members of Protestant churches, and membership offered them a connection to the world outside their ethnic community. Women were drawn to religious organizations because they provided them with opportunities to network and socialize outside the home.

Anti-Japanese Legislation. By 1924 roughly two hundred thousand Japanese had migrated to the Hawaiian Islands and one hundred eighty thousand to the continental United States. By this time, anti-Asian legislation had a long history in the United States. The 1870 Naturalization Act, which extended citizenship to African Americans, defined Asian immigrants as "aliens ineligible to citizenship," a category from which other forms of discrimination stemmed. The limitation on Japanese immigration began in 1907 with the gentlemen's agreement, which reduced the pool of eligible migrants to nonlaborers or those coming to be reunited with family members. Movement between Hawai'i and the continental United States was also banned. In reaction to the increasing number of Issei agriculturalists on the West Coast, in 1913 the California legislature passed a law that barred "aliens ineligible to citizenship" from owning property in the state and limited to no more than three years the leasing of agricultural property to them. Similar laws were also passed in several other states, including Washington and Arizona. Despite this legal setback, the Issei found ways to work around the laws, such as by placing land under the names of their Nisei children. ("Nisei," literally "second generation," is used to refer to the American-born children of Issei.)

Anti-Japanese sentiment continued to grow on the West Coast and spread across the United States. In 1924, Congress passed an immigration law that severely restricted the number of people who could enter the country. Although the new law set quotas for most nationalities, none was set for Japan or for any other nations whose peoples were "ineligible to citizenship." The law remained in force until the passage of the 1952 Immigration and Naturalization (McCarran Walter) Act, which granted Japanese an immigration quota of 185 persons a year and allowed Issei to be naturalized.

Perhaps the greatest episode of racially motivated legislation against the Japanese American community was the 1942 forced incarceration of some one hundred twenty thousand Japanese Americans, more than two-thirds of them U.S.-born American citizens. On 19 February 1942, President Franklin D. Roosevelt issued Executive Order 9066, which provided the initial authority for the mass incarceration of all Japanese immigrants and Japanese American citizens living in designated areas of Arizona, California, Oregon, and Washington. They were moved into sixteen assembly centers and ten concentration camps located in sparsely populated parts of California, Arizona, Idaho, Wyoming, Colorado, Utah, and Arkansas. The last of the internment camps closed in March 1946.

During World War II, roughly twenty thousand Japanese Americans served in the U.S. armed forces in the racially segregated 100th Infantry Battalion and 442d Regimental Combat Team. The 100th and the 442d were sent to the worst areas of fighting in the European theater. By the early twenty-first century they were still the most decorated unit in the history of the U.S. military.

Resettlement and the Nisei and Sansei Generations.

Beginning in 1942, college-age Japanese Americans were allowed to leave the camps and attend school east of the West Coast. Other Nisei were released to find work in places such as Minnesota, Colorado, and New Jersey. After the end of the war in 1945, a much different Japanese American community emerged from the internment. In the camps, leadership had shifted from the Issei to the Nisei, and the task of community rebuilding fell to the Nisei. Some of the Japanese Americans who had resettled in the Middle West and the East Coast returned west during the late 1940s and early 1950s. When they returned, Japanese Americans tended to settle in urban and suburban neighborhoods. Though Japanese Americans had tended to cluster together in ethnic enclaves in the years prior to World War II, the population became much more dispersed in the postwar years. As an ethnic group, Nisei achieved middle-class status and gave way to the third generation, the Sansei, who continued this trend of economic mobility, educational attainment, and dispersal.

The movement for redress and reparations for wartime incarceration proved to be one that invigorated the Japanese American community. The 1981 hearings of the Commission on Wartime Relocation and Internment of Civilians proved to be a cathartic event. More than seven hundred witnesses testified, many of whom spoke in public about internment for the first time. In 1988, President Ronald Regan signed the Civil Liberties Act, which provided redress of $20,000 for each surviving detainee. The redress movement sparked an interest in younger generations of Japanese Americans. In the early 1970s Sansei activists began making a yearly memorial pilgrimage to Manzanar, the site near the Sierra Nevada in California where one of the ten concentration camps was located. The pilgrimage has since become an annual event, and in the early twenty-first century many young Yonsei (fourth generation) and Gosei (fifth generation) continued to make the journey. Although Japanese American institutions no longer played an integral part in Yonsei and Gosei lives, a community presence continued in youth basketball leagues, religious institutions, and civil organizations such as the Japanese Americans Citizens League (JACL).

[*See also* **Asian Americans; Immigration; Japanese Americans, Incarceration of; Nativist Movement; Race and Ethnicity; Racism; Religion; Women and Religious Institutions;** *and* **World War II, Home Front.**]

BIBLIOGRAPHY

Daniels, Roger. *Asian America: Chinese and Japanese in the United States since 1850.* Seattle: University of Washington Press, 1988.

Hirabayashi, Lane Ryo, Akemi Kikumura-Yano, and James A. Hirabayashi, eds. *New Worlds, New Lives: Globalization and People of Japanese Descent in the Americas and from Latin America in Japan.* Stanford, Calif.: Stanford University Press, 2002.

Ichioka, Yuji. *Before Internment: Essays in Prewar Japanese American History.* Stanford, Calif.: Stanford University Press, 2006.

Ichioka, Yuji. *The Issei: The World of the First Generation Japanese Immigrants, 1885–1924.* New York: Free Press, 1988.

Matsumoto, Valerie. *Farming the Home Place: A Japanese American Community in California, 1919–1982.* Ithaca, N.Y.: Cornell University Press, 1993.

Okihiro, Gary. *Cane Fires: The Anti-Japanese Movement in Hawai'i, 1865–1945.* Philadelphia: Temple University Press, 1991.

Spickard, Paul. *Japanese Americans: The Formation and Transformations of an Ethnic Group.* Rev. ed. New Brunswick, N.J.: Rutgers University Press, 2009.

Christen Sasaki

JAPANESE AMERICANS, INCARCERATION OF

The forced removal from the West Coast in the spring and summer of 1942 of nearly one hundred twenty thousand Japanese Americans, more than two-thirds of them native-born U.S. citizens, and their subsequent incarceration in ten desolate concentration camps has been called America's worst wartime mistake. It is better understood as the culmination of a long history of discriminatory treatment of Asian immigrants and their descendants by the federal government. After 1870, Asian immigrants were defined as "aliens ineligible to citizenship," a category from which other forms of discrimination stemmed.

During the first several decades of the twentieth century, anti-Asian and specifically anti-Japanese legislation continued. By 1924, all Asians—except for Filipinos, who were then American nationals because the United States controlled the Philippines—were barred from immigrating to the United States. Despite these initiatives, when Japanese military forces attacked Pearl Harbor and other American bases on 7 December 1941, some one hundred twenty-seven thousand persons of Japanese ancestry or birth were living throughout the continental United States. Of these one hundred twenty-seven thousand persons, roughly ninety-three thousand lived in rural farming communities in California. An additional nineteen thousand lived in the northwestern states of Oregon and Washington.

Within hours of the attacks, agents from the Federal Bureau of Investigation arrested leaders of the Japanese American communities in the continental United States and Hawai'i and sent them to detention camps. This group included Japanese-language schoolteachers, consular officials, Buddhist priests, and fishermen. A few thousand German and Italian immigrants were also targeted. The sudden arrest of the Issei (first generation) leaders left the Japanese American community in chaos.

On 19 February 1942, President Franklin D. Roosevelt issued Executive Order 9066, which provided the initial authority for the mass incarceration of all Japanese immigrants and Japanese American citizens living in designated areas of Arizona, California, Oregon, and Washington. The order did not affect the few thousand Japanese Americans living on the East Coast or the majority of the hundred fifty thousand Japanese Americans in Hawai'i. Roughly two thousand citizens and residents of Japanese ancestry were arrested from thirteen Latin American countries and interned in the camps by the United States.

Although the removal was carried out by the U.S. Army, a separate wartime agency, the War Relocation Authority (WRA), operated the sixteen assembly centers and ten concentration camps located in sparsely populated parts of California, Arizona, Idaho, Wyoming, Colorado, Utah, and Arkansas. Many legal scholars anticipated that the U.S. Supreme Court would strike down Roosevelt's order and the actions that stemmed from it, but the justices refused to do so in the Japanese American cases of 1943–1944—*Hirabayashi v. United States* (June 1943), *Korematsu v. United States* (December 1944), and *Ex parte Endo*, issued the same day as *Korematsu*. The

decision in the *Endo* case did, however, end the government's authority to incarcerate or otherwise limit the freedom of "loyal" American citizens. The last of the internment camps closed in March 1946.

One of the changes that internment brought to the Japanese American community was a breakdown in family life and organization. Issei patriarchs lost their place as the family provider, while women, freed from most household chores, became active in camp organizations and worked in a variety of jobs. Meals were served at large communal mess halls, and inmates often ate in social groups rather than with family members. Because of their position as American citizens and their command of the English language, the Nisei (second generation) came to occupy leadership positions in camp. WRA officials often assigned the Nisei to positions as teachers, nurses, cooks, and firefighters.

As early as the summer of 1942, some Japanese Americans were released to do farm work or attend college in the Middle West and East Coast. A few with language skills were recruited by military intelligence. In 1943, Japanese American male citizens were encouraged to enlist in the U.S. Army, and in 1944 many were actually drafted for military service from behind barbed wire. Some thirty-six hundred young men were inducted into the army from the camps, and more than twenty thousand others served in the racially segregated 100th Infantry Battalion and 442d Regimental Combat Team.

A few Japanese Americans challenged the government unsuccessfully in the courts. A significant minority participated in peaceful protests, including resisting the draft. For resisting the draft, two hundred sixty-three young men were tried, convicted, and sent to federal prisons.

After the end of the war, a much different Japanese American community emerged from the concentration camps. The task of community rebuilding fell to the Nisei generation. Some of the Japanese Americans who had resettled in the Midwest and East Coast returned to the West during the late 1940s and early 1950s. When they returned, they tended to settle in urban and suburban neighborhoods.

After a presidential commission in 1982 identified "race prejudice, war hysteria, and a failure of political leadership" as the underlying causes of the incarceration, Congress passed the Civil Liberties Act of 1988, which awarded 81,974 individuals $20,000 each and apologized to them on behalf of the nation; President Ronald Reagan and George H. W. Bush also apologized. In 1999 a memorial to the ordeal of the Japanese Americans was approved for a small park near the Capitol in Washington, D.C.

[*See also* Asian Americans; Immigration; Nativist Movement; Racism; *and* World War II, Home Front.]

BIBLIOGRAPHY

Commission on Wartime Relocation and Internment of Civilians. *Personal Justice Denied: Report of the Commission on Wartime Relocation and Internment of Civilians.* Washington, D.C.: Government Printing Office, 1983.

Daniels, Roger, ed. *American Concentration Camps: A Documentary History of the Relocation and Incarceration of Japanese Americans, 1941–1945.* 9 vols. New York: Garland, 1989.

Hansen, Arthur A., ed. *Japanese American World War II Evacuation Oral History Project.* 5 vols. Westport, Conn.: Meckler, 1991–1995.

Inada, Lawson Fusao, ed. *Only What We Could Carry: The Japanese American Internment Experience.* Berkeley, Calif.: Heyday Books, 2000.

Matsumoto, Valerie. "Japanese American Women during World War II." *Frontiers: A Journal of Women Studies* 8 (1984): 6–14.

Spickard, Paul. *Japanese Americans: The Formation and Transformations of an Ethnic Group.* Rev. ed. New Brunswick, N.J.: Rutgers University Press, 2009.

Christen Sasaki

JESUITS

On 15 September 1566 when three Jesuit missionaries led by the Spaniard Pedro Martinez dropped anchor at what is now the border between Florida and Georgia, the Society of Jesus, founded formally in 1540, had already established itself in India, Japan, and South America, particularly in Brazil, where Jesuits had put in place the missionary method employed in both North and South America: make the colony a bastion of civilized culture, establish schools for colonists and native children, and then branch out to the jungles or the frontier to teach, baptize, and establish parishes with schools that might eventually grow into universities.

Killed immediately by the Indians, Martinez was the first Jesuit to die on what is now American soil. But his successors established themselves in Mexico and on the Pacific coast. In 1634 a group of colonists from England that included Jesuits settled in Maryland, in the 1640s French Jesuits poured down from Canada, and in the 1680s an Italian Jesuit with Spanish background arrived in Arizona and southern California. The French Jesuits Isaac Jogues, Jean de Brébeuf, and their six companions toiled among the Hurons and Mohawks until they were captured, tortured, and killed in New York State in the mid-1640s. Their successor, young Jacques Marquette, in 1673 explored the Great Lakes and paddled down the Mississippi River. From 1687 to his death in 1711, Eusebio Kino explored and worked in Baja

California, baptizing forty-five hundred souls in twenty-one years. A tough but humble entrepreneur, he became one of the first great horse and cattle kings of the West.

The Catholic Church was born as a permanent American institution on 25 March 1634 when a hundred and fifty men, women, and children on the *Ark* and the *Dove* waded ashore on Saint Clement's Island at the mouth of the Potomac and the Jesuit Andrew White offered Mass in Maryland. Though some worked with the Indians, converting few, the Jesuits supported themselves as gentlemen farmers and served the scattered Catholics as circuit riders. Though 113 Jesuit priests served over the years and only 25 remained in 1773, this group was the roots and trunk of the colonial American Catholic Church, and one of their number, John Carroll, became the first American Catholic bishop. His fellow priests elected him bishop in 1789, the same year in which he founded Georgetown University

In the first part of the nineteenth century, American Jesuits were mostly foreign-born. Jesuit education fanned across the country in staging areas, first in a border state, Maryland, then in the Mississippi valley at Saint Louis, then in urban centers with large Catholic populations. Jesuits from Georgetown founded institutions in in New England, Baltimore, and New Jersey, and then in the Midwest. Italian Jesuits settled on the West Coast; French Jesuits took over a seminary and founded what is now Fordham University in the Bronx and Manhattan, New York City, and on the Gulf Coast; and German Jesuits dominated the missions in Buffalo, New York, and Cleveland, Ohio.

In 1869—after the Civil War, during which Jesuits served as chaplains on both sides—Woodstock College in the Maryland woods was established to give all American Jesuits a strong theological education. It thrived through the 1960s and through the Second Vatican Council, with Jesuit professors including John Courtney Murray (1904–1967), Gustave Weigel (1906–1964), and the scripture scholar Joseph Fitzmyer (b. 1938). In 1940, Jesuit scholars introduced *Theological Studies*, the most influential Catholic theological quarterly in the country.

Following World War II, Jesuit colleges expanded, adding professional programs in fields including business, nursing, education, law, and medicine. In the 1960s and 1970s Jesuit institutions separately incorporated their Jesuit communities from their universities, and schools made themselves nonsectarian in order to qualify for state and federal aid. They established lay-dominated boards and adopted the norms of the American Association of University Professors for the hiring and promotion of faculty. Opponents considered these steps a sellout, though many supported them. Gradually, as Jesuits left during the 1960s and 1970s, novitiates and the major seminaries moved from the isolated countryside to the campuses of Jesuit universities in order to develop a more effective system of formation.

Jesuits engaged in contemporary public issues in a variety of ways. To broaden the society's intellectual and social missions, Jesuits began publishing the weekly magazine *America* on 17 April 1909; it reviews the problems of the day from a Catholic Christian standpoint. For instance, the Jesuit John LaFarge joined the staff in 1926 and pioneered the rights of black people. Meanwhile LaFarge's contemporary and fellow Jesuit Daniel Lord, author of some ninety books and a flood of pamphlets, as well as an adviser to Hollywood on moral standards, established the Summer Schools of Catholic Action. Most Jesuit chaplains supported World War II as a just cause, including dropping the atomic bombs on Hiroshima and Nagasaki.

The labor schools of the 1940s and 1950s taught parliamentary procedure and Catholic social doctrine to workingmen to ward off Communist takeovers of their unions. At Loyola University in New Orleans in the 1950s, the Jesuit Louis Twomey published the newsletter *Christ's Blueprint for the South*, and the Jesuit sociologist Joseph H. Fichter researched the southern parish, including its racial attitudes. Representing the convictions of many, but not all, Jesuits, in 1968 the priest and poet Daniel Berrigan showed his opposition to the Vietnam War by leading a raid on a draft board in Catonsville, Maryland; he spent three years in prison. In 1970 the Jesuit dean of the Boston College Law School, Robert F. Drinan, was elected to Congress because he opposed the war, and he served on the House Judiciary Committee that impeached President Richard M. Nixon.

In those years the major goal of the society was to make its mission relevant to the suffering of the world. In 1975 the Thirty-Second General Congregation of the Society of Jesus passed its statement on the relationship between faith and justice: "Since evangelization is proclamation of that faith which is made operative in love of others, the promotion of justice is indispensable to it." In response, American Jesuit high schools and colleges introduced service projects at home and in Latin America and reformed their curricula to educate "men and women for others."

In 2011, compared to 8,338 in 1960, there were 2,650 American Jesuits, organized into ten provinces to be combined into four administrative units. The Jesuit-run high schools numbered about fifty, depending on how the network of Catholic Cristo Rey and Nativity middle schools, not all of which are sponsored by Jesuits, are described. Of the twenty-eight Jesuit colleges and universities, Boston College and Georgetown are world-rated among the best. Nationally Georgetown,

Boston College (founded in 1863), Fordham (1841), Marquette in Milwaukee, Wisconsin (1881), Saint Louis (1818), and Loyola Chicago (1870) are among the 191 top universities. More than half of the Jesuits in 2011 were at least sixty years old, some Jesuit universities had only a dozen Jesuits on the faculty, and some Jesuit high schools had only a few. In 2011, consistent with an ongoing trend, nine Jesuit universities had lay, not Jesuit, presidents. Jesuit training stresses "indifference": this means that a Jesuit legacy does not depend on Jesuit priests being in charge of educational institutions, but that the society is flexible enough to continue its work wherever it is needed.

[*See also* Clergy; Education; Exploration, Conquest, and Settlement in North America; Franciscans; Missions, in America; Religion; *and* Roman Catholic Orders in Early America, Female.]

BIBLIOGRAPHY

Schroth, Raymond A. *The American Jesuits: A History*. New York: New York University Press, 2007.

Raymond A. Schroth

JEWISH AMERICANS

Although the 2010 U.S. Census showed that Jews made up less than 3 percent of the American population, their history in America is long and rich. As members of the most visible non-Christian faith throughout America's history, Jews have always influenced American ideas about pluralism. Their skin color allowed them greater acceptance in America than in other countries, but the persistence of anti-Semitism in the United States is often credited as one of the major reasons for American Jewish sympathy to liberal causes. Milton Himmelfarb, a prominent twentieth-century American Jewish thinker, is generally credited with the observation that Jews earn like Episcopalians (rich) and vote like Puerto Ricans (poor). This socioeconomic and political bifurcation of American Jews is distinctive of American Jewry and is emblematic of which aspects of American culture have been valued by Jewish immigrants. That so many American Jews do not practice the religion of Judaism but nonetheless consider themselves Jewish has challenged American conceptions about religious and ethnic groups and is not unconnected to Jewish support of America's separation of church and state.

Immigration.

Massachusetts and Connecticut stand out among early colonies in America for their intolerance toward those outside the Protestant faith, although greater animus was directed at Catholics and Quakers than at Jews. This fact that Jews were not the only ones discriminated against in the United States also made their experience very different from that of Jews in other countries. Rhode Island and Pennsylvania had strong Jewish communities as early as the mid-seventeenth century. Jews in Charleston made South Carolina the state with the largest Jewish population until the 1830s, but New York City is the oldest Jewish community in the United States.

The Jews who first came to North America in the seventeenth century were mostly Sephardic Jewish immigrants of Spanish and Portuguese descent, and they were denied the vote or ability to hold office except in the states where they formed a more sizable community. These Sephardic Jews had been victims of the Spanish Inquisition. Beginning in the eighteenth century, Ashkenazic Jews—Jews from eastern and central Europe—began to outnumber Sephardic Jews. In the early days the Sephardic elite were not entirely welcoming of the Ashkenazic Jews, but they did uphold Jewish commandments to give charity by providing material aid to the Ashkenazic Jews, and in time the divisions between the two communities eroded, particularly because of marriage: religious Jews considered intermarriage anathema, and the number of available Jewish marriage partners was small.

Between 1820 and 1840 the American Jewish population increased fivefold. Most of these immigrants were central European Jews who had faced obstacles to their economic advancement in Europe. Thus economic opportunity and religious freedom were strong motivations for immigrating. The era of highest immigration of Jews to America was between 1820 and 1924—also a period of Russian pogroms that targeted Jews. World War I ended the era of mass Jewish immigration to the United States, first because of wartime conditions and then because of restrictive quotas.

The very poorest and the very richest of Russian Jews did not make the trip to the United States. Young men were much more likely to travel to America on their own than young women were. Jews nonetheless participated in the Eastern European migration to America in disproportionate numbers to their population in Eastern Europe. There were distinct reasons for Jews to make the trip to the United States. The desire to practice Judaism without persecution led many to immigrate in order to transplant eastern European Judaism. Such Jews chose professions that allowed them freedom to observe the Sabbath and holidays. Others came with the goal of making money and consequently abandoned their Judaism in the United States. Another group consisted of radical freethinkers, such as socialists, unionists, and religious skeptics.

Locations and Occupations. In choosing places to live in the United States, Jews gravitated toward cities, congregating especially in port cities like New York, Philadelphia, Newport in Rhode Island, Charleston, and Savannah in Georgia. They did not distribute evenly across the country. Jews also earned a living in distinctive ways. Instead of farming like most Americans, Jews tended to work in areas of commerce. Thus the nineteenth century saw the rise of the Jewish peddler who fanned out across the United States. Jewish peddlers tended to become sedentary shop-owners once they married, and by the mid-nineteenth century a quarter of all American Jews lived in New York City, Philadelphia, and Baltimore.

In the nineteenth century, garment making and cigar making became industries with high levels of Jewish employees and employers. The garment industry had its center in New York City, and by 1910, New York produced 70 percent of the country's female apparel. It offered unique work opportunities for young, Jewish women immigrants, who often immigrated to the United States from eastern Europe, accompanied by a male relative and having the goal of finding work in the garment industry. Jewish women played a large role in the International Ladies' Garment Workers' Union, founded in 1900, including in its most famous strike, the historic Uprising of 20,000 in 1909, in which the Ukrainian-born Jewish woman Clara Lemlich emerged as a leader. In the Triangle Shirtwaist Company fire of 1911, the deadliest industrial disaster in New York City's history, Jewish and Italian women formed the majority of the fire's victims.

With Jews clustered in Eastern Seaboard port cities, it is not surprising that by 1820, most Americans had never seen a Jew. What most Americans knew about the Jews came from the Hebrew Bible. Because they were trying to convert them, it was the Christian evangelicals who were the most familiar with Jews. The intensity of these evangelicals led Jews to redouble their own efforts to educate their young in their religion. Jewish women were particularly active in the enterprise of Jewish education. Rebecca Gratz, an innovator in American Jewish education, also founded—in 1801, when she was just twenty years old—the Female Association for the Relief of Women and Children of Reduced Circumstances in Philadelphia and, in 1819, the Female Hebrew Benevolent Society. In the mid-nineteenth century, Rabbi Isaac Leeser published the first instruction books for Jewish children and the first American translation of the Torah in order to keep Jews knowledgeable about their own tradition.

Religious Life. The religious lives of American Jews often bore some relation to their sense of belonging in the United States. In the seventeenth and eighteenth centuries, Jews led quiet religious lives that were confined to the synagogue. Although cemeteries preceded synagogues in most Jewish communities, the synagogue eventually took on a range of functions, with its provision of kosher meat an especially important service because many Jews took the ritual purity of their meat more seriously than they did the detailed observance of the Sabbath and holidays. Synagogues also served as religious schools for the young. The rise of Reform Judaism in the nineteenth century, with its resemblance to Protestantism and its insistence on decorum in the sanctuary, suggested less than full confidence in being openly and distinctively Jewish.

Two rabbis competed for leadership of American Judaism: Rabbi David Einhorn and Rabbi Isaac Mayer Wise. Wise ended up being the leader of Reform Judaism when he accepted a pulpit in Cincinnati in 1854; he remained there until his death in 1900. His influence was large; he directed the first association of rabbis, and in 1875 he organized the Hebrew Union College, America's first—and still continuing—seminary to train rabbis. Although his hope to unite all American Jews was not realized, Wise had much influence on Reform Judaism.

Rabbi David Einhorn's son-in-law, Kaufmann Kohler, became the leader of radical Reform Judaism in America. Kohler was strongly motivated by Ethical Culture, a movement founded in 1876 by Felix Adler, the son of a rabbi. Kohler wanted to prevent educated and affluent Jews from defecting by providing a Judaism that accommodated their intellectual understanding of the world. Of the three main Jewish denominations, Reform was founded earliest and Orthodox Judaism last, in the 1890s, for it was not until the rise of Reform and Conservative Judaism that more traditional Jews found it necessary to establish a movement.

Anti-Semitism and Politics. Jews immigrated to escape persecution, and although the United States was not free from anti-Semitism, the anti-Semitism there paled in comparison with that experienced by Jews in other countries. Still, Jews' confidence and security in their Americanness was shaken by the more serious episodes of anti-Semitism in America. These include Ulysses S. Grant's 1862 order that expelled Jews from Tennessee because of their supposed profiteering, the Leo Frank lynching of 1915, and American anti-Jewish sentiment that built to an apex during the Great Depression and was reinforced by the radio-borne ranting of Father Charles Coughlin of Detroit and the public pronouncements of Henry Ford.

Politically, Jews have been involved in both the Republican and the Democratic Parties, and presidents of both sides have appointed Jews to important positions. It was not until the 1920s that Jews became visibly identified with the Democratic Party. Jews' commitment

to the United States and their nervousness of being suspected of dual loyalty meant that at first, Zionism did not attract many Americans. Zionist leaders picked up on these cues from American Jews by promoting Zionism as a means of rescuing and providing a home for persecuted Jews from other countries. Indeed, American Jewish membership in Zionist organizations rose as European Jews' situation worsened in the 1930s and 1940s. It was Hadassah, the largest women's Zionist organization in America, that drew the most energy from American Jews toward the cause of a Jewish homeland, thus continuing a tradition of Jewish women in America combining the American tradition of women involved in benevolent work and the Jewish tradition of philanthropy.

[*See also* Anti-Semitism; Central and Eastern European Americans; Labor Movements; Race and Ethnicity; Strikes and Industrial Conflict; *and* Women and Religious Institutions.]

BIBLIOGRAPHY

Diner, Hasia R. *The Jews of the United States, 1654 to 2000.* Berkeley: University of California Press, 2004.

Joselit, Jenna Weissman. *The Wonders of America.* New York: Hill and Wang, 1994.

Raphael, Marc Lee. *Judaism in America.* New York: Columbia University Press, 2003.

Sarna, Jonathan D. *American Judaism: A History.* New Haven, Conn.: Yale University Press, 2004.

Sarna, Jonathan D., and David G. Dalin. *Religion and State in the American Jewish Experience.* Notre Dame, Ind.: University of Notre Dame Press, 1997.

Rachel Gordan

JIM CROW ERA

African Americans emerged from slavery with enormous hope for the future. In the final decade of the nineteenth century, however, a rising tide of white supremacy blocked their efforts to actualize their freedom. In the late nineteenth century a formal structure of racial discrimination and marginalization, known as Jim Crow, emerged. Racial Segregation was a system of tightly enforced racial controls that mandated the physical separation of the races and oppressed African Americans economically, politically, and socially. Segregation laws separated African Americans and whites in many spheres, including work, housing, public transportation, and education. Jim Crow also consisted of a set of rules governing interactions between whites and African Americans. This system of racial etiquette required blacks to step aside for whites on city sidewalks and denied African Americans formal titles of respect. Despite all this, African Americans refused to let Jim Crow define their lives. They resisted segregation in many ways, including partisan politics, labor organizing, and informal daily resistance.

Origins. Although some forms of racial segregation existed in the urban North during the antebellum era, Jim Crow was not institutionalized through law until the 1890s. This process began in the South immediately after the Civil War when white elites regained control of state governments and imposed a system of severe racial restrictions, known as the black codes, that sought to mitigate the impact of emancipation. After 1867 the Radical Republicans took control over Reconstruction and embarked on a far more egalitarian agenda of racial reform; as a result African Americans made substantial gains in politics and education. Although federal support for racial equality declined after the end of Radical Reconstruction in 1877, the racial order remained fluid through the 1880s. That fluidity eroded after 1890 when African Americans were politically disenfranchised

in the South. In 1896 the Supreme Court decision in *Plessy v. Ferguson* established the doctrine of "separate but equal." In the wake of the *Plessy* decision, states across the South passed laws mandating the physical separation of the races in public spaces and facilities.

A combination of factors fueled this development of Jim Crow in the 1890s, including agrarian radicalism in the South and the West and Progressivism. Radical agrarian movements, including the Farmers' Alliances and the Populist Movement in the 1880s and 1890s, represented a challenge to the political power of southern elites and their northern industrial allies. Southern Redeemers used violence, intimidation, and a bevy of disenfranchisement measures, including the poll tax, literacy test, and white Democratic primary, to put down this threat to the southern political economy. Additionally, the Progressive Era was an important factor in fueling the rise of formal segregation law. Proponents of segregation drew on the Progressive Era emphasis on order and regulation to frame the physical separation of the races as a modern solution to the problem of racial disorder.

Whites relied on both violence and the law to enforce segregation. Between 1889 and 1932, a total of 3,745 lynchings took place in the South. White southerners spoke of lynchings as a punishment for black men who had raped white women; in reality lynch mobs targeted their victims because they had challenged the boundaries of segregation. Additionally, whites used the law to enforce white supremacy. In the late 1890s southerners formally wrote segregation into the law with new state constitutions.

Resisting Jim Crow. Although African Americans had little choice but to face segregation in their daily lives, they refused to let it define their existence in this way, and as

Earl Lewis has put it, "segregation became congregation" (Earl Lewis, *In Their Own Interests: Race, Class, and Power in Twentieth Century Norfolk* [Berkeley: University of California Press, 1991], p. 90). African Americans in the Jim Crow era found emotional and material sustenance in kinship, mutual aid associations, labor unions, and political organizations. They infused their daily lives with resistance, practicing their politics beyond the formal partisan structures.

Transportation.   The first segregation laws involved public transportation. In 1881, Tennessee was the first state to pass segregation laws on the railroad. Georgia followed in 1891 with the passage of the first streetcar segregation law. African Americans—including Ida B. Wells-Barnett, also a leader of the antilynching movement—resisted segregation on trains and streetcars through boycotts and legal suits. African Americans staged boycotts of segregated streetcars in twenty-five cities between 1900 and 1907, reflecting the vital role that ordinary African Americans played in protesting Jim Crow.

Education.   The history of African American education demonstrates the ways in which African Americans navigated Jim Crow by simultaneously protesting inequalities and claiming segregated spaces as their own. Although whites had established segregation in the majority of schools by the mid-1870s, African Americans refused to accept inequality of facilities. They fought to hire black teachers and petitioned legislators for additional funding.

Although there were enormous material inequalities between white and black schools, financial resources alone did not define the quality of the black educational experience in segregated schools. Black schools received substantially less funding from local and state governments, the physical school buildings were in poor physical condition, and African American teachers earned much less than their white counterparts did. Despite this material inequality, African American schools represented a space of empowerment and opportunity for African Americans in the otherwise repressive Jim Crow order.

Community.   Along with the family, the church has always been one of African Americans' most significant sources of support and resistance. African American churches filled many roles in the community. They served as spaces for political organization, education, leadership development, cultural and recreational events, and racial uplift. African American women performed a crucial role in building the racial-uplift arm of the church. The church provided social welfare services, such as support for the poor, sick, elderly, and abandoned children, denied to blacks under Jim Crow.

Mutual aid and fraternal organizations provided African Americans with material and emotional support to resist Jim Crow. African Americans made small contributions to the mutual aid organizations, and in return the organization provided health, death, and unemployment benefits to its members. In addition, mutual aid and fraternal organizations served as a space for the development of racial pride and to build leadership. African American women played a significant role in resisting Jim Crow through their activism in the Women's Club Movement, forming in 1896 the National Association of Colored Women, which provided child care for working mothers, aid for the elderly and sick, and educational facilities.

Migration between the Wars.   Migration was a tool of resistance against racism during the Jim Crow era. In a clear demonstration of their rejection of Jim Crow, from 1915 to 1945, 1.75 million African Americans moved from the rural South to southern, midwestern, northern, and western cities as part of what is called the Great Migration. A combination of factors motivated migration, including greater economic and educational opportunity and the right to vote. Many migrants also moved to escape the pervasive violence against African Americans. For African American women the desire to escape sexual violence was a very important motivator.

African American migrants to the North did not wholly escape Jim Crow. Although northern states had fewer formal segregation laws, northern whites routinely discriminated against African Americans—in employment and housing, for example. African American men and women found many fields of work closed to them because of Jim Crow. Before World War I the vast majority of African American women worked as domestic workers or laundresses, and African American men were excluded from well-paying industrial jobs.

Although life in the North was far from racially egalitarian, the Great Migration brought about tremendous political gains for African Americans. The Great Migration brought about an explosion in the number of black voters and the development of political institutions like the National Association for the Advancement of Colored People (NAACP), founded in 1909, and the National Urban League, founded in 1910. Taken together, this expanded voting power and institutional development laid the groundwork for the black freedom movements of the post–World War II era.

With the greater numbers of African American workers in northern cities, African Americans began to forge alliances with leftist and labor organizations connected with the Communist Party. In the 1920s and 1930s African Americans challenged the economic foundation of segregation at the local level with "don't buy where you can't work" campaigns, as well as in national organizations like the Brotherhood of Sleeping Car Porters, led by A. Philip Randolph.

During the 1930s and 1940s the NAACP saw significant growth in its membership and developed expanded legal campaigns against segregation in education, housing, and employment. In the 1930s the NAACP developed an extremely well-coordinated campaign against segregated schools and unequal pay for white and black teachers. Under the astute leadership of Charles Hamilton Houston and Thurgood Marshall, the NAACP achieved a series of legal victories from 1936 to 1954, beginning with *Murray v. Maryland* (1936) and culminating in *Brown v. Board of Education of Topeka* (1954). Although *Brown* was a major victory, some African Americans critiqued the emphasis on integration, arguing that integration would undermine autonomy and black educational traditions.

World War II and the Cold War. World War II and the Cold War provided an opening for an unprecedented challenge to Jim Crow. Ultimately the activism of millions of ordinary African Americans against Jim Crow came to fruition with the dismantling of the legal structure of segregation. The combination of greater electoral power, institutional development, economic gains, and international pressures made Jim Crow more vulnerable during the 1940s. African Americans capitalized on these advantageous conditions and, under the leadership of A. Philip Randolph, launched the so-called Double V campaign, which called for both victory abroad against Fascism and victory at home against Jim Crow. Randolph drew upon the expanded political and institutional power of African Americans to force President Franklin D. Roosevelt to issue Executive Order 8802

(25 June 1941), which desegregated wartime industries and federal government work and established the Fair Employment Practices Commission. Although Randolph did not succeed in forcing Roosevelt to desegregate the military in 1941, this goal was ultimately achieved in 1948. Eager to retain African American support and boost the image of the United States abroad, President Harry S. Truman ceded to Randolph's pressure and signed Executive Order 9981 (26 July 1948). Taken together, the desegregation of wartime industry and the desegregation of the military marked a major victory in African Americans' fight against segregation.

The Cold War had a significant, although dualistic, impact on the fight against segregation. Beginning in the 1940s the Red Scare pushed civil rights organizations to the right to avoid the taint of radicalism and forced them to alter their strategies and goals. Although anti-Communism limited the fight against Jim Crow, it also provided an opening for activists. In the Cold War competition for the hearts and minds of the Third World, the federal government knew that the unfair treatment of African Americans undermined America's image abroad. Such international pressures were one of many factors that prompted the government to become more responsive to African Americans' fight against segregation. African Americans, in turn, took advantage of the changing post–World War II climate by launching a grassroots movement through sit-ins, boycotts, marches, and voter-registration campaigns. Known altogether as the Civil Rights Movement, this campaign brought about significant victories in *Brown* (1954), the Civil Rights Act (1964), and the Voting Rights Act (1965).

Legacy. Although the legal and legislative victories of the mid-twentieth century are significant accomplishments by any measure,

segregation did not disappear from American life in 1964. Segregated schools and neighborhoods, along with racialized economic inequality, remained deeply entrenched. In the face of these obstacles, African Americans have drawn upon the inspiration of their activist forebears to continue their fight against Jim Crow and its legacy into the twenty-first century.

[*See also* **Desegregation; Internal Migration,** *subentry on* **African Americans; Labor Movements; Law and Society; Lynching; Racism; Reconstruction Era; Religion; Voluntary Associations,** *subentry on* **African American;** *and* **Women and Religious Institutions.**]

BIBLIOGRAPHY

Anderson, James D. *The Education of Blacks in the South, 1860–1935.* Chapel Hill: University of North Carolina Press, 1988. An excellent discussion of this early period of African American education.

Barkley Brown, Elsa. "Womanist Consciousness: Maggie Lena Walker and the Independent Order of Saint Luke." *Signs* 14 (1989): 610–633. A crucial discussion of the important role of mutual aid societies at the turn of the twentieth century.

Dailey, Jane. *Before Jim Crow: The Politics of Race in Postemancipation Virginia.* Chapel Hill: University of North Carolina Press, 2000. Argues for the racial fluidity of the postemancipation period.

Gilmore, Glenda Elizabeth. *Gender and Jim Crow: Women and the Politics of White Supremacy in North Carolina, 1896–1920.* Chapel Hill: University of North Carolina Press, 1996. An important discussion of the role of gender in racial politics during Jim Crow.

Lewis, Earl. *In Their Own Interests: Race, Class, and Power in Twentieth-Century Norfolk, Virginia.* Berkeley: University of California Press, 1991. Provides an excellent discussion of African Americans' lives and communities during Jim Crow.

Litwack, Leon F. *Trouble in Mind: Black Southerners in the Age of Jim Crow.* New York: Alfred A. Knopf, 1998.

Rabinowitz, Howard N. *Race Relations in the Urban South, 1865–1890.* New York: Oxford University Press, 1978. Challenges Woodward's arguments that the racial order was fluid in the period from 1877 to 1900 and that segregation did not emerge until 1900.

Trotter, Joe William, Jr., ed. *The Great Migration in Historical Perspective: New Dimensions of Race, Class, and Gender.* Bloomington: Indiana University Press, 1991.

Tushnet, Mark V. *The NAACP's Legal Strategy against Segregated Education, 1925–1950.* Chapel Hill: University of North Carolina Press, 1987.

Woodward, C. Vann. *The Strange Career of Jim Crow.* New York: Oxford University Press, 1955. Referred to by Martin Luther King Jr. as the "historical bible of the Civil Rights Movement," Woodward's work remains one of the central studies in the field.

Tess Bundy

JOHNSTOWN FLOOD

The Johnstown flood of 1889 was a natural disaster that devastated much of Johnstown, a steelmaking center in the Conemaugh River valley of southwestern Pennsylvania. In the hills above the city, the industrial elite of nearby Pittsburgh had built a private resort, including an artificial lake contained by a poorly designed and poorly maintained earthen dam. On 31 May 1889, weakened by torrential rain, the dam collapsed, sending a wall of water crashing down the valley. When it struck an unsuspecting Johnstown—having already overwhelmed four smaller towns—the deluge had risen to a height of forty feet. Some 2,200 of Johnstown's 30,000 people died, and much of the city was leveled.

The nation responded with a spontaneous charitable outpouring. Within weeks, some $4 million was collected and turned over to a commission established by the governor. Thousands of volunteers cleared wreckage and built temporary housing. Clara Barton, president of the American Red Cross, personally supervised the relief effort. In this laissez-faire age, the federal government limited its role to supplying a few temporary bridges. By year's end, Johnstown was nearly rebuilt. The wealthy resort owners escaped legal liability for their neglect.

Though the Galveston hurricane and flood of 1900 took more lives—some six thousand—the Johnstown flood remained for decades the paradigmatic American disaster. The episode illustrated the depth of national compassion and the ability of the emerging industrial order to organize a vast relief and reconstruction effort with little government involvement. But it also demonstrated the power of that order to evade the negative consequences of its acts.

[*See also* **Galveston Hurricane and Flood; Gilded Age;** *and* **Hurricane Katrina.**]

BIBLIOGRAPHY

McCullough, David G. *The Johnstown Flood.* New York: Simon & Schuster, 1968.

Alan Clive

JONES, ABSALOM

(1746–1818), slave who later cofounded the first African American church in North America and became the first ordained black minister in the Episcopal Church. As one of the leaders of Philadelphia's Free African Society, a mutual aid organization, and the pastor of the city's Saint Thomas's Church, Jones felt that African Americans needed to construct autonomous institutions beyond white interference. However, he pragmatically made alliances and concessions to whites who possessed the political clout or material resources necessary to make those institutions possible. Jones also set the tone of much early nineteenth-century black abolitionist rhetoric by forwarding the notion that if blacks publicly displayed their intelligence, resilience, and morality, then white racism would not have justification. This approach was adopted by black abolitionists such as Samuel Cornish and John Russwurm—who in the late 1820s founded *Freedom's Journal*, the first black newspaper— and strongly appealed to the growing black middle-class in cities such as Philadelphia and New York.

Jones was born a slave in Sussex County, Delaware, on 6 November 1746. Having learned to read as a child, Jones was hired out by his master to packinghouses in Philadelphia, where he learned to write and attended night school. He married a slave in 1770 and bought her freedom with loans that he raised with her father. In 1784 he bought his own freedom and adopted the surname Jones, but he continued to work for his master as a laborer. Jones belonged to Saint George's Methodist Church in Philadelphia and became close associates with Richard Allen, an unordained black preacher. Dissatisfied with white Methodists' contempt and the Quakers' patronizing attitudes, Jones and Allen both agreed that Philadelphia's growing black population needed an organization that could promote religion, literacy, and self-sufficiency. In 1787, Jones helped found the Free African Society, a group that assisted widows, orphans, and people with medical costs. By the 1780s the organization had also expanded its scope to more spiritual matters, with Jones heading a visiting committee meant to look after the moral conduct of its members.

By the 1790s, Jones and members of the Free African Society decided to erect their own church and school. They enlisted the help of Benjamin Rush, Philadelphia's most prominent physician, who launched a public relations campaign. Modest donations trickled in, but it was not until John Nicholson gave two $1,000 loans that church construction could actually begin. Throughout the process, Jones faced heavy resistance from Philadelphia's white religious leaders, who resented that the black community was not using their institutions. This resistance led Jones and Allen to respond to Rush's plea to nurse the sick and dispose of the dead during Philadelphia's 1793 yellow fever epidemic: Rush was erroneously confident that blacks could not contract yellow fever, and Jones and Allen felt that their community could demonstrate its qualities by helping the city's white population. Unfortunately, after the epidemic, the Irish American publisher Matthew Carey wrote a pamphlet vilifying the blacks' contributions.

In 1794, Jones's African Church joined the Episcopal Church of North America as the African Episcopal Church of Saint Thomas, and ten years later Jones was ordained as a minister. Jones, who passed away in 1818, helped to create one of the most vibrant and organized black communities in the early republic, a legacy that continues in Philadelphia to this day.

[*See also* **African Americans; Allen, Richard; Benezet, Anthony; Clergy; Early Republic Era; Free Communities of Color; Philadelphia; Religion;** *and* **Rush, Benjamin.**]

BIBLIOGRAPHY

Douglass, William. *Annals of the First African Church, in the United States of America*. Philadelphia: King & Baird, 1862. Available at http://quod.lib.

umich.edu/g/genpub/AGV8875.0001.001?
view=toc. Provides a wonderful collection of
primary-source material, including the Free
African Society's constitution and minutes, along
with Jones's own brief recollections of his life.

Jones, Absalom. *A Thanksgiving Sermon, Preached
January 1, 1808, in St. Thomas's, or the African
Episcopal Church, Philadelphia: On Account of the
Abolition of the African Slave Trade, on That Day, by
the Congress of the United States.* Philadelphia, 1808.
Available at http://antislavery.eserver.org/religious/
absalomjones/absalomjones.pdf. A widely anthol-
ogized sermon that provides an excellent look at
how Jones skillfully employed biblical language for
the abolitionist cause.

Nash, Gary B. " 'To Arise out of the Dust': Absalom
Jones and the African Church of Philadelphia,
1785–95." In his *Race, Class, and Politics: Essays
on American Colonial and Revolutionary Society*,
pp. 323–355. Urbana: University of Illinois Press,
1986. An excellent investigation of how Jones
and other prominent Philadelphia blacks balanced their desire for autonomy with strategic
alliances with powerful whites.

Jared Demick

JUVENILE DELINQUENCY

Although children and youth have always
misbehaved, the concept of juvenile delinquency as a distinct social phenomenon arose
in the United States only in the early nineteenth century, when it was associated with
the breakdown of traditional familial controls
in a period of emerging industrialization,
urbanization, and immigration. Delinquency
included both criminal acts, such as theft, and
noncriminal activities such as "incorrigibil-
ity" and "stubbornness." Reflecting a new faith
in the power of the environment to curb delin-
quent tendencies, philanthropists in the 1820s
founded the first "houses of refuge" in northern cities. By the late nineteenth century, most

states had established juvenile reformatories,
most of which quickly degenerated into repressive, overcrowded institutions.

After 1900, a new generation of Progressive
reformers, lauded as "child savers," sought
innovative means to save children from a life
of crime. In Illinois they established the first
juvenile court in 1899. Other states followed.
In juvenile courts, designed to be informal,
defendants lacked the legal rights accorded
to adult defendants, including the right to
a lawyer; social workers, psychologists, and
psychiatrists were to guide the judge. Juvenile
courts never lived up to their founders' ideals,
however. Few had specialized treatment services, and most defined delinquency in highly
gendered ways, routinely sentencing girls to
reformatories for sexual behavior for which
boys were rarely punished.

Scholars have offered many competing
theories of juvenile delinquency. Progressive Era sociologists stressed environmental
causes such as poverty. Biological determin-
ists regarded juvenile delinquents as physically and mentally degenerate. From the 1920s
to the 1950s, social and psychological explanations of delinquency predominated, with
sociologists focusing on family breakdown,
social strains, deviant subcultures, and class
and racial discrimination.

Treatment of juvenile delinquents changed
radically after the 1967 Supreme Court decision in *In re Gault*, which gave juveniles
unprecedented legal rights. Congress's landmark 1974 Juvenile Justice and Delinquency
Prevention Act encouraged states to define
delinquency far more narrowly, removing
truants and runaways from court jurisdiction.
As a result, juvenile courts became more
formal and legalistic institutions. In the 1980s
and 1990s, fueled by perceptions of spreading gang warfare and drug-related inner-city
violence, states became much more punitive,

"criminalizing" or "adultifying" their juvenile-justice systems by imposing longer sentences, transferring juveniles to adult court, and holding them in adult prisons and jails.

Widespread anxiety over juvenile delinquency characterized nearly every twentieth-century decade. During World War II, with many fathers at war and many mothers working, fears of escalating delinquency mounted. The 1950s witnessed a juvenile-delinquency panic—captured by Hollywood in such films as *The Wild One* (1954), *Rebel without a Cause* (1955), and *Blackboard Jungle* (1955)—and the protests, riots, and counterculture of the 1960s sparked new concerns. Whether delinquency changed significantly over the twentieth century remains unclear. Crime statistics, affected by changes in police practice and reporting, must be treated with caution; increasing numbers of arrests do not necessarily indicate an increase in delinquency rates. In the 1990s, police were more likely to arrest juveniles than they had been in earlier decades. Nevertheless, only 6 percent of juvenile arrests in the 1990s involved serious, violent offenses. Though public attitudes toward juvenile delinquents became more punitive after the 1960s, most so-called juvenile delinquency continued to consist of petty larceny, disorderly conduct, underage drinking, truancy, and running away from home.

[*See also* Adolescence; Counterculture; Drugs, Illicit; Family; Life Stages; *and* Prisons and Penitentiaries.]

BIBLIOGRAPHY

Bernard, Thomas J. *The Cycle of Juvenile Justice.* New York: Oxford University Press, 1992.

Sutton, John R. *Stubborn Children: Controlling Delinquency in the United States, 1640–1981.* Berkeley: University of California Press, 1988.

L. Mara Dodge

K

KATRINA

See **Hurricane Katrina.**

KELLEY, FLORENCE

(1859–1932), social reformer. Florence Kelley was born into a patrician Philadelphia Quaker and Unitarian family, the daughter of William Darrah Kelley, a leading Republican Party politician, and Caroline Bonsall Kelley. Graduating from Cornell University in 1882, Kelley then studied at the University of Zurich, where in 1884 she married Lazare Wischnewetzky, a Russian Jewish socialist medical student, and forged a lifelong identity as a socialist. Between 1885 and 1888 she gave birth to three children. Returning to New York City in 1886, she found it impossible to continue the political commitments begun in Zurich. In 1891, after Lazare began beating her, she fled with their children to Chicago, residing at Jane Addams's Hull-House until 1899. In 1895 she completed a law degree at Northwestern University.

Kelley established her national reputation during a three-year tenure as Illinois's Chief Factory Inspector (1893–1896), enforcing the state's pathbreaking eight-hour law for working women and children. In 1899 she assumed the position that she occupied until her death, secretary-general of the newly formed National Consumers League (NCL).

Returning to New York City, she lived at the Henry Street Settlement on Manhattan's Lower East Side.

Building sixty-four local leagues by 1906, Kelley, in cooperation with other women's organizations, worked to make American government more responsive to the needs of working people, especially wage-earning women and children. Using gender-specific legislation as a surrogate for class legislation, Kelley defended the constitutionality of legislation limiting the hours of working women, then successfully extended those protections to men. Similarly, the NCL pioneered the passage of state minimum-wage laws for women that in 1938 led to a federal minimum-wage law for women and men.

[*See also* **Child Workers; Consumer Movement; Feminist Reforms in the Progressive Era, Maternal; Labor Movements; Living-Wage Movement; Progressive Era; Settlement Houses;** *and* **Women Workers.**]

BIBLIOGRAPHY

Sklar, Kathryn Kish. *Florence Kelley and the Nation's Work: The Rise of Women's Political Culture, 1830–1900.* New Haven, Conn.: Yale University Press, 1995.

Sklar, Kathryn Kish, ed. *Notes of Sixty Years: The Autobiography of Florence Kelley.* Chicago: C. H. Kerr for the Illinois Labor History Society, 1986.

Kathryn Kish Sklar

KING, MARTIN LUTHER, Jr.

(1929–1968), civil rights leader. Martin Luther King Jr. was born on 15 January 1929 in Atlanta, Georgia, the son and grandson of Baptist ministers and leaders of the National Association for the Advancement of Colored People (NAACP). King's relatively privileged background prepared him for prominence as a national civil rights leader and international symbol of nonviolent resistance. But King also adopted his father's democratic commitment to minister to poor people—those whom Jesus called "the least of these"—and to mobilize them for political action. He was a youthful critic of capitalism, troubled by seeing Depression-era bread lines and by observing fierce competition between blacks and whites for low-wage jobs in a mattress factory where he worked as a teenager. King's religious and educational mentors exposed him to several philosophies of social change: the African American social gospel, Gandhian nonviolence and egalitarianism, labor unionism, and social-democratic New Deal liberalism. King received a BA from the historically black Morehouse College (1944–1948), a bachelor of divinity degree from Crozer Theological Seminary (1948–1951), and a PhD in theology from Boston University (1951–1955).

Early Civil Rights Leadership, Nonviolence. By 1955, King had returned south to pastor Dexter Avenue Baptist Church in Montgomery, Alabama, where he became active in the NAACP. When in December 1955 the NAACP official Rosa Parks refused to relinquish her bus seat to a white man, women staged a mass boycott of Montgomery's bus system. Montgomery's black leaders formed the Montgomery Improvement Association (MIA) and elected King their president. King helped galvanize a local cross-class coalition against the system of legal segregation. More than forty thousand black workers boycotted the buses until December 1956 when, thanks to the boycotters' Supreme Court victory over local segregation ordinances, the buses were integrated. During the boycott King endured multiple death threats and the bombing of his home. While ridding his home of guns, King committed himself to absolute nonviolence. Sustaining the morale of local black workers, King drew resources from northern liberals, churches, synagogues, and interracial labor unions. Appealing to Christian, Gandhian, and American civic ideals, he became the international symbol of a new southern militancy that favored direct-action protest over the litigation and lobbying strategies of the NAACP.

In 1957, King helped found the Southern Christian Leadership Conference (SCLC), serving as its president until his death. Despite a formal commitment to direct action, King steered the SCLC toward voter registration, and the MIA model of mass protest was not repeated in other southern cities with other issues as expected. King's caution was understandable in light of the violence and economic reprisals directed against protesters in the South. He moved to Atlanta in 1960 to copastor his father's church and devote himself full-time to the SCLC. In travels to Ghana and India, King saw the southern black struggle as part of a global movement against white supremacy, which he said was built upon "political domination," "economic exploitation," and racial "humiliation."

Mass Action and the Rights Revolution.
In 1960–1961, black student activists staged sit-ins at lunch counters, rode interstate buses in interracial teams, and ignited the largest wave of protest since the 1930s. The newly formed Student Nonviolent Coordinating Committee (SNCC) openly challenged King to practice his own doctrine of "jail, no bail"— that is, protesting and accepting lengthy jail sentences in lieu of posting bail. King submitted to arrest in Atlanta during protests against segregation at downtown department stores in October 1960. Initially skeptical of the Freedom Riders who challenged segregation

in interstate busing, King nonviolently rose to their defense in a dramatic confrontation with a white mob in May 1961—though he did not join them as they continued on to imprisonment in Mississippi. King inspired hundreds to go to jail in Albany, Georgia, in December 1961, drawing widespread press attention. But mysteriously, King bailed himself out when arrested, to the great disappointment of students. Facing "nonviolent" police repression, the Albany protests failed to achieve local desegregation and did not become the publicized national crisis that increasingly seemed essential to the success of nonviolence and national reform.

King's criticism of the failure of the Federal Bureau of Investigation (FBI) to protect civil rights protesters in Albany provoked the ire of the bureau's powerful director, J. Edgar Hoover. Until King's assassination in 1968, Hoover inaugurated a campaign of intimidation and disinformation about King's alleged Communist connections. Nevertheless, King increasingly appreciated that poor people's daily needs for economic justice had to be incorporated in antiracist organizing. He brought into the SCLC community organizers such as Septima Clark, who designed the Citizenship Education Program (CEP); the CEP linked campaigns for adult literacy and voter registration to efforts to secure an equal share of services, job training, and welfare benefits.

King became internationally renowned as a mass-protest leader again in 1963 when the SCLC joined in organizing local protests in Birmingham, Alabama. Marches for desegregated downtown stores, lunch counters, and job opportunities met widely publicized violent police repression. Hundreds of black communities across the nation joined in protests that compelled President John F. Kennedy to introduce legislation to outlaw discrimination in public accommodations, voting, and employment. King became a major strategist of the so-called Negro revolution and its principal symbol. He defended civil disobedience in his "Letter from Birmingham Jail" (16 April 1963) and stirred the nation with his "I Have a Dream" speech at the 28 August 1963 March on Washington for Jobs and Freedom. With less publicity King also joined in organizers' demands for public works employment and higher wages for workers. In the spring of 1964, King led demonstrations in Saint Augustine, Florida, maintaining pressure on President Lyndon B. Johnson and Congress to pass much strengthened legislation that became the Civil Rights Act of 1964. "Mobilizing" for dramatic short-lived protest was not the same as "organizing" for long-term politics and leadership development—a strategy favored by the young members of SNCC and their older advisers such as Ella J. Baker. But on such a scale, protest had a profound impact on the national agenda and the dismantling of southern legal segregation.

In Alabama in early 1965, King led a dramatic march from Selma to Montgomery for voting rights. In response, President Johnson introduced and Congress passed legislation that put federal registrars in southern counties. King also promised to "march on poverty" all across America, advocating full employment and decent integrated housing for all Americans. When in August the Watts neighborhood of Los Angeles rose up in violent revolt against police, King flew to the city to counsel nonviolence and to pressure the mayor to release into the neighborhoods pent-up dollars from President Johnson's new federal War on Poverty.

Poverty, Human Rights, Urban Crisis. King took the SCLC to Chicago in 1966 to join a coalition of neighborhood organizations calling for an end to slums. He also hoped to build national support for a civil rights act that would make housing discrimination illegal and protect civil rights workers from local intimidation; ultimately such legislation was passed only in the wake of his assassination in 1968. King and the SCLC organized open-housing marches in white neighborhoods, where residents brutally attacked marchers. King extracted only small concessions from the realtors' association and Mayor Richard Daley's political machine. But these protests dramatized everyone's right to choose a decent home in any neighborhood. And with King's support, Chicago activists built tenants' unions and won jobs through mass boycotts. King denounced big-city segregation and poverty as a form of "internal colonialism" that rested upon the exploitation of inner-city black workers, consumers, and tenants. Meanwhile he mediated between moderate integrationist leaders and radical Black Power activists in an increasingly divided black freedom movement.

As King explained to Congress in 1966, the struggle for "human rights" included the right "to live in a decent house" and the right to earn or receive "an adequate income." In December 1967, after a fourth summer of urban violence and the election of conservatives to Congress, King announced the multiracial Poor People's Campaign. Its aim was to pressure the government to strengthen the War on Poverty and wind down the war in Vietnam. In March 1968, thirteen hundred Memphis sanitation workers demanded higher wages, safe working conditions, and municipal recognition of their union. A cross-class black coalition as remarkable as that of Montgomery in 1956 supported the workers, drawing national attention and the support of interracial unions. King lent his prestige and resources to their quest for economic justice. He was assassinated there on 4 April.

[*See also* African Americans; Civil Rights Act (1964); Civil Rights Movement; Clergy; Desegregation; Great Society Reform Programs; March on Washington; Poverty; Riots, Urban; Segregation, Racial; *and* South, The.]

BIBLIOGRAPHY

Branch, Taylor. *Parting the Waters: America in the King Years, 1954–63.* New York: Simon & Schuster, 1988. The best of a three-volume social biography of King in social and political context.

Carson, Clayborne, et al., eds. *The Papers of Martin Luther King, Jr.* 6 vols. Berkeley: University of California Press, 1992–2007. King's hitherto unpublished works, along with introductions and annotations of letters, sermons, and speeches transcribed from audiotapes.

Fairclough, Adam. *To Redeem the Soul of America: The Southern Christian Leadership Conference and Martin Luther King, Jr.* Athens, Ga.: University of Georgia Press, 1987. Best on King in the context of his organization.

Garrow, David J. *Bearing the Cross: Martin Luther King, Jr., and the Southern Christian Leadership Conference.* New York: William Morrow, 1986. Authoritative and exhaustive on every aspect of King's daily public ministry.

Honey, Michael K. *Going Down Jericho Road: The Memphis Strike, Martin Luther King's Last Campaign.* New York: W. W. Norton and Company, 2007. Interweaves a bottom-up labor history and discussion of King's commitment to labor unionism.

Jackson, Thomas F. *From Civil Rights to Human Rights: Martin Luther King, Jr., and the Struggle for Economic Justice.* Philadelphia: University of Pennsylvania Press, 2007. An in-depth discussion of King's lifelong commitment to economic equality in the context of the many constituencies he sought to bring into coalition.

The Martin Luther King, Jr. Research and Education Institute. Stanford University. http://mlk-kpp01. stanford.edu. Home of the King Papers Project, a multivolume compendium; see especially the Online King Records Access database.

Ralph, James R., Jr. *Northern Protest: Martin Luther King, Jr., Chicago, and the Civil Rights Movement.* Cambridge, Mass.: Harvard University Press, 1993.

Thomas F. Jackson

KINSEY REPORTS

"Kinsey Reports" is the popular collective name for two massive sex surveys, *Sexual Behavior in the Human Male* (1948) and *Sexual Behavior in the Human Female* (1953), conducted by the Indiana University biologist Alfred C. Kinsey and his team and based on interviews with thousands of Americans. The studies' findings made them controversial best sellers: Kinsey demonstrated that much of Americans' sexual activity took place outside marriage and that the majority of the nation's citizens had violated accepted moral standards, as well as state and federal laws, in their pursuit of sexual pleasure.

Responses to both volumes were swift and impassioned. Although some authorities welcomed the reports as shedding light on previously taboo realms of human experience, many dismissed Kinsey's findings as improbable and dangerous, expressing fear that his statistics would lead men and women to abandon traditional marriage and even marriage and parenthood. Pundits related Kinsey's findings to a wide range of contemporary worries, including worries about increasing homosexuality, changes in American marriage, and shifting gender roles, often identified as increasing male weakness and female aggression. Many even believed that by exposing postwar Americans as weak and pleasure seeking, the researchers' findings threatened the nation's reputation and its tenuous position in the Cold War.

Kinsey's findings revealed a dramatic gap between accepted sexual norms and actual behavior—or, in Kinsey's words, between the "overt" and the "covert" of American sexuality. The national furor over the reports demonstrates both a rising postwar discourse of sexual entitlement and also acute anxieties about the implications of openly discussing and assigning importance to an increasing array of sexual acts. Commentators' shared belief that they lived in an era of rapid and often distressing sexual change challenges the widely held perception that the nation did not experience a "sexual revolution" until the 1960s, and the controversial status of the studies attests to the ongoing linkage of sexual behavior with anxieties about gender roles, family stability, and national identity.

[*See also* **Fifties, The; Marriage and Divorce;** *and* **Sexual Reform and Morality.**]

BIBLIOGRAPHY

Morantz, Regina Markell. "The Scientist as Sex Crusader: Alfred C. Kinsey and American Culture." *American Quarterly* 29, no. 5 (1977): 563–589. This brief but thorough overview of Kinsey's intentions and the reports' context, findings, and reception is invaluable to anyone interested in the reports.

Reumann, Miriam. *American Sexual Character: Sex, Gender, and National Identity in the Kinsey Reports.* Berkeley: University of California Press, 2005. Examines Kinsey's work and its reception, focusing on postwar debates about marriage, hetero- and homosexuality, and nationalism.

Miriam Reumann

KNIGHTS OF COLUMBUS

The Knights of Columbus is the world's largest fraternal association of Roman Catholic men. Founded in 1882 in New Haven, Connecticut, in a context of economic instability and pervasive anti-Catholicism,

the Knights of Columbus was originally formed as a mutual aid organization offering death benefits to surviving widows and children. The organization's founder, Father Michael J. McGivney, modeled the Knights on contemporaneous Catholic fraternal insurance organizations—the Massachusetts Catholic Order of Foresters and the Catholic Benevolent League of New York, in particular—but added unique components of secret ritual, Catholic religious piety, and American patriotism. Whereas competing fraternal organizations such as the Ancient Order of Hibernians celebrated ethnic distinctiveness, the Knights of Columbus encouraged Catholic men—many of them first- and second-generation Irish immigrants—to assimilate to dominant norms of Victorian manhood and to claim full participation in American cultural and political institutions. Though the founding generation of Knights was overwhelmingly Irish, membership in the organization gradually expanded to include Catholic men of diverse ethnicities, though Catholic men of African descent were informally excluded until well into the 1960s. The Knights of Columbus expanded quickly, establishing councils along the East Coast in the 1880s and into the South and Midwest by the 1890s. Concerned that expanding membership increased the liability of the organization's insurance programs, in 1892 the Knights bifurcated membership status into insurance and "associate" categories.

As the Knights of Columbus grew, the cultural functions of the organization gradually eclipsed its insurance program. Columbian Knighthood offered Catholic men a public identity that reflected prevailing notions of middle-class respectability, while it simultaneously affirmed a Catholic preference for stable, defined gender roles. Rituals and publications of the Knights of Columbus emphasized that true Catholic manhood required self-discipline, temperance, religious piety, responsible fatherhood, and civic duty. In contrast to recurrent anti-Catholic assertions that Catholics lacked the moral substance and political autonomy to participate successfully in a democratic polity, the Knights of Columbus insisted that Catholic faith was compatible with patriotic American citizenship.

Throughout the twentieth century the Knights of Columbus undertook public programs designed to counteract anti-Catholic stereotypes. In World War I the Knights secured permission from General John J. Pershing to provide recreation and comfort services both to soldiers in the United States and to those stationed overseas. Knights of Columbus secretaries—called "Caseys" by American soldiers—distributed cigarettes, playing cards, chewing gum, and postcards to soldiers through "huts" located throughout the eastern and western war zones, and under the motto "Everybody welcome, everything free," they sponsored athletic contests and moving pictures in recreation centers both in France and, later, in occupied Germany. Building on this foundation of public service, the Knights continued public activism in pro-Catholic and conservative causes after the war, opposing the resurgent Ku Klux Klan, assisting the legal defense of Catholic schools against legislation related to compulsory public education, building playgrounds for children in Rome, advocating that the words "Under God" be added to the Pledge of Allegiance, and opposing the legalization of abortion.

[*See also* **Antiabortion Movement; Anti-Catholicism; Fraternal Organizations;** *and* **Irish Americans.**]

BIBLIOGRAPHY

Brinkley, Douglas, and Julie M. Fenster. *Parish Priest: Father Michael McGivney and American Catholicism.* New York: William Morrow, 2006.

Kauffman, Christopher J. *Faith and Fraternalism: The History of the Knights of Columbus, 1882–1982.* New York: Harper & Row, 1982.

Koehlinger, Amy. "'Let Us Live for Those Who Love Us': Faith, Family, and the Contours of Manhood among the Knights of Columbus in Late Nineteenth-Century Connecticut." *Journal of Social History* 38, no. 2 (Winter 2004): 455–469.

Amy L. Koehlinger

KOREAN AMERICANS

The year 2003 marked the hundredth-year anniversary of Korean immigration to the United States. The centennial history of courage, hardships, and achievements goes back to 1903 when the first boatload of one hundred Koreans landed on Hawai'i as plantation contract workers. The Hawaiian Sugar Planters' Association was seeking an alternative cheap labor force to replace and control increasing numbers of Japanese laborers. This is known as the first wave of Korean immigration, although a small number of Koreans had already arrived in the United States as students, merchants, diplomats, or political exiles after the United States and Korea signed the Treaty of Amity and Commerce in 1882. According to the American Community Survey, by 2009 the Korean American community had grown to 1.3 million constituting 0.4 percent of the U.S. population. According to the 2010 U.S. Census, the Korean American community had grown to 1.4 million, constituting 0.5 percent of the U.S. population, and Korean Americans were the fifth-largest ethnic group among Asian populations in the United States, following Chinese, Indians, Filipinos, and Vietnamese.

Immigration. Historically the migration flow from Korea to the United States has been deeply tied to political situations in Korea, such as Japanese colonialism (1910–1945) and the Korean War (1950–1953). In 1905 when Japan deprived Korea of its diplomatic sovereignty, it prohibited Korean labor migration to Hawai'i. Until Korea's liberation, the Japanese colonial government regulated Korean emigration to the United States. Deteriorating political conditions in their motherland profoundly affected the lives of early Korean immigrants. They had to endure double injustice: not only did they suffer the common anti-Asian racial discrimination that prohibited naturalization and home and land ownership in the United States, but they also had to bear the insult of being assumed to be Japanese by a majority of Americans who could not distinguish the ethnic and cultural differences between Koreans and Japanese. Such experiences exacerbated the psychological damages of being a "people of no country." Yet Korean communities in the United States united under the patriotic cause of Korea's independence movement against Japanese colonialism, until Korea finally achieved liberation on 15 August 1945. They founded numerous political organizations to collect funds, established military-training programs, and produced influential political leaders. The first generation of Korean immigrants fought for Korean independence, and the next generation—American-born Koreans—eagerly supported America's war against Japan, many of them serving in the military.

With the end of World War II and Japanese colonialism, the Korean peninsula was soon divided into two separate political regimes under the Cold War ideology: the Republic of Korea (South Korea) and the People's Republic of Korea (North Korea). Korean immigration to the United States, which had been halted because of the Asian Exclusion Act of 1924, resumed during this time. The second wave of Korean immigration was mostly made up of college students, professionals, the wives of U.S. servicemen—women known as "Korean War brides"—and Korean War orphans adopted by Americans. Since the Korean War, South Korea has remained a political and military ally for the United States, and the designation "Korean American" generally refers to immigrants from South Korea. Yet by 2010 a hundred North Korean refugees resided in the United.

The third wave of Korean immigration began with the passing of the Immigration and Nationality Act of 1965, which abolished the national-origins quota system in the United States. The 1970s and 1980s were the peak of Korean immigration: more than six hundred thousand Koreans flew to the United States, mainly through family sponsorship. However, since the 1990s there has been a gradual shift in Korean immigration patterns as the U.S. immigration bureau has changed its priority from family reunion to investment- or employment-based immigration. This has resulted in the emergence of wealthy investors and highly skilled, well-educated professionals as the dominant force in twenty-first-century Korean immigration, including those who switch their visa status from temporary student or business visas to permanent residents.

Though these new immigrants appear to fit the prevalent notion of Asian Americans as a "model minority," they do not fairly represent the significant discrepancies in wealth within Korean American communities. In addition, the concept of the model minority itself is controversial. The economic and social standing of Korean Americans varies notably depending on class background, educational level, English proficiency, generation, length of residency, legal status, and profession. It becomes more difficult to measure the sociopolitical success of Korean Americans when taking into consideration the rapidly growing population of undocumented immigrants.

Experience in America. The most pivotal moment in Korean American history is the Los Angeles riots of 1992. When four white Los Angeles Police Department officers were acquitted of beating the African American motorist Rodney King, outrage over the verdict quickly led to violence and civil unrest. Massive arson and looting destroyed sections of South Central and nearby Koreatown, and as a result, fifty-five people died, thousands were injured, and a billion dollars in property damage was incurred (statistics vary). Korean Americans were the major victims of the riots, losing more than two thousand businesses. Though it is still debatable what caused the Los Angeles riots and why Koreans became the prime targets, this tragic event served as a wake-up call for Korean Americans who until then generally remained within their ethnic communities, isolating themselves from the outside world. Because Korean American communities continue to be large in cosmopolitan areas such as Los Angeles, New York City, Chicago, and San Francisco—areas where other minority groups are comparable in size—it is the pressing challenge of the Korean Americans to establish harmonious multiethnic relations, even while maintaining strong and prosperous ethnic communities.

By the twenty-first century, having learned lessons from the Los Angeles riots—the importance of political empowerment and the need for integration into mainstream society—Korean Americans of every generation actively participate in all aspects of American sociopolitical and civic life, including politics, law, the economy, the military, science, journalism, music, theater, film, literature, sports, and academia. The South Korean government has attempted to benefit from the assets of Korean Americans by amending its nationality law to allow dual citizenship, and in 2008 the U.S. government added South Korea to its Visa Waiver Program, which allows Korean citizens to travel and stay in the United States for up to ninety days without a visa. These political moves reflect the frequent transnational flow of people, capital, and cultures between the two nations across the Pacific. Transpacific migration will surely be further expedited in the future. How it will shape the next century for Korean Americans will be well worth observing.

[*See also* **Asian American Movement; Asian Americans; Hawai'i; Immigration; Los Angeles; Riots, Race;** *and* **Riots, Urban.**]

BIBLIOGRAPHY

Chang, Edward T., and Jeannette Diaz-Veizades. *Ethnic Peace in the American City: Building Community in Los Angeles and Beyond*. New York: New York University Press, 1999.

Jo, Moon H. *Korean Immigrants and the Challenge of Adjustment*. Westport, Conn.: Greenwood Press, 1999.

Kim, Ilpyong J., ed. *Korean-Americans: Past, Present, and Future*. Elizabeth, N.J.: Hollym International, 2004.

Patterson, Wayne. *The Korean Frontier in America: Immigration to Hawaii, 1896–1910*. Honolulu: University of Hawai'i Press, 1988.

Mina Shin

KU KLUX KLAN, FIRST

The Ku Klux Klan emerged in the years following Confederate defeat as a mode for whites from a range of backgrounds to express their dissatisfaction with the social changes brought about by the end of slavery and the other changes in the South after the Civil War. It drew upon a wide range of practices and forms and spread quickly, adapting to local circumstances, but its end came at different times and for different reasons across the South. Although the Ku Klux, as they were generally called at the time, often served the political purposes of the Democratic Party, they were far more than simply the paramilitary arm of the Democratic Party, as earlier historians described them. The Ku Klux Klan was both an expression of and a major influence on social relations after the war, shaped by the folk culture of the South and the popular culture of the nation.

The mid-nineteenth century contained many organizations and cultural forms somewhat similar to those of the Ku Klux Klan. Communities across the nation, and perhaps especially in the South, had folk traditions of social regulation through group activity that danced on the edge between theatricality and violence. Charivari, or "rough music," had been used for centuries as a warning or mild punishment for those people considered to be transgressing a community's norms— adulterers, wife beaters, alcoholics. It seems almost inevitable that such tactics would be turned against freedpeople. The early Ku Klux also drew heavily on costumes, behaviors, and language from popular culture, especially the minstrel stage. A visit from the Ku Klux was usually an assault, but it was frequently also a strange kind of performance. The secret oaths, the strangely named hierarchy, the vestments—all these reflect the influence of the secret societies and fraternal organizations that were at the peak of their popularity in the United States at this time.

Once the original Ku Klux Klan was formed by a group of young men in Pulaski, Tennessee, during the winter and spring of 1865–1866, it spread around the South, slowly at first but much faster after the Reconstruction era state governments began to take shape in early 1868. Some of this expansion was orderly and official, with the leaders of the movement in Tennessee sending emissaries to fertile grounds in other parts of the South to teach the secret rites, induct new members, and establish local and state Ku Klux hierarchies. More of the organization's spread, though, was ad hoc, a sort of freelance franchising of the idea and the name of the "Ku Klux Klan" even without formal connection to the original group. The widespread news coverage of the Ku Klux and depictions in popular culture made this type of expansion possible. By summer 1868, there were groups known as, or calling themselves, "Ku Klux" in all the former Confederate states.

There are few easy generalizations to be made about the membership of the Ku Klux Klan except that it was male and, almost without exception, white. The truth is that the membership profile of the Ku Klux almost certainly varied with the local circumstances. Unsurprisingly, young men seemed to be more involved than older men. Young men working as store clerks sometimes were key members in the small towns and railroad crossings that were increasing across the South. Lawyers and newspaper editors may have been overrepresented in comparison to men of other nonagricultural professions, perhaps because of their greater involvement with local politics and the kinds of communication networks that popularized the idea of the Ku Klux Klan. Much of the contemporary justification for the Klan argued that it was necessary to prevent property crime by freedpeople; although earlier scholars dismissed this as a self-serving smokescreen, more careful analysis shows that there may have been some truth to the claim, especially for hard-pressed yeomen trying to recover from the destruction of the war. On the one hand, a study of Alabama concluded that a majority of Ku Kluxers were young men who had grown up expecting to be small but comfortable slaveholders but who found themselves, after the war and emancipation of slaves, struggling to make a living and facing severely diminished prospects. On the other hand, a study of one of the busiest Ku Klux counties in South Carolina found that most members there were part of a tavern-based demimonde, the same brawlers, drinkers, and petty criminals who had been raising hell there since the 1850s.

The targets of the Ku Klux Klan varied as much as its membership did, although some broad patterns can be discerned as they developed over time. The earliest activities of the original Pulaski Klan, and many others, consisted of threatening performances, such as costumed parades, before evolving into full-fledged violence. Many early victims of Klan violence were African Americans whose economic activity made them seem threatening to whites who wanted to maintain traditional social structures and boundaries. In Spartanburg County, South Carolina, for instance, black coachmen working for white women were especially targeted. Similarly, as railroads came through the Piedmont region of North Carolina and South Carolina, the black men they hired to build the roads and work on them came in for attack by the Ku Klux because they were independent of local white employers and landlords, earning cash wages that they could spend as they pleased. In addition to the political freedom this gave the black men, this economic independence threatened white employers whose prosperity rested on exploitation of black workers. Labor control generally was a central theme of Klan attacks across the South.

As Reconstruction empowered African Americans as citizens, more Ku Klux Klan attacks took on political implications, and African American community leaders were targeted. By attacking such figures, the Klan disrupted black society on all levels at once, making freedpeople less connected to institutions that might help them and casting them onto their own resources, atomized and alone, much easier for whites to control. Another part of this sustained attack on black leadership was the use of terror, and especially sexual assault, against female family members of black community leaders. This tactic not only threatened to dissuade even the bravest activist, but also challenged his claim to manliness by showing that he could not defend vulnerable members of his household. Likewise, the Klan also attacked white supporters of black rights and some whites who allowed African Americans too many opportunities for economic independence. These attacks not only forced white allies to renounce their earlier "sins" of racial transgressions but showed African Americans that no one could help them.

The Klan's demise was as variable as its origins. In most locations it disappeared as the political conditions that brought it into existence disappeared. When the federal government finally took decisive action with the Enforcement Acts of 1870 and 1871, the congressional investigation across the South in 1871, the use of the army and the suspension of the writ of habeas corpus in South Carolina in October 1871, and the ultimately half-hearted prosecutions in 1872, they eventually brought Ku Klux Klan terrorism to an end.

[*See also* **Clothing; Ku Klux Klan, Second; Racism;** *and* **Terrorism, Domestic.**]

BIBLIOGRAPHY

Fitzgerald, Michael W. "The Ku Klux Klan: Property Crime and the Plantation System in Reconstruction Alabama." *Agricultural History* 71, no. 2 (Spring 1997): 186–206.

Nelson, Scott Reynolds. *Iron Confederacies: Southern Railways, Klan Violence, and Reconstruction.* Chapel Hill: University of North Carolina Press, 1999.

Nelson, Scott. "Livestock, Boundaries, and Public Space in Spartanburg: African American Men, Elite White Women, and the Spectacle of Conjugal Relations." In *Sex, Love, Race: Crossing Boundaries in North American History*, edited by Martha Hodes, pp. 313–327. New York: New York University Press, 1999.

Parsons, Elaine Frantz. "Midnight Rangers: Costume and Performance in the Reconstruction-Era Ku Klux Klan." *Journal of American History* 92, no. 3 (December 2005): 811–836.

Trelease, Allen W. *White Terror: The Ku Klux Klan Conspiracy and Southern Reconstruction.* New York: Harper & Row, 1971.

Bruce E. Baker

KU KLUX KLAN, SECOND

D. W. Griffith's landmark film, *The Birth of a Nation*, spawned a revival of the Ku Klux Klan when it premiered in Atlanta in 1915. The enormous popularity of Griffith's deeply racist fable, which cast Reconstruction era Klansmen as heroic saviors of American civilization, inspired a struggling fraternal organizer, William Simmons, to create a modern patriotic Klan devoted to upholding the social order and thwarting wartime dissent. Before 1920, Simmons's "second" Klan attracted only a small following in Georgia and Alabama. Then, in a climate of postwar racial, political, and economic tumult, Simmons hired two unheralded public relations entrepreneurs, Edward Clarke and Elizabeth Tyler, who devised a wildly successful plan to promote the Klan nationwide. Together, Simmons, Clarke, and Tyler raised an army of paid recruiters and distributed Klan newspapers and other literature across the nation.

By 1925 they had attracted perhaps 5 million dues-paying men and women—a separate organization, the Women of the Ku Klux Klan, emerged in 1923—throughout the United States and parts of Canada. The Klan movement was strong in the South but achieved even more success in the Middle West and the West, and it gained a significant presence in parts of the Northeast as well.

The new Klan flourished amid widespread concern that ordinary white Protestants were losing their place of dominance in American life. The perceived threat came not as it had during Reconstruction, from a real challenge to the political foundations of white supremacy, but from a broad range of interconnected, contemporary social, cultural, and economic conditions: the mass migration of African Americans to northern cities; the growing presence of southern and eastern European, Latino, Asian, and other immigrants in society; changing gender roles and sexual attitudes; an ascendant youth culture; intense concerns over violations of Prohibition and other vice and crime-related issues; a sense of declining devotion to religion; and a booming national culture of commerce, consumption, and entertainment that appeared to elevate economic, intellectual, and cultural elites at the expense of the individual, the family, and community. Klan recruiters and newspapers wrapped nearly every aspect of their message in ethnic bigotry, against Catholics and Jews as much as African Americans. At the same time, they addressed a long list of concerns about crime, morality, education, taxes, and other issues, tailoring their message to local circumstances and painting the movement as a means of achieving popular control over public life.

In many communities, particularly in the South and the Southwest, vigilante activities, intimidation, and violence marked the Klan's presence, most often in the form of extralegal

Prohibition enforcement and other attempts to impose respect for traditional values. Klan groups raided stills, blocked roads to search vehicles for alcohol, and warned errant husbands and fathers not to shirk family responsibilities. Violent confrontations between Klan and anti-Klan groups occurred in many locations; major riots erupted in Ohio, Indiana, and Illinois. There were also episodes of racial violence that did much to perpetuate the Klan's original heritage as the Jim Crow era and civil rights movement continued to unfold in the twentieth century.

By far, however, the Klan's greatest influence came from its ability to function as a vehicle for mainstream, right-wing populism. Men and women who joined the Klan represented a wide cross section of white Protestant society—affluent professionals, middle- and working-class people, urban and rural residents, and members of virtually all Protestant religious denominations. Klan members and supporters took part in frequent social activities such as barbecues and Sunday picnics, and they staged spectacular public parades, celebrations, and demonstrations. The movement came to wield extraordinary political power. In many areas, Klan-backed candidates took control of city governments, school boards, and especially district attorney and sheriff posts. Klan influence reached deep into state legislatures, Congress, and both major political parties. Klan insurgents challenged old-guard Republicans in many locations and assumed control of state governments in Indiana, Colorado, and Oregon. Klan populism roiled state Democratic parties, particularly in Texas, Oklahoma, Georgia, and Alabama. Support in southern states was powerful enough to rupture the Democratic National Convention in 1924 when northern delegates insisted on condemning the Klan in the national platform.

By the late 1920s the Klan was in steep decline. The decade's draconian immigration restrictions had eased xenophobic fears. At the same time, no amount of effort—by the Klan or any other group—seemed capable of making Prohibition work. The Klan's leadership also failed miserably. Simmons, Clarke, and Tyler fell into a series of alcohol-infused scandals and financial conflicts. The Dallas dentist Hiram Evans unseated Simmons in 1922 and brought some stability for a time, but ultimately he, too, was unable to deliver on the Klan's agenda. The Indiana Klan leader D. C. Stephenson attracted crippling national publicity in 1925 after he raped and murdered an Indianapolis woman. Although the second Klan could not sustain its explosive popularity, it added a significant, complex chapter to the Klan's larger history and—perhaps even more important—revealed the national scope and inherent power of right-wing populism in modern America.

[*See also* Anti-Catholicism; Anti-Semitism; Populist Movement; *and* Racism.]

BIBLIOGRAPHY

Blee, Kathleen M. *Women of the Klan: Racism and Gender in the 1920s.* Berkeley, Calif.: University of California Press, 1991.

MacLean, Nancy. *Behind the Mask of Chivalry: The Making of the Second Ku Klux Klan.* New York: Oxford University Press, 1994.

Moore, Leonard J. *Citizen Klansmen: The Ku Klux Klan in Indiana, 1921–1928.* Chapel Hill: University of North Carolina Press, 1991.

Pegram, Thomas R. *One Hundred Percent American: The Rebirth and Decline of the Ku Klux Klan in the 1920s.* Chicago: Ivan R. Dee, 2011.

Leonard J. Moore

L

LABOR MOVEMENTS

The origins of workers' protective organizations go back to the mid-eighteenth century. By the 1830s, wage earners' combinations, which often had both economic and political dimensions, were flourishing, despite their precarious their legal status. Throughout the remainder of the nineteenth century, the labor movement fluctuated in membership, ideology, and institutional character. The American Federation of Labor (AFL), founded in 1886, emerged as the dominant force, surviving challenges from rival labor centers. In the first third of the twentieth century the AFL remained largely an organization representing skilled, white, male workers. In the 1930s and 1940s, however, a rival national federation, the Congress of Industrial Organizations (CIO), succeeded in organizing thousands of unskilled workers of diverse ethnic backgrounds in mass-production industries. In the early post–World War II era, both the AFL and the CIO exerted considerable political influence, and unions achieved notable collective-bargaining gains. Beginning in the 1970s, a changing economy and a hostile political climate sharply eroded overall union representation, despite some success in organizing public employees and service-sector workers.

The Nineteenth Century.   In the expanding economy of the 1820s and 1830s, labor activism was highly localized and often characterized by informal organizations. Skilled native-born males dominated the early labor movement, but women, immigrants, and the unskilled also engaged in strikes and protests against unfair treatment. Demands for a ten-hour day were widespread, especially in large, industrializing cities such as New York, Boston, and Philadelphia.

Local coordinating bodies attempted with sporadic success to mobilize workingmen in the political arena as well. An economic downturn in the late 1830s and early 1840s, however, devastated this first general trade-union movement, which never did develop an overall national coordinating structure.

During the 1850s the labor movement revived. Unions of skilled iron molders, puddlers, textile workers, printers, shoemakers, and tailors emerged, some of them developing national coordinating organizations. A large-scale shoemakers' strike in eastern Massachusetts in 1860 revealed a labor movement poised between an older workplace regime that relied on skilled craftsmen and the immigrant and female workers who were replacing them. Ethnic, gender, and skill-level divisions, along with harsh repression by employer-influenced public authorities, smashed the strike, characterized by the historian Bruce Laurie as "possibly the first major work stoppage on the part of artisans-turned-workers" (p. 111).

During the Civil War, labor organization in the North exhibited diverse tendencies. Because nonagricultural workers constituted about 42 percent of the 2 million men who served in the armed forces, many fledgling local unions lost membership and in some cases disappeared. At the same time, wartime manpower shortages and rising prices spurred union growth and worker activism. The first permanent national union among railroaders, the Brotherhood of the Footboard, was founded in 1863 (it was renamed the Brotherhood of Locomotive Engineers, 1864–1865). Militant regional coal miners' unions emerged in Illinois and Pennsylvania, although both collapsed in the face of government repression and declining markets in the immediate postwar period.

In 1866 the western Pennsylvania iron molder William Sylvis led in the creation of the first truly national organization, the National Labor Union (NLU). In addition to demanding an eight-hour day and the right to organize, this new body also challenged what nineteenth-century laborites called "wage slavery"—that is, a system of compensation that made freeborn American workers dependent on capitalists for their families' sustenance. NLU leaders also urged the adoption of liberal land policies to enable wageworkers to become self-sufficient farmers and encouraged the formation of producers' cooperatives wherein workers could escape wage dependency. Broad in its appeal to the so-called productive classes, the NLU was at best ambivalent in its defense of African American and female workers. For their part, in 1869, freedmen founded the Colored National Labor Union, which was active primarily in the upper South and which echoed the NLU's denunciation of wage slavery.

By 1873 the NLU had collapsed. In 1869 a group of Philadelphia garment cutters founded the Noble and Holy Order of the Knights of Labor (KOL) as a secret fraternal society. After the 1877 railroad strikes and especially in the 1880s, the KOL grew rapidly. With the Pennsylvania metalworker and politician Terence V. Powderly as its Grand Master Workman, it became a dynamic force. The Knights organized all sectors of workers, regardless of skill, and also actively recruited women and African Americans, although its leaders shared the all-but-universal disdain for workers of Asian extraction.

Sharing the NLU's hostility to the wage system, the Knights formally embraced producers' cooperatives as the chief means of rescuing American workers from dependency and subordination. Powderly and other top leaders regarded strikes as a distraction from the KOL's cooperative agenda. Even so, thousands of those joining the KOL were less concerned with its official goals than with its use as a vehicle for improving wages and working conditions. For a time, despite these internal divisions, the Knights participated in a broad popular insurgency among workers, spawning worker-led political coalitions in scores of cities and towns around the country. The labor movement reached its nineteenth-century peak in 1886 with more than 700,000 workers in the Knights and another 250,000 in trade unions. By 1890, however, KOL membership was in rapid and terminal decline.

Trade unions rejected the KOL's increasingly tenuous program of promoting worker cooperatives. Organizations such as the United Brotherhood of Carpenters and Joiners (UCBJ; founded in 1881), the International Association of Machinists (IAM; 1888), and the Cigar Makers' International Union (1864) became affiliated with the AFL. Under the leadership of its cofounder and long-term president Samuel Gompers, the AFL accepted the wage system. Unions affiliated with it sought gains for their members within the capitalist economy. They pressed for recognition from employers so as to negotiate on wages and working conditions through a process that came to be termed "collective bargaining." This process usually involved the signing of a written contract containing the terms agreed upon. The AFL and its affiliated unions struggled to survive the dismal conditions that prevailed during the massive depression that began in 1893.

1900–1930. During the heyday of American industrialism (c. 1870–1950), unions among railroad workers and building tradesmen promoted the material interests and buttressed the social identities of native-born white males. At the same time, some unions, notably the United Mine Workers of America (UMWA; 1890), pursued biracial and multiethnic strategies of recruitment and collective bargaining. Still other unions that emerged during this period reflected the concerns of black, immigrant, and women workers and sought to represent the unskilled. Examples of these include the International Ladies' Garment Workers' Union (ILGWU; 1900) and the Brotherhood of Sleeping Car Porters (BSCP; 1925). All these organizations acknowledged the permanency, if not necessarily the ethical legitimacy, of America's capitalist-republican political economy. Other organizations, notably the KOL and the Industrial Workers of the World (IWW; 1905), put forth alternative visions of a just and efficacious social order.

Although the AFL regarded itself as the voice of all wage earners, in fact it privileged the concerns of relatively skilled, white, male workers. Its craft unions charged high entry fees and adopted high dues structures, in part because they typically provided members with union-funded training, job referral, and sometimes health care and death benefits. These organizations sought to limit the supply of skilled workers through advocacy of immigration restriction, apprenticing agreements, state and local licensing laws, and racial and gender exclusion.

Despite sporadic organizing efforts by the AFL, mass-production industries remained largely unorganized. In 1919, emboldened by membership gains and by apparently supportive federal labor policies during World War I, the AFL launched a campaign to organize half a million steelworkers of diverse ethnic identities and skill levels. But this effort, along with similar efforts in Chicago's multiethnic meatpacking hub, ended in failure, in part because of ethnic and racial tensions among the labor force in these industries. Despite its politically conservative orientation, the AFL suffered also from antiradical hysteria triggered by the success of the Bolshevik revolution in Russia. In the 1920s the decimation of the United Mine Workers, weakened by the opening of nonunion southern coalfields, added to the widespread sense that organized labor was in permanent, if not terminal, decline.

Great Depression and World War II.
During the era of the Great Depression and World War II (c. 1930–1946), however, the labor movement revived. As of 1930, there were about 3.5 million union members, representing less than a tenth of the nonagricultural labor force. By the end of World War II, the labor movement could count nearly 15 million members, about one-third of nonagricultural workers. Much of this expansion took place in mass-production industries such as steel, automotives, electrical appliances, papermaking, meatpacking, and manufacturing. Central to this dramatic expansion was the emergence of the Congress of Industrial Organizations (CIO).

The origins of the CIO were rooted in events in the first administration of Franklin D. Roosevelt (1933–1937). Thousands of previously unorganized workers responded to New Deal legislation, notably Section 7(a) of the National Industrial Recovery Act (1933), by creating new unions, initially under the auspices of the AFL. This surge also revived the UMWA and immigrant-led unions in the clothing and apparel industries. The UMWA president John L. Lewis, along with Sidney Hillman of the Amalgamated Clothing Workers of America (ACWA; 1914) and David Dubinsky of the ILGWU, sought at first to persuade AFL leaders of the need to capitalize on this explosion of interest

in union creation. In 1935, however, Lewis broke with the AFL leadership and promoted aggressive organizing in mass-production industries. By the fall of 1936 the CIO was effectively established as an independent labor federation, although it was not until 1938 that it formalized this status, adopting the name "Congress of Industrial Organizations."

The CIO unions differed from most of those in the AFL in terms of organizing strategies, openness to left-wing influences, and attitudes toward government's role in labor relations. In 1936 the new CIO launched a campaign to organize the steel industry through a centralized organization called the Steel Workers Organizing Committee (SWOC). Dozens of organizers, many of them recruited from Communist and Socialist organizations, were sent into the mills, where they were to establish rank-and-file groups. In the auto and meatpacking industries, both early CIO targets, rank-and-file militants led protests against racial discrimination, arbitrary disciplinary procedures, and company-imposed speedup of the work pace. These new CIO organizations, reflecting in part the heritage of interracial and interethnic membership characteristic of the UMWA, often made special efforts to attract African American workers.

In its early organizing efforts, the CIO benefited from the support of federal authorities, especially the National Labor Relations Board (NLRB), established under the terms of the 1935 Wagner, or National Labor Relations, Act. In 1936 the CIO aligned itself with the campaign to reelect Roosevelt and to support Democratic candidates in industrial states, which reinforced its link to federal agencies. Especially after the Wagner Act's validation by the U.S. Supreme Court in May 1937, a friendly NLRB played a significant role in the establishment of industrial unionism in the nation's industrial heartland.

During World War II (1939–1945), government policies assumed an even larger role in the labor movement's organizing and bargaining programs. By the time of the Japanese attack on Pearl Harbor in December 1941, the SWOC had completed organization of the steel industry, the United Auto Workers (UAW; 1935) had brought the holdout Ford Motor Company to the bargaining table, and significant gains had been made in meatpacking, farm equipment, appliances, pulp and paper, aeronautics, and other industrial sectors. At the time of U.S. belligerency the AFL, the CIO, and the railroad unions counted about 10 million members, around 20 percent of the nonagricultural labor force.

Once the United States entered the war, both the dynamics and the demographics of union recruitment changed. Soon after the attack on Pearl Harbor, leaders of both the AFL and the CIO publicly pledged to refrain from strikes during the war. Early in 1942, Roosevelt created a new agency, the National War Labor Board (NWLB), charged with resolving labor disputes and restraining inflation. Regarding competently led unions as a positive factor in efforts to increase military production, the NWLB soon devised a policy, known as "maintenance of membership," designed to stabilize union membership and compensate organized labor for its voluntary adoption of the no-strike pledge. By this arrangement, newly hired workers automatically became members of those unions with a collective-bargaining contract unless they chose quickly to opt out.

Maintenance of membership helped boost membership in both labor federations. By the end of the war, almost 15 million workers were enrolled in unions, representing a 40 percent increase over 1940 and a 400 percent increase since 1933. Particularly notable was the large influx of women into such unions as the UAW, in which the number of female workers grew from under 50,000 to over 300,000 during the war. Membership among African Americans also expanded dramatically during the war, with over 900,000 black union members by 1945, as compared with under 100,000 fifteen years earlier.

Labor's Golden Age, 1946–1973. After the war, emboldened by membership gains during the 1930s and the war years, both labor federations resolved to continue the momentum. Believing that low southern wages undermined union-achieved standards in the northern states, both the AFL and the CIO particularly targeted the South. Laborites believed that so long as the southern states excluded most blacks—and many lower-income whites—from the political process, fulfillment of the liberal New Deal political agenda in the postwar period would be impossible, and organized labor's newly won victories would be in jeopardy.

The postwar political climate, however, quickly proved less friendly to labor expansion than that of the Depression and World War II years. The CIO's campaign to organize southern textiles quickly lost momentum, while the more modest AFL effort in the South yielded only limited gains. The passage in 1947 of the Taft-Hartley Act, which encouraged states to outlaw contractual provisions for union security, provided antiunion employers with new weapons of resistance to organization. During the heightened tensions of the early Cold War, political divisions in the CIO led to the ouster of eleven pro-Soviet affiliates, some of them among the CIO's most vigorous and effective organizations.

In the 1950s the labor movement appeared to have reached the limits of its organizational expansion. Membership in unions stood at about one-third of the nonagricultural labor force, but sporadic efforts to expand into the growing clerical, technical, and white-collar sectors enjoyed little success. The strong, stable unions in the nation's central industrial and transportation core were successful in negotiating contracts that boosted wages, particularly at the lower end of the compensation scale, and in gaining pension and health-insurance benefits. Union successes in turn set standards that employers seeking to avoid unionization felt constrained to emulate. Sophisticated political and legislative operations made organized labor a significant factor in the political arena, especially within the Democratic Party. In 1955 the AFL and the CIO merged, ending two decades of rivalry and, some laborites hoped, providing the impetus for renewed organizing campaigns.

In reality, however, the merger wrought no surge of activism. George Meany, elected as first president of the AFL-CIO, opposed funneling the new federation's resources into risky mass-organizing campaigns. Instead the AFL-CIO focused its energies on political and legislative activity, seeking to position itself as the spokesman for lower-income Americans. Meany and his chief advisers cooperated eagerly with government officials in the formulation and implementation of the anti-Communist foreign and military policies of both Republican and Democratic presidents of the postwar era. Beset by negative publicity emanating from congressional investigations of corruption in the Teamsters and other unions, Meany rejected calls by the UAW chief Walter Reuther for renewed organizing activity, content with the AFL-CIO's role as a promoter of economic growth, expanded military spending, and liberal tax, social welfare, and civil rights legislation.

The Recent Past. Between 1955 and about 1980, although total union membership continued to rise, the percentage of workers in the nonagricultural labor force who belonged to unions showed steady decline. International competition in manufacturing industries, expansion of employment in the largely unorganized service sector, and a successful effort by major construction firms to undermine the unions in the building trades all contributed to this pattern. Efforts to organize southern textile and garment workers enjoyed some local success, but a protracted campaign throughout the 1970s at the J. P. Stevens & Company, the South's second-largest textile firm, yielded few permanent gains. In 1981 the administration of the Republican president Ronald Reagan smashed an illegal strike by members of the Professional Air Traffic Controllers (PATCO; 1968), an action that stiffened the determination of employers everywhere to attack organized labor. Throughout the 1980s and 1990s, along the country's interstate bus routes, in the Arizona copper mines, in the pulp and paper mills of New England and the South, and in the Midwest's heavy-equipment and food-processing industries, employers broke strikes, recruited permanent replacement workers, forced unions to accept harsh contract concessions, and used bankruptcy laws and other legal devices to destroy once-strong local unions and to escape contractual obligations.

This onslaught continued into the early years of the twenty-first century. Thus by 2010, union representation in the private nonagricultural labor force had shrunk to about 7 percent. There were bright spots in this otherwise dismal picture. Even as employment and union membership in mining, manufacturing, transport, and construction shrank, workers in the public sector, hitherto a largely union-free field, began to organize. Meanwhile, unions such as the Service Employees International Union (SEIU; 1921) and the Hotel Employees and Restaurant Employees (HERE; 1891) were developing innovative organizing strategies that recruited thousands of service workers, many of them women and people of color, in both the public and the private sectors.

Unionism by public employees surged in the 1960s and 1970s and sustained these membership gains into the twenty-first century. The American Federation of State, County, and Municipal Employees (AFSCME; 1932), the American Federation of Teachers (AFT; 1916), and other AFL-CIO affiliates representing federal employees, postal workers, firefighters, and health-care workers continued to thrive. In addition, once-genteel professional associations, notably the National Education Association (NEA; 1857), became de facto labor unions. The surge in activism by public workers was spurred in part by the civil rights and women's rights movements of the 1960s and by growing awareness of the inferiority of wage levels and benefits provisions experienced by public workers in comparison with those attained by unionized blue-collar workers. Whereas public employees traditionally had been encouraged to regard themselves as humble public servants, a younger, better-educated generation of teachers, clerks, custodians, and public-safety workers increasingly adopted a vocabulary of rights consciousness and entitlement.

Moreover, unions of public employees were able to sustain their gains into the new century. In 1955, about four hundred thousand public workers belonged to unions. By the early 1970s the number had increased eightfold, and 2010 found more than 7 million workers in public-employee unions. Over the period from about 1980 to 2010, the proportion of public employees who were members of unions held steady at about 35 percent. Indeed, in 2010 the U.S. Bureau of Labor Statistics reported that for the first time, the number of unionized public workers exceeded the number of unionized private-sector workers.

In the 1990s and early twenty-first century, the labor movement made headway in the traditionally hard-to-organize service sector as well. Restaurants, retail establishments, medical facilities, and janitorial services employed disproportionate numbers of workers of color, many of them women. Thousands of recent immigrants, some of them undocumented, toiled in this highly decentralized, low-wage sector. To be successful, unions such as HERE and the SEIU devised innovative methods of recruitment and new ways to persuade employers to accept union representation. In the late 1960s and into the 1970s and early 1980s, HERE reached out to students, faculty, and alumni in an eventually successful campaign to organize hundreds of Yale University food service, custodial, and clerical workers. The campaign in the 1960s and 1970s of the United Farm Workers (UFW; 1962), led by its charismatic president Cesar Chavez, to organize Hispanic and Filipino agricultural workers provided another example of how public outreach and innovative tactics could achieve gains for particularly vulnerable and ill-treated workers. The UFW's boycott of table grapes in the late 1960s and early 1970s aroused public sympathy for farmworkers throughout the United States and Canada and was instrumental in gaining changes in California labor laws and in achieving collective-bargaining contracts.

The UFW crusade was important also because Chavez recruited and trained a new generation of young organizers, many of whom went on to other, more established unions. In 1987 the SEIU launched the Justice for Janitors (JFJ) campaign in an effort to organize custodial workers, many of whom were recent immigrants from Mexico and Central America. This campaign borrowed techniques developed initially by the UFW. Workers held street parades, performed skits to demonstrate their grievances and demands, and sometimes personally confronted corporate executives. These campaigns enlisted community-action groups in pressuring employers to raise wages, provide health-insurance benefits, and recognize the union. In a different campaign, in 1999 the SEIU won collective-bargaining rights for seventy-four thousand California home-care workers, most of them women of color, in what was hailed as organized labor's largest representation victory in more than fifty years. In the 1990s and into the new century, HERE used a combination of aggressive confrontation and offers of cooperative relations with casinos and hotels to build a sixty-thousand-member local union in Las Vegas, one that provided its largely female and minority membership with a wide range of educational and support services.

Innovative approaches by no means guaranteed success. Still, this new-model, community-based approach to organizing did help mobilize vulnerable immigrants and other workers of color. Thus, for example, Los Angeles emerged in the 1990s as one of the country's most union-friendly cities. Indeed, in 2005, Hispanic-Latino unionists played a key role in electing Antonio Villaraigosa, who began his activist career as a teenager in the UFW grape boycott, mayor of the city. In such campaigns, women and people of color, once marginal figures in the traditionally white, male, blue-collar labor movement, now took center stage.

In the new century, these modest successes were accompanied by sharp internal controversies. In 2005 the SEIU abandoned the AFL-CIO to form an alternative labor center, called Change to Win. Moreover, internal conflicts wracked several large unions. This internecine conflict festered at a time when politicians in states that were once union strongholds were attacking the very existence of public employee unions. As the nation entered the second decade of the century, it remained uncertain whether a crippled and divided labor movement could fight off these attacks and resume its place as a powerful and respected force in American life.

[*See also* **Automation and Computerization; Chavez, Cesar; Child Workers; Community Organizing; Deindustrialization; Domestic Workers; Fraternal Organizations; Huerta, Dolores; Living-Wage Movement; Perkins, Frances; Southern Tenant Farmers' Union and National Farm Labor Union; Strikes and Industrial Conflict; United Farm Workers of America; Women's Trade Union League; Women Workers; Work;** *and* **Working-Class Life and Society.**]

BIBLIOGRAPHY

AFL-CIO. "About Us." http://www.aflcio.org/aboutus. This official website contains information about ongoing activities of the labor movement, as well as links to a number of labor-history sites.

Arnesen, Eric. "'Like Banquo's Ghost, It Will Not Down': The Race Question and the American Railroad Brotherhoods, 1880–1920." *American Historical Review* 99, no. 5 (1994): 1601–1633. A brilliant examination of the influential railroad unions and of organized labor's early twentieth-century race policies and practices.

Bernstein, Irving. *The Lean Years: A History of the American Worker, 1920–1933.* Boston: Houghton Mifflin, 1960. A vivid and authoritative account of organized labor's decline in the 1920s and in the Great Depression.

Bernstein, Irving. *The Turbulent Years: A History of the American Worker, 1933–1941.* Boston: Houghton Mifflin, 1969. The classic account of organized labor's resurgence in the 1930s.

Brody, David. *Workers in Industrial America: Essays on the Twentieth Century Struggle.* New York: Oxford University Press, 1980. Insightful essays on organized labor's institutional and political course.

Dean, Amy B., and David B. Reynolds. *A New New Deal: How Regional Activism Will Reshape the American Labor Movement.* Ithaca, N.Y.: ILR Press, 2009. What union activists must do—and to some extent are doing—to revitalize the labor movement in the twenty-first century.

Dubofsky, Melvyn. *We Shall Be All: A History of the Industrial Workers of the World.* Chicago: Quadrangle Books, 1969. The standard history of the Industrial Workers of the World, whose radical ideology challenged the early twentieth-century labor movement and whose innovative tactics have continued to inspire organizers and activists.

Early, Steve. *The Civil Wars in U.S. Labor: Birth of a New Workers' Movement or Death Throes of the Old?* Chicago: Haymarket Books, 2011. A detailed examination of the Andy Stern–led Service Employees International Union and of the challenges facing the beleaguered twenty-first century labor movement.

Getman, Julius G. *Restoring the Power of Unions: It Takes a Movement.* New Haven, Conn.: Yale University Press, 2010. Stresses the importance of rank-and-file activism and community outreach in the hostile organizing climate of the early twenty-first century.

Laurie, Bruce. *Artisans into Workers: Labor in Nineteenth-Century America.* New York: Hill and Wang, 1989. An insightful overview of the diversity of nineteenth-century union development.

Lichtenstein, Nelson. *State of the Union: A Century of American Labor.* Princeton, N.J.: Princeton University Press, 2002. A trenchant examination of organized labor's achievements and, especially, limitations between the New Deal and the onset of the twenty-first century.

Montgomery, David. *Beyond Equality: Labor and the Radical Republicans, 1862–1872.* New York: Alfred A. Knopf, 1967. An influential account of the interrelationship between emerging unionism and the post–Civil War black freedom struggle.

Montgomery, David. *The Fall of the House of Labor: The Workplace, the State, and American Labor Activism, 1865–1925.* Cambridge, U.K.: Cambridge University Press, 1987. A richly informed account of the struggles of working people's efforts to resist the hegemony of corporate capitalism.

Shaw, Randy. *Beyond the Fields: Cesar Chavez, the UFW, and the Struggle for Justice in the 21st Century.* Berkeley: University of California Press, 2008. Documents the importance of the UFW's struggle in the inspiration and training of labor and community activists in the late twentieth and early twenty-first centuries.

Taft, Philip. *Organized Labor in American History.* New York: Harper and Row, 1964. A detailed account of the mainstream labor movement's institutional development, based in part on Taft's privileged access to the AFL's archives.

Voss, Kim. *The Making of American Exceptionalism: The Knights of Labor and Class Formation in the Nineteenth Century.* Ithaca, N.Y.: Cornell University Press, 1993. Stresses the role of employer and state repression in blunting the Knights' challenge to the rise of corporate capitalism.

Zieger, Robert H. *The CIO, 1935–1955.* Chapel Hill: University of North Carolina Press, 1995. A detailed examination of perhaps the most significant episode in twentieth-century U.S. labor history.

Robert H. Zieger

LAS VEGAS

For decades Las Vegas had been little more than a desert oasis for local Indians, white ranchers, and travelers when in 1905 William Clark laid out a division town for his railroad connecting Los Angeles with Salt Lake City. Unlike western mining towns that mostly contained white single men, in 1910 only 63 percent of the 937 inhabitants were men and nearly one-fifth were children. The town was more than 90 percent Euro-American, with the largest racial minority being the fifty-six Hispanics who worked mostly for the railway. These demographic tendencies continued into midcentury, but they began to change with World War II and the influx of female and African workers.

World War II, the construction of Hoover Dam (1931–1936), and the re-legalization of gambling in Nevada shifted the economy toward tourism. The Strip began in 1941 with the debut of the El Rancho Vegas, followed by the Last Frontier and later Bugsy Siegel's Flamingo. White men dominated the industry as hotel and casino managers and dealers. Although women gamblers were always welcome, female employees were usually relegated to the "girl's ghetto" of cocktail waitress, keno running, and showgirl jobs. African American employees faced even worse discrimination. White clubs traditionally had no black dealers, although a few black-run clubs in the Westside ghetto did. In 1960, Asians and Latinos still represented a small portion of the local population, and therefore they held less than 3 percent of the resort jobs.

Downtown Las Vegas had been largely integrated from 1905 until the late 1930s, but pressure from many southern white dam workers led city officials in 1938–1939 to begin herding black businesses and residents into the city's old run-down Westside neighborhood. The process continued into the 1940s as city leaders and gaming executives curried favor with thousands of white soldiers, defense workers, and tourists. Blacks gradually lost the right to enter hotel casinos. During the 1940s and 1950s, even such popular black headliners as Nat King Cole, Lena Horne, and Sammy Davis Jr. were forced by their hotels to sleep in Westside rooming houses; the practice finally stopped only after Nat King Cole led a revolt. Conditions changed dramatically for all blacks in March 1960 when the local chapter of the National Association for the Advancement of Colored People threatened a protest march on the Strip if resorts there and downtown did not open their showrooms, restaurants, casinos,

and hotel rooms to minority patrons. The standoff ended quickly as resort executives, worried that negative publicity and televised confrontations would hurt tourism, agreed to the group's demands. From then on, all minorities were welcome.

Ending discrimination in employment proved to be much more difficult because of resistance from both the Nevada Resort Association, whose members were the employers, and the Culinary and other unions. After blacks had endured years of frustration, in 1971 the U.S. Justice Department obtained a federal consent decree that required the hotels to hire minority men and forced the unions to give them apprentice positions in all areas . In 1970, African Americans made up more than 10 percent of the metropolitan population, but they held only 19 percent of hotel jobs (mostly menial) and almost no casino jobs. The casino jobs edged up slowly for the rest of the century. Women fared better. By 1978, just seven years after the Plaza Hotel hired the first women dealers, more than 25 percent of the Strip's twenty-six hundred roulette, blackjack, and baccarat dealers were women. In 1981 women obtained their own federal consent decree requiring the resort industry to hire them, but it was rescinded just a few years later because of compliance.

Not until the late 1970s did large numbers of Latinos begin to veer off their traditional migration pathways through California and Arizona to enter Las Vegas, attracted by a growing number of resort jobs, as well as by landscaping and other service-sector businesses that fed off Las Vegas's explosive growth. By 2000, Latinos made up almost 22 percent of the population. Between 1986 and 2007, Las Vegas was the fastest-growing metropolitan area in the nation, and this boom eventually created a business class of Latinos, Asians, and Pacific islanders.

The economic recession of 2008–2010, along with the mortgage foreclosure crisis, substantially thinned out the Latino population. Indeed, nearly two hundred thousand people had left the metropolitan area by 2010, and new building came to a virtual halt. In 2010, Las Vegas experienced the highest unemployment rate of any city in the country —15 percent—and the highest foreclosure rate. By this time, however, the local population was the most diverse in history and the battle for equality in jobs, housing, education, and public places was largely over.

[*See also* Leisure; Prostitution; Segregation, Racial; Southwest, The; Sunbelt; *and* Tourism and Travel.]

BIBLIOGRAPHY

Gottdiener, M., Claudia C. Collins, and David R. Dickens. *Las Vegas: The Social Production of an All-American City.* Malden, Mass.: Blackwell, 1999.

Kraft, James P. *Vegas at Odds: Labor Conflict in a Leisure Economy, 1960–1985.* Baltimore: Johns Hopkins University Press, 2010.

Moehring, Eugene P. *Resort City in the Sunbelt: Las Vegas, 1930–2000.* 2d ed. Reno: University of Nevada Press, 2000.

Eugene Moehring

LAW AND SOCIETY

The very idea of the study of law and society implies some understanding about the nature of the two categories of analysis. How, after all, can one discuss the critical questions regarding the relationship between law and society—the ways in which social movements shape the law, for instance, or the effects of legal requirements on social behavior—without some agreement about the distinction between the two? One of the first challenges in telling the story of law and society in American history, then, is to consider what it means to talk about "law."

Defining the Law. Definitions of law tend to fall into one of three categories. A narrow definition would focus on courts and litigation: law is the work of trained lawyers and judges; it centers on doctrine, precedent, and interpretive practices; its central texts are court opinions and certain foundational documents, such as state and federal constitutions. Law here is premised on the idea that the world of law and the world of politics are largely distinct. This is the understanding of law that has dominated—and to a large extent continues to dominate in the twenty-first century—legal education in the United States. A broader definition of law would encompass not just litigation and court rulings, but also the actions of nonjudicial governing institutions. This would include the work of legislatures, administrative agencies, and countless local, state, and federal officials charged with rule making, enforcement, and dispute resolution. Under this definition, the divide between law and politics has little applicability. The focus is on the exercise of government authority in its various manifestations. A still broader understanding of law would include any form of authoritative rule and enforcement process, regardless of whether that rule is directly attributable to the power of the state. Under this functionalist conception of law, legal authority might derive from government, but it might also come from social institutions, such as the family, private associations, and trade groups, or even from established customs and cultural practices.

Recognition of these overlapping conceptions of law provides a window into the single most important development in sociolegal scholarship since the later twentieth century: the expansion of the study of law beyond the world of litigation and courts. Historians have written social histories of the law—sometimes described as legal histories "from below"—that offer rich and nuanced portraits of the role of everyday citizens in shaping the meaning of the law on the ground. They have explored both the "legal" work that is often done by ostensibly nonlegal actors and also the "nonlegal" work that has been done by lawyers. The focus here is on what James Willard Hurst, a pioneering figure in integrating social and legal history, described as the "working principles" of law. Hurst sought to explain "law not so much as it may appear to philosophers, but more as it had meaning for workaday people and was shaped by them to their wants and vision" (p. 5). Relatedly, sociolegal scholars in various disciplines have explored themes of popular legal consciousness, law as a form of discourse, and rights claiming as a tool of social mobilization, all of which call for broader, more functionalist conceptions of law. A broadening of the conception of law has allowed interdisciplinary legal scholars to consider the ways in which legal rules, norms, and processes permeate all aspects of society. Although the bifurcated terminology of "law" and "society" remains useful because it allows for a discussion of relations between "legal" (however defined) and "nonlegal" phenomena, it is important to recognize the assumptions about the meaning of law on which this terminology necessarily relies.

The Growth of Government Lawmaking.

When the major developments in law and society over the course of American history are examined, several themes stand out. First is the general expansion of government's lawmaking authority. Constraints on behavior previously regulated by informal collectives, such as families, communities, and churches, have become increasingly the responsibility of government. Legal historians have traced a robust tradition of state and local government regulation dating back to the beginning of the nation. And beginning in earnest during the Progressive and New Deal periods, the federal government has assumed more responsibility for the material and physical well-being of its citizens. With the assumption of government responsibility arrived a panoply of official regulations and remedial processes, displacing nongovernmental systems of authority and dispute resolution. This is not to say that informal systems have disappeared. Indeed, much sociolegal scholarship has been dedicated to considering the persistence of "order without law." Nonetheless, the growth of state-backed legal requirements and processes has steadily marginalized informal networks of social control. One need look no further than the exponential increase in the number of statutes, ordinances, and government regulations, the chronic backlog in the nation's courts, or the dramatic spike in the nation's prison population since the mid-twentieth century to see that law (in its formal sense) plays more of a role in the lives of American citizens than ever before. This same observation could have been made at any point in the nation's history.

Though there has there been a general growth of formal legal institutions and their influence throughout American history, this growth has not been evenly distributed across the various levels of governance in the United States. All forms of government have responded to the increased demands of a growing, modernizing society, but it has been the federal government that has seen the most dramatic increases in its power. States retain considerable control over the lives of their citizens, with vast swaths of law—including most of the laws relating to crime, family, and education—still falling under state jurisdiction. Yet the trend has been for the power of the national government to expand, generally at the expense of state power. The same demands that in 1787 motivated the adoption of a stronger central government under the Constitution have over the years led the American people steadily to deposit more and more sovereignty in the national government. These include the demand for unity in foreign affairs, particularly during times of international conflict (wars have been one of the most consistent spurs to increases in federal power); the benefits that national standards bring to commerce and economic growth; and national majoritarian opposition to practices that might have majority support in a particular state or region but are outliers from a national perspective (the prohibition of alcohol fits this description, as does civil rights in the post–World War II period). In response to these national crises and demands, law in the United States has become more national and more uniform.

Executive and Judicial Power.

The expansion of the responsibility of the federal government has fueled the growth of executive and judicial power in particular. Congress has played a less dominant role in defining the course of national policy making in the twentieth and twenty-first centuries than it did previously. The growth of executive power can be seen in the rise of what has come to be termed the "imperial presidency." Although concerns with presidential power over foreign and domestic affairs became particularly prominent with the Cold War and the creation of the national security state in the post–World War II era, the trend toward expanding executive power is as old as the presidency. Some of the most consequential legal statements of American history have come in the form of executive orders, including Abraham Lincoln's Emancipation Proclamation, the Japanese American internment order during World War II, and the desegregation of the military in 1948. There have been relatively few direct, committed efforts by the other branches of government to limit executive authority, and what efforts there have been have either failed or been generally ineffective.

The power of the executive is also evident in the emergence of the administrative state. The administrative state has its roots in the nineteenth century, but it was in the twentieth century that it took its modern form, with much government regulatory power exercised through agencies. Federal administrative agencies owe their existence to acts of Congress but are largely under the control of the executive. These agencies, which often exercise power to make rules, enforce them, and adjudicate disputes, first engaged with the most pressing needs of late nineteenth-century industrial society—industrialization, urbanization, and immigration. If for most Americans the face of the national government is the president, it is through administrative agencies that individual citizens are most likely to receive the benefits or be confronted with the constraints of federal law.

Another notable trend in American law has been the growing prominence of the judiciary as a central policy-making institution. Courts have always played an influential role in regulating American life. In the late eighteenth and nineteenth centuries, judges exerted a powerful influence on American society through the adjudication of private law disputes. Judges in early America drew on the British common law in the areas of property, torts, and contracts, while adapting doctrine to fit the American scene, particularly its system of chattel slavery and its explosive economic growth. Though legislative codification of the common law in the nineteenth century limited judicial discretion, thanks to their power to interpret statutes and to strike down laws through the exercise of constitutional judicial review, judges retained considerable authority over the course of law.

Judicial review proved a particularly potent and controversial weapon for the courts. As far back as the early years of the republic, state courts struck down acts of their legislatures for straying from constitutional principles. Beginning in the early nineteenth century, the U.S. Supreme Court policed the boundaries of federal power by striking down state laws and state court rulings that conflicted with the Constitution. By the end of the century the Court was also regularly striking down acts of Congress, something that it had done on only rare occasions in the antebellum period. Although judicial review was always a controversial practice—particularly when for a period from the 1890s through the 1930s the Court used it to strike down various efforts to regulate economic relations—over the course of American history it became increasingly accepted as one of the basic functions of the courts.

With the acceptance of judicial review has also come a general willingness on the part of both public officials and private citizens to accept judicial claims of interpretive supremacy over the meaning of the Constitution. The Constitution itself contains no guidelines for resolving disputes over constitutional interpretation, and into the twentieth century all three branches of the federal government, and in certain instances the states, regularly made claims about constitutional meaning. Although this decentered tradition of constitutional interpretation certainly did not disappear, by the middle of the twentieth century the Supreme Court had emerged as the clear winner, with other institutions of government generally deferring to its authority on questions of constitutional meaning.

The Role of Law in American Society. After the major developments in American legal history have been considered, a final fundamental question about law and American society remains: What have been Americans' attitudes toward their legal system and the role of law in their lives? Any kind of sweeping statement about the legal sensibilities of such a diverse society is difficult, even impossible. Nonetheless, this question has been a recurrent concern for those who have sought to understand American society, and their varied conclusions offer additional perspective into the place of law in American society.

America has often been described as a distinctly legalistic society. Alexis de Tocqueville wrote admiringly of the legalistic bent of the young nation in the first volume of his *Democracy in America* (1835), noting the dominant role of lawyers in American society and the "immense political power" vested in judges. "Scarcely any political question arises in the United States that is not resolved, sooner or later, into a judicial question," Tocqueville famously concluded. The prominence of lawyers and courts remains as much a defining characteristic of modern American society as it was when Tocqueville wrote in the 1830s. The judiciary continues to hold a special place in the American legal consciousness: public opinion polls find the Supreme Court to be the most respected branch of the federal government. Also commonly cited as evidence of a national commitment to law is Americans' reverence for their Constitution. Though there have always been deep divisions over its meaning, virtually from the moment of its adoption Americans have embraced the Constitution as the foundation of the American system of government.

Yet some scholars and commentators tell a quite different story about American attitudes toward the law, emphasizing a tradition of skepticism toward government power and a persistent willingness to defy the dictates of the law. Fears about the threat that government and legal regulations pose for individual liberty have created a steady undercurrent of resistance to the ever-expanding reach of the state. There have also been recurrent bouts of concern toward the willingness of Americans to flout the law or to resort to extralegal remedies. For example, in the midst of the failed Prohibition experiment, the popular historian James Truslow Adams wrote a widely noted article titled "Our Lawless Heritage." When in the late 1930s the Swedish sociologist Gunnar Myrdal came to the United States to write a report on its race relations, he was struck by the "low degree of law observance"—a problem that he saw not only in the lynch law of the Jim Crow South, but throughout the nation. In 1970, after a decade marked by unprecedented street protests and urban riots, the New York City Bar Association held a symposium to consider the question: "Is law dead?"

Much like American society itself, the place of law in American society is resistant to easy categorization. Although there are identifiable trends in the development of law and legal institutions, the most fundamental questions of the role of law in America yield little in the way of clear answers. Who has ultimate authority to assign meaning to the nation's foundational legal texts? Do Americans respect their law? What do Americans even mean when they discuss the "law"? It is in the struggle to come to terms with these kinds of questions that one finds the story of American law.

[*See also* **Everyday Life** *and* **Prisons and Penitentiaries.**]

BIBLIOGRAPHY

Ellickson, Robert C. *Order without Law: How Neighbors Settle Disputes.* Cambridge, Mass.: Harvard University Press, 1991.

Forbath, William E. *Law and the Shaping of the American Labor Movement.* Cambridge, Mass.: Harvard University Press, 1991.

Friedman, Lawrence M. *American Law in the 20th Century.* New Haven, Conn.: Yale University Press, 2002.

Friedman, Lawrence M. *A History of American Law.* 3d ed. New York: Simon & Schuster, 2005.

Goluboff, Risa L. *The Lost Promise of Civil Rights.* Cambridge, Mass.: Harvard University Press, 2007.

Gross, Ariela J. *What Blood Won't Tell: A History of Race on Trial in America.* Cambridge, Mass.: Harvard University Press, 2008.

Hall, Kermit L., and Peter Karsten. *The Magic Mirror: Law in American History.* 2d ed. New York: Oxford University Press, 2009.

Horwitz, Morton J. *The Transformation of American Law, 1780–1860.* Cambridge, Mass.: Harvard University Press, 1977.

Hurst, James Willard. *Law and the Conditions of Freedom in the Nineteenth-Century United States.* Madison: University of Wisconsin Press, 1956.

Kammen, Michael. *A Machine That Would Go of Itself: The Constitution in American Culture.* New York: Alfred A. Knopf, 1986.

McCann, Michael W. *Rights at Work: Pay Equity Reform and the Politics of Legal Mobilization.* Chicago: University of Chicago Press, 1994.

Myrdal, Gunnar. *An American Dilemma: The Negro Problem and Modern Democracy.* New York: Harper & Brothers, 1944.

Novak, William J. *The People's Welfare: Law and Regulation in Nineteenth-Century America.* Chapel Hill: University of North Carolina Press, 1996.

Rostow, Eugene V., ed. *Is Law Dead?* New York: Simon & Schuster, 1971.

Tomlins, Christopher L. *Law, Labor, and Ideology in the Early American Republic.* New York: Cambridge University Press, 1993.

Welke, Barbara Young. *Law and the Borders of Belonging in the Long Nineteenth Century United States.* New York: Cambridge University Press, 2010.

Christopher W. Schmidt

LEAGUE OF UNITED LATIN AMERICAN CITIZENS

In 1929, Mexican American political activists gathered in Corpus Christi, Texas, to unite various south Texas civil rights organizations for Mexican Americans under a single banner. With the leadership of Ben Garza Jr. and Alonso Perales, representatives from existing civil rights groups, including the Sons of America, the League of Latin American Citizens, and the Order of Knights of America, formed what ultimately became the largest and most influential Mexican American civil rights organization in the country, the League of United Latin American Citizens (LULAC). Eleven councils were formed, each in a separate town or city. The call to combat discrimination against Mexican Americans by asserting the rights of citizenship struck a responsive chord, and the organization expanded throughout the 1930s. LULAC made education, health care, housing, voting rights, juvenile delinquency, low wages, and citizenship its priorities.

LULAC was a new kind of Mexican American political organization. Its most prominent members were owners of small businesses, managers, lawyers, doctors, and other professionals. LULAC members were economic and social conservatives. They envisioned a world where everyone should be allowed to find their place in the social hierarchy if freed from the constraints of racism. LULAC officers were required to take an oath swearing that they would be "loyal to the government of the United States of America, support its Constitution, and obey its laws."

After World War II, LULAC grew in size and influence. The group conducted citizenship and English-language classes and raised money for local charities. It campaigned for the desegregation of restaurants, swimming pools, and other public facilities. LULAC councils also created Boy Scout and Girl Scout troops, 4-H clubs, Little League baseball teams, and fund-raisers for the March of Dimes and the Red Cross. Some LULAC councils sponsored tutoring programs in which schoolchildren were taught basic English and about American history and government. The group petitioned local school officials and led boycotts of public schools that refused to integrate. They also pursued educational reforms in court. From 1950 to 1957, LULAC was a party to approximately fifteen suits or complaints filed against school districts throughout the Southwest.

During the 1960s LULAC's prominence was challenged by other organizations vying to speak on behalf of Mexican Americans. Yet paradoxically, LULAC's public profile rose even as its membership dropped. The leadership leveraged the organization's name into social service programs sponsored by business and government. Their most notable achievements include the creation of SER Jobs for Progress (1965) and the Mexican American Legal Defense and Educational Fund, known as MALDEF (1968). SER Jobs for Progress grew into the largest job-training and placement service in the nation. In 1973, LULAC activists created the LULAC National Educational Service Centers to disburse scholarship monies and provide counseling and literacy services. The National LULAC Housing Commission owns two thousand units of low-income housing units in nine states. Other LULAC affiliates offer advocacy and services in areas such as health care for the elderly, credit and mortgages, Internet access, and computer skills. By the early twenty-first century the organization's national profile hinged on the ability of its national leaders to develop a relationship with the media and articulate its views.

LULAC steps into the national limelight every four years when it hosts forums for presidential candidates.

[*See also* 4-H Club Movement; Immigrants' Rights Movement; Mexican American Civil Rights Movement; *and* Scouting.]

BIBLIOGRAPHY

García, Mario T. *Mexican Americans: Leadership, Ideology, and Identity, 1930–1960*. New Haven, Conn.: Yale University Press, 1989.

Orozco, Cynthia. *No Mexicans, Women, or Dogs Allowed: The Rise of the Mexican American Civil Rights Movement*. Austin: University of Texas Press, 2009.

Benjamin Márquez

LEARNED SOCIETIES

"Learned society" is a term that ordinarily refers to a private, nonprofit association dedicated to furthering the interests of scholars in a specific field of scholarly inquiry. The typical learned society is an open-membership organization that has two basic functions: the publication of one or more scholarly journals in the field and the organization of an annual meeting of members for the purpose of delivering scholarly papers. The majority of members of learned societies are academics employed in tertiary education, although primary and secondary schoolteachers and other practitioners are frequently members. By the early twenty-first century the learned society was perhaps the most important reference point for academics, competing with their employing universities for their professional loyalty.

The historical progenitor of such societies in the English-speaking world was the Royal Society of London, founded in 1660 and typical of the products of the first scientific revolution in Europe. The first North American academy of this sort, the American Philosophical Society, was established by Benjamin Franklin in Philadelphia in 1743 for the purpose of "producing useful knowledge." It was joined in 1780 by the American Academy of Arts and Sciences, based in Cambridge, Massachusetts, created for "the cultivation and promotion of Arts and Sciences." The academy, like the Philosophical Society, was committed to the "forming and incorporating of men of genius and learning into public societies for . . . beneficial purposes." Like the Royal Society, both societies were selective in their membership, products of the Enlightenment commitment to the notion that "men of genius" could improve the world through the cultivation of their talents, but in a period of rudimentary higher education they had few institutional mechanisms for reaching their goals.

The early nineteenth century saw the creation of a number of societies that were "learned" by the standard of the times, but their knowledge creation was not professionally organized. The American Oriental Society, for instance, was formed in 1842, and it is usually described as the oldest learned society devoted to a particular field of scholarship—in this case the languages and literatures of Asia, already one of the traditional European fields of learning. There were also numerous urban academies such as the New York Academy of Sciences (1817), the Boston Society of Natural History (1830), and numerous historical societies (the Massachusetts Historical Society was founded in 1791), museums, and other cultural institutions with at least some commitment to scholarship. More consequentially for the development of modern learned societies, the American Association for the Advancement of Science, founded in 1848, was in many ways the precursor of the disciplinary societies that began to appear a generation later. But most of these organizations were created by and for wealthy and cultivated amateurs.

Learned societies as they are known in the twenty-first century are artifacts of the late nineteenth century when the academic disciplines first took on separate identities, the product of the second scientific revolution and the emergence of the modern university and the PhD degree built on the basis of the separation of fields of knowledge. As the university came to be organized around disciplinary departments, the new communities of scholars looked for ways to organize themselves regionally and nationally. The result was the formation of disciplinary learned societies across the range of fields of knowledge recognized at the time.

In the humanities, among the earliest learned societies were the American Philological Society (1869), the Society of Biblical Literature and Exegesis (1880), the Modern Language Association (1883), the American Historical Association (1884), and the American Philosophical Association (1900). The oldest learned society tradition is that of the humanities. In the natural sciences, the American Chemical Society was founded in 1876, followed by the Geological Society of America (1888), the American Mathematical Society (1889), the American Psychological Association (1892), and the American Physical Society (1899). But in the nineteenth century the scientific societies were weak, and a long time passed before they developed into the publication-rich organizations known in the twenty-first century. With the exception of the American Economics Association (1885), the societies for the social sciences were the product of the early twentieth century: the American Anthropological Association (1902), the American Political Science Association (1903), the Association of American Geographers (1904), and the American Sociological Association (1905). These, along with a few others, were the first in what became a tremendous proliferation of learned societies throughout the second half of the twentieth century as the pace of knowledge creation expanded exponentially, and subdisciplines, cross-disciplines, and new disciplines emerged.

There has also been a parallel development of national organizations designed to serve the learned academic disciplines. The remarkably private character of American social organization has meant that few of these organizations were formed in the public sector, although the National Academy of Sciences—established during the Civil War, in 1863—could be described as quasi public. But the national organization in the humanities, the American Council of Learned Societies (ACLS), is a nonprofit organization created in 1919, just after World War I, to advance the interests of the humanistic disciplinary societies and to represent the United States to international cultural organizations. The Social Science Research Council broke away from the ACLS in 1923 to give voice to the needs of the newly emergent disciplines of the social sciences. But of the three, the ACLS is the only organization formally constituted by learned societies, which play an important role in its governance.

Thus the scene of scholarship in the twenty-first-century United States is richly populated by learned societies, national organizations, and universities, all sustained by both government and private funding. This constitutes a richer and more complex environment for organized scholarship in the United States than in the rest of the world.

[*See also* Education *and* Libraries.]

BIBLIOGRAPHY

Furner, Mary O. *Advocacy and Objectivity: A Crisis in the Professionalization of American Political Science, 1865–1905.* New ed. New Brunswick, N.J.: Transaction, 2011.

Haskell, Thomas L. *The Emergence of Professional Social Science: The American Social Science Association and the Nineteenth-Century Crisis of Authority.* Urbana: University of Illinois Press, 1977.

Hawkins, Hugh. *Banding Together: The Rise of National Associations in American Higher Education, 1887–1950.* Baltimore: Johns Hopkins University Press, 1992.

Oleson, Alexandra, and Sanborn C. Brown, eds. *The Pursuit of Knowledge in the Early American Republic: American Scientific and Learned Societies from Colonial Times to the Civil War.* Baltimore: Johns Hopkins University Press, 1976.

Oleson, Alexandra, and John Voss, eds. *The Organization of Knowledge in Modern America, 1860–1920.* Baltimore: Johns Hopkins University Press, 1979.

Veysey, Laurence R. *The Emergence of the American University.* Chicago: University of Chicago Press, 1965.

Worcester, Kenton W. *Social Science Research Council, 1923–1998.* New York: Social Science Research Council, 2001. http://www.ssrc.org/workspace/images/crm/new_publication_3/%7B1f20c6e1-565f-de11-bd80-001cc477ec70%7D.pdf.

Stanley N. Katz

LEE, ANN

(1736–1784), leader of the Shakers. Ann Lee, born in 1736 in Manchester, England, the daughter of a blacksmith, married a blacksmith, Abraham Standerin, in 1762. They had no surviving children. Details concerning Lee's early adult life are limited. At some point she began associating with a religious sect led by James and Jane Wardley known as the Shakers, or Shaking Quakers, because of their ecstatic mode of worship. Lee emerged as a leader in this community, which increasingly came into conflict with authorities because the members disturbed worshipping congregations. In 1773 she was arrested and imprisoned for a time because of these confrontational activities. The following year Lee, her husband, and several followers sailed from England to America.

By 1776 a small group headed by Ann Lee was living at Niskayuna outside Albany, New York, but these so-called Shakers did not gain public attention until 1780. Then their worship meetings, which included dancing and whirling, drew criticism and opposition; they were also accused of immorality and heresy. The group at Niskayuna evolved into a community that supported itself through its own agriculture and labor. Lee's charisma dominated, and she also attracted increasing numbers of new members. Because Lee and the Shakers did not support the American War of Independence, Lee was arrested and incarcerated for more than four months, events that brought growing attention and opposition to her group. Opponents attacked her and the beliefs and practices of the community. The Shakers' most striking practices were acceptance of the "cross," namely, the practice of celibacy, which was required of all members, and the collective ownership of all resources including land. Their most troublesome belief affirmed that Ann Lee, called Mother Ann, was the mother of the elect spoken of in the Book of Revelation. Some also called her "the queen of heaven, Christ's wife." Shaker worship included singing, dancing, running, laughing, and a host of other ecstatic activities.

In May 1781, Lee and her closest associates set out on a missionary journey of more than two years' duration traveling across Massachusetts and Connecticut, visiting locations where Shaker converts lived. This journey inspired positive responses, solidifying emerging Shaker communities, but also fierce opposition from opponents. Lee's presence was critical to the society's expanding success. Her image as spiritual mother was powerful. She called for her followers to forsake sin and sexual relations. Lee's journey created a growing society made up of scattered Shaker communities. Many of the converts gathered into these communities came as families—some possessing substantial assets, including land, that they turned over to the society—and others came as impoverished individuals in need of financial assistance. Inside the communities, all members were theoretically equal, economically and socially.

One year after returning to Niskayuna, on 8 September 1784, Ann Lee died. The published obituary identified her as "Mrs. Lee, known by the appellation of the *Elect Lady*, or *Mother of Zion*, and head of that people called Shakers." The sayings attributed to her were not collected systematically until 1816 when they were published as *Testimonies of the Life, Character, Revelations, and Doctrines of Our Ever Blessed Mother Ann Lee, and the Elders with Her*, a text that exercised a formative influence upon the expanding Shaker community. Lee's influence within the society continued powerfully throughout the nineteenth and twentieth centuries, and it remains powerful for the handful of Shakers in the twenty-first century.

[*See also* **Colonial Era; Itinerant Preachers; Religion; Revivals; Sexual Reform and Morality; Utopian and Communitarian Movements;** *and* **Women and Religious Institutions.**]

BIBLIOGRAPHY

Blinn, Henry Clay. *The Life and Gospel Experience of Mother Ann Lee.* Canterbury, N.H.: Shakers, 1883. A view from inside the Shaker community.

Stein, Stephen J. *The Shaker Experience in America: A History of the United Society of Believers.* New Haven, Conn.: Yale University Press, 1992. A general history of the Shakers.

Stephen J. Stein

LEISLER'S REBELLION

Lasting from May 1689 to March 1691, Leisler's Rebellion was a political uprising in colonial New York that began with the collapse of royal government and ended with the arrival of a new governor and the execution of the rebellion's titular leader, Jacob Leisler. England's James II, the proprietor of New York, ruled with a heavy hand, leaving many colonists discontent with his rule and that of his governors. When news of England's Glorious Revolution of 1688, in which William III and Mary II replaced James's rule, reached America, it sparked a series of revolts in the colonies. In Boston, colonists reacted to the news of James II's downfall by imprisoning Sir Edmund Andros, the governor of the Dominion of New England, which included New York. Emboldened by the rebellion in Boston, colonists in Queens, Suffolk, and Westchester Counties in New York denounced the lieutenant governor Francis Nicholson for failing to recognize the new English sovereigns. On 31 May 1689 the rebellion spread to New York City when members of the local militia seized Fort James in the name of the new sovereigns. By June 1689 the provisional government, known as the Committee of Safety, elected Jacob Leisler, a captain of the local militia, as the captain of the fort. By December, Leisler had assumed the role of lieutenant governor of New York.

Historians have variously characterized Leisler's Rebellion as an ethnic, class, religious, or political movement. Each of these interpretations has its merits and failings, and no single explanation can account for the complex nature of the uprising. Though the ranks of both the supporters and the opponents of the rebellion defy simple categorization, the Leislerians were generally from Dutch, French, and German backgrounds and were farmers, artisans, or middling merchants. Meanwhile, elite merchants and former officeholders of English, Scottish, and Dutch backgrounds were less likely to support the rebellion, as were members of religious orders that had benefited from the former government's official policy of religious toleration.

Though the majority of the colonists supported the rebellion, the policies of Leisler's government soon frustrated its initial supporters. Leisler responded to opposition by imprisoning several of his critics without trial. When a new colonial assembly met in 1690, some counties refused to send representatives. Leisler's failed expedition against Canada, in which Massachusetts Bay, Plymouth, and Connecticut took part, further eroded his support. In June 1690 a small riot broke out between the rebellion's critics and its supporters. Nonetheless, Leisler and his supporters maintained their hold on New York until 1691.

The rebellion ended with the arrival in March 1691 of Henry Sloughter, King William's newly commissioned governor of New York. Upon his arrival, Leisler and his troops surrendered the fort. Leisler and his principal allies were immediately imprisoned for treason and murder. Though all of them were convicted of treason, only Leisler and his son-in-law, Jacob Milborne, were executed.

Though Leisler's Rebellion came to an end in 1691, its consequences were long-lasting. For more than two decades, politics in New York were characterized by a deep division between supporters of the rebellion's ideals and their opponents. By 1719, however, Governor Robert Hunter was able to say that the "very name of Party or Faction seems to be forgot," and the memory of Leisler's Rebellion was laid to rest in New York.

[*See also* **Colonial Era** *and* **New York City.**]

BIBLIOGRAPHY

Reich, Jerome R. *Leisler's Rebellion: A Study of Democracy in New York, 1664–1720.* Chicago: University of Chicago Press, 1953.

Voorhees, David William. "'In Behalf of the True Protestants Religion': The Glorious Revolution in New York." PhD diss., New York University, 1988.

Megan Lindsay Cherry

LEISURE

Leisure practices are deeply embedded in social, cultural, economic, and religious contexts, and ideas about leisure have varied widely throughout American history. Leisure has historically both reflected and constructed its larger society, and as a result it has evolved alongside the broader culture from the colonial period onward.

Leisure in Colonial Societies. Colonial leisure practices varied widely because the colonies were so socially, religiously, and economically diverse. Nevertheless, a common thread ran throughout colonial experience: leisure activities were deeply woven into the fabric of society. Colonists did not draw sharp distinctions between leisure and the activities of everyday life, and as a result, colonial leisure practices were expressions of the societies' religious, social, and political structures.

In New England, Puritan political and religious leaders generally believed that "sober mirth," or innocent, moderate recreation, was not only permissible but necessary for godly living. They associated asceticism with Catholicism, but they also warned that an excess of pleasure led directly to sin, so they sought to split the difference. Especially before the 1680s, "sober mirth" was found in the family and the church. The wide availability of religious texts, combined with historically high literacy rates, made reading and religious music central to Puritan leisure. Puritans' covenanted community created regular opportunities for social gatherings that, though sober in purpose, nevertheless offered the opportunity for recreation. These gatherings were often segregated by gender; men and women sat separately in church, and men's secular social lives revolved around civic events like elections and militia musters, whereas women gathered for work bees and childbirth.

Notwithstanding the ethic of "sober leisure," daily leisure practices often exceeded the boundaries of official sanction. Servants and slaves drank immoderately, engaged in extramarital sexual activity, and played sports on Sundays. At the end of the seventeenth century, leisure for all New Englanders began to secularize and become more gender-integrated. Early leaders had been suspicious of dancing, but by the eighteenth century it was a regular feature of weddings and parties, despite continuing official skepticism about its morality. Courtship practices also liberalized, as popular practices like the goodnight kiss and bundling became increasingly acceptable. Some leisure spaces stayed gender-segregated; for example, Puritans had always been comfortable with the moderate consumption of alcohol, so taverns remained important spaces of male sociability. Hunting and fishing were also popular recreations for New England men. Although "sober mirth"

remained a powerful ideal, it did not describe the entire universe of leisure practice.

In the southern colonies, staple-crop agriculture, indentured servitude, and slavery quickly created a wealthy planter class whose members had the time and resources to devote to an active life of leisure, and as a result southern planters quickly became the leading leisure class of the American colonies. Many organized their lives around seasonal social rounds that included balls, plays, horse racing, militia musters, gambling, and blood sports. Local and informal, athletic contests were often primarily venues for gambling. These leisure activities brought together a colonial elite that was dispersed on distant plantations; they entertained each other with legendary hospitality, and they gathered in colonial capitals like Williamsburg and Charleston for court sessions, which were social as well as political events. Some of the earliest theaters in British North America were built in southern provincial capitals. Above all, colonial planters sought to imitate the leisured lives of English country gentlemen, and they devoted a considerable portion of their agricultural wealth to this pursuit.

However, the vast majority of southerners led lives filled with far more work than play. The leisured lives of the colonial elite were supported by the labor of poor English people and, increasingly, African slaves. Poor whites participated in many of the same leisure activities that the wealthy planters did, albeit in more limited ways. Militia muster days in particular provided an opportunity for men of different social statuses to drink and engage in sport. A wide range of white men also hunted and fished. Such occasions were hardly socially leveling; indeed, leisure served to reinforce hierarchical relationships between white men.

As slavery increasingly replaced indentured servitude at the end of the seventeenth century, African slaves were explicitly excluded from English leisure life. So instead they developed a distinctive hybrid leisure life that mixed diverse African customs of music, dance, and storytelling with European influences like Christianity. Slaves carefully protected their limited leisure time, and they used their distinct cultural practices to create and transmit a distinct social identity that denied the legitimacy of racial bondage. In the colonial South, then, leisure was used to create relationships of social inclusion and exclusion, as well as to both reinforce and subvert dominance, in what were the most explicitly hierarchical colonial societies.

Leisure practices in the middle colonies were shaped by the region's dual identity as the most commercial and the most diverse British colonies. The wealthy mercantile elite of port cities like Philadelphia and New York came closest to emulating London society. They spent their time in coffeehouses, formed private clubs and philosophical societies, and established suburban pleasure grounds for horse races and picnics. The concentration of urban wealth meant that theater thrived in New York, though it was slowed in Philadelphia by the opposition of the Quaker leadership. In rural areas the Scotch-Irish, Germans, and Dutch lived, worked, and played in distinct, tight-knit ethnic communities. Leisure in these communities followed patterns similar to those of rural New England: leisure time revolved around the religious calendar and the rhythms of the agricultural year. For example, the Scotch-Irish Presbyterian religious year was centered on the Lord's Supper, a weeklong late-summer communion that combined religious services with feasting. And all rural communities in the middle colonies held bees, barn raisings, sporting contests, and other events that combined collective labor and leisure. Although specific leisure practices varied from one community to the next, they were all characterized by the close integration of work and play.

Industrialization and the Creation of Leisure Time.

Beginning in the early nineteenth century, the northern economy began a gradual but wide-ranging Industrial Revolution that fundamentally reshaped the relationship between work and leisure. If colonial societies had been characterized by a close integration of leisure, work, religion, and politics, then the industrializing society of the nineteenth-century North segregated these activities into different parts of the day, week, and year. The landscape of American leisure was transformed as a result.

Industrialization remade space as it moved production off small farms and out of family workshops and into mills and factories. Men and women led more and more distinct lives: men left the home to work and when they returned expected it to be a space of retreat and relaxation, whereas women continued to mix work and leisure in the same domestic setting. Industrialization shifted work to towns and cities, leading to unprecedented urbanization in the years after 1820. Many Americans left the rural communities that had been the context for their work and leisure lives for generations.

The regulation of time was also fundamental to industrialization. Industries deployed new machinery and division of labor to achieve efficiency and scale, and this required a workforce that was reliable and focused during extended working hours. Workers could no longer mix labor with socializing, drinking, and play; more and more, these leisure activities were confined to off-hours. Factories made this new labor discipline possible, and as a result workers' days were increasingly structured by the factory bell, which demarcated work hours from leisure hours. For workingmen, these leisure hours were often spent in homosocial leisure spaces like taverns and theaters. All but the poorest workingwomen generally left the industrial workforce upon marriage, so although their young adulthoods could be shaped by sharply distinguished leisure time, their adult lives were often lived according to more preindustrial patterns. These women integrated leisure with labor through shopping, visiting, children's recreation, and crafting, as well as by orchestrating family leisure activities at home. This industrialization of time and space was a gradual and halting process; although it began as early as the 1790s in New England, bosses struggled to purge leisure practices from working hours throughout the nineteenth century.

Indeed, as the slow spread of industrial discipline implies, many workers chafed under its demands. One important rallying point for labor resistance was the protection of leisure time. Skilled male workers began to win the right to ten-hour workdays in the 1840s. Protections for the poor women and children who increasingly worked as machine operatives were slower to come; in many states, child labor was not regulated until late in the century. In the 1880s and 1890s, nascent industrial labor unions began to fight for an eight-hour workday: their slogan "Eight hours for what we will" claimed the right to a workday that would also allow eight hours of daily leisure. This goal was achieved industry by industry in the early twentieth century, culminating in national legislation during the New Deal. The sharp division between labor and leisure that is characteristic of industrial society was created by the interplay between the logic of industrial production and workers' demands for time of their own.

The managerial classes were not eager to concede control over their workers' hard-won leisure time. They were concerned that

the divide between labor and leisure had created opportunities for working people to enjoy themselves in ways that were detrimental to their productivity. In the 1820s, efforts to regulate workers' leisure time had religious overtones, including moral reform, the Sunday-school movement, and antiprostitution action. The most aggressive and successful attempt to control workers' leisure was the temperance movement, which sought to convince men to forswear drinking and to close down taverns, saloons, and other spaces where workingmen socialized. Elite women, seeking to enclose men's leisure practices within female-gendered domestic space, often served as the foot soldiers in these moral-reform movements. By midcentury the middle class began to reimagine sports: instead of being a local recreation often closely tied to drinking and gambling, sports became a venue in which participants built healthy bodies and developed disciplined minds. As a result, gymnastics and ball sports became more organized and rule-bound, and industrial elites sought to transform workers' informal games into useful recreations.

Beginning with the literary and musical societies of the mills of Lowell, Massachusetts, in the 1820s, wealthy industrialists also sought to provide alternative "rational recreation" to tempt their workers away from drinking and gambling. This movement accelerated in the 1850s, with urban leaders pushing for the construction of parks and the establishment of YMCAs, and reached its pinnacle at the turn of the century with Andrew Carnegie's massive public-library campaign and the Progressive movement's push for playgrounds and organized recreation through settlement houses. This tension between workers' desire to guard their own leisure time and their bosses' desire to make it productive remained throughout the nineteenth century.

Urban Leisure in an Industrial Society.

Leisure took multiple forms in industrial and commercial cities. Middle-class families, as well as those who aspired to that status, spent more and more of their leisure time at home, which they imagined as a domestic "haven in a heartless world" with the wife and mother at its center. They retreated into the parlors of refined townhouses in the 1830s and 1840s and, in the postbellum period, increasingly into garden suburbs. Family life centered on reading, children's play, and newly domesticated holidays like Christmas and the Fourth of July. Cycling became a family sports fad in the 1890s, which made it the first sporting activity that encouraged women's participation as well as men's. In each of these cases, the Victorian middle class's emphasis on domesticity turned what had formerly been homosocial leisure pursuits into opportunities for family togetherness, supposedly insulated from the competitive pressures of market society.

However, the middle-class family's retreat from the market was more rhetorical than actual, because it was balanced by a much more powerful countervailing trend: the commercialization of leisure. The same social and economic processes that revolutionized the production of industrial goods also transformed Americans' pursuit of leisure. The first great entrepreneur of commercial leisure was P. T. Barnum, who built the craft of traveling showmanship into a commercial enterprise between the 1830s and the 1850s. He revolutionized museums, theaters, and circuses, transforming them from family operations into highly organized businesses that competed on a national and international scale. Despite the middle class's rhetoric of domesticity, Americans increasingly purchased entertainment in the commercial marketplace—purchased it from sophisticated business organizations that profited handsomely from the provision of leisure.

Although Barnum was the best-known entertainment entrepreneur of the nineteenth century, his techniques were widely applied. Early in the nineteenth century, entrepreneurs in towns featuring mineral springs began establishing commercial tourist destinations, and by the 1870s and 1880s a potent commercial combination of railroads, hotel operators, and guidebooks publishers had built an extensive tourist infrastructure designed to provide summer leisure to a national middle class. By the early twentieth century, closer, cheaper destinations began providing weekend recreation to working people, most famously Coney Island in Brooklyn, New York. At Coney Island and its imitators, leisure entrepreneurs constructed fantasylands that combined the latest mechanical and electrical technology with the techniques of mass entertainment in order to sell exuberant leisure to a mass audience.

Commercial leisure opportunities also multiplied within cities themselves. In the 1880s the antebellum theatrical traditions of minstrelsy and variety entertainment became commercial vaudeville, which strung together short acts into low-priced, on-demand entertainment that was widely available through the 1920s and 1930s. After it was formalized in the 1840s and 1850s, baseball became professionalized and transformed into commercial entertainment in the 1870s and 1880s. In the same decades, dance halls began to provide opportunities for heterosocial leisure to young working people, which led to a growing dance craze in the 1910s and 1920s. These commercial leisure venues became the dominant places where working people spent their hard-won leisure time.

Although Barnum's circuses and the big-time vaudeville circuits successfully commercialized live performance, it was the birth of electronic media that assured the ascendancy of commercial leisure. Moving pictures found their first mass audience in kinetoscope parlors and as entr'actes for vaudeville houses in the 1890s, but by the early twentieth century they became a dominant form of commercial leisure in their own right. Movies functioned both as cheap, quick diversions, in nickelodeons and other casual neighborhood spaces, and also as special-occasion entertainment in the movie palaces that sprang up in the 1910s. The relatively low cost and easy reproducibility of electronic media made them ideal for the provision of mass leisure to urban people across the class spectrum.

Commercially produced leisure was not immediately and uniformly embraced by all Americans at the turn of the century, however. Some groups resisted what they worried would be its homogenizing effects; well into the twentieth century, urban immigrant working-class communities, for example, maintained an annual cycle of events, often organized around saint's days and national anniversaries. These communities also supported strong ethnic associations that organized fairs and teams outside the leisure marketplace. Other groups were partially or completely excluded from mainstream leisure. Since it took place in public spaces like boardwalks, dance halls, theaters, and ballparks, commercial leisure reflected the boundaries that contemporaries drew around public participation. Leisure crowds were generally heterosocial, so women's participation could be fraught with danger because of the historic connection between women in public and prostitution. Commercial leisure venues were often sharply segregated by race, in both the North and the South, so African Americans created their own forms of commercial leisure, particularly jazz music. Alternative leisure spaces sprang up in black enclaves such as New York City's Harlem and certain neighborhoods of Chicago, Atlanta, and Los Angeles, which allowed musicians and patrons to avoid direct encounters with the indignities of segregation.

Whites had a complicated relationship to segregated leisure space. On the one hand, community leaders feared that commercial leisure would erode local and ethnic traditions and identities. On the other hand, participation in whites-only commercial leisure helped consolidate the white racial identity of first- and second-generation immigrants from southern and eastern Europe. Meanwhile the leisure industry increased the prominence of African American entrepreneurs and entertainers as white patrons sought out black leisure spaces, especially jazz clubs and boxing venues, which they regarded as "exotic." Thus the great commercial venues of the turn of the century brought together a public that was inclusive and exclusive at the same time.

From Producer to Consumer Society. Providers of commercial leisure in the nineteenth century faced a fundamental challenge in marketing recreation and relaxation. The culture that grew out of the Industrial Revolution was structured to create a society of efficient producers; indeed, this was precisely the subtext of the struggle for control over working people's leisure time. By the twentieth century, American business faced a new challenge in fostering enough consumption to keep the nation's factories—and leisure venues—working full-time.

Early twentieth-century mass-leisure phenomena like Coney Island and movie palaces began the process of legitimizing large-scale purchasing of pleasure. In the 1920s, the explosive popularity of jazz music and its associated dance styles, combined with the novel technology of the radio, drove an unprecedented expansion of leisure consumption. The construction of a consumer leisure culture was slowed by Prohibition, which drove commercial leisure venues underground and into the hands of organized crime, and also by the Depression. Widespread unemployment made commercial leisure unavailable and unappealing to the large numbers of people who needed more work, not more free time. But during the Depression, seeds were planted that after World War II flowered into a culture of leisure consumption. Organized labor took advantage of the economic crisis to build vacation time into labor contracts, and deferred consumption from the 1930s and 1940s created an extended period of postwar economic expansion that provided even the working class with disposable income for leisure.

Like many aspects of postwar society, leisure became increasingly family-centered. But postwar families did not simply resuscitate the Victorian middle class's sentimental domesticity, supposedly insulated from the immoral market. Instead, they embraced the market for consumer leisure and used it to enhance family togetherness. One of the archetypal technologies of postwar life was the television. Like radio before it in the 1920s, early television of the 1940s brought communities together around evening broadcasts, because sets were rare and expensive. But also like its broadcast predecessor, the proliferation of TV quickly had the opposite effect, isolating nuclear families in their living rooms and supplanting public leisure activities. This process moved much more quickly with television than it had with radio: television achieved dominant market penetration within a decade after the war. The market for consumer leisure moved out of public spaces and into the private living rooms of suburban nuclear families.

The other archetypal technology of mid-century leisure was the automobile. Cars became ubiquitous in the 1920s, and the postwar suburbs were built on this ubiquity. They enabled the construction of sprawling subdivisions in which houses had private backyards and basement rec rooms: there families could consume the fruits of the mass-leisure industry, like backyard barbecues and TV Westerns, in comfort and privacy. Cars fostered the replacement of downtown shopping districts and movie palaces with privately controlled malls and drive-ins. Cars also fundamentally reshaped tourism, because they decoupled vacations from train schedules and allowed families to bring their private domestic space on the road with them. They created a new industry of roadside attractions and brought vacationers to giant new theme parks like Disneyland, which opened in 1955. The automobile made a wider array of leisure experiences available to a broader swath of the population, but they hastened the decline of the great public commercial leisure spaces of the early twentieth century and replaced them with privatized spaces that insulated individual nuclear families from each other and from the wider world.

Generations of Leisure: Youth Culture and the Rise of Retirement.

Alongside and within the postwar culture of family togetherness, an alternative leisure culture based on generational segregation grew in importance. The term "youth culture" was coined during World War II to describe a phenomenon that had existed since the turn of the century, in dance halls and at Coney Island for working-class youth and, for young members of the middle class, at college fraternities and football games. But as the coining of the neologism suggests, youth culture achieved particular vibrancy and cultural power in the 1950s and 1960s. Buttressed by the increased discretionary spending power of teenagers, postwar youth culture formed in middle-class high schools and working-class street gangs. By the mid-1950s both of these youth cultures became organized around the new hybrid musical form of rock and roll. Like previous generations of white youth, especially during the jazz craze of the 1920s, postwar white youth embraced and appropriated African American forms of music and dance in order to declare generational independence. By the late 1950s, however, rock and roll was largely produced and consumed by whites, and its African American originators had largely been sidelined from what had become a booming business. Nevertheless, it retained its association with racial transgression, so it loomed large in the consciousness of adults for whom it represented a distinct youth culture that threatened the coherence of the nuclear family.

By the late 1960s, however, this generational leisure culture had triumphed. With the coming-of-age of the first baby boomers, the youth counterculture radically expanded the boundaries of socially accepted leisure practices, with its most radical members openly embracing drugs and recreational sex as legitimate and even valuable forms of leisure. Although most young people of the late 1960s did not, as Timothy Leary put it, "turn on, tune in, drop out," the commercial exploitation of countercultural style effectively cemented the idea that leisure time was to be spent in the company of peers, not family.

By the 1970s and 1980s the parents of the baby boomers had wholeheartedly embraced the practices of peer-group leisure. Supported by social programs like Social Security and Medicare, as well as by the generous corporate welfare programs of the prosperous postwar period, middle-class retirees increasingly viewed the years after age sixty-five as a distinct period devoted to full-time leisure. Unlike earlier generations of retirees, who had usually remained in their old neighborhoods near their children, prosperous members of the World War II generation often relocated to communities dedicated to the

leisure pursuits of the elderly, in warm-weather states like Florida and Arizona. There they played tennis and golf, traveled extensively, and constructed social networks consisting almost entirely of their peers. Although many aging Americans could not afford to devote entire decades to leisure in a resort-like environment, at least some degree of leisured retirement was available to an increasing number of Americans, thanks to postwar prosperity and generous government support. Thus by the late twentieth century, leisure time was often spent largely with peers according to a life cycle dictated by the rhythms of the late capitalist economy.

[*See also* **Amusement Parks and Theme Parks; Circuses; Coffeehouses and Coffee; Courtship and Dating; Dance Halls; Disney Amusement Parks; Film; Gambling; Health and Fitness; Holidays and Festivals; Life Stages; Militias, Early American; Music; Parades; Radio; Reading; Retirement Communities; Social Class; Sports, Amateur; Sports, Professional; Taverns and Bars; Television; Theater; Tourism and Travel; Vaudeville; Work;** *and* **YMCA and YWCA.**]

BIBLIOGRAPHY

Aron, Cindy S. *Working at Play: A History of Vacations in the United States.* New York: Oxford University Press, 1999.

Butsch, Richard, ed. *For Fun and Profit: The Transformation of Leisure into Consumption.* Philadelphia: Temple University Press, 1990.

Daniels, Bruce Colin. *Puritans at Play: Leisure and Recreation in Colonial New England.* New York: St. Martin's, 1995.

Grover, Kathryn, ed. *Hard at Play: Leisure in America, 1840–1940.* Amherst: University of Massachusetts Press, 1992.

Kasson, John F. *Amusing the Million: Coney Island at the Turn of the Century.* New York: Hill and Wang, 1978.

Mazur, Zbigniew. *The Power of Play: Leisure, Recreation, and Cultural Hegemony in Colonial Virginia*. Lublin, Poland: Wydawn. UMCS, 2010.

Mumford, Kevin J. *Interzones: Black/White Sex Districts in Chicago and New York in the Early Twentieth Century*. New York: Columbia University Press, 1997.

Nasaw, David. *Going Out: The Rise and Fall of Public Amusements*. New York: Basic Books, 1993.

Peiss, Kathy Lee. *Cheap Amusements: Working Women and Leisure in Turn-of-the-Century New York*. Philadelphia: Temple University Press, 1986.

Rader, Benjamin G. *American Sports: From the Age of Folk Games to the Age of Televised Sports*. 6th ed. Upper Saddle River, N.J.: Pearson, 2009.

Will B. Mackintosh

LESBIAN, GAY, BISEXUAL, AND TRANSGENDER RIGHTS MOVEMENT

See **Gay and Lesbian Rights Movement.**

LETTERS AND LETTER WRITING

Letter writing, and the technologies and institutions on which it depended, blossomed in the eighteenth-century American colonial era and the early republic era. Although letter writing and literacy had expanded from the Renaissance onward, in the eighteenth century letter writing became newly accessible not only to middling-status and rural men but also to women and children. Indeed, learning how to write properly became nothing less than an obsession among the upwardly mobile. Letter-writing manuals, which were directed at the middling sort, were among the most often reprinted books in eighteenth-century America and could even be obtained through subscription libraries in most colonies by midcentury. They contained advice on the appropriate content of letters to different recipients, on correct address, spelling, grammar, and even on how to fold and seal letters.

The eighteenth century saw a dramatic rise both in population and wealth and also in trade and travel around the British Empire. More people were moving to more places, more families were separated by great distance, and transatlantic export and import required close communication (and trust) between merchants who could be thousands of miles apart. It was in this time of rapid expansion that people increasingly turned to letter writing as a means of retaining the bonds of family and community. Furthermore, the increased need for the British government to control its colonial territories, as well as the imperial wars of the eighteenth century, further highlighted the necessity of closer communications. By midcentury the volume of transatlantic and intercolonial letter exchange had prompted the institution of packet services among England, New York City, South Carolina's port Charleston, and Kingston, Jamaica, which cut the time in which letters traversed the Atlantic to just over four weeks.

Letter writing did more than just connect people who were increasingly far from home and acquaintances: it also revolutionized the physical lives of those who could access it, and it created a huge gulf between those who could write letters and those who could not. To write a correct letter in this period, one needed not only paper—higher-quality paper was whiter than cheaper materials and therefore asserted the wealth of the writer—but also ink, inkstands, quills, desks, lamps, seals and wax, and manuals or schooling in letter-writing etiquette, as well as connections with people who might carry the letters onward.

Although these materials were more accessible than they had been in the seventeenth century, they were still out of the reach of those who were disadvantaged by social class or race. Recent scholarship has shown that letter writing grew in tandem with, and consolidated the power of, the middle class, and in so doing it placed those who were not wealthy or literate enough to write into an even more subordinate position. The inequities that were already evident in colonial American society meant that very few African Americans, for example, could learn to write or obtain the necessary letter-writing materials, and therefore most could not use letter writing as a means of creating networks and presenting themselves as agents. Those who did acquire these skills were notable in overcoming such seemingly insurmountable difficulties.

[*See also* **Atlantic World; Communication Networks; Everyday Life;** *and* **Reading.**]

BIBLIOGRAPHY

Bannet, Eve Tavor. *Empire of Letters: Letter Manuals and Transatlantic Correspondence, 1688–1820.* Cambridge, U.K.: Cambridge University Press, 2005.

Dierks, Konstantin. *In My Power: Letter Writing and Communications in Early America.* Philadelphia: University of Pennsylvania Press, 2009.

Pearsall, Sarah M. S. *Atlantic Families: Lives and Letters in the Later Eighteenth Century.* Oxford: Oxford University Press, 2008.

C. Ruth Watterson

LEWIS AND CLARK EXPEDITION

In a message to Congress in January 1803, President Thomas Jefferson called for an expedition up the Missouri River and west to the Pacific. With the Louisiana Purchase later that year, the project took on even greater significance. Jefferson chose the army captain Meriwether Lewis (1774–1809) to lead the expedition. Lewis selected as his partner a fellow officer, William Clark (1770–1838). More than forty men, including York, Clark's slave, composed the Corps of Discovery as it started up the Missouri in a keelboat and three canoes on 14 May 1804. By late October the expedition had reached present-day central North Dakota, where the members established their winter quarters, Fort Mandan.

In April 1805, Lewis and Clark sent the keelboat downriver before resuming their journey west, accompanied by a young Shoshone woman, Sacagawea (1786?–1812), and her French Canadian husband. They reached the source of the Missouri and advanced up a tributary, the Jefferson, before having to abandon their boats. Using horses obtained from Sacagawea's Shoshones, the expedition crossed the Continental Divide at Lemhi Pass and surmounted the Bitterroot Mountains via the Lolo Trail. At the Clearwater River they entrusted their horses to the Nez Percés, built canoes, and floated down the Clearwater, Snake, and Columbia Rivers to the Pacific, which they reached on 18 November 1805. They named their winter quarters Fort Clatsop.

In late March 1806 the corps started home. At the mouth of Lolo Creek the expedition split, Clark's contingent returning as they had come and Lewis's group advancing directly east to the Great Falls of the Missouri, where the units were reunited. On 23 September 1806, after an absence of twenty-eight months, the Corps of Discovery arrived at Saint Louis.

The Lewis and Clark expedition, which produced extensive published records and journals, was one of the most successful in the annals of world exploration. It destroyed the concept of an all-water route to the Pacific and helped fix in the public mind the vast extent of the Louisiana Purchase territory and the Pacific Northwest.

[*See also* **Early Republic Era; Exploration, Conquest, and Settlement in North America; Frontier, The; Native American History and Culture,** *subentry on* **1800 to 1900;** *and* **West, The.**]

BIBLIOGRAPHY

Ambrose, Stephen E. *Undaunted Courage: Meriwether Lewis, Thomas Jefferson, and the Opening of the American West.* New York: Simon & Schuster, 1996.

Moulton, Gary E., ed. *The Journals of the Lewis and Clark Expedition.* 13 vols. Lincoln: University of Nebraska Press, 1983–2001.

Richard A. Bartlett

LIBERIA, COLONIZATION OF

In December 1816 a group of men interested in addressing America's ongoing dilemmas of race and slavery met in Washington, D.C., to form the American Colonization Society (ACS). The new organization's purpose was, in its own words, "to promote and execute a plan for colonizing (with their consent) the Free People of Color residing in our Country, in Africa, or such other places as Congress shall deem most expedient." Although it had a single goal—namely, the removal of free African Americans to Africa—the motivations of the society's members were quite diverse.

There were slaveholders among the founders of the ACS who feared that free blacks set a bad example for their slaves—that is, they made slaves aspire to be free—and wanted the number of free African Americans in the country reduced. Actually, the free black population, largely because of the ending of slavery in northern states following the American Revolution, had grown in size more rapidly than the slave population had. In 1790 there were 59,000 free blacks in the United States and 700,000 slaves. In 1810 the slave population had increased only 70 percent, from 700,000 to 1.2 million people, while the free black population had increased from 59,000 to 186,000, a 215 percent increase for the same twenty-year period. Slaveholding members of the ACS insisted that the organization not mention general emancipation of slaves or even limited abolition in its charter. The ACS, not wanting to alienate white southern supporters, obliged.

In addition to slaveholders, the ACS attracted people who were genuinely interested in ameliorating the conditions of blacks, both slaves and free people of color. Some simply did not believe that free blacks or liberated bondspeople would ever be accepted by a majority of whites as fellow citizens sharing the same rights and immunities and thus thought it best to relocate them outside the United States. There were those members who saw the organization as an instrument for liberating slaves, and a number of slave masters eventually agreed to free their slaves for the express purpose of sending them to the ACS's colony of Liberia on the West African coast.

From its founding in 1822 until the end of the century, about sixteen thousand American blacks settled in Liberia. The vast majority were from southern states, such as Virginia, Georgia, North Carolina, and Maryland. Additionally, about six thousand African recaptives—people rescued by the U.S. Navy from (now illegal) transatlantic slave ships—were settled in Liberia during the nineteenth century. In general the conditions of life were difficult for American immigrants in Liberia. The vast majority of people who migrated were poor, and many had been slaves prior to leaving the United States. Few were prepared for life in a tropical frontier where ailments of various sorts flourished, including a virulent strain of malaria that killed 20 percent of all immigrants during the first generation of colonization. Along with disease, Liberia's founding was marked by incessant conflicts with indigenous Africans, who were dispossessed of land and sovereignty. Ironically, although the African American settlers had come to Liberia for freedoms and rights that were denied to them in the United States, the settlers constructed a colony (which became an independent republic in 1847) that largely excluded Africans—whom many settlers believed to be uncivilized and heathen—from the political and social life of Liberia.

The voices, aspirations, and goals of most Liberian immigrants have not been preserved in the historical record, with the exception of major political figures such as Lott Carey, Joseph Jenkins Roberts, and John Russwurm. However, the records of the ACS do contain a rich array of letters written by selected immigrants that provide a window into their experiences. Coursing through much of this correspondence is the notion of diaspora— that is, a salient sense that blacks in America felt that they had been uprooted, via the slave trade, from some pristine ancestral origin. Many immigrant writers portrayed Africa as their natural homeland and wrote in romantic ways about the continent and its people. Only after experiencing the hardships of life in tropical Africa did some become disabused of notions that they were "black" or "African" in any essential way.

In the United States, the idea of colonizing Liberia ultimately had limited appeal to African Americans or whites who were dedicated to the abolitionist movement. Their opposition to the Liberian experiment was further galvanized by the prominence of slaveholders among the ACS's supporters, as well as the halfhearted support that the U.S. government sporadically provided for Liberian colonization. At any rate, for some African Americans, Liberia proved a potent foil for imagining their identities in ways that connected them politically and psychically to Africa and its far-flung diasporic progeny.

[*See also* African American Emigration *and* Colonization Movement, African.]

BIBLIOGRAPHY

Burin, Eric. *Slavery and the Peculiar Solution: A History of the American Colonization Society.* Gainesville: University Press of Florida, 2005. A recent account of the ACS.

Clegg, Claude A., III. *The Price of Liberty: African Americans and the Making of Liberia.* Chapel Hill: University of North Carolina Press, 2004. Examines the ramifications of Liberian colonization on both sides of the Atlantic.

Shick, Tom W. *Behold the Promised Land: A History of Afro-American Settler Society in Nineteenth-Century Liberia.* Baltimore: Johns Hopkins University Press, 1980. Explores the social contours of the communities constructed by African American immigrants in Liberia.

Staudenraus, P. J. *The African Colonization Movement, 1816–1865.* New York: Columbia University Press, 1961. Though dated, this is the seminal study of Liberian colonization from the perspective of the ACS and its supporters.

Claude A. Clegg III

LIBRARIES

Though the earliest colonists brought a few books with them and established small libraries, it was not until 1731 that Benjamin

Franklin founded the Library Company of Philadelphia, the precursor of today's public library. An apprentice, he persuaded other young men of modest means who were interested in self-improvement to pool their money to buy books that none could afford alone. Other social libraries followed, spurred by an understanding of the importance of an informed electorate to the new republic. Library founders sought not only to increase knowledge but to promote virtue. Workers, brought to the cities by the Industrial Revolution, founded mechanics' or mercantile libraries to educate themselves and to provide wholesome leisure pursuits. Self-education and constructive use of leisure continued to create an impetus for libraries and the move toward tax-supported, truly public ones. New York State allowed taxation for school libraries beginning in the 1830s, but Boston Public Library became the first tax-supported public library in 1854. Such libraries then grew up rapidly, numbering 257 when the U.S. Bureau of Education published its 1876 special report, *Public Libraries in the United States of America: Their History, Condition, and Management.*

The special report was one of several events that marked 1876 as pivotal in the growth of libraries. Melvil Dewey, an ambitious Amherst College librarian, published *A Classification and Subject Index, for Cataloguing and Arranging the Books and Pamphlets of a Library*, first laying out his famed and ubiquitous Dewey decimal classification. The first journal pertaining to libraries, aptly called *Library Journal*, was born. And Dewey, with Boston Public Library's Justin Winsor, R. R. Bowker of *Publishers Weekly*, and Charles Ammi Cutter, the librarian of the Boston Athenaeum and an author of the 1876 special report, together founded the American Library Association (ALA). Since that time the ALA has had a profound influence on defining which reading

is "appropriate" and how the public library fosters literacy.

Advancing the public library as a means of uplift for the masses, the founders of the profession of librarianship encouraged the reading of useful nonfiction; fiction they regarded as frivolous or worse. Dewey recruited young women for library work, touting their greater manual dexterity and attention to detail. In 1887 at Columbia in New York City, where he was college librarian, Dewey founded the first school to educate librarians. Debates over the role of women in librarianship have persisted in the profession ever since, with some arguing, among other things, that their prevalence has kept salaries and status low.

Philanthropy and Expansion of Service.

Not only librarians, but philanthropists as well, saw libraries as important to the development of individuals as productive citizens. Most prominent was the steel magnate Andrew Carnegie. Self-educated through libraries himself, between 1886 and 1920 he provided more than $40 million (well over $1 billion in 2011 dollars) to build some 1,679 libraries in U.S. communities that would agree to support them. He was not alone. In Wisconsin, for example, aided by the Free Library Commission and its indefatigable Lutie Stearns, the lumber baron and state senator J. H. Stout funded traveling libraries starting in 1896 in an effort to reach rural readers of all ages with "wholesome" books. Women's clubs in many states joined comparable efforts, instigating the development of libraries. Reading rooms founded by women's groups became Carnegie libraries in some communities as a result of the advocacy of those groups, who pushed local officials to agree to the required support. A later, less widespread effort to develop literacy through libraries was that of the Julius Rosenwald Fund, established by a founder of Sears,

Roebuck. In addition to building schools for African Americans in the South, from the 1920s to the 1940s the fund supported library collections for these schools, where reading materials had been virtually nonexistent.

Although service to African Americans was rarely adequate anywhere in the country in the first half of the twentieth century, city libraries worked hard to provide services to immigrants. Library programs for immigrants and their children ranged from English and citizenship classes to early literacy instruction and talks about important current events. Librarians also used adult-education programs to engage all citizens in public issues. During World Wars I and II, libraries conducted book drives for servicemen under the aegis of the ALA, provided information about such subjects as blackouts and rationing, and even purged books in German or those that gave a favorable impression of the enemy. The use of libraries skyrocketed during the Depression, even as resources shrank. Through New Deal programs, however, librarians delivered books to rural communities by bookmobiles, rowboats, and even horseback. When the 1950 Public Library Inquiry revealed that most library users were white and middle class, some librarians questioned whether they should strive to serve the entire community. Others felt that they should and thus engaged in outreach to underserved groups and lobbied for federal legislation that would help rural communities receive library services.

Politics. In the 1930s, libraries increased their promotion of discussion of controversial issues, and as they tried to keep up with trends in literary publishing, it was inevitable that libraries would become contested sites. In 1939 the ALA resolved that libraries should collect materials of many points of view, and the concept of librarians as defenders of

"good" literature and readers' morals began to shift. In 1948 the ALA revised its Library Bill of Rights (first adopted in 1939), pledging to fight censorship of library materials, and it resisted the efforts of so-called committees who exposed un-American activities and other groups across the country to label or remove books considered pro-Communist. With the 1953 publication by librarians and publishers of the *Statement on the Freedom to Read*, libraries cemented their commitment to intellectual freedom. In the 1960s, groups seeking to restrict library materials focused their efforts on policing "unsuitable" materials for children and young adults, while libraries continued to assert the necessity of having a wide range of materials.

Economic constraints have tested libraries in the twenty-first century, even as they have responded to public needs such as Internet training and job-search assistance, early literacy, and support for homeschoolers and book clubbers, as well as providing a wide range of community-building activities. Loss of tax dollars, coupled with the rise of digital resources, has forced libraries to make difficult choices in order to continue to provide their communities with access to materials.

[*See also* **Education; Philanthropy;** *and* **Reading.**]

BIBLIOGRAPHY

Garrison, Dee. *Apostles of Culture: The Public Librarian and American Society, 1876–1920*. New York: Free Press; London: Collier Macmillan, 1979. Argues that women's dominance has been detrimental to the library's role in society.

Pawley, Christine. *Reading Places: Literacy, Democracy, and the Public Library in Cold War America*. Amherst: University of Massachusetts Press, 2010. Examines the contested nature of the library and the reading it provides through a case study of an experimental regional library service.

Robbins, Louise S. *The Dismissal of Miss Ruth Brown: Civil Rights, Censorship, and the American Library.* Norman: University of Oklahoma Press, 2000. Explores how Cold War tensions, civil rights, and censorship came together at a crucial time in American library history.

Van Slyck, Abigail A. *Free to All: Carnegie Libraries and American Culture, 1890–1920.* Chicago: University of Chicago Press, 1995. Exposes the complicated history of Carnegie libraries and the communities that wanted or did not want them.

Wiegand, Wayne A. *Irrepressible Reformer: A Biography of Melvil Dewey.* Chicago: American Library Association, 1996. Reveals a founding father of librarianship with all his warts.

Louise S. Robbins

LIFE EXPECTANCY

One of the greatest achievements of the contemporary era has been the reduction of death rates and the prolongation of human life. One way of summarizing this mortality transition is life expectancy, which expresses the average number of years of life remaining to a person at some age, often at birth. This measure is derived from life tables and can be calculated from data at a point in time for persons of different ages (period life expectancy) or by following the same groups of people over time as they age (cohort life expectancy). The data used usually come from census counts by age and sex, as well as from vital statistics of deaths, also by age and sex. But other data, such as genealogies and family reconstitutions, can be used, as can other methods.

Life expectancy in the United States has evolved through several stages. During the early colonial period, life expectancy was relatively short, death rates were high and variable, and epidemics of infectious disease were common. Life expectancy at birth generally ranged from twenty to thirty years. By the late seventeenth century, things had begun to improve, and by the late eighteenth century, mortality conditions were quite favorable by world standards. Thomas R. Malthus commented in 1798 that mortality conditions were quite benign in the new United States and had been for a while. Mortality was lowest in New England, with life expectancy at birth, abbreviated as "e(0)," at 35–60 years; was more severe in the middle colonies, where the e(0) was 30–45 years; and was highest in the South, where the e(0) was 25–35 years. Gradually, epidemic diseases such as measles and smallpox became endemic and joined malaria, dysentery, pneumonia, and bronchitis and tuberculosis as major causes of endemic, baseline mortality. Infectious and parasitic diseases accounted for most deaths and continued to do so until the twentieth century, when degenerative diseases such as cancer, cardiovascular diseases, and diabetes became dominant.

The Mortality Transition. The sustained mortality transition did not commence in the United States until about the 1870s. Life expectancy likely reached a high point in the late eighteenth century and then declined until the later nineteenth century. For example, genealogical data yield an expectation of life at age 10 (abbreviated "e(10)") of almost 57 years for white males in 1790–1794, but that expectation had declined to 48 years by 1855–1859. These results are supported by data on human stature, another indicator of physical well-being. Heights of Civil War military recruits, West Point cadets, college students, and others (mostly males) declined from those born in the 1830s to those born in the 1870s, consistent with a deteriorating disease environment. Information on specific cities with adequate vital statistics (New York, Boston, Philadelphia, Baltimore, New Orleans) reveals constant or rising mortality prior to the Civil War, with substantial mortality peaks as a result of cholera—which first appeared in the United States in 1832—typhoid, and yellow fever.

During the nineteenth century, sources of data improved. The U.S. Census, a federal mandate, was taken decennially from 1790. Questions about mortality in the year prior to the Census were asked in the Censuses of 1850–1900. But collection of vital statistics was left to state and local governments and consequently was uneven. In 1842, Massachusetts became the first state to commence comprehensive registration of births, deaths, and marriages. Quality was good by about 1855. Several states followed suit, but in 1900 the Death Registration Area was formed with only ten states and the District of Columbia. The entire United States was not covered until 1933.

By the middle of the nineteenth century there is enough information to make reasonable national estimates of life expectancy. By 1850, $e(0)$ for the white population was about 38 years, $e(10)$ was about 47 years, and the infant mortality rate (deaths below age one per 1,000 live births) stood at 217. The sustained mortality transition for the nation as a whole began only in the 1870s. The $e(0)$ for whites overall changed little between 1850 and 1880 and then began to rise from about 40 years in 1880 to about 52 years in 1900, about 69 years in 1950, and about 78 years in 2006. Much of the change in the first half of the twentieth century was caused by the continued decline in infectious and parasitic diseases. Infectious and parasitic diseases declined from 43 percent of total deaths in 1900/02 to just 7.5 percent in 1949/51.

A considerable portion of the increase in expectation of life in the later twentieth century was the result of improvements in longevity at older ages. For example, expectation of life at age 60 improved from 17 years in 1949/51 to 22.4 years in 2006.

Variations between Groups. The black population suffered a substantial mortality disadvantage, although blacks were protected somewhat by their more rural residence earlier in the twentieth century. (About 80 percent of the black population lived in rural areas in 1900, in contrast to 58 percent of the white population.) In 1900 the $e(0)$ for blacks was about 20 percent lower than that for whites, and their infant mortality rate was about 54 percent higher. The situation had been even worse around 1850, when blacks, mostly slaves, had an estimated $e(0)$ of 23—40 percent lower than that for whites—and an estimated infant mortality rate of about 350—61 percent higher than that for whites. Although between 1850 and 1900 the absolute differences in the infant mortality rate between blacks and whites had narrowed to about 8 infant deaths per 1,000 live births, the relative difference had grown. The black infant mortality rate, 13.4, was twice as high as that for whites, 5.6. In terms of $e(0)$, by 2006 the difference between whites and blacks had narrowed, though the $e(0)$ for the black population, 73 years, was still five years below that of the white population.

Overall, the United States does not stand well in the world in terms of its ranking of expectation of life and the infant mortality rate. According to World Bank data for 2006, the United States ranked forty-fourth in the world for $e(0)$ and forty-sixth for the infant mortality rate. Even if the whole American population had the same infant mortality rate as the white population (5.6), the rank would improve only to thirty-eighth. The reasons are multiple, but a lack both of widely distributed, basic medical care and of public-health interventions, especially prenatal care, have played a role. Nonetheless, the absolute differences between the United States and the rest of the world are not too large.

In terms of other mortality differentials, women have tended to live longer than men. In 1850, women had an e(0) that was 6 percent higher than that of men, a gap that had narrowed to only about 2 percent by 1900. But women outlived men by almost 7 percent, or five years, by 2006.

Differences between rural people and urban people were historically also large. In the nineteenth century, cities were distinctly less healthy places to live. Around 1830, the e(10) was 51 years in forty-four New England towns, 42 percent higher than the average for Boston, New York City, and Philadelphia (at 35.9 years). By 1900, the probability of a child surviving to age five was 22 percent worse in urban than in rural areas. This urban penalty disappeared by 1920, when the improved public-health programs and investments in urban America overcame the disadvantages of crowding, problems with water supplies and sewerage disposal, food contamination, lack of rubbish removal, and the large influx of immigrants. Among the foreign-born, life expectancy historically had usually been lower than that of native-born whites, partly because the foreign-born tended to have a lower socioeconomic status and partly because they tended to concentrate in urban areas.

Finally, regional variations in mortality were substantial at the first point for which they can be observed for the nation as a whole—around 1900. The lowest mortality areas were in the Midwest, and the highest mortality was found in the South and New England. These regional differences converged during the twentieth century thanks to the spread of public-health programs and medical care.

[*See also* **Demography; Disease; Health and Healing, Eighteenth and Nineteenth Centuries;** *and* **Public Health.**]

BIBLIOGRAPHY

Bell, Felicitie C., Alice H. Wade, and Stephen C. Goss. *Life Tables for the United States Social Security Area 1900–2080.* Actuarial Study No. 107. Baltimore: U.S. Department of Health and Human Services, Social Security Administration, Office of the Actuary, 1992.

Easterlin, Richard A. "The Nature and Causes of the Mortality Revolution." In his *Growth Triumphant: The Twenty-First Century in Historical Perspective,* pp. 69–82. Ann Arbor: University of Michigan Press, 1996.

Haines, Michael R. "The American Population, 1790–1920." In *The Cambridge Economic History of the United States,* vol. 2, edited by Stanley L. Engerman and Robert E. Gallman. Cambridge, U.K.: Cambridge University Press, 1998.

Haines, Michael R., ed. "Vital Statistics." In *Historical Statistics of the United States,* edited by Susan Carter, Scott Sigmund Gartner, Michael R. Haines, Alan L. Olmstead, Richard Sutch, and Gavin Wright, vol. 1, chapter Ab. Millennial ed. Cambridge, U.K.: Cambridge University Press, 2006.

Kunitz, Stephen J. "Mortality Change in America, 1620–1920." *Human Biology* 56, no. 3 (September 1984): 559–582.

Pope, Clayne L. "Adult Mortality in America before 1900: A View from Family Histories." In *Strategic Factors in Nineteenth Century American Economic History: A Volume to Honor Robert W. Fogel,* edited by Claudia Goldin and Hugh Rockoff, pp. 267–296. Chicago: University of Chicago Press, 1992.

Preston, Samuel H., and Michael R. Haines. *Fatal Years: Child Mortality in Late Nineteenth-Century America.* Princeton, N.J.: Princeton University Press, 1991.

Michael R. Haines

LIFE STAGES

Research on the historical meaning and importance of different life stages is relatively recent. From the 1960s on, a growing interest in family history resulted in studies of the evolution of childhood, the progression to adolescence and young adulthood, and the transition from adulthood to old age. The development of specialized subfields devoted to the status and roles of the youngest and oldest members of society produced a greater understanding of the aging process.

Childhood and Adolescence. An important landmark in the study of specific life stages was the 1962 English translation of Philippe Ariès's *Centuries of Childhood*. In western Europe prior to the sixteenth century, Ariès argued, children were quickly socialized into the adult world; childhood, he contended, was a concept that evolved only in recent centuries. Although few historians shared Ariès's nostalgia for a time when children enjoyed greater freedom but few institutionalized protections, his view of childhood as in many ways a social construction proved very influential.

Historians of colonial America generally portrayed childhood as a period lasting no later than the age of eight. At this relatively young age, most children began a sort of apprenticeship that encompassed their integration into the religious, social, and economic world of adults. Early research on colonial New England also indicated that the strong affective bonds that typically characterize modern parent-child relations were conspicuously absent. However, this depiction of childhood in early America has undergone some revision. Research on the Chesapeake region indicated that parents outside Puritan New England were more likely to have stronger emotional attachments to their children. Other scholars have argued that even in New England, relations between parents and children were probably closer than once thought.

Nonetheless, childhood has clearly changed in profound ways since the colonial era. The nineteenth century, for example, witnessed the increasing recognition of children's vulnerability and the need to protect children from undesirable moral influences. This recognition contributed to the expansion of compulsory public-school education, Progressive Era child-labor legislation, and social-welfare services designed to deal with delinquency, poverty, and child abuse.

The reasons for these changes remain under discussion. Some research, for example, has focused on demographic effects, linking the apparent lack of affection for children in early America to high child mortality. According to this view, the relatively high death rate among children resulted in a psychological reaction whereby parents avoided deep emotional attachments to offspring who quite possibly would not survive to adulthood. The large size of families, a consequence of women continuing to give birth past the age of forty, meant that many families ultimately contained children ranging from infants to young adults. This tended to blur the distinctions among the various stages of early life that eventually became sharply distinguished.

Other scholars link the emergence of childhood as a distinct life stage to the Industrial Revolution. The necessity of training a skilled industrial workforce contributed to the expansion of formal schooling as an important part of childhood, and the demise of family-based economies made the early socialization of children the exclusive domain of mothers. This transition, some argue, increased awareness of the emotional value of children.

Demographic and economic change also played a more indirect role in the development of modern childhood. The reform movements of late nineteenth- and early twentieth-century America were in many ways a response to increased levels of immigration, urbanization, and industrialization. A key component of the Progressive Era was the emergence of specialists—medical and health professionals, educators, social scientists, and social-welfare advocates—who increasingly used specific age groupings as an organizing framework. In addition, many of these professionals focused on the problems and developmental needs of children.

The recognition of adolescence as a specific developmental stage shows how specialists played a role in the evolution of modern childhood. Early in the twentieth century, psychologists popularized the notion that the onset of puberty marked the beginning of a stressful time in terms of identity formation. The discovery of adolescence—often dated from the publication in 1904 of a book of that title by the psychologist G. Stanley Hall—played a major role in reorganizing the lives of American teenagers. Compulsory high school attendance and the growth of youth organizations added adult-sanctioned structures not present before. This fundamental change helped lay the groundwork for the development of a pervasive youth culture in the twentieth century.

Although these changes in American childhood were profound, their timing varied. The need to contribute to the family economy is often credited with lower school-attendance rates for many ethnic groups and working-class youths during the nineteenth and early twentieth centuries. The lack of facilities and racial segregation resulted in lower school attendance among African American children, especially in the South. Gender differences in education were also evident. Young women's education was seen as preparation for their anticipated role as homemakers and mothers. Although gendered socialization and the influences of race and social class all remain influential, by the post–World War II period these distinctions generally diminished.

Ironically, even as the experience of childhood became more homogenized, childhood as a protected stage of life eroded over the last decades of the twentieth century: children were exposed to mass-media depictions of sex and violence, and the rise in divorce forced many children to confront adult realities at relatively young ages. In addition, two distinct child-rearing models based largely on social class emerged. Middle- and upper-class parents strove to provide a nurturing environment that included access to better educational facilities. This achievement-oriented style contrasted with that of parents who lacked the means, time, or energy to improve their children's probability of success later in life.

Much of the impetus for achievement-oriented parenting came from research done by developmental psychologists and social scientists, as well as from the central assumption that a child's environment and experiences have profound effects on later life. Glen H. Elder Jr.'s *Children of the Great Depression* (1974), an important historical study using this approach, examined the impact of the Depression of the 1930s on the lives of successive cohorts of California children. Elder's research model, often referred to as the "life-course approach," influenced historians studying life stages. According to this model, the timing of significant life-defining transitional events—leaving home, leaving school, marriage, and entry into the labor force—varies both from individual to individual and also according to gender, class, and culture, and the timing of a specific event in turn affects the timing of subsequent events.

Marriage and Adulthood. The transition to adulthood, most historians believe, proceeded more gradually in the past. In 1900, men and women typically left home, married, and established independent households later in life. Gradually, young adults accomplished these transitions at younger ages, and this trend accelerated after World War II. By the end of the twentieth century, most young adults accomplished the transition to adulthood in a far shorter period of time than they had a century earlier.

Why did the transition to adulthood become a more rigidly age-defined process? One theory is that in the past the timing of these transitions was articulated more by the family's collective needs. Children remained at home because they had an obligation to contribute to the family income. In addition, marriage and the establishment of an independent household were often contingent on attaining a minimum resource level, which for the urban working class could be a lengthy process. Over the twentieth century, as the economic well-being of most families became less dependent on the contributions of children, young adults increasingly accomplished these transitions not because of collective family needs, but rather according to specific age norms. However, the post-1970 era saw a slight reversal of this trend. As postsecondary education became a more protracted process, young men and women tended to leave home at later ages, and the marriage age increased. Nonetheless, the experience of young adulthood, like that of childhood and adolescence, was acutely affected by an increasing consciousness of age.

Old Age. The development of a more age-regimented society also affected older Americans. In the preindustrial past, according to a widely held view, the elderly enjoyed an exalted status. In agrarian-based, traditional economies, they maintained control of land and were repositories of knowledge acquired over a lifetime of productive work. In colonial America, historians have found, the elderly enjoyed a respected place in society but were often a focus of generational conflicts over family and community authority and the transfer of economic assets. By 1900, however, the elderly were seen, no longer merely as older adults, but rather as a distinct group with special needs. Like children, they drew the attention of reformers and social scientists, who claimed that many older Americans suffered from poverty and isolation from their kin.

Historical research suggests that the alarmist warnings at the end of the nineteenth century concerning the state of the elderly were exaggerated. Little evidence exists that their economic position was deteriorating. Older men maintained high rates of participation in the labor force, while homeownership—often the result of relatively high rates of savings—provided many widows with an important economic asset. In addition, most older Americans lived with kin—either a spouse or, in the case of widows and widowers, an adult child.

Nonetheless, the perception that the elderly needed public assistance instigated a variety of lobbying efforts on their behalf, which contributed to the passage of the Social Security Act in 1935. The provisions for old-age assistance reduced poverty among the elderly, but it also set in motion two significant trends. Earlier reformers had claimed that industrialization had increased unemployment among older men, yet labor-force participation rates among the elderly declined sharply after the 1930s. Social Security benefits also significantly affected the living arrangements of the elderly. Whereas in 1900 most formerly married elderly men and women lived with an adult child or other relative, by the end of the twentieth century most lived independently in single-person households. Social Security began this trend, some researchers believe, by providing widows and widowers with the resources to maintain an independent residence after the death of a spouse.

Demographic trends have also profoundly affected the lives of older Americans. A lower age at marriage and declining fertility rates—specifically the ending of childbearing at earlier ages—combined with increased life expectancy, resulted in the so-called empty-nest syndrome: the increasing time span experienced by parents after their youngest child leaves home. Increased longevity also contributed to a fundamental population shift, with approximately 13 percent of the American population over the age of sixty-five in 1990, compared to 4 percent a century earlier. In their multiplying numbers, the elderly became a potent force in American politics through various lobbying organizations. Although the twenty-first-century United States remains a youth-oriented society, the needs and concerns of the elderly, including the provision of health and retirement services, have important economic implications and are likely to loom even larger in the future.

[See also Adolescence; American Association of Retired Persons; Birth Control and Family Planning; Child Workers; Courtship and Dating; Death and Dying; Demography; Juvenile Delinquency; Life Expectancy; Marriage and Divorce; Retirement Communities; Social Security; and Work.]

BIBLIOGRAPHY

Chudacoff, Howard P. *How Old Are You? Age Consciousness in American Culture.* Princeton, N.J.: Princeton University Press, 1989.

Demos, John. *Past, Present, and Personal: The Family and the Life Course in American History.* New York: Oxford University Press, 1986.

Elder, Glen H., Jr. *Children of the Great Depression: Social Change in Life Experience.* Chicago: University of Chicago Press, 1974.

Haber, Carole, and Brian Gratton. *Old Age and the Search for Security: An American Social History.* Bloomington: Indiana University Press, 1994.

Hawes, Joseph M., and N. Ray Hiner, eds. *American Childhood: A Research Guide and Historical Handbook.* Westport, Conn.: Greenwood Press, 1985.

Modell, John. *Into One's Own: From Youth to Adulthood in the United States, 1920–1975.* Berkeley: University of California Press, 1989.

Van Tassel, David, and Peter N. Stearns, eds. *Old Age in a Bureaucratic Society: The Elderly, the Experts, and the State in American History.* Westport, Conn.: Greenwood Press, 1986.

Ron Goeken

LIVING-WAGE MOVEMENT

The living-wage movement developed in the first decade of the twentieth century as part of the Progressive reform effort to find legislative solutions to social problems. Inspired by late nineteenth-century social-justice movements, by the growth of a consumer-based class consciousness among U.S. workers, and by the Catholic social doctrine that every worker has a right to a decent livelihood, the movement sought to establish legal minimum wages that guaranteed all workers a living wage.

Florence Kelley, the general secretary of the National Consumers League (NCL), and Father John A. Ryan, an economist and Catholic priest who was the chief living-wage theorist in the United States, worked with activists in more than twenty states to investigate working conditions and to write and lobby for laws that would establish legal minimum wages for women and children in industrial and retail work. The NCL and the Women's Trade Union League provided key organizational support. The American Federation of Labor, however, opposed minimum-wage legislation. Between 1912 and 1933 sixteen states, Puerto Rico, and Washington, D.C., succeeded in passing the first minimum-wage laws in the United States. Living-wage proponents sought gender-based rather than class-based laws because the prevailing "freedom of contract" legal doctrine held that state regulation of labor conditions violated the due process clause of the Fourteenth Amendment. Supporters of minimum wages argued that women needed the state's special protection because of their disadvantaged position in the job market, their lack of political representation, and their social position and physical constitution as potential mothers of the next generation. In its 1917 decision in *Stettler v. O'Hara*, the U.S. Supreme Court affirmed that minimum-wage laws were a legitimate exercise of a state's police power: low wages, like long hours, potentially damaged the health and morals of women and children. Kelley and Ryan hoped that the *Stettler v. O'Hara* precedent would pave the way for class-based wage legislation.

The post–World War I backlash against Progressivism dealt a blow to the living-wage movement. In 1923 the Supreme Court's decision in *Adkins v. Children's Hospital* rendered Washington, D.C.'s minimum-wage law for women unconstitutional: because the Nineteenth Amendment, ratified in 1920, had given women the right to vote, women supposedly had freedom of contract and thus no longer needed special protection. Living-wage advocates continued their efforts and were rewarded in the 1930s when the Depression revived interest in minimum-wage laws. In 1933, New York and seven other states passed wage laws. Throughout the New Deal years, living-wage proponents worked with U.S. Secretary of Labor Frances Perkins, herself a longtime living-wage advocate, to achieve a universal federal living-wage standard. After a long political battle, the Fair Labor Standards Act (FLSA) of 1938 set federal minimum-wage and maximum-hours standards. The FLSA established a federal responsibility to protect workers from extremely low wages, but it failed to establish a living-wage standard, did not index the minimum wage to inflation, and excluded many nonindustrial workers. The law has since been amended to include more occupations, but it is still not universal.

Beginning in the 1990s, in response to growing income inequality, a coalition of religious, labor, community, and student groups built a new living-wage movement. Since 1994 more than 120 cities and counties and the state of Maryland have passed living-wage ordinances, and several universities have established living-wage agreements in response to campaigns coordinated by grassroots organizations such as ACORN and Let Justice Roll.

[*See also* **Child Workers; Kelley, Florence; Labor Movements; New Deal Social Reforms; Perkins, Frances; Progressive Era; Women Workers;** *and* **Work.**]

BIBLIOGRAPHY

Glickman, Lawrence B. *A Living Wage: American Workers and the Making of Consumer Society.* Ithaca, N.Y.: Cornell University Press, 1997.

Murphy, Laura. "An 'Indestructible Right': John Ryan and the Catholic Origins of the U.S. Living Wage Movement, 1906–1938." *Labor* 6, no. 1 (Spring 2009): 57–86.

Sklar, Kathryn Kish. "Two Political Cultures in the Progressive Era: The National Consumers' League and the American Association for Labor Legislation." In *U.S. History as Women's History: New*

Feminist Essays, edited by Linda K. Kerber, Alice Kessler-Harris, and Kathryn Kish Sklar. Chapel Hill: University of North Carolina Press, 1995.

Laura Murphy

LOS ANGELES

Although in 2010 the second-largest city in the United States, with an estimated population of 3.79 million residents (15 million in the metropolitan area) spread over 503 square miles, Los Angeles spent much of its first century of existence as a backwater. First populated at least a thousand years ago by the Tongva (Gabrieleño) people, the Los Angeles basin hosted perhaps ten thousand people by the time of the arrival of the Spanish explorers in 1769. As a result of the disastrous effects of colonization, the city that was christened *Nuestra Señora la Reina de los Angeles de Porciúncula* (Our Lady the Queen of Angels of the Little Portion) did not approach that population level again for more than a hundred years.

Under Spanish and Mexican control, the local economy relied primarily on raising cattle. The city began to expand through a series of booms and busts under American rule in the late nineteenth century, while native Californians and Latino Californios were gradually deprived of their land through sale, fraud, and biased courts. By the dawn of the twentieth century, the city was poised for explosive growth, spurred by the arrival of the railroad in 1876 and the construction of a deepwater port in 1899. The lure of "Mediterraneanism"—circulated widely by the Sunkist cooperative's marketing of oranges throughout the nation—began to draw wealthy eastern settlers. Meanwhile, an expansive interurban transit network, along with ambitious schemes to bring water to the metropolis, provided the infrastructure for rapid development. New industries of oil extraction, aviation, and, most famously, filmmaking emerged in the region. Hollywood's influential images of scenic southern California proved another powerful tool to the booster industry, which promised pleasant bungalows as alternatives to eastern cities' crowded and heterogeneous slums.

The subsequent influx of midwestern migrants during the boom years of the 1920s—when the city's population passed a million—reinforced a carefully orchestrated reputation of Los Angeles as a "white" city. This impression was enforced by a notoriously violent police department and a rigid system of restrictive deed covenants, covering as much as 95 percent of the city's residential property, that restricted Latino, Asian, and African American settlement to what Carey McWilliams termed an "archipelago" of enclaves near the downtown core.

By the late 1920s an influential group of local city planners began an alliance with land developers that ultimately resulted, although not quite as anyone had imagined, in a novel urban topography for the region. Deemphasizing the congested and multiethnic downtown district, planners hoped to remake the city as a low-density cluster of "garden cities." Although the idea ultimately failed, Los Angeles did subsequently develop a novel urban structure, highly dependent on the automobile, that distributed commerce, residence, and recreation over a vast area. The resulting multicentered, deconcentrated metropolitan pattern provided a new model of urban topography in the decades to come, even as many observers derided it as "sprawl."

During World War II, the growth of a lively African American community and the gradual resurgence of the city's Latino population were met with escalating racial prejudice, most notably illustrated in the wartime internment of Japanese American citizens and 1943's zoot-suit riots, in which servicemen rioted for three days against Mexican American youth.

In the aftermath of the war, civic leaders began to search for new ways to restore legibility to the sprawling metropolis, such as the iconic freeway system. Yet a new, unauthorized, grassroots vision of urban modernity had also been developing in Los Angeles. During the war, Central Avenue, home to many African Americans, had defined a new modern jazz scene. Subsequently, the rise of rock and roll brought together many different communities of Angelenos. By the time of the race riots in the Watts neighborhood in 1965, the rigidly enforced image of Los Angeles as a white city was gradually eroding.

By 1973, with the election of the African American Tom Bradley as mayor, the character of the metropolis had changed. Bradley promulgated a new definition of the city as a gateway to the Pacific Rim, and soon greater Los Angeles, the nation's preeminent manufacturing center, became the primary entry point to the United States for immigrants. Although many wealthy Angelenos, as Mike Davis has argued, have retreated into gated suburban communities and Los Angeles remains the archetypal horizontal metropolis, since the late twentieth century there has also been increasingly intensive inward development. The election of Antonio Villaraigosa as mayor in 2005 marked the ascendance not just of the Latino community—which constituted more than 48 percent of the population—but also of the grassroots multiethnic coalitions that mark Los Angeles as the most diverse large city in the nation.

[*See also* **Automobiles; California; Cities and Suburbs; Film; Internal Migration; Riots, Race;** *and* **Riots, Urban**.]

BIBLIOGRAPHY

Axelrod, Jeremiah B. C. *Inventing Autopia: Dreams and Visions of the Modern Metropolis in Jazz Age Los Angeles.* Berkeley: University of California Press, 2009.

Banham, Reyner. *Los Angeles: The Architecture of Four Ecologies.* New York: Harper & Row, 1971.

Davis, Mike. *City of Quartz: Excavating the Future in Los Angeles.* London and New York: Verso, 1991.

Fogelson, Robert M. *The Fragmented Metropolis: Los Angeles, 1850–1930.* Cambridge, Mass.: Harvard University Press, 1967.

McWilliams, Carey. *Southern California Country: An Island on the Land.* New York: Duell, Sloan & Pearce, 1946.

Pitt, Leonard, and Dale Pitt. *Los Angeles, A to Z: An Encyclopedia of the City and County.* Berkeley: University of California Press, 1997.

Starr, Kevin. *Americans and the California Dream, 1850–1915.* New York: Oxford University Press, 1973.

Jeremiah B. C. Axelrod

LOWELL TEXTILE MILLS

A partnership of Boston-based manufacturers later known as the Boston Associates, intending to bring industrialization to northern New England without the social ills that accompanied the process in Great Britain, founded Lowell, Massachusetts, in 1822 on former farmland at the junction of the Merrimack and Concord Rivers. At their inception, the factories of Lowell represented the height of technological and social advancement in cotton production. Francis Cabot Lowell, aided by the engineer Paul Moody, copied machines that he observed during tours of British factories in 1810 and 1811 and proposed a new method for organizing manufacturing. Tried on a small scale in Waltham, Massachusetts, before Lowell's

1817 death, the Waltham-Lowell system housed every stage of cotton production from cleaning to finishing in one massive establishment. When the initial experiment at Lowell proved successful, more associates began construction. By 1836, eight separate firms were being run on the same system operating in Lowell.

To staff the factories, Lowell manufacturers recruited farmers' daughters from across New England, women whose traditional family role in home textile production was becoming obsolete. Though many women were eager to move to Lowell, parental concerns and negative impressions of Britain's mills, combined with the economic fact that daughters' wage earning was not essential to many families' survival, meant that innovations in Lowell had to extend beyond the technological. To attract and retain their desired labor force, the Lowell firms provided boardinghouses, a strict set of regulations over social and workplace conduct, and educational opportunities for the workers. Early mill workers were required to attend worship services and conform to curfews. They also attended evening lectures, patronized the city library, and frequently wrote about their experiences. *The Lowell Offering*, written and edited by Lowell workers, was first produced in 1840. Though many mill girls used their wages to aid their families, they also had surplus to buy clothes, sit for photographs, and otherwise engage in the market economy. Many found it to be a liberating and empowering experience.

Competition in the textile industry combined with increasing numbers of immigrants in the United States to change working conditions in Lowell. The firms proposed a wage cut in 1834, and board charges were raised in 1836. The mill girls protested these changes with strikes. In the 1840s, Lowell mill workers joined New England–wide labor activism in the movement for a ten-hour workday. Manufacturers nevertheless continued to intensify work requirements to meet competitive demand, and migrant mill workers dissatisfied with conditions were more likely to return to (or never leave) family homes than to engage in protest. After about 1850, American-born migrants to Lowell were more likely to be experiencing economic hardship than seeking adventure beyond the farmyard walls. Like most manufacturers in the Northeast, the Lowell mills shifted to an immigrant workforce with families in the city rather than independent migrants. New England–born female migrants living in boardinghouses remained a minority among Lowell workers, but in most respects Lowell after the Civil War was indistinguishable from any other northeastern mill town.

[*See also* **Antebellum Era; Labor Movements; Rural Life and Society; Strikes and Industrial Conflict; Women Workers;** *and* **Work.**]

BIBLIOGRAPHY

Dublin, Thomas. *Women at Work: The Transformation of Work and Community in Lowell, Massachusetts, 1826–1860*. 2d ed. New York: Columbia University Press, 1993. Still the most comprehensive study of the social world of the New England migrants to Lowell, based on corporate records, mill girls' letters, and extensive local archives around New England.

Moran, William. *The Belles of New England: The Women of the Textile Mills and the Families Whose Wealth They Wove*. New York: Thomas Dunne, 2002. Effectively places Lowell's unique origins and workforce into the broader context of industrialization, immigration, and labor activism in New England.

Robinson, Harriet H. *Loom and Spindle, or Life among the Early Mill Girls, with a Sketch of "The Lowell Offering" and Some of Its Contributors.* Rev. ed. Kailua, Hawai'i: Press Pacifica, 1976. In this most famous memoir by a Lowell mill girl, Robinson describes the work and intellectual pursuits of the early workers in the city.

Wendy M. Gordon

LOYALISTS

More than half a million Americans rejected the Revolution and advocated reunion with the British Empire. The loyal Americans included European immigrants and their descendants, Native Americans, African American slaves, and free blacks. Black loyalists saw greater potential for freedom with the British, the Indians hoped to preserve their middle ground between the British Empire and the American settlers, and white loyalists wanted to prevent the collapse of their known world. These Americans associated Britain with Protestantism, commercial prosperity, naval power, and freedom.

Between 1774 and 1776, overt pressure from hostile rebel neighbors and militia committees compelled Americans to identify themselves as loyalists or rebels. An unprecedented test oath became a qualifier for American citizenship, for voting, and for holding property. The rebel tactics of tarring and feathering, imprisonment, and banishment that were used to suppress opposition forced people to abandon a neutral stance. Together, the oaths and violence eroded the middle ground between loyalism and rebellion. After 1775 when the British first established military headquarters in the city of Boston, the loyalist position became triangulated between rebel persecution and British protection.

Loyalist spokesmen circulated essays in pro-British newspapers during the crisis of 1774–1776 and in more than ten loyalist newspapers published in garrison towns between 1776 and 1783. These included the *Royal American Gazette* in New York City, the *Newport Gazette* in Rhode Island, the *Pennsylvania Evening Post*, and other papers in southern garrisons. The loyalist newspapers provided a forum for circulating loyalist arguments and promoting loyalist perceptions. Publicly offering their allegiance and military assistance, the loyalists prodded Britain to intensify its struggle against the rebels.

During the first three years of the war, the British suspicion of loyalist military potential disappointed many who considered themselves the King's most loyal friends. Unlike in previous wars, the British government had no foreign allies to share the burden of suppressing the American rebellion. Still, the British did not devise a formal policy for joining their three sources of potential strength: arming white loyalists, supporting powerful Native Americans along the Appalachian border, and freeing the large African American population along the southern coast. For the most part, individual commanders and leaders acted independently, depending on local circumstances.

In 1778 when the French Empire openly became an enemy of Britain both in North America and in Asia, the British were pressed for manpower and began to reconsider the place of loyalists in suppressing the rebellion. But the British promotion of loyalist militias in the southern backcountry backfired. The militias failed to pacify the South, and worse, they mobilized rebel resistance on a massive scale. Effectively, the clash of rebel and loyalist militias fomented a vicious civil war that tested the loyalty of farmers and frontiersmen.

More slaves became involved when the war switched from the North to the plantation colonies in the South and the Caribbean. Starting in 1775, British offers of freedom to rebel-owned slaves emboldened thousands. An estimated twenty-five thousand to fifty-five thousand slaves escaped to find protection behind British lines. The majority of runaways did strenuous and time-consuming work. They dug trenches, buried bodies, served as orderlies in hospitals, hauled provisions, collected firewood, and cared for animals.

Choosing loyalism united some Indian communities but created disunity among groups such as the Iroquois Six Nations and the Delawares. The internal fissures deepened as both British and rebel leaders advocated using friendly Indians to wage war against hostile ones. The warfare in Indian country was not decisive in shaping the outcome of the Revolution; the outcome of the Revolution, however, decisively affected the Indian world in North America. The British government abandoned the Indians who had fought and died on its behalf. The disputed "middle ground" of the natives, preserved tenaciously for almost two hundred years, came to be American ground.

The fragmentation of Britain's North American empire in 1783 led to the mass displacement of sixty thousand American loyalists, an estimated one in forty Americans at that time. In the short term, there was no future in the new United States for thousands of white colonists identified as loyalists. When known loyalists tried to return to their homes and resume their former lives, they faced insults, threats, and banishment from neighbors who accused them of massacring friends, desolating lands, and starting fires.

More than half of the white loyalists migrated to British Canada. Of the 3,225 loyalists who submitted a request for reparations from the British government, 468 were American refugee women. The women received lower pensions because they had not actively served in the royal cause. The loyalists who evacuated British garrisons in the South re-created slave plantations in the British Caribbean. The majority of slaves remained loyalist property and worked to rebuild the lost wealth of their owners. The British honored their promises of freedom to three thousand blacks who migrated to Nova Scotia after the war. More than 40 percent were female. Ignored and maltreated by both the British and the loyalists, a third of these black loyalists left Nova Scotia in 1792, hoping for a better life in British Sierra Leone.

[*See also* **Militias, Early American; Revolution and Constitution Era;** *and* **Voluntary Associations,** *subentry on* **British Colonies and Early Republic.**]

BIBLIOGRAPHY

Chopra, Ruma. *Unnatural Rebellion: Loyalists in New York City during the Revolution.* Charlottesville: University of Virginia Press, 2011.

Frey, Sylvia R. *Water from the Rock: Black Resistance in a Revolutionary Age.* Princeton, N.J.: Princeton University Press, 1991.

Jasanoff, Maya. *Liberty's Exiles: American Loyalists in the Revolutionary World.* New York: Alfred A. Knopf, 2011.

Smith, Paul H. *Loyalists and Redcoats: A Study in British Revolutionary Policy.* Chapel Hill: University of North Carolina Press for the Institute of Early American History and Culture at Williamsburg, Va., 1964.

Ruma Chopra

LYNCHING

A form of illegal execution, lynching was usually perpetrated against a person accused of a crime or some type of deviant behavior.

Historically, most lynching victims in the United States have been African American men. However, women, native-born white men, and members of other minority groups—including European immigrants, Chinese, and Hispanics—were also lynched, though in much smaller numbers. Although lynchings are often equated with hanging, other methods that have been used include shooting, burning, and drowning, sometimes followed by the mutilation or public display, or both, of the corpse. Some lynchings were carried out by large mobs, while others involved groups of only three or four people. White-supremacist or nativist groups like the Ku Klux Klan perpetrated some lynchings, but the informal and spontaneous organization of citizens into lynch mobs was more common. Most lynch victims had been accused, but not convicted, of such serious crimes as murder, assault, or rape. Other victims were killed because of transgressions of racial codes, such as insulting a white person or using inflammatory language.

Lynchings have occurred throughout U.S. history but have been concentrated more heavily in specific time periods. The number of African Americans lynched in the South increased sharply during Reconstruction as southern whites reacted to the federal occupation of the former Confederacy and to the increasing political and economic power of blacks. Lynchings peaked during the 1890s, when the annual total number of victims regularly exceeded eighty. The rate declined during the next four decades, with temporary upswings between 1905 and 1910, and again immediately following World War I. After 1930, lynchings became relatively rare, though some of the most highly publicized incidents occurred in the 1940s, 1950s, and even as late as the 1960s: examples include the 1955 lynching of the fourteen-year-old Emmett Till near Greenwood, Mississippi, and the lynchings of Claude Neal in 1934, Charles Mack Parker in 1959, and the civil rights activists James Chaney, Andrew Goodman, and Michael Schwerner in 1964. The number of lynchings of whites followed a different trend, declining through the late nineteenth century and virtually disappearing by the twentieth century.

Lynching was primarily a southern phenomenon. Mississippi and Georgia claimed significantly more victims than any other states, though the rate of lynching in relation to the size of the black population was highest in Florida. Outside the Southeast, lynchings were most likely to occur in the Southwest and West, though in considerably smaller numbers. Lynchings in the Southwest differed in important respects from those in the Southeast. For example, victims were more likely to be white or Latino and were more often accused of being horse thieves, bandits, or outlaws. Lynchings in the north-central and northeastern states were rare.

Because most lynching victims had been accused of serious crimes, lynching has sometimes been viewed, particularly by southern newspapers and commentators, as a form of popular justice, substituting for or reinforcing the formal criminal justice system. Since the later twentieth century, explanations for lynching have drawn from social-scientific theories. One theory describes lynchings as a form of aggression resulting from southern whites' economic frustrations. And, indeed, larger numbers of lynchings did occur during years when the southern economy faltered. Another theoretical perspective views lynching as a form of social control practiced by southern whites when they felt threatened by African Americans. According to this "racial threat" perspective, whites felt threatened when blacks competed with them for political power, economic security, or social status.

The sharp decline in lynchings after the mid-1920s is attributed by some to improved law enforcement, especially the increased use of patrol cars and radios. Another explanation emphasizes southern newspapers' increasingly negative treatment of lynch-mob behavior. Some claim that antilynching organizations played a critical role. The National Association for the Advancement of Colored People (NAACP) fought vigorously against lynching, as did the Association of Southern Women for the Prevention of Lynching and the Committee on Interracial Cooperation. Activists such as the NAACP's Walter White, Jessie Daniel Ames, and Ida B. Wells-Barnett were especially visible opponents of lynching. Still others have suggested that increasingly fierce resistance, sometimes armed, by African Americans discouraged mob behavior in whites. Finally, the decline of lynching has also been linked to major social and economic transformations in the South that fundamentally altered the relations between whites and African Americans.

At their peak, lynching and the fear of lynching had a profound effect on the African American population. Lynching posed a deadly danger to those who challenged the privileged position of whites in southern society. It also motivated many blacks to leave the South. Though some southern whites persisted in defending lynching as a necessary evil, increasing numbers of whites in all regions came to view the phenomenon as a barbaric national embarrassment and moral disgrace. The ample representation of lynching in American fiction, such as in Lillian Smith's *Strange Fruit* (1944), and frequent allusion to lynching—real and metaphorical—in discussions of contemporary race relations attest to its lasting influence.

[*See also* Antilynching Movement; Civil Rights Movement; Homicide; Racism; Rape; South, The; *and* Wells-Barnett, Ida B.]

BIBLIOGRAPHY

Brundage, W. Fitzhugh. *Lynching in the New South: Georgia and Virginia, 1880–1930*. Urbana: University of Illinois Press, 1993.

McGovern, James R. *Anatomy of a Lynching: The Killing of Claude Neal*. Baton Rouge: Louisiana State University Press, 1982.

Raper, Arthur F. *The Tragedy of Lynching*. Chapel Hill: University of North Carolina Press, 1933.

Tolnay, Stewart E., and E. M. Beck. *A Festival of Violence: An Analysis of Southern Lynchings, 1882–1930*. Urbana: University of Illinois Press, 1995.

Wright, George C. *Racial Violence in Kentucky, 1865–1940: Lynchings, Mob Rule, and "Legal Lynchings."* Baton Rouge: Louisiana State University Press, 1990.

Zangrando, Robert L. *The NAACP Crusade against Lynching, 1909–1950*. Philadelphia: Temple University Press, 1980.

Stewart E. Tolnay and E. M. Beck

M

MALCOLM X

(1925–1965), African American leader. Born Malcolm Little in Omaha, Nebraska, and later also known as El-Hajj Malik El-Shabazz, Malcolm X towers over what has been called the "long sixties," the critical period of social and political upheaval stretching from the late 1950s to the early 1970s, first as the national spokesman for the Nation of Islam (NOI), then briefly as the founder of the short-lived Organization of Afro-American Unity (OAAU), and finally, in death, as the patron saint of black radicalism in its Black Power phase. Other than his posthumous autobiography, which bears the imprint of his collaborator and editor, Alex Haley, Malcolm left no written work. Because he was assassinated just eight months after founding the OAAU in 1964, he did not leave an organizational legacy, either, save for turning an obscure NOI sect that in the 1950s had only hundreds of members into a national organization that by the early 1960s claimed tens of thousands of members. His principal contribution, rather, was evangelical: in face-to-face encounters on the streets of New York City's Harlem, in interviews on radio and television, and especially in speeches at churches, in lecture halls, and on street corners in Detroit and Cleveland, Malcolm X, one of the twentieth century's great masters of the spoken word, proselytized generations of African Americans. Unlike the civil rights movement icon Martin Luther King Jr., whose legacy includes the landmark Civil Rights Act (1964) and Voting Rights Act (1965), Malcolm's success lay in the realm of black consciousness, not in the U.S. Congress.

His philosophy evolved over time, from the uniquely American brand of racialist Islam of the NOI prophet Elijah Muhammad to an eclectic and rapidly changing blend of black nationalism, Pan-Africanism, proto-socialist internationalism, and orthodox Islam in his last days. His preaching also evolved. Especially in his later years, his preaching was rigorously historical: he insisted on analyzing the causes, nature, and possible solutions to contemporary problems through a close reading of the past (especially of past revolutions), always emphasizing the role of ordinary people in making history. He found a receptive audience among urban blacks in the North, and especially among a younger generation of black activists in the North and the South who were increasingly frustrated with the pace of change; most of this younger generation came to know him only after his death in early 1965, reading and hearing his speeches through reprints and recordings. His paradigm of the "field slave" and the "house slave" of the Old South, for example, in which he counterposed a "black revolution" and a "Negro revolution," heralded a tectonic shift in black activism. Malcolm's stance was part of a larger shift in activism from late 1963 to early 1965—precisely the period of Malcolm's break from the NOI—and what ultimately became known as the Black Power movement heralded Malcolm as its progenitor. Despite their many differences, groups like the Revolutionary Action Movement, the Republic of New Africa, the League of Revolutionary Black Workers, and especially the Black Panthers (who referred to themselves as the "heirs of Malcolm"), in addition to the disaffected in civil rights groups like the Student Nonviolent Coordinating Committee and the Congress of Racial Equality, found in Malcolm X's preaching a goal ("revolution"), a constituency (the "grassroots"),

and a method ("by any means necessary"). That the revolution fell short of the acolytes' desires does not diminish the significance of Malcolm's imprint on that historic moment.

[*See also* **Sixties, The.**]

BIBLIOGRAPHY

Breitman, George, ed. *Malcolm X Speaks: Selected Speeches and Statements*. New York: Merit, 1965.

Marable, Manning. "Malcolm X's Life-after-Death: The Dispossession of a Legacy." In his *Living Black History: How Reimagining the African-American Past Can Remake America's Racial Future*. New York: Basic Civitas, 2006.

Sales, William W., Jr. *From Civil Rights to Black Liberation: Malcolm X and the Organization of Afro-American Unity*. Boston: South End Press, 1994.

Jama Lazerow

MARCH ON WASHINGTON

The March on Washington for Jobs and Freedom took place on 28 August 1963 and was a rally of 250,000 people to demand passage of civil rights legislation and programs for economic opportunity. The rally—which marked the only time that all factions of the civil rights movement came together with a common agenda—climaxed with Martin Luther King Jr.'s "I Have a Dream" speech, considered by many the greatest speech of the twentieth century. The rally featured a wide range of leading lights from politics, civil rights, labor, religion, and the arts. Speakers included Roy Wilkins of the National Association for the Advancement of Colored People, Whitney Young of the National Urban League, John Lewis of the Student Nonviolent Coordinating Committee, and Walter Reuther of the United Auto Workers. Performers included the folk singers Bob Dylan and Joan Baez, the gospel singers Odetta and Mahalia Jackson, and the opera singer Marian Anderson. The film stars Charlton Heston and Marlon Brando also appeared.

The idea of a march on Washington originated in 1941 when A. Philip Randolph, the leader of the Brotherhood of Sleeping Car Porters, organized as many as one hundred thousand people to march down Pennsylvania Avenue to demand an end to discrimination in wartime industries. Randolph called off the rally when President Franklin D. Roosevelt answered his demands by signing Executive Order 8802. In December 1962, Bayard Rustin, a leading organizer in the antiwar, peace, labor, and civil rights movements, and Randolph discussed holding a massive rally to commemorate the centenary of the Emancipation Proclamation. Originally conceived as a rally for jobs and economic opportunity, the rally expanded to include civil rights.

President John F. Kennedy attempted to get march leaders to call off the rally, worried that it would endanger efforts to pass the civil rights bill he had introduced in June. But the leaders said that the movement needed a constructive outlet for activists frustrated by the slow pace of reform and violence in their demonstrations. As it happened, many likened the march's atmosphere to a church picnic, so gentle and agreeable was the atmosphere. But as they marched from the Washington Monument to the Lincoln Memorial, marchers demanded an end to racial segregation, full voting rights, and economic opportunity.

The highlight of the day was King's speech. King challenged America to honor the "promissory note" of the Declaration of Independence—the promise of "life, liberty, and the pursuit of happiness." King said that "we will not be satisfied" until blacks were granted civil rights. He challenged his followers to hold fast to a strategy of nonviolence. At a time

when young civil rights activists were growing disillusioned with the twin values of nonviolence and integration, King hoped to hold the center of the movement. He warned that progress would come only with struggle but promised that "unearned suffering is redemptive."

Some historians argue that the rally helped attract public support for the Civil Rights Act (1964), but others attribute that law to President Lyndon B. Johnson's legislative mastery and the national coming-together after Kennedy's assassination on 22 November 1963. The march offered the first time for mainstream America to witness the movement unfiltered by mainstream media. CBS covered the whole march live on television, and the three networks all covered King's speech. The event was broadcast globally via satellite TV.

[*See also* **King, Martin Luther, Jr.;** *and* **Sixties, The.**]

BIBLIOGRAPHY

Euchner, Charles. *Nobody Turn Me Around: A People's History of the 1963 March on Washington.* Boston: Beacon, 2010.
Hansen, Drew D. *The Dream: Martin Luther King, Jr., and the Speech That Inspired a Nation.* New York: Ecco, 2003.

Charles Euchner

MAROON SOCIETIES

Maroon communities, formed by escaped slaves, existed throughout the Americas and were most prevalent during the eighteenth century. The brutalities of plantation slavery persuaded many imported Africans that they had little to lose by flight into woodlands or mountains where they could fend for themselves.

Some of these escaped slaves banded together to form communities that offered an alternative to life on the plantations. The largest of these communities—in the mountains of Jamaica and Hispaniola, in the jungles of Suriname and Brazil, and in the swamps of South Carolina and Louisiana—were home to thousands of Maroons. These semipermanent settlements contained both homes and communal buildings, while nearby cleared areas were planted with crops.

Maroons were most often drawn from first-generation African-born slaves who possessed the hunting and field-craft skills necessary to survive in the harsh environments where Maroon settlements were usually located. Those born in Africa perhaps had a particularly keen sense of the freedom they had lost and wished to regain; thus Maroon societies were most common in regions that imported the most Africans, such as the West Indies and Brazil. Even in North America, however, which saw comparatively little direct importation from Africa, small Maroon communities were formed in remote regions.

New fugitives regularly replaced Maroons who had died or been captured, but some Maroon groups augmented their numbers by forcibly kidnapping slaves, especially women. Nearby plantations could also be raided for food and weapons, but every venture into the settlements increased the risk that whites would react. Planters sometimes turned a blind eye to Maroon settlements in remote areas that had little impact on plantation regions, but when Maroons began to affect the production of cash crops, then it was far more likely that military expeditions would be sent against them.

The longest-lived Maroon settlements exploited their geography to ensure their survival against military assaults. The inaccessible and mountainous part of central Jamaica known as the cockpit country, for instance, was very difficult to navigate by those hunting

Maroons, even without the ever-present threat of ambush or attack. Maroons quickly became adept at laying false trails for their pursuers, replete with traps and hidden dangers. Even when Maroon settlements could be located, regular troops found them defended by well-armed men who fought with the desperation of those who had nothing to lose. The large number of casualties among colonial troops, combined with the expense of fighting an unending guerrilla war, persuaded many local governments to sign peace treaties with well-entrenched Maroons. So-called treaty Maroons in Jamaica and Suriname in the mid-eighteenth century received official recognition of their freedom in return for a promise to capture new fugitives from slavery and hand them over to their masters. Maroons in North America were never offered treaty terms by colonial or state governments, even though some communities, such as those in the Great Dismal Swamp, persisted throughout both the colonial era and the antebellum era.

[*See also* **Atlantic World; Caribbean; Free Communities of Color; Slave Families and Communities;** *and* **Slavery,** *subentry on* **Colonial and Revolutionary Era.**]

BIBLIOGRAPHY

Lockley, Tim, ed. *Maroon Communities in South Carolina: A Documentary Record.* Columbia: University of South Carolina Press, 2008.
Price, Richard, ed. *Maroon Societies: Rebel Slave Communities in the Americas.* 2d ed. Baltimore: Johns Hopkins University Press, 1979.

Tim Lockley

MARRIAGE AND DIVORCE

Marriage, seen historically as the preferred form of legal cohabitation, has been widely thought to promote social stability and individual well-being and to be the most desirable setting in which to procreate and to raise children. When, who, and how one marries and what constraints affect those choices have varied over time by social, legal, cultural, and economic circumstances. Anglo-American attitudes traditionally embraced the inviolability of marriage and family, fostering social attitudes and laws that, in the past, made divorce difficult.

History. During the colonial era and into the early nineteenth century, marriage functioned primarily as a pragmatic, economic, and procreative alliance, binding couples and their extended families together. Choosing a partner wisely was important, especially for a woman, since divorce was difficult and one's future welfare depended on that choice. New England Puritans saw marriage as a civil contract based on mutual consent, and to this end, they closely monitored courting practices to ensure sound decisions. Puritans believed that well-ordered families fostered a well-ordered society, and they were vigilant in trying to uphold their ideals.

The duration of marriage has varied significantly. In the past, death usually was the limiting factor to a long marriage. In the seventeenth-century Chesapeake region, marriages lasted an average of only seven years, owing to the high mortality resulting from the prevalence of both disease and the death of women in childbirth. Serial marriages were common as successive spouses died, resulting in complex stepfamily relationships. In the healthier New England climate, colonial couples experienced longer marriages, resulting in more stable family situations.

Divorce was rare in the colonial period because it was considered disgraceful and was difficult to obtain, especially for women. Expectations regarding marriage partners and what

marriages could mean tended to be realistic, and most men and women did not marry for love. Because well-functioning families were basic to their ideals, Puritans did permit marital dissolution when couples proved incompatible. They believed that marriage and family life should be happy. Adultery, bigamy, and desertion were acceptable legal grounds for divorce in most colonies. Acquiring an absolute divorce that permitted each spouse to remarry was complicated and expensive. Many unhappy spouses simply ran away or sought a legal separation. Before 1800, most divorce petitioners were male, but after the Revolutionary War, more women filed for and succeeded in obtaining divorces. Until the mid-nineteenth century, colonial and state legislatures handled divorce proceedings, but gradually states began to turn divorce petitions over to the courts. They also began to codify laws rather than handle cases on an ad hoc basis.

Each colony and later each state established marriage and divorce laws that determined property rights, residency requirements, minimum age for marriage, and other rules relating to marriage and divorce. For instance, in most southern states, marriages between first cousins were legal, whereas in New England they were forbidden. In the antebellum era, South Carolina prohibited divorce entirely. A few colonies and states, primarily in the South, adopted fairly conservative policies concerning divorce. The unhappy partner had to petition the legislature or court to plead his or her case.

According to British law—which the colonies and most states followed—women upon marriage forfeited any property rights that they had enjoyed as single women. Unless a woman signed a prenuptial contract, everything she brought into a marriage or acquired during that time belonged to her husband. This situation did not begin to change until

1839 when Mississippi became the first state to pass a law to protect married women's property rights. This was enacted, not by an enlightened state legislature eager to expand women's rights, but instead by a pragmatic legislature that sought to protect family property by separating wives' assets when creditors came calling. Setting aside a wife's property meant that the family would have something to live on. New York and Pennsylvania followed with similar laws nine years later. By the early twentieth century, most states had granted wives the right to claim their own property and earnings.

Slaves faced a different situation. Although not allowed to marry legally, since this would have interfered with masters' rights to sell their slaves and to separate couples, slaves often formalized their marital relationships. Finding a partner, though, could be difficult, and many slave couples lived apart on separate plantations. When residing on the same farm or plantation, a man and woman moved in together, with or without a formal ceremony. Slave breeding that forced couples to procreate did happen, but this practice was rare. When slave couples decided to terminate their relationships, they did so merely by moving out.

Marriage rituals have varied from informal exchanges of vows before a judge or preacher to elegant, full-scale church weddings. In some cases, individuals drew up prenuptial contracts to protect their personal property. Slaves ritually jumped over a broomstick or listened to words read by their masters or preachers. Common-law marriages, which typically occurred among those living far from any community, allowed couples who had lived together for several years to claim legal marital status.

A number of variables have influenced the age at which men and women married. In colonial New England, most women married in their early twenties, men in their late twenties.

Seventeenth-century indentured servants in the South, because they were required to remain single while fulfilling their indentures, usually married late. By the second and third generations after initial settlement of the colonies, southern men were marrying in their mid- to late twenties and women in their late teens. Economic factors affected age at marriage. Struggling immigrants in the eighteenth and nineteenth centuries tended to marry later than did the native-born because poverty made it difficult to set up a household. Without an inheritance or adequate income, many young men could not afford to marry. Age at marriage remained relatively stable until the late 1940s and 1950s when it declined. It rose again in the 1960s, as more women pursued higher education and took paid jobs. By the early twenty-first century the age at marriage was at an all-time high.

Gauging marital happiness both past and present is virtually impossible. That few marriages in the past ended in divorce does not mean couples then were any more compatible than they are today: in the past, laws, traditions, and religious beliefs made divorce difficult, and few women had the means to live independently. There was also a stigma about divorce. Despite what is often assumed, the past was not a golden era of marital bliss, as numerous separations, public notices for runaway spouses, and private lamentations in letters and diaries attest.

Parental involvement in children's marital choices has varied over time. In the colonial period, property often influenced who and when one married. Daughters who needed dowries and sons who needed land to set up independent households depended on parents who thus could exert some influence over, if not actually dictate, their choice of partners. Strict rules governed young women's courtship behavior because of the fear of becoming pregnant outside marriage and the importance of a prudent choice. Parental involvement declined by the mid-eighteenth century, evidenced in part by siblings marrying out of birth order. In the nineteenth century, more women remained single, owing to the shortage of men, especially after the Civil War, as well as to more educational and work opportunities for females who could survive on their own. By the late twentieth century, parents usually played only minor roles, if any, in their children's choices, though this has varied among different cultural and ethnic groups.

Another change by the nineteenth century was the growing importance of marrying based on mutual attraction, love, and a desire to achieve personal happiness in marriage. Women in particular began to favor men likely to fulfill their ideal of a companionate marriage. As romantic ideals of marriage spread, especially among middle-class women, disappointment regarding marriage inevitably increased as well, and from 1840 on, the divorce rate climbed steadily. By the late nineteenth century, as some women became better educated and gained financial independence, divorce became a likelier option. States expanded the legal grounds for divorce as well, thus contributing to the rising divorce rate. This phenomenon cut across social classes as both wealthy and working-class couples sought divorces. A 1909 Census Bureau study on marriage and divorce showed a significant increase in the divorce rate. In 1870 there were 81 divorces per 100,000 of the nation's married population; by 1900 this number had risen to 200 divorces per 100,000.

Twentieth-Century Trends. By the early twenty-first century, divorce played the role that death once did in determining the length of marriage. During the twentieth century the divorce rate rose noticeably after each major war and dropped during the Depression of the 1930s when many couples stayed together in order to survive tough times. The divorce rate rose sharply after 1965, peaking around 1980 and stabilizing thereafter. In the 1990s, about half of all marriages ended in divorce, giving the United States the highest divorce rate of any western nation. Frequent divorces and remarriages have fostered complex extended family relationships involving stepparents and stepchildren, half brothers and half sisters—a situation that in some respects makes modern households resemble colonial households.

Some observers point to easier divorce laws, especially the initiation of so-called no-fault divorces passed by several states in the 1970s, to explain a decline in the traditional family and an increase in divorce rates. Others, however, view this phenomenon as less a result of changing laws and more a reflection of higher expectations about marriage and the need for a safety valve for the more emotionally charged nuclear-family setting. The high divorce rate may also reflect women's greater autonomy and ability to live on their own, with a corresponding lessening of tolerance for unrewarding relationships or spouses' bad behavior.

In a legal sense, most twentieth-century marriages involved monogamous, heterosexual relationships, but exceptions exist. In the past, some Native American tribes and Mormons practiced polygamy, but legislation largely ended this practice by the late nineteenth century. The 1990s ushered in a movement to legalize same-sex marriages, which initially met much resistance and enjoyed little success. In response to public concerns, Congress passed the Defense of Marriage Act in 1996 that bars federal recognition of same-sex marriages. By the second decade of the twenty-first century, the debate over this issue was occurring at the state level, for a handful of states had legalized same-sex marriages, and gay and lesbian couples had taken advantage of the opportunity to affirm their relationships legally. But the issue was heated, and both proponents and opponents expected the Supreme Court would have to adjudicate this matter, taking to the federal level a marriage-related issue that states traditionally have handled on their own.

In the twenty-first century a growing, popular alternative or precursor to marriage was cohabitation. From the 1960s on, increasing numbers of couples have chosen to live together without legally binding ceremonies or contracts, especially before they have children. More couples were also delaying marriage or deciding not to legalize their relationship at all. In the early 2000s the rate of marriage was the lowest it had been in several decades, while the divorce rate, though high, had stabilized. A major demographic shift was the age at which young men and women marry. Whereas in 1970 only 16 percent of Americans in their late twenties had never been married, by 2010 that proportion had risen to 55 percent. By 2010 the mean age of marriage was thirty, which also influenced the age at which couples started families.

Race and ethnicity have an impact on marriage. By the late twentieth century, a noticeable decline in rates of marriage occurred among African Americans. Married couples constituted less than half of all early twenty-first-century African American families, and women headed the majority of African American families with a single parent. Studies have shown that a shortage of African American men and an increase in the number of underemployed or unemployed black men have had a significant impact on falling marriage rates. Divorce rates among African Americans were also higher than in the general population. Meanwhile, marriages between couples of mixed races were increasing. Studies in

the early twenty-first century showed that nearly 15 percent of new marriages were between spouses of a different race or ethnic group, a doubling of that statistic since 1980. The highest rate of these interracial marriages occurred among Asians, then Hispanics, followed by African Americans and then whites.

[*See also* **Courtship and Dating; Demography; Gay and Lesbian Love and Relationships; Gay and Lesbian Rights Movement; Law and Society; Life Stages; Multiracial and Multiethnic Americans; Pregnancy; Sexual Reform and Morality; Slave Families and Communities;** *and* **Stanton, Elizabeth Cady.**]

BIBLIOGRAPHY

Basch, Norma. *Framing American Divorce: From the Revolutionary Generation to the Victorians.* Berkeley: University of California Press, 1999.

Cherlin, Andrew J. *Marriage, Divorce, Remarriage.* Rev. ed. Cambridge, Mass.: Harvard University Press, 1992.

Coontz, Stephanie. *The Way We Never Were: American Families and the Nostalgia Trap.* New York: Basic Books, 1992.

Cott, Nancy F. *Public Vows: A History of Marriage and the Nation.* Cambridge, Mass.: Harvard University Press, 2000.

Lystra, Karen. *Searching the Heart: Women, Men, and Romantic Love in Nineteenth-Century America.* New York: Oxford University Press, 1989.

May, Elaine Tyler. *Great Expectations: Marriage and Divorce in Post-Victorian America.* Chicago: University of Chicago Press, 1980.

Mintz, Steven, and Susan Kellogg. *Domestic Revolutions: A Social History of American Family Life.* New York: Free Press, 1988.

Pleck, Elizabeth. *Domestic Tyranny: The Making of American Social Policy against Family Violence from Colonial Times to the Present.* New York: Oxford University Press, 1987.

Riley, Glena. *Divorce: An American Tradition.* New York: Oxford University Press, 1991.

Salmon, Marylynn. *Women and the Law of Property in Early America.* Chapel Hill: University of North Carolina Press, 1986.

Simmons, Christina. *Making Marriage Modern: Women's Sexuality from the Progressive Era to World War II.* Oxford: Oxford University Press, 2009.

Stevenson, Brenda E. *Life in Black and White: Family and Community in the Slave South.* New York: Oxford University Press, 1996.

Weiss, Jessica. *To Have and to Hold: Marriage, the Baby Boom, and Social Change.* Chicago: University of Chicago Press, 2000.

Sally G. McMillen

MASONIC ORDER

The Ancient and Accepted Order of Freemasons originated in London in the early 1700s and spread to colonial America. The all-male secret organization flourished among colonial leaders, who were attracted to its deistic religion and its ideology of equality and fraternity. George Washington, Benjamin Franklin, John Hancock, and Paul Revere were among the prominent American Masons of the Revolutionary era. An Anti-Masonic furor in the 1820s nearly destroyed the order, however. Opponents accused the Masons of subverting democracy and orthodox Protestantism. When William Morgan, who threatened to expose Masonic secrets, disappeared in Batavia, New York, in 1826, suspicions of the order's conspiratorial nature seemed confirmed. Anti-Masonry became embroiled in partisan politics and decimated the order's ranks.

Shortly before the Civil War, the order regrouped and became the model for dozens of other fraternal organizations that enjoyed tremendous popularity in the late nineteenth and early twentieth centuries. With the leadership carefully assuaging fears about its secrecy, religious ideas, and effects on politics, the Masonic Order flourished. The organization claimed to stand for morality, piety, and charity. And although it consisted primarily of white skilled workers and middle-class Protestants, it boasted that in the lodge room, all men were equal. The order's most egregious lapse from its egalitarian ideal was its steadfast refusal to acknowledge the Prince Hall Freemasons, a black version of the order begun in Boston in 1775. White and black Masonry continued as separate organizations throughout the twentieth century.

Roman Catholics were absent from Masonic lodges primarily because of a papal interdiction against Masonic membership. Masons, however, also were influenced by the anti-Catholicism that pervaded much of Protestant America.

With more than 3 million members, Freemasonry reached a high point in the 1920s, but it never completely recovered from the devastation of the Great Depression. Though many men continued to enjoy membership in the twenty-first century, the organization proved too static and old-fashioned to sustain its popularity.

[*See also* Antebellum Era; Anti-Catholicism; **Fraternal Organizations;** *and* **Voluntary Associations,** *subentry on* **British Colonies and Early Republic.**]

BIBLIOGRAPHY

Dumenil, Lynn. *Freemasonry and American Culture, 1880–1930.* Princeton, N.J.: Princeton University Press, 1984.

Lipson, Dorothy Ann. *Freemasonry in Federalist Connecticut.* Princeton, N.J.: Princeton University Press, 1977.

Lynn Dumenil

McPHERSON, AIMEE SEMPLE

(1890–1944), evangelist and founder of the International Church of the Foursquare Gospel. Aimee Kennedy was born in Canada near the southern Ontario village of Salford, where her early religious impressions were shaped by her father's Methodism and her mother's enthusiasm for the Salvation Army. In 1908, Aimee embraced Pentecostalism and married Robert Semple, the evangelist who converted her. They sailed as missionaries to Hong Kong in 1910. Six weeks later, Robert died of malaria and other complications. Married again in 1912 to Harold McPherson, a bookkeeper, Aimee could not settle into a housewife's routine. In 1915, living in Providence, Rhode Island, she left Harold and dedicated her life to Robert Semple's work of evangelism. The couple divorced in 1921.

Aimee enjoyed instant success as an evangelist. In 1917 she began publishing *The Bridal Call*, a monthly magazine that helped her build an international network. Late in 1918 she moved to Los Angeles, where she opened the fifty-three-hundred-seat Angelus Temple and a Bible school in 1923 and her own radio station in 1924. Her charismatic sermons, often illustrated with visual props, attracted thousands. Fame turned to notoriety in 1926 when McPherson disappeared for six weeks. The district attorney's office sought to disprove her widely doubted claim that she had been kidnapped, but eventually all charges against her were dropped. Rumors persisted that she had spent the time with a male staff member of Angelus Temple. Her third marriage, in 1931, ended in divorce two years later. Bad health curtailed McPherson's activities thereafter, but her son Rolf McPherson carried on her ministry with considerable success.

[*See also* **Religion; Revivals; Twenties, The;** *and* **Women and Religious Institutions.**]

BIBLIOGRAPHY

Blumhofer, Edith L. *Aimee Semple McPherson: Everybody's Sister*. Grand Rapids, Mich.: Eerdmans, 1993.
Epstein, Daniel Mark. *Sister Aimee: The Life of Aimee Semple McPherson*. New York: Harcourt Brace Jovanovich, 1993.

Edith L. Blumhofer

MEDICINE, POPULAR AND NON-WESTERN

Medicine, like sculpture or music, is a material expression of culture. So it is not surprising that a multicultural society like America would foster a system of medical pluralism in which patients can choose from a variety of therapeutic alternatives. Indeed, from Ayurveda to Zen-inspired psychotherapy, from chiropractic to yoga, twenty-first-century Americans can—and do—select from an array of complementary and alternative medical (CAM) options. Nor is such remarkable diversity of choices a modern phenomenon; variety has always been a hallmark of American health care.

Early America. Arriving in a land where Native Americans possessed a medical tradition that included centuries of knowledge about the curative properties of local flora, the earliest European settlers brought their own heritage of herbal and folk medicine. Slaves, in turn, brought Afro-Caribbean healing traditions. In a few years, barber-surgeons, apothecaries, and other healers were added to this mix. And in roles from herbalists to midwives, women were key providers in this health-care delivery system. Formally educated physicians were few; most doctors were products of apprenticeships. The type of care that colonists received depended upon their station in life and where they lived. A poor person in New Orleans might well be treated by a folk healer using an herbal cure that drew on Native American knowledge and African animist tradition, whereas a Tidewater aristocrat or a wealthy Boston merchant might be administered to by a physician educated in Europe.

Among American revolutionary leaders was Dr. Benjamin Rush (1745–1813), a signer of the Declaration of Independence and the principal force behind the founding of the College of Philadelphia Medical School in 1765. Rush epitomized an effort to improve medical education in America, placing it upon a solid rational and scientific footing and in the process establishing an elite class of medical practitioners. Though at the time a current of empiricism flowed through medicine—that is, a belief that treatment should be based upon observation of past therapeutic success—there was also a very strong rationalist tradition. The rationalists believed that physicians must understand the theoretical basis of disease and develop treatments based upon that understanding. If success was meager, then a more vigorous application of a therapy was called for. This led to heroic measures such as copious bloodletting to treat everything from insanity to fevers and giving large doses of mercurous chloride (calomel) to treat cholera.

These heroic measures were often more injurious than curative and fueled a growing public suspicion of the medical elite, a suspicion in keeping with the overall spirit of Jacksonian democracy as frontiersmen challenged the establishment. Medical sects dedicated to rival understandings of health and illness emerged. Wooster Beach (1794–1868) organized the Reformed Medical Society of the United States in 1829 to advocate for botanically based medicine. This group morphed into the nucleus of the eclectic medical movement. But it was the New England farmer Samuel Thomson (1769–1843) and his followers

who most brazenly challenged the physician elite. Thomson developed a system that included use of herbal medicines, steam baths, emetics, and enemas. He patented his system and began selling rights that allowed an authorized agent to use the system to treat himself and his family. Ultimately, differences in ideas about business and therapeutics splintered Thomson's followers into rival groups, and the movement faded away.

Vital Matters of the Spirit. Wooster Beach received his initial medical training from an herbal doctor and then earned a medical degree in New York City. A nonconformist, Beach refused simply to follow the heroic measures advocated by many leading authorities. With a strong empiricist bent, he drew from both his early botanical training and his formal education. His aim was to use the least invasive therapeutic strategies that benefited patients. It was an approach that earned Beach and like-minded physicians the name "eclectics." Their premier institution, the Eclectic Medical Institute (EMI) of Cincinnati, Ohio, lasted nearly a century before closing in 1939.

As a group, eclectics were rooted in an empirical botanical model of medicine, but they were not impervious to the influence of the spiritual and vitalistic movements sweeping America in the 1800s: a tradition of fervent and esoteric religion was blossoming into the Second Great Awakening. Areas most touched by these revivals became breeding grounds for movements and leaders who blended spiritual awakening with impulses for social, political, and other types of reform.

This milieu of revival and reform fostered several alternative movements seeking to reshape medical practice and perfect the health of Americans. Homeopathy, although European in origin, gained a devoted American following. Another European import—hydropathy, the use of therapeutic baths to treat illness—also became popular. The American Sylvester Graham (1794–1851) combined an ascetic form of Presbyterianism with vegetarianism and abstinence from alcohol to create what he described as a science of life. Andrew Taylor Still (1828–1917) developed osteopathy, a system that sought to cure without use of medicine or surgery. And Mary Baker Eddy (1821–1910) transformed her own healing, which occurred while she was studying the Bible, into a system she called Christian Science.

Some of these movements, like Graham's, collapsed under the weight of their own dogmatism. Osteopathy eventually reached a rapprochement with allopathy, incorporating both medicine and surgery into its therapeutic alternatives. Others, like hydropathy, were transformed from medical intervention into complementary therapy to foster health and well-being. A few systems, like Christian Science, carried forward essentially intact into the twenty-first century. But all of them shaped the landscape of American medicine in the nineteenth century, perpetuating a mosaic of medical pluralism.

Women in Alternative Medicine. With the professionalization of allopathic medicine in the nineteenth century, the role of women in American health care was largely transformed from healers to helpers. All too often, the medical establishment cast them in the role of compassionate attendants who stood at the hearth and bedside executing the directives of male physicians.

Though not entirely free of the prejudices of their time, alternative medical movements were generally more open to women. Indeed, a fascinating aspect of nineteenth-century medical reform in America is the prominent role played by women. The feminist Elizabeth Cady Stanton (1815–1902), for example, was a lay practitioner and advocate of homeopathy.

Furthermore, sectarian medical schools often opened their doors to women in greater numbers than did conventional allopathic schools. In the second half of the nineteenth century, homeopathic schools alone graduated almost seventeen hundred female physicians. Even in the twenty-first century, women were still strongly represented in various CAM modalities, and women tended to be more likely than men to use CAM services.

In 1910 the Carnegie Institute published Abraham Flexner's stinging indictment of American medical education. Many medical schools, especially non-allopathic schools, were financially unable to meet the accreditation standards advocated in this report. Of the 131 medical schools operating in America when the Flexner report was released, fifty had closed their doors by 1922. Many of those that closed had admitted women, and not until the 1970s were women again admitted in appreciable numbers to American medical schools.

The Twentieth Century and Beyond. The quest for a medical system minimizing the use of medicine and relying instead on the curative power of nature continued in the twentieth century—even though allopathic medicine was making its greatest scientific advances.

After experimenting with magnetism, the self-taught healer D. D. Palmer (1845–1913) began focusing on spinal manipulation to treat disease, developing chiropractic medicine. His son, B. J. Palmer (1882–1961), built a chiropractic college and practice in Davenport, Iowa. Thanks in part to effective use of his own radio station, a powerhouse capable of broadcasting across the United States, B. J. Palmer turned chiropractic medicine into a nationally known therapy.

Naturopathy. One of the most important twentieth-century medical movements was naturopathy. Arising from the European nature cure movement at the end of the nineteenth century, naturopathy emphasized *vis medicatrix naturae*, a belief in the healing power of nature. The movement gained popularity in the early 1900s. Then, faced with a withering assault from the American Medical Association, hampered by state laws restricting naturopathic physicians' right to practice, and weakened by internal dissension, naturopathy almost disappeared. Later, however, naturopathy was rejuvenated thanks to renewed interest from the public, the establishment of sound, accredited naturopathic medical colleges, and legislative victories granting licensed naturopathic physicians the right to practice primary-care medicine in more than a dozen states. By the early twenty-first century naturopathy was one of the most dynamic areas of CAM in the United States.

The Age of Aquarius.

The emergence of the counterculture—and subsequent popular interest in holistic health—had a profound impact on medical pluralism in the late 1960s and 1970s. The public was once again suspicious of elites and began turning in new directions to take charge of their health. Asian influences on the New Age movement fueled interest in Ayurvedic medicine. Traditional Chinese medicine, once largely limited to ethnic communities, gained wider recognition. Public interest soared when President Richard M. Nixon visited China in 1972 and when in 1971 the *New York Times* journalist James Reston wrote of the Chinese herbs and acupuncture used on him after he had an emergency appendectomy in Beijing.

Contemporary Practice.

By the early twenty-first century, so-called alternative medicine had become a prominent current in the mainstream of American health care. A 2004 study by the Centers for Disease Control and Prevention estimated that 123 million Americans used some form of complementary and alternative medicine in the past twelve months. Even the term "alternative" had become something of a misnomer; most CAM users combined alternative therapies with conventional medical treatment. The allopathic medical establishment had followed suit. At least forty-six of the nation's leading academic medical centers had integrative medicine programs combining the best of alternative and conventional therapies. Once-exotic forms of care such as acupuncture had become staples of popular magazines. From urban enclaves to suburbia to rural hamlets, in the second decade of the twenty-first century, Americans continued their tradition of medical pluralism.

[*See also* **Great Awakenings; Health and Fitness; Health and Healing, Eighteenth and Nineteenth Centuries; Hospitals and Dispensaries; Midwifery;** *and* **Religion.**]

BIBLIOGRAPHY

Baer, Hans A. *Biomedicine and Alternative Healing Systems in America: Issues of Class, Race, Ethnicity, and Gender*. Madison: University of Wisconsin Press, 2001.

Barnes, Patricia, Eve Powell-Griner, Kim McFann, and Richard L. Nahin. "Complementary and Alternative Medicine Use among Adults: United States 2002." *Advance Data from Vital Health and Statistics* 343 (2004): 1–19. Based upon interviews with thirty-one thousand adults, this is perhaps the most definitive survey to date of Americans' use of complementary and alternative medicine.

Berman, Alex, and Michael A. Flannery. *America's Botanico-Medical Movements: Vox Populi*. New York: Pharmaceutical Products Press, 2001. Provides a definitive history of American botanical medicine from the colonial period to the twentieth century.

Eisenberg, David M., Roger Davis, Susan L. Ettner, Scott Appel, Sonja Wilkey, Maria Van Rompay, and Ronald C. Kessler. "Unconventional Medicine Use in the United States: Prevalence, Costs, and Patterns of Use." *New England Journal of Medicine* 328 (1993): 246–252. The article that shocked the biomedical establishment into realizing how widespread the use of alternative medicine was among their own patients; this article has been cited in at least thirty-four hundred works.

Grossinger, Richard. *Planet Medicine: Origins.* 7th ed. Berkeley, Calif.: North Atlantic Books, 2005. A remarkable source by an anthropologist-turned-publisher for the reader who seeks background by way of immersion in alternative medicine.

Haller, John S., Jr. *Swedenborg, Mesmer, and the Mind/Body Connection: The Roots of Complementary Medicine.* West Chester, Pa.: Swedenborg Foundation, 2010. Traces the influence of Emanuel Swedenborg and Franz Anton Mesmer through the spiritualists, socialist-utopian, and medical movements of the nineteenth century to the various therapies advocated by New Age healers.

Kaptchuk, Ted J., and David M. Eisenberg. "Varieties of Healing. 1: Medical Pluralism in the United States." *Annals of Internal Medicine* 135, no. 3 (2001): 189–195. A brilliant analysis of medical pluralism in America; suggests that the nature of pluralism has fundamentally changed from one of antagonism to a sort of postmodern medical diversity.

Kirschmann, Anne Taylor. *A Vital Force: Women in American Homeopathy.* New Brunswick, N.J.: Rutgers University Press, 2004. A fascinating history of the role that women have played in American homeopathy from its earliest days to a rejuvenation certainly fueled in part by its connections to the women's health movement of Second Wave feminism.

Shryock, Richard H. "Empiricism versus Rationalism in American Medicine, 1650–1950." *Proceedings of the American Antiquarian Society* 79 (1969): 99–150. This classic article articulates an epistemological history of American medicine.

Whorton, James C. *Nature Cures: The History of Alternative Medicine in America.* Oxford: Oxford University Press, 2002. A remarkable history of alternative medicine in America from the eighteenth century forward.

Cullen Clark